BILL   PHILIP
JONES NORTON

With additional material by: **Oliver Daddow, Mark Garnett, Michael Moran, Richard Kelly, Russell Deacon, Colin Copus, Harry Cowen, Wyn Grant, Peter Byrd, Andrew Flynn, Nicholas Rees**
And concluding essays by: **Andrew Gamble, Steve Richards, Chris Mullin, Andrew Heywood, Peter Riddell, Jonathan Freedland**

Politics UK

SEVENTH EDITION

Longman
is an imprint of

Harlow, England • London • New York • Boston • San Francisco • Toronto • Sydney • Singapore • Hong Kong
Tokyo • Seoul • Taipei • New Delhi • Cape Town • Madrid • Mexico City • Amsterdam • Munich • Paris • Milan

Pearson Education Limited
Edinburgh Gate
Harlow
Essex CM20 2JE
England

and Associated Companies throughout the world

Visit us on the World Wide Web at:
www.pearsoned.co.uk

First published 1991
Second edition published 1994
Third edition published 1998
Fourth edition published 2001
Fifth edition published 2004
Updated fifth edition published 2006
Sixth edition published 2007
Seventh edition published 2010

ISBN: 978-1-4058-9996-3

British Library Cataloguing-in-Publication Data
A catalogue record for this book is available from the British Library

Library of Congress Cataloging-in-Publication Data
A catalog record for this book is available from the Library of Congress

10 9 8 7 6 5 4 3 2 1
13 12 11 10

Typeset in 10/12.5pt ITC Century by 35
Printed and bound by Rotolito

The publisher's policy is to use paper manufactured from sustainable forests.

Brief contents

Part 6   The policy process   483

Appendix

Contents

Part 2   Defining the political world   57

Part 3   The representative process   119

Part 5   The executive process   383

Appendix

Supporting resources
Visit **www.pearsoned.co.uk/Jones** to find valuable online resources:

Companion Website for students
- A revision guide to help you consolidate your learning
- Multiple choice questions to test your understanding
- Guides to referencing and essay writing
- Regular monthly updates on current events in British politics

For instructors
- PowerPoint slides that can be downloaded and used for presentations
- Suggestions for group work and presentation assignments

Also: The regularly maintained Companion Website provides the following features:
- Search tool to help locate specific items of content
- Online help and support to assist with website usage and troubleshooting

For more information please contact your local Pearson Education sales representative or visit **www.pearsoned.co.uk/Jones**

Contributors

Colin Copus is Professor of Local Politics and Director of the Local Governance Research Unit in the Department of Public Policy, De Montfort University. His main research interests are: local party politics, local political leadership, the changing role of the councillor, and small party and independent politics. He also researches and writes on English national identity and English governance. He has recently concluded two major research projects: the first a Leverhulme-funded project exploring the role and impact of small political parties, independent politics and political associations in local government; the second, a Nuffield-funded comparative project examining the roles, responsibilities and activities of councillors across Europe. Colin is the author of two major books: *Leading the Localities: Executive Mayors in English Local Governance* (Manchester University Press 2006); and *Party Politics and Local Government* (Manchester University Press 2004). He has also served as a councillor on a London Borough council, a county and a district council and three parish councils.

Harry Cowen was born in Manchester and has taught on social science courses and degrees in Manchester, Salford, Liverpool and Gloucestershire. He has also worked in regional development and planning for the Ontario Government, Canada. His publications include: *The Human Nature Debate: Social Theory, Social Policy And The Caring Professions* (Pluto Press 1994); *Community Care, Ideology and Social Policy* (Pearson 1999); and contributions to Alcock, Daly and Griggs, *Introduction to Social Policy*, 2nd edn (2007). He has carried out contract research for a range of public bodies such as the former Commission For Racial Equality, local health authorities and housing associations. He was Honorary Research Fellow at the University of Gloucestershire.

Oliver Daddow is Senior Lecturer in the Department of Politics, History and International Relations, Loughborough University. He edited *Harold Wilson and European Integration* (2003); and is the author of *Britain and Europe since 1945* (2004), *International Relations Theory* (2009) and *New Labour and the European Union* (2010).

Russell Deacon is a Reader in Welsh Governance and Modern Political History in the Department of Humanities in the University of Wales Institute, Cardiff. He has also been a civil servant in the former Welsh Office and a senior researcher in the National Assembly of Wales. Dr Deacon has published widely on devolution and written a number of books including: *Devolution in Great Britain* (2006) and *Devolution in the United Kingdom* (2007) (with Dr Alan Sandry) on this subject. He is also a political historian who specialises on the Welsh Liberal Party and the wider Liberal Democrats. His most recent publication in this respect is *A History of Welsh Liberalism* (2010). Dr Deacon is chair of the British Liberal Political Studies Group.

Jonathan Freedland writes a weekly column for the *Guardian*. He is also a regular contributor to the *New York Times* and the *New York Review of Books*, and presents BBC Radio 4's contemporary history series, *The Long View*. He was named 'Columnist of the Year' in the 2002 'What the Papers Say' awards and in 2008 was awarded the David Watt Prize for

Journalism. He has also published five books, including three best-selling thrillers under the name Sam Bourne.

Andrew Gamble is Professor of Politics at the University of Cambridge and joint editor of *The Political Quarterly*. He is the author of *The Spectre at the Feast: Capitalist Crisis and the Politics of Recession* (Palgrave Macmillan 2009).

Mark Garnett is Lecturer in Politics at the University of Lancaster. His many books on British politics and society include *From Anger to Apathy: The British Experience since 1975* (Jonathan Cape 2007).

Wyn Grant is Professor of Politics at the University of Warwick and is the author of *Economic Policy in Britain* (2002). He is a regular commentator for radio and print media on economic policy issues.

Andrew Heywood is a leading writer of politics textbooks and an A Level chief examiner. His publications include: *Essentials of UK Politics* (2008), *Politics*, 3rd edn (2007), *Political Ideologies*, 4th edn (2007), *Political Theory*, 3rd edn (2004) and *Key Concepts in Politics* (2000). His main research interests are political ideologies and global politics.

Bill Jones joined the Extra-Mural Department at Manchester University in 1972 as the person in charge of politics and government, serving as Director 1987–92. His books include *The Russia Complex* (on Labour and the USSR); *British Politics Today* (which ran through seven editions before being republished with the suffix *The Essentials* in 2010); *Political Issues in Britain Today* (five editions); *Debates in British Politics* (with Lynton Robins, 2001); and *The Dictionary of British Politics* (2nd edition 2010). He was Vice Chair and Chair of The Politics Association 1979–85, being made a Life Fellow in 2001. He suffered a stroke while jogging in 1992 and took medical retirement from Manchester. In 2006 he took up a part-time teaching position at Liverpool Hope University being made a professor in 2009. He also occasionally broadcasts on radio and television and runs a political blog: *Skipper*.

Richard Kelly is Head of Politics at Manchester Grammar School. His publications include *British Political Parties Today* (Manchester University Press 1998), *Conservative Party Conferences* (Manchester University Press 1989) and *Changing Party Policy in Britain* (Blackwell 1999).

Michael Moran is Professor of Government at the University of Manchester. His publications include *Politics and Governance in the UK* (Palgrave 2005, 2nd edn, 2011) and *Business, Politics and Society* (Oxford University Press 2009).

Chris Mullin is a former minister and select committee chairman. His recently published diaries, *A View from the Foothills*, have been described by Peter Riddell of *The Times* as 'the central text for understanding the Blair years'.

Philip Norton (Lord Norton of Louth) is Professor of Government and Director of the Centre for Legislative Studies at the University of Hull, as well as being a member of the House of Lords. He is the author or editor of 28 books.

Nicholas Rees is Professor of International Politics and Contemporary History at Liverpool Hope University. His research interests include European integration, Europeanisation, EU external affairs and international relations. He has authored or edited four books, as well as having published numerous book chapters, and refereed journal articles.

Steve Richards is chief political commentator for the *Independent* and a contributing editor on the *New Statesman*.

Peter Riddell is Chief Political Commentator of *The Times* and a Senior Fellow of the Institute for Government (where he has co-written a report on 'Transitions: preparing for changes of government'). He chairs the Hansard Society and has been actively involved in the debate over parliamentary reform. He has written six books on British politics. He holds two honorary degree and is an Honorary Fellow of Sidney Sussex College, Cambridge.

Guided tour

The seventh edition of **Politics UK** is packed with features expressly designed to enhance your under-standing and enjoyment of British politics. Here are just a few:

BIOGRAPHY

Joseph Stalin (1879–1953)

Soviet dictator. Trained as a priest before becoming a revolutionary in Georgia, Russia. Was secretary to Lenin's Communist Party and after his death deviously manipulated his enemies out of power while placing his own supporters in key positions. Became unchallenged dictator in 1930s and tried to neutralise Hitler by doing a deal with him. Hitler broke the agreement and attacked the USSR in 1941. After initial reverses the Soviets fought back under Stalin's leadership and defeated Hitler. Despite his brutal behaviour Stalin won friends on the left in Western countries, who persisted in believing his propaganda and seeing him as a force for progress.

USSR. Members managed to survive the astonishing volte-face when Stalin ceased to oppose Hitler as first priority and signed a deal with him in 1939 to partition Poland. Once Hitler had invaded Soviet Russia in 1941, British communists breathed a sigh of relief; they were at last able to luxuriate in a vast amphitheatre of approving views as the whole country applauded the heroic Soviet effort. After the war, the party won two seats – Mile End and West Fife – but Stalin's expansion into Eastern Europe, his blockade of Berlin in 1948 and the crushing (after his death) of the Hungarian rising in 1956 by the Soviet military machine, not to mention Khrushchev's denunciation of Stalin in his secret speech to the 20th Party Congress, substantially disillusioned communists and Moscow 'fellow travellers' alike. The Cold War effectively ruined the chances of communist parties achieving power anywhere in Europe, and they began to wither and atrophy.

Trotsky – advocate of 'worldwide revolution' – was Lenin's heir apparent, but the dogged, apparently un-intellectual Joseph Stalin, Secretary of the Party, was cleverer than his brilliant colleague. He urged 'socialism in one country' rather than working for an unlikely international conflagration; he out-manoeuvred his rivals and plotted ruthlessly, succeeding in presenting Trotsky as a traitor to the revolution. Stalin eventually drove Trotsky into exile in Mexico, where his agents succeeded in assassinating him in 1940 (see Biography).

Stalin, by then, had become a brutal dictator, both paranoid and obsessed with power, claiming to be implementing **communism** but in reality imposing industrialisation, collective farming and his own tyrannical rule on a reluctant and starving peasantry. Anyone less than obsequiously worshipful of their leader was imprisoned, exiled or shot. Overseas communist parties were employed essentially to assist the development of the 'home of socialism', and any deviation from the party line was punished by expulsion or worse.

This is the legacy inherited by extreme left-wing parties in Britain. The Communist Party of Great Britain (CPGB) was founded in 1920 and became the willing tool of Moscow's message in this country, interpreting all the shifts in the official line and condemning anyone perceived as an enemy of the

BIOGRAPHY

Leon Trotsky (1879–1940)

Leon Trotsky was a Russian Jewish revolutionary politician born in the Ukraine. He was arrested for being a Marxist at the age of 19 but escaped from Siberia in 1902. After teaming up with Lenin, he became president of the first soviet in St Petersburg after the abortive 1905 revolution. He escaped to the West but returned to Russia in March 1917 to assist Lenin in organising the Bolshevik Revolution in November of the same year. He conducted peace negotiations with the Germans and led the Red Army of five million men in the ensuing civil war. An inspiring and charismatic leader as well as brilliant intellectually, Trotsky should have succeeded Lenin in 1924, but his theories of permanent world revolution were less well suited to the times than Stalin's pragmatic 'socialism in one country'; he was eventually exiled in 1929, being assassinated in Mexico with an ice pick in 1940 by Ramon del Rio, an agent of Moscow. His ideas live on, but mostly on the radical intellectual fringe in developed countries.

Each chapter opens with a set of **Learning objectives**, which list the topics covered and outlines what you should understand by the end of the chapter.

Biography boxes, found throughout the book, focus on particular individuals who have helped develop our understanding of what politics is, or who have played a significant role in British politics.

Ideas and Perspectives boxes focus in on specific questions, events or issues and suggest a range of responses.

Towards the end of each chapter you will find the new **Britain in Context** feature, which looks at the issues covered within a chapter in the context of global politics and provides a useful comparative angle on the key issues in British politics.

Chapter summaries come at the end of each chapter, to provide a resumé of the issues that have been under the microscope. **Discussion points** are listed at the end of each chapter, prompting you to consider and develop your own responses to the issues at hand. You will find annotated suggestions for **Further reading** at the end of each chapter.

Each chapter also ends with a list of **Useful websites**. While the web should be approached with caution it can be a tremendous tool for deepening your understanding of politics.

Throughout the text you will find certain terms and phrases highlighted in bold; you will find definitions for these terms and phrases in the **Glossary**, which comes towards the end of the book.

And another thing . . . is a feature that you will find at the end of each of the six parts of the book. These interpretive essays by leading political thinkers take a sideways glance at some of the key issues under debate in contemporary British politics.

Preface

Politics is an exciting subject. We, the authors, are naturally biased in thinking it offers students very special attractions. It is a subject you digest with your breakfast each morning; its complex canvas unfolds with the daily papers, the *Today* programme, the broadcast news, not excluding possible viewings of blogs; by the evening new details have been painted in and the picture subtly, sometimes dramatically, has changed.

Politics is unpredictable, dynamic; it affects us, it is about us. In one sense the canvas *is* us: a projection of ourselves and our aspirations, a measure of our ability to live together. Given what can happen when it goes wrong – a ruler like Pol Pot or Saddam Hussein, for example – politics is arguably the most important focus there is in the study of the human condition. We hope that this volume on the politics of the United Kingdom does the subject some kind of justice.

This book is designed to provide a comprehensive introduction to British politics for both the general reader and the examination candidate. With the latter group in mind, we fashioned a text for the first edition that was unusual by British standards. When we studied A-level politics, all those years ago, the transition from O-level to A-level was quite difficult. This was hardly surprising, because many of the A-level texts were the same as those we went on to study at university, partly because of shared assumptions about A-level and university students. It was believed that we should be treated as mature intellects (good), but also that it was up to us to extract meaning from the texts which, in the name of standards, made few concessions to our possible

unfamiliarity with the subject (not so good). In these circumstances it is hardly surprising that so many aspiring university students gave up before the intrinsic interest of the subject could capture them.

Things have improved since then, in the world of textbooks remarkably so. Syllabuses have become much wider and now embrace stimulating new areas such as political sociology and current political issues. This has helped authors produce more interesting work but a revolution has also taken place on the production side. *Politics UK*, when it came out in 1990, was arguably the first book to embrace the American approach of providing a comprehensive course textbook with a plethora of new features such as photographs, diagrams, tables and illustrative figures.

Since then most of our rival textbooks on British politics have adopted similar styles, and if imitation is the highest form of flattery, we are greatly flattered. The book has moved through six successful editions and this is the seventh. The key features of this new edition are as follows.

- The fourth edition was comprehensively 'Europeanised': each chapter was looked at and amended to take account of the EU impact and influence – all this material has been accordingly updated for the seventh edition.

- 'Updating' means covering developments over the four years since the last edition, of course – including the 2010 election – but older examples are still cited in some cases; there are continuities in British politics and the whole of the postwar period is used as a kind of laboratory in which political behaviour is observed.

■ Many of the chapters have been completely rewritten, and all chapters not rewritten have been comprehensively updated up to, where possible, spring 2010.

■ A chapter on the recent 2010 election was the last to be included.

■ The book contains an alphabetical Glossary defining all the key terms highlighted in the text.

■ The comparative approach to politics has become increasingly popular over the last decade and, while this is not expressly a comparative text, we have included a 'Britain in context' box for each chapter which provides a limited version of this kind of input.

■ *Politics UK's* companion website contains the best available guide to useful websites, as well as many other additional features, including a specially written set of revision notes for each chapter.

■ The book's presentation has been augmented by the inclusion of many tables, diagrams and up-to-date cartoons from the quality press.

The comment and debate essays at the end of each major part have been written, as before, by distinguished guest writers. This time they are:

■ **Professor Andrew Gamble** – distinguished Cambridge scholar and an authority on recent political history and the world economic crisis 2007–9.

■ **Jonathan Freedland** – much admired *Guardian* columnist and broadcaster.

■ **Steve Richards** – chief columnist at the *Independent* newspaper as well as radio and television broadcaster.

■ **Andrew Heywood** – the most successful author of politics textbooks in the country.

■ **Chris Mullin MP** – The MP for Sunderland South was a distinguished select committee chair as well as author of a much praised volume of diaries, *A View from the Foothills*.

■ **Peter Riddell** – another contribution to the book by this doyen of British political analysts: columnist and assistant editor of *The Times* as well as broadcaster and author of several books on British politics.

The original line-up of principal authors diminished from six to four by the sixth edition; we were sorry to lose Michael Moran (though we retain one chapter by him in this edition) and Dennis Kavanagh though pressure of work, leaving just myself and Philip Norton as main authors/editors. Colin Copus, Nick Rees, Andrew Flynn, Harry Cowen, Mark Garnett, Wyn Grant, Oliver Daddow and Russell Deacon all contribute towards this volume with discrete chapters. Professor Philip Cowley of Nottingham University was intended to become a 'main author', but hectic pressure of work (including a burgeoning media career) prevented this from happening; however, Philip Norton and I are very grateful for the valuable input he made to the planning of the present edition of a book which has continued to evolve since its first appearance in 1991.

The chapters on parliament in this book have always been authoritative and up to date; they are even more so since Philip Norton became a member of the House of Lords himself in 1998. Thanks are due to all the contributors and to the staff at Pearson Education who have proved remarkably helpful and professional, especially Kate Ahl who has been central to the book's preparation and, during its later stages, Georgina Clark-Mazo. We have to thank (chiefly) Chris Riddell for the brilliant cartoons, borrowed from his weekly contributions to the *Observer*. Special thanks are offered to those reviewers who commented so usefully on draft chapters of this book and thereby helped to improve them. Lecturers and teachers are reminded that if they adopt the book they will receive, free of charge, the Instructor's Manual, written by Bill Jones (and Graham Thomas). We hope teachers and students find the book as useful and stimulating as previous editions.

Bill Jones
Philip Norton
June 2010

Acknowledgements

We are grateful to the following for permission to reproduce copyright material:

Figures

Figure 10.1 from 'Pressure groups and the policy process', *Social Studies Review*, 3(5) (Grant, W., 1998), California Council for Social Studies; Figure 10.2 from 'Insider and outsider pressure groups', *Social Studies Review*, 1(1) (Grant, W., 1985), California Council for Social Studies; Figure 13.1 from 'The constitution in flux', *Social Studies Research*, 2(1) (Norton, P., 1986), California Council for Social Studies; Figure 19.1 from *British Politics Today* (Jones, B. and Kavanagh, D., eds), Manchester University Press (Gray, A., 1970) 'Local government in England and Wales', Manchester University Press; Figure 21.1 from *British Politics Today* (Jones, B. and Kavanagh, D., eds), Manchester University Press (Burch, M., 1979) 'The policy making process', Manchester University Press; Figure 21.3 from *Pressure Groups Today*, Manchester University Press (Baggott, R., 1995) p. 24, Manchester University Press; Figure 26.3 from *Spotlight on Business: Ten years of improving the environment*, The Environment Agency (2008) p. 20; Figure 26.4 from *Spotlight on Business: Ten years of improving the environment*, Environment Agency p. 21; Figure 27.1 from *European Barometer 71: Public Opinion in the European Union – National Report, United Kingdom*, European Commission (Spring 2009) p. 34.

Tables

Tables 3.1, 3.2 and 3.3 from the Office for National Statistics, Crown Copyright material is reproduced with the permission of the Controller, Office of Public Sector Information (OPSI); Table 8.2 from *Britain Decides* (Geddes, A. and Tonge, J., eds), Palgrave (Wring, D. and Deacon, D., 2005) 'The election unspun'; Table 9.1 from *Political Participation and Democracy in Britain*, Cambridge University Press (Parry, G., Moyser, G. and Day, N., 1992) p. 44; Table 9.4 from 'Social capital and urban governance: adding a more contextualised "top down" perspective', *Political Studies*, 48(4), 802–20 (Maloney, W., Smith, G. and Stoker, G., 2000), Blackwell Publishing Ltd; Table 12.6 from *Eurobarometer (2007) Attitudes towards the EU in the United Kingdom*, European Commission (FlashEurobarometer 2007 May 2007); Table 12.7 from the Office of National Statistics, Crown Copyright material is reproduced with the permission of the Controller, Office of Public Sector Information (OPSI); Tables 14.1, 15.8 and 15.10 from Ipsos/MORI; Table 15.1 from *The British General Election of 2005* (Kavanagh, D. and Butler, D., eds), Palgrave Macmillan (Criddle, B., 2005) 'MPs and candidates; Table 15.2 from *The British General Election, 2005* (Kavanagh, D. and Butler, D., eds), Palgrave Macmillan (Criddle, B., 2005) 'MPs and candidates', p. 159; Table 15.3 from 'The victorious legislative incumbent as a threat to democracy', *Legislative Studies Newsletter*, 18(2) (Somit, A. and Roemmele, A., 1995); Table 15.4 from *House of Commons Sessional Information Digests, 2001–8*, HMSO (2008) Parliament, Crown Copyright material is reproduced with permission under the terms of the Click-Use License; Table 15.5 from *House of Commons Sessional Information Digest, 2007–8*, HMSO (2008) Parliament, Crown

Copyright material is reproduced with permission under the terms of the Click-Use License; Table 15.9 from *Electronic Media, Parliament and the Media*, Hansard Society (Coleman, S., 1999) p. 20; Table 16.1 from www.parliament.uk; Table 19.2 adapted from Chris Game, 'Lost! 90% of councillors in 35 years: are county-wide unitaries effectively the end of UK local government?', paper presented to the PSA Local Politics Specialist Group, University of Birmingham, 20 January 2009; Table 19.5 from 'The New Local Government Network', nlgn.org.uk; Table 19.6 from nlgn.org.uk; Table 20.1 from *Judicial and Court Statistics 2007*, Cm 7467, HMSO (2008); Table 20.2 adapted from Ministry of Justice website, http://www.judiciary.gov.uk/keyfacts/statistics/ethnic.htm, HMSO, Crown Copyright material is reproduced with permission under the terms of the Click-Use License; Table 26.3 from *Spotlight on Business: Ten years of improving the environment*, Environment Agency (Environment Agency 2008) p. 18, Environment Agency; Table 26.4 from *Spotlight on Business*, Environment Agency, p. 18; Table 27.2 from *European Barometer 71: Public Opinion in the European Union – National Report, United Kingdom*, European Commission (Spring 2009) p. 7.

Text

Box 1.1 adapted from 'A doctor writes: politicians' pride is a medical disorder', *Guardian*, 28 March 2009 (Boseley, S.), Guardian News and Media Ltd; Box 6.3 from *Sex and Power: Who Runs Britain?*, Equal Opportunities Commission (2006); extract on pages 147–8 from 'Commons sketch', *Guardian*, 1999 (Hoggart, S.), Guardian News and Media Ltd; extract on pages 157–8 from 'Commons sketch', *Guardian*, 3 November 2009 (Hoggart, S.), Guardian News and Media Ltd; Box 6.5 from 'Feminist debates, ideology: feminism', *Politics Review*, 12(4) (Bryson, V. 2003), Philip Allan Updates, reproduced with permission of Philip Allan Updates; Box 8.5 from *Guardian*, 6 April 2009 (Pilkington, E.), Guardian News and Media Ltd; Box 9.1 from 'Editorial', *Guardian*, 17 June 1999, Guardian News and Media Ltd; Interview 10.8 from Tyne Tees TV programme (1986); extract on page 269 from *Hansard*, 18 December 2002, Vol. 642, col. 692, www.publications.parliament.uk/pa/ld200203/ldhansard/vo021218/text/ 21218-05/htm; Box 22.1 from 'What really causes crime?', *Guardian*, 12 July 2002 (Toynbee, P.), Guardian News and Media Ltd.

Photographs

The publisher would like to thank the following for their kind permission to reproduce their photographs:

(Key: b-bottom; c-centre; l-left; r-right; t-top)

Action Plus Sports Images: Neil Tingle 98; Alamy Images: archstock 598, Tim Gander 565, Steven Gillis hd9 imaging 429, Tim Graham 383, Johnny Greig 595, Ellen Isaacs 532, Janine Weidel Photolibrary / Alamy Images 41, Justin Kase z01z 387, David Levenson 457, One-Image Photography / Alamy 351, Tim Ayers Photography 249, Pictorial Press Ltd 526, Rolf Richardson / Alamy 354, Jack Sullivan 533; BBC Motion Gallery: 30; Corbis: Adam Woolfitt / Corbis 314, Angelo Hornak / Corbis 546, Bettmann 323, Peter Nicholls / Pool / Reuters / Corbis 134, Pool / Tim Graham Picture Library / Corbis 279, Tim Graham / Corbis 170; Getty Images: 1, 28, 217, 220, 483, AFP 110, 142l (inset), 258 (replacement), 396, AFP 110, 142l (inset), 258 (replacement), 396, AFP 110, 142l (inset), 258 (replacement), 396, Daniel Berehulak 604, Cocoon 57, CARL DE SOUZA / AFP 531, Anthony Devlin / WPA 392, Tim Gidal / Picture Post 549, David Gould 119, Indigo 215, 578l, Indigo 215, 578l, Peter Macdiarmid 221, JIM WATSON / AFP 577, Wireimage 578r; Guardian News and Media Ltd: Chris Riddle 123, Chris Riddle / *Observer* 180, 200, 497, 501, David Parkins 80, Chris Riddell 133, Chris Riddle / *Observer* 180, 200, 497, 501; http://www.un.org/Docs/sc/unsc_functions.html: 21; nisyndication.com: © The Sun 18 / 3 / 1997 142r, © The Sun 30 / 9 / 2009 142l; Pearson Education Ltd: Philip Langeskov 166, Royalty free image from CD 'Discovering the British Isles' 14; Press Association Images: Associated Press 491, Chris Radburn / PA / EMPICS 188, Empic Sports Photo Agency 258 (OUT), 410, EMPICS / Associated Press 289, © The Labour Party 527, PA Wire / EMPICS 45, 233, 257, 409; Rex Features: 461, Rex Features / Nils Jorgensen 144; Courtesy of Socialist Worker: 106; © Steve Bell / All Rights Reserved: 436, 504, 547, 559.

All other images © Pearson Education

In some instances we have been unable to trace the owners of copyright material, and we would appreciate any information that would enable us to do so.

PART 1
CONTEXT

CHAPTER 1

Politics in perspective

Bill Jones

There has never been a perfect government, because men have passions; and if they did not have passions, there would be no need for government.

Voltaire, *Politique et legislation*

The love of power is the love of ourselves.

William Hazlitt

I love fame; I love public reputation; I love to live in the eye of the country.

Benjamin Disraeli

Learning objectives

- To establish some understanding of the discipline of politics so that the subsequent contents of the book can be absorbed within its context.

- To explain and illustrate the concept of politics.

- To discuss the nature of politicians and the reasons why they choose their profession.

- To explain the importance of certain key concepts.

- To provide a brief overview of topics covered in the book.

■ The concept of politics defined and discussed

Politics is far from being a popular area of activity; politicians rank below those modern bêtes noire, estate agents, in some opinion polls. They are often held to be, among other failings: self-serving, venal, dishonest, power-obsessed people who are more likely to be a danger to society rather than its salvation. Politics and its politicians have changed over the years, both in its practices and the way it is regarded. Originally, it is fair to say, politicians were mostly people who had seized control by force and exercised it in their own interests. **Power** was often used merely to reflect the will and the glory of the chief conqueror and the changing nature of his whims.

Since those days a number of changes have occurred:

1 Rulers who are interested only in power for themselves, have become a recognised phenomenon against whom society must protect itself. Aristotle, the Greek philosopher argued that 'man is by nature a political animal' who required a robust system of law to be kept in check.

2 He also argued that government was best undertaken by a relatively disinterested group of well educated men, in effect a stratum of cultured gentlemen.

3 Two groups, long assumed to be excluded from the governing class – the very poor (originally slaves) and women – are no longer regarded as beyond the pale, though neither are as well represented as their numbers might justify.

4 Democracy – or a system whereby every citizen is entitled to some kind of say in their own government – has become widely accepted as desirable, especially in developed countries in Europe, North America and increasingly large parts of the rest of the world.

Defining politics

What precisely did Aristotle mean when he said man is by nature a *political* animal? The word is much used and most people think they know what it means but usually they cannot give a clear explanation. A typical reply might be that it's concerned with: 'Political parties, you know, Labour and Conservatives'.

Clearly this is factually correct but it does not take us very far towards a definition as many things have connections to political parties. No, to extract a clear definition we have to examine what things occur when 'politics' is definitely present.

For example, the following made-up news items can all be said to involve 'politics' at some level:

1 Father seeks to influence soccer manager to give his son a place in the team.

2 Chancellor ignores union claims for increased salaries.

3 Oil prices continue to rise as war spreads in Middle East.

4 Thousands demonstrate in favour of climate change measures.

The first example illustrates that politics operates at a 'micro' level; we speak of the 'politics' of the family or 'small groups'. The second is drawn from the mainstream of what we regard as 'political': a government minister taking a decision on something.

From these and the other two examples it can be seen that 'politics' entails:

■ a strong element of conflict and its resolution;

■ a struggle for scarce and finite resources;

■ the use of various methods of persuasion or pressure, to achieve a desired outcome.

So, if we can move towards a definition, it might be constructed as:

Politics is a process that seeks to manage or resolve conflicts of interest between people, usually in a peaceful fashion. In its general sense it can describe the interactions of any group of individuals, but in its specific sense it refers to the many and complex relationships that exist between state institutions and the rest of society.

■ Politicians and their ambition

'Politics is a spectator sport', writes Julian Critchley (1995: 80). An enduring question that exercises us spectators is 'Why are they doing it?' Dr Johnson, in his typically blunt fashion, said politics was 'nothing more nor less than a means of rising in the world'. But we know somehow that mere self-interest is not the whole truth. Peter Riddell of

BOX 1.1 IDEAS AND PERSPECTIVES

What does government do?

If politics is largely about government then what are the things that governments do? Anthony Giddens, in his *The Third Way*, provides the following analysis:

■ provide means for the representation of diverse interests;

■ offer a forum for reconciling the competing claims of those interests;

■ create and protect an open public sphere, in which unconstrained debate about policy issues can be carried on;

■ provide a diversity of public goods, including forms of collective security and welfare;

■ regulate markets in the public interest and foster market competition where monopoly threatens;

■ foster social peace through the provision of policing;

■ promote the active development of human capital through its core role in the education system;

■ sustain an effective system of law;

■ have a directly economic role, as a prime employer, in macro and micro intervention, plus the provision of infrastructure;

■ more controversially, perhaps, have a civilising aim – government reflects the widely held norms and values, but can also help shape them, in the educational system and elsewhere;

■ foster regional and trans-national alliances and pursue global goals.

Source: Giddens (1998: 47–8)

The Times, in his wonderfully perceptive book *Honest Opportunism*, looks at this topic in some detail. He quotes Disraeli, who perhaps offers us a more rounded and believable account of his interest in politics to his Shrewsbury constituents: 'There is no doubt, gentlemen, that all men who offer themselves as candidates for public favour have motives of some sort. I candidly acknowledge that I have and I will tell you what they are: I love fame; I love public reputation; I love to live in the eye of the country.'

Riddell also quotes F.E. Smith, who candidly gloried in the 'endless adventure of governing men'. For those who think that these statements were merely expressions of nineteenth-century romanticism, Riddell offers the example of Richard Crossman's comment that politics is a 'never ending adventure – with its routs and discomfitures, rushes and sallies', its 'fights for the fearless and goals for the eager'. He also includes Michael Heseltine, whom he once heard, irritated, asking at one of Jeffrey Archer's parties in 1986: 'Why *shouldn't* I be Prime Minister then?'

The tendency of politicians to explain their taste for politics in terms of concern for 'the people' is seldom sincere. In the view of Henry Fairlie this is nothing more than 'humbug'. William Waldegrave

agrees: 'Any politician who tells you he isn't ambitious is only telling you he isn't for some tactical reason; or more bluntly, telling a lie – I certainly wouldn't deny that I wanted ministerial office; yes, I'm ambitious.' As if more proof were needed, David Owen once said on television that 'Ambition drives politics like money drives the international economy.' Ambition, of course, is good for society only if it works for the general good; if it is purely self-inclined we end up with the likes of Saddam Hussein. As Edmund Burke noted: 'Ambition can creep as well as soar.' Politics is also an all-consuming obsession for some people. Writing in *The Guardian*, 11 March 2006, Michael Heseltine, that famously ambitious Conservative politician who narrowly missed gaining the top prize, probably spoke for all those bitten by the political bug when he said: 'Politics is a life sentence. It's an obsessive, all demanding, utterly fascinating, totally committing profession – stimulating, satisfying, stretching.'

Riddell goes on in his book – now dated but important as it discerned an important trend – to analyse how the ambitious political animal has slowly transformed British politics. He follows up and develops Anthony King's concept of the 'career politician', observing that a decreasing number of

BOX 1.2	The Hubris Syndrome

Symptoms of the 'hubris' syndrome are as follows:

- A narcissistic propensity to see one's world primarily as an arena in which to exercise power and seek glory.
- A disproportionate concern with image and presentation.
- A messianic manner.
- Excessive confidence in one's own judgement and contempt for advice.
- Exaggerated self-belief, bordering on omnipotence.
- A belief that one is accountable solely to history or god.
- Loss of contact with reality; often associated with progressive isolation.
- Restlessness, recklessness and impulsiveness.

*Extracted from Sarah Boseley's 'A Doctor Writes: Politicians' Pride is a Medical Disorder', The Guardian, 28 March 2009

MPs had backgrounds in professions, or 'proper jobs' in Westminster parlance, compared with those who centred their whole lives on politics. The jobs of these people were of secondary importance, merely anticipating or supporting the Westminster career. In 1951 the figure was 11 per cent; by 1992 it was 31 per cent. By contrast, the proportion of new MPs with 'proper jobs' fell from 80 per cent to 41 per cent.

Many of this new breed begin life as researchers for an MP or in a party's research department, then proceed to seek selection as a candidate and from there into parliament and from then on, ever onwards and upwards. The kind of MP who enters politics in later life is in steep decline; the new breed of driven young professionals has tended to dominate the field, proving firmer of purpose and more skilled in execution than those for whom politics is a later or learned vocation. The kind of businessman who achieves distinction in his field and then goes into politics is now a rarity rather than the familiar figure of the nineteenth century or the earlier decades of the twentieth century.

■ Ambition to hubris: a short journey?

Lord David Owen trained as a doctor and became an MP in 1966. He was made Labour Foreign Secretary at the precocious age of 38. His subsequent resignation from the party and involvement in the short-lived Social Democratic Party, denied him the senior role in government which many had predicted. There is little doubt his career was adversely

affected by the perception that he was an arrogant man, impatient with views with which he did not agree. So his 2007 book *The Hubris Syndrome: Bush, Blair and the Intoxication of Power* (he also wrote a paper on the same subject for the journal of the Royal Society of Psychiatrists in March 2009), made interesting reading for students of politics. He identifies the tendency to be intoxicated with power as an occupational hazard in politics and names as 'sufferers', Lloyd George, Neville Chamberlain, Thatcher, Blair and George Bush.

Owen, who admits to have exhibited elements of the syndrome himself, believes he has discerned a medical condition:

I have seen the isolation – this extraordinary pressure under which leaders in business or in politics live, with shortages of sleep – a generally very high-pressured existence. I'd liken it to . . . a long-distance runner. You go through a pain threshold and something changes. The public are way ahead. The man in the street starts to say the prime minister has 'lost it'. They put it all down to adrenaline. They see these people as supercharged.

■ Are politicians viewed generally with too much cynicism?

Certainly politics and its practitioners, according to many opinion polls, are seen in the present day, variously, as untrustworthy, self-seeking, power mad or cynical manipulators. My own view is that the cynicism has been excessive. Most politicians are quite decent people, trying hard to make a difference for the better. One of the problems is that in a 24-7 news age the media know that negative stories about political transgressions, whether sexual, financial or merely concerning incompetence, will attract great interest. The public loves to have someone to blame for things they do not like – high prices, poor public services, inflation, or whatever – and too often politicians are on the receiving end.

For example, Labour Home Secretary Jaqui Smith received a terrible press in late March 2009 when it transpired her husband had bought two 'blue' movies and charged them to his wife's Parliamentary expenses. The media really went to town; the minister was not directly involved but was at the same time embroiled in another well publicised dispute as to which was her 'main home' for expenses purposes. The accumulation of such stories tends to construct a default negative image of MPs, garnished perhaps by a national tradition or habit of sometimes savagely non-deferential, satirical criticism of our rulers. There is much evidence to suggest we are excessively cynical about our politicians but the history of their own behaviour makes it clear that they should be treated with, at minimum, a cautious discrimination. I think the closest to the truth I have found was encapsulated by Estelle Morris, a Labour Education Secretary who resigned in 2002. Upon being elevated to the Cabinet she asked a colleague what its members were 'really like' and received the reply:

The good news they are just like all the rest of us; but the bad news is . . . they are just like all the rest of us.

■ Key concepts in the study of politics

What is a concept?

A concept is usually expressed by a single word or occasionally by a phrase. Concepts are frequently general in nature, representing a specific function or category of objects. For example, the word 'table' usually refers to an individual human artefact, but it also embodies the whole idea of a table, which we might understand as a flat platform usually supported by legs and designed to have objects rested upon it. Without this definition a table would be a meaningless object; it is the concept that gives it purpose and function. As Andrew Heywood (1994: 4) explains:

a concept is more than a proper noun or the name of a thing. There is a difference between talking about a chair, a particular and unique chair, and holding the concept of a 'chair', the idea of a chair. The concept of a chair is an abstract notion, composed of the various features which give a chair its distinctive character – in this case, for instance, the capacity to be sat upon.

It follows, therefore, that the concept of a 'parliament' refers not to a specific parliament in a given country but to the generality of them – the abstract idea underlying them. By the same token, as we grow up, we come to attribute meaning and function to everyday objects through learning the appropriate concepts – plates, cups, windows, doors and so forth. Without these concepts we would be totally confused, surrounded by a mass of meaningless phenomena. In one sense concepts are the meaning we place on our surrounding world, impose on it, to enable us to deal with it. Similarly, we come to understand the political world through concepts that we learn from our reading, the media and our teachers. Over the years we come to extend them and refine them in order to achieve a sophisticated understanding, to become 'politically literate'. To use a slightly different analogy, concepts are like the different lenses opticians place in front of us when attempting to find the one that enables us to see more effectively. Without them we cannot bring a blurred world into focus; with them we achieve, or hope to achieve, some clarity and sharpness.

Power and authority and other ideas

These are two central ideas in the study of politics and need to be understood from the outset.

Power In essence this means the ability to get someone else to do what they otherwise would not have done. This could be achieved through direct coercion: threatening or delivering violence; pointing a gun at someone. While this relationship might be widely reflected in relations between states, it is rare, except in brutal tyrannies, for it to occur within organised states. Here there is a system for the management of disputes and usually this precludes the use of force or coercion, except as a background resort if all else fails.

Bachrach and Baratz (1981) argued that power is more subtle than this: decisions made by politicians not to do things were just as important as those actually made. If a matter is marginalised or ignored completely through the ability of someone or a group to exclude it, then considerable power is being exercised. Marx argued that those with control over wealth and its production effectively ruled society as they were able, through their control of the main institutions of society, to permeate it with the values upon which their own power rested. Thus, in his view, rich capitalists were able to win acceptance for their economic system as unarguable 'commonsense'.

Authority is the acceptance by someone of another's right to tell them what to do, for example a policeman or a judge. In other words this is power with the crucial added ingredient of legitimacy. For it to work the means whereby authority is granted – a process of discussion in an elected parliament – the related institutions must also be regarded as legitimate and authoritative. Few governments can survive without this characteristic.

Interests This term relates to what politicians are concerned to achieve. It could be more resources for a specific group in society, or more generally a class of people. It could be the reversal of a political decision – for example withdrawal from the EU – or it might be the obtaining of a place of status and power in government or merely an honour like a knighthood or a peerage. George Orwell in his dystopic novel, *Nineteen Eighty-Four*, suggests politicians are basically concerned to accumulate power, often for its own sake (see above, Politicians and their ambition). Certainly history can offer up any number of despots and tyrants – Hitler, Stalin, Saddam Hussein – who would fit this bill, but in a democracy, to some extent an antidote to political tyranny, safeguards are usually built in to prevent such a leader from gaining power.

Actors This term is often used to describe people who participate in politics: the *dramatis personae* of the process, which has often been likened to a performance or a game. Indeed senator Eugene McCarthy once wittily suggested that:

Being in politics is like being a football coach. You have to be smart enough to understand the game and dumb enough to think it's important.

Legislature This is the element of government in a democracy which is usually elected by a society to discuss and pass the laws by which it wishes to be governed. It is the election which provides the democratic authority the government needs to govern effectively. So in the case of the UK, it is Parliament, comprising the Commons, Lords and the Queen. It hardly needs saying that, at the time of writing, only the first element is democratically elected.

Executive This element is responsible for implementing the policies and laws produced by the legislature. In the Westminster model of government, the government is formed by the party winning a majority at a general election. In the US model, the President is elected separately and has a legitimacy similar to that of the legislature, producing a relationship between them which is essentially one of conflict and cooperation through negotiation.

Judiciary This is the part of government which interprets the laws, running the legal system of courts and the machinery of justice. It also handles appeals against alleged miscarriages of justice and rules whether laws are compatible with EU law which, since 1972, has taken precedence over domestic law by virtue of the terms of the Treaty of Paris.

Some political concepts are merely descriptive, for example 'election', but others embody a 'normative' quality – they contain an 'ought'. Such a concept is:

Democracy This notion of citizen involvement in government goes back to the Greeks who pioneered it in their city states. Churchill famously said of democracy that:

No one pretends that democracy is perfect or all wise. Indeed, it has been said that democracy is the worst form of government, except for all the others that have been tried from time to time.

In Britain it evolved out of conflicts between an absolute monarchy and an advisory council-cum-parliament reflecting the wealth all monarchs needed to rule. After centuries of gradually emerging authority the latter refused to endorse the royal will and a short but bitter civil war – in which parliamentary forces took the field under Oliver Cromwell against royalist armies – saw the king deposed and executed in 1649. In 1660 the monarchy was restored but had lost its supremacy to Parliament which was now set on a trajectory of increasing and decisive control over government business. The 1832 Reform Act laid the foundations for the democratic representation that has continued to evolve to the present day.

There can be no doubt our system is flawed:

1 Most voters are bored by current affairs and are functionally politically illiterate.

2 There is currently widespread distrust of politicians in the UK, scarcely allayed by the continuing behaviour of some of them.

3 Rousseau pointed out that the British electorate only has power on election days; once they have voted power is virtually immune from popular influence.

4 As Robert Michels observed with his 'iron law of oligarchy' outwardly democratic forms are usually subverted by small elites who come to control all the major institutions.

5 Voters' willingness to participate has been weakened by the complexity of some modern issues, for example, whether the UK should join the euro.

6 The media now dominates the conduct of democratic politics and politicians, with their media manipulators or 'spin doctors' have been able to disguise and obfuscate the real issues when it has suited them.

Representation This is another normative idea, central to democracy in that it enables large societies to be ruled to a degree, admittedly tenuous when few are interested in politics, by every citizen. The authors of the American Revolution adopted Reverend John Mayhew's resonant 1750 phrase – 'No Taxation without Representation' – as the banner of their cause because they believed the right to levy taxes could legitimately be obtained only through the consent of the American peoples' elected representatives.

Precisely what form representation takes is another matter as there is more than one possibility.

1 Altruistic: here someone will seek to protect and advance the interests of those represented. Whether such stated objectives, for example by MPs, are genuine, however, will always be a matter of judgement for voters.

2 'Delegate representative': this is when someone is obligated to represent voters' views in a defined way.

3 'Judgement representative': this version, wholly antithetical to item 2 above, is forever connected to the orator and theorist, Edmund Burke who, in 1774, told his electors in Bristol:

Your representative owes you, not his industry only, but his judgement; and he betrays, instead of serving you, if he sacrifices it to your opinion.

This approach risks being elitist in that it assumes the representative better knows what is good for his/her electors than they do.

4 'Revolutionary or "class" representative': this is usually associated with Marxist notions that bourgeois capitalism so blinds voters to the fact of their own exploitation, that only those revolutionaries who are aware of the proletariat's genuine interests can truly represent them.

5 'Educated representative': this is the view that voters require substantial knowledge of current affairs before they can properly vote. But if education is to be the criterion for representation, then why not select those who excel in competitive exams to represent us in government, like the mandarins of imperial China? (see Heywood 1994: 178–9).

6 Representation as microcosm: American President John Adams (1735–1826) argued that the legislature should be as exactly as possible 'a portrait in miniature of the people at large, as it should think, feel, reason and act like them'. This is a rather narrow view, however, which suggests a man cannot represent a woman or someone of one social class represent a voter from another.

In the British system representation is accepted as a fundamental requirement but no single interpretation is entrenched. Rather – perhaps in tune with Britain's pragmatic traditions – aspects of several of the above can be discerned. Apart from the occasional exceptions, British politicians are relatively non-corrupt and take their representative duties seriously; Tony Benn has argued for the delegate approach to representation, but for his fellow parliamentarians the Burkean view is the more accepted; the revolutionary approach has never been widely supported in Britain; and, while most MPs are well educated, it is not thought that a high level of education is an essential prerequisite either for an MP or for a voter.

Human nature This idea is central to the study of politics, that how human beings behave depends on their essential natures, so philosophers have speculated upon its essence. Thomas Hobbes, for example, was pessimistic: he felt that without the protective constraints of civilised society, the selfish nature of human beings would make life 'solitary, poor, nasty, brutish and short'. There would be no security of property, 'no thine and mine distinct; but only that to be everyman's, that he can get; and for so long as he can keep it'. Others did not agree. Rousseau argued that it was the evils of modern society which were responsible for its own dysfunctions. Karl Marx too was an optimist on this topic, arguing that mankind was much better than it appeared because of the corrupting effects of the harsh economic system of privately owned capital. Marx believed that human nature was a rogue product of a sick society asserting: 'Environment determines consciousness'. It followed that changing the social environment for the better would improve human nature too.

Charles Darwin's theory of evolution encouraged some, like Herbert Spencer to argue that this notion of the 'survival of the fittest' justified capitalism as the way in which the species was developing itself and to argue against government interference with the 'natural order' of things. But then came Sigmund Freud.

Freud argued that man is driven by instinctual urges underlying the desire to experience pleasure and the, often conflicting, need to adjust to social reality. To live any kind of ordered life excludes the continuance of the pleasure principle, so drives are repressed and sublimated into socially useful activities like work and achievement:

Sublimation of instinct is an essentially conspicuous feature of cultural development: it is what makes it possible for the higher psychical activities, in [the] scientific, artistic or ideological, to play such an important part in civilised life.

Herbert Marcuse agreed with Freud about repression but argued that modern society, especially class differences, generated too much of it and that a revolution was needed to correct the imbalance.

Nationalism It would be wrong to assume that nationalism has always been around. The extension of loyalty to a common ethnicity within a common territory, all sharing a common history and culture, including struggle against common foes arrived around 250 years ago and was facilitated greatly by industrialisation and modern economies. In the case of England it probably arrived earlier, around Elizabethan times; in Shakespeare's *Henry V* we have the king exhorting, 'Cry God for Harry, England and St George!'

The French Revolution allied the notion that everyone is endowed with certain natural rights with the right to self-determination for a national 'community' of people and this helped breath fire into a number of national movements in the nineteenth century including those of Belgium, Greece and Poland, not to mention the unifying nationalism of Italy and Germany. England, and its wider expression, Britain, has tended to pride itself on not

---

BOX 1.3   IDEAS AND PERSPECTIVES

Human nature – Milgram's experiment

The experimental psychologist Stanley Milgram conducted a historic experiment which suggested that – even though we might think it's the last thing we might do – everyone is capable of being sadistically cruel in response to presumed authority. He set up a situation in which people, more or less at random, were invited to join an alleged test involving someone tied to a chair. The participant was asked by a man in a white coat who appeared to have scientific authority to ask the pinioned person some questions and to administer electric shocks if the answers were wrong. The subject of the test was, in fact, an actor who shouted and writhed in response to the shocks. The participant, however, was told to continue with the shocks notwithstanding the subject's screams right up to an allegedly fatal level of 450 volts. Most of them did so without serious complaint. This experiment, essentially into human nature, showed, somewhat bleakly, that most of us are capable of behaving like guards in concentration camps if we accept the authority of the person directing us to apply the sadistic or even fatal force.

being especially nationalistic and on this side of the Atlantic, American patriotism is often seen as rather too overt and crude. Yet fierce sentiments do exist just below the surface, as the raucous support for the national football team and the 'Euro-scepticism' expressed towards the EU demonstrate.

Class Every society becomes stratified sooner or later into those with power and those without. The Greeks and Romans had slaves; Saxon and Norman nobility in England had serfs and peasants working their estates; and by the nineteenth century there were great masses of people working in factories owned by a small group of super-rich business men. For Karl Marx the formation of different classes and the consequent conflict between them was the motive force of history, constantly changing the present society into the future one. Studying British society in the industrial era, he discerned a small property-owning middle class (or *bourgeoisie*) controlling the lives of a vast new working class (or *proletariat*). His analysis was so profound, detailed and acute he immediately influenced thinking on society all over Europe, yet he did much more.

Marx believed the duty of a philosopher was not just to study society but to *change* it. He went on to argue that in the age of capitalism the rich would so exploit the poor that in the end the latter would rise up, cast off their shackles and commence a process whereby members of the working class would seize control of their own destinies. It followed, according to Marx that the duty of progressive people everywhere was to assist this historical process and help provide the vanguard of the working-class revolution.

Today the working class has halved in size since the early twentieth century and the middle class has burgeoned. John Major, when he became Prime Minister in 1990, tried to argue that Britain was now 'classless', but few accept this complacent analysis which so favours the group in power. Andrew Adonis and Stephen Pollard, in their book *A Class Act* (1997), show how a new 'super class' has emerged on US-style salaries and how another group – sometimes called an 'underclass' – has emerged at the bottom, living in poverty. Attempts by New Labour since 1997 to remove class inequalities have entailed massive expenditures on welfare services but the evidence is that the inequalities remain huge: only the rate of change has been arrested. Class is still very much a live political issue in the UK.

Freedom This elusive concept divides into 'freedom from' and 'freedom to': negative and positive freedom. It is imperative that people are free from the fear, persecution and imprisonment of a tyrannical regime but also important that people are not prevented by circumstances – birth, education, poverty – from having the chance to realise their potential as human beings. While both left and right can agree on the avoidance of the former, they differ sharply over the latter.

It was the liberal philosopher T.H. Green (see Wemde 2004) who first argued, in modern times, for 'positive freedom'. He believed that anyone prevented from realising his or her full potential was in a real sense unfree. He defined freedom as the ability of people to 'make the best and most of themselves'. If they were not able to do this then they were not free. This definition, so attractive to socialists, in theory opened up the whole field of government intervention, especially via welfare services. Such a formulation of the concept also carries with it the clear implication that wealth should be redistributed to give more chances to more people.

Opponents of this approach, echoing classical liberals, claim that it is self-defeating: the government takes away the individual's freedom to improve his or her lot; it takes away the freedom of employers to employ workers at rates the market requires; it is part, in fact, of a subtle, incremental tyranny. In the twentieth century, Friedrich Hayek (2001) and the economist Milton Friedman (1962) argued this case passionately, insisting that such a position was the 'road to servitude'. Sir Keith Joseph, a disciple of both thinkers, stated flatly that 'poverty is not unfreedom'.

Defenders insist that unless individuals are empowered to realise their personal potential, then they are not truly free. They also argue that the kind of freedom right-wingers and classical liberals want is the freedom of the strong to dominate the weak, or, as R.H. Tawney (1931) vividly put it, 'the freedom of the pike is death to the minnows'.

Equality This is another two-pronged concept, comprising 'equality of opportunity' and 'equality of outcome'. The left prefer the latter, the right the former. Both agree on the need for equality of opportunity and both sign up to it in respect of the law, gender, race and career choices; the problem lies with the 'outcome' bit. The right maintain that we already have full equality in respect of all the items mentioned. They cite the fact that anyone can proceed educationally, whatever their circumstances, provided they are dedicated and put in the effort. The left counter that the claim is disingenuous in that, while the odd one or two might manage to climb to the top from very humble beginnings, the majority fail miserably.

Meanwhile, those born in comfortable and supportive middle-class families, not only do much better in terms of education and career but also in terms of gaining positions of power in society: director's boardrooms, senior ranks of the armed forces, journalism, civil service and academe not to mention Parliament and the Cabinet. If the analogy of a race is used children from poor backgrounds, with less caring parents, start it from some distance behind those from privileged backgrounds.

Left-wingers have argued that the 'playing field' should be level for everyone and have urged more equal salaries or redistribution via taxation and state benefits. This wins the right-wing riposte that such actions remove incentives: if people can survive easily on benefits, they will not feel the need to work and improve themselves. In consequence society will be the poorer and those who have worked hard will see their reward highly taxed so that the lazy can benefit.

Social justice Who should get what in society? This concept causes as much disagreement and very similar debate as that over equality. Marx's ideal communist society was supposed to deliver: 'From each according to his ability, to each according to his needs.'

At the heart of this notion of social justice is that large accumulations of wealth, juxtaposed by poverty and ill health, are not justifiable. It follows, according to this approach, that wealth should be redistributed in society and, indeed, between nations. On the other hand, even left-wing theorists agree that some economic inequality is necessary to make the economic system work, so the real debate concerns how much redistribution is needed to achieve justice.

One influential thinker on the Left has been John Rawls, whose book *A Theory of Justice* (1999) has occasioned much debate. He asked us to consider what distribution of goods we would endorse if we were rational people planning a society but, crucially, were unaware of our own capacities. In this way it would be possible to prevent people from

favouring their own talents and strengths, for example preventing a clever person from advocating a meritocracy or a physically strong person a free-for-all society. This ensures that any decisions reached would be neutral. Rawls argues that all would agree on the greatest possible degree of liberty in which people would be able to develop their talents and life plans. In addition, however, Rawls posits the 'difference principle', whereby he maintains that social and economic inequalities – differences in wealth, income and status – are only just if they work to the advantage of the most disadvantaged members of society and only if they can be competed for fairly by all. Rawls argues that in such a situation rational people would choose, through a sense of insecurity, a society in which the position of the worst-off is best protected; this would be a market economy in which wealth is redistributed through tax and welfare systems up to the point when it becomes a disincentive to the economic activity. (It has to be said, however, that some poor people oppose high taxation and the benefits public expenditure can give to the poor because they hope one day to be rich and do not wish their bounty to be reduced by the depredations of the taxman.)

On the right Robert Nozick (1974) has been an influential theorist, arguing that wealth is justifiable if it is justly acquired in the first place (for example has not been stolen) and has been justly transferred from one person to another. He goes on to argue that if these conditions have not been met the injustice should be rectified. Nozick rejects the notion of 'social justice', the idea that inequality is somehow morally wrong. If transfers of wealth take place between one group in society and another, it should be on the basis of private charity, made on the basis of personal choice. But Nozick's views do not necessarily bolster right-wing views on property as the rectification principle could imply the redistribution of much wealth, especially when it is considered that so much of the wealth of the West has been won at the expense of plunder and slavery in Third World countries.

■ Analysing the political process

To illustrate some of the concepts used in the understanding of the political process a hypothetical situation is posited below and its implications considered.

BOX 1.4 BRITAIN IN CONTEXT

Conceptual dissonance

The former publisher and infamous fraud, Robert Maxwell, once wrote a series of hagiographic studies of East European leaders which sold extremely well in their own countries but showed a strange disinclination to fly from the shelves anywhere else. In the book he wrote about the notorious Romanian leader, Nicolae Ceaușescu, Maxwell, in an interview incorporated into the text, asks 'Mister President, tell me, why do your people love you so?' This question and its unperturbed reply illustrate the fact that different people have different takes on commonly understood ideas. Maxwell, driven by self-interest, probably knew the man was a vicious autocrat; Ceaușescu in turn probably genuinely believed he was loved, as his famous look of incomprehension indicated when crowds in front of his palace began angrily to interrupt one of his interminable speeches in 1989, a short time before he was deposed and shot. Both men, totally absorbed in their own false worlds, no doubt perceived the world differently from the people they exploited. But such 'conceptual dissonance' tends to occur between nations as well as between different kinds of people.

In many cases this flows from the vastly different histories experienced by countries. France, for example, has never quite recovered from its 1789 revolution founded upon the great ideas of 'Liberty, Equality and Fraternity'. Consequently, new arrivals to France have become citizens of the republic on an equal standing with everyone else. Such legal even-handedness is wholly admirable, one might think, but in the autumn of 2005 its limits were exposed when French leaders, especially Jacques Chirac, seemed to refuse to believe that the young men of the Muslim faith, many of North African provenance, who were rioting in the suburbs of Paris and other big cities, suffered from severe racial discrimination and disproportionate economic hardship. So deeply ingrained was this belief in equality that no separate social statistics were available regarding France's constituent minorities. They were just the same so there were no separate figures.

Another example of conceptual dissonance is provided by the difference between Western and Muslim societies. In the West free speech is a hallowed principle, defended even if it offends some people holding deep religious beliefs. For fundamentalist Muslims such tolerance is not possible. Anything which reflects what they see as disrespect for the prophet Mohammed they interpret not as merely a difference of viewpoint or maybe satirical humour, but as unforgivable blasphemy. The case of the Danish cartoons published in a right-wing newspaper in November 2005 well illustrated this difference in perception, only one of many between the two cultures.

In Japan, still influenced by its ancient culture, the world is also perceived in a different way from in the West. For example, social hierarchy is deemed in some situations to be as important as equality, so that people seated at a dinner table will place the person believed by a group to be the most senior and important in the place of honour while other guests will be placed according to their perceived rank and place in society.

The USA, created in the heat of a revolution against the perceived tyranny of George III, places huge stress on the need for democracy. This helps explain why the USA elects far more public officials than the UK; for example, dog and rat catchers, as well as mayors and sheriffs, are elected in America but not in the UK. It might also explain why President George W. Bush and his advisers believed so passionately in disseminating democracy in the Middle East. They believed it would lead to greater moderation, acceptance of the West and happiness for the Arab citizens concerned. For a long while it seemed this assumption had tragically misfired in the case of Iraq, invaded in 2003, whereupon it descended into chaos for several years. At the time of writing (2009) Iraq seems relatively peaceful but the cost has arguably been prohibitive.

The Mother of Parliaments: a model for many other legislatures
Source: Steve Allan/Brand X Pictures

A major national newspaper breaks a story that Kevin Broadstairs, a Conservative cabinet minister, has been having an affair with an actress. The PM issues a statement in support of his colleague and old friend from university days. However, more embarrassing details hit the front pages of the tabloids, including the fact that the same actress has also been carrying on with a senior member of the Opposition. The 1922 Committee meets, and influential voices call for a resignation.

This not unfamiliar situation can be analysed as follows:

■ *Interests*: The PM needs to appear above suspicion of 'favouritism' but also needs to show that he is loyal and not a hostage to either groups of backbenchers or the press. Broadstairs obviously has an interest in keeping his job, retaining respect within his party and saving his rocky marriage. The governing party needs to sustain its reputation as the defender of family values. The press wishes to sell more newspapers.

■ *Actors*: In this situation are potentially numerous: the PM, Broadstairs, the actress, her former lovers, backbench MPs, editors, television producers, the Opposition, Mrs Broadstairs and (unfortunately) her children, the Church, feminists and anyone else willing to enter the fray.

■ *Power*: The power relationship in these circumstances is naturally influenced by the ability of each side to enforce threats. The PM has the power of political life or death over the minister but would like to show his strength by resisting resignation calls; Broadstairs effectively has no power in this situation and is largely dependent on the PM's goodwill and possible press revelations.

■ *Authority*: No one questions the PM's right to sack Broadstairs. However, the press's right to force resignations is very much resisted by politicians. The ultimate authority of the governing party to call for the minister's head is also not questioned.

■ *Political process*: Will Broadstairs survive? Our minister in this situation is a hostage to the discretion of his mistress and other people either involved or perceiving an interest in the affair.

The outcome will depend on the following:

■ *Political will*: How prepared are the PM and Broadstairs to stand firm against resignation calls? How long could he hold out once the 1922 Committee has given the thumbs down? How long would this committee stay silent as it saw the issue eroding voter support? How effective would Broadstairs' enemies in his own party be in hastening his downfall?

■ *Influence*: How much influence does the PM have in Fleet Street? The evidence suggests that political sympathies of a paper count for nothing when a really juicy scandal is involved. Even right-wing papers carried full coverage of sleaze stories relating to John Major's government. Does Broadstairs have a body of support on the back benches, or is he a 'loner'?

■ *Manipulation*: How good is the minister at coping with the situation? Can he make a clean breast of it, like Paddy Ashdown regarding his extramarital affair in January 1992, and survive with reputation arguably enhanced? Can he handle hostile press conferences and media interviews (as David Mellor did with aplomb – though much good it did him)? Can the minister call up old favours on the back benches?

Let's suppose that things quieten down for a few days, the PM defends his friend at Question Time and the wife says she'll stand by her man. If this was all there was to it, Broadstairs would survive and live to fight again, albeit with his reputation and prospects damaged. We saw that in the somewhat similar David Mellor case the revelations kept on coming (much to public amusement and his embarrassment), but the crucial revelations concerned acceptance of undeclared favours by the minister. After this, backbench calls for a resignation and an excited press ensured that Mellor had to go.

The political process in this case is a little haphazard and depends to some extent on each day's tabloid headlines. It will also depend on the PM's judgement as to when the problem has ceased to be an individual one and has escalated to the point when his own judgement and the political standing of his party are in question. Alastair Campbell, Blair's famously powerful press secretary, reckoned that if public criticism of a minister continued after fourteen days then, even if blameless, the minister would have to resign as such publicity prevents the minister from functioning as the government requires. Once that point has been reached it is only a matter of time before the minister's career is over. There was much in ex-Prime Minister Harold Wilson's tongue-in-cheek comment that 'much of politics is presentation, and what isn't, is timing'.

■ Plan of the book

This opening chapter has discussed the meaning of politics, the nature of politicians and key concepts in the study of politics. The rest of the book, organised in six parts, follows directly from the definition we adopted on page 4.

Politics is about conflicting interests: Part 1 provides the historical, social and economic contexts from which such conflicts emerge in Britain; Part 2, on ideology, examines the intellectual basis of such conflicts. Politics is centrally concerned with how state institutions manage or resolve conflicts within society: Parts 3, 4 and 5 deal respectively with the representative, legislative (law making) and executive (law implementing) processes whereby such management takes place or is attempted. Finally, Part 6 examines how these institutions handle the major policy areas.

Chapter summary

This introductory chapter has explained that politics is about the management and resolution of conflicts by what people want to do and achieve. The study of the subject focuses on how this process is performed, especially the way individuals relate to the state. Key concepts in the study of politics are explained: power, authority, equality, representation, democracy and social justice.

Discussion points

■ Why do you think people go into politics and make it their life's work?

■ Think of a typically political scenario and analyse it in the way demonstrated in the chapter.

■ Which interpretation of equality and social justice seem most appealing to you?

Further reading

Crick's classic work (2000) is essential reading, as is Duverger (1966). Leftwich (1984) is worth reading as an easy-to-understand initiation, and Laver (1983) repays study too. Renwick and Swinburn (1989) is useful on concepts, though Heywood (1994) is by any standards a brilliant textbook. Axford *et al.* (1997) is also well worth looking into. Riddell (1993) is both highly perceptive and very entertaining – a must for anyone wondering if the subject is for them. O'Rourke (1992) is a humorous but insightful book. Oliver (1992) is an amusing collection of silly quotations from politicians. Michael Moran's book (Moran 2005) offers a subtle and authoritative introduction.

Bibliography

Adonis, A. and Pollarch, S. (1997) *A Class Act: The Myth of Britain's Classless Society* (Hamish Hamilton Ltd).

All, A.R. and Peters, B.G. (2000) *Modern Politics and Government* (Macmillan), Chapter 1.

Axford, B., Browning, G.K., Huggins, R., Rosamond, B. and Turner, J. (1997) *Politics: An Introduction* (Routledge).

Bachrach, P. and Baratz, M. (1981) 'The two faces of power', in F.G. Castles, D.J. Murray and D.C. Potter (eds) *Decision, Organisations and Society* (Penguin).

Crick, B. (2000) *In Defence of Politics* (Continuum).

Critchley, J. (1995) *A Bag of Boiled Sweets* (Faber and Faber).

Dearlove, J. and Saunders, P. (2000) *Introduction to British Politics* (Polity Press), Chapter 1.

Duverger, M. (1966) *The Idea of Politics* (Methuen).

Friedman, M. (1962) *Free to Choose: A Personal Statement* (Secker and Warburg).

Gamble, A. (2000) *Politics and Fate* (Polity Press).

Giddens, A. (1998) *The Third Way* (Polity Press).

Hague, R., Harrop, M. and Breslin, S. (2000) *Comparative Government and Politics* (Palgrave).

Hayek, F.A. (2001) *The Road to Serfdom* (Routledge Classics).

Healey, D. (1990) *The Time of My Life* (Penguin).

Heywood, A. (1994) *Political Ideas and Concepts* (Macmillan).

Jones, B. (2005) *The Dictionary of British Politics* (Manchester University Press).

Kingdom, J. (1999) *Government and Politics in Britain* (Polity Press).

Lasswell, H. (1936) *Politics, Who Gets What, When, How?* (McGraw-Hill).

Laver, M. (1983) *Invitation to Politics* (Martin Robertson).

Leftwich, A. (1984) *What is Politics? The Activity and its Study* (Blackwell).

Minogue, K. (2000) *Politics: A Very Short Introduction* (Oxford University Press).

Moran, M. (2005) *Politics and Governance in the UK* (Palgrave).

Nozick, Robert (1974) *Anarchy, State and Utopia* (Blackwell).

Oliver, D. (1992) *Political Babble* (Wiley).

O'Rourke, R.J. (1992) *Parliament of Whores* (Picador).

Orwell, G. (1955) *Nineteen Eighty-Four* (Penguin).

Owen, David (2007) *The Hubris Syndrome: Bush, Blair and the Intoxication of Power* (Politicos).

Rawls, John (1999) *A Theory of Justice* (Revised edn) (Belknap).

Renwick, A. and Swinburn, I. (1989) *Basic Political Categories*, 2nd edn (Hutchinson).

Riddell, P. (1993) *Honest Opportunism* (Hamish Hamilton).

Robins, S. (2001) *The Ruling Asses* (Prion).

Tawney, R.H. (1931) *Equality* (Unwin).

Wemde, Ben (2004) *T.H. Green's Theory of Positive Freedom: From Metaphysics to Political Theory* (Imprint Academic).

Zakaria, F. (2004) *The Future of Freedom* (Norton).

Useful websites

British Politics page: www.ukpol.co.uk

Euro Consortium for Political Research: www.essex.ac.uk/ecpr

International Political Science Association: www.ipsa-aisp.org/

Political Science resources: www.socsciresearch.com/r12html

UK Political Studies Association: www.psa.ac.uk

Blogs

Bill Jones's blog: http://skipper59.blogspot.com/

Norman Geras: http://normblog.typepad.com

Guido Fawkes: http://5thNovember.blogspot.com/

CHAPTER 2

Britain, the world, and Europe[1]

Oliver Daddow

Learning objectives

- To understand the nature of Britain's key international relationships.
- To understand the key ideas that have shaped British foreign policy.
- To understand contemporary debates about Britain being a 'force for good' in the world.

[1] Thanks to Jeremy McIlwaine at the Bodleian Library Oxford for helping me access Churchill's 1948 Party Conference speech.

Introduction

Britain is a global political, diplomatic and economic actor by virtue of its imperial history, membership of key international organisations and London's position as a leading financial centre. With its vast web of connections, however, have come real and lasting debates about the most appropriate role for Britain in the world, especially since decolonisation after the Second World War and the turn to Europe as a forum in which Britain tries to exercise global influence through its foreign policy. Some suggest Britain should safeguard its national interest by working more closely with its partners in the European Union. Others suggest Britain should continue to think and act globally, particularly through cultivating the 'special relationship' with the United States. In reality very few British leaders have wanted to make a decision in favour of one over the other. Although their language may change, it is clear that Prime Ministers of all the main political parties continue to see Britain as a 'force for good' in the world by virtue of working the country's Commonwealth, US and EU connections.

■ Britain's global outlook

Membership of many of the leading regional and global international organisations gives Britain a prominence and influence that very few other states can match. The Foreign and Commonwealth Office currently manages 260 diplomatic posts in 145 countries around the world, ranging from large embassies to smaller consulates (FCO 2009a). France is the only other state apart from Britain that is a member of all the institutions shown in Figure 2.1. However, being a member of a given international organisation is not necessarily the same thing as being able to exert great influence over that international organisation. Nor do the British seem as comfortable working with their partners in some international organisations as they do in others. For example, Britain was a founder member, and enthusiastic advocate, of the United Nations (UN) and the North Atlantic Treaty Organization (NATO) but was rather more hesitant about joining what since 1993 has been the European Union (EU), formerly the European Economic Community (EEC) to which Britain acceded in 1973. Understanding the organisational framework within which Britain's global relationships play out helps us to understand both the scope and limits of Britain's role in the world. It also provides crucial insights into the debates that surround the nature and conduct of British foreign policy today.

The United Nations

Britain was one of the founder members of the UN in October 1945 and has an Ambassador permanently stationed at the UN headquarters in New York, heading the UK's Mission to the United Nations. Along with France, the US, Russia and China, Britain is one of five Permanent Members of the UN Security Council (the P5 of the UNSC), giving it a crucial role in helping the UN maintain peace and security around the globe, through diplomacy, investigation and the deployment of military force. Ten other states are voted onto the Security Council for a period of two years each, making for a total of fifteen states on the UNSC at any one time: the core or permanent members circled by ten non-permanent members (UN 2008–9) (Figure 2.2).

Each member of the P5 has an effective veto over substantive issues that come before the Security Council, giving each of them huge sway in core UN discussions and debates (Table 2.1). Since the establishment of the P5 the heaviest users of the veto (Global Policy Forum undated a) have been Russia (124 times) and the US (82 times). This reflects the global politico-strategic context of the Cold War which played out between the two blocs led by each power for nearly fifty years after the establishment of the UN. Britain has used the veto 32 times, the last time in December 1989 along with France and the US over a resolution on the situation

UN

Afghanistan	India*	Somalia	Syria	Uganda*
Algeria	Indonesia	South Africa*	Tanzania*	Uruguay
Angola	Iran	St Kitts and Nevis*	Thailand	Vanuatu*
Antigua and Barbuda*	Iraq	St Lucia*	Togo	Venezuela
Argentina	Israel	St Vincent and the Grenadines*	Tonga*	Vietnam
Bahamas*	Ivory Coast	Sri Lanka*	Trinidad and Tobago*	Yemen
Bahrain	Jamaica*	Sudan	Tunisia	Zambia*
Bangladesh*	Jordan	Suriname	Tuvalu*	Zimbabwe*
Barbados*	Kenya*	Swaziland*	UAE	
Belize*	Kiribati*			
Benin	Kuwait			
Bhutan	Laos			
Bolivia	Lebanon			
Botswana*	Lesotho*			
Brazil	Liberia			
Brunei*	Libya			
Burkina Faso	Madagascar			
Burma	Malawi*			
Burundi	Malaysia*			
Cambodia	Maldives*			
Cameroon*	Mali			
Cape Verde	Marshall Islands			
Central African Republic	Mauritania			
Chad	Mauritius*			
Chile	Micronesia			
China	Mongolia			
Colombia	Morocco			
Comoros	Mozambique*			
Congo	Namibia*			
Congo (DR)	Nauru*			
Costa Rica	Nepal			
Cuba	Nicaragua			
Djibouti	Niger			
Dominica*	Nigeria*			
Dominican Republic	North Korea			
East Timor	Oman			
Ecuador	Pakistan*			
Egypt	Palau			
El Salvador	Panama			
Equatorial Guinea	Papua New Guinea*			
Eritrea	Paraguay			
Ethiopia	Peru			
Fiji*	Philippines			
Gabon	Qatar			
Gambia*	Rwanda			
Ghana*	Samoa*			
Grenada*	São Tomé and Principe			
Guatemala	Saudi Arabia			
Guinea	Senegal			
Guinea-Bissau	Seychelles*			
Guyana*	Sierra Leone*			
Haiti	Singapore*			
Honduras	Solomon Islands*			

OECD

Australia*   Mexico
Japan ▲   New Zealand*
               South Korea

Switzerland   Holy See

NATO

		EU
Canada*▲	Belgium	Austria
Iceland	Denmark	Finland
Norway	**France**▲	Ireland
Turkey	**Germany**▲	Sweden
United States ▲	Greece	
	Italy ▲	
	Luxembourg	
	Netherlands	
	Portugal	
	Spain	
	United Kingdom*▲	
	Czech Republic	
	Hungary	
	Poland	
	Slovakia	

Bulgaria	Estonia	Cyprus*
Romania	Latvia	Malta*
	Lithuania	
	Slovenia	

Albania	Kazakhstan	San Marino
Andorra	Kyrgyzstan	Serbia and Montenegro
Armenia	Liechtenstein	Tajikistan
Azerbaijan	Macedonia	Turkmenistan
Belarus	Moldova	Ukraine
Bosnia and Herzegovina	Monaco	Uzbekistan
Croatia	**Russia ▲**	
Georgia		

OSCE

* = Commonwealth Countries   ▲ = G8 Countries   **Bold red type** = Permanent Members of the UN Security Council
.... For EU and NATO enlargements in 2004

Figure 2.1 Membership of international organisations as at March 2006

Source: Foreign and Commonwealth Office (2006) *Active Diplomacy in a Changing World*,
http://collections.europarchive.org/tna/20080205132101/fco.gov.uk/Files/kfile/ozintpriorities2006Chapt2.pdf

UN SECURITY COUNCIL | Functions and Powers

UN Home | Security Council Home | Daily Programme | Webcast

Under the Charter, the functions and powers of the Security Council are:
- to maintain international peace and security in accordance with the principles and purposes of the United Nations;
- to investigate any dispute or situation which might lead to international friction;
- to recommend methods of adjusting such disputes or the terms of settlement;
- to formulate plans for the establishment of a system to regulate armaments;
- to determine the existence of a threat to the peace or act of aggression and to recommend what action should be taken;
- to call on Members to apply economic sanctions and other measures not involving the use of force to prevent or stop aggression;
- to take military action against an aggressor;
- to recommend the admission of new Members;
- to exercise the trusteeship functions of the United Nations in 'strategic areas';
- to recommend to the General Assembly the appointment of the Secretary-General and, together with the Assembly, to elect the Judges of the International Court of Justice.

Figure 2.2 UN Security Council: functions and powers
Source: http://www.un.org/Docs/sc/unsc_functions.html

Table 2.1 Use of the veto in the P5

Period	China*	France	Britain	US	USSR Russia	Total
Total	6	18	32	82	124	261
2008	1	–	–	–	1	2
2007	1	–	–	–	1	2
2006	–	–	–	2	–	2
2005	–	–	–	–	–	–
2004	–	–	–	2	1	3
2003	–	–	–	2	–	2
2002	–	–	–	2	–	2
2001	–	–	–	2	–	2
2000	–	–	–	–	–	0
1999	1	–	–	–	–	1
1998	–	–	–	–	–	0
1997	1	–	–	2	–	3
1996	–	–	–	–	–	0
1986–95	–	3	8	24	2	37
1976–85	–	9	11	34	6	60
1966–75	2	2	10	12	7	33
1956–65	–	2	3	–	26	31
1946–55	(1*)	2	–	–	80	83

* Between 1946 and 1971 the Chinese seat on the Security Council was occupied by the Republic of China (Taiwan), which used the veto only once, to block Mongolia's application for membership in 1955.

in Panama. Other resolutions vetoed by the UK in the 1980s included such issues as sanctions against South Africa, where Britain exercised its veto on several occasions, and over the Falkland Islands (Global Policy Forum undated b). We can see that P5 members tend to use the veto where they deem resolutions to be potentially damaging to their vital national interest, usually but not always defined in security terms.

The European Union

Like many of the international organisations considered in this chapter, the origins of the EU lay in the determination of leading nation states after 1945 to avoid another slide into war that had occurred twice in the first half of the twentieth century. The wider security context was also an important stimulus and was noticeable in American policy-making circles (see Ruane 2000). With the emerging Cold War between the superpowers, Russia and the US, Washington strategists wanted to see Europeans building up their defences as a means of deterring a potential attack from the East, in the event that the 'cold' war turned to 'hot' war. Attention became fixed on how to solve the 'German question' and in particular how to tie Germany into an institutional framework that would allow it to recover economically and politically without becoming once more an aggressive, expansionist power destabilising the continental landmass of Europe. In each of the key steps on the road to closer integration in western Europe we see economic means being used for political ends. The assumption of this 'functionalist' approach to integration (Haas 1958) is that creating interdependence between nation-states is a good way of helping them see how damaging the selfish actions of one state can be to a whole community of states; furthermore, by working together in institutions states can achieve collectively what they would not be able to achieve alone.

Various British Conservative and Labour governments decided to remain aloof from Europe's integrationist experiments for over twenty-five years, finally joining in 1973. Despite giving rhetorical support to the general idea of a 'United Europe', they were reluctant to involve themselves in a project they saw leading to a progressively more constrictive process leading to supranational political union. Britain was, however, a founder member of the intergovernmental Council of Europe, which it established in May 1949 with nine other

- to protect human rights, pluralist democracy and the rule of law;

- to promote awareness and encourage the development of Europe's cultural identity and diversity;

- to find common solutions to the challenges facing European society: such as discrimination against minorities, xenophobia, intolerance, bioethics and cloning, terrorism, trafficking in human beings, organised crime and corruption, cybercrime, violence against children;

- to consolidate democratic stability in Europe by backing political, legislative and constitutional reform.

Figure 2.3 Aims of the Council of Europe
Source: Council of Europe 2008

states: Belgium, Denmark, France, Ireland, Italy, Luxembourg, the Netherlands, Norway and Sweden (Figure 2.3). In September 1959 the European Court of Human Rights was established in Strasbourg to ensure that states meet the obligations they sign up to when they join the Council.

In Britain, support for the Council of Europe was cross-party and came from such influential figures as wartime leader Winston Churchill (1946) and Labour's Foreign Secretary at the time of its establishment, Ernest Bevin, who said it would inspire 'something new and hopeful in European life' (Bevin 1949).

Steps to create a supranational European entity that would challenge the sovereignty of member states to make their own legal, political and economic decisions did not meet with such support from Britain. The Clement Attlee Labour government of 1945–51 decided not to take Britain into the European Coal and Steel Community (ECSC). The brainchild of French Foreign Minister Robert Schuman and formally created by the Paris Treaty of April 1951, the ECSC aimed to take the two industries vital to a nation's war-making capacity out of national hands and put it under control of a European decision-making body, the High Authority. Its founder members were 'the Six': France, Germany, Italy, Belgium, the Netherlands and Luxembourg. When the Conservatives were returned to power under Winston Churchill in 1955 there were high hopes in western Europe that he would alter Labour's negativity towards European integration. However, the Conservatives continued the extra-European focus in the nation's postwar foreign policy by keeping Britain out of the European Economic Community (EEC), which under the Treaty of Rome in March 1957 expanded co-operation to other sectors of their economies. Instead, in 1960, Britain helped found the European Free Trade Association along with Austria, Denmark, Norway, Portugal, Sweden and Switzerland. While the Conservative administration in London saw EFTA as a means of protecting the British economy from the potentially harmful impact of being outside the trading bloc created by the Six, to the EEC Europeans this move looked like a hostile effort to torpedo the EEC at birth. Britain consequently lost a lot of good will it had built up among the countries of western Europe, even while remaining outside their efforts at closer integration (Ellison 2000). By 1960 it was fair to say that Europe

was at 'sixes and sevens': the six of the EEC against the seven of EFTA.

The creation of EFTA could not paper over the cracks in the British economy, however, and civil servants and politicians in London soon began to notice a marked divergence between the performance of the British economy and that of economies inside the EEC. Not just this, but Britain's trade patterns were perceptibly shifting from Commonwealth states to states in western Europe. During the 1960s Britain applied twice to join the EEC. First Harold Macmillan and then Harold Wilson saw their applications fail at the hands of French President Charles de Gaulle in 1963 and 1967 respectively (Ludlow 1997; Daddow 2003). After the second 'non' the British left their application on the table and the Conservatives under Edward Heath were finally able

This art installation in the Council of Ministers building in Brussels caused something of a stir when it was unveiled in January 2009 to mark the beginning of the Czech Presidency of the EU. It looks like a huge plastic modelling kit, with each of the 27 pieces representing a stereotype of the EU member states. France was on strike ('grève') and Sweden an item of flatpack furniture, while the Bulgarian sculpture had to be covered up (middle right of the image above left) because of complaints about the country being depicted as a 'Turkish toilet' (Gavrilova, 2009). Britain, meanwhile, was an empty space (above right). Twelve years after Tony Blair came to power aiming to help Britain more comfortable working with Europe, key planks of his strategy, such as joining the single currency, had never been put in place. As one former government insider put it: 'By the general election of 2005 Britain was no closer to joining the euro than it had been in 2001 and arguably further away than in 1997' (Price, 2005: 366). Psychologically as well as politically it is doubtful if many in Britain feel truly at home in Europe.

Entropa, David Cerny, Justus Lipsius Building Brussels, 1 January to 31 June 2009.
Source: Author's photos.

to take Britain into the EEC in 1973. These troubled decades in Britain's European policy set the tone for much of what has followed and the British have routinely struggled to accept the idea of a European future, tending to stay out of new plans for integration, notably the single European currency the Euro.

The North Atlantic Treaty Organization

Britain was a founder member of the North Atlantic Treaty Organization which was set up in April 1949 to fulfil the goals of the Atlantic Charter: freedom, security and prosperity for signatory countries, built on the principles of democracy, individual liberty and the rule of law (NATO 1949). The UK delegation to NATO is based in Brussels, headed by an Ambassador and staffed by civil servants from the Foreign Office, the Ministry of Defence and the three armed services. NATO membership was attractive to the British Labour government for two principal reasons.

The first and most immediate concern facing British foreign policy makers when NATO was created was to safeguard the country's security against the threat of a potentially revanchist Germany and perhaps more urgently Russia, which was then flexing its military muscle in the early years of the Cold War. Article 5 of the North Atlantic Treaty set down the principle that 'an armed attack against one or more of [the signatories] in Europe or North America shall be considered an attack against them all' and that in such circumstances all other NATO members would come to the aid of the party under attack, using armed force if necessary (NATO 1949). The second reason why NATO was attractive to Britain was that the US was a co-signatory. Having the US on board gave the organisation military as well as diplomatic credibility and played to the natural Atlanticism of British Foreign Secretary Bevin and Prime Minister Attlee. Essentially a product of the Cold War, since the collapse of the Soviet bloc in 1989 NATO has spent a good deal of time defining and redefining its role for the twenty-first century (Medcalf 2008). Since 2003 NATO has expanded both its membership and its military infrastructure so that it can play a constructive part in what are known as 'out-of-area' operations in places such as the Balkans, Afghanistan and the Darfur region of Sudan. In the Foreign Office's words NATO is now a 'global manager of security' rather than just a regional one (FCO 2009b).

The Organization for Security and Cooperation in Europe

The Organization for Security and Cooperation in Europe (OSCE) was founded by the Helsinki Act of 1975 at the Conference on Security and Co-operation in Europe (CSCE) which aimed to promote dialogue between states of the East and states of the West. At the end of the Cold War the CSCE helped the newly independent states in central and eastern Europe make the transition to democracy and free market economies, as well as dealing with internal and external threats to their security and stability (OSCE, undated: 1). The CSCE was renamed the OSCE in 1994 and now has a comprehensive threefold definition of security, working across these dimensions to fulfil its missions: traditional political–military security, economic security and environmental and human security. The methods it uses are suitably wide-ranging, from dialogue and security-building, across election monitoring, through to arms control and environmental activities. You can see in Figure 2.1 that the OSCE is the largest of the specifically security-focused international organisations with 56 members (as of March 2009). Crucially, it is the only organisation outside of the UN that brings the US and Russia to the same table.

As with the other international organisations covered here, the UK has a formal delegation based at the OSCE headquarters in Vienna and this represents the UK at the weekly meetings of the Permanent Council, works on arms control, and works with the OSCE's human rights institutions notably the Office for Democratic Institutions and Human Rights (ODIHR) 'to promote human rights and democracy through project work, election observation missions and legislative advice in participating States'. The ODIHR has observed some 150 elections over the past ten years or so and Britain provides up to 10 per cent of all election observers (FCO 2009c).

The Organisation for Economic Cooperation and Development

Britain has been a member of the Organisation for Economic Co-operation and Development (OECD) since 1961. The forerunner to the OECD was the Organisation for European Economic Co-operation, set up in 1948 to administer Marshall Aid funds from the US to help western European states recover from the ravages of the Second World War. The aim of the OECD is to help its members achieve sustainable economic growth and employment and in a wider context to contribute to global economic stability and expansion by encouraging free trade practices in the developed and developing worlds (OECD undated a). The OECD also gathers together a huge amount of economic statistics, reports and publications that help London's decision-makers shape the country's foreign economic policy (OECD undated b).

■ Empires, circles and bridges: ideas about British foreign policy

The practice of British foreign policy has been critically influenced by shifting ideas about Britain's place in the world, as well as the rise of new challenges to British national security and interests. These ideas have in turn been moulded by perceptions of the seriousness of events at home and abroad that impinge on Britain's ability and willingness to play out its role on the world stage. In something of an ongoing cycle, the ideas shape the practice which in turn shapes the ideas about British foreign policy. Disentangling the one from the other can be difficult and somewhat overplays the distinction between the theory and the practice of British foreign policy. Here, we will trace the evolution of the thinking about British foreign policy by studying two periods. In the first and by far the longer of the two periods we see the big ideas about Britain's role in the world taking shape and entrenching themselves within the political class and public mind at large. This is the imperial period which lasted roughly from the end of the American War of Independence in 1783 to the middle of the twentieth century when Britain developed managed a sprawling global Empire only to see it disintegrate after the Second World War. The second period began with the election of the Labour government of 1997 which tried, perhaps more than any of its predecessors, to help Britain come to terms with its post-imperial hangover and reduced global status following the Second World War in 1945, and privileged the ethical, communitarian dimensions of British foreign policy in an interdependent world.

Paradoxically, however, we will find that ideas about Empire and Britain's status as a major global player have died hard in Establishment Britain and it is doubtful whether New Labour successfully managed to implement a truly post-imperial foreign policy for Britain.

Britain as imperial power

At its height in the nineteenth and early twentieth centuries, the one idea that dominated British foreign policy thinking was the importance to Britain of possessing and expanding the British Empire. This Empire was the one built after the United States Congress declared in July 1776 that the thirteen American colonies which were then at war with Britain would henceforth be independent from Britain, that is, not formally part of the British Empire. Instead of concentrating on its transatlantic Empire, the British threw themselves into fresh imperialist expansion in key strategic locations such as India and the countries of sub-Saharan Africa, such that by the years between the First and Second World Wars the British Empire stretched over one-quarter of the land surface of the earth and contained one-fifth of its population. As Andrew Gamble has observed:

Empire for more than a century was the most important transnational space inhabited by the British and it had a profound impact on British politics, particularly on the way British people thought about race, and about the role of the British state in the world.

(Gamble 2003: 62)

It was both a formal and informal Empire. It was formal in that the British controlled the various colonies which made up the Empire and locked them into an informal economic sphere 'dominated by British companies, and a currency sphere in which the pound sterling was the accepted master currency'. The British maintained their domination of global trade by encouraging worldwide acceptance of the principle of the liberal economic order – the free movement of goods, capital and people (Gamble 2003: 79–80) backed by 'a sufficient exertion of power to secure an open market in which contracts would be enforceable' (Clarke 1996: 13–14). It may seem anachronistic today, but politicians such as Lord Curzon, Viceroy of India 1899–1905, could contentedly claim in the Victorian era that the British Empire was 'the greatest force for good the world has ever seen' while academic historians such as J.R. Seeley of Cambridge could publicly talk of Britain's civilising 'destiny' without fear of contradiction or dissent from the governing elites in Establishment Britain (Schama 2002: 262).

In the years 1950–4 the Empire–Commonwealth accounted for some 49 per cent of Britain's imports and took 54 per cent of British exports (Kennedy 1985: 335); in 1956 there were still some 45 separate governments controlled by what was then the Colonial Office (Cross 1968: 325). By 1960, however, Conservative Prime Minister Harold Macmillan identified the growing strength of what he called 'this African national consciousness' which became in the minds of London's foreign policy makers a symbol that attitudes towards the necessity and desirability of Empires were changing at home and abroad. Macmillan observed that: 'The wind of change is blowing through this continent, and whether we like it or not, this growth of national consciousness is a political fact . . . and our national policies must take account of it' (Macmillan 1960). One year later Macmillan applied to take Britain into the EEC, citing structural shifts in Britain's trading patterns from Commonwealth to Empire as a significant factor in the government's thinking about Britain's policy towards European integration (Camps 1964: 231). Continuing economic crises culminating in the devaluation of sterling in 1966 helped prompt a second, and again unsuccessful, application under Harold Wilson. Britain was only accepted into the European club in 1973, but this process appeared to show that the country's leaders and public had come round to accepting the role and status of regional power, commensurate with its economic capabilities. On the way the Labour government of Harold Wilson had made swingeing defence cuts which included withdrawing British forces from bases east of Suez in 1967 (Alexander 2003), a very public demonstration of the inability and unwillingness of the British to cling to Empire as an outlet for its global power and prestige; indeed in one interpretation it 'symbolized Labour's determination to leave the Empire behind' altogether (Gamble 2003: 209). However, while the rapid dissolution of Empire over a period of little more than twenty years from the retreat from India and Burma in 1947–8 may have signalled the end of the 'formal' Empire, the values and national purposes Britain had tried to inculcate through the possession of its overseas territories as far afield as

Canada, Africa, Asia and Australia left a legacy. Echoes of Empire continue to be heard in British foreign policy thinking to this day (Calvocoressi 2009: 177). The 'winds of change' might have blown through the Empire, but had they blown through the corridors of the Foreign Office in London?

Churchill's 'three circles'

The Second World War exposed Britain's inability and growing unwillingness to hold on to far-flung territories which drained its damaged economy at a time when moves to national self-determination in Asia and Africa were bringing the ethics of the existence of formal empires into the realm of public and political debate. Britain had already suffered serious economic upheaval with the end of the gold standard in September 1931 when the link between the one-to-one exchange value of the pound and gold was finally broken for good. For an economic system that had been in operation since the early eighteenth century and which had survived (just) the upheaval of the First World War, it was a sign of the economic turbulence of the times that the British had to admit defeat and that the pound was no longer held to be as valuable as gold. A more immediate and, in national security terms, potentially more devastating challenge to British power and prestige came from the rise of the Axis powers, Germany, Italy and Japan in the 1930s. The Second World War (1939–45) drained Britain economically. Simon Schama estimates that fighting the war cost Britain £7,000 million ($7 billion), or a quarter of its economy, with defence spending accounting for some 10 per cent of gross domestic product by 1945 (Schama 2002: 540). By the end of hostilities the demise of the national economy in Britain typified the situation across Europe where all the major players were deemed to be on the verge of economic, not to mention political and social, collapse (Ellwood 1996).

How would the British react to being forced into relying on a now superior economic power, the US, to bail it out of its economic travails and help provide for its continuing national security against a possibly resurgent Germany and an apparently hostile Russia? One idea that took hold came from then Opposition leader Winston Churchill, in his speech to the Conservative Party Conference in 1948, the theme of which was how to provide for national security when 'the state of the world and the position

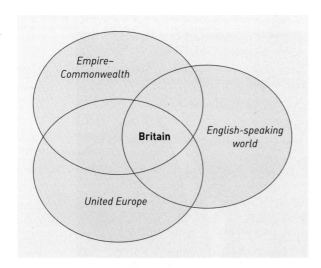

Figure 2.4 Churchill's three circles

of our country in it, have sunk to levels which no one could have predicted' (Churchill 1948: 149). In a short passage midway through the speech, Churchill suggested that the British had a unique role to play in the world by virtue of being 'the only country which has a great part to play in every one' of 'three great circles among the free nations and democracies' (all quotations in this section are from Churchill 1948: 153) (Figure 2.4).

Churchill's first circle, 'naturally', was the British Commonwealth and Empire which he had earlier in the speech described as 'the foundation of our Party's political belief'. The second circle was 'the English-speaking world in which we, Canada, and the other British Dominions play so important a part'. The third and apparently final circle was 'United Europe'. The ordering of the circles, with Europe very much last of the three, could be taken as symbolic, especially given the time Churchill spent in his speech more generally on the need for close British ties with the US and his comments on the importance of Empire. But what gets forgotten about this speech is that prior to setting out his model Churchill had eulogised the principle of European integration and stressed that 'there is absolutely no need to choose between a United Empire and a United Europe. Both are vitally and urgently necessary.' More evident in the speech than any denigration of the European ideal was Churchill's view that, of all the countries in the world, Britain was uniquely placed to play an active global role by virtue of its worldwide diplomatic entanglements, its European connections providing a prop to,

rather than the end of, the nation's outward-looking foreign policy agenda.

Updating the three circles model: Blair's 'bridge'

Tony Blair reshaped Churchill's three circles model to take account of the geostrategic context of British foreign policy at the turn of the twenty-first century. Blair replaced Empire with the US but made much the same kinds of claim as Churchill about Britain occupying a special place in the world, an arbiter between Europe, the US and the wider world. Blair's thinking on foreign policy came to centre on the idea that Britain could act as a 'bridge' between Europe (meaning the EU) and the US. In this vision for British foreign policy Britain maintains its centrality in world affairs by being a Churchill-esque point of contact, the privileged interlocutor, between Brussels and the national capitals in Berlin, Paris, Rome and so forth on the one hand, and Washington on the other. Already in 1997 Blair's thinking was clear and the concept was stated as a blunt fact of international life: 'We are the bridge between the US and Europe. Let us use it. When Britain and America work together on the international scene, there is little we can't achieve' (Blair 1997).

Note that Britain is *the* bridge, not *a* bridge, or one of several the US may wish to use as a route into the EU. Even in speeches where he was pushing the British to accept a European future he could not resist the bridge analogy: 'we are stronger in Europe if strong with the US. Stronger together. Influential with both. And a bridge between the two' (Blair 1999b). Blair's unwavering public support for George W. Bush's decision to undertake military operations to overthrow Saddam Hussein in March 2003 caused huge controversy within European–American relations and Britain's decision to support the US aroused great hostility in key EU countries such as France and Germany. Undeterred, Blair was still expounding the 'bridge' idea in November 2004, albeit with slightly less confidence than he had done in previous years:

We have a unique role to play. Call it a bridge, a two-lane motorway, a pivot or call it a damn high wire, which is often how it feels; our job is to keep our sights firmly on both sides of the Atlantic.

(Blair 2004) (Figure 2.5)

Source: Getty Images

'I come in friendship to renew, for new times our special relationship that is founded on our shared history, our shared values and, I believe, our shared futures.' (Brown 2009)

'The disparity in strength meant that the relationship was always more important for the British than the American partner' (Cradock 1997: 52)

How do we judge whether or not the 'special relationship' exists in anything other than the language used to express this certain quality to Anglo-American relations? As one critic of the term has put it, 'Politicians are so well practised in massaging each other's egos that the rhetoric about the relationship is poured out automatically regardless of the reality' (Dickie 1994: Preface, 10). Is this relationship built on enduring features such as shared history, values, language, economic outlook, and strategic proximity in times of war and conflict? Or are the short-term effects of personal relations between Prime Ministers and Presidents and their respective teams just as important? Do the obvious periods of synchronicity between the countries, for example under Winston Churchill and Franklin D. Roosevelt, Margaret Thatcher and Ronald Reagan, outweigh the periods of turbulence in the relationship, for example between Harold Wilson and Lyndon B. Johnson?

Thinking more widely, is there a certain 'X-Factor' that marks the Anglo-American relationship apart from America's relations with other states in and outside the EU, such as Germany and Japan? Is the relationship more a feature of British foreign policy discourse than American, and therefore too one-sided to be deployable as a valid concept that captures the nature of the true relations between these two countries which are, as Dimbleby and Reynolds pointed out in the title of their 1988 book, literally 'oceans apart' in so many ways? At the heart of this question lies the problem of how we measure the quality of diplomatic relations between the two states and then how we compare that outcome against measures for other such state-on-state relations. Henry Kissinger suggested in 1982 that Anglo-American relations are better off being described as a 'durable partnership' (Kissinger 1982) – do you agree?

How 'special' is 'special'?
Source: http://mtblog.newyorker.com/online/blogs/newsdesk/ObamaBrown.jpg

■ A 'force for good': New Labour's post-imperial foreign policy?

In the previous section we saw how Tony Blair tried to update Churchill's idea of the three circles of British foreign policy for the twenty-first century.

This went hand-in-hand with a whole host of other ways in which the New Labour government from May 1997 set about preparing Britain for life in the twenty-first century by modernising its domestic and foreign policy agendas. 'New' Labour as the governing party liked to be known wanted to fashion a 'New' Britain which could build on the best aspects

Tony Blair spent a lot of time trying to convince the British people and a global audience that Britain was uniquely well placed to act as a bridge between the US and the EU. Not everyone was convinced that his approach was either feasible or desirable. Here are some of the main criticisms levelled at the 'bridge' idea:

1 **A product of New Labour's 'third way' style of thinking which sets up artificial binaries and seeks to synthesise them by heading down the middle – part of a 'big tent' political strategy.** One exponent of this view was Robin Cook, Foreign Secretary 1997–2001 who noted: 'The concept of a bridge is perfectly tailored for New Labour, as a bridge cannot make choices, but by definition is in the middle' (Cook, 2003: 133). Ian Bache and Andrew Jordan are of the same view that Blair's positioning of Britain 'did not eliminate the Atlanticism of the past. Rather, the third way involved transcending such dilemmas' (Bache and Jordan, 2006: 8).

2 **Avoids making a difficult decision between a more transatlantic or more European direction for British foreign policy: the view from Europe.** Gerhard Schröder, German Chancellor 1998–2005, made the point at an EU–US summit in June 2001 that the problem with Blair's bridge was that the traffic only seemed to flow in one direction (in Seldon, 2005: 615). In this view the US had disproportionate influence over the policies and suggestions Blair tried to convince the Europeans to take on board, but Blair did not put European thinking to Washington with anything like the same gusto. Nor did Blair spend enough time selling his strategy to France or Germany or conversely persuading the Americans that the Europeans should be brought on board with regard to decision making in the 'war on terror' (Garton Ash, 2003).

3 **Blair said it but didn't mean it, and when push came to shove over Iraq Blair showed his true, Atlanticist, colours.** Like Robin Cook, Clare Short is another ex-government minister turned critic. Short was Head of the Department for International Development, DfID, from May 1997 to May 2003 when she resigned over British policy on Iraq. In her memoirs she writes that 'Blair insists that the UK is a bridge between the US and the EU but over Iraq he demonstrated a total incapacity to act as a bridge' and in the end Britain became nothing more than 'a mouthpiece of the US' (Short, 2005: 273 and 296). Christopher Meyer was British Ambassador to the US at the time of the Iraq invasion. His judgement is that already by January 2003 'Blair's famous bridge between Europe and America was sinking beneath the waves' (Meyer, 2006: 261).

4 **Blair said and meant it but was unable to put the words into practice: British over-confidence.** By the beginning of 2003, his biographer Anthony Seldon writes, 'While the bridge support was crumbling on the far side of the Atlantic, the always insecure base on the European side was simultaneously disintegrating' (Seldon, 2005: 589). In this interpretation Blair failed to convince either the Europeans *or* the Americans that Britain could be a viable go-between. Nor, crucially, could he match the 'hawks' in Washington for influence over Bush's foreign and defence policy thinking. As one former State Department official put it regretfully: 'we typically ignore them and take no notice – it's a sad business' (quoted in Baldwin and Webster, 2006).

Figure 2.5 Blair's 'bridge' collapses?

of the country's past but also move beyond that in terms of a fresh appreciation of the country's role in the world. Churchill's 'three circles' were not quite forgotten but they were thought about in a new light. The question is: did Blair and his team succeed in forging a post-imperial foreign policy? We will take each plank of the New Labour foreign policy agenda in turn, assessing on the way how the government set about modernising British foreign policy by devising new ways of conceptualising and speaking about Britain's role in the world.

The 'ethical' dimension

Just ten days into New Labour's governance of Britain, on 12 May 1997, Foreign Secretary Robin Cook launched a New Mission Statement for the Foreign Office, part of New Labour's wider approach to government which sought to be 'businesslike'. The New Mission Statement went hand-in-hand with

a Strategic Defence Review (SDR) published in July 1998 that sought to align British military capabilities and defence posture more closely with its foreign policy objectives (McInnes 1998), and was built on the characteristic New Labour promise of 'radical change and solid planning' (Robertson 1998: 4). The SDR was updated in 2002 to take account of the impact of the events of '9/11' on the global security environment (Cm 5566 Vol. I, 2002). Cook's Mission Statement set down four goals for British foreign policy, what Cook called his 'contract with the British people on foreign policy' (Cook 1997). The first goal of British foreign policy should be to safeguard national security, particularly but not exclusively through NATO membership. Cook's second goal was to promote British prosperity by promoting 'UK plc' abroad and encouraging exports. The third goal was to protect the environment and improve the quality of life in Britain. The fourth goal was the most commented upon: 'to secure the respect of other nations for Britain's contribution to keeping the peace of the world and promoting democracy around the world . . . Our foreign policy must have an ethical dimension . . .' with human rights at its centre (Cook 1997). This latter goal went to the very heart of what New Labour felt 'modern' Britain should be about: the country should command respect from other states in the international arena not because of its superior coercive power (the tenets of an imperial foreign policy) but because Britain stands out as a beacon, a 'force for good in the world' (Cook 1997). This idea of 'Cool Britannia' rather than 'Rule Britannia' was what Cook and New Labour had in mind for Britain's post-imperial foreign policy.

Doctrine of the international community

Cook's idea of the 'ethical dimension' never really took off in a serious and sustained way, not least because Prime Minister Blair hesitated to give it his full backing. In time the 'ethical dimension' was quietly dropped but New Labour remained committed to the idea of Britain playing the part of a 'force for good' in the world. Blair's regular commitment of UK armed forces to military interventions for humanitarian purposes, for example in Kosovo in 1999 and Sierra Leone in 2000, stand out as hard examples of the expeditionary impulse in British foreign policy under New Labour (Daddow 2009). They were conceptualised by Blair as instances of the 'international community' in operation. His assumption was that in an era of increased globalisation and interdependence British national interests can be negatively affected by evil or destabilising goings on in apparently remote parts of the globe. For example, drugs cultivated from poppies in Afghanistan can appear on Britain's streets because of the speed of modern day travel and the problems of policing porous national borders. In this situation, collective action can and should be undertaken to sort out those problems at source, if such action is viable and likely to succeed. He went on to set out

During the Kosovo conflict Blair met refugees at a camp in Macedonia to hear their experiences. Both he and Cherie Blair 'were clearly moved by the whole experience' (Campbell 2007: 387) and according to many observers this visit marked a key turning point in his commitment to intervention for humanitarian purposes (Seldon 2005: 401). Over Kosovo, Blair became widely regarded as the leader of the Western alliance, much to the chagrin of the Americans.
Source: http://news.bbc.co.uk/1/hi/uk_politics/407709.stm; BBC Photo Library

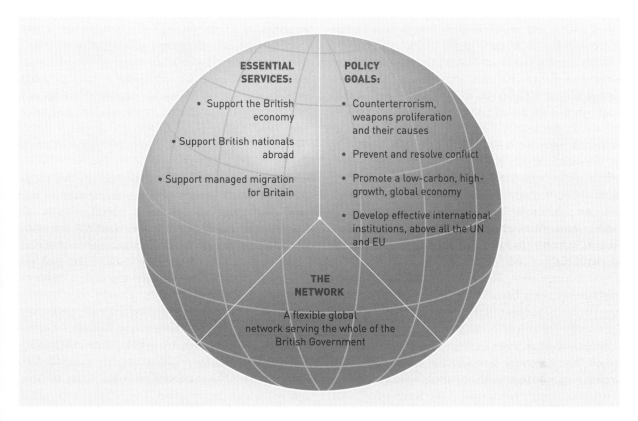

ESSENTIAL
SERVICES:

• Support the British
economy

• Support British nationals
abroad

• Support managed migration
for Britain

POLICY
GOALS:

• Counterterrorism,
weapons proliferation
and their causes

• Prevent and resolve conflict

• Promote a low-carbon, high-
growth, global economy

• Develop effective international
institutions, above all the UN
and EU

THE
NETWORK

A flexible global
network serving the whole of the
British Government

Essential services / Policy goals / The network.
Source: FCO 2008: 2, http://www.fco.gov.uk/resources/en/pdf/pdf1a/fco_strategicframework_2008

the 'circumstances in which we should get actively involved in other people's conflicts': Are we sure of our case? Have all diplomatic options been exhausted? Can military operations be 'sensibly and prudently undertaken'? Are we in it for the long term? And are there national interests involved? (Blair 1999a).

The British doctrine of international community remains up for debate: it is one theory of when, where and how to intervene among many. It has, though, garnered a lot of support 'as the best way of defending our interests and the moral way of promoting our values' (Powell 2007). In the Foreign Office's 2008 Mission Statement, 'Better World, Better Britain' the original Cook–Blair tenets have been updated and refined but continue to shape New Labour's foreign policy thinking under Prime Minister Gordon Brown and Foreign Secretary David Miliband.

The current strategy is divided into three strands. The first is the 'service' element: promoting British business and attracting investment, supporting British nationals abroad and managing migration

in Britain with its EU partners and further afield. The second strand incorporates the key policy focus of the Foreign Office. Top of the list is now countering terrorism together with weapons proliferation, the terrorism aspect very much a product of the post-9/11 focus on Islamic extremism and the threat to international peace and stability from Al Qaeda. Moving down the list we have conflict prevention and resolution, work on the environment and finally reform of the leading international institutions of which Britain is a member. All this work is carried out by 'the network' of British civil servants at home and diplomats abroad. In the latest Mission Statement we see elements of continuity (the focus on promoting UK plc), new emphases (terrorism is now top of the list of policy priorities) and the most memorable facet of the 1997 agenda, the 'ethical dimension', given a lower overall priority.

The 'British genius'

Foreign Secretary Cook and Prime Minister Blair both wanted to refashion British foreign policy for the twenty-first century by helping the British people rethink what it means to *be* British. Recasting British foreign policy in ethical terms, they hoped to secure British national interests in new ways, principally by making the world safe for democracy and heading off potential threats before they could physically do damage to Britain the island or British nationals abroad. What sometimes gets forgotten is the part Gordon Brown, Chancellor of the Exchequer between 1997 and 2007, played in adding intellectual ballast to this reworking of Britain's foreign policy priorities. He was particularly taken with George Orwell's 1941 idea of the 'English genius' (Orwell 1941) but simply renamed it, in true imperial fashion, the 'British genius'.

In Brown's view, Britain's post-imperial foreign policy would only be fashioned, paradoxically, when the British rediscovered the qualities that had made Britain great during the Victorian years of Empire. As he described them in May 1997 these qualities were: 'inventiveness, adaptability, hard work, love of learning, fairness and openness' (Brown 1997). Two years later Brown was of the same mind, that the essence of Britishness was defined 'not by ancient institutions but by living values that British people shared'. He evoked the idea of the British genius to call for the British people to be more outward-looking, to embrace multiculturalism, and to reclaim the global vision that had apparently deserted them and which had led to jingoistic expressions of nationalism and noticeable scepticism towards the European project (Brown 1999). This sense of being outward looking, 'internationalist not isolationist' as New Labour foreign policy makers were wont to call it, was summed up in a repeated theme in Brown's speeches as Chancellor that the English Channel was not a 'moat' but a 'highway' for ideas and commerce (for example Brown 2005).

As Prime Minister Brown has had greater scope to range over Britain's foreign policy priorities and since the onset of the global 'credit crunch' his attention in foreign policy speeches has naturally been on the reform of global financial institutions. Nonetheless, with echoes of Cook, Blair and his speeches as Chancellor, at the Lord Mayor's Banquet in November 2008, Brown set out four tenets for British foreign policy: internationalist not protectionist; interventionist not isolationist; progressive not paralysed by events; forward-thinking not trapped in the solutions of the past (Brown 2008). In sum, New Labour's foreign policy posture has been an eclectic mix of the old and new, some ideas have endured and others have been forgotten or quietly dropped. New Labour has called on the British people to move on from the past while using memories of that exact same past to inform their foreign policy thinking. Churchillian ideas will, it seems, live on in British foreign policy-making circles for many years to come.

Chapter summary

This chapter begins by exploring the history and legacy of Britain's key international relationships, focusing on its involvement in key international organisations: the UN, EU, NATO, the OSCE and OECD. It moves on to explore the key ideas that have shaped contemporary British foreign policy thinking, centring on Empire, Winston Churchill's alluring 'three circles' model of Britain's place in the world and on New Labour's updating of that line of thought through its concept of Britain acting out the role of a 'bridge' on the world stage. The final part surveys the New Labour governments' wider contribution to British foreign policy by examining its efforts to introduce an 'ethical' dimension to foreign policy, Tony Blair's 'doctrine of international community' and Gordon Brown's concept of the 'British genius'. Throughout, the chapter encourages students to think critically about the received orthodoxies surrounding British foreign policy and will help them interrogate the thinking behind the Conservative government's foreign policy as it develops after the 2010 election.

Discussion points

- Do you think Britain still warrants its place as a Permanent Member of the UN Security Council?

- How much global influence does Britain gain from its membership of (a) NATO and (b) the OSCE?

- Do you agree that Britain is Europe's 'awkward partner'?

- What are the principal ideas that have helped shape British foreign policy since 1945? Are these ideas relevant today?

- Did the 2003 invasion of Iraq show that Britain still places too much emphasis on its 'special relationship' with the United States?

- Explain how Britain has tried to act as a 'force for good' in the world since 1997. Has it succeeded?

- Have New Labour politicians successfully helped recast Britain's foreign policy posture in terms of identity and mission for the twenty-first century?

Further reading

Coverage of the most prominent themes and issues in British foreign policy can be found in John Dickie (2007), David Sanders (1990), Robert Holland (1991), David Reynolds (1991) and Paul Kennedy (1985), with a useful focus on the impact of decolonisation on Britain's image of itself as a Great Power in Heinlein (2002). On the strategic, political and economic dimensions of the British Empire see P.J. Cain and A.G. Hopkins (1993) and Eric Hobsbawm (1990); on the notion of the 'two' British Empires see Marshall (2001) and Bayly (2001). Ferguson (2004) gives a good overview of Britain's wider imperial experiences. On the 'special relationship' and the myths that surround it see John Charmley (1995) and David Dimbleby and David Reynolds (1988), and especially John Baylis (1997) on the slipperiness of the concept. Britain's troubled attempts to come to terms with the idea of European unity are documented in John Young (2000) and Hugo Young (1998), while Daddow (2004) traces the part

economic factors have played in government thinking on Europe back to the 1960s. Stephen George's famous thesis (1998) is that Britain has been Europe's 'awkward partner' – even after joining the organisation. Good accounts of New Labour's foreign policy include Richard Little and Mark Wickham-Jones (2001) and Paul Williams (2005). Rhiannon Vickers shows the party political roots of this foreign policy trajectory (2003), while Anne Deighton (2005) shows the strong links between Blairite and Churchillian thinking on British foreign policy. On the 'ethical' foreign policy see Nicholas Wheeler and Tim Dunnne (1998) and for critiques of this agenda see Christopher Hill (2001) and especially David Chandler (2003). William Wallace (2005) critiques Blair's endeavour to place Britain as a 'bridge' between Europe and America.

On the causes and conduct of the American Revolution see Wood (2003). The history, structure and functions of the UN are detailed in Baehr and Gordenker (2005) and Thomas Weiss (2008) considers how to improve the UN machine. NATO's post-Cold War identity crisis is well covered in Moore (2007) and the contributors to Smith (2006). For an alternative approach to the OSCE's role in promoting security see Sandole (2007).

Bibliography

Alexander, P. (2003) 'Commonwealth Crises and the Second Application', in Daddow, O.J. (ed.) (2003) *Harold Wilson and European Integration: Britain's Second Application to Join the EEC.* (Frank Cass) pp. 188–210.

Bache, I. and Jordan, A. (2006) 'Britain in Europe and Europe in Britain', in I. Bache and A. Jordan (eds) *The Europeanization of British Politics.* (Palgrave Macmillan) pp. 3–16.

Baehr, P.B. and Gordenker, L. (2005) *The United Nations: Reality and Ideal*, 4th edn (Palgrave Macmillan).

Baldwin, T. and Webster, P. (2006) 'US State Department official – relationship is one-sided', *The Times*, 30 November, http://www.timesonline.co.uk/tol/news/politics/article1088295.ece, first accessed 23 March 2009.

Baylis, J. (1997) *Anglo-American Relations since 1939: The Enduring Alliance* (Manchester University Press).

Bayly, C.A. (2001) 'The Second British Empire', in Winks, R.N. (ed.) (2001) *The Oxford History of the British Empire: Historiography* (Oxford University Press) pp. 54–72.

Bevin, E. (1949) Opening address at Council of Europe, 5 May, http://www.coe.int/t/dc/av/audio_archive_bevin_en.asp, first accessed 16 March 2009.

Blair, T. (1997) Speech at the Lord Mayor's Banquet, 10 November, http://www.number10.gov.uk/Page1070, first accessed 1 September 2005.

Blair, T. (1999a) 'Doctrine of the International Community', Economic Club, Chicago, 22 April, http://www.number-10.gov.uk/output/Page1297.asp, first accessed 6 September 2005.

Blair, T. (1999b) Speech about Britain in Europe, 14 October, http://www.number-10.gov.uk/output/Page1461.asp, first accessed 7 September 2005.

Blair, T. (2004) Speech at the Lord Mayor's Banquet, 15 November, http://www.number10.gov.uk/Page6583.asp, first accessed 15 September 2005.

Brown, G. (1997) 'Exploiting the British genius – the key to long-term economic success', speech to the Confederation of British Industry, 20 May, http://www.hm-treasury.gov.uk/speech_chex_200597.htm, first accessed 4 July 2006.

Brown, G. (1999) Speech at the Smith Institute, 15 April, http://www.hm-treasury.gov.uk/speech_chex_150499.htm, first accessed 4 July 2007.

Brown, G. (2005) 'The Hugo Young Memorial Lecture', 13 December http://www.hm-treasury.gov.uk/speech_chex_131205.htm, first accessed 4 July 2007.

Brown, G. (2008) Speech to the Lord Mayor's Banquet, 10 November, http://www.number10.gov.uk/Page17419, first accessed 18 March 2009.

Brown, G. (2009) Speech to US Congress, 4 March, http://www.number10.gov.uk/Page18506, first accessed 23 March 2009.

Cain, P.J. and Hopkins, A.G. (1993) *British Imperialism: Crisis and Deconstruction 1914–1990* (Longman).

Calvocoressi, P. (2009) *World Politics since 1945*, 9th edn (Pearson Education Limited).

Campbell, A. (2007) *The Blair Years: Extracts from the Alastair Campbell Diaries* (Hutchinson).

Camps, M. (1964) *Britain and the European Community 1955–1963* (Oxford University Press).

Chandler, D. (2003) 'Rhetoric Without Responsibility: The Attraction of Ethical Foreign Policy', *British Journal of Politics and International Relations*, 5, 3, pp. 295–316.

Charmley, J. (1995) *Churchill's Grand Alliance: The Anglo-American Special Relationship 1940–1957* (Hodder and Stoughton).

Churchill, W. (1946) Speech in Zürich, 19 September, http://www.coe.int/T/E/Com/About_Coe/DiscoursChurchill.asp, first accessed 16 March 2009.

Churchill, W. (1948) Official proceedings of Conservative Party Conference, Bodleian Library Special Collections, shelf mark NUA 2/1/56, pp. 149–56.

Clarke, P. (1996) *Hope and Glory: Britain 1900–1990* (Allen Lane/The Penguin Press).

Cm 5566 Vol. I (2002) 'The Strategic Defence Review: A New Chapter', July, http://www.mod.uk/NR/rdonlyres/79542E9C-1104-4AFA-9A4D-8520F35C5C93/0/sdr_a_new_chapter_cm5566_vol1.pdf, first accessed 17 March 2009.

Cook, R. (1997) 'Robin Cook's speech on the government's ethical foreign policy', Guardian Unlimited, http://www.guardian.co.uk/world/1997/may/12/indonesia.ethicalforeignpolicy, first accessed 20 October 2006.

Cook, R. (2003) *The Point of Departure* (Simon and Schuster).

Council of Europe (2008) http://www.coe.int/T/e/Com/about_coe/, first accessed 16 March 2009.

Cradock, P. (1997) *In Pursuit of British Interests: Reflections on Foreign Policy under Margaret Thatcher and John Major* (John Murray).

Cross, C. (1968) *The Fall of the British Empire 1918–1968* (Book Club Associates).

Daddow, O.J. (ed.) (2003) *Harold Wilson and European Integration: Britain's Second Application to Join the EEC* (Frank Cass).

Daddow, O.J. (2004) 'Economics in the Historiography of Britain's Applications to Join the EEC in the 1960s', in R. Perron (ed.). *The Stability of Europe: The Common Market: Towards European Integration of Industrial and Financial Markets? (1958–1968)* (Presses de l'Université de Paris-Sorbonne) pp. 81–97.

Daddow, O. (2009) '"Tony's War"?: Blair, Kosovo and the Interventionist Impulse in British Foreign Policy', *International Affairs*, 85, 3, pp. 547–60.

Deighton, A. (2005) 'The foreign policy of British Prime Minister Tony Blair: radical or retrograde?', Centre for British Studies, Humboldt University, Berlin, 11 July, http://www.gcsp.ch/e/publications/ Issues_Institutions/Europe/Academic_Papers/ Deighton-CBS-07.05..pdf, first accessed 3 March 2009.

Dickie, J. (1994) *'Special' No More: Anglo-American Relations, Rhetoric and Reality* (Weidenfeld and Nicolson).

Dickie, J. (2007) *The New Mandarins: How British Foreign Policy Works* (I.B. Tauris).

Dimbleby, D. and Reynolds, D. (1988) *An Ocean Apart: The Relationship between Britain and America in the Twentieth Century* (BBC Books).

Ellison, J. (2000) *Threatening Europe: Britain and the Creation of the European Community 1955–58* (Macmillan).

Ellwood, D.W. (1996) *Rebuilding Europe: Western Europe, America and Postwar Reconstruction* (Addison Wesley Longman Limited).

FCO (2006) *Active Diplomacy for a Changing World: The UK's International Priorities*. FCO Command Paper, CM 6762, March, Chapter 2, p. 26, http://collections.europarchive.org/tna/ 20080205132101/fco.gov.uk/Files/kfile/ 02intpriorities2006chapt2.pdf, first accessed 26 February 2009.

FCO (2008) Mission Statement, 'Better World, Better Britain', http://www.fco.gov.uk/resources/en/pdf/ mission-statement, first accessed 17 March 2009.

FCO (2009a) 'FCO global network', http:// www.fco.gov.uk/en/fco-in-action/ global-network/, first accessed 4 March 2009.

FCO (2009b) 'Britain in NATO', http:// www.fco.gov.uk/en/fco-in-action/institutions/ nato/, first accessed 15 March 2009.

FCO (2009c) 'Organisation for Security and Co-operation in Europe', http://www.fco.gov.uk/ en/about-the-fco/what-we-do/building-strong- relationships-ol/international-partners/osce, first accessed 16 March 2009.

Ferguson, N. (2004) *Empire: How Britain Made the Modern World* (Penguin).

Gamble, A. (2003) *Between Europe and America: The Future of British Politics* (Palgrave Macmillan).

Garton Ash, T. (2003) 'Blair's bridge', *Guardian*, 4 September, http://www.guardian.co.uk/politics/ 2003/sep/04/iraq.iraq, first accessed 23 March 2009.

Gavrilova, D. (2009) 'Entropa: art of politics, heart of a nation', 'Open Democracy', 19 January, http://www.opendemocracy.net/article/ entropa-art-of-politics-heart-of-a-nation, first accessed 8 February 2009.

George, S. (1998) *The Awkward Partner: Britain in the European Community*, 3rd edn (Oxford University Press).

Global Policy Forum (no date a), 'Changing patterns in the use of the veto in the Security Council', http://www.globalpolicy.org/security/data/ vetotab.htm, first accessed 4 March 2009.

Global Policy Forum (no date b), 'Subjects of UN Security Council votes', http://www.globalpolicy.org/ security/membship/veto/vetosubj.htm, first accessed 4 March 2009.

Haas, E.B. (1958) *The Uniting of Europe: Political, Social and Economic Forces, 1950–1957* (Stanford University Press).

Heinlein, F. (2002) *British Government Policy and Decolonisation 1945–1963: Scrutinising the Official Mind* (Frank Cass).

Hill, C. (2001) 'Foreign Policy', in Anthony Seldon (ed.), *The Blair Effect: The Blair Government 1997–2001* (Little, Brown and Company) pp. 331–53.

Hobsbawm, E.J. (1990) *Industry and Empire* (Penguin).

Holland, R. (1991) *The Pursuit of Greatness: Britain and the World Role, 1900–1970* (Fontana).

Kennedy, P. (1985) *The Realities Behind Diplomacy: Background Influences on British External Policy 1865–1980* (Fontana).

Kissinger, H. (1982) Speech at Royal Institute of International Affairs, *Executive Intelligence Review*, 11 January, http://www.larouchepub.com/ other/2002/2901_kissinger.html, first accessed 9 July 2002.

Little, R. and Wickham-Jones, M. (eds) (2000) *New Labour's Foreign Policy: A New Moral Crusade?* (Manchester University Press).

Ludlow, N.P. (1997) *Dealing with Britain: The Six and the First UK Application to the EEC* (Cambridge University Press).

Macmillan, H. (1960) Speech to South African
Parliament, 3 February, http://africanhistory.
about.com/od/eraindependence/p/wind_of_
change2.htm, first accessed 26 March 2009.

Marshall, P.J. (2001) 'The First British Empire', in
Winks, R.N. (ed.) (2001) *The Oxford History of
the British Empire: Historiography* (Oxford
University Press) pp. 43–53.

McInnes, C. (1998) 'Labour's Strategic Defence
Review', *International Affairs*, 74, 4, pp. 823–45.

Medcalf, J. (2008) *Going Global or Going
Nowhere?: NATO's Role in Contemporary
International Security* (Peter Lang).

Meyer, C. (2006) *DC Confidential* (Phoenix).

Moore, R.R. (2007) *NATO's New Mission: Projecting
Stability in a post-Cold War World* (Praeger).

NATO (1949) 'The North Atlantic Treaty', 4 April,
http://www.nato.int/docu/basictxt/treaty.htm,
first accessed 15 March 2009.

OECD (undated a) 'History', http://www.oecd.org/
pages/0,3417,en_36734052_36761863_1_1_1_1_
1,00.html, first accessed 16 march 2009.

OECD (undated b) 'Statistics Portal', http://www.
oecd.org/statsportal/0,3352,en_2825_293564_1_1_
1_1_1,00.html, first accessed 16 March 2009.

Orwell, G. (1941) *The Lion and the Unicorn*, Part 1,
http://orwell.ru/library/essays/lion/english/, first
accessed 18 March 2009.

OSCE (undated) 'The OSCE at a Glance', http://
www.osce.org/publications/sg/2006/04/
18784_591_en.pdf, first accessed 17 March 2009.

Powell, J. (2007) 'Why the West should not fear
to intervene', *Observer*, 18 November,
http://www.guardian.co.uk/commentisfree/2007/
nov/18/comment.foreignpolicy, first accessed
11 September 2008.

Price, L. (2005) *The Spin Doctor's Diary: Inside
Number Ten with New Labour* (Hodder and
Stoughton).

Reynolds, D. (1991) *Britannia Overruled: British
Policy and World Power in the Twentieth
Century* (Longman).

Robertson (1998) Introduction to Strategic Defence
Review (1998), http://www.mod.uk/NR/rdonlyres/
65F3D7AC-4340-4119-93A2- 20825848E50E/0/
sdr1998_complete.pdf, first accessed 17 March
2009.

Ruane, K. (2000) *The Rise and Fall of the European
Defence Community: Anglo-American Relations
and the Crisis of European Defence, 1950–55*
(Macmillan).

Sanders, D. (1990) *Losing an Empire, Finding
a Role: British Foreign Policy since 1945*
(Macmillan).

Sandole, D.J.D. (2007) *Peace and Security in the
Postmodern World: The OSCE and Conflict
Resolution* (Routledge).

Schama, S. (2002) *A History of Britain, Vol.3: The
Fate of Empire 1776–2000* (BBC Worldwide Ltd).

Seldon, A. (2005) *Blair* (The Free Press).

Short, C. (2005) *An Honourable Deception?:
New Labour, Iraq, and the Misuse of Power*
(The Free Press).

Smith, M.A. (ed.) (2006) *Where is NATO Going?*
(Routledge).

UN (2008–9) 'Charter of the United Nations,
Chapter V', http://www.un.org/aboutun/charter/
chapter5.shtml, first accessed 4 March 2009.

Vickers, R. (2003) *The Labour Party and the World,
Vol. 1: The Evolution of Labour's Foreign Policy
1900–51* (Manchester University Press).

Wallace, W. (2005) 'The Collapse of British Foreign
Policy', *International Affairs*, 82, 1, pp. 56–68.

Weiss, T.G. (2009) *What's Wrong with the United
Nations (and how to fix it)* (Polity Press).

Wheeler, N.J. and Dunne, T. (1998) 'Good
International Citizenship: A Third Way for
British Foreign Policy', *International Affairs*,
74, 4, pp. 847–70.

Williams, P.D. (2005) *British Foreign Policy under
New Labour, 1997–2005* (Palgrave Macmillan).

Wood, G.S. (2003) *The American Revolution:
A History* (Weidenfeld and Nicolson History).

Young, H. (1998) *This Blessed Plot: Britain and
Europe from Churchill to Blair* (Macmillan).

Young, J.W. (2000) *Britain and European Unity
1945–1999*, 2nd edn (Macmillan).

Useful websites

Council of Europe: http://www.coe.int/T/e/Com/
about_coe/

EFTA: http://www.efta.int/content/efta-
secretariat/content/about-efta/aboutefta

EU: http://europa.eu/

Global Policy Forum: http://www.globalpolicy.org/

NATO: http://www.nato.int/

ODIHR: http://www.osce.org/odihr-elections/
  17781.html, plus election monitoring report:
  http://www.osce.org/publications/odihr/2005/
  11/17148_478_en.pdf
OECD: http://www.oecd.org/home/0,3305,en_
  2649_201185_1_1_1_1_1,00.html

OSCE: http://www.osce.org/
OSCE YouTube channel:
  http://www.youtube.com/osce
UK Delegation to NATO:
  http://uknato.fco.gov.uk/en/
UN: http://www.un.org/

CHAPTER 3

Social and economic contexts

Mark Garnett

Learning objectives

- To outline the social and economic contexts of British politics.

- To identify the major trends in the social and economic setting.

- To show how Britain is affected by the wider European and global context.

Introduction

In the twenty-first century, 'the condition of Britain' has been a major preoccupation for commentators and politicians. The Conservative Party leader, David Cameron, has echoed some of his senior colleagues by speaking of Britain as a 'broken' country. For his own part, Gordon Brown was discussing the concept of 'Britishness' long before becoming Prime Minister in 2007. Coming from a key figure in the governing party, this was no less significant than Cameron's more eye-catching comments. It suggested that Britain had changed so radically in recent decades that the essence of the country needed to be re-defined; and not even the most enthusiastic supporter of recent governments could claim that all the changes had been positive.

For some commentators, the most notable changes in Britain over the twentieth century were social (and visible); in particular, immigration had promoted a radical change in the ethnic composition of the country. However, it can be argued that other developments have been more far-reaching in their effects – in particular, there had been a remarkable rise in the proportion of women in the workplace, and the old dominance of manufacturing industry as a source of employment had disappeared. These trends show that social change in Britain cannot be understood in isolation from the economic context. Equally, social and economic change in Britain takes place within wider contexts; Britain's membership of the EU has an increasing impact on the domestic affairs of the country, but arguably the effect of 'globalisation' is even more potent. The main purpose of the present chapter is to provide an overview of the current social and economic situation of Britain, and to outline the complex relationship between this context and the dilemmas facing British policy makers.

■ Society, economy and politics

All students of politics ought to be aware of the wide scope of the subject. In the past, it seemed possible to restrict the subject-matter of politics to certain key institutions, like political parties and bureaucracies, while paying only fleeting attention to the social context. Whatever its validity at the time, this approach can no longer provide a satisfactory picture of politics within any country. It is particularly unsuitable to the task of explaining political life within a diverse state like the UK.

Fortunately for the student of British politics, some social and economic developments are more obviously relevant than others. Major changes in society or the economy almost invariably give rise to complex calculations on the part of decision makers. Here are just two briefly-sketched scenarios of contemporary relevance:

1 A change in the age profile of the population

On the face of it, an increase in the proportion of elderly people within the population of any country could be seen as a cause for national celebration. Among other things, it might indicate the success of the healthcare system in treating illness, or providing good advice on matters such as diet and exercise. Alternatively, a change of this kind has serious repercussions for the political agenda. The prospect of longer life opens the possibility of a relatively prolonged period of retirement for a country's citizens. If retired people are likely to constitute an ever-increasing proportion of the population as a whole, politicians have to take a new look at the cost of any state provision for the elderly, notably pensions and care homes. Also, if greater life-expectancy is mainly the result of better healthcare, decision makers have to anticipate a corresponding increase in demand for such services.

Some politicians might be inclined to take tough decisions in the face of such evidence. They might, for example, want to propose a cut in the value of the state pension, or a radical revision of the retirement age. If so, they will have to confront the fact that elderly people have votes like all other adults, and the evidence suggests that, in Britain, they are more likely than younger people to exercise this right (in 2005, three-quarters of those aged 65 and above cast a vote, compared to less than half of those aged between 25 and 34). Thus, whatever their original feelings about state provision for old age, decision makers are likely to find themselves having to compromise in the face of sharply contrasting demands.

2 A sudden increase in immigration

Immigration is often seen as one way of tackling the problems associated with an ageing population. If significant numbers of young, highly-skilled and hard-working people can be persuaded to move to Britain (even on a temporary basis), there should be obvious economic benefits which will help the country meet the bills for higher pensions and healthcare.

However, a significant surge in immigration brings its own social problems. Often the immigrants will bring young families with them, putting pressure on local services (particularly education and housing). Immigrants may also face hostility from the existing population, especially when unemployment is high. In turn, these social problems can give rise to political dilemmas. Even politicians who believe in the principle of open borders will be tempted to introduce new immigration controls, perhaps by insisting that newcomers produce evidence of particular skills (and have a reasonable grasp of the language). A cool, rational response is unlikely to satisfy the public on such a controversial topic; elements of the media are always ready to exaggerate the 'threat' of immigration, and to present the arrival of relatively large contingents as a drain on the taxpayer rather than an economic asset. Politicians from the main parties are always aware of the potential for a backlash against immigrants, leading to a rise in support for parties of the extreme right. Thus, even liberal-minded parties are likely to ramp up their rhetoric in response to large-scale immigration.

■ Britain in statistics

These thumbnail sketches of contemporary issues are sufficient to indicate that social, economic and political developments can be interlinked in a relatively complex way. With this in mind, we can discuss some of the leading social and economic features of Britain today.

Table 3.1 Estimated population of the UK, mid-2008

	Population (thousands)	UK percentage
England	51,446	84
Scotland	5,169	8
Wales	2,993	5
Northern Ireland	1,775	3

Source: Office for National Statistics

Population

Official population figures for the UK are produced by a census which is held every decade (the next one is due in 2011). However, the Office for National Statistics produces regular estimates of changes in the population. On its calculations, the population of the UK in mid-2008 was 61.4 million. Of the constituent parts of the UK, England was by far the most populous (see Table 3.1); indeed, its population density (395 per square kilometre) made it the most densely-populated European country of any significant size. It had roughly double the population density of Germany, and quadruple the density of France.

As so often with statistics, these figures conceal significant contrasts which have serious political consequences. Thus, for example, the 2001 census found that the population density of the Greater London Urban Area was 5,100 people per square kilometre. This has obvious policy implications in the field of housing; how, for example, can relatively low-paid workers in vital public services like health and education afford suitable accommodation (whether rented or purchased) in an area where property prices are so much higher than in the rest of the country?

Another significant detail refers to our earlier example. The British population is ageing at a rapid rate. In 1983, there were around 600,000 people of 85 years and older. By 2008 it was estimated that this figure had more than doubled, to 1.3 million. It has also been estimated that the number will more than double again by 2033, reaching about 3.2 million (around 5 per cent of the projected population as a whole). At the same time, the proportion of young people has been falling, so that there are now at least as many Britons aged 65 and above as those aged 16 or less. In view of these figures, it was no surprise that in the summer of 2009 the government announced a review of the law which allowed employers to force workers into retirement at 65; already more than a million people had decided to continue working after the official retirement age.

Immigration and ethnicity

Another significant detail for policy makers was the net level of migration into the country. In 2007, the number of people who arrived in Britain to live for at least a year was 577,000. The estimated number of people leaving Britain was 340,000. Thus the net increase in the UK population due to arrivals and departures was 237,000 in 2007. Much of this increase was due to the expansion of the European Union, allowing easier entry for people from several Eastern European countries. For example, in 2007 almost 100,000 Polish citizens arrived in the UK. Having under-estimated the likely demand from the new EU entrant countries, the government had already introduced some restrictions. One difficulty was to estimate how many of these people were likely to want to stay in the country, rather than returning home after a relatively short time.

Predictably, though, some elements of the media presented the figures as a demographic disaster for an already-overcrowded country, and senior politicians issued regular warnings about a possible rise in support for the British National Party (BNP) in response.

The arrival of significant numbers from Eastern Europe added a new complication to the debate on immigration. Since the 1950s, discussion of immigration had been dominated by the alleged impact of settlers from the so-called 'New Commonwealth'. Opposition to large-scale immigration, in other words, was inextricably mixed with attitudes towards 'race'. According to the 2001 census, 7.9 per cent of the UK population was 'non-white'. In numerical terms, 4.6 million were classed as members of ethnic minorities, compared to more than 54 million 'whites'. Among the minorities, 2.3 million described themselves as 'Asian British'; 1.1 million were 'Black British'. Other ethnic groups had incurred hostility in the past; this was especially true of Irish-born people, of whom there were almost 700,000 according to the 2001 census.

In the last fifty years Britain, especially England, and even more especially London, has been transformed into a multi-ethnic society
Source: Janine Wiedel Photolibrary / Alamy

Religion is another factor which adds complexity to the debate on immigration. In the 2001 census, 1.59 million Britons described themselves as 'muslim'. Some commentators treated this as a worrying figure, since islam was clearly the fastest-growing faith in Britain. After the terrorist attacks on London on 7 July 2005, media attention understandably turned towards members of the islamic community, whether or not they were recent immigrants (notoriously, the London bombers were British-born). The ensuing debate proved that the overwhelming majority of British muslims accepted mainstream British values; and, in any case, followers of the islamic faith remained a tiny minority of the UK population. Although media coverage of the '7/7' attacks was relatively responsible, it was not sufficiently noted that the victims provided remarkable testimony of the degree to which (in London, at least), people from an amazing range of backgrounds – including muslims – had integrated within British society.

As Table 3.2 shows, the number of people who claim adherence to non-Christian faiths in Britain is massively outweighed by those who either keep their religious views to themselves, or openly state that they have no religious beliefs. Even so, it proved all too easy for elements of the media (and some politicians) to give the impression that islam would soon become a dominant force within UK society. Significantly, the 2001 census found that the unemployment rate among muslims was 14 per cent, compared to 4 per cent among Christians; and young muslims were twice as likely as their Christian counterparts to be without a job. On this basis, rather than predicting that islam would become dominant it was more plausible to assume that muslims would continue to be a highly disillusioned minority in Britain.

Table 3.2 Religious affiliation in the UK, 2001

Christian	42,079,417
Muslim	1,591,126
Hindu	558,810
Sikh	336,149
Jewish	226,740
Buddhist	151,816
Other religions	178,837
No religion/no answer	13,626,299

Source: Office for National Statistics

■ Crime: 'Broken Britain'?

For observers who are concerned about the 'condition of Britain', crime statistics are an obvious reference-point. This debate is sometimes confused by the fact that criminal activity is counted in two different ways: one set of figures is produced by the UK's police forces, while a British Crime Survey (BCS) is based on the experiences of people who might or might not report the activities which they experienced to the police. On the latter measure (preferred by the government), 10.1 million crimes were committed in England and Wales in 2007/8. In the same year, the number of crimes recorded by the police was 5 million. Although such headline figures could easily spread alarm among the readers of tabloid newspapers, the BCS had actually recorded a consistent fall in crime since 1995, when 19.4 million offences were reported by the public. One difficulty with the BCS was that it only covered the experiences of adults, which left sections of the media with ample scope for speculation at a time when the criminal propensities of children were a cause of serious public concern.

Whether or not crime has been falling in recent years, politicians always have to brace themselves for public demands for more police. Being seen as 'soft on crime' was regarded as a major electoral weakness for 'Old Labour', which Tony Blair was keen to redress even before he became party leader in 1994. His government duly increased police numbers – although critics alleged that bureaucratic tasks absorbed much of their time – and also introduced 'Community Support Officers' who wore uniforms but lacked many of the powers of the police. Another New Labour initiative was the Anti-Social Behaviour Order (ASBO), a way of addressing chronic social nuisances which might otherwise have escaped prosecution.

Another major headache caused by crime is the prison population. This issue can make law and order 'successes' into a source of negative headlines, because when serious offenders are caught and prosecuted they increase the number of people in custody. The prison population rose under New Labour, after years of relative stability, and new records were regularly established. In September 2009 the number of prisoners was 84,000 (against a maximum capacity of just over 85,000). By contrast, in 1993 the prison population was just 45,000. This remarkable increase partly reflected the government's desire to assuage public demand for heavier sentences in the most serious cases. At the same time, though, there were regular media accusations that judges were still being too soft, and that convicted criminals were often released long before they had served their original sentences. The main result of this statistical oddity – far less crime according to the figures, but many more incarcerated criminals – has been to increase the extent to which British politicians are distrusted by the public.

■ The economic context

This brief survey of social developments in Britain might paint an unduly mournful picture. It would have been possible to pick out more hopeful statistics. However, it is reasonable to suggest that the context in which British politics has been played out in recent years has been underlain by a significant element of unease about the state of society. Judged against the bald economic facts, this feeling seems surprising. Britain has declined relative to other countries since its Victorian heyday: it was being rivalled by nations like the USA and Germany at the beginning of the twentieth century. Even so, by international standards it remains a very wealthy nation, and unlike some newly enriched countries such as China, the individual prosperity of its citizens (calculated as 'Gross Domestic Product per head') is high.

For some observers, the British propensity for grumbling is actually a product of its prosperity. On this view, high living standards (and a system of state education which is uneven but generally satisfactory) give citizens the means and the leisure time to arm themselves with a range of grievances, and to make their views known. This 'post-materialistic' outlook does help to explain the rise of pressure groups in recent decades – particularly those that protest against the very economic developments upon which prosperity depends.

However, on its own this can hardly explain why Britons seem more dissatisfied than most of their European counterparts. Almost certainly, British truculence can also be traced to a nagging sense of decline – an emotion which extends beyond society and economics to sporting activities like football and cricket. Both of those games, after all, were invented by the British; but now although the national teams perform adequately they are certainly not world-beaters. Britain's economic history is similar. In the mid-nineteenth century it was unrivalled, not just for its productivity but for the inventiveness of its citizens. Those days are long gone; and, seemingly, the British regard the achievements of the past as a source of regret rather than glad commemoration.

■ The decline of manufacturing

In the Victorian era British economical supremacy was encapsulated in its remarkable manufacturing prowess. Cities like Manchester and Birmingham grew enormously during the Industrial Revolution, thanks at least in part to Britain's possession of considerable reserves of coal. Although commentators have questioned the overall economic benefit of Britain's overseas empire, this added to the country's stock of raw materials as well as underlining its prestige on the world stage.

However, British pre-eminence was unlikely to last. The two World Wars of the twentieth century sapped a strength which was already waning as other nations developed industries of their own. Victory in the Second World War – at enormous cost – turned out to be a mixed blessing in economic terms. Britain's industrial base was seriously damaged, but not devastated like that of Germany. This meant that the latter country was forced to renew itself almost from scratch, at a time of rapid technological change and with generous American assistance. Although the British people made notable economic sacrifices in the early postwar period, their competitive position was undermined because there was no equivalent need to return to the economic drawing board. Critics of the 1945–51 Labour governments have also argued that after the war Britain took the 'soft option', loading itself with the economic burden of a welfare state, and nationalising key industries which would henceforth be run in the interests of the workers rather than the need for profitability.

For whatever reason, by the late 1950s it was clear that Britain was sinking in the global economic league tables; hence its repeated attempts to join what was then the European Economic Community (EEC) and later became the European Union (EU). But even after Britain gained entry to 'Europe' in 1973, its economic plight worsened. More than its main competitors, its weaknesses were exposed by the oil crisis of the mid-1970s, when the price of this precious commodity more than quadrupled. Britain was widely regarded as failing to meet the economic challenges of the times, not least because of the strength of its trade union movement which exercised powerful influence over Labour governments and had rebuffed attempted reforms by the Conservatives. The trade unions were strongest within manufacturing industry, particularly those sectors which had been taken into state ownership after 1945.

■ The impact of Thatcher

When Margaret Thatcher took office in 1979 she was determined to reverse Britain's economic decline. In one important respect she came to power at a fortunate time; Britain was about to become a net exporter of oil, thanks to the reserves in the North Sea. However, rather than seizing on this as a way of protecting Britain from the effect of tough decisions, Thatcher immediately embarked on a radical course. The detail of her policies is discussed elsewhere in this book. Here we need only note that one of their major effects was an acceleration of the decline in British manufacturing industry. This was not necessarily deliberate (although, of course, Thatcherites were aware that a decline in manufacturing was likely to reduce the power of the trade unions). Afterwards it was easy for Thatcherites to rationalise the impact of their policies, saying that in an era of globalisation (see below) the decline of manufacturing was inevitable. However, it is more likely that at the time the Thatcherites hoped that British manufacturing would regain much of its old potency, thanks to a radical reduction of ill-advised state intervention.

Whatever its original motivations, the impact of Thatcher's policy was dramatic, and the trend established at that time has continued under New Labour (see Table 3.3 for the effect on employment). Within the manufacturing sector, certain changes have been even more remarkable. For example, there are now more professional footballers in Britain than coal-miners.

Table 3.3 The changing balance of selected economic sectors in Britain (millions employed)

	June 1979	March 2009
Financial and business	2.9	6.4
Manufacturing	7.1	2.9
Agriculture and fishing	0.6	0.5

Source: Office for National Statistics

Optimistic observers – who were certainly not confined to Mrs Thatcher's Conservative Party – took this development in their stride. More than two decades after Thatcher came to power, it could be argued that the British had actually benefited from the change. The millions of lost jobs in manufacturing were replaced by new work available within the service sector – notably within finance and business, but also in retail and hospitality. Some of these jobs might be repetitive, and involve quite demeaning dealings with members of the public. But at least they were not life-threatening, as work in the mines had been. Meanwhile, Britain's balance of payments – its trade with other countries – began to show massive deficits. But whereas these figures had once been vital economic indicators for governments, from 1979 onwards even Thatcher's media critics took little notice of them. It was assumed that the bill for imported goods was somehow being paid by the value of Britain's 'invisible earnings' – from its overseas investments, and, increasingly, from its thriving banking sector.

Nevertheless, the decline in manufacturing left many scars. It meant that the old industrial areas of Britain, notably those in Scotland, Wales and the north and Midlands of England, offered few prospects to young people apart from long-term unemployment or migration to more prosperous regions. In the 1980s, the disparity between the old industrial areas and the buoyant south-east of England led to much talk of a 'north–south' divide, although this was an over-simplification since some parts of the south (notably the south-west of England) suffered economic hardship at the time. The variation in the fortunes of various parts of the UK was reflected in the political fortunes of the main parties. By 1997, the Conservatives had lost all of their seats in Wales and Scotland, and were thinly represented in Britain's inner cities. This process had begun after 1979, but until 1997 the party managed to win overall parliamentary majorities on the basis of constituencies in the more prosperous parts of Britain. Whether justified or not, many residents of the areas suffering economic hardship felt that the Conservatives did not care enough to take more than token remedial measures.

■ Economic inequality

Under Mrs Thatcher, official unemployment reached a series of record levels; it peaked at over 3 million,

Royal Ascot is one of the few occasions when aristocrats and the newly enriched use old-fashioned clothes to distinguish themselves from less wealthy people who just like horse-racing
Source: Press Association Images / PA Wire / Empics

and even this figure was widely disbelieved because the government had repeatedly changed the basis of calculation. Unemployment contributed significantly to an increase of economic inequality, in terms both of income and wealth. In the latter respect, the gap between the best and the worst off in Britain has widened markedly since the 1970s. In 1976, the poorest 50 per cent of the British population owned 8 per cent of the wealth. By 2001, this had dropped to 5 per cent. By contrast, the richest 1 per cent owned 23 per cent of the wealth in 2001.

These statistics are particularly significant since Labour came to office in 1997 with the avowed aim of making Britain a fairer place. Some of its measures have been directed towards the reduction of child poverty – a key goal if Britons are ever to enjoy something like 'equality of opportunity'. However, progress even on this score was limited under New Labour. In part, this was because the government was firing at a moving target. Official definitions of poverty are based on *relative*, rather than *absolute* measures: so that as the better-off become more prosperous, others will be defined as 'poor' unless they enjoy a comparable improvement in their living standards. Thus campaigners against poverty were able to attack evidence of serious inequality even though the vast majority of British households possessed washing machines and central heating. Even so, significant disparities remained in what had come to be regarded as 'necessities' for a civilised existence; thus, for example, while almost 80 per cent of those earning at least £1,000 per week had internet access, the corresponding figure for those on £100–£200 per week was around 10 per cent.

As a result, New Labour's record in this field can be judged as no better than patchy, and after more than a decade in office the party had failed to make significant inroads into the 'Thatcher effect' on society, which its leaders had denounced so passionately when they were in opposition. The scene was set for the supposedly 'uncaring' Conservatives to claim that they, rather than Labour, best represented the interests of the poor.

■ Class and consumerism

Evidence that inequality remained serious after the advent of New Labour provided a strange contrast with the widely-prevailing view that Britain was far less 'class-ridden' than it had been in (say) the

1950s. Thus, when the Conservative John Major became Prime Minister in 1990 he stated that the creation of a 'classless society' was one of his key ambitions. In the eyes of some observers, Major's goal was not unrealistic; after all, he himself had risen from relatively humble origins, like his four immediate predecessors in Downing Street (Harold Wilson, Edward Heath, James Callaghan and Margaret Thatcher).

Actually, the fact that it was now possible to become Prime Minister without having attended public school gave a misleading impression of class as a social factor in British life. A cynic might say, in fact, that politics was one of the very few professions in which an affluent background was no longer a crucial advantage (and even in politics it continued to be very helpful). The top lawyers, for example, were still largely the products of public school and either Oxford or Cambridge Universities, which were rightly regarded as bastions of privilege.

The most noteworthy development in Britain since the 1960s is that the *outward trappings* of class have been changing. In the past, the rich had been unmistakable due to things like clothing and speech. These emblems of affluence were no longer so important; the rich sometimes dressed casually, or spoke with regional accents, because the old 'Establishment', which prided itself on appearance and a certain style of speech, had been subjected to media ridicule since the 1960s. More seriously, a person's *occupation* was no longer an infallible guide to his or her social outlook. The most spectacular examples of 'upward mobility' were footballers, who were relatively ill-rewarded in the 1960s, even if they were worshipped on the terraces. From the 1980s, they were elevated to the status of national icons, largely because of the financial rewards they could expect to receive. Other people, like plumbers, had once been regarded as fairly humble functionaries; but by the 1990s it was possible to hear of individuals who had abandoned 'respectable' careers within the traditional professions to take up plumbing, because the latter had become a more lucrative career option.

As a result of such changes, the traditional categorisation of social classes has been changed for official purposes (see Box 3.1). As well as being more complex, the categories are now more fluid than they were in the days when 'white-collar' workers (who made their living by using their brains) could be assumed to enjoy higher social status than manual workers who also used their muscles.

BOX 3.1	Classification of social categories (used in official statistics)

1 Higher managerial and professional (e.g. company directors, doctors and lawyers).
2 Lower managerial and professional (e.g. nurses, journalists and junior police officers).
3 Intermediate occupations (e.g. secretaries).
4 Small employers (e.g. farmers).
5 Lower supervisory occupations (e.g. train drivers).
6 Semi-routine occupations (e.g. shop assistants).
7 Routine occupations (e.g. waiters, refuse collectors).
8 The long-term unemployed.

Nevertheless, while traditional understandings of class have been eroded, new social barriers are constantly being erected. As the above examples suggest, the new measure of a person's social worth is the amount of money she or he earns, whatever its source. This is not necessarily a development which could improve social harmony; if anything, it has introduced a new element of social tension in Britain. While British 'deference' towards one's social superiors was regarded in some quarters as a sign that the country had yet to embrace the ideals of 'meritocratic' liberal democracy, it could be argued that the automatic veneration of wealth (rather than, say, personal integrity) is not an improvement. At the same time, in a 'consumerist' society status is linked as never before to the ostentatious display of expensive items. Even children could be made to feel outcast unless they wear specific items of footwear, or lack the latest kind of mobile telephone. Overall, there are reasons for serious concern that the disappearance of the old, relatively rigid class boundaries have merely unleashed an impulsion towards consumerist conformity.

■ The public sector

Another source of social tension, which pre-dated New Labour but became far more noticeable after 1997, was the difference between those who worked in the 'private sector', and those who were employed by the state. Mrs Thatcher had proclaimed her intention to 'roll back the frontiers of the state'; but (leaving aside the effects of the Thatcherite programme of de-nationalisation within state-run industries) over the 18 years of Conservative government after 1979 the numbers employed in 'Public Administration, education and health' increased by more than a million, from 5,687,000 to 6,676,000.

The rhetoric deployed by Conservative governments between 1979 and 1997 arguably did more harm to the public sector than the employment policies of those years. Convinced Thatcherites took the view that all individuals were motivated by economic self-interest, and from this perspective a nurse (for example) deserved no higher moral status than a bookmaker. The impact of this officially endorsed attitude towards public servants since the 1980s can hardly be exaggerated, and it has been reinforced by the tendency of successive governments to recruit top public servants from the private sector. The notion that serving one's country, in whatever capacity, is a higher ambition than the unadulterated desire to enrich oneself has comprehensively been undermined. Apart from a noticeable effect on the quality of decision making in government – top civil servants could no longer stand up against the ideas of ministers on the grounds that they represented the long-term national interest – the persistent denigration of public sector workers by the Conservatives and New Labour meant that it was difficult to justify the remaining financial benefits of working for the state, most notably the relatively generous pension arrangements.

If anything, the public view of people employed by the state deteriorated under New Labour. Prominent figures, including Tony Blair himself, attacked public servants for their opposition to state-driven reform proposals. The assumption behind such strictures was that most voters would applaud the rhetoric, whether or not the government's proposed changes were well-founded. At the same time, though, New Labour greatly expanded the state sector; public administration, education and health employed 8.14 million people in March 2009, compared to 6.68 million in June 1997.

On their own, these figures prove the continuing importance of the state's economic role in Britain. However, compared to 1979 the attitude of the state towards this economic role has been transformed. Most of the 8.14 million employees are well aware of the need to *behave* as if they work for private business, even if their wages (and pensions) are provided by the taxpayer. As a result, by 2009 poor motivation was very common among the public employees who, according to their critics, had reasons to rejoice thanks to their generous pensions and relative job security.

When the economic downturn (see below) began to bite in 2008, the first effects were felt within the private sector. This opened state servants to additional attack, on the grounds that the people who created wealth in Britain were suffering while those who worked within the public sector were continuing to thrive on the proceeds of taxation. In reality, the spread of the ethos of private business continued to be encouraged by government, so that totemic state institutions like the postal service seemed ripe for privatisation, and it was widely alleged that even the National Health Service (NHS) was thoroughly infested with the profit-motive. After the general election to be held in 2010, there is a strong likelihood of a radical reduction in the state sector, whether or not New Labour is re-elected.

■ A dependency culture?

During the 1980s, Conservative supporters often talked of a 'dependency culture' which had been created by an over-generous welfare state in the postwar period. On this view, a substantial group in society (usually inhabiting run-down inner-city areas) depended entirely on the state for their sustenance. For them, living on a variety of benefits had become a way of life which they were very likely to transmit to their children. The obvious answer, for such social commentators, was to make state benefits much less generous. This approach would actually improve the prospects for the long-term unemployed, for whom the gradual withdrawal of benefits could be seen as 'liberating', leading to a more prosperous future in employment and the inculcation of much needed self-esteem. Equally, though, such arguments were bound to appeal to hard-working but low-paid voters, who simply resented others who were apparently enjoying equivalent lifestyles without even trying to find jobs for themselves.

Under New Labour, the strategy of denying people the chance to spend their whole lives on benefits was given an aggressively positive 'spin'. Typically, government spokespeople argued that disadvantaged individuals should be given the opportunity to move 'from welfare to work'. In the United States, such policies were generally given the name 'workfare', and in that country there was an unmistakable element of compulsion (for example, if a person did not perform work of some kind he or she would not be entitled to taxpayer-funded benefits). For understandable reasons, Labour was not keen to advertise its acceptance of this approach: but over the years it gradually edged towards it, building on the previous Conservative decision to re-brand 'unemployment benefit' as 'the jobseekers' allowance'.

Despite such governmental initiatives, it was difficult to deny that a substantial sector of society was failing to derive any benefit from consumerism. While many observers took it for granted that Britain was a genuine 'meritocracy', the very idea of equal opportunities would have left members of the country's 'underclass' utterly mystified. Immediately after the 1997 general election, Tony Blair paid a visit to one area whose inhabitants were apparently faced with a lifetime of 'social exclusion'. Four years later, just before Labour was re-elected, a series of riots broke out in similar areas. However, whereas the Conservatives had sustained lasting criticism after the widespread inner-city riots of 1981, the violent outbreaks of 2001 were soon forgotten. This suggested that most people now felt that although specific instances of social exclusion could be remedied by government action, the problem as a whole was too deeply rooted to be eradicated from Britain.

■ Gender

Another trend which has persisted since the Thatcher years is the changing economic status of women. In June 2009, a total of 13.4 million British women were in employment of some kind, compared to 15.5 million men. This marked a significant improvement from the situation in 1971, when only 36.5 per cent of the workforce was female. Even in 1991, the proportion was only 43.2 per cent. However, when examined in detail the figures are less impressive. More than 5.6 million (over 42 per cent) of employed women in 2009 only worked part time. Among men, the corresponding figure was 1.9 million (just over 12 per cent of the male workforce). In this context a continued disparity in earnings, and in workplace rights, is obvious. Even among women who work full time, earnings tend to be significantly less, largely because of career breaks.

Finally, women are barely represented at the top of the hierarchy in institutions within civil society, such as privately-owned businesses or professions like the law. Politics, ironically, is an exception – or at least, it is becoming more equal after many decades in which females were only promoted as 'token women'. One of the latter, Margaret Thatcher, did manage to reach the top, thanks to luck as well as her undeniable abilities and dynamism. Notoriously, Thatcher did little to promote the careers of other Conservative women. Since then, however, all of the major parties have made concerted efforts to improve the representation of women within parliament, with significant success compared to the situation in the 1980s.

From this mixed picture, a few tentative conclusions may be drawn. Due to different life-expectancy there are more women than men in Britain. A more significant fact is that young women consistently outperform males in education. Everything else being equal, one would expect women to be at least as well-represented in the workforce as men, especially at the higher levels. But, of course, 'everything else' is far from equal. While men are more willing nowadays to accept a child-nurturing role, women are still much more likely to have their careers interrupted if they decide to start a family. Those who try to 'have it all', i.e. by having children but resuming their careers at the first opportunity, sometimes express regret when reflecting on their choice in later years. While much of the media publicity has concerned individuals in lucrative jobs, the expectation that women should find work of some kind has had a mixed effect at all levels. Many families have struck an acceptable 'work–life balance', with both partners making a roughly equal contribution to the economy of the household as well as the child care. In other cases, though, the stress resulting from an unequal balance has had a damaging effect on children as well as parents. More controversially, it can be argued that the greater economic expectations from women have helped to increase the incidence of single-parent families. In the past, the assumption that the male would always

be the chief bread-winner added to the moral pressure on a father to stay within the family unit. Now a father wishing to escape responsibility has social expectation on his side when he claims that the mother should find some kind of work to help support the children. On the other hand, women trapped in unsatisfactory relationships are less likely nowadays to be deterred from a break-up by the fear of destitution.

The changed economic situation of British women has undoubtedly helped to reduce the prominence in public debate of feminist arguments which captured much media attention in the 1960s and 1970s. Some observers, indeed, argue that the debate over feminism is over, and that even if absolute equality has not been achieved the major battles have been won. We have seen, however, that the remaining inequalities in the economic sphere are significant, and that the undoubted progress of recent decades has left new and unresolved social problems. The rude health of the pornography business introduces another difficulty, even though some 'post-feminists' seem to regard this as yet another way in which women can achieve 'empowerment'. The supposed link between the use of women as objects for gratification and the prevalence of sexual violence has certainly not been disproved, even if British society seems to have accepted that magazines and newspapers which rely on sex for their sales can be displayed prominently on supermarket shelves.

■ The changing nature of government intervention

In the course of our discussion we have noted a strong connection between economic and social developments. Furthermore, we have seen that changes within the economy and society often generate political dilemmas. One phenomenon which has outlasted the years of 'postwar consensus', indeed, is the general feeling that if a problem comes to public notice, 'the government should do something about it'. Mrs Thatcher and her ideological allies were particularly keen to change this commonplace view, but at best they reduced expectations in specific areas (e.g. the alleviation of poverty or the need to subsidise economic activities even if they were not profitable).

In many ways, the history of British politics since 1979 can be seen as an attempt by governments of both main parties to change the social and economic problems which they should have responsibility for tackling. Thus, after coming to office in 1979 senior Conservatives gave the impression that Britain's economic difficulties were the fault either of the trade unions or of previous governments. Far from intervening to halt the decline of Britain's manufacturing industry, they asserted that their job was to convince world markets that the days of intervention were over. There were some things that governments could do, and in future they would perform them with greater success, thus restoring the prestige of the British state. Other developments, however, were the product of 'market forces', and even if their short-term effects were very damaging the market should be allowed to resolve them one way or another, without interference by the state.

It is often argued that this change was necessary, since by the mid-1970s the government had become 'overloaded' in its socio-economic responsibilities. But successive governments have not lost the itch for intervention, even in the most bizarre circumstances. Tony Blair and Gordon Brown both took every opportunity to send their good wishes to British sporting teams – as if their intervention could affect the result in any way – and on one occasion Blair was even cited in support of a fictitious character in a television soap opera who had been sent to prison.

Unfortunately for the parties which win general elections in Britain, the public has good reason to demand action when the country is faced with real rather than imaginary problems. British governments still have considerable power to affect economic and even social developments. For example, they can pass laws, or manipulate the tax system to affect the behaviour of the people who have voted for them. However, there are constraints on this power, which have become more powerful in recent decades.

■ 'Europeanisation' and 'globalisation'

According to some critics, since the early 1970s British governments have been hampered of their own volition, through the country's repeated applications for membership of the EEC. Undoubtedly membership of what is now the EU has limited the

British freedom of action, especially since Mrs Thatcher's decision to push for a single European market in 1985. To make this vision into a concrete reality, European institutions had to enforce uniform standards across a range of economic activities, often to the considerable irritation of British businesspeople. Membership of the EU has also affected British social policies, for example on retirement age and immigration (although it must be noted that Britain was not a signatory to the border-relaxing Schengen Agreement which is usually cited in the media as the cause of Eastern European immigration to Britain; in any case, Schengen was not a formal EC initiative).

However, it can be argued that, far from being a serious limitation of Britain's right to make social and economic policies, the EU is actually a defence against the more pervasive process of 'globalisation'. On this analysis, when Mrs Thatcher took office Britain was faced with a stark choice: it could either adopt a 'siege economy', excluding imported goods from other countries, or it could open its economy to global forces, relying on the adaptability of its citizens to make a living in a new, more uncertain world. In taking the second option, it could be argued, the Thatcher government left itself highly vulnerable to fluctuations in the global economy, so that Britain would in future be subjected to periods of economic 'bust' as well as 'booms'. However, this uncertain prospect was seen as being far better than the inevitable decline which would ensue if the country tried to seal itself away from the global marketplace. Meanwhile, the Conservatives could hope that their radical policies would fuel an underlying improvement in the British economy, notably by privatising state-owned industries and reducing the power of the trade unions. The resulting economic system would be fitter and leaner, and thus better equipped to ride out any future storms in the global marketplace. Its prospects would be much better if Britain was part of a Europe-wide free-trading area, ensuring a large potential market for its goods whatever other countries might do to protect their own industries.

■ From 'boom' to 'bust': the economy under 'New' Labour

As we have noted, the Thatcherite approach to economics was convenient for ministers, who were able to shed numerous responsibilities (not least for the nationalised industries) which had caused regular political headaches in the postwar period. During the 1980s it also appeared that governments could survive serious economic difficulties, so long as the majority of the electorate remained prosperous and could be persuaded that global developments, rather than domestic decisions, were to blame. Thus the Conservatives won the 1992 general election, when many British families were still suffering from the effects of a serious recession.

It would be too simplistic to say that New Labour merely continued the Conservative approach after it took office in 1997; as we have seen, for example, the new government did try to alleviate child poverty. But we have also seen that the major socio-economic trends of the 1980s and early 1990s persisted without much abatement. In particular, Britain's prosperity became increasingly reliant on the financial sector of the economy. Sensing that this, rather than manufacturing, would be the main motor of the British economy in future, Labour politicians had been anxious to cultivate friendships within the City of London. This calculation seemed sensible, not least because the good opinion of the financial markets is a key factor in the economic viability of any country. Thus, for example, an incoming Labour government would not need to worry about an adverse reaction to its victory among international financiers, even if Britain's balance of 'visible' trade with the rest of the world was permanently in deficit.

For ten years, Labour's pact with the forces of globalisation had apparently paid off. Thanks to the buoyancy of the service sector, it even seemed that the government had restored something like 'full employment' (defined during the postwar period as a level not exceeding 3 per cent of the population). Senior government ministers began to lecture their EU colleagues about the supposed benefits of 'flexible labour markets', which in practice meant minimal state regulation of economic activity and laws which made it easier for firms to dismiss their employees. However, even at the height of the government's popularity its achievements needed qualification; for example, many people had left the workforce because they had registered for 'invalidity' rather than 'unemployment' benefit, and as we have seen many of the new jobs in the British economy were part time.

More seriously, those who worried about the decline of manufacturing could claim that they had been right all along. The economy was too dependent on the success of the financial sector, which in turn was heavily dependent on the desire of individual consumers to accumulate debts rather than waiting until they could afford their purchases. When the inevitable downturn came, it began with American financial institutions (which were closely linked to those in Britain) and spread almost immediately across the Atlantic. Having been relatively frugal in its economic management between 1997 and 2000, the New Labour government had followed the example of its electorate, by spending in excess of its revenue. Thus for a variety of reasons Britain was always likely to suffer badly from an economic downturn, compared to its neighbours. It was no longer possible for governments to absolve themselves from responsibility for the economic hardship suffered by the voters; and, as Britain entered a new era of tough economic decisions, it was difficult to calculate the social and political consequences with any confidence, in a country with so many underlying tensions.

BOX 3.2   BRITAIN IN CONTEXT

Britain's current economic situation is an open invitation to speculate about the position of the country in a wider context. On the one hand, as we have seen, the UK remains relatively prosperous. However, in recent decades it has retained this privileged status while the original basis for its economic strength (manufacturing) has been in a steep decline. The optimistic assessment of this position rests on the idea that the health of Britain's service sector (especially finance) has provided sufficient economic compensation. Yet it was always clear that the UK would suffer more than other countries from the effects of an economic downturn which began within the financial sector. Hopes of a sustainable economic recovery rest crucially on Britain's ability to equip its workforce with relevant skills, in a globalised economy which is likely to set a high premium on 'green' technology which causes minimal environmental damage.

In global terms, the difference between Britain and emerging industrial giants like China and India is difficult to put into context – at least without resorting to generalisations about the tendency of people to reject harsh working conditions once their country's average standard of living reaches a certain level, and they can compare their own situation to that of similar workers in other countries. It can even be argued that the impact of globalisation has been so different in various regions of Britain that it is difficult to make generalisations about economic conditions *within* the country. Differences were always likely to be accentuated by the effect of an economic recession. Thus, even within the supposedly prosperous Greater London area, in July 2009 the borough of Newham had the lowest rate of employment for the whole of the UK (60 per cent). Meanwhile, residents of the City of London had one of the highest rates (85.6 per cent) – although the latter figure was likely to decline due to the effects of the recession, especially on lower-paid workers.

Chapter summary

The chapter illustrates the complex relationship between society, economy and politics in the UK. Britain is densely populated even by European standards, although there are important regional variations. In themselves, these variations lead to difficulties for policy makers. Furthermore, Britain has an increasingly diverse society, and immigration is often seen as a key issue for voters (even if politicians are sometimes unwilling to address it). Fear of immigration (and hostility towards recent arrivals) tends to increase during times of economic uncertainty; and although Britain is hardly alone in hosting a large immigrant community, the debate in the UK can become particularly heated, not least because of the common view that the country is already 'overcrowded'.

The chapter goes on to discuss economic change. For most observers, the story here is one of protracted decline, punctuated by attempts on the part of UK governments and their media supporters to assert that the country has experienced an economic 'miracle'. Whatever the quality of these arguments, one economic trend is indisputable: compared to its status in the nineteenth century, Britain has ceased to be a dominant force in manufacturing. This decline, underway long before the Second World War, has accelerated since 1945 (and especially since Margaret Thatcher's Conservatives took office in 1979). The service sector is now the main element in UK economic activity. Some critics argue that this leaves Britain more vulnerable than ever before to fluctuations in the global economy, and its heavy reliance on financial services (banking etc.) has certainly helped to worsen the effects of the global economic downturn which began in 2007.

Nevertheless, most British politicians remain enthusiastic champions of 'globalisation', taking the view that free trade between nations is the best way of ensuring prosperity for all. At the same time, though, this development reduces the ability of British policy makers to influence the country's economic fortunes; and, since social and political change is so clearly linked to economic patterns, it is not surprising that the overall effect of globalisation has been to make voters and politicians alike feel more insecure.

Discussion points

■ Do you think that the reduction of direct government intervention in the UK economy since 1979 has been a welcome development?

■ 'Since 1945, there has been a tendency for opposition parties to exaggerate British economic decline, and for governments to look on the bright side'. Do you agree, and if so, has this tendency helped the British public to appreciate the dilemmas facing their country?

■ Has immigration brought benefits to British society, or would it have been better if the country had closed its borders after 1945?

■ Do you agree with the contention that 'Britishness' is best defined as a common enjoyment of a consumerist culture?

Further reading

The key text on this subject is A.H. Halsey and J. Webb (eds), *Twentieth Century British Social Trends* (Macmillan, 2000), which contains expert appraisals of the major developments over a century of rapid social and economic change. Annual editions of *Social Trends* are available online, at www.statistics.gov.uk/statbase; reviews of regional change are available from the same source. On specific subjects, R. Lister's *Poverty* (Oxford University Press, 2004), and J. Solomon's *Race and Racism in Britain* (Palgrave, 3rd edn, 2003) are more detailed studies.

On economic developments in Britain since 1945, contrasting arguments are presented by A. Gamble, *Britain in Decline: Economic Policy, Political Strategy and the British State*, Macmillan (4th edn, 1994), and G. Bernstein, *The Myth of Decline: The Rise of Britain since 1945* (Pimlico, 2004). On the impact of Thatcherism, see especially Ian Gilmour, *Dancing with Dogma: Britain under Thatcherism* (Simon & Schuster, 1992). On class, see the provocative thesis advanced by A. Adonis and S. Pollard in *A Class Act: The Myth of Britain's Classless Society* (Hamish Hamilton 1997).

Websites

The government's National Statistics Online (www.ons.gov.uk) is an invaluable resource for students of social and economic change. It is regularly updated with new statistical information, so it is advisable to browse through its contents rather than simply searching for specific items. Information concerning income and wealth can also be obtained from www.hmrc.gov.uk. A respected source of data and comment on economic matters is the Institute for Fiscal Studies, whose website is www.ifs.org.uk. Comparative data can be accessed through the website of the Organisation for Economic Co-operation and Development (OECD), at www.oecd.org/.

And another thing . . .

The legacy of empire

Andrew Gamble

Empires are transient affairs. In Shelley's poem, *Ozymandias*, a traveller from an antique land tells of finding a shattered statue in the desert. Its inscription read:

'My Name is Ozymandias, king of kings:
Look on my works, ye Mighty, and despair.'
Nothing beside remains. Round the decay
Of that colossal wreck, boundless and bare
The lone and level sands stretch far away.

Some think the British empire is a bit like that. At the last night of the Proms, the promenaders still bellow out the words of that great imperial anthem, *Land of Hope and Glory*: 'Wider still and wider shall thy bounds be set. God who made thee mighty, make thee mightier yet.' Their meaning has become rather obscure in the first decade of the twenty-first century. But one hundred years before it was different. The British empire was at the height of its powers and still expanding.

For several hundred years the English and then British state controlled an empire, and one of the largest the world had ever seen. This was the empire on which the sun never set. At its height, after the end of the First World War, it stretched across every continent, and incorporated a quarter of the world's population and about one-fifth of the land area of the globe. After 1945 the whole imposing edifice was dismantled with remarkable speed, and relatively little bloodshed, although the British had to fight insurgencies in several territories, including Malaya, Cyprus, Kenya and Aden, and had their authority defied by the white settlers of Rhodesia. By the end of the first decade of the twenty-first century very little was left. The remnants of the British empire were a scattering of islands across the oceans of the world, with a population of less than 200,000.

Yet the empire continues to shape British politics. The Britain we inhabit today was made what it is by the empire, and the signs of it are all around us.

Central to the project of empire was the expansion of England, and this expansion did not just involve far-flung dependencies in exotic places. The expansion of England began first in the islands of Britain and Ireland, and led to the incorporation of all these territories into one British state, a United Kingdom. This was the heart of all the empires that were to follow – in North America, in India, in Australasia, and in Africa. The British were to lose their first great territorial empire, in North America, after the American Revolution, but it proved far from a mortal blow. Instead it helped greatly to extend British power in another direction, towards trade and the creation of a vast open trading network which covered the greater part of the world in the course of the nineteenth century. This informal empire of trade, investment and finance was more valuable in many respects than the formal empire of territory, although the two were often combined.

The success of its policies of continual external expansion both through the acquisition of territories and the growth of trade and industry gave Britain a position of acknowledged supremacy by the middle of the nineteenth century. Britain was not just the ruler of the most populous and extensive territorial empire but also the centre of an expanding capitalist economic order, based on relatively open flows of capital, goods and people, which by the end of the nineteenth century had created a new kind of world economy, and the start of that diffusion of Western institutions, technologies, ideas and culture which has continued up to the present.

The demands of its territorial empire and the demands of its commercial empire meant Britain often appeared both authoritarian and liberal. The tension between these two, and the huge wealth that accrued to the British upper classes, set British society and institutions in a mould which is still visible. Many characteristic British institutions including the BBC, the universities, the public schools, the Church of England, the City of London, the Armed Forces, the Civil Service, the Law, the Monarchy, and Parliament itself were remade at the zenith of empire, and although now battered still retain a great deal of their familiar shape, and still exude the confidence that came from knowing that London was the financial capital of the world, that a quarter of the map was coloured pink, and that Britain set the standard. The British were leaders and pioneers and British ways of doing things were assumed to be the best.

Withdrawal from the empire was traumatic for many, but had in the end to be accepted. For a time it deeply divided opinion in Britain. By 1970 the greater part of the formal empire had gone, only a few major colonies like Hong Kong remaining in British hands. There were still, however, a number of unresolved issues, such as the existence of white supremacist governments in two former British colonies in Africa, Rhodesia and South Africa; and the problem of Palestine and the Middle East. As countries gained their independence they mostly joined the Commonwealth, but this has never been a very effective body in international affairs.

Among the many legacies of empire was immigration. The influx of citizens from the black Commonwealth was initially made possible by the right of all citizens from the empire and Commonwealth to work and reside in Britain. Gradually tighter controls were imposed, but by then the extent of black immigration from the Caribbean and from India and Pakistan into the UK in the decades after 1945 had changed Britain irreversibly, and made it a multi-ethnic and a multicultural society. This had profound consequences for schooling, for housing, for welfare, for employment, and also for politics too.

A second legacy was that the Union of the four nations in Britain and Ireland began to weaken. New troubles of an old kind erupted in Northern Ireland, but there was also an upsurge of support for nationalist parties in Scotland and Wales campaigning for independence. Empire had supplied a powerful project and created institutions which bound the nations of the United Kingdom together. With the empire gone the point of the Union no longer seemed so obvious. There were many small countries that were independent states within the European Union. Nationalists argue that this is a possible and desirable future for Scotland and for Wales. In this way the end of empire has brought into question the continuation of the United Kingdom, one of Europe's oldest states which was forged by the imperial designs of England.

A third legacy of empire was the choice between Europe and America. It has divided the main parties. Britain was a close ally of the United States in the Second World War, and this alliance continued after 1945 with the setting up of NATO and a range of military, diplomatic, financial, economic and intelligence collaboration. All parties in Britain were committed to the continuation of the American Alliance but they were divided as to whether Britain should participate in the new institutions promoting economic and political integration in Europe. This conflict over Britain's future, and how deeply involved it should become in Europe could be (and was) argued both ways from an imperial perspective. There were those who believed Britain should join Europe and lead Europe. The European Union would become the new vehicle for British power and influence in the world. There were others who thought Britain should remain separate from Europe, preserving its own sovereignty and independence. A diminution of power was better than absorption into something Britain could not control. For Eurosceptics Europe is no substitute for empire. Britain had other choices – to remain in splendid isolation, or to cleave ever more closely to the United States.

The ambivalence over Europe, which might seem the obvious international grouping for a post-imperial Britain, can in part be explained by the continued British commitment to that other legacy of empire, the open liberal world economic order, responsibility for which after 1945 was assumed by the United States. For many in the British political class the sense of imperial mission that had been so strong in the first part of the twentieth century did not die with the passing of Empire, but was transferred to the United States. The European Union for many former imperialists of all parties has never seemed a credible vehicle for that mission. Successive British Governments have seen the continued global leadership of the United States to be essential for securing Britain's major strategic interests. This explains why Britain participated alongside the United States in wars in Iraq and Afghanistan, and worked with the United States to coordinate international efforts to solve the 2008 financial crisis. Despite everything that has happened to them in the last 60 years, the British still think of themselves as an important nation, a nation that should be engaged in international affairs, and should be helping to shape the way the world is governed. That is perhaps the most powerful imperial legacy of all.

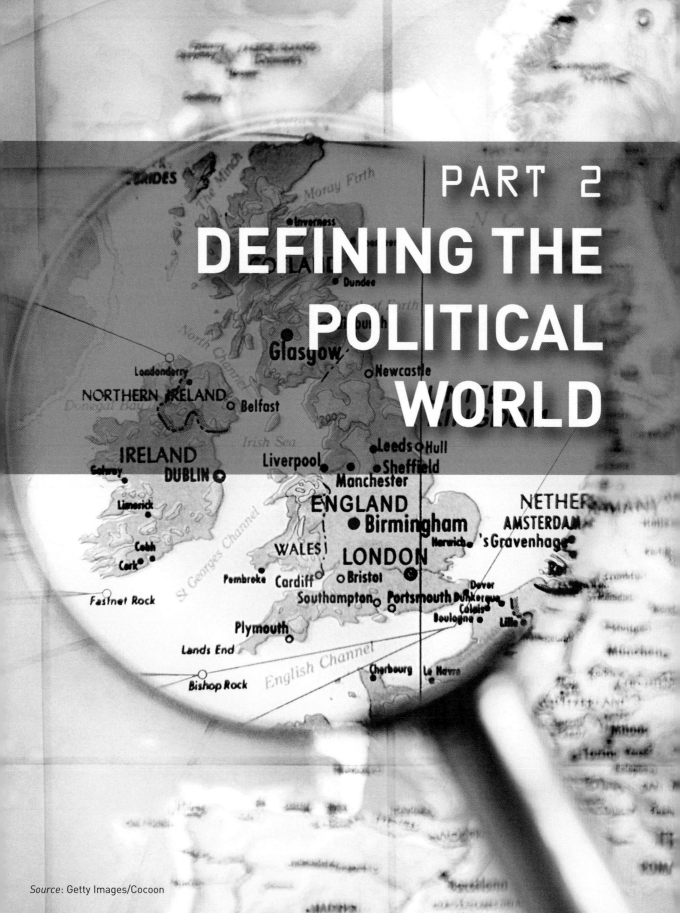

PART 2
DEFINING THE POLITICAL WORLD

Source: Getty Images/Cocoon

CHAPTER 4
Ideology and the liberal tradition

Bill Jones

Learning objectives

- To clarify the concept of ideology.

- To trace the transition of new ideas from their 'revolutionary' inception to accepted orthodoxy.

- To show how classical liberalism developed into new liberalism, the creed that set the social agenda for the next century.

Introduction

This chapter begins by discussing what we mean by the term 'ideology'. It goes on to explain how 'liberal' ideas entered the political culture as heresies in the seventeenth and eighteenth centuries but went on to become the orthodoxies of the present age. Classical liberalism in the mid-nineteenth century is examined together with the birth of modern liberalism in the early twentieth century. So-called 'liberal' ideas therefore provide the architecture of our beliefs in a democratic society; we hold our political views views, discuss and debate them within the framework of ideas acquired hundreds of years ago.

■ What is ideology?

For up to two decades after 1945 it seemed as if ideology as a factor in British politics was on the wane. The coalition comradeship of the war had drawn some of the sting from the sharp doctrinal conflicts between the two major political parties, and in its wake the Conservatives had conceded – without too much ill grace – that Labour would expand welfare services and nationalise a significant sector of the economy. Once in power after 1951, the Conservatives presided over their socialist inheritance of a mixed economy and a welfare state. Both parties seemed to have converged towards a general consensus on political values and institutions: there was more to unite than to divide them. By the end of the 1950s, some commentators – notably the American political scientist Daniel Bell – were pronouncing 'the end of ideology' (see Bell 1960) in Western societies.

However, the faltering of the British economy in the 1960s, exacerbated in the early 1970s by the rise in oil prices, industrial unrest and raging inflation, reopened the ideological debate with a vengeance. A revived Labour Left hurled contumely at their right-wing Cabinet colleagues for allegedly betraying socialist principles. Margaret Thatcher, meanwhile, Leader of the Opposition after 1975, began to elaborate a position far to the right of her predecessor Edward Heath (Prime Minister, 1970–4 – see Biography). The industrial paralysis of the 1978–9 'winter of discontent' provided a shabby end for Jim Callaghan's Labour government and a perfect backcloth against which Thatcher's confident assertions could be projected. From 1979 to 1990, ideology in the form of Thatcherism or the New Right triumphed over what has subsequently been labelled the 'post-war consensus'.

BIOGRAPHY

Edward Heath (1916–2005)

Conservative Prime Minister. Educated at Oxford in the 1930s, when he was deeply concerned about unemployment and the threat of fascism. He fought with distinction in the war and entered politics in its wake. He was a prominent younger member of Macmillan's governments and became leader of the Conservatives a year after their defeat of 1964. He became Prime Minister in 1970 on a right-wing ticket but resorted to 'left-wing' reflation when unemployment began to soar. During his four years in power, his greatest achievement was taking the country into Europe. He was replaced by Margaret Thatcher as leader in 1975 and could not hide his resentment at her 'disloyalty' (i.e. to him) or her extreme right-wing policies. He remained a bitter critical figure, defending his record and Europe, attacking his successor until the end of his career.

Ideology as a concept is not easy to define. Perhaps it is helpful to regard ideology as 'applied philosophy'. It links philosophical ideas to the contemporary world, it provides a comprehensive and systematic perspective whereby human society can be understood, and it provides a framework of principles from which policies can be developed.

Individuals support ideologies for a variety of reasons: moral commitment – often genuine, whatever cynics might say – as well as self-interest. It is entirely possible for a businessman, for example, to believe quite genuinely, that a pro-business set of policies by a party is good not only for him but for the nation as a whole. Clearly, ideology will mean more to political activists. It has to be recognised that most people are ill-informed on political matters, nor especially interested in them. But the broad mass of the population is not completely inert. During election campaigns they receive a crash course in political education, and leaving aside the more crass appeals to emotion and unreason, most voters are influenced to some extent by the ideological debate. The party with the clearest message that seems most relevant to the times can win elections, as Labour discovered in 1945, the Conservatives in 1979 and Labour again in 1997.

■ Classifying ideologies

This is a difficult and imperfect science, but the following two approaches should help to clarify it.

The horizontal left–right continuum

Left	Centre	Right

This is the most familiar classification, used and abused in the press and in everyday conversations. It arose from the seating arrangements adopted in the French Estates General in 1789, where the aristocracy sat to the right of the King and the popular movements to his left. Subsequently the terms have come to represent adherence to particular groups of principles. Right-wingers stress freedom, or the right of individuals to do as they please and develop their own lives and personalities without interference, especially from governments – which history teaches are potentially tyrannical. Left-wingers believe that this kind of freedom is only won by the strong at the expense of the weak. They see equality as the more important value and stress the collective interest of the community above that of the individual.

The implications of these principles for economic policy are obviously of key importance. Right-wingers champion free enterprise, or capitalism: the rights of individuals to set up their own businesses, to provide goods and services and to reap what reward they can. Left-wingers disagree. Capitalism, they argue, creates poverty amid plenty – much better to move towards collective ownership so that

workers can receive the full benefit of their labour. Politicians in the centre dismiss both these positions as extreme and damaging to the harmony of national life. They tend to argue for various combinations of left and right principles or compromises between them: in practice a mixed economy plus efficient welfare services. The left–right continuum therefore relates in practice principally to economic and social policy.

Left	Centre	Right
Equality	Less inequality	Freedom
Collectivism	Some collectivism	Individualism
Collective ownership	Mixed economy	Free enterprise

The vertical axis or continuum

The inadequacies of the left–right continuum are obvious. It is both crude and inaccurate in that many people can subscribe to ideas drawn from its whole width and consequently defy classification. H.J. Eysenck suggested in the early 1950s that if a 'tough' and 'tender' axis could bisect the left–right continuum, ideas could be more accurately plotted on two dimensions. In this way ideological objectives could be separated from political methodology – so tough left-wingers, e.g. communists, would occupy the top left-hand quarter, tough right-wingers, e.g. fascists, the top right-hand quarter, and so on.

The vertical axis can also be used to plot other features:

1 An authoritarian–libertarian axis is perhaps a more precise variation on the tough and tender theme.

2 A status quo–revolutionary axis is also useful. The Conservative Party has traditionally been characterised as defending the established order. However, Margaret Thatcher was a committed radical who wanted to engineer major and irreversible changes. It was Labour and the Conservative 'wets' who defended the status quo in the 1980s.

Political parties and the left–right continuum

Despite its inadequacies, the left–right continuum is useful because it is commonly understood (though see Box 4.1). It will be used as a guide to the

BOX 4.1	IDEAS AND PERSPECTIVES

Left and right discussed

In his book *The Third Way* (1998), Anthony Giddens suggests left and right are less than adequate terms. He points out that what was once left can now be right – such as nineteenth-century free-market views. He quotes the Italian writer Bobbio, who argues that politics is adversarial and that 'left and right' encapsulates the familiar idea of bodily opposites, i.e. the left and right arms. He goes on to say that when ideas are evenly balanced most people accept the dichotomy, but when one ideology seems 'the only game in town' neither side finds the terms suitable. The strong ideology seeks to claim it is the 'only' alternative, while the weaker tries to strengthen its position by absorbing some elements of the stronger side and offering them as its own, producing a 'synthesis of opposing positions with the intentions in practice of saving whatever can be saved of one's own position by drawing in the opposing position and thus neutralising it'. Both sides then present their views as beyond the old left/right distinction and as something totally new and exciting. Giddens comments that 'the claim that Tony Blair has taken over most of the views of Thatcherism and recycled them as something new is readily comprehensible from such a standpoint'. Giddens insists that the 'left' is not just the opposite of 'right': the core of the former is concerned with social justice or 'emancipatory' politics, while the right has shifted to anti-global and even racist positions.

He goes on to accept that socialism is no longer valid as a 'theory of economic management' and that in consequence the right/left distinction has lost relevance. Now people face 'life politics' decisions such as those connected with nuclear energy, work, global warming, devolution and the future of the EU, none of which fits easily into the old dichotomy. By talking of the 'radical centre', Giddens suggests that 'major gains' can be derived as it 'permits exchange across political fences which were much higher'. So to look at welfare reform, it is not merely an argument about high or low spending but comprises 'common issues facing all welfare reformers'. The question of how to deal with an ageing population isn't just a matter of setting pension levels. It requires more radical rethinking in relation to the changing nature of ageing.'

Source: Giddens (1998: 37–46)

following sections, but first a word on the way in which political parties relate to the political spectrum.

For most of the postwar period, the major ideological divisions have not occurred between the two big parties but within them. The Labour Party has covered a very wide spectrum from the revolutionary Left to the cautious social democrat Right. Similarly, two major Conservative schools of thought developed in the late 1970s: traditional ('wet') conservatism and the New Right or Thatcherite conservatism. The centre ground was dominated for many years by the Liberal Party, but during the 1980s it was first augmented by the Social Democratic Party (which split off from the Labour Party in 1981) and then was fragmented when the merger initiative following the 1987 general election resulted in the awkward progeny of the Social and Liberal Democrats plus the rump Social Democratic Party led defiantly by David Owen until May 1990, when the party formally folded.

■ The liberal tradition

Since then, like so many other political labels coined as forms of abuse ('tory' was once a name given to Irish outlaws), the word 'liberalism' has lost its derogatory connotations and fully traversed the ground between vice and virtue. Now liberalism denotes opinions and qualities that are generally applauded. Most people would like to think they are liberal in the sense of being open-minded, tolerant, generous or rational. This is partly because the ideas of the English liberal philosophers from the mid-seventeenth to the mid-nineteenth centuries became accepted as dominant elements in our political culture. These were the ideas that helped to create our liberal democratic political system in the late nineteenth century and since then have provided its philosophical underpinning.

Interestingly, in the USA the term came to assume a pejorative meaning in the early 1980s, when the Republicans successfully linked it to being 'soft on communism' and therefore anti-American (see Box 4.2); in March 2006 the film actor George Clooney's statement that he was indeed a 'liberal' consequently contained a note of defiance.

An important distinction clearly has to be made between liberal with a small 'l' and the Liberalism associated with the party of the same name until the 1987 merger. The Liberal Party always claimed a particular continuity with liberal philosophical ideas; but so deeply ingrained have these views become that most political parties also owe them substantial unacknowledged philosophical debts. For their part, liberals have made contributions to political, social and economic thinking that have been hugely influential and have been plundered shamelessly by other parties. It makes sense, therefore, to begin with some consideration of the liberal tradition of both the philosophical 'l' and party political 'L' variety.

Philosophical liberalism

Bertrand Russell attributes the birth of English liberal thought in part to the French philosopher René Descartes (1596–1650). His famous proposition 'I think, therefore I am' made 'the basis of knowledge different for each person since for each the starting point was his own existence not that of other individuals or the community' (Russell 1965: 579). To us such propositions seem unexceptional, but in the mid-seventeenth century they were potentially revolutionary because they questioned the very basis of feudal society. This relied on unquestioning acceptance of the monarch's divine right to rule, the aristocracy's hereditary privileges and the Church's explanation of the world together with its moral leadership. Feudal society was in any case reeling from the impact of the Civil War (1642–9), the repercussions of which produced a limited constitutional monarchy and the embryo of modern parliamentary government. Descartes had inaugurated a new style of thinking.

BIOGRAPHY

Bertrand Russell (1872–1970)

British philosopher and mathematician. *Principia Mathematica* was his most influential philosophical work but he wrote many popular books as well, including *The History of Western Philosophy* (1946). A radical member of the Liberal Party, he opposed the new creed of communism and after the Second World War threw himself into opposing nuclear weapons as a passionate pacifist.

Rationality

John Locke (1632–1704) did much to set the style of liberal thinking as rational and undogmatic. He accepted some certainties, such as his own existence, God and mathematical logic, but he respected an area of doubt in relation to most propositions. He was inclined to accept differences of opinion as the natural consequences of free individual development. Liberal philosophers tended to give greater credence to facts established by scientific enquiry – the systematic testing of theories against reality – rather than to assertions accepted as fact purely on the basis of tradition.

Toleration

This lack of dogmatism was closely connected with a liberal prejudice in favour of **toleration** and compromise. Conflicts between crown and Parliament, Catholicism and Protestantism had divided the country for too long, they felt: it was time to recognise that religious belief was a matter of personal conscience, not a concern of government.

Natural rights and the consent of the governed

This idea emerged out of the 'contract' theorists of the seventeenth and eighteenth centuries. These thinkers believed that each individual had made a kind of agreement to obey the government in exchange for the services of the state, principally 'security' or protection from wrong-doing. It was not suggested that anything had actually been signed;

the idea was more of an application of the legal concept of rights to the philosophical realm. It was all a far cry from Sir Robert Filmer's doctrine that the divine authority of monarchs to receive absolute obedience could be traced back to Adam and Eve, from whom all monarchs were originally descended.

Individual liberty

The idea of natural rights was closely allied to the concept of individual **liberty**, which had already been established by the eighteenth century: freedom for arbitrary arrest, search and taxation; equality before the law; jury trials, freedom of thought and expression, freedom to buy and sell.

Such liberties in practice were protected by constitutional checks and balances, limited government and representation. John Stuart Mill established the classic liberal view on liberty when he argued that anyone should be free to do as they wish unless their actions impinge on the freedom of someone else (see Box 4.2).

Constitutional checks and balances

Locke argued something destined to influence all future democratic government: that to ensure that executive power was not exercised arbitrarily by the monarch, the law-making or legislative arm of government should be separate, independent and removable by the community. This doctrine of the 'separation of powers' informed liberal enthusiasm for written constitutions (although, ironically, Britain has never had a written constitution or, indeed, an effective separation of powers).

Limited government

Instead of the absolute power that Filmer argued the monarch was free to exercise, liberal philosophers, mindful of past abuses, sought to restrict the legitimacy of government to a protection of civil liberties. It was held to be especially important that government did not interfere with the right to property or the exercise of economic activity.

Representation

It followed that if the legislature was to be removable then it needed to be representative. Many liberal Whigs – inclined to support parliament rather than the monarch – in the eighteenth century believed that Parliament was generally representative of the nation, even though the franchise was small and usually based on a highly restrictive property qualification. However, such positions were destined to be

---

BOX 4.2   IDEAS AND PERSPECTIVES

Libertarianism

For some people the central aim of political activity should be the defence of freedom, that everyone owns their own body, life and property and has the right to do as they please with them. This is essentially the J.S. Mill position, but the assertion of the individual right to freedom above all else leads to some unusual political positions. For example, some argue that the state needs to defend the freedom of others to certain rights – welfare support, for example – but for libertarians this involves an unacceptable imposition of taxes by the government, demands backed by force.

They also argue against any kind of censorship, the military draft, the minimum wage, laws on sexual behaviour, drug use and immigration controls while supporting free trade and prostitution. Robert Nozick's much admired 1974 work, *Anarchy, State and Utopia*, elaborated some of these positions including the view of taxation as 'forced labour'. Translated into the more conventional political world, libertarianism appeals partly to the anarchic left who resent any controls but perhaps more powerfully to the right and, because it implicitly entails disobedience to the law and a complete 'rolling back' of the state, the far right. In the USA some groups have established themselves as libertarian enclaves in conventional society, seeking to be true to their visions and in the process rejecting the whole concept and machinery of government with its controls, regulation and impositions. At this point left-wing anarchism and right-wing libertarianism meet in a variety of intriguing ways.

eroded by the inherent logic of natural rights: if everyone had equal rights then surely they should have an equal say in removing a government not of their liking?

The influence of the liberal philosophers perhaps seems greater in retrospect than it was because they were often seeking to justify and accelerate political trends that were already well under way. Nevertheless, such liberal notions were of key importance and provide ideas still used as touchstones in the present day.

Some commentators, such as Eccleshall (1984, 1986) and Gamble (1981), see liberalism as providing the philosophical rationale for modern capitalist society. Certainly the idea of individual freedom, property rights and limited government suited the emergent entrepreneurial middle classes destined to come of political age in the next century. However, liberal views on government have enjoyed a general acceptance not just in Britain but also in the USA, Western Europe and elsewhere. They have provided the commonly accepted ground rules of democratic behaviour, the 'procedural values' of toleration, fair play and free speech that Bernard Crick, the great modern advocate of citizenship, argued should be positively reinforced in our society via our classrooms. They have provided in one sense an 'enabling' ideology that all major parties have accepted. Indeed, it is in some ways surprising that a creed originating in an agrarian, largely non-industrialised country should have provided a political framework that has survived so tenaciously and indeed triumphantly into the present day.

Classical liberalism

The American and French Revolutions applied liberal principles in a way that shocked many of their more moderate adherents. The Napoleonic interlude caused a period of reaction, but during the mid- to late-nineteenth century classical liberalism took shape. Claiming continuity with the early liberals, this new school was based on the economic ideas of Adam Smith and the radical philosophers Jeremy Bentham, James Mill and his son John Stuart Mill. Liberalism with a capital 'L' then took the stage in the form of the Liberal Party, a grouping based on the Whigs, disaffected Tories – the group in the eighteenth-century parliament which supported the king – and the Manchester Radicals led by Richard Cobden and John Bright.

Classical liberalism was characterised by the idea of the independent, rational and self-governing citizen as the basic unit of society. For liberals, this concept now represented a goal or vision to be worked for. Liberals hoped that through the erosion of aristocratic privilege and the moral transformation of the working class, social differences would give way to a new society of equals.

Human nature

The liberal view of human nature was fairly optimistic. John Stuart Mill, for example, doubted whether working for the common good would induce citizens to produce goods as efficiently as when self-interest was involved. His awareness of human selfishness perhaps underlay his advice against too rapid a rate of social progress. However, at the heart of liberal philosophy was a belief in the potential of human nature to change into Locke's civilised reasonable human being, capable of being educated into responsible citizenship. Many liberals felt that such an education would take a great many years but that it was possible, especially through direct involvement of citizens in the economy and the political system.

BIOGRAPHY

John Stuart Mill (1806–73)

British philosopher. Influenced by his father, James, he became a leading advocate of representative government. Sat as an MP in the 1860s and supported votes for women. Wrote *Principles of Political Economy* (1848), *On Liberty* (1859), *Representative Government* (1861) and *Utilitarianism* (1863).

Freedom

Classical liberalism retained the emphasis on freedom. In his essay *On Liberty*, for example, Mill felt: 'It was imperative that human beings should be free to form opinions and to express their opinions without reserve.' The only constraint should be that in the exercise of his freedom, an individual should not impinge upon the freedom of others.

Utilitarianism

Jeremy Bentham (1748–1832) took the rationality of liberal philosophy to new levels with his science of utilitarianism. His approach was based on what now seems an extraordinarily simplistic view of human psychology. He argued that human beings were disposed to seek pleasure and avoid pain. While they sought what was best for themselves they frequently made mistakes. The role of government therefore was to assist individuals in making the correct choices, in enabling the achievement of the 'greatest happiness for the greatest number'. While Bentham embraced the *laissez-faire/capitalist* economic system as highly utilitarian, he believed that most laws and administrative arrangements reflected aristocratic privilege and therefore were in need of reform. His ideas were criticised as simplistic and his Panopticon – a model prison based on his philosophy – was generally seen as risible by other philosophers, but he had a pervasive influence on Liberal legislators in the nineteenth century.

Minimal government – middle-class values

Bentham's influence paradoxically led to far-reaching legal and administrative reforms: for example, the regulatory framework for mines and factories. However, other liberals were strongly opposed to such regulation both as a violation of laissez-faire principles and as an interference in the moral education of the poor. Liberals such as the social Darwinist Herbert Spencer (1820–1903) argued that welfare provision was wrong in that it sheltered the poor from the consequences of their behaviour. 'Is it not manifest', he argued, 'that there must exist in our midst an immense amount of misery which is a normal result of misconduct and ought not to be dissociated from it?' State support for the poor was therefore a dangerous narcotic likely to prevent the right lessons being learned. The stern lesson that classical liberals wished to teach was that the poorer classes would face the penalties of poverty unless they adopted the values and lifestyles of their economic superiors: thrift, hard work, moderate indulgence and self-improving pastimes.

Representative government

Bentham and James Mill (1773–1836) introduced arguments in favour of representative government. Bentham dismissed the natural rights argument as 'nonsense on stilts'. His own utilitarian reasoning was that such a form of government was the most effective safeguard for citizens against possibly rapacious rulers or powerful 'sinister interests'. As both men believed individuals to be the best judge of where their own interests lay, they favoured universal franchise (although Mill sought to restrict it to men over 40). His son, J.S. Mill (1806–73), is probably the best-known advocate of representative government. He urged adult male and female suffrage, but to guard against a 'capricious and impulsive' House of Commons he advised a literacy qualification for voting and a system of plural voting whereby educated professional people would be able to cast more votes than ill-educated workers. Mill also believed that a participatory **democracy** and the sense of responsibility it would imbue would contribute towards the moral education of society: 'Democracy creates a morally better person because it forces people to develop their potentialities.'

Laissez-faire economics

Laissez-faire economics was predicated on the tenet of individual freedom: it asserted that the ability to act freely in the marketplace – to buy and sell property, employ workers and take profit – was central to any free society. Adam Smith's (1723–90) broadsides against the trade protection of the eighteenth-century mercantilist system provided the clearest possible statement of the case for economic activity free from political restrictions. According to Smith, producers should be allowed to supply products at the price consumers are willing to pay. Provided that competition was fair, the 'invisible hand' of the market would ensure that goods were produced at the lowest possible price commensurate with the quality consumers required. Producers would be motivated by selfish pursuit of profit but would also provide social 'goods', through providing employment, creating wealth and distributing it in accordance with the energy and ability of people active in the economic system. Smith believed that government intervention and regulation would impede this potentially perfect self-adjusting system. Liberals were not especially worried by the inequalities thrown up by laissez-faire economics or claims that employers 'exploited' employees. Classical liberals were opposed to inherited financial advantages but not so concerned with the differences created by different performances in relation to the market. They favoured the meritocracy of the market: they were the high priests of capitalism.

Peace through trade

Liberals, especially the so-called Manchester Radicals, also applied their free-trade principles to foreign affairs. Richard Cobden, for example, regarded diplomacy and war as the dangerous pastimes of the aristocracy. His answer to these perennial problems was 'to make diplomacy open and subject to parliamentary control', eliminate trade barriers, and encourage free trade worldwide. Commerce, he argued, was peaceful and beneficial, and it encouraged co-operation and contact between nations. If the world were a completely open market, national economies would become more integrated and interdependent and governments would be less likely to engage in conflicts or war.

The new liberalism

The emphasis of classical liberalism was on laissez-faire, wealth production, toleration of inequality, minimal welfare, individual responsibility and moral education. Towards the end of the nineteenth century, however, liberals themselves began to move away from their own ascetic economic doctrines. John Stuart Mill had argued that government intervention was only justified to prevent injury to the life, property or freedom of others. To some liberals it appeared that capitalist society had become so complex and repressive that the freedom of poor people to develop their potential was being restricted: even if they were inclined to emulate their middle-class betters their capacity to do so was held back by poverty, poor health and education, and squalid living and working conditions. Liberal thinkers began to shift their emphasis away from 'negative' freedom – freedom from oppression – towards providing 'positive' freedom – the capacity of people to make real choices regarding education, employment, leisure and so on.

State responsibility for welfare

T.H. Green (1836–82) helped to initiate this movement for positive action to assist the poor by calling for a tax on inherited wealth. Alfred Marshall (1842–1924) believed that capitalism now provided such material plenty that it had the capacity to redistribute some of its largesse to the disadvantaged so that they would be able genuinely to help themselves to become self-reliant. But it was L.T. Hobhouse (1864–1929) who perhaps marked the key shift of Liberals towards paternalism:

The state as over-parent is quite as truly liberal as socialistic. It is the basis of the rights of the child, of his protection against parental neglect, of the equality of opportunity which he may claim as a 'future citizen'.

Hobhouse insisted that his version of paternalism should not be oppressively imposed; he favoured a basic minimum standard of living that would provide 'equal opportunities of self-development'. He followed Green in proposing taxation to finance such welfare innovations as health insurance and pensions. The great Liberal victory of 1906 enabled the government to implement many of these new measures. Thereafter Liberals became firm advocates of **welfarism**; in 1942, the Liberal William Beveridge produced his famous blueprint for the postwar welfare state.

The mixed economy: Hobsonian and Keynesian economics

Government intervention of a different kind was proposed by J.A. Hobson (1858–1940). He was the first major liberal economist (he later became a socialist) to argue that capitalism was fatally flawed. Its tendency to produce a rich minority who accumulated unspent profits and luxury goods meant that the full value of goods produced was not consumed by society. This created slumps and, indirectly, the phenomenon of economic imperialism. Capitalists were forced by such under-consumption to export their savings abroad, thus creating overseas interests with political and colonial consequences. Hobson argued that the state could solve this crisis with one Olympian move: redirect wealth from the minority to the poor via progressive taxation. The section of society most in need would then be able to unblock the mechanism which caused overproduction and unemployment, thus making moral as well as economic sense.

J.M. Keynes (1883–1946) (see Biography) completed this revolution in liberal economic thought by arguing that demand could be stimulated not by redistribution of wealth to the poor but by government-directed investment in new economic activity. Confronted by a world recession and massive unemployment, he concentrated on a different part of the economic cycle. He agreed that the retention of wealth by capitalists under a laissez-faire economic system lay at the heart of the problem, but he believed the key to be increased investment, not increased consumption. Instead of saving in a crisis,

John Maynard Keynes (1883–1946)

Born in Cambridge, Keynes was the son of an academic. He was educated at Eton and King's College, Cambridge, where he mixed in avant-garde intellectual circles, such as the 'Bloomsbury group', and taught sporadically. He served in the India Office (1906–8) and later wrote his first book on this subject. In the First World War he advised the Treasury and represented it at the Versailles Treaty negotiations but resigned over the terms proposed. His essay *The Economic Consequences of the Peace* (1919) brought his powerful radical intellect to the notice of the country's ruling élite. He attacked Churchill's restoration of the gold standard in 1925, and the unemployment caused by the Depression inspired his most famous work, *A General Theory of Employment, Interest and Money* (1936). His views won support on the left and in the centre as well as helping to inspire the New Deal policies of Roosevelt in the USA.

Keynes married a Soviet ballerina and with her father founded the Vic-Wells ballet. In 1943 he established the Arts Theatre in Cambridge. In the same year he played a leading role in the Bretton Woods agreement, which set up a new international economic order, the establishment of the International Monetary Fund and negotiations following the ending of lend-lease (a financial agreement whereby aid was channelled to the UK during the war) after the war to secure a major loan to help Britain to survive the rigours of the immediate postwar world. Most people achieve only a fraction in their lifetimes of what Keynes managed to do. He was one of the truly great figures of the century, and his influence lives on today.

would intervene with a whole range of economic controls to achieve full employment and planned economic growth. Keynes was not just concerned with the cold science of economics: his view of the mixed economy would serve social ends in the form of alleviated hardship and the extension of opportunity. But while Keynes was unhappy with capitalism in the 1930s he did not propose to replace it – merely to modify it. He was no egalitarian, unlike socialist economists, and disagreed with Hobsonian calls for wealth redistribution, which he felt would adversely affect the incentives to achieve that human nature required: 'for my own part I believe there is social and psychological justification for significant inequalities of income and wealth' (Keynes 1985: 374).

Internationalism

Radical liberals such as J.A. Hobson, Norman Angel, E.D. Morel, C.R. Buxton, H.N. Brailsford, Lowes Dickinson and Charles Trevelyan produced an influential critique of the international system, arguing that the practice of secret diplomacy, imperialist competition for markets, haphazard balance-of-power policies and the sinister role of arms manufacturers made war between nations tragically inevitable. The First World War appeared to vindicate their analysis and encouraged them to develop the idea of an overarching international authority: the League of Nations. The idea was picked up by political parties and world leaders, including the US President, Woodrow Wilson, and through the catalyst of war was translated into the League of Nations by the Versailles Treaty. Most of the radical liberals joined the Labour Party during and after the war, but the Liberal Party subsequently remained staunchly internationalist and in favour of disarmament proposals throughout the interwar period. Despite the failure of the League, Liberals passionately supported the United Nations which emerged in the wake of the Second World War.

Further development of democratic government

The New Liberals were no less interested than their predecessors in the development of representative democracy through extension of the franchise and the strengthening of the House of Commons. Lloyd George's device of including welfare proposals in his 1909 Budget – a measure that the House of Lords had traditionally passed 'on the nod' – precipitated a

governments should encourage businessmen to invest in new economic activity. Through the creation of new economic enterprises wealth would be generated, consumption increased, other economic activities stimulated and unemployment reduced. He envisaged a mixed economy in which the state

conflict between the two chambers that resulted in the House of Lords' power being reduced from one of absolute veto over legislation to one of delay only. In the early 1920s, the Liberal Party gave way to Labour as the chief opposition party, returning 159 MPs in 1923, 59 in 1929 and only 21 in 1935. The dramatic decline in the party's fortunes coincided with its support for a change in the electoral system from the 'first-past-the-post' system, which favoured big parties, to alternatives that would provide fairer representation to smaller parties, such as the Liberals, with thinly spread national support.

This chapter has sought to emphasise the centrality of the liberal (note small 'l') tradition in the evolution of modern British political thought. In the eighteenth century, it helped to establish reason,

---

BOX 4.3 BRITAIN IN CONTEXT

Liberal values

It is seductively easy to believe that the beliefs underpinning one's own system of government are somehow 'natural', 'universal' and superior to those of other cultures. Probably the most famous statement of liberal values is enshrined in the Declaration of Independence made by the 'thirteen united states of America' in 1776, beginning:

We hold these truths to be self-evident, that all men are created equal, that they are endowed by their Creator with certain unalienable Rights, that among these are Life, Liberty, and the pursuit of Happiness. That to secure these rights, Governments are instituted among Men, deriving their just powers from the consent of the governed.

These few words embody much of the liberal thinking of Hobbes (his views were a mixture of the liberal and illiberal), Locke, Paine, Rousseau and other thinkers associated the impending French Revolution. 'Life, liberty and the pursuit of happiness' were considered to be 'self-evident' truths, reflecting universal rights owned by all humans. At the time, when it was believed monarchs ruled with the authority of God who had decreed a natural order and social hierarchy, such views were wholly unorthodox and revolutionary; as much as the armies of Napoleon they unseated the established order in Europe and set the movement towards democracy in train.

As the new order took shape, what once was heretical became at first acceptable and then, by degrees, the new unchallenged orthodoxy. Citizens in Britain and the USA do not question these 'inalienable rights' which are enshrined in law and constitution; though in the USA the term 'liberal' has acquired pejorative overtones through the efforts of Repub-licans to identify Democrats with 'Un-American' (and hence unpatriotic) socialist ideas.

However, elsewhere in the world, such liberal values did not pass unchallenged. Communist countries claimed such beliefs were merely one of the means whereby property-owning capitalists fooled the exploited working classes into accepting gross inequalities. In more recent times fundamentalist Muslim movements have condemned Western liberalism as a sign of the West's decadence and corruption. They do not subscribe to notions of free speech but believe government should be a direct extension of their religion. This has given birth to a 'theocracy' in Iran, powerful internal movements in Muslim states and worldwide movements like al-Qaeda which seek to destroy the West; all this reinforcing the analysis of Samuel P. Huntington's exceptional book *The Clash of Civilizations and the Remaking of World Order* (Touchstone Books, 1997).

We should not, therefore, assume that liberal values are automatically right, and we should remember that:

1 Even cherished values – such as freedom of speech – are not absolute; Western countries all legislate to place limits of some kind.
2 Some Muslim countries do not accept liberal values but regard religious values as absolute, thus producing powerful conflicts with secular views of government (read Orhan Pamuk's novel *Snow* for excellent insights into these conflicts).
3 Before we reject such opposing views we should remember that even in 1776 (our Christian) God's name was invoked as the source of liberal values.

toleration, liberty, natural rights and the consent of the governed in place of religious dogma, feudal allegiance and the divine right of monarchs to rule. In the nineteenth century, it added representative, democratic government with power shared between various elements. Having provided key guidelines for our modern system of government, classical liberalism argued for minimal government intervention in social policy and an economy run essentially in harmony with market forces.

The New Liberals, however, engineered a new intellectual revolution. They argued for government intervention to control an increasingly complex economy that distributed great rewards and terrible penalties with near-random unfairness. They also saw commerce not as the healing balm for international conflicts but as the source of the conflicts themselves. The irony is that the Liberals Keynes and Beveridge proved to be the chief architects of the postwar consensus between Labour and Conservatives, while, as we shall see, Margaret Thatcher wrought her revolution not through application of traditional conservatism but through a rediscovery of classical liberalism.

■ Fukuyama and the end of history

No account of the development of the liberal tradition in politics can end without some reference to Francis Fukuyama, the formerly obscure official in the US State Department who argued in articles and a book (1992) that the liberal tradition had developed to the extent that, allied to free-enterprise economics, it had eclipsed all its rivals on the left and right – communism, fascism, socialism – thus producing the 'universalisation of Western Liberal democracy as the final form of human government'.

He founded his reasoning on the Hegelian notion that civilisations successively develop, resolve internal conflicts and change for the better. The 'end of history' is when a point is reached whereby conflict is eradicated and the form of society best suited to human nature has evolved.

The importance of the article lay partly in its timing. The British Empire took a couple of decades to expire, but Stalin's collapsed in a few years at the end of the 1980s. The intellectual world was deafened by the crashing of rotten regimes and astonished by the apparent vibrancy of their democratic successors. Moreover, after decades of defending liberal values against a grey and predatory communist bloc, the Western intelligentsia responded warmly to a thesis that appeared to say 'we've won'. Fukuyama's bold thesis fitted the facts and suited the mood of the times. Even in Britain the triumph of Thatcher in three successive elections between 1979 and 1987 seemed to reflect the thrust of the argument and her stated resolve to destroy socialism in her country. However, Fukuyama's thesis seems to ignore the exponential forces for change that are transforming society at breakneck speed: computer technology and the information revolution; the huge pressure on finite world resources; the spread of nuclear weapons; and the increasing concentration of wealth in a few hands, leading to the huge and growing gap between rich and poor. Who is to say that these forces will not undermine the liberal consensus and positions and possibly usher in a new authoritarianism? Moreover, as Samuel P. Huntington's book, *The Clash of Civilizations and the Remaking of World Order*, suggested, the world could now be engaged in a struggle between the values of the West and the more traditional and narrow values of Islam.

To assume that the liberal underpinnings of many of the world's political systems will survive can be seen as at best naive and at worst complacent.

Chapter summary

Ideology is a kind of applied philosophy. It can be classified on the right–left continuum, a flawed but still much-used form. The liberal tradition, based on rights, freedom and representation, developed from the seventeenth century and set the ground rules for political activity during the nineteenth and twentieth. Classical liberalism elevated the market economy, but the New Liberalism, which was concerned to protect society from its excesses, still provides the rationales for the welfare state and the mixed economy.

Discussion points

■ Are there better ways of classifying ideology than the left–right continuum?

■ What are the grounds for thinking that all human beings have rights?

■ Should government resist interfering in the economy?

■ Have the Liberals been exploited/robbed in ideological terms by the other two big parties?

■ Defend the Fukuyama thesis that the evolution of political systems has reached its end-point in liberal democratic free enterprise.

Further reading

Two excellent books are available that introduce politics students to ideology: Adams (1999) is well written and subtly argued, while Heywood (1998) is also essential reading. Useful in general terms are Eccleshall (1984) and Gamble (1981). Plant (1991) is more difficult but no less rewarding. On utilitarianism and liberalism, the texts by J.S. Mill (1971, 1975, 1985a, 1985b) are as good a starting point for understanding liberalism as any. Eccleshall (1986) lays some claim to be the definitive text, but Arblaster (1984) and Manning (1976) address wider readerships. Fukuyama (1992) elaborates the 'end of history' theory. Fareed Zakaria's *The Future of Freedom* (2004) is a quite brilliant book on threats to liberal democracy.

Bibliography

Adams, I. (1999) *Political Ideology Today*, 2nd edn (Manchester University Press).

Arblaster, A. (1984) *The Rise and Fall of Western Liberalism* (Blackwell).

Bell, D. (1960) *The End of Ideology* (Free Press).

Eccleshall, R. (1984) *Political Ideologies* (Hutchinson).

Eccleshall, R. (1986) *British Liberalism* (Longman).

Fukuyama, F. (1992) *The End of History and the Last Man* (Hamish Hamilton).

Gamble, A. (1981) *An Introduction to Modern Social and Political Thought* (Macmillan).

Giddens, A. (1998) *The Third Way* (Polity Press).

Hattersley, R. (1989) 'Endpiece: nous and nostalgia', *The Guardian*, 30 September 1989.

Heywood, A. (1998) *Political Ideologies: An Introduction*, 2nd edn (Macmillan).

Huntington, S.P. (1996) *The Clash of Civilizations and the Remaking of World Order* (University of Oklahoma Press, also in paperback published by Touchstone Books, 1997).

Keynes, J.M. (1971) *The Economic Consequences of the Peace*, Vol. II of his *Collected Works* (Palgrave Macmillan; first published 1919).

Keynes, J.M. (1985) *A General Theory of Employment, Interest and Money*, Vol. VII of his *Collected Works* (Macmillan; first published 1936).

Manning, D.J. (1976) *Liberalism* (St Martin's Press).

Mill, J.S. (1971) *Utilitarianism* (Everyman; first published 1863).

Mill, J.S. (1975) *Representative Government* (Oxford University Press; first published 1861).

Mill, J.S. (1985a) *On Liberty* (Penguin; first published 1859).

Mill, J.S. (1985b) *Principles of Political Economy* (Penguin; first published 1848).

Nozick, R. (1974) *Anarchy, State and Utopia* (Blackwell).

Pamuk, O. (2004) *Snow* (Faber and Faber).

Plant, R. (1991) *Modern Political Thought* (Blackwell).

Russell, B. (1965) *The History of Western Philosophy* (Unwin).

Sutherland, J. (1999) 'How Blair discovered defeat by definition', *The Guardian*, 25 October 1999.

Zakaria, F. (2004) *The Future of Freedom* (Norton).

Useful websites

http://libertarianism.com

CHAPTER 5

Political ideas: the major parties

Bill Jones

Party spokesmen say not what they mean but what they have agreed to say.

Michael Portillo, *The Observer*, 2 March 2003

Learning objectives

- To explain the provenance of Conservatism and the ideology of capitalist free enterprise, to explain the difference between 'one nation' and neo-liberal Conservatism, and to assess the impact of Margaret Thatcher on her party's ideas.

- To trace the origins of Labour thinking to the rejection of nineteenth-century **capitalism**, to describe its maturing into corporate **socialism** and revisionism plus the left-wing dissent of the 1970s and 1980s, and to analyse the impact of Labour's rapid move into the centre and the apparent embrace of neo-Thatcherite and communitarian ideas by Tony Blair.

- To sum up the message of the Liberal Party over the years, including its alliance with the SDP and its evolution into the Liberal Democrats.

Introduction

I n the aftermath of the Second World War, some commentators felt that the two major political parties in Britain were 'converging' ideologically. Daniel Bell, the American sociologist, wrote of 'the end of ideology', and in the 1970s a postwar 'consensus' was discerned between the two parties on the desirability of a welfare state and a mixed economy. Britain's relative economic decline inclined both parties to adopt more radical remedies that drew on their ideological roots. Margaret Thatcher swung the Conservatives violently to the right, while Labour went radically to the left in the early 1980s. Once Thatcher had gone, Major adopted a less overtly ideological stance, while Labour, following the failed experiment of Michael Foot as leader, successively under Neil Kinnock, John Smith and Tony Blair moved rapidly into the centre. This chapter analyses the evolution of the ideas of the major parties and brings up to date their most recent changes.

■ The Conservative Party

Source: Courtesy of the Conservative Party
(www.conservatives.com)

Key elements of Conservatism

Lord Hailsham (1959) has described 'Conservatism' as not so much a philosophy as an 'attitude'. However, it is possible to discern a number of key tenets on which Conservative policies have been based:

1 *The purpose of politics is social and political harmony*: Conservatives have traditionally believed that politics is about enabling people to become what they are or what they wish to be. They also believe in a balance, a harmony in society, a measured **pragmatism** that has always kept options open. Like Edmund Burke, they have tended to believe that 'all government . . . is founded on compromise'.

2 *Human nature is imperfect and corruptible*: This quasi-religious notion of 'original sin' lies at the heart of Conservatism, leading its supporters to doubt the altruism of humankind beyond close family, to perceive most people as more interested in taking rather than giving, and to see them as fairly easy to corrupt without the external discipline of strong government.

3 *The **rule of law** is the basis of all freedom*: Law restricts freedom, yet without it there would be no freedom at all, but instead – given humanity's selfish, aggressive nature – anarchic chaos. Accepting the authority of the law is therefore the precondition of all liberty.

4 *Social institutions create a sense of society and nation*: Social and political institutions help to bind together imperfect human beings in a thing called society. Living together constructively and happily is an art, and this has to be learned. At the heart of the learning process lies the family and the institution of marriage. The royal family provides an idealised and unifying 'micro-model'. At the macro level is the idea of the 'nation', ultimately a cause worth dying for.

5 *Foreign policy is the pursuit of state interests in an anarchic world*: States exhibit all the dangerous characteristics of individuals plus a few even more unpleasant ones of their own. A judicious defence of national interests is the best guide for any country in the jungle of international relations.

6 *Liberty is the highest political end*: Individuals need freedom to develop their own personalities and pursue their destinies. Conservatives agree with Mill that it should entail freedom from oppression and be allowed to extend until it encroaches upon the freedom of others. It should not embrace the 'levelling' of wealth, as advocated by socialists, as this redistribution would be imposed upon a reluctant population by the state (see also Chapter 1).

7 *Government through checks and balances*: 'Political liberty', said Lord Hailsham, 'is nothing else than the diffusion of power.' This means in practice institutions that divide power between them, with all having a measure of independence, thus preventing any single arm of government from being over-mighty.

8 *Property*: Conservatives, like David Hume, believe that the right to property is the 'first principle of justice' on which the 'peace and security of human society entirely depend'. Norton and Aughey (1981) take this further, arguing that it is an 'education. It enlightens the citizens in the value of stability and shows that the security of small property depends upon the security of all property' (p. 34). The Conservative policy of selling council houses reflected this belief in that it is assumed, probably rightly in this case, that people will cherish their houses more once they enjoy personal ownership.

9 ***Equality of opportunity*** *but not of result*: Conservatives believe everyone should have the same opportunity to better themselves. Some will be more able or more motivated and will achieve more and accumulate more property. Thus an unequal distribution of wealth reflects a naturally unequal distribution of ability. Norton and Aughey (1981) maintain that the party is fundamentally concerned with justifying inequality in a way that 'conserves a hierarchy of wealth and power and make[s] it intelligible to democracy' (p. 47). To do this, Conservatives argue that inequality is necessary to maintain incentives and make the economy work; equality of reward would reward the lazy as much as the industrious.

10 *One nation*: Benjamin Disraeli, the famous nineteenth-century Conservative Prime Minister, added a new element to his party's philosophy by criticising the 'two nations' in Britain, the rich and the poor. He advocated an alliance between the aristocracy and the lower orders to create one nation. His advice was controversial and has come to be seen as synonymous with the liberal approach to Conservatism.

11 *Rule by élite*: Conservatives have tended to believe the art of government is not given to all; it is distributed unevenly, like all abilities, and is carefully developed in families and outside these most commonly in good schools, universities and the armed forces.

12 *Political change*: Conservatives are suspicious of political change as society develops organically as an infinitely complex and subtle entity; precipitate change could damage irreparably things of great value. Therefore they distrust the system builders such as Marx, and the root-and-branch reformers such as Tony Benn. But they do not deny the need for all change; rather they tend to agree with the Duke of Cambridge that the best time for it is 'when it can be no longer resisted', or with Enoch Powell that the 'supreme function of a politician is to judge the correct moment for reform'.

The impact of Thatcherism

This collection of pragmatic guides to belief and action was able to accommodate the postwar Labour landslide, which brought nationalisation, the managed Keynesian economy, close cooperation with the trade unions and the welfare state. The role of Harold Macmillan was crucial here. In the 1930s he wrote *The Middle Way*, a plea for a regulated laissez-faire economy that would minimise unemployment and introduce forward economic planning. He was able to accept many of the reforms introduced by Labour and reinterpret them for his own party.

The postwar consensus continued with little difference over domestic policy between Macmillan and Gaitskell, Wilson and Heath. But when the economy began to fail in relation to competitors in the late 1960s and early 1970s a hurricane of dissent began to blow up on the right of the Conservative Party – in the person of Margaret Thatcher. She had no quarrel with traditional positions on law, property and liberty, but she was passionately convinced of a limited role for government (although not necessarily a weak one); she wanted to 'roll back' the socialist frontiers of the state. She was uninterested in checks and balances but wanted to maximise her power to achieve the things she wanted. She was opposed to contrived 'equality' and favoured the functional inequalities required by a dynamic economy. She had scant respect for the aristocracy as she admired only ability and energy, qualities she owned in abundance. She was not in favour of gradual change but wanted radical alterations, *in her lifetime*. She was a revolutionary within her own party, which still, even in 2010, had not stopped reverberating from her impact.

Thatcherite economics

1 Margaret Thatcher was strongly influenced by Sir Keith Joseph, in turn influenced by the American economist Milton Friedman. He urged that to control inflation it was merely necessary to control the supply of money and credit circulating in the economy.

2 Joseph was also a disciple of Friedrich von Hayek, who believed that freedom to buy, sell and employ, i.e. economic freedom, was the foundation of all freedom. Like Hayek, he saw the drift to collectivism as a bad thing: socialists promised the 'road to freedom' but delivered instead the 'high road to servitude'.

3 Hayek and Friedman agreed with Adam Smith and the classical liberals that, if left to themselves, market forces – businessmen using their energy and ingenuity to meet the needs of customers – would create prosperity. To call this 'exploitation' of the working man, as socialists did, was nonsense as businessmen were the philanthropists of society, creating employment, paying wages and endowing charities. When markets were allowed to work properly they benefited all classes: everyone benefited, even the poor: 'the greatest social service of them all', said Thatcher, 'is the creation of wealth.'

4 Thatcher believed strongly that:

(i) state intervention destroyed freedom and efficiency through taking power from the consumer – the communist 'command' economies were inefficient and corrupt, protecting employment through temporary and harmful palliatives, and controlling so much of the economy that the wealth-producing sector became unacceptably squeezed, and that

(ii) state welfare was expensive, morally weakening in that it eroded the self-reliance she so prized, and was, in addition, monopolistic, denying choice as well as being less efficient than private provision.

5 Trade unions were one of Thatcher's bêtes noires. She saw them as undemocratic, reactionary vested interests that regularly held the country to ransom in the 1970s. She was determined to confront and defeat them.

6 Her defence of national interests was founded in a passionate patriotism, which sustained her support for the armed forces and the alliance with the USA. During the Falklands War she showed great composure and courage in taking risks and ultimately triumphing. The reverse side of this was her preference for the US link over the European Union, which she suspected of being a Trojan horse for German plans to dominate the whole continent.

Margaret Thatcher therefore drove a battering ram through traditional Conservatism, but economically it was a return to the classical liberalism of the early to mid-nineteenth century (see Chapter 4). Many claimed to have been converted to her ideas, but the 1980s witnessed a tough internal battle, which the Prime Minister eventually won, between her and the so-called 'wet' wing of the party, which still hearkened back to the inclusive 'one nation' strand of the party's thinking.

The Major years

When John Major succeeded Margaret Thatcher following the virtual 'coup' in November 1990, many thought he would be the best hope of stern and unbending Thatcherism, but he seemed much more conciliatory, more concerned with the un-Thatcherite aim of achieving unity even at the cost of compromise. As the years passed, however, it became apparent that this initial analysis is far away from what happened. Major's government was almost wholly circumscribed by the ideas of his predecessor. As Heywood has pointed out, the Major government accepted her ideas; there was no conflict with 'wets', and even Heseltine, Clarke and Patten had accepted the unchallenged supremacy of markets by the mid-1990s. Moreover, he took her ideas further even than she dared in her day, privatising British Rail and introducing the market principle into many hitherto forbidden areas of the welfare state. The changes were in style rather than substance. In the 1980s, Thatcherism adopted a 'heroic' mode, smashing socialism and the power of the trade unions; it was like a continuous war or revolution as the Prime Minister tried to change 'the hearts and minds of the nation'. Major replaced that style with a 'managerial' version. However, he also added another element: a return to 'neo-conservatism' with a renewed emphasis on morality (the 'back to basics' campaign), obligation and citizenship. Conservatives have long been worried by the downside of market forces: growing inequality, the emergence of an underclass, insecurity at work and the loss of the 'feel-good factor', or the sense of the nation 'being at ease with itself' to use Major's phrase. There was a feeling in the mid-1990s that the nation's social fabric was in dire need of repair. Added to this market individualism plus neo-conservatism had been a shift towards a 'Little Englandism'. Most commentators did not believe Major was this kind of politician by instinct, but that he was forced to adjust his position on Europe quite drastically by the determined Eurosceptic minority, which, through his tiny majority, held the balance of power.

Major was criticised from many parts of the party: 'poor judgement and weak leadership' (*The Sun*); 'drifting with the intellectual tide' (Thatcher); 'He is not a natural leader, he cannot speak, he has no sense of strategy or direction' (Lord Rees Mogg); 'a nice bloke but not up to the job' (Kenneth Clarke); and, the cruellest cut, 'the government gave the impression of being in office but not in power' (Norman Lamont).

Hague's new start

As soon as the Conservatives lost the 1997 election so calamitously Major resigned and a contest was held for a new leader. In the end, genial ex-Chancellor Kenneth Clarke was judged too pro-EU and MPs chose the relatively unknown and untested William Hague. He was at least, for those who regretted the demise of Thatcher, firm on the subject of Europe: he would have very little of it and would not join the emergent European single currency for at least a parliamentary term, if ever. Those who mocked this narrow, Little England perspective were checked when his party won the European elections handsomely in June 1999. Subsequently Michael Portillo, the right-winger many felt would have won the leadership had he not astonishingly lost his huge majority to novice Labour candidate Stephen Twigg, had effectively reinvented himself as the quintessence of the 'Compassionate Conservatism' its leaders now claimed to embrace. However, this flirtation with a softer image did not last for the party as a whole; the Conservative High Command – alarmed by polls flat-lining at one-third of the vote – were worried that the party's core vote was about to crumble. In October 1999 Hague unveiled his 'Commonsense Revolution', a bundle of right-wing measures focusing on five 'guarantees': to cut taxes as a share of the national income; to keep out of the single currency

until at least the end of the next parliamentary session and to demand opt-outs on measures not in the national interest; a 'parents guarantee' whereby inefficient heads could be dismissed; a 'patients guarantee' setting maximum times for treatment; and a get-tough guarantee on work dodgers, who would lose all benefit if refusing work after eight weeks. In fact the conference represented a surprising swing back towards Thatcherism. The lady herself appeared and was cheered to the echo by the ageing delegates as well as praised in speeches that pointedly and hurtfully ignored the contributions made by the premier of seven years, John Major. Most of the right-wing press applauded the party's rediscovery of its identity – being right-wing, Eurosceptic and proud of it. But others were not so sure. That shrewd commentator Peter Riddell wrote that

The more William Hague roused his party faithful in Blackpool, the more he led them away from power . . . [his] main achievement . . . may have been to deepen the divisions within his own party and to reduce still further its chances of winning the next election.

(*The Times*, 12 October 1999)

BIOGRAPHY

William Hague (1961–)

English Conservative politician. Made his debut with a precocious speech at the 1977 conference. After Oxford, he worked as a management consultant and then became MP for Richmond in his native Yorkshire. He was seen as suitably opposed to Europe in 1997 and was preferred to Kenneth Clarke as leader. His early years were difficult with successes inside the Commons but rarely in the country. In the election of 2001 he stuck to his Eurosceptic guns throughout the campaign but could only persuade the nation to return one more Conservative MP. He resigned, with remarkably good grace, shortly after the election defeat. After that he busied himself with after-dinner speaking, an acclaimed biography of the Younger Pitt and occasional broadcasting. David Cameron, however, in December 2005 summoned him back to his party's front bench as Shadow Foreign Secretary and unofficial Deputy Leader.

Riddell, not for the first time, proved remarkably prescient: in June 2001 Labour's second landslide occurred. Hague resigned and a contest for the leadership of the Tories took place amid some acrimony. According to the new rules for electing a leader, the parliamentary party held a series of ballots to find the two candidates between whom the party faithful would choose. Portillo soon fell by the wayside, foundering, it seemed, on his admission of a homosexual experience when a student at Cambridge. It was left to Kenneth Clarke, again, to battle it out with the inexperienced right-winger Iain Duncan Smith. The latter's Euroscepticism, tough line on crime and general Thatcherite orthodoxy proved much more attractive, in the judgement of the ageing party membership, compared with the liberal one-nation approach of Clarke – despite his obvious political gifts – who lost by a two-to-one majority.

The Iain Duncan Smith effect

'IDS', as he is known, began his tenure as leader by striving to make an impression in the Commons, but Blair proved too dominant and his opponent too unsure of his ground to 'win' even a few of the weekly Prime Minister's Question Time encounters. What made it worse was that so many of the well-known Conservatives either had retired (e.g. Tebbit, Baker, Fowler), had not been keen on serving under Duncan Smith (e.g. Clarke, Hague), or were still stigmatised by association with the 'bad old days' of the Conservative's eighteen years in power (e.g. Howard, Gummer). Despite his defeat for the leadership, Portillo's influence remained as a voice calling for 'modernisation' of the Conservative message: a more inclusive attitude to women, gays and ethnic minorities; a distancing from anything resembling racism on immigration policy; an acceptance of the need to modernise and improve public services; and a less dogmatic hostility to all things European. Once again the dead weight of lumpen party opinion on key policy issues served to retard any progress. Duncan Smith's ineffectual orthodoxy was soon found to be out of touch in the polls, and in the spring of 2002, at the party's Harrogate conference, IDS effected a neat volte-face on policy, calling for a compassionate attitude towards the 'vulnerable' in society, a decentralisation of power to the regions and a supportive attitude towards the public services. However, shifting towards a new policy position is one thing; communicating it, via an unknown Shadow Cabinet, is another: the polls still flat-lined

at just over 30 percentage points. The new leader faced immense difficulty in convincing voters that his party was not, as he complained, 'nasty, extreme and strange' (*Observer* 2 July 2002). At the party conference later in the year, the new party chairman, Theresa May, urged the party to lose its 'nasty' image: evidence of her support for the modernisation camp. However, the *éminence grise* of this tendency featured again in February 2003 when Michael Portillo complained bitterly at the peremptory sacking of the chief executive of the party, Mark MacGregor. The outbreak of war against Iraq the following month enabled Duncan Smith to occupy familiar Conservative territory – pro-armed forces and pro-USA – although such a position precluded political exploitation of Prime Minister Blair's discomfort in prosecuting a war unpopular in the country and even more so in his own party; Kenneth's Clarke's backing of an 'anti-war' horse over Iraq scarcely helped to strengthen the embattled leader's position. Discontent with IDS grew in the run-up to the 2003 party conference and soon afterwards he lost a crucial party vote of

BIOGRAPHY

Michael Portillo (1953–)

Conservative politician. Educated at Cambridge. Worked for the Conservative Research Department, 1976–9, and as junior minister in various departments until he became a Cabinet minister in the early 1990s. Was defeated in the 1997 election and missed his chance to lead the party then. Worked hard at being an advocate of 'caring Conservatism' before becoming adopted as a candidate in the safe seat of Kensington. Made Shadow Chancellor in late 1999. 'Reinvented' himself as a caring, inclusive one-nation Conservative with speeches, television programmes and an admission of student-day homosexual experience. This last caused trouble with older Conservatives; when Portillo stood for the leadership after Hague's resignation, Norman Tebbit made a thinly veiled attack on his sexuality, and the modernisers' hope was defeated at the Commons stage (according to the new procedure) before party members were able to vote on the two nominees.

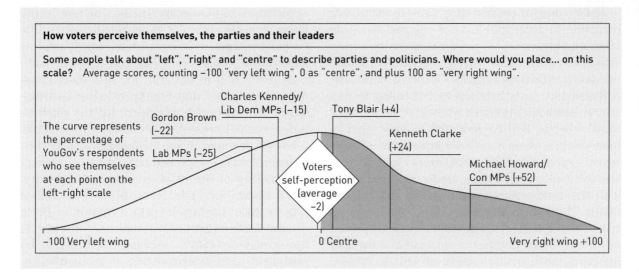

How voters perceive themselves, the parties and their leaders

Some people talk about "left", "right" and "centre" to describe parties and politicians. Where would you place... on this scale? Average scores, counting –100 "very left wing", 0 as "centre", and plus 100 as "very right wing".

Charles Kennedy/
Lib Dem MPs (–15)   Tony Blair (+4)

Gordon Brown
(–22)

Kenneth Clarke
(+24)

The curve represents
the percentage of
YouGov's respondents   Lab MPs (–25)
who see themselves
at each point on the
left-right scale

Michael Howard/
Con MPs (+52)

Voters
self-perception
(average
–2)

–100 Very left wing   0 Centre   Very right wing +100

Figure 5.1 How voters perceive themselves, the parties and their leaders
Source: From Policy Exchange (2005) *The Case for Change*, May 2005. Reproduced with permission

confidence. Michael Howard, the right-wing former Home Secretary, was selected in his place.

The era of Michael Howard

On Thursday 6 November 2003 the man who came sixth in the 1997 leadership challenge was, remarkably, elected unopposed to the leadership of his party. Despite his reputation for being a right-winger, Howard stressed his desire to continue IDS's emphasis on social justice with policies aimed at helping the disadvantaged. This was accompanied by calls for zero tolerance policing, more spending on drug treatment for addicts and an increase in the basic state pension. His concerns regarding Europe were underlined by renewed calls for a referendum on the proposed new constitution for the EU.

From the outset, Howard proved reasonably effective at Prime Minister's Questions but found it hard to resist the need to bolster up the core vote and did little to move the party into the electorally crucial centre ground. The party continued to languish in the polls as the general election approached in 2005. The party continued to lack a distinctive message right up to polling day on 5 May and duly paid the price when the votes were counted. The Conservatives won 33 more seats but had to sit back and watch an unpopular government led by a gifted but mistrusted Tony Blair maintain its hold on the Commons to the extent of an overall majority of 66. Howard, the old professional, seasoned politician, had hoped to lead a renaissance of Toryism but had proved to be merely a stop-gap leader of a party

which some perceived to be in terminal decline. Howard resigned quite soon but stayed on to preside over the election of his successor. This period – May to October – saw much soul searching during which most party members came to realise that drastic change was necessary. The Conservative Policy Exchange think tank produced a devastating report on the party highlighting its unpopularity, lack of contact with modern society and hopeless image as a party favouring middle-class people in the shires and the south-east. Figure 5.1, drawn from the report, reveals how people viewed their own political position on the left–right continuum and then superimposed their estimates of where leading politicians stood. Inevitably the majority of people occupy the centre ground, indicating where any party wishing to win an election needs to project its messages. Howard was perceived as being quite far to the right – his MPs also. Kenneth Clarke, on the other hand, was seen as substantially closer to the centre. Gordon Brown was located slightly to the right of Labour MPs and to the left of Charles Kennedy. And Tony Blair? His brilliant sense of where the centre of political gravity lies enabled him to sit astride the middle of the graph, four points to the right of dead centre.

The election of David Cameron, December 2005

The Conservative Party conference in October 2005 at Blackpool indicated that the party had finally realised that major change to the party and its thinking was necessary before an election win could be contemplated. The declared leadership candidates were able to address the delegates and make an initial pitch. Howard had influenced his own succession by placing members of the new young liberal or 'moderniser' group in his party to major positions in the Shadow Cabinet – George Osborne (34) to Shadow Chancellor and David Cameron (39) to Education – and allowing them to make an impression before the leadership contest in the autumn. Osborne, it seemed, had already decided not to run but to manage the campaign of his old Etonian friend, Cameron. Parallels with Tony Blair's rise to power were already being made before Cameron delighted the conference with a speech he had learnt by heart and delivered, apparently spontaneously, without notes. David Davis, the former minister in his mid-50s, who had assembled what many thought to be an impregnable lead among declared MPs, tried to follow suit but, compared with the sparkling, inspiring rhetoric of his rival, appeared lacklustre and dull. Cameron went on to win easily the MPs' ballot and then to win over the party for the membership ballot on 5 December which he won by a margin of two to one. On 6 December he took on Blair at PMQs and, in an excellent, witty debut performance, told him 'you were the future once'.

Cameron seeks to 'rebrand' and move into the centre ground

Cameron, while copying the informal, media-friendly style of the younger Tony Blair, was careful to steer clear of specific policy commitments, though it was clear his period in power would see a jettisoning of the party's much beloved positions on a number of issues. Cameron and his coterie of 'Notting Hill Set' colleagues were very keen to change the brand image of the party. During the 2005 election, focus groups had revealed that members who liked a policy position when it was explained to them changed their mind when they discovered it was a Conservative party policy. Concerted efforts were made to banish the notion of the 'nasty party', the idea of a bigoted, intolerant group of richer, older people who wanted power merely to advance their own interests and outdated way of life. Consequently Cameron let it be known his name was not David but 'Dave'; that he cared deeply about special-needs childcare (his NHS-cared-for disabled son, Ivan, died in February 2009); that he cared about the environment (cycling to the Commons, appointing environmentalist Zac

Goldsmith to an advisory position); that he cared about world poverty (Bob Geldof's turn to be included); and that the party no longer hated gays and opposed civil partnerships.

In late December Oliver Letwin declared his party favoured redistribution of wealth, and shortly afterwards Cameron shifted its position on immigration from opposition to qualified support for those incomers essential to the economy. Cameron also addressed the key area of tax cuts. It seemed Conservatives now would basically accept the 4 per cent increase in basic taxation since 1997 as necessary to sustain public services at requisite levels. He also declared that cuts would have to come in the wake of economic stability, a reversal of the Thatcherite view that the latter is a condition for the achievement of the former. And the party would no longer be the natural adjunct of the free enterprise economy: henceforward, the party would 'stand up to as well as for business'.

The new boy was careful, however, to keep the core vote onside with a judicious dash of Euro-scepticism. True, he wished to bury the party's civil war over the EU, which he deemed irrelevant now that the proposed new constitution had been rejected by France and Holland. But he nevertheless wanted the Conservative party to end its membership of the European People's Party, a right-wing grouping which nevertheless favoured rather too much integration. Perhaps his biggest break with the past, however, was to declare that the litmus test for social policies should be what they could do for the disadvantaged: many older Tories must have felt a twinge of apoplexy at that.

Like Blair in the mid-90s he set up a number of study groups to review policy areas. Opinion polls almost immediately registered a lead for Labour, albeit a slender one at that early stage. Blair must have realised at once that the political situation had been drastically changed and that he no longer could expect a free ride in his domination of the centre ground. But Cameron too did not face an easy ride; right-wing commentator, Melanie Phillips, writing in the *Daily Mail*, believed his prospectus 'leaves millions of natural conservatives effectively disenfranchised – and even worse demonized as dinosaurs by the party that is supposed to represent them'.

Wise old commentators judged such opposition to be precisely what Cameron needed. Blair had risen to public prominence over his brilliant defeat of party traditionalists over Clause 4. Lacking any similar dragons to slay, Cameron needed to overcome opposition from the older cohorts as represented,

Bob Geldof helps accelerate the Conservatives' new momentum by agreeing to become a consultant for them on world poverty
Source: Copyright © David Parkins. From the *Guardian*, 29 December 2005. Reproduced with permission

for example, by Lord Tebbit, one of Thatcher's most loyal and true-blue Conservative followers; it would be by overcoming such opposition that his party would be seen to have changed. As the 2010 election approached Cameron and his advisers sought to position themselves on the major questions of the day:

1 The need drastically to reduce government debt of £175 bn in 2009 so that international markets would not lose faith in the UK's ability to repay what it owed and increase interest rates for any future lending.

2 The political aim was to blame Labour for the recession triggered by the US banking crisis in 2007.

3 To offer protection for the NHS and education but to insist on deep cuts in public spending elsewhere to reduce debt and the size of the state.

4 Policy on the EU was made difficult by the insistence of the party rank and file on a referendum on the Lisbon treaty which they saw as strengthening moves towards a federalist Europe. On this issue Cameron faced a dilemma once the Lisbon Treaty had become ratified by all EU members and become a fait accompli. He solved it by abandoning the referendum idea.

■ The Labour Party and socialism

Source: Courtesy of the Labour Party (www.labour.org.uk)

Socialism

Socialism developed as a critique and alternative to capitalism and its political expression, Conservatism. It focused on economics as the key activity, but the full sweep of its message provided guidance on virtually all aspects of living.

Critique of capitalism

Socialism asserted that capitalism 'exploited' the working masses by selling the fruits of their labour, taking the lion's share of the revenue and paying only subsistence wages. This produced huge disparities in income between the suburban-living rich and the urban-based poor. Because the ruling capitalists dominate all the institutions of the state, argued Karl Marx, whose analysis was more influential in Britain than his prescriptions, they subtly intrude their values into all walks of life, and a complex web of mystifications produces a 'false consciousness' in which the working class believes wrongly that its best interests are served by supporting capitalist values. Capitalist championing of 'individualism' and 'freedom' are mere cloaks for the exploitation of the weak by the strong. The ruthlessness of the system induces similar qualities within society. Wage labour merely relieved employers of any residual obligations they might have felt towards their workers. By living in large urban settlements working men were alienated from each other, while the automating of industry denied workers any creative satisfaction. A final criticism was that capitalism with its booms and slumps was inevitably inefficient and inferior to a planned economy. Socialists argued that two large antagonistic classes emerge in capitalist societies: a small wealthy ruling class and a large impoverished proletariat, living in the cities, which actually created wealth.

Underlying principles of socialism

Socialism developed out of this critique of nineteenth-century capitalism. The principles underlying the new creed included the following:

1 *Human nature is basically good*: People wish to live together peacefully and cooperatively, according to this view; it is only the selfish competitive economic system of capitalism that distorts it.

2 *'Environment creates consciousness'*: It followed from this Marxist axiom that a superior environment will create a superior kind of person.

3 *Workers create the wealth*: They are entitled to receive the full fruits of their efforts and not the small fraction that the rich, bourgeois factory owners pay them.

4 *Equality*: Everyone has the right to start off in life with the same chances as everyone else; the strong should not exploit their advantage and impose themselves on the weak.

5 *Freedom*: The poor need more resources for the playing field of life to be level and thus be truly free.

6 *Collectivism*: Social solidarity should take the place of selfish individualism.

The Labour Party

Labour in power

Labour held power briefly in the 1920s and began to formulate a more pragmatic, less emotional and more coherent version of socialism. During the 1930s and the war years socialist thinkers such as Hugh Dalton (1887–1962) and Herbert Morrison (1888–1965) developed what has since been called 'corporate socialism', comprising:

1 *Keynesian economics*: Management of the economy, using investment to cure slumps and squeeze out unemployment.

2 *Centralised planning of the economy*: This was the corollary of the Keynesian approach; it had worked brilliantly during the 1939–45 war and would do the same for the peace, promised Labour.

3 *Nationalisation*: Morrison devised this approach based on bringing an industry out of private and into public control via a board accountable to Parliament. Once in power, Labour nationalised 20 per cent of the economy, including the major utilities.

4 *Welfare state*: Labour established the National Health Service and expanded universal social services into a virtual 'welfare state' in which the state had obligations to citizens 'from the cradle to the grave'.

5 *Mixed economy*: The extent of nationalisation was not defined but, unlike the Soviet command economies, it was intended to maintain a private sector, albeit one subordinate to the public.

6 *Socialist foreign policy*: The trauma of two world wars convinced Labour that a new approach was needed based on disarmament and international collective security. The USSR, however, proved resistant to fraternal overtures from a fellow left-wing government, and ultimately Labour's combative Foreign Secretary, Ernest Bevin (1881–1952), was forced to encourage the USA into the NATO alliance.

Revisionism

Anthony Crosland (1918–77), along with others like Gaitskell, Healey and Jenkins, was not content, like Morrison, to declare that 'socialism is what the Labour government does'; in his *The Future of Socialism* (1956), he asserted that Marx's predictions of capitalist societies polarising before revolutions established left-wing government had been proved hopelessly wrong; the working class had ignored revolutions and had been strengthened by full employment. The business class had not fought the advance of socialism but had been *tamed* by it. Crosland argued that the ownership of the economy was no longer relevant, as salaried managers were now the key players.

He attacked another sacred cow by maintaining that nationalisation was not necessarily the most effective road to socialism and that other forms of collective ownership were more effective. He concluded that Labour should now concentrate its efforts on reducing inequality through progressive taxation and redistributive benefits and – the key proposal – reducing class differences through an end to selection in education. In practice, revisionism was Labour's policy for the next thirty years, but when in government in the 1970s its fatal flaw was exposed: it was dependent on an expanding economy, and when this fell into decline public expenditure cuts became inevitable.

The left wing of the party, however, never accepted revisionism, and first Aneurin (Nye) Bevan, then Michael Foot, opposed the new drift towards a diluted ideology. In the 1960s, Wilson defied the Left in the parliamentary party, but when it teamed up with the trade unions trouble was in store for the 1970s administrations under both Wilson and Callaghan. Led by Tony Benn, the Left now offered an alternative economic strategy based on workers' control, extended state control of the economy, **participatory democracy** at all levels of national life, fresh injections of funds into the welfare state, encouragement of extra-parliamentary activity,

and unilateral abandonment of nuclear weapons. The revisionist leadership tried to ignore the Left, but when the 1979 general election was lost to a new and militantly ideological leader, Margaret Thatcher, the Left insisted that a similar return to the roots of socialist ideology was necessary. With the revisionist leadership defeated and discredited, the Left made its move, managing to translate its candidate, Michael Foot, into leader in 1980, plus imposing a radically left-wing set of policies on the party, which resulted in the 1983 manifesto being dubbed by Gerald Kaufman 'the longest suicide note in history'. More significantly, the Left's ascendancy led to the defection of an important centre-right section of the party to form the Social Democratic Party (see Box 5.1). The conventional view is that the new party split the anti-Tory vote and helped to keep Thatcher in power for a decade. However, the party's history as written by Ivor Crewe and Anthony King (1995) concluded that this transient new force, if anything, reduced the Tory majority.

Neil Kinnock, elected as Foot's successor, was a child of the Left but soon recanted, dismissing its prescriptions as 'Disneyland thinking'. He assiduously began to nudge his party towards the centre ground via a series of policy reviews, which essentially accepted the 'efficiency and realism' of the market as the best model of economic organisation. It was implicit in this new analysis – although hotly denied – that socialism was no longer relevant; even the word disappeared from party policy documents. When he lost the crucial 1992 election, he resigned and John Smith continued this 'desocialising' work. When Smith died tragically of a heart attack in May 1994, Tony Blair was elected leader and soon placed his stamp on a party denied power for nearly fifteen years.

Views of Labour leaders

As for Tony Blair, I still think, as I thought when I first met him, we're lucky to have him – both the Labour Party and the nation. He might have gone off and joined the Social Democrats and no-one would have heard of him again.

Michael Foot, *The Observer*, 6 September 1996

My view of Christian values has led me to oppose what I perceived to be a narrow view of self-interest that Conservatism – particularly in its modern, more right-wing form – represents.

Tony Blair, September 1995

BOX 5.1 Social Democratic Party

On 1 August 1980 Shirley Williams, David Owen and Bill Rodgers published their famous 'Gang of Three' statement: an open letter in the *Guardian* 'rejecting class war, accepting the mixed economy and the need to manage it efficiently'. After the Wembley conference of 1981 which passed rule changes strengthening the power of left-wing activists over candidate selection and the party leadership, the Gang of Three joined Roy Jenkins to form the Social Democratic Party (SDP). Over the next few months over two dozen Labour MPs made the same journey, joined by a solitary Conservative. The SDP fought the 1983 election in 'Alliance' with the small Liberal Party, garnering 26 per cent of the vote but less than 4 per cent of the seats. The much wished for breakthrough in 1987 failed when they mustered only 22 per cent. A formal merger of the two parties was delayed by personality problems posed largely by David Owen but by 1988 the future Liberal Democrats had emerged, albeit for a while with a defiant Owenite rump. The SDP was formed in a blaze of publicity and 'breaking the mould' rhetoric, but a genuine alternative was probably not on offer. In one sense its message represented an amalgam of policies picked up across the political spectrum. Decentralisation was close to the Liberal, Bennite and Green position; SDP views on the market economy and trade unions were close to Margaret Thatcher's position – she actually praised Owen for being 'sound' on both – and on social policy and defence the SDP was close to the position of the Callaghan government, to which the SDP leaders had once belonged. This is not to say that the SDP lacked a carefully worked out and detailed programme, merely that it lacked a distinctive alternative or even radical quality. History will judge the SDP as a party of protest with a limited appeal outside the middle classes.

Having already abandoned its former policies of opposition to the European Community/Union, unilateral nuclear disarmament and nationalisation, Blair shifted the party even further to the right by attacking the power of trade unions in the party. He waged a spectacularly successful war against the 'collective ownership' Clause Four in the party's constitution, drafted by Sidney Webb in 1917:

To secure for the workers by hand or by brain the full fruits of their industry and the most equitable distribution thereof that may be possible upon the basis of the common ownership of the means of production, distribution, and exchange, and the best obtainable system of popular administration and control of each industry or service.

Clause Four rewritten

The iconic clause, so fundamental that it was inscribed on membership cards, was replaced in April 1995 at a special conference by a massive majority. The new clause endorsed a 'dynamic economy, serving the public interest'; a 'just society which judges its strength by the condition of the weak as much as the strong'; 'an open democracy, in which government is held to account by the people';

and where 'decisions are taken as far as practicable by the communities they affect'.

Not content with this Blair later drew the party away from the social democratic heartland of full employment and welfare spending: it was deemed that the requisite high taxation would never be endorsed by middle-class voters – remember that Labour was caught out badly by the Conservatives over tax in 1992 – and it was believed that the world's economy had changed. With modern technology the economy has become globalised so that flows of capital can break companies and even currencies in minutes. To maintain policies of high taxation, it was believed, risks massive withdrawals of capital by speculators and investors from any economy contemplating such socialistic measures.

There was now no alternative to Thatcher's economics; 'New Labour' had effectively embraced tax cuts, low inflation, a market economy plus encouragement of entrepreneurial activity and some privatisation. Tony Blair flirted for a while with the idea of a 'stakeholder society', that everyone, individuals and groups, should have some investment in society, and everyone should feel part of their community at all levels, economic, cultural and social; the idea withered through business opposition to any wider role. The other biggish idea supported by Blair was constitutional reform; Labour embraced devolved assemblies for both Scotland and Wales plus reform of the House of Lords and a referendum on the electoral system. However, the changes were pitted with flaws, none more so than the unresolved, so-called 'West Lothian question', whereby Scottish MPs would have the ability to vote on English issues but English MPs do not have the ability to reciprocate as the internally elected assembly would assume this role (see Chapter 14). The Lords reform agenda stalled after the virtual abolition of hereditary peers and the chamber continued in its half-reformed way. As for reforming the voting system, the results of the Jenkins Report continued to gather dust as the party swung against the idea.

Blairism

The massive endorsement of New Labour in the general election of 1 May 1997 was fulfilment of the strategy conceived and implemented by Tony Blair and his close collaborator Peter Mandelson to move the Labour Party into a position where it embraced the market economy and removed the fear of old-style socialism felt by the middle-class occupants of 'Middle England'. 'Blairism' was vaguely expressed and lent itself to wide interpretation, but some commentators disagreed and claimed that Blairism boasted a coherent philosophical framework and was a well worked-out 'project'. Socially it is based on the idea of communitarianism. At university, Blair was very interested in the ideas of John McMurray, a Scottish philosopher who took issue with the modish idea of 'individualism', that the individual has choices and freedoms and is an autonomous unit. McMurray argued the contrary, that, as Adams puts it:

People do not exist in a vacuum; in fact, they only exist in relation to others. The completely autonomous self of liberal theory is a myth. People's personalities are created in their relationships with others, in the family and the wider community. By pursuing the interests of society as a whole we benefit individuals including ourselves.

Adams (1998: 148–9)

Blair argued that people should build communities based on the idea of responsibility, a sense of duty towards others maybe less fortunate and a recognition that one's actions have repercussions and may require reparation. Old Labour tended to see poor people as 'victims of the system'; to speak

of them having responsibilities is to borrow from another right-wing lexicon. Blair has also subscribed to the idea of a *Third Way*. Apart from being an alternative to socialism and pro-capitalist ideology, it was never clearly defined. Another participant has been the eminent sociologist Anthony Giddens, highly regarded by Blair, who has written a book, *The Third Way: The Renewal of Social Democracy*. This argues that the old definitions of left and right are obsolete (see Chapter 4) and that in the world of globalisation a new approach is required. He defines the overall aim of Third Way politics as helping citizens to:

pilot their way through the major revolutions of our time: globalisation, transformations in personal life and our relationship to nature . . . One might suggest as a prime motto for the new politics, 'No rights without responsibilities'.

Giddens (1998: 64–5) (see also Box 5.2)

Blair in power

For the first two years in power, Gordon Brown kept the brake firmly on expenditure but after the 2001 election, Labour embarked in 2002 on the spending of over £100 billion over the following years, marking for many a welcome return to Old Labour orthodoxy. However, the event that transformed Labour during the early months of 2003 was the war on Iraq. Tony Blair had decided to stand 'shoulder to shoulder' with George W. Bush after the horrific attacks on the World Trade Center on 11 September 2001, but the extent of his loyalty to a right-wing president advised by Republican hawks was anathema to many Labour MPs. When it proved impossible to muster a United Nations Security Council majority for the war in March, 139 MPs supported a hostile motion and Robin Cook resigned from the Cabinet. Left-wing critics spoke of a leadership contest. Such speculation proved premature but Blair's blind support for US foreign policy was squeezing support in his own New Labour power base (see also Chapter 28).

Blair's legacy

As it became obvious there was not much time left, Blair seemed to obsess with leaving a lasting 'legacy'. While he would have loved it to include a shiny new health and education service, polls showed voters relatively unimpressed and Labour

BOX 5.2   IDEAS AND PERSPECTIVES

How 'new' is New Labour?

A number of scholars have considered this question but the approach of Steven Fielding of Salford University (2003) is perhaps the most useful for this chapter's purposes. Fielding argues that New Labour is in reality part of the continuous development of social democratic thinking over the last century and a half. He denies the claim, associated with Roy Hattersley for one, that New Labour was a kind of 'coup' involving Blair, Mandelson and Gould and also denies the idea that New Labour was, in fact, all that new. His case is that New Labour was less to do with high-profile personalities and more to do with social democratic adaptations to the constantly fluid nature of international economics. As he sees it New Labour was an attempt to reconcile a system which produced winners and losers with the ideas of equality, justice and efficiency. This last was the crucial lacuna in socialism as Attlee's nationalisation produced overmanned loss-making state behemoths. Labour began to view the economy not so differently from Conservatives as something where growth and productivity had to be encouraged.

When this apparent attempt failed in a welter of strikes in 1979, the left swung back to bedrock and a right-wing Conservative government was elected. When voters rejected the left in 1983 and 1987 new thinking was set in train which nudged ever closer to an acceptance of market forces and a capitalist economy.

Writing some years into Labour's period in power, Fielding concluded:

The party at the start of the twenty-first century may be a highly cautious social democratic organization; but recognizably social democratic it remains. If the state has advanced modestly and in novel ways since 1997 Labour's purpose in office is the same as it ever was: to reform capitalism so that it may better serve the interests of the majority.

Source: Fielding (2003: 217)

critics furious at his encouragement of private sector invasion of such public sector citadels. For so many people, whatever their party loyalties, the debacle of the Iraq war will be emblazoned on Blair's grave. But this would be unfair. His tireless efforts in Northern Ireland, arguably proved crucial in winning an admittedly fragile settlement which saw a new Executive formed before he left office. Secondly, Blair caused the Conservatives to desert the aridities of Thatcherism. He had stolen Tory clothes to an extent but had subtly re-attired his party as liberal, tolerant and dedicated to improving the place of the less well-off majority. As leader followed leader the Conservatives finally got the message: they would have to change, just as Labour did from the mid-80s. David Cameron was the result. Now the litmus test for a new policy is, ostensibly at least, what it can do for the disadvantaged. Homophobia is out; environmentalism is very much in; pro-business yes, but at a distance; tax cuts maybe but not until the economy can sustain them.

Already the signs of Blair's greatest legacy perhaps are evident in our present politics: Thatcher finished off left-wing socialism but Blair has put paid to right-wing Conservatism: a legacy of which any left-leaning politician can be proud.

Gordon Brown's period in power
Brown's period as Prime Minister lasted only from June 2007, so he did not have much time to implant any characteristic elements. Indeed his critics claimed he lacked any real vision of what his party should offer the country.

Economy
Their voices were partially stilled by his reaction to the banking crisis of 2007 and the subsequent recession. He took confident strides in a Keynesian direction, channelling huge amounts of money into the banking system as a 'fiscal stimulus' to ensure the threatened collapse did not occur. There is some justification for believing his claim that other nations

followed his lead. The problem with such a policy was that it built up huge levels of debt which imposed heavy interest repayment obligations. In the run up to the election Labour argued that continued investment in the economy was necessary to avoid an even deeper recession. His arguments were undermined to an extent, in autumn 2009, when it became clear the UK economy was not emerging from recession like other developed nations like the USA, Germany, France and Japan. Labour argued strongly that they were not to blame for the recession and that the expenditure cuts proposed by the Tories would cause a fragile recovery to collapse into even deeper recession.

Public expenditure

Labour insisted in late 2009 that it would maintain public spending to sustain recovery and protect recipients of services. This was undermined however by Treasury plans indicating severe cuts in planned Labour expenditure from 2011 onwards.

Foreign policy

Labour took a positive view on the EU, supporting the Lisbon Treaty and seeking to ridicule Conservative hostility. On Afghanistan they offered continued support to the war but were damaged by accusations that British troops had not been properly equipped to fight the Taliban.

Long period in power: 1997–2010

As for the Tories in 1997, Labour suffered from the fact that they had been in power for three terms (over 12 years) and voters were tired of them. Frequent examples of poor or incompetent government received considerable publicity and fuelled fears of a major rejection at the 2010 election.

■ The Liberal Democrats

Source: Courtesy of the Liberal Democrats Party (www.libdems.org.uk)

After the war the Liberal Party continued to decline politically but still offered an alternative to voters in the centre of political ideas. At heart the party still adhered to the ideas of 'new liberalism' covered in Chapter 4, with emphases on individual liberty, equality, a mixed economy, a developed welfare state and a reformed, democratised system of government. Under the skilful successive leaderships of Jo Grimond, Jeremy Thorpe and David Steel, the party survived the postwar decades but hardly prospered. Then in 1981, as we have seen, it joined forces with the breakaway SDP to form the 'Alliance'. It was not difficult to unite on policies, which were very close; rather it was personalities who caused the foundering of this short-lived collaboration (see Box 5.1). In 1987, the two elements of the Alliance formally merged and fought the 1992 election as the Liberal Democrats. Its manifesto, *Changing Britain for Good*, called for a shift of power to the consumer and ordinary citizen, the development of worker shareholding and a market economy in which the market is the 'servant and not the master'. In addition, the party repeated the traditional call for reform of the voting system and **devolution** of power to the regions. Following the 1992 general election its new leader, Paddy Ashdown (elected in 1988), made steady progress with a replacing of 'equidistance' between the two big parties with a policy of open cooperation with Labour; in 1996, a joint Labour/Lib-Dem committee was set up to liaise on constitutional reform.

BIOGRAPHY

Paddy Ashdown (1941–)

Former leader of Liberal Democrats. Formerly captain in the Marines, he saw active service in Borneo. He also learned to speak Mandarin Chinese as part of the diplomatic corps 1971–6. Won Yeovil in 1983 as a Liberal and became leader of merged party in 1988. He worked hard to build a close relationship with Labour. Lib-Dems won 46 seats in the 1997 general election, after which Ashdown retired as leader. Charles Kennedy took over in 1999. Ashdown was appointed by the UN as International High Representative in Bosnia in May 2002.

The strong showing by the Liberal Democrats in the 1997 general election buttressed the claim of that party to be the de facto left-of-centre conscience of the new Blair order regarding constitutional reform and the nurturing of the welfare state, especially the educational system. The Lib Dems joined a Cabinet committee tasked with studying the future of constitutional reform – a tempting whiff of power perhaps for a party starved of it since the paltry sniff provided by the Lib–Lab pact of 1977–9. In 1999, Paddy Ashdown stood down after a distinguished period as leader of Britain's third party. His successor was the amiable Charles Kennedy, popular on quiz shows and a witty, clubbable man. He rejected suggestions to take up a left of Labour stance as the kind of *cul de sac* that had ruined Labour in the early 1980s. Instead he chose a 'business as usual' policy of 'constructive opposition' to Tony Blair with a view to replacing the Conservatives as the official opposition to the Labour government. In an interview with the US magazine *Talk*, Blair said that his biggest mistake in May 1997 had been not to ask Ashdown to join his Cabinet, although with such a huge majority it was politically impossible to deny even a single post to his own party.

In the 2005 election Kennedy fought his usual relaxed campaign, offering an anti-war stance over Iraq, increased taxation for the very rich, and no tuition fees for university students. This worked well in constituencies where Labour was the Lib-Dem target, and twelve seats were won in this way. However, what attracted former Labour voters did not work the same magic in the close Lib-Dem–Conservative seats: only three were won while five were lost.

This election of 62 MPs, though welcome, still carried a sense of feeling of a missed opportunity; in addition there developed sense that the party was losing what momentum it had gained at the election and all this contributed towards a whispering campaign against Kennedy. Complicating the situation, by the time of the autumn party conference a new wing was identified in the expanded 62-strong ranks of the Lib Dems: a group leaning more to the right, epitomised by *The Orange Book* of essays written by MPs and activists favouring a greater acceptance of market forces. Kennedy found his attempts to keep both factions happy were failing and by November senior party colleagues were said to be briefing against him.

Kennedy finally admitted the chief accusation against him – that he had a drinking problem – and a few days later, when the pressure did not abate, stood down in early January 2006. In the resultant, chaotic contest Simon Hughes and Chris Huhne waged a lively campaign, but the veteran Sir Menzies (Ming) Campbell won quite easily in the end, March 2006. When he in turn proved unable to offer a new direction and higher poll ratings, he too resigned in October 2007. Another contest took place and this time the young, good-looking Nick Clegg was the choice. He too had difficulty making an impact but he led the way in his 2008 conference in suggesting tax cuts; a nudge perhaps in the direction likely to win seats in the south-east from the Conservatives However, the Lib Dems have much for which to hope and fight; psephological predictions of a hung parliament in the 2009–10 election raised much talk of which side he would swing in any resultant coalition negotiations. The political positions of the Lib Dems have never seemed to matter very much as power has always seemed so far away. However, the possible prospect of a hung parliament, made their evolving policy positions for once into matters of intense interest.

■ The financial crisis of 2008

The worldwide financial crisis signalled by the collapse of the prestigious Lehman's investment Bank, in September 2008, presaged a desperate time in which leading governments tried a variety of remedies to a patient well into intensive care. It soon became apparent that a divide was opening up in party political reaction to the crisis. Prime Minister Gordon Brown, sought to blame the 'subprime' mortgage selling of US banks in the early years of the new century as the cause of the crisis and argued forcefully for a massive Keynesian 'fiscal stimulus' of borrowed money to kick start the world economy back into life. The Lib Dems, led by their formidable finance spokesman, Vince Cable – popular for his prescience in foreseeing the crisis and his wit in analysing it – tended to offer critical support to this approach. The Conservatives however, decided more lavish borrowing to solve a crisis caused by unwise borrowing was to take out a mortgage on the nation's future which our children will have to repay. In the wake of the G20 summit in London, 2009, the world could see that injections of vast funding saved the banking system but could not prevent a deep recession in most Western economies.

BOX 5.3   BRITAIN IN CONTEXT

Mainstream ideas and the political spectrum

As explained in Chapter 4, the political spectrum is usually represented from left to right, with unregulated free enterprise on the right and an anarchic or a communally owned economy on the left. Many of the ideas on the fringes – anarchism on the left or fascism on the right – would be regarded as extreme in the present day and unlikely to hold centre stage. Ideas likely to feature in the 'mainstream' of politics will usually be in the centre ground, that group of ideas which at any one time represents the general consensus of what people believe to be reasonable or legitimate political objectives.

Objectives which fall outside the mainstream are not automatic lost causes: repeated advocacy or changed circumstances can draw them into the centre – like anti-union legislation and privatisation during the early 1980s in the UK. During that same period the political spectrum was at its broadest in Britain with a near command economy being urged on Labour's left and a minimalist free enterprise state on the Thatcherite right. Since then ideological differences have narrowed significantly but they are still wider in Britain than in the USA.

Naturally right-wing pro-capitalist ideas are powerful in the USA, often seen as the 'headquarters' of world free enterprise thinking. By the same token 'left-wing' ideas, together with the US mainstream, are further to the right than in the UK. Americans have traditionally regarded any left-wing idea as the thin end of a communist wedge and therefore to be resisted as 'unpatriotic', not sufficiently 'American'. So even state-funded health services, commonplace in Europe, are seen from across the Atlantic as 'socialist' and therefore slightly sinister. Some theorists explain the weakness of US left-wing thinking as the consequence of 'hegemonic'

right-wing ideas: ideas so deeply ingrained and powerful they squeeze the life out of any alternatives. It is certainly true that both major parties in the USA stoutly support free enterprise economics: even the Democrats urge economic growth and support business, though not with the passion of the true believing Republicans.

Within Europe political spectrums, as in Britain, have tended to shift rightwards. Capitalism was no longer seen as a system which necessarily disadvantages large groups of people, but rather as the motor of dynamic economic growth from which all can benefit. Consequently communism faded away in the wake of the Cold War and most brands of left-wing socialism tended to follow suit. Former communist countries display a fascinating mix of ideas in their spectrums. During communism, as in most authoritarian regimes, the political spectrum was very narrow, containing virtually no options for genuine change.

But once the old pro-Moscow regimes imploded they were replaced by volatile new democracies in which, as in Russia, wild nationalism was present together with some surviving residual old-style communism. Many Russians, relieved at the passing of communism, were alarmed by their new combustible democracy and associated social dislocation. They gratefully accepted the promise of security which the former KGB chief Putin offered as president, even if political choices were once again heavily circumscribed. It would seem to be the case that a wide political spectrum, offering the chance of usually limited change at any particular time, is a characteristic of democracies. Authoritarian regimes do not tend to offer much choice and seek to shrink their spectrums into an unchanging narrowness.

Chapter summary

Conservatism is more than mere pragmatism in the ruling interest but includes a concern for unity, harmony and balance in a society based on property, equal opportunity, élite rule and gradual change. Margaret Thatcher gave major prominence to the neo-liberal strand in Conservatism, which stressed the primacy of markets in economics. Major returned to the rhetoric of 'one nation' Conservatism but contained the practice of Thatcherism. Labour began as a socialist party dedicated to the replacement of capitalism by a collectively owned economy, but in government translated this into nationalisation, a policy of doubtful success. In opposition during the 1980s it gradually shed its socialist clothes and donned those of the free market and restricted public spending: in effect a compromise with Thatcherism. Liberal Democrats inherited the 'new liberal ideas', of the early twentieth century to which they added an initial disposition to work with the Labour Party in office, something which faded after the invasion of Iraq in 2003.

Discussion points

■ To what extent was Margaret Thatcher a Conservative?

■ Did John Major contribute anything distinctive to Conservative thinking?

■ Did Labour sell out its principles during the 1980s?

■ Is there room for a distinctive third set of political ideas in Britain, and do the Lib-Dems offer them?

Further reading

Andrew Heywood's *Political Ideologies* (1998) is a valuable source, as is the similar book by Ian Adams (1998). The Giddens book, *The Third Way*, has been criticised as too vague, but it is chock full of interesting ideas and more than repays a careful reading.

Bibliography

Adams, I. (1998) *Ideology and Politics in Britain Today* (Manchester University Press).

Ashbee, E. and Ashford, N. (1999) *US Politics Today* (Manchester University Press).

Beer, S.H. (1982) *Britain Against Itself* (Faber).

Crewe, I. and King, A. (1995) *SDP: The Birth, Life and Death of the Social Democratic Party* (Oxford University Press).

Crosland, C.A.R. (1956) *The Future of Socialism* (Jonathan Cape).

Driver, S. and Mantell, L. (1998) *New Labour: Politics after Thatcherism* (Pluto Press).

Field, F. (1995) *Making Welfare Work* (Institute of Community Studies).

Fielding, S. (2003) *The Labour Party* (Palgrave).

Foley, M. (1994) *Ideas that Shape Politics* (Manchester University Press).

Foote, G. (1997) *The Labour Party's Political Thought* (Manchester University Press).

Giddens, A. (1998) *The Third Way: The Renewal of Social Democracy* (Polity Press).

Gould, B. (1989) *A Future for Socialism* (Jonathan Cape).

Gould, P. (1998) *The Unfinished Revolution* (Little, Brown).

Hailsham, Lord (1959) *The Conservative Case* (Penguin).

Heywood, A. (1998) *Political Ideologies*, 2nd edn (Macmillan).

Howell, D. (1980) *British Social Democracy* (Croom Helm).

Hutton, W. (1998) *The Stakeholding Society* (Polity Press).

Kelly, R. (1999) 'The Third Way', *Politics Review*, September.

Kelly, R. (1999) *British Political Parties Today* (Manchester University Press).

Marshall, P. and Laws, D. (2004) *The Orange Book: Reclaiming Liberalism* (Profile Books).

Norton, P. and Aughey, A. (1981) *Conservatives and Conservatism* (Temple Smith).

Policy Exchange (2005) *The Case for Change* (Policy Exchange).

Russell, A. (2004) *Neither Left nor Right – the Liberal Democrats and the Electorate* (Manchester University Press).

Smith, C. (1998) *Creative Britain* (Faber and Faber).

Tressell, R. (1965) *The Ragged Trousered Philanthropists* (Panther; first published 1914).

Tucker, K. (1998) *Anthony Giddens and Modern Social Theory* (Sage).

Whiteley, P. and Seyd, P. (1992) *Labour's Grass Roots: the Politics of Party Membership* (Clarendon).

Useful websites

Centre for Policy Studies: www.cps.org.uk/
Conservative Party: www.conservatives.com/
Institute of Economic Affairs: www.iea.org.uk/
Institute of Public Policy Research:
   www.ippr.org.uk
Labour Party: www.labour.org.uk/
Liberal Democrats: www.libdems.org.uk/

CHAPTER 6

Political ideas: themes and fringes

Bill Jones

Learning objectives

■ To explain and put into context the themes of:
  - feminism;
  - national identity;
  - environmentalism.

■ To identify, analyse and elucidate the political fringe on the far left and far right.

■ To explain the intellectual source of ideas characterising the political fringe.

Introduction

The first three chapters in this section looked at ideology, political concepts and party political ideas. This fourth chapter addresses three major themes – **feminism**, **national identity** and **environmentalism**. This is followed by the rarefied world of the political fringe, represented by a colourful assemblage of small parties that are not always easy to identify; they may be seen selling their newspapers on the street or taking part in street demonstrations or even contesting national elections. However, their intellectual roots are often connected to major philosophical themes and are therefore of interest.

■ Gender issues

Any woman whose IQ hovers above her body temperature must be a feminist.

Rita Mae Brown, author

In 1980, a United Nations report stated:

While women represent 50 per cent of the world's population, they perform nearly two-thirds of all working hours, receive one-tenth of world income and own less than 1 per cent of world property.

Despite the existence of a worldwide feminist movement, the position of women worldwide has improved very slightly, if at all, since the dawn of feminism in the late eighteenth century. The rights of women were implicit in the recognition of the rights of 'men', but thinkers such as Locke did not include women in their scheme of things. Rousseau did, however (while treating his own wife very badly), and in 1792 Mary Wollstonecraft's *A Vindication of the Rights of Women* (see Wollstonecraft, 1967) articulated their rights explicitly (see Biography) just as the French Revolution was asserting the rights of oppressed people everywhere. Whether women were 'oppressed' or not was a moot point. Most men assumed that women existed to perform domestic roles: producing and rearing children and caring for their husbands as well as doing all the household chores. Probably most women at the time would have agreed, had they ever thought themselves important enough to be consulted. They had no possibility of pursuing careers, voting or participating in public life. Their consolation was the power they exercised through this domestic role, influencing their menfolk, maybe even dominating them, behind the scenes. But the legal position of women at this time was dire: they had no right to divorce (unlike their husbands); they had no right to marital property; and their husbands could beat them quite legally – even rape them should they wish. Moreover, men regularly used prostitutes while preaching fidelity for their wives and divorcing them when this failed, on their side, to be upheld. In 'exchange' women were praised for their femininity and sensitivity and were idealised by the notion of romantic love. An unequal relationship indeed.

Emergent socialist ideas supported the position of women. Friedrich Engels argued in his book *The Origin of the Family, Private Property and the State* (1884) that the pre-historical position of

BIOGRAPHY

Mary Wollstonecraft (1757–97)

Mary Wollstonecraft was an Anglo-Irish writer and is often cited as the first modern feminist. At the age of 28 she wrote a semi-auto-biographical novel, *Maria*. She moved to London to become the 'first of a new genus' of women, a full-time professional writer and editor specialising in women and children. She was closely associated with the group of radical reforming writers called the English Jacobins, where she met her future husband, the philosopher William Godwin. In her book *A Vindication of the Rights of Women* (1792) she argued for equal rights for women in society, especially regarding educational opportunities. Her daughter with Godwin was Mary Shelley, the author of *Frankenstein*.

women had been usurped by men so that property now was passed on through the male line instead of the female because men wished to pass on property to their sons. The exploitative relationship between the propertied class and the proletariat was mirrored within the family by the relationship between men and women. A socialist revolution would sweep away private property and remove the economic basis of the exploitative monogamous marriage.

During the nineteenth century the women's movement, such as it was, concentrated on gaining the vote, the belief being that, once this citadel had fallen, the other injustices regarding the imbalance of political and legal rights compared with men would soon be remedied.

To an extent these early feminists were operating with the grain of history, as the franchise for men was being progressively extended at this time. Nevertheless, it took a bitter and militant struggle for the 'suffragettes', led by Emmeline and Christabel Pankhurst, to win through: in 1918 women received the vote, but only if they fulfilled certain educational and property qualifications and were, bizarrely it now seems, over the age of 30. They finally achieved equal political rights in 1928, but this did not automatically transform their position, or make any difference at all in the short and medium term. The women's movement subsided for a number of decades, but the impact of another world war, where women once again played leading roles on the home front, advanced their claims for better treatment. Simone de Beauvoir's *The Second Sex* (1952) attacked the asymmetry whereby men were defined as free independent beings and women merely in terms of their relationships with men.

But the so-called 'second wave' of feminism began with Betty Friedan's *The Feminine Mystique* (1963). This major work rejected the myth that women were different and were happy being the domestic adjuncts of their men. Having nominally equal rights did not deliver real equality in a world controlled by men and discriminating against women. In the late 1960s and 1970s, the work of Germaine Greer (*The Female Eunuch*, 1971) and Kate Millett (*Sexual Politics*, 1969) moved the focus of debate from the wider world of career and public life to the micro-worlds that we all inhabit. Greer developed some of the ideas of Herbert Marcuse (1964, 1969a, 1969b), who argued that Western society was sexually repressed. She suggested that women had absorbed the male idea of their sexuality as soft and yielding – a kind of sex image stereotype – while their true and possibly quite different nature was not allowed to be expressed and fulfilled. Concomitant with this went an assertion of lesbianism as a socially demonised activity. Instead of their living out expected roles, Greer was insisting that people could be true to themselves, being 'male' or 'female' according to their own natures. Millett's emphasis was on how women are brainwashed into accepting a given image of themselves regarding their role and even their appearance. This image, according to her, was a reflection of 'patriarchy': constructed by men with their interests in mind. What was attributed to gender roles was in fact no more than a socially constructed role that women were induced to accept from birth via a battery of socialising agencies, including family, tradition, law, the media and popular culture. Women were forced to accept a narrow, constricting role of being gentle, caring mother figures whose job was to tend their men. Alternatively, they were seen as whores and temptresses, equally subservient but this time more dangerous. Millett also directed attention at the family and home, pointing out that here was the most important arena in which the male controlled the key sexual relationship, dominating the female; following from this is the key feminist phrase, that 'the personal is the political'.

In the 1970s it was observed that liberal feminists, who believed that reform and a high degree of equality were possible in society as it is, coexisted with socialist feminists, who believed that the main inequality was still between classes and not the sexes. They believed that major changes to the

BIOGRAPHY

Germaine Greer (1939–)

Australian feminist, author and journalist. Educated at Melbourne and Cambridge Universities. Lectured at Warwick University but best known for her book *The Female Eunuch* (1971), which attacked the institution of marriage as a form of slavery and the way women's sexuality was misrepresented and denied by males. She modified her militant position in later life but is still an active advocate for women's rights.

BOX 6.1	IDEAS AND PERSPECTIVES

Sexual inequality at work

According to LSE research reports in February 2000 and January 2001, a woman earns on average £250,000 less than a man during a lifetime. This is partly because women workers tend to be concentrated in low-paid jobs but also because they are paid less than men for doing the same work and routinely denied access to bonus payments and pension schemes. Figures released in autumn 2008 revealed the gap is getting wider with men earning on average £15.54 an hour and woman £12.88; this makes a gender pay gap of 17.1 per cent, up from 17 per cent a year earlier; the TUC point out the gap is 21 per cent in the private sector.

economy and society were necessary before women could be truly free. A third group soon emerged: the *radical* feminists. For them the problem lies not in society or the economy but in human nature, more precisely, male human nature. The problem with women, in other words, is men. In *The Dialectic of Sex* (1980, originally published 1971), Shulamith Firestone perceived a fundamental oppression of women by men as a result of their biological role. Sexual domination therefore both precedes and exceeds economic exploitation. What she advocates is a 'sexual revolution much larger than – inclusive of – a socialist one' to 'eradicate the tapeworm of exploitation'. She argues for a restructuring of society through science, whereby children would be produced artificially and looked after communally so that women's physical and psychological burdens would be removed and they would be free for the first time in history.

Susan Brownmiller – *Against our Will* (1975) – shifts the focus to the violence that men use to threaten women; the fear of rape is used to maintain male dominance, and rapists act for all men in demonstrating the consequences of non-compliance. Other feminist writers, such as Andrea Dworkin and Dale Spender – often called 'supremacists' – assert female moral superiority and argue that the world would be better if women were in control. Often this type of feminist will be separatist in relation to men; their lesbianism consequently has a political quality to it. For them men are not necessary for women, and women who live with men are 'man identified' instead of being 'woman identified'.

It is often said that since the 1970s the women's movement has lost momentum. Certainly the tone has become milder; Greer (1985) and Friedan (1982) have both disappointed radicals by writing approvingly of domesticity and childrearing. The New Right in the USA and UK, moreover, have

reinforced 'traditional values' of women's roles and the desirability of marriage (and by implication the subversive effects of one-parent families) to hold society together. In their book *Contemporary Feminist Politics* (1993), Lovenduski and Randall applauded the progress made by the women's movement in permeating institutions and professions and in disseminating feminist values so effectively that they have become widely accepted as orthodoxies. However, they lament the failure to replace activists when they bow out of activity, and the internecine squabbling and fragmentation that have weakened the movement. A report covered by *The Observer* (7 November 1999) questioned whether women have made much progress at all. The American Psychological Association's study concluded that 'even though the fight for equal rights widened opportunities for many, it failed to give women control over their lives'. Experts cited in the article suggested the same could be said of the UK too; two-thirds of the 1300 receiving electro-convulsive therapy each week for depressive illnesses are women. The strong showing of women candidates in the 1997 general election – women MPs virtually doubled from 62 to 120, most of them Labour – cheered campaigners for more female representation and those who defended the special Labour measures to favour women candidates in winnable seats. However, some feminists have criticised 'Blair's babes', as they have been dubbed, as performing a decorative but non-feminist role in the governing party. Comparisons are made on the Labour side with the fiercely effective Barbara Castle and on the Conservative side with the legendary Thatcher. Boxes 6.2–6.4 provide chapter and verse on employment and political life in the UK showing that, while much has been achieved in the recent past, women are still at a definite disadvantage compared to men.

BOX 6.2   FACT

Women in public and political life

Although women make up 46 per cent of the labour market, they are under-represented in many jobs and positions with power or influence:

- Only 18 per cent of MPs are women.
- 24 per cent of UK MEPs are women.

Members of Parliament 2004 (UK)

Political party	Women		Men	
	Number of MPs	% of party	Number of MPs	% of party
Conservative	14	9	149	91
Labour	94	23	313	77
Liberal Democrat	6	11	49	89
Other parties[a]	5	15	29	85
All parties	119	18	540	82

[a] Includes Speaker and deputies.
Source: House of Commons (2004)

Members of the European Parliament 2004 (UK)

Political party	Women		Men	
	Number of MEPs	% of party	Number of MEPs	% of party
Conservative	2	7	26	93
Labour	7	37	12	63
Liberal Democrat	6	50	6	50
Other parties and independents	4	21	15	79
All parties	19	24	59	76

Source: European Parliament website

BOX 6.3   FACT

Women and men in Great Britain

Employment

- 46 per cent of people in the labour market are women.
- In the 16–64 age group, two-thirds of women and over three-quarters of men are in employment.
- Nearly half of women (44 per cent) and about one in ten men who work are part time.

Parents and carers

- Of mothers of under-fives, 52 per cent were in employment, and two-thirds of those working as employees were part time.
- Since there are almost 4.7 million under-eights in England and just over a million places with childminders in full day care or in out-of-school clubs, there are four children for each place in these types of provision.

Pay and income

- Average hourly earnings for women working full time are 18 per cent lower than for men working full time, and for women working part time hourly earnings are 40 per cent lower.

Source: From Equal Opportunities Commission (2006) *Sex and Power: Who Runs Britain?*

BOX 6.4	FACT

Women's representation in the public and voluntary sectors

Women make up:

- 35 per cent of public appointments
- 17.5 per cent of local authority chief executives
- 0.8 per cent of senior ranks in the armed forces
- 10.2 per cent of senior police officers
- 25.5 per cent of Civil Service top management
- 45.2 per cent of chief executives of voluntary organisations
- 8.8 per cent of top judges (high court judge and above)

- 31.8 per cent of secondary school head teachers
- 28.6 per cent of FE college principals
- 11.1 per cent of university vice chancellors
- 28.1 per cent of health service chief executives
- 22.4 per cent of trade union general secretaries or equivalent
- 33.3 per cent of heads of selected professional bodies

Source: Equal Opportunities Commission (2006: 9)

As if this was not enough to worry about, an article (criticised by several feminist writers) by Professor Alison Wolf, of Kings College London, in a March 2006 edition of *Prospect* magazine, maintained that new attitudes in the workplace are in effect 'killing feminism':

In the past, women of all classes shared lives centred on explicitly female concerns. Now it makes little sense to discuss women in general. The statistics are clear: among young, educated, full-time professionals, being female is no longer a drag on earnings or progress.

Wolf goes on to argue that total commitment to career diverts the crucial resource of female talent away from the caring professions like teaching, prevents them from volunteering and thus minimises 'female altruism', and dissuades many women from having children.

Box 6.5 provides a useful summary guide of feminist ideas together with their authors.

■ National identity: the English/ British sense of who they are

All countries have some sense of identity – where they have come from, who they are, what they stand for – and, just like individuals, most encounter problems in finding satisfactory answers. The USA, for example, comprising a multitude of different elements, often recent arrivals, experiences a fragile sense of unity and coherence which constantly has to be reinforced by overt – and what to Europeans may seem like manic – statements of patriotism. France too has been undergoing an identity crisis recently, with its famed sense of equality, dating back to the 1789 revolution, being questioned especially by Muslim immigrant groups which declare they are not in any real sense equal when they suffer from racism and widespread unemployment. The British also are undergoing problems in deciding who they are, what they are for and to whom they belong.

Andrew Gamble, in his *Between Europe and America* (2003), addresses this topic and analyses the way in which this sense of identity has changed over the years. He argues that England was at the heart of this identity, expanding to absorb Wales, Scotland and, until 1922, Ireland. After losing the 13 colonies, the empire enjoyed its biggest expansion in the nineteenth century embracing one quarter of the world's population and one quarter of its territory.

The empire created an extensive ruling élite and a world-view which also embodied a degree of smug superiority that often irritated the rest of the world. But the massive losses of the First World War sapped the nation's power and, even though the postwar settlement expanded the empire, it had lost its stability. The Second World War involved the sacrifice of much of the wealth which the empire represented and by 1945 it was living on borrowed time. The refusal of the US to support Britain's involvement in the attempt to regain the Suez Canal in 1956 was the signal for the further winding up of the imperial dream which independence to India in 1947 had initiated. Those schoolchildren who had

BOX 6.5	IDEAS AND PERSPECTIVES

Feminist debates

This is a schematic summary of the main strands of feminist thought. It is important to understand that these strands are not rigidly separate, that some writers could be entered in more than one category, and that in recent years there has been a significant convergence of apparently competing approaches.

Type of feminism	Key concepts	Goals	Key writers
Liberal	Rights, equality	The same rights and opportunities as for men, with a focus on the public sphere	*Classic:* Mary Wollstonecraft John Stuart Mill *Recent:* Betty Friedan Naomi Wolf Natasha Walter
Radical	Patriarchy, 'the personal is political', sisterhood	Radical transformation of all spheres of life to liberate women from male power. Replace or displace men as the measure of human worth	Kate Millett Andrea Dworkin Catherine MacKinnon Germaine Greer
Socialist and Marxist	Class, capitalism, exploitation	An economically just society in which all women and men can fulfil their potential	*Classic:* William Thompson Friedrich Engels Alexandra Kollontai Sylvia Pankhurst *Recent:* Michelle Barrett Juliet Mitchell Sheila Rowbotham Lynne Segal Anne Phillips
Black	Interactive and multiple oppressions, solidarity, black	An end to the interconnecting oppressions of gender, 'race' and class	*Classic:* Maria Stewart Julia Cooper *Recent:* Patricia Hill Collins bell hooks Angela Davis Heidi Mirza
Postmodern	Fragmentation, discourse, deconstruction, differences	Overcoming binary oppositions. Free-floating, fluid gender identities. However, the idea of a final goal is rejected in principle	Judith Butler Julia Kristeva Joan Scott Denise Riley Michelle Barrett

Source: Valerie Bryson (2003) 'Feminist debates, ideology: feminism', *Politics Review*, Vol. 12, No. 4, April 2003. Reproduced with permission from Philip Allan Updates

felt a thrill of pride in seeing the 1950s map of the world coloured with so much red had soon to adjust to a much more humble role.

Along with imperial decline came its economic concomitant: a slow sinking of Britain from 'work-shop of the world' to 'sick man of Europe'. During the seventies the sour mood of the times infected a workforce which became increasingly uncooperative and demanding of higher wages just when the country could no longer afford them. The result

English football fans display their support for the national team
Source: Action Plus Sports Images / Neil Tingle

was a major upsetting of the postwar settlement whereby agreed increased taxes funded a welfare state and included trade unions as a valued partner of government. Margaret Thatcher set about enthroning the role of markets, removing the inefficient nationalised industries, curbing the overpowerful unions and rolling back the role of the state. But the effects of this harsh medicine on Scotland and Wales gave added power to the arguments for independence in these countries. When Tony Blair was elected in 1997 the stage was set for the partial dismantling of the constitution – devolution – posing a number of questions about the concept of Britain. 'England' is no longer synonymous with 'Britain' now new identities have been assumed by the nations of the Celtic fringe, each with their separate assemblies.

At the same time there is an internal questioning of identity caused by the inflow of immigrants, initially from the empire and Commonwealth after 1945, and latterly by economic and political refugees from poorer and strife-torn countries during the latter part of the century. This growing

band of ethnic minorities has changed the nature of British cities and arguably made the country a 'multicultural' society. But there are evident strains, sometimes violent, between immigrants and their British neighbours; many resist this loss of their old identity and argue that such people are at heart 'foreigners'. Lord Norman Tebbit controversially demanded that, when cricket teams arrived from their home countries, Commonwealth immigrants should support the English side. In practice, immigrants and their descendants now tend to assume a dual identity of 'black British' or 'British Asian'.

Yet another thread in this complex reworking of identities is the European Union. At the 'Congress of Europe' in May 1948 Winston Churchill made the chairman's address, including the words: 'I hope to see a Europe where men and women of every country will think of being European and wherever they go in this wide domain will truly feel, "I am at home".' The truth is that neither he nor Ernest Bevin, Labour Foreign Secretary from 1945 to 1951, actually believed all the warm words they said about a united Europe. Like US diplomats, they recognised a degree of unity as necessary to resist the Soviet threat and were not opposed to a closer coming together should the nations concerned wish it; the problem was that Britain, when it came down to it, did not.

Bevin had explained in 1946 that Britain saw herself as a 'great power', adding that 'the very fact we have fought so hard for liberty, and paid such a high price, warrants our retaining that position' (Gamble 2003: 189). So Europe was seen as something separate from Britain, which still sat at the 'big boys' table. When the European Iron and Steel Community was established in 1950 – the organisational template, as it turned out, for the later European Community – Britain loftily stood aside, refusing to allow any mere Europeans to decide how these nationalised concerns should be run. The same thing happened with the developments up to 1957 when the Treaty of Rome established the new experiment in supranationalism. Clement Attlee summed up a dominant British political class view of Europe when he said:

The so-called Common Market of six nations. Know them all well. Very recently, this country spent a great deal of blood and treasury rescuing four of 'em from attacks by the other two.

It is no surprise that Britain initially was not interested but then the devastating American rebuff of Suez, plus the signs that British capitalism was unable to keep pace with the new dynamic customs union based in Brussels, brought about a dramatic change of emphasis and potential allegiance. Britain applied in 1959 and received another rebuff, this time courtesy of General De Gaulle who repeated the trick in 1967. Running behind the bus trying to catch it and then being thrown off when we did was not the best early experience to have of this economically integrated Europe. We finally made it in 1972 when the General had left the stage and a staunchly Europhile Ted Heath was able to manufacture a majority Commons vote for entry.

But dissent was by no means stilled. At first it was the Labour left which cavilled at this 'capitalist club' but under Thatcher it was the right-wing Conservatives who gave full expression to an anti-European position. They could not begin to accept that the British identity, forged by a thousand years of history, a worldwide empire and heroic struggles against tyranny, could be meekly subsumed into what Margaret Thatcher liked to call 'The Belgian

Empire'. Against what proved to be her better judgement she acceded to measures of greater integration but then, after leaving office, became an avid and bitter cheerleader for the Eurosceptic cause. Polls showed that upwards of a third of Britons tended to agree with her.

The dilemma for Britain's changing sense of identity now emerged starkly during the 1980s and 1990s. The Tory right preferred America to Europe: the American attitude to economics, welfare and, indeed, the management of world order. When Labour entered government many felt this identification would swing back towards our partners in Europe. Certainly Blair subscribed to the Social Chapter upon which Conservative sceptics had poured so much vitriol and joined in the EU (as it was called after Maastricht in 1992) summits, but his desire for Britain to join the common currency, the euro, was prevented by his Chancellor Gordon Brown to whom Blair had conceded virtual control of the economy. So entry into the EU's inner counsels was prevented; EU opponents were pleased and hoped Labour would maintain the pro-American bias favoured by many Conservatives. Brown, in any case, is a warm admirer of the American economic model and had tried hard to keep employment 'flexible', unlike many EU countries where pro-worker employment laws hold down productivity. But the biggest shifting of Gamble's 'four spheres' occurred after the 9/11 attack on the World Trade Center in New York (see Figure 6.1).

At this point, when the world stood back in horror, Blair was quick to offer his 'shoulder to shoulder' support for the USA. Other EU partners expressed outrage but none could match the fervour of Blair's support. Later Blair sent in troops to Afghanistan and then, much more controversially, to Iraq. British public opinion was similar to that of most EU countries, even those who supported George W. Bush – very sympathetic to the USA in the wake of the 9/11 attack but two-thirds of voters were not prepared to envisage an invasion against Iraq, however dreadful its ruler might be. Bush and Defence Secretary Rumsfeld's apparent arrogant disregard for multilateral solutions alienated much of European and British opinion. Blair refused to be drawn towards the EU consensus and remained true to his earlier position, matching Bush's rhetoric with his own. But Blair did have an idea of the role his country should perform; as he said in January 2003: 'We can help to be a bridge between the US and Europe.' The problems associated with such a route

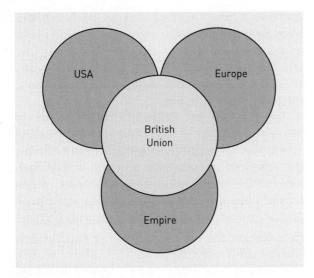

Figure 6.1 The Four Circles of England: in his *Between Europe and America* (2003), Andrew Gamble (pp. 30–4) quotes Churchill's view that Britain lay at the touching point of three circles – Empire, Europe and America. Gamble argues that since devolution, a fourth, that of the 'British Union', should be added

to a new identity were threefold. Firstly, Blair had shown a heavy bias towards the US, philosophically in terms of economic systems and politically in terms of its world role as a hyper-power. Secondly, Europe's two biggest and leading countries, France and Germany, both leaders and voters, were not as enamoured of the US as Tony Blair. Thirdly, on the major issues like Iraq, British public opinion was closer to America's European critics than to Blair's enthusiastic and uncritical support.

'Britishness'

Linda Colley (2005), in her book, *Britons: Forging the Nation 1707–1837*, argues that British people, known as such since the Act of Union 1707 with Scotland, tend to have a 'layered' sense of being British plus an often even closer identity like Scottish, Welsh, Northern Irish, Asian or Caribbean; oddly perhaps 'English' is more often regarded as interchangeable with 'British'. Some polling evidence suggests that the 'British' layer has given way to the connecting identity, so that many now feel more English, Scottish and so forth than the composite 'British'. Gordon Brown was clearly seeking to minimise his Scottishness by emphasising the importance of 'Britishness'. In January 2006 he even suggested a national day for 'Britain', explaining he

wished to 'recapture the union flag from the far right'. In a reference to the 7/7 bombings he added:

We have to face uncomfortable facts that while the British response to July 7th was remarkable, they were British citizens, British born apparently integrated into our communities, who were prepared to maim and kill fellow British citizens irrespective of their religion.

■ Green thinking

The ecological perspective rejects philosophies of the right, left and centre as more similar than dissimilar. Sir Jonathon Porritt (a senior environment adviser to the Blair government) characterises them collectively as '**industrialism**': this 'super-ideology . . . conditioned to thrive on the ruthless exploitation of both people and planet, is itself the greatest threat we face' (Porritt 1984). Conservatives, socialists and centre politicians argue about rival economic approaches – individualism versus collectivism and how the cake of national income should be sliced up and distributed – but they all agree that the size of the cake should be increased through vigorous economic growth. This is the central proposition that the Greens most emphatically reject. 'Industrialism', they say, is predicated on the continuous expansion of the goods and services and on the promotion of even more consumption through advertising and the discovery of an increasing range of 'needs'. It creates great inequalities whereby a rich and envied minority set the pace in lavish and unnecessary consumption while a substantial number – in many countries a majority – are either unemployed or live in relative, perhaps dire poverty. The Conservatives have presided over an increase in income differentials but have offered economic growth as a panacea: more for the rich and more for the poor. Porritt observes:

If the system works, i.e. we achieve full employment, we basically destroy the planet; if it doesn't, i.e. we end up with mass unemployment, we destroy the lives of millions of people . . . From an industrial point of view it is rational to . . . promote wasteful consumption, to discount social costs, to destroy the environment. From the Green point of view it is totally irrational, simply because we hold true to the most important political reality of all: that all wealth ultimately derives from the finite resources of our planet.

Porritt (1984: 46–7)

The Green view goes on to adduce a number of basic principles:

1 *A world approach*: All human activity should reflect appreciation of the world's finite resources and easily damaged ecology.

2 *Respect the rights of our descendants*: Our children have the right to inherit a beautiful and bountiful planet rather than an exhausted and polluted one.

3 *Sufficiency*: We should be satisfied with 'enough' rather than constantly seeking 'more'.

4 *A conserver economy*: We must conserve what we have rather than squander it through pursuit of high-growth strategies.

5 *Care and share*: Given that resources are limited, we must shift our energies to sharing what we have and looking after all sections of society properly.

6 *Self-reliance*: We should learn to provide for ourselves rather than surrendering responsibility to specialised agencies.

7 *Decentralise and democratise*: We must form smaller units of production, encourage cooperative enterprises and give people local power over their own affairs. At the same time, international integration must move forward rapidly.

Porritt maintains that this amounts to a wholly alternative view of rationality and mankind's existence. He contrasts the two world-views of industrialism and ecology in Table 6.1.

Inevitably, the other major parties have done all they can to climb aboard the Green bandwagon, cloaking their policies in light green clothes

Table 6.1 Two worlds: industrialism versus ecology

Industrialism	Ecology
The environment	
Domination over nature	Harmony with nature
Environment managed as a resource	Resources regarded as strictly finite
High energy, high consumption	Low energy, low consumption
Nuclear power	Renewable sources of energy
Values	
An ethos of aggressive individualism	Cooperatively based communitarian society with emphasis on personal autonomy
Pursuit of material goods	Move towards spiritual, non-material values
Rationality and packaged knowledge	Intuition and understanding
Patriarchal values, hierarchical structure	Post-patriarchal feminist values, non-hierarchical structure
Unquestioning acceptance of technology	Discriminating use and development of science and technology
The economy	
Economic growth and demand stimulation	Sustainability, quality of life and simplicity
Production for exchange and profit	Production for use
High income differentials	Low income differentials
A free-market economy	Local production for local need
Ever-expanding world trade	Self-reliance
Employment as a means to an end	Work as an end in itself
Capital-intensive production	Labour-intensive production
Political organisation	
Centralisation, economies of scale	Decentralisation, human scale
Representative democracy	Direct democracy, participative involvement
Sovereignty of nation-state	Internationalism and global solidarity
Institutionalised violence	Non-violence

Source: Adapted from Porritt (1984) *Seeing Green*, pp. 216–17

and shamelessly stealing the rhetoric of the environmentalists.

As it currently stands, the Greens' political programme is unlikely to fall within the 'art of the possible' (see below). It has established some support among students, and in 1994 it gained four council seats, but its best parliamentary performance was in 1989, when it managed 6.1 per cent of the vote in Lambeth, Vauxhall. In May 2003 Greens won seven seats in the Scottish Parliament. In 2005 the Greens fielded 202 candidates but not one got elected. Hardly a launching pad for power, but as Malcolm Muggeridge once pointed out, 'utopias flourish in chaos', and if global warming continues unchecked accompanied by more environmental chaos, it may well be the Greens who inherit politically what is left of the Earth, if it is not already too late by then.

BOX 6.6	IDEAS AND PERSPECTIVES

Global warming

Of all the many dangers facing the world's environment, it has been the problem of global warming that has most exercised environmentalists and governments in recent years.

The scientific argument on 'greenhouse' gases

It is an obvious fact that the earth receives its warmth from the sun. However, certain gases within the earth's atmosphere have been crucial in helping retain the sun's heat over the billions of years life has been evolving. Some of the sun's heat is reflected back into space but the retention of a portion of this heat, absorbed by the gases, has enabled the earth to achieve a temperature ideal for supporting life. Indeed, without such gases the average temperature of the world would have been −15°C instead of +18°C.

The first person to make the link between climate and greenhouse gases was the Swedish scientist Svante Arrhenius in 1898. He calculated that a doubling of CO_2 would increase world temperatures by 5–6°C. Other scientists observed that volcanic eruptions of sulphur dioxide into the atmosphere, which reflects sunlight, causes a degree of cooling. Some have attributed global warming to the lack of volcanic activity in the twentieth century. In 1988 the UN established the Intergovernmental Panel on Climate Change. The IPCC's latest estimate is of a warming of between 1.4 and 5.8°C by 2100 depending on what is done to curb gas emissions (IPCC 2001). Other studies suggest even higher rates of warming.

Consequences of global warming

The earth's temperature has provided the conditions in which humans have evolved and flourished, but rapidly rising temperatures would cause deforestation, the loss of fishing stocks, the collapse of many crops, outbreaks of many more destructive tropical storms, the melting of vast permafrosted areas (which would also release massive new stored reserves of CO_2) and the gradual melting of the ice-caps, causing catastrophic rises in sea level amounting to over 200 feet.

The developing world

The surging economies of China and India – often using CO_2-rich emitting energy production methods – hugely increase the threats, but it is hard for the developed world to insist that poorer countries forego the benefits and comforts which the West has enjoyed for many years. Awareness of the dangers grew throughout the latter half of the twentieth century, and in 1997 an agreement was reached at Kyoto whereby signatories agreed to reduce emissions to 5 per cent below the 1990 levels by 2010; in practice this means a reduction of 29 per cent in all greenhouse gases. Developing countries were excluded from this requirement, but the biggest problem lay with the reluctance of the USA to ratify the agreement.

With only 5 per cent of the world's population, the world's biggest economy emits a quarter of the world's CO_2. Energy lobbies in the USA vigorously disputed the thesis that the planet's climate is heating up.

George W. Bush, originally an oil man and advised by many more, refused to accept the Kyoto Protocol. One of his advisers, Myron Ebell, attacked the statement of David King, Britain's Chief Scientific Officer, that global warming was more of a threat to the future of the world than terrorism, on the grounds that King did not have the scientific expertise. He also claimed the whole global warming story was a scare tactic created by Europe to enable their ailing economies to compete more effectively against the USA. Barack Obama, elected in 2008, basically accepts the arguments and has pledged to reverse Bush's policy on this issue.

Scepticism about global warming remains despite the fact that 99 per cent of scientists in this area of study insist it is a fact. Some people argue that climate has always varied, with the Thames regularly freezing over in the Middle Ages, and Ice Ages occurring not infrequently. Scientists riposte that of the warmest 20 years ever experienced, 16 have happened during the last quarter-century and match almost precisely increases in CO_2 as a proportion of the atmosphere. Temperature increases of that kind are unprecedented and are conclusive evidence that we do have an acute problem which could conceivably lead to the ending of all human life.

The United Kingdom

The UK was an enthusiastic signatory of Kyoto and at first made good progress towards the agreed goal, assisted by a switch of power stations from coal to gas. The 2005 Labour manifesto set a target of 20 per cent, well above the required Kyoto level, but as the deadline has approached performance has declined. On 28 March 2006, Margaret Beckett, the then environment secretary, announced that reductions were likely to be in the range 15–18 per cent instead, blaming increased economic growth and the rise in oil prices which had caused many power stations to return to coal use. Since then recession-affected economic shrinkage will probably reduce emissions in the UK and worldwide. (See also Chapter 26.)

■ The political fringe

The political fringe is the name given to those small factions and groups that often do their political work outside the conference halls of the main parties rather than within them. Those who belong are often determined ideologues, given to regular argument in groups prone to splits and factions. They do have some intrinsic interest, however, as microcosms of political ideas and conflicts. It must also be remembered that in the early part of this century the Labour Party was just such a small faction, snapping around the heels of the Liberal Party. Yet within a couple of decades it was actually in power and destined to be there – with a huge majority – as the new millennium started.

Far left

Marx, Lenin and Stalin

Most far left groups owe their intellectual debts to Karl Marx. He argued that under a capitalist economy rich property owners would so drive down wages in pursuit of profits and a competitive edge that a vast army of impoverished workers would eventually rise up and sweep away the whole corrupt system. Once private property had been abolished, working people would begin to live new and better lives in an economy in which people would work willingly for each other and not reluctantly for an employer. It did not quite work out that way.

After the Marxist takeover of power in Russia in 1917, a period of great hardship and economic instability followed. Lenin established a political system based on centralised control supported by a network of secret police. He believed in the need for a 'vanguard party' of professional revolutionaries to lead the masses – who were deluded by agencies of capitalism into a 'false consciousness' – when the time came. There had to be rigid discipline and acceptance of the vanguard party's 'dictatorship of the proletariat' while it implemented socialism. Communists claimed that this was the transitional stage the USSR had achieved by the early 1920s, when Lenin died.

BIOGRAPHY

Joseph Stalin (1879–1953)

Soviet dictator. Trained as a priest before becoming a revolutionary in Georgia, Russia. Was secretary to Lenin's Communist Party and after his death deviously manipulated his enemies out of power while placing his own supporters in key positions. Became unchallenged dictator in 1930s and tried to neutralise Hitler by doing a deal with him. Hitler broke the agreement and attacked the USSR in 1941. After initial reverses the Soviets fought back under Stalin's leadership and defeated Hitler. Despite his brutal behaviour Stalin won friends on the left in Western countries, who persisted in believing his propaganda and seeing him as a force for progress.

Trotsky – advocate of 'worldwide revolution' – was Lenin's heir apparent, but the dogged, apparently un-intellectual Joseph Stalin, Secretary of the Party, was cleverer than his brilliant colleague. He urged 'socialism in one country' rather than working for an unlikely international conflagration; he out-manoeuvred his rivals and plotted ruthlessly, succeeding in presenting Trotsky as a traitor to the revolution. Stalin eventually drove Trotsky into exile in Mexico, where his agents succeeded in assassinating him in 1940 (see Biography).

Stalin, by then, had become a brutal dictator, both paranoid and obsessed with power, claiming to be implementing **communism** but in reality imposing industrialisation, collective farming and his own tyrannical rule on a reluctant and starving peasantry. Anyone less than obsequiously worshipful of their leader was imprisoned, exiled or shot. Overseas communist parties were employed essentially to assist the development of the 'home of socialism', and any deviation from the party line was punished by expulsion or worse.

This is the legacy inherited by extreme left-wing parties in Britain. The Communist Party of Great Britain (CPGB) was founded in 1920 and became the willing tool of Moscow's message in this country, interpreting all the shifts in the official line and condemning anyone perceived as an enemy of the USSR. Members managed to survive the astonishing volte-face when Stalin ceased to oppose Hitler as first priority and signed a deal with him in 1939 to partition Poland. Once Hitler had invaded Soviet Russia in 1941, British communists breathed a sigh of relief; they were at last able to luxuriate in a vast amphitheatre of approving views as the whole country applauded the heroic Soviet effort. After the war, the party won two seats – Mile End and West Fife – but Stalin's expansion into Eastern Europe, his blockade of Berlin in 1948 and the crushing (after his death) of the Hungarian rising in 1956 by the Soviet military machine, not to mention Khrushchev's denunciation of Stalin in his secret speech to the 20th Party Congress, substantially disillusioned communists and Moscow 'fellow travellers' alike. The Cold War effectively ruined the chances of communist parties achieving power anywhere in Europe, and they began to wither and atrophy.

BIOGRAPHY

Leon Trotsky (1879–1940)

Leon Trotsky was a Russian Jewish revolutionary politician born in the Ukraine. He was arrested for being a Marxist at the age of 19 but escaped from Siberia in 1902. After teaming up with Lenin, he became president of the first soviet in St Petersburg after the abortive 1905 revolution. He escaped to the West but returned to Russia in March 1917 to assist Lenin in organising the Bolshevik Revolution in November of the same year. He conducted peace negotiations with the Germans and led the Red Army of five million men in the ensuing civil war. An inspiring and charismatic leader as well as brilliant intellectually, Trotsky should have succeeded Lenin in 1924, but his theories of permanent world revolution were less well suited to the times than Stalin's pragmatic 'socialism in one country'; he was eventually exiled in 1929, being assassinated in Mexico with an ice pick in 1940 by Ramon del Rio, an agent of Moscow. His ideas live on, but mostly on the radical intellectual fringe in developed countries.

In the 1970s and 1980s opposition to communism in Eastern Europe intensified, and the accession of the liberal Mikhail Gorbachev to power in Moscow was the signal for bloodless revolutions throughout the former communist bloc, with only China, Cuba, Vietnam and Laos being spared. The CPGB split into a hard-line pro-Moscow rump and a liberal 'Euro-communist' wing, with the latter seizing control. It tried to transform itself into 'an open, democratic party of the new pluralistic and radical left'. In 1991 it ceased to be the CPGB and renamed itself the Democratic Left, though with little public support. Some of its former supporters, however, stuck with the party paper, *The Morning Star*, and founded the Communist Party of Britain – to little political effect: it has never fought a parliamentary election.

Trotskyism

A number of Trotskyite bodies sprang up during and after Trotsky's lifetime, calling for worldwide revolution. Ted Grant, a South African, was involved with some of them, such as the Militant Labour League, in the 1930s. With Peter Taafe, Grant set up the *Militant* newspaper and adopted the tactic of 'entryism', the idea being to infiltrate members of a 'Militant Tendency' (notice only a 'tendency' and not a separate party, which would have breached Labour rules) into the decaying structure of the 1960s Labour Party. The idea then was to seize leadership at the grass-roots level and, in theory, the country once the time for revolution arrived. The Tendency virtually controlled Liverpool City Council in the 1980s, and two members, Dave Nellist and Terry Fields, were elected MPs, plus Pat Wall for Bradford in 1987 (died 1990). They advocated a number of radical measures, including nationalisation of the top 200 companies, extension of state control over the whole economy, workers' control in state-owned industries, nationalisation of the media, a slashing of defence spending, withdrawal from the EC and abolition of the House of Lords. In 1992, the Tendency expelled its guru Ted Grant, ending its policy of entryism; the movement gave way to Militant Labour, still attempting to influence the Labour Party, but most of the prominent members had faded away and the MPs not only lost their seats but were first expelled from the party. However, Militant MPs, while exercising little influence during their time in the Commons, did impress with their dedication, hard work and refusal to accept more salary for themselves than a skilled worker.

The Workers' Revolutionary Party

Another Trotskyist thread into the colourful tapestry of the far left was provided by 'The Club', a grouping, led by Gerry Healy, which left the Revolutionary Socialist Party in 1947 to infiltrate the Labour Party. Healy was soon expelled from Labour for his Trotskyite views and put his energies into a new party to express and promote the views of his hero. The idea, as with all such parties, is to build up battle-hardened cadres to seize power when capitalism collapses, as it must, in its view. Its newspaper, *Newsline*, was rumoured in the seventies to be funded by Libya's Colonel Qadhafi. Membership was never high and suffered from Healy's imperious and eccentric leadership style, which led to the WRP actually splitting into two versions in the eighties and to his finally being deposed shortly afterwards. Celebrity members such as Vanessa Redgrave and her brother Corin, who stood as candidates in 1974 and 1979, gave the party a high media profile. The WRP still exists, led by Sheila Torrence, and still publishes *Newsline*.

The Socialist Workers' Party

Tony Cliff, who founded the Socialist Workers' Party, left the Labour Party at the beginning of the 1960s. His party has concentrated on international revolution, and international links are stressed. Paul Foot (1938–2004), nephew of Michael and a national columnist, was a high-profile and persuasive member. The SWP prints a newspaper, *Socialist Worker*, touted by young converts in many British cities and towns. It was also behind the Anti-Nazi League, set up to fight the growth of European Nazism in the 1970s and then revived in 1992 after the rise of the BNP in Britain. These initiatives won an influx of new members; since that heyday it has shrunk though remains active in fighting its causes and supporting Respect (see below) in local elections.

The Socialist Labour Party

This was formed in 1996 by miners' leader Arthur Scargill following his failure to prevent the rewriting of Clause Four at Labour's conference in 1995. 'We recognise only two classes in society, both of which are recognised by their relationship to the means of production', he explained. 'Our problems are the result of a rotten capitalist system.' Accordingly, his party favours common ownership of the economy,

Socialist Worker

www.socialistworker.co.uk

80p | No 1995 | 8 April 2006

THE DAY TO BURY BLAIR

MAY 4

SR
THE SOCIALIST REVIEW

MAGAZINE WITH SOCIALIST WORKER THIS WEEK

- ● **Strike to save our pensions**
- ● **Vote Respect in the local elections**

TONY BLAIR hopes he can ride out the storms of protest over the murderous war in Iraq. He hopes he can brush aside the resistance to the government's plunder of workers' pensions and the plans to make us all work longer.

He hopes he can insert private companies at the very centre of the NHS and schools before he leaves 10 Downing Street.

But on Thursday 4 May we can all do something to bring Blair down sooner rather than later. In the local elections we can campaign and vote for Respect.

If Respect councillors sweep into town halls it will be one of the most powerful weapons to pitch Blair out of office.

And trade union activists are pushing for 4 May to be part of a two-day strike that would repeat and extend the electrifying success of the 28 March strike over pensions.

We cannot afford to let Blair survive a day longer. Victories for Respect and massive strikes over pensions can make 4 May a day from which he never recovers.

Pensions action >>page 2
Respect election campaign >>page 5

US lied to cover-up massacres in Iraq

THE US has been caught trying to lay the blame for a massacre of Iraqi civilians on the resistance. The revelations come as reports of two new atrocities have surfaced.

The US claimed that one soldier and 15 Iraqi civilians—including seven women and three children—were killed by an insurgent attack on the town of Haditha in November.

But an investigation by Time magazine exposed the story as a lie. Time discovered that US troops went on the rampage through the town in revenge for the death of a Marine earlier that day.

Soldiers then tried to cover up the murders by claiming the civilians were killed by an insurgent bomb.

The revelation comes after the killing of 37 worshipers on

26 March during a US raid on a Shia Muslim mosque in eastern Baghdad.

The US claimed the men were killed after they fired on troops. But locals say that the men were executed by an Iraqi death squad under the control of a US officer.

The attack on the mosque came the day after Iraqi police published an official report on a massacre in the village of Abu Sifa, 37 miles north of Baghdad.

In that attack, which took place on 15 March, 11 civilians were killed, including four children and a six month old baby.

The report states, "US forces gathered the family in one room and executed 11 people, including five children, four women and two men, then they bombed the house, burned three vehicles and killed their animals."

A bad day out for Condi and Jack >>page 6

Egypt's year of resistance
Pages 8&9

Anne Alexander speaks to three women who took up arms against imperialism in 1956

A dirty little secret exposed
Page 3

Simon Basketter reveals the blacklists of union militants held by construction bosses

France at the crossroads
Pages 4&16

François Chesnais, Jim Wolfreys, Danièle Obono, Pierre Khalfa and **Basile Pot** report on days of hope in France

Beckett: a lust for despair?
Page 13

Sinead Kennedy looks at the life and work of the radical Irish playwright

Trotskyist left urges voters to dump Blair.

Source: Courtesy of *The Socialist Worker*

full employment, a four-day week, a ban on non-essential overtime, retirement at 56, restoration of union rights, abolition of the monarchy, House of Lords and public schools, and withdrawal from the EU. Only 500 attended the launch in May 1996. Scargill fought for the seat of Newport East against Alan Howarth in 1997 and for Hartlepool against Peter Mandelson in 2001 but polled negligibly.

The Socialist Alliance

This was a novel 'umbrella' organisation of left-wing parties that fought the 2001 general election. It was chaired by Dave Nellist, the former Militant MP, and its manifesto was both a scathing critique of New Labour as no better than Thatcherism and a hard-won (far left groups find it hard to agree) common

---

BOX 6.7   IDEAS AND PERSPECTIVES

The strange case of *Living Marxism*

This magazine, a descendant of the CPGB's *Marxism Today*, morphed into the more modern-sounding *LM* in the late 1990s when it published an article accusing ITN of fabricating the discovery of an apparently emaciated Muslim in a detention camp which in reality was a haven for such refugees. The magazine was sued, lost the action and was forced to close. But it is the provenance of the magazine and the movement it subsequently set in train which are so interesting for students of the far left. The story is traced to 1974 when a Trotskyist faction split from the International Socialists (now the Socialist Workers' Party) – which, in the words of David Pallister and colleagues (*Guardian*, 8 July 2000), 'used to spend most of its time in textual agonizing over the third volume of *Das Kapital*' – to form the Revolutionary Communist Group.

The RCG saw its role as training a 'vanguard elite to storm the citadels of capitalism'. However, Trotskyist groupings are notoriously both fickle and factional, and in 1976 one of the group's thinkers, David Yaffe, led out a like-minded section (broadly in favour of collaborating with certain other far left groups) called the Revolutionary Communist Tendency, later Party, or RCP. *Living Marxism* was its mouthpiece and, as such, it attracted notice for its intellectual energy and creativity. New RCP members were often recruited in 'up-market' places like Oxbridge and Covent Garden and after a period of 'political education' were encouraged to enter the professions, often those associated with the media or academe, and then donate a proportion of their salaries to the party.

In the wake of the Cold War's demise came a change of direction: the RCP was disbanded and *Living Marxism* became *LM*, the *raison d'être* for which was held to be 'freedom' – freedom to challenge, to offend, to say what one wanted. Under the influence of two thinkers, Frank Furedi (Professor of Sociology at the University of Kent) and former social worker Claire Fox, *LM* waged war on what was held to be government-manufactured panics over issues like GM foods, child rearing, AIDS as a heterosexual disease, and much else besides.

'The spirit of *LM*', in Furedi's words, 'is to go against the grain: to oppose all censorship, bans and regulations and codes of conduct; to stand up for social and scientific experimentation; to insist that we have the right to live as autonomous adults who take responsibility for our own affairs.'

The mission of the '*LM* Group' was alleged by some to be a permeation of the opinion-forming professions; Fox's Institute of Ideas and *LM* magazine were two facilitating agencies to these ends, organising seminars and conferences, involving 'Establishment' bodies like the Institute for Contemporary Arts and intellectuals like Blake Morrison, Lisa Jardine and Linda Grant.

This philosophy of 'ban nothing, question everything', unsurprisingly, found supporters on the libertarian right. Pallister *et al.* suggest that the grouping of right-wing **think tanks** and research institutes in the US known as the 'Freedom Network' offered a source of like-minded ideas, support and, indeed, quite possibly finance. So, we see a slightly weird evolution here of an extreme left faction morphing into new forms, imploding and then becoming a broader cultural movement which joined hands with groups that are sufficiently far to the right to make poor old Leon Trotsky revolve in his grave (see also Box 4.2 on Libertarianism for links with the far right, in Chapter 4).

agenda for an 'alternative to the global, unregulated free market'. However, the results did not augur well for future growth and success. The candidates who stood received very low percentages of the vote and the Alliance seemed to have closed down in 2005 but its website promises it is 'coming back'.

Respect: The Unity Coalition

This body was set up in 2004 as a result of collaboration between George Galloway, the SWP and members of the Muslim Association of Britain to campaign principally against the ongoing war in Iraq. Galloway was formerly the talented but maverick MP for a Glasgow constituency, expelled from Labour in 2004 for calling on British troops to disobey orders. He fought a clever, though much criticised, campaign in Hackney and Bethnal Green against the sitting MP, Oona King, and won a sensational victory. Apart from its anti-war stance, Respect offers a left-wing socialist prospectus including the end of privatisation and 'the bringing back into democratic public ownership of the other public services'.

John Callaghan, the authority on the far left, judges that 'far left politics is dying in its Leninist form and has moved into Green and anti-globalisation movements and has involved former militants from Muslim communities' (e-mail to author, 8 April 2006). But he makes a shrewd point when he points out that far left politics often act as an apprenticeship for future mainstream politicians, citing Alan Milburn and Stephen Byers (former Trotskyists) and John Reid (former member of the CPGB).

Far right

Fascism

This set of ideas, developed by Benito Mussolini in the 1920s and supplemented by Adolf Hitler in the 1930s, was founded on xenophobic nationalism and total submission to the state. Democracy was scorned as the language of weakness and mediocrity; a one-party totalitarian state led by a charismatic leader was the preferred alternative. The leader and his team were seen as the result of an evolving process whereby the best people and ideas won through. It followed that the same thing happened when nations fought; war was the means whereby nations grew and developed. Hitler added a racial twist: the Aryans were the founding race of

BIOGRAPHY

Adolf Hitler (1889–1945)

German dictator. Was originally an Austrian who tried to make a living as an artist. Fought in the First World War and set up the racist, expansionist Nazi movement in the 1920s. Came to power in the early 1930s and set about dominating Europe via threats, invasions and finally all-out war. In 1942 he dominated the continent but his decision to invade Russia and to declare war on the USA eventually proved his downfall. Still retains his admirers on the political fringe.

Europe, a race of conquerors, and the Germans their finest exemplars; all other races were inferior; the Jews in particular were lower than vermin and should therefore be destroyed. In the stressful inter-war years, racked by economic depression and unemployment, these unwholesome ideas seemed attractive and full of hope to many who faced despair as their only alternative. It is emotionally satisfying perhaps to blame one's troubles on a single group in society, especially one that is quite easily recognisable physically and very successful economically and culturally. It has also to be said that such ideas flourished in the fertile soil of a German culture sympathetic to anti-Semitism.

In Britain, Sir Oswald Mosley founded a party that evolved into the British Union of Fascists, offering himself as the strong charismatic national leader who would end the party bickering and lead the country into new successes. Mosley proposed that employers and workers should combine in the national interest and work in harmony; strikes and lock-outs should be banned; all major elements in the productive process should work together to plan the economy (corporatism). Moreover, he argued that the British Empire would provide all the things the country needed, and imports that could be made in Britain would be banned. Parliament and the old parties would be reformed and MPs would be elected according to occupational groups. Once elected, Parliament would pass on power to the leader to introduce the 'corporate state'. Parties and Parliament would be ended; everyone and everything would be 'subordinated to the national purpose'. Mosley's anti-Semitism was disguised in Britain, but his coded references to 'alien influences' were clear enough to most Britons; he favoured sending all the Jews in the world to a barren reservation. When it was revealed that Hitler's remedy to his self-invented 'Jewish problem' had been genocide of the most horrifying kind, a revulsion set in against fascist ideas. But they have proved unnervingly resilient and still appear in the present time in a different form.

The National Front and the BNP

In 1967 the National Front (NF) was formed. Its central message was a racist one, warning against dilution of the British race via intermarriage with other races of different colour which it believed would produce an inferior breed of Briton. Repatriation of black Britons was the answer offered. At the level of theory, however, the Jews were offered as the main threats, being characterised as an international conspiracy to subvert Western economies and introduce communism before setting up a world government based in Israel. This side of the NF and its utter contempt for democracy was disguised in public expressions, but it exercised considerable appeal to young men with a taste for violence and racial hatred. It later changed its name to the National Democrats. In 1983 the 'New' NF – later the British National Party – was born; this is dedicated to infiltration and is more secretive, having many contacts with neo-Nazi groups abroad and many terrorist groups too. Football supporters are often infiltrated by NF members, and in 1994 a friendly football match between Ireland and England was abandoned following thuggish violence instigated by the NF. A related body called Combat 18 (the number in the name relates to the order in the alphabet of Hitler's initials: AH) openly supports Nazi ideas and embraces violence as a political method.

The BNP at the 1997 general election

As previously, the general election of May 1997 saw the usual multicoloured rainbow of fringe joke candidates. But for the far left and far right as well as the pranksters the result was widespread loss of deposits; voters may flirt with the fringe from time to time, but when the election arrives they revert, perhaps fortunately, to 'sensible' voting. In May 2002, the BNP won three council seats in Burnley –

the biggest electoral victory for the far right in two decades. The party's new leader, Nick Griffin, with his articulate style and Cambridge education (see quotation from the *Observer* below), gave the party a credibility with arguments that exploited the feelings of poor indigenous voters that somehow immigrants were not only changing the nature of their localities but also receiving favoured treatment. This was argued with particular success in respect of asylum seekers, an issue much loved by the tabloids. These developments worried the mainstream parties, which were keen to nip this electoral upturn in the bud.

> The BNP has deliberately become increasingly sophisticated in the last few years to ensure ballot box success. . . . The irony is that it's New Labour who have shown us how to do it; we learnt from them that a party could change without losing its support base. New Labour dropped Old Labour in much the same way as we've moved on from the so-called 'skin head' era. We realized that the type of recruit we needed in the modern world was completely different to the sort we needed when we were engaging in street level activities.
>
> Kevin Scott, North-East Director BNP, quoted in the *Observer*, 20 April 2003

The same issue of *The Observer* also published the facts that:

- Thirteen of the BNP's twenty-eight regional directors or branch organisers in 2002 had criminal records for offences that included assault, theft, fraud, racist abuse and possession of drugs and weapons.

- Two thousand racial attacks were recorded by the Home Office up to 2003 after the dispersal programme for asylum seekers began in 2001.

- In 2003, 221 seats were targeted by the BNP, including councils in Lincolnshire, Cumbria, Surrey, Hampshire, Somerset, Wiltshire, Devon and Cornwall. In the event, on 1 May 2003 the party won thirteen seats nationwide, including eight in Burnley; however, Nick Griffin lost his fight for a seat, and his party won no seats in Sunderland despite fielding twenty-five candidates.

- In 2004 a BBC undercover reporter recorded a speech in Keighley by Nick Griffin in which he said: 'These 18-, 19- and 25-year-old Asian Muslims are seducing and raping white girls in this town right now.' He continued: 'It's part of their plan for conquering countries. They will expand into the rest of the UK as the last Whites try and find their way to the sea. Vote BNP so the British people really realize the evil of what these people have done to our country.' This speech, and a similar one by a former Leeds City Council candidate, both faced charges of behaviour likely to incite racial hatred in January 2006, but both defendants were sensationally acquitted when the cases came to court in 2006.

The BNP in 2009

The history of British fringe politics might well make 2009 a 'breakthrough year' for the far right. Immigration issues still rankled among those made unemployed by the recession of that year and the BNP benefited from the widespread backlash of distrust of politics. In the Euro-elections of June Labour came third behind UKIP but more worrying for many in the party was the fact that the lower turnout in the north-west had enabled the BNP to win two MEPs and therefore take a place of sorts on the national stage, rather than occupying its usual fringe position.

Following this the BBC felt obliged to invite the BNP leader Nick Griffin to participate in *Question Time*, the popular BBC show which provides something of a national showcase for different political viewpoints. The decision was fiercely contested by the likes of Peter Hain who claimed a 'clueless BBC is giving the BNP the legitimacy it craves' and quoted Griffin's own claim that his party aimed to 'defend rights for Whites with well-directed boots and fists'.

But it is hard to deny the BBC were acting within the democratic traditions of the country. In the event, the programme, on 22 October 2009, provoked much interest. Griffin was attacked by panel members (including Jack Straw and Chris Huhne) and the

BNP leader Nick Griffin celebrates his election as one of eight MEPs (Members of the European Parliament) for the north-west of England
Source: Getty Images / AFP

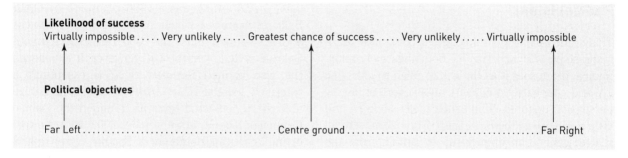

Likelihood of success

Virtually impossible . . . . . Very unlikely . . . . . Greatest chance of success . . . . . Very unlikely . . . . . Virtually impossible

Political objectives

Far Left . . . . Centre ground . . . . Far Right

Figure 6.2 The art of the possible

audience, and was generally felt to have been exposed as a second-rate politician. But his party had received a major publicity boost and it remains to be seen how beneficial it might prove to be.

The art of the possible

Politicians on the fringe have made a conscious or unconscious decision regarding the 'art of the possible', Bismarck's acute definition of politics. As Figure 6.2 illustrates, political objectives on the extremes have little chance of success; the best chances exist in the political centre. It is the big mainstream parties that tend to set the agenda and to go on to achieve items upon it. Changing Labour's Clause Four on common ownership was held to be beyond the art of the possible for a long time after Gaitskell's attempt failed in the late 1950s. Later, Callaghan referred to the issue as 'theological', but Blair decided that such a change was necessary to convince the public that Labour was no longer dangerously radical. His brilliant campaign in 1994 to change the clause to some extent redefined the art of the possible (Figure 6.2) in the Labour Party. Items on the far left or right are either unattainable or achievable only if circumstances change radically and, usually, rapidly.

Parties on the fringe have two possible strategies to pursue. First, they can eschew any real chance of winning power and seek merely to change the hearts and minds of citizens to provide the context in which radical change can occur. Early socialists effectively performed this role until the creed became a credible alternative in the mid-twentieth century. Even so, it took over 100 years for socialism to win an electoral victory in Britain, so activists of this type have to be genuinely dedicated to change in the future; few are so patient. Alternatively, the less patient can seek to short-circuit the normal

process of propagandising and winning over opinions by manipulating the democratic process. The really extreme activists on the right and left seek to set a revolutionary set of events in train and to seize power rather as the Bolsheviks did in Russia in 1917. As people usually need a substantial period to change their minds completely, this strategy usually requires the use of force, with all its attendant unpredictability and dangers. The early British communists and the Militants sought to reach the same objective through 'entryism': to drive their Trojan horse into a big party, Labour, and to win power through subterfuge. Seemingly underhand, this is not too disreputable a strategy given that the right-wing Conservatives led by Thatcher in the 1970s managed to achieve something similar by using the democratic machinery and then steering the party in a radical direction. Left-wing Labour tried a similar exercise in the early 1980s but was rebuffed so sharply by the electorate in 1983 that it left the way open for New Labour, maestros of the centre ground. So the radical socialist journalist Paul Foot sought to pursue the 'long haul' route of gradually changing social attitudes through education and exhortation. His uncle, Michael, also a fiery left-winger in his youth, decided to compromise a little and became a mainstream politician in the 1970s with a seat in the Cabinet and later a period as party leader. Time alone will tell how successful the agitators of the present will prove in the future, though those who articulate a 'green' perspective have seen their ideas move rapidly from the extreme left to somewhere much closer to the centre ground in a matter of only two to three decades. Moreover, the local and devolved assembly elections on 1 May 2003 saw one-in-eight voters casting their vote for parties on the political fringe, provoking the thought that maybe some of those groups on the fringe are destined in the near future to join the mainstream.

Radical Islam

This branch of 'fringe' thinking has come into sharp focus since 9/11 and the 7/7 bombings in London. Radical Islam sees it as the will of Allah to establish a world caliphate, to convert unbelievers either by persuasion or force. While such ideas seem to find little purchase in the USA, the 7/7 bombers were all second-generation immigrants to Britain from the Leeds area and ostensibly seemed well integrated into British society. It seems economically deprived areas of immigrant settlement nourishes radicalism with converts – like the Shoe Bomber, Richard Reid – particularly likely to take the extremist road.

Al Muhajiroun was a 1986 group led by Omar Bakri Muhammad which praised the 9/11 attacks and was banned under the 2006 Terrorism Act with Bakri expelled from the UK; however, it is believed the also banned *Saviour Sect*, is essentially a reformed version of *al Muhajiroun*. Abu Hamza al-Masri, a convicted terrorist, founded the Islamic Council of Britain, 11 September 2002, with the goal of 'implementing sharia law in Britain'. Other radical groups often are UK branches of transnational Islamic bodies like *Hizb ut-Tahrir*, an ostensibly peaceful grouping which some have claimed is a breeding ground for those who go on to adopt more extremist convictions.

BOX 6.8	BRITAIN IN CONTEXT

Themes and fringes

Box 5.3 in the last chapter focused on the political spectrum, my case being that in the USA it is not especially wide with very little support for left of centre positions or, indeed, for those right of centre as well. However, this should not be taken to imply that there are no groups occupying positions substantially to the left and right. Far from it.

The Socialist Party of America was born at the turn of the nineteenth century. Its leader, Eugene Debs, not only went to jail for his beliefs but stood for President on more than one occasion, yet never quite managed to poll a million votes. He was succeeded by Norman Thomas, a graduate of Princeton and a lay minister who also stood for the highest office but did no better than Debs in the end.

During the 1930s Roosevelt's New Deal, with its extensive government intervention in the economy, was implicitly socialist, but after the Second World War the backlash began with any left-wing idea being associated with communism and 'un-American' activities. The resultant McCarthyite witch hunts of the 1950s further weakened the left, but the socialist tradition survives in the form of The Socialist Party of the USA – not a major force, with affiliates in only 18 states. The Communist Party of the USA is even smaller and more ineffective. But there is, at the present time, the Progressive Coalition of House of Representatives members, numbering about sixty, who subscribe to a socialistic set of ideas. However, the only real force on the left is the Democratic Party, and this tends to deter those tending to the left from switching support to a small party with no chance of achieving power. Almost certainly, however, the groups on the far right are more powerful than those on the left.

One variety of socialism, the National Socialist Movement (NSM), is in fact on the far right, being admirers of Nazi Germany and the policies of Hitler. But the main blanket term for the far right is the 'Patriot Movement'. This takes in the militias which operate in well over half of the states together with the rifle clubs and survivalist clubs. These groups, many of them steeped in ultra-nationalism and anti-Semitism, were influential in motivating John McVeigh, the Oklahoma Bomber. The worrying aspect of such right-wing groupings is that they reject the *legitimacy* of government, its right to issue laws and levy taxes. Similarly, groups representing the Afro-American minority in the 1960s and 1970s, like the Black Panthers and the Weathermen, refused to accept government authority and were prepared to use violence as a method.

Another characteristic of US society not reflected to the same degree in the UK is the 'culture wars' within it. Here we see groups who believe that a changing society which includes a large number of single-parent families, a variety of races and people of contrasting sexual preferences requires a more liberal and flexible set of values, especially towards sexuality and abortion. Other groups, however, often motivated by religious convictions, hotly resist such a move and are determined, for example, to reverse the Supreme Court ruling which makes abortion legal.

Often supported by their churches, a large section of American society feel that family values are under severe attack and need to be defended against the compromised attitudes of current urban life, reinforced by the media and popular music. Almost 40 per cent of Americans regularly attend church and, under George W. Bush, such leanings have acquired political significance. In Britain only about 5 per cent of people attend church and religion generally has scant influence.

Chapter summary

Feminism is concerned with the unequal position of women in society and falls into liberal, socialist and radical categories. Nationalism emerged in the nineteenth century and, while it is now contested by internationalism, still retains much of its destructive force. Green thinking applies environmentalism to politics, calling for a revolutionary change in the way developed societies live. Far left fringe groups tend to draw on the ideas of Marx and Trotsky; their relevance has declined since the anti-communist revolutions, but many followers still keep up the struggle. Far right groups tend to be neo-fascist and racialist; their support is small but their influence subversive.

Discussion points

■ Has feminism achieved any major victories, and if so what are they?

■ What problems are there in defining the British identity?

■ Is nationalism more dangerous than terrorism?

■ What chance is there of the Greens ever winning power in the UK?

■ Why do you think people join fringe political groups?

Further reading

Lovenduski and Randall (1993) is a thorough review of feminism in Britain; the political ideas books by Adams (1993) and Heywood (1992) have good sections on nationalism; and Dobson (1990) and Porritt (1984) are good on ecology. An excellent study of totalitarianism is Arendt

(1951). On fascism, also recommended is Cheles *et al.* (1991); Thurlow (1986) is a history of British fascism to the present day.

Bibliography

Adams, I. (1993) *Political Ideology Today* (Manchester University Press).

Adams, I. (1998) *Ideology and Politics in Britain Today* (Manchester University Press).

Arendt, H. (1951) *The Origins of Totalitarianism* (Allen and Unwin).

Bentley, R., Dorey, P. and Roberts, D. (2003) *British Politics Update 1999–2002* (Causeway Press).

Brownmiller, S. (1975) *Against our Will: Men, Women and Rape* (Simon and Schuster).

Bryson, V. (2003) 'Feminist debates, ideology: feminism', *Politics Review*, Vol. 12, No. 4, April 2003.

Callaghan, J. (1987) *The Far Left in British Politics* (Blackwell).

Cheles, L., Ferguson, M. and Wright, P. (1991) *Neo-Fascism in Europe* (Longman).

Colley, L. (2005) *Britons: Forging the Nation 1707–1837* (Yale University Press).

de Beauvoir, S. (1968) *The Second Sex* (Bantam; first published 1952).

Dobson, A. (1990) *Green Political Thought* (Unwin Hyman).

Dowds, M. and Young, J. (1996) *13th British Social Attitudes Survey* (SPCR).

Engels, F. (2010) *The Origin of the Family, Private Property and the State* (Penguin Classics; first published 1884).

Equal Opportunities Commission (2006) *Sex and Power: Who Runs Britain? 2006* (Equal Opportunities Commission).

Ferguson, N. (2003) *Empire* (Allen Lane).

Firestone, S. (1980) *The Dialectic of Sex* (Women's Press).

Friedan, B. (1963) *The Feminine Mystique* (Norton).

Friedan, B. (1982) *The Second Stage* (Norton).

Gamble, A. (2003) *Between Europe and America* (Palgrave).

Giddens, A. (1998) *The Third Way* (Polity Press).

Greer, G. (1971) *The Female Eunuch* (Granada).

Greer, G. (1985) *Sex and Destiny* (Harper and Row).

Heywood, A. (1992) *Political Ideologies* (Macmillan).

House of Commons (200) *Weekly Information Bulletin*, 18 December 2004 (HMSO).

Hussein, E. (2007) *The Islamist* (Penguin).

Intergovernmental Panel on Climate Change (2001) *Climate Change 2001*, United Nations.

Lovenduski, J. and Norris, P. (2003) 'Westminster women: the politics of presence', *Political Studies*, Vol. 51, No. 1, March.

Lovenduski, J. and Randall, V. (1993) *Contemporary Feminist Politics* (Oxford University Press).

Marcuse, H. (1964) *One Dimensional Man* (Beacon).

Marcuse, H. (1969a) *An Essay on Liberation* (Penguin).

Marcuse, H. (1969b) *Eros and Civilisation* (Sphere).

Millett, K. (1969) *Sexual Politics* (Granada).

Nozick, R. (1974) *Anarchy, State and Utopia* (Blackwell).

Paglia, C. (2006) *Break, Blow, Burn* (Vintage).

Porritt, J. (1984) *Seeing Green* (Blackwell).

Reid, J.R. (2004) *The United States of Europe* (Penguin).

Thurlow, R. (1986) *Fascism in Britain* (Blackwell).

Wolf, A. (2006) 'Working girls', *Prospect*, April.

Wollstonecraft, M.A. (1967) *A Vindication of the Rights of Women* (Norton; originally published 1792).

Useful websites

Anti-Nazi League: www.anl.org.uk/campaigns.html

Green Party: www.greenparty.org.uk

National Democrats:
www.netlink.co.uk/users/natdems/

Searchlight Magazine:
www.searchlightmagazine.com/default.asp

Socialist Alliance: www.socialistalliance.net

Socialist Workers' Party: www.swp.org.uk

Workers' Revolutionary Party: www.wrp.org.uk

And another thing . . .

The long-term impact of the banking crisis on British politics – the optimistic and pessimistic scenarios

Steve Richards

Gordon Brown felt most at ease as Prime Minister for a few weeks in the autumn of 2008 when the economy went into meltdown. Suddenly he started to enjoy himself as he appeared to get a grip on the financial crisis. This was no time for a novice, he told the Labour conference in September of that year at a point when some in his cabinet were scheming to remove him. Shortly afterwards Brown was not only secure in his job, but the beneficiary of a bounce in the polls. The banking crisis had at least resolved for the time being the separate crisis over his leadership.

At last Brown had discovered a populist language to describe what he was doing. For months prior to the crisis he had admitted privately that he could not find accessible phrases and themes to convey his political purpose. That was partly because the purpose had become so ill defined that no phrase was available to capture the policies shaped increasingly by insecure expediency.

But by the end of September 2008 Brown was declaring with a robust self-confidence that the government would do whatever it took to help people in recession. He and other senior allies who had agonised for years over how to make the case for the state as a benevolent force were now doing so on every media outlet. Brown, Ed Miliband and Ed Balls all declared in interviews that this was a crisis that demanded a progressive response in which the government would be on the side of the people in the face of chronic market failure.

The mood at the Labour conference in the autumn of 2008 was on the whole even more euphoric. Fringe meetings were a noisy din of celebratory declarations about the crisis marking the end of Thatcherism and the beginning of social democracy. Brown made his moves accompanied by an uncharacteristically bold Bank of England. Banks were saved at great cost. International summits were called. Interest rates fell. David Cameron and George Osborne, normally self-assured and accomplished political artists, appeared to be thrown by the ideologically challenging events. One moment they declared they would support the government in a blitz-like spirit of national consensus. The next they were attacking Brown with a renewed intensity. Their lead in some opinion polls narrowed to a few points.

That brief period, which opened with Labour's conference in Manchester and ended with the pre-budget report delivered by the Chancellor, Alistair Darling, in December 2008, highlights the dangers of predicting the political consequences of the crisis. Those few weeks had a curiously unreal feel at the time and look even more dream-like in retrospect. There was always something slightly odd in the assumption that a government that had been in power for more than a decade would be the main political beneficiary of the biggest economic crisis since 1945. Of course there were precedents to back up the fleetingly giddy optimism of some ministers. John Major won amid economic gloom in 1992 and lost as the economy showed signs of booming in 1997. But with Brown having served as a uniquely dominant Chancellor for more than a decade explaining away steep decline was always going to be a challenge rather than an electoral opportunity.

The other optimistic scenario, as expressed by many senior figures in Labour and the Liberal Democrats, about the opening of a new progressive era also looks to be seriously misjudged, at least in the short term. The financial crisis brought about the end of lightly regulated markets, but the consequences of the reckless era mean that the government is broke. Darling's budget in April 2009 confirmed that public spending will be cut more drastically than it was in the 1980s.

For the next few years there will be no link between higher taxes and improvements in public services as there was in 2003 when Brown as Chancellor raised National Insurance Contributions to pay for higher levels of investment in the NHS. The budget in 2003 was the nearest Britain has come to dancing openly to the tunes of social democracy. The night before Brown announced the NIC rise I bumped into one of Tony Blair's most influential advisers who told me he thought the proposal would lose Labour the next election. In fact the budget proved to be the most popular Brown delivered in his eleven years in the Treasury. In the aftermath of the recession taxes will rise and services will decline, not exactly a vote-winning proposition.

There is though a cause for optimism about the likely nature of the political debate that will follow the recession. There will be an unavoidable focus on the role of the state. Such a debate should be welcomed across the political spectrum. New Labour never dared to instigate any public exchanges on the state partly because it had no fixed position of its own. My shelves creak with speeches by Blair and Brown on a thousand policy areas, but you will search in vain for defining comments on the size of the state and its purpose. They had famous and unresolved internal rows about the best way of delivering public services. Blair and Brown could never resolve the conundrum: how or why should central government hand over responsibility to local providers while taking the political and economic risks of raising taxes to pay for the provision of those services? But this is a secondary issue compared with the even bigger questions about what the state can and should be doing.

As the axe falls the debate will start. Will there be co-payments for NHS treatments? Is the private sector really more efficient in providing some public services? Should Britain rather pathetically seek to punch above its weight internationally by fighting wars and renewing trident when it cannot run a modern train service and still struggles to reach European standards in other public services, not surprisingly as funding has only come close to the EU average recently after decades of stinginess?

The recession will change British politics profoundly, but the change will be sluggish. In one of his last interviews before he died the former Labour prime minister, James Callaghan, told me that his generation had been slow to realise that the challenges of the 1970s demanded a different response to the ones they had been conditioned to give.

We were brought up politically in the 1930s when unemployment was the great social and economic evil. This included some Conservatives too. I think Ted Heath, Harold Wilson and I all felt we should do anything to prevent unemployment from rising. But we did not appreciate the global changes that limited what a government could do to insulate a country. We were too slow to appreciate that there would be jobs in new industries even if some of the less productive sectors in Britain would close. But we were working to avoid a repeat of the 1930s.

When Callaghan famously detected a 'sea change' in British politics during the 1979 election he was referring to a current which had been flowing for several years.

Callaghan, Wilson and Heath are not alone. When faced with tidal waves political leaders tend to stick with the strokes they learnt when they were younger. Brown's responses to the collapse of Northern Rock in 1997 were defined by what had happened in the 1970s and 1980s, his politically formative decades. He was terrified of nationalising the bank out of a fear of appearing to be 'old Labour'. Even when the *Economist* and the *Financial Times* advocated state ownership Brown resisted. Before he became prime minister he was tormented above all by taunts from the Conservatives and some internal critics that he would return to 'old Labour' policies. He resolved with his usual dogged determination to prove his opponents wrong, and in doing so landed himself in even more difficulty refusing to recognise that when ardently free-market magazines are calling for nationalisation it is politically safe to act.

The government's response has been slightly behind the curve throughout the crisis. Even Brown's widely hailed recapitalisation of the banks that took place in the autumn of 2008 was a confused initiative. The taxpayer was backing the banks, but the banks retained the freedom to do more or less what they liked. Only the Liberal Democrats' Treasury Spokesman, Vince Cable, has put the case for the temporary ownership of more banks in order to guarantee the flow of credit once more into the economy. The deification of Cable is illuminating. On one level he has the luxury of commenting from the sidelines, unburdened by power. But in his own quiet unassuming way he plays the role of Sir Keith Joseph in the 1970s, challenging orthodoxies that had been accepted for the previous two decades. In contrast David Cameron and George Osborne have tended to look to the 1980s for guidance, but as Callaghan and Brown discovered the past is a treacherous route map.

Political change will be shaped by the recession rather than the other way around. At some point a visionary will surface, or a political realignment will take place. The trigger will be the debate about the state as it was in different ways in 1979 and 1945.

THE REPRESENTATIVE PROCESS

CHAPTER 7
Elections

Mark Garnett

Learning objectives

- To understand the purpose and importance of elections in Britain.

- To evaluate the current voting system used for UK parliamentary elections, and examine the main alternatives.

- To describe recent changes in election campaigns.

Introduction

This chapter begins with a discussion of elections in general, before explaining key details of the voting system ('first-past-the-post' [FPTP], or 'simple plurality', as it is usually called) currently used for elections to the UK parliament. It goes on to outline the perceived problems regarding this system, and speculates about the prospects for change. Finally, it assesses recent changes in campaign techniques, and reforms of the laws regarding campaign finance.

■ The role of elections in liberal democracies

A basic tenet of liberal ideology is that government must be based upon the consent of the governed. This seems to be a fairly simple notion, involving few problems in practice. However, even the greatest liberal thinkers have found it difficult to decide what, exactly, should count as 'consent'. One of the very greatest, John Locke (1632–1704) ended up falling back on the idea of 'tacit consent', arguing that we are in some way expressing our acceptance of the prevailing system of government by merely walking along 'the King's highway'.

For most democrats, the principle of consent demands something much more meaningful than this. In Ancient Athens, citizens represented themselves when key decisions were taken, meeting and voting in a public assembly. This system is known as 'direct democracy'. While the citizen-body as a whole acted as an assembly making key decisions, governmental posts were filled by means of a 'ballot' – in modern parlance, the names of the 'winning' candidates for the necessary jobs were drawn at random out of a hat. In such conditions, office holding was seen as a duty rather than a means of personal advancement or enrichment.

However, in the modern era direct democracy seems wholly impracticable. Some enthusiasts see the Internet as a way of recapturing something approaching the Athenian system. However, the essence of Athenian democracy was that citizens should gather together physically, in a common space, and listen to the various arguments. Deliberations among isolated citizens, using technology rather than direct speech, would seem to be a pale and potentially dangerous imitation, leading to decision-making on the basis of emotion rather than constructive thinking.

Whatever the prospects of a return to direct democracy, most democrats are now reconciled to the idea that key political decisions should be taken by elected representatives. There are, though, two important provisos:

■ Elections should be 'free and fair'; that is, nobody should be prevented from submitting themselves as candidates; no-one should be disqualified from voting, unless for reasons which are themselves subject to common consent; every opportunity should be given to qualified persons to cast their votes; no-one should be subjected to intimidation or bribery; and all voters should have free access to information relevant to their choices, through media which are not subjected to state censorship.

■ Elections should be held at regular intervals, so that representatives can be held to account for decisions taken during their terms of office.

■ Elections in the UK

Until quite recently, few Britons were seriously concerned about the democratic system in the UK. No-one thought that the voting system for the Westminster parliament was perfect, but its verdicts commanded widespread support and the same system was used for all local government elections in Britain. That system is commonly known as '**first-past-the-post**' (**FPTP**, or 'simple plurality'). Under that system, the candidate who receives the most votes is elected – even if he or she is favoured by a relatively small minority of the voters. However, it is not the case that the party which wins the most seats on this basis could automatically form the next government. For that purpose, it is usually necessary

Tony Blair tries to bridge the 'trust gap' in the run-up to the 2005 general election
Source: Copyright © Chris Riddell. From the *Observer*, 20 February 2005. Reproduced with permission from Guardian Newspapers Limited

for a party to win more seats than all of its opponents in combination. In other words, individual seats are won on the basis of FPTP; but only if a party wins an absolute majority (more than 50 per cent) of the seats can it be reasonably sure of being able to form a government. If no single party secures an absolute majority of seats, the monarch as Head of State can become an important power-broker; but by convention he or she has to ask the leader of the party with the most seats if it is in a position to form a minority government, with the active support (or passive approval) of other parties.

The system escaped serious criticism even when it produced apparently anomalous results. Thus, for example, in the general election of 1951 Labour won a greater percentage of the national vote than the Conservatives; but the latter won enough seats to form a majority government, and when it duly did so there were few complaints. The underlying problems began to attract more comment after 1974,

when two general elections were held. In the first (held in February), Labour won fewer votes than the Conservatives, but four more seats. In the second (October), it won almost a million more votes than the Conservatives, and 42 more seats. However, in October 1974 other parties (including the Liberals) won 39 seats between them, meaning that Labour had an overall majority of only three. Labour had campaigned on the basis of a radical election manifesto in both of the elections of 1974, and although the prime minister Harold Wilson did his best to give the impression that he would govern on behalf of the whole nation, his party was heavily dependent on trade union support.

Some of the government's decisions were fiercely opposed by Conservatives, who claimed that the electorate had not given Labour a clear 'mandate' to implement radical policies. Among these critics was Lord Hailsham (1907–2001), who had been Lord Chancellor in the Conservative government

| BOX 7.1 | Britain's road to universal adult suffrage |

Until 1832, the British electorate was very small, and its general composition was determined by two characteristics: either the voters were quite substantial property-owners, or they lived in constituencies where (for historic reasons) the monarch had granted a Charter which gave the vote even to relatively poor inhabitants. After many years of agitation, a long process of electoral reform began in 1832 (under the auspices of the very aristocratic Whig party); but although that measure was hailed as 'The Great Reform Act', it left most males (and all women) disenfranchised. The main landmarks in the gradual move towards universal adult suffrage were as follows:

1832 The 'Great Reform Act' gives the vote to many middle-class property owners, but takes it away from many of the poor people (either in cities or rural areas) who had previously enjoyed the right to vote. Abolishes some seats ('rotten boroughs') which still could return MPs even if hardly anyone lived there any more.

1867 Second Reform Act: Extends the franchise to householders in towns and cities.

1872 Ballot Act: Qualified electors could now vote in secret.

1884 Franchise Act: Extends the vote to rural labourers, so that a quarter of the adult population can now vote.

1918 Representation of the People Act: All men of 21 and over can now vote, along with women of 30 and over. Electorate now more than 75 per cent of adult population.

1928 Representation of the People Act: Voting age equalised for men and women, at 21 years and over.

1948 Representation of the People Act: Abolishes 'plural voting', which allowed people with several properties to vote more than once.

1969 Representation of the People Act: Lowers the voting age to 18, for men and women.

2000 Representation of the People Act: Allows people without a permanent residence in the UK to vote, and opens the door to 'pilot schemes' which could give trial runs to different methods of voting (e.g. all-postal ballots, see below).

(1970–4) led by Edward Heath. In a broadcast lecture of 1976, Hailsham warned that Britain was in danger of becoming an 'elective dictatorship', since a party with very limited electoral support could still contrive to use the democratic forum of parliament to push through divisive policies. Hailsham argued in favour of a strengthened House of Lords which would be elected 'proportionately', as a defence against overmighty and unrepresentative governments (Hailsham 1978: 129). Among his other proposals, Hailsham advocated devolution to Scotland, Wales, Northern Ireland and England; and he urged greater use of referendums to gain an authoritative estimate of public opinion on key issues (see below).

| BOX 7.2 | Alternative voting systems |

A major difficulty facing would-be reformers of the system for parliamentary elections in Britain is that there are several alternatives, none of which can guarantee a perfect symmetry between the preferences of voters and the overall outcome. The scope for disagreement is increased by the fact that the suitability of the different systems varies according to existing political circumstances; thus, for example, while one system is used in Scotland, Wales and Greater London (see below), that method has not been adopted for the Assembly in Northern Ireland. Yet another system is used in elections to the European Parliament.

The **additional member system (AMS)** is best understood as a compromise between first-past-the-post (**FPTP**) and the more proportional systems. It has been adopted for the Scottish Parliament (see Table 7.1), the Welsh Assembly and the Greater London Assembly (GLA), which suggests that it is regarded with some favour by senior politicians – the 'least worst' option in their eyes, perhaps. The system is also used in Germany.

Under AMS, voters can make two choices. The first vote is cast for individual constituency representatives, as in FPTP. These constituency members make up at least half of the resulting assembly. The remaining members are elected on the basis of regional, multi-member constituencies. For this second contest, voters are asked to choose between competing party lists, and the seats are allocated to the successful parties broadly in proportion to the votes they receive. Supporters of the system argue that it retains the link between representatives and their constituents, while also making it less likely that individual electors will consider their votes to have been wasted.

The **single transferable vote (STV)** allows voters to list their choices in order of preference. They can vote for as many candidates as they like. Often, but not always, the constituencies are large and more than one member will be elected. To win a seat, a candidate needs to reach a specified 'quota'. When a candidate reaches this target, his or her remaining votes are redistributed among the other candidates (starting with the second preferences). If no candidate reaches the quota on the first ballot, the candidate with the *least* first preferences is eliminated and his or her votes are redistributed. This process continues until the required number of candidates has reached the quota.

This system is used in the Northern Ireland Assembly, where the quota is set at 14.3 per cent of the overall vote. Since 2007, STV has also been used in Scottish local elections. Supporters claim that the system is roughly proportional, and usually offers voters a very wide choice of candidates (they can, for example, expect to see several candidates from the same party on the ballot-sheet, which means that the outcome is not so tightly controlled by the central party which might favour one candidate over another). However, unlike AMS it does not guarantee a close link between members and a constituency of traditional size.

In the **alternative vote** system **(AV)**, voters also list their choices according to their preferences. The voting takes place in single-member constituencies, and a winner is declared when he or she achieves an overall majority of the votes cast. If no candidate secures more than 50 per cent of the vote when first preferences have been counted, the candidate with the fewest votes is eliminated and his or her second preferences are redistributed. This process continues until someone does achieve more than 50 per cent of the vote.

Supporters of this system argue that it retains the link between constituencies and members. Critics point out that it could lead to anomalies: for example, a candidate who wins clearly on the first ballot, but falls short of an overall majority, might end up being beaten by a rival who was the first preference of far fewer voters. However, it could be argued that this is actually an advantage of the system, since unlike FPTP it could prevent the election of divisive figures, who are loved by a large number of people but actively disliked by the majority.

A closely related system to AV is the **supplementary vote (SV)**. In this system the voter can indicate only two preferences. As with AV, the system is based on single-member constituencies. If no candidate wins an overall majority of first preferences, there is a 'run-off' between the candidates who come first and second. All of the ballots cast for the remaining candidates are examined, and the second preferences redistributed between the top two. At the end of this process, the candidate with the most votes is elected.

This system is used to elect many of England's mayors, including the Mayor of London (see Table 7.2). Like AV, if used in a parliamentary election it would ensure a link between the winning candidate and his or her constituency. However, unlike AV there is little chance than it could lead to a situation in which a candidate with very few first preferences could end up being elected, since only the candidates who come first and second in the initial ballot stand any chance of victory. On the other hand, this does mean that divisive or extravagantly populist figures have a good chance of prevailing.

The **regional list** system is used in the UK for elections to the European Parliament. Voters choose a particular party, rather than specified individuals, in multi-member constituencies. Seats are then allocated in close proportion to the size of the vote – i.e. if a party receives 40 per cent of the votes, it will get something like 40 per cent of the seats. Thus, in the 2009 European elections, the Conservatives won 27.7 per cent of the vote and received 25 of the available seats (in 2009 the UK elected 72 members of the European parliament [MEPs]). In sharp contrast to the situation in FPTP elections, the Liberal Democrats attracted 13.7 per cent of the vote, and were allotted 11 of the 72 seats.

Critics of the regional list system focus on two main issues: first, the constituencies tend to be very large, so that the individual voter feels little attachment to his or her representative; and second, it allows the various parties to decide which candidates are elected (e.g. if a party is allocated one seat on the basis of its electoral support, the party rather than the electorate decides which person should represent them).

Table 7.1 The effect of the additional member system (ams) on the election to the Scottish Parliament, 2007

Party	Share of constituency vote (%)	Constituency seats won	Share of regional list vote (%)	Regional list seats won	Total
Scottish National Party	32.9	21	31.0	26	47
Labour	32.2	37	29.2	9	46
Conservative	16.6	4	13.9	13	17
Lib Dem	16.2	11	11.3	5	16
Green	0.1	0	4.0	2	2
Others	2.0	0	10.6	1	1

Table 7.2 The effect of the supplementary vote (sv) on the London Mayoral election, 2008

Candidate	Party	First preference (%)	Second preferences (from other candidates)	Final percentage vote
Boris Johnson	Conservative	43.2	12.9	53.2
Ken Livingstone	Labour	37.0	15.1	46.8
Brian Paddick	Lib Dem	9.8	32.0	
Sian Berry	Green	3.2	16.6	
Richard Barnbrook	BNP	2.9	6.4	
Alan Craig	Christian Peoples Alliance	1.6	4.0	
Gerard Batten	UKIP	0.9	5.7	
Others		1.3	7.3	

Hailsham did not recommend proportional representation for the House of Commons itself, and after his party won the 1979 general election with a safe majority he seemed less worried about the UK political system. However, during the 18 years of Conservative rule (1979–97) the government's opponents became increasingly concerned. Now that they were in opposition, some Labour supporters suddenly realised that Britain might be an 'elective dictatorship' after all. Mrs Thatcher was able to push through controversial measures despite never coming close to winning an overall majority of votes cast in any of the three general elections which she won (see Table 7.3).

At the 1997 general election the pendulum swung the other way, and Labour began to benefit considerably from the distorting effects of FPTP. In the 2005 general election, Labour needed on average 26,900 votes to secure one MP; for the Conservatives, the necessary total was 44,500 votes. Generally speaking, senior figures in both main parties seemed content to live with these effects, on the grounds that if they did happen to win an election even by a tiny proportion of the vote they were

Table 7.3 Percentage vote share of winning parties at recent general elections (parliamentary majority in brackets)

1979, Conservatives	1983, Conservatives	1987, Conservatives	1992, Conservatives	1997, Labour	2001, Labour	2005, Labour
43.9 (43)	42.4 (144)	42.3 (102)	41.9 (21)	43.2 (179)	40.7 (166)	36.1 (67)

likely to have a 'workable' majority. However, within both Labour and the Conservative Party there were some people who could not forget the days when they had no chance of influencing political decisions even though their parties had won a very respectable share of the national vote. The greatest anger, though, was felt by supporters of the third electoral force – the Liberal–Social Democratic Alliance of the 1980s, which became the merged Liberal Democrat Party in 1988. In the 1983 general election, the Alliance won more than a quarter of the popular vote. Nationally, the gap between the votes for the Alliance and for Labour was less than three-quarters of a million. Nevertheless, thanks to the inbuilt bias of FPTP, the Alliance won just 23 parliamentary seats, compared to 209 for Labour! It was not surprising that Liberals were long-standing critics of the voting system, although this stance was based on principle as well as self-interest since sincere liberals have good reasons to be outraged by a system which places unequal values on the votes of citizens in different parts of the country.

■ The Jenkins Report

Before the 1997 general election, Labour and the Liberal Democrats agreed that a referendum should be held on the UK voting system. Again, cooperation between these parties arose from principle as well as opportunism; the Labour leader Tony Blair felt that the two parties represented 'progressive' politics in Britain, and were thus natural allies against the Tories. However, Blair's commitment to a referendum also reflected his fear that the current system might not deliver a workable majority to his party at the ensuing general election. As it turned out, the impact of FPTP transformed a relatively modest Labour vote into a crushing victory in 1997, so after he took office Blair had much less reason to advocate radical reform.

The former Alliance leader, Lord (Roy) Jenkins, was friendly with Blair and shared his view about the ultimate need for unity among progressive politicians. In October 1997 Blair appointed Jenkins to head a commission on the voting system. Significantly, despite Labour's electoral pledge of a referendum, Jenkins' commission was declared to be 'independent', so that the new government need not feel bound by its conclusions. Accordingly, when Jenkins reported after a year of deliberation, his proposals were quite cautious. He opted for a system under which most MPs (80–85 per cent) would be chosen by the **alternative vote** (see Box 7.2). However, the remaining MPs would be chosen in proportion to the electoral support for their respective parties. This compromise was generally known as 'AV-plus'. On paper, it was a clever idea; the 'AV' MPs would have to secure more than 50 per cent support in their constituencies, and even if they would usually have to rely on second preferences to achieve this proportion, they would still enjoy more legitimacy as constituency representatives than most MPs can currently command. Although the proportional element in Jenkins' system was relatively small, it was likely to act as a corrective to the existing system which gave too much parliamentary weight to the winning party and condemned the smaller parties to irrelevance.

Despite Jenkins' ingenious efforts, Blair could not persuade senior colleagues to endorse his conclusions and the promised referendum has never been held. The fact is that although electoral reform is an engrossing subject to some well-informed people, the average voter is not very interested. If Jenkins had proposed something simple to replace the current system, his chances of success would have been greater. However, he knew that a simple system would have been far too radical for most parliamentarians to accept. Hence, Jenkins decided to opt for complexity, hoping that existing MPs would be persuaded by his logic. It was no surprise that people who had been elected under the present system decided that, with all its undoubted faults, it was far superior to any alternative – especially one which had been proposed by a man who had once hoped to 'break the mould' of two-party politics.

There are, in fact, solid reasons for maintaining FPTP. The most important are:

■ FPTP is easy for voters to understand.

■ It is based on single-member constituencies, so that voters can identify with the representative of the area in which they live.

■ It usually (but not always) produces a clear-cut national verdict, so that the winning party can govern without cutting deals.

■ Alternative systems will almost invariably lead to coalition governments, which usually provide weak leadership for the country.

■ Many people like to simplify politics into a stark choice between the government and the main opposition party. FPTP encourages two-party politics, and thus gives these voters exactly what they want.

On the other side of the debate, critics of FPTP argue that:

■ The system usually gives a thumping majority to parties which have not persuaded a majority of the public that their policies are right.

■ Sometimes, though, it leads to a result in which no single party has an overall majority (as in the UK after the election of February 1974). Thus it can lead to political stalemate rather than strong government.

■ It encourages irresponsible opposition, since rather than rallying behind a government at a time of national crisis opposition parties will be tempted to make the most out of political difficulties.

■ While it can encourage the main parties to exaggerate their differences, at other times it makes them imitate each other, so that voters are deprived of a meaningful choice.

■ It depresses electoral turnout, because citizens are less likely to vote in constituencies where their preferred candidates have no chance of winning.

■ Although proportional systems might usually result in coalition governments, there is no reason to regard these as necessarily inferior from the democratic point of view to governments which impose policies which do not enjoy backing from a majority of the voting public.

In a democratic state, it would be reassuring to think that the eventual outcome of this debate would be settled by the quality of the arguments on either side – or, perhaps, by an objective review of the effects of different voting systems in Scotland, Wales and Northern Ireland. Regrettably, recent history shows that this is most unlikely to be the case. A system which produces a more 'proportional' outcome – or even one which persuades individual citizens that their votes will not be 'wasted' – is likely to be resisted by both of the main parties while they retain any hope of winning power at Westminster under FPTP. While this situation prevails, both of them will assert that their attachment to FPTP arises from principle rather than expediency. But if there is a closely-fought general election, after which the Liberal Democrats hold the balance of power, it would not be surprising if both Labour and the Conservatives announce a sudden conversion to any one of the various available systems, all of which are more closely compatible with the ideals of liberal democracy. Indeed, in the run up to the 2010 contest Gordon Brown suddenly announced an unexpected 'conversion' to the argument for electoral reform, even though he had been regarded as a stanch supporter of FPTP in the years when Labour's electoral prospects were much brighter.

■ Declining turnout

Whatever critics might say about FPTP, the system of election to the UK parliament does satisfy the basic criteria for the conduct of elections in a liberal democracy. That is, for example, new contests have to be called after a maximum of five years; citizens are free to stand for election (subject to nomination by ten local voters and the payment of a £500 deposit); opportunities to vote (in secret) are plentiful; and the counting of votes almost invariably proceeds without criticism. The task of the Boundary Commission, which makes regular changes to the geographical area of Westminster constituencies in line with demographic changes, is a difficult one. There are significant anomalies – at present constituencies in Wales have an average electorate of 56,000, compared to 70,000 in England. Even so, there have been few major public disagreements about the way in which seats are distributed around the UK.

On this basis, one might argue that the system in Britain has evolved in a fashion which satisfies the criteria of a liberal democracy in *procedural* terms. The remaining question, though, is whether the country is still animated by a democratic *spirit*. The chief concern here relates to the turnout at recent general elections. This is a serious matter, since if political parties no longer attract significant public support the legitimacy of government itself comes into question.

The 1992 general election gave no cause for serious disquiet. Although the Conservatives had been in power for more than a decade, under John Major they secured more votes in 1992 than any British party had achieved at a previous election. Ironically, thanks to the oddities of FPTP (and difficulties within his party) this was not enough to give Major a comfortable parliamentary cushion. By contrast, in 1997 Labour won an overwhelming majority, leading over-excited media commentators to talk of a new political mood in the country. On closer inspection, however, the 1997 general election was hardly a ringing public endorsement of the new government. Turnout was just 71.4 per cent, so that Labour won the support of less than a third of the eligible voters. In the next nationwide poll, the European parliamentary election of May 1999, the turnout slumped to a miserable 24 per cent.

It was just about possible to shrug off the latter statistic, since Britons are notoriously reluctant to vote in European elections. However, there was a dramatic development in the general election of 2001, when turnout was less than 60 per cent – easily the lowest figure recorded since Britain adopted universal suffrage. There was an improvement in the 2005 general election, but still only 61.2 per cent of qualified adults voted despite a steep increase in the number of citizens who cast their vote by post rather than taking the minimal trouble of visiting a polling station.

The political reaction to these disturbing figures was slightly ominous. In public, some ministers expressed concern. They could hardly avoid such comments, since the right to vote had been achieved slowly and painfully, and on paper at least it remained the most important channel through which ordinary members of the public could exercise influence over the political process. But ministers could also fall back on convenient alibis. In 2001, 2005 (and even 1997) the overall outcome of the election had been obvious for some time. This knowledge was likely to act as a serious disincentive to would-be voters – supporters of the opposition parties would be less likely to vote because they were certain of ending up on the losing side, while Labour voters might not take the trouble of voting because they knew their party was going to win regardless of their participation. Thus government supporters were able to claim that the turnout would have been higher if the overall result had been in doubt.

A second, and related excuse was that even people who had a vague attachment to opposition parties were not particularly bothered by the prospect of Labour victories, since the government had tried to avoid controversial decisions. This explanation for the low turnout was particularly convenient for the government, since it would imply that non-voting was actually a testament to its *success* in office. In seizing the 'middle ground' of politics, it might have taken away the fear of defeat which would have driven its own supporters to the polls; but, more importantly, it had deprived its opponents of their traditional incentive to cast a vote. On this view, then, a low turnout was actually a hidden vote of confidence in the government!

Whatever the merits of the Labour governments after 1997, this state of affairs could hardly be comforting to public-spirited Britons. At best, it denoted a general lack of public enthusiasm for elected politicians from all the major parties. Rather than seeing the low turnouts of 2001 and 2005 as evidence that the public was broadly content, it would be more realistic to see the mood of the time as foreshadowing the tidal wave of contempt which engulfed elected politicians in 2009, after revelations of the misuse of parliamentary expenses. In this context, a change in the voting system might not seem an obvious remedy for existing discontent. Alternatively, it could be argued that a new system, which was capable of persuading voters that their ballots would make some difference to the overall result, might encourage wider participation and thus inject a bit more life into a process which seems to be dying on its feet.

■ Election campaigns in contemporary Britain

It can be argued that one reason for the precipitate decline in turnout after New Labour's first term in office was a feeling of election-fatigue among the general public. After his party's 1997 victory, Tony Blair declared that he intended to 'govern as New Labour'. His purpose was to indicate that his government would confound those who hoped (or feared) that Labour was revert back to 'socialism' once the election was out of the way. However, in hindsight Blair's remark can be seen in a different light. Above all, New Labour was primarily an election-fighting outfit; and in government it continued to act as if a new poll was only one step away, for example by trying to ensure that none of its senior spokespeople gave any public expression of dissent.

General elections in Britain have been affected radically by the advent of television in the mid-twentieth century. Television made general elections into national media events, in which party leaders moved fairly rapidly to the centre of the stage. Increasingly, the main business for party strategists is to plan an itinerary for the leader which will showcase his or her strongest attributes; senior colleagues will be expected to tour the country, but their performances will attract limited media coverage (unless, as in the case of John Prescott in 2001, they punch an egg-throwing protestor in the course of their activities).

This focus on the leader at election time is itself of major importance, giving British parliamentary elections something of the flavour of US Presidential campaigns. This impression was reinforced before the 2010 general election by the agreement of the main party leaders to take part in televised debates. It also has a significant spill-over effect; anything that is seen to damage the credibility of the leader *between* elections can be taken by strategists as a blow to the governing party's chances of re-election. Equally, any defects in a party leader's conduct of an election campaign can be used as a reason to

change horses afterwards; thus, although Charles Kennedy was a highly popular leader of the Liberal Democrats, during the 2005 election campaign he was accused by colleagues of having been less than sober at media events. Whether or not the public noticed his lapses, members of his party took the view that he was too unreliable to remain as leader, to the widespread bemusement of the voters.

While the party leaders dominate media coverage, important work is still undertaken behind the scenes; and since general elections are won and lost as a result of votes cast in individual constituencies, it would be a mistake to suppose that all meaningful activity is now under the control of the central parties. However, strategists no longer place much value on face-to-face encounters with individual voters. Thanks at least in part to the lack of grassroots party members, voters tend nowadays to be contacted by telephone or email. The major parties take steps to identify 'target voters', who will be subjected to selling techniques which are more appropriate to the business world. Much of this effort will be directed towards key constituencies, rather than seats which look sure to provide overwhelming majorities for one party or another. Thus while some voters can receive the impression that they are being taken for granted, people living in the most important battlegrounds face almost constant disruption to their lives as senior politicians

BOX 7.3   'Primary' elections in UK politics

In July 2009, the Conservative Party attracted considerable publicity by holding a 'primary' election to decide on its candidate for the Totnes constituency. The Conservative candidacy at Totnes had fallen vacant because the incumbent MP, Anthony Steen, had decided not to contest the forthcoming general election after adverse publicity concerning his claimed expenses. Cynics might say that the circumstances of 2009 made Totnes a seat which the Conservatives could retain, but only if they took a step which 'cleansed' the party's image within the local community. On a less jaundiced view, the idea that local people should choose a party's candidate could only enhance the democratic process. Rather than restricting the vote to party members (or even known Conservative supporters), ballot papers were distributed to *every* eligible voter in the constituency, regardless of their party allegiance. This

procedure echoed the system of 'open primaries', used in some US states in the process of selecting party candidates for the national, presidential election. It is inherently risky, since in theory it allows the supporters of opposing parties to cast conspiratorial votes on behalf of the candidate who is least likely to win the ensuing general election. However, in the US open primaries have not been distorted in this way; and certainly after the verdict in Totnes was announced the Conservative leader, David Cameron, seemed to think that the experiment had worked well. The remaining dilemma for the party was whether open primaries would subsequently become the rule rather than the exception; whether they should only be used in unusual circumstances; or whether the 2009 event should be regarded as a one-off expedient, never to be repeated.

parade through their streets in search of photo-opportunities and positive headlines. As such, contemporary campaigning techniques can be regarded as another reason for increased public cynicism about the activities of the major political parties.

■ Reforms of the current system

If the slump in turnout after 1997 was a new development which caught most politicians by surprise, the New Labour years saw the re-emergence (albeit in more urgent form) of a well-established problem in British politics. As long ago as the 1920s, grave suspicions had been raised about an apparent link between the British honours system and the funding of political parties. The central figure in this scandal was the Liberal prime minister David Lloyd George, who amassed an electoral war-chest thanks to some dubious dealings with would-be earls and baronets.

The 1997 general election campaign was the most expensive in British history. Both of the main parties spent more than £25 million, which was a serious strain on their resources. Sources of funding had long provided ammunition for Labour and the Conservatives; the former were accused of being under the control of their trade union paymasters, while the contributions of business leaders to Conservative coffers was equally controversial (even if it attracted less hostile attention in the media).

Soon after the 1997 general election, the Labour government was hit by a scandal from an unexpected quarter. Far from being attacked yet again for its links with the trade unions, the party stood accused of accepting money from rich business-people who had not been known for their previous commitment to socialist values. Among these recent 'converts' to the Labour cause was the Formula 1 supremo, Bernie Ecclestone, who was revealed to have donated £1 million to Labour. Formula 1 had been exempted by the new government from legislation which banned the advertising of tobacco products at certain sporting events. Tobacco firms were important sponsors of Formula 1, so it was natural for Ecclestone to take an interest in the government's decisions on this subject.

In the wake of the Ecclestone affair, the Committee on Standards in Public Life headed by Lord Neill examined the question of party funding. The committee's findings were largely embodied in the Political Parties, Elections and Referendums Act (2000). As they affected elections, the main provisions were:

- Donations of over £5,000 to political parties at the national level would have to be publicly declared in future, whether the donations were in the form of money or services.

- The same 'transparency' would apply to donations made to individual constituency parties, above a value of £1,000.

- Donations from foreign nationals were no longer permissible.

- 'Blind trusts' (money donated to fund the activities of certain politicians without their direct knowledge) were outlawed.

- Parties would have to declare their donations either quarterly (at normal times), or weekly (during general election campaigns).

- Spending by parties would be limited according to a formula which allowed both of the main parties to spend no more than £19.38 million during the calendar year leading up to a general election.

- The new system would be policed by the independent Electoral Commission.

The new government could claim that the 2000 Act represented a substantial step towards 'cleaner' politics in Britain. In 2005, both major parties spent less than £18 million each on their campaigning activities – well within the limits laid down by the Act.

However, for the main parties the problems were just beginning. Even if campaigns could now be run within the official spending limits, a precipitate decline in contributions from ordinary members left them with inadequate resources. Business-people were the obvious sources of additional supply, and although some of these individuals were undoubtedly philanthropic, others were only bankrolling the parties in the hope of some kind of recompense. This kind of arrangement could still be made because the 2000 Act contained a loophole: although outright donations were more tightly policed, temporary loans were not affected.

In March 2006 the Metropolitan Police began an investigation into charges that honours were being traded in return for loans. The affair cast a shadow over British politics until July 2007, when the Crown Prosecution Service (CPS) finally decided that no criminal charges should be brought. However, several prominent people, including Lord Levy (Labour's chief fundraiser) had been arrested, while Tony Blair himself was interviewed twice by the investigators. It emerged that Labour had raised £14 million in loans for its 2005 election campaign, though the political impact of this news was reduced by the fact that the Conservatives had been even more successful in raising funds on this basis (they received £16 million), while even the Liberal Democrats were unable to boast of a clean bill of health.

State funding?

After the outbreak of the 'cash for honours' affair, the Blair Government established a new inquiry under Sir Hayden Phillips, a respected former civil servant. In March 2007 – before the Crown Prosecution Service had ended its work on 'cash for honours' – Phillips reported findings which were broadly similar to those of an earlier House of Commons committee. He argued that parties should receive up to £25 million per year from the state, depending on their performance. The rules on donations from private sources should be tightened further; the maximum allowed should be £50,000 (a very trifling sum compared to the generous provisions of people like Bernie Ecclestone).

To some observers, Phillips had come up with a reasonable solution to the dilemma of modern political parties, in Britain as elsewhere. On this view, organised parties were essential to the democratic process, but for one reason or another ordinary people were no longer prepared to pay for them on a voluntary basis. The only way round this problem was to get people to pay for them out of taxation. This would allow the state to keep the expense of elections under rigorous control, and to prevent incidents like the Ecclestone scandal from staining the political process in future.

However, the report was unlikely to impress anyone who was already sceptical about the condition of Britain's political parties. In their eyes, the parties had brought their financial problems on themselves, by spending too much on campaigns which were too often dominated by the abuse of opponents rather than constructive suggestions. This style of campaigning had helped to create a mood of serious dissatisfaction with party politics, so that ordinary citizens were no longer prepared to back the established organisations with voluntary donations. For critics of the existing system, state funding could

almost appear as a way of rewarding the political parties for their failure. Thus, while Sir Hayden Phillips had made the best possible case for state funding, the government was never likely to act on his proposals. To have the best chance of carrying public support, the idea of state funding would have to be implemented when parties were once again popular; but if they were truly popular, they would have no need of state support. In view of such considerations, the case for state funding in Britain seemed to be pretty hopeless, especially after the scandals about MPs' expenses which erupted in 2009.

Other proposals for reform

Short of a reform of the voting system itself, other ideas have been canvassed as ways of reviving British democracy:

■ *Compulsory voting*: This idea has been implemented in democratic states including Belgium and Australia. Electoral turnout in these countries is indeed much higher than it is in Britain. It could be argued that voting is a duty rather than a right, and (especially if participation is made as easy as possible) it could be argued that no citizen should be excused from taking part in the choice of a government. There are obvious civil liberty issues, but these are seemingly not insuperable: for example, a voter who disliked all of the options could plump for 'none of the above', or even deface the ballot paper. Nevertheless, a reform on these lines might end up disguising the underlying problems of British democracy, rather than solving them.

■ *Lowering the voting age*: Some optimistic observers have argued that the process would be healthier if the voting age were lowered from 18 to 16. While this might not increase turnout in the short term, it could pay dividends in the future if young people were allowed to think of themselves as possible participants at an earlier age, thus 'socialising' them into the idea of voting. However, survey evidence has suggested that while young people are interested in politics, they tend on balance to be even more disillusioned with the main parties than their elders. The Electoral Commission's carefully-worded report *Age of Electoral Majority* (2004) endorsed the existing age of 18, although it did recommend that the minimum age of people standing for parliament should be 18 rather than 21.

Michael Howard tries to woo voters of middle England in the 2005 election campaign
Source: Copyright © Chris Riddell. From the *Observer*, 6 March 2005. Reproduced with permission from Guardian Newpapers Limited

■ *All-postal ballots*: Between 2000 and 2003, the Electoral Commission oversaw more than 50 'pilot schemes' in which certain local government elections were conducted on the basis of all-postal ballots. This was in keeping with a general drive to make electoral participation as easy as possible: other ideas in this vein included changing the day of general elections to Saturday, rather than the traditional Thursday, or even allowing the polling stations to be set up in supermarkets. Initial trials of the all-postal system seemed promising, but fraud was always likely to be a problem. The resulting scandals meant that postal votes would have to be heavily scrutinised in future, leading to lengthy delays in the declaration of election results. By 2009 it looked as if the government was faced with a new dilemma – either return to the old system, under which postal ballots were only permissible for those who were chronically ill or on holiday, or accept a new situation in which votes could not be counted on election day – an outcome which would reduce the drama of British general elections, and probably reduce the turnout to the miserable level of 2001.

■ Tactical voting, and the rise of the independent candidate

The main parties have fared so badly in their efforts to mobilise public support that one almost suspects a degree of complacency in the face of falling turnout; the only thing that apparently matters to such parties is whether they win or lose, not whether their overall tally of seats reflects a significant degree of public support. The suggested remedies we have examined so far tend to be 'top-down' measures – that is, they have been mooted by

Tony Blair and Gordon Brown present a united front on the campaign trail, despite their well-documented difficulties
Source: Copyright © Peter Nicholls / Pool / Reuters / Corbis

members of the political 'establishment' rather than 'grass-roots' voters. In recent years, however, the voters themselves have tried to take the initiative in ways which have caused a degree of discomfort to the main parties.

Thus, for example, certain individuals (like the musician Billy Bragg) have tried to organise campaigns of 'tactical voting'. In itself, this is a negative comment on the state of British politics, since campaigners have tried to unseat specific candidates rather than promoting the virtues of opposing ones. In particular, before the 1997 general election tactical voting was urged as a way of getting rid of sitting Conservative MPs, by mobilising support behind the candidate best placed to topple them. In a typical case, this would involve Labour supporters voting for a Liberal Democrat – not because such voters actively sought the return of a Liberal Democrat government, but rather because they hated the Tories and a vote for the Liberal Democrats was the best way of getting rid of a sitting Conservative MP. Such campaigns have gone so far as to encourage 'vote swapping', which would entail (for example) a Labour supporter voting Liberal Democrat in a seat where this provided the best chance of removing a Conservative MP, in return for a Liberal Democrat in a different part of the country voting Labour if this promised to produce a similar result.

The overall impact of tactical voting is difficult to estimate with any certainty, but even in the volatile electorate of today it is unlikely to cause a shift in more than a handful of seats. More significant, perhaps, is the tendency of disillusioned voters to reject all of the major parties and seek out alternative candidates. Minor parties (e.g. the Greens in 1989, and the United Kingdom Independence Party [UKIP] in 2004 and 2009) have performed well in European parliamentary elections. But these elections do not attract a high turnout, and are conducted under the **regional** list voting system (see Box 7.2, above) which favours minor parties so long as their support exceeds a minimal level.

In elections to the Westminster parliament, candidates who are (at least formally) independent of *all* parties have caused a greater stir. Thus, in 1997 the former BBC reporter Martin Bell stood as an 'anti-sleaze' candidate in Tatton, Cheshire, and defeated the controversial Conservative MP, Neil Hamilton. In 2001 Dr Richard Taylor won the seat of Wyre Forest on the basis of his campaign to save a local hospital; he won again in 2005. In that election there were other Independent successes, although the father of a soldier killed in Iraq failed to make serious inroads into the majority won by Tony Blair in his constituency of Sedgefield. According to some media speculation, though, an election held in 2010 is likely to see the success of several Independents standing against MPs who have been implicated in various ways in the expenses scandals which hit Westminster in the summer of 2009. However, the candidates most likely to win as Independents tend to be celebrities rather than 'ordinary' citizens like Richard Taylor; and in any case the major parties have been quick to persuade headline-catching expenses offenders to step down at the next election, to create the impression that a new generation of 'clean' candidates is on its way to rescue the flagging system of party competition under FPTP.

■ Referendums

Until the 1970s, the British public enjoyed no formal opportunities to affect political decisions between elections. Other countries held referendums on particular policy issues, but in Britain this device was widely associated with the methods of dictators, who only held such polls in order to give some spurious legitimacy to decisions which they wanted to take, regardless of public opinion. Margaret Thatcher was not alone in using this argument when she attacked Labour's proposal to hold a referendum on continued British membership of the European Economic Community (EEC) in 1975.

However, on that occasion Mrs Thatcher's arguments were unsuccessful. In 1975 the Labour government was seriously divided over EEC membership, and the prime minister Harold Wilson saw a referendum on the issue as a way of resolving the question of membership without incurring any of the electoral penalties which normally affect parties that are seen to be divided. Having secured parliamentary approval for a public vote, he allowed his ministerial colleagues to campaign in accordance with their own beliefs, casting aside the usual restraint of 'collective cabinet responsibility'. In fact, once the better-funded 'Yes' campaign had won the EEC referendum of June 1975, Wilson exploited the opportunity to demote some of those who had campaigned for British withdrawal, notably the Industry Secretary Tony Benn.

The 1975 referendum was not actually the first time that members of the public had been asked for their opinion on a specific issue; but the precedent (the 1973 'Border Poll' held on the subject of the continued existence of Northern Ireland) is not exact, since that was not a nationwide ballot. However, since 1975 referendums have become part of the fabric of British political life – sometimes used, but more frequently refused. The governing principle in the UK is that such polls ought to be called when major constitutional changes are afoot. However, the definition of 'major constitutional changes' is in practice under the control of the existing government. Thus the Maastricht Treaty on European Union was ratified by parliament in 1993, without a referendum, and although Labour held referendums before implementing its policy of devolution to Scotland, Wales and Northern Ireland, it decided not to call votes on proportional representation (see above), membership of the euro-zone, or changes in EU practices arising from the abortive Constitutional Treaty of 2004.

On the face of it, enthusiasts for the referendum as a political device in Britain could be greatly cheered by the record of Labour governments after 1997. However, the evidence gives rise to more cautionary conclusions. Few of Labour's radical constitutional ideas (e.g. its reform of the House of Lords) have been subjected to a public vote. In theory, referendums are only advisory (i.e. parliament could reject the decision of the people if it wanted to); but few governments have actively sought unwelcome advice, and despite its controversial forays in foreign policy New Labour proved to be no exception to this rule.

It could be argued, in fact, that Labour's record actually confirms Mrs Thatcher's warnings back in 1975; that is, referendums have only been called on important questions when the government was confident that the result would be satisfactory, and its use in other cases (e.g. elected mayors outside London) has only been allowed because the government was unlikely to be deeply affected by the verdict. In this respect, the refusal to allow referendums on EU constitutional changes is seen in some quarters as a serious indictment of Labour's commitment to democratic values. Even more significant, perhaps, was the government's breach of its 1997 manifesto commitment to a referendum on electoral reform. From the perspective of those who support a change to a more proportional system of voting, the fact that after the 1997 general election Tony Blair felt strong enough deny the public a chance to endorse a more relevant way of expressing its preferences can only be regarded as the ultimate demonstration of the deleterious effects of FPTP on UK politics.

BOX 7.4   Referendums in the UK since 1973

1973: Border poll in Northern Ireland

A poll, restricted to qualified voters in Northern Ireland, which confirmed that the majority wished to remain part of the United Kingdom (although many members of the nationalist community refused to take part).

1975: Continued UK membership of the European Economic Community

This, the first UK-wide referendum, presented voters with a stark choice: either to stay in, or leave the EEC (later the European Union [EU]). The 'yes' campaign was far better funded, and supported by the majority of mainstream British politicians as well as celebrities. The result was overwhelmingly in favour of continued membership, though critics still complain (with justice) that the 'no' campaign never had a realistic chance to make its case.

1979: Devolution for Scotland and Wales

Voters in Scotland and Wales were asked if they wanted devolved institutions, with limited powers. In Scotland, a slender majority voted 'yes' but this was insufficient since legislation required at least 40 per cent of voters to accept the proposition (in practice the figure turned out to be 33 per cent). In Wales, devolution was rejected by an overwhelming majority.

1997: Devolution for Scotland and Wales

The vote of 1979 was radically revised eighteen years later, although the turnout in both Scotland and Wales was less than it had been first time round. The 'yes' vote in Scotland won 63.5 per cent. In Wales, where the devolved Assembly would have very limited powers, the 'yes' vote was only 50.3 per cent.

1998: Devolution for Northern Ireland

In May 1998 the electorate of Northern Ireland gave a resounding vote of confidence to the previous month's 'Good Friday Agreement', handing back devolved institutions to Northern Ireland after a quarter of a century of direct rule from Westminster. There was also a heavy majority in favour of the Agreement in a poll held south of the border.

2004: Regional assembly for the north-east of England

New Labour wanted to follow up devolution to Scotland, Wales and Northern Ireland with a plan to introduce regional assemblies (with limited powers) in the regions of England. Initially the idea was received with enthusiasm, but this gradually waned amidst fears that the assemblies would be mere 'talking shops'. Ultimately there was a referendum in only one of the regions – the north-east of England, where, significantly, opinion polls had registered high levels of support. In the actual vote, however, the proposal was heavily defeated: more than three-quarters of voters were against the plan.

Since 1998: Elected mayors

In May 1998 a referendum was held in London on the question of a directly-elected mayor and assembly. The proposal was comfortably carried (although turnout was barely more than one third). Labour hoped that many other towns and cities would decide to elect a 'chief executive' in the form of a mayor, but after a fairly auspicious beginning enthusiasm died away. By the beginning of 2008 only 13 mayors (including London's) had been elected; in October 2008 the voters of Stoke-on-Trent decided to scrap the experiment of an elected mayor after just six years.

Local referendums

One interesting aspect of the initiative for local mayors was that it allowed local residents to decide for themselves whether or not a referendum should be held; the poll could be called by the decision of councillors, or if a petition was signed by at least 5 per cent of local residents. Since the Local Government Act 1972, local voters have also enjoyed the power to call a vote on specific issues.

As in national referendums, the result is not officially binding on decision makers; but in practice few councils are prepared to go against a clear-cut decision. This power has been used more frequently in recent years, over things like proposed increases in local taxation, or schemes to alleviate traffic congestion. Thus, for example, in 2005 Edinburgh's citizens voted to reject the council's proposed scheme to levy charges to control city traffic.

BOX 7.5 BRITAIN IN CONTEXT

Although Britain is justly proud of its long history of representative institutions, as we have seen its progress towards universal suffrage was not exactly rapid (although it was not too far behind New Zealand, which became the first major country to give votes to all women as well as men in 1893, and France did not adopt the principle until 1944). Until recently, the general satisfaction with FPTP meant that senior British politicians did not pay much attention when other countries adopted alternative voting systems. If anything, the practical experiences of different systems, especially in European states, were held up as reasons *not* to change the way in which British MPs were elected, because they tended to result in unstable coalitions (Italy), or more stable coalitions in which members of parties with minimal support were able to win an almost automatic place in government (Germany).

However, it is reasonable to argue that the process of 'Europeanisation' has gradually affected opinion in the UK on this matter. All members of the European Parliament are now elected under a proportional system, of one kind or another. By the time the UK held its first European parliamentary election under the regional list system (in 1999),

alternatives to FPTP had already been adopted for the devolved institutions of Scotland, Wales and Northern Ireland. But elections to the European parliament were different because they were held across the whole of the UK. The importance of this change was not widely recognised, because the turnout in these elections was invariably low; few people understood the responsibilities of the parliament; and of the various alternative systems, the regional list arguably has the least attraction for would-be reformers of the Westminster system. Nevertheless, the change at least provided a practical toe-hold within British politics for people who were arguing for more radical reforms.

Another way in which the outside world has affected the conduct of British general elections is the impact of US-style campaigning. The major British parties have freely borrowed techniques from their US counterparts; in particular, critics argue, they have copied the tendency of American parties to concentrated on 'negative campaigning'. However, important differences remain; for example, while candidates for election in the US can buy advertising space on television, legal restrictions prevent this practice in the UK (and other West European states).

Chapter summary

In Britain, the traditional way of electing members of parliament is first-past-the-post (FPTP), where the candidate with the most votes wins the seat. This system has the virtues of simplicity, and of (usually) resulting in a clear overall majority for one party or another. However, the system always distorts public preferences. The Liberal Democrats (and predecessors) have criticised the system for many decades and in recent decades prominent members of the other main parties have echoed their criticisms.

The chapter sets out several alternative systems, which have their own virtues and defects. Overall, however, a chance from the present system seems timely, since it is obvious to most observers that FPTP depresses electoral turnout, because many people feel that their votes will be 'wasted' in one way or another. The logical case for reform seems so strong that the refusal of key politicians to endorse it has almost certainly acted as an additional reason for disillusion with the main parties. There have been some reforms in recent years, including an attempt to make voting as easy as possible; the relative failure of such measures (and the scandals surrounding the use of all-postal ballots) provides another reason for the acceptance of radical change.

On the face of it, since 1973 the referendum has been introduced in Britain as a device which allows members of the public a 'formal' way of influencing key government policies. However, the government, rather than the people, decides when referendums are applicable. Thus the history of the referendum in Britain can be said to lead us back to the initial problem – namely a voting system which hands overwhelming power over decision-making to a party that is unlikely to enjoy overwhelming public support. True, local inhabitants have the right to trigger referendums affecting the policies of their councils, but in a healthy democracy it is difficult to argue that the same right should not be extended to voters at the national level.

Discussion points

■ To what extent does the FPTP system really act as a disincentive to voters in elections to the UK parliament? Has the adoption of alternative systems for devolved institutions encouraged more people to vote?

■ What are the most effective arguments for and against the state funding of British political parties?

■ Under contemporary conditions, would the introduction of a right for British voters to demand referendums on key political issues be a more meaningful reform than any change to the system of voting for the Westminster parliament? If such a right were introduced, what problems might arise?

Further reading

For rigorous and insightful accounts of general elections since 1945, students should consult the 'Nuffield Studies' of each election. The latest of these is D. Kavanagh and D. Butler (eds), *The British General Election of 2005* (Palgrave, 2005). Apart from the Nuffield series, there are other very useful volumes which cover recent general elections; and the books about the election of 2001 are particularly relevant for students of recent trends. P. Norris (ed.), *Britain Votes 2001* (Oxford University Press, 2001), is particularly recommended, along with J. Bartle, R. Mortimore and S. Atkinson (eds), *Political Communications: The General Election Campaign of 2001* (Frank Cass, 2002).

For rival electoral systems, see especially D. Farrell, *Electoral Systems: A Comparative Introduction* (Palgrave, 2001), and P. Dunleavy and H. Margetts, 'Comparing UK Electoral Systems', in P. Norris and C. Wiezien (eds), *Britain*

Votes 2005 (Oxford University Press, 2005). D. Denver, *Elections and Voters in Britain* (Palgrave, 2nd edition, 2007) provides an admirable introduction for students of the electoral system and voting behaviour in Britain.

Bibliography

Hailsham, Lord (1978), *The Dilemma of Democracy: Diagnosis and Prescription* (Collins).

Useful websites

The key source for this subject is the Electoral Commission's website, www.electoralcommission.org.uk/. Other useful sites relating to electoral reform include www.electoral-reform.org.uk/ and the Constitution Unit's informative site at www.ucl.ac.uk/constitution-unit/.

CHAPTER 8

The mass media and political communication

Bill Jones

Learning objectives

- To explain the workings of the media: press and broadcasting.

- To encourage an understanding of how the media interact and influence voting, elections and the rest of the political system.

- To discuss how the pluralist and Marxist dominance theories help to explain how the media operate and influence society.

Introduction

Without newspapers, radio and pre-eminently television, the present political system could not work. The media are so all-pervasive that we are often unaware of the addictive hold they exert over our attentions and the messages they implant in our consciousness on a whole range of matters, including politics. This chapter assesses the impact of the mass media upon the workings of our political system, and some different theories about how they operate in practice.

■ The mass media

The term 'mass media' embraces books, pamphlets and film but is usually understood to refer to newspapers, radio and television. This is not to say that films, theatre, art and books are not important, but perhaps the influence of literature is usually less instant and more long-term. Since the 1950s, television has eclipsed newspapers and radio as the key medium. Surveys indicate that three-quarters of people identify television as the most important single source of information about politics. On average British people now watch over twenty hours of television per week, and given that 20 per cent of television output covers news and current affairs, a fair political content is being imbibed. Indeed, the audience for the evening news bulletins regularly exceeds 20 million. Surveys also regularly show that over 70 per cent of viewers trust television news as fair and accurate, while only one-third trust newspapers.

From the spoken to the written word

Television is now such a dominant medium that it is easy to forget that its provenance has been so recent. During the seventeenth and early eighteenth centuries, political communication was mainly verbal: between members of the relatively small political élite; within a broader public at election times; within political groups such as the seventeenth-century Diggers and Levellers; and occasionally from the pulpit. Given their expense and scarcity at the time, books, pamphlets and **broadsheets** had a limited, although important, role to play; they played a role during the Civil War (1640–49) and at the end of the eighteenth century pamphlets were very important in disseminating radical ideas.

The Industrial Revolution drew workers in from the land into crowded urban spaces where they arguably enjoyed a higher standard of living but were scarcely so contented they were not receptive to reformers and travelling speakers, like Orator Hunt, who delivered inspiring speeches in London and elsewhere including Peter's Fields in Manchester in August 1819, where the crowd was charged by mounted troops in the 'Peterloo Massacre'. The Chartists pursuing similar objectives attracted big audiences and also, like the Anti-Corn Law League, disseminated pamphlets via the new postal system.

Next came the inception of mass circulation newspapers – *The Times*, *Telegraph*, *Mail*, *Express* and *Mirror* – which provided information on current affairs for the newly enfranchised masses. The **Press Barons** – Northcliffe, Beaverbrook and Rothermere – became courted by politicians for the influence they were believed to wield; in consequence they were showered with honours and often given government jobs to further enhance their invariably enormous egos. Table 8.1 provides recent circulation figures for the national dailies.

By tradition the British press has been pro-Conservative. In 1945, the 6.7 million readers of Conservative-supporting papers outnumbered the 4.4 million who read Labour papers. During the 1970s, the tabloid *Sun* increased the imbalance to the right, and by the 1992 election the Labour-supporting press numbered only the *Guardian* and the *Daily Mirror*, with the vast majority of dailies and Sundays supporting the government party: 9.7 million to 3.3 million. However, Major's administration witnessed an astonishing shift of allegiance. It had been anticipated by press irritation with Thatcher's imperious style, continued with the criticism that Major received for being allegedly weak as a leader and insufficiently robust in relation to European issues, and intensified after the disastrous Black Wednesday, 16 September 1992, when Britain was forced out of the Exchange Rate Mechanism.

Table 8.1 Circulation of national dailies, September 2008

	September 2008	September 2007	% change	August 2008	September 2008 (without bulks)	April – September 2008	% change on last year
Sun	3,154,998	3,213,756	−1.83	3,148,792	3,154,998	3,133,776	0.68
Daily Mirror	1,440,651	1,584,742	−9.09	1,455,270	1,440,651	1,461,729	−6.61
Daily Star	731,433	803,726	−8.99	751,494	731,433	735,048	−7.92
Daily Record	380,849	412,332	−7.64	390,197	378,772	389,720	−4.43
Daily Mail	2,241,788	2,365,499	−5.23	2,258,843	2,123,186	2,267,502	−2.88
Daily Express	739,025	814,921	−9.31	748,664	739,025	738,924	−6.42
Daily Telegraph	851,254	890,973	−4.46	860,298	751,971	861,341	−3.43
The Times	638,033	654,482	−2.51	612,779	584,391	620,073	−2.91
Financial Times	429,381	441,219	−2.68	417,570	387,488	435,864	−1.10
The Guardian	348,878	367,546	−5.08	332,587	333,955	345,362	−5.27

Source: *Guardian*, 10 October 2008

Labour remained defiant despite the withdrawal of support from the *Sun* in the Labour Party Conference in 2009. The *Sun*'s backing of Labour was influential in their landslide victory in 1997

Sources: (Gordon Brown) Getty Images / AFP; (Tony Blair) *Sun* front cover, 30 September 2009, Carl De Souza / AFP, © News Group Newspapers Ltd

Stalwart Tory press supporters such as the *Mail*, *Times* and *Telegraph* aimed their critical shafts at the government and did not desist even after July 1995 when Major challenged his opponents to stand against him as party leader and won a none-too-

convincing victory. In addition to these factors Labour had become **New Labour**, led by the charismatic Tony Blair and shorn of its unpopular policies on unions, taxes and high spending. As the election was announced the *Sun* caused a sensation by emphatically backing Blair. Its Murdoch-owned stable-mate, the Sunday *News of the World*, followed suit later in the campaign. It should be noted that by this time a large proportion of the reading public had decided to change sides, and it could be argued that editors were merely making a commercial judgement in changing sides too (see Table 8.2 showing change of allegiances in the 2001 and 2005 general elections).

Table 8.2 Readership allegiances (%) of national daily newspapers, 2005 and (in brackets) 2001

	Labour	Con.	Lib Dem	Swing[a]
Guardian	43 (52)	7 (6)	41 (34)	8 (LD)
Independent	34 (38)	13 (12)	44 (44)	2 (LD)
Times	27 (28)	38 (40)	28 (26)	1.5 (LD)
Telegraph	13 (16)	65 (64)	17 (14)	2 (C)
Financial Times	29 (30)	47 (48)	21 (21)	–
Daily Express	28 (33)	48 (43)	18 (19)	5 (C)
Daily Mail	22 (24)	57 (55)	14 (17)	2 (C)
Sun	45 (52)	33 (29)	12 (11)	5.5 (C)
Mirror	67 (71)	11 (11)	17 (13)	4 (LD)
Star	54 (56)	21 (21)	15 (17)	1 (C)
Election result	36 (42)	33 (33)	23 (19)	3.1 (C)

[a] Percentage swings from Labour to (C) Conservatives, or (LD) Liberal Democrats.
Source: Wring and Deacon (2005)

Quality press and the tabloids

'All the instincts of the working class are Tory: on race, patriotism, you name it. It's just that they happen to vote Labour. Murdoch understands that which is why the Sun *has been so successful'*

(Lord) Bernard Donoughue, quoted in Chris Mullin (2009), *A View from the Foothills*, pp. 397–8

Anyone can see the UK press has 'quality' newspapers like *The Times*, *Telegraph*, *Guardian*, *Financial Times*, *Independent*, with their Sunday extensions, the 'mid-tabloids' like the *Mail* and *Express* and the tabloids like the *Sun*, *Mirror* and *Star*. Each type of product is aimed at and caters for a particular demographic: educated middle class, lower middle class and working class respectively.

Sunday paper sales declined from 17 million to 15 million in the period 1990–8, while dailies declined from 15 million to 13 million. Tabloids, less likely to attract loyal readerships, have tried every possible trick to win readers, from 'bimbos to bingo'. Marketing expert Winston Fletcher, writing in the *Guardian* (30 January 1998), pinpointed the formula, deplored by liberal opinion and politicians alike, that won readers: 'Publishers and editors know what is selling their newspapers with greater precision than ever before. And the figures show it is scandals, misfortunes and disasters.' In other words, 'sleaze sells'. Given the razor-sharp competition for audience share, it is surely regrettable but not so surprising that tabloids seize on scandalous stories like hungry dogs on bones. John Major's travails with sleaze stories have been well documented and helped to bring the Conservatives' eighteen years in power to an end in 1997. But Labour has been by no means immune either to sleaze or to the intrusive style of tabloid reporting which politicians and liberal-inclined opinion deplore but which is eagerly consumed. The foremost victim in recent years was David Blunkett, the remarkable blind Home Secretary who fell in love with a right-wing publisher, Kimberley Quinn, and who then discovered every detail of his relationship being read by the nation over its cornflakes for a number of weeks until evidence of undue favour having been shown to his mistress caused his downfall. After a period of 'purdah' he was brought back into the Cabinet in 2005 only to perish by tabloid once again when his business activities appeared to be in breach of the ministerial code. It is not strictly true to attribute this form of persecution to the tabloids alone; while they often start the process, the quality press watch

Reporters stand by during a typical media frenzy
Source: Rex Features / Nils Jorgensen

closely and join in the feeding frenzy as soon as they think it suitable and advantageous to sales.

But there is more to tabloids than lightweight stories; they sell by the million, and even if a vote is bought through blackening a politician's name, it counts as much as any other on election day. Media experts working for parties read the tabloids very carefully and react accordingly. In elections going back to the 1980s a close correlation was noted between issues run by the Conservatives and lead stories in the tabloids; it was known that certain tabloid editors had close links with Conservative Central Office. Tony Blair had long been convinced of the political importance of the tabloids. In 1997, he even wrote a piece pandering to their Euro-scepticism explaining why he had a 'love' for the pound. On May Day 2001, the *Sun* championed the case of a Norfolk farmer who had been imprisoned for shooting an intruder in his house. To counter it Blair personally wrote a 975-word rebuttal during a weekend at Chequers. The *Sun* concluded from this evidence of Blair's respect for the tabloids that he was 'rattled'.

Broadcasting

Hitler, Baldwin and Roosevelt exploited the radio successfully during the interwar years and during the war, Churchill's use of the radio must have been worth quite a few divisions to the war effort so inspiring did it prove. Some politicians, surprisingly including Neville Chamberlain, were adept speaking to the cameras of Pathe News; others, equally surprisingly, like Oswald Mosley, were not. During the war, films like *In Which We Serve*, starring Noel Coward, were effective vehicles for wartime propaganda. Broadcasts of the fledgling television service were stopped during the war and were slow to restart; not so in the USA where television was quickly recruited for political service. None more so than in 1952 when Richard Nixon bought 30 minutes of airtime to clear his name of financial impropriety with his famous 'Checkers' broadcast.

Offering himself as a hard-working honest person of humble origins, he finished his talk by telling viewers how his daughter had received a puppy as a present: he did not care what 'they say about it, we're gonna keep it!' (see quotation below). This blatant appeal to sentiment proved spectacularly successful and confirmed Nixon's vice-presidential place on the Eisenhower ticket. Later on, television ironically contributed to Nixon's undoing through the famous televised debates with Kennedy during the 1960 presidential election contest. Despite an assured verbal performance – those listening on the radio thought he had bested Kennedy – Nixon, the favourite, looked shifty with his five o'clock shadow and crumpled appearance. Kennedy's good looks and strong profile gave him a clear edge. Politicians the world over looked, listened and learned that how you appear on television counts for as much as what you say (see below on 'Television and the image').

Richard Nixon – the 'Checkers' speech

I should say this: Pat doesn't have a mink coat, but she does have a respectable Republican cloth coat. One other thing I should probably tell you, because if I don't they'll be saying this about me too. We did get something, a gift, after the election . . . a little cocker spaniel in a crate all the way from Texas . . . And our little girl, Trisha, the six-year-old, named it Checkers. And you know, the kids love that dog, and I just want to say this right now, that regardless of what they say about it, we're gonna keep it!

Richard Nixon, US Vice-President, in the 'Checkers speech' (cited in Green, 1982)

What they say about the papers

The gallery where the reporters sit has become the fourth estate of the realm.

Lord Macaulay 1828

As a journalist who became a politician . . . I formed rather a different view about the relations between government and the press. What shocked me when I was in government was the easy way in which information was leaked.

Norman Fowler, Ministers Decide: A Memoire of the Thatcher Years, 1991

I am absolved of responsibility. We journalists don't have to step on roaches. All we have to do is turn on the light and watch the critters scuttle.

P.J. O'Rourke on the duties of journalists in relation to politics, Parliament of Whores, 1992, p. xix

The British Broadcasting Corporation was founded in 1926 as a public corporation. John Reith, its first Director General, set a high moral tone – 'to inform, educate and entertain' – the vestiges of which can still perhaps be discerned. In 1955, however, the BBC's monopoly was broken when ITV came into being, followed by commercial radio in 1973.

The BBC was granted a second television channel (BBC2) in 1964; a second ITV channel (Channel 4) began broadcasting in 1982, and Channel 5 in 1997. In February 1989, Rupert Murdoch's Sky Television began broadcasting using satellite technology. After a quiet start the new technology took hold and was operating at a profit by 1993. Many of the channels offer old films and popular programme repeats from the USA, but Sky News has established itself in the eyes of the public and politicians as a respectable and competent 24-hour news channel which stands comparison with the BBC's equivalent rolling service.

■ Media organisations and the political process

Television has influenced the form of political communication

Broadcasting – especially television – has had a transforming impact on political processes. Two minutes of exposure on peak-time television enables politicians to reach more people than they could meet in a lifetime of canvassing, handshaking or addressing public meetings. Alternatively, speaking on BBC Radio 4's early morning *Today* programme gains access to a largely up-market audience of over one million opinion formers and decision makers (Margaret Thatcher always listened to it and once rang in, unsolicited, to comment). In consequence, broadcasting organisations have become potent players in the political game: the regularity and nature of access to television and radio has become a key political issue; interviewers such as John Humphrys, John Snow and Jeremy Paxman have become important – and controversial – national figures; and investigative current affairs programmes – especially during the Thatcher years – have been the source of bitter political controversy.

In the nineteenth century, it was commonplace for political meetings to entail formal addresses from great orators, such as Gladstone or Lloyd

George, lasting an hour or more. Television has transformed this process. To command attention in our living rooms politicians have to be relaxed, friendly, confidential – they have to talk to us as individuals rather than as members of a crowd. Long speeches are out. On television, orators are obsolete. Political messages have to be compressed into spaces of two to three minutes – often less. Slogans and key phrases have become so important that speech writers are employed to think them up. The playwright Ronald Millar was thus employed and helped to produce Margaret Thatcher's memorable 'The lady's not for turning' speech at the 1981 Conservative Party Conference.

Television and the image

Since the arrival of television, appearances have been crucial. Bruce (1992) quotes a study that suggested 'the impact we make on others depends on . . . how we look and behave – 55 per cent; how we speak – 38 per cent and what we say only 7 per cent. Content and form must therefore synchronise for, if they don't, form will usually dominate or undermine content' (p. 41). So we saw Harold Wilson smoking a pipe to pre-empt what his adviser Marcia Williams felt was an overly aggressive habit of shaking his fist to emphasise a point.

Margaret Thatcher was the first leading politician to take image building totally professionally under the tutelage of her media guru, Gordon Reece. Peter Mandelson, Labour's premier spin doctor of the 1980s and 1990s, commented that by the mid-1980s 'every part of her had been transformed: her hair, her teeth, her nose I suspect, her eyebrows. Not a part of Mrs Thatcher was left unaltered.' Every politician now has a career reason to be vain.

Blair v Brown

These two Labour prime ministers have hugely contrasting images. Blair's was chameleon to a degree; he was so keen to appeal to everyone he tried to be all things to all men: blokey with demotic speech, sipping a cup of tea in photo shoots; serious when reading the lesson at important funerals; aggressive and witty at PMQs; statesmanlike if addressing the UN; and on television he was a natural, able to convey relaxed good humour. He was also a little vain, seeking to dress young in tight jeans and allegedly using fake tan from time to time.

Brown was totally different: shy in public and often dishevelled; unable to project in public the warmth or wit his friends saw in private. At PMQs he was regularly bested by the more Blair-like Cameron and his speaking style, aggressive and incisive in opposition, proved lacklustre and pedestrian in government. Supporters claimed he was honest – not trying to be someone he was not like Blair – and serious in order to address the serious issues of the day. All the polling evidence, however, shows Brown failed to impress, charm or win over the majority of British voters who clearly respond to a little well-crafted wooing, even if it is at times a little obvious.

Broadcasters have usurped the role of certain political institutions

Local party organisation is less important now that television can gain access to people's homes so easily and effectively. However, the message is a more centralised national one, concentrating on the party leadership rather than local issues and local people. The House of Commons has lost some of its informing and educative function to the media. Ministers often prefer to give statements to the media rather than to Parliament – often on the Green just outside the House – and television interviewers gain much more exclusive access to ministers than the House of Commons can ever hope for. Even public discussion and debate are now purveyed via radio and television programmes such as the BBC's *Today*, *Newsnight* and *Question Time*.

The appointment of party leaders

Attlee was famously taciturn in front of the cameras and Churchill never took to it, but Macmillan flirted with television, conducting a stilted 'interview' in Number 10 in the run up to the 1959 election. From hereon, elections became televisual and the ability to shine on it a qualification for the top political jobs. So Wilson was good, Heath not so much so; Callaghan was competent, Thatcher became so. Major was average; Blair was brilliant. Gordon Brown tries hard but cannot overcome some kind of innate shyness and so struggles. David Cameron's 'without notes' speech in the 2006 Tory conference was the launch pad for his campaign and as leader he has proved a very good media performer.

Personnel

Unsurprisingly, the media and politics have become more closely interrelated, with media professionals such as David Steel, Tony Benn, Bryan Gould, Austin Mitchell and Peter Mandelson going into politics, and Robert Kilroy-Silk, Brian Walden, Michael Portillo and Matthew Parris moving out of politics and into the media. The apotheosis of this tendency was represented by former US President Ronald Reagan, who used his actor's ability to speak lines to the camera to compensate, arguably, for other political inadequacies.

Spin doctors

These fearsome-sounding new actors on the political stage focus their energies on ensuring that the media give the desired interpretation of events or statements. Their provenance is usually thought to have been during the eighties when the *New York Times* used the term in an October 1984 article to describe smartly dressed men and women who moved among crowds at political events and sought to explain what their political boss had *really* meant to say. Since then the popular idea is of somewhat shadowy figures moving around and choreographing press conferences or on the phone to television executives cajoling and bullying to get their way. The results are usually believed to be a distortion of the truth and to have fuelled the lack of trust in the political process.

The Labour Party, Tony Blair and 'spin'

For a generation . . . New Labour and spin doctors have been inseparable.

Editorial in the *Guardian*, 17 January 2003

One student of the media quoted a senior Labour spin doctor as saying: 'Communications is not an afterthought to our policy. It's central to the whole mission of New Labour' (Barnett and Gaber 2001: 116). So it is hardly surprising that Labour has been demonised as the party that invests too much in presentation, in 'spin'. Roy Greenslade, writing in the *Guardian* on 6 June 2002, argues that it all began in response to the way Neil Kinnock was treated by the right-wing press during the eighties. He was given no 'honeymoon' when elected in 1983, but from the start was attacked as a 'windbag', weak and incompetent. The *Sun, Mail* and *Express* pulled no punches and built up their coverage – much of it

BIOGRAPHY

Alastair Campbell (1957–)

Tony Blair's press secretary. Educated at Cambridge; had a career in tabloid journalism before joining Blair's personal staff. Often referred to as the 'real Deputy Prime Minister', he had constant access to his boss, and his words were held to carry the authority of the PM. He was well known to journalists and he used charm and threats to get his own way. Some Labour voices always believed him too powerful, but his appearance before a Commons Select Committee revealed that he can defend himself with gusto and effectiveness. In 2003 he was incensed when accused via a BBC interview of 'sexing up' the intelligence dossier used to justify the decision to go to war in Iraq. He was exonerated eventually but the ensuing media furore – during which he was accused of vindictiveness against the BBC – proved to be his swansong as he stepped down in the autumn of that year, still defiant and largely contemptuous of the nation's media.

based on no evidence – thoughout the decade. Leading up to the 1992 election, the *Sun*'s editor, Kelvin McKenzie, went to town two days before polling day, devoting nine pages to its 'Nightmare on Kinnock Street' feature. 'It's the *Sun* wot won it' was the triumphant headline following the result.

Maybe the reaction of Mandelson and his colleagues to this onslaught is understandable. Together with Alastair Campbell, Blair's press secretary, he insisted slurs were rebutted and retractions given. The right-wing media soon discovered they were being matched and criticisms of 'New Labour spin' became commonplace. Unfortunately this aggressive media policy continued into government and what had been an asset rapidly became a liability as voters began to doubt the veracity of government statements and statistics.

Mr Campbell lives and breathes for Tony Blair. He is the tough aggressive half of Tony Blair, the side of Tony Blair you never see in public. He writes most of what Tony Blair says. He writes almost everything that appears under Tony Blair's name. So sometimes, when Mr Blair is answering questions in the Commons, I like to watch Mr Campbell as he sits above his boss in the gallery. You sense his face is reflecting what the Prime Minister is thinking but cannot possibly reveal to MPs. When he comes up with a good line, and the loyal sycophants behind him applaud, Mr Campbell beams happily. Sometimes he rolls his head in pleasure at his own jokes. When Mr Blair is worsted, as happens quite a lot these days, Mr Campbell has two expressions. One is merely glum; the other a contemptuous grimace, which implies only a moron could imagine that Mr Hague had scored any kind of point.

Source: Simon Hoggart, 'Commons Sketch': the *Guardian*, 11 November 1999. © Guardian Newspapers Limited 1999, reproduced with permission

Labour tried to claim, after setting up the the Phillis Report in January 2003, that it had relaxed the rules whereby lobby (parliamentary correspondents) rules had been made more transparent but veteran spin doctor Bernard Ingham claimed he was not fooled; he did not believe spin had been banished. 'Spin is still everywhere', he wrote in the *Sunday Times* of 16 March 2003, 'and because of spin, Blair has forfeited the trust of the nation and . . . parliament.' Opinion polls gauging public trust in Blair certainly reinforced such a judgement, and some even attributed the shockingly low turnout in the 2001 election to a collapse of voter belief in what the government was saying.

It would be foolish to accuse New Labour of inventing spin; even before the advent of mass media, governments sought to offer the best possible interpretations of their actions. Yet, for all its expertise, Blair's operation lacked subtlety. Campbell acquired too high a profile as the demonic 'spinner' and even featured as the subject of a televised profile. Blair too once asked in a leaked 2000 memo for 'more eye-catching initiatives' to combat Conservative policy statements. After the non-discovery of Weapons of Mass Destruction in Iraq, after Blair had cited them as the justification for invasion in 2003, the association of New Labour with 'spin' was compounded.

The televising of Parliament

When the proposal that the proceedings of Parliament be televised was first formally proposed in 1966, it was heavily defeated. While other legislative chambers, including the House of Lords, introduced the cameras with no discernible ill effects, the House of Commons resolutely refused, chiefly on the grounds that such an intrusion would rob the House of its distinctive intimate atmosphere: its 'mystique'. By the late 1970s, however, the majorities in favour of exclusion were wafer thin and the case would have been lost in the 1980s but for the stance of Margaret Thatcher. In November 1985, it was rumoured that she had changed her mind, but at the last minute she decided to vote true to form and a number of Conservative MPs – known for their loyalty (or obsequiousness, depending on your viewpoint) – about to vote for the televising of the House instead rushed to join their leader in the 'No' lobby.

Finally, however, after a trial period, on 21 November 1989 the House appeared on television, debating the Queen's Speech. Margaret Thatcher reflected on the experience as follows:

I was really glad when it was over because it is ordeal enough when you are speaking in the Commons or for Question Time without television, but when you have got television there, if you are not careful, you freeze – you just do . . . It is going to be a different House of Commons, but that is that.

The Times, 24 November 1989

In January 1990 the broadcasting restrictions were relaxed: reaction shots of an MP clearly being referred to were allowed, together with 'medium-range' shots of the chamber some four rows behind the MP speaking or from the benches opposite. By the summer of 1990, it was obvious even to critical MPs that 'civilisation as we know it' had not come to an end. On 19 July, the Commons voted 131–32 to make televising of the chamber permanent. However, one unforeseen consequence of the cameras has been the reduction of members in the chamber. Now it is possible for MPs to sit in their offices and do their constituency business while keeping abreast of proceedings on their office televisions.

Television has transformed the electoral process

Since the 1950s, television has become the most important media element in general elections. Unlike in the USA, political advertising is not allowed on British television, but party political broadcasts are allocated on the basis of party voting strength. These have become important during elections and increasingly sophisticated, and some – like the famous Hugh Hudson-produced party political broadcast on Neil Kinnock in 1987 – can have a substantial impact on voter perceptions. More important, however, is the extensive news and current affairs coverage, and here US practice is increasingly being followed:

1 Professional media managers – such as Labour's Peter Mandelson – have become increasingly important. Brendan Bruce, Conservative Director of Communications 1989–91, comments: 'The survival of entire governments and companies now depends on the effectiveness of these advisers yet few outside the inner circles of power even know these mercenaries exist or what their true functions are' (Bruce, 1992, p. 128).

2 Political meetings have declined. Political leaders now follow their US counterparts in planning their activities in the light of likely media coverage. The hustings – open meetings in which debates and heckling occur – have given way to stage-managed rallies to which only party members have access. Entries, exits and ecstatic applause are all meticulously planned with the all-ticket audience as willing and vocal accomplices.

3 Given television's requirements for short, easily packaged messages, political leaders insert pithy, memorable passages into their daily election utterances – the so-called soundbite – in the knowledge that this is what television wants and will show in their news broadcasts and summaries throughout the day.

4 Party Political Broadcasts (PPBs) comprise slots allocated to the parties either on the basis of their voting performance at the previous election or on the number of candidates they are fielding. The first was made by Lord Samuel for the Liberals in 1951 but they were seldom skilfully made until 1987 when Hudson made that film of Neil Kinnock which impressively raised his personal ratings. In 1997 Major vetoed a PPB which represented Blair as a Faust-like figure, prepared to sell his principles for electoral victory. In recent years PPBs have declined further in importance. During the 1980s they averaged nine minutes in length but by 2005 this figure had come down to a mere two-and-a-half minutes.

The media and pressure groups

Just as individual politicians influence the media and seek their platforms to convey their messages, so do pressure groups as they seek to influence government policy. Pressure group campaigners such as Peter Tatchell of Outrage! and Tony Juniper of Friends of the Earth are expert in knowing about and massaging the form in which the press and television like to receive stories. Because it has been so successful, much pressure group activity now revolves around using the media. Anti-blood-sports campaigners use yellow smoke when trying to disrupt hunting events as they know television responds well to it.

■ The mass media and voting behaviour

Jay Blumler et al. wrote in 1978 that 'modern election campaigns have to a considerable extent become fully and truly television campaigns'. But what impact do the mass media have on the way in which citizens cast their votes? Does the form that different media give to political messages make any major difference? Substantial research on this topic has been undertaken, although with little definite outcome. One school of thought favours the view that the media do very little to influence voting directly but merely reinforce existing preferences.

Blumler and McQuail (1967) argued that people do not blandly receive and react to political media messages but apply a filter effect. Denver (1992, p. 99) summarises this effect under the headings of selective exposure, perception and retention.

1 *Selective exposure*: Many people avoid politics altogether when on television or in the press, while those who are interested favour those newspapers or television programmes that support rather than challenge their views.

2 *Selective perception*: The views and values that people have serve to 'edit' incoming information so that they tend to accept what they want to believe and ignore what they do not.

3 *Selective retention*: The same editing process is applied to what people choose to remember of what they have read or viewed.

Different media moreover, act in different ways as Table 8.3 suggests.

Table 8.3 The press, television and political influence

Television	Press
Balanced	Partisan
Trusted	Not trusted
Mass audience	Segmented audience
'Passive' audience politically	'Active' audience
Most important source of information	Secondary source

Source: Lecture by David Denver, September 1996

However, the filter-reinforcement thesis seems to accord too minor a role to such an all-pervasive element. It does not seem to make 'common' sense. In an age when party preferences have weakened and people are voting much more instrumentally, according to issues, then surely the more objective television coverage has a role to play in switching votes? Is it reasonable to suppose the filter effect negates all information that challenges or conflicts with established positions? If so, then why do parties persist in spending large sums on party political broadcasts? Some empirical data support a direct-influence thesis, especially in respect of television:

1 Professor Ivor Crewe maintains that during election campaigns up to 30 per cent of voters switch their votes, so despite the surface calm in 1983 and 1987 there was considerable 'churning' beneath the surface. These two elections may have been unusual in any case: the before and after campaign variations were much larger in 1979, 1974 and 1970 although not in the landslide 1997 election.

2 Many studies reveal that the four weeks of an election campaign provide too short a time over which to judge the impact of the media. Major shifts in voting preference take place between elections, and it is quite possible, or even probable that media coverage plays a significant role.

Assessing the effect of the media

Judging the effect of the media on voting behaviour is very difficult, because it is so hard to disentangle it from a myriad of factors such as family, work, region and class that play a determining role. However, it seems fair to say that:

1 *The media do reinforce political attitudes*: This is important when the degree of commitment to a party can prove crucial when events between elections, as they always do, put loyalties to the test.

2 *The media help to set the agenda of debate*: During election campaigns party press conferences attempt to achieve this, but the media do not always conform, and between elections the media, especially the print media, play a much more important agenda-setting role.

3 *It is clear that media reportage has some direct impact* on persuading voters to change sides, but research has not yet made clear whether this effect is major or marginal.

Focus groups

Much has been written about New Labour and focus groups, and a great deal of it has been uncomplimentary. They have been cited as evidence of Labour's concern with the superficial, with adapting policy on the basis of marketing expediency and not principle – in other words, as the thin end of the wedge that Old Labour critics argue has robbed the party of its moral purpose and integrity. This point of view is hotly refuted by the chief enthusiast for the technique in the Blairite party: Philip Gould, former advertising expert, who has written a fascinating book on the evolution of the 'new' party and its march to power (Gould, 1999). In the following extract he explains the technique and his own reasons for having faith in it:

I nearly always conduct focus groups in unassuming front rooms in Watford, or Edgware or Milton Keynes or Huddersfield, in a typical family room stacked with the normal knick-knacks and photos. The eight or so members of the group will have been recruited by a research company according to a formal specification: who they voted for in the last election, their age, their occupation . . . I do not just sit there and listen. I challenge, I argue back, I force them to confront issues. I confront issues myself. I like to use the group to develop and test ideas.
Gould (1999), pp. 327–8

The permanent campaign

In 2000, Ornstein and Mann edited a book entitled *The Permanent Campaign, and its Future*. The provenance of the phrase lay in 1982 with Sidney Blumenthal, who used it to describe the emergent style of media coverage in the USA. Assiduous USA watchers in New Labour's élite seem to have absorbed the new approach and made it their own: 'a nonstop process of seeking to manipulate sources of public approval to engage in the act of governing itself' (Hugh Heclo in Ornstein and Mann, 2000, p. 219). In other words, government and campaigning have become indistinguishable. The tendency now is for parties in government to view each day as something to be 'won' or 'lost'.

BOX 8.1   IDEAS AND PERSPECTIVES

John Lloyd's critique of the media, and a journalist's response

In his book *What the Media are Doing to Our Politics* (Lloyd, 2004), journalist John Lloyd diagnoses a parlous condition in the strained dealings between media and politics in Britain, not to mention other Western liberal democracies. He sees the relationship as one which has evolved from a fractious symbiosis to a damaging struggle for power in which the media have:

Claimed the right to judge and condemn; more, they have decided – without being clear about the decision – that politics is a dirty game, played by devious people who tell an essentially false narrative about the world and thus deceive the British people. This has not been the only, but it has been the increasingly dominant narrative which the media have constructed about politics over the past decade or so and, though it has suffered some knocks, remains dominant.

Lloyd (2004: 35)

In his Reuters lecture in October 2005, Lloyd discerned a 'parallel universe' which his colleagues inhabited and described but which bore little relation to the real world in which the real actors – politicians, corporate executives, trade union leaders, bishops, NGO heads – live and seek to do their jobs. But do these negative assumptions constitute a correct view or are these actors justified in complaining that what the media report is 'deeply inadequate'?

Various journalist reviewers of Lloyd's book were not impressed, but on 10 October 2005, *The Guardian* asked a number of these 'actors' to give their own views. Most felt the charges were justified. Tony Wright MP, academic and chair of the Public Administration Select Committee, felt the media should accept that they too had played a role in 'the collapse of trust in politics and politicians' which newspapers enjoy trumpeting in their pages, because they have helped to '. . . nourish a culture of contempt, engulfing the whole of public life'. Michael Bichard, one-time Permanent Secretary in the Civil Service and currently Rector of the University of the Arts, supported Lloyd's argument:

There is much evidence – especially in the press – of lazy, complacent and arrogant practice and the consequence of this is the parallel universe to which Lloyd refers.

Richard Eyre, the stage and screen director, observed:

Journalists often regard Daniel Ellsberg's maxim – 'all leaders lie and it's our duty to expose their lies' – as a vindication of, at least, deviousness and, at worst, blackmail, while blinding themselves to the fact zealous exposure of lies isn't always the same thing as revelation of the truth. And the motives of individual journalists are at least as venal and self-interested as those who they are indicting . . .

Anthony Sampson, who reviewed all these responses to Lloyd's critique, concluded:

Most respondents think [that Lloyd is right], and there can be no doubt about the genuine anguish of many distinguished people who feel aggrieved or simply resigned to the misrepresentations of the press.

So is the press malign and determined to distort perceptions of those in power? David Leigh, also of *The Guardian*, writing 'from the front line', as it were, contributes a powerful defence of the toiling hack. From his own experience he argues:

. . . when a journalist asks members of British institutions uncomfortable questions about what is going on, they respond with more or less polished evasions or with downright lies. They employ expensive PR teams to paint pictures that drift artistically away from reality. They try to intimidate with their lawyers. They conceal what they can and what they can't conceal, they distort.

He argues that all people in power are prone to this tendency: dictatorships try to suppress all dissent but democracies are not saved by elections every five years but by 'free speech coupled with a network of civic agencies which are truculent and unfettered. It's important that the various media behave as countervailing powers in a democracy; in fact it's absolutely necessary.' He went on to suggest that our leaders are often 'quite deranged'. Leigh concludes that on balance journalists do a necessary job pretty well but their performance is marred and debased by the fact that there is 'a race to the bottom in a declining market' and that it is true that 'some newspaper owners and newspaper people are venal, vain, cynical, sycophantic, low minded, partisan, unscrupulous or vindictive.' In *The Times* a few weeks earlier (8 December 2004), Simon Jenkins anticipated much of Leigh's case, writing that 'The British press is the most reptilian in the world', adding that 'it needs to be', given the weakness of Parliament in calling Blair to account and the way his government used spin to obfuscate every move it made.

Peter Oborne's critique of 'Manipulative Populism'

The well-known columnist, author and broadcaster Oborne, wrote a swingeing attack on the 'supplanting of parliamentary democracy' . . . 'a regime of media hype, spin doctors and skullduggery' (*The Triumph of the Political Class*). He recalls that Stanley Baldwin and Clem Attlee were prime ministers who worked through their ministers – who are the people who actually wield the legal power of government – and parliament. It followed that the Chief Whip was the person on whom the PM relied most heavily for support in his political battles.

But no more: the arrival of the 'celebrity prime minister' by which Oborne seems to mean Tony Blair (he doesn't mention Thatcher), has seen the emphasis shift to the chief spin doctor; he expresses this by reference to the eclipse of the fictional Francis Urquart – the epicene villain of Dobbs' *House of Cards* by the fictional Malcolm Tucker, the foul-mouthed hero-villain of Armando Ianucci's *The Thick of It* and *In the Loop*.

All the same black arts are at work; however, the battlefield has changed. Urquhart applied himself to parliament, Tucker bypassed the traditional institutions of the state and was only concerned with the media and its other methods of control: access, favouritism, information and the creation of an elite corps of client journalists.

Oborne recalls Brown's promise to:

'bring back cabinet government, respect civil service impartiality, restore the primacy of parliament and to abandon the dark political arts at which the team of political assassins around Blair had so excelled.'

However, Brown did none of these things and Cameron's appointment of Andy Coulson – former editor of *The News of the World* – does not suggest any real change if a new regime enters Downing Street. Oborne also explains that the elevation of Campbell and Coulson is due not necessarily to mere media strategies, but to the new nature of the media. It is now so all-encompassing, such a constant and demanding presence that it has become the instrument of a new kind of politics. Parliament is supposed to be the body which ultimately determines policy and decisions but the media is now so powerful it can apply a range of influences: certainly delays, sometimes vetos as well as urge courses of action. Oborne cites the vivid phrase coined by Anthony Barnett to describe this new way in which we are governed: 'manipulative populism'.

■ The mass media and the theory of pluralist democracy

If the mass media have such a transforming impact on politics, then how have they affected the fabric of British democracy? It all depends on what we mean by democracy. The popular and indeed 'official' view is that our elected legislature exerts watchdog control over the executive and allows a large degree of citizen participation in the process of government. This pluralist system provides a free market of ideas and a shifting, open competition for power between political parties, pressure groups and various other groups in society. Supporters of the present system claim that not only is it how the system ought to work (a normative theory of government) but it is, to a large extent, also descriptive: this is how it works in practice.

According to this view, the media play a vital political role:

1 They report and represent popular views to those invested with decision-making powers.

2 They inform society about the actions of government, educating voters in the issues of the day. The range of newspapers available provides a variety of interpretations and advice.

3 They act as a watchdog of the public interest, defending the ordinary person against a possibly over-mighty government through their powers of exposure, investigation and interrogation. To fulfil this neutral, disinterested role it follows that the media need to be given extensive freedom to question and publish.

This pluralist view of the media's role, once again both normative and descriptive, has been criticised under the following points.

Ownership and control influence media messages

Excluding the BBC, the media organisations are substantially part of the business world and embrace profit making as a central objective. This argument has more force since, following Murdoch's smashing of the trade union stranglehold over the press through his 'Wapping' revolution, newspapers now make substantial profits. This fact alone severely prejudices media claims to objectivity in reporting the news and reflecting popular feeling. In recent years ownership has concentrated markedly. About 80 per cent of newspaper circulation is in the hands of four conglomerates: Associated Newspapers, owned by the Rothermere family and controlling the *Daily Mail* and the *Mail on Sunday*; the Mirror Newspaper Group, owning the *Mirror*, *Sunday Mirror* and *Sunday People*; United Newspapers, owning the *Express*, the *Sunday Express*,

the *Star* and the *Standard*; and News International, owning *The Times*, *Sunday Times*, *News of the World* and the *Sun*. These latter-day press barons and media groups also own rafts of the regional press and have strong television interests: Murdoch, for example, owns Sky Television. Following the imprisonment of Conrad Black, the *Daily Telegraph* and *Sunday Telegraph* titles were taken over by the financier Barclay Brothers.

Nor is the press especially accountable: the Press Council used to be a powerful and respected watchdog on newspaper editors, but it has tended to acquiesce meekly in the concentration of ownership on the grounds that the danger of monopoly control is less unacceptable than the bankruptcy of familiar national titles. Moreover, since the *Sun* has regularly flouted its rulings, the council has lost even more respect and has been unable, for example, to prevent the private lives of public figures being invaded by tabloid journalists to an alarming degree.

BIOGRAPHY

Sir Christopher Meyer, Chairman of the Press Complaints Commission (1944–)

Oxbridge-educated Meyer is a career diplomat who stepped in to take over the PCC chair when Lord Wakeham became enmired in the 2002 Enron scandal. He served in Moscow, Brussels, Bonn and Washington and is fluent in all the relevant languages. In the 1980s, he was the chief Foreign Office spokesman under Geoffrey Howe and then took over as chief press officer. It is said that Meyer was pivotal in building a good relationship between Blair and Bush in the wake of the latter's controversial election – though much of this could be explained by good personal chemistry. In 2005 he published memoirs entitled *DC Confidential* which distributed insights into the way in which Blair operated (not good on detail), Prescott (poor on expressing himself), Jack Straw ('more to be liked than admired') and sundry other ministers whom he described as 'pygmies'. Apart from these personal swipes, however, there was little of substance in the book and Meyer survived calls for him to resign his PCC post.

Television evinces a much clearer distinction between ownership and control and fits more easily into the pluralist model. The BBC, of course, is government-owned, and in theory at least its board of governors exercises independent control. Independent television is privately owned, and this ownership is becoming more concentrated, but the Independent Broadcasting Authority (IBA) uses its considerable legal powers under the 1981 Broadcasting Act to ensure 'balance' and 'due accuracy and impartiality' on sensitive political issues. This is not to say that television can be acquitted of the charge of bias – as we shall see below – but merely that television controllers are forbidden by law to display open partisanship and that those people who own their companies cannot insist on particular editorial lines.

News values are at odds with the requirements of a pluralist system

In order to create profits media organisations compete for their audiences, with the consequent pursuit of the lowest common denominator in public taste. In the case of the tabloids this means the relegation of hard news to inside pages and the promotion to the front page of trivial stories such as sex scandals, royal family gossip and the comings and goings of soap opera stars. The same tendency has been apparent on television, with the reduction of current affairs programmes, their demotion from peak viewing times and the dilution of news programmes with more 'human interest' stories. As a result of this tendency it can be argued that the media's educative role in a pluralist democracy is being diminished. Some would go further, however, and maintain that the dominant news values adopted by the media are in any case inappropriate for this role. The experience of successful newspapers has helped to create a set of criteria for judging newsworthiness that news editors in all branches of the media automatically accept and apply more or less intuitively. The themes to which the public are believed to respond include:

1 *Personalities*: People quickly become bored with statistics and carefully marshalled arguments and relate to stories that involve disagreement, personality conflicts or interesting personal details.

2 *Revelations*: Journalist Nicholas Tomalin once defined news as the making public of something that someone wished to keep secret. Leaked documents, financial malpractice and sexual peccadilloes, e.g. the revelation that John Major had a four-year affair with Edwina Currie, are assiduously reported and eagerly read.

3 *Disasters*: The public has both a natural and a somewhat morbid interest in such matters.

4 *Visual back-up*: Stories that can be supported by good photographs (or film footage on TV) will often take precedence over those that cannot be so supported.

It is commonly believed that newspapers which ignore these ground rules will fail commercially and that current affairs television which tries too hard to be serious will be largely ignored and described, fatally, as 'boring'. There is much evidence to suggest that these news values are based on fact: that, perhaps to our shame, these are the themes to which we most readily respond. However, it does mean that the vast media industry is engaged in providing a distorted view of the world via its concentration on limited and relatively unimportant aspects of social reality.

'Tabloidisation' of television

Studies have shown the reduction of peak time current affairs television since the 1980s and some have argued there has been a progressive 'dumbing down' of the medium. Possible explanations for this, offered by Leach *et al.* (2003, pp. 164–5), are that:

1 Television competition has taken its cue from print journalism where falling sales have induced a 'race to the bottom'.

2 Newspapers are chasing younger readers and hope the snappy, abbreviated style, peppered with items about celebrities and the like, will prove attractive to this demographic.

3 Rupert Murdoch's influence of the mass media. For example, when Elvis Presley died *The Times* did not cover the funeral in 1977 as it was deemed inappropriate but after Murdoch took over in 1981 two journalists were sent to cover Bob Marley's last rites.

4 Increased competition from satellite and cable plus Internet-carried material has forced more populist policies.

BOX 8.2	IDEAS AND PERSPECTIVES

Bias, broadcasting and the political parties

Harold Wilson was notoriously paranoid about the media and believed that not only the press but also the BBC was 'ineradicably' biased against him, full of 'card carrying Tories', in the words of Michael Cockerell. Perhaps it is being in government that explains it, as in the 1980s it was Margaret Thatcher and her 'enforcer' Norman Tebbit who seemed paranoid. He launched ferocious attacks on the corporation, calling it 'the insufferable, smug, sanctimonious, naive, guilt-ridden, wet, pink, orthodoxy of that sunset home of that third-rate decade, the sixties'.

Answering questions in the House can be stressful amid all the noise, but ultimately the barbs can be ignored and the questions avoided easily. But on radio or television well-briefed interviewers can put politicians on the spot. This is why ministers of both parties have complained so vehemently about *Today* presenter John Humphrys and *Newsnight*'s Jeremy Paxman. Cockerell explains that Humphrys is not a 'politically motivated questioner; his aim is to strip away the public relations gloss and to use his own sharp teeth to counter pre-rehearsed soundbites' (*Guardian*, 28 May 1996).

This probably gets to the heart of the perennial conflict between politicians and the media. Politicians in power ideally would like to control the media – Mrs Thatcher once said she did not like short interviews but would like instead to have four hours of airtime on her own – and resent the criticism that they receive from journalists and interviewers. In a pluralist democracy it is indeed the job of the media to make government more accountable to the public, and perhaps it is when politicians do not like it that the media are doing their jobs most effectively.

The lobby system favours the government of the day

The pluralist model requires that the media report news in a truthful and neutral way. We have already seen that ownership heavily influences the partisanship of the press, but other critics argue that the lobby system of political reporting introduces a distortion of a different kind. Some 150 political journalists at Westminster are known collectively as 'the lobby'. In effect, they belong to a club with strict rules whereby they receive special briefings from government spokesmen in exchange for keeping quiet about their sources. Supporters claim that this is an important means of obtaining information that the public would not otherwise receive, but critics disagree. Anthony Howard, the veteran political commentator, has written that lobby correspondents, rather like prostitutes, become 'clients' or otherwise 'instruments for a politician's gratification' (Hennessy 1985: 9). The charge is that journalists become lazy, uncritical and incurious, preferring to derive their copy from bland government briefings – often delivered at dictation speed.

Television companies are vulnerable to political pressure

Ever since the broadcasting media became an integral part of the political process during the 1950s, governments of all complexions have had uneasy relationships with the BBC, an organisation with a worldwide reputation for excellence and for accurate, objective current affairs coverage. Margaret Thatcher, however, took government hostility to new lengths; indeed, 'abhorrence of the BBC appeared for a while to be a litmus test for the Conservativeness of MPs' (Negrine 1995: 125). Governments seek to influence the BBC in three major ways. First, they have the power of appointment to the corporation's board of governors. The post of chairman is especially important; Marmaduke Hussey's appointment in 1986 was believed to be a response to perceived left-wing tendencies (according to one report, he was ordered by Norman Tebbit's office to 'get in there and sort it out – in days and not months'). Second, governments can threaten to alter the licence system (although former Home Secretary Willie Whitelaw knew of no occasion when this threat had been used): Margaret Thatcher was known to favour the introduction of advertising to finance the BBC, but the Peacock Commission on the financing of television refused to endorse this approach. Third, government's attempt to exert pressure in relation to particular programmes – often citing security reasons. The range of disputes between the Thatcher governments and the BBC is unparalleled in recent history. In part this was a consequence of a dominant, long-established and relatively unchallenged Prime Minister as well as Thatcher's determination to challenge the old consensus – she long suspected that it resided tenaciously within the top echelons of the BBC.

Marxist theories of class dominance

The Glasgow University Media Group

On the basis of their extensive programme analyses, the Glasgow University Media Group suggest that television coverage of economic news tends to place the 'blame for society's industrial and economic problems at the door of the workforce. This is done in the face of contradictory evidence, which when it appears is either ignored [or] smothered' (1976: 267–8). Reports on industrial relations were 'clearly skewed against the interests of the working class and organised labour . . . in favour of the managers of industry'. The Glasgow research provoked a storm of criticism. In 1985, an academic counterblast was provided by Martin Harrison (1985), who criticised the slender basis of the Glasgow research and adduced new evidence that contradicted its conclusions.The Glasgow research is often cited in support of more general theories on how the media reinforce, protect and advance dominant class interests in society. Variations on the theme were produced by Gramsci, in the 1930s by the Frankfurt School of social theorists and in the 1970s by the sociocultural approach of Professor Stuart Hall (for detailed analysis see McQuail 1983: 57–70; Watts 1997), but the essence of their case is summed up in Marx's proposition that 'the ideas of the ruling class are in every epoch the ruling ideas'. He argued that those people who own and control the economic means of production – the ruling class – will seek to persuade everyone else that preserving status quo values and institutions is in the interests of society as a whole.

The means employed are infinitely subtle and indirect, via religious ideas, support for the institution of the family, the monarchy and much else.

Inevitably the role of the mass media, according to this analysis, is crucial. Marxists totally reject the pluralist model of the media as independent and neutral, as the servant rather than the master of society. They see the media merely as the instrument of class domination, owned by the ruling class and carrying their messages into every home in the land. It is in moments of crisis, Marxists would claim, that the fundamental bias of state institutions is made clear. In 1926, during the General Strike, Lord Reith, the first Director General of the BBC, provided some evidence for this view when he confided to his diary, 'they want us to be able to say they did not commandeer us, but they know they can trust us not to be really impartial'.

Which of the two models better describes the role of the media in British society? From the discussion so far, the pluralist model would appear inadequate in a number of respects. Its ability to act as a fair and accurate channel of communication between government and society is distorted by the political bias of the press, the lobby system, news values and the tendency of television to reflect consensual values. Moreover, the media are far from being truly independent: the press is largely owned by capitalist enterprises, and television is vulnerable to government pressure of various kinds. Does this mean that the dominance model is closer to the truth? Not really.

1 As former editor of ITN News, David Nicholas, observes (Tyne Tees TV, April 1986), 'trying to manipulate the news is as natural an instinct to a politician as breathing oxygen', but because politicians try does not mean that they always succeed. People who work in the media jealously guard their freedom and vigorously resist government interference.

2 The media may tend to reflect consensual views, but this does not prevent radical messages regularly breaking into the news – sometimes because they accord with news values themselves. Television also challenges and criticises the status quo: for example, at the humorous level in the form of *Bremner, Bird and Fortune* and *The Thick of It* and at the serious level in the form of the BBC's regular *Panorama* programme.

3 Programmes such as *Rough Justice* and *First Tuesday* in the past have shown that persistent and highly professional research can shame a reluctant establishment into action to reverse

Table 8.4 Summary table to show 'democrativeness' of media elements

Democratic criteria	Media and democrative tendency[c,d,e]				
	Broadsheets	Tabloids	Radio	BBC	Commercial TV
Easily accessible (for target audience)	+	+	+	+	+
Varied and plentiful	+	+	+	+	+
Concentration of ownership	–	–	–	+	–
Reliable factually	+	–	+	+	+
High-value political content	+	–	0	–	+
Accountability 1[a]	+	–	+	–	+
Accountability 2[b]	–	–	–	–	–
Low bias	0	–	+	+	+

[a] Accountability 1 = tendency for the media element to facilitate democracy.
[b] Accountability 2 = degree of accountability of medium to public.
[c] + = high tendency to encourage democracy.
[d] – = low tendency to encourage democracy.
[e] 0 = neutral effect (i.e. '0' is given for BBC radio as most of its five channels are music-based, and '0' for the bias of broadsheets as they tend to take give space to alternative opinions to their editorials).
Source: B. Jones (2000) 'Media and Government' in R. Pyper and L. Robins (eds) *United Kindom Governance*. Reprinted by permission of Palgrave Macmillan

injustices – as in the case of the Guildford Four, released in 1989 after fifteen years of wrongful imprisonment.

4 News values do not invariably serve ruling-class interests, otherwise governments would not try so hard to manipulate them. And even the most serious of the quality newspapers will join the feeding frenzy of a scandal like the one which submerged David Blunkett in 2004, once they deem the appropriate point has been reached.

Each model, then, contains elements of the truth, but neither comes near the whole truth. Which is the nearer? The reader must decide; but despite all its inadequacies and distortions the pluralist model probably offers the better framework for understanding how the mass media interact with the British political system. Table 8.4 reveals the complexity of the argument: some elements fit neatly into a supporting role, while others do not.

■ Language and politics

All this modern emphasis on technology can obscure the fact that in politics language is still of crucial importance. Taking the example of Northern Ireland, we have seen how the precise meaning of

words has provided a passionate bone of contention. When the IRA announced its ceasefire in 1994, its opponents insisted it should be a 'permanent' one. However, the paramilitary organisation did not wish to abandon its ability to use the threat of violence as a negotiating counter and refused to comply, insisting that its term 'complete' ceasefire was as good as the British government needed or would in any case get. Gerry Adams, president of the political wing of the IRA, Sinn Fein, had a similar problem over his attitude towards bombings. His close contact with the bombers made it impossible for him to condemn the bombing of Manchester in June 1996, so he used other less committing words like 'regret' or 'unfortunate'. Another aspect is tone of voice, which can bestow whole varieties of meaning to a statement or a speech. Sir Patrick Mayhew, for example, John Major's Northern Ireland Secretary, specialised in being 'calm'.

I went to the CBI conference in Birmingham to hear the Prime Minister speak, and there on a giant TV screen . . . was our very own Big Brother. This Big Brother smiles a lot in a self deprecating kind of way. He uses 'um' and 'well' as a rhetorical device, to convince us he's not reading out a prepared text, but needs to pause to work out exactly what he means. There is a prepared text of course but he adds to it phrases such as 'I really think' and 'you know I really have to tell you' and 'in my view'. This is the new oratory. The old politicians told us they were right, and that there was no room for doubt, the new politician is not telling us truths, but selling us himself . . . His message is that you should take him on trust; you should believe him because you love him.

Simon Hoggart, 'Commons Sketch: Blair lays on the therapy for the terracotta army', the *Guardian*, 3 November 1999. © Guardian Newspapers Limited, reprinted with permission

■ Media and the Internet

1 *Information*: It is now possible to download immense amounts of up-to-date information about political issues via the Internet.

2 *E-mail*: It is possible to communicate with politicians and the politically active all over the world, extending enormously the scope of political action.

3 *Interactive democracy*: By being hooked up to the Internet, it might be possible for politicians or government in democracies to seek endorsement for policies directly from the people. This would have all kinds of drawbacks, e.g. it could slow down the political process even more than at present in developed countries; it could give a platform to unsavoury messages like racism and power-seeking ideologues; it might enthrone the majority with a power it chooses to abuse. But these opportunities exist, and it is virtually certain that they will be experimented with if not adopted in the near future.

4 *Blogs*: It is now possible for anyone to set up their own website and issue opinions and information to the world on a regular basis. In the year 2005 it was calculated that 80,000 weblogs (blogs) were created and their rate of increase has now become exponential. Many younger people now use such sources as a matter of course, and some – like the US Drudge Report – break new stories or influence election campaigns. Fareed Zakaria offers this insight into the implications of the revolution currently taking place (see also Box 8.4):

Today's information revolution has produced thousands of outlets for news that make central control impossible and dissent easy. The Internet has taken this process another huge step forward, being a system where, in the columnist Thomas Friedman's words, 'Everyone is connected but no one is in control.'

Zakaria (2004)

However, the Internet still has some way to go before the existing media are usurped. Most blogs are manned by one or two people only; they do not have the same income as mainstream media; their scoops are still rare and often confined to fringe issues and political gossip. But, as Box 8.3 below suggests, in the USA things have maybe the locus of power is shifting much faster than in the UK.

5 *Mobile phones*: Virtually everyone now owns a mobile phone and this fact, together with the onrush of technology, has produced the transmission of more and more different types of information via their tiny screens. Some political parties have issued text messages to phone owners, but in 2006 more possibilities were opened up by the mobile provider which announced the results of an experiment whereby television had been broadcast direct to mobile phone subscribers. Despite the smallness of the screens, the trial was declared successful with thousands of mobile owners watching several hours of television a week – though most of it at home rather than on the move. Inevitably news and political content will in future be imbibed via this unlikely route and will become yet another facet of the political media.

BOX 8.3   The Huffington Post

Starting as a blog run by Arriana Huffington, Greek-born Oxbridge-educated and oil millionaire divorcee, the 'HuffPo' is making waves in the States. This is partly because its owner, once the scourge of the right, has swung to the left and now champions Obama. Moreover, while print journalism licks its wounds at redundancies and closures, the liberal blog had just announced, in April 2009, a $1.7m fund to help fill the gap left by the disappearing investigative news teams. The rise of the blog has been astonishing:

The fund also signals the website's ambition to move to a more central position in the media landscape – it began to call itself an 'internet newspaper' last year. April 2009 may well be seen as the moment the Huffington Post came of age. The HuffPo's rise has been impressive. Less than four years old and with fewer than 60 staff (including seven news reporters), it is now a competitor to the New York Times, *158 years old and with more than 1,000 journalists. According to the ratings website Comscore, in February the HuffPo drew more than a third of the* Times's *traffic: 7.3 million unique users to 18.4 million.*

Ed Pilkington, *Guardian, Media Guardian*, 6 April 2009

If the Drudge Report and the HuffPo as well as others continue to grow and the mainstream to contract, it might not be long before the new technology totally transforms the world of news reporting and commentary.

Political bloggers were delighted on 11 April 2009 when popular blogger Guido Fawkes received a link highly embarrassing to the government. It seemed that Damian McBride, a close aide of Gordon Brown, had been planning, with Derek Draper (former aide to Peter Mandelson) to launch a Labour blog which would disseminate smear stories (flagrant and untrue) damaging to the Conservatives. McBride resigned on 11 April, a day which might well mark a further shift in UK political communication from mainstream to cyberspace. But this day is still a long, long way off in the UK; most political blogs are one-man operations, even the big ones, like Iain Dale's Diary, Conservative Home and Guido Fawkes. All three of these, incidentally, are on the right; the left have not really begun to fire properly in the blogosphere.

BOX 8.4   BRITAIN IN CONTEXT

The media

The nature of the media in any country is usually a reflection of its political character. Democracies believe in freedom of speech and hence in open media, though politicians in democracies seek constantly to manipulate the media to their own advantage. In authoritarian systems the media are usually heavily controlled in terms of what newspapers can print or broadcasters can say on air.

The media in the UK play a similar role to those in the USA. The major difference is that in the latter, candidates can buy airtime to show their own political ads and to issue 'attack ads' to weaken opposing candidates. As such ads are very expensive, this gives an advantage to campaigns which are well funded. Indeed, many candidates in the US and incumbent legislators, governors and so forth, spend much of their energies raising campaign cash. The phenomenon of 'spin doctors' was more or less invented in the US where sculpting messages or media images for mass consumption has been something of a growth industry; they have since been disseminated worldwide to wherever democratic elections are regularly held. Much campaign output is either 'semi-mediated' like the presidential debates or 'mediated' in news broadcasts, but in the latter case candidates and their aides have become clever in gaining favourable media attention.

Many media critics claim that in the US the media favour the right in that they reflect and reinforce attitudes wholly accepting of the status quo. They point to Fox News, owned by Rupert Murdoch, which arguably leans towards a Bush interpretation of issues and news stories. As in the UK debate, others deny such bias and argue the media are essentially free. But this argument attains a worldwide dimension when ownership of the media is examined. Huge media conglomerates like Murdoch's News Corporation or Berlusconi's Mediaset control media in other countries and there is concern that some political control is thereby connected. Murdoch, for example, broadcasts satellite television into China and has agreed to some censorship controls demanded by the government of that country.

China has also sought to censor one of the fastest growing media forms: communication via the Internet. Here it is the search engine company, Google, which has attracted criticism for agreeing to controls over its activities in China. But such control cannot stop the burgeoning spread of such communication, especially the 'blogosphere'.

Blogs are online logs or diaries which are essentially forms of personal websites. They can be purely individual and carry all kinds of information from the person concerned – for example, 'I got up this morning and worked in the garden for two hours', about a business venture, about musical enthusiasms, about political issues, or, like the most successful and much visited ones, about celebrity gossip.

Writing in *The Guardian* on 9 February 2006, Charles Arthur reported that the blogosphere was 60 times its size of three years earlier and was doubling in size every five months; 75,000 are created every day and over 13 million were still active three months after their creation. Quite where this explosion of Internet communication will lead is unclear. It could prove to be a force for subversion – chipping away at the base of the status quo in a number of countries. Or it could be the object of government censorship in some countries, with governments hunting down these individuals hunched in front of their flickering screens. Or it could be neither and merely take its place as yet another logical element of globalisation.

Chapter summary

The spoken voice was the main form of political communication until the spread of newspapers in the nineteenth century. Broadcasting introduced a revolution into the way politics is conducted as its spread is instant and its influence so great. New political actors have emerged specialising in the media, and politicians have learned to master their techniques. Press news values tend to influence television also, but the latter is more vulnerable to political pressure than the already politicised press. Class dominance theories suggest that the media are no more than an instrument of the ruling class, but there is reason to believe that they exercise considerable independence and are not incompatible with democracy.

Discussion points

■ Should British political parties be allowed to buy political advertising on television?

■ Has televising Parliament enhanced or detracted from the efficacy of Parliament?

■ Does television substantially affect voting behaviour?

■ Do the media reinforce the political status quo or challenge it?

■ Should interviewers risk appearing rude when confronting politicians?

■ How important have blogs become in disseminating news and comment?

Further reading

A useful but now dated study of the media and British politics is Negrine (1995). Budge *et al.* (2007) provide two excellent chapters (13 and 14). The two most readable studies of leadership, the media and politics are both by Michael Cockerell (Cockerell 1988; Cockerell *et al.* 1984). Bruce (1992) is excellent on the behaviour of politicians in relation to the media. Blumler and Gurevitch (1995) is an essay on the crisis of communication for citizenship and as such is an interesting source of ideas. See Jones (1993) on the television interview. The most brilliant and funny book about the press is Chippendale and Orrie's history of the *Sun* (1992).

Bibliography

Barnett, S. and Gaber, I. (2001) *Westminster Tales: The 21st Century Crisis in Political Journalism* (Continuum).

Bilton, A., Bennett, K., Jones, P., Skinner, D., Stanworth, M. and Webster, A. (1996) *Introductory Sociology*, 3rd edn (Macmillan).

Blumler, J.G. and Gurevitch, M. (1995) *The Crisis of Public Communication* (Routledge).

Blumler, J.G. and McQuail, D. (1967) *Television in Politics* (Faber and Faber).

Blumler, J.G., Gurevitch, M. and Ives, J. (1978) *The Challenge of Election Broadcasting* (Leeds University Press).

Bruce, B. (1992) *Images of Power* (Kogan Page).

Budge, I., Crewe, I., McKay, D. and Newton, K. (2007) *The New British Politics* (Longman).

Chippendale, P. and Orrie, C. (1992) *Stick it Up Your Punter* (Mandarin).

Cockerell, M. (1988) *Live from Number Ten* (Faber and Faber).

Cockerell, M., Walker, D. and Hennessy, P. (1984) *Sources Close to the Prime Minister* (Macmillan).

Cohen, N. (1999) *The Observer*, 24 October 1999.

Cronkite, W. (1997) *A Reporter's Life* (Knopf).

Denver, D. (1992) *Elections and Voting Behaviour*, 2nd edn (Harvester Wheatsheaf).

Donovan, P. (1998) *All Our Todays: Forty Years of the Today Programme* (Arrow).

Fowler, N. (1991) *Ministers Decide: A Memoire of the Thatcher Years* (Chapmans).

Franklin, B. (1999) *Tough on Sound-bites, Tough on the Causes of Sound-bites: New Labour News Management* (Catalyst Pamphlet).

Geddes, A. and Tonge, J. (1997) *Labour's Landslide* (Manchester University Press).

Glasgow University Media Group (1976) *Bad News* (Routledge and Kegan Paul).

Gould, P. (1999) *The Unfinished Revolution* (Abacus).

Green, J. (1982) *Book of Political Quotes* (Angus and Robertson).

Harrison, M. (1985) *TV News: Whose Bias* (Hermitage, Policy Journals).

Hennessy, P. (1985) *What the Papers Never Said* (Political Education Press).

Hoggart, S. (1999a) 'Commons Sketch: Blair lays on the therapy for the terracotta army', *The Guardian*, 3 November 1999.

Hoggart, S. (1999b) 'Commons Sketch: no joke for No. 10 when Hague gag hits the target', *The Guardian*, 11 November 1999.

Ingham, B. (2003) 'The wages of spin', *Sunday Times*, 16 March (adapted from The *Wages of Spin*, John Murray, 2003).

Jones, B. (1993) '"The pitiless probing eye": politicians and the broadcast political interview', *Parliamentary Affairs*, January.

Jones, B. (2000) 'Media and government', in R. Pyper and L. Robins (eds) *United Kingdom Governance* (Palgrave Macmillan).

King, A. (ed.) (1997) *New Labour Triumphs: Britain at the Polls* (Chatham House).

Leach, R. *et al.* (1998) *British Politics* (Palgrave).

Lloyd, J. (2004) *What the Media are Doing to Our Politics* (Constable).

Marr, A. (1999) 'And the news is . . . electric', *The Observer*, 17 October.

McQuail, D. (1983) *Mass Communication Theory: An Introduction* (Sage).

Mullin, C. (2009) *A View from the Foothills* (Profile Books).

Negrine, R. (1995) *Politics and the Mass Media*, 2nd edn (Routledge).

Newton, K. (1992) 'Do voters believe everything they read in the papers?', in I. Crewe, P. Norris, D. Denver and D. Broughton (eds) *British Elections and Parties Yearbook* (Harvester Wheatsheaf).

Oborne, P. (2007) *The Triumph of the Political Class* (Simon & Schuster).

Ornstein, N. and Mann, T. (2000) *The Permanent Campaign, and its Future* (AET).

O'Rourke, P.J. (1992) *Parliament of Whores* (Picador).

▶

Sevaldsen, J. and Vardmand, O. (1993) *Contemporary British Society*, 4th edn (Academic Press).

Seyd, P. and Whiteley, P. (1992) *Labour's Grass Roots* (Clarendon Press).

Seymore-Ure, C. (1974) *The Political Impact of the Mass Media* (Constable).

Watts, D. (1997) *Political Communication Today* (Manchester University Press).

Whale, J. (1977) *The Politics of the Media* (Fontana).

Wring, D. and Deacon, D. (2005) 'The election unspun' in A. Geddes and J. Tonge, *Britain Decides* (Palgrave).

Zakaria, F. (2004) *The Future of Freedom* (Norton).

Useful websites

UK Media Internet Directory: Newspapers: www.mcc.ac.uk/jcridlan.htm

Daily Telegraph: www.telegraph.co.uk
The Independent: www.independent.co.uk
The Times: www.the-times.co.uk
Guardian: www.guardian.co.uk
The Economist: www.economist.co.uk
BBC Television: www.bbc.co.uk
BBC charter review: www.bbc.charterreview.org.uk
ITN: www.itn.co.uk
CNN: www.cnn.com

Blog sites

http://skipper59.blogspot.com/ (run by the author of this chapter)
http://5thnovember.blogspot.com/
http://normblog.typepad.com/
http://samizdata.net/blog/
http://chickyog.blogspot.com/
http://oliverkamm.typepad.com/

CHAPTER 9

Pathways into politics

Michael Moran

Learning objectives

- To understand the connection between the idea of democracy and **political participation** and recruitment in Britain.

- To understand why some people participate in politics and others do not.

- To understand why some people are recruited into positions of political leadership and some are not.

- To understand how participation and political recruitment have been changing in Britain.

Introduction

The great American President Abraham Lincoln (1809–65 and President 1861–5 during the American Civil War) offered what has probably come to be understood as the best-known definition of **democracy**: 'Government of the people, by the people, for the people'. But what does government by the people involve? The great traditions of republican government that helped to inspire American democracy originated in the city republics of ancient Greece – in communities where it was possible to gather all citizens together into a single forum to make important decisions. That is plainly not possible in a political system like the United Kingdom, governing as it does over 60 million people. Yet popular participation is central to democracy: that is signalled both in the Greek root of the word and in our everyday understanding as epitomised by Lincoln's definition. What sort of participation exists, and what sort is possible in a system claiming, as does the United Kingdom, to be democratic? That is the central question answered in this chapter. We look at three issues in particular: what patterns of popular participation exist; who is recruited into political leadership, and how; and what changes are taking place in patterns of participation and recruitment. These issues do not provide the full picture of participation, but seeking answers to them will illustrate two of its most important features: on the one hand, what opportunities exist for normal citizens, as distinct from professional politicians, to take part in political life; and on the other, who gets recruited into the very top levels of elected office, in the House of Commons and thus into government.

■ Democracy and participation

Democratic politics in Britain involves a complex mixture of direct and indirect participation: citizens can intervene directly in politics, or they can be represented indirectly by others whom they select.

The single most striking feature of direct participation is its rarity: in particular, only a tiny minority of the population are involved to a high degree in *conventional* political participation. (The importance of italicising this word to our understanding of the changing nature of participation will become clear by the end of the chapter; but for the moment we focus on this world of conventional participation.) Table 9.1 draws on the most authoritative study of conventional political participation to illustrate the point. The table shows popular participation to have two important features. First, the most common forms of participation are infrequent and/or sporadic: they take the form of voting in elections or signing petitions. Second, participation that takes a significant commitment of time and effort – for example canvassing in an election campaign – draws in only a tiny minority. The evidence in this table is now quite old; the original survey material was

gathered in the 1980s. But the passage of time has actually made the evidence more pointed, for over the last couple of decades these forms of participation – voting, canvassing for a candidate – have actually declined further.

Even these low figures overstate the extent of people's willingness to participate in politics. They report what a representative sample of the population claimed to do and, since participation is widely thought to be a good thing, there is evidence that people overstate what they do: for instance, the **turnout** in local elections and in elections for the European Parliament has never been anywhere near the numbers suggested by these figures, and in the most recent European elections in 2009 only just over 35 per cent of the electorate voted. (For the significance of recent turnout in UK parliamentary elections, see the section on the participation crisis near the end of the chapter.)

On this evidence the British are not political animals; only a minority, the **active minority**, give a substantial part of their lives over to political participation. Who are these people, and how do they differ from the majority of citizens? Some of the correlates of high participation are unsurprising:

Table 9.1 Percentage of population who have engaged in different forms of participation

	'Yes'/at least once (%)		'Yes'/at least once (%)
Voting in elections		*Contacting*	
Local	68.8	Member of Parliament	9.7
General	82.5	Civil servant	7.3
European	47.3	Councillor	20.7
		Town hall	17.4
Party campaigning		Media	3.8
Fund raising	5.2		
Canvassing	3.5	*Protesting*	
Clerical work	3.5	Attended protest meeting	14.6
Attending rally	8.6	Organised petition	8.0
		Signed petition	63.3
Group activity		Blocked traffic	1.1
Informal group	13.8	Protest march	5.2
Organised group	11.2	Political strike	6.5
Issue in group	4.7	Political boycott	4.3
		Physical force	0.2

Source: G. Parry, G. Moyser and N. Day (1992) *Political Participation and Democracy in Britain*, p. 44. Reproduced with permission from Cambridge University Press

---

BOX 9.1   IDEAS AND PERSPECTIVES

Apathy and British politics

Who cares about politics? The popular view is that it is dull, politicians are all the same and nothing changes. The preoccupation now is the pursuit of personal happiness – how much money you can earn and how well your personal life is going are Britons' main concern. To attend a political meeting or worry about politics is for anoraks and sad people with no other interests. Hence the fall in voter turnouts for last Thursday's European elections.

Yet politics represents the best of what it can mean to be a citizen. To gain power and to use it in the public interest are at the heart of democracy. The right to vote was hard won, and the wide agreement that politics and public affairs are increasingly dull, even purposeless, is to devalue our society. We are more than pleasure seekers.

It will be objected that the European elections, to a distant and controversial European Parliament, are scarcely a litmus test, but, if so, why was the turnout so much higher five years ago? Why are local election turnouts falling? Why are all branches of the media less and less confident that political coverage and analysis of public policy is what their audiences want?

Source: From an editorial in the *Guardian*, 17 June 1999. © Guardian Newspapers Limited, reprinted with permission

---

education, income and occupation are all implicated. The patterns of inequality in the distribution of resources outlined in Chapter 3 are partly reproduced in patterns of participation: those who participate most tend to have higher than average levels of education and higher than average income and are disproportionately from professional occupations. But the words 'tend to' and 'partly' are very important here; the study of participation in Britain by Parry and his colleagues cited above showed that there is no simple connection between wealth, education and participation (Parry *et al.*, 1992). At every level of British society, even among those groups most disposed to take an active part in politics, only a minority do so. More university professors than university porters take part in politics, but even among university professors politics is still a minority taste. Parry and his colleagues found that over half the population took part in only one activity, voting, which of course happens infrequently. By contrast, they identified a core of 'complete activists', who make up only 1.5 per cent of the population (just over 600,000). This is an absolutely large number of people. They are a minority, vital for the health of democracy, for whom politics is a consuming passion – the political system's equivalent of obsessive stamp collectors or snooker fanatics. But participation in snooker, billiards and pool is actually much commoner than political participation: about 20 per cent of men and 4 per cent of women report that they play. Viewed thus, politics counts as a small minority sport. Even opera – usually classed as a typical pursuit of the rich – is more popular among unskilled manual workers than is politics: 1 per cent of unskilled manual workers report that they attend opera. All these figures put into context the significance of participation in politics, and they are particularly worth bearing in mind when we consider how well politicians can claim to represent the popular will.

■ Democracy and non-participation

The politically active citizen is in a small minority, and that fact is a problem in achieving government 'by the people'. It is, however, a problem that may be soluble, because the overwhelming majority of the people participate sporadically, and through elections help to select some of the representatives who ensure indirect participation. But for the effectiveness of democracy an even more troubling feature is that part of the population – a minority – take no part in politics at all. It is not easy to get a clear picture of those who are completely excluded – or who exclude themselves – from all political participation, since one of the main means of studying who takes part in politics is the mass survey – and those who avoid politics are precisely those who are often difficult to contact by surveys.

Some of the totally inactive present a problem for any theory of democracy that demands the active involvement of all citizens, but their inactivity need not itself be taken as a sign that the British system is malfunctioning. There is a minority in the population – found in all classes – who are so obsessed with some other pursuit, be it train spotting or opera, that they have neither the desire nor the time to commit to politics in any form. They may be seen as the mirror image of the minority so obsessed by politics that they can commit to nothing else. Societies need these obsessives, otherwise train

A politically apathetic nation? A million indignant protestors take to the streets of London to protest against the Iraq war
Source: Pearson Education Ltd/Philip Langeskov

spotting, opera and democracy would die out. This random distribution of obsessives thus produces considerable social benefits.

Much more serious than the minority who rationally exclude themselves from all political participation are those who are excluded – particularly because the politically excluded also disproportionately suffer social, economic and cultural exclusion. We can begin to see why the problem is serious by considering some of the more obvious sources of exclusion. Consider the commonest form of conventional participation, voting. To vote, one must first be on an electoral register. An absolutely large number of adults are excluded by virtue of committal to institutions, notably prisons and mental hospitals. Britain has one of the largest prison populations in Europe: for some years now it has consistently exceeded 70,000. Most prisoners have been legally debarred from voting. In 2005 the European Court of Human Rights declared the ban on prisoners voting to be illegal. In April 2008 Jack Straw, the Justice Minister, announced that prisoners sentenced to less than four years (28,000) might get the vote. However, the necessary legislation had not been posted in time for the 2010 election. However, the practical effect of legal changes is unlikely to be great. This is because prisoners face considerable obstacles to participating in political life. The social mix of the prison population is not a cross-section of the population: prisons form a concentration of the poor, the least well educated (including the illiterate), the unskilled, those unable to get any sort of job, and those with mental and physical health problems. In the prison population, we see the most extreme and most visible (because confined in a state institution) bit of the iceberg of the politically excluded. Outside prison, another substantial excluded group until recently were the homeless. Voting requires registration, and to register required a fixed abode. The very nature of homelessness makes an accurate estimate of the numbers difficult. However, in a national survey in the mid-1990s, 6 per cent of all households reported some experience of homelessness in the preceding decade. In other words, being homeless is not a great rarity. The social profile of the homeless is also, unsurprisingly, distinctive: for instance, 30 per cent of lone parents with dependent children have reported some experience of homelessness. The requirement that a fixed abode is needed to register was relaxed in the Political Parties, Elections and Referendums Act of 2000. Nevertheless, given their condition of life it is unlikely that many of the homeless do actually register. Overall, Weir and Beetham have estimated that somewhere between 2 million and 3.5 million people are disenfranchised at any one time (Weir and Beetham 1999: 41).

All this adds up to a pattern that is problematic for democracy: exclusion from labour and housing markets goes with political exclusion. Exclusion from the system could lead to a build-up of frustration at not being heard, something to which some commentators attributed disturbances which have occurred periodically in some cities since the early 1980s. Beyond these visibly excluded groups is a less easily measurable world of political exclusion, but the weight of circumstantial evidence overwhelmingly points to the conclusion that those who take no part in politics are usually the poorest of the poor. Whether some other mechanisms of democratic politics can remedy these exclusionary features is considered later in this chapter.

■ Democracy and political recruitment

Political participation as an active citizen is one thing; being recruited into a full-time political position is another. But **political recruitment** of the latter kind is central to the workings of democracy in Britain for a reason we have already encountered: the scale and complexity of governing the United Kingdom means that, inevitably, there has to be some political specialisation; a minority has to make a career out of political leadership. That is the essence of representative democracy. How well the mechanisms of political recruitment function is therefore a critical matter as far as the evaluation of British democracy is concerned.

Getting citizens to participate voluntarily in politics is, as we have seen, a difficult business. But in the case of recruitment to full-time elected office, 'many are called but few are chosen' – there are far more aspirants than there are places. The most important gateway into this kind of political leadership is via a seat in the House of Commons, and the only realistic way into the House of Commons is through competing as the candidate of a leading political party. Competition for party nomination is intense. If we focus on the very top of the political tree – the leading positions in Cabinet, for instance – we find that, by the time people get there, a drastic process of selection has taken place.

How does this drastic selection process work? We will find that three features are important: politics at the top is now a full-time occupation; the selection process is brutal and gets more brutal the closer the top is reached; and right at the top, luck – good and bad – is very important.

The first of these features actually highlights the single most important fact about elected political leadership in Britain: it is a full-time profession, demanding total dedication. It is extremely difficult to combine with a serious, long-term commitment to any other job. That is a great change from a generation ago, when politics could be combined with another occupation. This is one of the keys to understanding the recruitment process. It is helpful to think of the road to the top as a bit like a long march by an army of hopefuls several thousand strong. They start out in their twenties wanting to reach the very top. By the time this young army reaches middle age all but the handful in or around the Cabinet have dropped out, exhausted or destroyed by the journey. The Labour Party leader (1963–76) and Prime Minister Harold Wilson was famously photographed as a child outside the door of No. 10 Downing Street; numberless others have been so photographed without coming near to entering through that door as Prime Ministers. They dropped out somewhere on the long march. Like an army losing soldiers, the process of elimination is governed by a number of features, ranging from the initial suitability of those who joined the march in the first place, to sheer luck. Broadly speaking, in the early stages of the march those who fall out are marked by consistent features; as the march reaches its close, luck starts to play an increasingly important part.

The best way to appreciate this is to start with those who have made a successful start on the long march – who have actually managed to become full-timers by virtue of being elected as Members of Parliament. This is the point at which most of those on the march to political leadership drop out, and for an obvious reason: there are only 646 seats in the House of Commons (650 in the 2010 election), and at any one election, because most incumbents are reselected, only a small number are actually available to new aspirants. With a few exceptions, election to the House of Commons has been the prime condition for achieving high political office in the United Kingdom. (The new devolved Parliament in Scotland and Assembly in Wales now offer an alternative route to governmental office.) But narrow though the passage is through which those on the long march to political leadership have to pass, it is narrower even than the figures for the size of the House of Commons would suggest. The chances of reaching and staying on the **front bench** are maximised by

securing, at an early age, a safe parliamentary seat – and the number of these is, naturally, considerably smaller than the total of parliamentary seats.

The 'gateway' into a seat in the House of Commons is very important to political recruitment, then, for a number of reasons. For all the evidence of the marginal role of the Commons itself to the making of policy, a seat in the House is virtually a condition of enjoying a career at the very top of national politics. The narrowness of the gateway makes this the key point at which most abandon the march to the top. Elections are dominated by parties. Only three members of the 2005–10 House of Commons could be considered political independents. Even one of these, George Galloway, was elected on an anti-Iraq war ticket for his Respect Party, though that party is essentially a Galloway vehicle. Thus, any realistic chance of entering the House of Commons depends on securing a party nomination. In the two leading parties, even nominations for hopeless seats are strongly contested, partly because contesting a hopeless seat is now a more or less compulsory apprenticeship for someone who aspires to nomination to a safe seat. Doing the rounds of local parties to secure nominations is the point at which some of the brutal realities begin further to weed out all but those most intensely committed. Although politics has become increasingly professionalised, it lacks many of the traditional features of a middle-class profession: hours of work are highly unsociable and difficult to reconcile either with family life or with most second occupations; it is a highly precarious source of income (despite the once generous expense allowances); and, while the national parties do try to exert some influence over candidate selection, the final say is still lodged with activists in individual constituency parties.

This last fact helps to explain some of the broad social characteristics of MPs as reflected in Table 9.2. Although some social skills – the ability to 'work a room', talking quickly and superficially to complete strangers – are important to potential MPs, most selection processes in constituencies put a high premium on speaking skills fostered by high levels of formal education and the practice of professions such as the law. Parliamentary politics is still a highly 'oral' occupation, and the ability to speak well in public is a highly valued skill. Those who make the selection at constituency level are able to make choices that reflect their preferences, both open and unacknowledged. These preferences go some way towards explaining the make-up of the House of

Table 9.2 Selected characteristics of Labour and Conservative Members of Parliament, 2005 general election (% of total for each party)

	Labour Party	Conservative Party
University education	64	81
Professional or business occupation	47	76
Manual worker	12	1

Source: Calculated from Criddle (2006: 164–5)

Table 9.3 Women's share of seats in a selection of popularly elected chambers*

	Women's share (%)
Sweden	45.3
Norway	38.2
Finland	37.5
Denmark	36.9
Netherlands	36.7
New Zealand	28.3
Austria	33.9
Germany	32.8
Iceland	30.2
UK (House of Commons)	19.7

* The figures are for popularly elected lower houses. Most are for elections during 2002–4; the UK figure is for the House of Commons elected in 2005.
Source: Adapted from the Inter-Parliamentary Union website (www.ipu.org/wmn-e/classif.htm). Reproduced with permission

Commons. As Table 9.3 shows, the representation of women in Parliament is low by international standards. Some of this is due to the fact that local selection committees often do not wish to select women as candidates – a prejudice that was both more open and more extensive in the past but which continues to influence the make-up of Parliament. Some is due to the sheer difficulty of combining a Parliamentary career with the demands of home-making and parenthood that even now still fall disproportionately on women (Norris and Lovenduski 1995). Likewise, open or unrecognised prejudice against some ethnic minorities, notably Afro-Caribbeans, helps to explain why the proportions of those in Parliament are well below the proportions in the wider population.

Once through the very narrow passage of a safe parliamentary seat – especially if it is acquired while someone is still in their thirties – the path to the top becomes considerably easier. The odds on reaching the front bench, especially in government, are not long. A government needs to fill over 100 ministerial offices. At any one time, a proportion of the parliamentary party will be ruled out – by manifest incompetence, some serious problem in private life, age (it is increasingly rare for someone to be given office for the first time once they have passed 50) or the fact that they have fallen foul of the leadership. The simple staying power guaranteed by a safe seat thus gives the ambitious an advantage. Beyond that, the pathway to the top starts to depend on a large number of difficult-to-control circumstances. Connections and patrons help, especially in getting a foot on the lower rungs of the ladder. Luck (being available when some accident, scandal or resignation causes a vacancy) plays a part. For instance, John Major (Conservative leader and Prime Minister, 1990–7) had his route to the top cleared by a succession of events in which he had no direct role: two important Cabinet resignations and then Mrs Thatcher's defeat in a leadership election within the Conservative Party. Finally, physical and mental robustness are very important. At the top political life is extraordinarily stressful. The successful need a physical constitution able to cope with long, odd hours, little leisure or exercise and the temptation to over-indulge in rich food and drink. It helps to be clever to survive at the top, but it is essential to be physically strong; any physical weakness will soon show itself, and any serious ill health is a virtually certain bar to office. At the very top, Prime Ministers tend to be highly robust: every postwar Prime Minister has survived into advanced old age (bar Major and Blair, who, of course, have yet to live that long). It is also essential in British government to have a particularly robust mental make-up: a large ego and enormous self-confidence. Political life is so intensely adversarial that anyone near the top will be subject to constant criticism and hard questioning. A tendency to self-doubt, or an inability to shrug off personal attacks, is almost as fatal to success as physical ill health. Getting to the very top – to be Prime Minister or Leader of the Opposition – is then heavily influenced by chance. Political life is full of ex-future Prime Ministers who looked certainties for the top job but who never made it; by contrast, it would have been impossible to predict the identity of the last six leaders of the Conservative Party

Prime Ministers in waiting? Eton College has provided 18 Prime Ministers, the last in 1963; but is this bastion of Old England about to provide another? And, if so, what does it tell us about modern British society?
Source: © Tim Graham / Corbis

(Thatcher, Major, Hague, Duncan Smith, Howard, Cameron) even a year before they took office. Indeed, David Cameron came unexpectedly up on the rails only a few short months before his victory in December 2005.

The importance of single-minded ambition in reaching the top is well illustrated by two figures who have dominated electoral politics during December 2005. David Cameron, the Leader of the Conservative Party after December 2005; and Gordon Brown, Chancellor since 1997 and Prime Minister since June 2007. Superficially they look dissimilar: Cameron is a quintessential product of the socially exclusive south of England upper class, educated at Eton

---

BOX 9.2   **IDEAS AND PERSPECTIVES**

How to get to the top in British politics

- Be born a male
- Be born white and English
- Go to university
- Start early: enter Parliament by the age of 35
- Get a safe seat
- Acquire a powerful patron, preferably in the cabinet

- Never suffer serious illness – if you must, conceal it
- Have a large ego – never experience self-doubt
- Spend every waking hour on politics and your career
- Above all, be lucky.

College and Oxford; Brown is the state-educated son of a church minister, educated at a Scottish state school and Edinburgh University. Actually they are very alike in their dedication to their political career: in their adult lives they have been virtually nothing but full-time politicians. The jobs they held before entering Parliament (both, as it happens, at one time working for TV companies) were just preparations for the life of full-time politics. Both entered Parliament early (Brown at 32, Cameron at 35) for safe seats, thus insulating themselves from the ups and downs of the electoral fortunes of their parties. Both live for politics and their career. And both are hugely skilled at the techniques of modern politics,

BIOGRAPHY

David Cameron (1966–)

David Cameron was elected leader of the Conservative Party in December 2005, defeating the one-time hot favourite David Davis. For over forty years the Conservative Party has generally preferred to choose leaders from comparatively modest social backgrounds. Cameron superficially represents a return to an older tradition: educated at the most élitist of all public schools, Eton, and at Oxford University. But in fact he is the very pattern of a modern politician. He has done little in his adult life other than full-time politics. He won the leadership because, unlike his rival, he showed immense talent in exploiting the tools of modern politics, notably communication via the mass media. This talent enabled to him to emerge within a few weeks from the position of outsider in the Conservative leadership contest to that of hot favourite – a position confirmed by his victory in the December 2005 election among Conservative Party members. The importance of presentation skills is emphasised by the fact that Cameron has no experience of government office, nor much even of public life (he only became an MP in 2001). Contrast his predecessor Michael Howard who had a long political career, including holding major public offices such as Home Secretary, before becoming leader.

notably at the rapid assimilation of information and its conversion into attractively packaged statements and soundbites suitable for the modern mass media, especially television.

■ Changing patterns of participation and recruitment

The preceding sections are designed to give a couple of 'snapshots' of pathways into politics: the pathways by which citizens who are not committed to a political career nevertheless participate in political life; and the pathways by which those with aspirations to full-time elected office make their way to the pinnacle. But as important as any snapshot is some sense of how things are changing over time. The evidence is that changes, both as regards participation and as regards political recruitment, are having contradictory effects – in some ways opening up new pathways to politics, while closing others off.

What features are weakening and what strengthening democratic participation?

Factors making democratic participation weaker

Some state policies have raised the barriers to participation. An obvious example is the aftermath of the **community charge**. In the late 1980s and early 1990s, large-scale popular resistance to the community charge (the 'poll tax', designed to replace rates on domestic property) was accompanied by widespread evasion – one of the commonest means of which was simply not to be recorded on the electoral register. Even after the repeal of the community charge, this has probably produced a permanently disenfranchised minority. The very fact that many of those who fail to register are engaged in hiding themselves from the state makes estimation of the numbers difficult, but there are almost certainly at least one million potential voters excluded in this way.

The decline of trade unionism, especially among manual workers, has also made participation more problematic for manual workers. Total membershi of trade unions has fallen sharply in recent yea Moreover, this fall has been disproportiona' concentrated in unions in heavy industries employing, predominantly, male manual workers. Active participation in unions was always confined to a small minority, but the decline of male manual worker trade unionism has significant implications for working-class political participation. For the participating minority, union activity was an exceptionally important channel not only in industrial relations but, through the unions' close connections with the Labour Party, in wider political life. The internal political life of unions was also a means by which groups of workers with little formal education acquired the skills that allow most effective participation – skills in public speaking, in running meetings and in organising groups. The decline of male manual worker trade unionism is probably the single most damaging social change as far as democratic participation in Britain is concerned.

Factors making democratic participation stronger

Although some public policies have made participation weaker, some have made it easier. The proliferation of candidates from minority parties at general elections is in part the result of a decline in the historic cost of running candidates. A parliamentary candidate in a general election must deposit £500 (refundable only if at least 5 per cent of the vote is received). The original amount was set in 1918, at £150: had that amount been increased in line with inflation the required deposit would now be in excess of £3,000. Yet another policy change which has widened opportunities to participate is described in detail in Box 9.3: the referendum, once of no importance in British political life, is becoming increasingly common and increasingly important.

BOX 9.3   **IDEAS AND PERSPECTIVES**

Referendums

A referendum is a vote allowing choice on a particular issue, as distinct from an election, which is a vote allowing choice between candidates. Traditional constitutional conventions were hostile to the referendum mechanism, and it was first used as a means of expressing popular views on a single important issue only in the 1970s; before that it had been used to decide comparatively minor issues like pub licensing laws in some localities. In 1975, a referendum was held to affirm approval or disapproval of the terms of our membership of the Common Market, which had been renegotiated by a new Labour government. At the time it was commonly argued that the referendum breached important constitutional conventions, such as that collective responsibility for major decisions should lie with a Cabinet answerable to the House of Commons. But the referendum proved its worth by settling a huge, and hugely divisive, political issue: after the 'yes' vote in 1975 Britain's continuing membership of the Common Market ceased to be a significant line of political division.

Since then, the referendum has become established as a major means of making decisions on historic political issues. In 1979, proposals to introduce devolved government in Wales and Scotland fell through failure to secure required majorities in referendums in the two countries. In 1997, by contrast, votes favouring the principle of devolution in the two countries led to major devolution Acts being passed in the following year. And in 1998, referendums in both Northern Ireland and the Republic of Ireland produced large majorities in favour of the Good Friday Agreement, the agreement by which the peace settlement in Northern Ireland is popularly known.

These examples also illustrate the ambiguous meaning of the referendum in modern Britain. It is now undoubtedly established as a means of expressing popular will – and thus of popular participation at historic moments. But as the most recent cases show, the people at large have typically been allowed to have a say only at the end of bargaining, as in the case of the Good Friday Agreement, when all kinds of ʳnatives that might have been popularly preferred have been closed off by the political élite. There ays been an argument about how far a referendum allows serious popular choice and how far it ans of giving a popular rubber stamp, or legitimacy, to policies worked out by the governing uncertainty continues to surround the referendum in Britain.

An even more significant factor encouraging participation is the accumulation of the '**social capital**' on which much democratic participation draws. 'Social capital' refers, in this connection, to the existence of a well-developed network of associations that underpin democratic politics. As the decline of manual worker trade unions shows, associations are critical to fostering participation in political systems – like that of the United Kingdom – where size and scale rule out much direct participation in decision making. The evidence both that associational life is becoming healthier and that associations are encompassing groups formerly excluded from participation is therefore important evidence in assessing the health of British democracy.

What is the evidence that these 'beneficial' changes are taking place? One striking sign is summarised in Table 9.4. This compares two surveys of associational life in Britain's second city, Birmingham. Two features of this table are noteworthy: the much larger number of associations when the 1990s are compared with the 1960s; and the striking rise in the number of religious groups. In part the latter change

is connected to immigration to Birmingham, but the experience of immigration is common to most of the large cities of the United Kingdom, so we can be pretty sure that we are picking up a national trend here. The connection between the renewal of 'social capital' and immigration also highlights another feature central to democratic participation: many of these groups cater precisely for those, like recent immigrants, who would otherwise find participation in conventional politics difficult. In other words, they are a powerful means of countering political exclusion.

The groups that are counted in estimates of 'social capital' more often than not have little to do with political participation directly – religious groups are a good example. But just as trade unions were historically 'schools' where members could learn the skills of organisation and participation, so the same can be said of religious denominations. More directly, we know that organised denominations have historically been important means of political mobilisation: famously, the origins of the Labour Party owed more to Methodism than to Marxism. And the same pattern seems to be repeating itself with the newer groups: the study of Birmingham by Maloney and his colleagues referred to in Table 9.4 showed that many of the new groups created since the 1960s are deeply involved in consultations over public policy, especially in the sphere of community relations.

The renewal of social capital has also brought into being other kinds of association that are mobilising the previously excluded. One of the most graphic examples is provided by the case of the sick – traditionally, a weak group often very difficult to organise for the purposes of participation in politics. The very group who might be thought to have the greatest interest in shaping health policy was the most likely to be excluded from it. However, Wood has shown that there has been a mushrooming of patient organisations: he paints a picture where numerous groups of patients, especially those suffering from long-term illnesses, are organising to an increasing extent; 88 per cent of the patient groups he identified had been formed since 1960 (Wood 2000).

What explains this apparent transformation of the landscape of participation? Three forces are important:

Table 9.4 Comparison of number of voluntary associations in Birmingham in 1970 and 1998

Type of association	Number in 1970	Number in 1998
Sports	2,144	1,192
Social welfare	666	1,319
Cultural	388	507
Trade associations	176	71
Professional	165	112
Social	142	398
Churches	138	848
Forces	122	114
Youth	76	268
Technical and scientific	76	41
Educational	66	475
Trade unions	55	52
Health	50	309
Not classified	–	75
Total	**4,264**	**5,781**

Source: From W. Maloney *et al.* (2000) 'Social capital and urban governance: adding a more contextualized "top-down" perspective', *Political Studies*, 48:4, pp. 802–20. Reproduced with permission of Blackwell Publishing Ltd

1 Long-term social changes have altered both the capacities and the outlook of the whole population. For instance, the long-term rise in the for

Table 9.5 The rise of the environmental movement: membership of selected groups (United Kingdom, thousands)

	1971	2004
National Trust	278	3,400
Royal Society for the Protection of Birds	98	1,010
Ramblers' Association	22	143

Source: For 1971, Office for National Statistics (1999), Table 11.4; for 2004, annual reports of the organisations

educational attainments of the population may be important, since the likelihood of participation rises with education: in the mid-1960s only about 5 per cent of 18-year-olds were in higher education; now the figure is above 40 per cent. Culturally, there has been an explosive growth in interest in the natural world and protecting the environment. As Table 9.5 shows, this has been reflected in a huge growth in membership of environment-related organisations. Of course, few people join organisations such as the Royal Society for the Protection of Birds to campaign politically; but the growing resources of these organisations are used to *represent* the concerns of members – thus contributing to the second (indirect) form of representation.

2 Advances in techniques of political organisation and in technology are making it easier to form and maintain groups. Pioneers in effective group organisation can be imitated very quickly: many of the campaigning groups of the 1990s – for instance, groups campaigning for the environment or for the disabled – are copying and adapting successful tactics, such as public demonstrations, developed in the 1960s and 1970s. Sometimes the transmission process is international: witness the success of the international environmental organisation Greenpeace, which did not even exist in the UK in the early 1970s. Meanwhile, the development of cheap desktop computing power makes the organisation of groups much easier than in the past: databases, mailing lists, and targeted mail shots to raise ~ort and money are all now within the reach ' relatively small, impoverished organisa- ~ing popular access to the Internet electronic organisation of political ~n easier in the future.

3 These electronic and social developments have given a considerable spur to the growth of **political entrepreneurship**. Political life, like economic life, is a kind of marketplace; and just as successful business entrepreneurs live by spotting and filling a gap for economic goods and services, the same can happen in political life. Entrepreneurs 'spot' groups that do not, or cannot, participate in political life and either organise them to participate or organise a group to lobby on their behalf. Political entrepreneurship is a very important development, since it is a key means by which the voice of the previously excluded, or the silent, can be heard in politics.

Changing patterns of recruitment

If we compare the present with a generation ago, two features dominate the pattern of change in political recruitment:

1 There has been a considerable narrowing of the social range in recruitment. A generation ago, two social groups now little represented in Parliament made up a sizeable proportion of the benches on both the Conservative and the Labour sides: on the former, a considerable group with established upper-class connections; on the latter, a considerable group who had spent part of their adult life as manual workers. The 'shorthand' signs of this were, on the one side, education at the most exclusive public school, Eton, and on the other occupation before entering Parliament. The 2005 general election saw only seventeen Etonians (fifteen of whom were Conservatives) returned to Parliament. While this was actually a small advance on the 2001 total (of fourteen), the Etonian contingent is in long-term decline. Although the percentage of Labour MPs who were once manual workers also showed a slight advance over 2001 (from 10 per cent to 12 per cent), this group too is in long-term decline (Butler and Kavanagh 2002: 202–4 and Criddle 2006 allow comparison of figures). Although strenuous efforts have been made in both leading parties in recent decades to 'democratise' their back benches, the effect, curiously, has been to mould MPs into something like a single prototype regardless of party. The typical MP, almost regardless of party, is now a middle-class professional.

2 This narrowing of the social range of political leaders is connected to a second development: the rise of the professional politician. The demands of most professional occupations – in business or elsewhere – are now so great that it is virtually impossible to make a long-term success while committed to politics. Even if an individual does not set out to be exclusively committed to one or the other, fairly early in a career a decision has to be made to concentrate either on politics or on a chosen profession. The demands of politics – especially parliamentary politics – now virtually rule out combining an active role in Parliament with a serious profession. Politics at this level is increasingly a full-time job, especially for the most ambitious MPs. The decline of the working-class MP has been hastened by other social forces. It partly reflects the declining influence of manual worker trade unionism in the Labour Party, because these unions were powerful patrons of manual workers. It partly reflects social change: although manual workers are in decline in Parliament, many of those with middle-class professional characteristics are 'meritocrats' from working-class families educated to university level. But the change is also due in part to the rise of politics as a full-time professional career. Professionalism makes early commitment to parliamentary ambitions even more important than in the past. The manual worker who made a mark in unions and then entered Parliament in fairly advanced middle age is much rarer than in the past.

A crisis of participation – or a crisis of conventional participation?

Democracy, however we define it, depends on extensive popular participation in important parts of political life. Yet there is a great deal of evidence that participation in many important political activities is falling. This was dramatised by the historically low turnout in the general election of 2001, and by the barely marginal recovery in the election of 2005, but there is other important evidence. One of the most important signs is the declining willingness of citizens to join, and take an active part in, political parties: parties now have about three million fewer

BOX 9.4   BRITAIN IN CONTEXT

Political participation in comparative context

This chapter makes abundantly clear that many forms of participation have declined in Britain in recent decades. But are the British unique in this respect? By some comparative measures participation is indeed low. Thus turnout in elections for local government and for the European Parliament are particularly low in Britain. But in the case of the former, at least, this is probably a perfectly rational response by voters, for British local authorities are especially powerless in comparison to most of their European neighbours. The British participation tradition is also especially restricted: compare the UK historically with the United States, where a wide range of local offices have been open to electoral choice and where the second Chamber – the Senate – has been popularly elected for nearly a century. (Contrast the case of the House of Lords.) As we have seen already in the chapter, this restricted participation tradition is changing: there is an increasingly wide range of opportunities to vote either for candidates for office, or in referendums governing policy choice. Many of the most important signs of 'participation decline' are common across the world of economically advanced democracies: for instance, the political party with a mass membership is losing its hold virtually everywhere, as a means of getting people either to vote or to become active in politics more generally. Most of the forces making for changes in participation in Britain are also common to other advanced industrial societies: for instance, the way innovative electronic technologies are spurring new forms of participation. Indeed, one of the marked features of many of the new groups who are drawing people into active politics is that they are linked in international networks: consider the examples of Amnesty International and Greenpeace International, both of which are virtually global movements. British political participation can thus no longer be considered simply a 'British affair'.

members than in the early 1950s. (The figures are approximate because until recently total membership figures were approximations.) Yet parties are the main institutions by which political competition is organised in Britain, and governments are overwhelmingly dominated by parties: that is why we routinely speak of the 'Labour' or the 'Conservative' government. Sharp falls in participation thus seem to suggest a wider crisis of democracy.

However, a more optimistic view would argue that we are just seeing a perfectly rational shift by citizens away from ineffective and often boring forms of participation – such as the tedium of local political party life – to more focused and effective participation: for instance, in special interest groups and in campaigning movements like those for the protection of the environment. We saw earlier (Table 9.5) that the membership of environmental groups has grown hugely in recent years. Of course, most people join the Royal Society for the Protection of Birds (the largest environmental organisation in Western Europe) because they are interested in nature, not because they are interested in politics. But in the heyday of political parties, members also joined parties for social reasons. The fall in the membership of the Conservative and Labour parties is partly because leisure possibilities are now richer and more interesting. In many parts of Britain in the 1950s life was so dull that the most exciting thing to do was to go to the local Conservative dinner dance.

When we join environmental groups we may not be consciously acting politically, but our action, and our subscription fee, help to make stronger an organisation that does campaign over a whole range of important political issues. The significance of the figures for environmental groups is that they may be part of a wider pattern of change in the nature of participation in Britain: a shift from what we have been calling 'conventional' to more unconventional kinds of participation. These patterns are detectable in the very latest surveys of the nature of participation (see, for example, Pattie *et al.* 2003, 2004). Based on national surveys Pattie and his colleagues unearthed a whole world of participation beyond the conventional range of parties and elections. To take a single example, over 30 per cent of those surveyed claimed to have boycotted purchase of some product within the preceding twelve months – in other words, tried to put pressure on a business to change its practices by using their power as consumers. Well-known campaigns of this kind have, for example, targeted producers of baby food on the grounds that their marketing practices in the developing world were injurious to the health of mothers and children, and targeted oil companies on the grounds that their production practices were environmentally damaging. We do not instinctively think of a visit to the supermarket or the petrol pump as involving a political action, but it is not hard to see that this kind of unconventional participation can be very significant indeed.

That there is a crisis of 'conventional' participation is thus pretty well established, and it is very worrying for those who control the best established institutions of conventional participation – which means those who lead the major political parties and fight parliamentary elections. But the rise of other modes of less conventional participation means that we should be cautious about concluding that there is a general crisis of participation, or that democracy is endangered by the decline of conventional participation. Democracy requires effective participation by the people; it is not obvious that direct action like boycotting products is less effective participation than being a rank and file member of a political party.

Chapter summary

What does evidence about political participation tell us about the health of British democracy? The evidence does not all point in the same direction: the pessimist would see the glass as half empty, the optimist as half full. The pessimist would see that mass popular participation in British politics is limited, mostly, to occasional voting in a general election; and there is some evidence that the appeal of this is declining. Only a small proportion of the population takes a sustained part in politics, and some forms of established participation – such as activism in a political party – are in steep decline. Sustained and high-level political activity has always been a bit like any other obsessive hobby, such as train spotting or an enthusiasm for opera: confined to a tiny minority. But whereas the disappearance of the train spotter or the opera buff would be a matter of regret, it would not fundamentally damage British democracy. The disappearance of the political activist, by contrast, would be very bad news for democratic politics in Britain. The optimist, on the other hand, would point out that, while the proportion of the total population participating in politics is small, the absolute numbers are still very large. What is more, many unconventional forms of activism, for example in various loosely organised political networks, have grown greatly in recent years. And in the new devolved institutions such as those in Scotland and Wales the opportunities to participate, by voting, have actually increased.

Discussion points

■ Can you think of any reforms that might make participation in politics more widespread?

■ What are the advantages, and what are the disadvantages, of the rise of the professional politician?

■ Is direct popular participation needed for effective democracy?

■ You are increasingly concerned about the environment and want to make government policy 'greener'. You do not have much spare time and can afford to take an active part in only one organisation. Discuss the pros and cons of what would be your most effective choice: joining a political party or joining an environmental pressure group.

Further reading

Parry *et al.* (1992) is the most authoritative study of popular participation in Britain. Pattie *et al.* (2004) paint a very different, more contemporary picture, while the article by the same authors (2003) gives a good thumbnail sketch of their core argument. Weir and Beetham (1999) is an attempt to sum up the present state of democracy; Norris and Lovenduski (1995) examine paths to the top in Britain.

Acknowledgement

Note: I am grateful to Byron Criddle of the University of Aberdeen for kindly allowing me a sight of the proof copy of his chapter on 'MPs and candidates' in Butler and Kavanagh (2006) – the latest in his invaluable snapshots of candidate and MP selection at successive general elections. Figures for the 2005 general election were calculated from his chapter.

Bibliography

Butler, D. and Kavanagh, D. (2002) *The British General Election of 2001* (Palgrave).

Criddle, B. (2006) 'MPs and candidates', in D. Butler and D. Kavanagh, *The British General Election of 2005* (Palgrave).

Maloney, W., Smith, G. and Stoker, G. (2000) 'Social capital and urban governance: adding a more contextualised "top-down" perspective', *Political Studies*, Vol. 48, No. 4, pp. 802–20.

Norris, P. and Lovenduski, J. (1995) *Political Recruitment: Gender, Race and Class in the British Parliament* (Cambridge University Press).

Office for National Statistics (1998) *Social Trends 28* (Stationery Office).

Office for National Statistics (1999) *Social Trends 29* (Stationery Office).

Parry, G., Moyser, G. and Day, N. (1992) *Political Participation and Democracy in Britain* (Cambridge University Press).

Pattie, C., Seyd, P. and Whiteley, P. (2003) 'Citizenship and civic engagement: attitudes and behaviour in Britain', *Political Studies*, Vol. 51, No. 3, pp. 433–68.

Pattie, C., Seyd, P. and Whiteley, P. (2004) *Citizenship in Britain: Values, Participation and Democracy* (Cambridge University Press).

Weir, S. and Beetham, D. (1999) *Political Power and Democratic Control in Britain* (Routledge).

Wood, B. (2000) *Patient Power? Patients' Associations and Health Care in Britain and America* (Open University Press).

Useful websites

An invaluable source of information about the rules governing participation, and of policy changes designed to encourage participation, is the website of the Electoral Commission, an official body established in 2000: www.electoral-commission.gov.uk. The web pages of two of the new elected bodies created by the devolution reforms are also very informative, providing lots of primary material that would be very useful for projects or dissertations: the Welsh Assembly at www.wales.gov.uk and the Scottish Parliament at www.scottish.parliament.uk. Some of the most important work on participation in recent years is at the time of writing being carried out via a research programme funded by the UK Economic and Social Research Council. To see the projects and researchers visit www.essex.ac.uk/democracy. The information in the chapter on the proportions of women members of legislatures in different countries is taken from the website of the international parliamentary union, a fund of information about all kinds of democratic participation: www.ipu.org. All the campaigning groups that, as the chapter shows, have become important to participation in recent years have websites. For a typical example, see www.greenpeace.org.

CHAPTER 10

Pressure groups

Bill Jones

Learning objectives

- To explain that formal democratic government structures conceal the myriad hidden contacts between government and organised interests.

- To analyse and explain the way in which groups are organised and operate.

- To introduce some familiarity with theories regarding this area of government–public interaction.

- To provide some specific examples of pressure group activity.

Introduction

The Norwegian political scientist Stein Rokkan, writing about his country's system, said 'the crucial decisions on economic policy are rarely taken in the parties or in Parliament'. He judged 'the central area' to be 'the bargaining table' where the government authorities meet directly with trade union and other group leaders. 'These yearly rounds of negotiations mean more in the lives of rank and file citizens than formal elections.'

British politics is not as consensually well organised or cooperative as the Norwegian model, but there is a central core of similarity regarding pressure group influence. Accordingly, this chapter examines the way in which organised groups play their part in the government of the country. Democratic government predicates government by the people, and politicians often claim to be speaking on behalf of public opinion. But how do rulers learn what people want? Elections provide a significant but infrequent opportunity for people to participate in politics. These are held every four years or so, but pressure groups provide continuous opportunities for such involvement and communication.

...ed a threat to his public sector pay policy from the stubborn refusal of the firefighters' union to reach

...ris Riddell. From the *Observer*, 17 November 2002. Reproduced with permission from Guardian

■ Definitions

Interest or **pressure groups** are formed by people to protect or advance a shared interest. Like political parties, groups may be mass campaigning bodies, but whereas parties have policies for many issues and, usually, wish to form a government, groups are essentially sectional and wish to influence government only on specific policies.

Historical background

The term 'pressure group' is relatively recent, but organised groups tried to influence government long before the modern age of representative democracy. The Society for Effecting the Abolition of the Slave Trade was founded in 1787 and under the leadership of William Wilberforce and Thomas Clarkson succeeded in abolishing the slave trade in 1807. In 1839, the Anti-Corn Law League was established, providing a model for how a pressure group can influence government. It successfully mobilised popular and élite opinion against legislation that benefited landowners at the expense of the rest of society and in 1846 achieved its objective after converting the Prime Minister of the day, Sir Robert Peel, to its cause. It proved wrong the cynical dictum that the interests of the rich and powerful will invariably triumph over those of the poor and weak and strengthened the supporters of Britain's (at that time nascent) representative democracy. In the twentieth century, the scope of government has grown immensely and impinges on the lives of many different social and economic sectors. After 1945, the development of the mixed economy and the welfare state drew even more people into the orbit of government. Groups developed to defend and promote interests likely to be affected by particular government policies. For its own part, government came to see pressure groups as valuable sources of information and potential support. The variety of modern pressure groups therefore reflects the infinite diversity of interests in society. A distinction is usually drawn between the following:

1 **Sectional** or **interest groups**, most of which are motivated by the particular economic interests of their members. Classic examples of these are trade unions, professional bodies (e.g. the British Medical Association) and employers' organisations.

2 **Cause** or **promotion groups**, which exist to promote an idea not directly related to the personal interests of its members. Wilberforce's was such a group, and in modern times the Campaign for Nuclear Disarmament (CND), the Child Poverty Action Group (CPAG) and the Society for the Protection of the Unborn Child (SPUC) can be identified. Of the environmental groups, the Ramblers' Association, Greenpeace and Friends of the Earth are perhaps the best known examples.

Other species of pressure group include:

■ *Peak associations*: These are umbrella organisations that represent broad bands of similar groups such as employers (the Confederation of British Industry, CBI) and workers (the Trades Union Congress, TUC).

■ *'Fire brigade' groups*: So called because they form in reaction to a specific problem and disband if and when it has been solved. They are often 'single-issue' groups; the Anti-Corn Law League could, at a pinch, be regarded as one such, and the contemporary coalition of environmental groups supporting the Road Traffic Reduction Campaign (see Box 10.1) is another.

■ *Episodic groups*: These are usually non-political but occasionally throw themselves into campaigning when their interests are affected: for example, sports clubs campaigning for more school playing fields.

Membership of sectional groups is limited to those who are part of the specific interest group, for example coal miners or doctors. In contrast, support for a cause such as nuclear disarmament or anti-smoking can potentially embrace all adults. However, the two types of group are not mutually exclusive. Some trade unions take a stand on political causes, for example (in the past) on apartheid in South Africa, or on poverty or sexual equality. Some members of cause groups may have a material interest in promoting the cause, for example teachers in the Campaign for the Advancement for State Education. It should be noted that pressure groups regularly seek to influence each other to maximise impact and often find themselves in direct conflict over certain issues, for example, and most obviously, 'Forest' which defends the rights of smokers and 'Ash', the anti-smoking body.

BOX 10.1 EXAMPLE

The Road Traffic Reduction Campaign

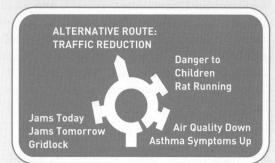

This campaign was a collaborative venture by groups perceiving a shared interest in reducing traffic congestion. If the campaign ever proves successful, it could be regarded as a 'fire brigade' grouping. Members of the Campaign Steering Group included Friends of the Earth, the National Asthma Campaign, the Civic Trust, the cycling group Sustrans and the Green Party, among many others.

In June 1999, they circulated an 'update' article to supporters that recorded their activities and noted their successes. Glenda Jackson, the transport minister, was congratulated for saying (7 May 1999) 'We will set national traffic reduction targets before the end of this parliament' and Michael Meacher, environment minister, for saying that 'overall traffic reduction remains a commitment'. Such plaudits are disingenuous in that their main purpose is to repeat stated commitments important to the movement so that the politicians involved will find it more difficult to ignore or disown them. On the reverse side of the article, transcripts of the ministerial statements are revealed to be the result of clever and sharp questioning at public meetings by campaign members. Indeed, a cynical reader of these transcripts might conclude that the commitments were extracted from somewhat reluctant politicians. Whatever the truth about the politicians' commitment, the result is effective pressure group action. Campaign supporters were enjoined to undertake actions such as writing to congratulate the ministers on their statements, to ask Labour groups on local councils to pass supporting resolutions, and to ask councillors to propose similar motions for the council to send.

Source: From the Road Traffic Reduction Campaign. Reproduced with permission from the Friends of the Earth

■ Civil society and groups

Civil society has a long provenance in political thought, being related to the seventeenth-century notion of a 'state of nature', which humans in theory inhabited before entering the protective confines of the state (see Chapter 4). The idea of such an independent social entity enabled the likes of Hobbes and Locke to argue that citizens had the right to overthrow a corrupt or failing government. Civil society was held to be the not overtly political relationships in society: those of family, business, church and, especially according to the modern sense of the term, voluntary organisations. These relationships help people to live together, cooperating, compromising; accepting both leadership and responsibility; providing the very basis of democratic activity; and training members in the art of democratic politics. Some commentators have argued

that, while citizen protest led to the overthrow of communist governments, the absence of a strong or 'thick' civil society in Eastern European countries has hindered their transition from totalitarian to democratic society. The ability to form organisations independent of the state is one of the hallmarks and, indeed, preconditions of a democratic society. A study by Ashford and Timms (1992) revealed substantial membership of groups in the UK, including 16 per cent in church or religious organisations, 14 per cent in trade unions, 17 per cent in sporting organisations and 5 per cent in environmental or ecological groups.

'Bowling alone'

One American student of civil society, Robert Putnam (1995), offers a depressing analysis in his essay 'Bowling alone'. He points out that despite rising levels of education – usually associated with increased participation – involvement with voluntary bodies was in decline: parent–teacher association membership had fallen from 12 million in 1982 to 5 million in 1995. Unions, churches and many other bodies reported similar declines. Moreover, people were less likely to socialise – the percentage who socialised with neighbours on more than one occasion during the year dropped from 72 per cent in 1974 to 61 per cent in 1993. The title of his book derived from the statistic that while the numbers involved in bowling between 1980 and 1993 increased by 10 per cent, the number playing in league teams plummeted by 40 per cent: Americans were 'bowling alone'. Putnam saw this as merely one symptom of 'disengagement': fading away of groups; the decline of solidarity and trust; and a detachment from the political process evidenced in falling turnouts at elections. Some bodies have huge memberships but, as Putnam shows in the USA, these are often 'passive memberships' where someone pays an annual subscription but attends no meetings. If Britain is anything like America – and it often mimics trends a few years removed – a slow decline in pressure group activity and a 'thinning' of civic society would seem to be a worrying possibility.

Research by Peter Hall (1999) has suggested that Britain has a much healthier pattern of voluntary group membership than the USA, but a report by the Institute of Education in February 2003 suggested worrying similarities with our transatlantic cousins. The study was based on three birth cohorts – 1946, 1958 and 1970. The first group produced a figure of 60 per cent membership of voluntary groups, the second only 15 per cent and those born in 1970 a mere 8 per cent.

More reassuringly, the 'Citizen Audit' programme at Sheffield University seemed to bear out Hall's findings. This report suggests that, despite the low turnout in the 2001 general election, the 'British public is politically engaged'. Its findings, based on interviews with 13,000 people, found that three-quarters had engaged in one or more political activities, more particularly:

■ 29 million had given money to a 'citizens' organisation;

■ 14 million had raised money for such an organisation;

■ 22 million had signed a petition;

■ 18 million had boycotted certain products in their shopping;

■ 17 million had bought certain goods for political reasons;

■ 2.5 million had taken part in a public demonstration.

Quite why a 'politically engaged' public should do all these things and yet not bother to vote in such massive numbers in 2001 is still unclear.

■ Pressure groups and government

The relationship between interest groups and government is not always or even usually **adversarial**. Groups may be useful to government. Ministers and civil servants often lack the information or expertise necessary to make wise policies, or indeed the authority to ensure that they are implemented effectively. They frequently turn to the relevant representative organisations to find out defects in an existing line of policy and seek suggestions as to how things might be improved. They sound out group leaders about probable resistance to a new line of policy. Moreover, an interest group's support, or at least acceptance, for a policy can help to 'legitimise' it and thus maximise its chances of successful implementation. If bodies involved in a new law refuse to cooperate and organise against it – as in the case of the poll tax in 1990 – a law can become unenforceable. The accession to power of Labour in May 1997 raised the spectre of union influence once again dominating policy, as in the 1970s. Blair was emphatic that unions, like any other group seeking influence, would receive 'fairness but no favours'. Indeed, Blair seemed more concerned to woo business groups than the electorally unpopular unions, so much so that Wyn Grant, an authority on pressure groups, has judged Blair's Labour government more pro-business than any other in his lifetime.

In the several stages of the policy process, groups have opportunities to play an important role (see Chapter 21):

1 At the initial stage they may put an issue on the policy agenda (e.g. environmental groups promoted awareness of the dangers to the ozone layer caused by many products and have forced government to act).

2 When governments issue Green Papers (setting out policy options for discussion) and White

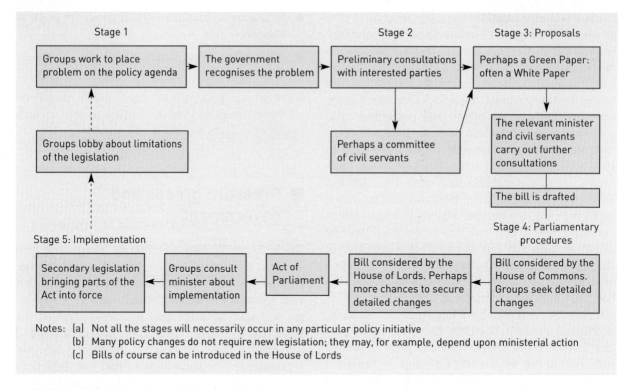

Figure 10.1 Pressure groups and the policy process
Source: From W. Grant (1988) 'Pressure groups and the policy process', *Social Studies Review*, Vol. 3, No. 5. Reproduced with permission from the California Council for Social Studies

Papers (proposals for legislation), groups may **lobby** back-benchers or civil servants.

3   In Parliament, groups may influence the final form of legislation. As we can see from Figure 10.1, groups are involved at virtually every stage of the policy process.

Insider–outsider groups

Groups are usually most concerned to gain access to ministers and civil servants – the key policy makers. Pressure group techniques are usually a means to that end. When government departments are formulating policies there are certain groups they consult. The Ministry of Agriculture, Fisheries and Food, when it existed under that name, was in continuous and close contact with the National Farmers' Union. Indeed, in 1989, in the wake of the salmonella food-poisoning scandal, it was alleged by some that the ministry neglected the interests of consumers compared with those of the producers. Wyn Grant (1985) has described groups that are regularly consulted as 'insider groups'; in the study

of pressure groups this has become possibly the most important distinction. A good example of a new insider group in The TaxPayers' Alliance (see Box 10.2), although some claim it is so close to the Conservative Party it is effectively a wing of it.

On the other hand, the Campaign for Nuclear Disarmament, for example, mounts public campaigns largely because it has no access to Whitehall; in Grant's language it is an 'outsider group'. Not only does it lack specialist knowledge on foreign policy or defence systems, but the policies it advocates are flatly opposed to those followed by every postwar British government. Grant's classification of groups is summarised in Figure 10.2.

To gain access to the inner sanctums of decision making, groups usually have to demonstrate that they possess at least some of the following features:

1   *Authority*, which may be demonstrated in the group's ability to organise a majority of its potential members. The National Union of Mineworkers spoke for nearly 100 per cent of miners for many years, but its authority was weakened not just by the fall-off in membership after the disastrous 1983–4 miners' strike but also by the formation

BOX 10.2   TaxPayers' Alliance: pressure group or Tory front?

'Since it was launched six years ago the Alliance has become arguably the most influential pressure group in the country . . .' So wrote the *Guardian*, 10 October 2009, in a major article on the new phenomenon, written in the wake of the Conservative Party conference in Manchester.

'The idea of tearing down the walls of big government as Cameron did in his speech on Thursday is something we have been talking about for years,' said its chief executive, Matthew Elliott, yesterday. 'The Tory party has moved on to our agenda.'

The TPA also claimed authorship of George Osborne's public sector pay freeze and that no public sector worker should earn more than the prime minister without the Chancellor approving it. The TPA also urge the wholesale abandonment of cherished Labour achievements: the secondary school building programme, child benefit and Sure Start centres for young children.

The media too – especially the right-wing press – have proved deliriously receptive to its messages:

'In the last year the *Daily Mail* quoted the TPA in 517 articles. The *Sun* obliged 307 times, once bizarrely on page 3 when a topless Keeley parroted the TPA's line against energy taxes. The *Guardian* mentioned the group 29 times.'

The term 'Alliance' suggests that the TPA has some kind of democratic legitimacy, that it represents the voting public in some kind of genuine fashion. Indeed, it claims to be: 'the guardian of taxpayers' money, the voice of the taxpayer in the media and their representative at Westminster'. The *Guardian* had investigated the TPA's sources for its £1m annual funding and discovered 60 per cent of it comprised donors giving £5000 or more to the Conservative Party. Moreover, one of the group's directors lives abroad and does not pay any UK tax.

Perhaps inevitably after this Labour sources called foul. Former Deputy Prime minister, John Prescott, denounced it as 'nothing more than a front for the Conservative Party', calling on the BBC – which regularly interviews TPA staff – to clarify its umbilical links to the Tories when its representatives are quoted or interviewed.

The Chief Executive of the TPA, Mathew Elliot, dismissed the attack, claiming it was as hard on the Conservative councils who wasted money as it was on Labour and pointing out its donors had once given to Labour in its earlier days.

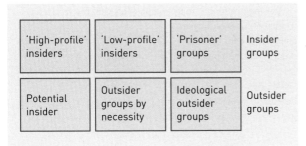

Figure 10.2 Grant's typology of pressure groups
Source: From W. Grant (1985) 'Insider and outsider pressure groups', *Social Studies Review*, Vol. 1, No. 1. Reproduced with permission from the California Council for Social Studies

in 1985 of the breakaway Union of Democratic Miners. Similarly, the authority of the teachers' unions has been weakened because of the divisions between so many different groups. Over-

whelming support by members for their group leadership's policies is another guarantor of authority.

2 *Information*: Groups such as the British Medical Association and the Howard League for Penal Reform command an audience among decision makers because of their expertise.

3 *The compatibility of a group's objectives with those of the government*: For example, trade unions traditionally received a more friendly hearing when pressing for favourable trade union legislation or state intervention in industry from a Labour than from a Conservative government. The TUC always received short shrift from Margaret Thatcher, who made no effort to disguise her hostility or even contempt. But even when likely to receive a friendly hearing, groups

seeking access to the policy process are not advised to put forward demands that the government regards as unreasonable.

4 *Compatibility of group objectives with public sympathies*: A group out of sympathy with public views – for example, advocating the housing of convicted paedophiles in residential areas – is unlikely to gain inner access to decision making.

5 *Reliable track record for sensible advice in the past and the ability, through knowledge of Whitehall, to fit in with its procedures and confidential ethos*: Most insider groups, like the BMA, CBI and NFU, fit this profile.

6 *Possession of powerful sanctions*: Some groups of workers are able to disrupt society through the withdrawal of their services. The ability of electricians to inflict injury on society was greater even than the miners', but after the privatisation of electricity their ability to 'close down' the nation was fragmented.

But becoming and remaining an insider group requires the acceptance of constraints. Group leaders, for example, should respect confidences, be willing to compromise, back up demands with evidence and

avoid threats (Grant 1989, 1990). Grant accepts that this typology is not quite as clear-cut as it at first seems. Some groups can be insider and outsider at the same time, for example Greenpeace. Also, insider groups, in the present day, are not invariably more influential than outsider ones: groups connected with the fuel crisis of 2000 brought the country to a standstill within days.

Being on the inside is still thought by many to be better than on the outside, though this does amount to a kind of Faustian pact that groups sign with government. If government fails to deliver the influence that group leaders expect, they can find themselves in trouble with their membership. Alternatively, they can become so closely associated with a particular government policy that they can lose credibility if that policy fails (but see below for Grant's recent thinking on the evolution of group relations with government).

Pressure group methods can be seen on a continuum running from peaceful methods to violent ones (see Figure 10.3). Anyone working for a pressure group, especially if it is a local one focusing on, say, a planning issue, will find themselves working hard at routine chores such as stuffing envelopes, ringing up supporters, delivering publicity and

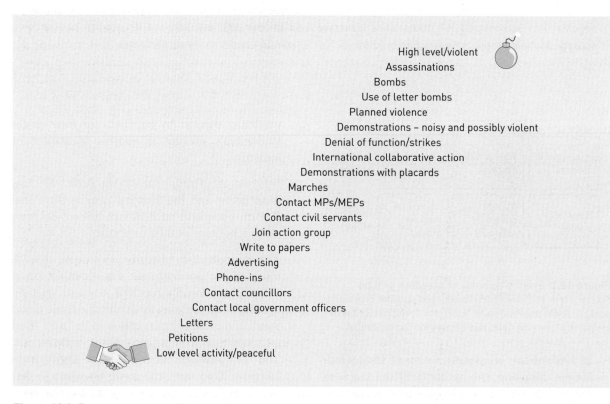

Figure 10.3 Pressure group methods continuum

collecting signatures on petitions. However, other groups use different techniques. Trade unions use or threaten to use the 'denial of function' approach; in practice, this means going on strike, a kind of holding to ransom of those who benefit from their labour. In some cases, however, such methods encounter moral restraints; for example, should nurses refuse to look after patients in support of a pay dispute? Few would find this easy. Other groups are concerned to test the law. The Ramblers' Association, for example, is quite happy to ignore notices from landowners denying them access if the notices are not legal; in such circumstances, its members are happy to assert their legal rights and to clear any obstructions that may have been put in place. However, they stop short of actually breaking the law. Other groups are prepared to go even further. Some anarchist groups deliberately break the law as part of a strategy of undermining law and order and existing civil society; others do so to attract the publicity of a court case and possibly a 'martyred' period in jail for an activist; for example Fathers 4 Justice.

Such groups and sentiments are still rare. Most groups concentrate their efforts at the peaceful end of the spectrum, but a change in the political culture is discernible over the last decade.

■ The growth (and increasing respectability) of direct action

Some groups either are so passionate or have become so impatient with the slow-moving wheels of government that they have deliberately used high-profile and illegal tactics. Brian Cass, the chief executive of Huntingdon Life Sciences, which conducts experiments on animals, was once beaten by animal rights activists wielding baseball bats and in April 2003 won a court injunction to prevent protesters from approaching within 50 yards of employees' homes. However, the best known of such extremists have probably been the protesters against the Newbury bypass and, later, the new runway at Manchester Airport. Unlike the stereotypical scruffy lefties, these are often respectable middle-aged, middle-class people or their nice children. In consequence, the protesters were often not criticised but lauded and turned into minor folk heroes like Daniel Hooper, who under his activist name of 'Swampy' featured in many protests.

Perhaps the endorsement of 'respectable' middle-class opinion is crucial in terms of how the media cover such stories. The Greenham Common women – often muddy, strident, badly dressed and with crew-cut hair – who camped outside US cruise missile bases in the UK during the 1980s were generally given negative coverage, especially by the right-wing press. Perhaps this new militancy is part of a growing awareness of political power among ordinary citizens. It also suggests that a sea-change has occurred regarding citizens' view of themselves (see Box 10.8 on p. 198).

> When he [Bertrand Russell, venerable philosopher and CND stalwart] attempted, Luther like, to hammer a petition to the very door of the Ministry it opened before him, only to reveal an official armed with a polite attitude and some Sellotape. The police watched with scarcely veiled amusement.
>
> Jonathan Green, *All Dressed Up: The Sixties and the Counterculture*, 1999

Terror tactics

The use of terroristic methods in Western societies has usually been strongly opposed by the general public, but they have been used, and not just by extremist political groups like the Baader-Meinhof group in Germany. In the USA, anti-abortion campaigners have shot doctors who undertake abortion work, and closer to home the Animal Liberation Front has regularly held hostile and sometimes violent demonstrations outside laboratories conducting experiments on animals (see Box 10.3). In some cases the group has also planted bombs.

On 18 June 1999, the group Reclaim the Streets and an alliance of environmental groups took over the City of London in an action that involved violence. In an article in the *Observer* (31 October 1999) entitled 'The New Revolutionaries', we see that some groups begin with limited aims focusing on one policy area, then widen their focus to take in wider targets for change. An activist for RTS is quoted as saying:

We tried all the tree hugging at the Newbury bypass. It did get some great publicity, but the road still got built. We lost. There are a lot of us who now recognise we can't pick individual battles; we have to take on the whole system.

BOX 10.3   EXAMPLE

The case of Darley Oaks Farm and Gladys Hammond

In October 2004, thieves stole the body of Gladys Hammond, mother-in-law to Christopher Hall, owner of a farm in Staffordshire which bred guinea pigs for scientific experimentation. In 2005 four activists were charged with conspiracy to backmail. The leader of the group was revealed as Jon Ablewhite, a clergyman's son, who had led a six-year campaign against the farm. He was a charismatic character, six feet plus, according to a fellow activist: motivated and organised – 'amicable and educated, just the type you need'. When the farm eventually stopped breeding guinea pigs he was ecstatic, saying: 'Factory farming is on the same moral level as the Holocaust because of the systematic abuse and killing of these animals. Don't forget that Goebbels learned from factory farmers and used their methods to execute the Jews.' Mrs Hammond's remains were recovered in 2006 and reburied on 31 May.

Jon Ablewhite, accused of desecration of Gladys Hammond's grave
Source: Chris Radburn / PA / Empics

At this point pressure groups are beginning to leave the world of merely influencing policy and are joining that of political parties.

A curious example of a pressure group which was undermined by members prepared to use extremist methods is Fathers 4 Justice. This was formed in December 2002 by marketing executive Matt O'Connor who had suffered from legal decisions denying him access to his children after divorce. His idea was to use high profile but basically amusing stunts to win public attention: 'ordinary dads doing extraordinary things'. After a number of harmless stunts, the organisation overstretched itself when on 18 January 2006 it transpired that a group connected with Fathers 4 Justice had planned to kidnap Tony Blair's five-year-old son Leo. The idea, it seemed, was to hold him for a while and then set

him free unharmed, but Matt O'Connor was dismayed: 'We do peaceful direct action with a dash of humour. We're in the business of uniting dads with their kids, not separating them.' He indicated that his group would cease to function. In April 2009, a member of climate change group, Plane Stupid, was cautioned by police after she threw green custard over Peter Mandelson in March. She commented:

Despite the harmless and comic nature of my antics, the police informed me that throwing custard over an unelected government minister could be seen as a public order offence and have cautioned me accordingly . . . Climate change is the greatest threat we have ever faced through which millions will lose their lives and livelihoods.

(*Guardian*, 10 April 2009)

BOX 10.4   IDEAS AND PERSPECTIVES

Violence as a political weapon

Writing in the *Guardian* on 14 November 2005, columnist Gary Younge discussed the riots devastating French suburbs and considered the efficacy of violent means to achieve political ends. He quoted African-American abolitionist Frederick Douglass's aphorism that 'Power concedes nothing without a demand. It never did and it never will.' He pointed out that the mostly unemployed ethnic minorities, living in rundown estates and suffering racial discrimination, had nothing to lose, but their actions immediately won concessions and government actions designed to alleviate their problems. Younge comments that 'none of this would have happened without the riots'. Any amount of peaceful measures would have attracted feeling attention but it was the damage to property and the threat to life which galvanised the French government. He went on to assert that 'When all non-violent, democratic means of achieving a just end are unavailable, redundant or exhausted, rioting is justifiable', but he goes on to add: 'Rioting should be neither celebrated nor fetishised, because it is a sign not of strength but of weakness. Like a strike, it is often the last and most desperate weapon available to those with the least power.' He warns that rioting easily becomes an end in itself and something which can polarise, divide and set loose murder and mayhem in society. He issues something like a partial endorsement of violence as a political weapon, urging that it be used with restraint and economy. Yet, critics might suggest to him, the problem is that using the threat of chaos to win concessions is perilously close to unleashing the real thing.

Also addressing this topic, Professor Timothy Garton Ash, writing in the *Guardian* on 2 March 2006, perceived the emergence of a 'group veto' by groups who say:

We feel so strongly about this that we are going to do everything we can to stop it. We recognize no moral limits. The end justifies the means. Continue on this path and you must fear for your life . . .

If the intimidators succeed, then the lesson for any group that strongly believes in anything is: shout more loudly, be more extreme, threaten violence, and you will get your way.

Inch by inch, paragraph by paragraph, we are becoming less free.

He concludes that any point of view which does not threaten harm should be tolerated – even right-wing historian David Irving's Holocaust denials – but that any person or group which urges 'kill the Jews!' or 'kill the Muslims!' should be 'met with the full rigour of the law'.

Aiming for the power points

Pressure groups seek to influence the political system at the most accessible and cost-effective 'power points'. The obvious target areas include:

1 *The public at large*: Groups seek to raise money, train staff, attract and mobilise membership, to assist in group activities and to apply pressure on their behalf.

2 *Other pressure group members*: Groups with similar objectives will often duplicate membership, e.g. Friends of the Earth members may also join Greenpeace. Moreover, such groups can combine forces over particular campaigns such as the Countryside Alliance, which coordinated a heterogeneous collection of groups against Labour's threatened ban on fox hunting (see Box 10.9 on p. 201).

3 *Political parties*: Groups will seek to influence the party that seems most sympathetic to its views. Inevitably trade unions – the historical crucible of the labour movement – look to Labour, and business groups tend to concentrate on the Conservatives (see below). Constitutional reform groups such as Charter 88 initially looked to the Liberal Democrats but, as such support was already solid, it embarked on a successful campaign to convert the Labour Party. Interestingly, the Campaign for Nuclear Disarmament achieved a similar conversion back in the 1960s and in the early 1980s but never achieved its objective, as Labour decided to abandon such a policy during the later part of the decade.

4 *Parliament*: Especially the House of Commons, but in recent years increasingly the House of Lords. The Commons is more attractive to groups as this is where the important debates on legislation occur. As Box 10.1 shows, groups often draft amendments for friendly MPs – often asked to hold voluntary office – to submit in Parliament. MPs are also sought – and this may be their most important function for some groups – for their ability to provide access to even more important people, such as the increasingly important Select Committees and

(especially) regular meetings with ministers and civil servants. This ability to provide access – sometimes at a price – has been at the centre of the rows over sleaze that dogged Major's government and has also affected Blair's administration. The academic Study of Parliament Group surveyed a number of groups, discovering that over three-quarters were in regular contact with MPs; some 60 per cent said the same of members of the Lords.

5 *Ministers and civil servants*: Clearly, ministers and their civil servants are natural targets for groups. Regular access provides 'insider' status and potentially composition of the policy-making 'triangle' also comprising ministers and civil servants (see Chapter 21). Baggott's (1988) research shows that 12 per cent of insider groups will see Cabinet ministers weekly, 45 per cent monthly; the figures for junior ministers were 14 and 67 per cent, respectively.

Groups anxiously seek membership of key bodies, which include:

■ Over 300 executive bodies with 4,000 members with the power to disburse financial resources.

■ Nearly 1,000 advisory committees with some 10,000 members.

■ Committees of inquiry into a myriad of topics (Labour, especially, have favoured such task forces since coming to power).

■ *Royal Commissions*: Not favoured by Conservative governments after 1979 but re-embraced by Blair's Labour government.

■ *Pre-legislative consultation*: It is established government practice that all interested parties should be asked to consult and give their views on proposed new legislation. For example, changes affecting universities are circulated not just to them but to groups with a strong interest in such education (such as the former Association of University Teachers). It was alleged that the Conservative governments after 1979 went through the motions of consulting but often allowed only a very short time and then ignored the advice anyway.

6 European Union (EU): Pressure group activity is like a river in that it seeks out naturally where to flow. Since power has shifted to Brussels so groups have automatically shifted their focus too. In the early days, when there was no elected European Parliament, their activities helped to reduce the '**democratic deficit**' (Greenwood 1997: 1), but since the Single European Act in 1986 groups have played an increasingly important role as the competence of EU institutions has expanded to include the environment and technology. The Maastricht Treaty of 1992 also extended EU powers into health and consumer protection. The Commission has calculated that there are 3,000 interest groups in Brussels, including more than 500 Europe-wide federations and employing 10,000 personnel (Greenwood 1997: 3). In addition there are over 3,000 lobbyists, a huge increase in just a few years. These lobbyists and groups – especially the business ones – invest the substantial resources needed to set up shop in the heart of Belgium because they feel the stakes are so high. The EU can make decisions that deeply affect, among others, the work and profits of fishermen, farmers and the tobacco industry, as well as the conditions of employment of trade unionists. Greenwood discerns five areas of EU activity that attract group pressure:

■ *Regulation*: Much of the EU's output of directives comprises rules governing the way the consumer is served. Indeed, in some sectors the bulk of new regulatory activities now takes place not in Whitehall but in Brussels.

■ *Promotion*: For example, the development of key technologies to support export drives.

■ *Integration*: Such as the measures to advance free and fair competition in the Single Market.

■ *Funding*: Such as the Structural Funds to reduce regional imbalances or funds for research activities.

■ *Enablement*: Such as measures to support environmental improvement.

The SEA and Maastricht Treaty expanded the power of the European Parliament and made it possible for it to amend legislation; pressure groups directed their attentions accordingly. But the major source of group interest remains the Commission, a relatively small number of officials who can be influenced via the usual processes of presentations, briefing documents, networks, lunches and so forth. Some directorates are more receptive than others, but on the whole the institutions of the EU expect to be lobbied and welcome such attentions on the grounds that people wishing to influence measures usually represent those who will be affected by them and hence are likely to make useful inputs. The cross-sectoral federations are often consulted as they are thought to be broadly representative: for example, UNICE (Union of Industrial Confederations of Europe), the highly influential EUROCHAMBRES (the association of European Chambers of Commerce), and ETUC (European Trade Union Confederation).

7 *The media*: The director of the charity Child Poverty Action once said that 'coverage by the media is our main strategy' (Kingdom 1999: 512). Such a statement could equally be made by virtually all pressure groups outside those few insider groups at the epicentre of government policy and decision making. Unless influence is virtually automatic, any group must maximise its ability to mobilise the public to indicate its authority, its power and potential sanction; influencing the public can be achieved only via the media. Therefore ensuring that group activities catch the eye of the media is the number one priority. Unsurprisingly, Baggott's findings (1995) revealed that 74 per cent of outsider groups contacted the media weekly and 84 per cent did so monthly. Interestingly, the percentages for the insider groups were even higher at 86 and 94 per cent, respectively, suggesting that media coverage serves important interest reinforcement functions even for those with a direct line to the government's policy-making process.

8 *Informal contacts*: So far the contacts mentioned have been ones that are in the public domain; it is quite possible that most would have a written minute of proceedings. However, the world does not function just on the basis of formal, minuted meetings. Britain is a relatively small island with a ruling élite drawn substantially from the 7 per cent of the population who are educated in public schools. It might be claimed that such a critique is a little old-fashioned but many argue that the deep connections of class, blood, marriage, shared education and leisure pursuits link decision makers in the country in a way that makes them truly, in the words of John Scott (1991), a 'ruling class'. It might also be claimed that the above analysis relates more to the Conservative political élite than to the more widely drawn and variegated New Labour equivalent.

But arguably political decision-making is only one aspect of power in society – economic and cultural decisions can be very important for millions of people. Glinga (1986) describes the manifold ways in which the upper-class British mix at their public schools, carrying the badge of their accent with them as an asset into the outside world, where they continue to enact school-like rituals in gentlemen's clubs such as the Athenaeum, Brooks's, White's and the Army and Navy. There they can exchange views and influence friends in the very highest of places. Jeremy Paxman points out (Paxman, 1991) that when Sir Robin Butler was made Cabinet Secretary he was at once proposed for membership of the exclusive Athenaeum, Brooks's and the Oxford and Cambridge clubs. It was almost as if the 'Establishment' had made the appropriate room at their top table for the new recruit. In addition, when not in their clubs they can meet in other élite leisure places such as the opera at Covent Garden, Glyndebourne and Henley. This form of the 'Establishment' still exists and still

BIOGRAPHY

Sir Robin Butler (1938–)

Former Secretary to the Cabinet. Educated at Oxford, from where he joined the Treasury. Worked in private offices of Wilson and Heath before rising to Permanent Secretary in the Treasury and then Secretary to the Cabinet 1988–97. Perhaps appropriately for Britain's top civil servant, Butler seemed to epitomise many of the ideals of the British ruling élite: he was the well-rounded man (he was also a rugby blue); he was apparently modest, articulate and effortlessly able while at the same time being 'infinitely extendable': able to cope with any crisis or any demands on his time or intellect. In 2005 he issued his report into the intelligence on which the decision to go to war in Iraq was based, a report which contained a degree of criticism rare for such a senior member of the Establishment, though his solution was scarcely revolutionary: a return to traditional Cabinet government where papers are tabled and discussed with minutes taken and circulated.

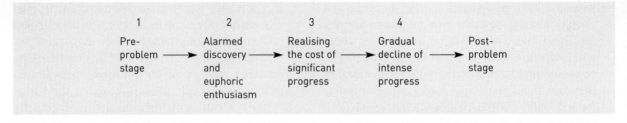

Figure 10.4 The issue attention cycle
Source: From A. McCulloch (1998) 'Politics and the environment', *Talking Politics*, Autumn 1998. Reproduced with permission from The Politics Association

exerts much influence; arguably the tendency for even New Labour to be agnostic over the social provenance of its élite members helps extend its influence. It is impossible to reckon the influence of such informal contacts, but some, especially the Marxists, claim that this is how the really big decisions are always made: in private and in secret between fellow members of the closely interlinked networks of the ruling élite. What follows in public is merely the democratic window dressing for self-interested fixing.

■ Factors determining effectiveness

The effectiveness of pressure groups is also a function of organisational factors. They need:

■ a coherent organisational structure;

■ high-quality and efficient staff (these days they recruit direct from the best universities);

■ adequate financial resources;

■ good leadership;

■ clear strategy.

Economic interest groups are usually well financed, but cause groups can often command significant annual income also; charities in 2008 managed to raise nearly £50bn. In addition, cause groups can compensate for shoestring resources by attracting high-quality committed leadership; for example, in the recent past, Jonathon Porritt (Friends of the Earth), Frank Field (CPAG), Mike Daube (ASH) and perhaps the most effective popular campaigner of them all, Des Wilson of Shelter and many other causes.

Good organisation is also of key importance, and the best pressure groups are as efficiently organised

as any business, with high-class staff recruited from the best universities.

■ Issue attention cycle

The American political scientist Anthony Downs has suggested that the media and the public's receptivity to pressure group messages is another potent factor influencing effectiveness. He pointed out that the new cause groups must run the gauntlet of the 'issue attention' cycle (see Figure 10.4). The pre-problem stage is followed by alarmed discovery, coupled with the feeling that something could and should be done. When it becomes clear, as it usually does, that progress will not be easy, interest declines and this is when the pressure group faces its toughest tests. This has certainly been true of environmental, nuclear disarmament and AIDS campaigns, but all three of these reveal that with new discoveries and fresh events the issue attention cycle can be rerun – possibly frequently over time.

■ Economic interest groups

The policies of the government in such areas as interest and exchange rates, taxation, spending, trading policy and industrial relations are important in providing the context for the economy. Two of the most powerful interest groups that try to influence these policies are business and trade unions.

Business

Business is naturally deeply affected by government economic policies, and it is understandable that its representatives will seek to exert influence. Many firms depend on government handouts, subsidies and orders and will seek to influence the awarding of contracts.

In one sense any sizeable business organisation acts like a pressure group. Multinational companies – many with turnovers larger than those of small countries – make their own regular and usually confidential representations to government. When conditions for trading appear more favourable in another country, they pack up and move their whole operation, often within months. The threat to do this and deny employment is a potent weapon which such large companies use to barter advantages from governments.

Strength in unity

Particular industries often form federations, such as the Society of Motor Manufacturers or the Engineering Employers' Federation, and seek strength in unity. The Confederation of British Industry (CBI) was formed in 1965 and since that date has acted as an overall 'peak' organisation to provide a forum for discussion – it holds an annual conference – and to represent the views of members to government. It has a membership of 15,000, employs several hundred staff and has an annual budget of some £5 million. The CBI is dominated by big companies, and this helps to explain the 1971 breakaway Small Business Association (later the Federation of Small Businesses). For much of Margaret Thatcher's first term of office her policies of high interest and exchange rates damaged manufacturing industry, and the CBI criticised her for it. On one famous occasion, the then Director General of the CBI, Sir Terence Beckett, called for a 'bare-knuckle' fight to make Margaret Thatcher change her deflationary policies, but his violent rhetoric abated after a stormy confrontation with that formidable lady Prime Minister. Under Tony Blair's business-friendly Labour administration the CBI under Adair Turner was generally supportive of government policy, whilst his highly extrovert, near demagogic successor, Digby Jones, was more critical of government. It is expected that Richard Lambert, appointed to the post in March 2006 and a more cerebral insider (as a Labour-supporting former editor of the *Financial Times*), will be more measured and possibly more effective.

The Institute of Directors is a more right-wing and political campaigning body. It opposed prices and incomes restraints, which the CBI was prepared to support in the 1970s, and it vigorously supported the Conservative government's policies of privatisation, cutting public spending and encouraging free-market economics. Other organisations, such as Aims of Industry, are used as means of raising support and indirectly revenue for the Conservative Party. Although no business group has a formal association with the Conservative Party, a number of major firms do make financial contributions. Many businesses utilise the informal contacts mentioned above, especially when the Conservatives are in power, as this tends to open up the channels of communication between government and business. These may take the form of whispers in the ears of government ministers at dinner parties, in gentlemen's clubs and elsewhere.

Trade unions

Trade unions perform two distinct roles. The first is political. Since they helped to form the Labour Party in 1900 they have played, and still play, a decisive role in the internal politics of that party (see Box 10.5). Trade unions are overtly involved in party politics more deeply than any other interest group.

The second role of individual trade unions is industrial bargaining, to represent the interests of their members on pay and working conditions in negotiations with employers. Three-quarters of all unions are affiliated to the Trades Union Congress (TUC), which speaks for the trade union movement as a whole. In the past this function has involved unions directly in the political life of the country.

Various attempts were made by Labour and Conservative governments to win the agreement of unions to pay policies that would keep inflation in check and the cost of British exports competitive in overseas markets. By the late 1960s, Harold Wilson had become so exasperated with striking trade unions that he proposed measures to curb their tendency to strike and cripple the economy. However, his White Paper 'In Place of Strife' was attacked by the unions, and James Callaghan led a successful revolt against it in the Cabinet, destroying the authority of Wilson's government. Ted Heath's administration after 1970 worked hard to solve the problem of union disruption and eventually tried a statutory (i.e. passing new laws) approach, but this foundered hopelessly and resulted in an election in 1974, which he lost. Labour back in power tried to stem the rocketing inflation by engineering a 'Social Contract' with the unions whereby they agreed to restrain wage demands in exchange for favourable policies

BOX 10.5 IDEAS AND PERSPECTIVES

Ever since February 1900, when the Labour Representation Committee, the embryo of the party, was formed, trade unions have played a key role and are the category of pressure group most closely involved in mainstream politics.

- *Affiliation*: Half of all trade unions are affiliated to the party including the majority of the big unions: Amicus, CWU, TGWU and USDAW. Other unions can have more complex relationships with the party: Unison has a general political fund as well as an affiliated one.
- *Money link*: A union's political fund receives money from members along with their subscriptions unless they specifically 'contract out'. Unions, if affiliated, decide how much to give to Labour from their funds. One calculation in 2005 was that contributions collected in this fashion and donated to Labour amounted to £24 million between 2002 and 2005, comprising half of the funding the party needs annually.
- *Membership*: Each union decides how many members it wishes to say pay the political levy. Those union members who pay the levy can join the party at a reduced rate:
- *Representation*: Union 'block votes' – leaders casting votes on behalf of affiliated members – used to dominate conference voting decisions, but the proportion allowed to count by the block votes was reduced to only 50 per cent in 1996, and the party's stated aim is to achieve 'one member, one vote' eventually.
- *Volunteers*: These provide the foot soldiers of the Labour Party; nearly three-quarters of trade unionists are party members and over half voted Labour at the last two elections.
- *Problems in Blair's second and third terms*: Blair's predilection for 'modernising' public services by involving private companies in their operations won him few friends in the unions, especially the new breed of leaders he now faced, who had not experienced the dog years of Labour's opposition to Thatcher.

on pensions, low pay and industrial legislation. This succeeded to an extent and for a while the UK had a pay regime that was almost Scandinavian in its harmony between business and workers, but in 1978 Callaghan's call for a 5 per cent limit was rejected by the unions, and his government descended into the ignominy of the 'winter of discontent' (January–February 1979) with, infamously, bodies left unburied and operating theatres without electricity.

Subsequently, Margaret Thatcher introduced a series of laws that emasculated union power: five Employment Acts and the 1984 Trade Union Act. These made unions liable for the actions of their members and rendered their funds liable to seizure by the courts, as the miners found to their disadvantage in 1984 when their lack of a strike ballot made them liable to sequestration of assets. Their bitter strike slowly ran out of steam and they suffered a humiliating defeat, which set the tone for union dealings with government for the rest of the decade. Days lost through strikes fell to an all-time low, and a kind of industrial peace held sway,

although at the cost of much bitterness. Margaret Thatcher refused to consult with the unions, and their occasional meetings proved to be cold and wholly unproductive. Unemployment helped to reduce the size of union membership by three million (a quarter) from 1979 to 1989. The growth of part-time work, mostly by women, did not help to swell membership much either, as such workers are notoriously difficult to organise. To minimise the impact of recession and shrinkage some unions decided to merge, such as Unison in 1993, the 1.3-million member public service organisation.

Margaret Thatcher, then, destroyed the power of the unions and John Major was the beneficiary, not to mention the leader of the incoming government, Tony Blair. In the run-up to the 1997 election the TUC sought to fashion an appropriate new role in relation to the government, which it expected to be a Labour one. Denying there had been any deal with Labour, John Monks said on 26 February 1997: 'We know there will be no special tickets to influence based on history or sentiment.'

BIOGRAPHY

John Monks (1945–)

Former General Secretary TUC, 1993–2003. Educated at Manchester University. Lifelong union official and made it to top TUC job when Norman Willis resigned in 1992. Moderate and conciliatory but – a sign of how the unions were moving against Blair – was moved to criticise the exclusion of unions from policy making under Blair. He sided with the Fire Brigades Union in autumn 2002 when it went on strike in support of a 40 per cent pay demand. He stood down in 2003 and was succeeded by Brendan Barber.

BOX 10.6 FACT

Union membership

- The TUC had 76 member unions, representing 7.62 million members in 1992 – a figure which dropped to 60 unions and 6.50 million members by 2009.
- Unite is the biggest union following the merger between Amicus, GMB and TGWU by 2007.
- 38 per cent of employees in their 40s are union members, but only 19 per cent of 19-year-olds.
- Women in full-time jobs are more likely to be union members than men in full-time jobs.
- 60 per cent of workers in the public sector are unionised, while only 20 per cent of private sector workers are members.

At the 1997 TUC Conference, Prime Minister Blair lectured the unions on their need to 'modernise': his favourite mantra. In 1999, he sought to charm them with a piece of doggerel verse. However, Blair has been careful not to encourage any thinking that the historical closeness of unions to Labour entitled them to any special treatment: 'fairness not favours' were the bluntly ungenerous terms to which he adhered. Some of his advisers were known to take seriously the possibility of severing the umbilical link with the unions. Blair showed every sign of wishing to maintain unions in the weakened state in which Thatcher had delivered them: reduced membership, limited ability to wage industrial conflict plus lowered morale and expectations after the trauma of the miners' strike. Despite some bitter conflicts like the firemen's strike in 2002, both Blair and Brown have enjoyed relative freedom from industrial conflict, and while they have not enjoyed their diminished status, union leaders have had to accept that most working people are much less militant now than during the 1970s and 1980s.

After the 2001 election victory, a new militancy seemed to emerge in the union movement with more outspoken leaders not prepared to keep quiet; these included Dave Prentis at Unison, Bob Crow at RMT and Mark Sewotka at PCS. But apart from the fireman's strike in 2002, unions have grumbled but not initiated any major industrial conflict. The victory won by Thatcher has left the unions still relatively emasculated.

Tripartism

This was the name given to Harold Macmillan's strategy of institutionalising contact between unions, employers and government in the form of the 1961 National Economic Development Council (NEDC). It was hoped this approach – similar to those used in Germany and Nordic countries – would improve Britain's notoriously volatile industrial relations. Critics accused such developments as unwelcome examples of **corporatism** when elites of government and interest groups unite to 'fix' decisions above the heads of ordinary voters.

Trade Union and Labour Party Liaison Organisation (TULO) and the Warwick Agreement, 2004

This forum exists to discuss policy issues of mutual concern. It comprises the general secretaries of the affiliated unions plus the Prime Minister, the deputy Prime Minister, the Chair of the Labour Party and other party officials. Regional and devolved national equivalents mirror the national committee. At the National Policy Forum in July 2004 in Warwick a series of agreements were achieved which succeeded in mending some of the fences between the unions and a Labour government contemplating a third term. The agreement covered improved working conditions including the guarantee of four weeks paid holiday, exclusive of bank holidays; protection of pension funds in company transfer or mergers; a series of guarantees for workers in public services; and a similar package for those in manufacturing, including extending the restrictions on sacking striking workers from eight to twelve weeks. 'Warwick changed the mood', one senior official was quoted (John Kampfner, 2 September 2004); 'we now have to see if these pledges are acted on.' Blair's strategy was to make limited concessions on employment rights while not budging on his public services reform agenda or on collective employment rights.

■ The growth of professional lobbying

One of the striking features of recent years has been the rapid growth of professional lobbying companies. These offer to influence policy and effect high-level contacts in exchange for large amounts of money. Often, the lobbyists are selling the excellent contacts they have made during a previous career in Parliament or the Civil Service. In this respect, Britain has once again moved towards the American model; on Capitol Hill, this kind of activity has been an accepted part of political life for decades.

In Britain, over sixty lobbying organisations have been set up, ranging from the small Political Planning Services to the large (now defunct) Ian Greer Associates. Most major public relations companies have lobbying operations, either in house or via an established lobbying company. Over thirty Conservative MPs worked for lobbyists before the Nolan Report; consultancies could pay anything up to and beyond £10,000 per year. There has been pressure for the regulation of such agencies (in Washington, they have to be registered). Westminster lobbyists can charge clients around £30,000 a year for a 'full service', including lobbying ministers, civil servants and MPs to push their case.

Lord Nolan and the removal of sleaze

Sleaze is not an invention of New Labour by any means and its roots go back at least a decade and a half. On 15 January 1990, the Granada TV programme *World in Action* broadcast its report on MPs and outside interests. It quoted Richard Alexander MP, who had placed an advertisement in the House of Commons magazine as follows: 'Hard working backbench Tory MP of ten years standing seeks consultancy in order to widen his range of activities.' The programme was only one of several investigations at that time and later of how MPs used 'consultancy', often for commercial interests; in effect they were paid to apply pressure through their network of contacts in Parliament and Whitehall. In 1994, the *Sunday Times* approached two MPs, under the guise of being a commercial interest, and asked them to place questions on its behalf in exchange for money. In the ensuing media row the newspaper was criticised by many Conservative MPs for its underhand tactics, but the two MPs concerned, Graham Riddick and David Tredinnick, were the object of much more widespread and impassioned obloquy. A commission on 'standards in public life' – 'sleaze' according to the popular media – was set up by John Major under the judge Lord Nolan. This reported in the autumn of 1995 and was debated in November. Nolan suggested curbs on the economic activity of MPs and urged that they be obliged to reveal the extent of their earnings. On 6 November, Nolan's proposals were agreed and a new system was introduced whereby MPs are:

■ obliged to disclose earnings, according to income bands;

■ forbidden from tabling questions and amendments on behalf of outside interests;

■ restricted in what they can say in the chamber on behalf of such interests;

■ obliged to register all details of contracts with a new and powerful Parliamentary Commissioner (since March 1996).

However, the subject of sleaze was not excluded from the news even after Nolan, much as Major would have appreciated this. The *Guardian* newspaper ran a story accusing a junior trade minister, Neil Hamilton, of accepting money when a backbench MP in exchange for asking questions and being in the employ of the well-known lobbying company Ian Greer Associates, the then agent of the owner of Harrods, Mr Mohamed Al Fayed. Al Fayed was running a campaign to prevent the tycoon Tiny Rowlands from regaining control of the store, and he also desperately wanted to win British citizenship.

Hamilton declared that he would sue (as he had successfully and sensationally against the BBC when *Panorama* had accused him of fascist tendencies).

However, in October 1996, in a major climbdown, he announced the withdrawal of his action on grounds of finance. The *Guardian* responded by calling him a 'liar and a cheat' on its front page. The story continued when the subject was referred to the Standards and Privileges Committee. Hamilton was trounced in the general election by the anti-corruption independent candidate Martin Bell. The memory of Conservative sleaze did not go away but Labour too came in for criticism. In March 2007 a number of people nominated for peerages were revealed to have loaned the Labour Party large sums of money at the suggestion of Labour's fund raiser Lord Levy. The resultant corruption scandal entailed a long running police inquiry, arrests of various people and even the interviewing of the prime minister, Tony Blair. In July 2007 it was announced by the Crown Prosecution Service that no action would be taken in connection with the allegations. In January 2009 Labour initiated an enquiry into allegations by the *Sunday Times* that four of its Members in the House of Lords had taken money for moving amendments to legislation passing through the chamber. Again the CPS decided to take no action.

■ Pressure groups and democracy

Do pressure groups contribute towards a healthier democracy? As in the debate over the media in Chapter 8, it depends on what is meant by 'democracy'. The commonly accepted version of British representative or pluralist democracy accords the media a respected if not vital role. According to this view:

1 Pressure groups provide an essential freedom for citizens, especially minorities, to organise with like-minded individuals so that their views can be heard by others and taken into account by government.

2 They help to disperse power downwards from the central institutions and provide important checks against possibly over-powerful legislatures and executives.

3 They provide functional representation according to occupation and belief.

4 They allow for continuity of representation between elections, thus enhancing the degree of participation in the democratic system.

5 They provide a 'safety valve', an outlet for the pent-up energies of those who carry grievances or feel hard done by.

6 They apply scrutiny to government activity, publicising poor practice and maladministration.

However, some claim that groups operate in a way that harms democracy. They claim the following:

1 The freedom to organise and influence is exploited by the rich and powerful groups in society; the poor and weak often have to rely on poorly financed cause groups and charitable bodies.

2 Much influence is applied informally and secretly behind the closed doors of ministerial meetings, joint civil service advisory committees or informal meetings in London clubs. This mode of operating suits the powerful insider groups, while the weaker groups are left outside and have to resort to ineffective means such as 'knocking on the door' through merely influencing public opinion.

3 By enmeshing pressure groups into government policy-making processes, a kind of 'corporatism' (see below) has been established that 'fixes' decisions with ministers and civil servants before Parliament has had a chance to make an input on behalf of the electorate as a whole.

4 Pressure groups are often not representative of their members and in many cases do not have democratic appointment procedures for senior staff.

5 Pressure groups are essentially sectional – they apply influence from a partial point of view rather than in the interests of the country as a whole. This tendency has led some political scientists to claim that in the 1970s Britain became harder to govern (King 1975b), exacerbating conflict and slowing down important decision-making processes.

■ Theoretical perspectives

Pluralism

This approach is both descriptive in that it claims to tell us how things are and normative in that it believes this is generally a good way for things to be. The importance of pressure group activity was first recognised by commentators in this country in the 1950s, taking their lead (as so often before and since) from an American scholar, on this occasion Robert Dahl, who believed that major decisions were taken in an American democracy – where power was widely dispersed and shared – through negotiation between competing groups. In 1957, British journalist Paul Johnson said pretty much the same thing about his own country, adding 'Cabinet ministers are little more than the chairmen of arbitration committees'. Samuel Beer, with his concept of 'new group politics', supported this view, believing the wartime controls, in which groups voluntarily aided the government in getting things done, to have survived the peace with the 'main substance' of political activity taking place between the 'public bureaucrats' of the government and the 'private bureaucrats . . . of the great pressure groups'. However, this pluralist approach was soon much criticised for claiming that power was equally dispersed and that access to government was open. Critics maintained that rich business interests would always exercise disproportionate influence and win better access.

Policy networks

This theory was constructed by political scientists Richardson and Jordan, with considerable help from Rhodes. It suggested that groups and other sources of advice were crucial to the formation of policy. They saw departments constructing 'policy communities' with stable membership of just a few insider groups; policy would flow from this community in consultation with ministers and officials. A looser collection of groups was discerned in 'issue networks'. These comprised a shifting membership of groups and experts who were only occasionally consulted and were – to use American parlance – 'outside the loop' (see also Chapter 21).

Corporatism

Corporatism – sometimes prefixed by 'neo-' or 'meso-' (Smith 1993: Chapter 2) – was in some ways a development of **pluralism** in that it perceived a contract of sorts taking place between the most powerful groups in the country, rather as Beer saw happening in the war, whereby the government exchanged influence with the groups for their agreement to deliver member compliance. In the

---

BOX 10.8   IDEAS AND PERSPECTIVES

The importance of citizen campaigning

Des Wilson was probably the best-known popular campaigner in the country – during the 1960s and 1970s – before he became a 'poacher turned gamekeeper' and joined the public relations staff of British Airports Authority. On a Tyne Tees TV programme in 1986 he explained his own philosophy on citizen campaigning and suggested ten guidelines for people wishing to become involved in such campaigns.

It is very important to remember that the very existence of campaigners, the fact that people are standing up and saying 'No, we don't want this, this is what we want instead', is terribly important because it makes it impossible for the political system to claim that there is no alternative to what they are suggesting.

Citizen organisations are about imposing citizen priorities on a system which we have set up which doesn't always act as well for us as it should. The more we can impose human values by maintaining surveillance, getting involved in organisations, being prepared to stand up and be counted, the better. Even if we are beaten the important thing is that the case has been made, the voice has been heard, a different set of priorities has been set on the table.

Our movement is, if you like, the real opposition to the political system because I believe all the political parties are actually one political system which runs this country. If we are not satisfied, it's no use just switching our vote around and it's no use complaining 'They're all the same, those politicians'. We can create our own effective opposition through our own lives by standing up and making demands on our own behalf.

Guidelines for campaigners

1 *Identify objectives*: Always be absolutely clear on what you are seeking to do. It is fatal to become side-tracked and waste energy on peripheral issues.

2 *Learn the decision-making process*: Find out how decisions are made and who makes them.

3 *Formulate a strategy*: Try to identify those tactics that will best advance your cause and draw up a plan of campaign.

4 *Research*: Always be well briefed and work out alternative proposals to the last detail.

5 *Mobilise support*: Widespread support means more political clout and more activists to whom tasks can be delegated.

6 *Use the media*: The media are run by ordinary people who have papers or news bulletins to fill. They need good copy. It helps to develop an awareness of what makes a good story and how it can be presented attractively.

7 *Attitude*: Try to be positive, but also maintain a sense of perspective. Decision makers will be less likely to respond to an excessively strident or narrow approach.

8 *Be professional*: Even amateurs can acquire professional research media and presentational skills.

9 *Confidence*: There is no need to be apologetic about exercising a democratic right.

10 *Perseverance*: Campaigning on local issues is hard work: this should not be underestimated. Few campaigns achieve their objectives immediately. Rebuffs and reverses must be expected and the necessary resilience developed for what might prove to be a long campaign.

Source: Jones (1986)

Scandinavian countries and Germany, something very like this contract had already become a regular part of the political process.

Corporatism, in one sense, was a means of bridging the gap between a capitalist economy and the socialist notions of planning and democratic consultation. To some extent this altered analysis matched the transition in Britain from a governing Conservative Party, whose ethos was against intervention, to a Labour one, whose ethos was in favour. The drift towards something called corporatism was perceived at the time and criticised by left-wingers such as Tony Benn and centrists such as David Owen.

The Marxist analysis of pressure groups

Marxists would argue that the greater role accorded to the state in corporatism is only an approximation of the real control exercised by business through the state; as Marx said, 'the state is nothing but an executive committee for the bourgeoisie'. The whole idea of pluralist democracy, therefore, is merely part of the democratic window dressing that the ruling economic group uses to disguise what is in reality its hegemonic control. Naturally, according to this view, the most potent pressure groups will be the ones representing business, while trade unions, for the most part, will be given a marginal role and will in any case act as 'duped' agents of the capitalist system, labouring under the 'false consciousness' that they are not being exploited.

New Right

According to the New Right analysis, shared by Margaret Thatcher, pressure groups do not enhance democracy as they are primarily interested in their own concerns and not those of wider society. They represent only a section of society, usually the producers, and leave large groups, such as the consumers, unrepresented. Also according to this view, pressure groups 'short-circuit' the proper working of the system by promiscuously influencing the legislature and the executive so that the former cannot properly represent the interests of all and the latter cannot implement what has been decided.

From the politics of production to the politics of consumption

At a conference at Salford University in March 2002, Professor Wyn Grant explained the evolution of pressure groups since the end of the Second World War. He perceived four phases:

1 *1945–60, establishment politics*: This occurred in response to the vast Keynesian extension of government intervention in the economy and the life of the country via the welfare state. Groups representing staff in these new public sector activities negotiated closely with governments of both colours and established rules as well as conventions of behaviour.

2 *1960–1979, tripartism*: Emergence of a new generation of cause groups. Government consultation with business and unions became formalised into tripartism, but cause groups were beginning to change with an explosion of membership for environmental groups.

3 *1979–1997, tripartite and professional groups downgraded*: Mrs Thatcher felt that she did not need advice from groups and resisted the close

contact they demanded. She also saw herself on a mission to dismantle the privilege and unfair practices that characterised many professions and their representative bodies. Insider groups still operated, but they were even less visible and were often disappointed.

4 *1997–, third way?* Tony Blair started by appearing willing to consult widely, although with definite care in respect of the unions. However, the rise of well-organised popular movements like the fuel protesters in September 2000, the Countryside Alliance and the Anti-War Movement in March 2003 revealed that 'outsider' groups were usurping the previously dominant role of insider groups: the former can now fill the streets and affect policy through delay or even effect reformulation. Grant assesses the Blair government as the most pro-business government (accepting of the disciplines of globalisation) since the war – more so even than Thatcher. He also suggests that a major

The hunting fraternity lamented the ban on their pastime, but did their best to get round its provisions

Source: Copyright © Chris Riddell. From the *Observer* 21 November 2004. Reproduced with permission from Guardian Newspapers Limited

shift has taken place from the 'politics of production' to the 'politics of collective consumption'. The former involved struggles over the 'fruits of the production process' via élite bargaining, tending to use 'corporatism' to affect sectional issues. The latter, by contrast, uses the Internet to organise dispersed support, tends to concentrate on 'public goods' and core social values (e.g. GM crops), and tends to be very media-driven (e.g. the fuel crisis of September 2000).

BOX 10.9 EXAMPLE

Banning fox hunting

In his 1997 manifesto, Tony Blair promised to ban fox hunting, and the Commons voted to do so in November 1997 by 411 votes to 151. However, the House of Lords rejected the bill and shortly afterwards the Countryside Alliance and its allies mobilised an impressive campaign involving a mass march to London. Lord Burns, former Treasury head, submitted a report in June 2000 which concluded that fox hunting 'seriously compromises the welfare of the fox'. Home Secretary Jack Straw then drew up a bill with three options: the status quo, a ban or a form of licensed hunting activity. The political problem for Blair was that his back-benchers saw the issue more as a 'class' issue and the advantages of a ban began to look less attractive once the pressure groups involved mounted a mass opposition, which also persuaded sceptical middle-class voters that maybe hunting was something which should be allowed after all.

In December of the same year, the Commons voted for a ban 373–158, but the Lords went for the status quo and the bill failed for lack of time in the Lords Committee stage. In June 2001, a commitment to a ban was repeated in Labour's manifesto; in March 2002, the Lords voted for the middle way 'licensed option'. Opponents of the legislation used clever public relations stunts, including a horse and dogs parade outside Parliament in May 2002. In July four Labour MPs, including the agriculture minister Elliot Morley, had their constituency offices attacked by balaclava-helmeted militants. The same group, the Real Countryside Alliance, disowned by the original body, defaced many public signs and buildings as part of its campaign in the north of England. Then in September 2002 an unusual approach was taken by the rural affairs minister Alun Michael. He invited a number of the protagonists in the debate to air their views over three days under his chairmanship. After the three days Michael announced that a bill would be drawn up shortly. It would bring fox hunting within the ambit of animal welfare legislation, which bans unnecessary cruelty. It was intended that local tribunals would decide where hunting performed a useful purpose to farmers or the landscape, outweighing suffering caused to animals.

On Sunday 22 September 2002, a huge demonstration was mounted by the Countryside Alliance in London. Called the Liberty and Livelihood March, it involved over 400,000 marchers: the biggest demonstration ever in the British capital at the time. It would seem that no government can ignore such a mobilisation of opinion in the 24/7 media age. Blair did ignore protesters over Iraq but paid a heavy political price. The government retreated from the outright ban for which many of its supporters craved, and the resultant Hunting Bill sought to allow hunting to proceed on a licensed basis. In the summer of 2003 Labour's Commons majority, on a free vote, overturned the government's preferred option of regulating fox hunting, and banned it completely. However, on 21 October the Lords rejected the ban and reinstated the regulated proposal. The legislative part of the saga was ended in November 2004 when Speaker Martin invoked the Parliament Act – used for only the fourth time since 1949 when it was passed – meaning that the ban on fox hunting came into force in February 2005. Pressure groups representing rural interests indulged in last-minute demonstrations and were galvanised to work against a Labour victory in the May election, but the political facts were that public opinion was generally in favour of a ban, so were a massive majority of Labour MPs, and Blair won a comfortable victory in May 2005. Since then the issue has subsided somewhat, though it seems some local hunts insist on riding out and stretching the law to its absolute limits, if not beyond on some occasions.

Writing in the *Observer* on 26 February 2006, Nick Cohen argued that:

The anti-hunting law that aroused so much passion is now producing contempt and indifference. Only one hunt has closed and hunters behave as if the 700 hours of parliamentary debate that preceded the ban was so much wasted breath . . . The difficulty was always that the anti-hunters weren't trying to protect foxes, but punish a particular kind of hunter: the Tory toff with red coat and redder face. . . . Today a farmer can still shoot or snare a fox, but if he goes after it with more than two dogs, the police will arrest him. That's the theory. In practice, the police have arrested hardly anyone.

BOX 10.10 BRITAIN IN CONTEXT

Pressure/interest groups

Most political systems contain concentrations of power which can exert some control over the system as a whole or over specific policies. This is true for democracies and autocracies alike, though the respective roles played by groups in both types of government differ greatly.

'Lobbies', as interest groups are called in the US – the most important of which are based in K St, Washington DC – have a particularly high profile for a number of reasons. Firstly, the three separate institutions of government – legislature, executive, judiciary – invite access in Washington and in their state-level equivalents, not to mention the primaries and related campaigns which groups can influence through financial contributions. Secondly, lobbyists are accepted as legitimate players in the political system, advancing views in a free society. Thirdly, interests surrounding presidents have tended to occupy favoured places in the White House. Thus civil rights bodies flourished and advanced their causes when Kennedy and Johnson were in office; while oil interests, especially the Halliburton company, won contracts and powerful executive offices for former employees under Bush.

The downside of all this activity is the constant suspicion that wealthy interests are winning favours in exchange for cash payments – either direct to politicians or indirectly via election campaign funds. Currently Jack Abramoff, a colourful and hugely influential Washington lobbyist, is on trial effectively for bribing powerful politicians to make decisions in the interests of his clients. Court cases are rare but serve to confirm the 'tip of the iceberg' suspicion that this has become almost an accepted part of the way in which American politics works.

Because US politics, not unlike those of the UK, are so open, the accusation of 'corporatism' – when state and interest groups combine to dominate decision-making – is seldom made. Countries regarded as much more corporatist are usually found in Europe, examples being Austria, Denmark, Germany, Finland and Ireland.

At the other end of the political scale autocratic governments do not usually allow formal access to groups. Less well developed countries, especially those in Africa, face the constant danger that the military – often the most powerful group in the country – will step in to take over, or at least do the bidding of a dictator who does not have national interests closest to his heart. But even a regime like that of the Chinese will consult widely with its doctors before changing its medical arrangements or with its businessmen and women before joining international trade organisations. Dictators should beware: if the needs of their people are constantly and flagrantly ignored, history suggests they will invariably rise up and cast off the shackles. Countless examples can be cited from Latin America, Africa and in the 1980s Eastern Europe where, for example, the Romanian leader Ceauşescu was overthrown and summarily executed.

In recent years the advance of globalisation has seen the emergence of hundreds of NGOs or 'non-government organisations' that may be associated with global bodies like the United Nations or the World Bank, with charities like Oxfam and Médecins sans Frontières, or with environmental issues like Greenpeace.

Chapter summary

Pressure groups seek to influence policy and not control it. 'Insider' groups, which have won acceptance by government, have traditionally had a privileged position compared with 'outsider' groups on the periphery, which tend to use high-profile techniques that serve to disguise their lack of real influence. Business groups seek to influence through the CBI and other channels, while trade unions have lost much power since 1979. Theoretical approaches include pluralism, corporatism and Marxism. The professional lobbying of Parliament and government has raised questions of democracy and legality, which the Nolan Committee was set up to address. On balance, pressure group influence has probably waned since 1979 but some groups, concerned with environmental and animal issues, have increased their influence and membership. Perhaps a shift has occurred in the way pressure groups interact with government, with widely popular movements now placing government under a kind of intense pressure it is loath to ignore.

Discussion points

■ Why do pressure groups emerge?

■ Why does government seek out groups and try to gain their cooperation?

■ Describe an example of pressure group activity from the recent past and consider what it tells you about the way groups operate.

■ Why do New Right thinkers dislike the influence of pressure groups?

Further reading

For the student the books and articles by Grant (1985, 1988, 1989, 2000) are the clearest and most useful, but Baggott (1995) is one of the most comprehensive current accounts and is very accessible. Smith (1993) is a study of some of the more theoretical aspects of the topic. On trade unions, see McIlroy (1995), Taylor (1993) and, on the impact of the Thatcher years, Marsh (1993). Baggott (1995) is good on European groups (pp. 206–19), and Greenwood (1997) offers a comprehensive study. Of the big textbooks, Kingdom (1999) provides excellent coverage (pp. 507–36), as does Coxall and Robins (1998) (pp. 167–86).

Bibliography

Ashbee, E. (2000) 'Bowling alone', *Politics Review*, September.

Ashford, N. and Timms, D. (1992) *What Europe Thinks: A Study of Western European Values* (Dartmouth).

Baggott, R. (1988) 'Pressure groups', *Talking Politics*, Autumn.

Baggott, R. (1992) 'The measurement of change in pressure group politics', *Talking Politics*, Vol. 5, No. 1.

Baggott, R. (1995) *Pressure Groups Today* (Manchester University Press).

Beck, U. (1992) *The Risk Society* (Sage).

Casey, T. (2002) 'Devolution and social capital in the British regions', *Regional and Federal Studies*, 12.3.

Coxall, B. and Robins, L. (1998) *Contemporary British Politics* (Macmillan).

Giddens, A. (1998) *The Third Way* (Polity Press).

Glinga, W. (1986) Legacy of Empire (Manchester University Press).

Grant, W. (1985, 1990) 'Insider and outsider pressure groups', *Social Studies Review*, September 1985 and January 1990.

Grant, W. (1988) 'Pressure groups and their policy process', *Social Studies Review*.

Grant, W. (1989) *Pressure Groups, Politics and Democracy in Britain* (Phillip Allan).

Grant, W. (2000) *Pressure Groups and Politics* (Macmillan).

Green, J. (1999) *All Dressed Up: The Sixties and the Counterculture* (Pimlico).

Greenwood, J. (1997) *Representing Interests in the European Union* (Macmillan).

Hall, P. (1999) 'Social capital in Britain', *British Journal of Political Science*, 29.3, pp. 417–61.

HMSO, *Modernising Government*, March 1999, Cmnd 4310.

Inglehart, R. (1977) *The Silent Revolution: Changing Values and Political Styles among Western Publics* (Princeton University Press).

Jones, B. (1986) *Is Democracy Working?* (Tyne Tees Television).

King, A. (1975a) 'Overload: problems of governing in the 1970s', *Political Studies*, June.

King, A. (1975b) *Why Is Britain Becoming Harder to Govern?* (BBC Books).

Kingdom, J. (1999) *Government and Politics in Britain* (Polity Press).

Marsh, D. (1993) *The New Politics of British Trade Unionism* (Macmillan).

McCulloch, A. (1988) 'Politics and the environment', *Talking Politics*, Autumn.

McIlroy, J. (1995) *Trade Unions in Britain Today*, 2nd edn (Manchester University Press).

McLeod, R. (1998) 'Calf exports at Brightlingsea', *Parliamentary Affairs*, Vol. 51, No. 3.

Moran, M. (1985) 'The changing world of British pressure groups', *Teaching Politics*, September.

Nye, J. (1997) 'In government we don't trust', *Foreign Policy*, Autumn.

Pahl, R. and Winkler, J. (1974) 'The coming corporatism', *New Society*, 10 October.

Paxman, J. (1991) *Friends in High Places* (Penguin).

Political Studies Association News, Vol. 13, No. 5, March 2003.

Putnam, R.D. (1995) 'Bowling alone', *Journal of Democracy*, January.

Reeves, R. (1999) 'Inside the violent world of the global protestors', *The Observer*, 31 October.

Scott, J. (1991) *Who Rules Britain?* (Polity Press).

Simpson, D. (1999) *Pressure Groups* (Hodder & Stoughton).

Smith, M. (1993) *Pressure Power and Policy* (Harvester Wheatsheaf).

Taylor, R. (1993) *The Trade Union Question in British Politics* (Blackwell).

Useful websites

Directory of 120 NGO websites: www.oneworld.org/cgi-bin/babel/frame.pl
Amnesty International: www.amnesty.org
Countryside Alliance: www.countryside-alliance.org/index.html
Friends of the Earth: www.foe.co.uk
Greenpeace: www.greenpeace.org.uk
Outrage!: www.outrage.org.uk
Trades Union Congress: www.tuc.org.uk
Blog: http://skipper59.blogspot.com/

CHAPTER 11

Political parties

Richard Kelly

Learning objectives

- Elucidate the unpopularity of British political parties.

- Explain the parties' unpopularity, with reference to both internal party politics and wider sociological, ideological and cultural changes.

- Examine the similarities and differences between the main parties' policies.

- Inspect the various ideas concerning the current shape of Britain's party system.

- Assess the implications of economic recession for British party politics.

- Prescribe reforms which may galvanise party politics in the years ahead.

Introduction

By the autumn of 2007, as Britain moved into a new economic era, it was already clear that British party politics was in a less than robust condition. Indeed, it seemed defined by profound crisis and chronic instability. Events during the next two years only deepened that impression. This chapter will dissect the crisis of British party politics from four related positions:

First, it will examine the relationship between parties and the electorate, highlighting the apparent breakdown between the two. In explaining this breakdown, it will examine the connection between parties and our wider democratic culture, but also touch upon more specific areas such as party organisation, party funding and the seismic journalistic revelations of May–June 2009.

Secondly, it will assess the shifting relationship between the policies of the main parties, particularly since the onset of recession, and ask whether it is still realistic to talk of an inter-party 'consensus'.

Thirdly, it will consider the changing shape of our party system, positing the view that no such 'system' actually exists.

Finally, it will ask whether the current crisis of political parties offers a redemptive opportunity, or whether it leaves the alternative notion – that the major parties are now impotent and redundant – looking grimly irresistible.

■ Disconnection from voters

The symptoms

For at least a decade, it had been plain that there was a widening gap between Britain's major political parties and the electorate. This struck at the heart of our representative democracy, which is dominated by party competition, party policies and party governments. If voters were indeed disenchanted with political parties then, by implication, they were disenchanted with the very basis of our political culture. As the Houghton Report noted as long ago as 1976, 'if the parties fail, then democracy fails' (see Fisher 2008). However, by the first decade of the new century, there were clear signs that the parties were failing chronically in the eyes of voters.

Declining turnout

The most obvious indication of this was diminishing turnout at elections – elections, after all being largely defined by political parties. At the 2005 general election, only 61.5 per cent of eligible voters cast their votes, the second worst turnout since 1918. This meant that the number of voters abstaining was greater than the number voting for any political party – including the party that now governs us. In fact, only 21.6 per cent of eligible voters supported

Labour – a record low for a governing party – while the number of people voting Labour in 2005 was lower than in 1987, when Labour lost by a landslide. Among first-time voters, fewer than 40 per cent again chose to vote, while in many urban constituencies only a minority of voters voted. (In Manchester Central, for example, the figure was just 43 per cent.)

Electoral reformers had sometimes argued that low turnout was an indictment not so much of the *party system* as of the *electoral system*, particularly first-past-the-post's tendency to produce 'safe' seats where voting may seem pointless. However, under New Labour a range of new electoral systems have been introduced for various 'secondary' elections; and turnout in these elections has not been impressive either. Turnout in the European elections of 2009 (conducted under the 'party list' system of proportional representation) was just 34 per cent – lower than in 1989 and 1994, when first-past-the-post was still being used. Turnout in the Scottish Parliament and Welsh Assembly elections of 2007 (conducted under the 'additional member system' of PR) was 52 per cent and 43 per cent respectively, while turnout in the various mayoral elections (conducted under 'supplementary vote') has averaged less than 40 per cent. Even in the London mayoral election of 2008, involving an unusual range of colourful and well-known candidates, only a minority of electors (44 per cent) cast their vote. In short, there is no hard evidence as yet that a change of electoral system will energise voters.

Declining identification

Underlying such figures has been a sharp decline in the number of voters who feel an allegiance to any political party. In 1964, 42 per cent of voters 'strongly identified' with a political party, but only 10 per cent did so by 2005 – and this excludes the 39 per cent who did not vote at all. Linked to this has been a growing tendency to support candidates with no party affiliation at all. At the 2005 general election, this was reflected in the election of Richard Taylor in Wyre Forest and Peter Law in Blaenau Gwent – once a Labour fiefdom. Indeed, in the by-elections held in Blaenau Gwent in 2006, independents triumphed in both the Parliamentary and Welsh Assembly contests. In the 25 mayoral elections held between 2000 and 2009, independents triumphed in 10 – and all went on to secure re-election.

This trend towards 'post-party' candidates was exemplified strongly in the local authority elections of 2008. In Wales, independents secured a quarter of council seats and thus constituted a majority on 22 council seats. Likewise, in Barnsley, independents held a third of the council's seats. After these elections, it was often suggested that many of the successful independents were covert Tories, unwilling to disclose their true colours. But, even if that were the case, it is significant that politicians wishing to exploit the governing party's decline are now likely to voice contempt for all parties rather than one in particular.

Declining membership

Meanwhile, party membership has continued to decline. Party leadership contests now provide a useful guide to how many members the parties have, given that all the main ones now enfranchise their grass-root members (it is reasonable to assume that all but the most torpid of party members have some interest in who leads them). In this respect, the three leadership contests since 2005 are revealing.

In the 1950s, Conservative Party membership peaked at over 3 million. Yet, in the 2005 Conservative leadership contest, fewer than 200,000 votes were recorded, despite a lively and well publicised campaign (see Box 11.1). The Liberal Democrats claimed up to 100,000 members during the first 10 years of their existence (1988–1998). Yet, in their 2006 leadership contest, fewer than 42,000 votes were recorded (see Box 11.2). The Labour Party, on coming to power in 1997, claimed around 400,000 members. Yet, in its deputy leadership contest of 2007, fewer than 97,000 votes were registered by its constituency members (see Box 11.3).

BOX 11.1 FACT

The 2005 Conservative leadership contest

David Cameron: 134,466 (67 per cent)
David Davis: 64,398 (32 per cent)
Ballot papers returned: 198,844 (78 per cent)

NB: In the 2 preliminary ballots, confined to Conservative MPs, first Ken Clarke and then Liam Fox were eliminated.

BOX 11.2 FACT

The 2007 Liberal Democrat leadership contest

Nick Clegg: 20,988 (50.6 per cent)
Chris Huhne: 20,477 (49.4 per cent)
Ballot papers returned: 41,465 (65 per cent)

The 2007 Labour deputy leadership contest

Final round[a]

	MPs/MEPs	Constituency members	Affiliated members[b]	*Total*
Harriet Harman:	15.42%	18.83%	16.18%	*50.43%*
Alan Johnson:	17.91%	14.50%	17.15%	*49.56%*
Votes cast:	367 (99%)	96,756 (54%)	215,604 (8%)	312,727 (54%)

[a] There had been four previous rounds of voting, each eliminating the bottom-placed candidate. In order, these had been: Hazel Blears, Peter Hain, Hilary Benn and Jon Cruddas.

[b] Each of the three sections constituted a third of the votes in an electoral college.

As the *Power* report noted in 2006, overall party membership is at just a quarter of its 1964 levels, with only about 2 per cent of voters now members of a political party. The income of the main parties also points to diminishing membership. Fewer members obviously mean fewer subscriptions; and fewer subscriptions mean that the parties become ever more reliant upon institutional funding and the generosity of a few wealthy supporters. By 2006, Labour derived only 8 per cent of its income from member subscriptions, the Conservatives 10 per cent (it had been around 40 per cent fifty years earlier), and the Liberal Democrats 30 per cent. Fewer members also mean a much lower profile in local communities – the number of Conservative Clubs fell by a third between 1980 and 2005, which, in turn, distances parties further from mainstream voters.

The demographic of party membership is also instructive, with the two main parties' youth wings having fewer than 30,000 members between them. It may be an over-gloomy prognosis, and an over-dramatic extrapolation of current trends, but unless the younger generation of voters become enthused by political parties in later life, the concept of 'party membership' could be virtually obsolete by the middle of the century.

Alternative forms of political participation

A further symptom of the party–voter disconnection is the shift from party-based activism to single-issue protest movements and pressure group campaigns. As the *Power* inquiry exemplified, Greenpeace had 30,000 members in 1981 but 221,000 members by 2006; the Royal Society for the Protection of Birds had 98,000 members in 1971 but over a million by 2005 (it is an oft-quoted statistic that membership of the RSPB is greater than that of the three main parties combined). In 2002, over half a million took part in the Countryside Alliance's various demonstrations; in 2003, following the start of the Iraq war, 1.5 m took part in 'Stop The War' protests; in 2005, over 150,000 attended the 'Live8' concert in Hyde Park ahead of the G8 summit. According to the *Power* report, 42 per cent of voters had signed some sort of petition during the previous two years, double the reported number for 1974.

All this points to an alternative, 'post-party' form of political participation, underpinned by a vibrant populism that parties can only envy. Voters have not become disconnected from politics per se; merely the type of politics represented by political parties.

The causes

Social and cultural change

The declining popularity of political parties is a long-term trend, linked to the long-term decline of class alignment upon which the two main parties once thrived. Society is now infinitely more eclectic and diverse, and it may be that a handful of parties cannot reflect the multidimensional society we now have. The multitude of pressure groups may well be a better vehicle for the multitude of interests in modern Britain.

This cultural and sociological shift has been reinforced by the decline of deference and the emergence of a new 'karaoke culture', fuelled by prolonged affluence and a revolution in communications – particularly widespread access to the Internet. These trends have served to empower many voters, while eroding the belief that elites and specialists (including party leaders) somehow 'know best'. Voters with a political interest are now less willing to take their cue from political parties and are more willing to set up their own ad hoc organisations, in which they can play a central role – hence the exponential growth of pressure groups and single-issue campaigns.

Ideological change

Since the end of the Cold War, the growth of pressure group politics has been helped by the demise of the old left–right battle and the subsequent particularisation of political debate. Parties are essentially 'big picture' forms of political activity, addressing the nature of society as a whole rather than its specific elements. Yet parties in the post-Thatcher era have not differed hugely on what that big picture should be – highlighted by a shared acceptance of capitalism plus high public spending, and symbolised by the advent of New Labour after 1994 and David Cameron's 'compassionate Conservatism' after 2005 (Jenkins 2006; Elliott and Hanning 2007). To a large extent, this consensus merely reflected how the bulk of voters felt. Nevertheless, it fuelled their impression that parties are 'all the same' and hastened voters' drift towards forms of political activity with a narrower focus.

Disempowerment

For much of the twentieth century, the cogency of party politics stemmed from an assumption that parties who secured office could, through the implementation of their policies, make a significant difference to society. As already indicated, the emergence of a post-Thatcher consensus has circumscribed that view. However, even if major parties had the *will* to be radically different in power, it is no longer clear that they have the *capacity*. Following the end of the Cold War, the UK economy has been increasingly shaped by global economic forces beyond the governing parties' control, prompting some writers to posit a 'silent takeover' of the British economy (Hertz 2002). By the start of the twenty-first century, any plan by ruling parties to macro-manage the British economy in classic Keynesian fashion – and thus make bold promises to voters – looked archaic and implausible. (Gordon Brown's attempt to alter this impression will be examined at the end of this chapter.)

The globalisation of the British economy was reinforced by the steady Europeanisation of British government. The Single European Act 1986 and the Maastricht Treaty of 1991 had further eroded the autonomy of UK governing parties, while the EU treaties endorsed by New Labour (Amsterdam, Nice, Lisbon) did little to reverse the loss of sovereignty. By 2003, almost four-fifths of the new regulations which annually affected UK voters came not from the policies of the governing party but from decisions made within the EU (Nugent 2003). In areas such as agriculture, fisheries, transport, health/safety regulations, retailing and the environment, a UK party coming into power has limited capacity to alter policies that affected millions of UK voters. By 2009, there was evidence that voters were increasingly aware of this and had formed their own conclusions in terms of the importance of both UK political parties and the elections they contested (*YouGov/Sunday Telegraph*, 16 May 2009).

In theory, this might underline the parties' European elections campaigns. Yet these elections are circumscribed by the limited role of the European Parliament within the EU and the impact of Britain's 72 MEPs (in a Parliament comprising over 600 representatives). This situation might be altered by the emergence of cohesive, pan-European party campaigns. But there were few signs of this in Britain's 2009 European elections, with voters continuing either to treat EU elections sceptically or as an opportunity to protest-vote against the Westminster government.

Reforms by recent governments have further undermined the parties' ability to effect change. The ongoing privatisation programme since 1979 – accelerated by New Labour's Private Finance Initiatives – has left governing parties with far less responsibility for the administration of vital public services. The Government's abdication of routine control of interest rates, transferring it to the Bank of England, has affected parties' ability to shape fiscal policy. And, thanks to legislation in 1998, a governing party's ability to shape human rights has been significantly surrendered to the judiciary. In short, the thesis offered by Richard Rose in 1980 – that parties had only limited scope to 'make a difference' – has been steadily reinforced by subsequent developments.

Party organisation

When explaining the parties' disconnection from voters, the above developments have been compounded by changes to party organisation. At a time when our culture has become less elitist and

BOX 11.4 FACT

Selecting Conservative candidates[a]

1 Associations (constituency parties) in 'target' seats with fewer than 300 members must choose Parliamentary candidates via 'primary' ballots open to non-party members.[b]
2 In larger associations, members choose a shortlist, half of whom must be women. The association's executive makes the final selection.[c]
3 An association's executive must consider only applicants from the National Approved List.[d]

[a] These amendments to the selection process were introduced by the Party's Constitutional College in 2006.
[b] This idea was pioneered by the Reading East and Warrington South associations prior to the 2005 general election.
[c] This reverses the previous arrangement, whereby the executive shortlisted and the membership selected. The 'positive discrimination' clause was also introduced in 2006.
[d] The National Approved List comprises about 500 candidates selected by national party officials. Prior to the Bromley and Chislehurst by-election 2006, there was some friction between national and local officials after the latter resisted the advice of the former to choose an A-list candidate.

Source: Conservative Party

more democratic, the main parties appear to have become more elitist and less democratic in their own structures.

As Minkin's classic study of *The Labour Party Conference* showed, ordinary Labour members once exercised real influence through the party's various blocs – notably trade unions and constituency parties (CLPs). Yet, during the Blair era, these blocs were diluted by the doctrine of 'one-member-one-vote' (OMOV) which, though anti-elitist in theory, seems to have had the opposite effect in practice: individual members, separated from such blocs, had reduced power to avert and correct the wishes of the leadership (Jackson 2009).

As such, the spread of OMOV inside Labour was accompanied by its rising reputation for autocratic leadership and heavily centralised management – both of which resulted in the demotivation of ordinary members. The *Power* inquiry found that 61 per cent of CLP members had attended no party meetings in a year and, as one CLP member told the *Power* inquiry: 'The power we have locally is negligible, and I don't think we have any say over national policy at all' (underlined by their hostility to the Iraq war). When former MPs Clare Short and Alice Mahon left the Party after 2005, they both cited the erosion of CLP autonomy and the loss of grass-root influence over policy. The present author's study of Labour's 'policy forums' (set up in the late 1990s) found that, in terms of altering Government policy, they were a weak alternative to Labour's conference in the Wilson–Callaghan era (Kelly 2001a).

Despite the introduction of OMOV for its leadership contests in 1998, there have been similar trends within the Conservative Party since 2005 (Denham and O'Hara 2008). Constituency party autonomy in candidate selection has been threatened by the advent of 'A-List' candidates and positive discrimination (see Box 11.4). Constituency party campaigning has also become more centrally controlled following the creation of Lord Ashcroft's 'Marginal Seats Unit' – in return for financing campaigns in such seats, Ashcroft's team has secured much more influence over local Tory parties. Likewise, the 'Conservative conference system', which allowed ordinary members a subtle and discreet influence over policy detail, has been quietly dismantled in favour of the Conservatives' own 'policy forums'. Like Labour's, these seem more open to manipulation by party apparatchiks (Kelly 1989, 2001a).

Redolent of New Labour between 1994 and 1997, Cameron's Conservative Party has thus acquired a 'vanguard' character, driven by a clique of London-based politicians and advisers with an unswerving loyalty to the leader (see Box 11.5). As with Labour's OMOV ballot on its 1997 manifesto, individual Tory members may have been given a vote over broad issues (*vide* the *Fresh Future* reforms of 1998 and the *Built to Last* policy statement of 2006). But, as numerous comments on the *Conservative Home* website testify, they have been stripped of influence over the evolving minutiae of party policy.

There seems to be an 'iron law' here, linking inter-party consensus with elitist party structures.

BOX 11.5 FACT

David Cameron's 'Inner Circle' 2006–9

George Osborne – Shadow Chancellor
Edward Llewellyn – Chief of Staff
George Bridges – Head of Campaigns
Andy Coulson – Head of Press
Steve Hilton – Director of Communications*
Danny Kruger – Chief speechwriter
Desmond Swayne – Cameron's Parliamentary Private Secretary
Oliver Letwin – Head of Policy
Nicholas Boles – Head of *Policy Exchange* (think-tank)

* Coulson resigned in 2007, but retained a 'covert and significant influence' (*Sunday Telegraph*, 25 January 2009).

This link was identified as long ago as 1955 by McKenzie's seminal study of *British Political Parties*. McKenzie noted that party leaders seeking to woo centrist voters would have to sideline their typically non-centrist members, and thus transform their parties into overt or covert oligarchies. This theory has lately been refined by the importance of political marketing: as both main parties have become more 'market-driven' and 'consumerist', they have further converged in terms of policy (Lees-Marshment 2008).

As Lees-Marshment explained, parties that are evangelical (or 'product-orientated') tend to have a polarising effect on inter-party policy and may end up with a manifesto that is 'exclusive' in the eyes of floating voters (*vide* Labour 1983). But such parties often tend to be quite 'inclusive' in their style of party management. If the party is going to 'evangelise', and seek to 'convert' voters, it makes sense for as many party members as possible to feel a stake in its policies. When Labour in the early 1980s had a decidedly 'product-driven' approach, it also had a reputation for decentralising power from Parliamentary leaders towards extra-Parliamentary activists (Shaw 2007). Likewise, Thatcher's Conservatives after 1983 seemed more inclined to shape rather than reflect public opinion; and this was accompanied by a subtle but steady growth of grass-root policy influence via the party's 'conference system' (Kelly 1989).

However, when a party becomes 'market-driven', the relationship between its leaders and members seems to change. Leaders start to attach less importance to their own members and more importance to external marketing agencies and voter focus groups, helping them ascertain what voters 'want'. The task of processing the resulting data, and thus interpreting exactly what voters *do* 'want', is often an 'elitist' activity that excludes all but a handful of party members. The task complete, a party's managers wish its members merely to absorb and carry out the 'message'. In such an environment, intra-party discussion becomes nugatory, confined to the communication rather than formulation of policy. The role of party members then becomes ancillary, supporting but not challenging the decisions of 'management'. In our present 'karaoke culture', this sort of role has decreasing appeal to the politically active.

There is further reason why market-driven parties are likely to end up with undemocratic, and potentially unpopular, styles of management. Party leaders who seem to follow, rather than lead, public opinion run the risk of seeming weak and uncertain in the eyes of voters. To compensate for this, there is a temptation for those same leaders to adopt macho forms of intra-party management – 'bravely' clamping down on dissent, 'ruthlessly' driving through their own agenda, 'facing down' those in the party who 'resist change', and generally suppressing party democracy to advertise their 'strong leadership' to voters. Tony Blair's assault on Labour's original Clause IV (1994–5) is probably the definitive example of this, while David Cameron's allies have urged him to find his own 'Clause IV moment', allowing him to crush publicly opposition inside his own party (Heffernan 2007; Jones 2008). Paradoxically, such tactics may only alienate further the 'post-deferential' generation of politicised adults.

Party funding

The way in which the main parties have generated income is another recent example of their self-harming tendencies. During the last decade or so, parties have become increasingly reliant upon the largesse of a few individuals, thus strengthening the idea that they are 'plutocratic' in character and divorced from the wishes of ordinary voters.

In 2006, it emerged that about £14 m of the £17 m Labour spent on its 2005 general election campaign came from about 12 businessmen, while 60 per cent of Conservative costs were financed by about 20 individuals (see Box 11.6). The image this created was made worse by the fact that this funding was often furtive and at odds with the spirit of the 2000 Political Parties, Elections and Referendums Act (Fairclough *et al.* 2007). Although the Act had brought greater transparency to donations given by individuals, parties by 2005 were circumventing it through the acceptance of 'loans' – usually at rates which implied they were nothing more than donations in disguise.

In 2006, Labour Party Treasurer Jack Dromey revealed he had known little about these loans and that party officials had been 'kept in the dark' about Labour's fundraising – a reference to the fact that Lord Levy had been mandated by Blair to solicit huge loans (or de facto donations) for Labour. Labour's rivals seemed far from innocent in this area (see Box 11.6). Details of the Conservatives' own loans were only revealed after an exhaustive inquiry by the Electoral Commission in 2006, when it transpired that some of these loans came from overseas residents – another example of how the spirit of the 2000 Act (which forbade such residents to make donations) was being transgressed.

To compound the problem, such loans were often associated with favouritism. In 2006, it was revealed that Capita – owned by Labour lender Rod Aldridge (see Box 11.6) – had benefited from the Government's public sector contracts, including the management of London's congestion charge. This had clear echoes of the Government exempting motor racing from its ban on tobacco advertising in sport, shortly after Formula 1 chief Bernie Ecclestone gave Labour a hefty donation in 1997.

In 2006, party funding was again brought into disrepute by the 'cash for peerages' scandal, when Scotland Yard investigated claims that senior Labour figures had contravened the Honours (Prevention of Abuses) Act 1925 by promising peerages in return for loans to the party. This led to the arrest of Levy and the possibility that a Labour leader and Prime

---

BOX 11.6   FACT

Substantial loans to the Labour/Conservative parties 2005

Labour

Sir David Garrard	Founder, Minerva property group	£2.3 m
Lord Sainsbury	Chief executive, supermarket dynasty	£2 m
Richard Caring	Clothing magnate	£2 m
Chai Patel	Executive, Priory health group	£1.5 m
Rod Aldridge	Chairman, Capita	£1 m
Nigel Morris	Founder, Capital 1	£1 m
Andrew Rosenfeld	Executive, Minerva	£1 m
Barry Townsley	Stockbroker	£1 m
Christopher Evans	Founder, Merlin Bioscience	£1 m

Conservative

Lord Ashcroft	Former Party Chairman	£3.5 m
Michael Hintze	Hedge fund consultant	£2.5 m
Robert Edmiston	Car dealer	£2 m
Arbuthnot Latham	City banker	£2 m
Johan Eliasch	Sportswear magnate	£1 m

Source: Guardian, 19 September 2006

BOX 11.7 **FACT**

The reform of party finance: recommendations of the Phillips Report

In March 2006, the Prime Minister commissioned Sir Hayden Phillips to undertake 'the most comprehensive analysis of party funding for over 30 years'. His proposals were published in March 2007.

- *Donations*: Phillips argued that the status quo was 'unsustainable', and agreed with the Conservative Party that donations should be capped at £50,000. Mindful of its narrow but hefty range of donations from trade unions, Labour objected to this proposal.
- *Campaign spending*: Criticising 'excessive and unnecessary' spending, Phillips called for a new cap on campaign spending and agreed with Labour that caps should also apply to constituency spending both during and between campaigns. Mindful of its targeting of marginal seats, the Conservatives objected to this proposal.
- *Further state aid*: Phillips foresaw an extra £25 m of state aid, based on two separate formulae – 'pence per vote' (linking state funding to electoral performance) and 'pence per member' (linking state funding to member recruitment). No party voiced serious objection to this proposal.

The lack of cross-party agreement to these proposals meant they were effectively shelved. According to Matthew Norman, 'The whole exercise was a hopeless waste of time' (*Independent*, 16 March 2007)

Minister would himself be detained by police in the course of a criminal investigation (Levy 2008). Small wonder that, in the wake of Levy's arrest, a *YouGov* poll found that the number of voters who thought the Government 'sleazy and corrupt' was greater than in 1997 – almost 10 years after Labour promised to 'clean up politics', after the last Conservative government had been discredited by 'cash for questions' and other scandals (*Daily Telegraph* 15 July 2006).

The parties might argue that the problems of funding stem from factors beyond their control, particularly the growing number of elections they have to contest. But, here again, voters may not be impressed by this argument, sensing that the parties' lack of income is mainly a result of needless spending. In recent years, parties have financed opulent offices, huge secretariats and lavish campaigns, exemplified by Labour's engorged party payroll (£13 m by 2007), the cost of its 2005 campaign HQ (£3 m compared to its normal HQ costs of £1.6 m), and its spending spree during the year of the 2005 general election (£14.5 m, compared with £2.6 m the year before). The Conservatives have been no less profligate, moving from their old Smith Square Central Office into state-of-the-art offices in London's Millbank without selling or renting Smith Square before leaving, leading to losses of £5.5 m by the end of 2006.

It was hoped by some that the Philips' Report on party finance (2007) would lead to a cleansing of the party funding issue. However, its lack of cross-party support meant that the problem lingered (see Box 11.7). Meanwhile, it later emerged that the parties had become even more reliant upon funding from institutions and a handful of individuals. By May 2009, Labour was again receiving almost 80 per cent of its funds from trade unions, while the Conservatives received over £11 m from just four benefactors (*Daily Telegraph* 27 May).

'Endemic' impropriety

Since the 1990s, the parties' integrity has been generically compromised by scandals affecting numerous party luminaries (Garnett 2008). By 2007, two journalists were able to produce a *Bumper Book of British Sleaze* – a forensic account of how hundreds of party politicians had behaved in a morally questionable way (Morton Jack and O'Rorke 2007).

When dissecting the unpopularity of parties, the *Power* report had avoided any reference to specific individuals, preferring to claim that the problem was 'systemic not personal'. However, a breathtaking piece of investigative journalism carried out by the *Telegraph* newspapers in May–June 2009 – concerning MPs' exploitation of Parliament's Additional Costs

BOX 11.8 FACT

The *Daily Telegraph* investigation of MPs' expenses: a selection of exposures

- *Jacqui Smith* (Lab): Claimed her sister's house was her main home, allowing claim for second home allowance on her family's home in Redditch.
- *Hazel Blears* (Lab): *Geoff Hoon* (Lab, Transport Secretary), *James Purnell* (Lab, Works and Pensions Secretary), *David McLean* (Con): *John Bercow* (Con): Avoided capital gains tax on sale of second homes by telling the Inland Revenue they were main residences.
- *David Chaytor* (Lab): *Elliot Morley* (Lab), *Ben Chapman* (Lab), *Bill Wiggin* (Con): Claimed interest payments on properties no longer mortgaged – a potential breach of Fraud Act 2007.
- *Ruth Kelly* (Lab): Claimed £31,000 of expenses on renovation and repair work on second home (in Bolton), despite much of work being covered by private insurance policy.
- *Shahid Malik* (Lab): Breached ministerial code by renting out second home at below market rate. Forced to resign as Justice Minister.
- *Peter Viggers* (Con): Claimed £1,645 from second home allowance to build floating duck island.
- *Andrew McKay*, *Julie Kirkpatrick* (Con): Husband and wife MPs who simultaneously claimed second home allowances on two different properties.
- *Margaret Moran* (Lab): 'Flipped' second home days before claiming, on new second home, £22,500 for dry rot treatment.
- *Keith Vaz* (Lab): Claimed £75,000 for second home, despite living in family home 12 miles away.
- *Douglas Hogg* (Con): Claimed £2,200 for cost of cleaning moat of second home (a mansion in Lincolnshire).
- *David Davis* (Con): Claimed £5,700 for portico.
- *Cheryl Gillan* (Con): Claimed £4.47 for dog food.
- *Gerry Adams*, *Martin McGuiness* (Sinn Fein): Claimed for second homes in London despite not taking up seats at Westminster.
- *Kitty Usher* (Lab, Work and Pensions Minister): Claimed for cost of removing Artex ceilings for reasons of 'taste'.
- *Charles Kennedy* (Lib Dem): Claimed for cost of sweets and teddy bears.

Source: Daily Telegraph, 11 May–9 June 2009

Allowance – suggested the problem was not so much systemic as endemic, pointing to general amorality on the part of innumerable party figures (see Box 11.8).

By June 2009, the *Telegraph* investigation had inflicted almost terminal damage upon voters' respect for political parties and their MPs. As one voter wrote, 'We are constantly told, by MPs of all parties, that they could earn much more outside politics. I don't think so: they would be in jail.' Another wondered (in respect of MPs' abuse of second home allowances), 'How can we trust political parties to run the country when many of their MPs don't even know where they live' (*Daily Telegraph* 16 May 2009). Britain's representative

democracy – underpinned by party politics – was widely felt to have reached its nadir.

■ Consensus and after

'Avant le deluge': the Thatcher/Blair/Brown settlement (1997–2007)

As indicated earlier, a key reason for voter disenchantment was a sense that parties were 'all the same'. To a large extent, this resulted from the centre-left acknowledging Margaret Thatcher's legacy after 1997 (Shaw 2007; Giddens 2007; Beech and Lee 2008). But the consensus was also shaped by Conservatives conceding aspects of the centre-left agenda, especially in respect of public spending. This 'social market' consensus, underpinning party politics from 1997–2007, is summarised here:

- There was a general acceptance that only markets and capitalist economics could deliver prosperity. There was a related acceptance that market economics should be extended wherever possible (hence Labour's enthusiasm for PFI schemes) and that the era of greater state ownership was over.

- There was a general acceptance that low inflation should be the 'holy grail' of economic policy and that monetary discipline (what Chancellor Brown called 'prudence') was the key to achieving it. To this end, there was a general acceptance of Brown's decision to transfer routine control of interest rates to the Bank of England's Monetary Policy Committee, and general support for Brown's Treasury 'rules', supposedly constraining Government borrowing.

- There was a general acceptance that income tax rates should be much lower than those of the pre-Thatcher era. In his final Budget (2007), Brown made a further gesture to Thatcherism by reducing the basic rate of income tax by 2 per cent.

- There was a general acceptance that public services should no longer have a 'one-size fits all' character, but instead promote 'diversity' and 'choice'. Labour in power duly rejected comprehensive schools in favour of various educational institutions (city academies, trust schools, specialist schools etc.) and allowed more variation within the NHS via the encouragement of 'foundation hospitals'.

- There was a general acceptance that the main purpose of economic growth was substantial increases in public spending rather than tax cuts. As the 2005 Tory manifesto stated 'We will increase government spending by 4 per cent a year, compared to Labour's plans to increase spending by 5 per cent a year.' The Conservatives duly promised tax cuts of just £4 bn – seen as 'chicken feed' by some free-market economists (Kelly 2006).

- There was a general acceptance that Britain's approach to the EU should be one of cautious integration. Labour had come a long way from its

David Cameron: Tory triangulator?
Source: Getty Images/Indigo

1983 position of withdrawal, and had strengthened Britain's links with the EU by incorporating its Social Chapter. The Conservatives, while remaining Eurosceptic, still spoke the language of reform rather than abandonment. Furthermore, neither party showed enthusiasm for the UK joining the EU single currency (although the Liberal Democrats still demanded entry at the earliest opportunity).

Cameron's 'Third Way' (2005–7)

This consensus was strengthened by David Cameron's leadership of the Conservative Party between 2005 and 2007. During his first two years as Opposition leader, Cameron seemed to be 'triangulating' the core principles of Conservatism with the embedded effects of New Labour (Kelly 2008a; Bale 2008). Although this upheld certain aspects of Thatcherism – such as the call for a 'looser and larger Europe' and a pledge to restore marriage tax allowance – it generally tilted towards more liberal-centrist positions. It acknowledged, for example:

■ That (*contra* Lady Thatcher's alleged claim) 'there is such a thing as society', and that action was needed to 'mend the broken society'.

■ That poverty was an urgent issue and that some wealth redistribution was required.

■ That 'stability' was the priority of economic policy – and that it could be threatened by cuts in taxation and government spending.

■ That short-term tax cuts would be modest, and that a Conservative government would 'share the proceeds of growth' with increases in public spending.

■ That the Conservatives would back New Labour's expansion of higher education by no longer opposing tuition fees.

■ That the Conservatives would back New Labour's city academies by shelving their commitment to more grammar schools.

■ That 'global warming' and 'carbon footprints' were now key issues for Conservatives (hence the message 'Go Blue, Get Green').

■ That crime arose not just from individual wickedness but from socio-economic deprivation (hence journalists' quip that Cameron wished to 'hug a hoodie').

■ That same-sex relationships were 'equally valid' and that Labour's civil partnership and 'gay adoption' laws would be respected.

■ That Labour's constitutional reforms would be broadly accepted: devolution, the new electoral systems, elective mayors and the quest for a more democratic second chamber would all be continued.

'Apres le deluge': a new polarisation? (2007–9)

Consensus politics are usually the product of prosperity: when most voters are satisfied with the economic status quo, it is hard for an Opposition to be radically different. Conversely, when voters are economically insecure, parties are inclined to offer divergent views as to why things went wrong and how things can be improved. As the economy worsened after 2007, it was therefore unsurprising

that the inter-party consensus became brittle. Indeed, by 2009, some classic left–right arguments had resurfaced.

(i) Public ownership or private ownership?

Having ditched its historic commitment to public ownership in 1994, it seemed during 2007–2008 that Labour was returning to first principles. The failing Northern Rock and Bradford and Bingley building societies were taken under state control, while the Government brokered a merger between the HBOS-Lloyds-TSB banking groups. By 2008, the Government was countenancing the effective nationalisation of the entire UK banking system – a notion once confined to the wildest reaches of the British left.

Though not explicitly opposed to this emergency measure, many Conservatives recognised that they might soon have to re-join the battle for free-market ideas. Interestingly, it was a view shared by Nick Clegg who, after his election as Lib Dem leader, nudged his party away from its left-of-Labour position and towards the free-market liberalism of the party's *Orange Books*, which Clegg and his Treasury spokesman Vince Cable had co-authored a few years earlier (Oaten 2009).

(ii) Keynes or prudence?

Brown's 'prudent' Treasury rules (see above) were meant to show that New Labour heeded Thatcherism's message about the perils of debt and borrowing. The 'sustainable investment rule', for example, stated that Government debt should not exceed 40 per cent of gross domestic product. With hindsight, such rules may have been more about image than reality. National debt had already risen from £350 bn in 1997 to £581 bn in 2007. By 2008, the Institute of Fiscal Studies warned that, when the Government's PFI debts were included, national debt stood at £110 bn, 45 per cent of GDP (Nelson and Hoskin 2008).

By 2009, the Government appeared to be galloping away from neo-liberal economics towards an emphatic form of neo-Keynesianism. Having spent £20 bn on a 'fiscal stimulus' package in November 2008, the Government's Budget of 2009 defied 30 years of economic orthodoxy. Borrowing in 2009–10 alone would rise to £175 bn, with national debt set to reach £1.4 trillion by 2013–14 – an expected 80 per cent of GDP. Conservatives, again

Leader of the Liberal Democrats, Nick Clegg, looks to the delegates as he is applauded after he made his leadership speech at the Lib Dems Party Conference
Source: Getty Images

backed by Clegg's front bench, attacked the policy, claiming that Labour had 'failed to repair the roof while the sun shone' and ditching their promise to match Labour's spending increases. Baroness Thatcher was said to 'feel very much at home with the new political battle-lines . . . though saddened that the lessons of the 1970s must again be learnt' (*Daily Telegraph* 25 April 2009).

(iii) Raise income tax?

Despite Labour's promise in 2005 not to 'raise the basic or top rates of income tax in the next Parliament', the 2009 Budget introduced a new top rate of 50 per cent for those earning $150,000 or more each year. When national insurance increases and personal allowance reductions were included, Britain was left with the highest marginal tax rate of any G7 country. Conservatives again protested and received some support from Clegg and Cable (who had committed their party to a lower standard rate, financed by a $20 bn reduction in public spending).

Although the main opposition parties were guarded about their own remedies, inter-party argument by 2009 thus had a clear ideological flavour. While Labour had re-adopted Keynesian ideas of 'tax, spend and borrow' (with a dose of Clause IV socialism), both Tories and senior Liberal Democrats stayed respectful of Thatcher's legacy, claiming the priority was to reduce debt, cut spending and avert any further tax rises. At the start of 2007, voters were said to be unhappy about the lack of conspicuous differences between the parties: by 2009, they seemed to have been appeased.

■ Which party system?

Given the turmoil of party politics after 2005, it was unsurprising that the shape of our party system remained uncertain. As Box 11.8 shows, it is hard to argue that the classic two-party system still exists. But there is confusion as to what, if anything, has replaced it.

BOX 11.9 FACT

The decline of a two-party system

The classic two-party system existed in Britain between 1945 and 1974. It had a number of features, all of which are less applicable today:

- *Duopoly of electoral support*: At the 1951 general election, the Labour and Conservative combined vote was 97 per cent. By the general election of 2005 it was just 67 per cent; in the Euro elections 2009 it was 45 per cent.
- *Duopoly of Parliamentary seats*: At the 1951 general election, all but nine MPs were Labour or Conservative. By 2005 the figure was 92.
- *Parity of electoral support*: Between 1945 and 1974, the average vote gap between the main parties was 3 per cent. Since 1979 it has been 9 per cent.
- *Loyal, class-based support*: Between 1945 and 1974, about two-thirds of the working class and three-quarters of the middle class regularly voted Labour and Conservative respectively. By 2005 a majority of working-class voters did not vote Labour and a majority of middle-class voters did not vote Conservative.
- *A nationwide two-party contest*: In the 1951 general election the Labour and Conservative parties came first and second in all but 12 seats, while both parties won substantial numbers of seats throughout the country. By 2005 one of the parties did not come first or second in over 200 seats, the Conservatives won only one seat in Scotland, while Labour won less than a quarter of the votes in southern England (outside London).

A three-party system?

Liberal Democrats are obviously fond of this claim, pointing out that they too have substantive experience of government. Since the introduction of devolved government in Britain, the party has been part of ruling coalitions in both Wales and Scotland. By 2009, they controlled 23 English councils (such as Stockport and Eastbourne) outright and held over 300 more council seats than Labour. At the 2005 general election, the party was the main opposition to the Conservatives in southern England (outside London) and the most popular party in the southwest. The increased likelihood of a hung Parliament at Westminster, even under first-past-the-post, could copper-fasten the third party's importance, while the political and personal empathy between Cameron and Clegg further increased the chance of a Lib Dem presence in a future coalition.

A multi-party system?

It is not just the Lib Dems who profited from the decline of the two-party system. The advent of proportional representation for many of the UK's

elections has accelerated the progress of Britain's other parties. Following the devolution elections of 2007, the Scottish National Party took control of the Scottish executive, while Plaid Cymru became part of the Welsh Assembly coalition. In the 2009 European elections, the United Kingdom Independence Party came second, while the Greens and British National Party each won seats. Indeed, one of the striking features of those elections was the fact that the collapse of Labour's vote did not overwhelmingly benefit the Conservatives: a range of alternative opposition parties – from the SNP in Scotland, to the BNP in northern England and to the Greens in the south – were beneficiaries of the anti-Labour swing.

A dominant party system?

This type of party system, similar to that seen in Japan, involves a plurality of parties contesting elections but only one succeeding – a stark contrast to a two-party system, where each party tastes success regularly. During the last 30 years in Britain, one of the main parties has enjoyed a lengthy spell in power while its main rival crashed to a series of ignominious defeats and looked generally hopeless. The 2009 European elections, when the Government polled just 16 per cent of the popular vote, and was eclipsed even in its traditional heartlands like Wales, seemed to portend an equally long period in the political wilderness for New Labour.

A variable party system?

According to the 'variable' model, Britain has not just one-party system but several party systems working concurrently. In the midlands, for example, there is still a mainly Lab–Con battle; in the south (outside London) a mainly Lib–Con battle; and in northern cities a mainly Lib–Lab battle. In Scotland and Wales, meanwhile, there is a four-way battle involving all three British parties and nationalists. Meanwhile, the 2009 European elections showed that the party battle in England could be complicated further by a resurgent UKIP and BNP.

A defunct party system?

The idea of a 'defunct party system' was first advanced after the 2001 general election (Kelly 2001b). This theory states that any 'system' – political or otherwise – must inherently have a strong measure of consistency and uniformity. Such 'systematic' features certainly existed in the 1950s and 1960s, when a Labour–Conservative battle obtained throughout the country, when tribal class support for the two parties existed in all regions, and when any electoral swing in one seat was replicated in most of the others.

In recent years, however, such clear patterns have been absent. At the 2005 general election, Labour's vote fell by 8 per cent in London, but by 'only' 4 per cent in Scotland; the Conservatives added 2 per cent to their support in the south-east, but lost 2 per cent in the north-east. The pattern of voting behaviour in marginal seats was similarly erratic: for example, the Conservatives enjoyed a swing of 6 per cent in Putney, but suffered a 4 per cent reverse in Cheadle. At the 2009 European elections, Labour added to its support in Leicester, despite catastrophic losses elsewhere.

It may be argued that these figures fit the 'variable party system' thesis described above. However, there are now variations of party support not just *between* but *within* certain areas. In north Wales in 2005, the Conservatives took Clwyd West on a swing of 1.3 per cent – yet their vote fell by 11 per cent in Anglesey. Within Greater Manchester's marginal seats, there was a Lab–Con battle in Bury South and Bolton West, a Lib–Con battle in Hazel Grove and Cheadle, and a Lib–Lab battle in Withington and Rochdale. So, even within a single metropolis, there is nothing 'systematic' about modern party competition.

In summary, today's party battles are marked by trendless voting patterns, irregular swings, infinite fluctuations and large-scale abstentions. The expected effects of the Parliamentary expenses scandal – namely, the growth of support for independents and the targeting of particular MPs – will only strengthen the non-systematic nature of modern elections. The 'British party system' has not just changed: it has apparently ceased to exist.

■ The crisis of political parties: collapse or catharsis?

By the summer of 2009, it was clear that Britain's political parties were in the midst of a serious crisis. This crisis was underpinned by a long-standing disconnection from voters, reinforced by the onset of economic recession, and cemented by disclosures of rapacity (and, in some cases, criminality) among MPs. In the eyes of many voters, at least, Britain's political parties were unfit for purpose.

But what is that purpose? During the twentieth century, one of the supposed functions of political parties was to effect radical and far-reaching change, with Attlee's Labour government and Thatcher's Conservatives usually cited as prime examples. However, by the end of the twentieth century, various factors (globalisation, privatisation, European integration) conspired to suggest that parties could no longer have such a cataclysmic effect. In response to the economic crisis after 2007, Gordon Brown's government aimed to correct this impression, promising to 'save' the country through bold, proactive government and a range of sweeping macro-economic measures.

For a while, left-leaning journals like the *New Statesman* saw such measures as a vindication of state power and, by implication, the governing parties that made it democratically accountable. During the period 2007–9, it was possible to argue that the age of 'particularistic' politics (represented by pressure groups) was waning, while a fresh era of 'generalistic' politics (represented by big government and major

Gordon Brown: re-empowered party government
Source: Getty Images

parties) was about to dawn. The politics of neo-liberalism, reflecting a minimal role for governing parties, was said to be over; the politics of supranational social democracy, where governing parties had to be radically *dirigiste*, was said to be ascendant.

Yet, by mid-2009, it seemed that a British Government had again overestimated its abilities. The International Monetary Fund's survey found that New Labour's fiscal stimulus had 'not done the trick' and that the Chancellor's projections for renewed growth were 'simply unrealistic'. The IMF warned that, unless UK public spending was cut

dramatically, the prospects of avoiding depression were 'slim' (*Financial Times* 22 May 2009). Put another way, unless the governing party pruned its ambitions, the country would suffer; instead of being a cure, hyperactive party government was part of the problem. The pan-continental swing against centre-left parties in the 2009 European elections was, perhaps, an indication that voters sensed this.

It was poignant that the IMF's report came when voters were concluding that the parties' chief spokesmen – their Parliamentarians – were morally ill-equipped to be hyperactive on their behalf. In the midst of the expenses scandal, a *YouGov* poll found a majority of voters thinking all the main parties were 'discredited' and 'could not be trusted' (*Sunday Telegraph* 31 May 2009). With an increasingly self-confident electorate increasingly sceptical of elites, this view had been simmering for some time. But it took a combination of economic and constitutional traumas to bring it powerfully to the surface.

Yet, in the wake of these traumas, it would be wrong to conclude that political parties were now otiose. The parties' most basic task – to govern by aggregating society's diverse interests – remains valid. Indeed, given the complexity of modern society, this task is more pertinent than ever. Nevertheless, if parties are to have enough credibility to carry it out, there will have to be a recasting of party politics, as iconoclastic bodies like *Jury Team* and the *National Union of Voters* were founded to point out.

Some prescriptions

If British party politics is to recover, a number of conditions may be necessary – three of which are considered below.

Localisation/democratisation of government

Although New Labour has extolled 'decentralisation', it is widely felt among voters that the new regional bodies (in Scotland, Wales and London) simply represent another tier of self-serving bureaucracy and inaccessible government. It is telling that, when voters in north-east England had a chance to endorse their own regional assembly (via a referendum in 2004), only 22 per cent did so on a turnout of 48 per cent. It may thus be argued that 'localisation' will not be meaningful unless it substantively empowers bodies that are *actually* local – such as county councils and city-wide authorities. This might be

Numerous MPs were forced to quit after the expenses scandal
Source: Getty Images/Peter Macdiarmid

followed by greater provision for local referendums and 'initiative' ballots – allowing voters to effect reforms proposed by public petitions – and 'recall' ballots, held if enough voters felt a local public official was unsatisfactory (Carswell and Hannan 2008).

Localisation/democratisation of party structures

The localisation of government might then allow the localisation of political parties. National party leaders would have to eschew any 'control freak' tendencies and accept more federal party organisations, allowing local parties to function in a way that suited local circumstances and empowered local party members. Local members, for example, would no longer have to choose candidates from national party lists, while party policy might also acquire an asymmetrical character.

Within their local organisations, parties might consider enfranchising not just ordinary members but also ordinary voters. 'Primary' elections, in which

voters chose party candidates, would therefore become commonplace – and thus mitigate complaints about diminished party membership and 'safe' seats.

An individualistic/intelligible electoral system

By May 2009, some prominent figures (like Labour's Alan Johnson) were suggesting proportional representation as a panacea. But the issue of electoral reform should be handled with care. The two systems of PR now used in England and Wales both incorporate 'closed' party lists, where voters cannot explicitly support or condemn individual party candidates. As such, there have been complaints that PR leads to 'stitch-ups', guaranteeing the election of senior party figures and further alienating voters from the political system (Kelly 2008b). Particularly after the expenses scandal, it is vital that voters feel able to target, negatively or otherwise, individual politicians. A *YouGov* poll found that only a minority of voters saw the expenses crisis as an indictment of our constitutional system, while just a third called for radical constitutional reform. A clear majority thought the crisis was an indictment of individual party MPs – and the priority was for those individuals to be punished (*Daily Telegraph* 1 June 2009).

■ Conclusion: American dream or back to the future?

It could be argued that some of the above ideas – notably dispersed government and looser party structures – point to the Americanisation of our political system. It could also be argued that such an arrangement, while appropriate to a vast democracy like the USA, is less suited to smaller and more homogenous European societies.

Yet there is nothing inherently un-British about such a new constitutional and party system. In fact, it has strong echoes of British politics over a century ago when government was less centralised, parties less regimented and party governments less hubristic in their ambitions. This was a period, in other words, when local government was more significant, variations in local administration more marked, intra-party rules more relaxed and the remit of government more modest and prosaic.

Given the recent economic and constitutional crisis, and with doubts now growing about the efficacy of 'big government', it may be worth considering whether such pre-democratic arrangements could be adapted to a modern, democratic setting. For all their recent difficulties, political parties would be indispensable to such a dramatic upheaval of our polity. In this respect, British political parties – far from being redundant – could be more important than ever in the years ahead.

BOX 11.10   BRITAIN IN CONTEXT

The problems besetting parties in the UK are far from uncommon elsewhere. Indeed, there is a case for arguing they are endemic throughout the world's democratic societies. Fukuyama's 'end of history' thesis (1992) foresaw a narrowing of party differences across the post-Cold War world which has generally served to de-energise voters. Despite Samuel Huntington's warning (1996) that the twenty-first century would be marked by a global 'clash of civilisations', on account of emergent religious fundamentalism, there were few signs by 2009 that this had polarised party debate, or galvanised voters, in most Western polities. In the USA, various studies (e.g. Maisel 2007) have confirmed the long-term trend away from party politics towards pressure group and protest movements, while the 2008 presidential election – featuring perhaps the most charismatic challenger in decades – still failed to raise turnout much above 60 per cent (similar to the figure at the UK general election of 2005, which was widely considered risible). Even more interesting, perhaps, is the limited interest in party politics within the newly democratised European societies (Cular 2005; Wasilewski 2009). Far from providing a contrast to the UK at the 2009 European elections, many of these countries showed even less enthusiasm for party prescriptions. Turnout in Poland, Slovenia and Slovakia, for example, was just 27 per cent, 28 per cent and 20 per cent, while turnout across the EU generally was just 43 per cent. Neither did it seem clear in these elections that party government had been vindicated in the eyes of voters: there was a marked swing against the centre-left, 'big government' parties almost everywhere. In short, one of the key questions posed in this chapter – 'do parties matter?' – continued to receive a globally obtuse response.

Chapter summary

As the first decade of the new century drew to a close, Britain's political parties remained in a state of crisis, stricken by voter disinterest, increasing public hostility, tumbling membership and dubious sources of income. The 2010 general election served to underline this crisis, with the main parties unable to offer the kind of distinctive approaches that once gave party politics traction. The nature of the British party system also stayed unresolved, the traditional two-party system having been succeeded by something altogether more volatile and oblique. However, the depth of the crisis – allied to the onset of recession – also gave parties a redemptive opportunity, encouraging them to reconsider their internal structures, the extent to which they empower their own members, the extent to which they decentralise and their relationship with alternative forms of political activity. It remains to be seen whether the main parties grasp this opportunity – or continue to atrophy in the face of rapid economic, cultural and sociological change.

Discussion points

■ Why have UK political parties alienated so many voters?

■ In what sense are UK political parties at odds with social, economic and cultural developments?

■ Is it now possible to speak of any 'British party system'?

■ Is there a post-credit crunch consensus among the main parties?

■ Do radical parties like the BNP represent a long-term challenge to the nature of party politics?

■ How much can parties in the twenty-first century learn from the those of the nineteenth century?

Further reading

Beech, M. and Lee, S. (eds) (2008) *Ten Years of New Labour* (Palgrave Macmillan).

Beech, M. and Lee, S. (eds) (2009) *The Conservatives Under David Cameron* (Palgrave Macmillan).

Elliott, F. and Hanning, J. (2007) *Cameron: the Rise of the New Conservative* (Harperpress).

Jury Team (2009) *The End of the Party* (JTPublications).

O'Hara, K. (2007) *After Blair: David Cameron and the Conservative Tradition* (Icon Books).

Shaw, E. (2007) *Losing Labour's Soul: New Labour and the Blair Government* (Routledge).

Bibliography

Bale, T. (2008) 'Qualifying the Common Wisdom: David Cameron and Conservative Party Change', *E-Pol* 3,1 www.politicaleducationforum.com.

Baston, L. and Herring, S. (2005) 'The Labour Party' in Seldon, A. and Kavanagh, D. (eds) *The Blair Effect* (Cambridge University Press).

Beech, M. and Lee, S. (eds) (2008) *Ten Years of New Labour* (Palgrave Macmillan).

Broughton, D. (2008) 'Electoral Change in Britain 2005–2008' *E-Pol* 1,1 www.politicaleducationforum.com.

Carswell, D. and Hannan, D. (2008) *The Plan: 12 Months to Renew Britain*, www.Lulu.com.

Cular, G. (2005) *Elections and the Consolidation of Democracy in Croatia* (Zagreb).

Denham, A. and O'Hara, K. (2008) *Democratising Conservative Leadership Selection* (Manchester University Press).

Dorey, P. (2008) 'The Conservatives: from Collapse to Cameron-led recovery', *E-Pol* 1,2 www.politicaleducationforum.com.

Elliott, F. and Hanning, J. (2007) *Cameron: The Rise of the New Conservative* (Harperpress).

Fairclough, P., Kelly, R. and Magee, E. (2007) 'Funding Political Parties: An Intractable Problem' in *UK Government and Politics: Annual Survey 2007* (Philip Allan).

Fisher, J. (2008) 'Party Finance Since 2005', *E-Pol* 1,2 www.politicaleducationforum.com.

Fukuyama (1992) *The End of History and the Last Man* (Penguin).

Garnett, M. (2006) 'Is the Conservative Party conservative?', *Politics Review*, Vol. 15, No. 3.

▶

Garnett, M. (2008) 'Sleaze and British Politics', *E-Pol* 1,1 www.politicaleducationforum.com.

Giddens, A. (2007) *Over To You, Mr Brown* (Polity).

Goodwin, R. (2008) *Innovating Democracy* (Oxford University Press).

Grant, M. (2005) 'Is Labour still a socialist party?', *Politics Review*, Vol. 15, No. 1.

Heffernan, R. (2007) 'Tony Blair as Labour Party Leader' in Seldon, A. (ed.) *Blair's Britain* (Cambridge University Press).

Hertz, N. (2002) *The Silent Takeover: Global Capitalism and the Death of Democracy* (Simon and Schuster).

Huntington, S. (1996) *The Clash of Civilisations and the Making of World Order* (Simon and Schuster).

Jackson, N. (2009) 'All the fun of the seaside', *E-Pol* 2,1 www.politicaleducationforum.com.

Jenkins, S. (2006) *Thatcher and Sons* (Allen Lane).

Jones, D. (2008) *Cameron on Cameron* (Fourth Estate).

Jury Team (2009) *The End of the Party* (JT publications).

Kelly, R. (1989) *Conservative Party Conferences* (Manchester University Press).

Kelly, R. (2001a) 'Farewell Conference, Hello Forum', *Political Quarterly*, Vol. 72, No. 3.

Kelly, R. (2001b) 'The Defunct Party System' *Talking Politics*, Vol. 14, No. 1.

Kelly, R. (2006) 'The Leadership Battle: Turning Point for the Tories?', Fairclough, P., Kelly, R., Magee, E. *UK Government and Politics: Annual Survey 2006*.

Kelly, R. (2008a) 'Conservatism Under Cameron: The New Third Way', *Politics Review*, Vol. 17, No. 3.

Kelly, R. (2008b) 'It's only made things worse: a critique of electoral reform in Britain', *Political Quarterly*, Vol. 79, No. 2.

Kelly, R. (2008c) 'The Battle for the Labour Leadership', Fairclough, P., Kelly, R., Magee, E. *UK Government and Politics: Annual Survey 2008* (Philip Allan).

Kelly, R. (2008d) 'The End of Ming' in Fairclough, P., Kelly, R., Magee, E. *UK Government and Politics: Annual Survey 2008* (Philip Allan).

Kelly, R. (2008e) 'The 2008 Elections and the British Party System', *E-Pol* 1,3 www.politicaleducationforum.com.

Kelly, R. (2009) 'Cameron's Third Way: A Redundant Project', *E-Pol* 2,1 www.politicaleducationforum.com.

Lees-Marshment, J. (2008) *Political Marketing and British Political Parties* (Manchester University Press).

Levy, Lord (2008) *A Question of Honour* (Simon and Schuster).

Maisel, L.S. (2007) *American Political Parties and Elections* (Oxford University Press).

McKenzie, R.T. (1955) *British Political Parties* (Heinemann).

Minkin, L. (1978) *The Labour Party Conference* (Allen Lane).

Morton Jack and O'Rourke (2007) *The Bumper Book of British Sleaze* (Foxcote).

Nelson, F. and Hoskin, P. (2008) 'The Great Debt Deceit: how Gordon Brown Cooked the Nation's Books', *Spectator*, 20 September.

Nugent, N. (2003) *The Government and Politics of the European Union* (Palgrave Macmillan).

Oaten, M. (2009) 'Lib Dem Ministers Ahoy?', *E-Pol* 2,2 www.politicaleducationforum.com.

O'Hara, K. (2007) *After Blair: David Cameron and the Conservative Tradition* (Icon Books).

Power Inquiry (2006) *Power To The People* (Rowntree Charitable Trust).

Rose, R. (1980) *Do Parties Make a Difference?* (Macmillan).

Shaw, E. (2007) *Losing Labour's Soul? New Labour and the Blair Government 1997–2007* (Routledge).

Wasilewski, J. (2009) *Political Leadership in Polish Counties* (Warsaw).

Wheatcroft, G. (2005) *The Strange Death of Tory England* (Penguin/Allen Lane).

Webb, P. (2005) 'The Continuing Advance of the Minor Parties', *Parliamentary Affairs*, Vol. 58, No. 4.

Useful websites

www.labour.org.uk
www.conservatives.com
www.conservativehome.blogs.com
www.libdems.org.uk
www.snp.org
www.plaidcymru.org
www.ukip.org
www.greenparty.org.uk
www.bnp.org.uk
www.zyra.org/uk
www.bubl.ac.uk/bublukpoliticalparties

This chapter is dedicated to Rod Martin (1950–2009), founder and Head of Manchester Grammar School's Politics Department, 1977–2009.

CHAPTER 12

Devolution

Russell Deacon

Learning objectives

- To define devolution and note the various devolutionary models.

- To explain the background and role of nationalism and the subsequent drive towards political devolution within the UK.

- To cover the story of how devolution evolved across the United Kingdom and Northern Ireland.

- To assess some of the key events and developments in devolutionary politics in the first decade of devolution.

- To explore some of the major impacts on the politics of the UK from the advent of devolution.

Introduction

The topic of devolution is not as modern as it may sound. It has dominated politics at various periods over the last 120 years, causing wars, the splitting of political parties and the downfall of governments. Since wide-scale political devolution arrived in the United Kingdom and Northern Ireland, at the end of the last century, the whole nature of British politics itself has undergone an evolutionary change. As the media in the United Kingdom tends to be dominated by that based around London, many people may not be aware of the extent of the changes to our political system or the variation in policy output over the last decade.

What then is devolution? At a basic level, devolution is simply the devolving of powers from the centre to the periphery. Importantly, this does not involve transferring sovereignty from Westminster, which therefore makes it distinctly different from federalism. In the case of the United Kingdom devolution therefore means transferring powers from Westminster and Whitehall to the devolved bodies and administrative offices across the United Kingdom. The process of devolution can be categorised as three discrete processes:

1 *Administrative*: The process by which power is transferred to allow specific functions to be carried out.

2 *Executive*: The process by which power is transferred to enable policy decisions to be made.

3 *Legislative*: The process by which the power to make laws is conferred on another body.

The United Kingdom and Northern Ireland has had administrative devolution for over a century. This expanded over time so that by the 1990s it covered all of the UK. Executive and legislative devolution, outside of Northern Ireland, however, are of a more recent occurrence. This type of devolution has had a far greater impact on the politics of the UK. It is this sort of devolution (often referred to as political devolution) that is examined in this chapter.

■ Theory

In 2005, Jennifer Todd, drawing upon the work of around twenty of the most prominent academics who had commented on devolution since the mid-1970s, highlighted three models of territorial politics which provide us with a way to assess devolutionary change.

The first model is that of 'state realism'. Within this model the state has adapted its state power and state sovereignty to take account of changing political realities. This new form of devolution is therefore simply the older dual polity whereby the centre allowed a certain practical autonomy on local issues to its peripheries, while retaining control over high politics. Under this model, however, the divide between the centre and the periphery is not clear-cut and therefore the older 'mainframe' of the unitary state may be under intolerable strain and crack.

The second model considers devolution to be driven by 'European regionalism'. This model indicates that nations within the UK move from 'state-centred' to 'European-determined linkage politics'. This means that within a European context, nations such as Scotland, Wales and Northern Ireland need the UK Parliament less and less as they are able to interact directly with the European Union without needing to go through Westminster. In turn, the European Union and European Commission require regions or nations in order to determine their policy output, such as the establishment of European regional development funding or support for cultural and linguistic policies. In the case of the United Kingdom part of this packaging involves the identification and recognition of the constituent nations.

The final model sees devolution as a 'renewal of imperial legacies'. Here the Westminster government, just as it did with its colonies in the last century, transfers more and more sovereignty and powers to the devolved nations. The strategy behind this is that in time they will become dominions independent in their own right. Those advocating this model point to Northern Ireland as an example of this. Here the Westminster government would be glad to be rid of its responsibilities for this troubled province. The main drawback to this theory, however, is that all mainstream British political parties constantly advocate their commitment to maintaining the union.

■ Nationalism and the drive towards political devolution

Nationalism in the United Kingdom is normally related to those groups that believe that either the nation or a putative nation is at the centre of a political system of government. Due to the fact that political boundaries in the British Isles have been fairly constant for the last five centuries, national identities have had time to develop and take firm, historical root. Even in Ireland, where the political boundaries were only firmly established in 1922, the national identity focuses on whether its citizens feel themselves to be Irish or British Irish nationals. And each side forms its own brand of nationalism, accordingly.

One of the common misconceptions of both academics and historians is to label only those groups that desire independence for their own nation, such as Plaid Cymru in Wales or the Scottish National Party in Scotland. This extends to *Mebion Kernow* in Cornwall or, in the case of Ireland, desiring union with another nation, either the Irish Republic or the UK. As many of us know nationalism in the British Isles is both wider and more complex than this. In the nineteenth century the Liberal Prime Minister, William Gladstone, was the originator of 'Home Rule – all round'; meaning in essence devolution for all of the nations of the British Isles. After this was defeated by the Liberal Unionists, who split from their own party and the Conservatives' liberal nationalism emerged once more in Scotland and Wales in the late Victorian and Edwardian era. The Young Scot's Society and *Cymru Fydd* (Wales to be) were both Liberal Party nationalist movements that pursued devolutionary policies which sought to place their own nations at the centre of their own political systems. Nationalism has continued in the Liberal Party and subsequently in the Liberal Democrat Party with a desire for a federal system of government for

the United Kingdom. Within the Labour Party, initially supportive of devolution, this desire was much reduced, particularly after the Russian Revolution and the First World War produced left-wing proponents who advocated the need for international socialism. It nevertheless maintained a distinct presence within the Labour Party from then on, despite the strong unionist tendency that existed in the Labour Party after the First World War. British and English nationalism have been ever-present in the Conservative party. There have even on occasions been elements of support for Scottish nationalism within the party. This, however, was never the case in Wales and for most of its history the Conservative Party has remained staunchly unionist there (British nationalist).

In Ireland, nationalism has always been viewed from a different perspective when compared to perceptions in England, Wales and Scotland. This is the nationalism which on both sides had blood on its hands, through centuries of religious warfare and rebellions against the British crown. This did not occur anywhere else in Great Britain after the last Jacobean revolt in Scotland in 1745. Firstly, Irish nationalism simply and unwaveringly demanded home rule. As this desire was rejected, so Irish nationalism became more violent. Irish nationalism then developed into Catholic nationalism pursuing the ideal of a united and independent Ireland. This was in turn countered by Protestant nationalism (Unionism) which sought to keep Ireland within the United Kingdom. The two then opposed each other in a bloody Irish civil war that lasted nearly the whole of the twentieth century.

In Wales and Scotland a new type of nationalism developed in the years before the Second World War. This was the nationalism of independence rather than home rule. By the end of the century, it would eclipse the nationalism which exists within the three mainstream UK parties. In 1925, Plaid Cymru was formed and then in 1934 the Scottish Nationalist Party (SNP) was created. Both had had their origins in other nationalist organisations but it was these parties that came to represent the mainstream independence nationalism of their respective nation states. Political scientists, however, do not always refer directly to them as nationalist parties. This label they reserve for those anti-immigrant parties, normally on the far political right such as the BNP. Instead Plaid Cymru and the SNP are referred to by them as ethnoregionalist parties. This means that they represent a specific regional/national group within a larger nation state, in this context the Welsh and the Scottish peoples in the United Kingdom. In the political world and in the media, however, they remain defined as nationalist parties but students of politics should be aware there is a clear distinction between nationalist and ethnoregionalist parties. Having stated this, however, they are still referred to by their commonly known label – 'nationalist party' in this chapter.

While in Northern Ireland the nationalist parties displaced the mainstream British political parties this has never been the case in Scotland or Wales. Here, for decades after their foundation, both Plaid Cymru and the SNP struggled to make any political progress. It was only with Plaid Cymru's by-election win in Carmarthen in 1966 and the SNPs similar by-election win in Hamilton in 1967 that the modern period of Scottish and Welsh nationalism associated with a drive towards independence started. This nationalist impact was seen to be so sudden and potentially damaging electorally to the Labour Party, which traditionally relied on their Scottish and Welsh seats to counteract the Conservatives' majority of the English seats, that they set up a Royal Commission under Lord Kilbrandon to examine the issue of devolution. When Lord Kilbrandon reported back in 1973 it was to a Conservative government under Edward Heath. It was some five years later, under the Labour government of James Callaghan and after much political turmoil, that the referendums on Scottish and Welsh devolution were held. The devolution referendum was defeated in Wales, in 1979, and in Scotland an insufficient majority was gained to carry it forwards. The Labour government then fell due to a vote of no confidence, being the first government to fall on an issue of devolution since Gladstone's Liberal government had split on Irish Home Rule almost a century before.

Two months later, that year, in the general election the Conservatives won and the pro-devolution Liberals, Plaid Cymru and the SNP lost between them 13 of their 29 MPs. The SNP was reduced from 11 to just two seats in the process. The victorious Conservatives had honed their campaigning skills in the Scottish and Welsh elections and increased their seats in these nations at the pro-devolutionists' expense. The new government under Margaret Thatcher was unashamedly pro-unionist. A month after their victory the Conservatives reversed the devolutionary mechanisms. The political fortunes of the pro-devolutionists were now put on hold for two decades.

Ireland

The historical events that resulted in the formation of the province of Northern Ireland (Ulster) fill many volumes. Bearing this in mind, the historical elements so instrumental in understanding the politics of Northern Ireland can only be touched upon here. Ulster has been a constant reminder of the British Isles' violent, sectarian and turbulent past transported into modern times. The religious wars between Catholics and Protestants that faded from the British mainland more than four centuries ago have yet to die in Northern Ireland. Politics there today therefore remains almost totally divided between political parties which were formed on a religious basis. The Catholic nationalists are republicans who seek a union with the Catholic Irish Republic, while the Protestants seek to maintain the union with the protestant United Kingdom (unionists). The only party that is non-sectarian is the 'Alliance Party', which is linked to the British Liberal Democrats but attracting only marginal support in Northern Ireland. In short, therefore after the Anglo-Irish Treaty of 1922, Northern Ireland broke away from Southern Ireland (Eire) and from then onwards has developed a separate political identity. It was given its own Parliament, known by the place in which it was prominently located – Stormont. Until 1972 Stormont ran the province, with near autonomy, as part of the United Kingdom with its own prime minister, the last being Brian Faulkner.

Stormont, however, was a Protestant-controlled Parliament that supported the mechanisms of a Protestant state which maintained a strict segregation similar to that between black and white citizens in the southern United States until the late 1960s. The Catholics, inspired by the American black civil rights movement, sought their own civil rights during the 1960s, mainly through their own political party called the Social Democratic and Labour Party (SDLP). This movement was heavily resisted by the Stormont government and enforced by the almost exclusively Protestant-manned Royal Ulster Constabulary (RUC) and their auxiliary policemen (B Specials). This produced a situation that got ever more violent and started a period known as 'the Troubles'. At its height in 1972, 467 people were killed, 323 of them civilians. The atrocities of that year became infamous in Irish history and included events such as: Bloody Sunday, Bloody Friday, McGurk's Bar, Kelly's Bar, Callender Street and

Abercorn. For the next three-and-a-half decades, while the British Army and Royal Ulster Constabulary fought the IRA, and the various other paramilitary organisations, the politicians (sometimes closely connected to paramilitaries, in particular Sinn Fein with the IRA) British and Irish Prime Ministers and the occasional American President, tried every 'carrot and stick' method they could conceive of to end the Troubles.

The current Northern Ireland peace process began with the signing of the Good Friday Agreement (named after the day on which it was signed) and its subsequent approval by a Northern Ireland referendum in May 1998. This created the devolved Northern Ireland Assembly, which officially started in December 1999. Because of the previous problems with Northern Ireland politics, such as the gerry-mandering of boundaries, the Assembly's elections were under STV, the most proportional system possible. The Good Friday Agreement meant that all of the main political parties would in future have to power share in any Northern Ireland government. The largest political party would take the First Minister post and the second largest that of Deputy First Minister. But within a short space of time the peace process ground to a halt once more. A row in February 2000 between the political parties over weapons decommissioning led to a four-month suspension of the Assembly.

A further crisis came in July 2001 when David Trimble, the Assembly's first minister and leader of the moderate Ulster Unionist Party (UUP), resigned out of frustration at the IRA's failure to decommission their weapons. He returned later that year when the IRA began to put its 'weapons beyond use'. The Northern Ireland Assembly then resumed business for a short period. Then, in July 2002 the IRA made an unprecedented apology for 'non-combatant' deaths. But Mr Trimble resigned again three months later after the discovery of incriminating documents in Sinn Fein's offices. Britain then resumed direct rule of Northern Ireland with the Prime Minister postponing the next Assembly elections until November 2003. In these elections, the more radical unionist Ian Paisley's Democratic Unionist Party (DUP) – which opposed the Good Friday agreement – displaced the UUP as the biggest party in the Assembly. At the same time, Sinn Fein replaced the moderate SDLP as the main Catholic (republican) party. As the rest of British politics was moving towards the political centre, Northern Ireland's was moving to the political extremes.

For a long while after the elections there was stalemate once more. In December 2004, remarkably, it seemed as though Mr Paisley might become the new First Minister, with Sinn Fein's Martin McGuinness (the former head of the IRA) as Deputy First Minister. But a bank raid and a brutal murder, both blamed on the IRA, wrecked the deal.

In Britain's general election in May 2005, the Democratic Unionists gained parliamentary seats at Mr Trimble's expense, and Sinn Fein escaped punishment for the IRA's misdemeanours by also increasing their share of the vote. But the British government's hasty welcome to the IRA's promise in July 2005 to 'end the armed campaign' enraged Unionists and pushed them further away from cooperation. Consequently, there was no devolved Assembly between the 2003 and 2007 elections. When the 2007 Northern Ireland Assembly elections occurred, the DUP and Sein Fein were now the main political parties in Northern Ireland (Table 12.1). It would therefore only be with their cooperation that Northern Ireland's Assembly would restart. Political progress was now stuck on the thorny issue of law and order in Northern Ireland. By now, the RUC had been disbanded and replaced with the Police Service of Northern Ireland (PSNI), which had a much larger number of Catholic officers in it. Yet this still lacked the required Republican support, something that was essential for Ulster's future.

In January 2007 Sinn Fein voted to support policing in Northern Ireland for the first time in the party's history. This broke the political log jam and enabled the DUP to remove a vital political barrier and join government with them. At the same time Tony Blair was using the 'stick' of introducing water charges for Northern Ireland, which all Northern Irish parties opposed, and Gordon Brown, then

Table 12.1 Northern Ireland Assembly results 1998–2007 (108 seats)

Party	1998	2003	2007
Social Democratic and Labour Party (SDLP)	24	18	16
Ulster Unionist Party (UUP)	28	30 (33)*	18
Democratic Unionist Party (DUP)	20	27 (24)*	36
Sinn Fein	18	24	28
Alliance	6	6	7
Others	12	3	3

* Three UUP defections to the DUP

Chancellor, offered the 'carrot' of £1bn extra funding if an Executive was formed. The strategy worked and the DUP leader Ian Paisley, at the age of 81, now saw his moment in history and finally joined with his lifelong republican foes in a joint administration. He became the First Minister and Martin McGuiness the Deputy First Minister. It seemed as though the threat of the gun had finally been removed from Northern Irish politics.

Then in May 2008 Northern Ireland got a new First Minister – Peter Robinson, the long-time deputy leader of the DUP, acceded, as Ian Paisley stood down. Sinn Fein then refused to nominate Martin McGuiness as Deputy First Minister unless the DUP agreed to the devolution of justice. Gordon Brown intervened and Gerry Adams was called to Number 10 to try and make a compromise. Between May and November the Executive did not meet and during this period the image of devolution took a nosedive with the general public. An accommodation was eventually reached in which the DUP agreed with Sinn Fein to make the police answerable to an Irish justice minister in time but both Sinn Fein and the DUP ruled themselves out of this post. The issue on policing was only resolved after another lengthy period of political posturing which also at one stage involved the temporary resignation of Peter Robinson, albeit on unrelated issues connected to a financial scandal involving his wife. Devolution in Northern Ireland always appears to be on a knife edge, the key issues contributing to this instability are as follows:

■ There still remain a number of problems in Northern Irish politics which could cause the process to break down at any time.
■ Some paramilitaries such as the Real and Continuity IRA continue to mount operations. Their actions, or those of the security services in seeking to tackle them, cause tensions among Unionists and Republicans which could split the Assembly once more.
■ Some DUP members such as the MEP Jim Allister remain anti-power sharing and are still popular among their party and the public. Their views could once more stop power sharing. In addition much of the DUP's own membership and support base remain opposed to power sharing.
■ The DUP's decision to back Labour in the 42-day detention of terror suspects in the Westminster Parliament's 2008 vote made the Ulster Unionists oppose the detention period and join with traditional forces, the Conservatives. They now field joint candidates' in Westminster general elections,

resulting in the Conservatives no longer being able to remain neutral from Northern Irish politics.
■ The southern Irish political party Fianna Fail now has a grassroots organisation in Northern Ireland particularly in South Armagh. The involvement of southern Irish political parties in Northern Irish politics remains something of an unknown quantity.

Scotland

Scotland, Wales and England became joined at the start of the seventeenth century. In March 1603 the English Queen Elizabeth I died and King James of Scotland became king of England and Ireland. This happened in a smooth transition of power quite different from most previous changes of monarch in both Scotland and England. James now concentrated his reign in England and for the rest of his life he only visited Scotland once, in 1617. This showed the start of a transition of power to England that went on for the next century.

When the Scottish Parliament was abolished with the Act of Union in 1707, the event was described by the Scottish Lord Chancellor, James Ogilvy, as like the 'end of an old song'. Yet the distinctive tune of Scotland and Scottishness did not end with the demise of its parliament. The Scottish church, education and legal systems remained separate from those in England and Wales. From 1885 onwards there was also a separate government department and minister for Scotland. Unlike the positions of Northern Ireland and Wales there was never any doubt over Scotland's existence as a country separate from England. Over time much of the government's business in Scotland was transferred from London to the Scottish Office in Edinburgh. From 1926 the Scottish Secretary also sat in the Cabinet. Therefore by the time the Second World War arrived, the Scottish Office already represented a substantial devolved administrative department.

For the first seven decades of the twentieth century there were sporadic attempts to push forward political devolution for Scotland among all of the parties in Scotland. This was strongest in the Scottish Liberals and the Scottish National Party (SNP) but there were also politicians in the Labour and Conservative (Unionist Party) who supported political devolution. They were, however, kept in check by a far more powerful unionist tendency in their respective parties that endured in Labour's case into the late 1970s and in the Conservatives into the late 1990s. The rise of the SNP as a political threat to Labour, in particular, and the recommendations of the Kilbrandon Commission in 1973 which led in turn to the failed devolution referendum of 1979. Albeit a referendum was won but failed to reach a vital 40 per cent threshold of the total Scottish population needed to vote in favour of a Scottish Parliament. In the event only 36 per cent of the total electorate had voted 'Yes'. During this period some interesting questions were raised in respect of Scottish devolution that were never effectively answered, see Box 12.1.

The 1980s and 1990s saw a succession of unionist Thatcherite Scottish secretaries who proved both unpopular and a boom for Scottish nationalism. The introduction of the hugely controversial and unpopular community charge (poll tax) in Scotland, a year before it occurred in England, also fuelled the feeling that the nation had become something of a testing ground for Thatcherism. Attempts by the last Conservative Scottish Secretary, Michael Forsyth, to increase and improve administrative devolution, while also giving a greater role to Westminster's Scottish Committees, did little to reduce the public and political mood for increased political devolution. From the mid-1980s onwards poll after poll indicated that the Scottish population wanted a Scottish parliament, and as time went on, this idea became more rather than less popular.

In March 1989 the Scottish Labour and Liberal Democrat Parties, together with a number of minor parties, trade unions, the churches and civil organisations formed the Scottish Constitutional Convention. As the body was only concerned with political devolution rather than independence, the SNP refused to join it. John Smith, George Robertson and Donald Dewar for the Labour Party and David Steel and Jim Wallace for the Scottish Liberal Democrats were the key political figures behind the move towards a Scottish parliament. The Convention published its report setting out the ground for a proportionally elected primary law-making and tax-raising Scottish parliament in November 1995 entitled *Scotland's Parliament, Scotland's Right*. With the Conservatives and Unionists totally removed from Scottish Westminster politics after the 1997 general election, a referendum was held in the September which saw a massive majority in favour of a Scottish Parliament (of those who voted 74.3 per cent were for the Parliament and 60.2 supported tax raising powers). The combined anti-devolutionist forces of both Scottish Labour

---

BOX 12.1 Scottish influence on UK politics and the West Lothian question

From the introduction of the *Authorised King James's Version of the Bible* (1611), the standard text for the Church of England for more than 250 years, to the succession of Scottish Prime Ministers such as Sir Henry Campbell Bannerman, Ramsey MacDonald, Andrew Bonar Law, Sir Alex Douglas Hume and Gordon Brown, Scottish influence on British politics has been substantial. There have been an even greater number of Scottish Cabinet ministers at Westminster and leaders of other British political parties such as the Liberals/Liberal Democrats (four of their seven postwar leaders). Yet the Scottish influence hasn't always been welcomed. In 1978 the anti-devolutionist Scottish Labour MP Tam Dalyell posed what became known as the West Lothian question. This concerned what right he had to vote on laws related to England and Wales, when English and Welsh MPs could not vote on issues related to West Lothian. This was because they are devolved from the Westminster Parliament to the Scottish Parliament. This issue has remained contentious to this day. It even concerned Gordon Brown, the Prime Minister, as his Kirkcaldy and Cowdenbeath constituency is in Scotland. This means that he is unable to vote on devolved issues in Scotland. In January 2004 the government only won a vote on top-up fees for England by the use of its Scottish MPs, Gordon Brown being one of these. This had also happened before on the creation of foundation hospitals, despite the fact that the Scottish Parliament had decided not to introduce these fees itself.

In 2005 the number of Scottish MPs at Westminster was reduced from 72 to 57, as part of the attempts to address the situation. This, however, didn't end the problem only reduce it. None of the three main political parties would end the right of Scottish MPs to vote on English bills. The Conservatives, however, plan to end Scottish MPs' right to take part in and vote on the line-by-line consideration of English parliamentary bills.

and Conservative MPs present in 1979 had now gone, which was reflected in the size of the 'Yes' vote.

Financially, the Scottish Parliament still relies on Westminster for its annual block grant and does not have significant tax-raising powers. It can raise income tax levels by up to 3 pence in the pound. This limits its autonomy for fiscal spending and this limited variation in income tax has only been suggested once. This was by the SNP government in 2007 when they suggested raising it in order to introduce a local Scottish income tax to replace the local government council tax. The SNP, however, dropped the idea in the face of fierce business opposition, pressures from Westminster and by the actual practicality of the three pence rise being insufficient to fund a replacement to council tax.

The first Scottish elections were on 6 May 1999 and saw a turnout of 58 per cent. Some 73 Members of the Scottish Parliament (MSPs) were elected by the traditional Westminster style first-past-the-post system and an additional 56 MSPs elected through AMS (the proportional electoral additional member system), in eight Scottish regions. The results were significant because:

■ These were the first elections to a Scottish Parliament in three centuries.

■ No one party gained a majority, which was not unexpected from the new proportional election, therefore a coalition government would operate in future.

■ It saw the UK's first Green Party parliamentarian, on the regional list for the Lothians.

■ The first Scottish Militant Party member was also elected – Tommy Sheridan – in the Glasgow region.

■ The rebel Labour MP Denis Canavan was elected in Falkirk West. He had been deselected by his own party, then stood against them and won. His success would encourage other Labour members not selected to do the same, not only in Scotland but also in Wales and London.

After the election was held, the process of forming the first Scottish government for almost three centuries occurred. The government in Scotland was initially referred to as 'The Scottish Executive' but is now widely known as 'The Scottish Government'. It is legally separate from the legislature and similar to the position in the Westminster Parliament. No one political party has every gained an overall majority at a Scottish Parliamentary election, see Table 12.2. Therefore after the 1999 and 2003 Scottish elections it was a Labour–Liberal Democrat coalition which formed and signed a four-year cooperation agreement in each instance. The first was called *Partnership for Scotland* followed by the unimaginatively titled *A Partnership for a Better Scotland* in August 2003.

Labour's Donald Dewar became the first politician to take the title of First Minister in Scotland and the Scottish Liberal Democrats' Jim Wallace, was his deputy. Dewar, who was seen as one of the 'fathers of Scottish devolution' died suddenly of a brain haemorrhage on 11 October 2000. He was replaced by Henry McLeish in April 2001. McLeish, however, resigned on 8 November 2001 due to the so-called 'Officegate' expenses row, which centred on the sub-letting of his constituency office in Glenrothes. He, in turn, was replaced by the the Motherwell and Wishaw Member of the Scottish Parliament, Jack McConnell. For the next five-and-a-half years the Scottish coalition executive worked effectively together through a series of policy and

Table 12.2 Scottish general election parliamentary elections results 1999–2007

Party	1999 Constituency	1999 List	2003 Constituency	2003 List	2007 Constituency	2007 List
Labour	53	3	46	4	37	9
Scottish National Party	7	28	9	18	21	26
Conservative and Unionist	0	18	3	15	4	13
Scottish Liberal Democrat	12	5	13	4	11	5
Scottish Green Party	0	1	0	7	0	2
Scottish Socialists	0	1	0	6	0	0
Independents	1	0	2	1	1	0
Others	0	0	0	1	0	0

Holyrood, seat of the Scottish Parliament, cost ten times the original estimate, a worthwhile investment?
Source: PA Wire / Empics

legislative changes which saw Scotland pursuing significantly different policies to those in England. The problems over the introduction of university tuition fees with both sides taking differing views (Labour for them, Scottish Liberal Democrats against) led to an independent commission being established that determined in favour of them not being introduced. The new Parliament building at Holyrood also became something of a scandal, costing ten times its original estimate. Both the architect Enric Miralles and the First Minister Donald Dewar who had been responsible for the original proposals, however, were dead by the time Lord Fraser's inquiry into the building had been undertaken.

From the outset the Scottish Parliament had been established with the power to create its own (primary) laws. This meant that laws could be made in three different ways: namely via Executive Bills, Committee Bills and MSP's Bills. The vast majority of legislation, as with the Westminster Parliament, is through Executive Bills. These Acts have helped provide Scotland with laws as diverse as those giving free long-term care for the elderly to those abolishing fox hunting and establishing STV as a method of election for Scottish local government.

Whereas the 2003 Scottish general election had been significant for continuing the Lab–Lib coalition government and widening the number of political parties present in the Parliament to six political parties, the 2007 election saw an end to this. In that election the SNP gained 20 seats. Its leader, Alex Salmond, returned to the Parliament after a four-year gap during which he had been leading his party at Westminster. The SNPs' gains had been at the expense of the other political parties, in particular the minority parties who had lost 12 of their 14 MSPs. The Conservatives and Labour, however, would not consider going into coalition with the SNP. The Scottish Liberal Democrats also refused to join them in coalition, due to their stance on not supporting a pro-independence party. The SNP formed a minority government with Scottish Green Party support but still 16 seats short of a majority. The centrepiece of the SNP government's programme is its commitment to having a referendum on independence, its so-called 'National Conversation' (see Box 12.3). There was, however, already a debate on Scotland's devolved future. This had arrived following a debate in the Scottish Parliament on 6 December 2007 where those developing it had resolved to set up an independently chaired commission to review devolution in Scotland. This was under Sir Kenneth Calman, Chancellor of the University of Glasgow. The remit of the Commission on Scottish Devolution was:

To review the provisions of the Scotland Act 1998 in the light of experience and to recommend any changes to the present constitutional arrangements that would enable the Scottish Parliament to serve the people of Scotland better, improve the financial accountability of the Scottish Parliament, and continue to secure the position of Scotland within the United Kingdom.

The Commission had the subsequent endorsement of the Scottish Secretary and UK Westminster government in March 2008. While it consulted, the SNP government rose in the opinions polls to as high as 48 per cent in August 2007 and constantly above Labour's share of around 30 per cent. In July 2008, the party triumphed in the by-election in Glasgow East, one of Labour's safest seats, by 365 votes and in the process overturned a Labour majority of 13,507 to win with a swing of 22.54 per cent. It seemed as though the SNP would sweep all before them. The arrival of the credit crunch, however, and subsequent discrediting of the Scottish banks and building societies, including Alex Salmond's former employer, the Royal Bank of Scotland, led to a fall in the SNPs fortunes. In November 2008 Labour won the Glenrothes by-election, with a comfortable majority of 6,737 over the SNP. The constituency bordered Gordon Brown's own seat and therefore the result acted as something of a boost to his own flagging status as Prime Minister. After this victory the distance between the SNP and Labour in the Scottish opinion polls showed the SNP still to be ahead but often only by one or two per cent. Ten years after devolution had arrived, Scotland once more was very much a two-party dominated system albeit with Labour or the SNP having to find another party in order to gain absolute power.

When the Calman Commission reported back in June 2009 it indicated that after 10 years Scottish devolution could be declared to be a 'success'. In declaring this Calman also recommended that it should further evolve and that Holyrood should take charge over much more of its own revenue raising. In future half the income tax raised in Scotland as well as stamp duty, landfill tax and air passenger duty would be collected by the Scottish government and form a third of its budget. The Calman Commission also said the Scottish Parliament should control other areas such as national speed limits, drink-driving laws and airgun legislation. While the SNP Government criticised Calman for not giving the Scottish Parliament full fiscal powers the other political parties welcomed its recommendation as naturally extending devolution. With a Westminster election on the horizon the Scottish Parliament then set about seeing how Calman could be implemented in practice. Shortly after this the SNP Justice Secretary Kenny MacAskill freed the terminally-ill Lockerbie bomber Abdelbasset Ali al-Megrahi in August, on compassionate grounds. This caused a storm of protest across the political spectrum but in particular in the United States, from President Obama downwards. On 2 September 2009 the SNP was overwhelmingly defeated in a vote on its handling of Ali al-Megrahi's release. Although the SNP continued as a minority government it was felt that Scotland's international standing had been damaged and that the lessons of the Ali al-Megrahi affair would have to be looked at carefully if Scotland was ever itself to become an independent sovereign nation.

Wales

Prior to the Acts of Union between 1536–42 under Henry VIII, Wales was not one nation but a patchwork quilt of crown lands and Marcher lordships. Therefore, until Welsh nationalism emerged in the latter half of the nineteenth century, Wales had been integrated closely into England. To all intents and purposes Wales ceased to be a nation and instead became a series of counties almost fully assimilated into England. During the late nineteenth century the Liberal Prime Minister William Gladstone was the first British leader to accept that Wales was a nation distinct from England. Liberal MPs such as Tom Ellis and David Lloyd George pushed forward Welsh nationalism and consequently the Liberal governments between 1905 and 1916 saw the establishment of many of the trappings of nationhood including a National Library and National Museum.

Despite the founding of Plaid Cymru (Party of Wales) in 1925, Welsh nationalism at a Parliamentary level remained mainly in the Welsh Liberal or Liberal National Party. The Labour Party, which under the Merthyr Tydfil MP Keir Hardie (1900–1916), had been pro-devolution after the First World War, turned almost against it. Those few Labour MPs who were pro-devolution did so against a rising tide of unionism. Nevertheless, despite this strong unionist stance, Jim Griffith, the deputy leader of the Labour Party, who was pro-devolution was able to persuade Harold Wilson and the wider Labour Party to establish both a Welsh Office and a Welsh Secretary in the Cabinet in 1964. This began a period of significant executive devolution in Wales.

The Conservatives in Wales always remained hostile to Welsh devolution with no significant figure emerging as pro-Welsh devolution, during the twentieth century. Thus with the vast majority of Welsh MPs being hostile or indifferent to Welsh devolution and the Welsh Liberals disappearing to just one MP (Emlyn Hooson) by 1966, Welsh nationalism was only reignited in 1966 when the Plaid Cymru President and their political hero, Gwynfor Evans, was elected to Carmarthen in 1966. From now on Plaid Cymru was seen as a direct threat to the Labour Party in Wales and they realised they had to do something to combat the appeal of the rising nationalist tide. As we noted earlier this resulted in the establishment of the Kilbrandon Commission in 1968 and the subsequent failure of the St David's Day devolution referendum in 1979. The referendum had only

occurred in the first place because of the minority Labour government's reliance on Welsh Liberal and Plaid Cymru MPs to stay in power.

A few months after the referendum result, a general election saw Margaret Thatcher's Conservative government elected which then controlled politics in Wales for the next 18 years. Although they always remained against political devolution, the various Conservative Welsh Secretaries enhanced administrative devolution. This included establishing the use of the Barnett formula (Box 12.2) which determined government funding for Wales, the extension of devolved powers in Wales and the reforming of Welsh local government into a system of 22 unitary authorities. Only Nicolas Edwards (1979–87), the first of the Thatcher–Major period Welsh Secretaries, however, was actually a Welsh MP. During the last ten years of Conservative rule in Wales therefore the succession of Welsh Secretaries with English constituencies, including Peter Walker, John Redwood and William Hague, fuelled resentment of a new era of English colonialism by 'unaccountable quasi colonial governors' who ruled via a series of unelected quangos. During this period the Welsh Labour Party continued to win the majority of Welsh seats but remained powerless against their Conservative foes. This was enough to persuade many within the Labour Party to support devolution and therefore by the general election of 1997, the party had become committed to introducing an elected Welsh Assembly in its first term.

When the Labour Party included an element of proportional representation in its plans (the additional member system), it was enough to persuade Plaid Cymru and the Welsh Liberal Democrats to endorse their plans in the referendum. With the Conservatives routed in the 1997 general election, losing all of their Welsh seats, and the Labour anti-devolution MPs silenced there was no effective opposition to the 'Yes' campaign. This helped them

BOX 12.2 Barnett formula

The Barnett formula was brought in as a funding mechanism for the devolved administrations prior to their expected arrival in 1979. The funding formula from the Westminster government to the proposed devolved bodies was established by Joel Barnett, then the Labour Chief Secretary to the Treasury. It was based loosely on the population sizes of

Scotland, Wales and England (10:5:85). The Barnett Formula remains controversial, in that various political parties state that it is either too generous or not generous enough and needs revision. Despite these claims the Barnett Formula has only undergone slight alterations since it was introduced in 1979.

BIOGRAPHY

Rt Hon Ron Davies (1946–)

Secretary of State for Wales 1997–98, leader of the Wales Labour Party 1998. At the age of 24 leader of Bedwas and Machen Urban District Council, youngest in the UK. Elected MP for Caerphilly in 1983 and joined the Opposition front bench in 1987 as Agriculture spokesman. Shadow Welsh Secretary from October 1992. Drew up most of the Welsh devolution policy and successfully led the 'Yes for Wales' referendum. Regarded as the 'father of Welsh devolution'. He resigned as Welsh Secretary and the Welsh Labour leader in 1998, after a sexual scandal on Clapham Common. Elected as the Assembly Member for Caerphilly in 1999 he resigned from that position in 2003 after another sexual scandal. In 2008, he was elected as an Independent councillor and then served as a Cabinet Member in the Plaid Cymru-led Caerphilly County Council. In the process he became the first New Labour Cabinet member to serve the cause and policy aims of another political party. Davies' evolution from New Labour Cabinet Member and 'father of devolution' to Council Cabinet Member of Plaid Cymru-led council in ten years is perhaps one of the most unusual changes in career path in Welsh political history.

win a narrow victory, by just 6,721 votes (0.3 per cent of the total vote). Wales was then given a national assembly of some 60 elected members (40 constituency members and 20 proportional members – list members). This assembly, unlike that in Scotland and Northern Ireland, would only have the power to amend secondary, rather than to originate its own primary legislation.

The Labour leader, Ron Davies, who led the 'Yes' campaign did not become the First Secretary (changed in 2001 to First Minister) as envisaged. Davies had been forced to resign and so a new leader was needed (see Biography). Thus when the dust settled after the 1999 Welsh Assembly elections it was Alun Michael, Ron Davies replacement as Welsh Secretary, and Tony Blair's loyal right-hand man in Wales who became the First secretary. He had won a controversial Labour party election competition against Rhodri Morgan to become Davies' replacement. Michael led a minority government in the Welsh Assembly and had initially refused to go into coalition with the Welsh Liberal Democrats, preferring to govern alone. As his party lacked a majority by three seats, it was only a matter of time before they were defeated. This came over a vote of 'no confidence' concerning his ability to gain matched-funding from the Westminster government's Treasury to secure European Objective One funding to Wales. Gordon Brown, then Chancellor, did not give his support in time and Michael resigned. He was replaced by Rhodri Morgan in an unelected leadership contest. Morgan then gained the required finance from the Treasury

and formed a coalition government with the Welsh Liberal Democrats led by Michael German.

The Lab–Lib Welsh Assembly coalition (2000–2003) was significant for five main things:

1 It gave both Wales and the Liberal Democrats their first taste of coalition government since 1945. In the process it showed that coalition government could be stable and that the identity of those political parties within it could remain distinct.

2 It revitalised the Welsh Assembly government's policy outputs by introducing a raft of Welsh policies such as limitation on top-up fees for students and free entry to museums that could be seen to be distinctly Welsh.

3 It started the process of changing the Assembly from one based on the vision of a corporate body, in which the opposition and government were both members of the legislature, to develop into one where the Assembly Members were divided into the executive and legislature.

4 The Assembly became a truly bilingual institution, whereby its business was conducted through both Welsh and English, led by the Presiding Officer – Lord Elis Thomas (the former leader of Plaid Cymru and Chairman of the Welsh Language Board).

5 It established a number of commissions which examined controversial aspects of Welsh Assembly coalition policy. The Rees Commission, for instance, provided a compromise solution

of student tuition fees, and the Sunderland Commission looked at the future of Welsh local government. It was the Richard Commission (chaired by the Labour Peer Lord Ivor Richard) which was established to examine the Assembly's current powers and the adequacy of its electoral systems.

The 2003 Welsh Assembly elections had seen Labour gain exactly half of the Assembly seats with the opposition gaining the other half. Lord Dafydd Elis Thomas immediately accepted the Presiding Officer's post once more. He had been the Presiding Officer (the Assembly's equivalent of the House of Commons Speaker) in the 1999–2003 Assembly. As the Presiding Officer can only vote in the Assembly's plenary sessions as a casting vote in the event of a tie, Thomas's decision meant that Labour now had an effective majority of one. They did not need to form a coalition. Rhodri Morgan was once more elected the First Minister and the Assembly set out to follow a Labour policy agenda, which, among other things, included the abolition of prescription fees in Wales.

When the Richard Commission reported back, it was after the Lab–Lib Coalition government had finished. They recommended that the Assembly be given full law-making powers and that it increase the number of Assembly Members to 80, to be elected by STV. Richard also recommended that the Welsh Assembly be formally divided on a parliamentary legislature and executive basis. While the Labour Party was happy to accept the last recommendation, it did not want to accept the first two. Therefore the electoral arrangements were ignored and the law-making powers were reduced to a complicated staged implementation of primary powers which still had to go through Westminster.

At the start of 2005, amid much controversy about rising costs, as it had risen in price from £12 million to £24 million pounds, the Assembly moved into a purpose-built legislative chamber on Cardiff Bay's waterfront. Then in May the Labour Assembly Member Peter Law contested his own Bleanau Gwent seat against the official Labour 'all-women shortlist' candidate. Law won the seat but in the process was expelled from the Labour Party. The Labour Party was now in a minority in the Assembly but limped on in government for the next two years suffering a number of defeats and having to come to 'arrangements' with the other political parties in order to get their policies and budget through. This provided an important reminder to the Labour Party of the instability of one-party minority government.

The 2007 Assembly elections, now entitled the 'Welsh General Election' once again saw no one party gain a majority, with Labour remaining the largest party but with five seats short of a majority (see Table 12.3). It was then a whole month before the parties fully examined the various possible combinations possible and the result was somewhat of a surprise for everyone including the political parties themselves. Labour joined together with its bitter political foe, Plaid Cymru, in what was termed the Red–Green Alliance (Red being the colour of Labour and Green that of Plaid Cymru). Rhodri Morgan once more became the first Minister and Plaid Cymru's leader Ieuen Wyn Jones the Deputy Minister. At the centre of the agreement between the parties was the establishment of another commission – the All Wales Convention – to examine how the proposed referendum in Wales on obtaining full primary law making would be best won. The Commission was chaired by the former British Ambassador to the United Nations, Sir Emyr Jones Parry. The desire for full law-making powers in Wales has risen over 2007, 2008 and 2009 (see Table 12.4).

Initially, the Labour government in Westminster under Tony Blair had tried to control the policy outputs of the Welsh Assembly. Over time, however, this desire to control had diminished and Wales was allowed very much to go its own way. Here Labour

Table 12.3 Welsh Assembly election results 1999–2007

Year	Constituency 1999	List 1999	Constituency 2003	List 2003	Constituency 2007	List 2007
Labour	27	1	30	0	24	2
Plaid Cymru	9	8	5	7	7	8
Conservatives	1	8	1	10	5	7
Welsh Liberal Democrats	3	3	3	3	3	3
Independents/others	0	0	1	0	1	0

BOX 12.3 Independence

Whereas there are no political parties advocating independence for Northern Ireland, there are those who advocate it for Wales, Scotland and even England. In a BBC Wales/ICM poll on 24 February 2009, some 13 per cent of Welsh people supported an independent Wales either inside or outside of the European Union. In similar polls in 1997, this figure had stood at 14.1 per cent and in 2003 at 13.9 per cent. Even in Plaid Cymru opinion is split as to whether the party should pursue independence or not. This is not the case in Scotland, however. Here the SNP, as the government there have committed themselves to bringing forward a Referendum Bill in 2010, offering the options of the status quo, enhanced devolution or full independence. The process leading up to this has been entitled the 'National Conversation'. All of the main

UK parties reject independence for Scotland, although in May 2008, Labour's former Scottish leader Wendy Alexander backed a referendum while Gordon Brown did not.

In November 2006, an ICM opinion poll for the *Sunday Telegraph* set the desire for independence among Scots at 52 per cent. By February 2009, however, it was down to 33 per cent, indicating the changeability on the issue. The more surprising element of the *Sunday Telegraph* poll was the fact that 48 per cent of English voters also wanted complete independence from the rest of the UK. This is also the view of the English National Party which frequently contests elections, albeit with little success, with English independence as its central policy agenda.

Table 12.4 The desire to see primary law-making powers for Wales

Institution	2007	2008	2009
In favour of turning assembly into full law-making parliament	47	49	52
Against turning assembly into full law-making parliament	44	42	39
Don't know	9	9	9

Source: BBC Wales/ICM polls, June 2007, February 2008, February 2009

Table 12.5 Who has the most influence on Wales?

Institution	1999	2003	2009
Assembly government	26	22.4	40
UK Government	25	57.9	29
Local councils	7	15	15
European Union	37	4.7	8
Don't know	6	0	7

Sources: 1999 poll *The Economist* Newspaper Limited, London (6 November 1999); 2003 poll Richard Commission; 2009 poll, BBC Wales/ICM poll (24 February 2009)

worked with both the Welsh Liberal Democrats and later Plaid Cymru to pursue agreed policy agendas in a way that was still alien to the Labour governments of Westminster. The ten years of Welsh devolution had also shown that there was a demand from within the Welsh Assembly and across the Welsh public for greater devolution. This, however, had been resisted and limited by the more unionist elements within the Welsh Labour Party rather than the British Labour Party in the ways it had previously used. The Welsh Labour MPs, conscious of their loss of power and status, continued to resist further advances in devolution. Yet the demands for increased powers remained solid in Wales and it is therefore likely that the Welsh Assembly will develop into a Parliament more similar to the Scottish model. By 2009 opinion polls were already indicating that the Welsh people thought that the Welsh Assembly government had

the greatest influence on their lives, itself an indication of just how much it had embedded itself into Welsh life (Table 12.5).

■ Devolution and the European Union (EU)

Jennifer Todd's models of devolution, cited at the start of this chapter, see devolution in the UK in part as a need to adapt to the EU's desire of 'European regionalism'. In turn, opinion polls across the United Kingdom have sometimes stated that the EU is the most important influential political institution on their lives (see Table 12.5). The level of trust in the EU across the UK has also increased over time. The *Eurobarometer*, that judges public

Table 12.6 Interest in EU affairs in the devolved nations/region

	Wales	Scotland	Northern Ireland	Greater London	UK average
Interested/fairly interested in European affairs	54.7	53.7	54.9	59.2	52.8
Voted in the last European elections	33.5	39.2	48.3	34.4	33.8
Believe that the EU should take a role in tackling:					
Climate change	86.1	81.2	83	79.3	80.4
Terrorism	92.2	86.3	86.3	83.4	85.6
Protecting human rights	88.4	88.6	85	86.7	84.8

Source: Eurobarometer (2007) Attitudes towards the EU in the United Kingdom, FlashEurobarometer 207, May 2007

opinion across the EU, has indicated that the awareness and interest in the EU among the devolved nations is considerably higher than the UK average, see Table 12.6.

Prior to political devolution to the non-English nations in the United Kingdom, there were three territorial departments' (Northern Ireland, Scottish and Welsh Offices) connections to the European Commission. This was mainly through four different processes:

1 The direct links and setting up of administrative processes required by the process of administering the Common Agricultural Policy and the European structural funds (European Social Fund and European Regional Development Funds).

2 The establishment of or support of territorial offices in Brussels, such as the Wales Information Centre. These acted as information gathering and lobbying organisations.

3 The secondment of territorial departments' civil servants to the European Commission and UKrep (the United Kingdom's Embassy to the European Commission).

4 The territorial departments' ministers attending Council of Ministers meetings and their inclusion in the Westminster government's Cabinet European Committee.

The EU referred to the territorial departments when they existed and later on to the English Regional Assemblies as sub-national authorities (SNAs). As those SNAs that covered the territorial departments gained political devolution the Westminster government committed itself to include them in the EU policy process. Although the UK government was keen to retain a single UK position on all EU issues, it did allow the non-English devolved bodies con-

siderable access to the UK's EU policy-making mechanisms. It also allowed Scotland and Northern Ireland primary legislative competence over those areas of responsibilities that had been devolved which were affected by EU policy. Wales, lacking the primary legislative powers, did not gain this same responsibility.

The relationship between the three devolved bodies and the Westminster government was developed through an inter-administration memorandum of understanding (MoU) in 2001 between the Office of the Deputy Prime Minister, then John Prescott, and the three devolved bodies. The MoU laid down a concordat for coordinating EU policy across the United Kingdom. In essence, the relationship meant that the Westminster government allowed the devolved bodies full integration into the process provided that the devolved bodies respected the confidentiality of the process and kept any discussions concerning this EU policy process within the designated processes. It took some while for the Whitehall Departments to fully remember that they had a duty to consult about relevant EU issues with the devolved bodies. Ultimately, as the UK lacks a constitutional court to resolve differences, the devolved SNAs can only get their own EU policy desires satisfied by successfully lobbying the Westminster government. As we saw earlier, this happened in Wales in 2000 when the Assembly successfully lobbied the Westminster government for additional resources to match-fund EU structural funds. This was too late, however, to save the career of the Labour First Secretary, Alan Michael, who lost a vote of no confidence over this issue.

The main area of access to and influence on EU policy making therefore remains the Westminster government. The SNAs also have a representation of the EU's Committee of the Regions which represents all 74 for the EUs designated regions. This body acts a mechanism for the regions to influence overall policy. All of the political devolved SNAs have offices in Brussels to serve as their eyes and ears with the Commission and Parliament. These offices, however, are not used on the whole to bypass the Westminster government but instead to act as an additional resource and information gatherer for each body. Officially therefore, the UK government regards them as part of the extended UKrep family rather than as independent agencies and they have consequently been given the requisite diplomatic status.

There are a number of differing characteristics of the devolved bodies and EU policy making. As the UK has what is known as asymmetrical (unequal) devolution and differing national interests or attitudes to the EU, policy creation differs. Thus, whereas fishing is an important issue in Scottish–EU relations, it is of little importance in Wales. Whereas the issue of ensuring that the European Parliament accepts Welsh as a fully recognised language is important to Wales–EU relations but acknowledges it is of no importance to the other devolved nations. At the same time the Westminster government will also often listen more to the opinions of one nation it regards as having more expertise in that area. Asymmetrical devolution also means that the English regions do not have the same impact on the EU process as do the other three nations. Within the SNAs, also the specific attention paid to EU issues varies. Therefore despite the fact that the Mayor of London is responsible for administering the European Structural Funds there is no specific committee on the GLA to scrutinise European issues directly. Instead it goes through the other committees. The case is similar in the Northern Ireland Assembly. Scotland and Wales, however, have both committees and ministers responsible for EU policy making.

The devolved bodies have also been able to interpret EU policies according to their own criteria, on occasions, setting the rules even if they have not been sanctioned by the European Commission. In February 2009, for instance, the Northern Ireland Assembly allocated farm modernisation payments on a 'first come, first served' basis which saw thousands of farmers waiting outside the Department of Agriculture's offices for days. Although the European Commission stated the projects should only get funding on 'objective criteria, rather than a first come, first served basis', the Northern Ireland Assembly still interpreted matters in its own way. This has caused considerable confusion which may not have occurred had there existed a centralised UK policy.

■ England and its regions

England under the flag of St George is seen from the outside as being one homogenous nation. There are, however, strong regional identities which politicians can only ignore at their peril. People in numerous English towns, cities and councils have their own distinct identities as strong as any national ones. Politicians have been long aware of this English regional distinctiveness which is particularly acute in counties such as Cornwall and Yorkshire and cities such as Liverpool, Manchester and London. Politicians, however, have been split as to how to deal with the distinctiveness. Over the last decade they have sought to tackle it by supporting it with regional political and administrative devolution. They have embraced local identity through the local government authority reorganisation with the re-establishment of old counties such as Rutland and old county borough councils such as Reading and Oxford. Unionists within both the Labour and Conservative parties, however, have sought to have minimum English regional identity and instead retain a strong unitary parliament in Westminster.

The origins of English devolution go back to a Speaker's conference in 1920 which decided the best solution to the problems of the devolutionary pressures in Ireland was 'Home Rule all round' for all of the British Isles nation states. The Labour and Conservative governments of that period did not agree with this notion, however and devolution of administrative power in England made slow progress. In the 1930s came the embryos of devolved government from the Special Areas Act 1934 which classified specific areas of the England according to their economic deprivation. Then during the Second World War England was divided into regional government areas for defence and other administrative purposes under regional governors. In the 1960s, the Regional Economic Planning Councils and Regional Economic Planning Boards were set up under Harold Wilson's Labour government. In the 1970s the Kilbrandon Commission had suggested regional elected authorities for England but the measure had not gone forward after the failure of Scottish and Welsh devolution in 1979. Then, under Margaret Thatcher's Conservative government, Urban Development Corporations were set up in the 1980s. All devolved some elements of administrative power from Whitehall to the regions but the boundaries of the different organisations often did not coincide. At the same time the Thatcher government had become increasingly frustrated by the Labour-controlled metropolitan authorities and the Greater London Council (led by Ken Livingstone) acting as alternative centres of power and undermining their own administration. They therefore abolished them all in 1986 leaving the large English metropolitan areas without an elected layer of government to control cross-borough activities.

Implementing the so-called 'European regionalism' model of devolution, it was the arrival of the EU's reforms to its Structural Funds (which provide economic assistance to specified regions) that required set and administratively integrated regional offices. Therefore in 1994, under Prime Minister John Major, the ten Government Offices of the Regions were established with the purpose of bringing together those elements of central government that needed to be integrated in order to make use of the EU's structural funds. When Labour came into power they turned these Government Offices into Regional Development Agencies which had Regional Chambers (RCs) above them. The RCs in the English regions were made up of appointed local government councillors, people from business and industry and other notables. When they were established at the start of the century it was thought that this would be a temporary measure and that in time they would be replaced by democratically elected members. In the event this did not occur and they were in time disbanded. The thrust beyond English devolution in Tony Blair's government came almost wholly from John Prescott, the Deputy Prime Minister. English devolution fell under his direct remit.

When Jack Straw had been the Labour Home Secretary in charge of the devolutionary process at the start of New Labour's 1997 term in office, he had defined what was called 'the triple lock' on the progress of English political devolution. This stated that if an English region wanted political devolution:

■ They would have to petition to become a directly elected assembly.

■ Parliament would have to legislate for this.

■ The electorate in the region would have to approve these measures in a referendum.

With Wales, Scotland and then Northern Ireland gaining devolution, England became one of the few countries in Europe without a form of regional government. This changed marginally in 2000 when a referendum was passed which established an elected mayor for London and an elected London Regional Authority, see Box 12.4. This did not apply for the rest of England, however. Prescott was therefore keen to see this spread to other English regions even if it didn't comply with Jack Straw's triple lock. Opinion polls had indicated that there was a demand for English regional government. This was highest in the north-east and north-west. In 2002 Prescott brought out the White paper: Your Region, Your Choice: Revitalising the English Regions which was followed by the White paper Your Region, Your Say. This set out the case for elected regional chambers in the English regions but not all at once, instead, it would be a step-by-step approach with the regions with the strongest identity going first. The Regional Assemblies (Preparations) Act 1993 went through Westminster and it was then planned to hold postal referendums in the north-west, north-east and Yorkshire and Humberside. Problems with postal voting during the European elections in June 2004 meant that the referendum on English devolution was scaled down to just one region – the north-east – and on 4 November 2004 a referendum was held there.

Support for the concept of a regional assembly in the north-east failed by almost five to one. The two 'No' campaigns, which ran there, had successfully defeated the 'Yes' campaign on similar issues to those that had resulted in the Welsh people rejecting their Assembly referendum in 1979. These revolved around the perception that they didn't want any more politicians, the assembly wasn't powerful enough, their regional identity wasn't strong enough, most Labour and Conservative politicians remained against it, as did local government which feared being scrapped.

The negative vote in the north-east in effect killed off English devolution. The Regional Chambers were scrapped although the RDAs were kept. Government ministers were now allocated to the nine English regions to run the RDAs. The Westminster Parliament set up eight English Regional Select Committees on an experimental basis in November 2008 to monitor the ministers and the RDAs. As part of the national strategy on the recession Gordon Brown also linked the RDAs and their government ministers into a Regional Economic Council to help plan government strategy. There were, however, no plans to make this an elected body, although the Conservatives still plan an English-only voting Parliament for Westminster.

BOX 12.4   Personality politics: The Mayor of London

There is one area of England that does have its own devolved government. That is London, with the Greater London Authority (GLA). The GLA is made up of a directly elected mayor and a separately elected authority. The Mayor of London controls a number of the capital's major public bodies. He sets the budget for the Metropolitan Police Service (MPS), Transport for London (TfL), The London Fire and Emergency Planning Authority (LFEPA), the London Development Agency (LDA) and the Greater London Authority (GLA).

Even before its inception the position of elected mayor of the authority became one of personality politics. Ken Livingstone, the former Labour leader of the GLC saw himself as the rightful heir to the mayor of the GLA. He was not selected by Labour in its controversial selection contest and then stood and won as an Independent against the official Labour candidate. For the next eight years Livingstone ran London with both success and personal controversy, often in the process ignoring the role of the GLA as a scrutinising body. It was Livingstone who introduced the successful traffic congestion

charge and also helped gain the Olympics for London in 2012.

Livingstone was defeated in 2008 by a Conservative politician as colourful in character as himself, Boris Johnson. The former MP for Henley-on-Thames and editor of *The Spectator*, Johnson had established a reputation for political mishaps and general buffoonery. Nevertheless this only added spice to his appeal as a candidate and he was duly elected by a majority of 139,772 votes.

The London-based media had engaged with the London mayoral election to a degree unparalleled in British politics, outside of the British general elections. Combined with the Conservative candidate victory this now enthused the Conservative party to introduce elected mayors across England. This was despite the fact that Labour's plans to introduce elected mayors had already widely failed and the Conservatives themselves had scrapped the metropolitan counties in the 1980s when council leaders such as Ken Livingstone had been seen to challenge their authority in central government.

Table 12.7 Public spending as share of GDP UK countries and London 2006

Nation/region	2005–06
United Kingdom	43.0%
England	40.9%
London	33.4%
Wales	62.4%
Scotland	54.9%
Northern Ireland	71.3%

Source: Office for National Statistics, 2008

Table 12.8 GDP per inhabitant UK countries and London 2006

Nation/region	GDP per inhabitant (euros)	GDP as a percentage of the EU average
United Kingdom	32,000	120.4
London	52,900	198.8
Wales	24,000	90.4
Scotland	30,800	115.9
Northern Ireland	26,000	97.1

Source: *Eurostat*, February 2009 (there is no separate figure for England)

■ Conclusions on devolution

After a decade of devolution in the United Kingdom we can conclude that it has had a number of impacts on the British political system. The foremost of these are:

■ Devolution has not helped the nations and regions of the regions converge (Tables 12.7

and 12.8). Disparities have remained as wide as under the strictly unionist state.

■ The constituent parts of the United Kingdom have not broken away from each other as was predicted by the anti-devolutionists. Even in Scotland where the SNP has pursued this policy it still looks fairly remote. The Union therefore has remained intact.

- Most of the political parties who are represented in the devolved bodies are not happy with the status quo. There have therefore been constant revisions and proposals for revisions of the constitutional devolution settlements.

- No one political party has ever gained the majority of the seats in a devolved government election. Coalition government and/or electoral pacts have become the norm now outside of Westminster politics. The Scottish Parliament and Northern Ireland Assembly have for their entire existence consisted of coalition governments. The Welsh Assembly has consisted of coalition governments for two of its three terms. This has moved the devolved governments and British politics closer to the European style of politics.

- The stability of the executives in Scotland and Wales has proved that proportional representation does not lead to unstable government, as has always been claimed would be the case, if it was introduced in Westminster.

- A whole new generation of young and female politicians who would have been unable to progress through the existing political system to Westminster have emerged. This has greatly reduced the gender imbalance in British politics. At the same time there has been the opportunity for the advancement of minor parties such as the Greens that have not been represented at Westminster thereby increasing the diversity of the political system.

- The quality of the elected representatives to the devolved institutions, however, has not always been of the level expected at the outset of devolution. Sometimes these have been unfavourably compared with those going to Westminster. This has led to accusations that devolved institutions have had to make do with 'second eleven' with the 'first eleven' going to Westminster. Many of those elected come from a local government,

public services or political party administrative background. What is forgotten, however, is that there are also equally poor Westminster MPs but because the media highlights only the most able Westminster politicians the poorer ones tend to go unnoticed.

- Relations between central and devolved governments have seen minimal change from predevolution arrangements for dealing with Scottish, Welsh and Northern Irish matters, relying on departmental concordats, bilateral and informal links largely among officials and not ministers. As a result the constitutional deadlock, also widely predicted, between the centre and devolved government has not occurred.

- With a lack of their own tax-raising powers, the devolved institutions are still under the considerable influence of Whitehall, the Chancellor of the Exchequer and the Treasury. Frustrations over the adequacy of the Barnett Formula remain, with non-English nations requiring greater funding. In time, however, particularly this may change. This is especially true in Scotland with the Calman Report advocating much larger taxraising power there.

- Policy and service differences between the devolved nations and England have intensified, particularly in certain aspects of healthcare. This has caused regional jealousy and animosity to occur.

- Not all politicians at Westminster have been prepared to accept the devolution in their own political powers and there often remains resistance or hostility to losing these powers. This has become most apparent in Wales as the nation moves towards a referendum on gaining full primary law-making powers for its Assembly. While most Assembly Members support the transfer of powers, most Westminster MPs do not.

- Personality politics, particularly in London, has caught the attention of the media creating unprecedented interest in devolved politics.

Chapter summary

At the start of this chapter we looked at Todd's three models of devolution. The type of devolution in Britain appears to have occurred along a version of Todd's 'state realism' model, within elements of the 'European regionalism' model. Devolution has resulted in modest and incremental change, with some minimal adaptations to cope with the demands devolution has created, in both Westminster and Whitehall. Westminster still maintains a strong legislative role in the devolved nations. This is true even in Scotland where the Sewell convention enables Westminster to legislate for devolved matters with the Scottish Parliament's consent. Westminster maintains a strong presence over taxation, international affairs, commerce and the economy and many social welfare issues. At the same time the Home Civil Service remains loyal to no single devolved government but instead to the crown. The much heralded break up of the United Kingdom therefore seems not a great deal closer than it was when the devolution process started in 1997, despite the threat of an independence referendum in Scotland. Relations between the devolved institutions and the Westminster government have also remained good even when there has been a difference of party political government in Scotland and Westminster. The fiscal restraint caused by the banking crisis and the role of a future Conservative government in its relationship with the devolved institutions may test this relationship once more. At the moment though it appears that devolution has been a further stage of political evolution rather than the revolution some sceptics predicted.

Discussion points

■ How have the policy differences affected the lives of the citizens in the respective nation states in terms of issues such as education and health?

■ Has devolution resulted in the end of the concept of Britishness?

■ Why do you think that English nationalism still remains a relatively minor political force?

■ Have the London-based political parties fully accepted their lack of control over events in the devolved nations?

■ Has devolution caused British politics to become more European and less Anglo-Saxon in nature?

■ What will be the likely shape of devolution by 2020?

Further reading

Those who wish to have brief overall picture of devolution and its developments should read

Devolution in the United Kingdom by Russell Deacon and Alan Sandry. A more comprehensive coverage of devolution can be found in *Devolution in Britain Today* by Russell Deacon. Those students who wish to examine the devolved politics of a particular region or nation now have a wealth of texts to choose from, including official publications and reports of the devolved bodies themselves. Edinburgh University Press, Manchester University Press and the University of Wales Press specialise in these, as do Welsh Academic Press. In particular, the reports produced by the Institute of Welsh Affairs and The Constitution Unit of the University of London are particularly useful.

Bibliography

Bulmer, Simon, Burch, Martin, Hogwood, Patricia and Scott, Andrew 'UK Devolution and the European Union: A Tale of Cooperative Asymmetry?', *Publius: The Journal of Federalism*, Vol. 36, No. 1, pp. 75–93.

Deacon, Russell (2002) *The Governance of Wales: The Welsh Office and the Policy Process 1964–99* (Welsh Academic Press).

Deacon, Russell (2006) *Devolution in Britain Today* (Manchester University Press).

Deacon, Russell and Sandry, Alan (2007) *Devolution in the United Kingdom* (Edinburgh University Press).

Devine, Tom (ed.) (2008) *Scotland and the Union 1707–2007* (Edinburgh University Press).

Eurobarometer (2007) Attitudes towards the EU in the United Kingdom, FlashEurobarometer 207, May 2007.

McEvoy, Joanne (2008) *The Politics of Northern Ireland* (Edinburgh University Press).

Osmond, John (2007) *Crossing the Rubicon: Coalition Politics Welsh Style* (Institute of Welsh Affairs).

Palmer, Rosanne (2008) *Devolution, Asymmetry and Europe: Multi-Level Governance in the United Kingdom* (Peter Lang).

Todd, Jennifer (2005), 'A New Territorial Politics in the British Isles?' in John Coakely, Brigid Laffan and Jennifer Todd, *Renovation Or Revolution? New Territorial Politics in Ireland and the United Kingdom* (University College Dublin Press).

And another thing . . .

The great parliamentary expenses crisis

Chris Mullin, MP

'THEY'RE ALL AT IT,' screamed the front page of the *Daily Mirror* over a story about MPs allowances.

Actually, we're not. The only place where I have ever worked where they were 'all at it' was Mirror Group Newspapers in the 1970s where, at the end of my first week, my expense claim was rejected by the man who was supposed to vouch for its accuracy on the grounds that it was so low that it would be an embarrassment to my colleagues.

I was then treated to a lesson in how to construct a fraudulent expense claim which, when no one was looking, I threw away.

One is not obliged, however, to believe every tabloid lie to recognise that MPs have brought much of their current travail upon themselves. It has been obvious for years that the system of remuneration and allowances is deeply flawed, that there have been wholesale abuses and that many opportunities for reform have been either avoided or actively resisted.

The flaws are threefold. First, to the huge embarrassment of many of us, we get to decide how much we should receive in pay and allowances. This has been justified on the grounds that Parliament is sovereign and, therefore, even though the issue is referred to the Senior Salaries Review Body, it is up to us to decide whether or not to accept their recommendations. So far as salaries are concerned, MPs have, in recent years at least, been generally restrained, often voting for lower than recommended increases in keeping with government pay policy. There have been notable exceptions, however. In 1996 MPs voted by a large majority (some of us were opposed) to award themselves a whopping 26 per cent pay increase.

So far as allowances are concerned, we have been generous to ourselves. In 2001 we voted through (again some of us, I am glad to say, voted against) an outrageous 42 per cent increase in the Additional Costs Allowance that enables those of us who represent constituencies beyond commuting distance of Westminster to maintain a second home, either in London or the constituency. From that moment onwards it became a target to be aimed at, rather than recompense for expenses legitimately incurred.

The second major flaw is that there has been no effective system of audit. For years officials of the House of Commons Fees Office encouraged Members to maximise their claims, rather than regulating how the allowances were spent. When I was first elected and for many years afterwards, it was not uncommon for a Member asking for advice to be told, 'it's your money, spend it as you see fit'. Some members came to regard the allowance as an extension of their salary, simply dividing the maximum amount claimable by 12 and claiming in monthly instalments, without ever being asked to provide any serious evidence of outgoings. Gradually, in recent years, the rules have been tightened, but old habits die hard.

Third, there was an absence of transparency and, therefore, no pressure on Members to justify their use of public money. When the Freedom of Information Act became law in 1999, it took a while for MPs to grasp the likely consequences. But the consequences were foreseeable. As long ago as May 2002 the then Leader of the House, Robin Cook, remarked presciently that 'few members have yet tumbled to the juggernaut heading their way'. How right he was.

Once the penny did drop, instead of cleaning up the system, the House of Commons authorities moved heaven and earth to avoid having to comply. The whips on both sides conspired to introduce a Private Members' Bill that would have exempted

MPs from the provisions of the Act. In fairness, it must be said that many Members refused to go along with this and as a result the proposed bill was swiftly abandoned.

By now requests for information were flooding in from journalists and members of the public. The House authorities initially responded by publishing headline figures for different categories of each MP's expenses. At the same time the rules were tightened, requiring the provision of receipts – but only for expenditure over £250. Unsurprisingly, this did not satisfy inquirers, whose appetite had by now been whetted by attempts to avoid disclosure. Unwisely, the House authorities chose to resist, employing lawyers to argue that the limited disclosure already conceded was sufficient to meet the demands of the Freedom of Information Act. Needless to say the Information Commissioner, Richard Thomas, was having none of this. Neither were the judges who, in due course, ruled that MPs should have to account in full for their use of public money.

At which point the House authorities caved in and agreed to provide full details of expenses claims for each of the previous four years, minus addresses and personal details such as bank account numbers and credit card details. It was a massive task. More than a million documents had to be scanned and MPs were given a chance to comment and to suggest deletions. While this was underway, someone apparently stole the computer disc containing the unedited details and sold it to the *Daily Telegraph* for a six-figure sum.

The results were devastating. For day after relentless day the *Telegraph* published details of some of the more exotic claims for the maintenance and repairs of swimming pools, tennis courts and even a moat. Home Secretary Jacqui Smith's husband was found, unknown to her, to have claimed for the hire of a pornographic video; more seriously she was found to be claiming the second home allowance against her family home. She was not the only one.

A new phenomenon – which quickly became known as 'flipping' – was identified. Some MPs, it appeared, were changing homes frequently in order to exploit to the full the second home allowance. Some were, at the same time, temporarily designating second homes as principal residences in order to avoid Capital Gains Tax when they sold up. Several were found to be claiming for mortgages that no longer existed. One was found to be claiming for a home on the south coast, over 100 miles from her constituency.

Almost immediately heads began to roll. Several ministers – including the Home Secretary – resigned or stepped down voluntarily from the government. Half a dozen Tory grandees who had been using the second homes allowance to maintain their country estates announced that they would not be contesting the next election. A number of Labour MPs announced – or were instructed by their party to announce – that they, too, would not be seeking re-election. One stood down immediately, triggering a by-election.

Party leaders vied with each other to demonstrate to an outraged public that they were dealing firmly with miscreants. Gordon Brown publicly disowned a member of his Cabinet who had avoided paying Capital Gains Tax. The Labour Party set up a 'Star Chamber' to deal with the most blatant examples of abuse. Tory leader David Cameron ordered the worst offenders in his party to repay excess claims – he himself repaid the cost of trimming the wisteria (Tory excesses were so much more elegant than Labour's) on his constituency residence and some of the big Tory offenders were simply ordered to announce that they would not contest the next election or face expulsion. One of Cameron's close aides, Andrew McKie, was among the casualties, along with his wife, Julie Kirkbride. Not to be out-done, the Liberal leader Nick Clegg called for constituents to be given the right to recall, mid-term, misbehaving MPs.

On 19 May 2009, the scandal consumed its most prominent victim. The Speaker, Michael Martin, announced his retirement. Fairly or unfairly, Speaker Martin had become widely regarded as an obstacle to reform and in the end pressure on him to stand down became irresistible.

The tabloids were in heaven. Tabloid journalism requires a constant supply of victims, be they mis-behaving footballers, errant soap stars or dodgy politicians – and here, courtesy of the *Telegraph*, was an unlimited supply. Even the most minor infringements suddenly became front page news.

The political impact was considerable. For the first time opinion polls rated MPs as lower in public esteem than even the bankers who had brought the world economy to the brink of destruction. All the main parties were contaminated, but Labour came off worst, partly because it was the governing party and it happened on their watch. The impact was reflected in the results of European elections in June 2009 when the Labour vote all but collapsed. Even the Tories, who had been riding high in the opinion polls, did not do particularly well. The beneficiaries were fringe parties, unrepresented at Westminster: the United Kingdom Independence Party, the Greens and – ominously – the British National Party.

The impact on the self-confidence of the political classes was devastating. For weeks the House of Commons was traumatised as members sat around awaiting the call from the *Daily Telegraph*. An unprecedented number of sitting Members, innocent and guilty alike, decided to stand down come the election. The damage to politics in general and the democratic process as a whole is incalculable.

As for the future, the key reforms have already been made. Transparency and proper audit will ensure that the abuses of the past can never be repeated. The damage to the political system as a whole will, however, take much longer to repair.

Chris Mullin was the MP for Sunderland South from 1987 to 2010. In 2009 he published a volume of diaries entitled *A View From the Foothills*. Two further volumes are in the pipeline.

PART 4
THE LEGISLATIVE PROCESS

Source: Alamy Images / Tim Ayers Photography

Introduction to Part 4

Bill Jones

So far this book has addressed the non-institutional elements of British politics; the remainder of the volume deals with the institutional aspects together with specific policy areas. Institutions can often seem confusing to students, who tend to study them individually and find it difficult to grasp how they relate to and interact with each other. Accordingly, this short section gives two contrasting overviews of how the system works.

■ Two overviews of the British political system

The functions of government

It is helpful to contrast the British political system with that of the USA. It is well known that the eighteenth-century framers of the US constitution wrote into their 1787 document a strict separation of powers. The legislature (Congress) and the executive (the Presidency) were to be elected separately for terms of differing length, with the **judiciary** (the Supreme Court) appointed by the President for life. In diagrammatic form, the functions can be represented by three separate and independent circles (see Figure 1).

The purpose of this arrangement was to disperse power to institutions that would check each other and ensure that no branch of government became over-mighty. In Britain, however, there never was such a separation. The three functions overlap significantly. To change or re-elect a government there is only one election and that is to the legislative chamber, the House of Commons. After the election, the majority party in that chamber invariably forms the executive. The crucial overlap between the

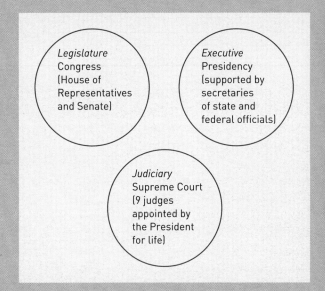

Figure 1 Functions of government: USA

legislative and executive spheres therefore comprises Prime Minister, Cabinet and the other seventy or so junior ministers. Until 2006, the judiciary was similarly appointed by the executive: not by the Prime Minister but by the Lord Chancellor, the government's chief law officer, who sat in the Cabinet and presided over the House of Lords (see Figure 2).

The US constitution ensures that the President cannot be overthrown by Congress – except through impeachment – but looser party discipline means that the President cannot regularly command congressional support for his policies; indeed, like Presidents Bush, for a while, and Clinton, his party may be in the minority in Congress. The British Prime Minister, in contrast, has more power: provided that the support of the majority party is sustained, he or she leads both the executive and legislative arms of government. However, loss of significant party

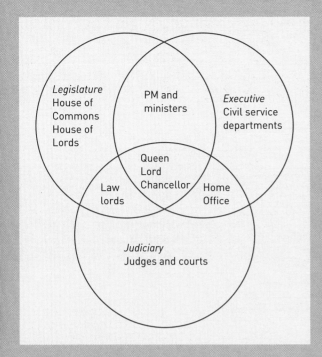

Figure 2 Functions of government: UK

support can bring down the British Prime Minister, as it did Chamberlain in May 1940 and Thatcher in 1990. This possibility clearly acts as a constraint upon potential prime ministerial action, but the fact is that parties in government very rarely even threaten to unseat their leaders, because they fear the electoral consequences of apparent disunity.

The executive's power is further reinforced by the doctrine of parliamentary sovereignty, which enables it to overrule any law – constitutional or otherwise – with a simple majority vote; and considerable residual powers of the monarch via the royal prerogative. The power of the House of Lords of legislative delay only (other than for bills originating

in the Lords), and local government's essentially subservient relationship to Westminster, complete the picture of an unusually powerful executive arm of government for a representative democracy.

Representative and responsible government

Represented in a different way, the British political system can be seen as a circuit of representation and responsibility. Parliament represents the electorate but is also responsible to it via elections. In their turn, ministers represent majority opinion in the legislature (although they are appointed by the Prime Minister, not elected) and are responsible to it for their actions in leading the executive. Civil servants are not representatives but as part of the executive are controlled by ministers and are responsible to them. Figure 3 illustrates the relationship.

This, of course, is a very simplistic view, but it does express the underlying theory of how British government should work. The reality of how the system operates is infinitely more complex, as Figure 4 – itself highly simplified – seeks to illustrate. Earlier chapters have explained how the different elements of British government operate in practice:

1 Parliament provides the forum, the 'playing field' on which the ordered competition of democratic government is publicly conducted.

2 Political parties dominate the system, organising the electorate, taking over Parliament and providing the ministers who run the Civil Service.

3 The Prime Minister as leader of the majority party can exercise considerable personal power and in recent years has become more akin to a presidential figure.

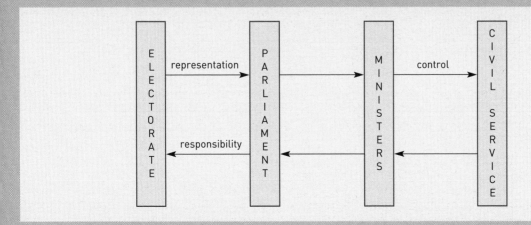

Figure 3 Representative and responsible government

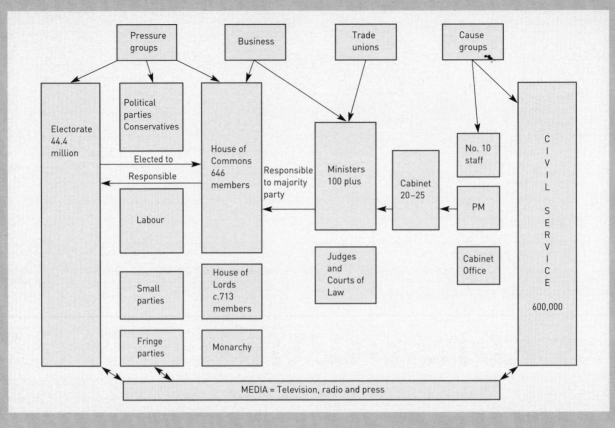

Figure 4 Elements of UK central government

4 The judiciary performs the important task of interpreting legislation and calling ministers and officials to account if they act without statutory authority.

5 Civil servants serve ministers, but their permanence and their professionalism, their vested interests in searching for consensus and defending departmental interests raise suspicions that they occasionally or even regularly outflank their ministerial masters.

6 Pressure groups infiltrate the whole gamut of government institutions, the most powerful bypassing Parliament and choosing to deal direct with ministers and civil servants. (See Chapter 11.)

7 The media have increasingly usurped the role of Parliament in informing the public and providing a forum for public debate. Television is a potent new influence, the impact of which is still to be fully felt. (See Chapter 10.)

Does the reality invalidate the theory? It all depends upon how drastically we believe Figure 4 distorts Figure 3. Indeed, Marxists would declare both to be irrelevant in that business pressure groups call the shots that matter, operating behind the scenes and within the supportive context of a system in which all the major actors subscribe to their values. Former cabinet minister Tony Benn would argue that the executive has become so dominant at the expense of the legislature that the PM's power can be compared with that of a medieval monarch. As we have seen, Britain's constitutional arrangements have always allowed great potential power – potential that strong Prime Ministers like Margaret Thatcher have been keen and able to realise when given the time. But I would maintain, and cite in support the analyses offered by the authors of this book, that the essential features of the democratic system portrayed in Figure 3 just about survive in that:

■ party-dominated governments are removable;

■ Parliament still applies watchdog controls (and just occasionally reminds the executive by biting);

■ the electorate has a choice between parties;

■ civil servants ordinarily seek to obey their political masters;

■ pressure groups influence but do not dictate.

Part 4 explains how the legislative system works; Part 5 explains the executive process; and Part 6 looks at a number of policy areas.

CHAPTER 13

The changing constitution

Philip Norton

Learning objectives

- To identify the sources and key components of the British constitution.

- To analyse the nature of the debate about the British constitution.

- To consider the major changes and modifications made to the constitution in recent years.

- To detail the arguments for and against some of the major changes that have taken place or are proposed to the constitution, including electoral reform.

- To address the problems faced by political parties as a consequence of constitutional change.

Introduction

In the quarter-century following the Second World War, the constitution rarely figured in political debate. It was seen as the preserve more of lawyers than of politicians. In the last three decades of the century, it became a subject of political controversy. Demands for reform of the constitution grew. Many of those demands were met by the Labour government elected in May 1997, with major changes being made to the constitutional framework of the country. Some critics demand further change. The changes that have taken place have created problems for the three main political parties.

■ The constitution

What, then, is a **constitution**? What is it for? What is distinctive about the British constitution? Where does it come from? What are the essential constituents of the 'traditional' constitution? What challenges has it faced in recent years? What changes have been made to it? What are the problems posed to the political parties by such changes? And what is the nature of the debate taking place about further constitutional change?

Definition and sources

What is a constitution? A constitution can be defined as the system of laws, customs and **conventions** that defines the composition and powers of organs of the state (such as government, Parliament and the courts) and regulates the relations of the various state organs to one another and of those state organs to the private citizen.

What are constitutions for? Constitutions vary in terms of their purpose. A constitution may be constructed in such a way as to embody and protect fundamental principles (such as individual liberty), principles that should be beyond the reach of the transient wish of the people. This is referred to as **negative constitutionalism** (see Ivison 1999). This tends to be reflected in presidential systems of government (see Bradley, Ziegler and Baranger 2007); the United States is a notable example. A constitution may be constructed in order to ensure that the wishes of the people are paramount. This is referred to as **positive constitutionalism**. Here, there are few, if any, restraints on the people's elected representatives. This tends to be reflected in parliamentary systems of government (Bradley, Ziegler and Baranger 2007). The UK falls primarily in this category.

What form do constitutions take? Most, but not all, are drawn up in a single, codified document. Some are short, others remarkably long. Some embody provisions that exhort citizens to act in a certain way ('It shall be the duty of every citizen . . .'); others confine themselves to stipulating the formal structures and powers of state bodies. Processes of interpretation and amendment vary. Most, but not all, have entrenched provisions: i.e. they can only be amended by an extraordinary process beyond that normally employed for amending the law.

The British constitution differs from most in that it is not drawn up in a single codified document. As such, it is often described as an 'unwritten' constitution. However, much of the constitution does exist in 'written' form. Many Acts of Parliament – such as the European Communities Act 1972, providing the legal basis for British membership of the European Community, and the Constitutional Reform Act 2005, creating a Supreme Court – are clearly measures of constitutional law. Those Acts constitute formal, written – and binding – documents. To describe the constitution as unwritten is thus misleading. Rather, what Britain has is a part-written, uncodified constitution.

Even in countries with a formal, written document, 'the constitution' constitutes more than the simple words of the document. Those words have to be interpreted. Practices develop, and laws are passed, that help to give meaning to those words. To understand the contemporary constitution of the United States, for example, one has to look beyond the document to interpretations of that document by the courts in the USA, principally the US Supreme Court, and to various acts of Congress and to practices developed over the past 200 years. The constitutions of most countries thus have what may be termed a primary source (the written document)

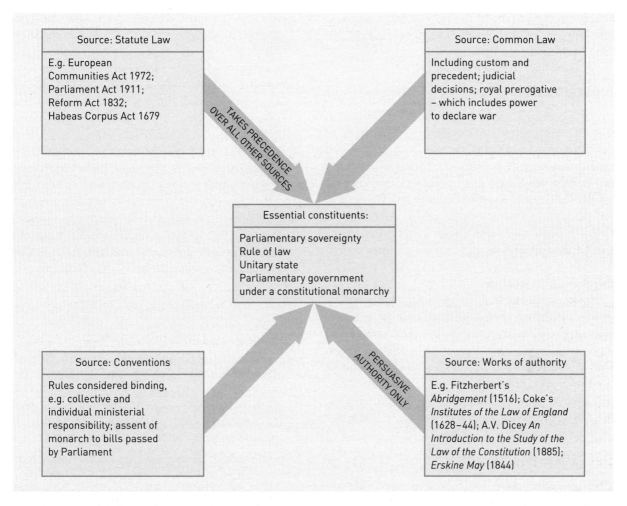

Figure 13.1 The traditional constitution: sources and constituents
Source: From P. Norton (1986) 'The constitution in flux', *Social Studies Review*, Vol. 2, No. 1. Reproduced with permission from the California Council for Social Studies

and secondary sources (judicial interpretation, legislative acts, established practice). The UK, without a written document, lacks the equivalent primary source. Instead, the constitution derives from sources that elsewhere would constitute secondary sources of the constitution. Those sources are four in number (see Figure 13.1). They are:

1 *statute law*, comprising Acts of Parliament and subordinate legislation made under the authority of the parent Act;

2 *common law*, comprising legal principles developed and applied by the courts, and encompassing the prerogative powers of the crown and the law and practice of Parliament;

3 *conventions*, constituting rules of behaviour that are considered binding by and upon those

who operate the constitution but that are not enforced by the courts or by the presiding officers in the Houses of Parliament;

4 *works of authority*, comprising various written works – often but not always accorded authority by reason of their age – that provide guidance and interpretation on uncertain aspects of the constitution. Such works have persuasive authority only.

Statute law is the pre-eminent of the four sources and occupies such a position because of the doctrine of **parliamentary sovereignty**. Under this judicially self-imposed concept, the courts recognise only the authority of Parliament (formally the Queen-in-Parliament) to make law, with no body other than Parliament itself having the authority to set aside that law. The courts cannot strike down a law as being contrary to the provisions of the constitution. Statute law, then, is supreme and can be used to override common law.

Amendment

No extraordinary features are laid down in Parliament for the passage or amendment of measures of constitutional law. Although bills of constitutional significance usually have their committee stage on the floor of the House of Commons, rather than in a public bill committee (see Chapter 15), there is no formal requirement for this to happen. All bills have to go through the same stages in both Houses of Parliament and are subject to simple majority voting. As such, the traditional constitution is, formally, a **flexible constitution**.

However, as we shall see, there are two recent developments that challenge this flexibility: membership of the European Community/Union and the incorporation of the European Convention on Human Rights into British law. The devolution of powers to elected assemblies in different parts of the United Kingdom may also be argued to limit, in effect, the capacity of Parliament to pass any legislation it wishes.

■ The traditional constitution: essential constituents

The traditional constitution existed for most of the twentieth century. It had four principal features. Although, as we shall see, these features have been challenged by changes in recent years, each nonetheless remains formally in place:

1 *Parliamentary sovereignty* has been described as the cornerstone of the British constitution. As we have seen, it stipulates that the outputs of Parliament are binding and cannot be set aside by any body other than Parliament itself. The doctrine was confirmed by the Glorious Revolution of 1688 and 1689, when the common lawyers combined with Parliament against the King. Since the Settlement of 1689 established that the King was bound by the law of Parliament, it followed that his courts were also so bound.

2 *The rule of law* was identified by nineteenth-century constitutional lawyer A.V. Dicey as one of the twin pillars of the constitution and is generally accepted as one of the essential features of a free society. However, it is logically subordinate to the first pillar – parliamentary sovereignty – since Parliament could pass a measure undermining or destroying the rule of law. It is also a matter of dispute as to what the term encompasses. In terms of the law passed by Parliament, it is essentially a procedural doctrine. Laws must be interpreted and applied by an impartial and independent **judiciary**; those charged under the law are entitled to a fair trial; and no one can be imprisoned other than through the due process of law. However, there is some dispute as to how far the doctrine extends beyond this, not least in defining the extent of the power of the state to regulate the affairs of citizens.

3 *A unitary state* is one in which formal power resides exclusively in the national authority, with no entrenched and autonomous powers being vested in any other body. In federal systems, power is shared between national and regional or state governments, each enjoying an autonomous existence and exercising powers granted by the constitution. In the UK, state power resides centrally, with the Queen-in-Parliament being omnicompetent. Parliament can create and confer certain powers on other bodies – such as assemblies and even parliaments in different parts of the UK – but those bodies remain subordinate to Parliament and can be restricted, even abolished, by it.

4 *A parliamentary government under a* **constitutional monarchy** refers to the form of government established by, and developed since, the Glorious Revolution. That revolution established the supremacy of Parliament over the King. The greater acceptance of democratic principles in the nineteenth and twentieth centuries has resulted in the enlargement of the franchise and a pre-eminent role in the triumvirate of Queen-in-Parliament (monarch, Commons, Lords) for the elected chamber, the House of Commons. 'Parliament' thus means predominantly – although not exclusively – the House of Commons, while 'parliamentary government' refers not to government by Parliament but to government through Parliament. Ministers are legally answerable to the crown but politically answerable to Parliament, that political relationship being governed by the conventions of collective and individual **ministerial responsibility**. A government is returned

in a general election and between elections depends on the confidence of a majority of Members of Parliament both for the passage of its measures and for its continuance in office.

Three of these four features (parliamentary sovereignty, unitary state, parliamentary government) facilitated the emergence of strong, or potentially strong, government, a government secure in its majority in the House of Commons being able to enact measures that were then binding on society and that could not be set aside by any body other than Parliament itself. There were no other forms of government below the national enjoying autonomous powers (the consequence of a unitary state); no other actors at national level were able to countermand the elected House of Commons, be it the crown or the House of Lords (the consequence of the growth of parliamentary government under a constitutional monarchy) or the courts (the consequence of the

doctrine of parliamentary sovereignty). The United Kingdom thus enjoyed a centralised system of government.

That system of government, made possible by the essential features of the constitution, was variously described as the Westminster system of government. At the heart of the system was the Cabinet, sustained by a party majority in the House of Commons. Each party fought a general election on the basis of a party manifesto and, if elected to office, it proceeded to implement the promises made in the manifesto. Parliament provided the legitimacy for the government and its measures, subjecting those measures to debate and scrutiny before giving its approval to them. *Party* ensured that the government almost always got its way, but the *party system* ensured that the government faced the critical scrutiny of the party in opposition.

The traditional constitution can, as we have seen, be traced back to the Glorious Revolution of the

Twenty-first century or not, debates cannot ensue in the House of Commons chamber unless the Mace is properly in position
Source: PA Wire / Empics

Lord Jenkins, former Labour Chancellor and Home Secretary, as well as co-founder of the shortlived SDP, was asked to chair a commission on voting reform which reported in 1998 but was subsequently ignored by the Labour Government. *Source*: Getty Images.

seventeenth century, but it emerged more fully in the nineteenth century with the widening of the franchise. It emerged in the form we have just described – the Westminster system – essentially in the period from 1867, with the passage of the second Reform Act (necessitating the growth of organised parties), and 1911, when the Parliament Act (restricting by statute the powers of the House of Lords) was passed. From 1911 onwards, power in the UK resided in the party that held a majority of seats in the House of Commons. In so far as the party in government expressed the will of the people and it achieved the measures it wanted, then the UK acquired, in effect, a limited form of positive constitutionalism.

■ Challenges to the traditional constitution

The traditional constitution was in place from 1911 to 1972. Although it was variously criticised in the years between the two world wars, especially in the depression of the 1930s, it went largely unchallenged in the years immediately after the Second World War. The nation's political institutions continued to

function during the war, and the country emerged victorious from the conflict. In the 1950s, the nation enjoyed relative economic prosperity. There appeared little reason to question the nation's constitutional arrangements. That changed once the country began to experience economic recession and more marked political conflicts. The constitution came in for questioning. If the political system was not delivering what was expected of it, was there not then a case for changing the system itself? The issue of constitutional reform began to creep onto the political agenda.

Since 1970, the traditional constitution has faced two major challenges. Both have had significant consequences for the nation's constitutional arrangements. The first was membership of the European Community (now the European Union). The second was the constitutional changes introduced by the Labour government elected in May 1997.

Membership of the European Community/Union

A judicial dimension

The United Kingdom became a member of the European Community (EC) on 1 January 1973. The Treaty of Accession was signed in 1972 and the legal basis for membership provided by the European Communities Act 1972. The motivation for joining the Community was essentially economic and political. However, membership had significant constitutional consequences, primarily because it:

■ Gave the force of law not only to existing but also to all future EC law. As soon as regulations are made by the institutions of the EC, they have binding applicability in the UK. The assent of Parliament is not required. That assent has, in effect, been given in advance under the provisions of the 1972 Act. Parliament has some discretion as to the form in which EC directives are to be implemented, but the discretion refers only to the form and not to the principle.

■ Gave EC law precedence over UK law. In the event of a conflict between EC law and UK law, the European law takes precedence. The full effect of this was only realised with some important court cases in the 1990s (Fitzpatrick 1999). In the *Factortame* case of 1990–1, the European Court of Justice held that the courts in the UK could suspend the provisions of an Act of Parliament, where it appeared to breach EC law, until a final determination was made. In the case of *Ex Parte EOC*, in 1994, the highest domestic court, then the appellate committee of the House of Lords, struck down provisions of the 1978 Employment Protection (Consolidation) Act as incompatible with EC law (Maxwell 1999).

■ Gave the power to determine disputes to the courts. Where there is a dispute over European law, the matter is resolved by the courts. Questions of law have to be decided by the European Court of Justice (ECJ). Where a question of European law reaches the highest domestic court of appeal (until 2009 the House of Lords, since then the Supreme Court), it has to be referred to the ECJ for a definitive ruling; lower courts may ask the ECJ for a ruling on the meaning of treaty provisions. All courts in the UK are required to take judicial notice of decisions of the ECJ.

The effect of these changes has been to challenge the doctrine of parliamentary sovereignty. The decisions of Parliament can, in certain circumstances (where they conflict with EC law), be set aside by a body or bodies other than Parliament itself – namely, the courts. In sectors that now fall within the competence of the European Union, it can be argued that the UK now has something akin to a written constitution – that is, the treaties of the European Union.

The doctrine of parliamentary sovereignty remains formally in place because Parliament retains the power to repeal the European Communities Act. The ECJ is able to exercise the power it does because an Act of Parliament says that it can. However, the effect of repealing the 1972 Act would be to take the UK out of the European Union. The claim that Parliament retains the power to repeal the 1972 Act appears to be accepted by most constitutional lawyers, although some now question this, and the longer the Act remains in force the more the doctrine of parliamentary sovereignty will be challenged and may eventually fade away.

A political dimension

As a consequence of membership, the constitution thus acquired a new judicial dimension, one that challenged the doctrine of parliamentary sovereignty. At the same time, it also acquired a new political dimension, one that challenged the decision-making capacity of British government. Under the terms of entry, policy-making power in various sectors of public policy passed to the institutions of the European Community. Subsequent treaties have served both to extend the range of sectors falling within the competence of the EC and to strengthen the decision-making capacity of the European institutions.

The Single European Act, which came into force in 1987, produced a significant shift in the power relationship between the institutions of the Community and the institutions of the member states, strengthening EC institutions, especially through the extension of qualified majority voting (QMV) in the Council of Ministers. The Act also brought about a shift in the power relationships within the institutions of the Community, strengthening the European Parliament through the extension of the cooperation procedure, a procedure that provides a greater role for the Parliament in Community law making. Further shifts in both levels of power relationship were embodied in the Treaty on European Union (the Maastricht Treaty), which took effect in November 1993. This established a European Union with three pillars (the European Community, common foreign and security policy, justice and home affairs), extended the sectors of public policy falling within the competence of the European Community and established a new co-decision procedure for making law in certain areas, a procedure that strengthened again the position of the European Parliament. It now became a partner, with the Council of Ministers, in law making. A further strengthening of the position of the EC, now the European Union, took place with the implementation in 1999 of the Amsterdam Treaty. This extended the range of subjects falling within the competence of the EU and widened the range of issues subject to the co-decision procedure. The Nice Treaty, which took effect in 2003, introduced reforms to the Council and Commission in preparation for the enlargement of the EU that took place in 2004. The Convention on the Future of Europe developed further proposals for major reforms, including the introduction of a constitution for the EU. Though the constitutional treaty fell foul of 'no' votes in referendums in France and Holland, a number of member states pressed for further institutional change. This pressure resulted in the Lisbon treaty, drawing on most of the provisions of the constitutional treaty and seeking to consolidate existing treaties into one. The Lisbon treaty encountered a 'no' vote in Ireland, but in a second vote was approved and took effect on 1 December 2009. The European Union is thus characterised by the absence of any steady state in constitutional terms: there is almost continual pressure for further change, with attendant consequences for the member states.

As a result of membership of the European Union, the British government is thus constrained in what it can do. The Government and Parliament could block new treaty provisions (primary legislation) – which require unanimous approval of the member states – but are constrained in seeking to block or change legislation introduced under the existing treaties (secondary legislation). Where proposals for secondary legislation are laid before the Council of Ministers, the UK minister may be outvoted by the ministers of the other member states. A decision may thus be taken that is then enforced within the UK, even if it does not have the support of the British government and Parliament. (Under the Luxembourg Compromise, agreed in 1966, a government may veto a proposal if it conflicts with the nation's vital national interests. Some governments, including the British and French, have argued that the compromise can still be used, but it has not been cited since the Single European Act was agreed, and various authorities question whether it could now be invoked.) If the government takes an action that appears to conflict with EU law, it can be challenged in the courts and then required to bring itself into line with EU law. An Act of Parliament, as we have seen, does not take precedence over European law. Membership of the European Community – now the European Union – has thus added a new element to the constitution, one that does not fit easily with the existing features of that constitution.

Constitutional reform under the Blair government

Background to reform

The 1970s and 1980s witnessed growing demands for reform of the existing constitution. The system of government no longer appeared to perform as well as it had in the past. The country experienced economic difficulties (inflation, rising unemployment), industrial disputes, civil unrest in Northern Ireland and some social unrest at home (riots in cities such as Bristol and Liverpool). There were problems with the political process. Turnout declined in general elections. The proportion of electors voting for either of the two major parties fell. Two general elections took place in one year (1974), with no decisive outcome. A Labour government elected with less than 40 per cent of the vote in October 1974 was able to implement a series of radical measures.

Critics of the constitution argued the case for change. Some politicians and lawyers argued the case for an entrenched Bill of Rights – putting rights beyond the reach of simple majorities in the two Houses of Parliament. The case for a Bill of Rights was put by Lord Hailsham in a 1976 lecture, subsequently published in pamphlet form under the title *Elective Dictatorship*. Some politicians wanted a new electoral system, one that produced a closer relationship between the proportion of votes won nationally and the proportion of seats won in the House of Commons. The case for a new electoral system was made in an influential set of essays, edited by Professor S.E. Finer in 1975. Finer argued that a system of proportional representation would put an end to partisanship and help get rid of the policy discontinuity that results when one party replaces another in government.

There were also calls for power to be devolved to elected assemblies in different parts of the United Kingdom and for the use of referendums. Both changes, it was argued, would push decision making down from a centralised government to the people.

The Labour government elected in 1974 sought, unsuccessfully, to pass measures providing for elected assemblies in Scotland and Wales. The government did make provision for the first UK-wide referendum, held in 1975 on the issue of Britain's continued membership of the European Community.

The demands for change were fairly disparate and in most cases tied to no obvious intellectually coherent approach to constitutional change. However, as the 1980s progressed, various coherent approaches developed (Norton 1982, 1993). These are listed in Box 13.1. Each approach had its advocates, although the high Tory and Marxist approaches were essentially overshadowed by the others. The corporatist, or group, approach was more to the fore in the 1970s, when a Labour government brought representatives of trade unions and business into discussions on economic policy. It retained some advocates in the 1980s. The socialist approach, pursued by politicians such as former Labour cabinet minister Tony Benn, had a notable influence in the Labour Party in the early 1980s, the Labour manifesto in the 1983 general election adopting an essentially socialist stance. The New Right approach found some influential supporters in the Conservative Party, notably cabinet minister Sir Keith Joseph; it also influenced the Prime Minister, Margaret Thatcher.

However, the two most prominent approaches were the liberal and the traditionalist. The liberal approach was pursued by the Liberal Party and then by its successor party, the Liberal Democrats. It also attracted support from a much wider political spectrum, including some Labour supporters and even some ex-Marxists. In 1988, a constitutional reform movement, Charter88, was formed (the year of formation was deliberate, being the tercentenary year of the Glorious Revolution) to bring together all those who supported a new constitutional settlement.

The liberal approach made much of the running in political debate. However, the traditional approach was the more influential by virtue of the fact that it was the approach adopted by the Conservative government. Although Prime Minister Margaret Thatcher supported reducing the public sector, she nonetheless maintained a basic traditionalist approach to the constitution. Her successor, John Major, was a particularly vocal advocate of the traditional approach. Although the period of Conservative government from 1979 to 1997 saw some important constitutional changes – such as a constriction of the role of local government and the negotiation of new European treaties (the Single European Act and the Maastricht Treaty) – there was no principled embrace of radical constitutional change. The stance of government was to support the existing constitutional framework.

As the 1990s progressed, the debate about constitutional change largely polarised around these two approaches. The collapse of communism, the move from Labour to New Labour in Britain and the demise of Margaret Thatcher as leader of the Conservative Party served to diminish the impact of several of the other approaches. As the liberal approach gained ground, so supporters of the traditional approach began to put their heads above the parapet in support of their position.

BOX 13.1　IDEAS AND PERSPECTIVES

Approaches to constitutional change

High Tory

This approach contends that the constitution has evolved organically and that change, artificial change, is neither necessary nor desirable. In its pure form, it is opposed not only to major reforms – such as electoral reform, a Bill of Rights and an elected second chamber – but also to modifications to existing arrangements, such as the introduction of departmental select committees in the House of Commons. Its stance on any proposed reform is thus predictable: it is against it. The approach has been embraced over the years by a number of Conservative MPs.

Socialist

This approach favours reform, but a particular type of reform. It seeks strong government, but a party-dominated strong government, with adherence to the principle of intra-party democracy and the concept of the mandate. It wants to shift power from the existing 'top-down' form of control (government to people) to a 'bottom-up' form (people to government), with party acting as the channel for the exercise of that control. It favours sweeping away the monarchy and the House of Lords and the use of more elective processes, both for public offices and within the Labour Party. It is wary of, or opposed to, reforms that might prevent the return of a socialist government and the implementation of a socialist programme. It is thus sceptical of or opposed to electoral reform (potential for coalition government), an entrenched Bill of Rights (constraining government autonomy, giving power to judges) and membership of the European Union (constraining influence, sometimes viewed as a capitalists' club). For government to carry through socialist policies, it has to be free of constitutional constraints that favour or are dominated by its opponents. The most powerful advocate of this approach has been former Labour cabinet minister Tony Benn.

Marxist

This approach sees the restructuring of the political system as largely irrelevant, certainly in the long run, serving merely to delay the collapse of capitalist society. Government, any government, is forced to act in the interests of finance capital. Changes to the constitutional arrangements may serve to protect those interests in the short term but will not stave off collapse in the long term. Whatever the structures, government will be constrained by external élites, and those élites will themselves be forced to follow rather than determine events. The clash between the imperatives of capitalism and decreasing profit rates in the meso-economy determines what capitalists do. Constitutional reform, in consequence, is not advocated but rather taken as demonstrating tensions within the international capitalist economy. This approach has essentially been a 'pure' one, with some Marxists pursuing variations of it and some taking a more direct interest in constitutional change.

Corporatist

The corporatist, or group, approach seeks the greater incorporation of groups into the process of policy making in order to achieve a more consensual approach to public policy. The interdependence of government and interest groups – especially sectional interest groups – is such that it should be recognised and accommodated. A more integrated process can facilitate a more stable economic system. Supporters of this approach have looked to other countries, such as Germany, as examples of what can be achieved. This approach thus favours the representation of labour and business on executive and advisory bodies and, in its pure form, the creation of a functionalist second chamber. It was an approach that attracted support, especially in the 1970s, being pursued in a mild form by the Labour government from 1974 to 1979 and also being embraced, after 1972, by Conservative Prime Minister Edward Heath.

New Right

This approach is motivated by the economic philosophy of the free market. State intervention in economic affairs is viewed as illegitimate and dangerous, distorting the natural forces of the market and denying the consumer the freedom to choose. The state should therefore withdraw from economic activity. This viewpoint entails a contraction of the public sector, with state-owned industries being returned to the private sector. If institutions need reforming in order to facilitate the free market, then so be it: under this approach, no institution is deemed sacrosanct. Frank Vipert, the former deputy director of the free-market think-tank the Institute of Economic Affairs, has advocated a 'free market written constitution'. It is an approach associated with several politicians on the right wing of the Conservative Party, such as John Redwood.

Liberal

Like the New Right approach, this is a radical approach to constitutional change. It derives from traditional liberal theory and emphasises the centrality of the individual, limited government, the neutrality of the state in resolving conflict and consensual decision making. It views the individual as increasingly isolated in decision making, being elbowed aside by powerful interests and divorced from a governmental process that is centralised and distorted by partisan preferences. Against an increasingly over-mighty state, the individual has no means of protection. Hence, it is argued, the need for radical constitutional change. The liberal approach favours a new, written constitution, embodying the various reforms advocated by Charter88 (now part of a wider reform movement, Unlock Democracy), including a Bill of Rights, a system of proportional representation for elections, an elected second chamber, and a reformed House of Commons. In its pure form, it supports federalism rather than devolution. Such a new constitutional settlement, it is argued, will serve to shift power from government to the individual. The only reform about which it is ambivalent is the use of referendums, some adherents to this approach seeing the referendum as a device for oppression by the majority. It is an approach pursued by Liberal Democrats, such as Shirley Williams, and by some Labour politicians.

Traditional

This is a very British approach and derives from a perception of the 'traditional' system as fundamentally sound, offering a balanced system of government. It draws on Tory theory in its emphasis on the need for strong government and on Whig theory in stressing the importance of Parliament as the agent for setting the limits within which government may act. These emphases coalesce in the Westminster model of government, a model that is part descriptive (what is) and part prescriptive (what should be). Government, in this model, must be able to formulate a coherent programme of public policy – the initiative rests with government – with Parliament, as the deliberative body of the nation, subjecting the actions and the programme of government to rigorous scrutiny and providing the limits within which government may govern. This approach recognises the importance of the House of Commons as the elected chamber and the fact that the citizen has neither the time nor the inclination to engage in continuous political debate. There is thus a certain deference, but a contingent deference, to the deliberative wisdom of Parliament. The fact that the Westminster model is prescriptive means that traditionalists – unlike high Tories – will entertain change if it is designed to move present arrangements towards the realisation of that model. They also recognise with Edmund Burke that 'a state without the means of some change is without the means of its conservation' and are therefore prepared to consider change in order to maintain and strengthen the existing constitutional framework. Over the years, therefore, traditionalists have supported a range of incremental reforms, such as the introduction of departmental select committees in the House of Commons, but have opposed radical reforms – such as electoral reform – which threaten the existing framework. There is wariness about membership of the European Union, with involvement accepted as long as it does not pose a major threat to the existing domestic arrangements for decision making. It is an approach pursued by many mainstream Conservative politicians and by some Labour MPs.

Supporters of the liberal approach argued that a new constitution was needed in order to push power down to the individual. Power was too heavily concentrated in public bodies and in special interests. Decentralising power would limit the over-mighty state and also be more efficient, ensuring that power was exercised at a more appropriate level, one more closely related to those affected by the decisions being taken. Supporters of the traditional approach countered this by arguing that the traditional constitution had attributes that, in combination, made the existing arrangements preferable to anything else

on offer. The attributes were those of coherence, accountability, responsiveness, flexibility and effectiveness. The system of government, it was argued, was coherent: the different parts of the system were integrated, one party being elected to office to implement a programme of public policy placed before electors. The system was accountable: electors knew who to hold to account – the party in government – if they disapproved of public policy; if they disapproved, they could sweep the party from office. The system was responsive: knowing that it could be swept from office at the next election, a government paid attention to the wishes of electors. Ministers could not ignore the wishes of voters and assume they could stay in office next time around as a result of post-election bargaining (a feature of some systems of government). The system was flexible: it could respond quickly in times of crisis, with measures being passed quickly with all-party agreement. The system was also effective: government could govern and could usually be assured of parliamentary approval of measures promised in the party's election manifesto. Government could deliver on what in effect was a contract with the electors: in return for their support, it implemented its promised package of measures.

The clash between the two approaches thus reflected different views of what the constitution was for. The liberal approach, in essence, embraced negative constitutionalism. The constitution was for constraining government. The traditional approach embraced a qualified form of positive constitutionalism. The Westminster system enabled the will of the people to be paramount, albeit tempered by parliamentary deliberation. The qualification is an important one.

Reform under a Labour government

In the 1970s, Labour politicians tended to adopt an essentially traditionalist stance. There was an attempt to devolve powers to elected assemblies in Scotland and Wales and the use of a national referendum, but these were not seen as part of some coherent scheme of constitutional reform. The referendum in particular was seen as an exercise in political expediency. In the early 1980s, the influence of left-wing activists pushed the party towards a more socialist approach to the constitution. Under the leadership of Neil Kinnock, the party was weaned off this approach. It began to look more in the direction of the liberal approach. The longer the party was denied office, the more major constitutional reform began to look attractive to the party. It was already committed to devolution. In its socialist phase, it had adopted a policy of abolishing the House of Lords. It moved away from that to committing itself to removing hereditary peers from the House and introducing a more democratic second chamber. Having previously opposed electoral reform, some leading Labour MPs began to see merit in introducing proportional representation for parliamentary elections. John Smith, leader from 1992 to 1994, committed a future Labour government

to a referendum on the issue of electoral reform. The party also began to move cautiously towards embodying rights in statutory form: in 1992 it favoured a charter of rights. It also committed itself to strengthening local government.

The move towards a liberal approach was apparent in the Labour manifesto in the 1992 and 1997 general elections. In both elections, the Conservatives embraced the traditional approach and the Liberal Democrats the liberal approach. The constitution was one subject on which it was generally acknowledged that there was a clear difference in policy between the parties.

Looking in greater detail at the Labour Party's proposals in the 1997 manifesto, the party advocated:

- devolving power to Scotland and Wales;
- removing hereditary peers from the House of Lords;
- incorporating the European Convention on Human Rights into British law;
- appointing an independent commission to recommend a proportional alternative to the existing electoral system;
- holding a referendum on the voting system;
- introducing a system of proportional representation for the election of UK members of the European Parliament;
- legislating for an elected mayor and strategic authority for London;
- legislating to give people in the English regions power to decide by referendum, on a region by region basis, whether they wanted elected regional government;
- introducing a Freedom of Information Bill;
- holding a referendum if the government recommended joining a single European currency;
- setting up a parliamentary committee to recommend proposals to modernise the House of Commons.

Following its election to office in 1997, the new Labour government moved to implement its manifesto promises. In the first session (that is, the first year) of the new parliament, the government achieved passage of legislation providing for referendums in Scotland and Wales. In these referendums, electors in Scotland voted by a large majority for an elected parliament with legislative and some

Table 13.1 Referendum results in Scotland and Wales, 1997

Scotland

	A Scottish Parliament	Tax-varying powers
Agree	1,775,045 (74.3%)	1,512,889 (63.5%)
Disagree	614,400 (25.7%)	870,263 (36.5%)

Turnout: 60.4%

Wales

	A Welsh Assembly
Yes	559,419 (50.3%)
No	552,698 (49.7%)

Turnout: 50%

tax-varying powers. Voters in Wales voted narrowly for an elected assembly to determine spending in the Principality of Wales (see Table 13.1). The government then introduced measures to provide for an elected parliament in Scotland and an elected assembly in Wales. Elections to the new bodies were held on 6 May 1999, and Scotland and Wales acquired new forms of government. The government also introduced legislation providing for a new 108-member assembly in Northern Ireland with a power-sharing executive. This, along with other unique constitutional arrangements – including a North/South Ministerial Council and a Council of the Isles – had been approved by electors in Northern Ireland in a referendum in May 1998.

In the first session, the government also achieved passage of the Human Rights Act, providing for the incorporation of most provisions of the European Convention on Human Rights into British law – thus further reinforcing the new judicial dimension of the British constitution – and a bill providing for a referendum in London on whether or not the city should have an elected mayor and authority. The referendum in London, in May 1998, produced a large majority in favour of the proposal: 1,230,715 (72 per cent) voted 'yes' and 478,413 (28 per cent) voted 'no'. The turnout, though, was low: only 34.1 per cent of eligible electors bothered to vote. The House of Commons appointed a Select Committee on Modernisation. Within a year of its creation, it had issued seven reports, including one proposing various changes to the way legislation was considered in Parliament. The government also introduced a bill providing for a closed member list system for the

election of British Members of the European Parliament (MEPs). The House of Lords objected to the provision for closed lists (electors voting for a list of party candidates, with no provision to indicate preferences among the party nominees) and pushed for an open list system, allowing electors the option to indicate preferences. The government resisted the Lords and eventually the Bill had to be passed, in the subsequent session of Parliament, under the provisions of the Parliament Act.

The introduction of a regional list system for elections to the European Parliament was complemented by the use of the additional member system (AMS) for elections to the Scottish parliament and the Welsh assembly, and by the use of the single transferable vote (STV) for the Northern Ireland Assembly (see Ministry of Justice 2008).

At the end of 1997, the government appointed a Commission on the Voting System to make a recommendation on a proportional alternative to the existing first-past-the-post system for electing the House of Commons. The commission was asked to report within a year. The five-member body, chaired by Liberal Democrat peer Lord Jenkins of Hillhead, reported in October 1998. It considered a range of options but recommended the introduction of an electoral system known as the alternative vote plus ('AV Plus'). Under this system, constituency MPs would be elected by the alternative vote but with top-up MPs, constituting between 15 and 20 per cent of the total number of members, being elected on an area-wide basis (such as a county) to ensure some element of proportionality.

In the second session of Parliament, the government achieved passage of the House of Lords Act. Taking effect in November 1999, the Act removed most hereditary peers from membership of the House of Lords. At the same time as introducing the House of Lords Bill, the government established a Royal Commission on the Reform of the House of Lords, under a former Conservative minister, Lord Wakeham, to make recommendations for a reformed second chamber once the hereditary peers had gone. The commission was asked to report within a year and did so. It recommended that a proportion of the membership of the second chamber be elected by popular vote.

The government also achieved passage of three other measures of constitutional significance during the parliament. The Greater London Authority Act brought into being an elected mayor and a strategic authority for the metropolis. The additional member electoral system was employed for election of Assembly members and the supplementary vote (SV) for election of the mayor. (The successful candidate in the first election for mayor was Ken Livingstone.) The Freedom of Information Act opened up documents held by public authorities, with certain exceptions, to public scrutiny. The Political Parties, Elections and Referendums Act created a new Electoral Commission, stipulated new rules governing donations to political parties and introduced provisions to cover the holding of referendums. Given that referendums had been promised on various issues, the measure was designed to ensure some consistency in the rules governing their conduct.

After a reforming first Parliament, constitutional change appeared to take a back seat to other measures introduced by the Blair government. However, a further major change was enacted at the end of the second Parliament, one not envisaged in the party's manifesto. The Constitutional Reform Act 2005 provided that the Lord Chancellor (a Cabinet minister at the head of the judiciary) need not be a lawyer or a peer. It also transferred the judicial powers of the Lord Chancellor (a political appointee) to the Lord Chief Justice (a senior judge) and created a new supreme court. Instead of the highest court of appeal being law lords sitting in a judicial committee of the House of Lords, it was now to be an independent body sitting separately from a legislative chamber. The court came into being in October 2009, housed in the old Middlesex Guildhall in Parliament Square. The change was described by the new President of the Court, Lord Phillips of Worth Matravers, as 'essentially one of form, not of substance' (*Financial Times*: 10 September 2009). It involved principally a transfer of personnel, the law lords moving from the House of Lords to the new court.

Further change came about as a result of political settlement in Northern Ireland in 2007 – Democratic Unionist leader Ian Paisley agreeing to go into a power-sharing government in the province with Sinn Fein member Martin McGuinness – and with Gordon Brown becoming prime minister in succession to Tony Blair. Whereas Blair had emphasised wider constitutional change, largely external to Parliament – though having significant consequences for Parliament – Brown focused on changes designed to strengthen Parliament in calling government to account and in enhancing its links with the public (Norton 2008). He introduced a *Governance of Britain* agenda, with Parliament at the heart of it.

There were various initiatives, including citizens' juries to discuss policy proposals and early publication each year of the draft programme for the next legislative session – enabling Parliament to debate proposals well ahead of the annual Queen's Speech. However, the principal legislative manifestation was the introduction in 2009 of the Constitutional Reform and Governance Bill, designed to transfer the prerogative power of treaty making from the Crown (in effect, the government) to Parliament. It also made certain changes to the House of Lords (for example, allowing the expulsion of members) as well as putting the civil service on a statutory basis. Separately, the government proposed that Parliament agree a resolution that in future the assent of the House of Commons would be necessary to commit UK armed forces in action abroad (the war-making power). The government also pressed for further reform of the House of Lords.

In a little over a decade, the Labour government thus saw through major changes to the country's constitution. These changes variously modified, reinforced or challenged the established tenets of the traditional constitution. Each tenet was affected in some way by the changes shown in Table 13.2.

Parliamentary sovereignty, already challenged by British membership of the European Community, was further challenged by the incorporation of most provisions of the European Convention on Human Rights (ECHR). This gave the courts an added role,

Table 13.2 Changes to the established tenets of the traditional constitution

Tenets	Affected by
Parliamentary sovereignty	Incorporation of ECHR Ratification of Amsterdam and Nice Treaties
Rule of law	Incorporation of ECHR Creation of a supreme court
Unitary state	Creation of Scottish Parliament, Welsh Assembly and Northern Ireland Assembly
Parliamentary government under a constitutional monarchy	Use of referendums New voting systems in different parts of the UK Removal of hereditary peers from the House of Lords Freedom of Information Act Modernisation of the House of Commons Transfer of prerogative powers

in effect as protectors of the provisions of the convention. If a provision of UK law was found by the courts to conflict with the provisions of the ECHR, a court could issue a declaration of incompatibility. It was then up to Parliament to act on the basis of the court's judgement. The ratification of the Amsterdam Treaty further strengthened the European Union by extending the area of its policy competence, thus putting various areas of public policy beyond the simple decision-making capacity of national government and Parliament. The Nice Treaty limited existing member states by creating a new system of weighted voting for when new members joined.

The rule of law was strengthened by the incorporation of the ECHR. The effect of incorporation could be seen as providing a little more balance between the twin pillars of the constitution identified by Dicey (parliamentary sovereignty and the rule of law). The courts could now protect the rule of law against Parliament in a way that was not previously possible. The transfer of powers from the Lord Chancellor to the Lord Chief Justice, and the creation of a new supreme court, was also designed to demonstrate judicial independence.

The unitary state was challenged by the creation of elected assemblies in Scotland, Wales and Northern Ireland. In Scotland, the new Parliament was given power to legislate on any matter not reserved to the UK Parliament. It was also given power to vary the standard rate of taxation by 3p in the pound. The UK Parliament was expected not to legislate on matters that fell within the competence of the Scottish Parliament. The powers previously exercised by the Welsh Office were devolved to a Welsh Assembly. Provision for the transfer of more powers was made by the Government of Wales Act 2006. Legislative and administrative powers were also provided for a new Northern Ireland Assembly: elections to the assembly were held in 2007. The devolution of such powers raised questions as to the extent to which Parliament should intervene in matters that were exclusive to a part of the UK other than England. As such, devolution may be seen to limit, in effect, the flexibility of the traditional constitution. As we shall see (Chapter 12), devolution also serves to reinforce the judicial dimension to the constitution, giving the courts a role akin to constitutional courts in determining the legal competence of the new assemblies.

The creation of these new assemblies also challenged some of the basic tenets of a parliamentary government under a constitutional monarchy. Decision-making power was being hived off to bodies other than the British Cabinet. Some decision-making competences had passed to the institutions of the European Union, others to elected bodies in different parts of the United Kingdom. There was also an enhancement of the powers of the courts at the expense of the government and Parliament. The coherence inherent in central parliamentary government was being challenged. Parliamentary government was also challenged by the use of referendums. Referendums provide for electors, rather than Parliament, to determine the outcome of particular issues. Opponents of a new electoral system also argued that, if the proposals for electoral reform were implemented, the capacity of the political system to produce accountable government would be undermined. The removal of most hereditary peers proved controversial – not least, and not surprisingly, in the House of Lords – although the full consequences for parliamentary government were not apparent: in the event, it proved to be a more independent House, willing to challenge the House of Commons. Reforms proposed to strengthen the House of Commons had some, albeit limited, effect.

The collective effect of these changes has been to modify, rather than destroy, the Westminster constitution. Formally, each of the elements of the constitution remains in place:

1 The doctrine of parliamentary sovereignty may be challenged by incorporation of the ECHR, but formally Parliament is not bound by the rulings of the courts. The courts may issue declarations of incompatibility, but it is then up to Parliament to act on them. Parliament retains the formal power not to take any action (even if the reality is that it will act on them).

2 The minister responsible for introducing the Human Rights Act – the Lord Chancellor, Lord Irvine – conceded that the Human Rights Act 'may be described as a form of higher law' but stressed that the Act decrees that the validity of any measure passed by Parliament is unaffected by any incompatibility with the ECHR. 'In this way, the Act unequivocally preserves Parliament's ability to pass Bills that are or may be in conflict with the convention' (House of Lords *Hansard*, written answer, 30 July 2002).

3 Devolution may challenge the concept of a unitary state, but ultimate power still resides with

the centre. Devolved powers – indeed, devolved assemblies – may be abolished by Parliament. The Westminster Parliament can still legislate for the whole of the UK, even in areas formally devolved. (Indeed, it variously does legislate for Scotland in devolved areas, albeit at the invitation of the Scottish Parliament.)

4 Formally, referendums are advisory only. Although it would be perverse for Parliament, having authorised a referendum, to ignore the outcome, it nonetheless has the power to do so.

5 The creation of a supreme court has entailed moving law lords out of the House of Lords but confers no new powers to strike down Acts of Parliament.

6 Although a new electoral system may destroy the accountability inherent in the present system, no new electoral system has been introduced for elections to the House of Commons. Instead, new systems have been employed for other assemblies.

Although the practical effect of some of the changes may be to challenge and, in the long run, undermine the provisions of the Westminster constitution, the basic provisions remain formally in place. The fact that they have been modified or are under challenge means that we may be moving away from the traditional constitution: however, as yet, no new constitution has been put in its place. The traditional approach to the constitution has lost out since 1997, but none of the other approaches can claim to have triumphed.

■ Parties and the constitution

In the wake of the general election of 1997, the stance of the parties on constitutional issues was clear. The Labour Party had been returned to power with a mandate to enact various measures of constitutional reform. The party's election manifesto was frequently quoted during debate on those measures, not least during debate on its House of Lords Bill. The Conservative Party remained committed to the traditional approach to the constitution. It had proposed no major constitutional reform in its election manifesto and was able to take a principled stand in opposition to various measures introduced by the Labour government. However, the measures

brought forward by the government created problems for both major parties and, to a lesser extent, for the Liberal Democrats.

The Labour Party

For the Labour Party, there were two problems. One was practical: that was, trying to implement all that it had promised in its election manifesto. A three-figure parliamentary majority in the period from 1997 to 2005 was not sufficient to stave off problems. The narrowness of the vote in the referendum in Wales in 1997 appeared to deter ministers from moving quickly to legislate for referendums in the English regions. When, in 2002, Deputy Prime Minister John Prescott published a White Paper on regional government, the proposals were cautious, providing for regional referendums on a rolling basis. It was recognised that not all regions would necessarily vote for a regional assembly. Initially, referendums in three regions were planned, but this was then reduced to one. When, in the first regional referendum, in the north-east in 2004, there was a decisive 78 per cent 'no' vote, the policy was effectively put on hold. The proposal for a referendum on a new electoral system encountered opposition. The report of the Commission on the Voting System in 1998 attracted a vigorous response from both Labour and Conservative opponents of change – one report suggested that at least 100 Labour MPs, including some members of the Cabinet, were opposed to electoral reform – and this appeared to influence the government. No referendum was held during the parliament and none was promised in the party's 2001 and 2005 election manifestos. The House of Lords Bill encountered stiff opposition in the House of Lords and the government was unable (and in this case largely unwilling) to mobilise a Commons majority to carry through further change. The Freedom of Information Bill ran into opposition from within the ranks of the government itself, various senior ministers – including Home Secretary Jack Straw – not favouring a radical measure. When the Bill was published in 1999, it was attacked by proponents of open government for not going far enough.

There was also a practical problem in that not all those reforms that were implemented had the desired effect. Far from stifling support for nationalist parties, devolution in Scotland provided the basis for the SNP to emerge as the largest single party in the 2007 elections to the Scottish Parliament and form a minority administration. Following the indecisive outcome of the 2007 elections to the National Assembly for Wales, a Labour–Plaid Cymru coalition was formed. Some of the judgments of the courts, interpreting the Human Rights Act, were heavily criticised by ministers (Norton 2007a). And, as we have noted, the House of Lords proved more assertive following implementation of the House of Lords Act (Russell and Sciara 2007), the Government suffering a string of defeats.

The constitution thus did not change in quite the way that the party had intended. This practical problem also exacerbated the second problem. The party was unable to articulate an intellectually coherent approach to constitutional change. It had moved away from both the socialist approach and the traditional approach and some way towards the liberal approach. However, it only partially embraced the liberal agenda. It was wary of a new system for elections to the House of Commons and appeared to have dropped the idea by the time of the 2001 election. The government hesitated to pursue regional assemblies in England. It set up a Royal Commission to consider reform of the House of Lords but – until a vote by MPs in 2007 favouring a largely or wholly elected House – it was reluctant to embrace demands for an elected second chamber. Some ministers opposed any change that might challenge the primacy of the House of Commons, in which the government had a parliamentary majority. In respect of both devolution and the incorporation of the European Convention on Human Rights, the government ensured that the doctrine of parliamentary sovereignty remained in place.

Although the Labour government was able to say what it was against, it was not able to articulate what it was for, at least not in terms of the future shape of the British constitution. What was its approach to the constitution? What did it think the constitution was for? What sort of constitution did it wish to see in place in five or ten years? When these questions were put to ministers, they normally avoided answering them. The Prime Minister, Tony Blair, avoided making speeches on the subject (Theakston 2005: 33). However, in a debate on the constitution in the House of Lords in December 2002, the Lord Chancellor, Lord Irvine, did concede that the government did not have an overarching approach, arguing instead that the government proceeded 'by way of pragmatism based on principle'. The three principles he identified were:

- ■ *To remain a parliamentary democracy, with the Westminster parliament supreme and within that the Commons the dominant chamber.*
- ■ *To increase public engagement with democracy, 'developing a maturer democracy with different centres of power, where individuals enjoy greater rights and where the government is carried out close to the people'.*
- ■ *'To devise a solution to each problem on its own terms.'*

House of Lords Hansard, 18 December 2002, Vol. 642, col. 692; www.publications.parliament.uk/pa/ld200203/ldhansrd/vo021218/text/21218-05.htm

The problem with these 'principles' is that they are not obviously compatible with one another: the first two are in conflict as to where power should reside – should it be in Westminster or in other centres of power? – and the third is a let-out clause, enabling policy to be made up as one goes along.

The government thus lay open to the accusation that it had no clear philosophical approach, nothing that would render its approach predictable or provide it with a reference point in the event of things going wrong. Opponents were thus able to claim that it has been marching down the path – or rather down several paths – of constitutional reform without having a comprehensive map and without any very clear idea of where it is heading. Tony Blair took one path and Gordon Brown another, but with neither articulating a clear destination.

The Conservative Party

The Conservative Party encountered a problem, although one that was essentially in the future. In the short term, it was able to adopt a consistent and coherent position. It supported the traditional approach to the constitution. It was therefore opposed to any changes that threatened the essential elements of the Westminster system of government. It was especially vehement in its opposition to proposals for electoral reform, mounting a notable campaign against the recommendations of the Commission on the Voting System in 1998. It published a defence of the existing electoral system at the same time as the commission report was launched. It opposed devolution, fearing that it would threaten the unity of the United Kingdom. It opposed the House of Lords Bill, not least on the grounds that the government had not said what the second stage of reform would be.

The party encountered some practical problems. It took time to organise itself as an opposition, having difficulties marshalling its forces to scrutinise effectively the government's proposals for referendums. The Conservative leader in the Lords, Lord Cranborne, negotiated a private deal with the government to retain some hereditary peers in the second chamber: he was sacked by the party leader, William Hague, for having negotiated behind his back. There were also some Conservative MPs who inclined towards a more liberal approach to the constitution, favouring an elected second chamber and an English Parliament. Some, especially after the party's third consecutive election defeat in 2005, favoured electoral reform.

However, the most important problem facing the party was long-term rather than short-term. How was a future Conservative government to respond to the constitutional changes made under the Labour government? The constitution would no longer be the traditional constitution the party had been defending up to 1997. Should a future Conservative government go for the reactionary, conservative or radical option (Norton 2005)? That is, should it seek to overturn the various reforms made by the Labour government, in effect reverting to the status quo ante (the reactionary option)? Should it seek to conserve the constitution as it stood at the time the Conservatives regained power (the conservative option)? Or should it attempt to come up with a new approach to constitutional change (the radical option)?

The Conservative leader, William Hague, recognised the conundrum facing the party and, in a speech in London in February 1998, challenged the party to address the issue. 'What happens to the defenders of the status quo', he asked, 'when the status quo itself disappears?' The party could not simply shrug its shoulders, he said, and accept whatever arrangements it inherited. Nor could the party reverse every one of Labour's constitutional changes. The clock could not be put back. 'Devolution or the politicisation of the judiciary are not changes that can easily be undone. Attempting to return the constitution to its status quo ante would be a futile task.' The party, he declared, would need to adopt its own programme of constitutional reform. He accepted that devolution was a fact and he committed the party to fighting for seats and working in the new assemblies. He outlined some of the issues, such as the relationship between Parliament and the judiciary and between Parliament and government,

which the party would have to address. He later appointed commissions to address various aspects of constitutional change – on reform of the House of Lords, on a single currency and on strengthening Parliament. In 1999, he spoke of the need to address the 'English question' in Parliament: how should legislation relating exclusively to England be dealt with by a Parliament made up of members from all parts of the United Kingdom? He sought to make some of the running in considering constitutional change. In so doing, he explicitly acknowledged the basic problem facing the party. As he pithily put it: 'you can't unscramble an omelette'.

In 2005, the new party leader, David Cameron, appointed a Democracy Taskforce to consider how democracy could be strengthened. However, the chair of the Taskforce, former cabinet minister Kenneth Clarke, admitted that its members could not reach agreement on all issues of constitutional reform. Its report did not embrace any particular approach. Although successive party leaders have occasionally come out with proposals for specific change, none has produced a clear, intellectually coherent approach. Some Tory MPs have advocated a conservative approach, opposing for example further changes to the House of Lords. Some favour a reactionary approach, advocating repeal of the Human Rights Act. Some embrace a radical approach, supporting such measures as a wholly elected second chamber and electoral reform. The party, in this respect, appears to be emulating its opponents.

Liberal Democrats

The Liberal Democrats could claim to be in the strongest position on issues of constitutional change. They embraced the liberal approach to constitutional change. They therefore had a clear agenda. They were able to evaluate the government's reform proposals against that agenda. Given that the government fell short of pursuing a wholly liberal agenda, they were able to push for those measures that the government had not embraced. Their stance was thus principled and consistent.

In so far as they encountered problems, they were practical problems. Because they favoured the reform measures espoused by the Labour government, they accepted an invitation to participate in a Cabinet committee comprising ministers and leading Liberal Democrats to discuss constitutional change. There was close, private contact between the Prime Minister, Tony Blair, and the leader of the

Liberal Democrats, Paddy Ashdown. The party thus had some input into deliberations on the future of the constitution. This cooperation engendered some debate within the party as to how far it might be taken. It also threw up problems for the party in terms of how far the government was prepared to go. Was the party sacrificing its principles for the sake of some peripheral involvement in government, receiving very little in return? It was widely reported that one condition of Liberal Democrat agreement to cooperate was a government commitment to a referendum on electoral reform. However, the failure of the government to act on this promise following publication of the report of the Commission on the Voting System – chaired by a leading Liberal Democrat – resulted in no notable action on the part of the party leader. Ashdown's successor, Charles Kennedy, elected in 1999, appeared less keen on maintaining close links with the government. The Cabinet committee remained formally in existence in the 2001 Parliament, but did not meet, and in 2005 was wound up. The party could claim that various reforms had been achieved, but it had carried little weight in pressing government to achieve some of its key goals. The bottle of constitutional reform may be half full but it was also half empty.

■ The continuing debate

The constitution remains an issue of debate. It does so at two levels. One is at the wider level of the very nature of the constitution itself. What shape should the British constitution take? How plausible are the various approaches to constitutional change? The Liberal Democrats, along with various commentators, advocate the liberal approach. The other parties have yet to articulate what sort of constitution they want to see in the future. The Conservatives have favoured the traditional approach but have yet to articulate how they propose to respond in government to the constitutional framework they inherit from the Labour government. They continue to defend certain features of the Westminster model, such as the existing electoral system, but not others, the party leadership having made a case for a predominantly elected second chamber. The Labour Party wants to move away from the Westminster model but not to the extent that it prevents a Labour government from governing.

The other level is specific to various measures of constitutional change. Some changes have been made to the constitution. Other changes are advocated, not least – although not exclusively – by advocates of the liberal approach. Electoral reform remains an issue on the political agenda. Supporters of change want to see the introduction of a system of proportional representation for parliamentary elections. Opponents advance the case for the existing first-past-the-post method of election (see Box 13.2). The use of referendums, and the promise of their use on particular issues, has spurred calls for their more regular use. Opponents are wary of any further use; some are opposed to referendums on principle (see Box 13.3). The role of the second chamber also generates considerable debate. Should there be a second chamber of Parliament? Most of those engaged in constitutional debate support the case for a second chamber but do not agree on the form it should take. Should it be wholly or partly elected? Or should it be an appointed House? (See Chapter 18.) The reforms pursued by a Labour government under Tony Blair and Gordon Brown did not put an end to debate about the future of the British constitution. If anything, it gave it new impetus, leaving the issue of the constitution very much on the political agenda.

BOX 13.2   DEBATE

Electoral reform (proportional representation)

The case for
- Every vote would count, producing seats in proportion to votes.
- It would get rid of the phenomenon of the 'wasted vote'.
- It would be fairer to third parties, ensuring that they got seats in proportion to their percentage of the poll.

- On existing voting patterns, it would usually result in no one party having an overall majority – thus encouraging a coalition and moderate policies.
- A coalition enjoying majority support is more likely to ensure continuity of policy than changes in government under the existing first-past-the-post system.
- A coalition enjoying majority support enjoys a greater popular legitimacy than a single-party government elected by a minority of voters.
- Coalitions resulting from election by proportional representation can prove stable and effective.
- There is popular support for change.

The case against
- Very few systems are exactly proportional. Little case to change to a relatively more proportional system than the existing system unless other advantages are clear.
- A system of proportional representation would give an unfair advantage to small parties, which would be likely to hold the balance of power.
- The government is most likely to be chosen as a result of bargaining by parties after a general election and not as a deliberate choice of the electors.
- It would be difficult to ensure accountability to electors in the event of a multi-party coalition being formed.
- Coalitions cobbled together after an election – and for which not one elector has definitively voted – lack the legitimacy of clear electoral approval.
- There is no link between electoral systems and economic performance.
- Coalitions resulting from election under a system of proportional representation can lead to uncertainty and a change of coalition partners.
- Bargaining between parties can produce instability, but coalitions can also prove difficult for the electorate to get rid of.
- There is popular support for the consequences of the existing electoral system – notably a single party being returned to govern the country.
- 'Proportional representation' is a generic term for a large number of electoral systems: there is no agreement on what precise system should replace the existing one.

The relationship between the debate about the constitution and about particular measures of constitutional reform throws up a vital question. Should specific reforms derive from a clear view of what the constitution, as a constitution, should look like in five or ten years? Or should the shape of the constitution be determined by specific changes made on the basis of their individual merits?

BOX 13.3   DEBATE

Referendums

The case for
- A referendum is an educational tool – it informs citizens about the issue.
- Holding a referendum encourages people to be more involved in political activity.
- A referendum helps to resolve major issues – it gives a chance for the voters to decide.
- The final outcome of a referendum is more likely to enjoy public support than if the decision is taken solely by Parliament – it is difficult to challenge a decision if all voters have a chance to take part.

- The use of referendums increases support for the political system – voters know they are being consulted on the big issues. Even if they don't take part, they know they have an opportunity to do so.

The case against
- Referendums are blunt weapons that usually allow only a simple answer to a very general question. They do not permit explanations of why voters want something done nor do they usually allow alternatives to be considered.
- Referendums undermine the position of Parliament as the deliberative body of the nation.
- There is no obvious limit on when referendums should be held – if one is conceded on the issue of Europe, why not also have referendums on Scottish independence, immigration, and capital punishment? With no obvious limit, there is the potential for 'government by referendum'.
- Referendums can be used as majoritarian weapons – being used by the majority to restrict minorities.
- There is the difficulty of ensuring a balanced debate – one side may (indeed, is likely to) have more money and resources.
- There is the difficulty of formulating, and agreeing, a clear and objective question.
- Research shows that turnout in referendums tends to be lower than that in elections for parliamentary and other public elections. In the UK, for example, there have been low turnouts in Wales (1997) and London (1998).
- Referendums are expensive to hold and are often expensive ways of not deciding issues – if government does not like the result it calls another referendum (as has happened in both Denmark and Ireland over ratification of European treaties).

BOX 13.4   BRITAIN IN CONTEXT

A distinctive constitution

The United Kingdom is distinctive for having an uncodified constitution. The laws, rules and customs determining how it is to be governed are not drawn up in a single document. This is a distinction it shares with only two other countries: Israel and New Zealand. Other states have drawn up codified documents as a consequence of being newly formed or having to start afresh, having broken away from a colonising power or having been defeated in battle. Britain has not suffered a distinctive constitutional break since the seventeenth century. An attempt to impose a codified, or 'written', constitution during the period of the Protectorate was abandoned with the restoration of the monarchy in 1660. When James II fled the country in 1688, he was deemed to have abdicated and those responsible for inviting his daughter and son-in-law, Mary and William of Orange, to assume the throne were keen to stress continuity in the nation's constitutional arrangements. The nation's constitutional

foundations thus pre-date the creation, starting with the USA in the eighteenth century, of formal codified constitutions.

There are other distinctive features of the nation's constitutional arrangements. Many countries have entrenched constitutions: that is, they are amendable only through some extraordinary process, such as a two-thirds majority in the legislature and/or approval by the people in a referendum. In the UK, laws that change the nature of the constitution – such as the Human Rights Act 1998 – go through the same process as those that determine that it is an offence to leave the scene of an accident.

In terms of the basic structure of government, the UK is also distinctive, but not unique, in having a particular form of parliamentary government. Some systems are presidential, where the head of government and the legislature are elected separately and where neither depends on the other for continuation in office. In a parliamentary system, the head of government and other ministers derive their positions through election to the legislature – they are not elected separately – and they depend for their continuation in office on the confidence of the legislature. There are two basic types of parliamentary government: the Westminster parliamentary system and the continental. The Westminster model stresses single-party government, elected normally through a first-past-the-post electoral system, with two major parties competing for the all-or-nothing spoils of electoral victory. The continental parliamentary system places stress on consensus politics, with coalition government derived from elections under electoral systems of proportional representation. The Westminster model has been exported to many Commonwealth countries, though a number have departed from it; New Zealand, for example, has adopted a system of proportional representation. There are also various hybrid presidential–parliamentary systems, where the president is directly elected but a government, under a prime minister, is formed through elections to the legislature. France has a hybrid system; hybrid systems have been adopted by a number of democracies in central and eastern Europe.

Chapter summary

The British constitution remains distinctive for not being codified in a single document. It is drawn from several sources and retains the main components that it has developed over three centuries. Although little debated in the years between 1945 and 1970, it has been the subject of dispute – and of change – in the years since. Proponents of reform have argued that existing constitutional arrangements have not proved adequate to meet the political and economic challenges faced by the United Kingdom. They have pressed for reform, and various approaches to change have developed. Debate has polarised around two approaches: the liberal, favouring a new constitutional settlement for the United Kingdom; and the traditional, favouring retention of the principal components of the existing constitution.

The constitution has undergone significant change as a result of British membership of the EC/EU and the return of a Labour government in May 1997. The judicial dimension of the constitution has been strengthened as a result of the incorporation of the European Convention on Human Rights into British law; by the devolving of powers to elected bodies in different parts of the UK, the courts acting in effect as constitutional courts for the devolved bodies; and by the creation of a supreme court. New European treaties have resulted in more policy-making power passing upwards to the institutions of the European Union. Devolution has seen some powers pass downwards to elected bodies in Scotland, Wales and Northern Ireland. The consequence of these changes has been to change the contours of the 'traditional', or Westminster, model of government, although not destroying the model altogether.

The constitution remains a subject of political controversy, posing problems for each of the main political parties. The Labour government has pursued a reform agenda but has done so on a pragmatic basis, embracing no particular approach to change. It has, in effect, fallen somewhere between the liberal and traditional approaches. For the Conservative Party, there is the challenge of determining how a future Conservative government will respond to the new constitutional arrangements. For the Liberal Democrats, there is the dilemma of determining how far to go along with a government that supports some of its goals but is unwilling to embrace a new constitutional settlement for the United Kingdom.

The British constitution has changed significantly in recent years and continues to be the subject of demands for further change, but its future shape remains unclear.

Discussion points

■ How does the constitution of the United Kingdom differ from that of other countries? What does it have in common with them?

■ Which approach to constitutional change do you find most persuasive, and why?

■ How convincing are the principal arguments against holding referendums?

■ Is electoral reform desirable?

■ What are the main obstacles to achieving major constitutional change in the United Kingdom?

Further reading

For a valuable overview of constitutional change in the twentieth century, see the contributions to Bogdanor (2003). For the principal features of the contemporary constitution, see, for example, Alder (2005).

Recent works addressing constitutional change under the Labour government are King (2007) and Bogdanor (2009). King tends to take a more critical view; the constitution, in his view, is 'a mess'. Bogdanor sees the old system being replaced by a new one. Also useful is Oliver (2003) providing a comprehensive overview of constitutional change, providing the context of change and looking at citizen-centred reforms and institutional reforms. Johnson (2004) and Marquand (2004) offer critical reflective analyses. On Conservative and Labour approaches to the constitution, see Norton (2005, 2007b, 2008).

Articles covering aspects of constitutional change can also be found in scholarly journals, not least *Public Law* and *Parliamentary Affairs*, as well as in student magazines such as *Politics Review*.

There are various useful publications that address specific issues. Most of these are identified in subsequent chapters (monarchy, Chapter 16; House of Commons, Chapter 17; House of Lords, Chapter 18; the judiciary, Chapter 23). Chapter 23 also addresses issues arising from membership of the European Union, the incorporation of the European Convention on Human Rights, devolution and the Constitutional Reform Act. On electoral reform, see Ministry of Justice (2008). On referendums, see Butler and Ranney (1994) and Qvortrup (2005).

Bibliography

Alder, J. (2005) *Constitutional and Administrative Law*, 5th edn (Palgrave Macmillan).

Benn, T. (1993) *Common Sense* (Hutchinson).

Bogdanor, V. (ed.) (2003) *The British Constitution in the Twentieth Century* (Oxford University Press/British Academy).

Bogdanor, V. (2009) *The New British Constitution* (Hart Publishing).

Bradley, A.W., Ziegler, K.S. and Baranger, D. (2007) 'Constitutionalism and the Role of Parliaments', in K.S. Ziegler, D. Baranger and A.W. Bradley (eds) *Constitutionalism and the Role of Parliaments* (Hart Publishing).

Brazier, R. (1994) *Constitutional Practice*, 2nd edn (Oxford University Press).

Butler, D. and Ranney, A. (1994) *Referendums Around the World* (AEI Press).

Finer, S.E. (ed.) (1975) *Adversary Politics and Electoral Reform* (Wigram).

Fitzpatrick, B. (1999) 'A Dualist House of Lords in a Sea of Monist Community law', in B. Dickson and P. Carmichael (eds) *The House of Lords: Its Parliamentary and Judicial Roles* (Hart Publishing).

Foley, M. (1999) *The Politics of the British Constitution* (Manchester University Press).

Hailsham, Lord (1976) *Elective Dictatorship* (BBC).

Institute for Public Policy Research (1992) *A New Constitution for the United Kingdom* (Mansell).

Ivison, D. (1999) 'Pluralism and the Hobbesian Logic of Negative Constitutionalism', *Political Studies*, Vol. 47, No. 1.

Johnson, N. (2004) *Reshaping the British Constitution* (Palgrave Macmillan).

King, A. (2007) *The British Constitution* (Oxford University Press).

Labour Party (1997) *New Labour: Because Britain Deserves Better* (Labour Party).

Marquand, D. (2004) *The Decline of the Public: The Hollowing Out of Citizenship* (Polity Press).

▶

Maxwell, P. (1999) 'The House of Lords as a Constitutional Court – the Implications of Ex Parte EOC', in B. Dickson and P. Carmichael (eds) *The House of Lords: Its Parliamentary and Judicial Roles* (Hart Publishing).

Ministry of Justice (2008) *Review of Voting Systems: The Experience of New Voting Systems in the United Kingdom since 1997*, Cm 7304 (The Stationery Office).

Norton, P. (1982) *The Constitution in Flux* (Blackwell).

Norton, P. (1993) 'The Constitution: Approaches to Reform', *Politics Review*, Vol. 3, No. 1.

Norton, P. (2005) 'The Constitution', in K. Hickson (ed.) *The Political Thought of the Conservative Party Since 1945* (Palgrave Macmillan).

Norton, P. (2007a) 'The Constitution: Fragmentation or Adaptation?' in M. Rush and P. Giddings (ed.) *The Palgrave Review of British Politics 2006* (Palgrave Macmillan).

Norton, P. (2007b) 'Tony Blair and the Constitution', *British Politics*, Vol. 2.

Norton, P. (2008) 'The Constitution under Gordon Brown', *Politics Review*, Vol. 17, No. 3.

Oliver, D. (2003) *Constitutional Reform in the UK* (Oxford University Press).

Qvortrup, M. (2005) *A Comparative Study of Referendums: Government By the People* (2nd edn, Manchester University Press).

Ranney, A. and Butler, D. (1994) *Referendums Around the World. The Growing Use of Democracy* (AEI Press).

Royal Commission on the Reform of the House of Lords (2000) *A House for the Future*, Cm 4534.

Russell, M. and Sciara, M. (2007) 'Why Does the Government get Defeated in the House of Lords? The Lords, the Party System and British Politics', *British Politics*, Vol. 2.

Theakston, K. (2005) 'Prime Ministers and the Constitution: Attlee to Blair', *Parliamentary Affairs*, Vol. 58, No. 1.

Useful websites

Organisations with an interest in constitutional change

Constitution Unit: www.ucl.ac.uk/constitution-unit
Electoral Reform Society: www.electoral-reform.org.uk
Campaign for Freedom of Information: www.cfoi.org.uk
Unlock Democracy: www.unlockdemocracy.org.uk/

Reports

Independent Commission on the Voting System (the Jenkins Commission):   www.archive.official-documents.co.uk/document/cm40/4090/4090.htm
Ministry of Justice, *The Governance of Britain*, Cm 7170:   www.official-documents.gov.uk/document/cm71/7170/7170.asp
Ministry of Justice, *Review of Voting Systems: The Experience of New Voting Systems in the United Kingdom since 1997*, Cm 7304:   www.official-documents.gov.uk/documents/cm73/7304/7304.asp
Royal Commission on the Reform of the House of Lords (the Wakeham Commission):   www.archive.official-documents.co.uk/document/cm45/4534/4534.htm

Government departments with responsibility for constitutional issues

Ministry of Justice: www.justice.gov.uk
Home Office: www.homeoffice.gov.uk

Other official bodies

The Electoral Commission: www.electoralcommission.org.uk

European bodies

European Convention on Human Rights: www.echr.coe.int

CHAPTER 14

The crown

Philip Norton

Learning objectives

- To identify the place of the monarchy in British constitutional history.

- To detail the political significance of 'the crown'.

- To outline the roles that citizens expect the monarch to fulfil and the extent to which they are carried out.

- To outline criticisms made of the monarchy – and the royal family – in recent years.

- To look at proposals for change.

Introduction

I t is an extraordinary fact, often overlooked, that Britain's representative democracy evolved over a thousand years out of an all-encompassing monarchy underpinned by the religious notion of the divine right of kings. The monarchical shell remains intact, but the inner workings have been taken over by party political leaders and civil servants. The shell itself has been the subject of critical comment, especially in recent years. This chapter analyses the emergence of the modern monarchy and considers its still important functions together with the arguments of the critics.

■ The monarchy

The crown is the symbol of all executive authority. It is conferred on the monarch. The monarchy is the oldest secular institution in England and dates back at least to the ninth century. In Anglo-Saxon and Norman times, the formal power that the crown conferred – executive, legislative and judicial – was exercised personally by the monarch. The King had a court to advise him and, as the task of government became more demanding, so the various functions were exercised on the King's behalf by other bodies. Those bodies now exercise powers independent of the control of the monarch, but they remain formally the instruments of the crown. The courts are Her Majesty's courts and the government is Her Majesty's government. Parliament is summoned and prorogued by royal decree. Civil servants are crown appointees. Many powers – prerogative powers – are still exercised in the name of the crown. The monarch exercises few powers personally, but those powers remain important. However, the importance of the monarchy in the twenty-first century derives more from what it stands for than from what it does.

The monarchy has been eclipsed as a major political institution not only by the sheer demands of governing a growing kingdom but also by changes in the popular perception of what form of government is legitimate. The policy-making power exercised by a hereditary monarch has given way to the exercise of power by institutions deemed more representative. However, the monarchy has retained a claim to be a representative institution in one particular definition of the term. It is this claim that largely defines the activities of the monarch today.

The monarchy predates by several centuries the emergence of the concept of representation. The term 'representation' entered the English language through French derivatives of the Latin *reprae-*

sentare and did not assume a political meaning until the sixteenth century. It permits at least four separate usages (see Birch 1964; Pitkin 1967):

1 It may denote acting on behalf of some individual or group, seeking to defend and promote the interests of the person or persons 'represented'.

2 It may denote persons or assemblies that have been freely elected. Although it is not always the case that persons so elected will act to defend and pursue the interests of electors, they will normally be expected to do so.

3 It may be used to signify a person or persons typical of a particular class or group of persons. It is in this sense that it is used when opinion pollsters identify a representative sample.

4 It may be used in a symbolic sense. Thus, individuals or objects may 'stand for' something: for example, a flag symbolising the unity of the nation.

The belief that free election was a prerequisite for someone to claim to act on behalf of others grew in the nineteenth century. Before then, the concept of 'virtual representation' held great sway. This concept was well expressed by Edmund Burke. It was a form of representation, he wrote

in which there is a communion of interests, and a sympathy in feelings and desires, between those who act in the name of any description of people, and the people in whose name they act, though the trustees are not actually chosen by them.

It was a concept challenged by the perception that the claim to speak on behalf of a particular body of individuals could not be sustained unless those individuals had signified their agreement, and the way to signify that agreement was through the ballot box. This challenge proved increasingly successful,

Royal ceremonial is symbolic of continuity with the past and of national unity
Source: Copyright © Pool / Tim Graham Picture Library / Corbis

with the extension of the franchise and, to ensure elections free of coercion, changes in the method of election (the introduction of secret ballots, for example). By the end of the 1880s, the majority of working men had the vote. By Acts of 1918 and 1928, the vote was given to women.

The extension of the franchise in the nineteenth and early twentieth centuries meant that the House of Commons could claim to be a representative institution under the first and second definitions of the term. The unelected House of Lords could not make such a claim. The result, as we shall see (Chapter 16), was a significant shift in the relationship between the two Houses. However, it was not only the unelected upper house that could not make such a claim. Nor could the unelected monarch. Nor could the monarch make a claim to be representative of the nation under the third definition. The claim of the monarch to be 'representative' derives solely from the fourth definition. The monarch stands as a symbol. The strength of the monarch as symbol has been earned at the expense of exercising political powers. To symbolise the unity of the nation, the monarch has had to stand apart from the partisan fray. The monarch has also had to stand aloof from any public controversy. When controversy has struck – as during the abdication crisis in 1936 and during periods of marital rift between members of the royal family in the 1990s – it has undermined support for the institution of monarchy and called into question its very purpose.

■ Development of the monarchy

The present monarch, despite some breaks in the direct line of succession, can trace her descent from King Egbert, who united England under his rule in AD 829. Only once has the continuity of the monarchy been broken, from 1642, when Charles I was deposed (and later executed) until the Restoration in 1660, when his son Charles II was put on the throne, restoring the line of succession. The principle of heredity has been preserved since at least the eleventh century. The succession is now governed by statute and common law, the throne descending to the eldest son or, in the absence of a son, the eldest daughter. If the monarch is under eighteen years of age, a regent is appointed.

Although all power was initially exercised by the monarch, it was never an absolute power. In the coronation oath, the King promised to 'forbid all rapine and injustice to men of all conditions', and he was expected to consult with the leading men of his realm, both clerical and lay, in order to discover and declare the law and before the levying of any extraordinary measures of taxation. Such an expectation was to find documented expression in Magna Carta, to which King John affixed his seal in 1215 and which is now recognised as a document of critical constitutional significance. At the time, it was seen by the barons as an expression of existing rights, not a novel departure from them.

The expectation that the King would consult with the leading men of the realm gradually expanded to encompass knights and burgesses, summoned to assent on behalf of local communities to the raising of more money to meet the King's growing expenses. From the summoning of these local dignitaries to court there developed a Parliament – the term was first used in the thirteenth century – and the emergence of two separate houses, the Lords and the Commons.

The relationship of crown and Parliament was, for several centuries, one of struggle. Although formally the King's Parliament, the King depended on the institution for the grant of supply (money) and increasingly for assent to new laws. Parliament made the grant of supply dependent on the King granting a redress of grievances. Tudor monarchs turned to Parliament for support and usually got it; but the effect of their actions was to acknowledge the growing importance of the body. Stuart kings were less appreciative. James I and his successor, Charles I, upheld the doctrine of the **divine right** of kings: that is, that the position and powers of the King are given by God, and the position and privileges of Parliament therefore derive from the King's grace. Charles' pursuit of the doctrine led to an attempt to rule without the assent of Parliament and ultimately to civil war and the beheading of the King in 1649. The period of republican government that followed was a failure and consequently short-lived. The monarchy was restored in 1660, only to produce another clash a few years later.

James II adhered to the divine right of kings and to the Roman Catholic faith. Both produced a clash with Parliament, and James attempted to rule by **royal prerogative** alone. A second civil war was averted when James fled the country following the arrival of William of Orange (James's Protestant son-in-law), who had been invited by leading politicians and churchmen. At the invitation of a new

Parliament, William and his wife Mary (James's daughter) jointly assumed the throne. However, the offer of the crown had been conditional on their acceptance of the Declaration of Right – embodied in statute as the 1689 Bill of Rights – which declared the suspending of laws and the levying of taxation without the approval of Parliament to be illegal. As the historian G.M. Trevelyan observed, James II had forced the country to choose between royal absolutism and parliamentary government (Trevelyan 1938: 245). It chose parliamentary government.

The dependence of the monarch on Parliament was thus established, and the years since have witnessed the gradual withdrawal of the sovereign from the personal exercise of executive authority. Increasingly, the monarch became dependent on ministers, both for the exercise of executive duties and in order to manage parliamentary business. This dependence was all the greater when Queen Anne died in 1714 without an heir (all her children having died) and yet another monarch was imported from the continent – this time George, Elector of Hanover. George I of Britain was not especially interested in politics and in any case did not speak English, so the task of chairing the Cabinet, traditionally the King's job, fell to the First Lord of the Treasury. Under Robert Walpole, this role was assiduously developed and Walpole became the most important of the King's ministers: he became 'prime minister'. Anne's dying without an heir and George's poor language skills facilitated the emergence of an office that is now at the heart of British politics.

George III succeeded in winning back some of the monarchy's power later in the eighteenth century. It was still the King, after all, who appointed ministers, and by skilfully using his patronage he could influence who sat in the House of Commons. This power, though, was undermined early in the nineteenth century. In 1832, the Great Reform Act introduced a uniform electoral system, and subsequent reform acts further extended the franchise. The age of a representative democracy, displacing the concept of virtual representation, had arrived. The effect was to marginalise the monarch as a political actor. To win votes in Parliament, parties quickly organised themselves into coherent and highly structured movements, and the leader of the majority party following a general election became Prime Minister. The choice of Prime Minister and government remained formally in the hands of the monarch, but in practice the selection came to be made on a regular basis by the electorate.

Queen Victoria was the last monarch seriously to consider vetoing legislation (the last monarch actually to do so was Queen Anne, who withheld Royal Assent from the Scottish Militia Bill in 1707). The year 1834 was the last occasion that a ministry fell for want of the sovereign's confidence; thereafter, it was the confidence of the House of Commons that counted. Victoria was also the last monarch to exercise a personal preference in the choice of Prime Minister (later monarchs, where a choice existed, acted under advice) and the last to be instrumental in pushing successfully for the enactment of particular legislative measures (Hardie 1970: 67). By the end of her reign, it was clear that the monarch, whatever the formal powers vested by the constitution, was constrained politically by a representative assembly elected by the adult male population, the government being formed largely by members drawn from that assembly. Victoria could no longer exercise the choices she had been able to do when she first ascended the throne.

The monarch by the beginning of the twentieth century sat largely on the sidelines of the political system, unable to control Parliament, unable to exercise a real choice in the appointment of ministers, unable to exercise a choice in appointing judges. The extensive power once exercised by the King had now passed largely to the voters and to politicians. The elective power was exercised by voters on election day: between elections it was the Prime Minister who exercised many of the powers formally vested in the monarch. By controlling government appointments, the Prime Minister was able to dominate the executive side of government. And as long as he could command majority support in the House of Commons, he was able to dominate the legislative side of government. Power thus shifted from an unelected monarch to what one writer later dubbed an 'elected monarch' (Benemy 1965) – the occupant not of Buckingham Palace but of 10 Downing Street.

The shift to a position detached from regular partisan involvement, and above the actual exercise of executive power, was confirmed under Victoria's successors. 'Since 1901 the trend towards a real political neutrality, not merely a matter of appearances, has been steady, reign by reign' (Hardie 1970: 188). The transition has been facilitated by no great constitutional act. Several statutes have impinged on the prerogative power, but many of the legal powers remain. There is nothing in law that prevents the monarch from vetoing a bill or from exercising personal choice in the invitation to form a government. The monarch is instead bound by conventions of the constitution (see Chapter 13). Thus, it is a convention that the monarch gives her assent to bills passed by Parliament and that she summons the leader of the largest party following a general election to form a government. Such conventions mean that the actions of the monarch are predictable – no personal choice is involved – and they have helped to ease the passage of the monarch from one important constitutional position to another.

These changes have meant that we can distinguish now between 'the crown' and 'the monarch'. The former denotes the executive authority that formally rests with the monarch but is in practice exercised in the name of the monarch, and the latter is the individual who is head of state and performs particular functions. The separation of the two is significant constitutionally and has major political consequences.

■ Political significance of the crown

The transfer of power from monarch to a political executive meant that it became possible to distinguish between head of state and head of government. It also ensured that great political power rested with ministers. Prerogative powers, as we have seen, remain important. They are powers that have always resided in the crown and that have not been displaced by statute. Many such powers remain in existence, though just how many is not clear. There is no definitive list, though a parliamentary committee in 2004 published a list supplied by the government, listing what it considered to be the main prerogatives. They include the summoning, prorogation and dissolution of Parliament; the appointment and deployment of armed forces; declarations of war; the giving of royal assent to Bills; the negotiation and ratification of treaties; the appointment of ministers, civil servants, senior figures in the church (the monarch is supreme governor of the Church of England) and in the judiciary; and the recognition of foreign states.

Prime Minister Gordon Brown, as part of his *Governance of Britain* agenda (see Chapter 13), proposed the transfer of a number of prerogative powers from Government to Parliament. The Con-

stitutional Reform and Governance Bill, introduced in 2009, contained provisions for Parliament to give assent to treaties. It also put the civil service on a statutory basis. The Prime Minister proposed that a parliamentary resolution be agreed, providing for the House of Commons to give its assent to committing armed forces to action abroad (the war-making power). He also raised the prospect of Parliament determining when it should be recalled.

Although these changes were designed to give Parliament a role determining important policy issues, most prerogative powers remained with ministers. It was also still Government that actually negotiated treaties and made the decision to go to war: what changed was that parliamentary approval was required to the Government's actions. Parliament was thus brought more into the process. The role of the monarch remained formal.

The monarch is thus the person in whom the crown vests, but the powers inherent in the crown are exercised elsewhere, in most cases by her ministers. Those powers are usually exercised directly by ministers. In other words, the monarch does not even announce the decisions taken by ministers in her name. Announcements of new ministerial appointments are made directly from Downing Street. Decisions as to military action have also been announced by No. 10. In 1939, the announcement that Britain was at war with Germany was made not by the King, George VI, but by the Prime Minister, Neville Chamberlain. The decision to send a task force to repel the Argentine invasion of the Falkland Islands in 1982 was taken by Margaret Thatcher and the Cabinet. The Chief of Naval Staff told her that a force could retake the islands. 'All he needed was my authority to begin to assemble it. I gave it to him . . . We reserved for Cabinet the decision as to whether and when the task force should sail' (Thatcher 1993: 179). Announcements about the conflict were subsequently made from Downing Street or the Ministry of Defence. In 2003, decisions about joining with the USA in an attack on Iraq were taken by the Prime Minister, Tony Blair. Media attention focused on 10 Downing Street, not Buckingham Palace. Treaties negotiated with other countries are signed by ministers. The Treaty of Accession to the European Community (now the European Union) was signed in 1972, not by the Queen but by the Prime Minister, Edward Heath.

As we have noted already, the appointment of ministers falls under the prerogative. The Prime

Minister thus decides who will be ministers – and who will not – and determines when the Cabinet shall meet and what it will discuss. He or she can also determine, within a five-year statutory limit, when Parliament shall be dissolved.

The prerogative is frequently exercised through rules, known as Orders in Council, that by virtue of their nature require no parliamentary authorisation. (Some Orders, though, are also made under statutory authorisation.) Orders in Council allow government to act quickly. Thus, for example, an Order in Council in 1982 allowed the requisitioning of ships for use in the campaign to retake the Falkland Islands. Not only are many prerogative powers exercised without the need for Parliament's approval, they are in many cases also protected from judicial scrutiny. The courts have held that many of the powers exercised under the royal prerogative are not open to judicial review.

Although the monarch will normally be kept informed of decisions made in her name, and she sees copies of state papers, she is not a part of the decision making that is involved. Nonetheless, the fiction is maintained that the decisions are hers. Peter Hennessy records that it was explained to him why the Table Office of the House of Commons would not accept parliamentary questions dealing with honours: 'It's the Palace', he was told (Hennessy 2000: 75). In other words, it was a matter for the Queen.

The maintenance of the royal prerogative thus puts power in the hands of the government. The government has, in effect, acquired tremendous powers, many of which it can exercise unilaterally. Parliament can question ministers about some aspects of the exercise of powers under the royal prerogative and could ultimately remove a government from office if dissatisfied with its conduct. However, so long as a government enjoys an overall majority in the House of Commons, it is unlikely to be much troubled about its capacity to exercise its powers. Parliament could curtail further the prerogative powers by statute but in so doing it would, in effect, be curtailing the powers of government.

Although the monarch now acts in a symbolic capacity, the country still has a form of medieval monarch – the Prime Minister. The monarch reigns, the Prime Minister rules. The Prime Minister enjoys the powers that he does because of the confluence of two things: a majority in the House of Commons and the royal prerogative.

■ The contemporary role of the monarchy

Given that the powers of the crown have almost wholly passed to the government, what then is the role of the monarch? Most people still believe that the monarchy has an important role to play in the future of Britain. In a MORI poll in January 2002, 80 per cent of those questioned said that the monarchy was important to Britain, as against 18 per cent who said that it was not.

What, then, is the monarch's contemporary role? Two primary tasks can be identified. One is essentially a representative task: that is, symbolising the unity and traditional standards of the nation. The second is to fulfil certain political functions. The weakness of the monarch in being able to exercise independent decisions in the latter task underpins the strength of the monarchy in fulfilling the former. If the monarch were to engage in partisan activity, it would undermine her claim to symbolise the unity of the nation.

Symbolic role

The functions fulfilled by the monarch under the first heading are several. A majority of respondents in a poll in the late 1980s considered six functions to be 'very' or 'quite' important. As we shall see, the extent to which these functions are actually fulfilled by members of the royal family has become a matter of considerable debate. Two functions – preserving the class system and distracting people from problems affecting the country – were considered by most respondents as 'not very' or 'not at all' important.

Representing the UK at home and abroad

As a symbolic function, representing the country at home and abroad is a task normally ascribed to any head of state. Because no partisan connotations attach to her activities, the sovereign is able to engage the public commitment of citizens in a way that politicians cannot. When the President of the United States travels within the USA or goes abroad he does so both as head of state and as head of government; as head of government, he is a practising politician. When the Queen attends the Commonwealth Prime Ministers' conference, she does so as symbolic head of the Commonwealth. The British government is represented by the Prime Minister, who is then able to engage in friendly, or not so friendly, discussions with fellow heads of government. The Queen stays above the fray. Similarly, at home, when opening a hospital or attending a major public event, the Queen is able to stand as a symbol of the nation. Invitations to the Prime Minister or leader of an opposition party to perform such tasks run the risk of attracting partisan objection.

At least two practical benefits are believed to derive from this non-partisan role, one political, the other economic. Like many of her predecessors, the Queen has amassed considerable experience by virtue of her monarchical longevity. According to one of her Prime Ministers, Tony Blair: 'she has an absolutely unparalleled amount of experience of what it's like to be at the top of a government' (Hardman 2007: 168). In 2002, she celebrated her fiftieth year on the throne. During her half-century on the throne, she had been served by ten Prime Ministers. Prime Minister Gordon Brown was a child when the Queen ascended the throne; his predecessor, Tony Blair, was born the year after she became Queen. Her experience, coupled with her neutrality, has meant that she has been able to offer Prime Ministers detached and informed observations. (The Prime Minister has an audience with the Queen each week.) As an informed figure who offers no challenge to their position, she also offers an informed ear to an embattled premier. 'After 50 years on the throne, the Queen harbours a greater store of political knowledge and wisdom than any prime minister whose length of career is at the mercy of fickle voters' (Hamilton 2002: 17). The value of the Queen's role to premiers has been variously attested by successive occupants of Downing Street (see Shawcross 2002). These have included Labour Prime Ministers Harold Wilson, James Callaghan, and Tony Blair, who were especially warm in their praise. Blair said at the time of the Queen's golden wedding anniversary that he enjoyed his weekly audience with the Queen, not simply because of her experience but because she was an 'extraordinarily shrewd and perceptive observer of the world. Her advice is worth having' (*The Times*: 21 November 1997). Her contact is not confined to the Prime Minister. The Chancellor of the Exchequer also sees her the night before a budget speech. As Gordon Brown recalled when he was Chancellor: 'She knows over the years what works and what doesn't. Sometimes you go back and change a bit of your speech' (Hardman 2007: 170).

The political benefit has also been seen in the international arena. By virtue of her experience and neutral position, the Queen enjoys the respect of international leaders, not least those gathered in the Commonwealth, a body comprising more than 50 countries with over 2 billion inhabitants. During the 1980s, when relations between the British government led by Margaret Thatcher and a number of Commonwealth governments were sometimes acrimonious (on the issue of sanctions against South Africa, for example), she reputedly used her influence with Commonwealth leaders 'to ensure that they took account of Britain's difficulties' (Ziegler 1996). There were fears that, without her emollient influence, the Commonwealth would have broken up or that Britain would have been expelled from it.

In terms of economic benefit, some observers claim – although a number of critics dispute it – that the Queen and leading members of the royal family (such as the Prince of Wales) are good for British trade. At home, royal palaces are major tourist attractions, though critics point out that Versailles – the royal palace in republican France – gets more visitors than Buckingham Palace. The symbolism, the history and the pageantry that surround the monarchy serve to make the Queen and her immediate family a potent source of media and public interest abroad. Royal (although not formal state) visits are often geared to export promotions, although critics claim that the visits do not have the impact claimed or are not followed up adequately by the exporters themselves. Such visits, though, normally draw crowds that would not be attracted by a visiting politician or industrialist. In 2001, the use of a member of the royal family to boost exports was put on a more formal footing when Prince Andrew, the Duke of York, was appointed as a special representative for international trade and development, working in support of British Trade International, a government body that encourages foreign investment and supports UK companies that trade overseas. In 2006, 293 of his 446 official engagements were trade related (Hardman 2007: 100).

Setting standards of citizenship and family life

For most of the present Queen's reign, this has been seen as an important task. The Queen has been expected to lead by example in maintaining standards of citizenship and family life. As head of state and secular head of the established Church, she is expected to be above criticism. She applies herself assiduously to her duties; even her most ardent critics concede that she is diligent (Wilson 1989: 190). In April 1947, at the age of 21, while still Princess Elizabeth, she said in a broadcast to the Commonwealth: 'I declare before you that my whole life, be it long or short, shall be devoted to your service.' She reiterated her vow in a speech to both Houses of Parliament in 2002. She and members of the royal family undertake about 4,000 public engagements each year (Hardman 2007: 15). The Queen lends her name to over 600 charities and voluntary organisations. Other members of her family involve themselves in charitable activities. The Prince of Wales founded eighteen out of twenty charities that form the 'Prince's Charities', a group of not-for-profit organisations. The Prince's Youth Business Trust has been responsible for funding the launch of 30,000 small businesses. The work of the Princess Royal (Princess Anne) as president of the Save the Children Fund helped to raise its international profile. Indeed, the name of a member of the royal family adorns the headed notepaper of about 3,000 organisations.

Up to and including the 1980s, the Queen was held to epitomise not only standards of good citizenship, applying herself selflessly to her public duties, but also family life in a way that others could both empathise with and hope to emulate. (Queen Elizabeth the Queen Mother – widow of George VI – was popularly portrayed as 'the nation's grandmother'.) Significantly, during the national miners' strike in 1984, the wives of striking miners petitioned the Queen for help. However, the extent to which the Queen fulfils this role has been the subject of much publicised debate since the late 1980s. The problem lay not so much with the Queen personally but with members of her family. By 1992, the Queen was head of a family that had not sustained one successful lasting marriage. The Prince of Wales, as well as the Princess, admitted adultery. The Duchess of York was pictured cavorting topless with her 'financial adviser' while her daughters were present. By the end of the decade, the divorced heir to the throne was attending public engagements with his companion, Camilla Parker-Bowles. In a MORI poll in January 2002, respondents were divided as to whether or not members of the royal family had 'high moral standards': 48 per cent thought that they did, and 44 per cent thought that they did not.

The claim to maintain high standards was also eroded by the collapse of a trial in 2002 involving the butler to Diana, Princess of Wales. The butler, Paul Burrell, was charged with stealing many items belonging to his late employer. The trial collapsed after it emerged that the Queen recalled a conversation with Burrell in which he said that he was storing items for safe keeping. This brought the Queen into controversy, but the consequences were greatest for the Prince of Wales after allegations were made about the running of his household, including the claim that staff were allowed to keep or sell gifts given to the Prince of Wales. The media interest led to an inquiry by Sir Michael Peat, the Prince's new secretary, and by a leading lawyer. Publication of their report in March 2003 was more critical than many observers expected. It identified flaws in the way the Prince's affairs had been conducted. The Prince's principal aide and confidant resigned. Following the collapse of the Burrell trial, a YouGov poll (17 November 2002) found that 17 per cent of respondents thought that 'recent revelations' had damaged the royal family 'a great deal' and 41 per cent 'a fair amount'. Following publication of the report, there was a marked increase in the number of people believing that Prince Charles should not succeed to the throne. In April 2002, 58 per cent of respondents thought he should succeed; following publication of the report, it was 42 per cent.

Uniting people despite differences

The monarch symbolises the unity of the nation. The Queen is head of state. Various public functions are carried out in the name of the crown, notably public prosecutions, and as the person in whom the crown vests the monarch's name attaches to the various organs of the state: the government, courts and armed services. The crown, in effect, substitutes for the concept of the state (a concept not well understood or utilised in Britain), and the monarch serves as the personification of the crown. Nowhere is the extent of this personification better demonstrated than on British postage stamps. These are unique: British stamps alone carry the monarch's head with no mention of the name of the nation. The monarch provides a clear, living focal point for the expression of national unity, national pride and, if necessary, national grief.

This role is facilitated by the monarch largely transcending political activity. Citizens' loyalties can flow to the crown without being hindered by political considerations. The Queen's role as head of the Commonwealth may also have helped to create a 'colour-blind' monarchy, in which the welfare of everyone, regardless of race, is taken seriously. At different points this century, members of the royal family have also shown concern for the economically underprivileged and those who have lost their livelihoods – ranging from the 'something must be done' remark in the 1930s of the then Prince of Wales (later Edward VIII) about unemployment while visiting Wales to the work of the present Prince of Wales to help disadvantaged youths.

This unifying role has also acquired a new significance as a consequence of devolution. The crown remains the one unifying feature of the United Kingdom. The UK traditionally comprises one constitutional people under one crown and Parliament. The position of the UK Parliament is circumscribed by virtue of devolving powers to elected assemblies in different parts of the UK. The royal family anticipated the consequences of devolution by seeking funding for an enhancement of the royal offices and residence in Scotland. The Queen opened the Scottish Parliament as well as the National Assembly for Wales. In the event of conflict between a devolved government and the UK government, the Queen constitutes the one person to whom members of both governments owe an allegiance.

The extent to which this unifying feature remains significant was exemplified by the funeral of Queen Elizabeth the Queen Mother, who died in 2002 at the age of 101. The number of people queuing up to pay their respects as the Queen Mother's coffin lay in Westminster Hall, as well as those lining the route for the funeral, far exceeded expectations. When questioned as to why they were queuing for hours to pay their respects, some people responded by saying that it was because it enabled them to express their sense of identity as being British. The Queen Mother's funeral and the Queen's Golden Jubilee celebrations (see Box 14.1) acted as a focal point for the expression of national identity, of bringing people together – a million people lined the Mall in London for the Queen's Golden Jubilee celebrations in June 2002 – in a way that no other national figure or institution could do.

BOX 14.1   IDEAS AND PERSPECTIVES

Golden Jubilee year, 2002

The Queen celebrated fifty years on the throne in 2002. Two major events affecting the royal family dominated the year. The first was the death of Queen Elizabeth the Queen Mother at the age of 101. The second was the celebration of the Queen's half-century on the throne. Both attracted crowds on a scale that far exceeded most expectations. The press was downplaying popular interest in the Queen Mother's funeral in the immediate wake of her death. Many in the media anticipated that the Golden Jubilee celebrations would fail to ignite popular interest. They were proved wrong.

The Queen Mother died at the Royal Lodge in Windsor Great Park on 31 March. Her body was transported to one of the chapels of St James' Palace in London. It was later moved from the chapel to lie in state at Westminster Hall. The journey to Westminster Hall was a short one of half a mile. Approximately 400,000 people lined the route for that journey. Over the next few days, more than 200,000 filed passed the coffin in Westminster Hall in order to pay their respects. It had been anticipated that probably no more than 70,000 would do so (if that), and in anticipation Westminster Hall was only to be open for certain hours each day. In the event, the hall stayed open almost round the clock as people queued for hours – some suffering from hypothermia during the cold nights – in order to walk past the coffin. The doors of the hall were only finally closed at 6.00 am on the morning of the funeral. The funeral took place at Westminster Abbey on 9 April. Parliamentarians gathered in Westminster Hall for the departure of the coffin. Members of the royal family walked behind it for the short journey to the abbey. After the service, the coffin was carried by hearse to its final resting place at Windsor. It is estimated that one million people lined the route, 400,000 of them in central London and the rest on the route to Windsor.

The numbers turning out to watch, and the number filing past the coffin, were not the only indication of how people reacted to the Queen Mother's death. An estimated 300 million viewers worldwide watched the funeral on television. Perhaps as tellingly, the National Grid recorded a significant drop in demand of 2,400 megawatts during the hour before the two-minute silence at 11.30 am. This was more than the fall recorded during the solar eclipse in 1999. It compares with a drop of 2,700 megawatts (the highest fall of all) during the three-minute silence in memory of those killed in the attacks in New York and Washington on 11 September 2001.

The popular reaction to the death of the Queen Mother took the mass media by surprise. The scale of the reaction resulted in a marked increase in coverage. It also appeared to galvanise the media to give greater attention to the celebrations of the Queen's Golden Jubilee. The Queen undertook a jubilee tour of the United Kingdom. It began on 1 May. On that day, about 6,000 anti-globalisation protesters descended on London. While they were protesting, the Queen visited Exeter in Devon: 30,000 people turned out to welcome her. During her tour, between May and August, she visited 70 cities and towns in England, Scotland, Wales and Northern Ireland, usually attracting large and enthusiastic crowds. The Jubilee culminated in a weekend of celebrations, including classical music and pop concerts in the grounds of Buckingham Palace. The pop concert, on 3 June, was followed by a massive firework display involving 2.5 tonnes of fireworks and attracted a television audience worldwide that was put at 200 million. An estimated one million people lined the Mall for the event, the area from Buckingham Palace to Admiralty Arch thronging with flag-waving celebrants. A similar number were in central London the following day when the Queen attended a service of thanksgiving in St Paul's Cathedral followed by a Golden Jubilee Festival in the Mall. And, over a six-month period, there were 28 million hits on the Golden Jubilee website.

Why did so many people turn out for, or watch on television, the Queen Mother's funeral and the Queen's Golden Jubilee celebrations? There are several possible explanations.

Personal respect for the Queen Mother and the Queen

The Queen Mother was often portrayed as the nation's 'favourite grandmother'. She was a strong, charismatic woman, driven by a sense of public duty. She refused to leave the country during the war. She took an interest in all the organisations of which she was a patron, in many cases visiting regularly. She continued to fulfil public engagements long after she turned 100. It has been argued that the crowds loved her largely because she loved the crowds. Her daughter, the Queen, inherited her sense of public duty. At 76, the Queen was the oldest monarch to celebrate a Golden Jubilee. The death of her mother so soon after the death of her sister (Princess Margaret) and the dignified way she coped with the funeral are argued by some to have increased public sympathy and support for her, encouraging people who might not otherwise have done so to turn out for the jubilee celebrations.

Respect for the institution of monarchy

It is difficult to separate the individual from the institution. The Queen Mother had become Queen Consort in 1936. She was the last Empress of India. Queen Elizabeth, as Queen Regnant, is head of state and the embodiment of the attributes that many look for in a monarch. Turning out for both the Queen Mother's funeral and the Queen's jubilee celebrations was seen by some as representing respect for the institution and the fact that both Queen Elizabeth the Queen Mother and Queen Elizabeth II were part of the nation's history. A MORI poll for the ITV programme *Tonight with Trevor MacDonald* in May found that 41 per cent of those questioned 'felt that the monarchy has strengthened following the deaths of Princess Margaret [the Queen's sister] and the Queen Mother'.

Expressing a sense of identity

The Queen is the one unifying element of the British constitution. Though some decision-making powers have been devolved to elected bodies in different parts of the United Kingdom, the Queen remains the sovereign of all the people or peoples of the United Kingdom. The Queen Mother's funeral and the Golden Jubilee celebrations provided occasions for people to come together at a time when fragmenting pressures were at work. The World Cup in 2002 allowed English supporters to support the England team and Scottish supporters the Scottish team. The Golden Jubilee brought everyone together. *The Times* (10 April 2002, special supplement) quoted one 54-year-old woman from Enfield who had turned out for the Queen Mother's funeral: 'We have to be here. We are Londoners and we are British.'

Media manipulation

Critics argue that much of the popular celebration was contrived by the media and by the royal family. The broadcast media gave the funeral and the jubilee celebrations blanket live coverage. The Director General of the BBC, Greg Dyke, was quoted as saying that the BBC had saved both itself and the monarchy. The Queen made a dignified broadcast, and the Prince of Wales a very personal one, following the death of the Queen Mother. Various members of the royal family, including the Duke of York and the Princess Royal, spent time meeting people who were queuing to pay their respects in Westminster Hall. The concerts at Buckingham Palace were carefully organised to ensure that people were chosen by ballot, not by social position. The firework display was a massive popular entertainment.

These explanations are not mutually exclusive nor are they necessarily exhaustive. There are not sufficient hard data available to prove which is correct. The least plausible is the last, in that it appears that the media were following rather than leading public opinion. In 2000, the BBC decided not to broadcast the birthday parade to celebrate the Queen Mother's 100th birthday. A MORI poll for the *Daily Mail* found that 56 per cent thought the decision was wrong; only 34 per cent thought it was right. A memo was also circulated in the BBC ahead of the jubilee celebrations indicating that the coverage should be more critical. The people lining the streets when the Queen Mother's coffin was moved to Westminster Hall alerted the media to the fact that they might have misjudged the popular mood and they responded accordingly. The BBC coverage of the funeral was judged by 64 per cent of respondents in one poll to be 'about right'.

The strength of the attachment to the monarchy is also reflected in one finding of a poll, carried out by Mediaedge: CIA for the *Daily Telegraph*. It found that 40 per cent of those questioned would alter their viewing habits and follow coverage of the Jubilee, compared with only 25 per cent who gave the same response for the World Cup.

However, the extent to which this role is fulfilled effectively does not go unquestioned. Critics, as we shall see, claim that the royal family occupies a socially privileged position that symbolises not so much unity as the social divisions of the nation. Although the royal household is known for having gays in its employ, and is an equal opportunities employer, critics have drawn attention to the dearth of employees in the royal household drawn from ethnic minorities. The 12,000 employees in the royal household are not especially well paid. In September 2009, for example, Buckingham Palace was advertising for a liveried helper at a starting salary of just over £17,000 a year. There have been attempts since to widen recruitment, but pay and conditions are not among the most competitive.

Allegiance of the armed forces

The armed services are in the service of the crown. Loyalty is owed to the monarch, not least by virtue of the oath taken by all members of the armed forces. It is also encouraged by the close links maintained by the royal family with the various services. Members of the royal family have variously served in (usually) the Royal Navy or the Army. Most hold ceremonial ranks, such as colonel-in-chief of a particular regiment. Prince Andrew was a serving naval officer and a helicopter pilot during the 1982 Falklands War. Prince Harry, as a serving army officer, saw action in Afghanistan in 2008. Prince William, the heir to the throne, is also a serving officer. The Queen takes a particular interest in military matters, including awards for service. In 2009, she instituted the Elizabeth Cross for widows of soldiers killed on active service or as a result of terrorist acts. Such a relationship helps to emphasise the apolitical role of the military and provides a barrier should the military, or more probably sections of it, seek to overthrow or threaten the elected government. (In the mid- to late 1970s, the press and some television programmes reported rumours that a number of retired officers favoured a coup in order to topple the Labour government.) In the event of an attempted military coup, the prevailing view – although not universally shared – is that the monarch would serve as the most effective bulwark to its realisation, the Queen being in a position to exercise the same role as that of King Juan Carlos of Spain in 1981, when he forestalled a right-wing military takeover by making a public appeal to the loyalty of his army commanders.

Maintaining continuity of British traditions

The monarch symbolises continuity in affairs of state. Many of the duties traditionally performed by her have symbolic relevance: for example, the state opening of Parliament and – important in the context of the previous point – the annual ceremony of Trooping the Colour. Other traditions serve a psychological function, helping to maintain a sense of belonging to the nation, and a social function. The awarding of honours and royal garden parties are viewed by critics as socially elitist but by supporters as helping to break down social barriers, rewarding those – regardless of class – who have contributed significantly to the community. Hierarchy of awards, on this argument, is deemed less important than the effect on the recipients. The award of an MBE (Member of the Order of the British Empire) to a

The Queen's interest in military matters extends, on this occasion, to overseeing her grandson as he finds a royal role for the twenty-first century
Source: Empics / Associated Press

local charity worker may mean far more to the recipient, who may never have expected it, than the award of a knighthood to a senior civil servant, who may regard such an award as a natural reward for services rendered. Investiture is often as important as the actual award.

To some it is a rather tiresome ordeal but to most a moving and memorable occasion. A fire brigade officer, who was presented with the British Empire Medal, spoke for many when he said: 'I thought it would be just another ceremony. But now that I've been, it's something I'll remember for the rest of my days'.

(Hibbert 1979: 205)

Each year 40,000 people are invited to royal garden parties, or to parties on behalf of charities, either at Buckingham Palace or Holyrood House in Edinburgh. Few decline the invitation. During the Queen's reign, more than one million people have attended the garden parties.

Again, this function does not go unchallenged. The award of honours, for example, is seen as preserving the existing social order, the type of honour still being determined by rank and position. It is also seen as a patronage tool in the hands of the Prime Minister, given that only a few honours (Knight of the Garter, the Order of Merit and medals of the Royal Victorian Order) are decided personally by the Queen. However, both Buckingham Palace and Downing Street have sought to make some changes while preserving continuity. Successive Prime Ministers have tried to make the honours system more inclusive – in recent years, for example, knighthoods have been conferred on head teachers – and the monarchy has sought to be more open. Since 1993, any member of the public has been able to nominate someone for an honour: nomination forms are available online.

Preserving a Christian morality

The Queen is supreme governor of the Church of England, and the links between the monarch and the church are close and visible. The monarch is required by the Act of Settlement of 1701 to 'joyn in communion with the Church of England as by law established'. After the monarch, the most significant participant in a coronation ceremony is the Archbishop of Canterbury, who both crowns and anoints the new sovereign. Bishops are, as we have seen, formally appointed by the crown. National celebrations led by the Queen will usually entail a religious service, more often than not held in Westminster Abbey or St Paul's Cathedral. The Queen is known to take seriously her religious duties and is looked to, largely by way of example, as a symbol of a basically Christian morality.

Preserving what are deemed to be high standards of Christian morality has been important since the nineteenth century, although not necessarily much before that: earlier monarchs were keener to protect the Church of England than they were to practise its morality. The attempts to preserve that morality in the twentieth century resulted in some notable sacrifices. Edward VIII was forced to abdicate in 1936 because of his insistence on marrying a twice-married and twice-divorced woman. In 1955, the Queen's sister, Princess Margaret, decided not to marry Group Captain Peter Townsend because he was divorced. She announced that 'mindful of the Church's teaching that Christian marriage is indissoluble, and conscious of my duty to the Commonwealth, I have resolved to put these considerations before others'. However, two decades later, with attitudes having changed, the Princess herself was divorced. Her divorce was followed by that of Princess Anne and Captain Mark Phillips and later by that of the Duke and Duchess of York and the Prince and Princess of Wales. Following the death of Diana, Princess of Wales, the Prince of Wales began to be seen in public with his companion, Camilla Parker-Bowles. Although attitudes towards divorce have changed, divorces and separations in the royal family – and the heir to the throne admitting to adultery – have nonetheless raised questions about the royal family's capacity to maintain a Christian morality. The capacity to do so has also been challenged explicitly by the heir to the throne, Prince Charles, who has said that he would wish to be 'a Defender of Faiths, not the Faith'.

The stance of the Prince of Wales also reflects criticism by those who do not think that the royal family *should* preserve a morality that is explicitly or wholly Christian. Critics see such a link as unacceptable in a society that has several non-Christian religions. The connection between the crown and the Christian religion may act against the crown being a unifying feature of the United Kingdom. The problem was exemplified in August 2002, when a Muslim traffic warden objected to the badge worn by police officers and traffic wardens. The badge comprised a crown with a cross, symbol of the Christian faith, on top of it.

Those who think the royal family should preserve a strict Christian morality appear to be declining in number. This was reflected at the start of the twenty-first century in popular attitudes towards the relationship of Prince Charles and Camilla Parker-Bowles. Mrs Parker-Bowles was divorced and her former husband was still living. She and Prince Charles engaged in an affair while both were still married. In a YouGov poll in August 2002, when asked what they believed should happen at the end of the Queen's reign, a majority of respondents – 52 per cent – said that Prince Charles should become King and be allowed to marry Mrs Parker-Bowles. No less than 60 per cent would approve of the Archbishop of Canterbury allowing them to have a Church of England wedding (*Evening Standard*: 15 August 2002). In the event, they married in a civil ceremony in April 2005.

Exercise of formal powers

Underpinning the monarch's capacity to fulfil a unifying role, and indeed underpinning the other functions deemed important, is the fact that she stands above and beyond the arena of partisan debate. This also affects significantly the monarch's other primary task: that of fulfilling her formal duties as head of state. Major powers still remain formally with the monarch. Most prerogative powers, as we have seen, are now exercised by ministers on behalf of the crown. A number of other powers, which cannot be exercised by ministers, are as far as possible governed by convention. By convention, as we have seen, the monarch assents to all legislation passed by the two Houses of Parliament; by convention, she calls the leader of the party with an overall majority in the House of Commons to form a government. Where there is no clear convention governing what to do, the Queen acts in accordance with precedent (where one exists) and, where a choice is involved, acts on advice. By thus avoiding any personal choice – and being seen not to exercise any personal choice – the monarch is able to remain 'above politics'. Hence the characterisation of the monarch as enjoying strength through weakness. The denial of personal discretion in the exercise of inherently political powers strengthens the capacity of the monarch to fulfil a representative – that is, symbolic – role.

However, could it not be argued that the exercise of such powers is, by virtue of the absence of personal choice, a waste of time and something of which the monarch should be shorn? Why not, for example, vest the power of dissolution in the Speaker of the House of Commons, or

simply – as suggested by Blackburn (1999) – codify existing practice in a way that requires no involvement by the monarch? There are two principal reasons why the powers remain vested in the sovereign.

First, the combination of the symbolic role and the powers vested in the crown enables the monarch to stand as a constitutional safeguard. A similar role is ascribed to the House of Lords, but that – as we shall see (Chapter 16) – is principally in a situation where the government seeks to extend its own life without recourse to an election. What if the government sought to dispense with Parliament? To return to an earlier example, what if there was an attempted military coup? The House of Lords could not act effectively to prevent it. It is doubtful whether a Speaker vested with formal powers could do much to prevent it. The monarch could. As head of state and as commander-in-chief of the armed forces, the monarch could deny both legitimacy and support to the insurgents. This may or may not be sufficient ultimately to prevent a coup, but the monarch is at least in a stronger position than other bodies to prevent it succeeding. Thus, ironically, the unelected monarch – successor to earlier monarchs who tried to dispense with Parliament – serves as an ultimate protector of the political institutions that have displaced the monarchy as the governing authority (see Bogdanor 1995).

Second, retention of the prerogative powers serves as a reminder to ministers and other servants of the crown that they owe a responsibility to a higher authority than a transient politician. Ministers are Her Majesty's ministers; the Prime Minister is invited by the sovereign to form an administration. The responsibility may, on the face of it, appear purely formal. However, although the monarch is precluded from calling the Prime Minister (or any minister) to account publicly, she is able to require a private explanation. In *The English Constitution*, Walter Bagehot offered his classic definition of the monarch's power as being 'the right to be consulted, the right to encourage, the right to warn'. The Queen is known to be an assiduous reader of her official papers and is known often to question the Prime Minister closely and, on other occasions, the relevant departmental ministers. Harold Wilson recorded that in his early days as Prime Minister he was caught on the hop as a result of the Queen having read Cabinet papers that he had not yet got round to reading. 'Very interesting, this idea of a new town in the Bletchley area', commented the Queen. It was the first Wilson knew of the idea. More significantly, there are occasions when the Queen is believed to have made her displeasure known. In 1986, for example, it was reported – although not confirmed – that the Queen was distressed at the strain that the Prime Minister, Margaret Thatcher, was placing on the Commonwealth as a result of her refusal to endorse sanctions against South Africa (see Pimlott 1996; Ziegler 1996); she was also reported to have expressed her displeasure in 1983 following the US invasion of Grenada, a Commonwealth country (Cannon and Griffiths 1988: 620). Indeed, relations between the Queen and her first female Prime Minister were claimed to be strained (see Hamilton 2002), although Mrs Thatcher said that her relationship with the Queen was correct. The Queen is also believed to have signalled her displeasure when Prime Minister Tony Blair failed to include her in the itinerary of a visit to the UK by US President Bill Clinton (Pierce 1999). Nonetheless, former Prime Ministers have variously attested to the fact that the Queen is a considerable help rather than a hindrance, offering a private and experienced audience. She also serves as a reminder of their responsibility to some other authority than political party. She also stands as the ultimate deterrent. Although her actions are governed predominantly by convention, she still has the legal right to exercise them. When the government of John Major sought a vote of confidence from the House of Commons on 23 July 1993 (following the loss of an important vote the previous evening), the Prime Minister made it clear that in the event of the government losing the vote, the consequence would be a general election. (By convention, a government losing a vote of confidence either resigns or requests a dissolution.) However, the government took the precaution of checking in advance that the Queen would agree to a dissolution.

■ Criticisms of the monarchy

Various functions are thus fulfilled by the monarch and other members of the royal family. There has tended to be a high level of support for the monarchy and popular satisfaction with the way those functions are carried out. The level of satisfaction was notable during the Queen's Golden Jubilee in 2002. However, a high level of support for the institution of monarchy has not been a constant in British political history. It dropped during the reign of Queen Victoria when she withdrew from public activity following the death of Prince Albert. It dropped again in the 1930s as a result of the abdication crisis, which divided the nation. It increased significantly during the Second World War because of the conduct of the royal family and remained high in postwar decades. It dipped again in the 1990s: 1992 was described by the Queen as her *annus horribilis* (horrible year). The monarchy was no longer the revered institution of preceding decades, and its future became an issue of topical debate. Even at times of high popular support, it has never been free of criticism. In recent years, the criticisms have been fuelled by the activities of various members of the royal family, the Prince of Wales coming in for especial criticism in 2002 and 2003.

Four principal criticisms can be identified: that an unelected monarch has the power to exercise certain political powers; that, by virtue of being neither elected nor socially typical, the monarchy is unrepresentative; that maintaining the royal family costs too much; and that the institution of monarchy is now unnecessary. The last three criticisms have become more pronounced in recent years.

Potential for political involvement

The actions of the sovereign as head of state are governed predominantly by convention. However, not all actions she may be called on to take are covered by convention. This is most notably the case in respect of the power to appoint a Prime Minister and to dissolve Parliament. Usually, there is no problem. As long as one party is returned with an overall majority, the leader of that party will be summoned to Buckingham Palace (or, if already Prime Minister, will remain in office). But what if there is a 'hung' parliament, with no one party enjoying an overall majority, and the leader of the third-largest party makes it clear that his or her party will be prepared to sustain the second largest party in office, but not the party with the largest number of seats? Whom should the Queen summon? Following the February 1974 general election, Edward Heath resigned as Prime Minister after his party lost its majority and he failed to negotiate a deal with the Liberal parliamentary party. The Queen then summoned Labour leader Harold Wilson. Labour constituted the largest party in the House of Commons, but it was more than 30 seats short of an overall majority. What if, instead of attempting to form a minority government, Wilson asked immediately for another general election? What should the Queen have done? Her advisers deliberated in case it happened, but in the event Wilson formed a government before seeking an election later in the year (see Hennessy 2000: Chapter 3). There is no clear convention to govern the Queen's response in such circumstances, and the opinions of constitutional experts as to what she should do are divided. Similarly, what if the Prime Minister was isolated in Cabinet and requested a dissolution, a majority of the Cabinet making it clear that it was opposed to such a move, would the Queen be obliged to grant her Prime Minister's request?

These are instances of problems that admit of no clear solution, and they pose a threat to the value that currently derives from the sovereign being, and being seen to be, above politics. She is dependent on circumstances and the goodwill of politicians in order to avoid such a difficult situation arising. When the Queen was drawn into partisan controversy in 1957 and 1963 in the choice of a Conservative Prime Minister, the obvious embarrassment to the monarchy spurred the party to change its method of selecting the leader. There remains the danger that circumstances may conspire again to make involvement in real – as opposed to formal – decision making unavoidable.

Given this potential, some critics contend that the powers vested in the monarch should be transferred elsewhere. Various left-of-centre bodies have advocated that some or all of the powers be transferred to the Speaker of the House of Commons. The proposal was advanced in 1996, in a Fabian Society pamphlet, by Labour parliamentary candidate Paul Richards, and again in 1998 by the authors of a pamphlet published by the left-wing think-tank Demos (Hames and Leonard 1998). Defenders of the existing arrangements contend that the retention of prerogative powers by the crown has created no major problems to date – one constitutional historian, Peter Hennessy, in a 1994 lecture, recorded only five 'real or near real contingencies' since 1949 when the monarch's reserve powers were relevant (Marr 1995: 234; see also Bogdanor 1995) – and it serves as a valuable constitutional long-stop. Giving certain powers to the Speaker of the Commons would be to give them to a member of an institution that may need to be constrained and would probably make the election of the Speaker a much more politicised activity. Furthermore, the Speaker or other such figure would be likely to lack the capacity to engage the loyalty of the armed forces to the same extent as the monarch.

Unrepresentative

The monarchy cannot make a claim to be representative in the second meaning of the term (freely elected). Critics also point out that it cannot make a claim to be representative in the third meaning (socially typical). The monarchy is a hereditary institution, based on the principle of primogeniture: that is, the crown passes to the eldest son. By the nature of the position, it is of necessity socially atypical. Critics contend that social hierarchy is reinforced by virtue of the monarch's personal wealth. The Queen is believed to be among the world's richest women. Many of the functions patronised by the Queen and members of the royal family, from formal functions to sporting events, are also criticised for being socially élitist. Those who surround the royal family in official positions (the Lord Chamberlain, ladies-in-waiting and other senior members of the royal household), and those with whom members of the royal family choose to surround themselves in positions of friendship, are also notably if not exclusively drawn from a social élite. In the 1950s, Lord Altrincham criticised the Queen's entourage for constituting 'a tight little enclave of British "ladies and gentlemen"' (Altrincham et al. 1958: 115). Various changes were made in the wake of such criticism – the royal family became more publicly visible, the presentation of débutantes to the monarch at society balls was abolished – but royalty remains largely detached from the rest of society. The closed nature of the royal entourage was attacked in the 1990s by the Princess of Wales, who had difficulty adapting to what she saw as the insular and stuffy nature of the royal court. Even at Buckingham Palace garden parties, members of the royal family, having mixed with those attending, then take tea in a tent reserved for them and leading dignitaries. Focus groups, commissioned by Buckingham Palace in 1997, concluded that the royal family was out of touch because of their traditions and upbringing as well as remote because of 'the many physical and invisible barriers thought to have been constructed around them' (quoted in Jones 1998). It was widely reported in 2002 that the most trusted aide to the Prince of Wales even squeezed his toothpaste onto his toothbrush for him. In a MORI poll in 2002, 68 per cent of those questioned thought that the royal family was 'out of touch with ordinary people'; only 28 per cent thought that it was not.

Pressures continue for the institution to be more open in terms of the social background of the

Queen's entourage and, indeed, in terms of the activities and background of members of the royal family itself. The public reaction to the death, in a car crash in 1997, of Diana, Princess of Wales – popular not least because of her public empathy with the frail and the suffering – and the findings from the focus groups (commissioned in the wake of the Princess's death) are believed to have been influential in persuading the Queen to spend more time visiting people in their homes and exploring how people live (for example, by travelling on the underground and by visiting a supermarket). Defenders of the royal family argue that it is, by definition, impossible for members of the family to be socially typical – since they would cease to be the royal family – and that to be too close to everyday activity would rob the institution of monarchy of its aura and charm.

Overly expensive

The cost of the monarchy has been the subject of criticism for several years. This criticism became pronounced in the 1990s. Much but not all the costs of the monarchy have traditionally been met from the civil list. The civil list constitutes a sum paid regularly by the state to the monarch to cover the cost of staff, upkeep of royal residences, holding official functions, and of public duties undertaken by other members of the royal family. (The Prince of Wales is not included: as Duke of Cornwall his income derives from revenue-generating estates owned by the Duchy of Cornwall.) Other costs of monarchy – such as travel and the upkeep of royal castles – are met by government departments through grants-in-aid from Parliament. In 1990, to avoid an annual public row over the figure, agreement was reached between the government and the Queen that the civil list should be set at £7.9 million a year for ten years. When the other costs of the monarchy – maintaining castles and the like – are added to this figure, the annual public expenditure on the monarchy was estimated in 1991 to exceed £57 million.

In the 1970s and 1980s, accusations were variously heard that the expenditure was not justified, in part because some members of the royal family did very little to justify the sums given to them and in part because the Queen was independently wealthy, having a private fortune on which she paid no tax. (When income tax was introduced in the nineteenth century, Queen Victoria voluntarily paid tax. In the twentieth century, the voluntary commitment was whittled down and had disappeared by the time the

Queen ascended the throne in 1952.) These criticisms found various manifestations. In 1988, 40 per cent of respondents to a Gallup poll expressed the view that the monarchy 'cost too much'. In a MORI poll in 1990, three out of every four people questioned believed that the Queen should pay income tax; half of those questioned thought the royal family was receiving too much money from the taxpayer. Certain members of the royal family became targets of particular criticism.

These criticisms became much louder in 1991 and 1992. They were fuelled by a number of unrelated developments. The most notable were the separation of the Duke and Duchess of York and – in December 1992 – of the Prince and Princess of Wales, following newspaper stories about their private lives. The result was that members of the royal family became central figures of controversy and gossip. In November 1992, fire destroyed St George's Hall of Windsor Castle, and the government announced that it would meet the cost of repairs, estimated at more than £50 million. Public reaction to the announcement was strongly negative. At a time of recession, public money was to be spent restoring a royal castle, while the Queen continued to pay no income tax and some members of the royal family pursued other than restrained lifestyles at public expense. A Harris poll found three out of every four respondents believing that ways should be found to cut the cost of the royal family.

Six days after the fire at Windsor Castle, the Prime Minister informed the House of Commons that the Queen had initiated discussions 'some months ago' on changing her tax-free status and on removing all members of the royal family from the civil list other than herself, the Duke of Edinburgh and the Queen Mother. The Queen herself would meet the expenditure of other members of the royal family. (This amounts to just over £1.2 million a year.) The Queen announced the following year that Buckingham Palace was to be opened to the public, with money raised from entrance fees being used to pay the cost of repairs to Windsor Castle. These announcements served to meet much of the criticism, but the controversy undermined the prestige of the royal family. Critics continued to point out that most of the costs of the monarchy remained unchanged, funded by public money, and drew attention to the fact that the Queen was using novel devices of taking money from the public (entrance fees to the Palace) in order to fund Windsor Castle repairs rather than drawing on her own private wealth.

Controversy was again stirred in January 1997 when Defence Secretary Michael Portillo announced plans for a new royal yacht, to replace *Britannia*, at a cost of £60 million. Public reaction was largely unfavourable, and Buckingham Palace let it be known that the government had not consulted members of the royal family before making the announcement. The plan to build a replacement yacht was cancelled a few months later by the new Labour government.

Supporters of the monarchy point out that savings have been made in recent years. The decommissioning of the royal yacht has saved £12 million a year. The royal family has made economies in travelling. By 2008–9, Head of State Expenditure was £41.5 million, a notable reduction in the costs compared with ten years previously. The cost of the contemporary monarchy, Buckingham Palace noted, amounted in 2008–9 to 69p per person in the country. Defenders contend that the country obtains good value for money from the royal family, the costs of monarchy being offset by income from crown lands (land formerly owned by the crown but given to the state in return for the civil list), which in 2008–9 amounted to £211 million, and by income from tourism and trade generated by the presence and activities of the Queen and members of her family. They also point out that much if not most of the money spent on maintaining castles and other parts of the national heritage would still have to be spent (rather like Versailles in France) even if there was no royal family. When such money is taken out of the equation, the public activities of the Queen and leading royals such as the Princess Royal are deemed to represent good value for public money. The cost of the monarchy in the United Kingdom, for example, is less than the cost of maintaining the presidency in Italy. However, despite the various savings made, people in the UK are split as to whether monarchy offers value for money. In a MORI survey in 2002, 45 per cent of respondents thought that it did offer value for money, as against 48 per cent who thought that it did not. In the same poll, 55 per cent thought that members of the royal family could be described as 'extravagant'.

Unnecessary

Those who criticise the monarchy on grounds of its unrepresentative nature and its cost are not necessarily opposed to the institution itself. A more open and less costly monarchy – based on the Scandinavian model, with the monarch mixing more freely with citizens and without excessive trappings – would be acceptable to many. However, some take the opposite view. They see the monarchy as an unnecessary institution; the cost and social élitism of the monarchy are seen as merely illustrative of the nature of the institution. Advocates of this view have included Tom Nairn in *The Enchanted Glass: Britain and its Monarchy*, Edgar Wilson in *The Myth of the British Monarchy*, Jonathan Freedland in *Bring Home the Revolution*, the contributors to Cyril Meadows, *Ending the Royal Farce*, Alastair Gray and Adam Tomkins in *How We Should Rule Ourselves*, and in 2009 *The New Statesman* magazine. Wilson contends that the various arguments advanced in favour of the monarchy – its popularity, impartiality, productivity, capacity to unite, capacity to protect democratic institutions of state, and ability to generate trade – are all myths, generated in order to justify the existing order. To him and similar critics, the monarchy forms part of a conservative establishment that has little rationale in a democratic society. They would prefer to see the monarchy abolished. 'The constitutional case for abolishing the Monarchy is based mainly on the facts that it is arbitrary, unrepresentative, unaccountable, partial, socially divisive, and exercises a pernicious influence and privileged prerogative powers' (Wilson 1989: 178). The monarchy, declared *The New Statesman*, 'sits like the spider at the centre of a web of wealth and privilege . . . Its continued existence gives legitimacy to the deeply unequal way in which British society is structured' (*The New Statesman*: 13 July 2009). Removing the monarchy, it said, would have huge symbolic value, 'confirming the people of Britain as citizens, not subjects'. Necessary functions of state carried out by the monarch could be equally well fulfilled, so critics contend, by an elected president. Most countries in the world have a head of state not chosen on the basis of heredity. So why not Britain?

Supporters of the institution of monarchy argue that, despite recent criticisms, the Queen continues to do a good job – a view that, according to opinion polls, enjoys majority support – and that the monarchy is distinctive by virtue of the functions it is able to fulfil. In a MORI poll in April 2006, 85 per cent of respondents were satisfied with the way the Queen was doing her job, a figure even higher than recorded at the time of the Golden Jubilee; only 8 per cent were dissatisfied. It is considered doubtful that an appointed or elected head of state would be able to carry out to the same extent the symbolic role, representing the unity of the nation. For a head of state not involved in the partisan operation of government, it is this role (representative in the fourth sense of the term) that is more important than that of being an elected leader. Indeed, election could jeopardise the head of state's claim to be representative in the first sense of the term (acting on behalf of a particular body or group). The monarch has a duty to represent all subjects; an elected head of state may have a bias, subconscious or otherwise, in favour of those who vote for him or her, or in favour of those – presumably politicians – who were responsible for arranging the nomination. The Queen enjoys a stature not likely to be matched by an elected figurehead in engaging the loyalty of the armed forces; and by virtue of her longevity and experience can assist successive Prime Ministers in a way not possible by a person appointed or elected for a fixed term. Hence, by virtue of these assets particular to the Queen, the monarch is deemed unique and not capable of emulation by an elected president. Although these assets may have been partially tarnished in recent years, it is argued that they remain of value to the nation.

■ Proposals for change

The monarchy has never been wholly free of critics. In the 1970s and 1980s, those critics were relatively few in number. In the early 1990s, they became far more numerous and more vocal. There were various calls for changes to be made in the institution of the monarchy and in the conduct of members of the royal family. Those most responsible for this situation arising were members of the royal family themselves. The marital splits, the antics of various royals, the public perception of some members of the royal family as 'hangers-on' (enjoying the trappings of privilege but fulfilling few public duties) and the failure of the Queen to fund the restoration of Windsor Castle herself contributed to a popular mood less supportive of the monarchy than before. This critical mood was tempered at the start of the new century.

Although the public standing of the monarchy improved, not least at the time of the Queen's Golden Jubilee, calls for change continue to be made. Various options have been advanced. These can be grouped under four heads: abolition, reform, leave alone and strengthen.

Abolition

The troubles encountered by the royal family in the late 1980s and early 1990s appeared to influence attitudes toward the monarchy itself. As we have seen, the Queen described 1992 as her *annus horribilis* – her horrible year. That was reflected in popular attitudes towards the monarchy. Until the middle of 1992, fewer than 15 per cent of people questioned in various polls wanted to see the monarchy abolished. A Gallup poll in May 1992 found 13 per cent of respondents giving such a response. By the end of the year, the figure had increased to 24 per cent. In 1994, those favouring abolition gained the support of a leading magazine, *The Economist*.

Not only was there an increase in the percentage of the population expressing support for the abolition of the monarchy; there was also an increasing agnosticism among a wider public. In 1987, 73 per cent of respondents in a MORI poll thought that Britain would be worse off if the monarchy were abolished. In December 1992, the figure was 37 per cent; 42 per cent thought it would make no difference. The same poll found, for the first time, more people saying that they did not think that the monarchy would still exist in fifty years' time than saying it would: 42 per cent thought it would not against 36 per cent saying it would.

However, those who argue the case for the retention of the monarchy appear still to have a considerable edge over those demanding abolition. The early 1990s represented the low point in terms of popular disaffection with royalty. The number of those thinking that Britain would be worse off if the monarchy were to be abolished has increased since 1992, although it is still not back to the level of the 1980s. (In June 2000, 50 per cent thought that Britain would be worse off; 37 per cent said it would make no difference and 10 per cent said better off.) Support for abolition of the monarchy has varied but usually no more than one in five express support for a republic. Those who do favour abolition are more likely to be found among the left-leaning members of the professional classes than the lower middle or working class: 'abolition of the monarchy is much more a demand of liberal intellectuals . . . than of the traditional working class left' (Mortimore 2002: 3). Although the proportion dipped in April 2005 (around the time of the marriage of Prince Charles), usually about seven out of ten people questioned favour retaining the monarchy (Table 14.1). Between 1992 and 2002, the proportion of the population

Table 14.1 Attitudes towards the monarchy

Q. If there were a referendum on the issue, would you favour Britain becoming a republic or remaining a monarchy? (%)

	April 1993	Dec 1994	Aug 1998	Feb 2002	Apr 2004[a]	Apr 2005	Apr 2006
Republic	18	20	16	19	20	22	18
Monarch	69	71	75	71	71	65	72
Don't know/Other	14	9	9	10	10	13	18

[a] Question differs slightly for the 2004 survey.

Sources: From Ipsos/MORI. Copyright © Ipsos MORI, reproduced with permission

believing the monarchy would not exist in fifty years' time outnumbered those believing that it would; since then, the proportion believing it will exist in fifty years' time has outnumbered those believing it will not. An Ipsos MORI poll in May 2002 found that 44 per cent believed it would exist in fifty years, against 33 per cent who believed that it would not. The equivalent figures in April 2006 were 41 per cent against 40 per cent.

Reform

Recent years have seen a growing body of support for some change in the nature of the monarchy and especially in the royal family. Some proposals for reform are radical. The authors of the Demos pamphlet, *Modernising the Monarchy*, argue the case not only for transferring the monarch's prerogative powers to the Speaker of the House of Commons but also for holding a referendum to confirm a monarch shortly after succeeding to the throne (Hames and Leonard 1998). There are some survey data to suggest that more people support the first of these proposals than oppose it. In a MORI poll in August 1998, 49 per cent thought that the powers should be removed, against 45 per cent who thought they should be retained.

There is also a desire for more general change in the way the monarch, and other members of the royal family, conduct themselves. This desire has been tapped by opinion polls as well as by the focus groups commissioned by Buckingham Palace. The public preference is for a more open and less ostentatious monarchy, with the Queen spending more time meeting members of the public, and with other members of the royal family, especially the 'minor royals', taking up paid employment (as some have) and blending into the community. A Granada TV deliberative poll in 1996, which involved interviewing people before and after discussing the subject with experts, found that the biggest percentage of affirmative responses was for the statement that 'members of the royal family should mix more with ordinary people'. The percentage agreeing was initially 66 per cent and, after discussion, it increased to 75 per cent. In a MORI poll in January 2002, 54 per cent of those questioned agreed with the statement that 'the monarchy should be modernised to reflect changes in public life'. Only 28 per cent felt that 'the monarch's role should remain broadly unchanged'.

There is also some support for a change in the order of succession. A small number of people favour the Queen abdicating in favour of Prince Charles, but the number is declining: it peaked in 1981 (48 per cent) and 1990 (47 per cent); since then, the proportion believing that she should remain Queen has exceeded 60 per cent. Some people also favour 'skipping a generation' and allowing Prince William, Prince Charles's elder son, to succeed to the throne in place of his father. In a MORI poll in September 1997, in the wake of the death of Diana, Princess of Wales, 54 per cent supported such a move: by November 1998, the percentage giving the same response was 34 per cent. The proportion increased markedly in March 2003 following the publication of the critical report on the way Prince Charles's household was run. By 2005, opinion was evenly divided. A MORI poll in April 2005 found that 43 per cent favoured such a move against 40 per cent opposed. However, the option of skipping a generation would require a change in the law. A decision by the Queen, or by Prince Charles upon or at the time of his succession to the throne, to abdicate is not one that can be taken unilaterally. Under the Act of Succession, Prince Charles will become King automatically on the death of his mother. There is no formal power to abdicate. That would require – as it did in 1936 – an Act of Parliament.

Another change that has variously been discussed, but which has less immediate relevance, is that of allowing the eldest child to succeed, regardless of gender. (Given that Prince Charles is the eldest child of the sovereign and his eldest child is a male, it will be at least two generations before any change becomes relevant.) In 1996, it emerged that the senior members of the royal family, apparently prompted by Prince Charles, had formed a small group (the 'Way Ahead Group' composed of senior royals and Buckingham Palace officials) to meet twice a year to consider various changes to existing arrangements. One proposal considered by the group was to allow the eldest child to succeed to the throne; another was to end the ban on anyone who marries a Roman Catholic succeeding to the throne.

The measures taken by the Queen in recent years – notably the decision to pay income tax, to limit the civil list and to spend more time meeting ordinary members of the public – appear to enjoy popular support. The deliberations of the Way Ahead Group were designed also to bring the institution up to date and enhance such support. The financial accounts (once highly secret) are now published, the jubilee celebrations in 2002 were carefully planned, and junior royals have a somewhat lower public profile than before as well as receiving no support from public funds. In 2002, the Queen became the first member of the royal family to receive a gold disc from the recording industry: 100,000 copies of the CD of the *Party at the Palace*, produced by EMI, were sold within a week of release.

Leave alone

The monarchy as it stands has some ardent admirers. Conservative MPs have generally moved quickly to defend the monarchy from criticism. When a Fabian Society pamphlet, *Long to Reign Over Us?*, was published in August 1996 (Richards 1996) advocating a referendum on the monarchy, a Conservative cabinet minister, Michael Portillo, immediately portrayed it as an attack on the institution of monarchy. 'New Labour should be warned that they meddle with the monarchy at the nation's peril', he declared. After 1997, some of the attempts by Prime Minister Tony Blair to encourage change also encountered criticism. In 1999, the leading historian, Lord Blake, declared: 'Reform has gone far enough . . . The monarchy is one of the fixed points of the British constitutional firmament. It cannot be subjected to constant change' (Pierce 1999).

Although this stance attracts support, it tends to be outweighed by those favouring some reform

(a fact acknowledged in effect by the royal family in the creation of the Way Ahead Group). As we have seen, most people questioned in the MORI poll in January 2002 favoured some change; only 28 per cent wanted to leave the monarchy broadly unchanged. Those favouring modest reform appear to be in a majority among voters. It is also the stance favoured by the Labour government. 'Palace officials have been told clearly by Downing Street that there is strong political pressure for a much leaner monarchy' (Pierce 1999). Although some of the proposals emanating from Downing Street, such as reducing the ceremony of the state opening of Parliament, have been resisted by Buckingham Palace (see Pierce 1999), the need for reform has generally been accepted by the royal family.

Strengthen

The final option is that of strengthening the role and powers of the monarchy. A Gallup poll in 1996 for the *Sunday Telegraph* tapped a body of support for giving the Queen a greater role. This was especially marked among working-class respondents and among the 16- to 34-year-old age groups: 57 per cent of working-class respondents thought that the Queen should be given 'a more substantial role in government'; and 54 per cent of respondents aged 16 to 34 also thought that she should have a more substantial role (Elliott and McCartney 1996). The nature of the role was not specified. As we have seen, the potential for the Queen to be drawn into decision making exists, and that potential may increase as a consequence of recent constitutional changes. The exercise of some of these powers may not prove unpopular to a section of the population. It was notable in the 1996 poll that many respondents regarded the Queen as having superior skills to those of the then Prime Minister, John Major: 46 per cent thought that the Queen would make a 'better Prime Minister than John Major'; 39 per cent thought that she would make a better Prime Minister than Tony Blair; and 47 per cent of working-class respondents thought that she would run the country 'more wisely than politicians'.

There is thus some body of support for the Queen exercising more power in the political affairs of the nation. However, that view is not widely held among politicians, nor – as far as one can surmise – among members of the royal family. As we have seen, the strength of the monarchy rests largely on the fact that it is detached from the partisan fray and is not involved in having to exercise independent judgement. Having to make independent decisions would be popular with some but, and this is the crucial point in this context, not with all people. Those adversely affected by a decision would be unlikely to keep their feelings to themselves. The monarchy would be drawn into the maelstrom of political controversy, thus ridding it of its capacity to fulfil the principal functions ascribed to it.

■ Conclusion

The monarch fulfils a number of functions as head of state. Some of those functions are not peculiar to the monarch as head of state: they are functions that are typically carried out by a head of state. Supporters of the monarchy argue that a number of functions are particularly suited to the monarch and, in combination, could not be fulfilled by an elected or appointed head of state. The monarchy was under strain in the early 1990s as a result of various disconnected events, and its public standing declined markedly. The nature of the monarchy was further called into question following the death of the popular Diana, Princess of Wales, in August 1997. The Queen and other members of the royal family have responded to criticism by implementing changes in structures and activities designed to create a more open and responsive monarchy. The actions of the Queen and her family appeared to bear fruit, especially in the celebration of the Queen's Golden Jubilee in 2002. There is no strong desire to get rid of the monarchy. However, there is scepticism about the future of the monarchy. Although most people (82 per cent in a 2006 IpsosMORI poll) think that the monarchy will still exist in ten years' time and, as we have seen, 41 per cent of respondents think that it will exist in fifty years' time, only 24 per cent think it will exist in 100 years' time. The monarchy, however, has proved remarkably adaptable, weathering some notable storms, and engaging popular support. It remains the most popular of the nation's political institutions.

BOX 14.2   BRITAIN IN CONTEXT

Presidents and monarchs

The United Kingdom is not unusual in having a monarchy. There are basically two types of head of state: presidents and hereditary rulers. Presidents are typically elected, though their role in government may vary. Some combine executive powers as head of government with formal ceremonial power as head of state; the President of the USA combines both. Some are predominantly ceremonial, that is, serving as head of state but not head of government; the President of Ireland is an example of this type. The same distinction can be drawn in terms of hereditary rulers. Some are both head of government and head of state. The number is now small, concentrated especially in the Middle and Far East, as powerful rulers over time have been overthrown, removed by popular vote or reduced to playing a largely ceremonial role. More than two-thirds of hereditary rulers have a predominantly or wholly ceremonial role, exercising few or no independent political powers. Most hereditary rulers take the title of king or queen, but some have the title of emir, grand duke, prince, sheik, or sultan; they are generally subsumed under the generic title of monarchs.

Monarchies account for less than one-quarter of the nations that now exist. There is a notable concentration of ceremonial monarchies in Western Europe – Belgium, Denmark, the Netherlands, Norway, Spain, Sweden and the United Kingdom are monarchies; Luxembourg is a Grand Duchy and Monaco a principality. The number of countries with a monarch exceeds the number of monarchs, as some monarchs reign over more than one country: the Queen of Denmark, for example, is also Queen of Greenland. None, though, can match the British monarch, who is Queen of fifteen Commonwealth countries and of a number of non-sovereign territories such as Bermuda, Gibraltar, the British Virgin Islands and the Falkland Islands.

Chapter summary

The monarchy remains an important institution in British political life. The monarch's transition from directing the affairs of state to a neutral non-executive role – with executive powers now exercised by ministers in the name of the monarch – has been a gradual and not always smooth one, but a move necessary to justify the monarch's continuing existence.

Transcending partisan activity is a necessary condition for fulfilling the monarch's symbolic ('standing for') role and hence a necessary condition for the strength and continuity of the monarchy. The dedication of the present monarch has served to sustain popular support for the institution. That support dropped in the 1990s, criticism of the activities of members of the royal family rubbing off on the institution of monarchy itself. Popular support for the institution remains and received a particular boost in the Golden Jubilee year of 2002. However, most people when questioned want to see some change, favouring the monarchy and royal family being more open and approachable.

Discussion points

■ What is the point in having a monarchy?

■ Does the royal family represent value for money?

■ What are the most important roles fulfilled by the Queen in contemporary society?

■ What public role, if any, should be played by members of the royal family, other than the Queen?

■ Should the monarchy be left alone, reformed or abolished?

Further reading

There are few substantial analyses of the role of the crown in political activity. The most recent scholarly analysis – that by Bogdanor (1995) – seeks to transcend recent controversy. The book provides a good historical perspective on the role of the monarchy as well as offering a defence of the institution. Hardie (1970) provides a useful guide to the transition from political involvement to neutrality; Hibbert (1979) also offers a useful overview. Lacey (1977, Golden Jubilee edition 2002) and Pimlott (1996, Golden Jubilee edition 2002) have produced useful and readable biographies of the Queen. Recent books about the monarchy include Douglas-Home (2000) and Shawcross (2002). Strober and Strober (2002) offer quotations from people who have been close to the Queen during her fifty-year reign. Hardman (2007) provides a guide to the royal family at work.

In terms of the debate about the future of the monarchy, the most recent reform tracts are those by Barnett (1994), Richards (1996) and Hames and Leonard (1998). The principal works arguing for abolition are Nairn (1988), Wilson (1989), Freedland (1999) and Meadows (2003). The issue of *The New Statesman*, 13 July 2009, advocating abolition, also provides a substantial critique. On the case for monarchy, see Gattey (2002).

In terms of the controversies of the early 1990s, the book that sparked media interest in the state of the Prince of Wales's marriage was Morton (1992), followed later by a revised edition (Morton, 1997). The biography of Prince Charles by Jonathan Dimbleby (1994) also contributed to the public debate. On the work undertaken by Prince Charles, see Morton (1998).

Bibliography

Altrincham, Lord, *et al.* (1958) *Is the Monarchy Perfect?* (John Calder).

Bagehot, W. (2009) *The English Constitution (Oxford World's Classics)* (Oxford Paperbacks; originally published 1867).

Barnett, A. (ed.) (1994) *Power and the Throne: The Monarchy Debate* (Vintage).

Benemy, F.W.G. (1965) *The Elected Monarch* (Harrap).

Birch, A.H. (1964) *Representative and Responsible Government* (Allen & Unwin).

Blackburn, R. (1992) 'The Future of the British Monarchy', in R. Blackburn (ed.) *Constitutional Studies* (Mansell).

Blackburn, R. (1999) 'Monarchy and the Royal Prerogative', in R. Blackburn and R. Plant (eds), *Constitutional Reform* (Longman).

Bogdanor, V. (1995) *The Monarchy and the Constitution* (Oxford University Press).

Cannon, J. and Griffiths, R. (1988) *The Oxford Illustrated History of the British Monarchy* (Oxford University Press).

Dimbleby, J. (1994) *The Prince of Wales. A Biography* (Little, Brown).

Douglas-Home, C. (2000) *Dignified and Efficient: The British Monarchy in the Twentieth Century* (Claridge Press).

Elliott, V. and McCartney, J. (1996) 'Queen Should have Real Power, say Britain's Youth', *Sunday Telegraph*, 21 April.

Freedland, J. (1999) *Bring Home the Revolution* (Fourth Estate).

Gattey, C.N. (2002) *Crowning Glory: The Merits of Monarchy* (Shepheard Walwyn).

Gray, A. and Tomkins, A. (2005) *How We Should Rule Ourselves* (Canongate Books).

Hames, T. and Leonard, M. (1998) *Modernising the Monarchy* (Demos).

Hamilton, A. (2002) 'Ten Out of Ten, Ma'am', *London Diplomat*, May/June.

Hardie, F. (1970) *The Political Influences of the British Monarchy 1868–1952* (Batsford).

Hardman, R. (2007) *Monarchy: The Royal Family at Work* (Ebury Press).

Hennessy, P. (2000) *The Prime Minister: The Office and its Holders since 1945* (Allen Lane/Penguin Press).

Hibbert, C. (1979) *The Court of St James* (Weidenfeld & Nicolson).

Jones, M. (1998) 'Queen to Appoint Royal Spin Doctor to Boost Ratings', *Sunday Times*, 22 February.

Lacey, R. (1977) *Majesty* (Hutchinson).

Lacey, R. (2002) *Royal: Her Majesty Queen Elizabeth II*, The Jubilee Edition (TimeWarner).

Marr, A. (1995) *Ruling Britannica* (Michael Joseph).

Meadows, C. (ed.) (2003) *Ending the Royal Farce* (Republic).

Mortimore, R. (2002) 'The Monarchy and the Jubilee', *MORI: British Public Opinion Newsletter*, Spring, Vol. XXV, No. 1.

Morton, A. (1992) *Diana: Her True Story* (Michael O'Mara Books).

Morton, A. (1997) *Diana, Her True Story – In Her Own Words* (Michael O'Mara Books).

Morton, J. (1998) *Prince Charles: Breaking the Cycle* (Ebury Press).

Nairn, T. (1988) *The Enchanted Glass: Britain and its Monarchy* (Century Hutchinson Radius).

Pierce, A. (1999) 'Spin Meister of Royal Reform Trips up', *The Times*, 4 September.

Pimlott, B. (1996) *The Queen* (HarperCollins).

Pimlott, B. (2002) *The Queen: Elizabeth II and the Monarchy*, Golden Jubilee edition (HarperCollins).

Pitkin, H.G. (1967) *The Concept of Representation* (University of California Press).

Richards, P. (1996) *Long to Reign Over Us?* (Fabian Society).

Shawcross, W. (2002) *Queen and Country* (BBC).

Strober, D. and Strober, G. (2002) *The Monarchy: An Oral History of Elizabeth II* (Hutchinson).

Thatcher, M. (1993) *The Downing Street Years* (HarperCollins).

Trevelyan, G.M. (1938) *The English Revolution 1688–9* (Thornton Butterworth).

Wilson, E. (1989) *The Myth of the British Monarchy* (Journeyman/Republic).

Ziegler, P. (1996) 'A Monarch at the Centre of Politics', *Daily Telegraph*, 4 October.

Useful websites

Official royal websites
Royal family: www.royal.gov.uk
Online monthly magazine of the above: www.royalinsight.gov.uk
Prince of Wales: www.princeofwales.gov.uk
Duke of York: www.thedukeofyork.org/Home/Home.aspx
Crown Estate: www.crownestate.co.uk

Nominations for public honours
Nomination process: www.direct.gov.uk/en/
    Governmentcitizensandrights/UKgovernment/
    Honoursawardsandmedals/index.htm

Organisations favouring reform
Republic: www.republic.org.uk
Centre for Citizenship: www.centreforcitizenship.org

Organisation supporting the monarchy
Constitutional Monarchy Association:
    www.monarchy.net

Survey data on attitudes towards the Royal Family
MORI: www.mori.com/polls/indroyal.shtml

CHAPTER 15

The House of Commons

Philip Norton

Learning objectives

- To explain the importance of the House of Commons in terms of its history and its functions.

- To identify and assess the means available to Members of Parliament to fulfil those functions.

- To describe and analyse pressures on the House and proposals for reform.

- To identify different approaches to parliamentary power.

Introduction

The House of Commons has evolved over seven centuries. At various times, it has played a powerful role in the affairs of the nation. Its most consistent activity has been to check the executive power. Its power has been limited by royal patronage and, more recently, by the growth of parties. It nonetheless remains an important part of the political process. It has to give its assent to measures of public policy. Ministers appear before it to justify their actions. It remains an arena for national debate and the clash of competing party views. It provides an important institutional constraint on the actions of government. However, its capacity to fulfil its functions has been the subject of debate. Criticism has led to various demands for change.

■ Origins of Parliament

Parliament has its origins in the thirteenth century. It was derived not from first principles or some grand design but from the King's need to raise more money. Its subsequent development may be ascribed to the actions and philosophies of different monarchs, the ambitions and attitudes of its members, external political pressures and prevailing assumptions as to the most appropriate form of government. Its functions and political significance have been moulded, though not in any consistent manner, over several hundred years.

Despite the rich and varied history of the institution, two broad generalisations are possible. The first concerns Parliament's position in relation to the executive. Parliament is not, and never has been on any continuous basis, a part of that executive. Although the Glorious Revolution of 1688 confirmed the form of government as that of 'parliamentary government', the phrase, as we have seen already (Chapter 13), means government through Parliament, not government by Parliament. There have been periods when Parliament has been an important actor in the making of public policy, not least for a period in the nineteenth century, but its essential and historically established position has been that of a reactive, or policy-influencing, assembly (Box 15.1; see Mezey 1979; Norton 2005); that is, public policy is formulated by the executive and then presented to Parliament for discussion and approval. Parliament has the power to amend or reject the policy placed before it, but it has not the capacity to substitute on any regular basis a policy of its own. Parliament has looked to the executive to take the initiative in the formulation of public policy, and it continues to do so.

The second generalisation concerns the various tasks, or functions, fulfilled by Parliament. Parliament is a multifunctional body. Not only does it serve as

---

BOX 15.1 IDEAS AND PERSPECTIVES

Types of legislature

- *Policy-making legislatures*: These are legislatures that not only can modify or reject measures brought forward by the executive but also can formulate and substitute policy of their own (e.g. the US Congress).
- *Policy-influencing legislatures*: These are legislatures that can modify and sometimes reject measures brought forward by the executive but lack the capacity to formulate and substitute policy of their own (e.g. UK Parliament, German Bundestag).
- *Legislatures with little or no policy effect*: These are legislatures that can neither modify nor reject measures brought forward by the executive, nor formulate and substitute policies of their own. They typically meet for only a short period each year to give formal approval to whatever is placed before them (e.g. former legislatures of Eastern European communist states, such as East Germany).

a reactive body in the making of public policy, it also carries out several other tasks. Its principal tasks were established within the first two centuries of its development. In the fourteenth century, the King accepted that taxes should not be levied without the assent of Parliament. The giving of such assent was variously withheld until the King responded to petitions requesting a redress of grievances. At the same time, Parliament began to take an interest in how money was spent and began to look at the actions of public servants. It became, in a rather haphazard way, a body for the critical scrutiny of government.

■ The development of Parliament

Knights and burgesses were summoned in the thirteenth century in order to give assent to the King's decision to raise extra taxes. They joined the King's court, comprising the leading churchmen and barons of the realm. In the fourteenth century, the summoning of knights and burgesses became a regular feature of those occasions when the King summoned a 'parliament'. At various times during the century, the knights and burgesses sat separately from the churchmen and barons, so there developed two chambers – the Commons and the Lords.

The House of Commons became more significant in subsequent centuries. It was an important political actor during the Tudor reigns of the sixteenth century and a powerful opponent of the Stuart monarchs, who asserted the divine right of kings to rule in the seventeenth. Clashes occurred between Parliament and Charles I – leading to the beheading of the King and a short-lived period of republican government under Oliver Cromwell – and, later, between Parliament and James II. The fleeing of James II in 1688 allowed leading parliamentarians to offer the throne to James's daughter and son-in-law (Mary and William) on Parliament's terms, and the supremacy of Parliament was established. Henceforth, the King could not legislate – or suspend laws – without the assent of Parliament.

Parliament nonetheless continued to look to the executive power – initially the King, and later the King's ministers assembled in Cabinet – to take the initiative in formulating measures of public policy. When measures were laid before Parliament, assent was normally forthcoming. In the eighteenth century, royal influence was employed, either directly or through the aristocratic patrons of 'rotten boroughs',

to ensure the return of a House favourable to the ministry. This influence was broken in the nineteenth century. The 1832 Reform Act enlarged the electorate by 49 per cent and abolished many, although not all, rotten boroughs. The effect of the measure was to loosen the grip of the aristocracy on the House of Commons and to loosen the grip of the monarch on the choice of government. The last time a government fell for want of the monarch's confidence was in 1834. MPs entered a period when they were relatively independent in their behaviour, being prepared on occasion to oust ministers and sometimes governments (as in 1852, 1855, 1856 and 1866) and to amend and variously reject legislation. Except for the years from 1841 to 1846, party ties were extremely loose.

This so-called **golden age** was to prove short-lived. At that time, there was little public business to transact and what there was of it was reasonably easy to comprehend. Members were not tied overly to party and could make a judgement on the business before them. The consequence of the 1867 Reform Act, enlarging the electorate by 88 per cent, and of later Acts reducing corrupt practices, was to create an electorate too large, and too protected by the law, to be 'bought' by individual candidates. Extensive organisation was necessary to reach the new voters, and organised political parties soon came to dominate elections. For a winning party to govern effectively, its members in the House of Commons needed to be united, and by the end of the century cohesive party voting was a feature of parliamentary life. Party influence thus succeeded royal patronage in ensuring the assent of MPs for measures brought forward by ministers of the crown.

The effect on Parliament of the rise of a mass electorate was profound. Governments came to be chosen by the electorate, not – as had occasionally happened in preceding years – by the House of Commons. Popular demands of government engendered not only more measures of public policy, but more extensive and complex measures. By the turn of the century, Parliament lacked the political will and the institutional resources necessary to subject increasingly detailed government bills to sustained and effective scrutiny. Albeit in a somewhat different form to earlier centuries, executive dominance had returned.

For the House of Commons, though, the developments of the nineteenth century served to confirm it as the pre-eminent component of the Crown-in-Parliament. The Glorious Revolution had established

Parliament's supremacy over the King. The rise of the democratic principle in the nineteenth century established the supremacy of the elected House over the unelected. The House of Commons was clearly a representative chamber in that it was freely elected and in that its members were returned to defend and pursue the interests of electors (see Chapter 16). The House of Lords could claim to be representative in neither sense. The subordinate position of the House of Lords was confirmed by statute in the Parliament Act of 1911.

The position so established in the nineteenth century continued into the twentieth. The House of Commons remained – and remains – the dominant chamber in a Parliament dominated by party, with the initiative for measures of public policy resting with the Cabinet and with a party majority in the House ensuring the passage of those measures.

That sets the historical context. What, then, is the contemporary position of the House of Commons? What are the essential characteristics of the House – its members and its procedures? What functions does it fulfil? What tools does it have at its disposal to fulfil them? And to what extent have developments in recent years strengthened or weakened its capacity to carry out those functions?

■ The House of Commons

The size of the House of Commons has varied over time, ranging in the twentieth century from a high of 707 seats (1918–22) to a low of 615 (1922–45). The number was reduced in 1922 because of the loss of (most) Irish seats; it has varied in postwar years and from 1945 to 1974 stood at 630; because of the increase in the size of the population, it was increased in 1974 to 635, in 1983 to 650, in 1992 to 651 and in 1997 to 659. In 2001, there was the first reduction since 1922: the number of seats in Scotland went down from 72 to 59 to take account of the fact that Scotland had its own parliament. As a result, the number of seats in the 2005 Parliament was 646. The number is set to increase to 650 in the Parliament of 2010.

Elections

The maximum life of a parliament is five years. Between 1715 and 1911, it was seven years. Members (MPs) are returned for single-member constituencies. These have been the norm since the Reform Act of 1885, although twelve double-member constituencies survived until the general election of 1950. The method of election employed is the 'first-past-the-post' system, with the candidate receiving the largest number of votes being declared the winner. This again has been the norm since 1885, although not until the general election of 1950 (with the abolition of university seats, for some of which a system of proportional representation was used) did it become universal. All seats nowadays are contested by two or more candidates. Again, this is a relatively recent development. In elections before 1945 a significant fraction of members – an average of 13 per cent – were returned unopposed. As late as the 1951 election, four Ulster Unionist MPs were returned in uncontested elections.

Each constituency comprises a defined geographical area, and the MP is returned to represent all citizens living within that area. (University seats

---

BOX 15.2   IDEAS AND PERSPECTIVES

The atmosphere of the House

By the standards of the Palace of Westminster, the House of Commons (Figure 15.1) is not a particularly ornate chamber. Relatively new compared with the rest of the Palace – rebuilt after being destroyed on 10 May 1941 by enemy bombing – it has a fairly functional feel to it. When it was rebuilt, there was a change in the style but not in the size. This meant that it was too small to accommodate every member. This has proved to be beneficial on two counts. First, on the rare occasions that the House is full, it conveys a sense of theatre: some members sit on the steps in the aisles, some crowd around the Speaker's chair, some stand in packed ranks at the bar of the House. Tension rises as the Prime Minister, or another senior minister, closes for the government and the Speaker rises to put the question. Members then troop into the voting lobbies either side of the chamber. If the outcome of the vote is uncertain, the tension is

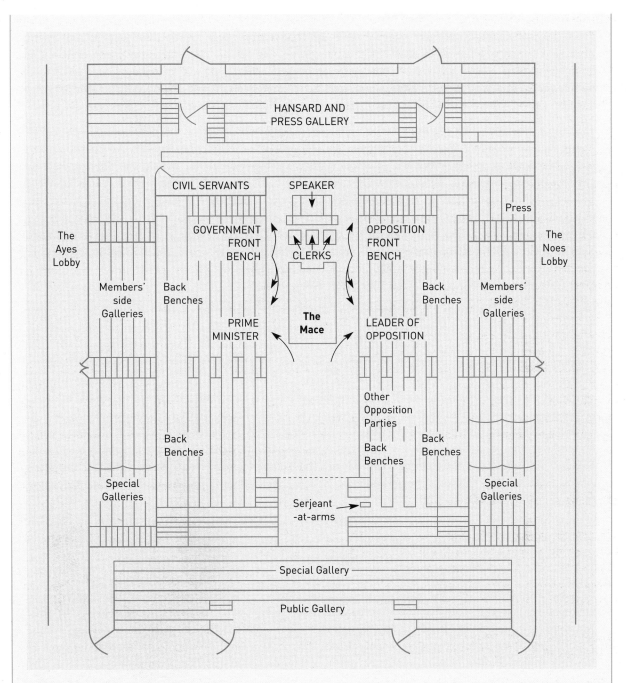

Figure 15.1 House of Commons seating plan

close to unbearable. After ten to fifteen minutes – sometimes longer – the tellers return and those representing the winning side line up on the right at the table, facing the Speaker. Once those on the winning side realise they have won, a massive cheer goes up. The most dramatic vote of recent history was on 28 March 1979, when the Labour government lost a vote of confidence by one vote. There have been dramatic votes in the twenty-first century when the Labour government has come close to defeat, as on the second reading of the Education Bill in 2003 – even the government whips were not sure who had won – or the the occasions when it was defeated: in 2005 on a provision to allow 90-day detention without trial and in 2009 on the resettlement rights in the UK of former Gurkha soldiers.

The second reason why the small chamber is better than a larger one is simply because such dramatic occasions are rare. Most of the time the chamber is notable for the rows of empty green benches as a handful of MPs sit around listening – or half-listening, or whispering to a neighbour – as one of their number delivers a speech from notes, sometimes quite copious notes. The chamber looks cavernous on such occasions. With a much larger chamber, the sheer emptiness of the place would be overwhelming.

The empty green benches are more apparent now than in previous decades. It is common to lament a fall in attendance. Most MPs have other things to do. There is little vital business in the chamber and nowadays there are very few members who will attract a crowd when they speak: the big speakers of yesteryear are either dead (Enoch Powell, Edward Heath, Robin Cook, Michael Foot), departed (Tony Benn) or in the House of Lords (Michael Heseltine, Margaret Thatcher). A change in the hours of sittings, allowing MPs to get away early on a Thursday evening, coupled with a tendency to schedule less important business for a Thursday, has meant that for some MPs it is now virtually a three-day week. They arrive in Westminster on the Monday – sometimes late in the day – and depart on Thursday. Neither parliamentary party meets now on a Thursday; indeed, very few meetings are organised on a Thursday. Most are now crowded into the day on Tuesday or Wednesday.

Proceedings in the chamber can be lively during Question Time, but even during that attendance – other than for Prime Minister's Questions – can be pretty poor. During debates, the proceedings can be notably dull. The government front bench will have one or two ministers listening, taking notes as necessary for the purpose of replying at the end. A government whip will be perched further along the bench, keeping an eye on proceedings, taking notes and liaising with the Chair about business. Their opposite numbers will be on the Opposition front bench. Notes or signals will variously pass between the whips, followed sometimes by a meeting behind the Speaker's Chair to fix some deal. Some MPs will wander in, look at what is going on and then depart. Some take their seats, stay a few minutes and go. A few will spend some time in the chamber and occasionally intervene to make a point. Some MPs (such as Labour MP Dennis Skinner) are regulars in the chamber, but they are the exceptions. Each tends to have a particular place where they like to sit, so even if there is plenty of space close to where they enter the chamber they move to the spot they are familiar with.

Visitors to the public gallery may be disappointed by the small number of MPs in the chamber, but at least nowadays the proceedings are easier to follow than they have ever been. One can work out the actual order of business in the chamber from the Order Paper, nowadays simplified to indicate the actual order of business. MPs still refer to one another in the third person and by constituency, but whenever an MP rises to speak or intervene the occupant of the Chair calls out the MP's name. Some exchanges can be enlightening as well as entertaining, but they tend to be exceptional. Proceedings tend to be predictable. Tensions can rise in an ill-tempered debate, and all the diplomatic skills – or disciplinary powers – of the Speaker or Deputy Speaker may be necessary to restore order. Some MPs try to get around the rules by raising partisan points on bogus points of order, much to the despair of the Speaker.

There are the exceptional debates, not just those when the chamber is packed but when an issue comes up in which some MPs have a genuine interest and of which they have some expert knowledge. On those occasions, those listening learn something and the minister takes the speeches seriously. One rough measure of how seriously the speech is being taken is the number of notes that pass between the minister and the civil servants in the official box.

For members of the public, proceedings are not only easier to follow than before but they are also now permitted to take notes. One inconvenience, however, is that they now sit behind a screen to watch MPs at work. The screen was installed for reasons of security – not so much to protect ordinary MPs but rather the Prime Minister and members of the Cabinet – and serves as a reminder of the difficult times in which public figures have to operate.

were exceptional: the constituencies comprised graduates of the universities, regardless of where they were living.) Constituency boundaries are at present drawn up and revised regularly by independent Boundary Commissions (one covering each country – England, Scotland, Wales and Northern Ireland); each commission is chaired formally by the Speaker of the House of Commons, although the essential work of leadership is undertaken by a deputy, who is a judge. Under existing legislation, boundary reviews are required every eight to twelve years. The commissions are enjoined to produce constituencies within each country of roughly equal size (in terms of the number of electors), although as far as possible retaining existing county and natural boundaries. An Electoral Commission, created by the 2000 Act, reports on elections and referendums, oversees the registration of, and donations to, political parties, and seeks to raise public awareness of elections.

Members

Although the House may constitute a representative assembly in that it is freely elected and MPs are returned to defend and pursue the interests of constituents, it is not a representative assembly in being typical of the socio-economic population that elects it. The members returned to the House are generally male, middle-class and white. These characteristics have been marked throughout the twentieth century. The House has tended to become even more middle-class in the years since 1945. Before 1945, and especially in the early years of the century, the Conservative ranks contained a significant number of upper-class and upper middle-class men of private means, while the parliamentary Labour Party (the PLP) was notable for the number of MPs from manual working-class backgrounds: they constituted a little over half of the PLP from 1922 to 1935 and before that had been in an overwhelming majority (Rush 1979: 69–123). Since 1945, the number of business people on the Conservative benches has increased, as has the number of graduates, often journalists or teachers, on the Labour benches.

The shift in the background of Conservative MPs since 1945 is reflected in education as well as occupation. In 1945, just over 83 per cent of Conservative MPs had been educated at public schools – 27 per cent at Eton. Almost two-thirds – 65 per cent – had been to university, with half having gone to Oxford or Cambridge. Sixty years later – in the

Table 15.1 University-educated MPs, 2005 (%)

Party	University (all)	Oxford and Cambridge
Labour	64	16
Conservative	81	43
Liberal Democrat	79	31

Source: B. Criddle (2005) 'MPs and candidates', in D. Kavanagh and D. Butler (eds) *The British General Election of 2005*. Reproduced with permission of Palgrave Macmillan

parliament elected in 2005 – 60 per cent were public-school educated, with just under 8 per cent having been at Eton; 81 per cent had been at university, the proportion having gone to Oxford or Cambridge comprising 43 per cent (see Table 15.1). The party has witnessed, particularly in the general elections in and since 1979, a growing number of newly elected candidates who have gone to state schools and then gone on to Oxbridge or some other university. The underlying trend continues to be for the proportion of university-educated MPs to be greater among the new intake of MPs than among the parliamentary party as a whole, and for a university education to be more prevalent among MPs than among unsuccessful candidates. The trend also continues of new MPs being less likely to have attended Eton than Conservative MPs as a whole. In the 2005 general election, 'the new Conservative intake was less elitist with fewer than half from private schools and fewer with the elitist pedigree of "public school and Oxbridge" – only 22 per cent of newcomers compared to 35 per cent in the entire Parliamentary Party' (Criddle 2005: 165–6). The members of the parliamentary party are not socially typical, but they are somewhat more middle-class than the members elected in the years before 1979.

On the Labour side, the notable change in educational background has been the rise in the number of graduates. In 1945, just over one-third of Labour MPs (34 per cent) had been to university. By 1970, just over half of the PLP were university graduates. In the parliaments of Labour governments from 1997 onwards, approximately two out of every three Labour MPs had been to university, though the figure dipped slightly in 2005. In 1997 the figure was 66 per cent, in 2001 it was 67 per cent and in 2005 it was 64 per cent (Table 15.1). Most of these were graduates of universities other than Oxford and Cambridge. The percentage of Oxbridge-educated Labour MPs has shown little change – the percentage educated at Oxbridge in 2005 (16 per cent) was almost identical to that of 1945.

These figures reflect the growing middle-class nature of the PLP. The percentage of manual workers in the party declined in each successive parliament until 1974, increased in 1979 and 1983, but then dropped back in subsequent elections. Only 17 per cent of new Labour MPs in 1992 were drawn from manual backgrounds. It declined further in subsequent elections, reaching its lowest percentage ever – 10 per cent – in 2005; only two of the new intake in 2005 came from a manual background. 'Labour MPs', as Byron Criddle noted in his analysis of the 2005 Parliament, 'were increasingly drawn from the ranks of professional politicians, who dominated the new intake and who had come to rival the weight of the teaching profession' (Criddle 2005: 166).

Indeed, there is something of a convergence between members on both sides in terms of education and background. Of new MPs elected to the House of Commons, the vast majority – on both sides of the House – are university-educated, and a large proportion drawn not only from some middle-class occupation but from an occupation that is in the domain of politics or communication. Teachers, journalists and political staffers have been notable among the new intake of Labour MPs in and since 1997; just over 20 per cent of Labour MPs returned in 2005 had been academics or teachers. Business and the professions continue to dominate on the Conservative benches, though 17 per cent of the Tory MPs elected in 2005 had been political organisers, publishers or journalists.

This convergence also reflects the growth of the 'career politician' – the individual who lives for politics, who seeks entry to the House of Commons as early as possible and who seeks to stay in the House for as long as possible, ideally holding government office along the way (King 1981; Riddell 1993). Career politicians are contrasted with old-style MPs, who used to make a mark in other fields before becoming involved in politics and who could – and variously did – leave the House of Commons to pursue some other interest (for example, heading a major company or the family firm). The old-style members may have been ambitious in terms of government office, but they recognised that there was more to life than politics. For career politicians, politics is their life. The career politician has always existed in British politics, but their numbers have grown in recent years. They often (though not in all cases) hold a job in an area related to politics before

seeking election. The consequence of the growth of the career politician is something we shall consider later.

Where there is a difference between the two sides is in terms of council experience and in terms of gender. Labour MPs are more likely to have served as local councillors. Of the new MPs elected in 1997, almost two-thirds of Labour MPs had served as councillors, compared with one-quarter of Conservative MPs. The new but relatively small Labour intake of 2001 also included a number of long-standing councillors, especially in safe Labour seats (Criddle 2002: 192). There are also many more women sitting on the Labour benches than on the Conservative (and Liberal Democrat) benches.

Women became eligible to sit in the House only in 1918. The number elected since then has been small. Between 1918 and 1974, the total number of women elected to the House was only 112 (including Countess Markievicz, the first woman elected but who, as a Sinn Fein candidate, did not take her seat). In the 1983 general election, 23 women were elected to the House; in 1987 the figure was 41 and in 1992 it was 60, still less than 10 per cent of the membership. The Labour Party in 1993 adopted a policy of all-women short lists in a number of constituencies in order to boost the number of female Labour MPs. Although the policy was struck down by an employment tribunal in 1996 on the grounds that it breached sex discrimination legislation, this did not affect seats where female candidates had already been selected. As a result, a record number of female Labour MPs were elected in 1997: no less than 101, 64 of them elected for the first time. Labour replaced all-women short lists with 50–50 short lists (half of the candidates female, the other half male) but this failed to push up the number of women candidates. In the 2001 election, the number of women MPs dropped to 118. However, more were adopted for safe seats in the subsequent Parliament and in 2005 the number increased to an all-time high of 128, just under 20 per cent of the total.

The number of women MPs on the Labour benches is more marked than on the benches of other parties. Although Conservative leaders have encouraged local parties to adopt female candidates, very few have done so. The result has been a notable disparity between the parties (see Table 15.2). In 2005, seventeen women were elected as Conservative MPs, three more than in 1997; although a record number, it still represented less than 9 per cent of

Table 15.2 Women elected to Parliament, 2005

Party	Number of women MPs (2001 figure in parentheses)	
Labour	98	(95)
Conservative	17	(14)
Liberal Democrat	10	(5)
SNP	0	(1)
United Ulster Unionists	1	(1)
Democratic Unionists	1	(1)
Sinn Fein	1	(1)
Other	0	(0)
Total	**128**	**118**

Source: From B. Criddle (2005) 'MPs and candidates', in D. Kavanagh and D. Butler (eds) *The British General Election of 2005*, p. 159. Reproduced with permission of Palgrave Macmillan

the parliamentary party. The Liberal Democrats have also had problems in getting more women elected; in 2005 they managed to double – from five to ten – the number of female MPs; again, an all-time high but one that represented only 16 per cent of Liberal Democrat MPs. The percentage of women MPs in the House of Commons in recent parliaments remains low compared to some other countries – especially the Nordic countries – but it is now above the average for national parliaments. Data compiled by the Inter-Parliamentary Union show that in 2005 the UK ranked fifty-first out of 187 national parliaments in terms of the proportion of women members.

The number of non-white MPs remains very small. For most of the twentieth century there were none at all. The first non-white MP was elected in 1892: Dadabhai Naoroji, an Indian, was elected as Liberal MP for Finsbury Central. Another Indian was elected as a Conservative three years later. A third sat from 1922 to 1929. There was then a 58-year gap. In 1987, four non-white MPs were elected. In 1992 the number increased to six (five Labour and one Conservative) and in 1997 to nine (all Labour), including the first Muslim MP and two Sikhs. In 2001, the figure reached twelve, again all sitting on the Labour benches (although the Conservatives did have one MP who was Anglo-Indian). In 2005, the number increased to fifteen, with thirteen on the Labour benches (four of them Muslims) and the Conservatives now having two MPs from ethnic backgrounds – one black and one Asian. The fifteen represent 2.3 per cent of MPs – another all-time high – but still less than half

of what would correspond to the proportion in the population.

One reason for the persistence of white, male MPs is the length of time that MPs typically serve in the House. Some MPs sit for thirty or forty years. In the 2005–10 Parliament, the Father of the House of Commons (the longest continuously serving MP), Labour MP Alan Williams, had been first elected in 1964. Another MP was elected in 1959 but did not have continuous service, losing his seat in 1964 and being returned for another in 1966. Seven MPs – including well-known figures such as Kenneth Clarke, John Prescott and Dennis Skinner – had served continuously since 1970. A typical member sits for about 20 years. Given the growth in the number of career politicians, it is unlikely that this figure will decrease; if anything, the reverse. Even if parties are keen to replace existing MPs with candidates from a wider range of backgrounds, the opportunity to replace them does not necessarily come up very quickly. The length of service of legislators is a particular feature of the British House of Commons: MPs tend to serve as members longer than legislators in other comparable legislatures (see Table 15.3). Even in the 1997 general election, which – as a result of a massive swing to the Labour party – brought in a record number of new MPs (no fewer than 253), more than 60 per cent of MPs had served in the previous parliament. More than 30 MPs had first been elected to parliament in 1970 or earlier. However, the figures suggest that even when the

Table 15.3 Average length of legislative service, 1994

Country	Average length of service (years)
Canada	6.5
France	7
Denmark	7.8
Germany	8.2
Israel	11
USA (Senate)	11.1
USA (House)	12.2
New Zealand	13.1
Japan	15
United Kingdom	20

Source: A. Somit and A. Roemmele (1995) 'The victorious legislative incumbent as a threat to democracy', *Legislative Studies Newsletter*, Vol. 18, No. 2, July. Reproduced by permission of A. Somit

opportunity exists to select a new candidate, local parties tend to select candidates in the same mould as their predecessors.

Members are paid an annual salary, but until 1912 they received no payment at all. Since then, they have been paid, but on a relatively modest basis. In 1954, for example, the salary was £1,250 and in 1964 it was increased to £3,250. In January 1996, an MP's salary was £34,086, fairly modest by international comparison – legislators in Italy, the USA, France and Germany were all paid considerably more (more than twice as much in Italy and the USA) – and by comparison with higher levels of management in the UK. (Ministers receive higher salaries.) In July 1996, MPs voted to increase their salaries by 26 per cent, to £43,000. The increase was controversial, and unpopular, but it still left MPs lagging behind the salaries of members of other comparable legislatures. The salary has increased since and, in April 2009, it was set at £64,766.

Since the 1960s, parliamentary facilities have also improved. In the mid-1960s, an MP was guaranteed only a locker in which to keep papers and received no allowance, whether for hiring a secretary or even to cover the cost of telephone calls. If an MP was lucky enough to have an office, it was usually shared with several other MPs. A secretary had to be paid out of the MP's own pocket. A secretarial allowance (of £500) was introduced in 1969. This allowance evolved into an office cost allowance, allowing an MP to hire one and sometimes two secretaries and in most cases a research assistant (more often than not, part-time). In 1999, the office cost allowance stood at £50,264. In 2001, the House agreed to a new system. The office cost allowance was split into two: a staff cost allowance and an incidental expenses provision. Each MP could claim a staff cost allowance, enabling them to employ up to the equivalent of three full-time staff, but with the staff paid centrally by the House authorities and on agreed rates with standard contracts. In 2008, the figure was increased to the equivalent of 3.5 staff. Each MP can also claim a further £20,000 towards incidental expenses. MPs can claim travel expenses and, for those living outside London (and thus having to maintain two homes), an additional costs allowance – known since 2009 as a personal additional accommodation expenditure – up to £24,222 (2009–10 figures). MPs with inner London constituencies receive a small London supplement. The additional cost allowance, as we shall see, became highly controversial in 2009 when details of claims made by MPs were published. A communications allowance was also introduced in 2007, 'to assist in the work of communicating with the public on parliamentary business'. It was initially set at £10,000 but was increased in 2008 to £10,400 and frozen at that figure until 2011.

The physical space available to MPs has also increased. Buildings close to the Palace of Westminster – including the former Scotland Yard buildings in Derby Gate, known as the Norman Shaw Buildings – were acquired for parliamentary use. More recently, buildings in Parliament Street – between Whitehall and Parliament Square – were taken over and redeveloped, retaining the exterior but with a modern and integrated complex of offices inside. They have the address of 1 Parliament Street. To these has been added a major purpose-built parliamentary building, known as Portcullis House, in Bridge Street, just across the road from the Clock Tower housing Big Ben and linked to the Palace by an underground passage. With the completion of Portcullis House, which includes rooms for committee meetings as well as suites of offices for MPs, each MP now has an office.

Sittings of the House

The House to which Members are returned meets annually, each parliamentary session running usually now from November to November. There is a long summer recess, but the session is not prorogued (formally adjourned) until shortly after the House returns in the autumn; that allows the House to meet and deal with bills which have not completed their passage. The effect of prorogation is to kill off unfinished public business; any bills that have not received the Royal Assent fall, though there is now provision for some bills to be carried over from one session to another. In the event of a general election being called, Parliament is dissolved, cutting short the session. If a general election is held in the spring, the new session will usually be a long one, running from the sitting of the new House through to the November of the following year.

The House usually sits for more than 150 days a year, a not unusual number compared with some other legislatures, such as those of the USA, Canada and France, although considerably more than most other legislatures. What makes it distinctive is the number of hours for which it sits: it sits usually for more than 1,200 hours a year. The figures for the period from 2001 to 2008 are given in Table 15.4. In

Table 15.4 The House of Commons: length of sittings, 2001–8

Session	Number of sitting days	Number of hours sat	Average length of sitting day
2001–2[a]	201	1,297	7 hours 40 minutes
2002–3	162	1,287	7 hours 57 minutes
2003–4	157	1,215	7 hours 44 minutes
2004–5[b]	65	535	8 hours 14 minutes
2005–6[a]	208	1,572	7 hours 33 minutes
2006–7	146	1,119	7 hours 40 minutes
2007–8	165	1,306	7 hours 55 minutes

[a] Long session following a spring general election.
[b] Short session, because of the calling of a general election.
Source: From the *House of Commons Sessional Information Digests, 2001–8.* © Parliamentary Copyright 2008. Parliamentary copyright material is reproduced with the permission of the Controller of Her Majesty's Stationery Office (HMSO) on behalf of Parliament

previous parliaments, the sittings were sometimes longer, averaging nearly 1,500 hours in non-election sessions in the 1987–92 parliament. Other elected chambers are not able to compete with these figures.

Until 1999, the House sat at 2.30 p.m. on the first four days of the week and at 9.30 a.m. on Fridays. On the first four days, it usually rose by 10.30 p.m. In an experiment started in 1999, it started meeting at 11.30 a.m. on Thursdays (rising earlier in the evening, usually by 7.00 or 8.00 p.m.). In 2002, the House agreed to meet at 11.30 a.m. on Tuesdays and Wednesdays as well, with the House rising by 7.00 p.m. (by 6.00 p.m. on Thursdays). The new sitting times took effect in 2003. However, they did not prove popular with all MPs (especially with MPs living long distances from London) and in 2005 the House voted to revert to a 2.30 p.m. start on a Tuesday, though agreeing to sit at 10.30 a.m. on a Thursday. The House thus has an uneven pattern of sitting times: 2.30 p.m. on Monday and Tuesday, 11.30 a.m. on Wednesday, 10.30 a.m. on Thursday, and (if sitting) 9.30 a.m. on Friday. Sittings may, in certain circumstances, be extended in order to transact particular business. Late or all-night sittings variously take place to get through the remaining stages of a bill. (If the House has an all-night sitting and is still sitting when the new day's sitting is scheduled to commence, then the business for that next day falls.) Late-night sittings became rare in the 1992–7 parliament but were employed again following the return of a Labour government in 1997 in order to get some of its major legislation through. On Fridays, when **private members' bills** are normally discussed, the House rises at 3.00 p.m. To give

MPs more time to be in their constituencies, the House does not sit every Friday: ten Fridays each session are designated as non-sitting Fridays.

As a result of a change agreed by the House in 1999, there is also a 'parallel chamber', or 'main committee', allowing MPs to meet and discuss issues separate from the main chamber (see Box 15.3). This allows for non-contentious issues to be debated. Meetings are held in the Grand Committee Room, just off Westminster Hall, and are known formally as meetings in Westminster Hall. The topics covered on Tuesdays and Wednesdays each week are proposed by private Members; the Thursday sitting is given over to a debate on a subject of general interest or a select committee report. All MPs can attend – as in the main chamber – although in practice few do so.

Functions

The principal function of the House is often seen as involvement in law making. It is, after all, classified as a legislature and the name means carrier, or giver, of law. In practice, as we have seen, the House essentially responds to the measures that the government brings forward. Furthermore, much of the time of the House is given over to business that has nothing directly to do with legislation. Question Time is now an established feature of the House. It is not part of the legislative process. When the House debates the economy or the government's industrial policy, those debates are not parts of the formal legislative process. The House has an important role to play in the legislative process, but it is clearly not its only role.

The Grand Committee is located just off Westminister Hall.

Source: Copyright © Adam Woolfitt / Corbis

Meetings in Westminster Hall

In December 1999, the House of Commons introduced a new form of meeting – meetings in Westminster Hall. These enable MPs to meet separately from the main chamber, and the gathering is sometimes described as a parallel chamber. (The parallel chamber is modelled on Australian experience.) Meetings in Westminster Hall are open to all MPs. They can come in as they can in the main chamber. The principal differences between the main chamber and the room used for the parallel chamber are of size and structure. The room used – the Grand Committee Room, located just off the cavernous Westminster Hall – is much smaller than the chamber of the House of Commons. (For part of 2006 another room was used while the Grand Committee Room was redeveloped.) It also differs in structure. MPs sit at desks arranged in a semicircle around a raised dais. The desks are fixed and have desktop microphones. Meetings are presided over by a Deputy Speaker or one of the MPs on the Chairmen's Panel (senior MPs who are drawn on in order to chair standing committees) and are usually used for discussing non-contentious business. Votes cannot be held. Meetings now take place from 9.30 a.m. to 2.00 p.m. on Tuesdays, from 9.30 to 11.30 a.m. and from 2.30 to 5.00 p.m. on Wednesdays, and from 2.30 to 5.30 p.m. on Thursdays. On Tuesdays and Wednesdays, there are short debates on topics raised by individual members. Thus, for example, on Tuesday 14 July 2009, the topics debated were healthcare services in Shropshire, rail service on the East Coast mainline, HM Prison Wellingborough, government funding for local authority support for adults with learning difficulties, and the effect on communities of government policy on gypsies and travellers. The following day, topics included abortion law in Northern Ireland, combat stress and the NHS, and local authorities' role in promoting apprenticeships. Thursday sittings are given over to debates on general topics or select committee reports. Thus, on Thursday 16 July 2009, the report of the Communities and Local Government Committee on 'Housing and the Credit Crunch', and the government's response to it, were debated. Attendance at meetings is low – usually a handful of MPs – not dissimilar to the chamber itself when private members' motions are taken.

The creation of the parallel chamber was controversial. Supporters see it as a way of allowing issues, for which there would otherwise be no time in the chamber, to be discussed. Most Conservative MPs voted against setting it up because they feared it would serve to distract attention from the chamber and absorb MPs' energies on minor issues. In the event, meetings of the new body have proved low-key, attracting virtually no media attention (the inaugural meeting was effectively ignored) and very little attention on the part of MPs. The chamber was initially employed on an experimental basis, but MPs subsequently voted to make it permanent. It was not seen as damaging to the main chamber and back-benchers have found it useful as a means of raising issues that they might not have the opportunity to raise in the main chamber. Each debate brings an issue to the attention of government, with a junior minister replying. The proceedings are published in *Hansard*.

The principal functions of the House can be grouped under four headings: those of legitimisation, recruitment, scrutiny and influence, and expression. Several other functions can be identified (see Norton, 2005) but these can largely be subsumed under these four broad headings.

Legitimisation

The primary purpose for which the representatives of the counties and boroughs (the communes) were first summoned was to assent to the King's demand for additional taxes. Subsequently, their assent also came to be necessary for legislation. The House has thus been, since its inception, a legitimising body.

The House fulfils the task of 'manifest legitimisation', that is, the overt, conscious giving of assent. In the UK the function has two elements: the giving of assent to bills and to requests for supply (money) and the giving of assent to the government itself. The government depends on the confidence of the House of Commons for its continuance in office. If the House withdraws its confidence, then by convention the government resigns or requests the dissolution of Parliament.

The House proceeds on the basis of motions laid before it: for example, to give a bill a second reading or to express confidence in the government. By approving such motions, the House gives its formal – manifest – assent. Members may vote on motions. The Speaker of the House asks those supporting the motion to say 'aye', those opposing to say 'no'. If no dissenting voices are heard, the Speaker declares that 'the ayes have it'. If some MPs shout 'no' and persist then members divide (that is, vote). A simple majority is all that is necessary. (This is subject to two basic requirements: that at least forty MPs – a quorum – are shown by the division to be present and that, in voting on a closure motion, at least 100 MPs have voted in favour.) Members vote by trooping through two lobbies, known as the division lobbies (an 'aye' lobby and a 'no' lobby), where they are counted and their names recorded. The result of the vote is then announced in the chamber.

It is this accepted need for the House to confer legitimacy through giving its assent that constitutes the basic power of the House in relation to government. Initially, the knights and burgesses summoned to the King's court were expected to give assent. Gradually, members began to realise that, as a body, they could deny assent to supply and later to legislation. This formed the basis on which they could ensure the effective fulfilment of other functions. It remains the basis of the power of the House of Commons. Without the assent of the House, no measure can become an Act of Parliament. The contemporary point of contention is the extent to which the House is prepared to use its power to deny assent. Critics contend that the effect of the growth of party and hence party cohesion has largely nullified the willingness of the House to employ it.

The House also fulfils what Robert Packenham has termed the function of 'latent legitimisation'. According to Packenham, this derives from the fact that 'simply by meeting regularly and uninterruptedly, the legislature produces, among the relevant populace and élites, a wider and deeper sense of the government's moral right to rule than would otherwise have obtained' (Packenham, in Norton 1990: 87). However, it can be argued that such activity is necessary but not sufficient to generate such an underlying sense of legitimacy. Latent legitimacy can be said to derive from the House fulfilling the other functions expected of it (Norton 2005: 10).

Given that Parliament not only sits regularly but has fulfilled a range of tasks expected of it for a considerable period of time, it is arguably a much stronger agent of latent legitimisation than many other legislatures. It would seem plausible to hypothesise that the function is weaker in a political system in which the legislature is a recent and conscious creation of resuscitation by the prevailing regime and fails to carry out tasks expected of it by the people.

Recruitment

Ministers are normally drawn from, and remain within, Parliament. The situation is governed solely by convention. There is no legal requirement that a minister has to be an MP or peer.

The practice of appointing ministers from those who sit in Parliament derives from expediency. Historically, it was to the King's benefit to have his ministers in Parliament, where they could influence, lead and marshal support for the crown. It was to the benefit of Parliament to have ministers who could answer for their conduct. An attempt was made early in the eighteenth century to prevent ministers from sitting in Parliament, but the legislation was superseded by another law allowing the practice to continue (Norton 2005: 43).

The convention that ministers be drawn from and remain within Parliament – predominantly now, by convention, the House of Commons – is a strong one inasmuch as all ministers are currently MPs or peers. It is extremely rare for a minister to be appointed who does not sit in either House and even rarer for that person to remain outside Parliament while in office: the person is either elevated to the peerage (nowadays the most used route) or found a safe seat to contest in a by-election. On occasion, one of the Scottish law officers – the Solicitor General for Scotland – was appointed from the ranks of Scottish lawyers and remained outside Parliament, but that was the exception that proves the rule. The post ceased to be part of the UK government following devolution.

The relationship between the House and ministers is governed by convention. Under the convention of individual ministerial responsibility, ministers are answerable to the House for their own conduct and that of their particular departments. Under the convention of collective ministerial responsibility, the Cabinet is responsible to the House for government policy as a whole. It is this latter convention that requires a request for the dissolution of Parliament or the resignation of the government in the event of the House passing a **motion of no confidence** in the government.

The fact that ministers remain in Parliament clearly has a number of advantages to government. Things have not changed that much from earlier centuries in that ministers can use their positions to lead and marshal their supporters. Ministers themselves add notably to the voting strength of the government, the so-called 'payroll vote' in the House. Just over eighty ministers serve in the Commons and just over twenty in the Lords. With ministers' unpaid helpers – parliamentary private secretaries – added to the number, the payroll vote usually comprises a third or more of the MPs sat on the government side of the House. The government thus has a sizeable guaranteed vote to begin with. Party loyalty – and ambition for office – usually ensures that the votes of **backbenchers** follow those of ministers.

The convention that ministers be drawn from the ranks of parliamentarians has certain advantages for Parliament. It ensures that members are close to ministers, both formally and informally. Ministers can be questioned on the floor of the House; members can waylay them in the corridors and the division lobbies for private conversations. The fact that ministers remain as members of the House means that they retain some affinity with other members. MPs elevated to ministerial office retain their constituency duties.

Above all, though, the convention renders the House of Commons powerful as a recruiting agent. The route to ministerial office is through Parliament. In some other systems, the legislature is but one route to the top. In the USA, for example, there are multiple routes: cabinet ministers – and presidents – can be drawn from the ranks of business executives, academics, state governors, former army officers and lawyers. The US Congress enjoys no monopoly on recruitment to executive office. In the UK, Parliament does have such a monopoly. Parliament is the exclusive route for those intending to reach the top of the political ladder. Those aspiring to ministerial office thus have to seek election to the House of Commons (or hope – often in vain – for a peerage) and have to make their mark in the House. The House also serves as an important testing ground for potential ministers and, indeed, for those on the ministerial ladder (see Norton 2005: 50–2). A poor performance at the despatch box can harm a minister's chances of further promotion. A con-sistently poor performance can result in the minister losing office. Conversely, a bravura performance at the despatch box may save a minister who is under pressure to go. For ambitious politicians, the chamber matters.

Scrutiny and influence

Scrutiny and influence are essentially conjoined functions. The House subjects both the measures and the actions of government to scrutiny. It does so through various means: debate, questioning and committee deliberations. If it does not like what is before it, it can influence the bill or the policy under consideration. It may influence solely by the force of argument. It may influence by threatening to deny assent (that is, by threatening to defeat the government). Ultimately, it may actually refuse its assent, denying the government a majority in the division lobbies.

These two functions are central to the activity of the House and absorb most of its time. Government business enjoys precedence on most days. The House spends most of its time discussing legislation and the policy and actions of ministers. Although the dominance of *party* has ensured that normally the government is assured a majority in divisions, the party *system* helps to ensure that government is subject to critical scrutiny from opposition parties in the House. The procedures of the House are premised on the existence of two principal parties, with each having the opportunity to be heard. Membership of all committees of the House replicates party strength on the floor of the House, thus ensuring that the opposition has an opportunity to offer critical comments and to force government to respond at all stages of the parliamentary process.

Furthermore, scrutiny and influence may also take place outside, or despite, the context of party. MPs sit for particular constituencies. Although elected on a party label, they are nonetheless expected to ensure that government policy does not damage constituency interests. They may also be influenced by moral and religious views that ensure they pay careful attention to bills and government policies that run counter to their personal convictions. They may also listen to bodies outside Parliament – charities, consumer groups, professional organisations, companies – that have a particular interest in, or knowledge of, the subject under debate.

However, the extent to which the House actually fulfils these functions is a matter of dispute. Critics contend that the government stranglehold, via its party majority, ensures that the House is denied the means for sustained and effective scrutiny, and that, inasmuch as it may exert some limited scrutiny, that scrutiny is not matched by the capacity to influence government. MPs may consider and find fault with a particular measure but not then prove willing to use their power to amend or reject it.

Expression

The House serves not one but several expressive functions. Members serve to express the particular views and demands of constituents. An individual constituent or a group of constituents may be affected adversely by some particular policy or by the actions of some public officials. Constituents may feel that a particular policy is bad for the constituency or for the country. Contacting the local MP will usually result in the MP passing on the views to the relevant minister and may even result in the member raising the issue on the floor of the House. The pursuit of such cases by MPs ensures that they are heard and their points considered by ministers.

MPs also express the views of different groups in society as a whole. A range of issues that do not fall within the ambit of party politics are taken up and pursued by private members. MPs may express the views of organised interests, such as particular industries or occupations. They may express the views of different sectors of society, such as students or the elderly. Many will give voice to the concerns of particular charitable, religious or moral groups. For example, some MPs press for reform of the laws governing abortion, some want to liberalise the laws concerning homosexuality, and some want to strengthen the laws on road safety. These issues can be pursued by MPs through a number of parliamentary procedures (see Cowley 1998). In some cases, members table amendments to government bills. Another route is through the use of private members' bills. Although the more contentious the issue, the less likely the bill is to be passed, the debate on the bill serves an important function: it allows the different views to be expressed in an authoritative public forum, heard by the relevant minister and open to coverage by the mass media.

MPs, then, serve to express the views of constituents and different groups to the House and to government. MPs may also serve to express the views of the House and of government to constituents and organised groups. The House may reach a decision on a particular topic. Members may then fulfil an important role in explaining why that decision was taken. Members individually may explain decisions to constituents. **Select committees** of the House may, in effect, explain particular policies through their reports, which are read not just by government but also by groups with a particular interest in the committee's area of inquiry. The House thus has a tremendous potential to serve several expressive functions. The extent to which it does so is a matter of considerable debate. MPs have limited time and resources to pursue all the matters brought to their attention. The attention given to their activities by the media and by government may be slight. Many groups may bypass Parliament in order to express their views directly to ministers. Furthermore, it is argued, the views expressed by MPs on behalf of others are drowned out by the noise of party battle. By limiting the resources of the House and by keeping information to itself, the government has limited the capacity of the House to arm itself with the knowledge necessary to raise support for public policies.

These are the most important functions that may be ascribed to the House. The list is not an exhaustive one. Other tasks are carried out by the House. These include, for example, a disciplinary role (punishing breaches of privilege and contempt) and a small quasi-judicial role, primarily in dealing with private legislation (legislation affecting private interests, not to be confused with private members' legislation). Other functions often ascribed to the House can, as we have explained, be subsumed under the four main headings we have provided. However, two other functions, identified by Walter Bagehot in *The English Constitution* in 1867, have been lost by the House. One, the 'elective' function – that is, choosing the government – was held only briefly during the nineteenth century. Before then it was a function exercised by the monarch. Since then, it has passed largely, although not quite exclusively, to the electorate. The electorate chooses a government on a regular basis at general elections. The House retains the power to turn a government out through passing a motion of no confidence; but it is not a power it has exercised regularly – in the past century, it was used only in 1924 and 1979, opposition parties combining to turn out a minority government.

The other function is that of legislating. Initially, the need for the House to give its assent was transformed by members into the power to initiate measures, first through the presentation of petitions to the crown and later through the introduction of bills. This power was important in the nineteenth century, when the House could be described as sharing the legislative power with government. Even so, its exercise was limited. Most legislation introduced into the House was private legislation. Since then, public legislation has expanded as parties have become more powerful. Parties have ensured that the power to formulate – to 'make' – legislation rests with government, with the House then giving its assent. In so far as the House has retained a residual legislative power, it is exercised through the medium of private members' legislation. However, even that legislative power can be described now as one shared with government. Since 1959, no private member's bill that has been the subject of a vote at second reading (the debate on principle) has made it to the statute book without government providing time for it.

■ Scrutiny and influence

The functions that the House retains can be described as modest but appropriate to a reactive legislature. They have developed over time. But how well are they currently carried out? The principal functions of the House in relation to the executive are those of scrutiny and influence. The means available to the House to fulfil those functions are also at the disposal of members for expressing the views of their constituents and of wider interests. They can be grouped under two headings: legislation and executive actions.

Legislation

For Parliament, the legislative process constitutes the consideration of a bill once it has been formally introduced. However, in recent years, some bills have been published in draft form and considered by a committee prior to formal introduction (Kennon 2004; Hansard Society 2004; Constitution Committee 2004; Norton 2005: 75–7). From 1997–8 to 2006–7, fifty-eight bills were published in draft and thus available for some pre-legislative scrutiny (Constitution Committee 2008: 6). The number peaked in the 2003–4 session, when 12 bills were published in draft, representing one in three of government bills for the session. Such scrutiny

enables members to examine and comment before the government has decided on the final wording, and hence may be more willing to make changes before it commits itself to the measure. Despite considerable time pressures, bills subject to pre-legislative scrutiny have been variously amended as a result of recommendations by the committees considering them (Norton 2005: 77). The committees engaging in such scrutiny have normally been departmental **select committees**.

When a bill is formally introduced into Parliament, it has to go through a well-established process involving debate and consideration in committee. About 30–40 per cent of the time of the House is taken up with debate on bills. In the 2007–08 session, for example, it was 38 per cent (see Table 15.5). The bulk of this time is given over to government bills. (Private members' legislation usually occupies just under, or occasionally just over, 5 per cent of time on the floor of the House.) Every bill has to go through three 'readings' plus a committee and (usually) a report stage. The stages are shown in Table 15.6.

The first reading marks the formal introduction. No debate takes place. Indeed, at this stage there is not even a printed bill. All that is read out is the bill's title. Following first reading, the bill is printed. The second reading comprises a debate on the principle of the measure. Most government bills will be allocated a half or a full day's debate for second reading. Major bills, especially of constitutional significance, may be given two or more days for debate. In the 1997–2001 Parliament, for example, the bills providing for devolution to Scotland and Wales, for an elected Greater London Authority, and for removal of most hereditary peers from membership of the House of Lords were each accorded a two-day debate.

The debate itself follows a standard pattern: the minister responsible for the bill opens the debate, explaining the provisions of the bill and justifying its introduction. The relevant shadow minister then makes a speech from the opposition front bench, outlining the stance of the opposition on the bill. After these two frontbench speeches, most members present tend to leave the chamber, usually leaving a small number of MPs to listen to the remaining speeches. Backbenchers from both sides of the House are then called alternately, plus usually a member from one or more of the minor parties, and the debate is then wound up with speeches from the opposition and government front benches. (The

Table 15.5 Time spent on the floor of the House, 2007–8

Business	Total time spent (hours : minutes)
Addresses, including debate on Queen's Speech	37.42
Government bills	
Second reading	116.01
Committee of the whole House	79.20
Report	116.06
Third reading	15.40
Lords amendments	38.29
Allocation of time orders (including programme motions)	7.14
Private members' bills (including ten-minute rule bills)	74.47
Government motions	
EC documents	5.35
Business motions	10.36
General	64.35
Opposition motions	125.22
Private Members' motions (substantive)	2.54
Adjournment	
Government debates	99.16
Topical debates	35.42
Last day before recess	16.12
Daily half-hour debates (at end of business)	82.40
Standing Order No. 24 debate (emergency debate)	3.14
Estimates	19.21
Money resolutions	0.22
Ways and Means resolutions (including Budget debate)	24.31
Statutory instruments	27.38
Question Time (including topical questions)	142.14
Urgent Questions	1.16
Statements (including business statements)	106.33
Miscellaneous	32.20
Daily prayers	13.25
Total	**1306.31**

Source: House of Commons Sessional Information Digest, 2007–08. © Parliamentary Copyright 2008. Parliamentary copyright material is reproduced with the permission of the Controller of Her Majesty's Stationery Office (HMSO) on behalf of Parliament

House tends to fill up again for the winding-up speeches.) If the bill is contested, the House then divides. Debates, though not always predictable in content, are generally so in outcome: only three times in the past 100 years has the government lost a vote on second reading (in 1924, 1977 and 1986). Speeches on occasion may influence some votes, even whole debates, but they are exceptional. A government sometimes loses the argument but not usually the vote.

Once approved in principle, the bill is then sent to committee for detailed scrutiny. Some bills, because of their constitutional significance or because of the need for a speedy passage, will have their committee stage on the floor of the House. In most sessions the number is very small. The majority of bills, though, are sent to a **public bill committee**. Up to 2006, bills were sent to standing committees. Standing committees were introduced in 1882 and became the norm in 1907. Despite the name, they were 'standing' only in name (Standing Committee A, Standing Committee B etc.): their membership changed for each bill. The committees were limited not only by the fact that there was no permanent membership but by their inability to take evidence. Witnesses could not be summoned and written evidence received. The committees could only consider the bills before them. They proceeded by way of discussing amendments to clauses before agreeing the clauses. Each committee was structured like the chamber in miniature; one side facing the other, with ministers, shadow ministers and whips among the membership and with debate following party lines. Government backbenchers were encouraged to keep quiet to facilitate the passage of the bill and opposition MPs encouraged to speak in order to challenge the government. Government defeats in committee were rare.

Because of the limitations of standing committees, their utilisation came in for considerable criticism. In 2006, following a report from the Select Committee on the Modernisation of the House of Commons, the House agreed a new procedure: the public bill committee (PBC). In dealing with private members' bills and certain other bills, they are similar to the old standing committees. However, they differ significantly in respect of Government bills that have been introduced in the Commons and have been subject to a programme motion (stipulating the times at which stages have to be completed), but which have not had pre-legislative scrutiny (in other words, been before an evidence-taking committee):

Table 15.6 Legislative stages

Stage	Where taken	Comments
First reading	On the floor of the House	Formal introduction: no debate
Second reading	On the floor of the House[a]	Debate on the principle
[Money resolution	On the floor of the House	Commons only]
Committee	In public bill committee in the Commons unless House votes otherwise (certain bills taken on the floor of the House); in Grand Committee or on the floor of the House in the Lords	Considered clause by clause; amendments may be made
Report[b]	On the floor of the House	Bill reported back to House; amendments may be made
Third reading	On the floor of the House	Final approval: no amendments possible in the Commons
Lords (or Commons) amendments	On the floor of the House	Consideration of amendments made by other House

[a] In the Commons, non-contentious bills may be referred to a committee.
[b] If a bill is taken in committee of the whole House in the Commons and no amendments are made, there is no report stage.

in dealing with these bills, public bill committees are empowered to take both oral and written evidence. Within the time it has to consider a bill, the committee can determine what proportion of sittings will be devoted to taking evidence. In its evidence-taking, a committee is supported by the Scrutiny Unit, a body of specialists employed by the House, which also prepares briefing material for the committee.

In the first two sessions of their operations (2006–07, 2007–08), 17 bills were sent to evidence-taking public bill committees for their committee stage. Out of a total of 199 sittings by the committees, 50 of them were devoted to taking evidence. In addition, 411 written pieces of evidence were accepted (Levy 2009: 26). As the use of public bill committees has developed, so MPs have tended to be better informed and more willing to engage in debating the provisions of the bill. As Jessica Levy has noted, 'Along with introducing the practice of direct questioning of witnesses (and the minister) in place of probing amendments, PBCs have proved more efficient than their standing committee predecessors' (Levy 2009: 49).

However, PBCs also have similarities with their predecessor standing committees. Each committee comprises between 16 and 50 members, though the norm is to appoint close to the minimum, other than for big bills like the Finance Bill. The membership is appointed anew for each bill. The membership thus lacks a corporate ethos. Each committee is chaired by a member of the Chairmen's Panel, whose role is to preside in a manner similar to the Speaker; there is thus no leadership of the committee as a collective body. The membership reflects the party composition of the House, and ministers, shadow ministers and **whips** are appointed, with the government whips present to ensure, as in the chamber, that the government gets its business. One of the biggest constraints remains one of time. Committees are under pressure because of the number of bills introduced each session and the need to get them through usually by the end of the session. Several committees may therefore be appointed at roughly the same time. The need to get the business transacted by a stipulated date limits the time available to hear witnesses and, equally importantly, digest what they have to say in time to influence debate on the amendments moved in committee.

After the committee stage, a bill returns to the House for the report stage. This provides an opportunity for the House to decide whether it wishes to make any further amendments and is often used by the government to introduce amendments promised during committee stage, as well as any last-minute (sometimes numerous) amendments of its own. There is, though, no report stage if a bill has been taken for its committee stage on the floor of the House and been passed without amendment.

There then follows the bill's third reading, when the House gives its final approval to the measure. Such debates are often short. If the bill is not contentious, there may be no debate at all. As can be seen from Table 15.5, debate on third reading occupies relatively little time. On completion of its third reading, the bill then goes to the House of Lords and, if the Upper House makes any amendments, the bill then returns to the Commons for it to consider the amendments. In most cases, the amendments are accepted. If not, the House of Lords usually gives way, though sometimes only after considerable behind-the-scenes negotiations. Once both Houses have approved the bill, it then goes to the Queen for the Royal Assent. Once that assent is given, then that, as far as Parliament is concerned, concludes the legislative process.

The process is fairly well established but much criticised (see, e.g., Brazier 2004), not only because of the inefficiencies of the committee procedure but also because of the time constraints imposed by government. In the past, after considerable time had been taken up by opposition MPs debating the early clauses of a bill in committee, the governments would resort to a timetable, or guillotine, motion, imposing a timetable for the remaining provisions of a bill. Guillotine motions had been variously employed since 1887 but their increased use in the last quarter of the twentieth century attracted frequent condemnation. Because of the criticism, the two principal parties agreed in 1994 to a voluntary timetabling of bills. This meant that each bill was subject to an agreed timetable from the beginning, thus avoiding the need for a guillotine to be introduced at a later stage. However, this agreement was not sustained in the new parliament returned in May 1997 and the Labour government variously resorted to the use of the guillotine, or what were termed programme motions, to get measures through. In 2000–1, new standing orders were introduced for programming motions, and programming is now a common and much disputed feature of business. Programme motions differ from the previous use of the guillotine in that they are introduced and agreed by the House following the second readings of bills. Most government bills are now subject to such motions. The most stringent part of programming tends to be for consideration of Lords amendments, where it is not uncommon for a programme motion to stipulate that debate on the amendments, however many or important they are, is limited to one hour.

Bills thus follow a fairly predictable route. There are some variations: some non-contentious bills, for example, can be sent to a second reading committee, thus avoiding taking up valuable debating time on the floor of the House. Private members'

bills are also treated differently, primarily in terms of timetabling. They have to go through all the stages listed, but time for their consideration on the floor of the House is extremely limited. Each session a ballot is held and the names of twenty private members are drawn. They are then entitled to introduce bills during the Fridays allocated to such bills, but only about the top half-dozen are likely to achieve full debates.

Bills constitute primary legislation. They often contain powers for regulations to be made under their authority once enacted. These regulations – known as delegated or secondary legislation and usually taking the form of what are termed statutory instruments – may be made subject to parliamentary approval. (Under the affirmative resolution procedure, the regulation must be approved by Parliament in order to come into force; under the negative resolution procedure, it comes into force unless Parliament disapproves it.) Some regulations, though, only have to be laid before the House and others do not even have to be laid.

Given the growth of delegated legislation in postwar years – sometimes more than 1,500 statutory instruments are introduced in a session – the House has sought to undertake scrutiny of it (Norton 2005: 91–3). Detailed, and essentially technical, scrutiny is undertaken by a Select Committee on Statutory Instruments. However, there is no requirement that the government has to wait for the committee to report on a regulation before bringing it before the House for approval, and on occasion – although not frequently – the government will seek approval before a regulation has been considered by the committee. Time for debate is also extremely limited, and much delegated legislation is hived off for discussion in a standing committee on delegated legislation. There is also a separate committee and procedure for dealing with regulatory reform orders, enabling primary legislation imposing a regulatory burden to be changed by order. There are also separate committees and procedures for dealing with draft European legislation: it is considered by a European Scrutiny Committee and, if recommended for debate, is discussed normally by one of three European committees.

Executive actions

Various means are employed to scrutinise and to influence the actions of government. These same means can be and usually are employed by MPs

House of Commons in session
Source: Corbis / Bettmann

to express the views of constituents and different interests in society. The means essentially are those available on the floor of the House (debates and Question Time), those available on the committee corridor (select committees) and those available off the floor of the House (early day motions, correspondence, the parliamentary commissioner for administration, party committees and all-party groups). Some individually are of limited use. It is their use in combination that can be effective in influencing government.

Debates and Question Time

Most of the time of the House is taken up debating or questioning the actions of government. *Debates* take different forms. They can be on a substantive motion (for example, congratulating or condemning the policy of the government on a particular issue) or, in order to allow wide-ranging discussion (especially on a topic on which the government may have no fixed position), on an adjournment motion ('That this House do now adjourn'). For example, prior to the Gulf War at the beginning of 1991, the situation

in the Persian Gulf was debated on an adjournment motion. After military action had begun, the House debated a substantive motion approving the action. Adjournment debates under this heading can be described as full-scale adjournment debates. They are distinct from the half-hour adjournment debates that take place at the end of every sitting of the House. These half-hour debates take the form of a backbencher raising a particular issue and the relevant minister then responding. After exactly half an hour, the debate concludes and the House adjourns.

Debates are initiated by different bodies in the House. Most motions introduced by government are to approve legislation. However, the government occasionally initiates debates on particular policies. These can range from major issues of public policy, such as war in Iraq in 2003, to debate on essentially parliamentary matters, such as select committee nominations and the installation of the security screen in the public gallery. More frequently, debates are introduced by opposition parties. Twenty days each year are designated as opposition days. On seventeen of these twenty days, the motion (or motions – a day's debate can be split into two) is chosen by the Leader of the Opposition. On the remaining three days, the topic is chosen by the leader of the third-largest party in the House (the Liberal Democrats). One or two additional days are usually found for other parties. There are also three estimates days each session, the choice of estimate for debate being made by a select committee of the House: the Liaison Committee, comprising the MPs who chair other select committees.

A recent innovation – introduced in 2007 – is the topical debate. Each week, a ninety-minute debate is held on a topical issue, of local, national or international importance suggested by an MP. Subjects are suggested by members to the Leader of the House – by letter, e-mail or in questions to the Leader on the weekly business statement (mostly the last of these) – and the Leader announces which topic has been selected. On 14 May 2009, for example, the topical debate was on Sri Lanka and on 4 June 2009 it was on 'The Economy: Supporting Business'.

Private members are also responsible for initiating the topics in the daily half-hour adjournment debates: on three days a week (four, if sitting on a Friday), members are selected by ballot, and on one the Speaker chooses the member. These backbenchers' occasions provide opportunities to raise essentially non-partisan issues, especially those of concern to constituents. Although such debates are poorly attended, they allow members to put an issue on the public record and elicit a response from government.

The half-hour adjournment debates involve a backbencher raising an issue, sometimes one or two other backbenchers making quick contributions, and then a response from a minister. Full-scale half-day or full-day debates initiated by government or opposition resemble instead the practice adopted in second reading debates. There are speeches from the two front benches, followed by backbench speeches alternating between the two sides of the House, followed by winding-up speeches from the front benches and then, if necessary, a vote. The term 'debate' is itself a misnomer. Members rarely debate but rather deliver prepared speeches, which often fail to take up the points made by preceding speakers. Members wishing to take part usually inform the Speaker in advance and can usually obtain some indication from the Speaker if and when they are likely to be called. There is a tendency for members not to stay for the whole debate after they have spoken. Members, especially backbenchers,

frequently address a very small audience – sometimes no more than half a dozen MPs. There is a prevailing view in the House that attendance has dropped over recent years. MPs now have offices they can spend time in. There are competing demands on their time, and as the outcome of most votes is predictable – and members know perfectly well how they intend to vote – there appears little incentive to spend time in the chamber. Major set-piece debates – as on a motion of confidence – and a debate in which the outcome is uncertain can still attract a crowded chamber, some members having to sit on the floor or stand at the bar of the House in order to listen to the proceedings. Occasionally a particularly good speaker, such as former Conservative leader William Hague, may attract members into the chamber. Such occasions are exceptional. On most days, MPs addressing the House do so to rows of empty green benches.

Debates take place on motions. However, there is one form of business taken on the floor of the House that departs from the rule requiring a motion to be before the House. That is *Question Time*. This takes place on four days of the week – Monday to Thursday – when the House is sitting. It is the first substantive order of business once the House sits: it commences once prayers and some minor business – announcements from the Speaker, certain non-debatable motions concerning private legislation – are completed. It concludes exactly one hour after the House has commenced sitting.

Question Time itself is of relatively recent origin (see Franklin and Norton 1993). The first recorded instance of a question being asked was in the House of Lords in 1721, and the first printed notice of questions to ministers was issued in 1835. Question time itself – a dedicated slot under the heading of 'Questions' on the order paper – dates from 1869. The institution of a dedicated slot for Prime Minister's Questions is of even more recent origin, dating from July 1961. From 1961 to 1997, the Prime Minister answered questions for fifteen minutes on two days of the week (Tuesday and Thursday). In May 1997, the new Labour Prime Minister, Tony Blair, changed the procedure, answering questions for thirty minutes once a week on a Wednesday.

The practice of asking questions is popular with MPs, and the demand to ask questions exceeds the time available. Members are thus restricted in the number they can put on the order paper: no more than one to any one department on any day and no more than two in total on the day. (It is thus possible to have a question to the department answering before Prime Minister's Questions and one to the Prime Minister.) Questions can be tabled up to three working days in advance (four for those to the secretaries of state for Northern Ireland, Scotland and Wales) and are selected by a random physical and computer shuffle. Questions must be precisely that – statements and expressions of opinion are inadmissible – and each must be on a matter for which the minister has responsibility. There is also an extensive list of topics (including arms sales, budgetary forecasts and purchasing contracts) on which government will not answer questions. Ministers may also decline to answer on grounds of 'disproportionate cost'. At the end of 2008, the cost of answering an oral question was estimated to be £410. If the cost of answering a particular question was calculated to be £750 or more, then the minister may decline to answer.

The normal practice of tabling questions seeking answers to clear and specific questions tabled in advance was complemented in 2007 by the introduction of a new type of question. Towards the end of questions to a particular department, there are now 'topical questions'. These are not dissimilar to Prime Minister's Questions in that a member asks a minister an 'open' question – 'If he will make a statement on his departmental responsibilities' – and then supplementary questions can be on any aspect of the responsibilities of the department. The procedure enables questions to be raised that are current and provides an opportunity for opposition members to test ministers to ensure that they are fully briefed on issues affecting their departments.

Ministers answer questions on a rota basis, most ministries coming up on the rota every five weeks. The larger departments, such as the Treasury, are each allocated a full question time. Smaller departments are allocated only part of a question time (some may get 30 minutes, or even 10 minutes.) All questions tabled by members used to be printed on the order paper, a practice that was costly and largely pointless. The number tabled often ran into three figures, but the number of questions actually answered in the time available was usually fewer than 20. Following changes approved by the House in 1990, only the top 25 – fewer if the department is not taking up the whole of Question Time – are now printed.

The MP with the first question rises and says 'Question Number One, Mr Speaker' and then sits down. The minister rises and replies to the question.

The MP is then called to put a follow-up – or 'supplementary' – question, to which the minister responds. Another member may then be permitted by the Speaker to put another supplementary. If an opposition **frontbencher** rises, he or she has priority. During Prime Minister's Question Time, the Leader of the Opposition is frequently at the despatch box and is permitted up to six interventions (and the leader of the Liberal Democrats three). The Speaker decides when to move on to the next question.

During an average session, about 2,000 to 3,000 questions will receive an oral answer. In the 2007–8 session, for example, the number was 2,645 (out of 5,151 that were published on the order paper). With supplementaries included, the figure is nearer 7,000: in 2007–8 it was 6,760.

Question Time is not the only opportunity afforded to MPs to put questions to ministers. Members can also table questions for written answer. These provide an opportunity to elicit more detailed answers than can be obtained through an oral question and are particularly useful for obtaining data from departments. The questions, along with ministers' answers, are published in *Hansard*, the official record of parliamentary proceedings. There is no limit on the number of written questions that an MP can table. The average MP tables just over 100 a session. Exceptionally, some members table well in excess of 1,000. The number tabled each year has risen over the decades (see Franklin and Norton 1993: 27). By the 1990s, some sessions saw more than 40,000 questions being tabled. This figure has been far exceeded in the twenty-first century. In the 2007–8 session, the number was 78,508.

Question Time itself remains an important opportunity for backbenchers to raise issues of concern to constituents and to question ministers on differing aspects of their policies and intentions. However, it has become increasingly adversarial in nature, with opposition frontbenchers participating regularly – a practice that has developed over the past 30 years – and with questions and supplementaries often being partisan in content. Some members view the proceedings, especially Prime Minister's Question Time, as a farce. However, it remains an occasion for keeping ministers on their toes (figuratively as well as literally), and it ensures that a whole range of issues is brought to the attention of ministers. It also ensures that much material is put on the public record that would not otherwise be available.

Select committees

The House has made greater use in recent years of select committees, appointed not to consider the particular details of bills (the task of public bill committees) but to consider particular subjects assigned by the House. Historically, they are well-established features of parliamentary scrutiny. They were frequently used in Tudor and Stuart parliaments. Their use declined in the latter half of the nineteenth century, the government – with its party majority – not looking too favourably on bodies that could subject it to critical scrutiny. For most of the twentieth century, the use of such committees was very limited. The position changed in the 1960s and, more dramatically, in the 1970s.

The House has a number of long-standing select committees concerned with its privileges and internal arrangements. However, for the first half of the twentieth century, the House had only two major select committees for investigating the policy or actions of government: the Public Accounts Committee (PAC) and the Estimates Committee. Founded in 1861, the PAC remains in existence and is the doyen of investigative select committees. It undertakes post hoc (i.e. after the event) scrutiny of public expenditure, checking to ensure that it has been properly incurred for the purpose for which it was voted. The Estimates Committee was first appointed in 1912 for the purpose of examining ways in which policies could be carried out cost-effectively. In abeyance from 1914 to 1921 and again during the Second World War, it fulfilled a useful but limited role. It was abolished in 1971 and replaced by an Expenditure Committee with wider terms of reference.

The PAC and Estimates Committees were supplemented in the 1940s by a Select Committee on Statutory Instruments and in the 1950s by one on nationalised industries. There was a more deliberate and extensive use of select committees in the latter half of the 1960s, when the Labour Leader of the House, Richard Crossman, introduced several reforms to try to increase the efficiency and influence of the House. A number of select committees were established, some to cover particular policy sectors (such as science and technology) and others particular government departments (such as education). One was also appointed to cover the newly created Parliamentary Commissioner for Administration (PCA), better known as the ombudsman. However, the experience of the committees did not meet the expectations of their supporters. They suffered from limited resources, limited attention (from backbenchers, government and the media), limited powers (they could only send for 'persons, papers and records' and make recommendations), the absence of any effective linkage between their activities and the floor of the House, and the lack of a coherent approach to, and coverage of, government policy. Some did not survive for very long. The result was a patchwork quilt of committees, with limited coverage of public policy.

Recognition of these problems led to the appointment in 1976 of a Procedure Select Committee, which reported in 1978. It recommended the appointment of a series of select committees, covering all the main departments of state, with wide terms of reference and with power to appoint specialist advisers as the committees deemed appropriate. It also recommended that committee members be selected independently of the whips, the task to be undertaken by the Select Committee of Selection, the body formally responsible for nominating members. At the beginning of the new parliament in 1979, the Conservative Leader of the House, Norman St John-Stevas, brought forward motions to give effect to the Procedure Committee recommendations. By a vote of 248 to 12, the House approved the creation of the new committees. Initially, twelve were appointed, soon joined by committees covering Scottish and Welsh affairs. In the light of their appointment, various other committees were wound up. The PAC and the Committee on the Parliamentary Commissioner were retained. In 1980, a Liaison Select Committee, comprising predominantly select committee chairmen, was appointed to coordinate the work of the committees.

The fourteen new committees began work effectively in 1980. Their number has fluctuated since, usually reflecting changes in departmental structure. Committees were also added to cover sectors or departments not previously covered, notably science and technology and, in 1994, Northern Ireland. In the parliament returned in 1997, sixteen departmental select committees were appointed. The number increased in the following parliament after changes in the structure of departments and by the end of the parliament eighteen were in existence: they were reappointed in the 2005 parliament. As a result of further changes in departments, the number increased to nineteen. There also exists the Committees on Arms Export Control (formerly known as the Quadripartite Committee), comprising four departmental select committees (defence, foreign affairs, international development, and business, innovation and skills) which meet on occasion in order to examine strategic export controls. There are also several non-departmental select committees. These comprise principally 'domestic' committees – such as the Committee on Standards and Privileges and the Finance and Services Committee – but they also include investigative committees, such as the PAC, Environmental Audit, Public Administration, European Scrutiny and Statutory Instruments Committees, and regional committees. In 2009, nine regional committees were appointed to examine the regional strategies and the work of the regional bodies for the regions of England.

The nineteen departmental select committees in existence at the end of 2009 are listed in Table 15.7. Each committee is established 'to examine the expenditure, administration and policy' of the department or departments it covers and of associated public bodies. As can be seen from the table, a committee has usually eleven, thirteen or fourteen members. The chairmanships of the committees are shared between the parties – usually in rough pro-portion to party strength in the House – although committee members are responsible for electing one of their own number from the relevant party to the chair. This power vested in committee members has variously resulted in the election of independent-minded chairmen, such as Nicholas Winterton (Conservative chairman of the Health Committee, 1991–2), Frank Field (Labour chairman of the Social Security Committee, 1990–7), Chris Mullin (Labour chairman of the Home Affairs Committee, 1997–9 and 2001–3) and Gwyneth Dunwoody (Labour chairman of the Transport Sub-Committee 1997–2002, Transport Committee 2002–2008).

Each committee has control of its own agenda and decides what to investigate. It has power to take evidence, and much of its time is spent questioning witnesses. Each committee normally meets once a week when the House is sitting in order to hold a public, evidence-taking session. Members sit in a horseshoe shape, MPs sitting around the horseshoe – not necessarily grouped according to party – with the witness or witnesses seated in the gap of the horseshoe. Each session will normally last between one and two hours.

Table 15.7 Departmental select committees, 2009

Committee (number of members in parenthesis)	Chairman
Business, Innovation and Skills (11)	Peter Luff (Con)
Children, Schools and Families (14)	Barry Sheerman (Lab)
Communities and Local Government (11)	Dr Phyllis Starkey (Lab)
Culture, Media and Sport (11)	John Whittingdale (Con)
Defence (14)	Rt Hon. James Arbuthnot (Con)
Energy and Climate Change (14)	Elliot Morley (Lab)
Environment, Food and Rural Affairs (14)	Rt Hon. Michael Jack (Con)
Foreign Affairs (14)	Mike Gapes (Lab)
Health (11)	Rt Hon. Kevin Barron (Lab)
Home Affairs (14)	Rt Hon. Keith Vaz (Lab)
International Development (11)	Rt Hon Malcolm Bruce (Lib Dem)
Justice (14)	Rt Hon Sir Alan Beith (Lib Dem)
Northern Ireland Affairs (13)	Sir Patrick Cormack (Con)
Science and Technology (13)	Phil Willis (Lib Dem)
Scottish Affairs (11)	Mohammad Sarwar (Lab)
Transport (11)	Louise Ellman (Lab)
Treasury (14)	Rt Hon. John McFall (Lab)
Welsh Affairs (11)	Dr Hywel Francis (Lab)
Work and Pensions (11)	Terry Rooney (Lab)

Committee practices vary. Some hold long-term inquiries, some go for short-term inquiries, and some adopt a mixture of the two approaches. Some will also summon senior ministers for a single session just to review present policy and not as part of a continuing inquiry. The Chancellor of the Exchequer, for example, appears each year before the Treasury Committee for a wide-ranging session on economic policy. Although committees cannot force ministers to attend, the attendance of the appropriate minister is normally easily arranged. So, too, is the attendance of civil servants, although they cannot divulge information on advice offered to ministers or express opinions on policy: that is left to ministers. Attendance by ministers and civil servants before committees is regular and frequent, although most witnesses called by committees represent outside bodies. In investigating a particular subject, a committee will call as witnesses representatives of bodies working in the area or with a particular expertise or interest in it. Figure 15.2 shows but part of the agenda of select committee meetings and witnesses in a typical week.

At the conclusion of an inquiry, a committee draws up a report. The report is normally drafted by the committee clerk – a full-time officer of the House – under the guidance of the chair. It is then discussed in private session by the committee. Amendments are variously made, although it is relatively rare for committees to divide along party lines. Once agreed, the report is published. The committees are prolific in their output. From their creation in 1979 through to the summer recess in 2004, they published a total of 1,932 reports. Among the subjects being examined in 2009 were the banking crisis, housing finance, teacher training, global security, carbon budgets, the future of aviation, alcohol, the cocaine trade, the Department of International Development's programme in Nigeria, students and universities, and policing and justice in Northern Ireland. Most reports embody recommendations for government action. Some of the recommendations are accepted. Others become subject to the 'delayed drop' effect: the government rejects or ignores a report but several years later, without necessarily acknowledging the work of the committee, implements some of the recommendations. Overall, only a minority of the recommendations emanating from committees will be accepted immediately and acted on by government. A more common response is to note a recommendation or to say that it is under review.

A select committee has no formal powers to force the government to take any action on a report. All that the government is committed to do is to issue a written response to each report within 60 days of the report being published. The target is not always met.

The departmental select committees, like the House itself, are multifunctional. They serve several purposes. They have added considerably to the store of knowledge of the House. They provide an important means for specialisation by members. They serve an important expressive function. By calling witnesses from outside groups, they allow those groups to get their views on the public record. The evidence from witnesses is published. Reports are published in paper form and on the Internet (www.parliament.uk, see under 'committees'). More time is now devoted to committee reports as a result of various Thursdays being devoted to debating them in Westminster Hall. The committees may take up the cases espoused by some of the groups, ensuring that the issue is brought onto the political agenda. The reports from the committees are read and digested by the groups, thus providing the committees with the potential to serve as important agents for mobilising support. Above all, though, the committees serve as important means for scrutinising and influencing government, especially the former. Ministers and civil servants know they may be called before committees to account for their actions. Committee sessions allow MPs to put questions to ministers in greater detail than is possible on the floor of the House. They give MPs the only opportunity they have to ask questions of officials. Not only will poor performances be noted – not least by the media – but also poor answers may attract critical comment in the committee's report. No minister or official wishes to be seen squirming in the face of difficult questions.

Select committees have thus developed as a major feature of parliamentary activity, with most MPs viewing that activity in a positive light. Their purview now even encompasses the Prime Minister. Prior to 2002, Prime Minister Tony Blair had refused requests to appear before the Public Administration Select Committee, citing the fact that his predecessors had not appeared before select committees. In 2002, he reversed his stance and agreed to appear before the Liaison Committee to answer questions. His first appearance, for two-and-a-half hours, took place on 16 July. It is now standard practice that the prime minister appears before the committee twice a year.

Tuesday 14 July 2009

Treasury

Subject: Appointment of Adam Posen to the Monetary Policy Committee, Bank of England

Witnesses: Adam Posen, External Member of the Monetary Policy Committee, Bank of England

Environmental Audit

Subject: Carbon Budgets

Witnesses: Sir David King, Director, and Dr Cameron Hepburn, Senior Research Fellow, Smith School of Enterprise and the Environment, University of Oxford; Professor Paul Ekins, Professor of Energy and Environment Policy, King's College London; Professor David MacKay, Professor of Natural Philosophy, Department of Physics, Cavendish Laboratory, University of Cambridge

Business and Enterprise

Subject: Exporting out of recession

Witnesses: Lord Davies of Abersoch CBE, Minister for Trade and Investment, Department for Business, Innovation and Skills, and Gareth Thomas MP, Minister of State, Department for International Development

Culture, Media and Sport

Subject: Press standards, privacy and libel

Witnesses: To be confirmed

Defence

Subject: ISTAR

Witnesses: Air Vice-Marshal Carl Dixon OBE, Capability Manager (Information Superiority), Air Commodore N J Gordon MBE, Air Officer ISTAR in Headquarters 2 Group, and Brigadier Kevin Abraham, Director Joint Capability, Ministry of Defence

Home Affairs

Subject: (i) The Work of Europol; (ii) The Cocaine Trade

Witnesses: (i) Rob Wainwright, Director, Europol (ii) Mitch Winehouse

Welsh Affairs

Subject: Ports in Wales

Witnesses: Paul Clark MP, Parliamentary Under-Secretary of State, Department for Transport; Ieuan Wyn Jones AM, Deputy First Minister and Minister for the Economy and Transport, Welsh Assembly Government

Joint Committee on Human Rights

Subject: Business and Human Rights

Witnesses: Rt Hon Michael Wills MP, Minister of State, Ministry of Justice, Ian Lucas MP, Parliamentary Under-Secretary of State, Department for Business, Innovation and Skills, and Rt Hon Lord Malloch-Brown KCMG, Minister for Africa, Asia and the UN, Foreign and Commonwealth Office

Home Affairs

Subject: The work of the Home Office

Witnesses: Rt Hon Alan Johnson MP, Secretary of State for the Home Department

Justice

Subject: Constitutional Reform and Renewal

Witnesses: Rt Hon Jack Straw MP, Secretary of State for Justice and Lord Chancellor

Figure 15.2   Meetings of select committees

Despite these various strengths and advances, limitations remain. Membership has usually been determined by the whips, though in 2010 the House voted for members to be elected by the House. The committees have limited powers and limited resources. They have the time and resources to investigate only a small number of issues. The number of reports they issue exceeds the time available on the floor of the House or in Westminster Hall to debate them. Most reports will not be mentioned on the floor of the House or even read by most MPs. Government is committed to providing a written response to committee reports but under no obligation to take action on the recommendations made in those reports. And although ministers and officials appear before committees, they do not necessarily reveal as much as the committees would like. Although the committees constitute a major step forward for the House of Commons, many MPs would like to see them strengthened.

Early day motions

Of the other devices available to members, early day motions (EDMs) are increasingly popular, although of limited impact. A member may table a motion for debate 'on an early day'. In practice, there is invariably no time to debate such motions. However, they are printed and other MPs can add their names to them. Consequently, they are used as a form of parliamentary notice board. If a motion attracts a large number of signatures, it may induce the government to take some action or at least to pause, or it may seriously embarrass the government. This happens occasionally. An EDM in 2002–3 expressing concern over possible military action against Iraq attracted the signatures of more than 150 Labour MPs, seen as a signal that the government might run into substantial opposition on its own side if it were pre-cipitate in agreeing to use force to topple the Iraqi regime; the government subsequently suffered the largest rebellious vote by backbenchers in the postwar era. Such occasions, though, are rare. EDMs are more often used for fulfilling a limited expressive function, allowing members to make clear their views on a range of issues, often reflecting representations made to them by people and groups outside the House. Examples of such EDMs are illustrated in Figure 15.3. The range of topics is extremely broad and the number of motions tabled an increasingly large one, exacerbated by motions unrelated to public policy, for example,

congratulating particular sporting teams or individuals on their achievements.

In the 1970s and 1980s, about 300–400 EDMs were tabled each year. In the 1990s, the number each year exceeded 1,000. In the 1992–7 parliament, a total of 7,831 were tabled – an average of just over 1,500 a session. The number dipped in the 1997–2001 parliament, when 3,613, an average of just over 900 a year, were submitted, but increased notably in the 2001–5 parliament when MPs put in a total of 6,767 – an average of 1,691 a session. The number has increased substantially since then, with over 2,000 a session being submitted. In the long 2005–06 session, 2,924 were tabled, in 2006–07 it was 2,385 and in 2007–08 the figure was 2,727. The consequence of excessive use of EDMs is that their value as a means of indicating strength of opinion on an issue of political significance is devalued. Their utility, which was always limited, is thus marginal, although not non-existent. Each is studied by the relevant government department and they still give MPs the opportunity to put issues of concern on the public record. An EDM which attracts more than 300 signatures – which rarely happens – will get noticed. Most of the rest will not.

Correspondence

The means so far considered have been public means by which MPs can scrutinise government and make representations to it. However, a number of private means exist, two official and two unofficial. One official means is through corresponding with ministers. Since the 1950s, the flow of letters to MPs from constituents and a range of organisations (companies, charities and the like) has grown enormously. The flow increased significantly in the 1960s and increased dramatically in subsequent decades. In the late 1960s a typical MP would receive something in the region of 2,000 to 3,000 items of mail every year. In 2008, 4.1 million items of mail were delivered to the Palace of Westminster, 85 per cent of them going to the House of Commons: that averages out at nearly 5,500 items of mail per MP. The usual method for an MP to pursue a matter raised by a constituent is by writing to the relevant minister, usually forwarding the letter from the constituent. At least 10,000 to 15,000 letters a month are written by MPs to ministers.

For an MP, writing to a minister is one of the most cost-effective ways of pursuing constituency casework (see Norton and Wood 1993: Chapter 3). A letter invites a considered, often detailed response, usually free of the party pressures that prevail in the chamber; by being a private communication, it

Asterisk figures show number of MPs to have signed the motion. The first six names to sign (the sponsors) are always listed, followed by the names of the latest Members to sign.

97   FLOOD MANAGEMENT   3:12:08
Miss Anne McIntosh
Mr Peter Ainsworth
Mr James Paice
Bill Wiggin
Mr Simon Burns
Mr David Drew

                                                                                          * 64

  Dr Julian Lewis
That this House notes the devastation caused by recent flooding and the institutional confusion and chaos that was exposed; regrets that responsibility for surface water flooding remains unclear, with no single body in charge; and urges the Government to bring responsibility for flood management under the remit of one body at the earliest opportunity.

113   PROVISION OF PUBLIC LAVATORIES   4:12:08
Tim Farron
Peter Bottomley
Dr Evan Harris
Mr Mike Hancock
Jeremy Corbyn
Mr David Drew

                                                                                          * 31

  Patrick Mercer
That this House believes that the provision of public lavatories is a vital public service and notes with regret the closure of public lavatories over recent years; recognises that these closures have a particular impact on older and disabled people and those with young families; and calls on the Government to make the necessary resources available to enable local authorities to provide public lavatories.

As an Amendment to Tim Farron's proposed Motion (Provision of Public Lavatories):
Bob Spink
Frank Cook
Mr Andy Reed

                                                                                          * 3

Line **5**, at end add 'and calls on local authorities which are considering closures of public lavatories to fully consult residents before any decisions are taken.'

                                                                                8:12:08   (a1)
174   FIREFIGHTER SAFETY   8:12:08
Mr Andrew Dismore
Mr Michael Clapham
John McDonnell
Mr David Drew
Ian Stewart
Mr Martin Caton

                                                                                          * 142

Mr Robert Marshall-Andrews   Steve Webb   Derek Twigg
Jim Sheridan
That this House notes the recent increased number of firefighter deaths highlighted in the Fire Brigades Union report In the Line of Duty; further notes the lack of safety-critical operational guidance for fire authorities highlighted in that report, and the absence of a properly resourced national body with overall responsibility for recording and investigating firefighter deaths and other serious incidents; and calls for work to be commenced with stakeholders leading to the creation of such a body with responsibility for developing and agreeing safety-critical operational guidance arising from those investigations.

258   ANIMAL TESTING AND HOUSEHOLD CLEANING PRODUCTS   11:12:08
Bob Russell
Mr Adrian Sanders
Mr David Drew
John McDonnell
Mr Andrew Dismore
David Simpson

                                                                                          * 115

  Mr Anthony Wright
That this House supports the campaign of the British Union for the Abolition of Vivisection to end the suffering of animals in tests for household cleaning products and their ingredients; and urges the House of Commons Commission to demonstrate support for this initiative by ensuring that cleaning products used throughout the parliamentary estate have been certified as not tested on animals.

Figure 15.3 Examples of early day motions to show how MPs use this device to draw attention to particular issues, July 2009

avoids putting a minister publicly on the defensive. Ministers are thus more likely to respond sympathetically in the use of their discretion than is the case if faced with demands on the floor of the House. Furthermore, there is no limit on the number of letters an MP can write, and those letters can usually be dictated at a time of the member's choosing. Letters from MPs to ministers are accorded priority in a department – each is circulated in a special yellow folder – and have to be replied to by a minister. If a letter fails to obtain the desired response, the member has the option of then taking the matter further, either by seeing the minister or by raising the matter publicly on the floor of the House.

Correspondence is a valuable and efficient means of ensuring that a matter is considered by a minister. A great many letters on a particular problem can alert a minister to the scale of that problem and produce action. Letter writing is also a valuable means of fulfilling an expressive function. Most constituents who write do so to express a particular viewpoint or in order to obtain an authoritative explanation of why some action was or was not taken; only a minority write to try to have a particular decision changed. Writing to the MP is a long-established, and now much used, means for citizens to have some input into the political process. Nonetheless, corresponding with ministers has a number of limitations (see Norton 2005: Chapter 9). MPs are not always well versed in the subjects raised with them by constituents. Some lack sufficient interest, or knowledge of the political system, to pursue cases effectively. Increasingly, they have difficulty finding the time to deal with all the matters raised by them.

Parliamentary commissioner for administration

Since the late 1960s, MPs have had another option at their disposal in pursuing particular issues raised by constituents. The Parliamentary Commissioner for Administration – or ombudsman – was established under an Act of 1967 to investigate cases of maladministration within government. The term 'maladministration' essentially covers any error in the way a matter is handled by a public servant: it does not extend to cover the merits of policies. The ombudsman considers only complaints referred by MPs: a citizen cannot complain directly. The Commissioner enjoys some protection in office in that he or she can only be removed by an address by both Houses of Parliament to the crown. (The first

female ombudsman – Ann Abraham – was appointed in 2002.) She has a relatively modest staff of just over fifty. She can summon papers and take evidence under oath. When an inquiry is completed, she sends a copy to the MP who referred the case as well as to the relevant department. Her recommendations are normally acted on. However, she labours under a number of limitations: she has a limited remit, limited resources and limited access to certain files – she has no formal powers to see Cabinet papers. Perhaps most notably, she has no powers of enforcement. If she reports that officials have acted improperly or unjustly in the exercise of their administrative duties, it is then up to government to decide what action to take in response; if it fails to act, the only remaining means available to achieve action is through parliamentary pressure.

The number of cases referred to the ombudsman has increased over the years. Most complaints are deemed not to fall within her remit. In 2008–09, 79 per cent of complaints received were not properly made or were premature. In the year, 401 cases for investigation were accepted. The Departments attracting the most parliamentary complaints were the Department of Work and Pensions, the Home Office, and HM Revenue and Customs. Many are not taken forward and in other cases inquiries are undertaken to see whether the body that is the subject of the complaint wishes to take action that meets with the approval of the complainant. This frequently happens. Although the relevant departments usually act on the ombudsman's recommendations – a failure to do so is rare – the government has since 2002 twice rejected recommendations that certain factual information should be released under the Code of Practice on Access to Government Information, in 2005 rejecting the findings in a case where some applicants to a scheme to compensate people interned by the Japanese in the Second World War were excluded because they or their parents were not born in the United Kingdom, and in 2006 rejecting the findings in a case on the handling of pension schemes.

The ombudsman reports to the Public Administration Committee in the Commons which can then pursue any matters that have not been resolved satisfactorily. In December 2005, for example, it held a hearing on the report concerning the treatment of those interned by the Japanese who were denied compensation. In appearing before the committee, the relevant minister announced that the issue was being urgently reviewed.

The Commissioner thus serves a useful service to MPs – and their constituents – but constitutes something of a limited last resort and one that has no direct powers of enforcement. MPs prefer to keep casework in their own hands and pursue it with government directly. For most members, the preferred device for pursuing a matter with a minister remains that of direct correspondence.

Party committees

An important unofficial means of scrutinising and influencing government is that of party committees. These are unofficial in that they are committees of the parliamentary parties and not officially constituted committees of the House.

Each parliamentary party has some form of organisation, usually with weekly meetings of the parliamentary party. The two largest parties – Conservative and Labour – have traditionally had a sufficient number of members to sustain a series of committees. Conservative backbench committees were first established in the 1920s and established a reputation for being politically powerful (Norton 1979, 1994). The committees had elected officers and usually met weekly to discuss forthcoming business and topics of interest, often with invited speakers. Any Tory MP could attend and if a controversial issue attracted a large audience, it signalled to the whips that there was a problem. However, the early 1990s witnessed a decline in attendance at meetings – members had many competing demands on their time – and the massive decline in the number of Conservative MPs in the 1997 general election meant that the party had insufficient numbers to maintain the committees on the scale of previous decades. As a result, the number of committees was scaled down and in 2003 a new practice instituted, with four omnibus committees sharing the same time slot and meeting on a rota basis.

Labour backbench committees traditionally lacked the clout of Conservative committees, but in the 1992–7 parliament the standing orders of the Parliamentary Labour Party (PLP) were changed in order to enhance the consultative status of the committees. Since 1997, Labour ministers have consulted with backbench committees, some achieving a reputation for being assiduous in doing so. The committees also serve another purpose: they allow MPs to specialise in a particular subject. They enable an MP, through serving as officer of a committee, to achieve some status in the parliamentary party. This is often especially helpful to new members, giving them their first opportunity to make a mark in parliamentary life. It may also serve as a way of getting noticed for the purpose of being promoted to ministerial office. However, despite their attraction to MPs and their influence within party ranks, the committees have to compete for the attention of members – there are many other demands on members' time.

All-party groups

All-party groups, like party committees, are not formally constituted committees of the House. They are formed on a cross-party basis, with officerships being shared among members of different parties. They have proved particularly popular in recent decades. In 1988 there were 103 all-party subject groups. The number has grown massively since. By 2009, the number had grown to 430. (There are also 140 country groups, each bringing together MPs – and peers – with a special interest in the country or territory concerned.) Some of the groups, known as all-party parliamentary groups, are confined to a parliamentary voting membership; some – known as associate parliamentary groups – include non-parliamentarians. The subjects covered by these groups are diverse, including, for example, AIDS, alcohol abuse, boxing, compassion in dying, electoral reform, folk arts, gas safety, girl guiding, hill farming, Irish in Britain, Islam, prison health, rowing, and tourism. Some exist in name only. Others are active in discussing and promoting a particular cause, some pressing the government for action. Among the more influential are the disability group, the long-established parliamentary and scientific committee, and the football group, which has been active in influencing policy on such issues as safety in sports grounds. The breast cancer group has been especially active in raising parliamentary awareness of the condition. Many of the all-party groups have links with relevant outside bodies – about two-thirds receive support, usually administrative, from interest groups (Norton 2005: 128) – and can act as useful means of access to the political process for such groups. Like party committees, all-party groups have to compete with the other demands made on MPs' time.

In combination, then, a variety of means are available to MPs to scrutinise and influence government and through which they can serve to make known the views of citizens. The means vary in effectiveness and viewed in isolation may appear of little use. However, they are not mutually exclusive, and MPs will often use several of them in order to pursue a particular issue. An MP may write privately to a minister and, if not satisfied with the response, may table a question or seek a half-hour adjournment debate. In order to give prominence to an issue, a member may table an EDM, speak in debate and bombard the minister with a series of written questions. The most effective MPs are those who know how to use these means in combination and – on occasion – which ones to avoid.

■ Members under pressure

MPs are called on to carry out the tasks of the House. As we have seen, the resources available to them to carry out those tasks have increased in recent years. MPs have more resources than before. They have a better salary than before, and they have office and support facilities far in excess of those available to their predecessors. However, the demands on the typical MP have increased massively in recent decades, on a scale that far surpasses the increase in the resources available to deal with them. The increase in demands on MPs' time can be ascribed to four sources: public business, organised interests, constituents and MPs themselves.

Public business

The volume of business has increased in recent decades. This is particularly pronounced in terms of legislation. The number of bills introduced by the government is nowadays not much greater than it was in earlier decades. What has increased is the volume. Bills are much longer than they used to be. They are also more complex. Before 1950, no more than 1,000 pages of public Acts were passed each year. Before 1980, no more than 2,000 pages were passed each year. Since 1980, the figure has usually been in excess of 2,500 pages and on occasion has surpassed 3,000 pages. Since 2000, some bills have been so big that they have had to be published in two parts. This increased volume places a significant strain on parliamentary resources. Most bills go to public bill committees. The longer and more complex the bill, the more time it needs in committee. The Education Reform Bill in 1987–8 received more parliamentary time (200 hours) than any other postwar measure. Given that several public bill committees will normally be in existence at the same time – bills frequently go for committee consideration at the same time in the session – there is a tremendous strain on the finite resources of MPs, in terms of both their number and the time they have at their disposal.

In addition to the greater volume of public legislation, there is also the burden of other business. This includes, for example, having to scrutinise EU legislation, a task that falls principally on the European Scrutiny Committee (which considers all EU documents submitted to the House) and three European committees, responsible for discussing documents that the House considers worthy of further consideration. It also includes the work of the select committees. As can be calculated from Table 15.7, the departmental select committees take up the time of 237 MPs. Committee work, which often requires reading a substantial amount of paperwork submitted by witnesses and outside bodies, can be time-consuming. Some of the material can be detailed and complex. All this work – in terms of both the European committees and the departmental select committees – represents a relatively recent increase in the workload of MPs; there were no European committees prior to the 1970s and, as we have seen, only a few investigative select committees. Then there are the other select committees, both investigative and domestic. Some MPs can be appointed to serve on three or four separate committees.

Organised interests

MPs have always been subject to lobbying by outside groups – groups wanting members to push for a particular outcome in terms of public policy. However, that lobbying has become pronounced in recent decades (Norton 2005: Chapter 10). Since 1979, organised interests – firms, charities, consumer groups, professional bodies, pressure groups – appear to have 'discovered' Parliament. Government appeared to adopt more of an arm's-length relationship with outside bodies. The departmental select committees came into being and provided particular targets for organised interests. The 1970s had also seen something of a growth in the voting independence of MPs. As a consequence of these several developments, the House of Commons looked far more attractive than ever before to organised interests wanting to influence public policy (Rush 1990; Norton 1999a). One survey of organised interests found that three-quarters had 'regular or frequent contact with one or more Members of Parliament' (Rush 1990: 280). Of the groups that had such contact, more than 80 per cent had asked MPs to table parliamentary questions, and almost 80 per cent had asked MPs to arrange meetings at the House of Commons. Over half had asked MPs to table amendments to bills and to table a motion. It is common to hear MPs in debates refer to material they have received from interest groups (see Norton 2005: 201). This contact between organised interests and MPs has a number of beneficial consequences. Among other things, Members are provided with advice and information that can prove useful in questioning government and in raising new issues. However, it also has some negative consequences. One is the demand on MPs' time. One survey of 248 MPs in 1992 found that on average an MP spent over three-and-a-half hours a week meeting group representatives (Norris 1997: 36–7). Further time is taken up by acting on the requests of such groups and by reading and, if necessary, responding to the mass of material that is mailed by the groups. MPs now have difficulty coping with the sheer volume of lobbying material that is sent to them.

Constituents

Organised interests have been responsible for a marked increase in the mailbag of MPs. So too have constituents. We have touched already on the volume of mail received in the House of Commons in the twenty-first century. For the MP, constituency work takes priority and can occupy a large portion of the day in dictating replies to constituents' letters. It can also occupy most of every weekend, through both appearances at constituency functions and holding constituency surgeries – publicly advertised meetings at which constituents can see the MP in private to discuss particular concerns.

When an MP receives a letter from a constituent that raises a particular grievance (failure to receive a particular state benefit, for example) or issue of public policy, the MP will normally pursue the matter with the government through writing to the relevant minister. Ministers answer in the region of 250,000 letters a year, mostly from MPs.

The burden of constituency demands continues to increase, and MPs have difficulty finding the time to cope with constituency demands and the demands of public business (see Norton and Wood 1993; Norton 2005: 189–91). By 1996 it was estimated that MPs devoted almost 40 per cent of their time to constituency business (Power 1996: 14). The problem is particularly acute for MPs with constituencies close to Westminster: constituents expect them to find the time to be at constituency events, even when the House is sitting. The burden has also increased as constituents – as well as pressure groups – have made increasing use of e-mail. In 2002, the Information Committee of the Commons reported that 10–20 per cent of an MP's correspondence might be received electronically, a figure which it noted was set to climb. E-mail is quick as well as cheap – unlike letters, no stamps are required. MPs are not only recipients of communications but are themselves generators of communications to constituents. Apart from particular correspondence, this may take the form of newsletters and, increasingly, websites. Most MPs have websites and some engage in interactive dialogue through the use of blogs (see Norton 2007). A number also now use Twitter.

MPs themselves

MPs are also responsible for adding to their own burden and to that of the resources of the House. As we have seen, recent years have seen the growth of the career politician. There is a greater body of members who are keen to be re-elected and to achieve office. They are keen to be noticed in the House. Achieving a high profile in the House helps them to be noticed locally. This may help, albeit at the margins, with re-election (see Norton and Wood 1993) and, indeed, may help with reselection by the local party. It is also considered necessary for the purposes of promotion, given the growing number of career politicians and hence the more competitive parliamentary environment. The tendency of the career politician is to table as many questions as is permissible: research assistants will variously be asked to come up with suitable drafts (see Franklin and Norton 1993). The career politician will try to intervene as often as possible in the chamber and will table early day motions to raise issues. There is also likely to be an allied tendency to attract media attention, not least with frequent press releases.

All these pressures add up to create a particular burden for MPs. Surveys by the senior salaries review body have shown that, over the decades, the amount of time devoted to parliamentary duties has increased. One study in the 1990s suggested that MPs typically work in excess of a seventy-hour week. It is difficult for MPs to keep pace with all the demands made of them. Their resources have improved in recent years, and they have been aided considerably by new technology, but the resources have not kept pace with the demands made of members. For many MPs, it is a case of running in order to stand still. For others, it is a case of slipping backwards. There is a particularly important conflict between trying to find time for constituency work and finding time for dealing with public business in the House (Norton and Wood 1993; Norton 2005: 189–91). So long as constituency work takes priority, then the time needed for public business is under particular pressure.

■ The House under pressure

The fact that MPs work hard for their constituents is frequently acknowledged by constituents. Assessments of the role of the local MP tend to be positive (twice as many people saying the local MP did a good job as the proportion saying the MP did a bad

job) and consistent, having shown little change over a number of years. However, the view held by citizens about the House of Commons appears more ambivalent, certainly more volatile, than the views they hold of the local MP. The proportion of people thinking that the House of Commons is doing a good job has varied over the years, sometimes quite substantially. In a 1991 MORI poll, for example, 59 per cent of those questioned thought that Parliament worked well or fairly well. Four years later, in 1995, that figure had gone down to 37 per cent. The number saying it worked fairly or very badly increased from 16 to 38 per cent. Since then, as shown in Table 15.8, the proportion saying it works well has increased slightly, but then slipped back before slumping in May 2009 to 20 per cent. The percentage fairly or very dissatisfied reached an unprecedented 63 per cent. Whereas the preceding polls had shown more people giving a positive than a negative response (albeit at times only just), the difference in 2009 was minus 43 per cent.

What, then, might explain why attitudes towards Parliament are not more positive? The House of Commons has seen major changes in recent decades. Some of these changes, such as the creation of the departmental select committees, have reinforced

Table 15.8 Views on the efficacy of Parliament 1995–2009
Q Are you satisfied or dissatisfied with the way that Parliament works?

	21 April–8 May 1995* %	17–21 August 2000* %	9–15 May 2001** %	6–17 December 2003 %	23–28 November 2006 %	29–31 May 2009*** %
Very satisfied	2	4	4	1	2	2
Fairly satisfied	32	39	41	35	33	18
Neither satisfied nor dissatisfied	27	19	16	27	24	11
Fairly dissatisfied	22	21	19	23	24	30
Very dissatisfied	9	8	11	9	9	33
No opinion	8	10	9	5	8	6
Satisfied	34	43	45	36	35	20
Dissatisfied	31	29	30	32	33	63
Net satisfied	+3	+14	+15	+4	+2	−43

*In 1995 and 2000, asked as 'To what extent are you satisfied or dissatisfied with the way each is doing its job these days? The way Parliament works'
**In 2001, asked as 'To what extent are you satisfied or dissatisfied with the way each is doing its job these days? The way the Westminster Parliament works'
***In 2009, asked as 'Q To what extent are you satisfied or dissatisfied with the way each is doing its job these days? The Westminster Parliament'
Source: Ipsos MORI

the capacity of the House to fulfil a number of its functions. However, other changes – internal as well as external to the House – have served to challenge its public standing and its capacity to fulfil the tasks expected of it. These can be summarised under the headings of partisanship, executive dominance, the creation of other policy-making bodies, and sleaze.

Partisanship

The clash between the parties is a characteristic of British political life. It is a long-standing feature of the House of Commons. There is a perception that, in recent years, it has become more intense. This is reflected, for example, in the nature of Prime Minister's Question Time, where the desire for partisan point-scoring has largely squeezed out genuine attempts to elicit information (see Franklin and Norton 1993). However, perhaps most importantly of all, partisanship is now more publicly visible. The introduction of the television cameras to the Commons means that, in a single news broadcast covering the House, more people will see the House in that single broadcast than could ever have sat in the public gallery of the House. Although there is general support for broadcasting proceedings among public and politicians, the focus on the chamber has tended to encourage a negative perception. A 1996 MORI poll revealed a very clear perception of politicians engaged in negative point-scoring (Table 15.9). As the author of a 1999 Hansard Society study of the broadcasting of Parliament noted, 'The overwhelming perception of parliamentarians as point-scoring, unoriginal and dogmatically partisan can not be blamed entirely on negative reporting by journalists. If one purpose of broadcasting Parliament was to allow people to judge it for themselves, the low esteem MPs are held in by the public has not been elevated by ten years of live exposure' (Coleman 1999: 21). When people see the House on television, they see either a largely empty chamber – MPs are busy doing things elsewhere – or a body of baying MPs, busy shouting at one another and cheering their own side. That is particularly noticeable at Prime Minister's Question Time. One Gallup poll in 1993 found that 82 per cent of those questioned agreed that what took place 'sounds like feeding time at the zoo'. As Peter Riddell noted of Prime Minister's Question Time, 'no other aspect of parliamentary life generates more public complaints' (*The Times*: 4 April 1994). For MPs who want to win the next election, supporting their own side in the cham-

Table 15.9 Perceptions of MPs

Response	%
Q. When you hear politicians from different parties on radio and television, do you have the impression that they are mainly concerned with reaching agreement or are they mainly concerned with scoring points off each other?	
Reaching agreement	3
Scoring points	93
Don't know	4
Q. When you hear politicians on television or radio, do you feel that they fairly often break new ground, or do you almost always feel you've heard it all before?	
New ground	4
Heard it before	92
Don't know	4
Q. When you hear politicians on television or radio, do you feel that they are usually saying what they believe to be true, or are they usually merely spouting the party line?	
Truthful	6
Party line	88
Don't know	6

Source: From S. Coleman (1999) *Electronic Media, Parliament and the Media*, p. 20. Reproduced with permission from the Hansard Society

ber takes precedence over maintaining public trust in the institution (see Norton 1997: 365). Given that the television coverage focuses on the chamber and not on the committee work of the House, the enduring perception that viewers have is of a House of noisy, point-scoring MPs, contributing little new to political debate.

Executive dominance

There has been a perception of a growth in executive dominance in the UK (see Allen 2001). The effect of this, it is argued, is a greater marginalisation of Parliament. Party dominates the House, and this stranglehold has been exacerbated as more and more power has been concentrated in Downing Street. This perception of executive dominance was marked when Margaret Thatcher occupied Downing Street and was revived under the premiership of Tony Blair. The extent to which Parliament is marginalised has been the subject of academic debate, but the perception of a peripheral legislature resonates with

Table 15.10 Perceptions of parliamentary control over government: Parliament does not have sufficient control over what the government does

	1991 (%)	1995 (%)	2000 (%)
Strongly agree	10	13	21
Tend to agree	40	39	32
Neither agree nor disagree	19	21	20
Tend to disagree	20	15	8
Strongly disagree	3	3	4
No opinion	9	9	15

Sources: MORI state of the nation poll 1995, ICM Research state of the nation poll 2000. Copyright © Ipsos MORI, reproduced with permission

the public. The MORI state of the nation polls in the 1990s and in 2000 found a growing body of respondents who believed that Parliament did not have sufficient control over what the government does (Table 15.10). By the mid-1990s, a majority of respondents – 52 per cent – agreed with the statement that Parliament does not have sufficient control over what the government does. Only 18 per cent disagreed. This perception appears to have been reinforced under the Labour government of Tony Blair. As can be seen from Table 15.10, by 2000 the biggest change was in the percentage of respondents who agreed 'strongly' with the statement.

The popular perception of Labour MPs slavishly voting as they are told was encapsulated by a *Guardian* cartoon showing a Labour MP holding an electronic voting device displaying two options: 'Agree with Tony [Blair]' and 'Strongly Agree with Tony'. As research by Philip Cowley (2002, 2005) and Cowley and Stuart (2008) has shown, this perception is overstated. The Blair and Brown governments have faced unprecedented rebelliousness from backbenchers. The three most notable occasions have been: in 2002 when 122 Labour MPs voted against government policy on Iraq, the biggest rebellion on foreign policy faced by any Labour government; in 2005 when the Blair government suffered its first defeat on a whipped vote, MPs voting down a government proposal to allow detention without charge for ninety days; and in 2009 when the Brown government was defeated on the rights of former Gurkha soldiers to settle in Britain. Labour MPs have been willing to vote against the government to a degree not popularly recognised. However, the perception of executive dominance persists – the Prime Minister governing with little regard to Parliament – and it remains the case that the government will almost always get its way in a parliamentary vote. The defeat in 2005 was

the first in more than 2,000 votes to take place in the Commons since the Labour government was returned in 1997. There remains a popular view of a House of Commons that it is not calling government to account. The House is weak in the face of a strong executive.

Creation of other policy-making bodies

The capacity of the House to fulfil its functions is undermined not only by executive domination of the House but also by the creation of other policy-making bodies. Even if MPs had the political will to determine outcomes, their capacity to do so is now limited by the seepage of policy-making powers to other bodies. There are three principal bodies or rather three collections of bodies involved: the institutions of the EU, the courts and the devolved assemblies.

The effect of membership of the European Union will be touched on in Chapter 27. We shall return to its legal implications in Chapter 20. Membership has served to transfer policy competences in various sectors to the institutions of the European Union: they have increased in number with subsequent treaty amendments. Other than being able, under the Lisbon Treaty, to challenge a proposal on the grounds that it breaches subsidiarity, parliament has no formal role in the law-making process of the EU. It seeks to influence the British minister prior to the meeting of the relevant Council of Ministers, but – if qualified majority voting (QMV) is employed – the minister may be outvoted. There is nothing that Parliament can do to prevent regulations having binding effect in the UK or to prevent the intention of directives from being achieved.

The courts have acquired new powers as a result of British membership of the EU as well now as a consequence of the incorporation of the European Convention on Human Rights (ECHR) into British law and as a consequence of devolution. The effect of these we shall explore in greater depth in Chapter 20. Various disputed issues of public policy are now resolved by the courts, which have the power to suspend or set aside British law if it conflicts with EU law. The courts are responsible for interpreting the provisions of the ECHR. The courts are also responsible for determining the legal limits established by the Acts creating elected bodies in Scotland, Wales and Northern Ireland. The capacity of the House of Commons to intervene or to overrule the courts is now effectively limited.

The devolution of powers to elected assemblies in different parts of the United Kingdom also limits the decision-making capacity of Parliament. Parliament is not expected to legislate on matters devolved to the Scottish Parliament. The Scottish Parliament has been given power to legislate in areas not reserved under the Scotland Act and has also been given power to amend primary legislation passed by Parliament. The powers of the National Assembly for Wales have been extended under the terms of the Government of Wales Act 2006. The creation of a power-sharing Northern Ireland Assembly in 2007 has also resulted in a shift of power from Westminster to Stormont. The scope of decision making by Parliament is thus constricted.

Sleaze

Throughout the twentieth century, there were various scandals involving politicians accepting illicit payments in return for some political favour. In the 1970s and 1980s, there was criticism of MPs for accepting payment to act as advisers to lobbying firms or hiring themselves out as consultants. One book, published in 1991, was entitled *MPs for Hire* (Hollingsworth 1991). At the time it was published, 384 MPs held 522 directorships and 452 consultancies. In 1994, the issue hit the headlines when a journalist, posing as a businessman, offered twenty MPs £1,000 each to table parliamentary questions. Two Conservative MPs did not immediately say no to the offer. The story attracted extensive media coverage. The two MPs were briefly suspended from the service of the House. The story was further fuelled later in the year when *The Guardian* claimed that two ministers had, when backbenchers, accepted money to table questions; one, Tim Smith, then promptly resigned as a minister and the other, Neil Hamilton, was eventually forced to leave office. The furore generated by the stories led the Prime Minister, John Major, to establish the Committee on Standards in Public Life, under a judge, Lord Nolan. In 1995, the House accepted the recommendations of the committee about payment from outside sources, though not without opposition from some Conservative Members. MPs went further than the committee recommended in deciding to ban any paid advocacy by MPs: members cannot advocate a particular cause in Parliament in return for payment. Members were also required to disclose income received from outside bodies that is paid to them because they are MPs (for example, money from a company for advice on how to present a case to government). The House also approved the recommendation to establish a

code of conduct and appoint a Parliamentary Commissioner for Standards to ensure that the rules are followed. The code was subsequently drawn up and agreed. It is accompanied by a guide to the rules of the House relating to members' conduct.

The effect of the 'cash for questions' scandal was reflected in opinion polls. In a 1985 MORI poll, 46 per cent thought that 'most' MPs made a lot of money by using public office improperly. In 1994, the figure was 64 per cent, and 77 per cent agreed with the statement that 'most MPs care more about special interests than they care about people like you'. Continuing allegations of breaches of the rules after the return of a new government in 1997 did nothing to help Parliament's reputation (see Doig 2001, 2002). However, what was to precipitate the slump in the reputation in the House of Commons in 2009 was a scandal over MPs' expenses. The House in 1971 introduced an additional cost allowance to assist MPs with maintaining a second home. Initially a modest sum, the amount that an MP representing a seat outside London could claim had reached £24,222 for 2009–10. Though the amount claimable was known, details about claims were not made public. In 2009, details were to be released under the Freedom of Information Act, but the *Daily Telegraph* got hold of advance and unexpurgated copies of the claims made by MPs and published details over a number of weeks. Publication of details of some of the claims – most prominently for a duck house, clearing a moat, in two instances claiming for mortgages that had already been paid off, and in another claiming for, even though not having, a second home – led to a public scandal. There was public dissatisfaction with the ease with which MPs could claim money for a whole range of items (furniture, household goods and repairs, food), often without receipts, and, in effect, supplement their salaries. The scandal led to the police investigating the actions of some MPs (such as those claiming to cover non-existent mortgages) and to the Speaker of the House of Commons, Michael Martin, resigning: he had resisted attempts to make public details of the claim and was the target of much of the criticism of how the House had responded to the crisis. Several MPs that had made claims that attracted particular public opprobrium announced that they would not be seeking re-election; some Labour MPs were brought before a party 'star chamber' and told that they would not be permitted to stand again as Labour candidates. The Government achieved enactment of the Parliamentary Standards

Act 2009, transferring responsibility for policing and paying allowances to an independent body. The Committee on Standards in Public Life was given responsibility for making other recommendations to address the problem. The public reaction was unprecedented in living memory, resulting in a marked collapse in trust in the House of Commons and leaving MPs unsure of how to respond.

■ Pressure for change

These variables combine to produce a House of Commons that is under pressure to restore public confidence and to fulfil effectively the functions ascribed to it. There are various calls for reform of the House in order to address both problems. However, there is no agreement on what should be done. Even in the wake of the scandal over MPs' expenses in 2009, not all those demanding reform are agreed on the scale of the problem, and they come up with very different proposals for reform. There are, put simply, three principal approaches to reform. Each derives from a particular perception of the role of the House of Commons in the political system. They can be related very roughly to the three types of legislature identified at the beginning of the chapter.

1 *Radical*: The radical approach wants to see Parliament as a policy-making legislature. Parliament is seen as weak in relation to the executive – and is seen to be getting weaker. Reform of the House of Commons within the present constitutional and political framework is deemed inadequate to the task. Without radical constitutional reform, the House of Commons will remain party-dominated and under the thumb of the executive. To achieve a policy-making legislature, the radical approach not only supports reform within the institution but also wants major reform of the constitution in order to change fundamentally the relationship between Parliament and government. Such change would include a new electoral system as well as an elected second chamber. As such, this radical approach can be seen to fit very much within the liberal approach to the constitution (see Chapter 13). The most extreme form of this view advocates a separation of powers, with the executive elected separately from the House of Commons. Only with radical

reform, it is argued, can high levels of public trust in Parliament be achieved.

2 *Reform*: This approach wants to strengthen the House of Commons as a policy-influencing body, the onus for policy-*making* resting with government but with the House of Commons having the opportunity to consider policy proposals in detail and to influence their content. As such, it falls very much within the traditional approach to constitutional change (see Chapter 15), although it is not exclusive to it. Traditionalists, for example, can find common cause with adherents to the socialist approach in respect of some reforms. Even adherents of the liberal approach will support reform, although arguing that it does not go far enough. (For traditionalists, reform is both necessary and sufficient. For liberals, it is necessary but not sufficient.) Reformers favour structural and procedural changes within the House. They want to strengthen committees. They want more time for legislative scrutiny. Given the collapse in trust in the Commons, they also want to enhance the relationship between Parliament and the public, with greater scope for members of the public to make their views known, for example through e-petitions and online consultations. Reducing the size of the House was also seen as making more efficient use of resources, not least through reducing the pressure created by members themselves. The sorts of reforms that are advocated are listed in Table 15.11.

3 *Leave alone*: This approach, as the name suggests, opposes change. It is the stance of a High Tory (see Chapter 13) although it is not exclusive to the High Tory approach. Some Labour MPs have opposed reform, wanting to retain the chamber as the central debating forum. Those who support this stance stress the importance of the chamber as the place where the great issues of the day are debated. Committees and greater specialisation detract from the fulfilment of this historical role, allowing MPs to get bogged down in the detail rather than the principle of what is proposed by government. Providing MPs with offices takes them away from the chamber. Although not quite envisaging a House with little or no policy effect, advocates of this approach see the role of the House as one of supporting government. They emphasise that there is no great public demand for change, with scandals such as those of MPs' expenses in 2009 constituting, in their view,

Table 15.11 Reform of the House of Commons: proposals to strengthen the House

- Make pre-legislative scrutiny the norm by publishing all bills, before their introduction into Parliament, in draft form and allowing select committees to study them.
- Require each bill at some stage during its passage to be subject to examination by an evidence-taking committee.
- Create more time for evidence-taking by public bill committees.
- Make greater use of online consultations for select committee inquiries.
- Give departmental select committees an annual research budget (Banham 1994: 50, suggested £2 million a year for each committee).
- Create new procedures for examining delegated legislation and give the House the power to amend statutory instruments.
- Give select committees, and the Speaker, powers to summon ministers.
- Introduce e-petitions and establish a petitions committee to consider issues of importance raised by the public.
- Reduce the number of MPs, creating a smaller and more professional House.

essentially transient and ultimately marginal events. Most people want a government that can govern, and the House of Commons is there to support that government in carrying out the programme it laid before the electors.

For radicals, the contemporary emphasis on constitutional reform gives them hope that their stance may be vindicated. The creation of new elected assemblies in Scotland, Wales and Northern Ireland – both elected for fixed terms – will, they hope, act as a spur to radical change in England. Not only do these parts of the UK have their own elected assemblies, they also have electoral systems that are different to that employed for the House of Commons. With the use also of different electoral systems for the Greater London Assembly and the European Parliament, the House of Commons remains the only legislative body in the UK elected by the first-past-the-post system. Those who adopt this radical stance view electoral reform as a crucial mechanism for revitalising the House of Commons.

For reformers, reform constitutes a practical as well as a desirable option. They point to what has happened in recent years as well as to various reform tracts identifying the case for further change. The introduction of the departmental select committees in 1979 showed what could be achieved in strengthen-

ing Parliament as a policy-influencing legislature. Some reforms have been carried out since 1997 as a consequence of reports issued by the Select Committee on Modernisation of the House of Commons (see Brazier *et al.* 2005). These have included the creation of the 'parallel chamber' in Westminster Hall, the creation of public bill committees, the election by the House of members of select committees and the introduction of regular post-legislative review. More modest changes have included the introduction of payment for those who chair both select and public bill committees.

Reformers want to see more significant changes, and recent years have seen the publication of various reform tracts, including the reports of the Conservative Party's Commission to Strengthen Parliament (the Norton Report) 2000, the Hansard Society's Commissions on Parliamentary Scrutiny (the Newton Report) 2001 and on the Communication of Parliamentary Democracy (the Puttnam Report) 2005, as well as reports from the Modernisation Committee in the Commons and the Constitution Committee in the House of Lords. The Constitution Committee's report, *Parliament and the Legislative Process* (2004), advocated not only reform of the legislative process, but also more extensive pre-legislative and post-legislative scrutiny. The report has led to the introduction of post-legislative review as a standard procedure, most Acts to be reviewed three to five years after enactment.

Those who want to leave the House of Commons alone take heart from the fact that they frequently succeed, not least by default (see Norton 1999b). Many ministers are not too keen on any significant reform that will strengthen the capacity of Parliament to criticise government or prevent it having its way. They want Parliament to expedite government business, not have it delayed. Robin Cook, when he was Leader of the House (2001–3), had notable difficulty in carrying his colleagues with him in pursuing a reform agenda. The whips have proved reluctant to see change and in 2002 were accused of encouraging Labour MPs not to agree to all the recommendations of the Modernisation Committee. Also, MPs – once a parliament is under way – become too tied up with the day-to-day demands of constituency work and public business to stand back and address the issue of parliamentary reform. The 'leave alone' tendency may not be strong in its advocacy but can be quite powerful in achieving the outcome it wants.

Parliamentary reform has been a feature of debates over the past forty years. However, the problem in achieving reform is the classic one. Most MPs are elected to support the party in government. At the same time, they are members of a body that is supposed to subject to critical scrutiny the very government they are elected to support. Are they going to vote to strengthen the House of Commons if the effect is to limit the very government they were elected to support? The options are not necessarily mutually exclusive – reformers argue that good government needs an effective Parliament – but perceptions are all-important. If ministers think a strengthened Parliament is a threat, will they not be inclined to call on their parliamentary majority to oppose it? In those circumstances, backbenchers may have to choose between party and Parliament. Some recent reforms have been important, but none challenges the basic capacity of government to get its way. At the end of the day, the government achieves passage of its measures.

■ Explaining Parliamentary power

As is apparent from the figures in Tables 15.8 and 15.10, as well as the demands for reform made by observers and many politicians, there is a widespread perception that Parliament is not doing as good a job as it should be doing. The House of Commons is seen as weak in the face of executive dominance. Yet Parliament has survived for several centuries; it is at the heart of our political system. Just how powerful is it? On the face of it, not very, yet much depends on how power is defined. There are different approaches. The three principal approaches derive from explaining the capacity to affect outcomes in terms of observable decision making (the pluralist approach), non-decision making (deriving from élite theory) and institutional constraints (Norton 2005).

Decision making

This approach focuses on how issues are resolved once they are on the political agenda. Once a government brings forward a proposal, what difference does Parliament make to it? Does the measure emerge in the form in which the government introduced it or at least in the form it wants it? From this perspective, Parliament exercises some power, but it is limited. Parliament has the coercive capacity to say 'no' to government. Legislation is dependent

on the assent of Parliament. If MPs vote down a bill, then it cannot proceed. However, as we have seen, the use of this coercive capacity is rare. MPs also have a persuasive capacity: that is, they may induce government not to proceed with a measure (or to change it) even though it has the option of proceeding. Ministers may be persuaded by the force of argument, by a desire to maintain goodwill on the part of their own supporters, by the desire to avoid embarrassing publicity (the public appearance of a divided party), or by the threat of defeat. Even with large majorities in the 1997 and 2001 parliaments, Labour ministers occasionally made concessions to their own backbenchers. Thus, for example, Jack Straw as Home Secretary made changes to the Criminal Justice (Terrorism and Conspiracy) Bill as well as to the Immigration and Asylum Bill in order to assuage the criticisms of Labour MPs (Cowley 2002: 32, 52–4). When one Labour MP opposed to provisions for incapacity benefit embodied in a welfare bill went to see the then Social Security Secretary, Alistair Darling, he was asked 'What's your price?' (Cowley 2002: 47). This persuasive capacity became more pronounced in the 2005–10 parliament, when – with a reduced overall majority – the threat of defeat became more potent.

MPs thus have the capacity to affect the outcome of measures, but that capacity is extremely limited. Most bills will clear the Commons in the form they were introduced or at least in the form preferred by government. Amendments made in response to backbench pressure – or from members of other parties – are few and far between. Concessions are occasionally offered in order to ensure that enough MPs are prepared to vote for the bill. Ministers generally opt for the minimum they can get away with in terms of concessions; in the 1997–2001 parliament, for example, negotiations 'rarely yielded anything that discontented backbenchers wanted' (Cowley 2002: 180). The House of Commons *can* make a difference and occasionally the difference is significant and high-profile, but on the whole it is usually at the margins. From this perspective, Parliament is not a particularly powerful body and certainly not as powerful as many would wish it to be.

Non-decision making

Non-decision making is the capacity to keep certain things off the political agenda. The pluralist, or decision making, approach is concerned with outcomes once an issue is on the agenda. The élitist, or non-decision making approach, focuses on how issues get on to the agenda in the first place. Non-decision making is when an issue is kept off the agenda. In élite theory, there is a body that acts as a gate-keeper, ensuring that certain fundamental matters never become the subject of political debate. Parliament is not seen as part of such an élite, but the concept of non-decision making is relevant in so far as it relates to anticipated reaction. An issue may be kept off the political agenda because those responsible for agenda setting realise that it would encounter significant and possible fatal opposition. There may be occasions, therefore, when the government decides not to bring forward a bill because it does not believe it could get it through Parliament. On occasion, the adverse reaction may be so obvious that ministers do not even need to discuss it. As a consequence, there are obvious problems in detecting instances of non-decision making. There have been cases, though, where a government has been known not to proceed with a measure because of anticipated reaction. When she was Prime Minister, Margaret Thatcher once said that she had not been as radical in economic policy as she would have liked: the reason, she said, was because she would not have been able to get the approval of Parliament. That may have been a post hoc rationalisation for not being more radical rather than the actual reason, but it points to the potential power of Parliament.

Anticipation of how MPs may behave thus has some influence on government. It is a feature not confined to the UK. As Cox and Morgenstern (2002: 446) have observed, 'the venerable "rule of anticipated reactions" makes even primarily reactive legislatures . . . relevant'. If government becomes too extreme, then Parliament may act to constrain it. Knowing that, government avoids the extremes. As such, Parliament is powerful, though the number of occasions when ministers have actually contemplated introducing a measure but then decided not to because of anticipated parliamentary reaction is likely to be very small. Given the problems of identifying non-decision making, that can only be surmised, but the existence of overall majorities for government and the willingness of MPs to vote loyally with their party make it plausible.

Institutional constraints

The institutional approach is not so much concerned with the substance of a measure but rather with the institutional structures and norms that determine how an issue is resolved. Here the concern is not with how MPs behave – whether they vote for a bill or not – but with the rules (and the acceptance of those rules) that determine how a bill becomes law. However large the government's parliamentary majority, it cannot simply get all the measures it wants passed by Parliament within a matter of days or weeks. Each bill, as we have seen, has to go through a set procedure. There are several stages each bill has to go through and there are gaps between each stage. As we have seen, there is limited parliamentary time available. The finite number of MPs available to serve on public bill committees may be seen as a problem for Parliament but it also limits the number of bills that can be considered at the same time. Government thus has to consider which bills it wishes to introduce each year. There is not sufficient parliamentary time to deal with all the bills it would like to introduce and only a minority of bills put forward by departments are accepted for introduction in a particular session. Even then, there is the problem of miscalculation and a bill may not get through in the time available. A bill is more likely to fail because of misjudgements about timing (or the calling of a general election, prematurely bringing a Parliament to an end) than it is because MPs have voted it down.

From this institutional perspective, Parliament is a notably powerful body. For bills to become law and be enforced by the courts, they have to be assented to by Parliament. There is no alternative process. The parliamentary *process* is thus crucial and that process is governed by a large body of often complex rules. The book embodying all the rules and precedents, known as *Erskine May* (the name of the clerk who first produced it in the nineteenth century), runs to more than 1,000 pages. Though the House of Commons is master of its procedure, and the government could use its majority to change the rules (and sometimes does), it cannot embark on wholesale change. Ministers are not procedural experts – they rely on the clerks, who are politically neutral – and the House proceeds on the basis of a common acceptance of the rules. There is a general acceptance that government is entitled to get its business done and the opposition is entitled to be heard.

Parliament thus functions on the basis of a consensus on the rules. If government tried to manipulate the rules excessively in its favour, opposition parties may refuse to continue playing by those rules. There is thus what has been termed an 'equilibrium of legitimacy' (Norton 2001a: 28), each side accepting the legitimacy of the other in what it seeks to do. That acceptance allows the process to function effectively. It is an acceptance that underpins the institutional power of Parliament. It is an acceptance that shapes ministers' behaviour. Bills have to be drawn up in a particular form for introduction to Parliament. Ministers are not only drawn from Parliament – and remain constituency MPs – they also have to appear in Parliament to justify their measures and their policies and to answer MPs' questions. There is no legal requirement for ministers to turn up at Question Time to answer questions, but the accepted rules of procedure ensure that they do. Whether they like it or not, Parliament shapes what they do. As an *institution*, Parliament is a powerful body.

BOX 15.4 BRITAIN IN CONTEXT

Ancient and large, but not unusual

The Westminster Parliament is distinctive because of its longevity. It is one of the oldest parliaments in the world. However, in terms of its place in the political system – especially in its relationship to the executive – it is not unusual. Of the types of legislature identified in Box 15.1, it is the first – that of *policy-making legislatures* – that is notable for not being a crowded category. Of national legislatures, only the US Congress has occupied the category for any continuous period of time. It is joined by the state legislatures of the USA and a few legislatures of more recent creation.

The category of *policy-influencing legislatures* is the crowded category and encompasses most legislatures in western Europe and the Commonwealth. It has also been swelled by the changes in the legislatures of the new democracies of southern, central and eastern Europe: previously they occupied the third category, that of *legislatures with little or no policy effect*, but – with democratisation– they have now moved up to occupy the second or even (sometimes briefly) the first category. The third category is now largely confined to dictatorships and one-party states, where legislatures exist for the purpose of giving assent to whatever is placed before them.

Within the category of policy-influencing legislatures, the UK Parliament is not ranked in the top reaches of the category; that is, there are other legislatures that utilise more extensively the capacity to amend or reject measures brought forward by the executive. The Italian parliament and the Scandinavian legislatures are among the strongest legislatures in the category. Westminster, and other Westminster-style legislatures, has less impact on public policy by virtue of the fact that it exists in a Cabinet-centred, two-party system, where the parties compete for the all-or-nothing spoils of electoral victory under a first-past-the-post electoral system. Continental parliamentary systems, utilising different electoral systems, place more stress on coalitions, with parliaments operating through committees on a more consensual basis.

The UK Parliament, however, is not seen as the weakest legislature in the category of policy-influencing legislatures. In western Europe, the weakest in this category are the French and Irish parliaments.

The categories identified in Box 15.1 cover legislatures in relation to public policy. Most legislatures fulfil a range of other functions. The UK Parliament is distinctive, but not unique, for the emphasis that its members give to constituency work. In common with other parliamentary – as opposed to presidential – systems, it serves as the route for advancement to executive office. It shares many of its functions with other policy-influencing legislatures. As with many other legislatures, it is under threat from the expansion of executive power. Where it is distinctive is in terms of its size. There are more than 1,400 parliamentarians (MPs and peers) at Westminster, making the UK Parliament the largest in the democratic world. (The US Congress, by contrast, has a total of 535 members; some legislatures in small states have fewer than 100 members.) Both chambers, in terms of sitting hours, are also among the busiest legislative chambers in the world.

Chapter summary

Parliament is an institution at the heart of the British political system. The principal role of the House of Commons is one of scrutinising government. Various means are available to MPs to undertake this role. Those means have been strengthened in recent years but have made only a modest contribution to improved scrutiny. Members and the House have been subject to pressures that have made it difficult for MPs to fulfil their jobs effectively. Some politicians see no need for change. Others advocate reform of the House, some through radical constitutional change, others through reform from within the institution. Inertia may prevent reform being achieved, but the issue is on the political agenda.

Discussion points

■ What are the most important functions of the House of Commons?

■ What purpose is served by select committees? Should they be strengthened?

■ Should, and can, the House of Commons improve its scrutiny of government legislation?

■ Is the increase in the constituency work of MPs a good or a bad thing?

■ Will reforming the practices and procedures make any difference to public perceptions of the House of Commons?

■ What should be done to restore public confidence in the House of Commons?

■ What would *you* do with the House of Commons – and why?

Further reading

The most recent texts on Parliament, useful for the student, are Riddell (2000), Rush (2005), Norton (2005), and Rogers and Walters (2006). Riddell analyses the pressures faced by Parliament. Rogers and Walters offer a good overview of Parliament, especially its procedures. Rush and Norton are designed for student use, the latter analysing Parliament from different theoretical perspectives and examining the relationship of Parliament to the citizen as well as to government. There is also a wide range of essays, by practitioners and academics, on different aspects of Parliament in Baldwin (2005).

The socio-economic background of MPs is covered by Rush (2001) and the behaviour of MPs in recent parliaments by Cowley (2002, 2005). The largely neglected relationship of Parliament to pressure groups is the subject of Rush (1990) and the report of the Public Administration Committee (2008). Parliamentary questions are considered extensively in Franklin and Norton (1993) and briefly in Giddings and Irwin (2005). The Procedure Committee of the House of Commons has also published a number of reports on parliamentary questions: the most recent, on written questions, was published in 2009 (Procedure Committee 2009a). MPs' constituency service is covered in Norton and Wood (1993), Power (1998) and Chapter 9 of Norton (2005). Parliamentary scrutiny of executive agencies is the subject of Giddings (1995). The relationship of Parliament to the law is discussed in Oliver and Drewry (1998). The relationship of Parliament to the European Union is covered comprehensively in Giddings and Drewry (2004). Many of these books are the products of research by study groups of the Study of Parliament Group (SPG), a body that draws together academics and clerks of Parliament. A reflective set of essays, by members of the SPG, on parliamentary change and the issues facing Parliament in the twenty-first century is to be found in Giddings (2005). The relationships of Parliament to the European Union, government, pressure groups and citizens are put in comparative context in Norton (1996), Norton (1998), Norton (1999a) and Norton (2002) respectively.

A critique of Parliament's scrutiny of the executive is to be found in Weir and Beetham (1999). On parliamentary reform since 1900, see Kelso (2009). On proposals for reform of the House of

Commons, see the Commission to Strengthen Parliament (2000), Norton (2001b), the Hansard Society Commission on Parliamentary Scrutiny (2001), the Constitution Committee of the House of Lords (2004), Brazier (2004) and the Modernisation Committee of the House of Commons (2006, 2007). On the proposal for e-petitioning of Parliament, see the Procedure Committee (2009b), On the consequences of attempts at modernisation, see Brazier *et al.* (2005).

Bibliography

Allen, G. (2001) *The Last Prime Minister* (Graham Allen).

Baldwin, N.D.J. (ed.) (2005) *Parliament in the 21st Century* (Politico's).

Banham, J. (1994) *The Anatomy of Change* (Weidenfeld & Nicolson).

Brand, J. (1992) *British Parliamentary Parties* (Oxford University Press).

Brazier, A. (2004) 'Standing Committees: Imperfect Scrutiny', in A. Brazier (ed.) *Parliament, Politics and Law Making* (Hansard Society).

Brazier, A., Flinders, M. and McHugh, D. (2005) *New Politics, New Parliament?* (Hansard Society).

Coleman, S. (1999) *Electronic Media, Parliament and the Media* (Hansard Society).

Commission to Strengthen Parliament (2000) *Strengthening Parliament* (Conservative Party).

Constitution Committee, House of Lords (2004) *Parliament and the Legislative Process*, 14th Report, Session 2003–4, HL Paper 173–I (The Stationery Office).

Constitution Committee, House of Lords (2008) *Pre-Legislative Scrutiny in the 2006–07 Session*, Session 2007–08, HL Paper 43 (The Stationery Office).

Cowley, P. (ed.) (1998) *Conscience and Parliament* (Cass).

Cowley, P. (2002) *Revolts and Rebellions* (Politico's).

Cowley, P. (2005) *The Rebels* (Politico's).

Cowley, P. and Norton, P. (1996) *Blair's Bastards* (Centre for Legislative Studies).

Cowley, P. and Stuart, M. (2008) 'A Rebellious Decade: Backbench Rebellions under Tony Blair, 1997–207', in M. Beech and S. Lee (eds) *Ten Years of New Labour* (Palgrave Macmillan).

Cox, G.W. and Morgenstern, S. (2002) 'Epilogue: Latin America's Assemblies and Proactive Presidents', in S. Morgenstern and B. Nacif (eds) *Legislative Politics in Latin America* (Cambridge University Press).

Criddle, B. (1992) 'MPs and Candidates', in D. Butler and D. Kavanagh (eds) *The British General Election of 1992* (Macmillan).

Criddle, B. (1997) 'MPs and Candidates', in D. Butler and D. Kavanagh (eds) *The British General Election of 1997* (Macmillan).

Criddle, B. (2002) 'MPs and Candidates', in D. Butler and D. Kavanagh (eds) *The British General Election of 2001* (Macmillan).

Criddle, B. (2005) 'MPs and Candidates', in D. Kavanagh and D. Butler (eds) *The British General Election of 2005* (Palgrave Macmillan).

Doig, A. (2001) 'Sleaze: Picking up the Threads or "Back to Basics" Scandals?', *Parliamentary Affairs*, Vol. 54, No. 2.

Doig, A. (2002) 'Sleaze Fatigue in "the House of Ill-repute"', *Parliamentary Affairs*, Vol. 55, No. 2.

Drewry, G. (ed.) (1989) *The New Select Committees*, revised edn (Oxford University Press).

Franklin, M. and Norton, P. (eds) (1993) *Parliamentary Questions* (Oxford University Press).

Giddings, P. (ed.) (1995) *Parliamentary Accountability* (Macmillan).

Giddings, P. (ed.) (2005) *The Future of Parliament* (Palgrave Macmillan).

Giddings, P. and Drewry, G. (eds) (2004) *Britain in the European Union* (Palgrave).

Giddings, P. and Irwin, H. (2005) 'Objects and Questions', in P. Giddings (ed.) *The Future of Parliament* (Palgrave Macmillan).

Griffith, J.A.G. and Ryle, M. (1989) *Parliament* (Sweet & Maxwell).

Hansard Society (1993) *Making the Law: Report of the Commission on the Legislative Process* (Hansard Society).

Hansard Society (2004) *Issues in Law-Making 5. Pre-Legislative Scrutiny* (Hansard Society).

Hansard Society Commission on the Communication of Parliamentary Democracy, *Members Only?* (Hansard Society).

Hansard Society Commission on Parliamentary Scrutiny (2001) *The Challenge for Parliament:*

Making Government Accountable (Vacher Dod Publishing).

Hollingsworth, M. (1991) MPs for Hire (Bloomsbury).

Kennon, A. (2004) 'Pre-legislative Scrutiny of Draft Bills', Public Law, Autumn, pp. 477–94.

Kelso, A. (2009) Parliamentary reform at Westminster (Manchester University Press).

King, A. (1981) 'The Rise of the Career Politician in Britain – and its Consequences', British Journal of Political Science, Vol. 11.

Levy, J. (2009) Strengthening Parliament's Powers of Scrutiny? (The Constitution Unit, University College London).

Mezey, M. (1979) Comparative Legislatures (Duke University Press).

Modernisation of the House of Commons Select Committee (2006) House of Commons, The Legislative Process, First Report, Session 2005–06, HC 1097 (The Stationery Office).

Modernisation of the House of Commons Select Committee (2007) House of Commons, Revitalising the Chamber: The Role of the Back-bench Member, First Report, Session 2006–07, HC 337 (The Stationery Office).

Norris, P. (1997) 'The Puzzle of Constituency Service', The Journal of Legislative Studies, Vol. 3, No. 2.

Norton, P. (1979) 'The Organization of Parliamentary Parties', in S.A. Walkland (ed.) The House of Commons in the Twentieth Century (Oxford University Press).

Norton, P. (ed.) (1990) Legislatures (Oxford University Press).

Norton, P. (1993) Does Parliament Matter? (Harvester Wheatsheaf).

Norton, P. (1994) 'The Parliamentary Party and Party Committees', in A. Seldon and S. Ball (eds) Conservative Century: The Conservative Party since 1900 (Oxford University Press).

Norton, P. (ed.) (1996) National Parliaments and the European Union (Cass).

Norton, P. (1997) 'The United Kingdom: Restoring Confidence?', Parliamentary Affairs, Vol. 50, No. 3.

Norton, P. (ed.) (1998) Parliaments and Governments in Western Europe (Cass).

Norton, P. (1999a) 'The United Kingdom: Parliament Under Pressure', in P. Norton (ed.) Parliaments and Pressure Groups in Western Europe (Cass).

Norton, P. (1999b) 'The House of Commons: The Half Empty Bottle of Reform', in B. Jones (ed.) Political Issues in Britain Today, 5th edn (Manchester University Press).

Norton, P. (2001a) 'Playing by the Rules: The Constraining Hand of Parliamentary Procedure', The Journal of Legislative Studies, Vol. 7.

Norton, P. (2001b) 'Parliament', in A. Seldon (ed.) The Blair Effect (Little, Brown).

Norton, P. (ed.) (2002) Parliaments and Citizens in Western Europe (Cass).

Norton, P. (2004) 'Parliament and Legislative Scrutiny: an Overview of Issues in the Legislative Process', in A. Brazier (ed.) Parliament, Politics and Law Making (Hansard Society).

Norton, P. (2005) Parliament in British Politics (Palgrave Macmillan).

Norton, P. (2007) 'Four Models of Political Representation: British MPs and the Use of ICT', The Journal of Legislative Studies, Vol. 13.

Norton, P. and Wood, D. (1993) Back from Westminster (University Press of Kentucky).

Oliver, D. and Drewry, G. (eds) (1998) The Law and Parliament (Butterworth).

Power, G. (1996) Reinventing Westminster (Charter 88).

Power, G. (1998) Representing the People: MPs and their Constituents (Fabian Society).

Procedure Committee, House of Commons (1990) The Working of the Select Committee System, Session 1989–90, HC 19 (HMSO).

Procedure Committee, House of Commons (2009a) Written Parliamentary Questions, Third Report, Session 2008–09, HC 859 (The Stationery Office).

Procedure Committee, House of Commons (2009b) e-Petitions: Call for Government Action, Second Report, Session 2008–09, HC 493 (The Stationery Office).

Public Administration Committee, House of Commons (2008) Lobbying: Access and Influence in Whitehall, First Report, Session 2008–09, HC 36–I (The Stationery Office).

Riddell, P. (1993) Honest Opportunism (Hamish Hamilton).

Riddell, P. (2000) Parliament Under Blair (Politico's).

Rogers, R. and Walters, R. (2006) How Parliament Works, 6th edn (Longman).

Rush, M. (ed.) (1979) 'Members of Parliament', in S.A. Walkland (ed.) The House of Commons in the Twentieth Century (Oxford University Press).

Rush, M. (1990) *Pressure Politics* (Oxford University Press).

Rush, M. (2001) *The Role of the Member of Parliament Since 1868* (Oxford University Press).

Rush, M. (2005) *How Parliament Works* (Manchester University Press).

Somit, A. and Roemmele, A. (1995) 'The Victorious Legislative Incumbent as a Threat to Democracy: a Nine Nation Study', *American Political Science Association: Legislative Studies Section Newsletter*, Vol. 18, No. 2, July.

Weir, S. and Beetham, D. (1999) *Political Power and Democratic Control in Britain* (Routledge).

Useful websites

Parliamentary websites

Parliament: www.parliament.uk

Parliamentary Committees: www.parliament.uk/
business/committees.cfm

Guide to parliamentary committees:
www.parliament.uk/about/how/committees.cfm

Factsheets: www.parliament.uk/parliamentary_
publications_and_archives/factsheets.cfm

Parliamentary education service:
www.parliament.uk/education/index.htm

Register of Members' Interests: www.publications.
parliament.uk/pa/cm/cmregmem.htm

Hansard: www.publications.parliament.uk/pa/cm/
cmhansrd.htm

Other related websites

Commission to Strengthen Parliament (the Norton Report):   www.conservatives.com/pdf/norton.pdf

Hansard Society for Parliamentary Government:
www.hansard-society.org.uk

CHAPTER 16

The House of Lords

Philip Norton

Learning objectives

- To describe the nature, development and role of the House of Lords.

- To identify the extent and consequences of fundamental changes made to the House in recent years.

- To assess proposals for further change to the second chamber.

Introduction

The House of Lords serves as the second chamber in a **bicameral legislature**. The bicameral system that the United Kingdom now enjoys has been described as one of asymmetrical bicameralism. That is, there are two chambers, but one is politically inferior to the other. The role of the second chamber in relation to the first moved in the twentieth century from being co-equal to subordinate. As a subordinate chamber, it has carried out tasks that have been recognised as useful to the political system, but it has never fully escaped criticism for the nature of its composition. It was variously reformed at different times in the twentieth century, the most dramatic change coming at the end of the century. Debate continues as to what form the second chamber should take in the twenty-first century.

The House of Lords is remarkable for its longevity. What makes this longevity all the more remarkable are two features peculiar to the House. The first is that it has never been an elected chamber. The second is that, until 1999, the membership of the House was based principally on the hereditary principle. The bulk of the membership comprised **hereditary peers**. Only at the end of the twentieth century were most of the hereditary peers removed. The removal of the hereditary peers was not accompanied by a move to an elected second chamber. Whether the United Kingdom is to have an elected or unelected second chamber remains a matter of dispute. It perhaps says something for the work of the House of Lords that the contemporary debate revolves around what form the second chamber should take rather than whether or not the United Kingdom should have a second chamber.

What, then, is the history of the House of Lords? How has it changed over the past century? What tasks does it currently fulfil? And what shape is it likely to take in the future?

■ History

The House of Lords is generally viewed by historians as having its origins in the Anglo-Saxon *Witenagemot* and more especially its Norman successor, the *Curia Regis* (Court of the King). Two features of the King's *Curia* of the twelfth and thirteenth centuries were to remain central characteristics of the House of Lords. One was the basic composition, comprising the **lords spiritual** and the **lords temporal**. At the time of the Magna Carta, the *Curia* comprised the leading prelates of the kingdom (archbishops, bishops and abbots) and the earls and chief barons. The main change, historically, was to be the shift in balance between the two: the churchmen – the lords spiritual – moved from being a dominant to being a small part of the House. The other significant feature was the basis on which members were summoned. The King's tenants-in-chief attended court because of their position. Various minor barons were summoned because the King wished them to attend. 'From the beginning the will of the king was an element in determining its make up' (White 1908:

299). If a baron regularly received a summons to court, the presumption grew that the summons would be issued to his heir. A body thus developed that peers attended on the basis of a strictly hereditary dignity without reference to tenure. The result was to be a House of Lords based on the principle of heredity, with writs of summons being personal to the recipients. Members were not summoned to speak on behalf of some other individuals or bodies. Any notion of representativeness was squeezed out. Even the lords spiritual – who served by reason of their position in the established Church – were summoned to take part in a personal capacity.

The lack of any representative capacity led to the House occupying a position of political – and later legal – inferiority to the House of Commons. As early as the fifteenth century, the privilege of initiating measures of taxation was conceded to the Lower House. The most significant shift, though, took place in the nineteenth century. As we have seen (Chapter 15), the effect of the Reform Acts was to consign the Lords to a recognisably subordinate role to that of the Commons, although not until the passage of

The statue of Richard the Lionheart stands outside the entrance to the House of Lords
Source: One-Image Photography / Alamy

the Parliament Act of 1911 was that role confirmed by statute. Under the terms of the Act, the House could delay a non-money bill for no more than two sessions, and money bills (those dealing exclusively with money, and so certified by the Speaker) were to become law one month after leaving the Commons whether approved by the House of Lords or not. Bills to prolong the life of a parliament, along with delegated legislation and bills originating in the House of Lords, were excluded from the provisions of the Act. The two-session veto over non-money bills was reduced to one session by the Parliament Act of 1949.

The subordinate position of the House of Lords to the House of Commons was thus established. However, the House remained a subject of political controversy. The hereditary principle was attacked by those who saw no reason for membership of the second chamber to be determined by accident of privileged birth. It was attacked as well because the bulk of the membership tended to favour the Conservative cause. Ever since the eighteenth cen-

tury, when William Pitt the Younger created peers on an unprecedented scale, the Conservatives enjoyed a political ascendancy (if not always an absolute majority) in the House. In other words, occupying a subordinate position did not render the House acceptable: the composition of the House, however much it was subordinated to the Commons, was unacceptable. There were some attempts in the period of Conservative government from 1951 to 1964 to render it more acceptable, not by removing hereditary peers or destroying the Conservative predominance but rather by supplementing the existing membership with a new type of membership. The Life Peerages Act 1958 made provision for people to be made members for life of the House of Lords, their titles – and their entitlement to a seat in the House of Lords – to cease upon their death. This was designed to strengthen the House by allowing people who objected to the hereditary principle to become members. Following the 1958 Act, few hereditary peerages were created. None was created under Labour governments, and only one

Conservative Prime Minister, Margaret Thatcher, nominated any (and then only three – Harold Macmillan, who became the Earl of Stockton; George Thomas, former Speaker of the House of Commons; and William Whitelaw, her Deputy Prime Minister). The 1963 Peerages Act made provision for hereditary peers who wished to do so to disclaim their titles. Prior to 1999, these were the most important measures to affect the membership of the House. Although both measures – and especially the 1958 Act – had significant consequences, pressure continued for more radical reform. In 1999, acting on a commitment embodied in the Labour manifesto in the 1997 general election, the Labour government achieved passage of the House of Lords Act. This removed from membership of the House all but ninety-two of the hereditary members. The effect was to transform the House from one composed predominantly of hereditary peers to one composed overwhelmingly of **life peers**. However, the removal of the hereditary peers was seen as but one stage in a process of reform. The House of Lords created by their removal was deemed to be an interim House, to remain in place while proposals for a second stage of reform were considered. The issue of what should constitute the second stage of reform has proved highly contentious.

■ Membership

Until the passage of the House of Lords Act, which removed most hereditary peers from membership, the House of Lords had more than 1,000 members, making it the largest regularly sitting legislative chamber in the world. Its size was hardly surprising given the number of peers created over the centuries by each succeeding monarch, although the largest increase was in the twentieth century. In 1906, the House had a membership of 602. In January 1999, it had 1,296. Of those, 759 were hereditary peers. (The figure includes one prince and three dukes of the blood royal.) The remaining members comprised 485 life peers, 26 peers created under the Appellate Jurisdiction Act 1876 (the law lords, appointed to carry out the judicial business of the House) and 26 lords spiritual (the 2 archbishops and 24 senior bishops of the Church of England). With the removal of all but 92 of the hereditary peers, the House remains a relatively large one. In the immediate wake of the removal of the hereditary peers, the House had 666 members. With new creations and deaths, the figure has fluctuated since, but with a clear upward trajectory. By July 2009, there were 739 members. (Though, of these, 12 were on leave of absence, 2 were suspended until the end of the session and 1 was disqualified while serving as an MEP.) Of these 739, 598 were life peers created under the provisions of the 1958 Act.

The membership of the House has thus been affected dramatically by the 1958 Life Peerages Act and the 1999 House of Lords Act. In many respects, the former made possible the latter, creating a new pool of members who could serve once hereditary peers were removed. Indeed, the creation of life peerages under the 1958 Act had a dramatic effect on the House in terms both of composition and activity. The impact of the 1999 Act will be considered in greater detail later.

■ Composition

In terms of composition, the 1958 Act made possible a substantial increase in the number of Labour members. Previously, Labour members had been in a notable minority. In 1924, when Labour first formed a minority government, the party had only one supporter in the Upper House. The position changed only gradually. In 1945, there were 18 Labour peers. Forty-four Labour peers were created in the period of Labour government from 1945 to 1951, but their successors did not always support the Labour Party. By 1999, there were only 17 hereditary peers sitting on the Labour benches. Life peerages enabled Labour's ranks to be swelled over time. Prominent Labour supporters who objected to hereditary peerages were prepared to accept life peerages, so various former ministers, ex-MPs, trade union leaders and other public figures were elevated to the House of Lords. At the beginning of 1999, there were more than 150 life peers sitting on the Labour benches. Apart from former ministers and MPs, they included figures such as the broadcaster Melvyn Bragg, film producer David Puttnam, crime writer Ruth Rendell, and TV presenter, professor and doctor Robert Winston. Further creations helped bring the number above 200 and by December 2005 there were 210 Labour peers as against 207 Conservatives. A combination of more Labour creations and the death of a number of Conservative peers has further widened the gap.

Table 16.1 Composition of the House of Lords, July 2009

By party Party	Life Peers	Hereditary: elected by party	Hereditary: elected office holders	Hereditary: * royal office holder	Bishops	Total
Conservative	145	39	9	0	0	193
Labour	211	2	2	0	0	215
Liberal Democrat	66	3	2	0	0	71
Cross-bench	169	29	2	2	0	202
Bishops	0	0	0	0	26	26
Other**	15	2	0	0	0	17
Total	606	75	15	2	26	724

NB Excludes 12 Members who are on leave of absence, 2 who are suspended and 1 disqualified as an MEP

By type	Men	Women	Total
Archbishops and bishops	26	0	26
Life Peers under the Appellate Jurisdiction Act 1876	22	1	23
Life Peers under the Life Peerages Act 1958	452	146	598
Peers under House of Lords Act 1999	90	2	92
Total	590	149	739

* These are: The Marquess of Cholmondeley, Lord Great Chamberlain (Crossbench), The Duke of Norfolk, Earl Marshal (Crossbench)

** These are:

Non-affiliated – L. Archer of Weston-Super-Mare; L. Black of Crossharbour; L. Brabazon of Tara; B. Clark of Calton; B. Ford; B. Hayman, Lord Speaker; L. Jacobs; L. Kalms; L. Roper; L. Smith of Finsbury; L. Triesman; L. Watson of Invergowrie; B. Young of Old Scone

L. Pearson of Rannoch: UKIP; L. Willoughby de Broke: UKIP; L. Stevens of Ludgate: Conservative Independent; L. Stoddart of Swindon: Independent Labour

Source: www.parliament.uk

The creation of life peers from 1958 onwards served to lessen the party imbalance in the House. In 1945, Conservative peers accounted for 50.4 per cent of the membership. In 1998, the figure was 38.4 per cent (Baldwin 1999). Before 1999, the second-largest category in the House comprised those peers who choose to sit independently of party ranks and occupy the cross-benches in the House. At the beginning of 1999 – that is, in the pre-reform House – the state of the parties was Conservative 473, Labour 168, Liberal Democrats 67 and cross-benchers 322. This left in excess of 250 other peers who did not align themselves with any of these groupings. The effect of the removal of most heredi-tary peers in 1999 was to create greater equality between the two main parties, leaving the balance of power being held by the cross-benchers and the Liberal Democrats. The composition of the House, in July 2009, is given in Table 16.1.

The creation of life peers drawn from modest backgrounds has also served to affect the social profile of the membership. Hereditary peers were typically drawn from the cream of upper-class society. Life peers were drawn from a more diverse social background. However, even with the influx of life peers, the membership remained, and remains, socially atypical. Life peerages are normally con-ferred on those who have achieved some particular distinction in society, be it social, cultural, sporting, economic or political. By the time the recipients have achieved such a distinction, they are, by definition, atypical. There was therefore little chance of the House becoming socially typical. Members of the House are drawn notably from backgrounds in the law, the Civil Service and the teaching profession, these three categories account-ing for nearly 40 per cent of the membership (Criddle *et al.* 2005: 34–5). The next largest category – accounting for just nearly 5 per cent of the membership – is that of trade union officials. The House is also atypical in terms of age and gender. Given that peerages tend to be given to those who have already achieved something in life and that they entail service for life, it is not surprising that the average age of the membership is 68. It is rare for people to be made life peers while in their 20s or 30s. Television mogul Lord Alli (born 1964) was elevated to the peerage in 1998 at the age of 34.

The Chamber of the House of Lords
Source: Rolf Richardson / Alamy

Lawyer and Conservative Party vice-chair Baroness Warsi (b. 1971) became a peer in 2007 at the age of 36. The hereditary peerage produced some young peers, succeeding their fathers at an early age, but they were small in number and largely disappeared as a result of the House of Lords Act, though not entirely: in 2009, of the ten youngest peers, five were hereditary peers. One of them, Lord Freyberg (born 1970), entered the House at the age of 23. Women, who were first admitted to the House under the provisions of the 1958 Life Peerages Act, also constitute a minority of the membership, but a growing one. In 1990, there were 80 women in the House, constituting 7 per cent of the membership. The removal of a large number of – overwhelmingly male – hereditary peers and the creation of more women life peers has meant that the number, and proportion, of women peers has increased notably. In July 2009, there were 149 women peers, constituting just over 20 per cent of the membership. Of these, all bar two held life peerages. Recent years have seen several black and Asian peers created, although they constitute a small proportion of the total. There are also a number of openly gay peers, including Lord Alli, Cabinet minister Lord Mandelson, former cabinet minister Lord Smith of Finsbury, and former head of BP Lord Brown of Maddingley.

There has been another consequence of life peerages in terms of the membership of the House. It has brought into the House a body of individuals who are frequently expert in a particular area or have experience in a particular field. This claim is not exclusive to life peers – some hereditary peers are notable for their expertise or experience in particular fields – but it is associated predominantly with them. This has led to claims that when the House debates a subject, however arcane it may be, there is usually one or more experts in the House to discuss it (Baldwin 1985). Thus, for example, in a short debate on the contribution of science, technology and engineering to the United Kingdom, held on 4 June 2009 and introduced by the President of the Environment Industries Commission, the speakers included the President of the Royal Society; a research neuroscientist and director of the Royal Institution of the UK; the honorary chairman of Cambridge University's technology transfer office and director of several high-technology companies; the director of the Warwick Manufacturing Group at Warwick University; the chairman of the Foundation for Science and Technology; and a peer who had spent more than 20 years in consulting engineering as an engineering designer and 25 years as an engineering journalist. The minister replying to the debate was himself a former development engineer with a PhD in robotics who had chaired the BioIndustry Association. This claim to expertise in many fields is often contrasted with membership of the House of Commons, where the career politician – expert in the practice of politics – dominates. The body of expertise and experience serves, as we shall see, to bolster the capacity of the House to fulfil a number of its functions.

■ Activity

The creation of life peers also had a dramatic effect on the activity of the House. In the 1950s, the House met at a leisurely pace and was poorly attended. Peers have never been paid a salary and many members, like the minor barons in the thirteenth century, found attending to be a chore, sometimes an expensive one: the practice, as in the thirteenth century, was to stay away. The House rarely met for more than three days a week, and each sitting was usually no more than three or four hours in length. For most of the decade, the average daily attendance did not reach three figures. Little interest was shown in its activities by most of its own members; not surprisingly, little interest was shown by those outside the House.

This was to change significantly in each succeeding decade (see Figure 16.1). Life peers were disproportionately active. Although they constituted a minority of the House, they came to constitute a

Session	Average daily attendance
2002–03	362
2003–04	368
2004–05	388
2005–06	403
2006–07	415
2007–08	413

Figure 16.1 Average daily attendance in the chamber, 2002–2008
Source: House of Lords (2008) *The Work of the House of Lords 2007–08*. © Parliamentary copyright 2008. Parliamentary copyright material is reproduced with the permission of the Controller of Her Majesty's Stationery Office (HMSO) on behalf of Parliament

majority of the most active members of the House. The effect of the increasing numbers of life peers was apparent in the attendance of members. Peers attended in ever greater numbers and the House sat for longer. Late-night sittings, virtually unknown in the 1950s and for much of the 1960s, became regular features. In the 1980s and 1990s, the average daily sitting was six or seven hours. By the end of the 1980s, more than 800 peers – two-thirds of the membership – attended one or more sittings each year and, of those, more than 500 contributed to debate. By the time of the House of Lords Act in 1999, the House was boasting a better attendance in the chamber than the House of Commons. The effect of the 1999 Act was to result in a House in which the active members dominated. Although the membership halved in 1999, the daily attendance hardly changed. Whereas the average daily attendance figure for 1992–3 constituted just under one-third of the membership, that for the post-reform 2003–4 session constitutes more than half. In the 2003–4 session, 50 per cent of the members attended 65 per cent or more of the sittings – a remarkable achievement given that many members had full-time posts outside the House, attending in order to give the benefit of their expertise. The House now witnesses an average daily attendance that exceeds 400 (Figure 16.1).

One other consequence of the more active House was that the number of votes increased. They were few and far between in the 1950s, about ten to twenty a year. By the 1980s and 1990s, the figure was usually closer to 200. The political composition of the House meant that a Labour government was vulnerable to defeat. In the period of Labour government from 1974 to 1979, the government suffered 362 defeats at the hands of the House of Lords. However, Conservative governments were not immune. The preponderance of Conservative peers did not always translate into a majority for a Conservative government. In the period of Conservative government from 1979 to 1997, ministers suffered just over 250 defeats in the House. The government was vulnerable to a combination of opposition parties, the cross-benchers and, on occasion, some of its own supporters. The Labour government elected in 1997 was vulnerable to defeat, at least for the first two sessions, because of the large number of Conservative peers. Since the removal of most hereditary peers in 1999, it cannot be defeated by the Conservatives alone but is vulnerable to defeat because of a combination of opposition parties or

of the opposition and cross-benchers or of all the opposition parties and a preponderance of cross-benchers. From 1997 through to May 2009, the government suffered 489 defeats; of these, 419 took place in the post-1999 reformed House. A future Conservative government will be as vulnerable to the same combination of forces as the Labour government; as such, both parties now enjoy equality in the House.

The House also became more visible to the outside world. In 1985, television cameras were allowed to broadcast proceedings. There was a four-year gap before the televising of Commons proceedings began: in those four years, the House of Lords enjoyed exclusive television coverage. In the 1990s, the House was also ahead of the House of Commons in appointing an information officer and seeking to ensure better public understanding of its role and activities. The Information Office of the House has been highly active in disseminating information about the work of the House, generating booklets and information packs for which the House of Commons has no equivalent.

■ Procedures

The House differs significantly from the Commons not only in its size, composition and remuneration (peers can claim allowances to cover travel, accommodation, subsistence and some secretarial support, but they still receive no salary) but also in its procedures. The presiding officer of the House, who sits on the Woolsack, has no powers to call peers to speak or to enforce order. The maintenance of the rules of order is the responsibility of the House itself, although peers usually look to the Leader of the House to give a lead. Peers wishing to speak in a set-piece debate, such as a second reading debate, submit their names in advance (they can now do so electronically), and a list of speakers is circulated shortly prior to the debate. Peers then rise to speak in the order on the list. At other times, as in Question Time, if two peers rise at the same time, one is expected to give way. (If neither does so, other peers make clear their preference as to who should speak by shouting out the name of the person they wish to hear.) If a speaker strays from what is permissible, other peers shout 'Order'. If a speaker goes on for too long, it is always open to another peer to rise and call attention to the fact (a task normally undertaken by the government whip on duty) or, in extreme cases, to move the motion 'That the noble peer be no longer heard', but this is a device rarely employed. The Lords remains a more chamber-oriented institution than the Commons, although – as we shall see – it is making more use of committees than before. Although the House votes more frequently than it used to, the number of divisions in the Lords is fewer than in the Commons. (There will usually be about three times as many votes each year in the Commons as in the Lords.) This in part reflects the recognition by peers of the political predominance of the elected chamber. Peers are often reluctant to press issues to a vote and rarely do so on the principle of a measure. By virtue of an agreement reached between the two party leaders in the Lords in 1945, the House does not divide on the second reading of any bill promised in the government's election manifesto and, by extension now, any bill appearing in the government's programme for the session. This is known as the Salisbury convention, named after the Conservative leader in the Lords who enunciated it.

There are also two other features where it differs from the Commons and which enhance its capacity to affect the outcome of legislation. First, the House discusses all amendments tabled to bills. In the Commons, the chair selects only a limited number for debate. Second, there are no timetable (guillotine) motions. Debate continues so long as peers wish to speak. There are also considerable opportunities for peers to raise issues in the House. Some debates are time-limited (although not the committee and report stages of bills) and a fifteen-minute time limit operates for backbench speeches in set-piece debates. Peers keep their speeches even shorter if a great many of them sign up to speak in a time-limited debate. Time limits force peers to think about what they want to say and to ensure that they focus on the main points. The results tend to be a series of short, informed and often highly educative speeches.

■ Functions

The debate about reform of the House of Lords has focused largely, though not wholly, on its composition. The functions of the House – the tasks that it carries out – have not generated as much controversy. There has been a wide body of agreement

that the functions it fulfilled in the twentieth century, and continues to fulfil in the twenty-first, are appropriate to a second chamber. As we shall see, this view is not necessarily held by all those expressing views on the House of Lords. Nonetheless, the view has tended to predominate among those engaged in the debate, including the government of the day. The functions are broadly similar to those of the Commons but not as extensive. The extent to which they differ derives from the fact that politically the House is no longer co-equal with the Commons.

Legitimisation

The House fulfils the functions of both manifest and latent legitimisation, but on a modest scale. It is called upon to give the seal of approval to bills, but if it fails to give that approval, it can be overridden later by the House of Commons under the provisions of the Parliament Acts. Only in very rare circumstances – as in the case of a bill to lengthen the life of a parliament, secondary legislation or (somewhat more significantly) bills originating in the Lords – is its veto absolute. By virtue of being one of the two chambers of Parliament and by fulfilling the functions it does effectively, the House may have a limited claim to fulfilling a function of latent legitimisation. It is a long-established part of the nation's constitutional arrangements. However, such a claim is offset by the House having no claim to being a representative assembly – neither speaking for particular bodies in society nor being socially typical – and by its limited legislative authority. A claim to traditional authority has been superseded by a claim to specialised knowledge, the House being able to draw on experience and expertise in considering the measures before it, but that 'technocratic' legitimacy is not on a par with the legitimacy of the elected chamber.

Recruitment

The House provides some of the personnel of government. As we have seen (Chapter 9), ministers are drawn from Parliament and, by convention, predominantly now from the elected House.

The Prime Minister appoints a number of ministers from the Upper House primarily for political and managerial reasons. Although the government is normally assured of getting its bills through the House, it is not necessarily guaranteed getting them through in the form it wants them. It is therefore prudent to have ministers in the Lords in order to explain bills and to marshal support. In addition, the House provides a pool from which the Prime Minister can draw in order to supplement ministers drawn from the Commons. The advantage offered by peers is that, with no constituency responsibilities, they are able to devote more time to ministerial work than is the case with ministers who do have constituency duties. It also has the advantage of widening the pool of talent available to the Prime Minister. Someone from outside Parliament can be elevated to the peerage at the same time as being appointed to government office. Both Tony Blair and his successor, Gordon Brown, made use of this power to enhance the ranks of their ministerial team, each bringing in a range of people from industry (Lord Sainsbury, Lord Simon of Highbury, Lord Jones of Birmingham, Baroness Vadera), the law (Lord Falconer of Thoroton), broadcasting (Lord MacDonald of Tradeston, Lord Carter of Barnes), the health service (Lord Darzi), finance (Lord Myners, Lord Davies of Abersoch), the military (Admiral Lord West), the EU (Lord Mandelson, Baroness Kinnock), the UN (Lord Malloch-Brown) as well as some Downing Street advisers (Baroness Morgan of Huyton, Lord Adonis), to serve as ministers.

Ministerial appointments in the Lords have also enabled women politicians to be promoted. Five women have served as Leaders of the House of Lords (Baroness Young 1981–2, Baroness Jay 1998–2001, Baroness Amos 2003–07, Baroness Ashton 2007–08, and Baroness Royall 2008–). Of the ministers in the Lords in mid-2009, approximately one-third were women. Baroness Amos was the first black woman to serve in the Cabinet. Baroness Scotland was the first woman and first black person to serve as Attorney General.

However, the number of ministers appointed in the Lords is relatively small. At least two peers have traditionally served in the Cabinet (Lord Chancellor and Leader of the House) but usually no more than four. Four is a rarity and two, until 2005, the norm. Under the Constitutional Reform Act 2005, the Lord Chancellor need no longer be a peer; Jack Straw was the first MP to be appointed to the post. There is thus now only the Leader of the House who sits automatically in the Cabinet. However, there have been occasions when a peer has been appointed to head a department. Gordon Brown appointed two peers to head departments: Business Secretary Lord Mandelson and Transport Secretary Lord Adonis. Usually about 20 other ministers are drawn from the Lords, supplemented by eight whips (including the Chief Whip). The number of ministers does not match the number of ministries, with the result that the whips have to take on responsibility for answering for particular departments – another difference from the House of Commons, where the whips have no responsibility for appearing at the despatch box. A frequent speaker at the despatch box is the government deputy chief whip, who often represents one or more senior departments without a junior minister. Even with a small number of posts to be filled, governments have on occasion had difficulty in finding suitable peers for ministerial office. It used to be the case that Conservative governments had sometimes to draw on young hereditary peers. Labour governments were limited by the relatively small number of Labour peers. The creation of life peerages in recent years, quantitatively and qualitatively, has widened the pool of talent. Both sides have tended to use the Whips' Office as a training ground for substantive ministerial office.

Scrutiny and influence

It is in its remaining functions that the House of Lords is significant. The House performs an important role as an agent of scrutiny and influence. The House does not undertake the task of scrutiny on behalf of constituents, as peers have none. Rather, the House undertakes a more general task of scrutiny. Three features of the House render it particularly suitable for the detailed scrutiny of legislation. First, as an unelected House, it cannot claim the legitimacy to reject the principle of measures agreed by the elected House. Thus, basically by default, it focuses on the detail rather than the principle. Second, as we have noted already, its membership includes people who have distinguished themselves in particular fields – such as the sciences, the law, education, business, industrial relations – who can look at relevant legislation from the perspective of practitioners in the field rather than from the perspective of elected party politicians. And, third, the House has the time to debate non-money bills in more detail than is usually possible in the Commons – as we have seen, there is no provision for a guillotine, and all amendments are discussed. The House thus serves as an important revising chamber, trying to ensure that a bill is well drafted and internally coherent. In order to improve the bill, it will often make amendments, most of which will be accepted by the Commons. In terms of legislative scrutiny, the House has thus developed a role that is viewed as complementary to, rather than one competing with (or identical to), that of the Commons.

The value of the House as a revising chamber is shown by the number of amendments it makes to legislation. Most of these are moved by the government itself, but a significant proportion of these are amendments promised by government in response to comments made by backbench members. Each session, the House will typically agree 1,000 to 4,000 amendments to bills. (In the 1999–2000 session, the number of amendments made totalled 4,761, constituting an all-time record.) In the 2007–08 session, of 7,259 amendments that were tabled, 2,625 were agreed (House of Lords 2008).

Even these figures do not do justice to the scrutiny undertaken by the Lords. The scrutiny is frequently constructive and is acknowledged as such by the government. Thus, for example, during the 1998–9 session, 108 non-government amendments were moved to the Access to Justice Bill. Of these, 71 received a ministerial response that was positive. The responses were important not only for their number but also for their range: they included promising to consider points raised in debate (28 occasions), accepting the principle of an amendment (21 occasions) and promising to draw a point to the attention of those responsible for drafting the bill (three occasions) (Norton 1999). Ten amendments were accepted as they stood. The constructive work undertaken by the House was conceded by the Lord Chancellor, Lord Irvine of Lairg, at the conclusion of the bill's passage through the House. The importance of these figures lay not only in the number of constructive responses from government but also in the fact that it is difficult to envisage scrutiny in the House of Commons producing such a response.

This role in scrutinising legislation – in so far as it constitutes a 'second look' at legislation – is of special importance given that it has been characterised as one of the two core functions of the House (Norton 1999), meaning that it is a function that is particular to the House as the second chamber. It is not a function that the House of Commons can carry out, since it is difficult if not impossible for it to act as a revising chamber for its own measures; that has been likened to asking the same doctor for a second opinion. The role of the House as a revising chamber is thus offered as being central to the case for retain-

ing a second chamber. It is also the role that occupies the most time in the House: usually about 50 to 60 per cent is devoted to considering legislation.

The House also scrutinises, and on occasion influences, government policy. Peers can debate policy in a less partisan atmosphere than the Commons and are not subject to the constituency and party influences that dominate in the elected House. They are therefore in a position to debate issues of public policy that may not be at the heart of the partisan battle and which, consequently, receive little attention in the Commons. Given their backgrounds, peers are also often – although not always – able to debate public policy from the perspective of those engaged in the subject. The House is able to debate higher education, for example, with considerable authority. The Lords contains several distinguished academics and members with experience in higher education (university chancellors, vice-chancellors and pro-vice-chancellors, masters of university colleges, peers who have chaired HE funding bodies, led inquiries into higher education, and former secretaries of state for education); although the House of Commons contains some former university lecturers, it does not have members with the same experience and status in education as those in the Upper House.

Expression

The House, like the Commons, also fulfils a number of expressive functions. It can bring issues onto the political agenda in a way not always possible in the Commons. MPs are wary of raising issues that may not be popular with constituents and that have little salience in terms of party politics. Peers are answerable to no one but themselves. They can raise whatever issues they feel need raising. The House may thus debate issues of concern to particular groups in society that MPs are not willing to address. Formally, it is not a function the House is expected to fulfil. Indeed, according to *Erskine May*, the parliamentary 'bible' on procedure, Lords may indicate that an outside body agrees with the substance of their views, but they should avoid creating an impression that they are speaking as representatives of outside bodies. Thus, not only is the House not a representative assembly, it should avoid giving the impression of being one! In practice, peers take up issues that concern them, often alerted to the issue by outside bodies. Peers are frequently lobbied by outside organisations. One extensive survey in the 1990s found that half of the groups surveyed were in touch with peers at least once a month, and almost one in five were in contact on a weekly basis (Baggott 1995: 93, 164). Each peer receives letters each year usually running into four figures, most from outside organisations. Some groups write to ask peers to move amendments to bills, some merely keep members informed of what is happening with the organisation, and some are keen that peers raise issues with government, if necessary on the floor of the House. Some peers are particularly active in raising the concerns of particular groups, such as farmers, the disabled, the terminally ill, or the people of Zimbabwe, or pursuing very particular issues, such as railways, the effects of smoking or the upkeep of war graves.

The House also has the potential to express views to citizens and influence their stance on public policy. The function is limited by the absence of any democratic legitimacy, the capacity to influence deriving from the longevity of the House and its place as one of the two chambers of Parliament, as well as from the authority of the individual peers who may be involved. However, the scope for fulfilling this function is somewhat greater than in the House of Commons, simply because more time is available for it in the House of Lords. Between 20 and 30 per cent of the time of the House is given over each session to debates on motions tabled by peers: about 20 per cent of time is given over to general debates, and between 4 and 10 per cent of the time is given over to questions for short debate (QSDs), each lasting for 60 or 90 minutes.

Other functions

To these functions may be added a number of others, some of which are peculiar to the Upper House. Foremost among these historically has been the judicial function. The House until 2009 constituted the highest court of appeal within the United Kingdom. Although formally a function residing in the House as a whole, in practice it was carried out by a judicial committee comprising twelve **law lords** – judges specially appointed to the House to enable it to fulfil its judicial role – and peers who have held high judicial office. The law lords, though members of the House, avoided speaking on any matters that may be deemed partisan or involve measures on which they may later have had to adjudicate in a judicial capacity. They also normally abstained from voting, though on occasion a law lord voted on

an issue that had been the subject of a free vote. However, this long-standing judicial function ceased to reside in the House in 2009, when a new supreme court, created under the Constitutional Reform Act 2005, came into being (see Chapter 13) and the law lords moved from the Palace of Westminster to form the justices of the new court.

Like the Commons, the House also retains a small legislative role, primarily in the form of private members' legislation. Peers can introduce private members' bills, and a small number achieve passage, but it is small – even compared with the number of such bills promoted by MPs. The introduction of such bills by peers is more important in fulfilling an expressive function – allowing views on the subject to be aired – than in fulfilling a legislative role. Time is normally found to debate each private member's bill and, by convention, the government – even if opposed to the measure – does not divide against it. Among contentious issues raised by such bills has been that of decriminalising the actions of those seeking to assist terminally ill individuals who wish to bring their lives to an end (assisted dying). The Assisted Dying Bill introduced by Lord Joffe in the 2004–05 session helped ensure that the issue was discussed and enabled people with views on the issue to make them known. The time given to private members' legislation is important but not extensive: as in the Commons, it occupies usually less than 5 per cent of the time of the House.

The House is also ascribed a distinct role, that of a constitutional safeguard. This is reflected in the provisions of the Parliament Acts. The House, as we have noted, retains a veto over bills to extend the life of a parliament. It is considered a potential brake on a government that seeks to act in a dictatorial or generally unacceptable manner: hence it may use its limited power to amend or, more significantly, to delay a bill. In practice, though, the power is a limited one, as well as one not expected to require action by the House on any regular basis. The House lacks a legitimate elected base of its own that would allow it to act, on a substantial and sustained basis, contrary to the wishes of an elected government. Even so, it constitutes the other core function of the House in that it is a function that the House alone, as the second chamber, can fulfil: the House of Commons cannot act as a constitutional check upon itself.

In combination, these various functions render the House a useful body – especially as a revising chamber and for raising and debating issues on which peers are well informed – but one that is clearly subordinate to the elected chamber. The fact that the House is not elected explains its limited functions; it is also the reason why it is considered particularly suited to fulfil the functions it does retain.

■ Scrutiny and influence

The means available to the House to fulfil the tasks of scrutiny and influence can be considered, as with the Commons, under two heads: legislation and executive actions. The means available to the House are also those available to fulfil its expressive functions.

Legislation

As we have seen, 50 to 60 per cent of the time of the House is given over to legislation. Bills in the Lords have to go through stages analogous to those in the House of Commons. There are, though, differences in procedure. First readings are normally taken formally, but there have been rare occasions when they have been debated: on four occasions (in 1888, 1933, 1943 and 1969) first readings were actually opposed. Second readings, as in the Commons, constitute debates on the principle of the measure. However, votes on second reading are exceptionally rare. Because of the Salisbury convention, the House does not vote on the second reading of government bills. A vote may take place if, as exceptionally happens, a free vote is permitted. This happened in 1990 on the War Crimes Bill and in 1999 on the Sexual Offences (Amendment) Bill to lower the age of consent for homosexual acts to 16. Both bills had been passed by large majorities in the House of Commons but both were rejected, on free votes, in the House of Lords. Both occasions were exceptional. Both measures were later enacted under the provisions of the Parliament Act.

The main work of the House takes place at committee and report stages. For some bills, the committee stage is actually dispensed with. After second reading, a motion may be moved 'That this Bill be not committed' and, if agreed to, the bill then awaits third reading. This procedure is usually employed for supply and money bills when there is no desire to present amendments. For those bills that do receive a committee stage, it is taken either on the floor of the House or in grand committee. Virtually all bills used to be taken on the floor of the House, but now in order to ensure that the House continues to examine all bills in detail, several are considered in grand committee.

The grand committee is, in effect, something of a parallel chamber. It comprises all members of the House and can meet while the House is in session. In practice, attendance is relatively small – comprising those with a particular interest in the measure – permitting sessions to be held in the Moses Room, an ornate committee room just off the Peers' Lobby. In 2007–08, 13 bills were considered in grand committee. Votes cannot take place in grand committee, so amendments can only be accepted if no member objects. (If objection is made, the matter has to be held over to report stage.) Of 1,769 amendments moved in grand committee in 2007–08, 357 were accepted.

More recently, the House has also experimented with sending a bill to a special procedure public bill committee, which is empowered to take oral and written evidence. Of longer standing is the power to refer a bill, or indeed any proposal, to a select committee for detailed investigation. It is a power that has been utilised when it has been considered necessary or desirable to examine witnesses and evidence from outside bodies. Between 1972 and 1991, seven bills were sent to select committees. All bar one of the bills were private members' bills. More recently, select committees have been appointed to consider a major government bill (the Constitutional Reform Bill) and a Private Member's Bill (the Assisted Dying for the Terminally Ill).

Committee stage in the Lords differs notably from committee stage in the Commons. In the Lords, all amendments tabled are debated and – whether on the floor or in Grand Committee – any peer can attend the proceedings. All peers with an interest or expertise in a measure can thus take part, be it for the whole of the committee stage or on particular amendments of interest to them. There is thus the potential for a more thorough consideration than is possible in the Commons. The emphasis is on ensuring that the bill is well drafted and coherent.

Report and third reading provide further opportunities for consideration. Again, all amendments tabled are debated. Report may be used by government to bring forward amendments promised at committee stage and also to offer new amendments of its own. It is also an opportunity for members to return to issues that received an inadequate response by government at committee stage (although amendments rejected by the House at committee stage cannot again be considered). It is also possible for amendments to be made at third reading, and this opportunity is variously employed. The motion for third reading is put formally and agreed to and then amendments are taken. Once they have been dealt with, the motion 'That the Bill do now pass' is put. The result is that some bills, especially large or contentious bills, can and do receive a considerable amount of attention at different stages in the House of Lords.

Executive actions

As in the House of Commons, various means are available for scrutinising the actions of the executive. The principal means available on the floor of the House are those of debate and questions. Off the floor of the House, there are select committees and, at the unofficial level, party meetings.

Debates

Debates, as in the Commons, take place on motions. These may express a particular view, or they may take the form of either 'take note' motions or motions calling for papers. 'Take note' motions are employed in order to allow the House to debate reports from select committees or to discuss topics on which the government wishes to hear peers' views: ministers use 'take note' motions rather than motions calling for papers because with the latter they are responsible for supplying the papers being called for. Motions calling for papers are used by backbenchers to call attention to a particular issue; at the end of the debate it is customary to withdraw the motion, the purpose for which it was tabled – to ensure a debate – having been achieved.

All peers who wish to speak in debate do so, and there is a greater likelihood than in the Commons that the proceedings will constitute what they purport to be: that is, debates. Party ties are less rigid than in the Commons, though nonetheless still strong (see Norton 2003), and peers frequently pay attention to what is being said. Although the order in which peers speak is determined beforehand, it is common practice for a peer who is speaking to give way to interventions. Within the context of the chamber, the chances of a speech having an impact on the thought and even the votes of others are considerably greater than in the more predictable

Lower House. Indeed, it is not unknown for peers when, uncertain as to how to vote, to ask 'what does X think about it?'.

One day each week, up until the Whit recess, is given over to two general debates. (The debate day used to be Wednesday but in 2005 the House agreed to change it to Thursday.) Once a month, the debates are determined by ballot. Peers wishing to have debates submit motions which then appear on the order paper and two are drawn at random by the clerk on a set day. The topics on the remaining debate days are allocated to each of the parties in turn and to the cross-benchers. The two debates last up to a total of five hours. The balloted debates are automatically each of two-and-a-half hours in length. On the party days, the time, within the five-hour maximum, is varied depending on the number of speakers. These general debates are occasions for issues to be raised by backbenchers rather than frontbenchers. The purpose of each short debate is to allow peers to discuss a particular topic rather than to come to a conclusion about it. Topics discussed tend to be non-partisan, and the range is broad. On 21 May 2009, for example, Lord Dixon-Smith moved a motion to call attention to the changes required of society to meet the 2050 carbon dioxide emissions target set by the Climate Change Committee and Lord Moynihan moved a motion to call attention to the impact of disease on the British bee population, the spread of the varroa mite and the consequences for the pollination of crops and fruit. Both motions provided the opportunity for interested peers to offer their views and for ministers to explain the government's position and to reveal what proposals were under consideration by the relevant department. The time devoted to each debate is divided equally among the number of backbench speakers (the opener and the minister replying have fixed time limits) and, in the event of many peers wishing to speak, the time available to each may be as little as four or five minutes.

Questions

Questions taken on the floor in the Lords are of two types: oral questions and questions for short debate (QSD). (Lords may also table questions for written answer, and nowadays they do so in increasing numbers: often more than 5,000 a session.) Oral questions are taken in Question Time at the start of each sitting: the House sits at 2.30 p.m. on Monday and Tuesday, 3.00 p.m. on Wednesday and 11.00 a.m. on

NOTICES AND ORDERS OF THE DAY

Tuesday 28 April 2009 at 2.30pm

Lord Collins of Mapesbury *will be introduced as a Lord of Appeal in Ordinary*

*Oral questions, 30 minutes

*Lord Dykes to ask Her Majesty's Government when they next expect to hold discussions on climate change issues with the Czech Presidency of the European Union.

*Baroness Warsi to ask Her Majesty's Government what is their position on polygamous marriage in the United Kingdom.

*Lord James of Blackheath to ask Her Majesty's Government what controls they will apply to ensure that Scottish banks printing money do not do so at a level that would disproportionately favour the Scottish economy.

*Lord Dubs to ask Her Majesty's Government how many homeowners will be helped by the recently announced Homeowners Mortgage Support Scheme; and what is the forecast cost of it.

Health Bill [HL] Report [Lord Darzi of Denham] *11th Report from the Joint Committee on Human Rights*

Baroness Howells of St Davids to ask Her Majesty's Government what steps they will take to ensure that the United Nations can act in accordance with the objectives outlined in the preamble to the Charter of the United Nations. *(Dinner break business, 1 hour)*

In the Moses Room at 3.30pm

Perpetuities and Accumulations Bill [HL] Second Reading Committee [Lord Bach]

The following two motions are expected to be debated together:

European Communities (Definition of Treaties) (United Nations Convention on the Rights of Persons with Disabilities) Order 2009 Consideration in Grand Committee [Lord McKenzie of Luton] *10th Report from the Joint Committee on Statutory Instruments*

Lord Lester of Herne Hill to move that the Grand Committee do consider the Report of the Joint Committee on Human Rights on the United Nations Convention on the Rights of Persons with Disabilities: Reservations and Interpretative Declaration (12th Report, HL Paper 70).

Figure 16.2 House of Lords order paper: in the House of Lords, questions are addressed to Her Majesty's Government and not to a particular minister

Thursday. (If sitting on a Friday, it sits at 10.00 a.m. but no questions are taken.) Question Time lasts for up to a maximum of 30 minutes and no more than four questions may be taken. Questions are similar to those tabled for oral answer in the Commons, although – unlike in the Commons – they are addressed to Her Majesty's Government and not to a particular minister (see Figure 16.2). Also, there is no departmental rota: the questions may be to different departments. A question to an environment minister, for example, may be followed by one to a defence minister. A peer rises to ask the question appearing in his or her name on the order paper, the relevant minister (or whip) replies for the government, and then supplementary questions – confined to the subject of the original question – follow. This procedure, assuming the maximum number of questions is tabled (it usually is), allows for seven to eight minutes for each question, the peer who tabled the motion by tradition being allowed to ask

the first supplementary. Hence, although Question Time is shorter than in the Commons, the concentration on a particular question is much greater and allows for more probing.

At the end of the day's sitting, or during what is termed the 'dinner hour' (when the House breaks in mid-evening from the main business), there is also usually a QSD (as, for example, Baroness Howell's question shown in Figure 16.2). If taken during the dinner hour, debate lasts for a maximum of 60 minutes. If taken as the last business of the day, it lasts for a maximum of 90 minutes. Peers who wish to speak do so – signing up in advance – and the appropriate minister replies to the debate. The advantages of QSDs are similar to those of the half-hour adjournment debates in the Commons, except that in this case there is a much greater opportunity for other members to participate. It is not unknown for the number of speakers to run into double-figures. The topics are generally varied and non-partisan. On

12 May 2009, for example, Lord Rodgers of Quarry Bank raised the role of privy counsellors; the following evening, Lord Jones of Cheltenham asked what assessment the Government had made of the future of St Helena, and the following night Lord Richard asked whether the Government would accord formal recognition to the men and women of Bomber Command during the Second World War.

Committees

Although the House remains a chamber-oriented institution, it has made greater use in recent years of committees. Apart from a number of established committees dealing, for example, with domestic function of the House, it has variously made use of ad hoc select committees. Some ad hoc committees have been appointed to consider the desirability of certain legislative measures. A number have been appointed to consider issues of public policy. (Some are also appointed to deal with essentially internal matters, such as the speakership of the House.) The House has also made use of its power to create sessional select committees, i.e. committees appointed regularly from session to session rather than for the purpose of one particular inquiry. The House has

three long-established committees with reputations as high-powered bodies. They have been joined by three more, plus a joint committee.

The most prominent of the established committees is the *European Union Committee* (known, until 1999, as the European Communities Committee). Established in 1974, it undertakes scrutiny of draft European legislation, seeking to identify those proposals that raise important questions of principle or policy and which deserve consideration by the House. All documents are sifted by the chairman of the committee – who also holds the formal and salaried position of deputy chairman of committees – with those deemed potentially important being sent to a subcommittee. The committee works through seven subcommittees (see Table 16.2), each subcommittee comprising two or more members of the main committee and several co-opted members. In total, the subcommittees draw on the services of 70 to 80 peers. Each subcommittee covers a particular area. Subcommittee E, for example, deals with law and institutions. Members are appointed on the basis of their particular expertise. Subcommittee E includes some eminent lawyers – it was, until 2009, chaired by a law lord – as well as members who have experience of government. A subcommittee, having

Table 16.2 Committees in the House of Lords, July 2009

Name of Committee	Chairman
Communications	Rt Hon. Lord Fowler (Con)
Constitution	Rt Hon. Lord Goodlad (Con)
Delegated Powers and Regulatory Reform	Lord Godhart QC (Lib Dem)
Economic Affairs	Lord Vallance of Tummel (Lib Dem)
Subcommittee on the Finance Bill	Lord Vallance of Tummel (Lib Dem)
European Union Committee	Rt Hon. Lord Roper (Non-affiliated)
Subcommittees:	
A. Economic and financial affairs, and international trade	Baroness Cohen of Pimlico (Lab)
B. Internal market	Rt Hon. Lord Freeman (Con)
C. Foreign affairs, defence and development policy	Lord Teverson (Lib Dem)
D. Environment and agriculture	Lord Sewel (Lab)
E. Law and institutions	Rt Hon. Lord Mance (Law Lord)
F. Home affairs	Rt Hon. Lord Jopling (Con)
G. Social policy and consumer affairs	Baroness Howarth of Breckland (Cross-bench)
Merits of Statutory Instruments	Lord Filkin (Lab)
Science and Technology	Lord Sutherland of Houndwood (Cross-bench)
[Joint Committee on Human Rights	Andrew Dismore MP (Lab)]

had documents referred to it, can decide that the document requires no further consideration, or can call in evidence from government departments and outside bodies. If it decides that a document requires further consideration, then it is held 'under scrutiny' – that is, subject to the scrutiny reserve. The government cannot, except in exceptional circumstances, agree to a proposal in the Council of Ministers if it is still under scrutiny by Parliament.

Written evidence to a subcommittee may be supplemented by oral evidence and, on occasion (though not often), a minister may be invited to give evidence in person. The subcommittees prepare reports for the House (in total, about 20 to 30 a year), including recommendations as to whether the documents should be debated by the House. (About 2 per cent of the time of the House is taken up debating EU documents, usually on 'take note' motions.) The EU Committee has built up an impressive reputation as a thorough and informed body, issuing reports that are more extensive than its counterpart in the Commons, and which are considered authoritative both within Whitehall and in the institutions of the EU. The House, like the chambers of other national legislatures, has had no formal role in the European legislative process (see Norton 1996) and so has no power, other than that of persuasion, to affect outcomes. The significance of the reports, therefore, has tended to lie in informing debate rather than in changing particular decisions (Norton 2005: 153).

The *Select Committee on Science and Technology* was appointed in 1979 following the demise of the equivalent committee in the Commons. (The Commons committee has since been re-created.) The remit of the committee – 'to consider science and technology' – is wide, and its inquiries have covered a broad range. The committee is essentially non-partisan in approach and benefits from a number of peers with an expertise in the subject. Recent chairmen have included the President of the Royal Academy of Engineers and a former rector of the Imperial College of Science, Technology and Medicine. For its inquiry into pandemic influenza in 2005 it co-opted Lord May, the President of the Royal Academy (a former chief scientific adviser to the government), and Lord Soulsby of Swaffham Prior, President of the Royal Institute of Public Health (and previously a professor of parasitology). In recent sessions it has investigated genomic medicine, nanotechnologies and food, pandemic influenza, personal Internet security, science and

technology research funding priorities, systematics and taxonomy, and waste reduction. The committee has raised issues that otherwise might have been neglected by government – and certainly not considered in any depth by the Commons – and various of its reports have proved influential (see Grantham 1993; Hayter 1992).

The *Delegated Powers and Regulatory Reform Committee*, previously known as the Delegated Powers and Deregulation Committee, looks at whether powers of delegated legislation in a bill are appropriate and makes recommendations to the House accordingly (see Himsworth 1995). It also reports on documents under the Regulatory Reform Act 2001, which allows regulations in primary legislation to be removed by secondary legislation. The committee has established itself as a powerful and informed committee, its recommendations being taken seriously by the House and by government. Indeed, it is standard practice for the government to accept its recommendations. At report stage of the Access to Justice Bill in February 1999, for example, the government moved 34 amendments to give effect to the recommendations of the committee.

These committees have been supplemented by three more. The *Constitution Committee* was established in 2001 to report on the constitutional implications of public bills and to keep the operation of the constitution under review. It regularly issues reports on the constitutional implications of bills and has published major reports on, among other topics, the process of constitutional change, devolution, inter-institutional relations in the UK, the regulatory state, Parliament and the legislative process, the surveillance state, and the relations between Parliament, the executive and the courts. The *Economic Affairs Committee* was also appointed in 2001. It has published reports on banking supervision and regulation, the impact of economic sanctions, the current state of monetary policy, apprenticeship, and the state of the British economy. It has also established a subcommittee to consider the annual Finance Bill. The *Communications Committee* is the most recent of the sessional committees, having been appointed in 2007. It succeeded an ad hoc committee on the BBC Charter Renewal. Since its creation, it has undertaken a number of in-depth studies, publishing reports on the chairmanship of the BBC, the ownership of the news, government communications, and public service broadcasting.

As a consequence of the passage of the Human Rights Act 1998, the two Houses have also created a

Joint Committee on Human Rights. The committee is chaired by an MP, but it follows Lords procedures. It has six members drawn from each House. It considers matters relating to human rights and has functions relating to remedial orders (bringing UK law into line with the European Convention on Human Rights) under the 1998 Act. Its main task is reporting to the House on bills that have implications for human rights. It was particularly influential, for example, in reporting on the Anti-Terrorism, Crime and Security Bill in 2001. In the light of the committee's report, and pressure from members in both chambers, the government agreed to make changes to the bill.

These permanent committees are variously supplemented by ad hoc committees, appointed to consider particular issues. Committees reporting in the twenty-first century have covered the monetary policy committee of the Bank of England (2001), stem cell research (2002), the crash of Chinook helicopter ZD576 (2002), animals in scientific procedures (2002), religious offences (2003), the Constitutional Reform Bill (2004), the Assisted Dying for the Terminally Ill Bill (2005), the speakership of the House (2006), economic regulators (2007), intergovernmental organisations (2008), and the Barnett Formula (2009). Most of these attracted considerable media attention. The report on the Chinook helicopter crash was debated in both Houses. Various ad hoc joint committees have also been appointed to consider draft bills; one was also appointed to consider the conventions applying to the Lords.

The committees thus constitute a valuable and growing supplement to the work undertaken on the floor of the House. They allow the House to specialise to some degree and to draw on the expertise of its membership, an expertise that cannot be matched by the elected House of Commons. Like select committees in the Commons, the committees choose their own topics of inquiry. However, unlike the Commons committees, there is no government majority. A typical 12-member committee will comprise four Labour peers, four Conservatives, two Liberal Democrats and two cross-benchers. The composition in terms of expertise and political affiliation encourages a notable bipartisan approach.

The committees also fulfil an important expressive function. They take evidence from interested bodies – the submission of written evidence is extensive – thus allowing groups an opportunity to get their views on the public record. Given the expertise of the committees, reports are treated as weighty documents by interested groups; consequently, the committees enjoy some capacity to raise support for particular measures of public policy. Committees also have the capacity to elicit a government response at the despatch box as well as in writing. The government provides a written response to each committee report – agreeing in 2005 to do so within two months, bringing it into line with the Commons – but if the committee recommends that a report be debated in the House, then time is found to debate it. The House has agreed that such debates should be in prime time, but this is not always possible to achieve.

Party meetings

The parties in the Lords are organised, with their own leaders and whips. Even the cross-benchers, allied to no party, have their own elected leader (known as the convenor) and circulate a weekly document detailing the business for the week ahead. (They even have their own website: www.crossbenchpeers.org.uk.) However, neither the Conservative nor the Labour Party in the Lords has a committee structure. Instead, peers are able to attend the Commons backbench committees or policy group meetings, and a number do so. Any attempt at influence through the party structure in the Lords, therefore, takes the form of talking to the whips or of raising the issue at the weekly party meeting.

Party meetings, as well as those of cross-bench peers, are held each week. (The meeting day has changed in recent years, following changes to the arrangement of business in the House.) Such meetings are useful for discussing future business as well as for hearing from invited speakers. For example, in meetings of the Association of Conservative Peers (ACP) – the Lords equivalent to the 1922 Committee – the business usually comprises a short talk by a member of the executive of the 1922 Committee about developments in the Commons, the Chief Whip announcing the business for the following week, and a discussion on a particular issue or a talk from a frontbencher or expert on a particular subject. When a major bill is coming before the House, the relevant member of the Shadow Cabinet (or, if in government, minister) may be invited to attend, along with a junior spokesperson, to brief peers on the bill. Sometimes party meetings have the characteristics of a specialist committee, since often peers with an expertise in the topic will attend and question the speaker. For a minister or shadow minister, or even an expert speaker, the occasion may be a testing one, having to justify a measure or proposal before an often well-informed audience.

Party meetings are useful as two-way channels of communication between leaders and led in the Lords and, in a wider context, between a party's supporters in the Lords and the leadership of the whole party. Given the problems of ensuring structured and regular contact between whips and their party's peers, the party meetings provide a useful means of gauging the mood of the regular attenders. They are also useful ways of enhancing communication with the Commons, former MPs often being active in the membership. In 2009, both the main party groups were chaired by ex-MPs.

■ Reform: stage one

Demands for reform of the House of Lords were a feature of both the late nineteenth century and the twentieth. As the democratic principle became more widely accepted in the nineteenth century, so calls for the reform of the unelected, Conservative-dominated House of Lords became more strident. Conservative obstruction of Liberal bills in the 1880s led the Liberal Lord Morley to demand that the Upper House 'mend or end', an approach adopted as Liberal policy in 1891. In 1894, the Liberal conference voted in favour of abolishing the Lords' power of veto. When the Lords rejected the Budget of the Liberal government in 1909, the government introduced the Parliament Bill. Passed in 1911, the preamble envisaged an elected House. An inter-party conference in 1918 proposed a scheme for phasing out the hereditary peers, but no time was found to implement the proposals. A 1948 party leaders' conference agreed that heredity alone should not be the basis for membership. Again, no action was taken. In 1969, the Parliament (No. 2) Bill, introduced by the Labour government led by Harold Wilson, sought to phase out the hereditary element. The bill foundered in the House of Commons after encountering opposition from Conservative MPs, led by Enoch Powell, who felt it went too far, and from Labour MPs, led by Michael Foot, who believed it did not go far enough. The willingness of the House of Lords to defeat the Labour government in the period from 1974 to 1979 reinforced Labour antagonism.

In 1983, the Labour Party manifesto committed the party to abolition of the Upper House. Under Neil Kinnock (leader 1983–92) this stance was softened. In its election manifesto in 1992, the party advocated instead an elected second chamber. This was later amended under Tony Blair's leadership to a two-stage reform: first, the elimination of the hereditary element; and, second and in a later Parliament, the introduction of a new reformed second chamber. The Liberal Democrats favoured a reformed second chamber – a senate – as part of a wider package of constitutional reform. Charter 88, the constitutional reform movement created in 1988 (see Chapter 13), included reform of the Upper House 'to establish a democratic, non-hereditary second chamber' as a fundamental part of its reform programme.

The Labour manifesto in the 1997 general election included the commitment to reform in two stages. 'The House of Lords', it declared, 'must be reformed. As an initial, self-contained reform, not dependent on further reform in the future, the rights of hereditary peers to sit and vote in the House of Lords will be ended by statute.' That, it said, would be the first step in a process of reform 'to make the House of Lords more democratic and representative'. A committee of both Houses of Parliament would be appointed to undertake a wide-ranging review of possible further change and to bring forward proposals for reform.

The Labour victory in the 1997 general election provided a parliamentary majority to give effect to the manifesto commitment. However, anticipating problems in the House of Lords, the government delayed bringing in a bill to remove hereditary peers until the second session of the parliament. The bill, introduced in January 1999, had one principal clause which ended membership of the House of Lords on the basis of a hereditary peerage. It was passed by the House of Commons by a large majority. In the House of Lords, peers adhered to the Salisbury convention and did not vote on second reading. However, they subjected it to prolonged debate at committee and report stage. In the Lords, an amendment was introduced – and accepted by the government – providing that 92 peers should remain members of the interim House. The 92 would comprise 75 chosen by hereditary peers on a party basis (the number to be divided according to party strength among hereditary peers), 15 to be chosen by all members of the House for the purpose of being available to serve the House, for example as

Deputy Speakers, and the Earl Marshal and the Lord Great Chamberlain, in order to fulfil particular functions associated with their offices. The government had indicated in advance that it would accept the amendment, on condition that the Lords did not frustrate passage of the bill. Although the House made various other amendments to the bill, against the government's wishes, the bill made it eventually to the statute book. All bar the 92 hereditary peers exempted by the Act ceased to be members at the end of the session. When the House met for the state opening of Parliament on 17 November 1999, it was thus a very different House from that which had sat only the week before. It was still a House of Lords, but instead of a House with a membership based predominantly on the heredity principle, it was now primarily an appointed House, the bulk of the members being there by virtue of life peerages.

■ Reform: stage two

After the return of the Labour government in 1997, opponents criticised ministers for not having announced what form stage two of Lords reform would take. The government responded by appointing a Royal Commission on Reform of the House of Lords to consider reform in the light of other constitutional developments while having regard to the need to maintain the Commons as the pre-eminent chamber. The Commission, chaired by a Conservative peer, Lord Wakeham (a former Leader of both the House of Commons and the House of Lords), was appointed at the beginning of 1999 and was required to report by the end of the year. It held a number of public meetings in different parts of the country and completed its report by the end of 1999: it was published in January 2000.

In its report, *A House for the Future* (Cmd 4534), the Royal Commission recommended a House of 550 members, with a minority being elected. It identified three options for the size of the elected element:

1 *Option A*: 65 elected members, the 'election' taking place on the basis of votes cast regionally in a general election.

2 *Option B*: 87 elected members, directly elected at the same time as elections to the European Parliament.

3 *Option C*: 195 elected members, elected by proportional representation at the same time as European Parliament elections.

Under options B and C, a third of the members would be elected at each European Parliament election. A majority of the members of the Commission favoured option B. It was proposed that the regional members – whatever their number and method of selection – should serve for the equivalent of three electoral cycles and that the appointed members should serve for fixed terms of 15 years. Under the proposals, existing life peers would remain members of the House.

The Commission's report was extensive, but the reaction to it focused on its recommendations for election. Supporters of an appointed second chamber felt that it went too far. Supporters of an elected second chamber argued that it did not go far enough. Many critics of the report felt that at least 50 per cent of the members should be elected. The report did not get a particularly good press.

Although not well received by the press, the Commission's report was received sympathetically by the government. Following its 1997 manifesto commitment, it sought to set up a joint committee of both Houses, but the parties could not agree on what the committee should do. The Labour manifesto in the 2001 general election committed the government to completing reform of the House of Lords: 'We have given our support to the report and conclusions to the report of the Wakeham Commission, and will seek to implement them in the most effective way possible.' In November 2001, the government published a White Paper, 'Completing the Reform', proposing that 20 per cent of the members be elected. It invited comments, and the reaction it got was largely unfavourable. In a debate in the House of Commons, many Labour MPs argued that the White Paper did not go far enough. Both the Conservative and Labour parties supported a predominantly elected second chamber. The Public Administration Committee in the Commons issued a report, *The Second Chamber: Continuing the Reform*, arguing that, on the basis of the evidence it had taken, the 'centre of gravity' among those it had consulted was for a House with 60 per cent of the membership elected. An early day motion favouring a predominantly elected second chamber attracted the signatures of more than 300 MPs.

Recognising that its proposals were not attracting sufficient support in order to proceed, the government decided to hand over responsibility to Parliament itself. It recommended, and both Houses agreed to, the appointment of a joint committee. After meeting twice, the committee issued a short report explaining how it intended to proceed. It indicated that it would proceed in two stages. The first would involve looking at all the existing evidence and outlining options for the role and composition of the second chamber. The second would involve seeing whether the opinions expressed by both Houses on the options could be brought closer to one another, if not actually reconciled. The committee would then address more detailed matters, along with any outstanding issues concerning the functioning of Parliament and any constitutional settlement that might be necessary in determining the relations of the two Houses. 'The Committee believes that such a settlement would need to be robust, practical and command broad support in Parliament and beyond if it is to have any chance to endure.'

The committee completed the first stage of its work at the end of 2002, when it published a report addressing functions and composition. It argued that the existing functions of the House were appropriate. On composition, it listed seven options – ranging from an all-appointed to an all-elected House – and recommended that each House debate the options and then vote on each one. Both Houses debated the joint committee's report in January 2003. Opinion in the Commons was divided among the several options. Opinion in the Lords was strongly in favour of an all-appointed House. On 4 February, both Houses voted on the options. MPs voted down the all-appointed option but then proceeded to vote down all the remaining options favouring partial or total election (see Maclean *et al.* 2003; Norton 2004). (An amendment favouring unicameralism was also put and defeated.) Peers voted by a three-to-one majority in favour of the all-appointed option and, by a similar margin, against all the remaining options. Of the options, that of an all-appointed chamber was the only one to be carried by either House. The outcome of the votes in the Commons was unexpected – commentators had expected a majority in favour of one of the options supporting election (the vote on 80 per cent of members being elected was lost by three votes) – and it was widely assumed in the light of the votes that there was little chance of proceeding with moves towards a second stage of reform involving election (see Norton 2004: 195–7).

Instead, the government decided to introduce a bill to remove the remaining hereditary peers from the House of Lords, establish a statutory appointments commission and provide that peers could be expelled if convicted of an offence subject to a certain term of imprisonment. However, the government abandoned the idea when it failed to craft an amendment-proof bill: it feared that MPs might try to amend it by introducing provisions for election. Some parliamentarians sought to keep the issue on the political agenda. The debate divided between those who were interested in reforming the powers of the Upper House and those who wanted to change its composition.

Labour peers in the Lords established a working party to review the powers, procedures and conventions of the House. Its report, published in 2004, favoured a new Parliament Act, embodying a time limit for bills in the Lords (and for bills starting life in the Lords to be brought within the scope of the Act), as well as a codification of conventions (Labour Peers Group 2004). The recommendations received a mixed response from peers, but in replying the Lord Chancellor, Lord Falconer, indicated sympathy with the argument for putting a time limit on bills in the Lords.

The debate then switched to those who favoured a reform of the composition of the House. In 2005, five prominent MPs – including former Conservative Chancellor Ken Clarke and former Labour Foreign Secretary Robin Cook – published a reform tract, *Reforming the House of Lords*, in which they argued the case for a 350-member second chamber, with 70 per cent elected, the elected members serving for the equivalent of three parliaments and with one-third of the membership being renewed at each general election (Clarke *et al.* 2005). Led by Liberal Democrat Paul Tyler, they introduced a private member's bill, the Second Chamber of Parliament Bill, designed to give effect to their recommendations. The bill made no progress.

Labour's 2005 election manifesto showed that the government was drawn more to a reform of powers than a major change in composition. Declaring that a reformed Upper House 'must be effective, legitimate and more representative without challenging the primacy of the House of Commons', it said that, following a review by a committee of both Houses, 'we will seek agreement on codifying the key conventions of the Lords, and developing alternative forms of scrutiny that complement rather than replicate those of the Commons; the review should also explore how the upper chamber might offer a better route for public engagement in scrutiny and policy making.' It also committed the party to legislate to place 'reasonable limits on the time bills spend in the second chamber – no longer than 60 sitting days for most bills'. The paragraph dealing with composition was short: 'As part of the process of modernisation, we will remove the remaining hereditary peers and allow a free vote on the composition of the House.'

In the new 2005 parliament, a joint committee on conventions was appointed – it essentially endorsed the existing conventions, but made clear they would not necessarily be able to survive any substantial reform of the House – and the Government published another white paper on Lords reform (HM Government 2007), this time indicating a preference for a House with 50 per cent of the members elected and 50 per cent appointed. In March 2007, both Houses were again invited to vote on various options. Peers repeated their votes of 2003, voting by three-to-one in favour of an appointed House and against all the other options. However, on this occasion, MPs voted in favour of an 80 per cent elected House (by 305 votes to 267) as well as for a wholly elected House (by 337 votes to 224), though the majority for a wholly elected House was inflated by a substantial number of Labour MPs who opposed an elected House voting for the option in order to sabotage election: they reasoned that the Government would find unacceptable a wholly elected House.

The Government responded by establishing a group of leading members of each party to discuss ways of implementing the decision of the Commons. The outcome was a white paper in July 2008 (Ministry of Justice 2008) which identified different options but which produced little by way of concrete recommendations: Justice Secretary Jack Straw conceded in the foreword that it was not 'a final blueprint for reform'. It was announced that the white paper would be debated in both Houses before the end of the session. The White Paper evoked a largely apathetic response and was overshadowed by a range of other contentious issues. The debates in the two chambers never materialised. The government conceded that it would not be possible to legislate in that Parliament in order to create an elected chamber.

Various participants in the debate on the future of the House noted that the House of Lords that followed the Parliament Act of 1911 had

been intended as an interim House until legislation could be passed to provide for a more democratic chamber. That interim House lasted for nearly 90 years. Some wondered whether the interim House that existed following the passage of the House of Lords Act might not now last a similar period of time.

■ The future of the second chamber?

The question of what to do with the House of Lords has thus been a notable item on the political agenda. Given that the removal of hereditary peers from membership of the House was intended as the first stage in a two-stage process, the future shape of the House remains a matter of debate. What are the options?

In the period leading up to the reform of the House in 1999, four approaches to reform were identified (Norton 1982: 119–29). These were known as the four Rs – retain, reform, replace or remove altogether. With some adaptation, they remain the four approaches following the passage of the House of Lords Act.

Retain

This approach favours retaining the House as a non-elected chamber. It argues that the interim House, comprising predominantly life peers, is preferable to an elected or part-elected chamber. The House, it is argued, does a good job. It complements the elected House in that it carries out tasks that are qualitatively different from those of the House of Commons. It is able to do so because its members offer particular expertise. By retaining a House of life peers, one not only creates a body of knowledge and experience, one also creates a body with some degree of independence. The cross-benchers in the House hold the balance of power and are able to judge matters with some degree of detachment. If the House were to be elected, it would have the same claim to democratic legitimacy as the Commons and would either be the same as the Commons – thus constituting a rubber-stamping body and achieving nothing – or, if elected by a different method or at different times, have the potential to clash with the Commons and create stalemate in the political system. Election would challenge, not enhance, the core accountability of the political system (see Norton 2007). Who would electors hold accountable if two elected chambers failed to reach agreement?

This approach has been taken by a number of MPs and peers, indeed by a clear majority of peers. Support for the retain option has also taken organisational form. In 2002, a campaign to argue the case against an elected second chamber was formed within Parliament. Led by an MP (Sir Patrick Cormack, Conservative MP for Staffordshire South) and a peer (this writer), it attracted a growing body of cross-party support in both Houses (Norton 2004). The group argued for some change, including closing off the by-election provision for peers, enabling peers to apply for permanent leave of absence, and putting the Lords appointments commission on a statutory basis – and supported a private member's bill to implement these changes, introduced by one of its supporters, Lord Steel of Aikwood; though not making much progress, the Bill garnered cross-party support and influenced the Government to introduce similar provisions in its Constitutional Reform and Governance Bill in 2009 though the provisions failed to be enacted. The changes advocated by the group were designed to strengthen, not destroy, the existing appointed House. For it, appointment was fundamental to maintaining the existing value of the House. It believes the House adds value to the political process; a partly or wholly elected House it views as value detracting.

Reform

This approach, advocated by the Royal Commission, favours some modification to the interim House, although retaining what are seen as the essential strengths of the existing House. It acknowledges the value of having a membership that is expert and one that has a degree of independence from government. At the same time, it argues that a wholly appointed chamber lacks democratic legitimacy. Therefore it favours a mix of appointed and elected members. The advantages of such a system were touched on in the government's 1998 White Paper, Modernising Parliament (pp. 49–50): 'It would combine some of the most valued features of the present House of Lords with a democratic basis suitable for a modern legislative chamber.' The extent of the mix of nominated

and elected members is a matter of some debate. Some would like to see a small proportion of members elected. The Royal Commission, as we have seen, put forward three options. The government, in its 2001 White Paper, recommended that 20 per cent of the membership be elected and in 2007 increased this to 50 per cent. Some reformers favour an indirect form of election, members serving by virtue of election by an electoral college comprising, say, members of local authorities or other assemblies.

Replace

This approach favours doing away with the House of Lords and replacing it with a new second chamber. Some wish to replace it with a wholly elected house. Election, it is contended, would give the House a legitimacy that a nominated chamber, or even a part-elected chamber, lacks (see Box 16.1). That greater legitimacy would allow the House to serve as a more effective check on government, knowing that it was not open to accusations of being undemocratic. It would have the teeth that the House of Lords lacks. Government can ignore the House of Lords: it could not ignore an elected second chamber. If members were elected on a national and regional basis, this – it is argued – would allow the different parts of the United Kingdom (Scotland, Wales, Northern Ireland and the English regions) to have a more distinct voice in the political process. This stance is taken by a number of organisations, including the Liberal Democrats and Unlock Democracy. Both favour an elected senate. It is also the stance taken by a former Labour Leader of the House of Lords, Lord Richard (see Richard and Welfare 1999) and, as we have seen, by some senior MPs (Clarke et al. 2005). It is also the stance taken by the Labour government following the vote of the House of Commons in 2007.

Others who favour doing away with the House of Lords want to replace it not with an elected chamber but with a chamber composed of representatives of different organised interests – a **functional chamber**. This, it is claimed, would ensure that the different groups in society – trade unions, charities, industry, consumer bodies – had a direct input into the political process instead of having to lobby MPs and peers in the hope of getting a hearing. The problem with this proposal is that it would prove difficult to agree on which groups should enjoy representation in the House. Defenders of the existing House point out that there is extensive de facto functional

---

BOX 16.1   **DEBATE**

An elected second chamber

The case for

- Democratic – allows voters to choose members of the chamber.
- Provides a limit on the powers of the first chamber.
- Provides an additional limit on the powers of government.
- Gives citizens an additional channel for seeking a redress of grievance or a change of public policy.
- Can be used to provide for representation of the different parts of the United Kingdom.
- Confers popular legitimacy on the chamber.

The case against

- Rids the second chamber of the expertise and the experience provided by life peers.
- Undermines accountability – who should electors hold accountable if the second chamber disagrees with the first?
- Superfluous if dominated by the same party that has a majority in the first chamber.
- Objectionable if it runs into frequent conflict with the popularly elected first chamber.
- Will not be socially representative – election tends to favour white, middle-aged and male candidates – and would thus, in any event, simply replicate the House of Commons.
- May prevent the elected government from being able to implement its manifesto commitments.
- Legitimacy of the political process will be threatened if conflict between the two chambers produces stalemate or unpopular compromise policies.

---

representation in any event, with leading figures in a great many groups having been ennobled.

There is also a third variation. Anthony Barnett and Peter Carty of the think-tank Demos have made the case for a second chamber chosen in part by lot (see also Barnett 1997). In evidence to the Royal Commission in 1999, they argued that people chosen randomly would be able to bring an independent view.

We want 'People's Peers' but they must come from the people and not be chosen from above, by an official body. It is possible to have a strong non-partisan element in the Second Chamber, and for this to be and to be seen to be democratic and lively.

The principle of public participation, they argued, should be extended to the national legislature.

Remove altogether

Under this approach, the House of Lords would be abolished and not replaced at all. Instead, the UK would have a **unicameral legislature**, the legislative burden being shouldered by a reformed House of Commons. Supporters of this approach argue that

there is no case for an unelected second chamber, since it has no legitimacy to challenge an elected chamber, and that there is no case for an elected second chamber, since this would result in either imitation or conflict. Parliament should therefore constitute a single chamber, like legislatures in Scandinavia and New Zealand. The House of Commons should be reformed in order that it may fulfil all the functions currently carried out by the two chambers.

Opponents of this approach argue that a single chamber would not be able to carry the burden, not least given the volume of public business in a country with a population of 60 million, many times larger than New Zealand and the Scandinavian countries with unicameral legislatures. Furthermore, they contend, the House of Commons could not fulfil the task of a constitutional safeguard, since it would essentially be acting as a safeguard against itself. Nor would it be an appropriate body to undertake a second look at legislation, since it would not be able to bring to bear a different point of view and different experience from that brought to bear the first time around.

Although abolition has on occasion attracted some support – including, as we have seen, at one point from the Labour Party – it is not an approach that has made much of the running in recent debate. It did, though, attract 163 votes when MPs voted on it in March 2007.

Polls reveal that opinion on the Lords is mixed. Supporters of change cite opinion polls showing that most respondents generally favour the reform or replace options, though with no clear majority for either. In a MORI poll in 1998, 24 per cent of respondents wanted to replace the House with a new second chamber elected by the public; 23 per cent wanted to replace it with a part-elected, part-nominated chamber; 20 per cent wanted to leave the House as it was (with the passage of the 1999 Act their preferred option fell by the way); 13 per cent favoured removing hereditary peers and having new peers nominated by government; and only 12 per cent favoured abolition. In a December 2001 ICM/Democratic Audit poll, 27 per cent favoured a wholly elected House, 27 per cent a House with most members elected, 14 per cent a House with a minority of members elected and 9 per cent a wholly appointed House. (Abolition was not offered as an option.) Almost a quarter of the respondents gave a 'don't know' response.

Supporters of an appointed chamber cite polls which show that people view the work of the House of Lords in a positive light and do not regard reform as a priority for government. An ICM poll for the think tank *Politeia* in March 2005 found that 72 per cent of respondents thought that the House of Lords did a very or fairly good job; only 23 per cent thought that it did a fairly bad or very bad job. A similarly large majority – 71 per cent – thought that the House provided an effective check on the power of the government. Almost two-thirds – 63 per cent – believed that the powers of the Lords should not be reduced. Though there may be support for change, it appears not to be very deep: 59 per cent of those questioned agreed that reform of the Lords was not a priority for the next five years.

A 2007 Ipsos MORI poll carried out for the Constitution Unit at University College London also revealed that members of the public believed that in determining the legitimacy of the Lords, trust in the appointments process was most important (76 per cent listed it as very important), followed by the House considering legislation carefully and in detail (73 per cent), members being experts in their field (54 per cent), and the House acting in accordance with public opinion (53 per cent). Having some members elected by the public came fifth in the list of priorities. When asked to select the two most important factors, election again came fifth. Those who claimed to be knowledgeable about Parliament ranked the inclusion of elected members even lower still (Russell 2007: 6). The survey also found that a slightly higher proportion of the public consider the House of Lords is carrying out its policy role well than say the same about the Commons. As Meg Russell concluded:

Contrary to expectations, given widespread support for elected members in many earlier surveys, this factor is not considered important in comparison with other factors such as careful legislative scrutiny, trust in appointments, and listening to public opinion. Even when offered two choices about what matters, relatively few members of the public pick election, with more supporting the factors already mentioned or inclusion of independent members . . . However, there is concern about the way in which members of the House of Lords are chosen. One solution to this problem is clearly to introduce elections for the upper house. But our results suggest that a reform to the appointments process might actually have more widespread support.

Russell (2007: 8)

The debate continues. The options in terms of the contemporary debate are those of retain, reform, replace or remove altogether. Each, as we have seen, has its proponents. The arguments for and against an elected chamber are considered in Box 16.1. The battle to determine the future shape of the second chamber continues. No side has emerged triumphant.

BOX 16.2 IDEAS AND PERSPECTIVES

The atmosphere in the House

The House of Lords is stunning in its grandeur. For some, it is awe-inspiring; for others, it is suffocating. The House combines crown, Church and a chamber of the legislature. The magnificent throne dominates the chamber. On entering the chamber, a peer bows to the cloth of estate – just above the throne – as a mark of respect. (Unlike the Commons, there is no bowing when leaving the chamber.) Look up and you see the magnificent stained glass windows. Look down and you see the red benches of a debating chamber. The House combines symbolism with the efficiency of a working body. From the bar of the House you see the throne: lower your eye-line and you see the laptop computer on the table of the House. The clerks sit in their wigs and gowns, using the laptop as well as controlling the button for resetting the digital clocks in the chamber.

On Mondays to Thursdays, the benches are usually packed for the start of business. The combination of increasing attendance and a relatively small chamber means that peers often have to get in early to get their preferred spot on the benches. (Unlike the Commons, one cannot reserve a seat in advance.) The Lord Speaker's procession mirrors that of the Speaker of the House of Commons in its pomp and dignity. Peers bow as the mace passes. Once the Lord Speaker has taken her place on the Woolsack, prayers are said. Once these are over, members of the public are admitted to the gallery and other peers come into the chamber. At the start of Question Time, the Clerk of the Parliaments, sitting bewigged at the table, rises and announces the name of the peer who has the first question on the Order Paper. The peer rises and declares, 'I beg leave to ask the question standing in my name on the Order Paper'. The answering minister rises to the despatch box and reads out a prepared response. The peer rises to put a supplementary, followed later by others. If two peers rise at the same time, one is expected to give way; otherwise, as a self-regulating chamber, it is members who decide – usually by calling out the name of the peer they wish to hear, or else by shouting 'this side', indicating that the last supplementary was put by someone on the other side of the House. If neither gives way, the Leader of the House usually intervenes, but the Leader can be overruled by the House. Normally, good manners prevail.

Peers take a lively interest in questions. There are approximately seven or eight minutes available for each question. If time on a question goes beyond that, peers shout 'next question'. Ministers need to be well briefed. It is usually obvious when ministers are out of their depth or have been caught out. Question Time can be educational. The topics are diverse and usually there is knowledge on the part of questioners and ministers. If a minister runs into trouble, the fact that the chamber is packed adds to the tension. Question Time can also be funny. When a minister, questioned about the use of mobile 'phones on aeroplanes, faced a supplementary about the perils of mobile telephones 'on terra firma', he did not hear the full supplementary and had to ask a colleague. Realising he had taken some time to return to the despatch box, he rose and said: 'I am sorry My Lords, I thought terra firma might be some obscure airline!' On another occasion, a question about the safety of a female chimpanzee that had been mistreated received a very detailed answer, which included the facts – as I recall – that the chimp was now in a sanctuary with other chimps, that the group was led by a male of a certain age and that the chimp was enjoying herself. Whereupon the redoubtable Baroness Trumpington got to her feet and declared: 'My Lords, she is better off than I am!'

The House of Lords is a remarkably egalitarian institution: members are peers in the true sense. The atmosphere of the House can be tense, sometimes exciting – the results of votes are frequently uncertain – and occasionally a little rough. Maiden speeches, given priority in debates and heard in respectful silence (peers cannot enter or leave the chamber while they are taking place), can be nerve-wracking, even for the most experienced of public speakers. Most of the time the House has the feel of what it is: a working body, engaged in debate and legislative scrutiny. The emphasis is on constructive debate and revision. Partisan shouting matches are rare. At times, especially at the committee stage of bills, attendance can be small, the main debate taking place between the two front benches, but the effect of the probing from the opposition benches ensures that ministers have to offer informed responses. Notes frequently pass from civil servants in the officials' box to the minister at the despatch box. The quality of ministers can be very good. Ministers who are well regarded and who take the House seriously can rely on the occasional indulgence of the House if they make a slip. The responsibilities of some ministers mean that they spend a great deal of time in the chamber. In the 2005–6 session, the Home Office minister, Baroness Scotland, was regularly at the despatch box, taking bills through the House, as was the constitutional affairs minister, Baroness Ashton of Upholland. In 2004, Baroness Scotland was voted peer of the year by the Political Studies Association, and in the 2005 *House Magazine* Parliamentary Awards ceremony, Baroness Ashton was voted minister of the year.

The only way to appreciate the atmosphere, and the productive nature of the House, is to be there. One certainly cannot glean it from television – the House is squeezed out by the Commons – or from the official report. *Hansard* is good at tidying up speeches, correcting grammar and titles. The tidying up can also have the effect of sanitising proceedings. During the passage of the Access to Justice Bill, Conservative Baroness Wilcox – a champion of consumers – moved an amendment dealing with consumer affairs. The Lord Chancellor, to the delight – and obvious surprise – of Lady Wilcox, promptly accepted the import of the amendment. Lady Wilcox rose and exclaimed 'Gosh. Thanks'. This appeared in *Hansard* as 'I thank the noble and learned Lord. He has pleased me very much today'! When the House collapses in laughter – as it did after the minister's terra firma remark or Baroness Trumpington's intervention – this either appears in *Hansard* as 'Noble Lords: Oh!' or else is ignored. No, one definitely has to be there to appreciate the atmosphere.

BOX 16.3 BRITAIN IN CONTEXT

A distinctive second chamber

The House of Lords is distinctive as a second chamber because of its existence as a second chamber, its membership and its size.

It is distinctive, but far from unique, in existing as a second chamber; that is, as part of a bicameral legislature. Almost two-thirds of countries have unicameral legislatures (Massicotte 2001). Bicameral legislatures are, however, common in Western countries, especially larger ones, and in federal systems.

It is distinctive, but again not unique, in that its members are appointed rather than elected. (It was unique in the period up to 1999, when most of its members served in the House by virtue of having inherited their seats; no other major national legislature had a chamber based on the hereditary principle.) Of the 66 second chambers that exist, 17 use appointment as the predominant method of selection: the most prominent in the Western world are the UK and Canada. Of the remaining countries with second chambers, 27 employ direct election as the predominant method of selection; the rest employ indirect election or some other method of selection (Russell 2000: 29–32).

The House of Lords is unusual in that it has no fixed membership – the membership varies as some members die and others are appointed at different times. Members are also exceptional in terms of their tenure. Though it is common for members of second chambers to serve longer terms than members of the first chamber, no other chamber is based predominantly on life membership. In the House of Lords, all members serve for life other than the Lords Spiritual, who cease to be members when they retire as Archbishops or Bishops. The House is remarkable also in terms of its size. Whereas it is common for second chambers to have a smaller membership than the first, the House of Lords is larger than the first and, indeed, has a claim to be the largest second chamber in the democratic world; the House of Commons has a claim to be the largest first chamber. Together, they form the largest legislature in the democratic world.

Chapter summary

The House of Lords serves as a notable body of scrutiny – both of legislation and of public policy – and as a body for giving expression to views that otherwise would not be put on the public record. As such, it adds value to the political process. The fact that it is not elected means that it has limited significance as a body for legitimising government and measures of public policy and as a body through which politicians are recruited to ministerial office. The fact that it is not elected also makes it a target of continuing demands for reform.

The question of what to do with the House of Lords has been a matter of debate for more than a century. The election of a Labour government in 1997, committed to reform of the House, brought it to the forefront of debate. The removal in 1999 of most hereditary peers from membership fundamentally changed the composition of the House. It became a chamber composed overwhelmingly of life peers. For some, that was a perfectly acceptable chamber. For others, it was not. The House of Lords serves not only as a forum to discuss political issues. It is itself a political issue. That is likely to remain the case.

Discussion points

■ What are the principal functions of the House of Lords? Are they appropriate functions for a second chamber of Parliament?

■ Does the House of Lords do a better job than the House of Commons in scrutinising government legislation? If so, why?

■ Should the institutions of the European Union pay attention to reports from the House of Lords?

■ Was the government right to get rid of most hereditary peers from the House of Lords? Should it have got rid of *all* of them?

■ Would a reform of the appointments process to the House of Lords be preferable to having an elected House?

■ What would *you* do with the House of Lords – and why?

Further reading

The main text on the House of Lords is Shell (2007). Crewe (2005) constitutes a fascinating anthropological study. On the work of the House, see also Part IV of Blackburn and Kennon (2003), Chapter 6 of Baldwin (2005), Norton (2005) *passim*. On peers' voting behaviour, see Norton (2003) and the work produced by the Constitution Unit at University College London (www.ucl.ac.uk/constitution-unit/research/parliament/house-of-lords.html). On the House prior to the reform of 1999 see Shell and Beamish (1993) and Dickson and Carmichael (1999), the latter providing useful material on the House in both its political and judicial roles.

On Lords reform, see Kent (1998), Tyrie (1998), Richard and Welfare (1999), the Report of the Royal Commission on the Reform of the House of Lords, *A House for the Future* (2000), the Government White Paper, The House of Lords: Completing the Reform (2001), the report from the Public Administration Select Committee, *The Second Chamber: Continuing the Reform* (2002), Norton (2004), Shell (2004), Clarke *et al.* (2005), Norton (2007), HM Government (2007), Ministry of Justice (2008), and Tyrie, Young and Gough (2009). Morrison (2001), Chapter 5, offers an overview enriched by extensive interviews. Useful comparative information is to be found in Russell (2000). There is also valuable material on the website of the Royal Commission, www.archive.official-documents.co.uk/document/cm45/4534/4534.htm

Bibliography

Baggott, R. (1995) *Pressure Groups Today* (Manchester University Press).

Baldwin, N.D.J. (1985) 'The House of Lords: Behavioural Changes', in P. Norton (ed.) *Parliament in the 1980s* (Blackwell).

Baldwin, N.D.J. (1999) 'The Membership and Work of the House of Lords', in B. Dickson and P. Carmichael (eds) *The House of Lords: Its Parliamentary and Judicial Roles* (Hart Publishing).

Baldwin, N.D.J. (ed.) (2005) *Parliament in the 21st Century* (Politico's).

Barnett, A. (1997) *This Time: Our Constitutional Revolution* (Vintage).

Blackburn, R. and Kennon, A. (2003) *Griffith and Ryle on Parliament: Functions, Practice and Procedures*, 2nd edn (Sweet & Maxwell).

Clarke, K., Cook, R., Tyler, P., Wright, T. and Young, G. (2005) *Reforming the House of Lords* (The Constitution Unit).

Constitution Unit (1996) *Reform of the House of Lords* (The Constitution Unit).

Constitutional Commission (1999) *The Report of the Constitutional Commission on Options for a New Second Chamber* (Constitutional Commission).

Crewe, E. (2005) *Lords of Parliament* (Manchester University Press).

Criddle, B., Childs, S. and Norton, P. (2005) 'The Make-up of Parliament', in P. Giddings (ed.) *The Future of Parliament* (Palgrave Macmillan).

Dickson, B. and Carmichael, P. (eds) (1999) *The House of Lords: Its Parliamentary and Judicial Roles* (Hart Publishing).

Drewry, G. and Brock, J. (1993) 'Government Legislation: An Overview', in D. Shell and D. Beamish (eds) *The House of Lords at Work* (Oxford University Press).

Grantham, C. (1993) 'Select Committees', in D. Shell and D. Beamish (eds) *The House of Lords at Work* (Oxford University Press).

Hayter, P.D.G. (1992) 'The Parliamentary Monitoring of Science and Technology', *Government and Opposition*, Vol. 26.

Himsworth, C.M.G. (1995) 'The Delegated Powers Scrutiny Committee', *Public Law*, Spring.

HM Government (2007) *The House of Lords: Reform*, Cm 7072 (The Stationery Office).

House of Lords: Completing the Reform (2001) Cmd 5291 (The Stationery Office).

House of Lords (2006) *House of Lords Annual Report and Accounts 2005–06*. (The Stationery Office).

House of Lords (2008) House of Lords: Public Bill Sessional Statistics for Session 2007–08 (Public and Private Bills Office, House of Lords).

House of Lords Information Office (2005) *The Work of the House of Lords* (House of Lords).

Kent, N. (1998) *Enhancing Our Democracy* (Tory Reform Group).

Labour Peers Group (2004) *Reform of the Powers, Procedures and Conventions of the House of Lords* (Labour Peers Group).

Maclean, I., Spirling, A. and Russell, M. (2003) 'None of the Above: the UK House of Commons Vote Reforming the House of Lords, February 2003', *Political Quarterly*, Vol. 74.

Massicotte, L. (2001) 'Legislative Unicameralism: A Global Survey and a Few Case Studies', *The Journal of Legislative Studies*, Vol. 7, No. 1, pp. 151–70.

Ministry of Justice (2008) *An Elected Second Chamber: Further reform of the House of Lords*, Cm 7438 (The Stationery Office).

Modernising Parliament: Reforming the House of Lords (1999) Cm 4183 (The Stationery Office).

Morrison, J. (2001) *Reforming Britain: New Labour, New Constitution?* (Reuters/Pearson Education).

Norton, P. (1982) *The Constitution in Flux* (Basil Blackwell).

Norton, P. (ed.) (1996) *National Parliaments and the European Union* (Cass).

Norton, P. (1999) 'Adding value to the political system', submission to the Royal Commission on the House of Lords.

Norton, P. (2003) 'Cohesion Without Voting: Party Voting in the House of Lords', *The Journal of Legislative Studies*, Vol. 9.

Norton, P. (2004) 'Reforming the House of Lords: A View from the Parapets', *Representation*, Vol. 40.

Norton, P. (2005) *Parliament in British Politics* (Palgrave Macmillan).

Norton, P. (2007) 'Adding Value? The Role of Second Chambers', *Asia Pacific Law Review*, Vol. 15.

Patterson, S.C. and Mughan, A. (eds) (1999) *Senates: Bicameralism in the Contemporary World* (Ohio State University Press).

Public Administration Select Committee (2002) *The Second Chamber: Continuing the Reform*, Fifth Report, Session 2001–2002, HC 494-I (The Stationery Office).

▶

Richard, Lord and Welfare, D. (1999) *Unfinished Business: Reforming the House of Lords* (Vintage).

Royal Commission on the Reform of the House of Lords (2000) *A House for the Future*, Cm 4534 (The Stationery Office).

Rush, M. (ed.) (1990) *Parliament and Pressure Politics* (Clarendon Press).

Russell, M. (2000) *Reforming the House of Lords: Lessons from Overseas* (Oxford University Press).

Russell, M. (2007) 'Peers and Public Attitudes to the Contemporary House of Lords', www.ucl.ac.uk/constitution-unit/files/research/parliament/lords/survey-results2007.pdf.

Shell, D. (1983) 'The House of Lords', in D. Judge (ed.) *The Politics of Parliamentary Reform* (Heinemann).

Shell, D. (2004) 'The Future of the Second Chamber', *Parliamentary Affairs*, Vol. 57.

Shell, D. (2005) 'The House of Lords: A Chamber of Scrutiny', in P. Giddings (ed.) *The Future of Parliament* (Palgrave Macmillan).

Shell, D. (2007) *The House of Lords* (Manchester University Press).

Shell, D. and Beamish, D. (eds) (1993) *The House of Lords at Work* (Oxford University Press).

Tyrie, A. (1998) *Reforming the Lords: A Conservative Approach* (Conservative Policy Forum).

Tyrie, A., Young, G. and Gough, H. (2009) *An Elected Second Chamber: A Conservative View* (The Constitution Unit).

White, A.B. (1908) *The Making of the English Constitution 1449–1485* (G.P. Putnam).

Useful websites

Parliamentary websites

Cross-bench peers: www.crossbenchpeers.org.uk

Government Whips' Office: www.lordswhips.org.uk (provides details on future business, including speakers)

House of Lords: www.parliament.uk/lords/index.cfm

House of Lords Select Committees: www.parliament.uk/business/committees/ld_select.cfm

The Work of the House of Lords: www.parliament.uk/documents/upload/HoLwork.pdf

What Lords do: www.parliament.uk/about/how/members/lords.cfm

Reform

HM Government, *The House of Lords: Reform*: www.official-documents.gov.uk/document/cm70/7027/7027.pdf

Ministry of Justice, *An Elected Second Chamber: Further reform of the House of Lords*: www.official-documents.gov.uk/document/cm74/7438/7438.pdf

Report of the Royal Commission on the Reform of the House of Lords (Wakeham Commission): www.archive.official-documents.co.uk/document/cm45/4534/contents.htm

Unlock Democracy: www.unlockdemocracy.org.uk/

And another thing . . .

Managing the Cabinet's big beasts

Andrew Heywood

All too often the Cabinet in the UK is portrayed as a single, collective force – something that Prime Ministers try to subdue and control for fear of succumbing to it. This, indeed, is the conventional image of the political executive as a battle ground between the personal power of the Prime Minister and the collective weight of the Cabinet. Prime Ministers exert influence to the extent that they are able to emancipate themselves from the constraints of Cabinet collegiality. However, in many, perhaps most, circumstances this image is misleading. Despite the fact that, thanks to collective responsibility, the Cabinet ministers stand or fall together, the Cabinet usually acts more as a collection of individuals than as a single collective force. The Prime Minister has no single relationship with the Cabinet, but rather a series of individual relationships with some 20 to 23 ministers. Most of these ministers, most of the time, can nevertheless be treated (should the Prime Minister so wish) with cavalier disregard. Quite simply, they need the Prime Minister much more than the Prime Minister needs them. The same, however, cannot be said about the Cabinet's major figures – its 'big beasts'.

Who are the Cabinet's big beasts? What is it that distinguishes the big beasts from, if you like, the small ducks? Three key factors stand out. First, big beasts have a significant power base within the party. They enjoy support within the parliamentary party, among backbenchers and, in all likelihood, among ministerial colleagues inside and outside the Cabinet, as well as in the party more widely. This means that they will be influential players in any future power struggle within the party, and may even be leadership contenders themselves. Second, big beasts are figures of a certain public standing. They not only attract media attention and have high

name-recognition, but also command a measure of public respect as 'Cabinet heavyweights', usually linked to perceived competence and a record of policy success. This means that their fate – their rise or their fall – has an electoral impact on the government itself.

Third, big beasts *project* themselves as big beasts. They develop and sustain independent political identities, albeit within the confines of Cabinet collegiality and party unity. Big beasts not only possess political leverage, but are also willing to use it. In other words, objective and subjective factors need to coincide. A prominent Cabinet minister who distinguishes himself or herself by scrupulous loyalty towards the Prime Minister – such as William (Willie) Whitelaw, home secretary and Deputy Prime Minister in Thatcher's first government, 1979–83 – is not a big beast. As Thatcher later, and gratefully, put it, 'Every Cabinet needs a Willie'. By the same token, political projection is not enough in itself if party and electoral leverage wane. For instance, John Prescott, Deputy Prime Minister under Blair, 1997–2007, probably ceased to be a big beast once Blair had secured a second landslide election victory in 2001, as this demonstrated the declining significance of the left-wing and trade union elements within the party that tended to identify with Prescott as the leading survivor of 'old' Labour.

Ultimately, a big beast is a minister whose resignation would seriously weaken the Prime Minister, either or both by undermining party support or by damaging the Prime Minister's public image. This does not, however, mean that big beasts are necessarily threats to, still less rivals of, the Prime Minister. Indeed, big beasts may benefit prime ministers as well as constrain them. No Prime Minister wants to be seen to preside over a Cabinet of minnows. To some extent, the standing of the Prime Minister is a reflection of the talent and ability in his or her Cabinet, so long as, of course, unity and loyalty are maintained. The key point, though, is that the loyalty and support of Cabinet heavyweights cannot be taken for granted: it must be worked for; big beasts must be 'managed'. But what does this mean? Balance-of-power theorists in international relations helpfully distinguish between two types of behaviour that subordinate states adopt in relation to dominant states. They may either 'bandwagon' (that is, side with a stronger power in the hope of increasing security and influence, meaning that they 'jump on the bandwagon') or 'balance' (that is, oppose or challenge a stronger or rising power for fear of leaving themselves exposed). In short, Prime Ministers manage the Cabinet's big beasts by encouraging them to 'bandwagon' rather than 'balance'.

The classic strategy for ensuring the loyalty of Cabinet heavyweights, inclining them towards 'bandwagoning' behaviour, is through patronage and preferment. Big beasts do not become big beasts because they hold senior Cabinet posts; they hold senior Cabinet posts because they are big beasts. Senior appointments work in two ways. In the first place, they prevent a potentially dangerous 'gap' opening up between a minister's Cabinet rank and his or her sense of their own importance. Non-preferment risks encouraging ministers to 'balance' by manoeuvring against the Prime Minister, either in pursuit of their own leadership ambitions or in the belief that their careers would prosper better under an alternative leader.

The second, and vital, consideration is that senior appointments ensure that big beasts are forced to remain politically 'close' to the Prime Minister. Ministers who hold senior posts – especially those of Chancellor of the Exchequer, Foreign Secretary and Home Secretary – are not only forced into closer and more regular contact with the Prime Minister (even perhaps being drawn into the Prime Minister's inner circle), but their greater public prominence also leaves very little scope for disloyalty. For senior-ranking ministers, open criticism of the Prime Minister is unthinkable, and even the hint of 'manoeuvrings' against the premier is likely to damage the minister concerned every bit as much as the Prime Minister. Nevertheless, patronage is the beginning of the process of managing big beasts, not the end. Prime Ministers must also be astute enough to recognise when big beasts need to be 'stroked' and when they need to be 'checked', as both strategies have their pitfalls. This is best illustrated by when things go wrong.

Margaret Thatcher claimed in her memoirs that she had been toppled by a 'Cabinet coup' (Thatcher 1993). In fact, the bulk of her Cabinet only advised her in a series of individual meetings in November 1990 to withdraw her candidacy in the second ballot of the Conservative Party's leadership election once her failure to secure victory in the first ballot had demonstrated that she was doomed to defeat. Nevertheless, the Cabinet did play a role in this process, but more through individual actions rather than collective ones. The preconditions for Thatcher's downfall were laid by three senior-level resignations from her Cabinet – those of the Defence Secretary Michael Heseltine in 1986, the Chancellor of the Exchequer Nigel Lawson in 1989, and the Deputy Prime Minister Geoffrey Howe in 1990. The cumulative impact of these resignations was to expose key policy divisions in the Conservative Party and the government (particularly over Europe) and to damage Thatcher's reputation and public standing. Together with unpopular policies such as the 'Poll Tax', they contributed to the developing impression that the Prime Minister had become an electoral liability.

Heseltine, Lawson and Howe were certainly more dangerous outside of the cabinet than they had been inside. The party leadership election in 1990 was precipitated by a challenge by Michael Heseltine, very publicly supported by Lawson and Howe – something that would have been impossible had they remained in the Cabinet. What is more, each of the resignations was avoidable, as each stemmed from a failure to 'stroke' a big beast who was in danger of 'balancing' rather than 'bandwagoning'. Heseltine resigned over the Westland Affair when he believed that the Prime Minister had sided with his rival, Leon Brittan; Lawson resigned over a policy clash with the Prime Minister's economic advisor, Alan Walters, who she continued to back; and Howe resigned over Thatcher's unilateral assertion that the UK would never enter a single European currency.

The relationship between Prime Minister Tony Blair and his Chancellor Gordon Brown offers a particularly instructive example of the successes and failures of managing big beasts. Aside from speculation about a possible deal in 1994 that allowed Blair to challenge for the leadership of the party while Brown stood aside, in return for a promise by Blair to step aside in favour of Brown in due course,

Blair's treatment of Brown bears all the classic hallmarks of a 'stroking' approach. As, with Blair, one of the two leading figures in the 'new' Labour project, an effective shadow Chancellor and the architect of Labour's 1997 landslide election victory, Brown was duly, and predictably, rewarded with control over the Treasury. Once the Prime Minister had consolidated 'new' Labour's control over key areas of policy making, it is no exaggeration to suggest that, for Blair, cabinet management largely boiled down to managing Gordon Brown. He did this consistently by encouraging 'bandwagoning' rather than 'balancing', allowing Brown, for instance, to build up an unprecedented power base in the Treasury which enabled him to exert control over large swathes of domestic policy. Brown came to operate almost as a 'second' Prime Minister responsible for domestic affairs.

This strategy proved to be highly effective for most of Blair's first two terms, even ensuring Brown's full and open support for the deeply controversial decision in 2003 to invade Iraq. Brown's backing for the policy helped to consolidate Cabinet support and at least reduced hostility to it on the Labour backbenches. Brown's 'bandwagoning' benefited both himself and the Prime Minister. However, as the Blair premiership extended, after 2005, into its third term, the drawbacks of 'stroking' became increasingly apparent. Brown's public prominence, his standing in the party and his power base in the Treasury, to say nothing of his record of policy success (based on years of stable economic growth), fuelled his ambitions as well as those of Brownite elements within the government and party who were increasingly frustrated by Blair's long tenure. In other words, 'stroking' strategies had ultimately produced a 'balancing' response. At the same time, however, precisely the same factors effectively ruled out a shift at this stage to a 'checking' strategy, in which Brown may have been marginalised, demoted or even sacked. The result of this was that Blair stood down as Prime Minister in June 2007 without having served his promised full third term and against a backdrop of barely concealed hostility between Blairites and Brownites, which damaged the images of both the outgoing and the incoming Prime Minister.

There are signs, nevertheless, that big beasts may be a species in decline. The Blair cabinets of 1997–2007 contained but a single, genuine big beast, while the Brown Cabinet after 2007 arguably contained none. By contrast, Harold Wilson's Cabinets in the 1960s featured such heavyweights as Anthony Crosland, Dennis Healey, Roy Jenkins and Dick Crossman. Where have all the big beasts gone? They appear to have succumbed to the changing nature of political careers and to the changing character of political parties. The trend in favour of 'career politicians', whose main, and sometimes only, professional experience has been within, or related to, the Westminster jungle, is certainly part of the explanation. Working outside of Westminster, especially in senior positions – in academic life, business, law, journalism, the trade unions, the civil service or wherever – gave politicians wider skills, knowledge and experience, making them, somehow, figures of greater substance. Similarly, as programmatic, mass-membership political parties have given way to modern 'catch-all' parties, political careers are increasingly built on the basis of presentational qualities and televisual skills, discouraging rising politicians from taking up 'serious' ideological stances and relieving them of the need to cultivate support within the factions and tendencies of the party. However, if the conveyer belt that produces big beasts now functions less reliably, much of the texture and vibrancy of cabinet government will be lost. It might also mark the point at which the task of checking Prime Ministerial power passed finally from the Cabinet to the electorate.

Reference

Thatcher, M. (1993) *The Downing Street Years* (HarperCollins).

10

PART 5
THE EXECUTIVE
PROCESS

FIRST LORD OF THE TREASURY

10

CHAPTER 17

The core executive: the Prime Minister and Cabinet

Philip Norton

Learning objectives

- To describe the development of the office of Prime Minister.

- To identify the nature of prime ministerial power and the significance of the individual in the office.

- To describe the development and role of the Cabinet.

- To assess different explanations of the location of power at the heart of British government.

Introduction

The fount of policy making in Britain has always been the executive. Initially the Crown was all-powerful but then the powers of the Crown came to be exercised by bodies on behalf of the Crown. The king's justice came to be dispensed by his courts. Generating measures of public policy moved to the king's ministers, especially in the eighteenth century with the arrival of the Hanoverian kings, who had little interest in domestic politics. As we have seen (Chapter 16), the monarch moved from being at the heart of public policy to being, by the twentieth century, above the political fray, giving assent to what is decided but not interfering in the process. Political power came to be exercised by the king's ministers, the leading ministers drawn together in a **Cabinet** and headed by the king's principal, or prime, minister. Though political power passed to the Prime Minister and Cabinet, the form of monarchical government remained and continues to provide the legal framework within which government is conducted.

The emergence of a powerful Prime Minister and Cabinet was marked in the nineteenth century. Collective responsibility became a convention of the constitution. Although the legal authority of ministers rested on their position as servants of the Crown, their political authority came to rest on the fact that they commanded a majority in the House of Commons. After the 1840s, the monarch's choice of ministry was constrained by the votes of the electors. The combination of legal and popular authority made for a powerful executive. The head of the party commanding a majority in the House of Commons was invited to become Prime Minister and, by the very reason he became Prime Minister, was able to exercise considerable power through the party's majority in the House. By virtue of the doctrine of parliamentary sovereignty (see Chapter 15), the outputs of Parliament were binding and could be set aside by no body other than Parliament itself. Who commanded a majority in the House of Commons could thus wield considerable power. The Prime Minister and Cabinet came to form the heart of government – the core executive – in the United Kingdom. Though recent pressures – the hollowing out of the state and multilevel governance (discussed later) – have led to the core executive operating in a more crowded and fragmented political environment, the Prime Minister and Cabinet remain at the heart of British government.

■ The Prime Minister

The first person generally held by historians to be the first Prime Minister was Robert Walpole. As Stephen Taylor has written,

Robert Walpole is one of the most remarkable figures of modern British politics. He is commonly regarded not only as the first prime minister, but also as the longest serving holder of that office, his twenty-one years far exceeding the tenure of any of his successors. He was the dominant figure of the early Hanoverian period.

(Taylor 1998: 1)

He also came to live in 10 Downing Street, a house given to him by George II. However, the term 'prime minister' had been employed before and it was not one that Walpole favoured. The term entered common use following Walpole's tenure but not until the twentieth century was it referred to in statute. The formal title held by the king's first minister was First Lord of the Treasury, a title still held by the occupant of 10 Downing Street.

Walpole established the basic features of the office and under him one can see the essential constitutional division between the monarch and the monarch's first minister: the former remained as head of state, but the latter became the head of government. For another century, the monarch was to exercise the freedom to select the Prime Minister, but it was the selection of someone who was to head the King's government. The Prime Minister had arrived. Since Walpole's lengthy tenure as the king's principal minister, the office has undergone some significant change. The office itself has also seen an array of office holders (Englefield, Seaton and White 1995). Up to 2010, 51 men and one woman have been appointed Prime Minister, serving a total of

Downing street
Source: Alamy Images / Justin Kase z01z

74 ministerial terms: some, of course, have held the office on more than one occasion. William Gladstone, for example, held the post on four separate occasions. Lord Derby and the Marquess of Salisbury each held it on three separate occasions in the nineteenth century, as did Stanley Baldwin in the twentieth. Some have been short-lived premierships. The Duke of Wellington's second term in office lasted less than one month (17 November to 9 December 1834). In the twentieth-century, Andrew Bonar Law served for the shortest period of time – seven months, from October 1922 to May 1923 (he was dying from throat cancer) – and the longest serving was Margaret Thatcher: a total of eleven-and-a-half years, from May 1979 to November 1990.

Some Prime Ministers have gone down in history as major figures: William Pitt the elder (the Earl of Chatham), William Pitt the younger (Prime Minister at the age of 24), William Gladstone, Benjamin Disraeli, David Lloyd George and Winston Churchill among them. Others, including some of the early occupants of the office, have faded into obscurity and some never really emerged from it. Seven Prime Ministers have died in office, though the last was Lord Palmerston in 1865. Of the seven, one was assassinated (Spencer Perceval, in 1812). In the eighteenth and nineteenth centuries, it was not uncommon for the Prime Minister to sit in the House of Lords. The last to do so was the Third Marquess of Salisbury, who left office in 1902 (being succeeded by his nephew, Arthur Balfour); since then, the convention has been that the Prime Minister must sit in the House of Commons. Most Prime Ministers have entered office having served an apprenticeship in other senior ministerial offices. A few have entered office with no previous ministerial experience, including the first Labour Prime Minister, J. Ramsey Macdonald. The most recent Prime Minister never to have held ministerial office before entering No. 10 Downing Street was Tony Blair.

The Prime Minister heads the government. To understand the premiership, it is necessary to look at the powers that inhere in the office, as well as the constraints that operate. However, while necessary, it is not sufficient. To understand how those powers are deployed, it is necessary to look at who holds the office.

The office of Prime Minister

In the eighteenth century, the person holding the premiership had little by way of a formal office: that is, a significant body of administrative support. The position became more significant in the nineteenth century with the development of a unified ministry, ministers becoming bound by the convention of collective ministerial responsibility. However, the body at the heart of government – the Cabinet – suffered from a lack of basic organisation. It was a collection of senior ministers, coming together for meetings; members took it in turn to be the host and the implementation of decisions was dependent on the individuals attending to remember what had been agreed. Civil servants had to approach ministers to see if they knew what had been decided. The waiters variously leaked what had been discussed and it was not unknown for some members to be asleep when important decisions were taken.

The situation changed notably in the twentieth century with the creation in 1916 of a Cabinet Secretariat and the appointment of a Cabinet Secretary. The impetus for the change was the need for efficiency in time of war, but the structure was maintained in peacetime. The use of the Secretariat initially attracted criticism.

The criticisms primarily grew out of the fact that the attachment of the Secretariat to the Cabinet had been carried out by Lloyd George and that he had then tied that body to his own person, thus effectively increasing his own power vis-à-vis the other members of the Cabinet.
(Carter 1956: 202)

The Secretariat served to ensure the recording and coordination of decisions, operating under the person who chaired the Cabinet – the Prime Minister. The position of the Prime Minister was also strengthened in 1919 with the creation of a unified civil service, under a Permanent Secretary as its head. A regulation 'laid down that the consent of the Premier (which in practice meant the head of the civil service) would be required in all departments to the appointment of permanent heads and their deputies' (Blake 1975: 46–7). It is a power that was to become a particularly important one under some

later Prime Ministers, notably Margaret Thatcher and Tony Blair.

Over time, Downing Street has expanded. In addition to the private office, linking the Prime Minister to Whitehall, the PM's Office has acquired a political office, linking the PM to the party, and a press office, linking the PM to the media. It has also acquired a body of policy advisers. Prime Ministers variously appointed advisers, or drew on the advice of the Cabinet Secretary or other senior civil servants. In 1970, a small body of advisers – the Central Policy Review Staff (CPRS), commonly known as 'the think tank' – was established. It comprised some political appointees and seconded civil servants to advise the Cabinet on policy issues. It answered to the Cabinet through the Prime Minister, but came to be overshadowed by a body of advisers answering solely to the PM, the No. 10 Policy Unit. The CPRS was wound up in 1983. The Policy Unit comprises a body of high-flying political advisers, including some policy specialists.

Margaret Thatcher also appointed a Chief of Staff. Tony Blair created a Chief of Staff, but with more extensive powers than those exercised by his predecessor in the Thatcher Government: these included the power to give directions to civil servants. Tony Blair also created various units, such as a Performance and Innovation Unit, Delivery Unit and the Forward Strategy Unit, which were formally housed in the Cabinet Office but in many cases reported directly to the Prime Minister. They were designed to enhance joined-up government. The Delivery Unit, for example, was created in 2001 to ensure that the Government achieved its objectives in key areas of public service. Gordon Brown rescinded some of the changes introduced by his predecessor (removing, for example, the Chief of Staff's power to give instructions to civil servants; and indeed doing away with the need for a Chief of Staff) but retained various units to provide advice. Key among these was the Strategy Unit, set up to carry out long-term strategic reviews of major policy areas, undertake studies of cross-cutting policy issues, and work with departments to promote strategic thinking and improve policy-making.

The expansion of the Prime Minister's Office has meant that there are now approximately two-hundred people working in 10 Downing Street. Though the Prime Minister's Office is formally a part of the Cabinet Office, it nonetheless now has its own Permanent Secretary. The size of the staff supporting the Prime Minister is such that not all can be accommodated in 10 Downing Street. The

Permanent Secretary, for example, is housed principally in 12 Downing Street.

The powers of the Prime Minister

The Prime Minister is the most powerful person in government, but exercises no statutory powers. Rather, his powers exist by convention. His power as the monarch's first minister confers considerable sway not only over Cabinet and all ministers, but also over the civil service, a raft of public bodies, and people seeking preferment through the award of honours. His principal powers can be listed as follows.

Appoints, shuffles and dismisses ministers. The Prime Minister chooses who else will be in Government. A new Prime Minister appoints over one hundred ministers. Which ministers will form the Cabinet, and their ranking within Cabinet, is a matter for the PM. The Prime Minister can also move or dismiss ministers. Some may be deemed to have earned promotion and others not to have lived up to expectations. Appointing and moving ministers may be undertaken not only for the purposes of reward (or indicating dissatisfaction in the case of demotion or dismissal) but also to reflect the PM's political values. Appointing ministers sympathetic to a particular philosophic strand within the party may reflect the PM's desire for that philosophy to dominate in a particular ministry. Margaret Thatcher, for example, appointed neo-liberal supporters to head the key economic ministries.

Chairs the Cabinet. The PM not only decides who will be in the Cabinet, but also decides when it will meet, what it will discuss, and what it has decided. The Cabinet normally meets once a week, but under some PMs it has met more frequently. Under Tony Blair, it rarely met more than once a week and even then it was for a brief meeting, sometimes lasting less than an hour. Gordon Brown was keen to place more emphasis on the role of Cabinet and, in order to distinguish his approach from that of Blair, moved Cabinet meetings from Thursdays to Tuesdays.

The agenda is determined by the PM. The inclusion or exclusion of certain issues can be politically contentious. The manner of discussion is also influenced by the PM. Some premiers encourage free-ranging discussion, others prefer more concise contributions. Cabinet under John Major was said to resemble a seminar. Under Tony Blair, the items tended to be for report rather than discussion. It is rare for votes to be taken. The PM normally sums up

a discussion and it is the PM's summary that forms the basis of the minutes. The summing up may not necessarily reflect the full tenor of the discussion and may not always coincide with some ministers' recollections of what was said, but it is the Prime Minister's summary that counts.

The PM not only decides the composition of Cabinet but also what Cabinet committees will be created. The Cabinet, a large body meeting once a week, is not in a position to transact all the business of government. Most policy proposals are considered by Cabinet committees. Only if there is disagreement in committee (and if the chair of the committee agrees) is an issue referred to Cabinet. The PM decides who will chair the committees as well as who will serve on them. Which minister is appointed to chair the most committees is often taken as a sign of which minister enjoys the PM's confidence.

Controls Whitehall. The Prime Minister not only decides who shall be the ministerial heads of departments, he can also create, abolish or merge departments, as well as determine who shall be the civil service heads of those departments. The structure of government is a matter for the PM and some have created giant departments. Under Gordon Brown, a massive Department, the Department for Business, Innovation and Skills, was created, with no less than ten ministers under a Secretary of State. Responsibility for transport policy is sometimes included in a large department, such as the Department for the Environment, and at other times is handled by a free-standing Ministry of Transport.

The senior civil service appointments are also the responsibility of the Prime Minister. The PM used to leave this responsibility to others and promotion was usually on the basis of seniority. More recent Prime Ministers have taken an interest in who occupies the top positions. Margaret Thatcher ensured that some senior civil servants were promoted over the heads of more senior officials because they were seen to be capable of effective policy delivery. Tony Blair was also keen to press for civil service change in order to enhance policy delivery and to combat what he termed 'departmentalitis' – the tendency for ministers and officials to act in the interests of their department rather than deliver what the PM wanted (see Chapter 21).

Dispenses honours and public appointments. The PM formally advises the monarch on who should receive particular honours and who should be appointed to public posts in the gift of the Crown. In effect, he thus determines who will be honoured.

The range of honours and appointments is substantial. It encompasses peerages. Though proposals for cross-bench (that is, non-party affiliated) peerages are now made by an independent appointments commission, the PM can still determine who shall be elevated on a party basis. He can appoint ministers from outside Parliament and make sure they are offered peerages, thus ensuring they are within Parliament. He can determine who shall hold various public appointments, including the heads of the security services, the armed forces, and the BBC. Even when appointments are formally in the gift of other ministers, the PM may intervene to make sure a favoured candidate is appointed. The Prime Minister's patronage extends even to certain professors (regius professors) at Oxford and Cambridge Universities and bishops of the Church of England. The archbishops and bishops of the Anglican Church are Crown appointments, with the appointments process traditionally handled by an official in No. 10. Though Gordon Brown signalled that he wished some appointments in the gift of PM to be hived off to dedicated or more appropriate bodies, much power of patronage remains in the hands of the occupant of Downing Street.

These are the main powers, but they are not the only ones. One particularly important power is to advise the monarch as to when a general election shall be held. Until 1918, this was a decision taken by the Cabinet, but since then the final decision has rested with the Prime Minister (Hennessy 2000: 68). A Parliament is limited to a maximum term of five years, but within that period the PM can ask Her Majesty to call an election. It is not unusual for a Prime Minister to seek an election four years after the previous election. However, if the governing party is trailing in the opinion polls, the PM may decide to go the full five years, as happened, for example, in 1992 and 1997. If the governing party is re-elected, this tends to enhance the reputation of the Prime Minister, who has led the party to victory, and this adds to the PM's political capital.

The PM's political capital is also enhanced by other aspects of his office as well as by the fact that he is party leader. As head of government, the PM attends various international gatherings, including the European Council and summits of heads of government of the leading economic nations. This gives him not only a voice in international deliberations but also raises his political profile. He can be seen to be striding the world stage, on behalf of the United Kingdom, in a way no other minister can. The Foreign Secretary or Chancellor of the Exchequer play essentially supporting roles when the Prime Minister is present to represent the UK.

The fact that the PM is head of government, and holder of an office held by a number of political greats, also enhances the media attention accorded the office holder. A report from outside 10 Downing Street is more likely to be carried by the broadcast media than one from outside a Government Department. Even if the report is of Cabinet proceedings, it will be broadcast in front of the place where the Cabinet meets – 10 Downing Street. There is no other obvious place. The backdrop of the Cabinet Office in Whitehall would have little resonance. The development of a rolling 24-hour news media increases the media focus on No. 10. Other developments also result in the PM being seen as standing apart from the rest of government. Security considerations mean that he travels with a security escort, setting him aside from others. Though some senior ministers have security protection, it is not on the scale accorded the Prime Minister.

These are all features deriving from the Prime Minister's status as Prime Minister. However, he also has political clout by virtue of the political position that propelled him to office and which he retains after he has entered No. 10: that of party leader. As party leader, he commands both a party apparatus, especially important when it is a Conservative Prime Minister, and can draw on the support of his parliamentary party. MPs want their party to succeed and it is the party leader who is crucial in delivering success. This can have its downsides for the PM if success is not forthcoming, but if it is (and if the party's standing in the opinion polls is strong) then the Prime Minister is usually unassailable within the party.

The Prime Minister is thus a powerful figure, standing at the apex of government. The powers that inhere in the office are considerable. However, the way in which those powers are exercised will not necessarily be the same under succeeding Prime Ministers. To understand how the powers are wielded, one has to look at *who* is Prime Minister.

The person in No. 10

The reasons why people become Prime Minister vary from PM to PM. The skills necessary to exercise the powers of the office also vary. One way of looking at why politicians become Prime Minister is to look at their purpose in being in office. Some seek office in order to achieve a particular programme of public policy. Some enter No. 10 out of a sense of public duty or simply because they are ambitious for office. To give some coherence as to the motivation for entering office, a fourfold typology of Prime Ministers has been created (Norton 1987, 1988). The four types of Prime Ministers are innovators, reformers, egoists, and balancers.

Innovators seek power – they fight to become Prime Minister – in order to achieve a particular programme, one that they have crafted. If necessary, they are prepared to push and cajole their party into supporting them in carrying out the programme. A leading example is Margaret Thatcher. She embraced a neo-liberal philosophy and pursued it with great vigour, sometimes in the face of much opposition from within her own party. She had a clear future goal.

Reformers seek power in order to achieve a particular programme of public policy, but one essentially dictated by the party itself. Prime Minister Clement Attlee led a reforming postwar Labour Government, but under him the programme that was carried out was that embodied in Labour's 1945 election manifesto, *Let Us Face the Future.*

Egoists seek power for the sake of having power. They are principally concerned with the here and now of British politics, operating in order to maintain their occupancy of No. 10. They will take whatever action they consider necessary to protect their position. Harold Wilson was a good example of an egoist, variously contending with what he saw as attempts by other ministers to oust him. Tony Blair also falls primarily in this category. His period as Leader of the Opposition suggested he may be an innovator, but once in office his prime goal, especially in his first term, was to continue his tenure of office. Gordon Brown also falls principally into this category. Though he entered office with policy goals, his principal focus once in office was to maintain power.

Balancers seek to maintain stability in society. They are concerned with the current state of society, seeking to ameliorate tensions and avoiding policies that may prove socially divisive. They fall into two types: those who seek power and those who are conscripted; the latter are usually compromise choices for party leader. Balancers by their nature tend to be Conservatives, such as Harold Macmillan, but the category also includes Labour Prime Minister James Callaghan. Both Macmillan and Callaghan were power-seekers. An example of a conscript was Sir Alec Douglas-Home (then the Earl of Home) chosen by the Queen, after taking advice, in preference to power-seeking rivals.

These categories are ideal types and some Prime Ministers have straddled categories or moved from one to the other: Churchill, for example, was very different as Prime Minister in peacetime (1951–55) to that which he had been in wartime (1940–45). He had been an innovator in wartime, having a very clear understanding of what he wished to achieve, and in peacetime was a balancer, keen to maintain social stability and having little comprehension of domestic policy.

How the Prime Minister operates in office will thus vary from PM to PM. So too does the extent to which they achieve their goals. They may know what they want to achieve, but that does not guarantee that they get their way. Prime Ministers need a range of skills in order to get what they want (Norton 1987). They have the powers of the office, but some may be more proficient than others in the exercise of those powers. Some PMs have been able to appoint ministers who have delivered what is expected of them. Some have been good in their management of government; others have not been. Sir Anthony Eden, for example, was notoriously bad in his management of his ministers. Some know when to provide leadership and when to go ahead with something – and when not to go ahead with a particular policy. For much of her premiership, Margaret Thatcher demonstrated effective political antennae. As one of her Cabinet colleagues put it, she knew what she wanted to achieve, but she also recognised a brick wall when she saw one (former Cabinet minister to author). If there was a clear obstacle, she sought to work round it or, if necessary, abandoned the policy. Others have sometimes just ploughed on.

Some Prime Ministers have adopted an oratorical approach in order to get their way – an approach favoured, for example, by Tony Blair – whereas others have tended to focus on detailed policy reflections and seeking to impose their decisions on Cabinet, an approach taken by Edward Heath. They have also differed in the extent to which they have left ministers to get on with their jobs or sought to micromanage the affairs of government. Some have proved good at seeing backbenchers regularly in order to ensure they remain supportive of the government's aims; others have tended to distance themselves from their supporters, sometimes – as in the case of Edward Heath (Norton 1978) – with disastrous

Cabinet meeting
Source: Getty Images / Anthony Devlin / WPA

consequences for their continuation as party leader.

The powers of the Prime Minister are thus substantial, though how and why they are utilised will differ from one Prime Minister to another. The extent to which a Prime Minister achieves desired outcomes will also be dependent on others. The occupant of 10 Downing Street does not live in a vacuum. The Prime Minister has to work in a political environment that includes a large number of political actors, and their number – as we shall see – has increased in recent years. One of those actors is the Cabinet.

■ The Cabinet

The king used to appoint people to key offices, such as Chancellor, Treasurer and Secretary of State. They came to meet in a council of the king, the Privy Council, though the number of people invited to it was such that it became too large for the purposes of maintaining secrets and moving quickly. In the latter half of the seventeenth century, the principal ministers came to be drawn together in the Foreign Committee of the Privy Council: this in time came to be known as the junto, or Cabinet Council, or Cabinet (Macintosh 1977: 35–7). By the end of the century, such a body was meeting frequently. The appointment of Whig leaders in 1694, when there was a Whig majority in the Commons, was seen by some historians as constituting the first modern Cabinet. The Cabinet developed in the eighteenth century and, under the Hanoverian kings, it met regularly without the king being present. There was also a smaller inner or working group of lords or an inner cabinet and at times, especially when the king withdrew from Cabinet, the influence of the Cabinet declined. Under George III, the name Cabinet came to be employed for the inner cabinet. Royal appointment was the crucial feature. 'Once a Cabinet was appointed and given royal support, it could normally rely on a majority in both houses and a victory at the next general election' (Macintosh 1977: 63). Though the Cabinet came to work as a distinct body, the membership nonetheless was determined by the king.

The political developments of the nineteenth century changed fundamentally the nature of politics. The extension of the franchise and the growth of mass-membership political parties served to transfer power from Crown to Parliament and, within Parliament, to confirm the supremacy of the House of Commons. The outcomes of general elections came to determine which party was in power and, hence, which party leader was to be Prime Minister and form a Cabinet. The Cabinet could not necessarily take the House of Commons for granted, though by the end of the century the hold of party on the House had grown. By the twentieth century, political control in the House was essentially top-down rather than bottom-up. The convention of collective ministerial responsibility had also developed: ministers were bound by the decisions taken by Cabinet. This applied to all ministers and not just those who formed the Cabinet.

The Cabinet, as we have seen, was not a highly organised body prior to the twentieth century. When the Cabinet developed as a recognisable body, the practice tended to be to keep minutes, but the practice was not maintained during the nineteenth century. As we have noted, the Cabinet met regularly at dinner, with members taking it in turn to be host. They were not the most efficient means of despatching business. One member thought 'we should have no Cabinets after dinner. We all drink too much wine, and are not civil to each other' (cited in Gilmour 1971: 221). Sleeping was common and it is claimed that most members were asleep when the decision to invade the Crimea was taken. There were problems with maintaining secrecy, not least as the body grew in size (to about fifteen members by 1850) and because waiters would hear what was discussed. The meetings themselves could be fairly discursive as there was relatively little business to discuss. 'The pressure of government business was slight . . . Even under Rosebery, at the end of the century, a large part of a Cabinet session could be spent discussing the exact text of one of Juvenal's satires' (Daalder 1964: 27). There was no infrastructure. Ministers had their own departments. There was no dedicated support structure and no consistent records were kept. Implementation rested on ministers' recollections of what had been decided. As one commentator, himself later to be a Cabinet minister, recorded 'The Lord of Chaos himself could hardly have devised more suitable arrangements for the furtherance of his own objectives' (Gilmour 1971: 222).

Some structure was provided, as we have seen, by the creation in 1916 of a Cabinet Secretariat. This ensured there was administrative support and a means of ensuring decisions were recorded and transmitted to Departments. The functions of the Cabinet were also authoritatively delineated two years later in the report of the Machinery of Government Committee (see Le May 1964: 237–42). These were listed as (a) the final determination of the policy to be submitted to Parliament; (b) the supreme control of the national executive in accordance with the policy prescribed by Parliament; and (c) the continuous coordination and delimitation of the authorities of the several Departments of State. The Cabinet is thus, formally, the collective body that determines the policy of government and has the machinery to ensure that its writ runs throughout Whitehall. It operates within limits set by Parliament, but that is a body in which it enjoys usually the support of most MPs. It is chaired by the Prime Minister, but the conclusions, as summarised by the PM, are deemed to be those of the Cabinet.

Though the work of the Cabinet was not unduly onerous in the nineteenth century, it became notably more demanding in the twentieth. There were particular demands placed on it in wartime: the need for secrecy and despatch led to the creation of inner, or war, Cabinets. The main permanent development in peacetime occurred after 1945. The state sector expanded considerably and more demands were made of government. The business of government grew, making it difficult for the principal policies to be decided in a body meeting only once or sometimes twice a week. The use of Cabinet committees became more extensive. Committees were variously employed in the nineteenth century and the first permanent committee – the Committee of Imperial Defence – was created in 1903; it was also the first to have a secretariat. Many committees were established in the First World War, but the number receded in peacetime: in an average year, about twenty would be in existence (Gordon Walker 1972: 39). The number burgeoned in the Second World War, but – unlike in the aftermath of the First World War – the basic structure was retained in peacetime. 'Attlee was thus the first Prime Minister to have in peacetime a permanent structure of Cabinet Committees' (Gordon Walker 1972: 41). The structure was maintained under succeeding Prime Ministers. The extent of the committees, both in terms of number and activity, was such that from the Attlee Government onwards there were concerns as to the sheer volume of work being undertaken by committees and the consequent problem of overload. In 1951 there were 148 standing committees and 313 ad hoc committees (Hennessy 1986: 45). In 1967, the Prime Minister, Harold Wilson, enhanced the status of the committees by saying that a matter could only be taken from committee to Cabinet with the agreement of the committee chairman. Previously, any member of the committee could insist a matter dealt with in committee be considered in Cabinet.

The stress on Cabinet committees, however, was to decline towards the end of the twentieth century. The number of committees came down under Margaret Thatcher (just over 30 standing committees and just over 120 ad hoc committees in the period up to 1986) and also under Tony Blair. There was a greater reliance on bilateral meetings, or ad hoc meetings with senior ministers, or the Prime Minister determining the matter without recourse to the Cabinet. This was seen by commentators as confirming a trend towards Prime Ministerial government and away from Cabinet government.

Despite the perceived emphasis on the role of the Prime Minister, the Cabinet nonetheless remains a core component of British government. The functions ascribed to it in 1918 remain relevant and, in practice, are complemented by important political roles. The principal roles are essentially five and can be listed as follows.

Approves policy. Though policy does not originate in Cabinet, it is nonetheless the body, operating through its committees, that approves the policies that are to be laid before Parliament. Ministers serving on Cabinet committees do not necessarily agree proposals without commenting on them and sometimes inviting the minister to come back with a re-worked policy. The Cabinet Committee on Legislation is especially important for determining which measures shall be laid before Parliament in the next session of Parliament. The Devolution Committee was also extremely important in the 1997–2001 Parliament in drawing up measures to give effect to the Government's policy on devolution. The then Cabinet Secretary, Sir Robin Butler, was later to say: 'I have always held out that the operation of the Devolution Committee which Lord Irvine chaired after the 1997 election, was a model of how cabinet committees ought to work' (Butler 2009). The Committee resolved most issues, which were then reported to Cabinet.

Resolves disputes. There are sometimes clashes between Departments. A dispute may sometimes go to the Prime Minister, but the role of Cabinet is to act as an arbiter. This role is usually carried out by the Cabinet Office. For example, if there are differences between some Departments as to the stance to be taken in an EU negotiation, the Cabinet Office seeks to iron out the differences and ensure – in the words of Cabinet Secretary Sir Gus O'Donnell – 'that the government goes with a single position' (O'Donnell 2009). However, serious policy disputes between ministers have to be ironed out in Cabinet or Cabinet Committee. As another former Cabinet Secretary, Lord Wilson of Dinton, put it:

There is still an enormous amount of decision-taking that is circulated to Cabinet or circulated to Cabinet committees and where someone is unhappy they have the opportunity to bring it up and for a discussion to take place, and that does happen.

(Wilson 2009)

Constrains the Prime Minister. Though the Prime Minister chairs the Cabinet and usually achieves desired outcomes, there are occasions when members may not be prepared to go along with the PM. Even powerful Prime Ministers such as Winston Churchill and Margaret Thatcher could not always get their way with Cabinet colleagues. Thatcher was notable in that she sometimes summed up discussions at the beginning. This could be portrayed as a sign of a dominating Prime Minister, but it was just as much a sign of weakness. She could not be certain that ministers would agree with her and so she had to try to steer them in the direction she favoured. Tony Blair kept meetings short, reducing the opportunity for discussion, but there were occasions when he ran into opposition from members. Thus, for example, the lead headline in *The Independent on Sunday* on 8 May 2005 was 'Cabinet defies Blair in power struggle'. Even the most persuasive of premiers cannot always ensure that the Cabinet will go along with the policy favoured by No. 10.

Unifies government. The Cabinet formally has responsibility, as we have seen, for coordinating government. The Cabinet Office is the key body for monitoring what goes on in Whitehall and ensuring that Cabinet decisions are relayed to officials. However, there is also an important political dimension. The Cabinet is the body through which the Prime Minister can reach out to the rest of government. It is essentially a means of conveying the collective will of government and not only informing departments but, in effect, enthusing them. An astute Prime

Minister can work through Cabinet to lead rather than direct.

Unifies the parliamentary party. The Prime Minister can work through Cabinet to reach the rest of government, but can also work through Cabinet to reach the party in Parliament. The Cabinet is described by some commentators as a committee of Parliament. It is not a committee of Parliament – it is a committee of Government – but it comprises parliamentarians. Cabinet ministers remain within Parliament and see backbench members on a regular basis. Ministers have offices in the Palace of Westminster as well as in their departments. Some Cabinet ministers may also have their own power base within the House, having the support of like-minded MPs. Cabinet discussions can help ensure that ministers feel that they have been involved and are thus willing to embrace the outcomes of Cabinet deliberations, taking those decisions back to party colleagues and persuading them to support them.

The Cabinet may thus be seen as a buckle between party leaders and Whitehall and between party leaders and Westminster. The extent to which it is an effective buckle depends in large measure on the extent to which it is fully utilised.

Under the Blair premiership in particular, it was open to accusations that it was not being fully utilised. Cabinet meetings were short and, according to one member, achieved little. 'Occasionally, people would express concern, or a little doubt about an issue raised, but only in a very mild way and others rarely took up such comments' (Short 2004: 70). Another, David Blunkett, wrote of Cabinet Committees: 'Some are more useful than others. Where something has to be collectively agreed, then they are worthwhile, but where it is just a rubber stamp or where people just read out their departmental brief, then they are a complete waste of time' (Blunkett 2006: 564). According to James Naughtie, 'No Prime Minister since the nineteenth century has spent more time avoiding formal meetings with cabinet colleagues than Tony Blair' (Naughtie 2001: 104). He was seen as distancing himself not only from Cabinet, but from the civil service and Parliament (Norton 2008: 92–100). His premiership seemed to epitomise the presidentialisation of British politics. Though Cabinet and Cabinet committees retained relevance – they were still the sites on occasion of collective deliberation – the Cabinet system has given way to a debate over the extent to which power in British Government is concentrated in No. 10 Downing Street.

■ Presidential government?

The debate as to whether Britain has Prime Ministerial or Cabinet Government is not new. It was being hotly debated forty years ago (see Norton 1982: Chapter 1). What is remarkable is that some commentators thought that there was anything approaching government by the Cabinet (see, for example, Jones 1965; Brown 1968; Gordon Walker 1972). By its nature, a body of over 20 people meeting once and sometimes twice a week is not in a position to engage in policy making on a consistent basis. The Cabinet can give assent to policy proposals, its committees fulfil important tasks of scrutiny and approval, but it is not a body for the initiation or formulation of measures of public policy. Some Prime Ministers have been more dependent on their Cabinets, or some of their Cabinet colleagues, than others, but the Prime Minister has usually been the central figure of government. If the PM has been overshadowed in government, it has not usually been by the Cabinet but by one or more senior members of the Cabinet.

The thesis of a presidential premiership in UK government has grown in recent years. The thesis has been challenged, but not on the grounds of a powerful Cabinet but rather because of a more crowded political environment. The Prime Minister has had to contend with more powerful political actors. The territory in which the Prime Minister's writ runs has contracted. The Prime Minister operates in a shrinking world.

Presidential or constrained?

The thesis of a *presidential premiership* rests on the Prime Minister becoming more detached from Cabinet, party and Parliament and operating as if the occupant of the office is elected directly by the people (see Foley 1993, 2000, 2004). The PM acts as the embodiment of the national will and intervenes within government to ensure a particular outcome is achieved (Thomas 1998: 79). Detachment, or what Bennister has termed 'institutional stretch', is not confined to the UK (Bennister 2007: 2–19) but under Tony Blair it was arguably taken to unprecedented levels (Norton 2003a, 2003b, 2008). Though Gordon Brown sought to distinguish his style of prime ministerial leadership from that of Tony Blair, decision making remained heavily concentrated in 10 Downing Street. The occupant of No. 10 is surrounded by key advisers, personally

Margaret Thatcher & Tony Blair
Source: Getty Images / AFP

appointed by the Prime Minister and thus owing their positions to him. He may occasionally consult with senior ministers, but ultimately it is the Prime Minister who determines the policy to be pursued; that policy is then announced or reported to Cabinet before being put in the public domain. The style of government under Tony Blair was characterised as 'sofa government', comprising informal meetings with other senior ministers and/or key advisers.

However, the thesis does not go unchallenged. The Prime Minister is dominant within British Government, but not all-powerful, and the territory within which he is powerful is becoming smaller. He is constrained to some degree within government and, increasingly outside government.

Constraints within government. The Prime Minister may exercise considerable powers. Ministers are dependent on him for their positions and some commentators see them as agents of the Prime Minister. We shall examine the claims of a *principal-agent* relationship in the next chapter. However, there are other studies which suggest that policy-making power is not concentrated in Downing Street. The *baronial* model posits that

much policy making is done by senior ministers. No statutory powers are vested in the Prime Minister, or in the Cabinet. The powers are vested in senior ministers. Though the Prime Minister may take an interest in particular sectors, he has limited time and is usually not a policy polymath. As a result, senior ministers are often left to generate policy initiatives within their departments. Again, we shall examine this model in the next chapter. We shall consider it alongside the *bureaucratic* model, which identifies the capacity of civil servants to shape policy outcomes. There are various means available to officials to influence what a minister sees and considers. Civil servants carry out the decisions of ministers, but they may have a considerable influence over those decisions. Indeed, in some cases, it was argued that 'in certain departments, for example the Home Office, it appeared that officials effectively ran the department, and ministers were seen as obstacles to its smooth running' (Richards and Smith 2002: 61).

The essential point is that the Prime Minister does not exist in a vacuum and, though some decisions may be taken unilaterally, nonetheless has to work with ministers and officials in order to deliver public policy. The different parts of government will normally work together, but there may be times when they are not in harmony. The Prime Minister may face resistance within Cabinet. Particular Cabinet colleagues may refuse to go along with a particular proposal. He may be advised by the Cabinet Secretary that a particular proposal may not work or may best be achieved by some other means. As former Cabinet Secretary, Lord Wilson of Dinton, put it: 'I think you may take it that we have all of us, in our time, had to be firm' (Wilson 2009). There may be times when the Prime Minister may not be able to take Parliament for granted. All Prime Ministers since Edward Heath onwards have suffered one or more defeats it the House of Commons (and considerably more in the House of Lords); Margaret Thatcher's Government actually lost a Bill – the Shops Bill in 1986 – when 72 Conservative MPs voted with the Opposition to defeat it. The Prime Minister may be able to achieve what he wants by adopting a detached and confrontational stance, but it is difficult to maintain that approach indefinitely without inciting a backlash. The Prime Minister is an integral part of Government rather than a free-standing and all-powerful office standing apart from it.

Constraints outside government. However, perhaps the most powerful constraint on the Prime

Minister in the twenty-first century is the fact that his capacity to achieve desired outcomes is limited by policy-making power becoming more dispersed. There has been what has been termed a hollowing-out of the state (see Rhodes 1997: 17–18). Whereas policy-making power was previously concentrated at the centre – that is, within the core executive at the heart of a unitary nation state – it is now shared among a number of bodies at sub-national, national and supranational level.

Prime Minister and Cabinet

Cabinet Secretary Sir Gus O'Donnell in evidence to the House of Lords Constitution Committee 2009:

'I worked with John Major who had a very collegiate style. He used the Cabinet committees in that way. Tony Blair, when he came in in 1997 – not that I was there at the time – had a strong emphasis on stock takes and delivery. He wanted to get specific deliveries on things like literacy and numeracy, specific items. That was his very big emphasis. With Gordon Brown coming in as Prime Minister, it is difficult to separate him coming in from global events. It has been dominated by an economic agenda and that has worked mainly through the National Economic Council. What this tells me is that it is partly the style of the Prime Minister, partly events. This is what I mean about being flexible.'

Constitution Committee, House of Lords, Cabinet Office Inquiry: Minutes of Evidence, Wednesday 4 November 2009

http://www.publications.parliament.uk/pa/ld/lduncorr/const041109ev10.pdf

Some policy-making competence has been transferred to elected bodies in Scotland, Northern Ireland and Wales. Some has passed to other bodies at national level, including regulators and the courts. The courts are now important actors in determining whether provisions of UK law are in conflict with European law or with the European Convention on Human Rights. Some has passed upwards to supranational bodies, such as the institutions of the European Union. The Government also operates as but one of several participants in international gatherings such as the meetings of leaders of the key economic nations (G7, G20, the World Trade Organisation). The capacity to achieve desired outcomes is also increasingly limited by globalisation, reducing the barriers that each country can erect to protect its own internal economic activity. The Prime Minister cannot dictate the flow of global markets. Policy is thus made by different bodies at different levels. Various terms have been utilised to describe this, but the most commonly-used phrase now is that of multi-level governance (see Bache and Flinders 2004).

The importance of this for British Government is that whereas the Prime Minister has been described (albeit ironically) as 'first among equals' in Cabinet, in international gatherings he is not first among equals, but at best an equal among equals. If anyone is pre-eminent in such gatherings, or first among equals as heads of government, it is the President of the United States. Whereas in Cabinet, the Prime Minister is dealing with members who are appointed by him, in summits of heads of government he is dealing with members who have their own national power base. Other than in bilateral meetings, he can find himself in a minority. Decisions may be taken with which the Prime Minister disagrees, but which he may find it politic to go along with. In the EU Council of Ministers, the UK minister may lose out through qualified majority voting, a decision being taken which has effect in the UK even though it lacks the support of the British Government and Parliament.

The consequence of these developments for the Prime Minister is encapsulated in the title of a study by Professor Richard Rose (2001): *The Prime Minister in a Shrinking World*. The world is getting smaller in terms of communication and economic developments. There is a growing interdependence and a growing trend towards seeking to address global problems through international meetings and agreement. When policy competences were concentrated in national government, the Prime Minister could exercise considerable power in determining outcomes. In the twenty-first century, he has to try to accumulate more powers to his office in order to cope with a rapidly changing political environment, one in which his political writ does not run as far as it once did. It is thus possible to characterise the Prime Minister as having to run in order to stand still. Given the extent and speed of globalisation, it may be seen by some as a losing battle. The world may, in Rose's terms, be shrinking: a corollary is that so is the Prime Minister's kingdom.

Chapter summary

The Prime Minister stands at the apex within British Government. The occupant of the office leads the Cabinet and heads the party that usually enjoys a clear majority in the House of Commons. A strong Prime Minister may thus be in a position to achieved desired outcomes. However, the extent to which Prime Ministers actually achieve what they want varies. Prime Ministerial power is variable and not a constant.

The extent to which Prime Ministers can achieve their goals depends in part on who the Prime Minister is: what they want to achieve, and their skills in getting their way, will – as we have seen – vary from premier to premier. The political climate, not least the relationship between different political bodies, can change. A Prime Minister may enjoy a good parliamentary majority and be returned at the next election with a small and potentially difficult majority. Events at an international or national level may blow a Government off course. John Major as Prime Minister led his party to victory in 1992, but with a much reduced majority: the same year, his Government was forced to withdraw from the European exchange rate mechanism, triggering a collapse in confidence in the Government's ability to handle the economic affairs of the nation. A 'no' vote in Denmark in a referendum on the Maastricht treaty emboldened Conservative MPs opposed to the treaty to try to defeat passage of the bill to give legal effect to it in the UK. Shortly after becoming Prime Minister, Gordon Brown was seen as a powerful Prime Minister, riding high in the opinion polls. His popular support plummeted later in the year when he decided not to call a general election. He reclaimed some support for his initial response to the global 'credit crunch' in 2008, but that then receded as the UK economy went into recession.

Prime Ministerial power thus varies not only from premier to premier but also within a premiership. There were times when Margaret Thatcher was dominant as Prime Minister and at other times, as during the Westland crisis in 1986 or in her last year in office (1989–90), when she was politically vulnerable. Tony Blair, similarly, was usually powerful but nonetheless experienced phases when he was politically weak. He was also at times constrained by his Chancellor of the Exchequer, Gordon Brown. 'For such a so-called presidential figure Blair was blocked in key areas. The Chancellor carved out a measure of autonomy hardly ever achieved by a minister' (Kavanagh 2007: 7).

The variability of Prime Ministerial power was well expressed in 2009 by former Cabinet Secretary, Lord Wilson of Dinton:

You may have times, as we had times, when prime ministers have been so strong that their colleagues accepted anything they wanted to do; they had a parliamentary back bench which was supportive of whatever they did; public opinion was happy; the economy was going well. Their ability to get their way was therefore unparalleled, but that does not alter the fundamental fact that if circumstances are different and a prime minister is in a weak position, his cabinet colleagues are debating the issues strongly, it is not possible for the prime minister to have his way and we are not in a country where the prime minister is a president and can just say 'This is what happens and this is what goes'. We are always fundamentally in a position where if cabinet ministers wish to assert themselves then the power of the prime minister will be checked and balanced in that way. (Wilson 2009)

The variability of Prime Ministerial power is further exacerbated by international developments, over which the Prime Minister may have little or no influence. The Prime Minister can be and frequently is powerful, but ultimately is dependent on what one Prime Minister, Harold Macmillan, summarised as 'events, dear boy, events'.

Discussion points

■ What are the main tasks of the Prime Minister? To what extent have they changed in recent decades?

■ To what extent does it matter *who* is Prime Minister?

■ Does the Cabinet still have a significant role in British Government?

■ What are the principal constraints on prime ministerial power?

■ Has the United Kingdom seen the growth of a 'presidential' Prime Minister?

■ To what extent is prime ministerial power variable?

Further reading

There are various books on Prime Ministers and the premiership. Among the most recent are Leonard (2005), Rose (2001) and Hennessy (2000). Foley (1993, 2000, 2004) examines the presidentialisaton of the premiership. For a comparative study, see Helms (2005). On the premiership of Tony Blair, see Riddell (2005), Beckett and Henke (2004), Seldon (2004), and Rentoul (2001). Campbell (2007) also gives a fascinating insight into what went on in Downing Street under Blair. On multilevel governance, see Bache and Flinders (2004). There is no one good recent work on the Cabinet: valuable material may be found in the diaries of former Cabinet ministers, such as Short (2004) and Blunkett (2006).

Bibliography

Bache, I. and Flinders, M. (2004) (eds) *Multi-Level Governance* (Oxford University Press).

Beckett, F. and Hencke, D. (2004) *The Blairs and their Court* (Aurum).

Bennister, M. (2007) 'Tony Blair and John Howard: Comparative Predominance and "Institution Stretch" in the UK and Australia', *British Journal*
of Politics and International Relations, Vol. 7, pp. 2–19.

Blake, R. (1975) *The Office of Prime Minister* (Oxford University Press).

Blunkett, D. (2006) *The Blunkett Tapes* (Bloomsbury).

Brown, A.H. (1968) 'Prime Ministerial Power (Part II)', *Public Law*, Summer, pp. 96–118.

Butler, Lord (2009) Evidence, Constitution Committee, House of Lords, *Cabinet Office Inquiry: Minutes of Evidence, Wednesday 24 June 2009*, http://www.publications. parliament.uk/pa/ld/lduncorr/const240609ev4.pdf

Campbell, A. (2007) *The Blair Years* (Hutchinson).

Carter, B.E. (1956) *The Office of Prime Minister* (Faber and Faber).

Daalder, H. (1964) *Cabinet Reform in Britain 1914–1963* (Stanford University Press).

Englefield, D., Seaton, J. and White, I. (1995) *Facts About The British Prime Ministers* (Mansell).

Foley, M. (1993) *The Rise of the British Presidency* (Manchester University Press).

Foley, M. (2000) *The British Presidency: Tony Blair and the Politics of Public Leadership* (Manchester University Press).

Foley, M. (2004) 'Presidential Attribution as an Agency of Prime Ministerial Critique in a Parliamentary Democracy: The Case of Tony Blair', *The British Journal of Politics and International Relations*, Vol. 6 (3), pp. 292–311.

Gilmour, I. (1971) *The Body Politic*, 3rd revised edn (Hutchinson).

Gordon Walker, P. (1972) *The Cabinet*, revised edn (Fontana).

Helms, L. (2005) *Presidents, Prime Ministers and Chancellors* (Palgrave Macmillan).

Hennessy, P. (1986) *Cabinet* (Basil Blackwell).

Hennessy, P. (2000) *The Prime Minister: The Office and its Holders since 1945* (Allen Lane The Penguin Press).

Jones, G.W. (1965) 'The Prime Minister's Powers', *Parliamentary Affairs*, Vol. 18, pp. 167–85.

Kavanagh, D. (2007) 'The Blair Premiership', in A. Seldon (ed.) *Blair's Britain 1997–2007* (Cambridge University Press).

Le May, G. (1964) *British Government 1914–1963*, 1964 edn (Methuen).

Leonard, D. (2005) *A Century of Premiers* (Palgrave Macmillan).

Macintosh, J.P. (1977) *The British Cabinet*, 3rd edn (Stevens).

Naughtie, J. (2001) *The Rivals* (Fourth Estate).

Norton, P. (1978) *Conservative Dissidents* (Temple Smith).

Norton, P. (1982) *The Constitution in Flux* (Martin Robertson/Basil Blackwell).

Norton, P. (1987) 'Prime Ministerial Power: A Framework for Analysis', *Teaching Politics*, Vol. 16 (3), pp. 325–45.

Norton, P. (1988) 'Prime Ministerial Power', *Social Studies Review*, Vol. 3 (3), pp. 108–15.

Norton, P. (2003a) 'Governing Alone', *Parliamentary Affairs*, Vol. 56 (4), pp. 543–59.

Norton, P. (2003b) 'The Presidentialisation of British Politics', *Government and Opposition*, Vol. 38, pp. 274–8.

Norton, P. (2008) 'Tony Blair and the Office of Prime Minister', in M. Beech and S. Lee (eds) *Ten Years of New Labour* (Palgrave Macmillan).

O'Donnell, G. (2009) Evidence, Constitution Committee, House of Lords, *Cabinet Office Inquiry: Minutes of Evidence, Wednesday 4 November 2009*, http://www.publications. parliament.uk/pa/ld/lduncorr/const041109ev10.pdf

Rentoul, J. (2001) *Tony Blair: Prime Minister* (Little, Brown and Company).

Rhodes, R.A.W. (1997) *Understanding Governance: Policy Networks, Governance, Reflexivity and Accountability* (Open University Press).

Riddell, P. (2005) *The Unfulfilled Prime Minister* (Politico's).

Richards, D. and Smith, M.J. (2002) *Governance and Public Policy in the UK* (Oxford University Press).

Rose, R. (2001) *The Prime Minister in a Shrinking World* (Polity).

Seldon, A. (2004) *Blair* (Free Press).

Short, C. (2004) *An Honourable Deception?* (Free Press).

Taylor, S. (1998), 'Robert Walpole, First Earl of Orford', in R. Eccleshall and G. Walker (eds) *Biographical Dictionary of British Prime Ministers* (Routledge).

Thomas, G.P. (1998) *Prime Minister and Cabinet today* (Manchester University Press).

Wilson, Lord (2009), Evidence, Constitution Committee, House of Lords, *Cabinet Office Inquiry: Minutes of Evidence, Wednesday 24 June 2009*, http://www.publications.parliament. uk/pa/ld/lduncorr/const240609ev4.pdf

Appendix

■ Prime Ministers since 1900

Marquess of Salisbury (Con)	1895–1902
Arthur J. Balfour (Con)	1902–1905
Sir Henry Campbell-Bannerman (Lib)	1905–1908
Herbert H. Asquith (Lib)	1908–1916
David Lloyd George (Lib) (1)	1916–1922
Andrew Bonar Law (Con)	1922–1923
Stanley Baldwin (Con)	1923–1924
J. Ramsay MacDonald (Lab)	1924
Stanley Baldwin (Con)	1924–1929
J. Ramsay MacDonald (Lab/Nat Lab)(2)	1929–1935
Stanley Baldwin (Con)	1935–1937
Neville Chamberlain (Con)	1937–1940
Winston Churchill (Con)	1940–1945
Clement Attlee (Lab)	1945–1951
Winston Churchill (Con)	1951–1955
Sir Anthony Eden (Con)	1955–1957
Harold Macmillan (Con)	1957–1963
Sir Alec Douglas-Home (Con)	1963–1964
Harold Wilson (Lab)	1964–1970
Edward Heath (Con)	1970–1974
Harold Wilson (Lab)	1974–1976
James Callaghan (Lab)	1976–1979
Margaret Thatcher (Con)	1979–1990
John Major (Con)	1990–1997
Tony Blair (Lab)	1997–2007
Gordon Brown (Lab)	2007–

(1) Led Conservative-dominated coalition from 1918
(2) Led Conservative-dominated coalition from 1931

■ The Cabinet November 2009

Prime Minister, First Lord of the Treasury and Minister for the Civil Service	Rt Hon Gordon Brown MP
Leader of the House of Commons and Lord Privy Seal	Rt Hon Harriet Harman QC MP
Secretary of State for Business, Innovation and Skills, First Secretary and Lord President of the Council	Rt Hon Lord Mandelson
Chancellor of the Exchequer	Rt Hon Alistair Darling MP
Secretary of State for Foreign and Commonwealth Affairs	Rt Hon David Miliband MP
Secretary of State for Justice and Lord Chancellor	Rt Hon Jack Straw MP
Secretary of State for the Home Department	Rt Hon Alan Johnson MP
Secretary of State for Environment, Food and Rural Affairs	Rt Hon Hilary Benn MP
Secretary of State for International Development	Rt Hon Douglas Alexander MP
Secretary of State for Communities and Local Government	Rt Hon John Denham MP
Secretary of State for Children, Schools and Families	Rt Hon Ed Balls MP
Secretary of State for Energy and Climate Change	Rt Hon Edward Miliband MP
Secretary of State for Health	Rt Hon Andy Burnham MP
Secretary of State for Northern Ireland	Rt Hon Shaun Woodward MP
Leader of the House of Lords and Chancellor of the Duchy of Lancaster	Rt Hon Baroness Royall of Blaisdon
Minister for the Cabinet Office, and for the Olympics and Paymaster General	Rt Hon Tessa Jowell MP
Secretary of State for Scotland	Rt Hon Jim Murphy MP
Secretary of State for Work and Pensions	Rt Hon Yvette Cooper MP
Chief Secretary to the Treasury	Rt Hon Liam Byrne MP
Secretary of State for Wales	Rt Hon Peter Hain MP
Secretary of State for Defence	Rt Hon Bob Ainsworth MP
Secretary of State for Transport	Rt Hon Lord Adonis
Secretary of State for Culture, Media and Sport	Rt Hon Ben Bradshaw MP

Also attend Cabinet meetings

Minister of State for Business, Innovations and Skills	Rt Hon Pat McFadden MP
Minister of State for Employment and Welfare Reform	Rt Hon Jim Knight MP
Minister of State for Housing and Planning	Rt Hon John Healey MP
Minister of State for Science and Innovation	Rt Hon Lord Drayson
Parliamentary Secretary to the Treasury and Chief Whip	Rt Hon Nicholas Brown MP

Attend Cabinet meetings when Ministerial responsibilities are on the agenda

Attorney General	Rt Hon Baroness Scotland of Asthal QC
Minister of State for Regional Economic Development and Co-ordination; Local Government	Rt Hon Rosie Winterton MP
Minister of State for Children, Young People and Families	Rt Hon Dawn Primarolo MP
Minister of State for Transport	Rt Hon Sadiq Khan MP

CHAPTER 18

Ministers, departments and civil servants

Philip Norton

Learning objectives

■ To promote an understanding of the place and significance of government departments in British government.

■ To identify the role and political impact of ministers in policy making.

■ To assess the relationship between ministers and civil servants.

■ To summarise and assess competing models of policy making.

Introduction

Departments form the building blocks of British government. Each is headed by a minister, who has responsibility for government policy in the sector covered by the department. Each is staffed by a body of professional civil servants, responsible for advising the minister on policy and for ensuring that policy is implemented. The capacity for ministers to determine policy has been increasingly constrained by external pressures, but ministers remain significant players in policy making.

■ Ministers

Ministers stand at the heart of British government. In legal terms, they are the most powerful figures in government. When an Act of Parliament confers powers on government to do something, it does not say 'The Prime Minister may by order . . . [do this or that]'; nor does it say 'The Cabinet may by order . . .'. What it says is 'The Secretary of State may by order . . .'. In other words, legal powers are vested in senior ministers, not in the Prime Minister or Cabinet. Senior ministers are those appointed to head government departments. Their formal designation is Ministers of the Crown. Most will be given the title of Secretary of State (Foreign Secretary, Secretary of State for Home Affairs – popularly known as the Home Secretary – and so on). Originally, there was only one Secretary of State to assist the King. The post was subsequently divided, but the fiction was maintained that there was only one Secretary of State, and that fiction is maintained to the present day. That is why Acts of Parliament still stipulate that 'The Secretary of State may by order . . .' or 'The Secretary of State shall by order . . .'. There is no reference to 'The Secretary of State for Transport' or 'The Foreign Secretary' but simply 'The Secretary of State'.

Each Minister of the Crown heads a government department. Each has a number of other ministers, known as junior ministers, to assist in fulfilling the responsibilities of the office. Each senior minister has one or more political advisers. Each has a body of civil servants – permanent, non-political professionals – to advise on policy and to ensure the implementation of policy once it is agreed on. The number of civil servants in each department will normally run into thousands.

Each Minister of the Crown is thus vested with important legal powers. Each has a department to assist in carrying out the policy or decisions that he or she has made. Each is thus, in formal terms, an important political figure, vital to the continuation of government in the United Kingdom. However, in the view of many commentators, the legal position does not match the political reality. Although legal power may be vested in senior ministers, the real power, it is argued, is exercised elsewhere. The capacity to determine policy has, on this argument, passed to other political actors, not least the European Union, the Prime Minister, civil servants, and the courts. One argument is that senior ministers are now not principals in terms of policy making but rather agents, be it of the Prime Minister, of the civil servants in their department or of the European Union.

What, then, is the structure and operation of government departments? What are the powers of a senior minister? What are the limitations? To what extent is a senior minister able to deploy the powers of the office to achieve desired outcomes? And what is the best model that helps us to understand the position of senior ministers in British government? Are they agents of other actors in the political system? Or are they powerful independent figures?

■ Departments

Each Minister of the Crown heads a **department**. The structure is essentially hierarchical. Those working in a department fall into one of two categories, the political or the official. At the head of the department is the minister, assisted by a number of junior ministers. The senior minister will have a parliamentary private secretary (PPS) as well as one or more special advisers to assist. Other ministers will also normally appoint a PPS and some ministers of state will also have special advisers. The minister and these other appointees constitute the political part of a department. The official part of the department comprises civil servants, headed by the Permanent Secretary. Civil servants in the department answer to the minister through the Permanent Secretary. There is now usually a management board, chaired by the Permanent Secretary and comprising the senior civil servants of the department. The department is usually divided into divisions, headed by a secretary-general or director. Each department will also usually have one or more executive agencies for which it is the sponsoring department. Figure 18.1 shows the actual organisational structure of the Department for Transport, in 2009. The structure differs from department to department. Some have far more extensive and complex structures than the Transport Department.

Political appointees

Junior ministers

There are three ranks of junior minister: ministers of state, parliamentary under-secretaries of state and parliamentary secretaries. (Because the acronym for the parliamentary under-secretaries of state is PUSS, they are known in Whitehall as 'pussies'.) They are appointed to assist the senior minister in carrying out the minister's responsibilities. They will normally be allocated particular tasks. Thus, for instance, in the Department for Culture, Media and Sports, one of the junior ministers is designated as Minister for Sport. In the Foreign and Commonwealth Office, one of the ministers of state is Minister for Europe. In the Department of Health, one of the ministers is Minister for Public Health.

Junior ministers are appointed by the Prime Minister, although sometimes after consultation with the minister heading the department. Their authority derives from the senior minister. It is the senior minister who decides what responsibilities they shall have and, in effect, how powerful they shall be in the department. They act on behalf of the senior minister. They have no formal line control over civil servants. A junior minister, for example, cannot overrule the the Permanent Secretary. A dispute between a junior minister and the Permanent Secretary would have to be resolved by the senior minister.

The number of junior ministers has grown over the past half-century. In the years after the Second World War, it was usual for a senior minister to be assisted by a single junior minister, normally a parliamentary secretary. The Foreign Secretary had two under-secretaries, as did the Scottish Secretary, but they were unusual. The number of junior ministers was thus similar to that of cabinet ministers. Since then, the number of junior ministers has tripled. In August 2009, there were 23 cabinet ministers and 71 junior ministers (as well as 27 whips). It is not unusual for a department to have four or five junior ministers; in 2009, the Department for Business, Innovation and Skills was created, with a total of eleven ministers – the secretary of state, six ministers of state, and four parliamentary under-secretaries. Seven of the ministers held joint appointments, six with other departments and one with serving as a whip in the House of Lords.

Serving as a junior minister is usually a prerequisite for serving as a senior minister. It is rare for an MP to be appointed to the Cabinet straight from the backbenches. An ambitious backbencher will normally hope to be appointed as a parliamentary under-secretary of state and then as a minister of state before being considered for appointment to the Cabinet. Not all aspiring politicians make it beyond the ranks of junior minister. Some are dismissed after two or three years; some serve for a decade or more without making it to the Cabinet.

The sheer number of junior ministers has been a cause of some controversy. Although their number helps to spread the workload within a department, some observers and former ministers have argued that there are too many of them. The increase in their number may be justified by the need for managerial efficiency (i.e. spreading the workload), but the reason for the growth may be the fact that the more junior posts there are the greater the size of the government's payroll vote in Parliament – and the more posts there are to be dispensed by prime ministerial patronage.

Parliamentary private secretaries

Traditionally, one route to reaching junior ministerial office has been through serving as a parliamentary private secretary (PPS). (The other principal route has been through serving as an officer of a backbench committee.) A parliamentary private secretary is appointed to assist a minister. The post is unpaid, the holder is not officially a member of the government and the tasks undertaken are largely determined by the minister. A PPS may serve as the minister's principal link with backbenchers, listening to what has been said and transmitting the views of MPs to the minister. The PPS will also normally

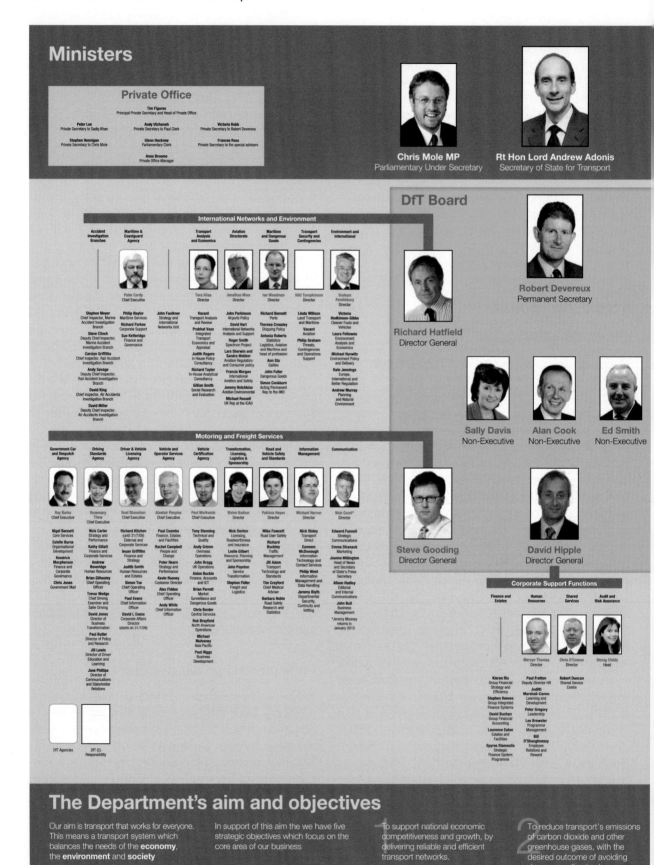

Figure 18.1 Structure of a government department

Rt Hon Sadiq Khan MP
Minister of State

Paul Clark MP
Parliamentary Under Secretary

Department for
Transport

July 2009

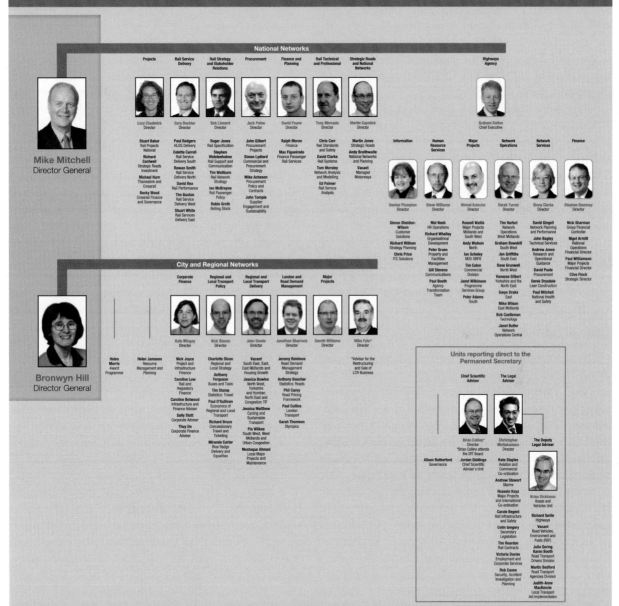

To contribute to better safety, security and health and longer-life expectancy through reducing the risk of death, injury or illness arising from transport, and promoting travel modes that are beneficial to health.

To promote greater equality of opportunity for all citizens, with the desired outcome of achieving a fairer society.

To improve quality of life for transport users and non-transport users, and to promote a healthy natural environment.

help with arranging friendly parliamentary questions and act as a message carrier between the minister and the officials' box in the House of Commons during a parliamentary debate.

The PPS is selected by the minister, although subject to confirmation by the Prime Minister. In some cases, ministers will use their PPSs as trusted advisers. They may also arrange for them to have desks in their departments and may include them in the regular meetings (known as 'prayers') held with junior ministers and senior civil servants in the department. They thus learn how a department works, and if they perform especially well the senior minister may recommend them for promotion to junior ministerial office.

The number of PPSs has grown over the decades. Whereas only senior ministers used to appoint PPSs, it is now the practice for other ministers to appoint them as well. Such appointments may be helpful to junior ministers. They are also helpful to government. Although PPSs are not paid, they are nonetheless usually treated as being part of the government when it comes to votes in the House of Commons. A PPS who votes against the government is liable to be dismissed. The result is, in effect, to increase by almost 50 per cent the block vote that the government whips can rely on in a parliamentary vote.

Special advisers

Unlike ministers and PPSs, special advisers are not drawn from the ranks of parliamentarians. There are two types of special adviser. One is the expert, appointed because of an expertise in a particular subject. The other – the more common type – is the political, appointed to act as an adviser to the minister on a range of issues, to assist with speech writing and to act as a political link between the minister and the party and with other bodies outside the department. They are typically young, bright graduates who are politically ambitious. (One of the special advisers appointed in 1992 by Conservative Chancellor Norman Lamont was David Cameron, later to become an MP and leader of the Conservative party.) Their loyalty is to the minister, who is responsible for appointing them and to whom their fortunes are linked: if the minister goes, the special adviser goes as well. A minister may, and frequently does, invite the special adviser to stay with them if they are moved to another post. Sometimes an incoming minister may invite the special adviser to

the previous incumbent to stay on. However, the link is normally with one minister. It is thus in the interests of the special adviser to be loyal to the minister and to work hard to ensure the minister's success.

Like junior ministers and PPSs, the number of special advisers has grown in recent years. By mid-2009, there were 42 (excluding those serving the Prime Minister in Downing Street). Special advisers have their origins in the 1960s, but they became important figures in the 1970s: then, only very senior ministers were permitted to have a special adviser, and no more than one. The number expanded in the 1980s and early 1990s and there was a further expansion with the return of a Labour government in 1997, with some departments permitted to have more than two special advisers. Two remains the norm, though with some senior ministers having more.

The appointment of special advisers has proved controversial. Some critics are wary of political appointees who are not answerable to Parliament having such a role close to ministers. Some see them as being too powerful and undermining the role of civil servants. 'They seem to have taken over the Prime Minister's office and largely run the Treasury' (Denman 2002: 254). Supporters point out that special advisers are actually of value to civil servants in that they can absorb political work that civil servants should not be asked to do (such as liaising with party bodies and replying to correspondence that has a partisan flavour). However, if they encroach on functions assigned to civil servants, or seek to give orders to civil servants, then problems may arise and, as we shall see, in recent years have arisen.

The officials

The bulk of the people working in government departments are **civil servants**. Since 1996, the most senior posts have been brought together to form the 'Senior Civil Service', presently comprising 4,700 officials. A new pay and performance management system was introduced in April 2002, with new salary bands introduced on the basis of recommendations from the Senior Salary Review Body. In 2008–09, the salary range for Permanent Secretaries was £139,740 to £273,250 and for Pay Band 3, occupied by those immediately below Permanent Secretaries, it was £99,960 to £205,000. Annual salary increases are performance related.

At the front line: Gus O'Donnell, the new Head of the Civil Service, meets the staff
Source: Press Association Images / PA Wire / Empics

Permanent Secretary

The Permanent Secretary is the permanent head of a department. He (very rarely she) will usually have spent his entire career in the Civil Service, rising up the ranks in the service before being appointed Permanent Secretary in a department. Formally, the Permanent Secretary has line control within a department. That is, all communication between civil servants and a senior minister is formally channelled through the Permanent Secretary. In practice, that is now administratively impossible. Instead, submissions will normally go straight to the minister, and the minister may call in the relevant civil servants to discuss particular issues for which they have responsibility. Nonetheless, submissions will be copied to the Permanent Secretary, and the Permanent Secretary will normally sit in on all discussions concerning important policy and administrative matters.

The Permanent Secretary is answerable to the minister for what goes on in the department. However, there is one exception. The Permanent Secretary is the accounting officer for the department. That means that responsibility for ensuring that money is spent for the purposes for which it has been voted by Parliament rests with the Permanent Secretary. The Permanent Secretary is answerable for the accounts, and if those accounts are the subject of an investigation and report by the National Audit Office, then it is the Permanent Secretary who appears before the Public Accounts Committee of the House of Commons to answer questions raised by the report.

The Permanent Secretary is, in effect, the chief executive of the department, but training for the role has usually been acquired over twenty or thirty years in the Civil Service. One study of 111 permanent secretaries in four periods between 1945 and 1993 found that all bar three were men (Theakston

Cambridge-educated Sir Kevin Tebbit is the Permanent Secretary at the Ministry of Defence
Source: Press Association Images / Empics Sports Photo Agency

Civil servants

A similar pattern is to be found for those below the rank of Permanent Secretary. The typical senior civil servant is a white male; recent years have seen an increase in the number of women entering the Senior Civil Service, though two-thirds of posts are held by men. In 2008, 33 per cent of senior civil servants were women, up from 18 per cent in 1999; 3.6 per cent were drawn from ethnic minorities.

Recent years have, however, seen major changes in terms of both roles and structures. A more open structure has been introduced, with greater emphasis on bringing in people with outside experience. **Civil servants** are increasingly being recruited by open competition. This is especially the case with the chief executives of government agencies, although it extends to other senior posts. Of the most senior posts in the Civil Service, about 30 per cent are open to external candidates.

The Civil Service has a less rigid hierarchy than it had in the 1970s and 1980s. There is less rigidity in terms of the positions held by senior civil servants (titles are now likely to be more managerial, such as director, than bureaucratic, such as assistant secretary) and responsibility for pay and recruitment is no longer centralised but instead delegated to individual departments. Each department also has responsibility for training, although courses have been provided centrally. These used to be provided by the Civil Service College. The college was incorporated by the incoming 1997 Labour Government in a Centre for Policy and Management Studies (the CPMS). The CPMS was itself incorporated in the National School of Government, established in June 2005 to help public sector organisations build capacity in good governance. The School links with academic bodies to provide training in management. It offers senior manager workshops for senior civil servants as well as programmes in, for example, people management, leadership, financial management and policy delivery.

The senior civil service accounts for less than one per cent of civil servants. At the end of 2008, there were 488,000 full-time equivalent posts in the civil service. Most of these were in executive agencies. These agencies, such as the Benefits Agency, began to be created in 1988 following publication of a report, *Improving Management in Government: the Next Steps*, by Sir Robin Ibbs. Most executive responsibilities of government have been hived off to such agencies, and today 78 per cent of civil

1995: 36–43). They were usually educated at public school or grammar school before going on to Oxford or Cambridge University. Most went straight from university into the Civil Service and spent 25 years in Whitehall before taking up their present positions. Most had also served in more than one department, a feature especially of the latter half of the century. They were also predominantly 'generalists' – with degrees in classics or the arts – rather than specialists in law or economics; occasionally, a Permanent Secretary would be appointed who had some specialist knowledge of the subject covered by the department, but such figures were – and remain – rare. Just as ministers are normally generalists rather than specialists in a subject, so too are the civil servants who run the department. Their specialist knowledge is of how the machinery of government operates.

servants are employed in executive agencies. The intention behind the agencies has been to separate the service-delivery responsibilities of government from policy making. Those senior civil servants responsible for policy advice to ministers remain at the heart of government departments.

Two features of the Civil Service over the past two decades are of particular relevance in studying government departments. The first is the greater emphasis on managerial and business skills. This emphasis developed under the Conservative governments of Margaret Thatcher and John Major. It has been continued under the Labour government returned in 1997. There is demand on the part of the government for the Civil Service to have much clearer goals, to operate in terms of performance indicators and to deliver on targets that are set for it. Prime Minister Tony Blair was particularly keen to shake up Whitehall and to ensure that civil servants were capable of delivering on the goals set by government. The various changes that have been introduced over the past twenty years have been brought together under the umbrella term 'new public management' (NPM). There has also been the introduction of 'prior options' testing to ensure that the services provided are necessary and best carried out by public bodies. The result has been the privatisation of various agencies. This, along with other changes (including the earlier privatisation of bodies in the public sector), has served to reduce the size of the Civil Service. In 1976, there were just over 750,000 civil servants; by 2008, as we have seen, there were just under half-a-million, though the figure has fluctuated over the years.

The second change is less often commented on but is more central to explaining the relationship between ministers and civil servants: that is, the less rigid structure within the 'core' of each department. The old hierarchical structure, policed and protected by senior civil servants who had been in place for years, has given way to a more flexible arrangement, not just in terms of formal structure but also in terms of the contact that ministers have with civil servants (see Page and Jenkins 2005: 112–4). Permanent Secretaries tend no longer to be the gatekeepers of what advice is or is not sent to a minister. The change in the structure of the Civil Service not only has made departments more open in terms of the people recruited to serve in senior posts but also has coincided with changes introduced by ministers. In recent years, ministers have been more prone to move away from a culture of paperwork – making decisions based on papers placed before them by officials – and towards a more open and interactive culture, calling in civil servants to discuss with them the proposals embodied in their papers.

Senior ministers thus head departments that have a more managerial and business-oriented ethos than before. Those departments, although they have shrunk in staff terms over recent years, can still be significant employers. Most civil servants work in one of four departments: the Department of Work and Pensions (employing 21.8 per cent of civil servants), HM Revenue and Customs (17.7 per cent), the Ministry of Justice (17.1 per cent) and the Ministry of Defence (15.8 per cent). However, the policy-making side of each department is relatively small. Those employed in the top echelons of the Civil Service – the senior civil service and the ranks immediately below them – comprise no more than 20,000 people.

■ Ministerial power

It has been argued that ministerial power – the power to determine particular outcomes – derives from several variables (Figure 18.2). One is specific to the office: the legal, departmental and political powers of the office deriving from the convention of individual ministerial responsibility. Two others are specific to the individual: the purpose of the incumbent in taking office, and the skills of the incumbent. And there are three that are essentially external to

The office
  Legal, departmental and political powers

The individual in the office
  Purpose in taking office
  Skills of the incumbent

External environment
  The power situation
  Climate of expectation
  International developments

Figure 18.2 The components of ministerial power
Source: Adapted from Norton (1997a) 'Leaders or led? Senior ministers in British government', *Talking Politics*, Vol. 10, No. 2, pp. 78–85. Reproduced with permission of The Politics Association

the office: the power situation, the climate of expect-ation and international developments.

The office

Ministers are powerful by virtue of the constitutional convention of individual ministerial responsibility (see Norton 1997b). The doctrine confers important legal, departmental and even parliamentary powers.

The legal dimension is central. We have touched on this at the beginning of this chapter. No statutory powers are vested in the Prime Minister or Cabinet. As Nevil Johnson has written, 'the enduring effect of the doctrine of ministerial responsibility has been over the past century or so that the powers have been vested in ministers and on a relentlessly increasing scale' (Johnson 1980: 84). Postwar years have seen a substantial increase in the volume of legislation passed by Parliament. Bills are not more numerous, but they are longer and more complex. It is common for bills to confer powers on ministers and to do so in broad terms.

The doctrine confers important departmental powers in that it asserts ministerial line control. The focus of much of the writing on the doctrine has often been the culpability of ministers for the actions of their civil servants, but more importantly and more pervasively the doctrine establishes that civil servants are answerable to the minister and to no one else. Civil servants answer to the minister formally through the Permanent Secretary. The creation of executive agencies has not destroyed this basic relationship. Agency heads have some degree of autonomy, but the agencies remain within government, under a sponsoring department, and the agency chief is responsible – answerable – to the minister in that department.

The doctrine may also be deemed important in that the minister is answerable to Parliament for the department. That may appear a limitation – in that the minister is the subject of parliamentary ques-tioning and attack – but it is also a power in that the minister alone is answerable to Parliament. Civil servants are not answerable to Parliament. They cannot appear at the despatch box. They may be summoned before a select committee, but they have no independent voice before that committee.

Parliamentary powers also derive from being Her Majesty's ministers. Since the crown alone can request money, money resolutions have to be moved by a minister. Parliamentary rules also provide that certain other motions, such as the motion to suspend the seven or ten o'clock rule – allowing debate to continue beyond the set time for the conclusion of business – can be moved only by ministers. Parliamentary business proceeds on the basis of an agenda set largely by government, and that business largely entails bills and motions brought forward by government. That business is normally departmen-tal business: bills are brought forward by individual departments and steered through Parliament by the ministers of that department. Ministers generally have a far greater opportunity to speak than is the case with other parliamentarians.

Ministers, then, enjoy considerable formal powers. They also enjoy some public visibility – itself a potential source of power – deriving from their position in government. A senior minister will have a greater chance of persuading a newspaper editor to come to dinner than will a member of the Oppo-sition front bench or a humble backbencher. A min-ister will be able to attract publicity by virtue of exercising the power of the office or by announcing an intention to exercise that power. Even if no formal power to act exists, a minister may attract publicity by making a statement or letting the press know informally what is planned. Departments have press officers, but ministers may also use their special advisers to brief journalists. Press officers are civil servants. Special advisers, as we have seen, are political appointees.

Senior ministers also have some power by virtue of their political position. That is, they will be drawn (by convention) from one of the two Houses of Parliament. Unlike ministers in some other coun-tries, they retain their seats in the legislature. More importantly, though also subject to much greater variability, they may also enjoy a power base in Parliament. They may seek to build that power base, for instance through regular contact with back-benchers. Under the Labour government of Tony Blair, the Chancellor of the Exchequer, Gordon Brown, acquired a reputation for assiduously court-ing backbenchers and newly appointed ministers. Such a power base may give them leverage in rela-tion to other ministers and to their departments. It may also make it very difficult for a Prime Minister to sack them.

The individual in the office

There are two dimensions to the individual in the office: purpose and skills. A minister may have important powers as a minister, but knowing that

Figure 18.3 Types of senior minister

fact tells us little about how and why those powers are exercised. For that, we have to turn to the person in the office. Ministers become ministers for a variety of reasons. Some simply want to be ministers. Some want to achieve particular policy outcomes. Some want to be Prime Minister. What they want will determine how they act.

Consequently, how ministers act varies considerably. As one former cabinet minister recorded in her memoirs, 'there are as many ministerial styles as there are ministers' (Shephard 2000: 105). However, it is possible to identify different types of minister. One study has identified five types of senior minister – team player, commander, ideologue, manager and agent (Figure 18.3) (Norton 2000). The types relate to different locations of decision-making power. With commanders, ideologues and managers, power-making power is retained in the office but exercised in different ways. With team players and agents, policy is 'made' elsewhere, either because ministers cannot prevent it or because they prefer to abdicate power to these locations.

Team player

A team player is someone who believes in collective decision making and wants to be part of that team. This correlates more or less precisely with the concept of Cabinet government. Proposals may be put by a minister to Cabinet, but it is the Cabinet or rather a Cabinet committee that deliberates and decides on the policy. In practice, there is very little evidence to suggest that many senior ministers see themselves primarily as team players. Ministers will normally have a clear policy they wish the relevant Cabinet committee to approve. Rather than acting collegially, they prefer to operate as discrete policy-makers.

Commander

Commanders are those who have very clear ideas of what they want to achieve, and those ideas derive from their own personal preferences and goals. (Preferences should be taken to include ambition.) These may derive from their own past experiences in business or government, or simply from their personal reflections. When they accept a particular office, they usually have some idea of what they want to achieve. Individuals may not be consistent commanders throughout their ministerial career. They may have a very clear idea of what they want to achieve in one or more particular office but not in another. For example, one politician who held five Cabinet posts during the Thatcher and Major premierships had a clear idea of what he wanted to achieve in three of them (one was the post he had always wanted); in another he had a general idea (even though it was a post he had not wanted) and in the other – a rather senior post – he had no clear perception of what he wanted to achieve. Rather, he assumed one of the other roles: that of 'manager'. There are normally commanders in each era of government. There have been a number of commanders in the Labour government since 1997, including Gordon Brown as Chancellor of the Exchequer as well as Education Secretary and Home Secretary David Blunkett, Foreign Secretary and Leader of the House of Commons Robin Cook, and International Development Secretary Clare Short.

Ideologue

An ideologue is someone who is driven by a clear, consistent philosophy. Thus, whatever office they occupy, the policies they pursue will derive from that philosophy. There were some ideologues – pursuing a neo-liberal philosophy – in the period of Conservative government from 1979 to 1997. These included Sir Keith Joseph, Nicholas Ridley and John Redwood. However, they were not as numerous as is often supposed. This, in part, reflects the fact that Prime Ministers have rarely appointed ministers on purely ideological grounds. Prime Minister Margaret Thatcher largely left junior ministerial appointments to others, thus restricting her choice when it came to choosing cabinet ministers. Some ministers who may appear to be ideologues are not; rather, their views in particular sectors coincide with those of a particular ideological strand. One minister who held office under Margaret Thatcher conceded that in one particular post he had what he described as 'Thatcherite priorities'; but when he occupied another more senior post later, he was certainly not seen as a Thatcherite but rather viewed by Thatcherites as having 'gone native'. There have been few ideologues in the Cabinet under Tony Blair and Gordon Brown, other than members with a preference to side with either Blair ('Blairites') or Brown ('Brownites').

Manager

Here the minister takes the decisions but is not driven by any particular ideology or personal world-view. Instead, the approach is pragmatic, sometimes Oakeshottian: that is, helping to keep the ship of state afloat and operating efficiently. Ministers may anticipate issues; more frequently they respond to them. They do not necessarily take the departmental line but decide it for themselves. When several competing demands are made of them, they act as brokers, listening and weighing the evidence and then taking a view. A good example of a manager during the period of Conservative government in the 1990s was Foreign Secretary Douglas Hurd. There have been a number of managers under Tony Blair and Gordon Brown. One minister who attended Cabinet, and was a former parliamentary private secretary to Tony Blair, confided in a colleague that, with a few exceptions, members of the Cabinet were 'managerial types – capable, efficient, but without an ideological anchor' (Mullin 2009: 526).

Agent

Here the minister essentially acts on behalf of another body. There are two principal types of agent: those of the Prime Minister and those of the Civil Service.

1 *Prime Ministerial*: Here the minister is appointed to ensure that the wishes of the Prime Minister are carried out. (This is distinct from an ideologue, who may share the Prime Minister's ideology but is an enthusiast for the ideology and will give that preference over the Prime Minister's wishes.) Occasionally, a Prime Minister may decide, in effect, to be their own Foreign Secretary or Chancellor of the Exchequer, although that depends on the willingness of the minister in question to comply: Margaret Thatcher had an easier time influencing economic policy with Sir Geoffrey Howe as Chancellor than

she did when that office was held by Nigel Lawson. During the Thatcher era, there were various media reports that some ministers were put in at middle-ranking level to act as the Prime Minister's eyes and ears in a department. Several 'Blairite' members of the Cabinet under Tony Blair were viewed as being there to deliver the vision of the Prime Minister.

2 *Civil Service*: Here the minister essentially adopts the departmental brief and does what the officials in the department want the minister to do. Ministers may adopt this role because they want a quiet life – some actually move up the 'greasy pole' of government despite being remarkably lazy – or because they do not have the personal will or intellect to resist the persuasive briefings of officials. Civil servants can be remarkably persuasive, and indeed devious (papers put in late, or among a mass of papers in the red box), and one or two departments, such as the Foreign Office, do have reputations for pursuing a particular departmental ideology. On some issues, ministers don't take a stand, and, as Gerald Kaufman recounts in *How To Be a Minister*, will read out their departmental brief in Cabinet committee (Kaufman 1997).

Ministers, then, have important powers and some of them want to exercise those powers. However, whether they do so successfully depends on their skills and the political environment they occupy.

Skills

In one study of prime ministerial power, it was argued that the essential skills needed by a Prime Minister, in addition to those of selection, were those of leadership, anticipation and reaction, and that a number of strategic options were available to them to achieve the desired outcome (Norton 1987: 325–45). The strategic options were those of command, persuasion, manipulation, and hiding. These skills and options also apply to senior ministers:

1 *Command*: Ministers may have a clear intellectual view of what they want to achieve, but actually taking decisions to ensure that view is realised may be difficult. One cabinet minister in the early 1980s, Sir Keith Joseph, was notorious for having difficulty making decisions to achieve his ideological goals. Despite being viewed as a strong minister, Gordon Brown as Chancellor of

the Exchequer had a reputation for procrastination. Conversely, some ministers have no difficulty making decisions: examples in the 2005 Parliament have included Defence Secretaries John Reid and John Hutton.

2 *Persuade*: Some ministers may know what they want to achieve and take a clear view. However, they need on occasion to be able to carry colleagues and others – MPs, outside organised interests, the public – with them. There are different devices that ministers may employ to bring the different actors onside: meetings with the relevant backbench committee, for example; a 'dear colleague' letter to the party's MPs; a press conference; private briefings for journalists; and 'keeping No. 10 briefed' ('No. 10' meaning principally the Prime Minister but also, on occasion, other actors in Downing Street, such as the prime minister's principal advisers). Some ministers will also spend time meeting affected bodies, for example by making an effort to attend their annual conferences and accepting invitations to speak. Some ministers in the Blair and Brown governments have had reputations as persuaders, being willing to see MPs privately to discuss their concerns and if necessary agree compromises. They have included Justice Secretary Jack Straw and Chancellor of the Exchequer Alistair Darling.

3 *Manipulate*: The Prime Minister is sometimes devious, and the same applies to senior ministers. On occasion, one may have to play off one body against another. Manipulation may entail 'kite flying' in the media, feeding a misleading story that can be denied and then using it as leverage to achieve a particular outcome. Manipulation may be met by manipulation. Downing Street may leak a story, only for a member of the Cabinet to then provide an alternative view or to deny the story, or a minister may leak details of discussions in order to invoke media coverage and generate public opposition to what has been discussed.

4 *Hide*: Ministers need to know when to avoid a particular problem. Sometimes it is better to keep one's head below the parapet rather than risk putting it above the parapet and getting shot at by the media and disgruntled MPs. One of the values of having junior ministers is that they can be put up to take the flak. In 2009, public criticism of the government's failure to extend settlement rights in the UK to all former Gurkha soldiers was fielded not by a Cabinet minister but by junior Home Office minister Phil Woolas.

These are strategic options. However, there are two other skills that ministers need in order to achieve their goals: they need to be good time managers, and they need to understand how the system – and their particular department – works.

1 *Effective time management*: The work of a senior minister is extraordinarily time-consuming. One Scottish Secretary was told by his private office that on average 1,000 items passed through the office every week, of which he saw 700 – in other words, 100 items a day (Lang 2002: 65). Dealing with such items is in addition to a range of meetings, preparation for speeches and being in the House. For ministers, it is therefore essential to organise their time effectively. Some former Cabinet ministers have admitted that they had difficulty prioritising their activities and saying 'no' to various activities. Some expressed admiration for their colleagues who managed to organise their time and stay on top of their departments. One minister was described as 'superbly professional. Those who worked with him . . . say that he was ruthless in doing only what he considered essential' (Shephard 2000: 118). One means of relieving some of the pressure is by delegation. Some ministers are good at delegating and making use of junior ministers. One Conservative Cabinet minister in the Thatcher government, for example, gave his junior ministers particular responsibilities and then had them draw up a work programme for the next two years, and every three months he had a meeting with each minister to discuss progress. Others are less well organised, and some have difficulty delegating tasks effectively.

2 *Understanding the system*: Ministers need to know how the process works.

The nature of a department and the tools at its disposal to achieve change are important factors in the exercise of power. Understanding them is necessary to achieve change, and to respond to pressure, whether of politics, circumstance or crisis.
(Shephard 2000: 114–15)

Very occasionally, some ministers are appointed without any prior experience of Parliament, but the experience has rarely been a happy one, those involved displaying a lack of sensitivity to the needs of a department and of the parliamentary environment. One way to understand the system – the most obvious and long-standing – is by ministerial apprenticeship. Holding junior ministerial office is useful as a way of seeing how the system works from the inside. One of the points made by one former minister was that in order to be effective in achieving your goals as a senior minister it helped, first, to have been a junior minister in the department that one was appointed to head; and, second, to have served in the Whips' Office. As a junior minister, one gets to know how the particular department works (departments differ enormously), and as a whip one gets to know how to handle MPs and to anticipate what is likely to cause trouble in the House. Understanding of a department may also derive from longevity in the office, but that is something largely beyond the control of the incumbent. Another, more recent, way is by study. Prior to the 1997 general election, seminars were organised for shadow ministers on the workings of government. Training is now available to ministers through the National School of Government. Such training provides access to sources and best practice that may not be achieved by personal experience in junior office.

Without some (ideally, all) of these skills, a minister – however intelligent and self-driven – is not likely to succeed and may find their ministerial career stunted or destroyed altogether.

External environment

Ministers may also find that their capacity to achieve desired outcomes is enhanced by the environment external to their department. This environment includes the power situation, the climate of expectations and international developments:

1 *Power situation*: The power situation overlaps with the powers and constraints of the office but provides a dynamic element. Power relationships are not static. And what the 'power situation' refers to is the relationship between different bodies in the immediate political environment. In terms of ministers, this covers especially Downing Street, Cabinet, Parliament, the Civil Service and the media.

   A previously popular Prime Minister may lose support among the parliamentary party or the public and start to seek support from particular ministers, doing so through being more supportive of their policies. A minister may find it easier to push a policy through as the authority of a Prime Minister wanes. There may be a shift in the power situation as a result of a Cabinet reshuffle. A minister may find that colleagues opposed to a particular policy have been moved or sacked. Elections of officers of backbench party committees may result in opponents of a minister's policy being replaced by supporters. Changes of ownership of particular newspapers may result in greater media support for a policy. Changes may occur that make the power situation unfavourable, but at times it may be highly favourable to a particular minister and the policies of that minister. Martin Smith sums up the difficulties faced by Prime Minister John Major compared with Margaret Thatcher not in terms of weak and strong personality but in terms of a changed power situation: 'Major had no majority in parliament, the government was divided, and the popular perception was that his government lacked economic competence – circumstances created Major's indecisiveness; it was not indecisiveness that led to the Conservative defeat' (quoted in Morrison 2001: 279). Prime Minister Gordon Brown also witnessed a significant shift in the power situation following his decision in 2007 not to call an election in that autumn and following the sudden economic downturn of 2008–09. He moved from being seen as an invulnerable premier to one that was highly vulnerable, with various ministers and backbenchers seeking to engineer his resignation.

2 *Climate of expectation*: The expectations of citizens are clearly important and change over time. The Conservative Party was the beneficiary of a particular climate of expectation in 1979 and the victim of a very different climate in 1997. The popular mood may initially be hostile to a particular proposal and then, perhaps induced by particular events, swing in support of it. Particular ministers may benefit from a particular climate of expectation, a popular mood favouring what they want to achieve. That mood can be a political resource for the minister, making it difficult for the Cabinet to resist a proposal for which there is clearly overwhelming popular support. Alternatively, the climate may change, constraining ministers in what they want to achieve. After 2003, there was a change of mood towards war,

with popular support for continued involvement in war in Iraq, and later Afghanistan, seeping away.

3 *International developments*: What happens elsewhere in the world may limit ministers in terms of what they wish to achieve but on occasion may also make it possible for ministers to achieve what they want. A natural disaster or civil war may strengthen the position of a minister who wishes to increase foreign aid or to intervene militarily in a conflict. A shift in power or in policy in another state may facilitate a minister achieving a particular outcome. A change of government in another EU country may enable a minister to get a particular proposal adopted by the EU Council of Ministers.

Two conclusions can be drawn from the foregoing analysis. The first is that senior ministers have the potential to be significant figures in determining public policy. The second is that ministerial power is variable, not constant. It can be subject to a wide range of constraints. Let us consider in a little greater depth the constraints.

Constraints

Ministers labour under a number of constraints. The most important are constitutional, legal and managerial. Constitutionally, they are constrained by the doctrine of collective ministerial responsibility. Major decisions have to percolate up for Cabinet approval, which means, in practice, Cabinet committee; and approval may not always be forthcoming. The constitutional power exercised by the Prime Minister to hire, fire and shuffle ministers may also be a powerful constraint on ministerial policies, and it may be exercised in order to reflect the Prime Minister's policy preferences.

At the individual level, there are two important constitutional constraints. One is the convention of individual ministerial responsibility. The other is the ministerial code. The convention of individual ministerial responsibility is one that, as we have seen, ensures that statutory powers are vested in ministers and that they have line control within their departments; it is also one that renders ministers answerable for what takes place within their departments. This is often assumed to mean that, in the event of an error within a department, the minister resigns. Although ministers may be deemed culpable for what goes on in their departments, this

has rarely meant having to resign if mistakes are made. Ministers have variously resigned because of personal scandal, such as David Blunkett in 2004 (allegations of seeking preferential treatment for a nanny in gaining a visa), or disagreement with government policy, such as Robin Cook in 2003 (over war with Iraq), or disagreement with the Prime Minister's style of leadership, as with Works and Pensions Secretary James Purnell and Europe Minister Caroline Flint in 2009, but very rarely because of a mistake made within their department (see Norton 1997b; see also Woodhouse 1994). A distinction is frequently drawn between policy and operation: if the policy is right but is not carried out, then those public officials who have failed to carry it out are the ones who are disciplined. However, the dividing line is not always clear. The creation of executive agencies has created officials more clearly identifiable as being responsible for delivering policies, but there have been various clashes between ministers and officials over responsibility for determining action by the agencies. Conservative Home Secretary Michael Howard dismissed the head of the Prison Service, Derek Lewis, in 1995 over prison escapes, but was accused by the Opposition of being responsible for a failure of policy. This reflects the weakness as well as the strength of the convention: ministers may not necessarily resign but they have to answer for what happens in their department. Even if the minister does not resign, the minister's career may be adversely affected.

Ministers are also constrained by the ministerial code. This is a code of conduct drawn up by the Prime Minister. The first modern version was drawn up by Clement Attlee in 1945 and was variously revised by his successors. It was formally a secret document until John Major agreed to its declassification in 1992. The code stipulates how ministers should conduct themselves in their dealings with others, including the Civil Service and Parliament, and how they should conduct their personal life in order to avoid conflicts of interest. The code shapes ministers' behaviour and breaches may be punished by the Prime Minister. It was a failure to comply with one of the recommendations of the code that led to David Blunkett's second resignation from the Cabinet in 2005. Following accusations that the Prime Minister was both prosecutor and jury in respect of the code, Tony Blair in 2006 announced that he was appointing an external adviser to assist in considering complaints about ministerial conduct. He appointed the Comptroller and Auditor General to assist him. His successor, Gordon Brown, appointed the former Parliamentary Commissioner for Standards, Sir Philip Mawer.

Legal constraints exist in that ministers may be limited by the powers conferred on them by Parliament. They have increasingly to be sensitive to the risk of acting *ultra vires* (beyond powers). A greater degree of judicial activism in recent decades may be the product of a change of judicial culture (or of those who are affected by government being more prepared to seek judicial review) or a change in the nature of government; but whichever it is, the courts are now more willing than previously to review the legality of ministerial actions.

The courts, as we shall see in Chapter 20, are also more active as a consequence of various constitutional changes. Ministers are constrained by the conditions of membership of the European Union, by the incorporation of the European Convention on Human Rights (ECHR) into British law, and by the devolution of powers to elected assemblies in different parts of the United Kingdom. In policy areas that fall within the competence of the EU, ministers can no longer exercise power unilaterally but rather form part of a collective decision-making body (the Council of Ministers) in which they may be overruled. As their responsibilities have increased as a consequence of the UK's membership of the EU, so their capacity to affect outcomes has decreased. Ministers are constrained by the provisions of the ECHR and in introducing bills now have to confirm that they comply with the provisions of the ECHR. Devolution has moved certain policy areas to the competence of elected assemblies, especially the Scottish Parliament, and a UK minister may have difficulty moving ahead with a policy without the support of one or more of the devolved executives.

Ministers are also subject to what may be termed managerial constraints. Ministers have a mass of responsibilities and duties: they are departmental ministers; they are members of the Cabinet; they are members of the appropriate EU Council of Ministers; they are party and political figures (invited to attend and address a mass of meetings); they are ministers answerable to Parliament; they are (except for those ministers who are peers) constituency MPs; and they are party MPs who have to attend Parliament to vote for their party. Ministers have difficulty managing their time. Their evenings are taken up reading and signing the papers that are crammed into their ministerial red boxes. Their days may be full of meetings with officials and representatives of outside bodies, leaving little time for sustained reflection. Time spent travelling between meetings is variously spent dictating constituency correspondence into a dictaphone.

Ministers are also public and political figures, driven increasingly by the demands of a 24-hour news service. The media demand instant comments, and there are now the means for immediate communication. Ministers – and those wanting to interview them – are rarely without their mobile telephones. Some ministers also maintain their own blogs.

The consequence of these demands is that ministers are frequently in a reactive, rather than a proactive, mode, having to rush to deal with problems and queries placed before them – on a relentless scale – and with little time to stand back and to think through what they want to achieve and whether they are on the path to achieving it.

■ Explaining ministerial power

Ministers are powerful figures in government. At the same time, they are subject to remarkable constraints. How, then, can one make sense of their role in British government? Various models have been created to help us to understand the role of ministers in policy making. Let us assess three that provide very different perspectives: the principal–agent model, the power-dependency model and the baronial model.

Principal–agent model

This stipulates that ministers are essentially the agents of a principal. Thus, although some ministers may be commanders, ideologues or managers, most fall under the category, identified earlier, of agents. One school of thought contends that the UK has **prime ministerial government**, and thus that ministers are agents of the Prime Minister. Another school of thought advances the proposition that the UK has Civil Service government, and thus that ministers are agents of civil servants.

The prime ministerial government school of thought argues that the powers of the Prime Minister are such that the Prime Minister is in a position to determine public policy. He or she makes policy preferences through the choice of senior ministers. If the Prime Minister wishes to achieve a particular policy outcome, he can effectively require a senior minister to agree to that policy. A minister failing to comply with prime ministerial wishes may cease to be a minister. Furthermore, the Prime Minister can ensure particular outcomes through control of the Cabinet agenda and through chairing the Cabinet. Tony Blair in particular was accused of marginalising his Cabinet in order to ensure he gets his way (see Kavanagh and Seldon 1999; Foster 2005). The Prime Minister can keep a tight rein on ministers through monitoring their speeches and through requiring the text of speeches to be cleared by Downing Street. Government policy, it is argued, is increasingly being made in Downing Street and not in the individual government departments.

The Civil Service school of thought argues that it is the Civil Service that determines policy outcomes. Working through departments, civil servants can help to shape, even determine, the minister's agenda. 'In practice', according to Weir and Beetham (1999: 167), 'ministers rely almost wholly on their departments, senior bureaucrats and private offices, and the resources and advice they can provide.' Civil servants have an advantage over ministers in terms of their numbers, permanence, expertise and cohesion. There is one senior minister heading a department. The number of senior civil servants in the department may run into three figures. A minister, even with the help of a number of junior ministers, cannot keep track of everything that is going on in a department. A senior minister will, on average, serve in one ministerial post for two years. (In the decades before the Second World War, the average was four years.) Civil servants will be in place in the department before a minister arrives and will usually still be in place once a minister has departed. A new minister provides civil servants with an opportunity to fight anew battles that may previously have been lost. One former minister recounted:

Lunch with my successor at Environment, Bob Ainsworth, who seems more at home in the job than I was. As I suspected, soon after I was out of the door, aviation officials came back to him with a modified version of the expensive and pointless research into night-flight sleep disturbance which I had refused to endorse . . .

Mullin (2009: 181)

Furthermore, their permanence also allows civil servants to build up a body of administrative expertise that is denied to a transient minister. Civil servants may be in a position to know what is achievable,

and what is not, in a way that ministers cannot. Civil servants, it is argued, are also more politically and socially cohesive than ministers: politically cohesive in that they imbue a particular Civil Service and departmental ethos, and their approach is shaped by that ethos; and socially cohesive in that they tend to be drawn from the same or similar social backgrounds and to be members of the same London clubs. Ministers, on the other hand, imbue no particular ethos and are drawn from somewhat disparate backgrounds. They do not tend to mix socially together in the way that senior civil servants do.

Civil servants are in a position to influence, even control, the flow of information to a minister. A minister may not always receive every piece of information relevant to a particular proposal. The minister's diary may be filled with meetings that are largely inconsequential or so numerous as to squeeze out time to do other things (see Shephard 2000: 119). The minister's red boxes may be filled with a mass of papers, the more important tucked away at the bottom. Officials may put up position papers, outlining various options, but omitting others or skewing the material in support of each in such a way that only one option appears to be viable. Indeed, ministers may have little chance to think and write anything of their own. One cabinet minister, deciding that he wanted to jot down some thoughts of his own, looked for some clean paper and found that there was none in his office. He asked his private secretary for some.

He went out and came back after a pause, holding in front of him like a dead rat, one single sheet of plain white paper, which he solemnly laid on the desk. After an apprehensive glance at me he left and I suddenly realised how civil servants controlled their masters: always keep them supplied with an endless supply of neatly prepared memoranda. Never give them time to think for themselves. Above all, never give them paper with nothing on it.

Lang (2002: 65)

Civil servants also monitor ministers' calls and may seek to limit formal contact between one minister and another and, indeed, between ministers and people outside the department. One minister encountered opposition when she decided to hold a series of breakfasts for businesswomen: 'The roof fell in. There was strong Treasury resistance – "But why, Minister?" – and a total inability to provide a tablecloth or anything to eat or drink, much less to get anyone else to do so' (Shephard 2000: 112). If a minister takes a view contrary to that adopted by civil servants in the department, the civil servants may ask civil servants in other departments to brief their ministers to take a contrary line when the matter comes before Cabinet committee. There is also extensive contact between officials in the UK government and in the EU Commission. Ministers, with little time to prepare for meetings, often have to be briefed on the plane to Brussels. On this line of argument, ministers have little scope to think about policy goals and to consider information and advice other than that placed before them by their officials. Sometimes the limitations are purely those of time. In other cases, they may be intellectual, ministers not having the mental capacity to challenge what has been laid before them. As one Chief Secretary to the Treasury once recorded, on complex issues ministers not directly involved in an issue would read the briefs, prepared by civil servants, the night before or as the argument proceeded. 'More often that not . . . they would follow the line of the brief' (Barnett 1982: 41). The dependence on the papers prepared by officials can occur at the highest levels. The Cabinet Office prepares a brief for the Prime Minister for Cabinet meetings indicating, on the basis of papers circulated and knowledge of those involved, the line the PM may wish to take ('Subject to discussion, the Prime Minister might wish to conclude . . . '). This is a form of prompt to the PM, who may or may not choose to utilise it. However, one senior civil servant records the occasion when Prime Minister Harold Wilson had to leave during a discussion and handed over to his deputy, Edward Short:

Short was a Bear of Little Brain and would have been as capable of understanding, let alone summarising, the previous discussion as he would have been at delivering a lecture on quantum mechanics. He presided wordlessly over the discussion for a further five minutes, then spoke. 'I find we have agreed as follows' – and read out the draft conclusions penned before the discussion had begun . . . Not without a modest satisfaction, the Secretariat recorded the conclusions read out by the Deputy Prime Minister.

Denman (2002: 169)

This view of the power of the Civil Service over ministers has been voiced by former ministers – among them Tony Benn – and was famously encapsulated in a popular television series, *Yes Minister*,

in the 1980s. The Permanent Secretary, Sir Humphrey Appleby, and other civil servants were able to out-manoeuvre the minister, Jim Hacker, in a way that finds resonance in the memoirs of some ministers.

However, both schools of thought have been challenged. The prime ministerial government model overlooks, according to critics, the limited time, resources and interest of the Prime Minister. The Prime Minister occupies a particular policy space – that of high policy (dealing with the economic welfare and security of the nation) – and has limited time to interfere in middle-level policy generated by ministers (see Norton 1997a, 2000). Furthermore, despite an extension of policy resources in Downing Street under Tony Blair, the resources available to a Prime Minister in Downing Street are limited. A senior minister has more advisers than the Prime Minister has in the minister's sector of public policy. Even though material must be cleared through Downing Street, some ministers are slow in submitting texts of speeches; some may never even reach Downing Street. Ministers may brief the press, or even give interviews, without clearance from No. 10 (see Short 2004: 177). Prime Ministers rarely have a grasp of, or a deep interest in, every sector of public policy. Instead, they leave it to ministers to get on with their jobs, frequently free of interference from Downing Street. Indeed, one of the most remarkable findings of recent research into senior ministers was that it is very rare for a Prime Minister, when appointing ministers to Cabinet office, to tell them what is expected of them (Norton 2000). The advice offered to John Major when he was appointed Foreign Secretary was brief and unrelated to specific policy: 'You had better hang on to your seatbelt' (Seldon 1997: 87). When Clare Short was offered the post of International Development Secretary by Tony Blair, they discussed who she wanted as her junior minister and what to call the new Department: 'I was then whisked off to my new department' (Short 2004: 56). It appeared to be a not dissimilar experience with John Prescott: 'We discussed briefly what the big new department would contain' (Prescott 2008: 212).

The Civil Service school of thought is challenged by the claim that civil servants are not as proactive and as cohesive as proponents of this thesis suggest. The demands made of civil servants are such that they too have little time for sustained thought and reflection. Although research suggests that civil servants in some departments imbue a particular departmental ethos, most civil servants seek to carry out the wishes of their ministers, regardless of their own views or prior departmental preferences. Indeed, recent research points to the extent to which civil servants are loyal to their ministers (Norton 2000). Far from seeking to impede them, they work hard to carry out their wishes. Furthermore, as Page and Jenkins found in their study of middle-ranking civil servants, 'where ministerial and departmental priorities conflicted, and the minister has expressed a clear view on the matter, there was no question but that the minister's view prevailed' (Page and Jenkins 2005: 133). Ministers are also now more likely to call civil servants in to quiz them about the papers they have submitted. Ministers themselves may also discuss matters privately, free from Civil Service involvement. Some of these meetings are bilateral rather than multilateral. One minister, interviewed by this author, recalled with wry amusement how his civil servants tried to limit his contacts with other ministers, largely oblivious to the fact that once he was in his minister's room in the Commons he could quite easily pop to see other ministers, in adjoining offices, to have a quiet chat.

Civil Service cohesion, and the ethos attached to the service and to particular departments, is also being eroded by the people from outside the Civil Service being brought in to senior posts and also by the greater emphasis being placed on managerial skills. Civil servants are being trained to deliver certain specified goals. A perceived failure to deliver under the Labour government of Tony Blair resulted in pressure being put on senior civil servants to improve their performance in meeting the government's targets (see Gray and Jenkins 2005). As civil servants are under greater pressure to deliver what ministers expect of them, so ministers are also bringing in more political appointees in order to provide advice and to handle their relations with the media (see Foster 2005: 207–22). That greater dependence on special advisers has been marked in recent years, generating public controversy and creating a grey area between civil servants and special advisers. Relations became especially strained in 2001–2 in the Transport Department between civil servants and the minister's special adviser, Jo Moore. Relationships broke down in the department, leading to the resignation of not only the special adviser but also the minister, Stephen Byers. Under the Blair government, his chief of staff (Jonathan Powell) and communications secretary (Alastair Campbell), both special advisers, were given executive powers, allowing them to give instructions to civil servants, a position that led to criticism and claims of a politicisation of the Civil Service. These powers were rescinded when Gordon Brown became Prime Minister. There has also been a tendency to seek advice from a range of bodies outside government – think tanks, advisory committees and task groups. In many cases, civil servants are not seen as being in the decision-making loop.

A seminal work on Cabinet ministers by Bruce Headey found that civil servants looked to ministers for leadership. They preferred ministers who could take decisions and fight (and win) departmental battles (Headey 1974: 140–53). That appears to remain the case. As one former Permanent Secretary put it, 'To some it might seem like heaven on earth to have a Minister who has no ideas and is endlessly open to the suggestions or recommendations of officials. But that is not the case. Officials need ministers with ideas . . . Officials need stimulus; need leadership; and, on occasion, conflict' (Holland 1995: 43). Middle-ranking civil servants work on policy detail, but they do so on the basis of a ministerial 'steer' (Page and Jenkins 2005: 136–40). This suggests that civil servants are more likely to welcome an effective commander, ideologue or manager as their minister than an agent or team player.

Power-dependency model

This model has been developed by R.A.W. Rhodes (1981, 1997). Although used to cover particularly, but not exclusively, centre–local relations, it is relevant for a study of the relationship between ministers and other actors in the political system. It is based on several propositions. One of the principal propositions is that any organisation is dependent upon other organisations for resources. Thus, the Prime Minister is dependent on the resources available in government departments; he does not have all the resources he needs in Downing Street. Ministers are dependent on their departments: they need civil servants to provide advice and to carry out their decisions. Civil servants need ministers to deliver resources through fighting battles with the Treasury and in Cabinet. Far from being in conflict with one another, the relationship may be closer to a partnership (Weir and Beetham 1999: 172–5). A second proposition is that in order to achieve their goals, organisations have to exchange resources. In other words, no body can operate as an exclusive and effective body. Actors within the political system need others in the system to help them to achieve their goals. There is a dependence on others (see Norton 2003). That means that alliances have to be created. The model recognises that there may be a body or group of bodies that dominate in the relationship but that the relationship may change as actors fight for position.

The relevance for understanding the role of senior ministers is that it stands as something of a corrective to the principal–agent model. Although there may be times when the Prime Minister or civil servants are to the fore in determining policy outcomes, ministers are not relegated to some supporting role. They need the Prime Minister and civil servants, but conversely the Prime Minister and civil servants need them: they are an important resource, and they cannot necessarily be taken for granted. A Prime Minister may thus need to build support in Cabinet to get a controversial measure approved: the support of senior ministers thus constitutes a vital, indeed a necessary, resource. It may be necessary, but it may not be sufficient. Statutory powers, as we have seen, are vested in senior ministers. The Prime Minister, and Cabinet, thus need to ensure that the relevant minister is willing to exercise those powers. Others may thus depend on the resources at the disposal of ministers. At the same time, ministers themselves are dependent on the resources of others. They need the political support of the Prime Minister. They need their civil servants to carry out their wishes. They also need different bodies outside government to accept and to help to implement their policies. The Justice Secretary, for example, may need to mobilise the support of the Bar in order to achieve reform of the legal system.

The power-dependency model thus suggests a more complex and less hierarchical political process than that advanced by the principal–agent model. Although the Prime Minister may predominate, it is not to the extent that we can claim the existence of prime ministerial government. Ministers are more important players in the process than the principal–agent model suggests. Although important, ministers themselves are not dominant either. They too depend on others in the political process. The process of policy making is thus an essentially crowded and interactive one.

The power-dependency model has been variously criticised (see Rhodes 1997: 37). In terms of understanding the place of senior ministers in government, it does not necessarily help to explain who is predominant at any one time. Extensive empirical research would be necessary to do that. It also runs foul of objections from advocates of the principal–agent model. They contend that senior ministers may be resources that a Prime Minister needs, but they are subordinate resources that can be drawn on by the Prime Minister without the need for persuasion. The power-dependency model does not help to explain cases where the Prime Minister has achieved a particular outcome by adopting a confrontational stance rather than an alliance-building one. As various Cabinet ministers noted, Margaret Thatcher as Prime Minister was not noted for seeking to build alliances in Cabinet. Similarly, Tony Blair was criticised for distancing himself from the Civil Service and others, substituting detachment and prime ministerial instructions for mutual dependence (Norton 2003: 543–59; Norton 2008). It also does not help to explain those cases where ministers can, and do, ignore civil service advice and act unilaterally and, on occasion, go beyond the bounds of normal ministerial powers. In the words of one former civil servant, 'We have to recognise that the assumption that the civil service is there to keep the government within the bounds of constitutional propriety is so threadbare it would be unwise to rely on it' (Jenkins 2004: 807).

Baronial model

This model has been developed by this writer. It posits that ministers are like medieval barons in that they preside over their own, sometimes vast, policy territory. Within that territory they are largely supreme. We have identified the formal and informal underpinnings of this supremacy. Ministers head their respective departments. They have the constitutional authority and the legal power to take decisions. No one else enjoys that power. Junior ministers have no formal power and can act only on the authority of the senior minister. Once the minister has taken a view – that is, made a decision – the civil servants in the department implement it. The ministers have their own policy space, their own castles – even some of the architecture of departments (such as the Ministry of Defence and the Ministry of Health, both in Whitehall) reinforces that perception – and their own courtiers. Indeed, recent years have seen a growth in the coterie of courtiers appointed by some senior ministers, some – such as Gordon Brown when Chancellor of the Exchequer – being seen almost as having an alternative court to that of the Prime Minister (see Naughtie 2001: 124–5). The minister's baronial position is also protected to some degree by what is termed a 'silo mentality' in the Civil Service (Page 2005): officials want to protect their particular departmental turf and will support the minister in seeking to protect or extend the responsibilities, and budget, of the department. The ministers fight – or form alliances – with other barons in order to get what they want. They resent interference in their territory by other barons and will fight to defend it.

The analogy is not altogether accurate in that the barons have no responsibility for raising taxes. (The exception is the Chancellor of the Exchequer, who has become more powerful than the original holders of the ancient office.) The Prime Minister also has greater power than a medieval monarch to dispense with the services of the barons, although the differences are not as great as may be supposed: a Prime Minister has difficulty dispensing with the services of powerful barons. He has his court and they have theirs. Despite the absence of a precise fit, the model has utility for understanding the nature and fluidity of power relationships within government. It has found resonance in various works on the Blair premiership, as in Francis Beckett and David Hencke's *The Blairs and their Court* (2004). Far from Cabinet being a homogeneous body of prime ministerial agents, it is a heterogeneous gathering and includes usually some powerful individuals.

Furthermore, reinforcing the baronial model is the approach taken by ministers to their jobs. Although Prime Ministers can use ministerial appointments as a way of changing or confirming their own policy preferences, they rarely choose a Cabinet of similar ministerial types. A Cabinet typically contains a mix of commanders, managers and ideologues, with the interests of the individual ministers around the table, and their particular departmental territories, taking precedence over any concept of altruistic collective decision-making.

This provides a new perspective on the relationship between senior ministers and the Prime Minister. Rather than being able to give directions, as in a principal–agent relationship, a Prime Minister has to be prepared to bargain with the more powerful barons in his government. He may be able to control some of the weaker members of the Cabinet, but others may be too powerful to be subject to prime ministerial direction. Reducing the power of the Cabinet may not necessarily have diminished the position of individual ministers, with whom the Prime Minister has to deal directly. At a minimum, ministers have an important gatekeeping role. To follow the analogy, they can close their departmental drawbridges and deny the Prime Minister entry to their policy domain. If the Prime Minister wants a particular policy implemented, the relevant minister has the formal power to say no, and a strong-minded commander or ideologue, even a determined manager may have the political will to exercise that power.

A Prime Minister has limited scope to act unilaterally. He has no departmental responsibilities. Furthermore, the Prime Minister has limited resources to ensure that ministers act in accordance with his wishes. His own court, as we have noted, is a relatively small one. Attempts by Tony Blair and Gordon Brown to strengthen the coordination and oversight of Downing Street are testimony to this limited capacity. The more cunning of senior ministers can frequently circumvent attempts to limit what they say and do. Speeches may be sent late to Downing Street. Backbenchers or the media may be mobilised in support of a particular policy. Cabinet ministers often have their favoured lobby journalists. Outside bodies may come to the defence of a minister they believe to be sympathetic to their cause.

The senior barons are thus able to plough their own furrows, making their own speeches, leaking – through their courtiers – their own side of a particular argument and their own perception of what has taken place in Cabinet or Cabinet committee. They can and do form alliances to achieve the approval of measures subject to Cabinet – which usually means Cabinet committee – approval (middle-level policy) and may operate unilaterally in laying orders that they are empowered by statute to make (low-level policy). Sometimes Prime Ministers – especially at times when their political authority is weakened – are in a constricted position, having to remind their ministers not to leak details of what has taken place and not to speak to the press without clearance.

Ministers develop their own ways of preserving their territorial integrity. Some adopt an isolationist stance, others a confrontational stance (see Norton 2000). The stances taken reflect both the variety of approaches taken by ministers and the fact that they cannot be characterised as agents. They are barons, and in order to get their way they sometimes have to fight other barons as well as the monarch.

Characterising senior ministers as barons is also appropriate in that, like medieval barons, they are powerful but not all-powerful. They are constrained by other powerful actors, including the monarch (Prime Minister) and other barons (senior ministers), and by a recognition that they have to abide by laws and conventions. Indeed, as we have seen, they are increasingly constrained as the political environment has become more crowded, with groups coming into existence and making more demands of them – groups that they may need to cooperate with in implementing policy – and with more actors with the power to take decisions of their own. Ministers may thus find their time consumed by fighting battles with other political actors, be it bodies within the European Union or within the UK. Consequently, to provide a dynamic of the present state of senior ministers in British government, one can offer a model of barons operating within a shrinking kingdom (Norton 2000).

This model is compatible with the power-dependency model, but it provides a greater emphasis on the role of ministers and encompasses the different strategies adopted by ministers, including fighting battles as well as alliance building. It is geared more directly than the power-dependency model to senior ministers. However, it has been criticised on the grounds that the fit with medieval barons is far from perfect – that the power and activity of the barons bears little relevance to senior ministers today. It can also be challenged on the grounds that it underestimates the power of the Prime Minister. As someone close to Tony Blair said while Labour was still in Opposition: 'You may see a change from a feudal system of barons to a more Napoleonic system' (Hennessy 2000: 478; Naughtie 2001: 96). Napoleon, though, needed his generals and his form of rule was, and is, difficult to sustain.

The model also has the same drawback as the other models in that they are models rather than theories. However, it stands as a useful counterpoint

---

BOX 18.1   BRITAIN IN CONTEXT

Bureaucrats and politicians

The distinction between ministers and civil servants – that is, elected politicians and full-time officials – is not distinctive to the UK. What is notable is the extent to which the integrity of the Civil Service is maintained. Despite accusations of a creeping politicisation of the Civil Service, the extent to which the Civil Service in the UK is a body of permanent public servants, there to serve the government whichever party is in power, is remarkable in comparative context. The distinction is one that has been exported to many Commonwealth countries, though not necessarily maintained to the same degree as in the UK.

In some countries, the senior administrative posts in government are essentially patronage posts. In the USA, not only are cabinet ministers, and their juniors, appointed by the President, but so too are the administrative posts below them; the President has more than 2,000 administrative posts in his gift. In some countries, such as France, the distinction is not always a clear one to draw, with senior civil servants sometimes being appointed to senior ministerial posts, including that of Prime Minister.

The relationship between the head of government and cabinet ministers also differs, especially depending on the type of government that exists. In presidential systems, Cabinet members are usually dependent solely on the patronage of the President. They typically enjoy no separate political legitimacy of their own, since – under the separation of powers – they are not members of the legislature. In parliamentary systems, Cabinet members may be drawn from and remain within the legislature; in some, they may be drawn from, but are precluded from remaining in, the legislature. The principal difference between the two systems, though, is that a President cannot usually be brought down by the legislature. In a parliamentary system, the head of government is dependent on the confidence of the legislature. That dependence may sometimes give other members of the leader's party a significant political clout, especially if they have a following of their own in the legislature. Relationships between the Prime Minister and Cabinet may thus be more complex, potentially rendering the Prime Minister vulnerable to a Cabinet coup or challenge by a senior member.

to the principal–agent model. It provides a new perspective on the role of senior ministers, emphasising the role played in government by ministers as ministers, rather than seeing them solely as a collective body, subsumed under the heading of government or Cabinet. This model suggests that senior ministers are more important figures in British government than is generally realised.

Chapter summary

Ministers of the Crown head government departments. Those departments are extensive and complex bodies. Ministers enjoy substantial formal as well as political powers. The extent to which they are able to utilise those powers will depend upon the purpose and skill of the individual minister as well as the power situation, the climate of expectation and international developments. Ministers face considerable constraints, especially in recent years as the domain in which they operate has been constricted.

Ministers operate in a complex political environment. Different models seek to locate the place of ministers in that environment. The principal–agent model contends that ministers are agents of the Prime Minister or of civil servants. The power-dependency model posits an environment in which ministers have to negotiate with other actors in order to achieve desired outcomes. The baronial model posits that ministers have their own policy territory, castles and courtiers and fight or build alliances in order to get their way. The last two models suggest that ministers enjoy a greater role in policy making than is generally realised in the literature on British politics.

Discussion points

■ Is there an ideal type of senior minister?

■ Why are departments the basic building blocks of British government?

■ What should be the relationship between a minister and civil servants?

■ What is the relationship between ministers and civil servants?

■ Which model best explains the position of senior ministers in British government?

Further reading

Former ministers variously publish memoirs or diaries. Among those by former Cabinet ministers are Lawson (1992), Hurd (2003), Cook (2003), Short (2004), Blunkett (2006) and Prescott (2008), though the last has relatively little of relevance to ministerial power and minister-civil service relationships. Shephard (2000) provides a succinct, and very readable, commentary in her section on 'Ministers and Mandarins'. Mullin (2009) provides excellent insights into the role of a junior minister. Kaufman (1997) provides a humorous but pertinent guide as to how to be a good minister. However, very few academic works have appeared that look conceptually at the role of ministers. Rose (1987) provides a functional analysis, and Brazier (1997) offers a more formal analysis. A broader analysis, encompassing the dynamics of ministerial office, is provided by Norton (2000). Junior ministers are covered by Theakston (1987). The relation of ministers to Parliament is dealt with by Woodhouse (1994, 2002). Political, and judicial, accountability is also covered by Flinders (2001).

There are various works on departments and, more especially, civil servants. A massive work, looking at departments and the civil servants that work in them, is that of Hennessy (2001). Other works include Theakston (1995, 1999), Barberis (1997), Richards (1997), Rhodes (2001), Gray and Jenkins (2005), Page and Jenkins (2005) and, for a useful historical overview, Bogdanor (2003); see also Chapter 15 of Foster (2005). Lipsey (2000) provides a useful analysis of relationships in the Treasury. Jenkins (2004) offers a useful and brief overview from the perspective of a former civil servant. Denman (2002) offers a wonderfully readable and insightful view from the perspective of a senior civil servant. Stanley (2004) provides the civil servant equivalent to Kaufman's book: Chapter 1 covers working with ministers. For more material, see Chapter 21 of the present volume.

Bibliography

Barberis, P. (ed.) (1997) *The Civil Service in an Era of Change* (Dartmouth).

Barnett, J. (1982) *Inside the Treasury* (André Deutsch).

Beckett, F. and Hencke, D. (2004) *The Blairs and their Court* (Aurum Press).

Blunkett, D. (2006) *The Blunkett Tapes* (Bloomsbury).

Bogdanor, V. (2003) 'The Civil Service', in V. Bogdanor (ed.) *The British Constitution in the Twentieth Century* (The British Academy/Oxford University Press).

Brazier, R. (1997) *Ministers of the Crown* (Clarendon Press).

Cook, R. (2003) *Point of Departure* (Simon & Schuster).

Denman, R. (2002) *The Mandarin's Tale* (Politico's).

Flinders, M. (2001) *The Politics of Accountability and the Modern State* (Ashgate).

Foster, C. (2005) *British Government in Crisis* (Hart Publishing).

Gray, A. and Jenkins, B. (2005) 'Government and Administration: Public Service and Public Servants', *Parliamentary Affairs*, Vol. 58.

Headey, B. (1974) *British Cabinet Ministers* (George Allen & Unwin).

Hennessy, P. (2000) *The Prime Minister: The Office and its Holders since 1945* (Allen Lane/Penguin Press).

Hennessy, P. (2001) *Whitehall*, revised edn (Pimlico).

Holland, Sir G. (1995) 'Alas! Sir Humphrey, I Knew him Well', *RSA Journal*, November.

Hurd, D. (2003) *Memoirs* (Little, Brown).

Jenkins, K. (2004) 'Parliament, Government and the Civil Service', *Parliamentary Affairs*, Vol. 57.

Johnson, N. (1980) *In Search of the Constitution* (Methuen).

Kaufman, G. (1997) *How to be a Minister* (Faber and Faber).

Kavanagh, D. and Seldon, A. (1999) *The Powers Behind the Prime Minister* (HarperCollins).

Lang, I. (2002) *Blue Remembered Years* (Politico's).

Lawson, N. (1992) *The View from No. 11* (Bantam Press).

Lipsey, D. (2000) *The Secret Treasury* (Viking).

Morrison, J. (2001) *Reforming Britain: New Labour, New Constitution?* (Reuters/Pearson Education).

Mullin, C. (2009) *A View from the Foothills* (Profile Books).

Naughtie, J. (2001) *The Rivals* (Fourth Estate).

Norton, P. (1987) 'Prime Ministerial Power: A Framework for Analysis', *Teaching Politics*, Vol. 16, No. 3, pp. 325–45.

Norton, P. (1997a) 'Leaders or Led? Senior Ministers in British Government', *Talking Politics*, Vol. 10, No. 2, pp. 78–85.

Norton, P. (1997b) 'Political Leadership', in L. Robins and B. Jones (eds) *Half a Century in British Politics* (Manchester University Press).

Norton, P. (2000) 'Barons in a Shrinking Kingdom? Senior Ministers in British Government', in R.A.W. Rhodes (ed.) *Transforming British Government*, Vol. 2 (Macmillan).

Norton, P. (2003) 'Governing Alone', *Parliamentary Affairs*, Vol. 56.

Norton, P. (2008) 'Tony Blair and the Office of Prime Minister', in M. Beech and S.D. Lee (eds) *Ten Years of New Labour* (Palgrave Macmillan).

Page, E.C. (2005) 'Joined-up Government and the Civil Service', in V. Bogdanor (ed.) *Joined-Up Government* (The British Academy).

Page, E.C. and Jenkins, B. (2005) *Policy Bureaucracy* (Oxford University Press).

Parkinson, C. (1992) *Right at the Centre* (Weidenfeld & Nicolson).

Prescott, J. (2008) *Prezza* (Headline Review).

Pyper, R. (1995) *The British Civil Service* (Prentice Hall/Harvester Wheatsheaf).

Rhodes, R.A.W. (1981) *Control and Power in Centre–Local Government Relationships* (Gower).

Rhodes, R.A.W. (1997) *Understanding Governance* (Open University Press).

Rhodes, R.A.W. (2001) 'The Civil Service', in A. Seldon (ed.) *The Blair Effect* (Little, Brown).

Richards, D. (1997) *The Civil Service under the Conservatives, 1979–1997* (Academy Press).

Rose, R. (1987) *Ministers and Ministries* (Clarendon Press).

Seldon, A. (1997) *Major: a Political Life* (Weidenfeld & Nicolson).

Shephard, G. (2000) *Shephard's Watch* (Politico's).

Short, C. (2004) *An Honourable Deception?* (The Free Press).

Stanley, M. (2004) *Politico's Guide to How to be a Civil Servant* (Politico's).

Tebbit, N. (1989) *Upwardly Mobile* (Futura).

Theakston, K. (1987) *Junior Ministers* (Blackwell).

Theakston, K. (1995) *The Civil Service since 1945* (Blackwell).

Theakston, K. (1999) *Leadership in Whitehall* (Macmillan).

Weir, S. and Beetham, D. (1999) *Political Power and Democratic Control in Britain* (Routledge).

Woodhouse, D. (1994) *Ministers and Parliament* (Clarendon Press).

Woodhouse, D. (2002) 'The Reconstruction of Constitutional Accountability', *Public Law*, Spring.

Useful websites

Ministers

List of government ministers: www.parliament.uk/mpslordsandoffices/government_and_opposition/hmg.cfm

Ministerial responsibilities: www.cabinetoffice.gov.uk/ministerial_responsibilities.aspx

Ministerial Code: www.cabinetoffice.gov.uk/propriety_and_ethics/ministers/ministerial_code.aspx

Civil Service

Civil Service: www.civil-service.gov.uk

First Division Association of Civil Servants: www.fda.org.uk

Cabinet Office: www.cabinetoffice.gov.uk/about_the_cabinet_office/organisation.aspx

National School of Government: www.nationalschool.gov.uk/

Related websites

Public Administration Committee of the House of Commons: www.parliament.uk/parliamentary_committees/public_administration_select_committee.cfm

Guide to being a civil servant: www.civilservant.org.uk

10

CHAPTER 19

Local government

Colin Copus

Learning objectives

- To consider the implications of the dual role of local councils in acting as politically representative institutions and as the providers of important public services.

- To explore whether widespread public apathy about local government undermines local democracy in Britain.

- To consider the impact on local government of the introduction of political executives: directly elected mayors and indirectly elected leaders and their cabinets.

- To examine whether local councils should have more freedom from central control.

- To examine whether councillors represent the community or their party.

- To explore the relationship between British local government and the European Union's policy-making network.

Leeds town hall
Source: Alamy Images / Steven Gillis hdg

Introduction

There are around 22,000 councillors in Britain of whom (at the beginning of 2006), 8,181 were Conservative, 6,514 were Labour, and 4,754 were Liberal Democrat. In addition, the Scottish National Party had 186 councillors elected, Plaid Cymru had 182, and there were some 2,206 who were independent of political parties, or who stood for election for a non-party organisation such as a residents' association or a community group. In Northern Ireland, which uses the Single Transferable Vote system, we find a broader range of political representation and the representation of different shades of unionist and nationalist opinion. The seats held by the various parties in Northern Ireland after the 2005 elections was: Democratic Unionist Party 182, Sinn Fein 126, Ulster Unionist Party 115, Social Democratic and Labour Party 101, Alliance Party 30 and others, 28 seats.

Local councils are political and democratically elected bodies and this chapter will explore the tensions that exist between local government as a politically representative set of institutions and a local authority as a body that manages and administers the provision of a complex range of local services. It will however, focus more closely on the political role of the local council, as, in discussions about the financing, organisational administration of large public bureaucracies, the management of public services and arguments about the amount of control central government should have over councils, it is easy to forget that they are elected bodies with their own policy agenda and their own special relationship with local voters. The politics of local government often become submerged under discussions about running schools, providing social care, the lighting, repairing and sweeping of the streets and the emptying of dustbins. All of which, of course, are vital public services, but, if all 22,000 councillors across Britain disappeared tomorrow, then these services would still continue to be provided. So, this chapter will deliberately concentrate on the politics of local government and the vital role councillors play as elected representatives and governors, rather than the role they often find themselves playing – that of an elected service manager!

The chapter will explore the long-term relationship between local government and local politics and, to do this, in first section it will examine the development and structure of British local government; in the second it will explore the relationships between local and central government; the third will consider the growth, impact and role of party politics at the local level; the fourth section will examine the changes made to the way in which political decisions are made by the Local Government Act 2000, which introduced directly elected mayors and executive council leaders into local government. It will also look at aspects of what has been known as the 'modernising agenda' for local government, as it relates to the politics and policy of local government; the fifth will consider the policy environment of local government; and the final section will look at the government's apparently ill-fated proposals for elected regional assemblies in England and the more successful devolution to Scotland and Wales. It will also look at the relationship between local government and the European Union.

■ Background

British local government has always been subordinate to central control. Unlike many of its continental counterparts, British local government remains constitutionally unprotected from the political ideologies, policies, priorities and, indeed, caprice of central government. The shape, size, structure, functions, powers, duties and very existence of local councils rest in the hands of central government to decide and the courts to interpret. Indeed, central government could abolish all local government and replace it with a system of central administration by the simple process of passing an Act of Parliament to that effect. Such a Bill for the abolition of local government would simply have to pass the same Parliamentary procedures as any other Bill on any other subject – it would not have to navigate some special constitutional procedure. Moreover, British councils can do only that which the law grants them permission or powers to do; any action not sanctioned by law is *ultra vires* (beyond the powers) and liable to be quashed or rendered null and void by the courts.

The constitutionally subordinate role of local government to the centre at Westminster and Whitehall has led many to regard the work of local councils as no more than an administrative process – devoid of its own political life. Indeed, as Gyford (1976: 11) points out, some maintain that it is management and administration that solves local problems, not the making of what are political, and party political, choices about the allocation of scarce resources. Moreover, central government concerns (justified or otherwise) about the efficiency of local government service provision and about variations in service standards within and across councils and across the country, coupled with central government regulation of local authorities and large-scale public apathy when it comes to local elections, raises questions about the continued existence of, or need for, independent local government (Byrne 1983: 24).

To the litany of criticism that has often been heaped upon local government can be added time-consuming and opaque decision-making structures; the supposedly poor calibre of many local councillors; party politics, leading to unnecessary conflict and confrontation; large and remote units of local government distant from many of the communities represented and served; the tension between political and community representation and notions of technical efficiency of service administration (the technocrat–democrat argument); and the constraint on local action and decision-making arising from wider economic and social factors (Stanyer 1976; Dearlove 1979; Elcock 1982; Hampton 1987; Wolman and Goldsmith 1992). Despite questions as to its value and relevance, local government and, indeed, local democracy and autonomy hold an important position in the political structure and processes of British governance. Indeed, democratically elected councils provide an all too vital safeguard against an over-powerful central government and ensure that political space and positions exist for those that do not share the political affiliation of the government of the day. While the British government is always assured of its own way, the usual practice in policy making has been for some degree of negotiation, compromise and bargaining to occur between central government and the localities. Local government and locally elected councillors are vital for any democratic country.

Local government, and the decisions made by councils and councillors, comes with a legitimacy that flows from the consequences of the electoral process. Local elections produce a layer of political representatives able to claim a mandate from local citizens for the decisions they make and the policies they pursue. Moreover, councillors operate in a greater proximity to the citizen than does the Member of Parliament and the government. While the local electoral mandate theory has been criticised by comparison with its national counterpart, councillors acting as duly elected representatives of the people provide an important legitimacy to the activities of local government (Wolman and Goldsmith 1992). It is the people's vote that prevents local government from being wholly an administrative arm of central government. But it is a vote that turn-out in local elections indicates the public are less and less willing to grant.

Yet, despite present-day local government being based on notions of representative democracy and one person one vote; this was not always the case. The development of the local franchise was originally concerned to ensure that the electorate, and the candidates from whom they could select, fulfilled some property qualification (Keith-Lucas 1952). Councillors, during the Victorian period, were often seen less as local politicians and more as keepers of the public purse (councillors today still have a fiduciary as well as political relationship to the voter), indeed, the development of local government has been described as less a search for representative democracy and more the development of a form of ratepayer democracy (Young 1989: 6). But today, councillors hold office as a consequence of the public vote, and the vast majority of councillors are affiliated to one of the national parties and often see their role not only as a local representative but also from a wider party political viewpoint (HMSO 1986b; Young and Davis 1990; Copus 2004).

■ British local government: from confusion to cohesion

The uniformity displayed by the current map of local government structure is a recent phenomenon. Indeed, it is the myth of the importance of uniformity that enabled the demands of service management and administration to sideline political representation as the driving force for local self-government. British local government has gone through a process of evolution interspersed with periodic revolution; growing from the naturally formed communities of Anglo-Saxon England; local government took on a shape, size and structure that reflected its roots in very local communities. Parishes, boroughs and counties developed over time, sharing the provision of services and local administrative matters with an often confusing mix of other statutory, non-statutory and private providers, alongside magistrates and sheriffs and other local offices appointed by the monarch.

As new problems and issues of government arose, dealing with the impact of an increasingly complex world became the local responsibility of a range of local bodies and appointed boards. Parishes, boroughs and counties overlapped in area and responsibilities with a host of boards and commissions such as those for; improvement, street paving, drainage, public health and, of course the Poor Law Guardians. The evolutionary development of local government saw administration and local decision making shared between single and multipurpose bodies, formed variously by statute, appointment, self-selection or election. The structures and arrangements for managing local affairs prior to 1835 would be barely recognisable when compared to today's local councils.

It was the reforming zeal and legislative whirlwind of activity during the Victorian period that began to give some national coherence to the shape and responsibilities of local government while continuing to deal, in an ad hoc fashion, with many of the problems generated by, and for, the developing capitalist system. Commencing with the 1835 Municipal Corporations Act, described by Wilson and Game (2002) as the 'foundation of our present day local government', and up to the 1899 reform of London government, the Victorians gave a basis to local government of popular – although not universal – election, financial responsibility and uniformity of purpose, shape and process. By the turn of the century, local authorities looked and felt like the 'governments' of their localities but were ironically being increasingly controlled by the centre (see Chandler 2007). The structure of counties, districts, non-county boroughs and all-purpose county boroughs, with parishes as a fourth sub-tier, promoted some uniformity. But it left unanswered the question of how many layers (or tiers) of local government there should be to meet the often conflicting requirements of political representation and effective and efficient service provision.

The legislatively enforced uniformity of local government continued throughout the twentieth century, as did the preoccupation of central governments, of all political colours, with the regulation of local activity and the diminution of local autonomy. It was in the period after the Second World War, when policy makers were grappling with rapidly changing demographic, political, social and technological developments, and a rapidly expanding welfare state, that the demands of efficient service administration and responsive, democratic local government needed to be reconciled (Young and Rao 1997). Yet, reconciling political representation with service provision proved a difficult task as one facet of local government could easily sideline the other. Technocratic and democratic needs are driven by different factors, with technocracy requiring bigger and bigger units of local government; and local democracy requiring smaller and more cohesive communities. Throughout the twentieth century, the technocracy of service provision, management and administration won a series of important battles over the needs of local democracy as a politically representative process. These victories become very apparent when looking at the shape, size and structure of local government.

The Herbert Commission Report on London Government (HMSO 1960) resulted in the replacement in 1965 of the London County Council (created in 1889) as the strategic authority by the geographically larger Greater London Council. In addition, 32 London boroughs and the City of London Corporation had responsibility for the provision of day-to-day services (replacing the 28 boroughs introduced in 1899) (see Pimlott and Rao 2002 and Travers 2004). As with other reorganisations, size mattered, and as a consequence local cohesion and community representation lost out. In 1966, the Labour government set up a Royal Commission on Local Government in England, with separate inquiries into the future of local government in Wales and Scotland. The Report of the Royal Commission

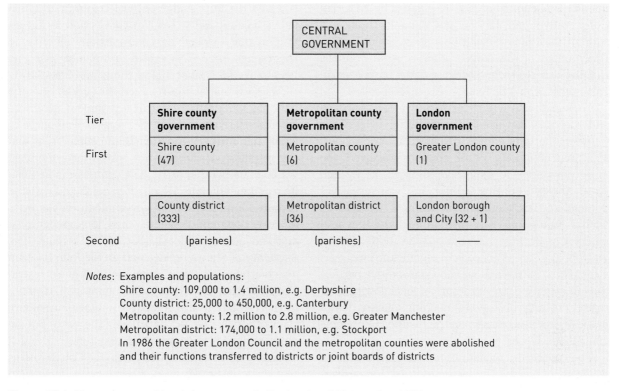

Figure 19.1 The structure of local government in England and Wales after 1974
Source: Adapted from Gray (1979).

(HMSO 1967a), while accepting the importance of democratic local government, expressed the belief that it was then too numerous and fragmented, but it was equally unable to agree unanimously a blueprint for change. The majority report suggested a unitary solution with 58 authorities outside London responsible for all local government services. However, a minority report argued for a two-tier division of function and structure based on city regions and 'shire' and 'district' councils. The Labour government accepted the majority report, but its Conservative successor elected in 1970, and mindful of its strengths in the shires, introduced a new two-tier structure through the 1972 Local Government Act.

As a consequence, on 1 April 1974 the map of local government changed dramatically (Figure 19.1). The systems of local government for the big cities and counties were the inverse of each other. In the major conurbations, six metropolitan counties were created alongside 36 metropolitan districts. The metropolitan counties were major strategic authorities, while the metropolitan districts had responsibility for the large-spending services such as education, social services and housing.

In the shires the situation was almost reversed; the counties – 47 of them – were the education and social service authorities as well as having a wider strategic remit. The districts were responsible for housing, with leisure as the other major spending service, alongside planning and waste-removal functions. In England and Wales, the number of counties was reduced from 58 to 47 and the districts from 1,249 to 333. As a result of the Wheatley Commission (HMSO 1969), local government in Scotland was also reorganised on a two-tier basis with nine large regional councils and 53 districts, alongside three island authorities. Thus, in 1974 British local government became less local and more subject to division of function between increasingly large and remote units.

The political debate behind the 1974 reorganisation is often overshadowed, and indeed obscured, by the technocratic versus democratic arguments of large efficient local government against small responsive self-governing communities. In the 1960s and 1970s, the Labour and Conservative parties saw the structure of local government, the allocation of services between tiers and the drawing of authority boundaries as important political considerations;

not a new phenomenon but one shared by Victorian Conservative and Liberal governments. Labour's support for a unitary solution – still current Labour Party policy – saw large, urban-centred councils running all services, and because of the party's urban base, these would be mainly Labour-controlled.

Conservative support for the two-tier approach and the 1970 government's allocation of services between the tiers equally displayed its party political preoccupations. Shire counties received the more powerful and expensive services, as by and large these counties would be Conservative-dominated. The metropolitan districts were given similar functional responsibilities, which would enable Conservatives in some of the more affluent metropolitan areas to control significant local services. Thus, for the Labour and Conservative parties, the importance of the structure of local government rested not only on the technocratic against democratic arguments but also on the realities of political control and power.

The political considerations concerning local government were at the fore in most of the reorganisations that occurred in the 1980s and 1990s, instigated again by a Conservative government. The metropolitan counties, and particularly the Greater London Council, led from 1981 by Ken Livingstone, had become troublesome for the Thatcher government. The Conservatives' 1983 manifesto had pledged to abolish these authorities, and after the publication of a White Paper, 'Streamlining the Cities' (HMSO 1983), this was duly accomplished in 1986. The responsibilities of the GLC and six metropolitan counties were transferred to the boroughs below them, or to a series of joint boards. While the Conservative government argued that the metropolitan counties had outlived their usefulness and were large, remote, unresponsive, bureaucratic and expensive, they had, at a stroke, removed from the local and national scene a source of acute political embarrassment and opposition.

The reorganisations of the 1990s display similar political and party political undercurrents as well as an interesting shift by the Conservatives towards favouring a unitary system of local government. In 1992, John Major's Conservative government established a Local Government Commission, chaired by Sir John Banham (former Director of Audit at the Audit Commission and Director General of the Confederation of British Industry) to review the structure of local government. Government guidance to the commission favoured the unitary system and

stressed the importance of local government efficiency, accountability, responsiveness and localness, criteria that display the contradictions inherent in the technocratic–democratic arguments that had been played out since 1945 (Young and Rao 1997).

Yet the commission rejected the production of a national blueprint for local government structure and instead recommended the creation of all-purpose, single-tier **unitary authorities** in some areas and the retention of the two-tier system or a modified version of it in other areas. The commission justified its recommendations, which often conflicted with the favoured approach of the government, on the basis of cost, community identity and local geography, and the degree of local support for change. The Secretary of State's replacement of Sir John Banham as chairman of the Commission with Sir David Cooksey, again from the Audit Commission, resulted in the formation of a few more unitary authorities than otherwise would have been the case, but no new nationwide reorganisation resulted.

However, it has not always been the Conservatives that have ushered in new unitary councils and Labour has shown its preference for unitary local government with the announcement in July 2007 of nine successful applications for unitary status made by councils. These applications – contested by some of the councils effected – resulted in April 2009 in 44 councils being replaced by 9 unitary councils, with a loss of over 1,300 councillors (for an excellent analysis of the latest review of local government, see Chisholm and Leach 2008) (see Table 19.1).

Local government in Scotland and Wales has fared somewhat differently from that in England. The 1992 Local Government Act abolished the county and district councils in Wales and the regional and district councils in Scotland, replacing them with 22 unitaries in Wales and 32 in Scotland. Local government in Northern Ireland had been reorganised in 1972, when 26 District councils were created. As a result of the 'review of public administration' in Northern Ireland, these 26 councils are to be replaced by 11 councils in 2011 – requiring the postponement of the elections due for 2009.

The Blair government elected in 1997 moved quickly on its promise to reintroduce elected local government for the whole of London and did so with the Greater London Authority Act 1999. The Act created the new Greater London Authority, consisting of the London Assembly and the directly elected mayor of London. The Assembly has 25 elected members, 14 of whom are members elected from

Table 19.1 New English unitary councils created in 2007

County area unitary proposal (number of districts in brackets)	New unitary structure	Change in number of councils
Bedford (3)	2 Unitary Bedford	4 reduced to 2
Chester (6)	2 Unitary Cheshire	7 reduced to 2
Cornwall (6)	County Unitary	7 reduced to 1
Durham (7)	County Unitary	8 reduced to 1
Northumberland (6)	County Unitary	7 reduced to 1
Shropshire (5)	County Unitary	6 reduced to 1
Wiltshire (4)	County Unitary	5 reduced to 1

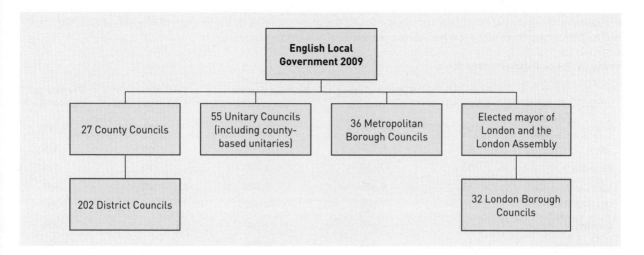

Figure 19.2 The structure of English local government
In addition there are some 9,000 parish and town councils across Britain and the Local Government and Public Involvement in Health Act made possible the formation of parish councils in London.

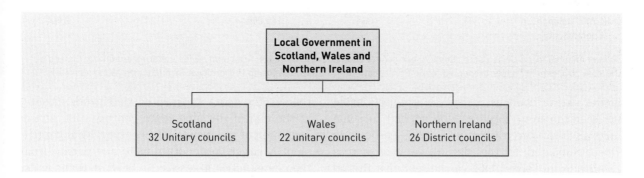

Figure 19.3 Local Government in Scotland, Wales and Northern Ireland

constituencies formed from the London boroughs and elected by the first-past-the-post system; eleven are members from across London, with no specific constituencies, elected from a party (or independent) list. The London mayor is elected by the supplementary vote system. The first elected mayor of London, who served two consecutive terms in office, was Ken Livingstone who was also the last leader of the GLC. He was defeated in the 2008 elections by the Conservative candidate: Boris Johnson.

The gradual creep towards an all unitary system of local government goes hand-in-hand with increase

Steve Bell cartoon of Boris Johnson and Mayors for War: Boris takes peace out of London (in 2008 Boris withdrew London's membership of the global Mayors for Peace initiative, founded by the mayors of Hiroshima and Nagasaki)
Source: Copyright © Steve Bell. From the *Guardian*, Reproduced with permission.

Table 19.2 Local government scale

	Population (millions)	Number of lower tier councils	Average population per council	Total number of councillors 000s	Persons per councillor
France	59	36,700	1,600	515	120
Spain	40	8,100	4,900	65	620
Germany	83	12,400	6,600	200	420
Italy	57	8,000	7,200	100	600
Belgium	10	589	18,000	13	800
Sweden	9	290	31,000	46	200
Netherlands	16	443	36,000	10	1,700
Denmark	5	98	51,000	5	1,200
UK 1974	56	520	108,000	26	2,150
UK 2008 (changes in England only)	60	468	128,000	22	2,730
UK 2009 (changes in England only)	61	433	140,000	21	2,900

Source: Adapted from: Chris Game, 'Lost! 90 per cent of councillors in 35 years: Are county-wide unitaries effectively the end of UK local government? paper presented to the PSA Local Politics Specialist Group University of Birmingham – 30 January 2009.

in the size of councils. Indeed, it is questionable whether the term 'local' can be applied to some units of local government in Britain, particularly when compared to the size of councils across Europe. From Table 19.2 it can be seen that Britain has the largest average population size but the fewest councillors per citizen (representative ratio); the situation remains more or less the same, whatever European nations are included in the table. England remains a mixed system of local government, with a two-tier, district and county structure existing alongside a range of unitary councils, the latter including, of course, the London Boroughs and metropolitan borough councils. The structure reflects the more fragmented patchwork existing at the end of the nineteenth century. But, at the beginning of the twenty-first century, local government is larger, and more remote and distant from the communities it serves. As Stewart reminds us: 'the average population of shire districts is over 10 times the average of the lower tier in Europe' (Stewart 2003: 181). It is likely that neither the Conservatives of Labour has finished with the unitarisation of English local government, nor with the increase in council size associated with it; English local government may not remain local at all. It is now necessary to consider whether we can indeed, call it 'government' either.

Table 19.3 Key Legislation in the creation/abolition of councils

Act	Effect of the Act
Municipal Corporations 1835	The right to petition for an elected council
Local Government Act 1888	51 county councils; 62 county boroughs (and the London County Council)
Local Government Act 1894	688 urban district councils; 692 rural district councils
London Government Act 1899	Creates 28 metropolitan boroughs within the LCC
London Government Act 1963	Greater London Council and 32 London boroughs
Local Government Act 1972	46 counties and 296 districts (excludes London)
Local Government Act 1985	Abolishes 6 metropolitan councils and the GLC
Local Government Act 1992	34 county councils; 36 metropolitan borough councils; 238 districts; 46 unitary councils
Greater London Authority Act 1999	Creates the London assembly and the directly elected mayor of London
Local Government and Public Involvement in Health Act 2007	Loss of 44 councils replaced by 9 new unitary councils

■ Inter-governmental relations: general competence or general dogsbody?

The chapter has already set out British local government's subordinate role to central government. Such an arrangement is not the only relationship between national and sub-national governments, and this section will consider, in the light of the Blair government's modernising agenda for local government, how the centre and the localities could interact on a more equal footing.

The British unitary state and unwritten constitution, resting on the doctrine of Parliamentary supremacy, ensures that the party with a majority in Parliament is able to legislate as it thinks fit, unhindered by any mechanisms for constitutional restraint. While the courts may interpret government legislation, they cannot hold it unconstitutional and unenforceable, effectively striking legislation down as the US Supreme Court may do. Thus, intergovernmental relations in Britain are conducted in an environment where political control of the machinery of central government allows national political concerns and policy to supersede local discretion.

Despite the supremacy of Parliament, much of the relationship between national and sub-national governments is conducted within a framework where bargaining between institutions is a norm. However, this bargaining occurs in an unbalanced context, with central government ultimately assured of its own way. Local authorities are able to redress some of that imbalance by challenge and seeking compromise (Rhodes *et al.* 1983). However, local authorities have no general competence to act for the citizens of their area. Thus they are not representative bodies that are able to govern their locality but may act only where Parliament has granted 'positive authority for their actions in a specific law' (Hampton 1987).

General competence, on the other hand, would see councils able to govern their localities within a broad framework of powers set out by Parliament. It would not necessarily mean that councils could take whatever action they wished, rather that they would not require specific legislative authority for each action and would be less constrained by the courts than at present. Much of the debate concerning general competence centres on the powers, roles and responsibilities of local government and how the discretion to act at the local level is defined and codified in relation to central government.

Should local councils be subordinate to central control and regulation? Should they only be able to act in cases where Parliament gives express authority? Or should local councils be granted a power of general competence to govern their own localities as they think fit and in accordance with the wishes of their electorate? Councils are elected bodies, comprising the local political representatives of the citizenry and councillors hold office by virtue of the public vote, should they not have the powers to act accordingly? Moreover, councils and councillors are closer to the people they represent than central government, MPs and civil servants. The issues they deal with often have a more immediate and greater specific impact on the day-to-day well-being of local citizens than the activities of central government. In addition, strong and independent local councils can act as a counterbalance to the political power of central government and are a means by which local voices can be heard at the heart of government. With this in mind, the question of general competence for local government becomes one of balancing the political power of the centre and localities.

British local government does not posses a general competence like that held by most other European countries (Wilson and Game 2002). But, section one of the Local Government Act 2000 gives councils a duty to promote the social, economic and environmental well-being of local communities (for a detailed exploration of how sub-national governments can affect the welfare or well-being of citizens, see Wolman and Goldsmith 1992). As Wilson and Game (2002) point out, section one of the Act enables local government to become involved in areas such as tackling social exclusion, reducing health inequalities, promoting neighbourhood renewal and improving local environmental quality. There is, however, still some reticence in local government about experimenting with the well-being aspects of the Act. Such reticence results from centuries of central control and court intervention and also from apparent central government reluctance to allow councils to experiment – councils which have tried to use the well-being powers to save rural post-offices threatened with closure have found the civil service throwing considerable obstacles in the way.

The government's policies for local government are displayed in a number of publications: *Renewing Democracy: Rebuilding Communities* (Labour Party 1995); the 1997 and 2001 Labour Party election manifestos; and the Green and White Papers Local Democracy and Community Leadership (DETR 1998a), Modern Local Government: In Touch with the People (DETR 1998c), Local Leadership: Local Choice (DETR 1999b), Strong Local Leadership: Quality Public Services (DTLR 2001) and Vibrant Local Leadership (ODPM 2005). While these documents can be seen as a blueprint for local government in the twenty-first century, they do not seek in any way to address the balance between the sovereign and supreme centre by giving local government the power of general competence. There is a counter-argument to local power and discretion that is becoming known as the 'post-code lottery'. That is, central government are less and less inclined to accept different standards of service existing in different parts of the country, even though the decisions that led to that difference were the result of

choices made by the voters at election time. The argument goes that basic services, education, housing, transport, health, etc. (not all services are provided by local government, of course) should not vary in quality and availability. Such arguments fundamentally undermine the notion of local choice about policy and spending priorities. Whether this debate is inspired by the government or the general public is interesting – are those living in Hartlepool really bothered about the service levels in Torbay and vice versa, unless they move there? Yet, a continued debate about the powers of local government, the relationship between central and local government and with the citizens they both seek to serve, govern and represent, would be beneficial to the health of our democracy. We are left to consider: should local government have more power and if so, what? Before answering this question we need to explore the nature of local politics.

■ Local government and local politics

Despite folklore to the contrary, local government and local and national politics have had a long and intertwined association, an association stretching back much further than the 1974 local government reorganisation, often wrongly identified as the point when national politics invaded local council chambers. Indeed, prior to the 1835 Municipal Corporations Act, local government was already politicised, controlled for the most part by what Fraser (1979) described as self-perpetuating Tory–Anglican elites. Moreover, the first municipal elections after the 1835 Act were essentially party battles between the holders of, and contenders for, local political power. Even in the towns that did not immediately incorporate after the 1835 Act, the campaign for new municipal status often divided along party lines. Similar party battles occurred throughout the nineteenth century over the reform, and control, of London government (Young 1975).

Gyford (1985) summarised the long-term process of the party politicisation of local government, identifying five distinct stages: Diversity (1835–65), Crystallisation (1865–1905), Realignment (1905–45), Nationalisation (1945–74) and Reappraisal (1974 onwards). The stages chart the gradual solidification of the party system in local government and indicate that while party politics has had a constant presence in the campaigns for control of local councils and in the conduct of council business, the context and texture of party activity have changed.

Local politics has moved from a time when candidates and councillors often disguised their national party allegiances (see also Grant 1973; Clements 1969) to today, where something like 80 per cent of all councils have been categorised as 'politicised'. Indeed, political party involvement in local government has been described as almost 'universal' (HMSO 1986b; see also Wilson and Game 2002: 276–80).

As representative bodies, with the ability to distribute scarce local resources and decide broad policy approaches to important local services, councils are inherently political bodies. It is therefore no surprise that members and supporters of national political parties have had an interest in securing representation on and control of councils. Hennock (1973), Jones (1969) and Lee (1963) indicate not only the long association between local government and political parties but also the different texture that party politics has taken and the varied relationships that have existed within and between parties.

Bulpitt (1967) has summarised these differences into a typology of local party systems as either negative or positive, the main distinction between the systems being the degree to which councillors act as coherent political groupings to accept responsibility for the control of council policy and the settling of patronage issues. What has varied over time and place is the nature of the relationship between the parties and the degree to which councillors sharing the same political allegiance cohere as distinct party groups. It is the rigidity with which party groups cohere to provide a council with a governing administration, or an opposition bloc, that distinguishes the conduct of party politics in council chambers from its more fluid predecessors (Young and Davis 1990).

Today the overwhelming majority of council elections are contested by members of national political parties, and most local elections have the flavour of a series of mini general elections (Newton 1976). That is, local elections reflect voters' national preoccupations rather than local concerns; thus local elections often turn on the national fortunes of the main political parties. Indeed, a casual glance at the election-night programmes will give you constant analysis by the experts of what this, or that, result means for the government, or for the recovery of the Conservative Party, or for the fortunes of the new Leader of the Liberal Democrats, and far less about

what the results in South Lakeland or Vale of White Horse, means for local citizens and for the way in which those councils had hitherto been run.

However, conflicting views exist as to the balance of local and national influences at local elections, with some evidence suggesting that local issues are important when voters cast a local ballot (HMSO 1986a; Green 1972). Indeed, as turnout declines, it is more likely that the voter going to the polls is more concerned about local issues and the running of the council, than national party fortunes, and recent local election results as a consequence are less reliable tools from which to try and extrapolate national election results.

Cross-national comparisons of local turnout are problematic because of elements of compulsory voting for nations at the top of the table and different structures and tiers of sub-national government. However, Britain can take little comfort, with local turnout bumping along at around 40 per cent. Indeed, in some by-elections turnout has fallen to single figures. Poor turnout raises serious questions about the democratic legitimacy of local government and the ability of councillors to claim an electoral mandate for their policies.

These elections however, were held on the same day as the General Election and also would have seen turnout benefit from experiments in some areas with increased use of postal voting (see Local Government Elections Centre at: www.research.plymouth.ac.uk/elections). The turnout in the 2008 local elections, where no other level of election was being held, was around 36 per cent.

Poor turnout no doubt damages local accountability and legitimacy. But, added to this is the party group system and the way in which groups organise to conduct their business and the business of the council, alongside the loyalty and discipline they expect of and by and large receive from councillors, that have the potential to further damage local accountability and representation (Copus 1998, 1999a, 1999b). The party group system sees councillors bound to the decisions of their groups, taken in private and closed meetings, and expected to publicly support, or at least acquiesce in, the outcomes of those meetings, irrespective of how he or she may have spoken or voted in those meeting and of the views of the voters.

The organisation and activity of party groups varies depending on the party concerned, but each of the three main national and two nationalist parties produces model standing orders for their council party groups. Standing orders are open to interpretation by individual groups, such interpretations depending on the personnel of the group, the nature of the relationship between the groups and the political composition of the council. Indeed, patterns of party interaction and competition will vary depending on the type of council concerned (Rallings and Thrasher 1997; Wilson and Game 2002). Largely, however, groups are well organised and structured, with a range of officers undertaking different tasks and clearly identified expectations of loyalty from their membership. In addition, party groups have a range of disciplinary procedures and sanctions available to use against recalcitrant members. The nature of and willingness to use such disciplinary mechanisms vary across the parties, as does the willingness to take a flexible interpretation of standing orders and allow councillors to act at variance with group decisions. The party group is now the most important theatre for the conduct of local representation and for council decision making (Hampton 1970; Saunders 1979; Stoker 1991; Game and Leach 1995).

The way in which party groups conduct council business can be problematic because local government is overwhelmingly dominated by the main three national political parties; in England alone, for example, almost 92 per cent of all councillors are from the Conservative and Labour parties or the Liberal Democrats. Some 93 per cent of England's almost 22,000 councillors are from the main three parties.

With such a deep penetration into local town halls by the main parties it is all the more important to emphasise the 'local' element of local government and, if parties continue in the town hall setting their wider national political battle, we are left asking again, where is the 'local' in local government (see Table 19.4)?

Yet, is it fair to say that local government and the parties that run the town hall are aware of the need to listen to the voice of the local citizenry and recognise that local politics are often driven by local concerns and issues that do not sit neatly into an ideological view of the world. But, the committee system through which local government operated and which had developed since the Victorian period, was seen by many commentators to be flawed. Radical change was necessary in the way the politics of the councils was carried out and that change came in 2000.

■ Creating a new form and approach to local politics

When elected in 1997, the Blair government was committed to a widespread review of the British constitution; much of the previous Conservative government's policies towards local government were to be scrapped or radically changed. Indeed, when in opposition Labour had recognised the importance to political pluralism of a vibrant, healthy and vigorous local government and local politics. The government's agenda for reform was displayed in a series of publications: a Green Paper, three White Papers, a discussion paper and two Acts of Parliament: Local Democracy and Community Leadership (DETR 1998a), Modern Local Government: In Touch with the People (DETR 1998c), Local Leadership: Local Choice (DETR 1999b) and Strong Local Leadership: Quality Public Services (DTLR 2001), Vibrant Local Leadership (ODPM 2005); and the 1999 London and 2000 Local Government Acts. While other documents have been published since, these contain the core of what the government still thinks is the political model of a modern council.

The Local Government Act 2000 radically transformed the structure of political decision making in local government and Part II of the Act required all councils, with populations above 85,000, to introduce one of three new-style executive political decision-making arrangements. Three executive options available under the Act were:

Table 19.4 Councillors by party

	Conservative	Labour	Lib Dem	Nationalists	Independents and smaller parties
England	9,229	3,738	7,491		1,503
Wales	173	346	161	207	377
Scotland	141	351	169	363	198

1 A directly elected executive mayor and cabinet.

2 A mayor and council manager (an option removed by the Local Government and Public Involvement in Health Act 2007; and,

3 An indirectly elected executive leader and cabinet.

The indirectly elected leader and cabinet option has been the one preferred by the overwhelming majority of councils, which is not surprising as this option represents the least change to existing practices and structures. Here, the council, but in reality the ruling party group, selects one of its members to be the leader of the council. A cabinet of up to nine councillors (plus the leader of the council) is formed, again normally from the majority party group unless the council has no overall control; the leader and cabinet form the council's political executive. The system is not dissimilar to that existing prior to the 2000 Act, when the ruling group would ensure that the council appointed its leader as council leader and went on to elect a number of committee chairs and vice-chairs from among its number. The main requirement of the Act is that all councils with populations over 85,000 must formally distinguish between those councillors forming an executive and the rest of the council membership, who are charged with holding the executive to account and scrutinising its activity.

Before introducing a directly elected mayor as the council's executive arrangement a binding referendum must be held, called either by the council or as the result of a petition containing signatures of 5 per cent of the local population. Much debate has centred on the directly elected mayor, a political office very different from the current ceremonial and largely non-partisan mayor that chairs council meetings. Despite many councillors complaining that the mayoral office would see the concentration of inordinate power in the hands of a single individual, the reality is different from that which is often claimed. The directly elected mayor has broadly similar powers to that of the indirectly elected leader. Indeed, as a result of the Local Government and Public Involvement in Health Act 2007, indirectly elected leaders are appointed by their councils for a four-year term.

The elected mayor is elected by all the voters of a council area, not just by councillors, and thus comes with a direct electoral mandate far more powerful and legitimate than the indirect one granted to an indirectly elected council leader by fellow councillors. The directly elected mayor is elected by the supplementary vote system, where voters place a cross in a first- and second-preference column against their preferred two candidates. After the first count, if no one candidate achieves 50 per cent of the votes cast, all but the top two candidates are eliminated and the second-preference votes redistributed to the remaining. The system ensures that any victorious candidate secures over 50 per cent of the vote.

The mayor becomes a highly visible political head of the council with responsibility for providing political leadership, proposing the policy framework for the council, preparing the council's budget and taking executive decisions. The council is responsible for scrutinising the work of the mayor and his or her cabinet and proposing amendments to policy and the budget. It is fair to say that giving the public the right to select directly the political head of the council, rather than having the choice made for them by councillors, has failed to ignite a blaze of interest in the mayoral option. So far, only eleven of the thirty referendums held outside London have returned a 'yes' vote. Table 19.5 displays the referendum results so far obtained.

In May and October 2002 the elections for directly elected mayors were held, and Table 19.6 shows the outcomes of these contests. What is clear from the results is that voters in at least half the mayoral contests have taken the opportunity the new arrangements have given them to reject candidates from political parties and often from the party that has long controlled the council.

In any of the above options, those councillors remaining outside the executive are charged with the duty of scrutinising, through a number of overview and scrutiny committees, the activities of the council's executive. These councillors would be expected to put party loyalty to one side and publicly criticise a council executive that may well comprise their own party colleagues, whom they themselves may have voted into executive office. The modernising agenda rests on councillors' willingness to scrutinise an executive in public, but so far it has underestimated the pull of party group loyalty. It is unlikely that the sort of scrutiny envisaged by the government will occur overnight when councillors are expected to scrutinise the activities of their party colleagues.

The introduction of new political arrangements into councils and a clear distinction between executive and scrutiny members is aimed at overcoming the secretive and opaque nature of much local

Table 19.5 Results in mayoral referendums, 2001–2

Council	Date	Result	For	%	Against	%	Turnout (%)	Type
Berwick-upon-Tweed	7 Jun 2001	No	3,617	26	10,212	74	64	poll with GE
Cheltenham	28 Jun 2001	No	8,083	33	16,602	67	31	all postal
Gloucester	28 Jun 2001	No	7,731	31	16,317	69	31	all postal
Watford	12 Jul 2001	Yes	7,636	52	7,140	48	24.5	all postal
Doncaster	20 Sep 2001	Yes	35,453	65	19,398	35	25	all postal
Kirklees	4 Oct 2001	No	10,169	27	27,977	73	13	normal
Sunderland	11 Oct 2001	No	9,593	43	12,209	57	10	normal
Hartlepool	18 Oct 2001	Yes	10,667	51	10,294	49	31	all postal
LB Lewisham	18 Oct 2001	Yes	16,822	51	15,914	49	18	all postal
North Tyneside	18 Oct 2001	Yes	30,262	58	22,296	42	36	all postal
Middlesbrough	18 Oct 2001	Yes	29,067	84	5,422	16	34	all postal
Sedgefield	18 Oct 2001	No	10,628	47	11,869	53	33.3	all postal
Brighton and Hove	18 Oct 2001	No	22,724	38	37,214	62	32	all postal
Redditch	8 Nov 2001	No	7,250	44	9,198	56	28.3	all postal
Durham	20 Nov 2001	No	8,327	41	11,974	59	28.5	all postal
Harrow	7 Dec 2001	No	17,502	42	23,554	58	26.06	all postal
Plymouth	24 Jan 2002	No	29,553	41	42,811	59	39.78	all postal
Harlow	24 Jan 2002	No	5,296	25	15,490	75	36.38	all postal
LB Newham	31 Jan 2002	Yes	27,163	68.2	12,687	31.8	25.9	all postal
Shepway	31 Jan 2002	No	11,357	44	14,438	56	36.3	all postal
LB Southwark	31 Jan 2002	No	6,054	31.4	13,217	68.6	11.2	normal
West Devon	31 Jan 2002	No	3,555	22.6	12,190	77.4	41.8	all postal
Bedford	21 Feb 2002	Yes	11,316	67.2	5,537	32.8	15.5	normal
LB Hackney	2 May 2002	Yes	24,697	58.94	10,547	41.06	31.85	all postal
Mansfield	2 May 2002	Yes	8,973	54	7,350	44	21.04	normal
Newcastle-under-Lyme	2 May 2002	No	12,912	44	16,468	56	31.5	normal
Oxford	2 May 2002	No	14,692	44	18,686	56	33.8	normal
Stoke-on-Trent	2 May 2002	Yes	28,601	58	20,578	42	27.8	normal
Corby	3 Oct 2002	No	5,351	46	6,239	53.64	30.91	all postal
LB Ealing	12 Dec 2002	No	9,454	44.8	11,655	55.2	9.8	combination postal and ballot
Ceredigion	20 May 2004	No	5,308	27	14,013	73	36	unknown
Torbay	14 July 2004	Yes	18,074	55	14,682	45	32.1	unknown

Source: The New Local Government Network website, April 2003: nlgn.org.uk

political decision making. It aims to make decision making open and transparent and thereby enhance local accountability, the committee system being seen as responsible for diffusing responsibility and thus making the holding of individuals to account almost impossible. Indeed, even a committee chair could not be said to be responsible for a committee decision.

June 2009 saw mayoral contests in Doncaster, Hartlepool and North Tyneside. In Doncaster the sitting Labour mayor was replaced as Labour candidate, which did Labour no good, as Peter Davies, the candidate for the English Democrats was elected mayor after the counting of second preference votes. The Doncaster result is a major victory for the English Democrats, a new party formed in 2002; it

Table 19.6 Mayoral election results, May and October 2002

Council	Winning candidate	Political affiliation	Elected on 1st or 2nd count	Electorate	Turnout
May 2002					
Doncaster	Martin Winter	Labour	2nd	216,097	58,487 (27.07%)
Hartlepool	Stuart Drummond	Independent	2nd	67,903	19,544 (28.78%)
LB Lewisham	Steve Bullock	Labour	2nd	179,835	44,518 (24.75%)
Middlesbrough	Ray Mallon	Independent	1st	101,570	41,994 (41.34%)
LB Newham	Robin Wales	Labour	1st	157,505	40,147 (25.49%)
North Tyneside	Chris Morgan	Conservative	2nd	143,804	60,865 (42.32%)
Watford	Dorothy Thornhill	Liberal Democrat	2nd	61,359	22,170 (36.13%)
October 2002					
Bedford	Frank Branston	Independent	2nd	109,318	27,717 (25.35%)
LB Hackney	Jules Pipe	Labour	2nd	130,657	34,415 (26.34%)
Mansfield	Tony Egginton	Independent	2nd	72,242	13,350 (18.48%)
Stoke-on-Trent	Mike Wolfe	Mayor 4 Stoke	2nd	182,967	43,985 (24.04%)

Source: New Local Government Network website: nlgn.org.uk

Table 19.7 Elected mayors 2009

Bedford	Frank Branston: Independent	re-elected 2007
Doncaster	Peter Davies: English Democrat	elected 2009
Hackney	Jules Pipe: Labour	re-elected 2006
Hartlepool	Stuart Drummond: Independent	re-elected 2009
Lewisham	Steve Bullock: Labour	re-elected 2006
Mansfield	Tony Eggerton: Independent	re-elected 2007
Middlesbrough	Ray Mallon: Independent	re-elected 2007
Newham	Robin Wales: Labour	re-elected 2006
North Tyneside	Linda Arkley: Conservative	elected (for a second time) 2009
Watford	Dorothy Thornhill: Liberal Democrat	re-elected 2006
Torbay	Nick Bye: Conservative	elected 2005

currently only has three councillors across the country and none in Doncaster. But the Doncaster result has given this new English party effective control of a major metropolitan borough. In Hartlepool, independent Stuart Drummond was re-elected to serve for a third term – he won notoriety at his first election in 2002 by standing as H'Angus the monkey' and wearing the costume of the mascot for Hartlepool Town Football Club; he was re-elected for a second term in 2005 with a 10,000 majority; his majority in 2009 was just 800 after the second preference count, but he was elected over another independent candidate; neither of the candidates from the two main parties made it to the second count. In North Tyneside, Conservative candidate Linda Arkley, who had lost the mayoralty in 2005, was elected for a second time, defeating the sitting Labour mayor (see Table 19.7).

On the surface directly elected mayors appear to be a radical change for local government, but the mayors and councils on which they serve were given no new real powers that would clearly distinguish them and their councils from any non-mayoral council. It is not so much the power of the mayor that is different, rather how they get the job, and here it is the voters that decide not a handful of councillors from the ruling group on the council. One thing is clear however, as the referendum results show: voters across the country do not appear all that interested in having that power!

A word about alternative arrangements

The real story of the Local Government Act 2000 is the story of political executives, but as a piece of political expediency to ensure the passage of the bill through the House of Lords, the government was forced to concede the alternative arrangement option. That is, authorities with populations of 85,000 or less could introduce a slimmed-down committee system instead of a political executive. Government regulations flowing from the 2000 Act set out how alternative arrangements can be configured within council chambers. The full council will set the policy framework and approve the budget and be supported by up to five 'policy committees'. One or more overview and scrutiny committees will hold the policy committees to account and assist them in their work (DETR 2000: para 9.8). Membership is limited by regulation to 15 for a committee and 10 for a subcommittee (DETR 2000: para 9.13). At the outset, of the 86 councils to which alternative arrangements could apply, 59 chose to go down that route.

■ Local government: a changing policy environment

While councillors have links to the external environment through their parties and communities, and business, professional and political organisations, the decisions they take rest heavily on the advice they receive from officers employed by the authority. These professionals and managers form an important antenna for councillors on the outside world.

Many alternative sources of information exist for councillors to that received from officers, but, as the paid employees and advisers to the council, senior officers are a potentially powerful influence on councillors' final decisions. Moreover, officers can influence councillors in their private discussions in the party group through the production of council minutes and reports that councillors consider in their group meetings, and, by attendance at those meetings, on request, to answer questions and give advice, which until quite recently was largely accepted. Young and Laffin (1990) indicate that party politics has radically altered the patterns of interaction between officers and councillors and that the task of advising councillors no longer comes with the certainty of officer influence that it once had. The fact remains that for the vast majority of councillors the advice received from officers is among the most important and influential they receive; securing alternative sources of advice and support comes at a premium. Even the new overview and scrutiny committees formed by councils under the 2000 Act have yet to provide councillors with much direct access to sources of information and advice apart from local government officers.

Local government officers coming from a range of professional backgrounds, mainly associated with the specialist services provided by local authorities or from the wider professions such as the law, interact with colleagues whose profession is management. The professional as expert and the professional manager now operate in what is the accepted principle of local government management: the corporate approach. This approach was championed in 1972 by the Bains Report, which challenged the then dominant functional approach to local government organisation and management.

The Bains Report took a managerial perspective towards the role of the officer, but as Stewart (1986: 132) reminds us, 'decisions made by a manager can have important and unexpected political consequences'. Indeed, it is senior officers and senior councillors acting as a 'joint elite' (Stoker 1991) that is at the heart of local government political management. While tensions may exist between the elite of senior councillors and officers, the carving out of spheres of influence enables an uneasy alliance between officers and members to contribute a dynamic tension to the local policy processes. The uneasy but dynamic tension existing between councillors and officers risks disruption by pressure from external sources for the council to respond to particular demands, or to interact with external bodies around various local issues and events. External pressure on local authorities comes from the local citizenry, regional institutions of governance and the European Union.

■ The citizenry: consultation and participation

Local government policy making is not inevitably informed by the citizenry simply because the council is closer to the people it represents than the national Parliament. Local people are only able to be part of the process of local decision making if two conditions are met: first, the council has a range of mechanisms by which the views of the citizen can be sought; second, the council, and councillors in particular, is willing to respond positively to the views of the citizen and indeed to change and develop council policy accordingly. Public involvement in local government is not a case of a council convincing the people it has the right answers but of developing those answers to ensure congruence between policy and the views of the citizen. Such a process is set within a representative framework where councillors will assess the outcomes of citizen consultation and participation but be responsible for making the final decisions on important local issues.

The Blair government's modernising agenda for local government recognises the inherent tension between local representative democracy and enhanced citizen participation. The modernising agenda does not set out to replace representative democracy with a participative variant; rather, it seeks to use citizen involvement to inform the outcomes of the representative processes as they link to local policy making. 'Local Democracy and Community Leadership' (DETR 1998a) exhorts councils to involve the public more in their decision-making processes and urges that such involvement be a regular rather than an episodic feature. The government has set out the virtues of enhanced public involvement thus:

The prize is an ever closer match between the needs and aspirations of communities and the services secured for them by their local authority, better quality services, greater democratic legitimacy for local government and a new brand of involved and responsible citizenship; in short, reinvigorated local democracy. Increasingly, the degree to which an authority is engaged with its stakeholders may become a touchstone for the authority's general effectiveness.

DETR (1997: 16)

It is clear that local government officers and councillors are expected to engage far more closely with the communities they serve and represent than has so far been the norm. So how can the public become more closely involved in the activities of the local council aside from standing for election and voting? Local Democracy and Community Leadership (DETR 1997) provides an answer by setting out a clear expectation that councils will use a number of specific mechanisms for seeking and responding to the views of the citizen. Moreover, it recognises that 'different forms of consultation may be appropriate to the different stages in the development of a policy or a strategy' (DETR 1997: 16).

Councils are encouraged to use the following methods for citizen involvement:

- citizen juries
- focus groups
- visioning conferences
- deliberative opinion polls
- citizens' panels
- community forums or area-based neighbourhood committees
- interest and user group forums
- referendums to test public opinion on specific local issues (councils can call local polls under section 116 of the 2003 Local Government Act).

The government has further developed and refined its idea of how councils should be engaging with their communities and how the role of the councillor should continue to meet the dual responsibilities of being involved in governing an area as a whole and representing and championing the communities in the wards or divisions they represent (ODPM 2005). Indeed, the government sees the councillor as being at the heart of the local neighbourhood, proving political leadership in a very local context. Yet, the government also sees a greater role for the citizen working alongside the councillor, particularly though area and neighbourhood forums.

The Local Government and Public Involvement in Health Act 2007 has given councillors greater powers to raise local issues with overview and scrutiny committees and to instigate a high-profile public debate around an issue. The Act also provides new powers for council scrutiny committees to review the actions and policies of a wide range of organisations outside of the council, which provide public services of one sort or another. Councils now have the opportunity to hold to account and to influence policy development across a swath of activities for which they are not the direct providers. Coupled with the scrutiny committees' ability to engage directly with local citizens, this provides a powerful framework for councils to ensure the voice of the public is heard not only at the council, but also by a number of bodies at all levels of governance. The key distinguishing factor for local government, from all the other agencies and organisations with which it has to interact – central government to one side – is its democratic base and its elected mandate – some organisations with greater powers, roles and responsibilities than elected councillors can not claim that direct mandate from the voters and regional government is a particularly good example of a powerful body with no direct electoral legitimacy.

■ The regional agenda

Regional government has existed in England for some time, with a number of **quangos**, or government offices, or other public organsiations, organising and operating on a regional basis and formulating and implementing regional policy and spending tax-payers money on regional initiatives. What is missing from the equation is any form of democratically controlled regional government (see the north-east result below).

As part of the package of constitutional reform introduced by the Blair government, eight English regional development agencies (RDAs) were launched on 1 April 1999, formed by the Regional Development Agencies Act 1998. These agencies were created to ensure that decisions about regeneration and regional policy and priorities, were made within the regions concerned and to address economic imbalances between regions. The RDAs cover the following areas: north-east, north-west, Yorkshire and the Humber, west Midlands, east Midlands, east of England, south-west, and south-east, with the London RDA, introduced in 2000 to link with the arrival of the London mayor and the Greater London Authority. With the agencies also formed for Scotland, Wales and Northern Ireland, the RDAs covered the whole of the UK.

The RDAs took over responsibility for the urban regeneration work (revival of areas made derelict, usually through industrial failure) and their main objectives are:

■ economic development and social and physical regeneration;

■ business support, investment and competitiveness;

■ enhancing regional skills;

■ promoting employment;

■ sustainable development.

The RDAs' role is to raise the average prosperity of their regions to that of the rest of the European Union. While the RDAs are clearly regional bodies, the focus for much of their work will be to integrate the economic prospects of the English regions with the European Union and its regions. The RDAs prepare regional economic development strategies which set out a five- to ten-year strategic vision for their regions, addressing the needs of wide and often socially, economically and geographically diverse areas and drawing in a wide range of partnership bodies from the private, public and voluntary sectors.

The RDAs are appointed bodies not elected chambers, but their work has been overseen by eight Regional Assemblies, however these Assemblies are also not directly elected. The Assembly membership is appointed from existing councillors and also can include local MPs and MEPs. The creation of these Assemblies was related to a European Union agenda for a Europe of the regions – which would weaken national parliaments in the EU structure. A Government White Paper, 'Your Region, Your Choice: Revitalising the English Regions' (DTLR 2002) set out plans for these Assemblies to be directly elected. But the plan was scuppered on 4 November 2004, when a first referendum on forming an elected regional assembly for the north-east was decisively defeated by voters, when of a possible 1.9 million voters, 197,310 voted 'yes' (22.1 per cent) and 893,829 voted 'No' (77.9 per cent).

At the same time voters were also told on the ballot paper than should they vote 'Yes', then local government in the area would be re-organised on a **unitary authority** basis Thus, existing councils would disappear should the referendum say 'Yes' to a regional chamber. The referendum 'No' result meant local government remained as it was. When, however, the nine new unitary councils referred to above were formed in April 2009 – three of these new councils were located in the area covered by the north-east referendum and were not too dissimilar to proposals in 2004 – the government eventually gets what it wants, one way or another, when it comes to the localities.

Table 19.8

1999 (seats)	2003 (seats)	2007 (seats)
Labour: (56)	Labour: (50)	Labour: (46)
SNP: (35)	SNP: (27)	SNP: (47)
Conservative: (18)	Conservative: (18)	Conservative: (17)
Liberal Democrat: (17)	Liberal Democrat: (17)	Liberal Democrat: (16)
Scottish Greens: (1)	Scottish Greens: (7)	Scottish Greens (2)
Scottish Socialists: (1)	Scottish Socialists (6)	Scottish Socialists: (0)

On 25 July 2007, Gordon Brown, making one of his first major decisions on becoming Prime Minister, announced the abolition of the Regional Assemblies by 2010 and the transfer of their responsibilities to the RDAs which they had worked alongside. Yet, the regionalisation of England has not stopped as Gordon Brown appointed nine regional premiers, or ministers for each of the English regions to oversee regional matters. Further, many government quangos are formed on a regional basis and discussions continue about transferring some responsibilities currently with local government to the regional level. So, what are these regions? England has nine of them; they are the:

- North-east
- North-west
- Yorkshire and the Humber
- East Midlands
- West Midlands
- South-west
- South-east
- East
- London

Only two of the nine have recognisable place names: Yorkshire and the Humber and London; the rest are just generic and meaningless compass points that reflect European and central government administrative convenience, rather than recognisable and definable regional communities and identities as regions in many other European nations do. England has no real tradition of regionalism in the same sense as other parts of Europe; it would make more sense for the English regions to be called: Northumbria, Mercia, Wessex, Essex, Kent, East Anglia and Sussex, the seven Anglo-Saxon kingdoms of

England – at least these have something more to say about the history and traditions of England than compass-point divisions. But there is a deeper story here that says much about successive British governments' attitudes towards England as distinct from Scotland and Wales, so let us look at the recent democratic innovations in Scotland and Wales.

The Scottish and Welsh dimensions

A vital part of the Blair government's constitutional reform package, and one quickly acted upon after the 1997 election victory, was the introduction of an elected Scottish Parliament and a Welsh Assembly, the first elections to which were held in May 1999. The election results for the three sets of elections held so far are shown in Table 19.8.

There are 73 members representing individual constituencies and elected under the traditional first-past-the-post system and another 56 members elected using a regional list system for eight electoral regions of Scotland. Currently, the Scottish National Party has formed a minority administration in the parliament. The SNP is pledged to Scottish separation from Britain and to hold a referendum on the issue.

The Welsh Assembly has 60 elected members: 40 members representing individual constituencies and elected under the first-past-the-post system; and 20 members selected from 'party list' from five electoral regions. The results of the first three elections are shown in Table 19.9.

The creation of the Scottish Parliament and the Welsh Assembly represent a major change in the structure and processes of British government and transference of political and legislative power from Westminster to alternative parliaments. Although the powers of the Scottish and Welsh devolved chambers continual pressure from both bodies to enhance their powers and the current government's willingness to

Table 19.9 Welsh Assembly elections

1999 (seats)	2003 (seats)	2007 (seats)
Labour (28)	Labour (30)	Labour (26)
Plaid Cymru (17)	Plaid Cymru (12)	Plaid Cymru (15)
Liberal Democrats (6)	Liberal Democrats (6)	Liberal Democrats (6)
Conservatives (9)	Conservatives (11)	Conservatives (12)
Independent (0)	Independent (1)	Independent (1)

listen to such arguments will no doubt see gradual increases in the powers and responsibilities of both developed bodies. It is already almost impossible to talk any longer of *British* transport, education, health and regeneration policy, with only foreign affairs having a distinctly British flavour and all this despite the Scottish Prime Minister of Britain's constant concerns about Britishness.

Prior to the creation of the devolved chambers for Scotland and Wales, local government had already been reorganised on a wholly unitary basis, with 32 unitary councils in Scotland and 22 in Wales, avoiding the need for the Blair government to re-organise local government while introducing the devolved political arrangements to Scotland and Wales. The two chambers have developed their own unique relationships with their local government and have introduced a distinct Scots and Welsh dimension to local government legislation emanating from the Westminster Parliament; both chambers have responsibility for local government matters.

While, generally, local government in England, Scotland and Wales now has features that distinguish it in each country, the most distinctive feature was the introduction of the single-transferable-vote system for the 2007 council elections in Scotland. The new voting system resulted in only five of 32 Scottish councils having a single group (or party) with an overall majority; three of which are independent groups. Local government in England and Wales continues to be elected by the first-past-the-post system.

What about England?

So, Scotland with a population of around five million has its Parliament, Wales, with a population of about three million and Northern Ireland with a population of over 1,600,000 (all figures from the 2001 census) both have their Assemblies. But England, the biggest country in the UK, with a population of just over 49 million (2001 census, but closer in 2009 to 51 million) and which contributes the most, by way of tax, to the UK government has neither its own Parliament or government to speak up for its interest; England was excluded by the government from the devolution process with the preferred option being, rather than to recognise England as a nation, to break it into nine regions. Moreover, legislation regarding English local government (and any English issues for that matter) is left to the UK Parliament, whereas on all legislation effecting England alone, Scottish and Welsh MPs can vote. Ironically, the government's devolution agenda has opened up a gaping democratic deficit of its own creation and left a clear piece missing in the UK constitutional and governing jigsaw; the 'Campaign for an English Parliament' is seeking to fill that gap. Perhaps the solution to the UK's democratic and representative arrangements is not regional government, but an English Parliament, sitting alongside the Scottish, Welsh and Northern Ireland bodies, in a Federal UK – that would be a constitutional revolution.

■ Local government and the European Union

The relationship between British local government and the EU has come a long way since a 1991 Audit Commission report drew attention to its often 'blinkered' approach to EU matters. Relationships between sub-national government such as British local councils and supranational bodies such as the EU will always be conducted in a complex environment and through a complex system. John (1996) describes this system as triadic, that is conducted between three groups of actors at each of the three levels of governmental interaction. Indeed, the relationship between the EU and local government is influenced by two major factors: European law and policy; and the relationships between local and national government. Moreover, some local governments see the EU as a way around problematic relationships with national government and economic and political constraints, a situation that applied particularly in the UK throughout the 1980s and early 1990s (John 1996).

The impact of the EU on local government is less clear than the impact of national government but just as important. The EU affects local councils through a range of policy initiatives and demands: environmental health, consumer protection, public protection and even social and human rights legislation. These all impact on the activities of local government, and many councils have expressed concerns about the level of resources involved.

Even so, many local authorities have recognised the importance of securing funding from the EU and contributing to the EU policy-making process, to the extent that many UK local councils employ specialist staff to deal with European issues and negotiate with the EU (Goldsmith and Sperling 1997). Indeed, some have formed special committees of the council to deal with European matters and have European liaison officers, often with an economic development specialism, and located within economic development departments (Preston 1992a, 1992b).

Some councils have established Brussels offices, either individually or as part of a consortium, and, while often small-scale affairs, they can disseminate information and establish links with the EU and other European national and sub-national governments. These offices are able to prepare funding bids, lobby for policy initiatives or changes, work with other bodies attempting to influence the EU, draw the private and voluntary sector closer into the EU policy network and place their local authority at the heart of the EU. John (1994) sees such Brussels offices as a cross-national marketplace to develop partnership funding bids and to indulge in informal lobbying of EU officials – a process in which many British councils lose out compared with their European counterparts, who place far more emphasis on resourcing such offices.

Local government placing itself at the heart of the EU serves three purposes:

1 Authorities can develop a range of funding partnerships with a diverse group of organisations.

2 It fosters inter-municipal learning.

3 It enables regions and councils to learn of, and shape, new EU policy initiatives (Ercole *et al.* 1997).

Preston (1992b) indicates why local government is anxious to develop good relationships with the EU, highlighting the financial and policy benefits that flow from successful applications for European Social Fund and European Regional Development Fund support. The financial resources available from these programmes have enabled British local councils to pursue expansionist economic development policies in spite of tight controls from central government. Indeed, something like 74 per cent of British councils have applied for EU structural funds (Goldsmith and Sperling 1997).

Another reason for the popularity of the EU within local government is that element of the Maastricht Treaty concerning subsidiarity. This is popularly taken to mean by local councils that decisions should be decentralised to the lowest appropriate level of government, thus locating functions and powers with sub-national governments. However, John (1996) points out that this is a matter of political interpretation, as the treaty itself refers to relations between member states and the EU, not between states and local government. On the other hand, the Council of European Municipalities and Regions is campaigning for changes to the treaty that will clarify the meaning of subsidiarity in relation to the role of sub-national governments in policy and decision making. The European Charter of local self-government, which the Blair government signed up to immediately after the 1997 election as a sign of commitment to local government, already recognises that many areas of public policy and political affairs are properly administered at the local or regional level.

The EU provides British local government with:

■ access to funding;

■ an opportunity to pursue its own policy agenda despite central government restrictions and direction – indeed, the possibility of a way around the unitary British state;

■ political influence in important EU policy networks, linkages with other European local governments and local government consortiums;

■ opportunities to strengthen its role, functions, powers and responsibilities.

As British local government comes to terms with devolved parliaments and chambers, it may find valuable resources in the EU that will enable it to ward off the possible centralising tendencies of yet more layers of government above local authorities.

BOX 19.1   BRITAIN IN CONTEXT

If you want to see what other countries say about their local government and the nature of the relationship between central government and local government and between central government and local government and the citizen, then go to: http://www.psr.keele.ac.uk/const.htm#U. Here, you can view the written constitutions of countries across the globe; note that after the UK the site refers to Magna Carta. Yet a random glance at some of the constitutions provides stark evidence of the context within which UK local government sits:

Ireland

Article 28A

■ The State recognises the role of local government in providing a forum for the democratic representation of local communities, in exercising and performing at local level powers and functions conferred by law and in promoting by its initiatives the interests of such communities.

Poland

Article 16

■ The inhabitants of the units of basic territorial division shall form a self-governing community in accordance with law.
■ Local government shall participate in the exercise of public power. The substantial part of public duties which local government is empowered to discharge by statute shall be done in its own name and under its own responsibility.

Croatia

■ Citizens shall be guaranteed the right to local self-government.
The right to local self-government shall include the right to decide on needs and interests of local significance, particularly on regional development and town planning, organisation of localities and housing, public utilities, childcare, social welfare, culture, physical culture, sports and technical culture, and the protection and promotion of the environment.

Germany

Article 28

■ Article 28 (Federal guarantee concerning Laender constitutions, guarantee of self-government for local authorities).
■ The constitutional order in the Laender must conform to the principles of republican, democratic, and social government based on the rule of law, within the meaning of this Basic Law. In each of the Laender, counties and communities, the people must be represented by a body chosen in universal, direct, free, equal and secret elections. In the communities the assembly of the community may take the place of an elected body.
■ The communities must be guaranteed the right to regulate on their own responsibility all the affairs of the local community within the limits set by law. The associations of communities also have the right of self-government in accordance with the law within the limits of the functions given them by law.

These, and the other constitutions you can access, give to local government in the countries concerned, something that is lacking in the UK: the constitutional right for local self-government to exist, in one form or another. Moreover, they provide a clear set of principles on which the relationship between the central government and local sub-national government will be conducted and what central government can and can not do to local government. In Britain, no such restraint exists on what central government can do to the localities, from rearranging responsibilities for certain services, to large-scale reorganisation of the size and shape of councils, to outright abolition of councils, such as in the 1974 reorganisation and the abolition of the metropolitan counties in 1986, as well as the forced merger and effective abolition of councils replaced by unitary authorities. Moreover, citizens have no say over the shape, size, responsibilities or powers of councils as for example exists in many US states. In Britain, local government is subservient to central government and the citizen subservient to both, at least in constitutional terms.

Unlike much, though by no means all, local government elsewhere, UK local government is heavily constrained by the law and the doctrine of *ultra vires*, that is, acting beyond powers specifically granted to it by statue. Before a council in Britain can do anything, it must be certain that there is legislation in existence saying it can do what it proposes to do. Other nations approach the power and role of local government differently by granting, often in a written constitution, the power of general competence. General competence means that local government can do whatever it wishes do to for the good of its citizens, so long as any actions are not prohibited by law. Put simply, British local government can do only what the law says it can do; elsewhere local government can do anything so long as the law does not say that it can not. But this picture is becoming cloudier as the relationship between local government in Scotland and Wales takes on a different form with the Scottish and Welsh devolved chambers to that between England and the UK government.

By looking at the UK it is often easy to conclude that the words 'local government' are a misnomer; perhaps we now have a situation where councils are too large to be local and have too little power to be government.

Different nations come to different constitutional settlements between the centre and the localities and we have an arrangement that emerged over time from our histories and traditions, but which was shaped to reflect the power of the centre; other nations, at various times, have had the opportunity to sit down and devise a system of government and to write a constitution and thus have created something different from our own approach to the power of government. Who is to say who has it right? But there is choice to be made between an all-powerful central government which can control the localities, and powerful councils that can react to the wishes of local citizens – even if they conflict with the government's policies. If your council wanted to double the level of council tax, you might want the government to be able to stop it; or, you might want your council to be able to spend as much as it likes on local services, whatever the tax. Or, you might want to be able to force a local referendum on the issue, or be able to remove your councillors from office before the next election. What do you think?

Chapter summary

The chapter has considered British local government as a politically representative set of arrangements designed to ensure responsiveness to the demands of local citizens. It has also outlined the constitutionally subordinate nature of local government to central control but indicated that this need not be the only constitutional settlement available between the localities and the centre. The chapter has investigated the role of political parties in local government and the wider political process of local democracy as they are enacted through local councils. As well as a political process, it has considered local government as a set of institutional relationships between citizens, the centre and the EU. It has also discussed the main elements of the government's modernising agenda.

The chapter has also emphasised the politically dynamic nature of local government, which exists not only as a means of providing services – important though that may be – but also as a means by which the will of local people can be expressed and realised.

Discussion points

■ Has the British system of local government been over-reformed since the early 1970s?

■ Should local government get bigger or smaller, or, stay the same size, and why?

■ Should we have a tiered or unitary structure of local government?

■ Should local government have more or less freedom to do what it wants to?

■ Given the increasing central control of local government, would it be best to run it from London?

■ Are directly elected mayors, elected by all the voters, a better way of running local government than a council leader chosen by councillors?

■ Is it better to have councils run by national political parties or by local groups and independents?

■ Should England have its own parliament?

Further reading

Copus, C. (2004) *Party Politics and Local Government* (Manchester University Press).

Leach, S. and Wilson, D. (2000) *Local Political Leadership* (The Policy Press).

Le Gales, P. (2002) *European Cities: Social Conflicts and Governance* (Oxford University Press).

Stoker, G. (2006) *Why Politics Matter: Making Democracy Work* (Palgrave Macmillan).

Wilson, D. and Game, C. (2010) *Local Government in the United Kingdom*, 5th edn (Palgrave Macmillan).

Bibliography

Audit Commission (1991) *A Rough Guide to Europe: Local Authorities and the EC* (HMSO).

Bains, M.A. (1972) *Working Group on Local Authority Management Structures, The New Local Authorities: Management and Structure* (HMSO).

Bulpitt, J.J.G. (1967) *Party Politics in English Local Government* (Longman).

Byrne, T. (1983) *Local Government in Britain* (Pelican).

Chandler, J.A. (2007) *Explaining Local Government: Local Government in Britain Since 1800* (Manchester University Press).

Chisholm, M. and S. Leach (2008) *Botched Business: The Damaging Process of Re-organising Local Government, 2006–2008* (Douglas McLean).

Clements, R.V. (1969) *Local Notables and the City Council* (Macmillan).

Copus, C. (1998) 'The Councillor: Representing a Locality and the Party Group', *Local Governance*, Vol. 24, No. 3, Autumn, pp. 215–24.

Copus, C. (1999a) 'The Political Party Group: Model Standing Orders and a Disciplined Approach to Local Representation', *Local Government Studies*, Vol. 25, No. 1, Spring, pp. 17–34.

Copus, C. (1999b) 'The Councillor and Party Group Loyalty', *Policy and Politics*, Vol. 27, No. 3, July, pp. 309–24.

Copus, C. (2000) 'Consulting the Public on New Political Management Arrangements: A Review and some Observations', *Local Governance*, Vol. 26, No. 3, Autumn, pp. 177–86.

Copus, C. (2004) *Party Politics and Local Government* (Manchester University Press).

Dearlove, J. (1979) *The Reorganisation of British Local Government: Old Orthodoxies and a Political Perspective* (Cambridge University Press).

DETR (1997) Local Democracy and Community Leadership.

DETR (1998a) Local Democracy and Community Leadership.

DETR (1998b) Improving Local Services through Best Value.

DETR (1998c) Modern Local Government: In touch with the People.

DETR (1999a) Implementing Best Value: A Consultation Paper on Draft Guidance.

DETR (1999b) Local Leadership: Local Choice.

DETR (2000) New Council Constitutions: Consultation Guidelines for English Local Authorities, C. Copus, G. Stoker and F. Taylor.

DTLR (2001) Strong Local Leadership: Quality Public Services.

DTLR (2002) Your Region, Your Choice: Revitalising the English Regions.

Elcock, H. (1982) *Local Government: Politicians, Professionals and the Public in Local Authorities* (Methuen).

Ercole, E., Walters, M. and Goldsmith, M. (1997) 'Cities, Networks, EU regions, European Offices', in M. Goldsmith and K. Klausen (eds) *European Integration and Local Government* (Edward Elgar).

Fraser, D. (1979) *Power and Authority in the Victorian City* (St Martins Press).

Game, C. and Leach, S. (1995) *The Role of Political Parties in Local Democracy*, Commission for Local Democracy, Research Report No. 11 (CLD).

Goldsmith, M. and Sperling, E. (1997) 'Local Government and the EU: The British Experience', in M. Goldsmith and K. Klausen (eds) *European Integration and Local Government* (Edward Elgar).

Grant, W.P. (1973) 'Non-partisanship in British Local Politics', *Policy and Politics*, Vol. 1, No. 1, pp. 241–54.

Gray, A. (1979) 'Local Government in England and Wales, in B. Jones and D. Kavanagh (eds) *British Politics Today* (Manchester University Press).

Green, G. (1972) 'National, City and Ward Components of Local Voting', *Policy and Politics* 1(1) September 1972, pp. 45–54.

Gyford, J. (1976) *Local Politics in Britain* (Croom Helm), p. 11.

Gyford, J. (1985) 'The Politicisation of Local Government', in M. Loughlin, M. Gelfand and K. Young *Half a Century of Municipal Decline*, (George Allen and Unwin).

Hampton, W. (1970) *Democracy and Community: A Study of Politics in Sheffield* (Oxford University Press).

Hampton, W. (1987) *Local Government and Urban Politics* (Longman).

Hennock, E.P. (1973) *Fit and Proper Persons: Ideal and Reality in Nineteenth-Century Urban Government* (Edward Arnold).

HMSO (1960) *Royal Commission on Local Government in Greater London, 1957–60* (The Herbert Commission), Cmnd 1164.

HMSO (1967a) *Report of the Royal Commission on Local Government* (Redcliffe-Maud Report), Cmnd 4040.

HMSO (1967b) *Committee on the Management of Local Government*, Research Vol. III, *The Local Government Elector*.

HMSO (1969) *Royal Commission on Local Government in Scotland* (The Wheatley Commission), Cmnd 4159.

HMSO (1983) *Streamlining the Cities*, Cmnd 9063.

HMSO (1986a) *Committee of Inquiry into the Conduct of Local Authority Business*, Research Vol. III, *The Local Government Elector*, Cmnd 9800.

HMSO (1986b) *Committee of Inquiry into the Conduct of Local Authority Business*, Research Vol. I, *The Political Organisation of Local Authorities*, Cmnd 9798, pp. 25, 197.

HMSO (1997) *Committee on Standards in Public Life*,Vol. II, *Standards of Conduct in Local Government in England and Wales*, Cmnd 3702 – II.

HMSO (1998) *Modern Local Government: In Touch with the People*, Cmnd 4014.

HMSO (1999) *Local Leadership: Local Choice*, Cmnd 4298.

HMSO (2001) Local Authorities (Model Code of Conduct) (England) Order 2001, Statutory Instrument 2001 No. 3575.

Institute for Public Policy Research (1991), *The Constitution of the United Kingdom*.

John, P. (1994) 'UK Sub-national Offices in Brussels: Diversification or Regionalism?', paper presented to the ESRC Research Seminar: British Regionalism and Devolution in a Single Europe, LSE.

John, P. (1996) 'Centralisation, Decentralisation and the European Union: The Dynamics of Triadic Relationships', *Public Administration*, Vol. 74, Summer, pp. 293–313.

Jones, G.W. (1969) *Borough Politics: A Study of Wolverhampton Borough Council 1888–1964* (Macmillan).

Keith-Lucas, B. (1952) *The English Local Government Franchise* (Basil Blackwell).

Labour Party (1995) *Renewing Democracy: Rebuilding Communities*.

Lee, J.M. (1963) *Social Leaders and Public Persons: A Study of County Government in Cheshire since 1888* (Clarendon Press).

Newton, K. (1976) *Second City Politics: Democratic Processes and Decision-Making in Birmingham* (Clarendon Press).

ODPM (Office of the Deputy Prime Minister) (2005) *Vibrant Local Leadership*.

Pimlott, B. and N. Rao (2002) *Governing London* (Oxford University Press).

Preston, J. (1992a) 'Local Government and the European Community', in George (ed.) *Britain and the European Community: The Politics of Semi-Detachment* (Clarendon Press).

Preston, J. (1992b) 'Local Government', in S. Bulmer, S. George and J. Scott (eds) *The United Kingdom and EC Membership Evaluated* (Pinter).

Rallings, C. and Thrasher, M. (1997) *Local Elections in Britain* (Routledge).

Regional Development Agencies and Regional Chambers (1999) (Ludgate Public Affairs).

Rhodes, R.A.W., Hardy, B. and Pudney, K. (1983) *Power Dependence, Theories of Central–Local Relations: A Critical Assessment* (University of Essex, Department of Government).

Saunders, P. (1979) *Urban Politics: A Sociological Interpretation* (Hutchinson).

Stanyer, J. (1976) *Understanding Local Government* (Fontana).

Stewart, J. (1986) *The New Management of Local Government* (Allen & Unwin).

Stewart, J. (2003) *Modernising British Local Government: An Assessment of Labour's Reform Programme* (Palgrave).

Stoker, G. (1991) *The Politics of Local Government* (Macmillan).

Travers, T. (2004) *The Politics of London: Governing an Ungovernable City* (Palgrave).

Wilson D. and Game, C. (2002) *Local Government in the United Kingdom*, 3rd edn (Palgrave Macmillan).

Wolman, H. and Goldsmith, M. (1992) *Urban Politics and Policy: A Comparative Approach* (Blackwell).

Young, K. (1973) 'The Politics of London Government 1880–1899', *Public Administration*, Vol. 51, No. 1, Spring, pp. 91–108.

Young, K. (1975) *Local Politics and the Rise of Party: The London Municipal Society and the Conservative Intervention in Local Elections 1894–1963* (Leicester University Press).

Young, K. (1989) 'Bright Hopes and Dark Fears; the Origins and Expectations of the County Councils', in K. Young (ed.) *New Directions for County Government* (Association of County Councils), p. 6.

Young, K. and Davis, M. (1990) *The Politics of Local Government Since Widdicombe* (Joseph Rowntree Foundation).

Young, K. and M. Laffin (1990) *Professionalism in Local Government* (Longman).

Young, K. and Rao, N. (1997) *Local Government Since 1945* (Blackwell).

Useful websites

Office of the Deputy Prime Minister: odpm.gov.uk

Local Government Association: lga.gov.uk

Improvement and Development Agency: idea.gov.uk

Local Government Information Unit: lgiu.gov.uk

New Local Government Network: nlgn.org.uk

National constitutions: www.constitution.org

For a directory of all local council websites, try: tagish.co.uk/tagish/links/localgov.htm

The Labour Party: labour.org.uk

The Conservative Party: conservativeparty.org.uk

The Association of Liberal Democrat Councillors: aldc.org.uk

The Green Party: greenparty.org.uk

Local Government Elections centre: research.plymouth.ac.uk/elections

The National Standards Board: standardsboard.co.uk

The Lyons Inquiry: lyonsinquiry.org.uk

CHAPTER 20

The judiciary

Philip Norton

Learning objectives

- To identify the relationship of the judicial system to other parts of the political process.

- To describe the basic structure of that system, and how it has changed in recent years as a result of a greater willingness of judges to undertake judicial review, and as a consequence of constitutional change.

- To consider demands for change because of perceived weaknesses in the system.

FIRST LORD OF THE TREASURY

Introduction

Britain does not have a system like the USA, where the Supreme Court acts as ultimate interpreter of the constitution and pronounces upon the constitutionality of federal and state laws together with the actions of public officials. Since 1688, British courts have been bound by the doctrine of parliamentary sovereignty. They have been viewed as subordinate to the Queen-in-Parliament and detached from the political process. However, the received wisdom has not always matched the reality, and recent years have witnessed a growth in judicial activism. British membership of the European Union has added a significant judicial dimension to the constitution. So too has the incorporation of the European Convention on Human Rights (ECHR) into British law and legislation providing for devolution of powers to elected bodies in different parts of the United Kingdom. The UK has also acquired a Supreme Court, which came into being in October 2009, replacing the appellate committee of the House of Lords as the highest domestic court of appeal. The United Kingdom now has a court that has a physical similarity to, though not the powers of, its US namesake. The courts have become important political actors. Recent years have also seen criticism of the way the courts dispense justice. This chapter explores the nature of the British judicial system and growing concern about its powers and competence.

■ The judicial process

The literature on the judicial process in Britain is extensive. Significantly, most of it is written by legal scholars: few works on the courts or judges come from the pens of political scientists. To those concerned with the study of British politics, and in particular the process of policy making, the judicial process has generally been deemed to be of peripheral interest.

That this perception should exist is not surprising. It derives from two features that are considered to be essential characteristics of the judiciary in Britain. First, in the trinity of the executive, legislature and judiciary, it is a subordinate institution. Public policy is made and ratified elsewhere. The courts exist to interpret (within defined limits) and apply that policy once enacted by the legislature; they have no intrinsic power to strike it down. Second, it is autonomous. The independence of the judiciary is a much vaunted and essential feature of the rule of law, described by the great nineteenth-century constitutional lawyer A.V. Dicey as one of the twin pillars of the British constitution. The other pillar – parliamentary sovereignty – accounts for the first characteristic, the subordination of the judiciary to Parliament. Allied with autonomy has been the notion of political neutrality. Judges seek to interpret the law according to judicial norms that operate independently of partisan or personal preferences.

Given these characteristics – politically neutral courts separate from, and subordinate to, the central agency of law enactment – a clear demarcation has existed for some time, the study of the policy-making process being the preserve of political scientists, that of the judiciary the preserve of legal scholars. Some scholars – such as J.A.G. Griffith, formerly Professor of Law at the University of London – have sought to bridge the gap, but they have been notable for their rarity. Yet in practice the judiciary in Britain has not been as subordinate or as autonomous as the prevailing wisdom assumes. The dividing line between politics and the law is blurred rather than rigid and it is becoming more blurred.

■ A subordinate branch?

Under the doctrine of parliamentary sovereignty, the judiciary lacks the intrinsic power to strike down an Act of Parliament as being contrary to the provisions of the constitution or any other superior body of law. It was not always thus. Prior to the Glorious Revolution of 1688, the supremacy of **statute law** was not clearly established. In *Dr Bonham's Case* in

The Middlesex Guildhall, Supreme Court entrance
Source: Alamy Images

1610, Chief Justice Coke asserted that 'when an Act of Parliament is against common right and reason, or repugnant, or impossible to be performed, the common law will control it, and adjudge such act to be void'. A few years later, in *Judge* v *Savadge* (1625), Chief Justice Hobart declared that an Act 'made against natural equity, as to make a man judge in his own case' would be void. Statute law had to compete not only with principles of common law developed by the courts but also with the prerogative power of the King. The courts variously upheld the power of the King to dispense with statutes and to impose taxes without the consent of Parliament.

The Glorious Revolution put an end to this state of affairs. Thereafter, the supremacy of statute law, under the doctrine of parliamentary sovereignty, was established. The doctrine is a judicially self-imposed one. The common lawyers allied themselves with Parliament in its struggle to control the **prerogative** powers of the King and the prerogative courts through which he sometimes exercised them. The supremacy of Parliament was asserted by the Bill of Rights of 1689. 'For the common lawyers, there was a price to pay, and that was the abandonment of the claim that they had sometimes advanced, that Parliament could not legislate in derogation of the principles of the common law' (Munro 1987: 81). Parliamentary sovereignty – a purely legal doctrine asserting the supremacy of statute law – became the central tenet of the constitution (see Chapter 15). However, the subordination of the common law to law passed by Parliament did not – and does not – entail the subordination of the judiciary to the executive. Courts retain the power of interpreting the precise meaning of the law once passed by Parliament and of reviewing the actions of ministers and other public agents to determine whether those actions are *ultra vires*, that is, beyond the powers granted by statute. The courts can quash the actions of ministers that purport to be, but that on the court's interpretation are not, sanctioned by such Acts.

If a government has a particular action struck down as *ultra vires*, it may seek parliamentary approval for a bill that gives statutory force to the action taken; in other words, to give legal force to that which the courts have declared as having – on the basis of existing statutes – no such force. But seeking passage of such a bill is not only time-consuming; it can also prove to be politically contentious and publicly damaging. It conveys the impression that the government, having lost a case,

is trying to change the rules of the game. Although it is a path that governments have variously taken, it is one they prefer to – and often do – avoid.

The power of judicial review thus provides the judiciary with a potentially significant role in the policy cycle. It is a potential that for much of the twentieth century was not realised. However, recent decades have seen an upsurge in judicial activism, judges being far more willing both to review and to quash ministerial actions. The scope for judicial activism has also been enlarged by three other developments: British membership of the European Union, the incorporation of the European Convention on Human Rights (ECHR) into British law and the devolution of powers to elected assemblies in different parts of the UK. Indeed, the first two of these developments have served to undermine the doctrine of parliamentary sovereignty, giving to the courts a new role in the political process. Whether they wanted to or not, the courts now find themselves playing a more central role in the determination of public policy. That role is likely to become more visible now that there exists a dedicated Supreme Court, housed in its own building in Parliament Square.

■ An autonomous branch?

The judiciary is deemed to be independent of the other two branches of government. Its independence is, in the words of one leading textbook, 'secured by law, by professional and public opinion' (Wade and Bradley 1993: 60). Since the Act of Settlement, senior judges hold office 'during good behaviour' and can be removed by the Queen following an address by both Houses of Parliament (see Jackson and Leopold 2001: 433–4). (Only one judge has ever been removed by such a process. Jonah Barrington, an Irish judge, was removed in 1830 after it was found that he had misappropriated litigants' money and had ceased to perform his judicial duties.) Judges of inferior courts enjoy a lesser degree of statutory protection. Judges' salaries are a charge upon the consolidated fund: this means that they do not have to be voted upon each year by Parliament. By its own resolution, the House of Commons generally bars any reference by MPs to matters awaiting or under adjudication in criminal and most civil cases. By convention, a similar prohibition is observed by ministers and civil servants.

For their part, judges by convention refrain from politically partisan activity. Indeed, they have generally refrained from commenting on matters of public policy, doing so not only of their own volition but also for many years by the direction of the Lord Chancellor. The Kilmuir guidelines issued in 1955 enjoined judges to silence, since 'every utterance which he [a judge] makes in public, except in the course of the actual performance of his judicial duties, must necessarily bring him within the focus of criticism'. These guidelines were relaxed in the late 1970s but then effectively reimposed by the Lord Chancellor, Lord Hailsham, in 1980. For judges to interfere in a contentious issue of public policy, one that is not under adjudication, would – it was felt – undermine public confidence in the impartiality of the judiciary. Similarly, for politicians to interfere in a matter before the courts would be seen as a challenge to the rule of law. Hence the perceived self-interests of both in confining themselves to their own spheres of activity.

However, historically the dividing line between judges and politicians – and, to a lesser extent, between judicial and political decision making – is not quite as sharp as these various features would suggest. In terms of personnel, memberships of the executive, legislature and judiciary are not mutually exclusive. Particularly in the higher reaches, there has been some overlap, though the degree of overlap has declined considerably in the twenty-first century. The most obvious and outstanding historical example of overlap is to be found in the figure of the Lord Chancellor. Prior to the passage of the Constitutional Reform Act 2005, he was head of the judiciary, the presiding officer of the House of Lords, and a member of the Cabinet. The 2005 Act changed this situation, providing for the transfer of his judicial role to the Lord Chief Justice – the transfer took place in 2006 – and enabling someone other than a peer and senior lawyer to hold the post. The post of Lord Chancellor remains, as a conjoined role with that of Secretary of State for Justice, and has responsibility for the management of the courts system.

Other executive office holders with judicial appointments are the Law Officers: the Attorney General and the Solicitor General. They serve as legal advisers to the government and lead for the Crown in major prosecutions, especially where state security is concerned. The consent of the Attorney General is required for certain prosecutions to be launched. Within government, the legal opinion of the Law Officers carries great weight and, by convention, is treated in confidence.

The highest court of appeal in the United Kingdom was, until 2009, the House of Lords. For judicial purposes, this constituted an appellate committee of the House, comprising the law lords – appointed to the House for the purpose of fulfilling its judicial functions – and peers who had held high judicial office. Some Members of Parliament serve or have served as recorders (part-time but salaried judges in the Crown Court) and several sit as local magistrates. Judges in the High Court, Court of Appeal and Court of Session are barred by statute from membership of the Commons, and any MP appointed to a judgeship becomes ineligible to remain in the House. In 2009, the prohibition was extended to the House of Lords, so that some peers who were senior judges, such as the Lord Chief Justice, were excluded from membership for the period that they held judicial office.

Although those holding political office seek as far as possible to draw a clear dividing line between political and judicial activity, that line cannot always be maintained. At times, they have to take judicial or quasi-judicial decisions. However, they remain members of an executive accountable, unlike judges, to Parliament. This remains the case with the Law Officers. (There are separate law officers for Scotland.) It used to be the case also with the Lord Chancellor and, to some extent, the Home Secretary, who exercised quasi-judicial functions, but the functions involved in both cases have now been transferred to the courts. The Attorney General may intervene to prevent prosecutions being proceeded with if she considers such action to be in the public interest. Under powers introduced in 1989, she may refer to the Appeal Court sentences that appear to the prosecuting authorities to be unduly lenient. She also has responsibility in certain cases for initiating proceedings, for example under the Official Secrets Act, and although she takes decisions in such matters independently of government colleagues, she remains answerable to Parliament for her decisions. These powers, along with the Attorney General's role as legal adviser to the government, can bring the Law Officers into the realms of political controversy. This was the case most notably with the Attorney General's advice to the government in 2003 that it was lawful for it to commit troops to the invasion of Iraq. Some lawyers questioned the legality of the war, and rumours that the Attorney's advice had raised some doubts about the legality generated demands that it be published – the advice is normally confidential – and led eventually to it being put in the public domain.

Judges themselves do not completely stand apart from public controversy. Because they are detached from political life and can consider issues impartially, they are variously invited to chair public inquiries into the causes of particular disasters or scandals and to make recommendations on future action. This practice has been employed for many years. Recent examples have included the inquiries into the collapse of the BCCI bank (Sir Thomas Bingham, 1991), into standards in public life (Lord Nolan, 1995), into the sale of arms-making equipment to Iraq (Sir Richard Scott, 1996), into the police handling of the murder of black teenager Stephen Lawrence (Sir William Macpherson of Cluny, 1999), into the shootings during 'Bloody Sunday' in Northern Ireland (Lord Saville of Newdigate, 2001–), and into the death of Dr David Kelly (Lord Hutton, 2003–4). The inquiries or the reports that they issue are often known by the name of the judge who led the inquiry (the Nolan Committee, the Scott Report, the Hutton Report). The reports are sometimes highly controversial and may lead to criticism of the judge involved (see McEldowney 1996: 138). One irate Conservative MP berated Lord Nolan outside the Palace of Westminster in 1995, and his report was the subject of heated debate in the House of Commons. Sir Richard Scott was heavily criticised by many Conservative MPs and by a former Foreign Secretary, Lord Howe of Aberavon, for the way he conducted his inquiry. Lord Hutton's report, which led to the resignation of the director general of the BBC (Greg Dyke), was largely discredited when a subsequent report (the Butler report) found that there had been significant changes to the government's dossier making the case for war with Iraq.

Judges themselves have also been more willing in recent years to enter public debate of their own volition. The past two decades have seen a tendency on the part of several judges to justify their actions publicly. In 1988 Lord Chancellor Mackay allowed some relaxation of the Kilmuir rules in order that judges may give interviews. One judge in particular – Judge Pickles – made use of the opportunity to appear frequently on television. A greater willingness to comment on issues of public policy has also been apparent on the part of the most senior judges. The appointment of Lord Justice Bingham as Master of the Rolls and Lord Justice Taylor as Lord Chief Justice in 1992 heralded a new era of openness. Both proved willing to express views on public policy, both advocating the incorporation of the European Convention on Human Rights into British law. Taylor not only gave press interviews but also used the floor of the House of Lords to criticise government policy. Their successors have maintained a similar degree of openness and this to some degree has become institutionalised: the Lord Chief Justice now publishes an annual report and usually appears annually before the Constitution Committee of the House of Lords to discuss any issues of concern. The judges have also appointed a spokesperson who can respond to public concerns or media criticism and explain the role of judges in the judicial process.

Thus, although the two generalisations that the judiciary constitutes a subordinate and autonomous branch of government – subordinate to the outputs of Parliament (Acts of Parliament) but autonomous in deciding cases – remain broadly correct, both are in need of some qualification. The courts are neither as powerless nor as totally independent as the assertion would imply. For the student of politics, the judiciary is therefore an appropriate subject for study. What, then, is the structure of the judicial system in Britain? Who are the people who occupy it? To what extent has the judiciary become more active in recent years in reviewing the actions of government? What has been the effect of membership of the EC/EU, the incorporation of the ECHR into British law, and of devolution? And what pressure is there for change?

■ The courts

Apart from a number of specialised courts and tribunals, the organisational division of courts is that between **criminal law** and **civil law**. The basic structure of the court system in England and Wales is shown in Figure 20.1. (Scotland and Northern Ireland have different systems.) Minor criminal cases are tried in the magistrates' courts, minor civil cases in county courts. Figure 20.1 (page 462) also shows the higher courts that try serious cases and the routes through which appeals may be heard. The higher courts – the Crown Court, the High Court and the Court of Appeal – are known collectively, as the Senior Courts of England and Wales. At the head of the system stands the Supreme Court.

Lord Phillips of Worth Matravers, President of the Supreme Court

Lord Phillips of Worth Matravers
Source: Rex Features

Born in 1938, Nicholas Phillips studied law at Cambridge, was called to the Bar in 1962 and practised as a barrister from 1962 to 1987. From 1973 to 1978, he was junior counsel to the Ministry of Defence and to the Treasury in Admiralty matters. He was made a QC in 1978. He served as a Recorder from 1982 to 1987 and became a Judge of the High Court (Queen's Bench Division) in 1987. In 1995 he was appointed to the Court of Appeal and made a privy counsellor. He chaired the inquiry into BSE (1998–2000). In 1999 he was made a law lord, being ennobled as Lord Phillips of Worth Matravers. The following year, he was appointed Master of the Rolls, that is, head of civil justice, and in 2005 he became Lord Chief Justice. In that capacity, in 2006 he became head of the judiciary, in place of the Lord Chancellor, under the provisions of the Constitutional Reform Act 2005. In 2008 he rejoined the law lords as the senior law lord. With the other law lords, he moved in 2009 to become a member of the new Supreme Court, entering the history books as the first President of the Supreme Court.

He has served on a number of bodies. He chaired the Law Advisory Council of the British Council from 1991 to 1997 and the Council of Legal Education from 1992 to 1997. He also chaired the Lord Chancellor's Advisory Committee on Public Records from 2000 to 2005 and, from 2005, the Criminal Procedure Rules Committee. He is President of the British Maritime Law Association. He also holds a number of honorary degrees.

Married with two children and two stepchildren, he lists his interests as mountains and – appropriately for someone who has specialised in maritime law – the sea.

Criminal cases

More than nine out of every ten criminal cases in England and Wales are tried in magistrates' courts. In some recent years this has constituted almost or just over 2 million cases, though the number has dropped with the use of out-of-court resolutions, such as the use of cautions and fixed-penalty fines for summary motoring offences. There were 1.74 million defendants proceeded against in criminal cases in 2007. The courts have power to levy fines, the amount depending on the offence, and to impose prison sentences not exceeding six months. The largest single number of cases tried by magistrates' courts are motoring offences. Other offences tried by the courts range from allowing animals to stray onto a highway and tattooing a minor to burglary,

assault, causing cruelty to children and wounding. On average it takes 147 days from commission of an offence to completion of a case. Once before a court, a majority of minor offences are each disposed of in a matter of minutes; in some cases, in which the defendant has pleaded guilty, in a matter of seconds.

Magistrates themselves are of two types: professional and lay. Professional magistrates are now known, under the provisions of the 1999 Access to Justice Act, as district judges (magistrates' courts); they were previously known as stipendiary magistrates. There are about 140 district judges and 170 deputy district judges. They are legally qualified and serve on a full-time basis. They sit alone when hearing cases. Lay magistrates, of which there are just under 30,000, are part-time and, as the name

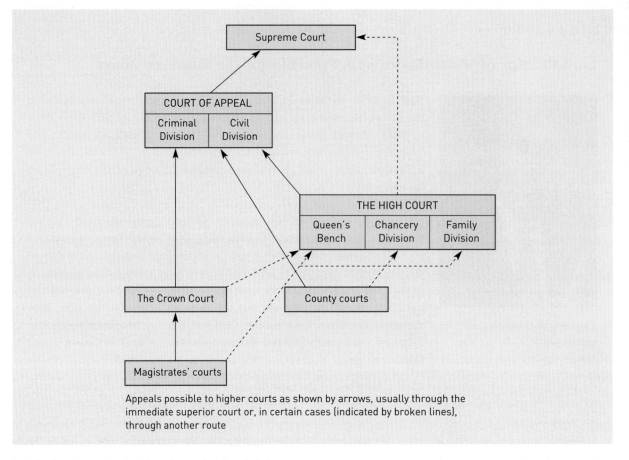

Appeals possible to higher courts as shown by arrows, usually through the immediate superior court or, in certain cases (indicated by broken lines), through another route

Figure 20.1 The court system in England and Wales

implies, are not legally qualified, although they do receive some training. Lay magistrates are drawn from the ranks of the public, typically those with the time to devote to such public duty (for example, housewives, local professional and retired people), and they sit as a bench of between two and seven in order to hear cases, advised by a legally qualified clerk. Cities and larger towns tend to have district judges (magistrates' courts); the rest of England and Wales relies on lay magistrates.

Until 1986, the decision whether to prosecute – and the prosecution itself – was undertaken by the police. Since 1986, the Crown Prosecution Service (CPS), headed by the Director of Public Prosecutions, has been responsible for the independent review and prosecution of all criminal cases instituted by police forces in England and Wales, with certain specified exceptions. In Scotland, responsibility for prosecution rests with the Crown Office and Procurator Fiscal Service. Members of this service – like the CPS in England and Wales – are lawyers.

Appeals from decisions of magistrates' courts may be taken to the Crown Court or, in matrimonial cases, to the Family Division of the High Court, or – on points of law – to the Queen's Bench Division of the High Court. In practice, appeals are rare: less than 1 per cent of those convicted appeal against conviction or sentence. The cost of pursuing an appeal would, in the overwhelming majority of cases, far exceed the fine imposed. The time of the Crown Court is taken up instead with hearing the serious cases – known as indictable offences – which are subject to a jury trial and to penalties beyond those that a magistrates' court can impose. In 2007, 153,000 defendants were dealt with in the Crown Court.

The Crown Court is divided into 92 courts. The most serious cases will be presided over by a High Court judge, the most senior position within the court; a circuit judge or a recorder will hear other cases. High Court and circuit judges are full-time, salaried judges; recorders are legally qualified but part-time, pursuing their normal legal practice when not engaged on court duties.

Appeals from conviction in a Crown Court may be taken on a point of law to the Queen's Bench Division of the High Court but usually are taken to the Criminal Division of the Court of Appeal. Appeals against conviction are possible on a point of law and on a point of fact, the former as a matter of right and the latter with the leave of the trial judge or the Court of Appeal. Approximately 10 per cent of those convicted in a Crown Court usually appeal. The Appeal Court may quash a conviction, uphold it or vary the sentence imposed by the lower courts. Appeals against sentence – as opposed to the conviction itself – are also possible with the leave of the Appeal Court and, as we have already seen, the Attorney General now has the power to refer to the court sentences that appear to be unduly lenient. In cases referred by the Attorney General, the court has the power to increase the length of the sentence imposed by the lower court.

The Court of Appeal consists of judges known as Lord Justices of Appeal and four judges who are members *ex officio* (the Lord Chief Justice, the Master of the Rolls, the President of the Family Division of the High Court and the Vice-Chancellor of the Chancery Division), although the composition varies from the criminal to the civil division. Appeals in criminal cases are usually heard by three judges, presided over by the Lord Chief Justice or a Lord Justice. Judges of the Queen's Bench may also sit on the court.

From the Court of Appeal, a further appeal is possible to the Supreme Court if the court certifies that a point of law of general public importance is involved and it appears to the court, or to the Supreme Court, that the point ought to be considered by the highest domestic court of appeal. The Supreme Court is presided over by a President and eleven Justices of the Supreme Court.

One other judicial body should also be mentioned. It does not figure in the normal court structure. That is the Judicial Committee of the Privy Council, essentially a product of the country's colonial history. This committee was set up in 1833 to exercise the power of the Privy Council in deciding appeals from colonial, ecclesiastical and admiralty courts. Three to five senior judges sit. It comprises essentially Justices of the Supreme Court and some other senior judges. Most of its functions have disappeared over time, though it has retained a limited role in considering particular appeals in certain criminal cases from a number of Commonwealth countries and from certain domestic bodies, such as

disciplinary committees in the medical, veterinary and other healthcare professions. It assumed a new – though, in the event, short-lived – significance as a consequence of devolution. Until 2009, legal challenges to the powers exercised by the devolved bodies were heard by the Judicial Committee. It lost these powers to the new Supreme Court.

Civil cases

In civil proceedings, some minor cases (for example, involving the summary recovery of some debts) are dealt with in magistrates' courts. However, most cases involving small sums of money are heard by county courts; more important cases are heard in the High Court.

County courts are presided over by circuit judges. The High Court is divided into three divisions, dealing with **common law** (the Queen's Bench Division), equity (Chancery Division) and domestic cases (Family Division). The Court comprises the three judges who head each division and just over one-hundred judges known as puisne (pronounced 'puny') judges. In most cases judges sit alone, although a Divisional Court of two or three may be formed, especially in the Queen's Bench Division, to hear applications for writs requiring a public body to fulfil a particular duty (*mandamus*), to desist from carrying out an action for which it has no legal authority (prohibition) and to quash a decision already taken (*certiorari*). Jury trials are possible in certain cases tried in the Queen's Bench Division (for example, involving malicious prosecution or defamation of character) but are now rare.

Appeals from magistrates' courts and from county courts are heard by Divisional Courts of the High Court: appeals from magistrates' courts on points of law, for example, go to a Divisional Court of the Queen's Bench Division. From the High Court – and certain cases in county courts – appeals are taken to the Civil Division of the Court of Appeal. In the Appeal Court, cases are normally heard by the Master of the Rolls sitting with two Lords Justices of Appeal.

From the Court of Appeal, an appeal may be taken – with the leave of the Court or the Supreme Court – to the Supreme Court. In rare cases, on a point of law of exceptional difficulty calling for a reconsideration of a binding precedent, an appeal may go directly, with the leave of the Supreme Court, from the High Court to the Supreme Court.

Cases brought against ministers or other public bodies for taking actions that are beyond their powers (*ultra vires*) will normally be heard in the Queen's Bench Division of the High Court before being taken – in the event of an appeal – to the Court of Appeal and the Supreme Court. The Government has suffered a number of reverses in the High Court as a result of ministerial decisions being judicially reviewed.

Tribunals

Many if not most citizens are probably affected by decisions taken by public bodies, for example those determining eligibility for particular benefits or compensation for compulsory purchase. The postwar years have seen the growth of administrative law, providing the legal framework within which such decisions are taken and the procedure by which disputes may be resolved.

To avoid disputes over particular administrative decisions being taken to the existing, highly formalised civil courts – overburdening the courts and creating significant financial burdens for those involved – the law provides for a large number of tribunals to resolve such disputes. There are now tribunals covering a wide range of issues, including unfair dismissal, rents, social security benefits, immigration, mental health and compensation for compulsory purchase. Those appearing before tribunals will often have the opportunity to present their own case and to call witnesses and cross-examine the other side. The tribunal itself will normally – although not always – comprise three members, although the composition varies from tribunal to tribunal: some have lay members, others have legally (or otherwise professionally) qualified members; some have part-time members, others have full-time members. Employment tribunals, for example, each comprise an independent chairman and two members drawn from either side of industry.

The activities of tribunals are normally dull and little noticed. On rare occasions, though, decisions may have political significance. In January 1996, an employment tribunal in Leeds held that the policy of the Labour Party to have women-only shortlists for some parliamentary seats breached sex discrimination legislation. Rather than pursue an appeal, which could take up to twenty months to be heard, the party decided not to proceed with such shortlists.

The judges

The most senior judges are the twelve members of the Supreme Court. They are eminent lawyers, normally drawn from the ranks of the Court of Appeal. The other most senior judicial appointments – the Lord Chief Justice (head of the judiciary and of the Appeal Court in criminal cases), Master of the Rolls (head of the Appeal Court in civil cases), President of the Family Division and the Lord Justices of Appeal – are drawn from High Court judges or from barristers of at least ten years' standing, although solicitors are now also eligible for consideration. Other judges – High Court judges, circuit judges and recorders – are drawn principally from barristers of at least ten years' standing, although solicitors and circuit court judges may be appointed to the High Court. Nominations for judicial appointments are made by an independent Judicial Appointments Commission.

The attraction in becoming a judge lies only partially in the salary (see Table 20.1) – the top earners among barristers can achieve annual incomes of several hundred thousand pounds. Rather, the attraction lies in the status that attaches to holding a position at the top of one's profession. For many barristers, the ultimate goal is to become Lord Chief Justice, Master of the Rolls or a Justice of the Supreme Court.

Judges, by the nature of their calling, are expected to be somewhat detached from the rest of society. However, critics – such as J.A.G. Griffith, in *The Politics of the Judiciary* (5th edn, 1997) – contend that this professional distance is exacerbated by social exclusivity, judges being predominantly elderly upper-class males.

Although statutory retirement ages have been introduced, they are generous in relation to the normal retirement age: High Court judges retire at age 75, circuit judges at 72. Less than 15 per cent of senior judges are female (see Table 20.2). In 2009, there was only one female Justice of the Supreme Court – Baroness Hale of Richmond, the first ever female to be appointed to the highest court of appeal (initially the House of Lords) – and three women among thirty-three Lord Justices of Appeal. And as Table 20.2 reveals, of 109 judges of the High Court, only 11 were women. Those from ethnic minority backgrounds are even scarcer: three High Court judges and twenty circuit judges.

In their educational backgrounds, judges are also remarkably similar. The majority went to public school (among Supreme Court Justices and Lord Justices, the proportion exceeds 80 per cent) and the vast majority graduated from Oxford and Cambridge Universities; more than 80 per cent of

Table 20.1 Judicial salaries, 2009–2010

Group	Annual salary (£) from	
	April 2008	**April 2009**
1 (Lord Chief Justice)	236,300	239,845
1.1 (Lord Chief Justice of Northern Ireland, Master of the Rolls, President of the Supreme Court)	211,000	214,165
2 (Justices of the Supreme Court, President of the Queen's Bench Division, President of the Family Division)	203,800	206,857
3 (Lord Justices of Appeal)	193,800	196,707
4 (High Court judges)	170,200	172,753
5 (Senior Circuit Court judges, certain Tribunal Presidents, certain senior Recorders)	136,500	138,548
6.1 (Circuit judges, certain Tribunal Presidents)	126,400	128,296
6.2 (Deputy Senior District Judge [Magistrates' Court])	119,000	120,785
7 (District Judges [Magistrates' Courts], Immigration Judges)	101,400	102,921

Source: Ministry of Justice, *Judicial and Court Statistics 2007*, Cm 7467 (The Stationery Office, 2008) © Crown Copyright 2008. Crown copyright material is reproduced with the permission of the Controller of Her Majesty's Stationery Office (HMSO)

Table 20.2 Gender of senior judges, April 2008

Position	Male	Female	Total
Lords of Appeal in Ordinary [now Justices of the Supreme Court]	11	1	12
Lord Justices of Appeal	33	3	36
High Court Judges	98	11	109
Circuit Judges	492	72	564
Total	**634**	**87**	**721**

Source: Adapted from the Ministry of Justice website (http://www.judiciary.gov.uk/keyfacts/statistics/ethnic.htm). © Crown Copyright 2009. Crown copyright material is reproduced with the permission of the Controller of Her Majesty's Stationery Office (HMSO)

circuit judges did so, and the proportion increases the further one goes up the judicial hierarchy.

Senior judgeships are the almost exclusive preserve of barristers. It is possible for solicitors to become judges, though few have taken this route: in 2008, only one Lord Justice of Appeal and one High Court judge were drawn from the ranks of solicitors. The proportion of solicitors is greater among the ranks of circuit judges: 89 out of 564.

Judges thus form a socially and professionally exclusive or near-exclusive body. This exclusivity has been attacked for having unfortunate consequences. One is that judges are out of touch with society itself, not being able to understand the habits and terminology of everyday life, reflecting instead the social mores of thirty or forty years ago. The male-oriented nature of the judiciary has led to claims that judges are insufficiently sensitive in cases involving women, especially rape cases. The background of the judges has also led to allegations of inbuilt bias – towards the government of the day and towards the Conservative Party. Senior judges, according to Griffith, construe the public interest as favouring law and order and upholding the interests of the state. The claim of deference to the executive is also one that has been pursued by Keith Ewing (Ewing 2004; Ewing and Tham 2008). Though accepting courts may be an irritant to the executive, he has argued that they are not an obstacle (Ewing and Tham 2008: 691).

Though Griffith's claim about political bias has not been pursued by many other writers, the effect of gender and social exclusivity has been a cause of concern among jurists as well as ministers. Such concern exists at a time when the judiciary has become more active. There has been a greater willingness on the part of judges to review the actions of ministers (Stevens 2003: 358–9). There has also been increased activity arising from the UK's membership of the European Community/Union. The incorporation of the ECHR into British law and the creation of devolved assemblies have also widened the scope for judicial activity. In combination, these developments have raised the courts in Britain to a new level of political activity – and visibility.

■ Judicial activism

The common law power available to judges to strike down executive actions as being beyond powers granted – *ultra vires* – or as contrary to natural law was not much in evidence in the decades prior to the 1960s. Courts were generally deferential in their stance towards government. This was to change in the period from the mid-1960s onwards. Although the judiciary changed hardly at all in terms of the background of judges – they were usually the same elderly, white, Oxbridge-educated males as before – there was a significant change in attitudes. Apparently worried by the perceived encroachment of government on individual liberties, they proved increasingly willing to use their powers of judicial review.

In four cases in the 1960s, the courts adopted an activist line in reviewing the exercise of powers by administrative bodies and, in two instances, of ministers. In *Conway* v *Rimmer* in 1968, the House of Lords ruled against a claim of the Home Secretary that the production of certain documents would be contrary to the public interest; previously, such a claim would have been treated as definitive. Another case in the same year involved the House of Lords considering why, and not just how, a ministerial decision was made. It was a demonstration, noted Lord Scarman (1974: 49), that judges were 'ready to take an activist line'.

This activist line has been maintained and, indeed, become more prominent. Successive governments have found ministerial actions overturned by the courts. There were four celebrated cases in the second half of the 1970s in which the courts found against Labour ministers (Norton 1982: 138–40), and then several in the 1980s and the 1990s, when they found against Conservative ministers.

Perceptions of greater judicial activism derive not just from the cases that have attracted significant media attention. They also derive from the sheer number of applications for **judicial review** made to the courts (Stevens 2003: 358). At the beginning of the 1980s, there were about 500 applications a year for leave to apply for judicial review. The figure grew throughout the decade, exceeding 1,000 in 1985, 1,500 in 1987 and 2,000 in 1990. In the 1990s, it generally exceeded 3,000 and in 1998 it reached 4,539. The annual figure has since remained in excess of 4,000, sometimes dramatically in excess of that figure. In 2004 there were 4,207 applications. In 2007 it reached 6,690. 'Judicial review was the boom stock of the 1980s', declared Lord Bingham in 1995.

'Unaffected by recession, the boom has roared on into the 1990s.' The figures show that it roared on into the new century.

Each year, a number of cases have attracted media attention and been politically significant. In 1993, Lord Rees-Mogg challenged the power of the government to ratify the Maastricht Treaty. His case was rejected by a Divisional Court of the Queen's Bench Division. The same month – July 1993 – saw the House of Lords find a former Home Secretary, acting in his official ministerial capacity, in contempt of court for failing to comply with a court order in an asylum case. The ruling meant that ministers could not rely on the doctrine of crown immunity to ignore the orders of a court. *The Times* reported (28 July 1993):

Five law lords declared yesterday that ministers cannot put themselves above the law as they found the former home secretary Kenneth Baker guilty of contempt of court in an asylum case. The historic ruling on Crown immunity was described as one of the most important constitutional findings for two hundred years and hailed as establishing a key defence against the possible rise of a ruthless government in the future.

Ironically, the case was largely overshadowed by attention given to the unsuccessful case pursued by Lord Rees-Mogg. Kenneth Baker's successor as Home Secretary, Michael Howard, also variously ran foul of the courts, the Appeal Court holding that he had acted beyond his powers. Indeed, tension between government and the courts increased notably in 1995 and 1996 as several cases went against the Home Secretary (Woodhouse 1996). In July 1996, the court found that he had acted unlawfully in taking into account a public petition and demands from members of the public in increasing the minimum sentence to be served by two minors who had murdered the two-year-old Jamie Bulger. Nor were cases confined to the period of Conservative government. After the return of the Labour government in 1997, successive Home Secretaries fell foul of the courts. In July 1999, for example, Jack Straw's attempts to retain his power to ban journalists who were investigating miscarriages of justice from interviewing prisoners was declared unlawful by the House of Lords. The same month, the Court of Appeal found against him after he sought to return three asylum seekers to France or Germany. In 2001, an order made by Mr Straw, and approved by Parliament, designating Pakistan as a country that presented no serious risk of persecution was quashed by the Court of Appeal. In a judgment at the end of 2004, in the *Belmarsh case*, the law lords held that powers in Part 4 of the Anti-Terrorism, Crime and Security Act 2001 were disproportionate and discriminatory because they applied only to foreign nationals. All these cases, along with several other high-profile judgments – including a number by European courts – combined to create a new visibility for the judiciary.

The courts, then, are willing to cast a critical eye over decisions of ministers in order to ensure that they comply with the powers granted by statute and are not contrary to natural justice. They are facilitated in this task by the rise in the number of applications made for judicial review and by their power of statutory interpretation. As Drewry (1986: 30) has noted:

Although judges must strictly apply Acts of Parliament, the latter are not always models of clarity and consistency . . . This leaves the judges with considerable scope for the exercise of their creative skills in interpreting what an Act really means. Some judges, of which Lord Denning was a particularly notable example, have been active and ingenious in inserting their own policy judgements into the loopholes left in legislation.

Judicial activism is thus well established. The courts have been willing to scrutinise government actions, and on occasion strike them down, on a scale not previously witnessed. Some commentators in the 1990s saw it as a consequence of the Conservative Party being in government for more than a decade. However, the courts maintained their activism under a Labour government, much to the displeasure of some ministers and resulting, as we shall see, in some high-profile clashes between ministers and the courts.

However, the extent and impact of such activism on the part of judges should not be exaggerated. There are three important caveats that have to be entered. First, statutory interpretation allows judges some but not complete leeway. They follow well-established guidelines. Second, only a minority of applications for judicial review concern government departments: a larger number are for review of actions taken by local authorities. Third, most applications made for judicial review fail. Of applications in 2007, only 21 per cent were granted leave to apply and of the 338 cases disposed of, only 162 were allowed.

Even so, activism on the part of the courts constitutes a problem for government. Even though the percentage of applications where leave is given to proceed has declined, the absolute number has increased. And even though government may win most of the cases brought against it, it is the cases that it loses that attract the headlines.

■ Enforcing EU law

The United Kingdom signed the treaty of accession to the European Community in 1972. The European Communities Act passed the same year provided the legal provisions necessary for membership. The UK became a member of the EC on 1 January 1973. The European Communities Act, as we have seen in Chapter 13, created a new judicial dimension to the British constitution.

The 1972 Act gave legal force not only to existing EC law but also to future law. When regulations have been promulgated by the Commission and the Council of Ministers, they take effect within the United Kingdom. Parliamentary assent to the principle is not required. That assent has already been given in advance by virtue of the provisions of the 1972 Act. Parliament may be involved in giving approval to measures to implement directives, but there is no scope to reject the purpose of the directives. And, as we recorded in Chapter 15, under the provisions of the Act, questions of law are to be decided by the European Court of Justice (ECJ), or in accordance with the decisions of that court. All courts in the United Kingdom are required to take judicial notice of decisions made by the ECJ. Cases in the UK that reach the Supreme Court are, unless the justices consider that the law has already been settled by the ECJ, referred to the European Court for a definitive ruling. Requests may also be made by lower courts to the ECJ for a ruling on the meaning and interpretation of European treaties. In the event of a conflict between the provisions of European law and those of an Act of Parliament, the former are to prevail.

The question that has most exercised writers on constitutional law since Britain's accession to the EC has been what British courts should do in the event of the passage of an Act of Parliament that expressly overrides European law. The question remains a hypothetical one. Although some doubt exists – Lord Denning when Master of the Rolls appeared to imply on occasion that the courts must apply EC law, Acts of Parliament notwithstanding – the generally accepted view among jurists is that courts, by virtue of the doctrine of parliamentary sovereignty, must apply the provisions of the Act of Parliament that expressly overrides European law (see Bradley 1994: 97).

Given the absence of an explicit overriding of European law by statute, the most important question to which the courts have had to address themselves has been how to resolve apparent inconsistencies or conflict between European and domestic (known as municipal) law. During debate on the European Communities Bill in 1972, ministers made clear that the bill essentially provided a rule of construction: that is, that the courts were to construe the provisions of an Act of Parliament, in so far as it was possible to do so, in such a way as to render it consistent with European law. However, what if it is not possible to construe an Act of Parliament in such a way? Where the courts have found UK law to fall foul of European law, the UK government has introduced new legislation to bring domestic law into line with EC requirements. But what about the position prior to the passage of such legislation? Do the courts have power to strike down or suspend Acts of Parliament that appear to breach European law? The presumption until 1990 was that they did not. Two cases – the *Factortame* and *Ex Parte EOC* cases – have shown that presumption to be false. The former case involved a challenge, by the owners of some Spanish trawlers, to the provisions of the 1988 Merchant Shipping Act. The High Court granted interim relief, suspending the relevant parts of the Act. This was then overturned by the House of Lords (predecessor of the Supreme Court), which ruled that the courts had no such power. The European Court of Justice, to which the case was then referred, ruled in June 1990 that courts did have the power of injunction and could suspend the application of Acts of Parliament that on their face appeared to breach European law until a final determination was made. The following month, the House of Lords granted orders to the Spanish fishermen preventing the Transport Secretary from withholding or withdrawing their names from the register of British fishing vessels, the orders to remain in place until the ECJ had decided the case. The case had knock-on consequences beyond EU law: having decided that an injunction could be granted against the crown in the field of EU law, the courts subsequently decided that it could then be

applied in cases not involving EU law (Jacobs 1999: 242). However, the most dramatic case in terms of EU law was to come in 1994. In *R. v Secretary of State for Employment, ex parte the Equal Opportunities Commission* – usually referred to as *Ex Parte EOC* – there was a challenge to provisions of the 1978 Employment Protection (Consolidation) Act. The House of Lords held that the provisions of the Act effectively excluded many part-time workers from the right to claim unfair dismissal or redundancy payments and were as such unlawful, being incompatible with EU law (Maxwell 1999). Although the *Factortame* case attracted considerable publicity, it was the *EOC* case that was the more fundamental in its implications. The courts were invalidating the provisions of an Act of Parliament. Following the case, *The Times* declared 'Britain may now have, for the first time in its history, a constitutional court' (5 March 1994, cited in Maxwell 1999: 197).

The courts have thus assumed a new role in the interpretation of European law, and the court system itself has acquired an additional dimension. The ECJ serves not only to hear cases that emanate from British courts but also to consider cases brought directly by or against the EC Commission and the governments of the member states. Indeed, the ECJ carries a significant workload, so much so that it has to be assisted by another court, the Court of First Instance, and both are under considerable pressure in trying to cope with the number of cases brought before them. In the twenty-first century, the ECJ alone receives 800 to 900 cases a year.

There is thus a significant judicial dimension to British membership of the European Union, involving adjudication by a supranational court, and the greater the integration of member states the greater the significance of the courts in applying European law. Furthermore, under the Maastricht Treaty, which took effect in 1993, the powers of the ECJ were strengthened, the court being given the power to fine member states that did not fulfil their legal obligations. Although the cases heard by the ECJ may not often appear to be of great significance, collectively they produce a substantial – indeed, massive – body of case law that constitutes an important constraint on the actions of the UK government. Each year, that body of case law grows greater.

Against this new judicial dimension has to be set the fact that the doctrine of parliamentary sovereignty remains formally extant. Parliament retains the power to repeal the 1972 Act. The decisions of the ECJ have force in the United Kingdom inasmuch as Parliament has decreed that they will. When Lord Rees-Mogg sought judicial review of the government's power to ratify the Maastricht Treaty, the Speaker of the House of Commons, Betty Boothroyd, issued a stern warning to the courts, reminding them that under the Bill of Rights of 1689 the proceedings of Parliament could not be challenged by the courts. (Lord Rees-Mogg, whose application was rejected, emphasised that no such challenge was intended.) And it was the British government that instigated the provision in the Maastricht Treaty for the ECJ to fine member states. The number of cases brought in the ECJ against the UK, alleging a failure to fulfil its obligations, is a relatively small one. Out of 207 cases brought before the ECJ in 2009 only 13 were brought against the UK and even this constituted a high number compared to previous years. In 2007, out of 212 cases, only 2 were brought against in the UK; in the previous year, it was 4 out of 193 cases. Even so, the impact of membership of the EC should not be treated lightly. It has introduced a major new judicial dimension to the British constitution. It has profound implications for the role of the courts in influencing public policy in the United Kingdom. That was emphasised by the ruling of the House of Lords in the *Ex Parte EOC* case. The courts now appear to have acquired, in part, a power that they lost in 1688.

■ Enforcing the European Convention on Human Rights

Reinforcing the importance of the courts has been the incorporation of the European Convention on Human Rights (ECHR) into British law. Although not formally vesting the courts with the same powers as are vested by the 1972 European Communities Act, the incorporation nonetheless makes British judges powerful actors in determining public policy.

The European Convention on Human Rights was signed at Rome in 1950 and was ratified by the United Kingdom in March 1951. It came into effect in 1953. It declares the rights that should be protected in each state – such as the right to life, freedom of thought and peaceful assembly – and stipulates procedures by which infringements of those rights can be determined. Alleged breaches of the Convention are investigated by the European Commission on Human Rights and may be referred to the European Court of Human Rights.

The convention is a treaty under international law. This means that its authority derives from the consent of the states that have signed it. It was not incorporated into British law, and not until 1966 were individual citizens allowed to petition the commission. In subsequent decades, a large number of petitions were brought against the British government. Although the British government was not required under British law to comply with the decisions of the court, it did so by virtue of its international obligations and introduced the necessary changes to bring UK law into line with the judgment of the court. By 1995, over 100 cases against the UK government had been judged admissible, and 37 cases had been upheld (see Lester 1994: 42–6). Some of the decisions have been politically controversial, as in 1994 when the court decided (on a ten–nine vote) that the killing of three IRA suspects in Gibraltar in 1988 by members of the British security forces was a violation of the right to life.

The decisions of the court led to calls from some Conservative MPs for the UK not to renew the right of individuals to petition the commission. Liberal Democrats and many Labour MPs – as well as some Conservatives – wanted to move in the opposite direction and to incorporate the ECHR into British law. Those favouring incorporation argued that it would reduce the cost and delay involved in pursuing a petition to the commission and allow citizens to enforce their rights through British courts. It was also argued that it would raise awareness of human rights. This reasoning led the Labour Party to include a commitment in its 1997 election manifesto to incorporate the ECHR into British law. Following the return of a Labour government in that election, the government published a White Paper, Rights Brought Home, and followed it with the introduction of the Human Rights Bill. The bill was enacted in 1998.

The Human Rights Act makes it unlawful for public authorities to act in a way that is incompatible with convention rights. It is thus possible for individuals to invoke their rights in any proceedings brought against them by a public authority or in any proceedings that they may bring against a public authority.

Courts will, from time to time, be required to determine if primary or secondary legislation is incompatible with Convention rights. They will decide if the acts of public authorities are unlawful through contravention, perhaps even unconscious contravention, of those rights. They may have to award damages as a result.

(Irvine of Lairg 1998: 230)

Although the courts are not empowered to set aside Acts of Parliament, they are required to interpret legislation as far as possible in accordance with the convention. They look to the jurisprudence of the European Court on Human Rights, but can build on it: the standards set out in case law by the Strasbourg court constitute a floor rather than a ceiling (Wright 2009). The higher courts can issue declarations of incompatibility where UK law is deemed incompatible with the ECHR: it is then up to Parliament to take the necessary action. The Act makes provision for a 'fast-track' procedure for amending law to bring it into line with the ECHR.

The incorporation of the ECHR into British law creates a new role for British judges in determining policy outcomes. In the words of one authority, 'it gives the courts an increased constitutional role, moving them from the margins of the political process to the centre and increasing the underlying tension between the executive and the judiciary' (Woodhouse 1996: 440). Indeed, the scale of the change was such that senior judges had to be trained for the purpose and, in order to give the courts time to prepare, the principal provisions of the Act were not brought into force until October 2000. (One effect, though, was immediate. The provision requiring ministers to certify that a bill complies with the provisions of the ECHR was brought in immediately following enactment.) By May 2007, the courts had issued 24 declarations of incompatibility, though six of these were overturned on appeal and one remained subject to appeal. Twelve were dealt with by legislation or remedial orders and the government had yet to decide how to remedy the incompatibility in the remaining cases.

In April 2003, for example, in the case of *Bellinger* v *Bellinger*, the courts held that section 11(c) of the Matrimonial Causes Act 1973 was incompatible with Articles 8 and 12 of the Convention. This led to Parliament enacting the Gender Recognition Act conferring rights on those who changed gender, including the right to a new birth certificate. Also in April 2003, the courts in *Blood and Tarbuck* v *Secretary of State for Health* issued a declaration in respect of a provision of the Human Fertilisation and Embryology Act 1990 which prevented the use of a dead husband's sperm to be used by the mother to conceive. A private member's bill was employed, with government assistance, to change the law. However, the most significant case was to come in December 2004, in the *Belmarsh case*, to which we have already referred, when the House of Lords held that powers in Part 4 of the Anti-Terrorism, Crime

and Security Act breached the provisions of the Convention in that they were disproportionate and discriminatory in applying only to foreign nationals. The decision, as we shall see, caused a political storm and contributed to a major clash between executive and judiciary. The government nonetheless introduced a Terrorism Bill with new provisions in place of those embodied in the 2001 Act. However, provisions in the new Act, providing for control orders on individuals, also fell foul of the courts, the House of Lords holding that impositions of 18-hour curfews constituted a deprivation a liberty under Article 5 of the Convention.

The Act has thus had a major effect on the relationship of Parliament and the executive to the courts. Parliament has, in effect, handed over its traditional power of protecting rights to the courts. One study, covering the period 1994 to 2007, found a notable increase in human rights cases being considered by the highest court of appeal (then the House of Lords) following enactment of the Act (Shah and Poole 2009). Enforcing the rights embodied in the Act has on occasion brought the courts into conflict with the executive. Though the courts have not gone as far as some critics would wish, they have used their powers to limit the executive (Kavanagh 2009). The position was summarised by Jeffrey Jowell, in writing that the Human Rights Act 'may on the face of it be just another unentrenched statute, but its effect is to alter constitutional expectations by creating the presumption across all official decision making that rights do and should trump convenience' (Jowell 2003: 597). It is the courts that decide when such trumping should take place.

■ The impact of devolution

The devolution of powers to elected assemblies in different parts of the United Kingdom (see Chapter 15) has also enlarged the scope for judicial activity. The legislation creating elected assemblies in Scotland, Wales and Northern Ireland – the Scotland Act, the Government of Wales Act and the Northern Ireland Act – stipulates the legal process by which the powers and the exercise of powers by the assemblies can be challenged.

There are complex provisions for determining whether a particular function is exercisable by a devolved body, whether it has exceeded its powers, whether it has failed to fulfil its statutory obligations or whether a failure to act puts it in breach of the ECHR. These are known as 'devolution issues'. A law officer can require a particular devolution issue to be referred to the Supreme Court (before 2009, it was to the Judicial Committee of the Privy Council). It is also open to other courts to refer a devolution issue to higher courts for determination. Devolution issues considered by the High Court or the Court of Appeal may be appealed to the Supreme Court, but only with the leave of the court or the Supreme Court. If a court finds that a devolved body has exceeded its powers in making subordinate legislation, it can make an order removing or limiting any retrospective effect of the decision, or suspend the effect of the decision for any period and on any conditions to allow the defect to be corrected. A law officer can also make a pre-enactment reference to the Supreme Court to determine whether a bill or a provision of a bill is within the competence of the devolved body. In other words, it is not necessary for the measure to be enacted: a law officer can seek a determination while the measure is in bill form.

The provisions of the devolution legislation create notable scope for judicial activity. There is scope for the courts to interpret the legislation in a constrictive or an expansive manner. The approach taken by the courts has major implications for the devolved bodies. There is also scope for the courts to move away from the intentions of the Westminster Parliament. The longer an Act of constitutional significance survives, the intent of Parliament in passing it gradually loses its significance (Craig and Walters 1999: 289). Policing powers of the devolved bodies by the courts has political as well as legal implications. The point has been well put by Craig and Walters. As they note, the Scotland Act, while giving the Scottish Parliament general legislative powers, also limits those powers through a broad list of reservations.

At the minimum, this means that the Scottish Parliament will have to become accustomed to living with the 'judge over its shoulder'. Proposed legislation will have to be scrutinised assiduously lest it fall foul of one of the many heads of reserved subject matter . . . The need for constant recourse to lawyers who will, in many instances, indicate that proposed action cannot be taken, is bound to generate frustration and anger in Scotland.
(Craig and Walters 1999: 303)

As they conclude,

The courts are inevitably faced with a grave responsibility: the way in which they interpret the SA [Scotland Act] may be a significant factor in deciding whether devolution proves to be the reform which cements the union, or whether it is the first step towards its dissolution.
(Craig and Walters 1999: 303)

As with the Human Rights Act, the cases may be more significant for their quality, and their deterrent effect, than for their number. The number of 'devolution issues' brought before the courts is relatively rare. From the inception of devolution and the transfer of responsibility for devolution issues to the Supreme Court in 2009, the Judicial Committee of the Privy Council decided 20 cases brought before it, some of them incorporating more than one appeal. In 2001, for example, the Judicial Committee dealt with ten appeals in five cases. All of them were brought under the Scotland Act, and all but one group involved claims made in Scottish criminal proceedings that the Lord Advocate (the Scottish equivalent of the Attorney General), as prosecutor, was infringing their human rights. One group related to proceedings arising from a law passed by the Scottish Parliament that prevented the discharge from hospital, where the safety of the public so required, of a patient suffering from a mental disorder even if not detained for medical treatment. Of the ten appeals, five were dismissed and five were allowed. Since then, the court had no more than three cases brought before it in any one year.

■ Demands for change

Recent years have seen various calls for change in the judicial process. Some of these have focused on the court's constitutional role in relation to government and the protection of rights. Others have focused on decisions of the courts in domestic criminal and civil cases.

Constraining the executive

In terms of the place of the courts in the nation's constitutional arrangements, there have been various demands to strengthen the powers of the courts, and some of these calls have borne fruit, primarily with the incorporation of the ECHR into British law. Some want to go further. Some want to see a more inclusive document than the ECHR. The ECHR, for example, excludes such things as a right to food or a right of privacy (see Nolan and Sedley 1997). The Liberal Democrats, Unlock Democracy and a number of jurists want to see the enactment of an entrenched Bill of Rights. In other words, they want a measure that enjoys some degree of protection from encroachment by Parliament. Formally, as we have seen, Parliament does not have to act on declarations of incompatibility issued by the courts. Under the proposal for an entrenched Bill of Rights, the courts would be able to set aside an Act of Parliament that was in conflict with the ECHR, rather in the same way that the courts have set aside the provisions of an Act deemed to be incompatible with EU law.

The powers acquired by the courts – and the calls for them to be given further powers – have not been universally welcomed (see Box 20.1). Critics view

---

BOX 20.1   DEBATE

More power to judges?

The European Convention on Human Rights has been incorporated into British law. This gives a new role to judges. Some proposals have been put forward to strengthen the courts even further by the enactment of an entrenched Bill of Rights, putting fundamental rights beyond the reach of a simple parliamentary majority. Giving power to judges, through the incorporation of the ECHR and, more so, through an entrenched document, has proved politically contentious. The principal arguments put forward both for and against giving such power to the courts are as follows:

The case for
■ A written document, such as the ECHR, clarifies and protects the rights of the individual. Citizens know precisely what their rights are, and those rights are protected by law.
■ It puts interpretation in the hands of neutral judges, independent of the political process.
■ It prevents encroachment by politicians in government and Parliament. Politicians will be reluctant to tamper with a document, such as the ECHR, now that it is part of the law. Entrenchment of the measure – that is, imposing extraordinary provisions for its amendment – would put the rights beyond the reach of a simple majority in both Houses of Parliament.
■ It prevents encroachment by other public bodies, such as the police. Citizens know their rights in relation to public bodies and are able to seek judicial redress if those rights are infringed.
■ It ensures a greater knowledge of rights. It is an educative tool, citizens being much more rights-conscious.
■ It bolsters confidence in the political system. By knowing that rights are protected in this way, citizens feel better protected and as such are more supportive of the political system.

The case against
■ It confuses rather than clarifies rights. The ECHR, like most Bills of Rights, is necessarily drawn in general terms and citizens therefore have to wait until the courts interpret the vague language in order to know precisely what is and what is not protected.
■ It transfers power from an elected to a non-elected body. What are essentially political issues are decided by unelected judges and not by the elected representatives of the people.
■ It does not necessarily prevent encroachment by public bodies. Rights are better protected by the political culture of a society than by words written on a document. A written document does not prevent public officials getting around its provision by covert means.
■ It creates a false sense of security. There is a danger that people will believe that rights are fully protected when later interpretation by the courts may prove them wrong. Pursuing cases through the courts can be prohibitively expensive; often only big companies and rich individuals can use the courts to protect their interests.
■ If a document is entrenched, it embodies rights that are the product of a particular generation. A document that is not entrenched can be modified by a simple majority in both Houses of Parliament. If it is entrenched – as many Bills of Rights are – it embodies the rights of a particular time and makes it difficult to get rid of them after their moral validity has been destroyed, as was the case with slavery in the United States.

the new role of the courts as a threat to the traditional Westminster constitution (see Chapter 15), introducing into the political process a body of unaccountable and unelected judges who have excessive powers to interpret the provisions of a document drawn in general terms. Instead of public policy being determined by elected politicians – who can be turned out by electors at the next election – it can be decided by unrepresentative judges, who are immune to action by electors. As we have seen, the powerful position of the courts has not commended itself to all ministers. In 2001, Home Secretary David Blunkett attacked the interference by judges in political matters and even raised the possibility of 'suspending' the Human Rights Act (Woodhouse 2002: 261). In December 2004, following the decision of the House of Lords to strike down certain provisions of the Anti-Terrorism, Crime and Security Act, Foreign Secretary Jack Straw said that the law lords were 'simply wrong' to imply that detainees were being held arbitrarily; it was for Parliament and not the courts to decide how best Britain could be defended from terrorism (see Norton 2006). Following terrorist bombings in London in July 2005, ministers wanted new anti-terrorist legislation but were worried it may fall foul of the courts. In announcing a series of measures to address the terrorist threat, Prime Minister Tony Blair in August 2005 stirred controversy by declaring 'the rules of the game are changing'. He conceded it was likely that the legislation would be tested in the courts. 'Should legal obstacles arise', he said, 'we will legislate further including, if necessary, amending the Human Rights Act in respect of their interpretation of the European Convention on Human Rights and apply it directly in our own law.' In 2008, Justice Secretary Jack Straw reiterated his 'great frustration' with the way the Act had been interpreted by the courts' and wanted to 'rebalance' the legislation with an emphasis on responsibilities. Both Prime Minister Gordon Brown, in his *Governance of Britain* agenda, and Conservative leader David Cameron raised the prospect of a British Bill of Rights of Duties and Responsibilities.

Tony Blair's comments were seen as a challenge to the judiciary. Critics of his statement contended that the courts were not the problem: they had simply been applying the law as passed by Parliament. Roger Smith, the Director of the pressure group JUSTICE, argued that, if the Prime Minister wanted to amend the ECHR, success would be unlikely; if he wanted to loosen its provisions, he would get little support. 'Mr Blair may want to amend the domestic implementation of the Convention: it is difficult to see how this might work. Finally, he may just want to intimidate the UK judiciary: that would be unworthy' (*The Times*, 20 September 2005). Portraying the courts as part of the problem, rather than as part of the solution, meant the government was drawing the courts into the political fray, essentially anticipating conflict and doing so at a time of major change in the highest echelon of the judicial system.

■ Applying the law

The courts have thus proved controversial in terms of their constitutional role. They have also been the subject of debate in terms of their traditional role in interpreting and enforcing the law. The debate has encompassed not only the judges but also the whole process of criminal and civil justice.

In 1999, the usually sure-footed law lords encountered criticism when they had to decide whether the former Chilean head of state, General Augusto Pinochet, who had been detained in the UK, should be extradited from Britain to Spain. The first judgement of the court had to be set aside when one of the law lords hearing the case was revealed to have been a director of a company controlled by a party (Amnesty International) to the case. It was the first time that the law lords had set aside one of their own decisions and ordered a rehearing. Especially embarrassing for the law lords, it was also the first case in which an English court had announced its decision live on television (see Rozenberg 1999).

Lower courts, including the Court of Appeal, came in for particular criticism in the late 1980s and early 1990s as a result of several cases of miscarriages of justice (see Mullin 1996; Walker and Starmer 1999). In 1989, the 'Guildford Four', convicted in 1975 of bombings in Guildford, were released pending an inquiry into their original conviction; in 1990, the case of the Maguire family, convicted of running an IRA bomb factory, was referred back to the Appeal Court after the Home Secretary received evidence that the convictions could not be upheld; and in 1991, the 'Birmingham Six', convicted of pub bombings in Birmingham in 1974, were released after the Court of Appeal quashed their convictions. The longest-running case was the Bridgewater case, in which several men had been convicted in 1979 of the murder of newspaper boy Carl Bridgewater. The Court of Appeal refused leave to appeal in 1981 and had turned down an appeal in 1987, before the case was again brought back in 1996. The men were released in 1997. In 1998, the Court of Appeal decided to set aside posthumously the conviction of Derek Bentley, hanged in 1953 for murder, after deciding that he had been deprived of a fair trial. Several previous attempts to get the conviction set aside had failed. Various lesser-known cases have also resulted in earlier convictions being overturned. By the end of August 2009, the Court of Appeal had quashed a total of 280 convictions referred to it by the Criminal Cases Review Commission.

The judges involved in the original cases were variously criticised for being too dependent on the good faith of prosecution witnesses – as was the Court of Appeal. The Appeal Court came in for particular criticism for its apparent reluctance even to consider that there might have been miscarriages of justice. As late as 1988, the court had refused an appeal by the 'Birmingham Six', doing so in terms that suggested that the Home Secretary should not even have referred the case to the court. When lawyers for the 'Birmingham Six' had earlier sought to establish police malpractice by bringing a claim for damages, the then Master of the Rolls, Lord Denning, had caused controversy by suggesting, in effect, that the exposure of injustice in individual cases was less important than preserving a façade of infallibility (Harlow 1991: 98). By the 1990s, that façade had been destroyed. Although the cases were few in number – and only a small proportion of the applications made to the Criminal Cases Review Commission result in cases being referred to the Appeal Court (by 1999, 440 out of 11,348 cases reviewed) – it has been the high-profile cases that have undermined the position of the courts.

Another criticism has been the insensitivity of some judges in particular cases, notably rape cases. In 1993, for example, the Attorney General referred to the Court of Appeal a lenient sentence handed out by a judge in a case where a teenager had been convicted of the attempted rape of a nine-year-old girl. The judge had said that he received evidence that the girl in the case was 'no angel herself'. The comment attracted widespread and adverse criticism. The Appeal Court, while asserting that the judge had been quoted out of context, nonetheless condemned the sentence as inappropriate and increased it. An earlier case, in which another judge had awarded a young rape victim £500 to go on holiday to help her to forget about her experience, attracted even more condemnation. Such cases highlighted a problem that appears pervasive. A survey published in 1993 revealed that 40 per cent of sentences by circuit courts in rape cases were of four years or less, even though Appeal Court guidelines recommend that five years should be the starting point in contested rape cases. (The maximum sentence possible is life imprisonment.) Lenient sentences in a number of cases involving other offences also fuelled popular misgivings about the capacity of the courts to deliver appropriate sentences.

In 2000, the European Court of Human Rights ruled that the minimum term of imprisonment (or 'tariff') for murder committed by juveniles should be set by the courts and not by the Home Secretary. In effect, the power thus passed to the Lord Chief Justice. It was first used in the case of two young men, Thompson and Venables, who as minors had abducted and killed two-year-old Jamie Bulger. Lord Woolf recommended a reduction in the tariff set by a previous Home Secretary, a reduction that meant that both became eligible for parole immediately. The case had aroused strong feelings, and the Lord Chief Justice's decision was unpopular. Equally unpopular was a subsequent granting by a senior judge of an injunction preventing publication of any information that might lead to the identity or future whereabouts of the two.

The result of such cases may have limited public regard for judges, albeit not on a major scale. MORI polls have tended to show that around 60 per cent of those questioned express satisfaction with the way judges do their job. In 2004, for example, it was 58 per cent. However, the figure is less than for most of the other professions mentioned. In 2004, although 58 per cent were satisfied or very satisfied with the way judges did their job – against 18 per cent who were fairly or very dissatisfied – the figure was notably below that for nurses (96 per cent), doctors (92 per cent), teachers (86 per cent), and dentists (82 per cent). The police (67 per cent) also came out ahead of the judges. Only lawyers (54 per cent), politicians generally (27 per cent), and government ministers (27 per cent) received lower satisfaction ratings. Nonetheless, the figures show more than three times as many people satisfied than dissatisfied. The figures have remained reasonably consistent, apart from a notable dip in 2003. Polls also show that, perhaps not surprisingly, most people trust judges to tell the truth.

Other aspects of the criminal justice system have also attracted criticism. The activity and policy of the Crown Prosecution Service have also been particular targets. The CPS has been largely over-worked and has had difficulty since its inception in recruiting a sufficient number of well-qualified lawyers to deal with the large number of cases requiring action. In 1999, it was revealed that stress was a particular problem for many CPS lawyers. The CPS has also been criticised for failing to prosecute in several highly publicised cases where it has felt that the chances of obtaining a conviction were not high enough to justify proceeding. Damning reports on the organisation and leadership of the CPS were published in 1998 and 1999. As a response to the latter report, the new Director of Public Prosecutions undertook to reform the service, providing a more organised and transparent system of public prosecutions.

Another problem has been that of access to the system. Pursuing a court case is expensive. In civil cases, there is often little legal aid available. Those with money can hire high-powered lawyers. In cases alleging libel or slander, or claiming invasion of privacy, only those with substantial wealth can usually afford to pursue a case against a well-resourced individual or organisation, such as a national newspaper. Millionaires such as motor racing executive Max Moseley have pursued cases successfully, but for anyone without great financial resources the task is virtually impossible. Cases can also be delayed. Many individuals have neither the time nor the money to pursue matters through the courts. That is likely to be exacerbated with the creation of the Supreme Court. The costs of the new body are greater than those of its predecessor, the appellate committee of the House of Lords (which was able to draw on many facilities already provided in the Palace of Westminster); the additional cost is being recouped through increasing the fees charged to litigants.

Implementing change

Various proposals have been advanced for reform of the judiciary and of the system of criminal justice. A number, as we have seen, have been implemented. There have been moves to create greater openness in the recruitment of senior judges as well as to extend the right to appear before the senior courts. In 1998, new judges were required to reveal whether they were freemasons. (It was feared that member-

ship of a secret society might raise suspicions of a lack of impartiality.) The 1999 Access to Justice Act created a community legal service (CLS) to take responsibility for the provision of legal advice and for legal aid. It also created a criminal defence service, to provide that those charged with criminal offences receive a high-quality legal defence. Legal language has also been simplified. The Crown Prosecution Service has undergone sinificant change. A Commissioner for Judicial Appointments, to oversee judicial appointments, was put in place in 2001. The Constitutional Reform Act 2005 created a Judicial Appointments Commission. There have also been various reforms to criminal law in terms of sentencing and the management of cases in the magistrates' courts. In 2002, the government published a White Paper, 'Justice for All', proposing further changes to the criminal justice system. These included changing the rules as to what evidence may be presented, having judge-only trials in serious and complex fraud cases, removing the double jeopardy rule (preventing someone from being tried twice for the same offence), and creating a Sentencing Guidelines Council to ensure more uniformity in sentencing. Some of these have been implemented, including the ending, in certain exceptional circumstances, of the double jeopardy rule and the creation of a Sentencing Guidelines Council. Attempts to reduce the number of jury trials have variously fallen foul of opposition in the House of Lords. And, as we have seen, the Lord Chancellor's position as head of the judiciary has been transferred to the Lord Chief Justice and, in 2009, the Supreme Court came into being.

The courts are undergoing significant change – the changes of the past decade probably surpassing anything experienced in the previous half-century – but the pressure for reform continues. As the constitution has acquired a new judicial dimension, so the courts have become more visible and embroiled in political controversy. The creation of a Supreme Court, in the eyes of some, strengthens the position of the judiciary. The court, according to former Lord Chancellor Lord Falconer, 'will be bolder in vindicating both the freedoms of individuals and, coupled with that, being willing to take on the executive' (BBC News Online, 8 September 2009; http://news.bbc.co.uk/1/hi/uk/8237855.stm). A law lord, Lord Neuberger, who declined to move to the new Supreme Court and was instead appointed Master of the Rolls, said in September 2009 that there was a real risk of 'judges abrogating to themselves greater power than they have at the moment' (BBC News Online, 8 September 2009). Others have argued that the court may actually become exposed and vulnerable to attack by ministers, lacking the buffer provided by the House of Lords (Norton 2005: 321–3). The presence of the law lords enabled peers to understand and appreciate their role, and provide something of a protective shield; the law lords, for their part, were able to understand the nature of the parliamentary system. The Lord Chancellor has also traditionally been in a position to protect the interests of the judicial system within government. The creation of a Supreme Court, and the ending of the traditional role of the Lord Chancellor, may leave senior judges isolated and hence more exposed to attack from senior ministers. The judges have become more important political actors and, as such, more significant targets of political attack. One cannot now study the making of public policy in the United Kingdom with the courts left out.

BOX 20.2   BRITAIN IN CONTEXT

Common law versus civil law

Courts in the UK differ from those in most other countries in that they do not have responsibility for interpreting a codified constitution. Their role has principally been that of engaging in statutory, not constitutional, interpretation; courts in other countries generally engage in both (though not always: there are countries with codified constitutions, such as the Netherlands, which maintain the principle of parliamentary sovereignty). The role of the courts in the UK has changed significantly as a consequence of the UK's membership of the EC/EU and the passage of the Human Rights Act 1998 – the treaties of the EU and the European Convention of Human Rights having the characteristics of higher law documents – but the basic distinction still remains. In so far as the courts are empowered to interpret such documents, they do so under the authority of Parliament and not a written constitution.

They also differ from their continental counterparts in that – along with the USA and most Commonwealth jurisdictions – they are based on the principles of common law rather than civil (or Roman) law. The common law tradition is based on law deriving from particular measures and their interpretation by the courts; much rests on judge-made law. The civil law tradition rests on a particular legal code stipulating the general principles of law that are to apply.

Not all systems follow the British in adopting an adversarial format – a feature of the common law tradition, the case being argued by competing counsel – nor in the presumption of being innocent until proven guilty. Some systems adopt a form of religious or socialist law, in some cases requiring the accused to prove their innocence or simply presuming guilt, with the accused having no real opportunity to put their case.

Though generalisations can be drawn about courts in the United Kingdom, these can only be taken so far. Scotland has its own legal system. Though the Act of Union 1707 resulted in a unitary state, Scotland nonetheless retained its legal system. There is thus one court system, and body of law, for England and Wales and another for Scotland.

However, though there are significant differences between the legal system (or rather systems) in the UK and those in other countries, there are also features that are increasingly common. The effect of international treaties is to create common obligations. Thus, for example, the United Kingdom is a signatory to the European Convention on Human Rights; so too are more than forty other countries. The European Court of Human Rights is ultimately responsible for the interpretation of the Convention. Though the British courts are now empowered to consider Convention rights, their interpretation can be challenged in the European Court in Strasbourg. The UK is one of 27 members of the European Union and each is bound by the treaties establishing the European Community and Union. The interpretation of the treaties lies ultimately with the European Court of Justice, which sits in Luxembourg. European countries are witnessing what, in effect, constitutes a common judicialisation of their political systems.

Chapter summary

Although not at the heart of the regular policy-making process in Britain, the courts are nonetheless now significant actors in the political system. Traditionally restricted by the doctrine of parliamentary sovereignty, the courts have made use of their power of judicial review to constrain ministers and other public figures. The passage of two Acts – the European Communities Act in 1972 and the Human Rights Act in 1998 – has created the conditions for judges to determine the outcome of public policy in a way not previously possible. Judges now have powers that effectively undermine the doctrine of parliamentary sovereignty, with the outputs of Parliament not necessarily being immune to challenge in the courts. The passage of devolution legislation, creating elected bodies in Scotland, Wales and Northern Ireland, has also enlarged the scope for judicial activity, with potentially significant constitutional and political implications. The Constitutional Reform Act 2005 has resulted in the creation of a Supreme Court. The greater willingness of, and opportunity for, the courts to concern themselves with the determination of public policy has been welcomed by some jurists and politicians while alarming others, who are fearful that policy-making power may slip from elected politicians to unelected judges. The courts are having to meet the challenge of a new judicial dimension to the British constitution while coping – not always successfully – with the demands of an extensive system of criminal and civil justice.

Discussion points

- Why should the courts be independent of government?

- What role is now played by judges as a result of Britain's membership of the European Union?

- Can, and should, judges be drawn from a wider social background?

- Is the incorporation of the European Convention on Human Rights into British law a good idea?

- Has the creation of a Supreme Court strengthened or weakened the position of the senior judiciary?

Further reading

Basic introductions to the legal system can be found in student texts on constitutional and administrative law, such as Alder (2005) and Bradley and Ewing (2007). The most recent and succinct analysis of the changing role of judges in the nation's constitutional arrangements is Stevens (2002); see also Stevens (2003). On independence and accountability, see Bradley (2008). On possible future developments, see Le Sueur and Malleson (2008).

On judicial review, see Forsyth (2000). On the impact of membership of the EC/EU on British law, see Fitzpatrick (1999), Maxwell (1999) and Loveland (2003). On the incorporation of the ECHR, see Woodhouse (2002), Klug and O'Brien (2002), Shah and Poole (2009), Kavanagh (2009) and Wright (2009); for a critical view, see Ewing (2004) and Ewing and Tham (2008). On the implications for the courts of devolution, see especially Craig and Walters (1999). On the implications of the creation of the Supreme Court, see Le Sueur (2004) for a detailed legal analysis of its role in the United Kingdom and Norton (2005) for a brief consideration of its constitutional implications. On the Constitutional Reform Act, see Windlesham (2005). On the abolition of the role of Lord Chancellor, see Oliver (2004).

Bibliography

Alder, J. (2005) *Constitutional and Administrative Law*, 5th edn (Palgrave Macmillan).

Banner, C. and Deane, A. (2003) *Off with their Wigs: Judicial Revolution in Modern Britain* (Imprint Academic).

Bingham, Lord (2002) *A New Supreme Court for the United Kingdom* (The Constitution Unit).

Blackburn, R. (1997) 'A Bill of Rights for the 21st Century', in R. Blackburn and J. Busuttil (eds) *Human Rights for the 21st Century* (Pinter).

Bradley, A.W. (1994) 'The Sovereignty of Parliament – in Perpetuity?', in J. Jowell and D. Oliver (eds) *The Changing Constitution*, 3rd edn (Oxford University Press).

Bradley, A.W. (2008) 'Relations Between the Executive, Judiciary and Parliament: an Evolving Saga?' *Public Law*, Autumn.

Bradley, A.W. and Ewing, K.D. (1997) *Constitutional and Administrative Law*, 12th edn (Longman).

Bradley, A.W. and Ewing, K.D. (2007) *Constitutional and Administrative Law*, 14th edn (Longman).

Craig, P. and Walters, M. (1999) 'The Courts, Devolution and Judicial Review', *Public Law*, Summer.

Drewry, G. (1986) 'Judges and Politics in Britain', *Social Studies Review*, November.

Drewry, G. (1991) 'Judicial Independence in Britain: Challenges Real and Threats Imagined', in P. Norton (ed.) *New Directions in British Politics?* (Edward Elgar).

Ewing, K. (2004) 'The Futility of the Human Rights Act', *Public Law*, Winter.

Ewing, K. and Tham, J. (2008) 'The Continuing Futility of the Human Rights Act', *Public Law*, Winter.

Fitzpatrick, B. (1999) 'A Dualist House of Lords in a Sea of Monist Community Law', in B. Dickson and P. Carmichael (eds) *The House of Lords: Its Parliamentary and Judicial Roles* (Hart Publishing).

Forsyth, C. (ed.) (2000) *Judicial Review and the Constitution* (Hart Publishing).

Griffith, J.A.G. (1997) *The Politics of the Judiciary*, 5th edn (Fontana).

Harlow, C. (1991) 'The Legal System', in P. Catterall (ed.) *Contemporary Britain: An Annual Review* (Blackwell).

Home Office (1998) *Rights Brought Home: The Human Rights Bill*, Cm 3782 (Stationery Office).

Irvine of Lairg, Lord (1998) 'The Development of Human Rights in Britain under an Incorporated Convention on Human Rights', *Public Law*, Summer.

Jackson, P. and Leopold, P. (2001) *O. Hood Phillips and Jackson, Constitutional and Administrative Law*, 8th edn (Sweet & Maxwell).

Jacobs, F. (1999) 'Public Law – the Impact of Europe', *Public Law*, Summer.

Jowell, J. (2003) 'Judicial Deference: Servility, Civility or Institutional Capacity?' *Public Law*, Winter.

Kavanagh, A. (2009) 'Judging the Judges under the Human Rights Act: Deference, Disillusionment and the "War on Terror"', *Public Law*, April.

Klug, F. and O'Brien, C. (2002) 'The First Two Years of the Human Rights Act', *Public Law*, Winter.

Klug, F. and Starmer, K. (2001) 'Incorporation Through the "Front Door": The First Year of the Human Rights Act', *Public Law*, Winter.

Le Sueur, A. (ed.) (2004) *Building the UK's New Supreme Court: National and Comparative Perspectives* (Oxford University Press).

Le Sueur, A. and Malleson, K. (2008) 'The Judiciary', in E. Hazell (ed.), *Constitutional Futures Revisited* (Palgrave Macmillan).

Lester, Lord (1994) 'European Human Rights and the British Constitution', in J. Jowell and D. Oliver (eds) *The Changing Constitution*, 3rd edn (Oxford University Press).

Loveland, I. (2003) 'Britain and Europe', in V. Bogdanor (ed.) *The British Constitution in the Twentieth Century* (British Academy/Oxford University Press).

Maxwell, P. (1999) 'The House of Lords as a Constitutional Court – the Implications of *Ex Parte EOC*', in B. Dickson and P. Carmichael (eds) *The House of Lords: Its Parliamentary and Judicial Roles* (Hart Publishing).

McEldowney, J. (1996) *Public Law* (Sweet & Maxwell).

McEldowney, J. (1998) 'Legal Aspects of Relations Between the United Kingdom and the Scottish Parliament: the Evolution of Subordinate Sovereignty?', in D. Oliver and G. Drewry (eds) *The Law and Parliament* (Butterworth).

Mullin, C. (1996) 'Miscarriages of Justice', *The Journal of Legislative Studies*, Vol. 2, No. 2.

Munro, C. (1987) *Studies in Constitutional Law* (Butterworth).

Munro, C. (1992) '*Factortame* and the Constitution', *Inter Alia*, Vol. 1, No. 1.

Nolan, Lord and Sedley, Sir S. (1997) *The Making and Remaking of the British Constitution* (Blackstone Press).

Norton, P. (1982) *The Constitution in Flux* (Blackwell).

Norton, P. (2005) 'Parliament and the Courts', in N.D.J. Baldwin (ed.) *Parliament in the 21st Century* (Politico's).

Norton, P. (2006) 'The Constitution: Selective Incrementalism', in M. Rush and P. Giddings (eds) *The Palgrave Review of British Politics* (Palgrave Macmillan).

Oliver, D. (2004) 'Constitutionalism and the Abolition of the Office of the Lord Chancellor', *Parliamentary Affairs*, Vol. 57.

Rozenberg, J. (1999) 'The *Pinochet* Case and Cameras in Court', *Public Law*, Summer.

Scarman, Lord (1974) *English Law – The New Dimensions* (Stevens).

Shah, S. And Poole, T. (2009) 'The Impact of the Human Rights Act on the House of Lords', *Public Law*, April.

Stevens, R. (2002) *The English Judges* (Hart Publishing).

Stevens, R. (2003) 'Government and the Judiciary', in V. Bogdanor (ed.) *The British Constitution in the Twentieth Century* (British Academy/ Oxford University Press).

Wade, E.C.S. and Bradley, A.W. (1993) *Constitutional and Administrative Law*, 11th edn A.W. Bradley and K.D. Ewing (eds) (Longman).

Walker, C. and Starmer, K. (1999) *Miscarriages of Justice* (Blackstone Press).

Windlesham, Lord (2005) 'The Constitutional Reform Act 2005: Ministers, Judges and Constitutional Change', *Public Law*, Winter.

Woodhouse, D. (1996) 'Politicians and the Judges: A Conflict of Interest', *Parliamentary Affairs*, Vol. 49, No. 3.

Woodhouse, D. (2002) 'The Law and Politics: In the Shadow of the Human Rights Act', *Parliamentary Affairs*, Vol. 55, No. 2.

Wright, J. (2009) 'Interpreting Section 2 of the Human Rights Act 1998: Towards an Indigenous Jurisprudence of Human Rights', *Public Law*, July.

Zander, M. (1989) *A Matter of Justice*, revised edn (Oxford University Press).

Useful websites

Judicial process in the UK

Court Service: www.hmcourts-service.gov.uk/
Criminal Cases Review Commission: www.ccrc.gov.uk/index.htm
Criminal Justice System – England and Wales: www.cjsonline.gov.uk/
Judicial Committee of the Privy Council: www.privy-council.org.uk/output/page5.asp
Judiciary of England and Wales: www.judiciary.gov.uk/index.htm
Magistrates' Association: www.judiciary.gov.uk/index.htm
Ministry of Justice: www.judiciary.gov.uk/index.htm
Supreme Court: www.supremecourt.gov.uk/index.html

Other relevant sites

European Court of Justice (ECJ):   http://europa.eu/ institutions/inst/justice/index_en.htm
European Court of Human Rights: www.echr.coe.int/echr/

And another thing . . .

The Rolls-Royce of government? A critique of the civil service

Peter Riddell

The civil service is often seen as an unchanging part of the British establishment – the permanent government which carries on ruling imperturbably whichever party is in power. That image, of the quietly efficient Rolls-Royce at the heart of government, never popular but respected, now looks distinctly dated. The metaphor needs changing: not to the old banger as *The Economist* wrote in 2007, or being in danger of failing its MoT as a Conservative MP argued in 2009.

A new description would be more complicated, and subtle. To a close observer, who talks with civil servants daily, the quality remains as high as before. There are still Rolls-Royce minds at the top of Whitehall. But there is no longer the self-confidence, the assurance of command of the past. Rather, there is doubt and uncertainty about the role of the civil service, and relationships both with ministers and the public.

These doubts reflect challenges to three of the pillars of the traditional civil service: first, as the dominant, if not sole, supplier of policy advice; second, in offering a lifelong career; and third, in being at the pinnacle of a unified state machine for delivering services.

The 'Rolls Royce' era was quintessentially the 1940s and 1950s. The civil service emerged from the Second World War as one of the agents of victory, and then of recovery, in an era when it was accepted that the state should plan many aspects of peoples' lives. This was when the phrase 'the man in Whitehall knows best' became widely used, though hardly as a term of affection. It was a misquotation from Douglas Jay, a Labour minister, who wrote in 1937, before the war, that 'in the case of nutrition and health, just as in the case of education, the gentleman in Whitehall really does know better what is good for people than people know themselves'. But it caught the spirit of the times.

The Conservatives successfully campaigned in the 1950 and 1951 general elections against excessive bureaucracy and regulations. The paradox was that the Tories criticised 'the man in Whitehall' but they still admired the professionalism and expertise of the senior civil service. That era lasted until the 1970s and was epitomised by the silky Sir Humphrey Appleby, the Permanent Secretary and then Cabinet Secretary always trying to manipulate the hapless minister Jim Hacker in the hit television series of the 1980s – first *Yes Minister* and, then, *Yes, Prime Minister*.

But the image of the effortlessly superior civil service had already been questioned – not least in the late 1960s by the Fulton report which criticised the alleged cult of the amateur, the Oxbridge classicist or historian, and urged the recruitment of more specialists, as well as outsiders.

The report was largely brushed aside at the time, but its assumptions were reflected in the Crossman and Benn diaries, depicting life in the Labour Governments from 1964 onwards. They portrayed the civil service as conservative and obstructive. Bernard, later Lord, Donoughue, head of the Downing Street Policy Unit from 1974 until 1979, was critical of the Treasury and of some civil servants for looking after their own interests, especially on pay and pensions, and for trying to bounce ministers. His diaries, published nearly three decades later, revealed the courtier-like manoeuvring at the centre of power, notably involving the late Lord Hunt of Tamworth, the then Cabinet Secretary, and in part the model for Sir Humphrey (not surprisingly since Donoughue advised the writers of *Yes, Minister.*)

Yet the existence of Donoughue as a politically appointed adviser showed how the old system was starting to fracture. From the 1940s until the 1970s, the civil service had enjoyed a monopoly of advice into which outsiders rarely intruded. Occasionally, respected bodies like Chatham House or the National Institute for Economic and Social Research were consulted. And partisan groups such as the Fabian Society or the Bow Group influenced the policies of Labour and the Conservatives respectively when the parties were in opposition. But the terms of the debate, and access to ministers, were tightly controlled by the permanent civil sercvice. That also reflected a general acceptance within Whitehall of a broadly consensual view of economic management, nationalised industries and the welfare state.

The breakdown of this consensus during the stagflation of the 1970s was linked with the emergence of new sources of policy advice. These took two forms: first, the appointment of a small number of special advisers, particularly after Labour took office in 1974. This was initially resisted by senior civil servants as a threat to their position, notably by creating a partial barrier between ministers and the civil service. Second, a big expansion occurred in the number of partisan think tanks, notably with the creation of the free market Centre for Policy Studies in 1974. This challenged the post-war Keynesian and welfare state consensus and heavily influenced the agenda of the Conservative Opposition, especially after Margaret Thatcher became leader in 1975.

In office, Thatcher was often critical of the civil service as an institution, notably at an embarassing dinner with Permanent Secretaries in 1980, but she relied upon, and had good relations, with indidivual civil servants. Special advisers played an important, but subordinate, role during her era. But they gradually gained acceptance from senior officials for their role in performing more partisan tasks – in speech writing, and contacts with MPs and the media – which civil servants could not do.

The big change came after 1997 when the Blair Government not only increased the number of special advisers but also put them in more prominent positions, notably in 10 Downing Street and the Treasury. Jonathan Powell became chief of staff at No. 10, and, along with Alastair Campbell, director of communications, had special powers to give orders to civil servants (under an order in council revoked when Gordon Brown became Prime Minister). They were as influential as any civil servants, apart from Jeremy Heywood, the key domestic policy official under Blair and then later, at more senior level, under Brown, and apart from the main foreign affairs advisers. In the Treasury, Ed Balls, Brown's senior adviser, became the main coordinator of advice from Treasury officials to the Chancellor, and was more important than successive Permanent Secretaries at the Treasury.

Civil servants often found themselves sidelined as special advisers became both the main channel, and source, of policy ideas. Such advisers became protective of their ministers, not only within departments but also in relations with 10 Downing Street where powerful advisers acted as both the eyes and enforcers for the Prime Minister. The cross-currents of these relationships were caught in the series *The Thick of It*.

At the same time, the civil service's role was challenged by the proliferation of think tanks, both non-partisan ones like the Institute for Fiscal Studies and more politically aligned ones such as IPPR for Labour and Policy Exchange for the Tories. A further challenge came from management consultants, many of whom did advisory work for the government from the late 1980s onwards. Such consultants were eager to win government contracts and often lent some of their talented staff to work in Whitehall, in the Policy Unit or as temporary civil servants.

The second big change is, as Lord Turnbull, the Cabinet Secretary and head of the Home Civil Service from 2002 until 2005 put it, while there is still a permanent civil service, there are no longer permanent civil servants working from their early 20s until 60. There is now much more movement in and out. Increasingly, there has been open competition for the top posts in the senior civil service so that outsiders, often from elsewhere in the public sector (notably local government), occupy top posts. Half a dozen of the current officials of Permanent Secretary rank came into Whitehall in their 40s and 50s, notably the heads of the departments for Children, Schools and Families, and of Communities and Local Government. They are still, of course, a minority but more outsiders have been brought in to run executive agencies.

That links with the third big change: the fragmentation of central government itself. Of course, there have been departmental and non-departmenal public bodies of various kinds and descriptions for many decades. But, from the late 1980s onwards, the creation, and expansion, in the number of executive agencies to run large chunks of government activities has challenged the conventional model. There has been much anguished debate about where the lines of accountability and responsibility lie, but, in administrative, if not political, terms the heads of agencies are in a different position from mainstream civil servants. In addition, many operations have been contracted-out, and, in some cases, privatised. Many services are now provided by third/voluntary or private sector groups, which have grown rapidly since the early 1990s. So there is no longer a monolithic public service delivering services on a universal basis.

Career civil servants face increased competition in many of their traditional tasks – notably in providing policy advice and in administration. They are having to learn new tasks and skills, in managing big projects and in delivering services. It is no longer enough to be an adept inside operator, working your way up through private office and policy jobs. The Rolls Royce operators still thrive – just look at the power of Jeremy Heywood at the centre of Whitehall. But they no longer rule unchallenged.

PART 6
THE POLICY PROCESS

CHAPTER 21

The policy-making process

Bill Jones

Learning objectives

- To define policy in government.
- To encourage familiarity with the most popular models of policy making.
- To examine the notion of the policy process.
- To give some examples of questionable policy making.

Introduction

This chapter examines the anatomy of policy and policy making in central government, focusing on its stages together with some theories relating to the process before concluding with a look at two case studies where outcome failed to match expectations and one of a policy currently in the making. Accordingly the chapter delves briefly into the complex area of policy studies, an area that has attracted attention, because it deals with political outcomes and draws together so many elements, embodying so much of the political universe: process, influence, power and pressure as well as the impact of personality. Consequently, policy studies has emerged as a kind of sub-discipline with some claim to be a focus for a social science approach to human interaction involving such subjects as psychology, sociology, economics, history, philosophy and political science. Policy studies was essentially born in the USA, so much of it focuses on American examples and policy environments; but more generally it draws on public policy in Western liberal democracies as a whole. The Bibliography provides an introduction to some of the voluminous literature in the field.

■ How policy is made

Policy can be defined as a set of ideas and proposals for action culminating in a government decision; to study policy, therefore, is to study how decisions are made. Government decisions can take many forms: Burch (1979: 108) distinguishes between two broad kinds, as follows:

1 Rules, regulations and public pronouncements (e.g. Acts of Parliament, Orders in Council, White Papers, ministerial and departmental circulars).

2 Public expenditure and its distribution: the government spends some £500 billion per annum, mostly on public goods and services (e.g. educa-

tion, hospitals) and transfer payments (e.g. social security payments and unemployment benefit).

Figure 21.1 portrays the government as a system that has as its input political demands together with resources available and its 'output' as the different kinds of government decision. The latter impact on society and influence future 'inputs', so the process is circular and constant.

Both Burch and Wood (1990) and Jordan and Richardson (1987) review a number of different analyses as 'models': possible or approximate versions of what happens in reality. Eight of these are summarised below. For a fuller account of the available models, see Parsons (1995), John (1998), Hill (2000) and Dorey (2006).

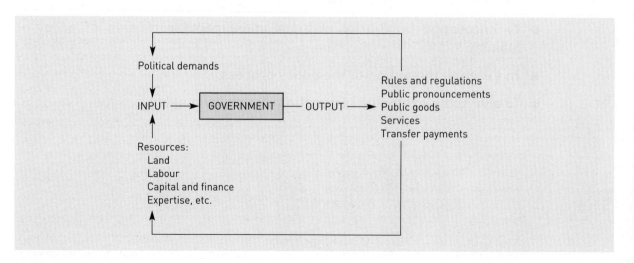

Figure 21.1 The policy process
Source: Burch (1979)

■ Models of policy making

1 *The conventional model*: This is the 'official' explanation of policy making found in Central Office of Information publications and the utterances of civil servants in public (though seldom in private). This maintains that Parliament represents and interprets the public will through its representatives, who support government ministers, who formulate executive policies, which are thereupon faithfully and impartially implemented by civil servants. The notion that a 'thin red line' of democracy connects voters with civil servants via the nominee of a political party in Parliament strikes many as tenuous but this is the officially sanctioned theory of how policy is made.

2 *The ruling-class model*: This is effectively the Marxist assertion, that those empowered with taking key decisions in the state – civil servants and politicians – subscribe consciously or unconsciously to the values of the dominant economic class, the property-owning upper middle classes. It follows that 'the executive of the modern state is but a committee for managing the common affairs of the whole bourgeoisie' (Marx and Engels 1848). According to this view, most policy outputs will have the effect of protecting dominant group interests. It also assumes that the superstructure of democracy is all false, hiding the true 'hegemony' of the economic class. Ralph Miliband (1969) provides a good analysis of this approach (though, ironically, two of his sons are now key people in this very system); for a summary of the argument see John (1998), Chapter 5.

The following two models attribute decisive importance to differing elements within the political system.

3 *The pluralist model*: This is often associated with the US political scientist Robert Dahl. It assumes that power is dispersed within society to the various interest groups that constitute it – business, labour, agriculture, and so forth – and that they can 'make themselves heard effectively at some crucial stage in the process of decision' (Jordan and Richardson 1987: 16). According to this view, interest groups interact and negotiate policy with each other in a kind of free market, with government acting as a more or less neutral referee.

4 *Corporatism*: This is associated with the work of Philippe Schmitter and is offered as an alternative to pluralism. This model perceives an alliance between ministers, civil servants and the leaders of pressure groups in which the last are given a central role in the policy-making process in exchange for exerting pressure upon their members to conform with or accept government decisions. In this view, therefore, interest groups become an extension – or even a quasi-form – of government. Corporatism has also been used pejoratively by British politicians of the left (Benn), right (Thatcher) and centre (Owen) to describe the decision-making style of the discredited 1974–9 Labour government.

The next two models ascribe key importance to two specific elements of the system.

5 *The party government model*: The stress here is on political parties and the assertion that they provide the major channel for policy formulation. Some, like Wilensky (1975), regard 'politics' as peripheral to the formation of policy, while others, like Castles (1989) maintain that the agenda is shaped by the processes of liberal democracy (Parsons 1995: section 2.11).

6 *The Whitehall model*: This contends that civil servants either initiate major policy or so alter it as it passes through their hands as to make it substantially theirs – thus making them the key influence on policy. Allison (1971) argued that bureaucracies do not meekly do the bidding of elected masters but are fragmented, competing centres of power: in John's words, 'Policy often arrives as the outcome of an uncoordinated fight between government bureaus' (John 1998: 44). Ministers discuss possible future actions with their very experienced and able advisers. If a trusted senior civil servant advises against a new initiative, this is bound to give the minister pause for more thought and adjustments might be made or the idea might even be dropped completely. Whitehall is not just 'in the loop' of policy making, *it is an essential part* of this loop.

The final two theories concentrate upon the way in which decision makers set about their tasks.

7 *Rational decision making*: This approach assumes that decision makers behave in a logical, sequential fashion. Accordingly, they will identify their objectives, formulate possible strategies, think through their implications and finally

choose the course of action that on balance best achieves their objectives. This approach is consistent with the traditional model in that civil servants undertake the analysis and then offer up the options for popularly elected politicians to take the decisions (see Parsons 1995: section 3.4; John 1998: Chapter 6).

8 *Incrementalism*: This approach, associated with the hugely influential work of Charles Lindblom, denies that policy makers are so rational and argues that in practice they usually try to cope or 'muddle through'. They tend to start with the status quo and make what adjustments they can to manage or at least accommodate new situations. In other words, policy makers do not solve problems but merely adjust to them. The case of privatisation argues against this 'adjusting' approach in that when Nigel Lawson came to consider it in the early 1980s the cupboard, in terms of relevant files and experience, was totally bare. Instead, Conservative ministers had to devise wholly new approaches and, whatever one's views on the outcome, it is perhaps to their credit that – even allowing for a determined Prime Minister and a large majority – they succeeded in a government culture so resistant to radical innovation.

It is clear that most of these models are basically descriptive, while others, like the rational choice and conventional models, are also partially prescriptive – they offer an ideal approach as to how policies should be made – but cannot necessarily tell us how decisions are actually made.

It is also obvious that echoing somewhere within each approach is the ring of truth. It would not be too difficult to find examples in support of any of the above models. The truth is that policy making is such a protean, dense area of activity that it is extremely difficult to generalise and be accurate in all cases. Nevertheless, the search for valid statements is worth the effort, otherwise our political system will remain incomprehensible. We will therefore look at the process in greater detail in a search for some generally true propositions about it.

■ The policy cycle

If they agree on nothing else, policy study scholars seem to agree that policy making can be understood better as a cycle; a problem arrives on the agenda and is processed by the system until an answer is found. Analyses of the cycle can be quite sophisticated. Hogwood and Gunn (1984) discern a number of stages: deciding to decide (issue search and agenda setting); deciding how to decide; issue definition, forecasting; setting objectives and priorities; options analysis; policy implementation, monitoring and control; evaluation and review; and policy maintenance, succession or termination. However, Lindblom disagrees. He argues that 'Deliberate or orderly steps . . . are not an accurate portrayal of how the policy process actually works. Policy making is, instead, a complexly interactive process without beginning or end' (Lindblom and Woodhouse 1993: 11, quoted in Parsons 1995: 22). However, policy studies can appear overly abstract and removed from reality at times; for the limited purposes of this chapter, three easily understood stages will suffice: initiation, formulation and implementation. These are considered below but first a brief look at how 'problems' come to be defined as such and how they come to be seen as requiring solutions.

'Social construction' of problems

This concept appears in Dorey (2006: 8–11) and relates to the evolving nature of things requiring action. In the nineteenth century women were denied certain basic rights and could even be beaten or raped by their husbands. It has taken a long while but societal values have changed so that women have acquired the vote and legal protection against what is now seen as abuse. Similarly homosexuals – once persecuted and imprisoned – are now allowed to be themselves outside the reach of the criminal law. Attitudes towards legal drug use (alcohol, nicotine) and illegal use (cannabis, heroin, cocaine) are also in a constant state of change and influence related frameworks (for example, smoking is now seen as seriously unhealthy and is banned in workplaces).

Dorey also points out how wider values and ideological changes influence political action. Poverty was once not seen as a problem – prosperity was a personal responsibility – but by the twentieth century Liberal ideology was becoming the new orthodoxy; tax funded state assistance began to be introduced to alleviate problems of old age, illness and unemployment. Moreover, the extension of the vote to lower socio-economic strata, meant 'inaction' – which favoured employers and owners of property – was no longer so easy to maintain.

Agenda setting

John Kingdon (1995, see Dorey 2006: 27–31) per-ceived it necessary for three 'streams' to conjoin for an item to be added to public policy: the recognition of something as a problem (problem stream); the identification of possible solutions (policy stream); and the requisite opportunities – time, accession to power of a party prepared to act and so forth (polit-ical stream). For example, poverty was not seen as a legitimate concern of government until Liberalism and Socialism emerged to suggest it might be and no action was taken until the Liberal and Labour parties gained power for periods in the twentieth century.

Policy initiation

Agenda setting

Each government decision has a long and complex provenance, but all must start somewhere. It is tempting to think that they originate, eureka-like, in the minds of single individuals, but they are more often the product of debate or a general climate of opinion involving many minds. Policy initiatives, moreover, can originate in all parts of the political system. Setting the political agenda is a curiously elusive process. Items can be deliberately intro-duced by government, and clearly it has many routes available to it, e.g. Tony Blair in the summer

of 1999 announcing in an interview that fox hunting really *would* be banned; or Blair again, announcing, in the wake of the 'cash for peerages' scandal in March 2006, that greater transparency would be introduced regarding loans to political parties. The media too have enormous power to set the agenda: Michael Buerk's reports from Ethiopia detailing a scale of famine that touched the nation and initiated assistance; Alan Milburn, in an interview on 9 April 2006, refusing to say he would not be a candidate for the leadership when Blair stood down.

Figure 21.2 depicts six groups of possible policy initiators placed on a continuum starting from the periphery and moving in towards the nerve centre of government in No. 10. The figure uses the idea of 'distance from the centre', capturing the truth that the routes into policy making are many and varied (see also Parsons 1995: section 2.4).

General public

The public's role in policy making is usually limited to (the democratically vital function of) voting for a particular policy package at general elections. They do have other occasional opportunities, however, for example the referendums on the EC and Scottish and Welsh devolution in the 1970s, and pressures can be built up through lobbying MPs, as when, in the mid-1980s, Sir Keith Joseph was forced to withdraw his proposals to charge parents for a proportion of

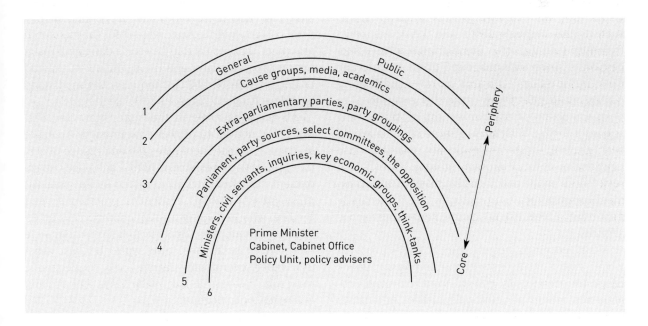

Figure 21.2 Policy initiatives

their children's university tuition fees. Occasionally, events occur that create widespread public concern, and governments often take action in the wake of them. For example, legislation on dogs was enacted after a spate of attacks by dogs on children one summer in the 1980s, and handguns were banned after the Dunblane shootings of March 1996. In many cases – as in the two just cited – such precipitate action, in reaction to the sudden rousing of public opinion, proves to be poorly framed and receives much criticism. In more recent years, public opinion has been roused by the proposed fox hunting ban and the war in Iraq in spring 2003. Both attracted huge demonstrations in London; in the former case they had some observable effect in delaying and altering proposed measures, but in the latter case Tony Blair carried on, convinced that he was right, and ignored the public outcry. However, the repercussions and damage of ignoring public and party opposition may take years to make themselves felt; what is without doubt is that Blair paid a heavy price in political support for ignoring the Iraq outcry.

Cause groups, media and academic experts

Many cause groups (see also Chapter 10) operate in the 'wilderness' – their values antithetical to government and not listened to – and many also stay there, but some do influence public opinion and decision makers and after years of struggle achieve action on issues such as abortion, capital punishment and the environment. Others achieve success on specific issues after an extended period of campaigning, such as Des Wilson's 1960s and 1970s campaign to reduce lead in petrol. Some groups achieve success via a single well-publicised event such as the Countryside Alliance's march on the Labour Party conference in 1999, which caused the government to postpone action on fox hunting during the coming session (despite Blair's assurances that he would act). Certain policy 'environments' will include a bewildering array of pressure groups, all of which seek to lean on the policy-making tiller. Local government associations, for example, are particularly important in areas like education, housing and social services.

Media coverage heavily affects the climate in which policy is discussed, and important policy proposals occasionally emerge from television programmes, newspaper editorials, articles in journals and so forth. One editorial on its own would have little effect, but a near consensus in the press might

well stimulate action. Occasionally ideas are picked up from individual journalists – Mrs Thatcher used to be advised regularly by right-wing journalists such as Woodrow Wyatt, Paul Johnson and Simon Heffer. Other media figures who used to be consulted regularly on policy matters by Margaret Thatcher included the press magnates Rupert Murdoch and Conrad Black. Murdoch was also rumoured to advise Blair whenever he chose to visit Downing Street and where, because of his massive media clout, he was assured of a warm welcome. One commentator even argued Murdoch was virtually an additional member of the Cabinet (Wilby 2006). We also know that a wide range of influential people were regularly invited to dine with the Blairs at the PM's official rural retreat, Chequers, and almost certainly dinner-table conversation occasionally results in some kind of action. Lord Levy, a tennis partner of Tony Blair, eventually found himself acting as Blair's emissary to the Middle East and later as a key fund raiser (in March 2006 controversially so, when the 'loans for peerages' row erupted) for the Labour Party.

Occasionally the media provide crucial information. The classic example of this was in 1987, when Nigel Lawson, as Chancellor, denied entry to the ERM by prime ministerial veto, had tried to achieve his object by other means, namely manipulating the value of the pound to shadow that of the deutschmark. When *Financial Times* journalists interviewed Margaret Thatcher, they questioned her about this policy. She denied any knowledge of it but when they produced definitive evidence in the form of charts she accepted, somewhat surprised, that they were correct, and the stage was set for the mammoth argument that resulted in Lawson's damaging resignation two years later and the beginning of the end of her reign in No. 10 (for more on the media and agenda setting, see Parsons 1995: section 2.3).

All these agencies in the 'outer rim' (see Figure 21.2) interact to provide that intangible climate of discussion that encourages the emergence of certain proposals and inhibits others. Each policy environment has its own climate created by its specialist press, pressure groups, academics, practitioners and the like, who frequently meet in conferences and on advisory committees. Specific policy environments therefore exist in their 'own' world but also exist in a wider, overarching reality – e.g. an economic recession, an overseas war – which sets limits to and influences policy content.

However, an interesting feature of these peripheral bodies is that from time to time they are blessed

David Hume (1711–73)

Scottish philosopher and historian. Studied in Edinburgh – where his depressive temperament meant it took time for him to settle – but went to live in France, where he wrote his *Treatise on Human Nature* (1739). He questioned the validity of principles, which he described as 'artificial', and challenged the notion of natural law as well as the social contract ideas of Hobbes, Locke and Rousseau. Hume was bitterly disappointed when his opus failed to make much impact, but his *Essays Moral and Political* (1743), produced shortly afterwards, were an instant success and confirmed his reputation as one of the founding, and greatest, British empiricist philosophers of his age.

with favour, their arguments listened to, their proposals adopted, their leaders embraced by government and given advisory or even executive status. It is almost as if, godlike, the government has reached down and plucked them up to place them – albeit temporarily – on high.

Part 2 of this book explained how policy emerged out of an ideological framework and pointed out how academics, philosophers and other thinkers had contributed towards these frameworks. The most obvious influences on the Left would include Karl Marx, R.H. Tawney, Harold Laski, William Beveridge and, incomparably in the economic sphere, J.M. Keynes. Right-wing writers would include figures such as David Hume and Michael Oakeshott and (on economics from the 1970s onwards) the two overseas academics Friedrich Hayek and Milton Friedman. Academics specialising in specific policy areas such as transport, housing, criminology and so forth also regularly come up with proposals, some of which are taken up or drawn upon. John Major welcomed the views of the so-called 'seven wise men'

Lord Anthony Giddens, Blair's sociologist guru on Third Way thinking
Source: Press Association Images / Associated Press

(selected academics) on economic policy. Blair and Brown established a formal committee called the Monetary Policy Committee comprising academics and financial experts who every month advise the Bank of England on interest rates. On other occasions, academics can suddenly be welcomed in by leading figures in government, as when sociologist Anthony Giddens was used by Blair as a kind of 'guru' regarding the formulation of 'Third way' thinking.

Extra-parliamentary parties and party groupings

Both the Labour and Conservative extra-parliamentary parties find it easier to influence their respective leaders in opposition than in government. As Chapter 10 noted, Labour's system of internal democracy gave a substantial policy-making role to the trade unions, the National Executive Committee and the party conference during the 1930s and up until the 1970s (New Labour somewhat emasculated conference during and since the 1990s). The Conservative Party is far less democratic, but conference can set the mood for policy formulation, the research department can initiate important proposals, and the Advisory Committee on Policy did much to reformulate the main outlines of Conservative policy in the late 1970s.

Party groupings – many of which have contacts with Parliament – can also exert influence. The Fabian Society, founded in 1884, has long acted as a kind of left-wing think tank (see Box 21.1), and in the 1980s the once left-wing Labour Coordinating Committee was influential in advising Neil Kinnock

as he shifted Labour's policies towards the centre. Similarly, the No Turning Back Group in the Conservatives sought to keep the party on the right-wing track indicated by their heroine Margaret Thatcher, both before and after her fall from power, and it took the 'Cameron uprising' in the autumn of 2005 to remove what many perceived as its dead hand. The Institute for Public Policy Research (IPPR) has established itself over the past decade as a kind of Blairite think tank, constantly on hand to feed in relevant ideas and research findings.

Parliament

The role of Parliament in initiating policy can be considered under two headings: party sources and party groups, and non-party sources. In government, parliamentary parties have to work through their backbench committees, although individual MPs seek to use their easy access to ministers to exert influence and press their own solutions. One Conservative MP, David Evans, pulled off the remarkable coup of convincing his Prime Minister that the identity card system introduced by Luton Town Football Club should be compulsorily introduced nationwide. His success was short-lived: the scheme was dropped in January 1990 (though it did not die – see the section on identity cards towards the end of this chapter).

The Opposition is concerned to prepare its policies for when and if it takes over the reins of government. Neil Kinnock wrested future policy making out of the party's NEC with his policy review exercise (1987–9), involving leading members of his frontbench team in the process. However, the Opposition also has to make policy 'on the hoof' in reaction to political events. It is their function and in their interests to oppose, to offer alternatives to government – but this is not easy. Opposition spokesmen lack the detailed information and support enjoyed by government; they need to react to events in a way that is consistent with their other policy positions; they need to provide enough detail to offer a credible alternative, yet avoid 'host-ages to fortune' and closing options should they come to power. The Conservatives after 1997 found it hard to perform as an effective opposition, through splits in their ranks and uncertain leadership. Most commentators judged that this was not good for the health of the nation's democracy; the election of the young and dynamic new leader, David Cameron, in December 2005 transformed this situation. Unsurprisingly,

BOX 21.1 IDEAS AND PERSPECTIVES

Think tanks

Mrs Thatcher regained her momentum partly because she discovered 'Thatcherism': a new set of ideas comprising the abolition of constraints in the economy, privatising state-owned enterprises and reform of the public sector. They were provided by the intelligentsia of the 'New Right', many of them working through think-tanks (*The Economist*, 18 November 1992).

After the demise of Thatcher in 1990, these American-style independent hot-houses of ideas receded. The Centre for Policy Studies (CPS) used to issue a report every fortnight, but with Major in power rather than its original patron, its output slowed to zero. The output of the Adam Smith Institute (ASI), once a pioneer in privatisation ideas, also slowed and with Blair in power it was reduced to producing a complimentary report on his first 200 days. The Institute for Economic Affairs (IEA) was the oldest right-wing think tank, but it also curtailed its activities once Thatcher had gone. It also has to be said that the disaster of the 'poll tax', a product of the ASI, contributed to their declining respect. And the splits did not help: Graham Mather left the IEA to form his own European Policy Forum, while David Willetts at the CPS left after criticism to become an MP and director of the Social Market Foundation.

Labour has been relatively light on think tanks, but the Fabian Society, set up by the Webbs in 1884, has effectively been a highly influential think tank for over 100 years. It still exists with an impressive membership from the public and the parliamentary party. It organises seminars and conferences and keeps up a good flow of pamphlets and serious studies, a post-1997 one being the work of a certain Tony Blair. In addition, at the current time there is the Institute for Public Policy Research (IPPR), which has produced a number of New Labour studies. Demos – initially headed by Geoff Mulgan before he became a No. 10 adviser is now led by Tom Bentley. Are think tank personnel merely seeking to enter politics and become MPs? According to Tom Clougherty, the young director of the ASI, during a student study group visit in March 2009, his role gave him far more influence than any MP might exert. Certainly many think tank personnel have made the journey into senior advisory or ministerial positions, for example David Miliband (IPPR), John Redwood (Centre Policy Studies) and Geoff Mulgan (Demos) (see Dorey 2006: 19–26)

he initially poured energy into changing the unpopular image and 'brand' of his party, and his policy statements were little more than statements of intent, designed to drag the party into the middle ground on social justice and the environment. Creating detailed policies, announced Oliver Letwin in April 2006, would take another eighteen months of focused effort. Received wisdom for oppositions is that such exercises are best left until close to the election; an abiding problem for oppositions is that any good ideas they might come up with can be stolen by government and represented as its own.

Party groups (some of which have membership outside Parliament) such as the Bow Group, Monday Club, Tribune and Campaign Group can all have peripheral – but rarely direct – influence on policy making.

The seventeen departmental select committees regularly make reports and recommendations, some of which are adopted. Most experts agree that these committees are much more important now that their proceedings can be televised, especially the Treasury Committee which summoned so many senior finance people for interrogation in the wake of the banking collapse in 2008. Most reports represent cross-party consensus on specific issues but others, such as the Social Services Committee, once chaired by the much admired (and briefly a minister) Frank Field, can offer wide-ranging and coherent alternatives to government policy. Individual MPs probably have a better chance of influencing specific, usually very specific, policy areas through the opportunities available to move private members' bills (see Chapter 15).

Failure to utilise the policy-making machinery provided by the governing party can lead to dissent. In May 2003, certain Labour MPs were complaining that the Prime Minister, set on ignoring Parliament, was now introducing policy – especially that relating to universities – that had originated wholly in his own office and not at all in the governing party. Party critics claimed 'top-up fees' in higher education in the autumn of 2003 was the product of Downing Street adviser Andrew Adonis – appointed and not elected, of course. After a cliff-hanging process of accommodation by the government of these internal criticisms, the bill eventually became an act on 27 January 2004 by a majority of only five. Adonis was later elevated to the peerage and made schools minister after the 2005 election.

Ministers, departments, official inquiries and 'think tanks'

Strong-minded ministers will always develop policy ideas of their own either as a reflection of their own convictions or to get noticed and further their ambitions. Michael Heseltine, in the wake of the Toxteth troubles, probably shared both motivations when he submitted a paper to the Cabinet called 'It Took a Riot', proposing a new and un-Thatcherite approach to inner city regeneration: the policy was not accepted by Cabinet but was partially implemented in Merseyside, though not elsewhere. Such major initiatives are not the province of civil servants, but through their day-to-day involvement in running the country they are constantly proposing detailed improvements and adjustments to existing arrangements. Such initiatives are not necessarily the preserve of senior officials: even junior officers can propose changes that can be taken up and implemented.

A Royal Commission can be the precursor to major policy changes (for example, the Redcliffe–Maud Royal Commission on Local Government, 1966–9), but Margaret Thatcher was not well disposed towards such time-consuming, essentially disinterested procedures – she always felt she knew what needed doing – and during the 1980s none was set up. Major, however, set up the Royal Commission on Criminal Justice, and Blair the Royal Commission on the House of Lords in 2000 chaired by Lord Wakeham. He has also initiated scores of task forces and inquiries to prepare the ground for new legislation. Departments regularly establish their own inquiries, often employing outside experts, which go on to make important policy recommendations.

Right-wing think tanks were especially favoured by Margaret Thatcher (see Box 21.1). *The Economist* (6 May 1989) noted how she spurned Oxbridge dons – the traditional source of advice for No. 10 – and suggested that 'the civil service is constitutionally incapable of generating the policy innovation which the prime minister craves'. Instead, as a reforming premier she instinctively listened to the advice of 'people who have been uncorrupted by the old establishment'. Think tank advice was often channelled to Margaret Thatcher via the No. 10 Policy Unit. Their radical suggestions acted as a sounding board when published and helped to push the climate of debate further to the right. If new ideas are received in a hostile fashion, ministers can easily disavow them. The 'privatisation' of government advice in the form of think tanks was a striking feature of Margaret Thatcher's impact upon policy making. The Institute for Public Policy Research (IPPR) has established itself over the past decade as a kind of Blairite think tank, constantly on hand to feed in relevant ideas and research findings (see Box 21.1).

Prime Minister and Cabinet

This is the nerve centre of government, supported by the high-powered network of Cabinet committees, the Cabinet Office, the No. 10 Policy Unit and policy advisers. After a period of ten years in office, it is likely that any Prime Minister will dominate policy making. Chapter 17 made it clear that while many sought to whisper policy suggestions in her ear, Margaret Thatcher's radical beliefs provided her with an apparently full agenda of her own. The evidence of her extraordinary personal impact on major policy areas is plain to see: privatisation, trade union legislation, the environment, the exchange rate, sanctions against South Africa, the poll tax and Europe – the list could go on. However, she was also unusual in taking a personal interest in less weighty matters such as her (ill-starred) attempt to clean up litter from Britain's streets following a visit to litter-free Israel. Harold Wilson saw himself as a 'deep lying halfback feeding the ball forward to the chaps who score the goals'. Thatcher was not content with this role: she wanted to score the goals as well. Wilson also said that a Prime Minister governs by 'interest and curiosity': Thatcher had insatiable appetites in both respects and an energy that enabled her to feed them to a remarkable degree. Under her, assisted by her own relentless energy and a constitution that delivers so much power to the executive, the office of Prime Minister took on a policy-initiating role comparable, perhaps, with that of the US President. John Major was also exceptionally hard-working, as premiers must be, but he was happy to delegate more than his predecessor and to listen to voices around the Cabinet table, especially that of his powerful deputy, Michael Heseltine. Blair proved to be a premier more in the Thatcher mould, bypassing Cabinet and making decisions in small groups of close advisers (allegedly sitting on the sofa in No. 10 Downing Street), especially his 'kitchen cabinet', which originally included Alastair Campbell, Jonathan Powell and, more often than not, unelected aides rather than elected politicians (see Chapter 17). Blair continued the 'presidentialising' tendency in British politics, dominating the spotlight of national attention and conducting a very personal style of government. The decision to back George W. Bush in his assault on Iraq in 2003 was very much the result of Blair's own passionate determination that this policy was the morally correct one. In her evidence to the Foreign Affairs Select Committee on 17 June 2003, Clare Short claimed a 'shocking collapse in proper government procedure' in that all the main decisions were made by Blair and a small unelected entourage of Blair, Alastair Campbell, Lady (Sally) Morgan, Jonathan Powell and adviser David Manning. Throughout the process, Foreign Secretary Jack Straw had been a mere 'cypher'. Gordon Brown claimed he would seek a return to more traditional policy-making but in practice – for example over the 2008 economic crisis – this did not appear to be the case (see Box 21.2 later in this chapter).

The concept of the core executive

This approach to understanding the nerve centre of British government has come into its own in recent years as it provides a clearer picture of how decision-making occurs while supplying a number of useful correctives to more traditional thinking (for a fuller discussion see Chapter 17). The basic idea of the core executive is that decision making takes place at the highest level, constituted by a body of leading figures drawn, depending on the issue, from the Prime Minister's Office, the Cabinet and Cabinet Office plus the head officials of the departments concerned with the particular issue. This is a more helpful concept in that it reduces the notion of a simple hierarchy and replaces the idea of a tip to the pyramid with that of a halo or circle of key people. This is also useful in that it avoids the diversion of the difference between the political and administrative, the minister and civil servant. Anyone who has been involved in policy making will describe how civil servants – in theory policy 'eunuchs' who merely stand by loyally while politicians undertake this democratically driven function – participate in its evolution as centrally as any politician. And the same goes, in recent years, for the top political advisers like Alastair Campbell. It also embraces the idea of a permanent core of central 'players' on the policy-making stage plus a regular cast who visit according to the issue on the agenda. One of the best short accounts of the core executive – Moran (2005), *Politics and Governance in the UK* – elaborates usefully on the modern PM's office:

The details [of the PM's Office] constantly change, partly because prime ministers constantly worry about whether they are being adequately served, and partly because life at the centre has a frenetic, hothouse quality: little empires are constantly being built (and dismantled) as different people struggle for the ear of the prime minister and for their own personal advancement. The atmosphere is rather like that of the court of a monarch, where the skill lies in catching the ear and the eye of the powerful one.

Moran (2005: 118)

So private secretaries will process the information and paper which goes before the top person; combinations of civil servants and political advisers will feed in policy advice; and the press office will seek to ensure that what disseminates out to the wider political system, and beyond that to voters themselves, is formulated – with great sensitivity and sophistication – in a way which will advance-policy objectives and not undermine them.

From this brief and admittedly selective description it is clear that:

■ Policy can be initiated at both the micro and macro levels from within any part of the political system, but the frequency and importance of initiatives grow as one moves from the periphery towards the centre.

■ Even peripheral influences can be swiftly drawn into the centre should the centre wish it.

■ Each policy environment is to some extent a world unto itself with its own distinctive characteristics.

■ The core executive, comprising the system's top decision makers, will be complicit in formulating high policy and directing it outwards and downwards to the relevant parts of the government machine.

Higher education policy making, for example, will include, just for starters, the Prime Minister, the Cabinet, the No. 10 Policy Unit, plus senior officials from Education (the core executive) assisted by think tanks, numerous parliamentary and party committees, more middle-ranking officials from the Departments of Education and Employment, the Treasury, the funding councils for the universities, the Committee of Vice-Chancellors and Principals, the University and College Union and other unions, and *The Times Higher Education Supplement*, together with a galaxy of academic experts on any and every aspect of the subject. Downing Street policy – not just the PM but his network of aides and advisers – is now of key importance in this high-profile policy area.

Policy formulation

Once a policy idea has received political endorsement it is fed into the system for detailed elaboration. This process involves certain key players from the initiation process, principally civil servants, possibly key pressure group leaders and outside experts (who usually are also political sympathisers) and, usually at a later stage, ministers. In the case of a major measure, there is often a learning phase in which civil servants and ministers acquaint themselves with the detail of the measure: this may require close consultation with experts and practitioners in the relevant policy environment. The measure, if it requires legislation, then has to chart a course first through the bureaucracy and then the legislature.

The bureaucratic process

This will entail numerous information-gathering and advisory committee meetings and a sequence of coordinating meetings with other ministries, especially the Treasury if finance is involved. Some of these meetings might be coordinated by the Cabinet Office, and when ministers become involved the measures will be progressed in Cabinet committees and ultimately full Cabinet before being passed on to parliamentary counsel, the expert drafters of parliamentary bills.

The legislative process

As Chapters 15 and 16 explained, this process involves several readings and debates in both chambers. Studies show that most legislation passes through unscathed, but controversial measures will face a number of hazards, which may influence their eventual shape. Opposition MPs and peers may seek to delay and move hostile amendments, but more important are rebellions within the government party: for example, determined backbench Labour opposition to the university top-up fees legislation in January 2004 produced a series of amendments to the measure which made the original proposal almost unrecognisable – though such examples are rare. The task of piloting measures through the legislature falls to ministers, closely advised by senior officials, and this is often when junior ministers can show their mettle and make a case for their advancement.

From this brief description it is clear that four sets of actors dominate the policy formulation process: ministers, civil servants, pressure group leaders and an array of experts appropriate to the subject. Some scholars calculate that the key personnel involved in policy formulation might number no more than 3,500. As in policy initiation, Margaret Thatcher also played an unusually interventionist role in this process. Reportedly she regularly called ministers and civil servants into No. 10 to speed things up, shift developments on to the desired track or discourage those with whom she disagreed. It would seem that Tony Blair was in the same mould and maybe more so, raging in public and private at the inertia of the public sector and the more general 'forces of conservatism' he criticised at the 1999 Bournemouth party conference. Dynamic politicians like Thatcher and Blair become impatient at the slowness with which the wheels of government turn and so seek to catalyse its progress through personal interventions. In her resignation speech Clare Short, who resigned in May 2003 over the role of the UN in reconstructing Iraq, bitterly attacked Blair's centralisation of policy making in a fashion which was still valid in 2006:

I think what's going on in the second term in this government, power is being increasingly centralised around the prime minister and just a few advisers, ever increasingly few. The Cabinet is now only a 'dignified'

Genghis the Tory. Riddell suggests right-wing forces exist behind Cameron
Source: Copyright © Chris Riddell. From the *Observer*, 30 August 2009. Reproduced with permission from Guardian Newspapers Limited

part of the constitution. It's gone the way of the Privy Council. Seriously, various policy initiatives are being driven by advisers [in No. 10] who are never scrutinised, never accountable.

Lord Butler of Brockwell, former Cabinet Secretary, was a well-known sceptic of Blair's methods involving political aides and meetings on the Number 10 sofa. His July 2004 *Review of Intelligence on Weapons of Mass Destruction*, arising from the decision to invade Iraq alongside US forces, contained a section on the machinery of government. In it the report cited evidence from two former Cabinet members who 'expressed their concern about the informal nature of much of the Government's decision-making process, and the relative lack of use of established Cabinet Committee machinery' (pp. 146–7). Specifically, the report pointed out that from April 2002 to the outbreak of hostilities, the Defence and Overseas Policy Committee did not meet once, yet there were 'some 25 meetings attended by key Ministers, officials and military officers most closely involved [who] provided the

framework of discussion and decision making within Government'.

Policy implementation

It is easy to assume that once the government has acted on something or legislated on an issue it is more or less closed. Certainly the record of government action reveals any number of measures that have fulfilled their objectives: for example, the Attlee government wished to establish a National Health Service and did so; in the 1980s, Conservative governments wished to sell off houses to council tenants and did so. But there are always problems that impede or sometimes frustrate implementation or that produce undesired side effects. Between legislation and implementation many factors intervene. Jordan and Richardson (1982: 234–5) quote the conditions that Hood suggests need to be fulfilled to achieve perfect implementation:

1 There must be a unitary administrative system rather like a huge army with a single line of

authority. Conflict of authority could weaken control, and all information should be centralised in order to avoid compartmentalism.

2 The norms and rules enforced by the system have to be uniform. Similarly, objectives must be kept uniform if the unitary administrative system is to be really effective.

3 There must be perfect obedience or perfect control.

4 There must be perfect information and perfect communication – as well as perfect coordination.

5 There must be sufficient time for administrative resources to be mobilised.

To fulfil wholly any, let alone all, of these conditions would be rare indeed, so some degree of failure is inevitable with any government programme. Examples are easy to find.

Education

The 1944 Education Act intended that the new grammar, technical and secondary modern schools were to be different but share a 'parity of esteem'. In practice this did not happen: grammar schools became easily the most prestigious and recruited disproportionately from the middle classes: the government could not control parental choice. To remedy this, comprehensive schools were set up in the 1950s and 1960s, but it was the middle-class children who still performed best in examinations. Reformers also neglected one crucial and in retrospect blindingly obvious factor: comprehensive schools recruit from their own hinterlands, so inner-city schools draw children from predominantly working-class areas with a culture tending to produce lower educational standards, while suburban schools are drawn from more middle-class families who place a high value on education and whose children consequently achieve higher standards. The government made policy on the basis of inadequate information and awareness.

Poll tax

The euphemistically named 'community charge' – known as the 'poll tax' – was the brainchild variously of right-wing think tanks, Kenneth Baker, William Waldegrave and others (although following its collapse most people were keen to disclaim parentage – political failures, unsurprisingly, are always

'orphans'). The rationale behind it was logical; local taxes – the 'rates' – were based on property but penalised the wealthy, who paid more on big properties. However, over half were either exempted or received rebates yet still enjoyed the benefits of local services; consequently they had no reason to vote for lower rates and were not 'accountable' for them in the opinion of Conservatives like Thatcher, a keen supporter of the scheme. The new tax was to be a flat-rate one and payable by all to some degree, even students and the unemployed. The obvious unfairness of taxing the poor as heavily as the rich was widely recognised, even by Conservative voters. Yet Thatcher's personal support, defiant style and the pusillanimous nature of many MPs and ministers – Michael Portillo informed conference that he was not daunted but 'delighted' to be placed in charge of it – let a clearly flawed law onto the statute book. In March 1990, polls showed a huge majority opposed it and on 7 April a riot erupted in London. When John Major succeeded Thatcher he quickly replaced the measure with one more closely resembling the old property-based rates, and the heat soon left the issue of local government finance (for more on the poll tax, see Chapter 19). Programme failure also often results from the operation of constraints that constantly bear upon policy makers.

Constraints upon policy makers

Financial resources

Policy makers have to operate within available financial resources, which are a function of the nation's economic health at any particular time, and the willingness of key decision makers, especially in the Treasury, to make appropriate provision from funds available to government.

Political support

This is initially necessary to gain endorsement for a policy idea, but support is also necessary throughout the often extended and complex policy-making process. Lack of it, for example, characterised the tortured birth of the poll tax as well as its ignominious demise. Support at the political level is also crucial, but it is highly desirable within the bureaucracy and elsewhere in the policy environment. Resistance to policies can kill them off *en route*, and anticipated resistance is also important; as Jordan and Richardson (1982: 238) hypothesised: 'There are probably more policies which are never introduced because of the anticipation of resistance, than policies which have failed because of resistance.' Some departments now seek to gauge levels of popular support through the use of focus groups, a technique borrowed from commercial and political marketing (see Chapter 18 and below).

Competence of key personnel

An able, energetic minister is likely to push policy measures through; a weak minister is not. Civil servants are famously able in Britain, but even they need to work hard to be up to the task of mastering rapidly the detail of new measures; their failure will impede the progress of a measure and limit its efficacy. Tony Blair has created (maybe necessary) waves in the Civil Service by emphasising the primacy of 'delivery'. Civil servants must be able to achieve practical things as well as advise ministers.

Time

New legislative initiatives need to carve space out of a timetable so overcrowded that winners of Private Members' ballots are lobbied by departments themselves to adopt bills awaiting parliamentary consideration. Moreover, the whole system is arguably over-centralised and, some would say, chronically overloaded.

Timing

Measures can fail if timing is not propitious. Just after a general election, for example, is a good time to introduce controversial measures. Margaret Thatcher, it will be recalled, was unable to secure the sale of British Leyland to an American company in the spring of 1986 because she had lost so much support over the Westland episode.

Coordination

Whitehall departments divide up the work of government in a particular way: proposals that fall between ministries are often at a disadvantage, and the job of coordinating diverse departments is not, in the view of critics, managed with particular efficiency. Burch (1979: 133) also notes that:

Too often policy making becomes a conflict between departments for a share of the limited resources available. This is . . . especially true of expenditure politics

when departments fight for their own corner at the cost of broader policy objectives.

Personality factors

Key decision makers are not as rational as perhaps they ought to be. They might have personal objectives – ambition, desire for image and status, and rivalries – which lead them to oppose rather than support certain policy objectives. The best recent examples concern rows between Prime Ministers and their Chancellors: Margaret Thatcher and Nigel Lawson in the late 1980s; Blair and Brown clashed bitterly over very many issues, for example entering the single currency – the euro, Blair was enthusiastic and Chancellor Brown cautious to the point of applying a veto to such a move.

Geographical factors

A bias in favour of the south-east is often detectable in government policies – for example, in the granting of defence contracts – partly because decision makers in our centralised system live in the home counties, partly because the south-east has a more buoyant economy and partly as a result of political factors: this after all is the heartland of the traditional party of government. (For a subtle and controversial analysis of territorial politics in the UK, see Bulpitt [1983].)

International events

The increasing interdependence of the large economies has made events such as the quadrupling of oil prices in the early 1970s major constraints upon policy making. In some cases these constraints are formal, as when the International Monetary Fund attached strict public expenditure conditions to its 1976 loan to Callaghan's Labour government. Political events such as the Falklands War can clearly have an enormous impact upon major policy areas, while the 1989 revolutions in the communist countries changed the whole context within which foreign policy is formulated. The greatest perturbations in the present century were caused initially by the terrorist attacks of 11 September 2001 followed by the successive US-led wars in Afghanistan and Iraq.

The influence of Europe

Treaty obligations and the growing power of Community institutions have imposed increasingly

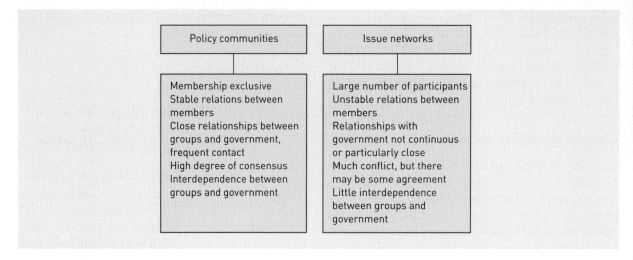

Figure 21.3 Policy networks
Source: Baggott (1995: 24)

powerful constraints upon the freedom of action that British policy makers have enjoyed (see Chapter 27). British policy making is now well embedded into the Brussels machinery with senior civil servants constantly travelling on the shuttle to Brussels, Strasbourg and Luxembourg.

Policy networks

Jordan and Richardson (1987) argued that policy making in Britain is not uniform; every aspect has its own specific characteristics. They lay less stress on manifestos or the activities of Parliament but point to the mass of interconnecting bodies that have an interest in the policy area: the 'policy community'.

To some extent this is a theory about how interest groups interact with government to help formulate policy. Access to the policy community is restricted to actors prepared to play the game: act constitutionally, accept that the government has the last word, keep agreements and make reasonable demands. These rules automatically exclude radical groups with high-profile campaigning styles in most cases, although the accession to power of a radical political message can alter this, as in the case of Thatcherism. To exercise real clout, a group has to become an 'insider' (see Chapter 10). Communities have a core and a periphery – rather like that suggested in Figure 21.3 – with the stable core continuously involved in the policy process and a secondary group, less stable in membership, involved from time to time but lacking the resources to be in the core.

Professor Rod Rhodes developed this idea but saw that often the policy community was not cohesive or sharply defined; he began to discern a more fragmented and more accessible form: a 'policy network' with a very large and constantly changing membership, often with conflicting views. Baggott's diagram (Figure 21.3) shows the contrast between the two ideas with some clarity. Baggott (1995: 26) criticises the approach for not explaining the provenance of the networks and over-concentrating on the group–government nexus to the exclusion of the broader political environment.

Comprehensive political marketing

Jennifer Lees-Marchment wrote a book in 2001 which argued that marketing had become so all-pervasive in modern politics that politicians now 'design' policies for the electoral market and then deliver them once in power. She claims parties no longer dispense 'grand ideologies' striving to convert voters to their faiths. Instead they have adjusted to the way we now vote: instrumentally, expecting parties to deliver on promises made in the marketplace of election campaigns. She argued that initially Labour was 'product-based' in the early 1980s when it persisted in selling something no one wanted. The result was failure. Then the party tried a 'sales-oriented' approach, improving its campaigning capacity through advertising, direct mailings and so forth. The result was better but still not enough to win. Then, as New Labour, it began to listen to 'market' demands via focus groups and polls, and fashioned a 'product' the market, i.e. voters, really wanted. The result was the 1997 landslide. The thesis has been criticised as showing politics as devoid of real passion, or any meaning at all; but the analysis is sufficiently acute for much of it to emit the ring of truth.

■ Case studies in policy making

This chapter concludes with two case studies: an examination of policy formulation and implementation in the Millennium Dome; and the ongoing issue of identity cards.

The Millennium Dome

A Conservative project

The provenance of this idea is to be found in John Major's 1992 administration: to celebrate the new millennium in a way that would capture the imagin-

ations of the British people, rather as the Festival of Britain had done in 1951. The Millennium Commission was set up in 1993 and received substantial funding from the National Lottery. Various ideas were mooted to celebrate the event, some located outside the capital – one in Birmingham being the strongest rival to the London region. Michael Heseltine was keen on an exhibition based on the site of an old gasworks on the Greenwich peninsula on the prime meridian (0 degrees longitude). He became the driving force behind it, being appointed to the Millennium Commission when it was set up in 1994 and continuing in this role after becoming Deputy Prime Minister in 1995. In 1996, he set up a Cabinet subcommittee to progress the idea and to raise capital from bankers and businessmen. Crick (1997: 430) tells how the DPM bullied and twisted arms, holding a series of weekly breakfast meetings to ensure that the project would be embraced by the government. The problem was that financing the project was very problematic, more so than the rejected Birmingham option. However, Heseltine was

Finding a use for the Millennium Dome continues to prove difficult
Source: Copyright © Chris Riddell. From the *Observer*, 10 September 2000. Reproduced with permission from Guardian Newspapers Limited

totally committed to the idea and steamrolled the doubters. In 1997, it seemed that the forthcoming election might imperil the project, so he personally lobbied Blair before the election (Heseltine 2000: 513) and won his agreement to continue with it (should he win the election), subject to a review.

New Labour adopts the Dome

New Labour considered the Dome in an early Cabinet. Blair, it seemed, was uncertain and dithered for a month over a decision. Peter Mandelson, grandson of Herbert Morrison, architect of the 1951 Festival, was the chief proponent of the project but was opposed by Gordon Brown, who scorned such PR approaches and was worried that the Treasury would have to bail out a possible failure. With a week to go, 'the costings were dubious; the sponsorship was absent; the contents were vague when not non-existent' (Rawnsley 2000: 54). Moreover, the press was mostly derisive and other ministers were highly sceptical, including Chris Smith, Frank Dobson (who said that the Dome should be 'fired into outer space'), Clare Short and David Blunkett. However, Blair was taken by Mandelson's flamboyant vision of a huge, symbolic, all-inclusive dome to celebrate the 'rebirth of Britain under New Labour'. It seems that the initial doubts of John Prescott had been won over by the regeneration aspects of the scheme. At a pre-Cabinet meeting on 19 June 1997, moreover, he insisted that abandonment of the project at this early stage would make them look 'not much of a government'. When Blair had to leave the meeting early, Prescott took over and faced so much criticism that he dared not take a vote. Instead, 'Tony wants it' was enough for the project to be approved. Blair chose to ignore the Dome's critics in the press, Parliament and Cabinet and to press on with the (destined) national 'folly'.

In a *Guardian* article (13 May 2003) following her resignation as International Development Secretary, Clare Short recalled the decision on the Dome being taken:

We went around the table and everyone spoke. I remember Donald Dewar saying you could have a party and free drink for everyone in the country and still save a lot of money. Then Tony said 'I've got to go' and went out and announced we were going ahead with the dome. John Prescott was left there to sum up and that's how we learned that Cabinet government was coming to an end.

Short added that this was too often the way in which bad decisions were taken.

The Dome

The structure was designed by the Richard Rogers Partnership and became the world's largest dome, covering, remarkably, nearly 20 acres. It was divided into six zones for the purposes of the exhibition, including a Learning Zone, a Body Zone, a Talk Zone and a Faith Zone. Mandelson was the first minister to be in charge of the project, Blair's former flatmate Lord Falconer the next in line. Jenny Page, a former civil servant, was made chief executive of the government-owned Millennium Experience Company. In 1997, the first of many public controversies was caused when Stephen Bayley, the somewhat volatile consultant creative director, resigned. Critics fastened onto the lateness of the project and the inaccessibility of the site plus the paucity of displays to fill the vast new arena. Mandelson's visit to Disneyland in January 1998 gave out all the wrong signals. Through the fog of government pronouncements the press delightedly began to discern something decidedly pear-shaped. Mandelson's 'it's going to knock your socks off' merely added fuel to negative expectations. The cost soon escalated from £200 million closer to £1 billion, and the undoubted quality of the Dome's structure – completed, astonishingly, on time – did not silence the critics, many of whom were invited to the opening celebration on New Year's Eve 1999. The evening's performances were rated as good but, by the greatest ill fortune, transport to the Dome broke down and huge crowds of key opinion formers were left waiting for three hours at a freezing East London station during which they sharpened their pens and then dipped them in vitriol for the next day's papers. Even New Labour's spin machine could not save the Dome from a comprehensive panning.

From then on it was downhill. The exhibitions were open to the public for the space of a year, and to meet financial targets twelve million members of the public were expected to pay the £20 entrance fee. However, actual attendance figures were half that, and while most who visited claimed that it was value for money, a vociferous minority insisted that it was not. Rawnsley comments acidly that 'The Dome was the vapid glorification of marketing over content, fashion over creation, ephemera over achievement . . . It was a folie de bombast' (2000: 327–30). Even a Dome supporter, Polly Toynbee in the *Guardian*, had to confess that it was 'a lemon'. Within weeks, the Dome had to be subsidised with a further £60 million of lottery money. In February

Jenny Page resigned, to be replaced by a Frenchman from Eurodisney, Pierre-Yves Gerbeau. The press assiduously reported the poor attendance and the breakdowns. In May, the chairman of the Millennium Company resigned. Poor 'Charlie' Falconer – the fall guy once Mandelson had departed – was forced to sustain a false enthusiasm for an unconscionable period. Eventually, the government came to sell the structure but found few takers. In the end, it gave the building away – in exchange for a share of putative profits – to a company which successfully turned it into a venue for rock concerts. A 'vacuous temple to political vanity' (Rawnsley 2000: 331) had lost the nation a sum of money that could have built many schools and hospitals.

What went wrong?

■ *Icon politics*: The government opted for a vanity project with little focus or meaning. Moran (2001) calls this 'icon politics', projects chosen merely for their symbolic significance. Inevitably it was decided by those occupying the inner sanctum of government – it was intended to be Blair's opening manifesto ploy in his re-election campaign.

■ *Entertainment ill-suited to government*: The project was entertainment-based, and governments are not designed or equipped to succeed in such a fickle area. Desperate attempts to please a huge audience almost inevitably turned into banality; whatever the media advisers might have sought to feed to the nation, no amount of spin could change this.

■ *Financial warnings*: From early days, warnings regarding uncertain finances were ignored.

■ *Cabinet doubts* were voiced but overruled because of the iconic significance of the project. Fear of damaging criticism from the Opposition meant that such high-level criticism failed to enter the public domain.

■ *Abandonment* of the project at an early stage might have minimised the damage but the government – Blair to the fore – determined not to admit defeat and to brazen out the hurricane of flak.

All these factors contributed to the digging of an ever deeper hole by the government: a classic case of policy making gone horribly wrong.

Postscript: a happier ending?

The future of the Dome itself hung in the balance for a while. John Prescott was associated with a scheme inspired by billionaire Philip Anshcutz to turn it into a mega casino but opposition to such establishments eventually scuppered it. The US businessman was behind Meridian Delta, the company which bought the Dome in 2001. If permission can be obtained, part of the Dome is still in theory available for a super casino but the rest of it has been converted into a leisure facilities centre and an arena for music concerts. Bon Jovi provided the opening concert in June 2007 but the O_2 arena has now become a well-recognised facility, meaning that not all of the Millennium Dome concept has crumbled into dust and ridicule.

Identity cards

This second case study is different because it is an ongoing policy issue which will not be finally resolved for some years yet. This policy saga – for that is what it has become – first entered the public domain in February 2002 when David Blunkett, the then Home Secretary, announced an 'entitlement card' to prevent benefit fraud and deter terrorism. The idea soon attracted vitriolic criticism for its estimated cost of over a billion pounds and its erosion of civil liberties. In consequence the idea was repackaged to be introduced in stages with a full decision on a compulsory scheme delayed until 2013. Many suggested the idea should be dropped, but instead of dropping the scheme after the 2005 election it was submitted to Parliament at the end of June. This time, however, the card was to include biometric information relating to the subject's face, fingerprints and iris; it was passed on its second reading but the government's slimmed majority was further reduced by rebels – mostly from the left-wing Campaign Group – to a mere thirty-one. In the *Guardian* on 28 June 2005 Martin Kettle discussed objections by David Davis, Charles Clarke's Conservative Shadow Home Secretary, who had suggested that the idea had to pass the test of four questions:

1 Will it work to achieve its stated goals? Certainly it would help prevent benefit and identity fraud but few believe, even in government, that it would deter terrorists, producing an (at best) opaque case for the innovation in the first place. Debates in the Lords during January made the

case seem more 'dubious' the longer they continued, according to the *Guardian* on 18 January 2006. In a letter to the same paper on 23 January 2006, the minister in charge, Tony McNulty, argued that the card would be a major blow against financial and benefit fraud: 'linking a unique biometric to personal data means people have control over access to their details'.

2   Is the government capable of introducing such a system? IT-based schemes have turned out to be notoriously difficult to introduce successfully and huge amounts had been wasted by the NHS on new data processing which had proved calamitous, as had the tax credit scheme which had resulted in huge overpayments being claimed back from recipients.

3   Is it cost-effective? Initial estimates of the cost exceeded £1 bn but that soon tripled, with the

government's best estimate of the cost to the public of the card – in combination with a passport – being £93 per person. Over half of respondents to an ICM poll supported the scheme at such a price in June 2005. The Home Office calculated the cost at £6 bn over ten years, but a careful study by the LSE placed the total cost at £19 bn or even £24 bn. While rebutting the LSE estimate as absurd, the government resisted giving detailed costings on the grounds that such commercially sensitive information would prevent the public from receiving the best possible deal when contracts were issued. Lord Crickhowell in the Lords debate inevitably accused the government of offering the taxpayer a 'pig in the poke'.

4   Can civil liberties be safeguarded? The Information Commissioner, Richard Thomas, thinks

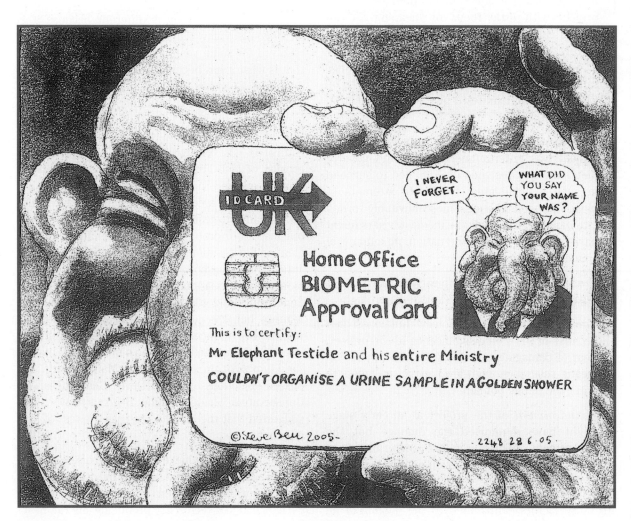

Steve Bell's caustic view on Charles Clarke's plans for ID cards
Source: Copyright © Steve Bell. From the *Guardian*, 28 June 2005. Reproduced with permission

not. He addressed the Home Affairs Select Committee in June 2004 and confessed himself 'increasingly alarmed' by the plan. He did not see a 'sufficient rationale' for recording for the whole population: their name, address, date of birth, gender, nationality and biometric details from finger and eye scans. The idea had 'potential for significant detrimental impact on the day-to-day lives of individuals'.

So, ID cards appear to be too expensive, too riskily experimental, and far too dangerous a violation of civil liberties. But the government – convinced that these judgements will all be proved wrong – was determined to push through a 'flagship' piece of legislation. On 29 March 2006 votes in both Houses appeared to end the conflict between the two Houses. Despite the opposition of the Liberal Democrats, the measure was passed in the House of Lords 287–60. MPs later approved it 301–84. From 2008 everyone renewing a passport will be issued an ID card and have their details placed on the National Identity Register. Through a legislative compromise, people will have the right, until 2010 not to be given a card; however, they will still have to pay for one and have their details placed on the NIR. Anyone seeking a passport after 2010 will be obliged to have an ID Card.

However, 'implementation' is subject to all kinds of pressures as we have seen. Public support for the idea was damaged by the loss of 25 million names by HMRC in November 2007. In March 2008 the Home Office announced that as a result of this loss plans had been put back by two years to 2012. In November it was announced that foreign nationals living in UK could apply for identity cards at a variety of centres throughout the country. Eventually all foreign nationals will have to have such cards and by 2015 90 per cent will have been issued with one. In March 2008 the Home Office announced future plans on ID cards.

From 2011–12 everyone over 16 who applies for a passport will have fingerprints and facial scans added to a National Identity Register. From 2010 students will be encouraged to acquire ID cards. The aim was that everyone would eventually carry an ID card and the government hoped the nation would come to accept this as normal, just as it is in other European countries. However, the Conservatives and Liberal Democrats were strongly opposed on civil liberties grounds and when they formed their coalition after the May 2010 election, their Queen's Speech contained an 'Identity Documents Bill' to cancel the programme and destroy all data on the national identity register. So this substantial piece of policy making had a somewhat tortured history and fell at the last through that oldest of democratic reasons: the election of a new government.

BOX 21.2 BRITAIN IN CONTEXT

Policy making in the USA

Each political system produces different patterns of policy making. To some extent this is a direct reflection of system 'mechanics', but political culture and personalities as well as international factors often play important roles. So we see that in the USA, policy emerges via a route very different from that in the UK. At heart the British Prime Minister dominates the executive, like the President, but as long as his party is behind him, he also dominates the legislature. The US chief executive, however, is separately elected and has responsibility for initiating and implementing policy: on the face of it a more powerful figure. However, the US system is complex with myriad checks and balances.

The President is Head of State, Commander in Chief of the Armed Forces, Chief Appointing Officer, Chief Diplomat and, effectively, Chief Legislator. The President can veto any Congressional bill with which he disagrees; in addition to this he has responsibility for the successful implementation of policy. But these powers are balanced by the sole ability of Congress to declare war, the requirement for many appointments to be confirmed by the Senate, the need for a two-thirds majority to ratify treaties, the power of Congress over the making of new laws and the raising of revenue, the ability of Congress to override the veto with a two-thirds majority, and the ability of Congress to impeach the President for 'high crimes and misdemeanors'.

The President faces substantial foreign policy constraints from the Senate, made even more restrictive after the War Powers Act in 1973 in the wake of the Vietnam War. He has more freedom of action domestically but cannot set interest rates and is dependent on Congress for revenue. For a long time after the Constitution deemed that Congress would check the President, Congress was perceived as the more powerful institution, but in 1933 Roosevelt successfully extended presidential powers in a bid to overcome the problems created by the Depression. Since then the relationship has ebbed and flowed. Presidential success is crucially dependent on the President's ability to negotiate successfully with Congress; he often has to persuade dissident legislators from his *own* party to give him the support he needs to push measures through; party discipline is nowhere near as strong as in the UK. Congress may also, of course, be of a different political complexion, as Clinton found to his cost towards the end of his time in power.

The President appoints Cabinet members to lead departments but shares one much criticised feature of British politics: he tends to rely a great deal on personal aides and advisers. Both Thatcher and Blair were criticised for allowing their 'kitchen cabinets' to assume too much power, as did Nixon, Carter, Reagan and Clinton. George Bush Jr has also attracted some criticism but has perhaps tended to give secretaries of state like Rumsfeld and Rice relatively more room in which to operate. So a constant tension exists between departments and White House advisers as to whom the President listens and whose advice he follows.

The President has two other powerful weapons at his disposal. Firstly, he can appoint to the Supreme Court judges who tend to reflect his political views, thus influencing the context in which laws will be made over the next two to three decades. Secondly, he has unrivalled access to public opinion which he uses to encourage or even bully Congress into passing his laws. Roosevelt, when negotiating with unsympathetic Congressional leaders, used to glance meaningfully at the microphone placed on his desk in the Oval Office – it often did the trick. Public opinion is a constant resource available to the President as voters can be thus mobilised to put pressure on Congress to follow the presidential lead. This explains why presidential ratings are often taken more seriously in the US than those of the Prime Minister in the UK.

Chapter summary

Policy can be defined as either rules and regulations or public expenditure and its distribution. There are various theories about or models of policy making, including the pluralist, corporatist, ruling-class and Whitehall models, plus the rational choice and incrementalist perspectives on decision making. Policy can be seen to pass through three stages: initiation, formulation and implementation. 'Core' decision makers have a constant control of the process, but elements from the 'periphery' are brought in from time to time. The concept of policy networks is useful in analysing policy making. Extra-parliamentary parties and think tanks can have considerable influence, depending on the issue and the situation. Implementation can be very difficult and result in policy objectives being missed or even reversed. Policy makers face many restraints upon their actions, including timing, coordination and international events.

Discussion points

■ Which model of policy making seems closest to reality?

■ Should there be more popular control over policy making?

■ How persuasive is Lindblom's theory of incrementalism?

■ What lessons can be learned from the process whereby the Millennium Dome project brought into being?

Further reading

Building on the foundation texts of Lasswell, Simon, Lindblom, Etzioni, Dror and Wildavsky, the field of policy studies has spawned a substantial literature over the past forty years or more. In recent decades, Burch and Wood (1990) and Ham and Hill (1993) have provided good introductions to the denser studies available. Hogwood and Gunn (1984) is well written and interesting, as is Jordan and Richardson (1987). For an up-to-date and penetrating analysis see Smith (1993). The best comprehensive study of policy studies used to be Wayne Parsons' *Public Policy* (1995), but that role has been thankfully superseded by Peter Dorey's excellent shorter and more accessible *Policy Making in Britain*. Peter John's *Analysing Public Policy* (1998) and Michael Hill's *The Policy Process in the Modern State* (2000) are both short, competent, clear, though now slightly dated treatments. For a very good shorter introduction to the topic, Moran's *Politics and Governance in the UK* (2005: 412–50) has not been bettered.

Bibliography

Allison, G.T. (1971) *The Essence of Decision: Explaining the Cuban Missile Crisis* (Little, Brown).

Ashbee, E. and Ashford, N. (1999) *US Politics Today* (Manchester University Press).

Bachrach, P.S. and Baratz, M.S. (1970) *Power and Poverty, Theory and Practice* (Oxford University Press).

Baggott, R. (1995) *Pressure Groups Today* (Manchester University Press).

Bulpitt, J. (1983) *Territory and Power in the United Kingdom* (Manchester University Press).

Burch, M. (1979) 'The Policy Making Process', in B. Jones and D. Kavanagh (eds) *British Politics Today* (Manchester University Press).

Burch, M. and Wood, B. (1990) *Public Policy in Britain*, 2nd edn (Martin Robertson).

Butler, Lord of Brockwell (2004) *Review of Intelligence on Weapons of Mass Destruction*, HC898, July.

Castles, F. (1982) *The Impact of Parties* (Sage).

Castles, F. (1989) *The Comparative History of Public Policy* (Oxford University Press).

Crick, M. (1997) *Michael Heseltine* (Hamish Hamilton).

Dorey, P. (2006) *Policy Making in Britain* (Sage).

Downs, A. (1957) *An Economic Theory of Democracy* (Harper & Row).

Easton, D. (1965) *A Framework for Political Analysis* (Prentice Hall).

Etzioni, A. (1964) *A Comparative Analysis of Complex Organisations* (Prentice Hall).

Etzioni, A. (1968) *An Active Society: A Theory of Societal and Political Processes* (Free Press).

Franklin, B. (1998) *Tough on Soundbites, Tough on the Causes of Soundbites, Catalyst paper* 3 (Catalyst).

Hague, R., Harrop, M. and Breslin, S. (1998) *Comparative Government and Politics* (Macmillan).

Ham, C. and Hill, M. (1993) *The Policy Process in the Modern Capitalist State* (Harvester Wheatsheaf).

Heseltine, M. (2000) *Life in the Jungle: My Autobiography* (Coronet).

Hill, M.J. (ed.) (1993) *New Agendas in the Study of the Policy Process* (Harvester Wheatsheaf).

Hill, M. (2000) *The Policy Process in the Modern State* (Prentice Hall).

Hogwood, B. (1992) *Trends in British Public Policy* (Open University Press).

Hogwood, B. and Gunn, L.A. (1984) *Policy Analysis in the Real World* (Oxford University Press).

Jessop, B. (1990) *State Theory: Putting Capitalist States in Their Place* (Polity Press).

John, P. (1998) *Analysing Public Policy* (Pinter).

Jones, B. (1986) *Is Democracy Working?* (Tyne Tees TV).

Jordan, G. and Richardson, J.J. (1982) 'The British Policy Style or the Logic of Negotiation', in J.J. Richardson (ed.) *Policy Styles in Western Europe* (Allen & Unwin).

Jordan, G. and Richardson, J.J. (1987) *Governing Under Pressure* (Martin Robertson).

Lee, G. (1989) 'Privatisation', in B. Jones (ed.) *Political Issues in Britain Today*, 3rd edn (Manchester University Press).

Lees-Marchment, J. (2001) *Political Marketing and British Political Parties: The Party's Just Begun* (Manchester University Press).

Lindblom, C.E. (1959) 'The Science of Muddling Through', *Public Administration Review*, Vol. 19.

Lindblom, C.E. and Woodhouse, E.J. (1993) *The Policy Making Process*, 3rd edn (Prentice Hall).

Marx, K. and Engels, E. (1848) *The Communist Manifesto* (Oxford University Press).

McKay, D. (2001) *American Politics and Society* (Blackwell).

Miliband, R. (1969) *The State in Capitalist Society* (Weidenfeld & Nicolson).

Moran, M. (2001) 'Not Steering but Drowning: Policy Catastrophes and the Regulatory State', *Political Quarterly*, Autumn, pp. 414–27.

Moran, M. (2005) *Politics and Governance in the UK* (Palgrave).

National Audit Office, *The Millennium Dome: report by the Comptroller and Auditor General*, HC936 1999–2000, accessible at www.open.gov.uk/nao

Naughtie, J. (2001) *The Rivals* (Fourth Estate).

Parsons, W. (1995) *Public Policy* (Edward Elgar).

Platt, S. (1998) *Government by Task Force*, Catalyst paper 2 (Catalyst).

Rawnsley, A. (2000) *Servants of the People* (Hamish Hamilton).

Rawnsley, A. (2010) *The End of the Party: The Rise and Fall of New Labour* (Viking).

Rowlands, D. and Pollock, A. (2004) 'Choice and Responsiveness for Older People in the "Patient Centred" NHS', *British Medical Journal*, January.

Schmitter, P.C. (1979) 'Still the Century of Corporatism', in P.C. Schmitter and G. Lembruch (eds) *Trends Towards Corporatist Intermediation* (Sage).

Schnattschneider, E.E. (1960) *The Semisovereign People* (Holt, Reinhart & Winston).

Simpson, D. (1999) *Pressure Groups* (Hodder & Stoughton).

Smith, M. (1993) *Pressure, Power and Policy* (Harvester Wheatsheaf).

Watts, D. (2003) *Understanding US/UK Government and Politics* (Manchester University Press).

Wilby, P. 'Rupert Murdoch is Effectively a Member of Blair's Cabinet', *The Guardian*, 1 July 2006.

Wildavsky, A. (1979) *Speaking the Truth to Power* (Little, Brown).

Wilensky, H. (1975) *The Welfare State and Equality* (University of California Press).

Useful websites

Fabian Society: www.fabian-society.org.uk
Demos: www.demos.co.uk
Catalyst: www.catalystforum.org.uk
10 Downing Street: www.number10.gov.uk
Anti-ID Card Group: www.no2id.net

CHAPTER 22

The politics of law and order

Bill Jones

Learning objectives

- To explain the connection between political ideas and the problem of law and order.

- To consider the causes of crime and its profile as a political issue.

- To examine some related issues like punishment.

- To explain and analyse the secret security services.

The mood and temper of the public with regard to the treatment of crime and criminals is one of the unfailing tests of the civilization of a country.

Winston Churchill, as Home Secretary, 1911, quoted in Jenkins (2001: 180)

A society should not be judged on how it treats its outstanding citizens but by how it treats its criminals.

Fyodor Dostoyevsky

Introduction

This chapter examines a political issue that affects everyone: crime and punishment. Opinion surveys show that concern on this topic has been steadily rising throughout the 1980s and 1990s as crime figures have soared and in some cases, for example property crime, even exceeded American levels. Anticipating a general election in 2005, Tony Blair packed his Queen's Speech in autumn 2004 with even more proposals to crack down on crime. This chapter examines the subject within the context of political ideas; assesses the extent of the current problem; discusses some of the probable causes of crime and concludes with a brief examination of the security services and other Home Office issues.

■ Law, order and political ideas

Ever since humankind began to live together over 9,000 years ago, the question of law and order has been of central concern. Solitary cave dwellers did not need a code of law, but any group of humans living as a community did. Fundamental to such a code was property. From the earliest times this included food, clothes, homes and utensils, joined later by money once it had become a medium of exchange. Also highly important was physical safety – one of the reasons, after all, why people lived together in the first place. The Babylonian king, Hammurabi (d. 1750 BC) established a body of law famously based on the notion of retribution: 'an eye for an eye, a tooth for a tooth'; Islamic ('*sharia*') law, in some respects, tends to perpetuate such principles.

Legal systems in developed Western countries still seek to defend property and the person, but an extremely large variety of considerations have been embodied in pursuit of that elusive concept, 'justice'. Political thinkers have also wrestled with these problems. Aristotle recognised the necessity of law and governments that apply it with wisdom and justice. In the wake of the English Civil War, the philosopher Thomas Hobbes rested his whole justification for the state on its ability to provide physical protection for its citizens. Without such protection, he argued, life would be a brutal process of destructive anarchy; Conservative philosophers have always stressed the need for such protection. Conservative Party policy still reflects this powerful emphasis: 'The Conservative Party has always stood for the protection of the citizen and the defence of the rule of law' (1992 election manifesto).

Another group of philosophers approach the problem from a different angle. They argue that people are naturally inclined to be law-abiding and cooperative. They only transgress, so the argument runs, when their social environment damages them and makes deviation both inevitable and understandable. Social reorganisation therefore, can alleviate the problem of crime. Foremost among these thinkers was Karl Marx, who attributed most of what was wrong with society to the corrupting and debilitating effect of a vicious capitalist economic system.

A kind of continuum is therefore recognisable: pessimists, who see criminals as reflections of man's innate imperfections; and optimists, who believe that crime has roots in society and can be attacked and remedied by social action. In British politics, the Tories have tended to occupy a position towards the pessimistic end of the spectrum and Labour the optimistic one.

In 1979, Margaret Thatcher made great play of how hers was the party of law and order. Studies showed this benefited her enormously in the election of that year. Moreover, there is reason to believe that most voters tend towards the pessimistic end of the spectrum and respond to tough remedies that hark back to Hammurabi (if not the American Wild West). The Thatcherite analysis – still very influential in the Conservative Party – is that humans are basically weak and sinful creatures who need all the support of Church, family, school and community to keep them on the straight and narrow. During the 1960s ('that third-rate decade', according to Norman Tebbit) Labour's over-liberal approach tipped the balance of socialisation towards an absence of individual responsibility: parents were encouraged to slough off their responsibility in favour of an insidiously vague concept of 'society', which took the blame for a whole portmanteau of things and destroyed the notion of 'personal accountability', that crucial binding quality in any functioning society. Consequently, children grew up expecting and exercising free licence – 'doing their own thing' in the argot of the time – moving on to become juvenile offenders and then hardened criminals. Back in 1993, The *Sunday Telegraph* neatly summarised the Thatcherite critique of the left's approach (15 August):

It is the very beliefs of those theorists [left-wing academics who maintain that crime is caused by social conditions] that are responsible for our present malaise. They preach, in a doctrine which first became prominent during the sixties but stretches back to Rousseau, that man is inherently good, and that he must cast off the chains of conventional behaviour and morality that enslave him.

The unlimited flow of immigrants, the argument continues, causes more tensions and contributes to crime, while the abrogation of personal responsibility which they alleged Labour accepted and encouraged, was nourishing a crime wave.

Labour rejected this view of the world. Their Home Office spokesmen and spokeswomen preferred to concentrate on the roots of crime, which they believed lay in poor economic and social conditions. The first element of this is seen as the huge inequality between rich and poor that the free-enterprise economic system invariably creates. Such social gulfs create anger and frustration: members of the favoured élite are able to progress smoothly through privileged education to highly paid and influential jobs. Meanwhile, poor people face vastly inferior life chances and huge, often insurmountable, challenges if they wish to succeed. They are surrounded by images that equate personal value with certain symbols such as expensive cars and clothes: when they cannot acquire them legally, it is a small step to breaking the law to redress the balance. So the system itself causes crime by encouraging people to want things that they have to steal to acquire. When they do not, the result is often poverty and hopelessness: the breeding ground of crime for successive generations of people at the bottom of the pile. Left-wingers also point to how the law favours the rich and protects their property, imprisoning petty burglars for long stretches yet letting off city fraudsters with suspended sentences or fines.

Interestingly, the positions of both major parties began to converge in the early 1990s. The Tories had long insisted that social conditions were not connected with crime: how else did figures stay stable during the Depression years of the 1930s? However, the massive increase in crime during the 1980s and early 1990s and a series of studies by the Home Office (especially those of Simon Field, who plotted graphs of property crime and consumption in 1900–88, finding a close correlation between unemployment and property crime) encouraged a change of heart. Eventually, the government abandoned this untenable position: on 28 October 1992 Home Office minister Michael Jack accepted that recession had played its part in pushing up the crime figures, saying that downturns in the economy were traditionally accompanied by increases in crime.

For its part, Labour responded to the spate of fearsome juvenile crime in 1993 – including the horrific murder of Jamie Bulger by two young boys – by expressing a tougher line on sentencing and the treatment of young offenders. The two big parties, especially with Kenneth Clarke as Home Secretary and Tony Blair as Shadow Home Secretary, found a surprising amount upon which to agree. Blair's soundbite 'tough on crime – tough on the causes of crime' was Labour's attempt to be true to its old social analysis of crime while exploiting the popular animus against law breakers. Arguably the former emphasis came to eclipse the latter as time went by.

As the 1997 general election approached, both parties targeted crime as a campaign priority, adopting tough postures on handguns and combat knives in the autumn of 1996, for example. Indeed Michael Howard, the populist Conservative Home Secretary,

BIOGRAPHY

Michael Howard (1941–)

Former Conservative Home Secretary. Educated at Cambridge. Became MP in 1983, minister of local government, Employment and Environment Secretary before Home Secretary (1993–7). Stood in leadership election in 1997 but, after being criticised in a Commons speech by former junior understudy Ann Widdecombe, saw the man he asked to run as his deputy go on to win. Left the Shadow Cabinet in 1999. In 2001 he returned as Shadow Chancellor under Iain Duncan Smith. When this period of leadership came to an undistinguished end, Howard was elected unopposed to take IDS's place. He led his party into the May 2005 election but when Labour won its third term, Howard resigned, leaving the field open for a new generation of younger Conservatives. He never quite lost the negative aura he acquired while Home Secretary.

sought to play to the right-wing gallery in his own party; what was more surprising was that his Labour shadow, Jack Straw, sought to match him and even exceed him in right-wing zeal, so sensitive had the opposition become to the need to attract floating votes, especially middle-class ones, in order to end 18 years out of power (see also Reiner 2006a).

■ Defining crime

Legal: In one sense crimes are anything which are so described by legal statute, but this is too broad-brush a classification:

1 Criminal law is itself a subdivision of the law, relating to those rules society as a whole have judged to be offences: burglary, assault, homicide for example. They are crimes against 'everyone' and so are dealt with separately from 'civil' law which concerns differences at a more private, individual level, for example disputes about contracts, landlords seeking back rent from tenants, divorce settlements and the like. For this reason criminal law has a stricter standard of evidence – 'beyond reasonable doubt' – than civil law's 'on the balance of probabilities'.

2 Definitions of law change over time. Reiner (2008) mentions a study of 3,514 people prosecuted by Essex quarter sessions 1628–32:

> . . . 144 were thefts and 48 were assaults. But these figures were dwarfed by the 480 prosecutions for allowing bridges or roads to fall into decay, 229 for keeping a disorderly alehouse, and, by far the biggest category – 684 prosecutions for failing to attend church. (p. 25)

3 If a law is considered 'unjust' it is possible to argue its invalidity, as champions of justice, like Luther-King or Mandela did in relation to laws discriminating on the grounds of race.

4 Moral values change slowly but sometimes massively over time, so laws discriminating against women and homosexuals for example, no longer feature on the statute book.

Types of crime: Some three quarters of crimes committed are property offences. At 22 per cent (2005–6 figures) violent offences have displayed a worrying increase while drug offences per se are a relatively small category.

■ Causes of crime

Some of the causes of crime have already been touched on. Politicians, it has been shown, argue either that people have become, or have been allowed to become, less law-abiding, more 'evil' even (though this is a much-contested concept), or that society has become a forcing ground for such deviancy. Causes inevitably reflect political prejudices, but there are other possible causes.

The huge gap between rich and poor

One view is that all forms of private property constitute a form of theft, that all property by rights belongs to everyone. According to this view, everyone who is rich has 'appropriated' their property from others, leading to the position espoused by the American radical Angela Davis: 'The real criminals in this society are not the people who populate the prisons across the state but those who have stolen the wealth of the world from the people.' It remains a fact that the gap between rich and poor in Britain over the last 20 years has grown faster than in any other developed Western country.

A vividly clear recent contribution to this literature was made by Richard Wilkinson and Kate Pickett (2009) in *The Spirit Level*. Their book, based on painstaking research across international borders, suggests that the greater the relative inequality within a country, the more acute is its range and intensity of social dysfunction. Their figures proved this to be true in relation to trust levels, education, teenage pregnancies, life expectancy, obesity and violence. Their scatter graph, Figure 22.1 illustrates how imprisonment rates closely follow this index from the least unequal countries – Japan, Scandinavia, northern Europe – to the most unequal: UK, Australia, Israel, Portugal, and, by a distance, the biggest imprisoner, the USA whose rate is four-and-a-half times that of the UK and 14 times that of Japan.

There are now many more potential crimes

In the old days, family arguments were ignored by police as 'domestics'. Since the law has changed, crimes of violence have registered an increase. Furthermore, the proliferation of consumer goods has increased the opportunity for crime: there are simply more things to steal, especially valuable portable objects like ipods and mobile phones.

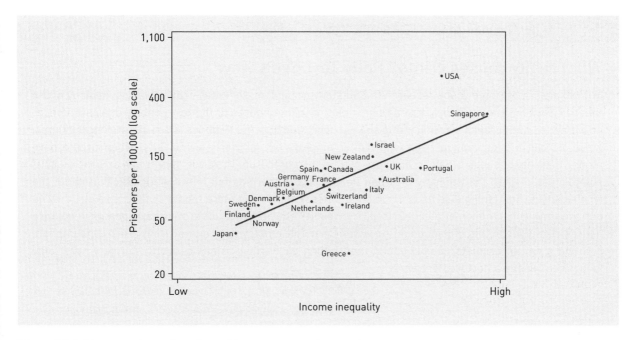

Figure 22.1 More people are imprisoned in more unequal countries

Young people are faced with a difficult world in which to grow up

1 Many young people are increasingly the products of fragmented families and have lacked the emotional security of a proper home.

2 Long-term unemployment – likely to increase following the deep depression beginning in 2009 – has replaced valuable socialisation through work with despair. As a consequence young people lose out, as American sociologist Charles Murray (1990) observes, 'acquiring skills and the network of friends and experiences enable them to establish a place for themselves – not only in the workplace but a vantage point from which they can make sense of themselves and their lives' (p. 25).

3 As a consequence of unemployment, youngsters find life infinitely grey and pointless. Crime can seem like the ultimate rebellion and excitement. John Purves, a solicitor who has defended many young joyriders in the north-west and the north-east, explains that it 'provides an escape from their humdrum existences. They are thrilled by the speed of these flying machines and the more dangerous it gets the more excited they become. It's an addiction . . . The press call them

"deathriders"; that's the real thrill' (*Observer*: 25 June 1994).

Growth of an underclass

Charles Murray, quoted above, has written that he thinks the UK is well on the way to developing its own underclass of disaffected poor living in the inner cities, often in council housing and unemployed, eking out their lives on benefits and crime. Any youngster living in such an area finds it very difficult to resist the allure and rewards of crime and the attractions of drugs, easy living and violence.

Values have declined

This view is especially popular with Conservatives, who hark back to a golden age when it was possible to live without fear of crime. Geoff Pearson's brilliant book *Hooligan* (1983) disposes of this myth:

Conservatives have enthused about this mythical law abiding society 20 years ago for decades. Twenty years ago, in fact, they were just as worried about crime and disorderly youth as they are now, panicked by hippies in the late sixties and early seventies, by Teds in the fifties and 'Americanised youth' in the forties.

BOX 22.1	IDEAS AND PERSPECTIVES

What really causes crime? Polly Toynbee's view

In 1988 a piece of Home Office research fell on stony ground, out of kilter with the ruling ideology of the times. *Trends in Crime and their Interpretation* plotted crime figures in the last century against the economic cycles, with graphs tracking crime against boom and bust. Its evidence is conclusive: in good times, when *per capita* consumption rises with higher employment, property crime falls. When people have money their need is less great, so burglary and theft trends drop. However, theft rises as soon as consumption falls when the economy dips and people on the margins fall out of work. But that is not the whole picture. Something else happens in good times. People have more money in their pockets, they go out and their consumption of alcohol rises. The result? They hit each other more and personal violence figures rise. Exactly this is happening now with near full employment and soaring drink consumption, creating a rise in assaults, mainly young men hitting each other at night (mainly not very hard, only 14 per cent visited a doctor afterwards).

Source: Polly Toynbee, 'What Really Causes Crime?', *Guardian*, 12 July 2002

© Guardian Newspapers Limited 2002, reprinted with permission

■ Drugs and crime

Much has been written about the complex connection between drugs and crime. Chris Nuttal, in charge of research at the Home Office, estimates that two-thirds of all property crime is drug-related. On average a heroin addict has to raise £13,500 annually to support the habit, £8,000 more if crack cocaine is also involved. Most of this is raised via shoplifting, and a series of drug tests in different parts of the country have revealed that over three-quarters of those arrested were under the influence of alcohol and two-thirds other drugs. In July 2005 the press revealed that a suppressed report on the war on drugs showed it was being lost. Traffickers made so much money out of their trade that seizures of 60–80 per cent were needed to turn the tide; in reality seizures amounted to a mere 20 per cent. An increasingly influential argument has emerged pressing for control of recreational drugs through legalisation, but most politicians shy away from a policy which superficially appears to advocate easier access to dangerous drugs.

■ Anti-social behaviour

Much has been written about the rise of anti-social behaviour or 'yob culture' of the kind which makes town and city centres unwelcome to families, women on their own or middle-aged people wishing to go to theatres and cinemas. For the general public, this is possibly the major cause of crime and source of apprehension. The source of the problem, most agree, is excessive consumption of alcohol and so the further liberalisation of drinking hours which took place in November 2005 was not thought to be an especially intelligent piece of government, though, to be fair, to date it seems to have had minimal impact.

■ Neo-liberal economic policies and 'anomie'

Reiner (2007) argues that the chief well spring of crime is the eclipse of consensus Keynesian welfare thinking by neo-liberal ideas from the mid-1970s onwards. In the 1980s this produced 'the massive social dislocations of deindustrialisation and resurgent mass unemployment . . . for increasing numbers of young men, especially among ethnic minorities and in inner city areas . . .' The unbridled turbo capitalism had 'devastating consequences for order that far outweighed the strong state measures introduced to control it in a Canute-like effort to stem the social tsunami' (pp. 95–96). Reiner cites Merton's idea of alienation or 'anomie': the conflicts generated by a desire to get on combined with lack of opportunity to do so. Being unemployed, for example, would be a good example of a condition likely to create such a state of mind. This problem is exacerbated in a consumerist society where values are rooted in materialism, the acquisition of goods, chattels and other inanimate articles. Such a society provides no finite limit whereby 'success' can be measured: the rich want to become the super rich who in turn aspire to exceed the wealth of Microsoft founder Bill Gates or finance wizard, Warren Buffet. But if someone at the bottom end of society cannot even reach the first rung of the materialist ladder, what are they to do? A Liverpudlian youth on *Weekend World* in December 1985 expressed his reaction simply but eloquently thus:

Some people have got jobs, they can go out and buy things they want. But we're on the dole, we haven't got the money so we go out robbing to get the money.

The work of Box, Erlich and the already mentioned Field, did much to establish the once disputed nexus between economic downturns and increases in crime, whether against property or indeed violence against the person. A distinction also needs to be made between 'core' employment where, for example, skilled workers enjoy relative employment and financial security and the 'secondary' or peripheral sector where workers are poorly paid and lack employment rights. The latter kind of employment is much less likely to reduce crime rates though there is evidence the introduction of the minimum wage in 1999 helped bring down crime in previously low wage areas (Reiner 2007: 101).

■ Conviction rates

Reiner (2007) explains how the volume of crime is much greater than that formally registered by the police. The British Crime Survey (BCS), based on 40,000 interviews with ordinary citizens provides a more reliable snapshot of how crime is being experienced 'at ground level':

Only 2 per cent of crimes measured by the BCS end up with a convicted offender, and another 1 per cent in a caution. The proportion of known crimes leading to someone being sentenced to custody is 0.3 per cent. And they are mainly for a variety of street crimes . . . The imbalance begins with what is reported (or more often not reported) by victims and more marked as the cases go through the criminal justice system.

Figure 22.2 illustrates this tendency vividly.

■ 'Dark crime figure'

Why are less than half of this true 'dark figure' of offences ever reported to the police? There are several reasons. Some victims are not aware they have become victims – especially children; some choose not to report the offence because they consider it too minor or entails insufficient loss to justify the trouble. In a fair number of violent crimes the victim saw the matter as 'private' to be resolved

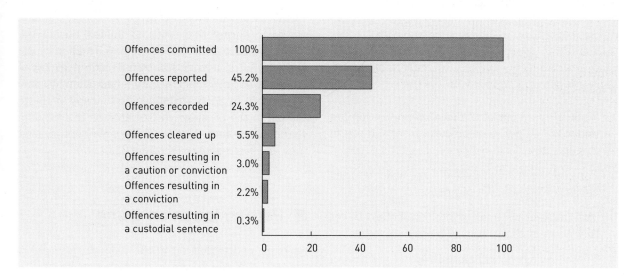

Figure 22.2 Attrition within the criminal justice system (percentage of offences committed)
Source: G. Barclay and C. Tavares, *Digest 4: Information on the Criminal Justice System in England and Wales* (London: Home Office, 1999: 29)

independently; in other cases victims might fear reprisals for going to the police. Some offences also do not have a victim in that the person against whom the 'offence' is committed – for example a drug or prostitution offence – are willing participants. Police officers, for their part, fail to record over half of all crimes reported to them, according to the 1981 BCS. Another consideration is the reclassifications of crime introduced by the Home Office on a fairly regular basis.

Who are the perpetrators?

One longitudinal survey of all people born in 1953 revealed that by the age of 30 one in three men had been convicted of a crime; one in sixteen had been to prison; and, significantly, the 7 per cent who had been convicted six or more times accounted for two-thirds of all offences. The survey also showed that violence was on the increase: one in eight men convicted of an offence had committed a crime of violence by the age of 20. For those born in 1963, the proportion had risen to one in five. Certainly young criminals seem to abound. Most crimes are committed by people aged 14 to 20; over 90 per cent of all 15- to 16-year-old offenders re-offend within four years. On 20 November 1996, the Audit Commission reported on juvenile justice. Its document, *Misspent Youth*, revealed that the 150,000 teenage offenders commit seven million crimes every year, only 19 per cent of which are recorded by police and only 5 per cent cleared up, with a mere 3 per cent resulting in arrest and action.

If those in prison are compared with society in general, as Table 22.1 reveals, a number of characteristics are made clear.

1 While 16 per cent of the general population are under 25, 40 per cent of those in prison are in this age group.

2 Forty-nine per cent of society are male yet they constitute 96 per cent of prisoners.

3 Two per cent were taken into care before 16 yet they provide 26 per cent of those behind bars.

4 Those leaving school before 16 are 11 per cent of society yet 40 per cent of prisoners.

5 Five per cent of the UK are from ethnic minorities yet this group provides 16 per cent of prisoners.

Table 22.1 Prison and general population compared

	Prison population (%)	General population (%)
Under 25	40	16
Male	96	49
Ethnic minority	16	5
Semi/unskilled occupation	41	18
Unemployed	33	8.7
No permanent home	13	0.3
Left school before 16	40	11
Frequent truancy	30	3
Lived with both parents till 16	62	83
Taken into care before 16	26	2

Sources: R. Walmsley, L. Howard and S. White, *The National Prison Survey 1991* (London: HMSO, 1992); *Social Trends 1993* (HMSO)

Crime trends

Figure 22.3 shows how crime figures maintained a steady plateau for nearly a century after the 1850s but began to rise after the Second World War until half a million a year were recorded during the 1950s. Then a steady increase occurred to around a million per year during the 1960s, 2 million during the 1970s and then a sharp spike up to 5.5 million by the early 1990s. Following this mid-decade peak crime gradually began to decline until it had fallen by some 40 per cent by 2008. Criminologists mostly attribute the fall to the prosperity associated with the 'boom years' of the first decade of the new century, but they also have doubts (see Box 22.3).

Getting tough on crime

As explained earlier on in the chapter, after 1979 crime, by virtue of its huge increase, became a potent factor in voter choice. The Conservatives under Michael Howard led the charge, as Box 22.2 explains.

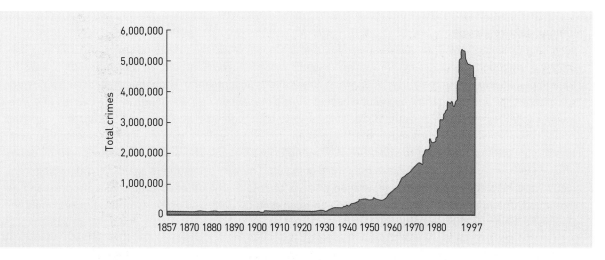

Figure 22.3 Crimes recorded by the police, 1857–1997
Source: G. Barclay and C. Tavares, *Digest 4: Information on the Criminal Justice System in England and Wales* (London: Home Office, 1999: 2)

BOX 22.2   **IDEAS AND PERSPECTIVES**

Howard's measures to curb crime

At the 1993 Conservative Party conference in Blackpool, Home Secretary Michael Howard unveiled 'the most comprehensive programme of action against crime' announced in Britain, including abolition of the right to silence for defendants; new measures against terrorism; tougher penalties for persistent young offenders; the building of six new prisons; new powers to evict squatters and for police to stop trespassers; automatic custody for anyone convicted of rape, manslaughter or murder or attempting the offence who is subsequently accused of any of these crimes; a review to toughen sentences in the community; and accepting all sixteen proposals of review on cutting paperwork to let police do more active duties.

Howard told the conference:

There is a tidal wave of concern about crime in this country. I am not going to ignore it. I am going to take action. Tough action.

However, the reaction to Howard's line was not as warm outside the conference chamber as it was within. Lord Justice Woolf threw in a firecracker when he said publicly that these 'get tough' policies would not work and were 'short-sighted and irresponsible'. On 17 October 1993, the *Observer* led with the views of no fewer than seven judges, all of whom attacked the idea asserted by Howard that 'prison works' through taking criminals off the street and providing a deterrent to others.

Lord Ackner said the causes of crime 'lay deep in society, in the deterioration of personal standards, the family and the lack of self-discipline'. Lord Justice Farquharson, chairman of the Judicial Studies Board said:

The idea that we are building more and more prisons appals me. I have never believed prison rehabilitates anyone.

Lord Bruce Laughland was even more explicit:

The effectiveness of the deterrent diminishes the more an individual goes to prison. People fear hearing the gates shut behind them for the first time. Prison may satisfy public opinion and the victims' understandable feelings, but it has no rehabilitation effect whatsoever . . . a great deal of dishonesty is contributed by politicians.

▶

Labour get even tougher

New Labour under Tony Blair was desperate to match Conservative toughness on crime and a virtual 'bidding war' on tough measures got under way. Reiner, writing in *The Guardian*, 25 November 2005, saw the tipping point occurring in the early 1990s when New Labour accepted the 'economic and social framework of Thatcherism', meaning that the second part of Blair's mantra on crime – 'tough on the causes of crime' – was likely to be vestigial; now the police had to try to be 'tough on crime' to substitute for the vanished social cohesion which had previously helped to keep crime at bay. Throughout Labour's tenure in power, prison populations continued to soar. Despite falling crime figures, the public, made sceptical by dodgy official statistics, continued to believe they were going up. The very precautions against crime, which ironically were helping to reduce it, encouraged citizens to retain a heightened awareness of crime and its likelihood. The onset of the economic recession beginning in 2008 saw property crime figures spike for the first quarter of 2009, but only mildly so.

BIOGRAPHY

David Blunkett (1947–)

Born in Sheffield and educated initially in his own city before going to the Royal Normal College for the Blind, Richmond College FE and then Sheffield University, where he studied politics. Worked for the Gas Board and then as a tutor in industrial relations. Became a councillor in 1970, going on to lead Sheffield Council (1980–7) before being elected MP for Sheffield Brightside in 1987. Shadowed Environment and Education before being appointed Secretary of State for Education in 1997, where he was generally reckoned to have had a successful period in office. In 2001 was made Home Secretary, where he became known for being tough on criminals and not overly tender towards asylum seekers. No doubt it was this alleged illiberalism that prompted Sir John Mortimer to declare in March 2003: 'It is so sad to learn, as a lifelong Labour voter, that our Home Secretaries are worse than the Conservative ones.'

■ Current crime figures

The huge explosion in crime figures occurred in the 1980s and was a consequence, argues Robert Reiner, of neo-liberal economic policies (see above). In 1921 a mere 193,000 **notifiable** (i.e. serious) **offences** were recorded; by 1979 the figure was 2.5 million and by 1993 had increased by a further

128 per cent to 5.7 million. Then crime figures began to decline steadily so that by the middle of the first decade of the new century Labour was claiming credit for a 40-plus percentage reduction in serious crime with the BCS figures reflecting similar falls. Reiner (see Box 22.3) rejects the increase in punitiveness which has characterised penal policy for the last two decades and, while he confesses criminologists have no definitive answer, he thinks it is related to the relatively high levels of prosperity during the 'consumer boom' years 1995–2007.

Crime figures October 2009

These quarterly figures showed a fall of 4 per cent on the second quarter of 2008. BCS figures revealed a similar picture with overall levels remaining relatively stable in the year to June 2009 (Travis 2009). The headline aspects of the figures included an overall fall of 4 per cent; a fall of murders with knives by 35 per cent; a 5 per cent fall in drug crimes and 4 per cent in drug offences. For the first time 50 per cent of respondents feel that councils and police are dealing with crime and anti-social behaviour – up from 45 per cent in 2008. However, the recession was thought to have been responsible for a spike in property crime, for example robberies and cycle theft, in the first quarter of 2009.

■ The security services and related Home Office matters

As well as the law enforcement agencies of the courts, supported by the police, there are the security services, much loved by novelists and screenwriters as sources for their plot lines. People who have worked for these services usually puncture the popular illusion of mystery, excitement and glamour by claiming that such work is mostly routine and often very boring. Most of us, perhaps, would be surprised that defending the state against enemies within or without is not inherently exciting.

Three pieces of legislation authorise the security services:

1 *Security Service Act 1989 (amended in 1996)*: This placed the services under the control of the Home Office and laid out the duties of the Director General.

2 *Intelligence Services Act 1994 (ISA)*: This established the Intelligence and Security Committee, a Commons Committee that oversees the expenditure, administration and policy of the intelligence and security services.

3 *Regulation and Investigatory Powers Act 2000 (RIPA)*: The Act that set up the Commissioner of Interception, a Commissioner for the intelligence services and a tribunal to hear complaints under the Human Rights Act.

The last two Acts allow warrants to be issued by the Home Secretary to intercept communications, interfere with property and undertake 'intrusive surveillance'.

There are four main elements to the security services: MI5, Special Branch, MI6 and GCHQ.

MI5

The existence of MI5 is well known, but until recently most of its activities were shrouded in secrecy. The most we knew officially was that it was set up in 1909 to counter the activity of German spies in the run-up to the First World War. We now know, since 1993, that it employs 2,000 personnel and has a budget of £150 million per year, most of which is spent on counter-terrorism and the bulk of the rest on counter-espionage. After the end of the Cold War, it was perhaps a little short of things to do and in 1992 it was tasked with gathering intelligence about the IRA. In 1996, it was given the further responsibility of helping to counter 'serious crime'. For most citizens the closest they are likely to get to the agency is if they are vetted for a sensitive post in government. Physically, however, they can now easily see from where this very secret work is controlled: from its headquarters on the banks of the Thames not far

from the Houses of Parliament. Political control falls to the Home Secretary.

Special Branch

This is a branch of the police force, ultimately under the Home Secretary, tasked with combating terrorism, espionage, sabotage and subversion. In addition it provides security for important people, watches the ports and airports and makes arrests for MI5. Like MI5, it employs 2,000 personnel but at £20 million per year spends much less.

MI6

MI6 deals with political and economic intelligence abroad. It works mostly through agents attached to British embassies overseas, although it maintains close liaison with the Defence Intelligence Service. It comes under the authority of the Foreign Secretary. From 1994, it has added serious crime to its portfolio of responsibilities, including money laundering and drug smuggling as well as illegal immigration.

Government Communications Headquarters (GCHQ)

This 'listening post' organisation originated from the famously successful code-breaking service based in Bletchley Park during the war. It operates under a treaty signed with the USA in 1947 and seeks to monitor international radio communications utilising communication satellites and listening posts worldwide. Its base in the UK is in Cheltenham and it has over 6,000 employees with an annual budget of £500 million. In 1984, the Thatcher government controversially banned membership of trade unions – allegedly at US request – on security grounds; trade union rights were restored by Labour in 1997.

Apart from the 1994 Act mentioned above, the security services are not accountable to Parliament; the Prime Minister is ultimately responsible for their actions, and the respective heads of the services report directly to him. The PM also chairs the Cabinet Committee on the Security and Intelligence Services. One of the six secretariats in the Cabinet Office is concerned with security and intelligence and serves to coordinate relevant information for feeding into Cabinet. This secretariat contains the

Coordinator of Intelligence and Security, who is another official in this important area who reports directly to the PM. The Joint Intelligence Committee comprises (among others) the secret service heads; it supplies the Cabinet with security information. The security services do not come under the jurisdiction of any complaints procedure, and they do not need to inform the police of their operations. When security service personnel have had to give evidence in court, they have done so with their identities concealed. Critics point out that those tasked with controlling these services have little time to do so and in practice know very little of what goes on. The Security Commission was established in 1964 and investigates security lapses and shortcomings.

The Home Affairs Select Committee in 1993 asked for the right to investigate the activities of the security services in order to guard against abuses of power. The government went some of the way towards meeting its critics in 1994 when it set up, via the Intelligence Services Act, the Intelligence and Security Committee. This comprises nine members drawn from both Houses of Parliament and is charged with scrutiny of the expenditure, administration and policy of MI5, MI6 and GCHQ. It meets weekly and occasionally issues critical reports like the one (1995) in which the service heads were criticised for not being aware of the adverse effects of the spying activities of CIA agent Aldrich Ames. Critics argue that the new committee has too few powers to be effective: it cannot call witnesses or relevant papers and is able to investigate only that which the security service heads allow.

■ Transfer of constitutional responsibilities to Lord Chancellor's department

After the 2001 general election, Tony Blair transferred a number of constitutional functions to the office of his former boss, the Lord Chancellor Lord Irvine. These covered human rights, House of Lords reform, freedom of information, data protection, the crown dependencies (Channel Isles, Isle of Man), royal, hereditary and Church matters, civic honours (city status and lord mayoralties) and the Cenotaph ceremony (an annual service to honour the war dead led by the Queen).

■ Terrorism Acts, 2000–2009

The 2000 Act preceded the attack on the World Trade Center, although those horrific events prompted some additional toughening up of the earlier measure. The act defined 'terrorism' as any threat to influence the government of the UK 'for the purpose of advancing a political, religious or ideological cause'. Civil rights campaigners point out that the Act's scope is dangerously wide. Taken with its detailed provisions, it empowers police to make arrests without warrants, enter buildings without court orders (if they reasonably suspect terrorists are to be found within) and prosecute people for holding information likely to be useful to terrorists. People can be stopped at random, and if they refuse to give their names can be sent to prison. Police can also seize any cash that they think 'is intended for the purposes of terrorism' without specific authorisation. The Liberal Democrats in the form of Simon Hughes MP attacked the definition of terrorism as 'far too wide'. In the event of someone being found in possession of something likely to be used for the purposes of terrorism, then it is up to the accused to prove his or her innocence. In April 2004 the government announced CONTEST, a new cross-departmental strategy aiming to counter sources of terrorism and related acts at home and abroad.

In June 2005 the European Commisioner of Human Rights, Alvaro Gil-Robles, published a damning report on Britain's anti-terror laws. He perceived an attitude in which 'human rights are frequently construed as, at best, formal commitments and, at worst, cumbersome obstructions'. He concluded that such rights were not luxuries but 'the very foundation of democratic societies'. Particularly in mind were the long-term detention of terrorist suspects in Belmarsh prison and their treatment while in custody. Then came the July bombings on the London Underground which launched another wave of get-tough initiatives against possible terrorists. In the autumn of 2005 Tony Blair launched yet another Terror Bill which sought to exclude from the UK any people 'glorifying' or inciting terrorist acts, disseminating publications to the same end, or preparing such acts and training others to do so. But the most draconian and controversial measure proposed was the detention of suspects for up to 90 days. Blair and Clarke, his Home Secretary, were warned this was more than their party could accept, but they pressed on regardless and in November 2005 the measure was defeated when 49 Labour MPs refused to support the government. Blair was unrepentant, saying sometimes it was right to lose if the issue was the right course of action. The eventual 28-day period of detention was still longer than most other EU countries had thought wise to impose. In the autumn of 2008 Home Secretary Jacqui Smith attempted to amend the detention time to 42 days but after a crushing defeat in the House of Lords on 13 October she made a humiliating about turn, announcing she was withdrawing the proposal.

■ The security services and 'dodgy dossiers' on Iraq

In September 2002, the government published a dossier on Iraqi 'weapons of mass destruction' that embodied a substantial amount of intelligence services information. Later, in February 2003, another dossier was published focusing on the Iraqi regime's concealment of such weapons. Neither dossier was considered convincing at the time, especially when the latter was damagingly revealed to include a plagiarised section of a twelve-year-old PhD thesis, but in the wake of the war, critical scrutiny intensified. In May 2003, it was alleged by a BBC journalist

Andrew Gilligan that senior intelligence officers were accusing New Labour's spinmeister, Alastair Campbell, of adding his own material to the September dossier to 'sex it up' to make more compelling the case for a war his master strongly favoured. In the ensuing furious row, which involved the suicide of Dr David Kelly, the MOD officer alleged to be Gilligan's source, many observed that the intelligence services had been involved closely, and unhealthily, in the presentation of what were in essence political arguments. Lord Hutton took extensive evidence in the ensuing inquiry, some of which seemed to support the Gilligan case, but his report surprisingly exonerated government and accused only the BBC, leading to several resignations. The Butler Report on the intelligence services' failure over the non-existent weapons of mass destruction in Iraq also cleared the government of any major wrong-doing but was critical of several areas of poor intelligence; it criticised Blair's description of the Iraq intelligence and warning that the country had weapons which could reach British-controlled areas within 45 minutes as 'authoritative'. Critics of the government were outraged that the man at the centre of much of the intelligence furore, John Scarlett, was allowed promotion to head of MI5. The Chilcot Inquiry into the Iraq war opened in July 2009.

BOX 22.3 BRITAIN IN CONTEXT

Crime and punishment

The Economist (23 August 2003) reacted to the news that 11.3 per cent of American boys born in 2001 will go to jail (33 per cent of black boys) with the comment that 'conservative politicians are on their way to creating a criminal class of unimaginable proportions'.

Every society on the planet suffers from problems of crime. Part of this is due to the fact that drugs are, albeit illegally, one of the world's major traded commodities. Crime in the USA has a well-known international profile, as so many Hollywood movies have chosen stories about gangsters, bank robbers or gang violence. Some sociologists have argued that countries with a very high Gini coefficient – relationship of rich to poor – were likely to attract the highest crime rates, as relative differences fuel

resentment and – when in the same society – opportunity. Figures available suggest there may be much in such calculations.

The nation with the best rating on this index is Japan with a ratio of richest 10 per cent to poorest 10 per cent of 4.5. The crime rate in Japan is, accordingly, relatively low. The equivalent ratio for the UK is 13.8, placing it 51st in the international rankings. The USA comes in at 15.9 and 92nd. Countries like Brazil and South Africa, both notorious for their crime rates, come even lower down at ratios of 33.1 and 68, respectively: 116th and 117th overall. Murder figures in the USA have been astonishingly high by British or European standards. For many years visitors to New York expected to encounter muggers on every street corner or a Los Angeles blazing with gang warfare.

Crime is still a major problem in the USA with, in 2002, nearly 5,000 cases of aggravated assault in Washington alone, a sexual assault every two minutes somewhere in the country, and 42 murders for every 100,000 people in Detroit. But then came a rather unexpected fall in crime levels. According to the FBI, the crime rate per 100,000 inhabitants was just under 2,000 in 1960, rose to nearly 6,000 in 1990, but began to fall in the nineties, ending up at about 4,000 in 2004. Why did crime increase?

Professor Robert Reiner, from the LSE (Reiner 2006b), analyses the changing patterns of crime, noting that similar patterns of crime occurred in the USA and industrialising European countries: an increase during the late eighteenth and early nineteenth centuries during the early Industrial Revolution followed by 'a long-term process of inclusion of the majority of the population in legal, political and, to a lesser extent, economic and social citizenship'. The late twentieth century saw a sharp upturn in crime in these same countries. Reiner identifies two explanations, one favoured by the Left and the other by the Right: the return to a tougher form of capitalism–neo-liberalism, replacing welfarism and causing hardship; and the erosion of social values by the 'permissiveness' of liberalism, expressed most typically during the sixties.

Reiner quotes Currie who attributed the rise to

great structural inequalities and community fragmentation and weakened ability of parents to monitor and supervise their children – and a great many other things all going on at once, all entwined with each other, and all affecting the crime rate – with the combination having an impact that is much greater than its parts.

Why did crime fall? Reiner dismisses 'zero tolerance' as other cities in the US experienced similar falls to the home of this approach: New York. He also dismisses the 'enormous expansion of punitiveness, above all the staggering and gross levels of imprisonment' as a major cause. Numbers of US citizens in jail are indeed horrendous – a higher percentage than in any other country: two million are in jail with nearly half of them drawn from the 12 per cent of the population which is black. More likely an explanation for the downturn, he thinks, was the upturn in the economies of these nations which reduced the need for property crime, but he has to conclude: 'The crime drop remains something of a mystery, defying any simple account.'

Chapter summary

Conservative thinkers have tended to base their law and order policies on a pessimistic view of human nature, while Labour has tended to be more optimistic. However, both views began to converge in the late 1980s and early 1990s. Crime figures suggest a crime wave, but there are many qualifications to bear in mind. It is doubtful whether the Conservatives substantially reversed the crime wave in the early 1990s. It seems likely that crime breeds in poor, rundown areas of big cities. Police attempts to control crime have not been very successful and have received much criticism, even from the Conservatives. Tougher prison sentences are favoured by the Conservatives, but experience suggests that this is no real answer.

The Home Office is the department in charge of the security services, although it has transferred constitutional responsibilities to the Lord Chancellor's Department. The 2000 Terrorism Act has offended those concerned with the defence of human rights.

Discussion points

■ Which analysis of human nature seems closer to the truth, the pessimistic or optimistic version?

■ How reliable are crime figures?

■ Would more widely spread prosperity solve the crime problem?

■ Are too many criminals locked up?

■ What alternative forms of punishment would you advocate?

Further reading

By far the best single book on this subject, and drawn on heavily in this chapter, is Reiner (2008); it is warmly recommended. On race riots, Michael Keith (1993) is worth a read; and on penal policy, Windlesham (1993) is still authoritative and interesting. *The Economist*'s reports on crime are always well informed and well written, as are those of the quality press whenever crime moves to the top of the political agenda.

Bibliography

Box, S. (1987) *Recession, Crime and Punishment* (Oxford University Press).

Dorling, D. (2005) 'Prime Suspect', in P. Hillyard *et al.*, *Beyond Criminology* (Pluto).

Dunning, E.G., Gaskell, G. and Benewick, R. (eds) (1987) *The Crowd in Modern Britain* (Sage).

IPPR (2006) *Crime-share: The Unequal Impact of Crime* (Institute of Public Policy and Research).

Jenkins, R. (2001) *Churchill* (Pan).

Jones, B. (1999) 'Crime and Punishment', in B. Jones (ed.) *Political Issues in Britain Today* (Manchester University Press).

Keith, M. (1993) *Race Riots and Policing* (UCL Press).

Lea, J. and Young, J. (1984) *What is to be Done About Law and Order?* (Penguin).

Mawby, R.I. (1999) *Policing Across the World* (UCL Press).

Murray, C. (1990) *The Emerging British Underclass* (IEA Health and Welfare Unit).

Pearson, G. (1983) *Hooligan: A History of Respectable Fears* (Macmillan).

Rawnsley, A. (2010) *The End of the Party: The Rise and Fall of New Labour* (Viking).

Reiner, R. (1993) *The Politics of the Police*, 2nd edn (Harvester Wheatsheaf).

Reiner, R. (2006a) 'The Social Democratic Criminology', in T. Newburn and P. Rock (eds) *The Politics of Crime Control* (Oxford University Press).

Reiner, R. (2006b) 'Law and Order', in *Current Legal Problems* (published via UCL by Oxford University Press).

Reiner, R. (2007) *Law and Order: An Honest Citizen's Guide to Crime and Control* (Polity).

Reiner, R. (2008) *Law and Order* (Polity).

Toynbee, P. (2002) 'What Really Causes Crime?' *Guardian*, 12 June 2002.

Travis, A. (2009) 'Crime Down 4%, Police Figures Show and Murders with Knives Decline 35%', *Guardian*, 23 October 2009.

Wilkinson, R. and Pickett, K. (2009) *The Spirit Level* (Allen Lane).

Windlesham, Lord (1993) *Responses to Crime*, Vol. 2 (Clarendon Press).

Useful websites

Home Office: http://www.homeoffice.gov.uk/

Prison Service: http://www.hmprisonservice.gov.uk/

Policed Service: http://www.police.uk/

CHAPTER 23
Social policy

Harry Cowen

Learning objectives

- To define the nature of social policy.

- To encourage an understanding of the long-term historical significance of social policy in the UK.

- To assess the political perspectives driving New Right and New Labour social policy strategies.

- To evaluate contemporary social policy issues and debates.

Introduction

I n this chapter we concentrate upon social policy, a central aspect of UK government and politics. To begin with, we present a definition of the term. We then trace the history and development of the modern welfare state, up to the mid-1970s, and analyse the impact of New Right and New Labour politics upon welfare state policies during the last quarter of the twentieth century and into the new century. To conclude, the chapter evaluates a series of contemporary issues.

■ The nature of social policy

Social policy is not easily definable, given the breadth of its fields of action: the problems it addresses, through government action, are rarely static. It represents a major sphere of state activity, dealing with social security; employment; housing; education and health (Hudson, Kuhner and Lowe 2008). Here, a significant role of the state is to raise taxes from the general populous. It also organises **transfer payments** through taxation, from groups in the community to other groups, with evident redistributive consequences. In this respect, social policy decisions mesh with those in related areas such as politics and economics. Overarching political perspectives shape government policies and decisions on matters such as the distribution of social resources, the extent of any requisite state intervention in the operations of welfare services, and the utilisation of markets in social spending and income generation. Clearly, a rather thin dividing line runs between governmental economic and social policies.

Accordingly, the 1980s' wholesale restructuring of the UK economy in response to a sea change in global capitalism, and the concomitant ideological shifts, proved crucial determinants in the history of the welfare state over the latter part of the twentieth century. Finally, a defining element is social policy's perpetual concern with society's array of social problems: social inequality; poverty; child abuse; health and sickness, and the purported breakdown of communities.

■ History and development of the welfare state: the growth of collectivism

Industrial capitalism as an economic system became most in evidence during the nineteenth century. Urban deprivation and squalor in the UK's major cities were uncomfortably transparent. In an attempt to manage and control the results, the UK state re-enacted the long-standing Poor Laws to locate those best able to work, so as to oil the wheels of the laissez-faire market system. Reforms were instituted to ameliorate the social outcomes of untrammelled competition. 'Public Health' appeared on the government agenda (and was vigorously pursued by such notable reform advocates as the Utilitarian Jeremy Bentham). The stimulus for reform derived in part from middle-class anxieties that putrid environmental conditions would be literally transported over to their own adjacent neighbourhoods. Elementary education for all was also introduced. Such policies constituted fragmentary, minimal state intervention to support private industrial production for profit, rather than the working-class labour force (Dean 2006). On the other hand, the beginnings of a collective consciousness appeared, alongside the development of welfare liberalism, the growth of the labour movement, the emergence of a British Labour Party and the accompanying activities and writings of the Fabians.

While social policy and the growth of collectivism was to be dominated in the first quarter of the twentieth century by the flourishing of social democratic ideas, one should not underestimate the role of the Liberal Party in the development of state social policy. The Liberal Government preceding the First World War achieved undisputed radical reform of state welfare. Lloyd-George's 1911 National Insurance Act advanced the principle of insurance as a state responsibility. School meals for malnourished children became a feature of early education – 1906 Education (Provision of Meals) Act, while the Old Age Pensions Act 1908 provided 25 pence per week for the over-70s, worth some £16 at 1999 prices (Lund 2002). Contributing to this push towards a state social policy were the Fabians and in particular the involvement of intellectuals Sydney and Beatrice Webb in the

1909 Royal Commission on the Poor Laws and the Relief of Distress (Alcock 2008). The new Labour Party, formed in 1906, pressurised the Liberals in 1907 as a riposte to unemployment with a bill over the workers' 'right to work', which was refuted by a liberal philosophy still clinging to the notion of the supremacy of market freedoms (Lund 2002).

However, the First World War destroyed any remnants of laissez-faire liberal beliefs, rejected as a realistic panacea for solving the periodic crises of capitalism. The enormous losses of men in the French trenches wreaked havoc upon the families left. Eventually, unemployment soared to mass proportions in the 1920s with worldwide depression.

The Depression culminated in the Second World War and the ubiquitous wholesale destruction of cities, homes and people across Europe. It had become doubly apparent that total destruction of a society's social fabric could not be rectified by private and voluntary enterprise. A renewed, heigh-tened role of the state in capitalism was required, a recognition articulated by the economist J.M. Keynes (1936) in his *General Theory of Employment, Interest and Money*, advocating government spending as the collectivist role for remedying widespread unemployment. This perspective exerted a huge influence on the social conditions of the time. Along similar lines, Sir William Beveridge's wartime (1942) 'Report on social insurance and allied schemes' acted as a beacon for what was to become the postwar **welfare state**.

Beveridge's seminal work was built upon a social democratic political philosophy of meeting human wants and basic needs, in an effort to eliminate what he termed the five giants of Want, Ignorance, Squalor, Disease and Idleness. His report advocated a social security system of flat-rate contributions and benefits; a national minimum standard of living, and established the idea of social care from the 'cradle to the grave'.

William Beveridge
Source: Alamy Images / Pictorial Press Ltd

Angela Eagle, Labour Minister, Pensions
Source: Press Association Images/© The Labour Party

The 1945 socialist government (the most radical Labour administration of the century) and the resultant comprehensive welfare state founded on Beveridgean principles, politically defined the immediate postwar period in the UK. Under Prime Minister Clement Attlee, Labour created the five policy giants of the welfare state (Timmins 2001): the National Health Service; free education for all; a comprehensive insurance and social security system; and a major programme of decent quality council housing. The overarching political perspective was social democratic, and culminated in the widening of citizenship: state welfare as citizenship rights (Marshall 1963).

The 1944 Education Act, in fact introduced by R.A.B. Butler, a Conservative Minister in the wartime cross-party coalition government, but supported by Labour and Liberal, brought in compulsory schooling, assembled a tripartite system of secondary modern, technical and grammar schools, and expedited the unprecedented possibility for pupils from low-income families to progress on to university with financial support from government.

The 1946 NHS Act brought into being the first comprehensive health service free at the point of consumption, and GPs under a national umbrella (although private practice was allowed to continue). The 1946 National Insurance Act, extended pensions to all of retirement age (65 for men; 60 for women). The National Assistance Act, 1948, introduced a scheme of assistance for those who completely fell outside of the net for insurance, such as sick, disabled or old people not qualifying for a pension. Responsibility for this cash help was taken over from local government by central government. The former became responsible for the new set of personal and social services for both adults and children. Under the 1948 Children Act, local authorities were invested with duties to advance the interests and opportunities of all children in public care (Lund 2002). With the 1949 Housing Act, local authorities' significance and the quality of public sector housing were enhanced, along with the promotion of 'social mix'. The government achieved high levels of building output, once more due to the energies and determination of Aneurin Bevan, now in charge of housing. But, it is argued by Cole and Furbey (1994), the universal principle assumed in other social welfare fields was absent in housing, where acquiescence to the private sector predominated. Nevertheless, by the late 1960s high-rise tower blocs transformed some of Europe's worst areas of slum housing in UK cities, most under Labour control.

Was there a real consensus galvanising the major political parties around the issue of postwar state welfare services? Considerable evidence points to a broadly shared social democratic perspective. The capitalist class had itself faced destruction in the interwar years; the resultant widespread poverty and misery stemming from economic collapse led to the shaping of a collective conscience, and an ostensible recognition among Conservatives and employers, as well as by Labour, of the central place of the state in civil society and of the progressiveness of the Keynesian and Beveridge principles. Those situated on the radical right, however, treated the consensus as real but misguided.

■ Social policy 1951–1975

During the years from the 1950s, with the interchange of Labour and Conservative governments, approaches to the welfare state were on the whole continuous until the mid-1970s – more consensus than conflict (Sullivan 1992), with increasing expenditure on social security; less agreement on comprehensive schooling; both Conservative and Labour overseeing the expansion of further and higher education and teacher training. The major political parties subscribed to the idea of a mixed economy NHS (in which private consultants operated within the hospitals) but with final state control. However, the general ebullience in state welfare spending was muted by the 1970s. A fundamental and accelerated restructuring of capital in the British economy, commenced in the 1960s in response to heavy international competition, soon produced its impact upon social expenditure. Serious inflation now accompanied rising unemployment: clearly, Keynesian principles were no longer effective. The International Monetary Fund (IMF) demanded huge reductions in public spending and public sector pay as the price for its loans to the government (Glyn and Sutcliffe 1972).

Ironically, as poverty, unemployment and economic inequalities persisted, the institution of the welfare state itself came under attack from both the political left and feminists (for promoting the capitalists' interests, and launching a benefits system which discriminated against women) and the political right (viewing the welfare state as wasteful and encouraging idleness). By 1979, the New Right felt ready to embark upon dismantling the traditional welfare state.

■ Social policy under the Conservatives: Thatcher and the New Right

UK Social policy, as with just about every other feature of the political environment, underwent a further revolutionary upheaval in the late 1970s, with a palpable ideological veer to the right. Basically, as far as the new perspectives towards social welfare were concerned, these were best characterised by Prime Minister Margaret Thatcher's early 'soundbite': 'There's no such thing as society.' This overttly individualistic worldview was an unequivocal reaction to the social democratic and arguably consensual state which had driven social policy from the 1940s to the 1970s: a total rejection of the implicit egalitarianism of the postwar welfare state and its collectivist ethos. The New Right government, elected in 1979, was suspicious of the state support in the social

sphere (although less so in the arena of defence and policing), drawing its legitimacy from the theories of market economists Friedrich Hayek (1944: *Road to Serfdom*) and Milton Friedman (1980: *Free to Choose*). The Thatcher policies towards social and economic welfare services revolved around marketisation and privatisation of amenities like social care, health and council housing.

The Thatcher social reforms

Employment policy

The Conservative government employment policies of the 1980s hinged upon deregulation, flexibility of labour markets, and enabling the market to work freely. Unemployment levels, already high due to the rapid restructuring of the UK's ageing industries, soared by dint of the government's 'lame duck' policies which pressed for company and factory closures. Social security benefits were only offered for six, instead of twelve months. More state attention was paid to youth unemployment with programmes such as YTS (Youth Training Scheme), and YOP (Youth Opportunities Programme). Yet these policies failed to deal with hidden unemployment among vulnerable groups, for example, ethnic minorities. Nor did they steer recipients into full-time jobs (Alcock 2008).

Health policy

Health represented the archetype of the New Right's market-orientated politics, although by her second term, Thatcher's original plans to virtually replace the NHS by private provision were shelved. The Conservatives' health policy consisted in redirecting the basis of health provision to private practice and insurance; the introduction of internal markets and competition *within* the NHS; contracting for services; and managerialism. This set of policies was eventually incorporated into the 1990 NHS and Community Care Act. The whole process, for both health and community care, had been orchestrated by Sir Roy Griffiths, imported by the Conservatives from the world of business and retailing. The reforms entailed the separation of purchasing and providing health services, so as to stimulate competition; the creation of NHS Health Trusts, self-financing from marketing their own services; and GPs becoming fund-holding practices. A new managerialist philosophy, coupled with the precept of 'consumer choice', underpinned the proposals, which implied the extended (and questionable) use of business methods in medical and nursing care in the drive for economic efficiency and lower costs (Cowen 1999).

Social and community care policy

New Right policies for social care were implemented in parallel with their health policies, and indeed the interconnections and levels of collaboration were enforced by the NHS and Community Care Act 1990. Notwithstanding, the traditional conflicts between the different 'cultures' of health and social care authorities accompanying the unavoidable delineation of the respective budgets, have tended to re-emerge. During their period of government, the Conservatives basically shifted the structures of service provision for disabled persons, incapacitated persons, and people suffering mental illness, from the public to the private and independent sectors, and transferred collective responsibilities to the local authority. Again, Griffiths was instrumental in deflecting the operation of social care services into the cauldren of market competition. Mental health provision was 'deinstitutionalised' through closure of the UK's giant mental hospitals and replaced by 'family' care (usually by women) in the community. General managers were increasingly brought in to oversee social services departments, while social work professionals found costing exercises were outweighing face-to-face contact with clients, with severe consequences particularly for child care services provision. Another integral part of the planned transition from public social care to community care was the pivotal expansion of the voluntary sector and its related responsibilities (an onerous burden, given the paucity of a remunerated, properly trained labour force).

Education policy

When the Conservatives had been in opposition during the 1970s, the privatising of education based on the ideas of the right-wing 'Black Papers' pressure group had served as a key plank in their manifesto. Once in power, their 1988 Education Reform Act proved as radical as its 1944 predecessor. Its goal was to reinforce hierarchical schooling by subjecting it to market forces in addition to central government control. As with the health reforms, consumer choice

and managerialism provided the driving force. First, the Act created a national curriculum and a rubric for standard assessment targets (SATs) in all state schools. Second, the legislation instituted local management of schools (LMS), meaning delegated budgets and professional managers, severe limitations on LEA functions and the weakening of teachers' representation, whereas delegating increased powers to the schools, the heads and the governing bodies. Third, city technology colleges and grant-maintained schools were introduced, all operating independently of local authorities (Chitty 1992). The New Right transposed its overarching managerialist and consumerist agenda onto educational policy, creating problems of highly stressful testing for young children, a de facto lack of choice for many parents, and accumulating workloads among teaching staff, intensified by the new formally published directly competitive, school league tables.

The demise of council housing

UK housing policy experienced a tectonic shift under the New Right Conservatives. Within a decade, under the stimulus of the iconic 1980 Housing Act, a huge programme of privatisation in the housing field transformed the UK landscape. The size of the council housing stock was drastically reduced and owner-occupation correspondingly increased. The government sharply curtailed capital spending by local authorities, and greatly reduced housing subsidies. It redefined the roles of local authority housing departments which became managers of the local housing stock. For example, the 1980 Housing Act facilitated mass sales of council houses and flats to tenants at huge discounts under the 'Right to Buy'. More than one million properties were sold by new towns and local authorities up to 1986 – exceeding one-sixth of the whole public housing stock (Forrest and Murie 1991; Cole and Furbey 1994).

During its second term of office the Thatcher Government introduced the 1988 Housing Act, which directed the transference of council properties by tenants into the ownership and management of private management companies (Sullivan 1994). Due to this Act and the 1989 Housing Act, so many dwellings had been transferred to housing associations that the proportion of dwellings rented from local councils had plummeted to 17 per cent; the remaining local authority stock was becoming a 'ghetto' for low income families (Lund 2005).

■ Social policy under New Labour

A lively debate in the early years of New Labour was, as noted previously, the extent to which Prime Minister Blair's claims to travelling a 'third way' between socialism and pro-capitalism were justified. Below, we explore whether New Labour's strategies for social policy shadowed those of the New Right.

Social policy

Employment policy under New Labour

New Labour's position on employment in the UK, known as the 'New Deal' or 'Welfare-to-work' strategy, was intrinsic to its general approach to welfare, and especially towards those who have relied upon the benefits system for income. It entailed a 'New Deal for Lone Parents' comprising advice, training and childcare, for steering them into the jobs' market; a compulsory New Deal programme for unemployed under-25s; a compulsory programme for 25-plus and unemployed, and work-based training for 16–18 year-olds without a job or not in full-time education. The training programmes covered a wide range of support. Receipt of benefits depends upon participation, aligned with New Labour's emphasis upon the recognition of citizen responsibilities in exchange for citizen rights (Bryson 2005). Many of the measures shadowed the 1996 US legislation on work opportunities (Deacon 2002), although in addition, New Labour inaugurated a statutory minimum wage.

Albeit the case that many people were moved off the benefits list, the 'New Deal' was less successful in securing longer-term jobs for them. The difficulties multiplied with the widening of the target groups to encompass lone parents, sick and disabled persons (Bryson 2005), and indeed the 2008/09 recession cast doubt on the adequacy of the programme for dealing with mass unemployment.

The new social welfare and managerialism

While it is debatable whether New Labour really was ploughing a third way, the continuities from the New Right have been irrefutable. This is certainly the case in the application of business models to welfare services. One might argue that the reconstruction of welfare and the welfare state was augmented by New Labour's vigorous managerialism, and its related public sector 'modernisation' programme. The reorganisation of the welfare state under New Labour operated on three fronts: producing 'mixed economies' of welfare involving the public, private and voluntary sectors; the extensive use of markets or quasi-markets in service provision, including areas such as health and social care which had not previously experienced them; and the changing organisational forms of government (quasi-government) for directing social services spending (Clarke *et al.* 2000).

The health service under New Labour

New Labour comprehensively restructured the traditional NHS, focusing on management and efficiency (the Thatcher 'continuum'), but devoting more attention than the Conservatives to performance and state monitoring. Essentially, the application of more efficient management throughout the public services aimed at the achievement of increased service provision at lower cost. An element of this managerialist strategy entailed the forging of partnership between the NHS and other health-related organisations, through the creation of Primary Care Groups, NHS trusts and the launching of clinical governance with the national watchdog NICE (National Institute for Clinical Excellence) (Poole 2000).

During the New Labour years, patient choice figured as a continuing strand of UK health policy users' orientation, although the strength of the providers' enthusiasm was uneven between the constituent nations of the United Kingdom. Tensions survived in the partnerships, while the strategy of cost effectiveness (Peckham 2007) came into question when Prime Minister Gordon Brown announced £2 billion extra for the NHS following crises of underfunding and under-resourcing in the hospitals and regular problems for patients in obtaining speedy appointments with the GP.

Personal social services under New Labour

The social services furnish an added example of the protraction of New Right managerialism into the 1990s and the first decade of the twenty-first century, mixed with New Labour's moral communitarianism, and the promotion of decentralisation. Indeed, the early espousal of communitarianism developed hand-in-hand with the decentralisation of social services, while extending centralised control by the formation of national monitoring agencies such as the Audit Commission and the Social Services Inspectorate.

Group of people outside a Job Centre
Source: Getty Images/Cart de Souza/AFP

In its transparent Thatcherist distrust of the professions, New Labour's social policy distanced itself from Old Labour (Johnson 1999). One may trace a continuity from the NHS and Community Care Act 1990 to the privatisation of local authority-based social services and the utilisation of social voluntary organisations and associations.

The 1998 White Paper 'Modernising Social Services' reflected New Labour's main principles for the public sector, coordinated by professional

Group of older people in conversation
Source: Alamy Images/Ellen Isaacs

managers. This meant a drive for *performance* in the social services through measures such as 'best value'; the overseeing of standards, via the regulatory bodies; the growing application of the notion of consumers in a marketplace to user involvement in service provision; and the concept of 'accountability' (Langan 2000). With the widening concern over matters of childcare, the paper 'Every Child Matters', 2003, and the 2006 Child Care Act heralded joint working between education, health and social services by the formation of local Children's Trusts (Alcock 2008).

Long-term care for elderly people and associated escalating costs has remained a controversial subject, given the escalating longevity of UK citizens. Indeed, New Labour had already rejected the recommendations of the Royal Commission on the Funding of Long-term Care for it to be financed out of general taxation (Alcock *et al.* 2008). The Wanless Report (2006) estimated a cost of £31 billion by 2026, portending momentous decisions

ahead for policy makers, politicians and users (Alcock 2008).

Social security and reforms under New Labour

Again, in its social security strategy, New Labour claimed to negotiate a third way between Old Labour and the New Right, yet prioritising work as opposed to benefits. New Labour's commitment was to maintain the policies of the New Right for affordable social security, actively encouraging participation in the workforce. On the other hand, New Labour produced a series of policies targeting those deemed to be socially excluded, including the setting up of a governmental Social Exclusion Unit, and the SureStart initiatives aimed at Education, Health and Employment Zones in areas of poverty (Hewitt 1999).

In 2006, New Labour introduced a set of social security reforms covering child support, pensions and out-of-work benefits. Future increases in the state pension have been tied to earnings and not just to price inflation; the state pension age will gradually increase, and only 30 rather than 44 years of contributions will be required by retirees. The child support system underwent a total overhaul, including a dismantling of the ineffective Child Support Agency, tougher measures for absent parents reneging on their financial responsibilities for their children; the promotion of parental responsibility, and an altogether more simplified system. Higher state pensions, it may be argued, do constitute a break from the past – both from Old Labour and Conservative; yet child maintenance levels were likely to remain inadequate (McKay 2007).

Housing policy under New Labour

In its earlier period of office (1997–2001), New Labour's treatment of housing was unequivocally more one of consistency with the Thatcher years than of any change of direction. Despite attempts to modify the 'Right to Buy' programme, the volume of sales did not fall until 2005. The period after 2001 was marked by a more productive approach, with devolution in Wales, Scotland and Northern Ireland encouraging more house building there, besides city revitalisation schemes in England.

Nevertheless, affordable home ownership remained a priority: a number of government schemes and packages were made available (for social housing tenants) to allow diverse groups access to home ownership by various types of loans and part-ownership schemes. Targets for increasing affordable housing in England were advanced from 70,000 to 120,000 per year. Clearly, despite privatisation and demunicipalisation, New Labour continued to intervene in the arena of housing provision, although the ownership of housing assets figured more prominently in New Labour's 'New Welfare State': housing assets were tethered to the market more than ever (Murie 2007). With the marked upsurge in buy-to-let properties, the housing system was inadvertently spiralling towards financial chaos.

In spite of a New Labour 'rough sleepers' initiative, growth in numbers of statutory homeless people mirrored house price inflation (Lund 2005). The average price of a house climbed from £70,000 in 1997 to £195,000 in 2007 (Alcock *et al.* 2008) and social housing remained as the 'residual' housing sector. Meanwhile, the UK requires an extra 2 million houses by 2016 (Alcock *et al.* 2008).

Education policy under New Labour

In 1997 the incoming Labour Prime Minister Blair pronounced 'education, education, education' as *the* leading social policy. Education policies drew special attention to the basic skills of numeracy and literacy, and to the project of 'lifelong learning'. This reflected an evident departure from previous Conservative government policies. However, New Labour failed to deliver a real challenge to the Tories' pre-occupation with standards, performance, measurement and testing (Bochel 2005). School league tables and OFSTED inspections proliferated, irrespective of persistent and widespread work-related stress and illness among primary and secondary school teachers. Labour also kept the model of an array of schools, including trust schools, and the

David Lammy, Labour Minister, Higher Education
Source: Alamy Images/Jack Sullivan

marginalisation of Local Education Authorities. The diminution of teacher representation on governing bodies was equalled by the growth of parent power and the additional creation of Academies free from LEA authority. All reinforced, indeed magnified Conservative education policies. New Labour's modernising agenda of managerialism orchestrated its education policies, encompassing numerous state intervention measures scarcely countenanced by the New Right (Fergusson 2000). Yet further market-style provision of schooling characterised New Labour's education policy after 2005: trust schools might possess their own assets and develop their own capital contracts. In the spirit of its 'widening participation' programme, New Labour set itself a target of increasing student numbers in universities and colleges of higher education by 50 per cent, to be funded outside of national taxation. The resulting rise of top-up fees on the basis of private provision meant a compete turnaround from the postwar Old Labour philosophy of free further and higher education for families on ordinary incomes. The new policy allowed universities to charge their own fees in 2008, re-awakening Old Labour fears that the higher education system's structures (whereby the older 'Russell Group' universities form an expensive 'top tier') were again simply reproducing UK social class differences. Significantly the Scottish universities initially adopted a stance *against* the introduction of privately funded fees (*THE* 2008, 2009).

BOX 23.1   International social policy and the UK

One expanding area of social policy as a discipline in recent years is the comparison of patterns and 'performance' in different economies, and the extent to which citizens enjoy access to state resources. A seminal study of the late 1990s is Esping-Andersen's *Three Worlds of Welfare Capitalism*. This presented three welfare state models: the social democratic state; the corporatist state, and the liberal state, according to the extent of state involvement in welfare protection. The UK, displaying higher levels of inequality, came under the market-orientated, liberal category. The Scandinavian economies were classified as 'social democratic', evincing higher levels of equality. The social democratic states also achieved the highest economic and employment growth rates. More recently, other categorisations noted by Giddens (2007) have included the Mediterranean economies as a group and those nations of the former Communist bloc now rapidly industrialising. However, the global nature of capitalist competition has altered the picture over the past 25 years, so that national state welfare strategies, incorporating cutbacks in social expenditure, the marketisation and privatisation of social and health care facilities, and managerialist practices in public services, have all tended to converge (Esping-Andersen, 1996; Flynn, 2002).

Figure 23.1 shows the proportion of social protection expenditure in the UK, in 2006, was close to the European Union average of 27.5 per cent, although lagging behind the Scandinavian economies and France; all in fact ranged between 25 and 31 per cent.

Similarly, from Figure 23.2 the annual spending on educational institutions per pupil for the UK in 2004 was close to the European Union average of some 6,000 euros, while clearly exceeded by the Scandinavian nations (7,000 euros), although considerably above a poorer Mediterranean country such as Portugal (4,250 euros).

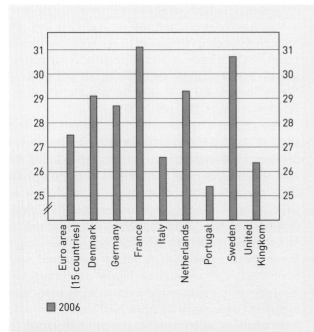

Figure 23.1 Total expenditure on social protection, per cent of GDP, 2006
Note: Social protection embraces social benefits in cash or kind, to reduce the burden of risk and need, plus administration costs of the scheme.
Source: Eurostat, 2009

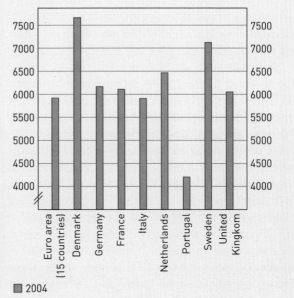

Figure 23.2 Annual expenditure on public and private educational institutions per pupil/student, in Euros 2004 (By level of education [PPS based on full-time equivalents])
Source: Eurostat, 2009

■ Contemporary issues

Child protection

Child protection is a perennial policy issue of the present century. The significant Children and Young Person's Act 1969 vested local authorities with responsibility for children deemed by the courts to be no longer subject to parental control, while the Children Act 1989, under the Conservative government, had emphasised the rights of children. But in 2001, the case of Victoria Climbie's brutal physical abuse and subsequent murder by her aunt was a resounding indictment of child care policy. New Labour introduced the Children's Act 2004 which directed local authorities to set up children's and young persons' departments, integrated with the local education departments. Nevertheless, details were revealed of yet another horrific case, the death of Baby Peter in Haringey, London. The baby, aged 17 months, died from abuse by his mother, her boyfriend and her lodger, in spite of 60 visits from social workers, doctors and police, all of whom had failed to notice the child's multiple injuries. The publicity led to mass accusations of state irresponsibility and statutory incompetence. Media attacks, largely directed at social workers, were furious and the politicians, cognisant of public anger, acted accordingly. The Director of Haringey Social services, Sharon Shoesmith, followed by others was dismissed from her post. However, in reply, voices from the profession pointed to unacceptable working conditions, namely under-staffing, managerialist and performative targets inappropriately applied to social services, and the time-consuming IT recording tasks, which were diverting valuable hours away from face-to-face contact with clients. (PSW November 2008; Lindsay 2009; Barnes 2009).

Surestart

However, New Labour professed considerable success in the very area of family policy and disadvantaged children with a major investment in its 'Surestart' joint departmental initiative setting up a host of Children's Centres (targeting 2,500 by 2008 and 3,500 by 2010). The Centres and the 'Surestart' project, modelled on US President L.B. Johnson's flagship Head Start programme of the 1960s, promoted parental involvement in the scheme; centres made available services like IT training and job-related skills training to parents intent on entering the job market.

'Surestart', though, was not without its critics. Toynbee and Walker (2008), on the whole enthusiastic, also observe a general lack of awareness around the programme, and the poor funding: the public case for social spending and the necessary redistributive taxes is only made half-heartedly in the UK. In the light of the shocking lack of pre-school provision in the UK, compared with a number of other countries, 'Surestart' represented a distinct improvement, yet child care in the UK, where pre-school provision is still part time, remains under-funded relative to, for example, other European Union nations. The UK spends 0.5 per cent of GDP on under-fives, while France spends twice as much, and Denmark four times as much (Toynbee and Walker 2008).

The Conservative Party Opposition under David Cameron was negative towards the scheme on the grounds of cost and on its belief that the state should not intervene in child care. Furthermore, as with various social policy activities, funding was endangered by the 2008/09 financial crisis.

Economic recession and its impact on social policy

The global recession of 2008/09, beginning in the United States, with the drastically curtailed supply of mortgages, affected the UK housing situation first. Further, the collapse of various insurance and pension corporations resulted in a sizable contraction of corporate contributions to employee pensions, in the wake of £ billions lost in the value of pension funds; public sector schemes faced huge deficits

exceeding hundreds of £billions (*Observer*: 12 April 2009). Also affecting the older population was the mounting shortage of places in financially unviable private care homes: a social services departments' survey found that by early 2009, 15 per cent of homes had closed in English local authority localities (*Guardian*: 10 April 2009).

The Labour Government's 2009 budget, the first since the global capitalist collapse, was a pointer to the expected impacts on welfare expenditure far into the next decade, including *actual* cuts from 2011 onwards. £2.3 billion out of £3.62 billion in expenditure cutbacks, were ear-marked for health services: by April 2011, the NHS was expected to find this extra sum in efficiency savings. The King's Fund (health policy 'think tank') speculated that after 2011, there would be hardly any growth in funding for the NHS, whichever political party was in power (*Guardian*: 24 April 2009).

In addition, £650 million cuts were allocated to children, schools and families. Speculations with respect to the future of 'Surestart' centres emphasised the vulnerability of the entire programme in the event of an incoming government uncommitted to their survival, especially as the running costs of the 3,500 centres would reach £1.3 billion by 2011 (*Guardian*: 24 April 2009). Education as a sector was to find £1 billion in savings on top of its diminished budgets. The £500 million advanced for building social housing was still considered inadequate for meeting the huge shortfall in housing supply by housing experts anticipating a massive rise in numbers on the waiting lists for social housing (*Guardian*: 23 April 2009). Despite the government's long-term trajectory planned for cuts in services, however, the Conservative opposition was intent on earlier and more extensive real expenditure cutbacks.

BOX 23.2   BRITAIN IN CONTEXT

Inequality and social policy

Numerous social commentators, most famously economist W.W. Rostow (1960) have long contended that economic growth 'trickles down' to the population at large, regardless of how wealth and incomes are distributed across an economy. Hence, one might surmise that enhanced wealth

per se is assuredly positive for minimising social problems (through reducing poverty levels) and maximising the effectiveness of social policy. Beneficiaries of substantial wealth may be construed as having no causal connection with the levels of poverty in the same society. Conservatives

Table 23.1 Distribution of personal marketable wealth 1986–2003

	Share of top:				
	1%	**5%**	**10%**	**25%**	**50%**
1986	18	36	50	73	90
1991	17	35	47	71	92
1996	20	40	52	74	93
2001	22	42	54	72	94
2003	21	40	53	72	93

Source: HMRC (2006); Hills, Sefton, Stewart (2009)

do not interpret part of their political remit as removing barriers to equality, while New Labour applied few constraints over the fortunes of the UK's super-rich (the *Sunday Times*' annual wealth surveys seem to sustain such an observation: its 2009 edition recorded Lakshmi Mittal and Family's wealth at £10,800 million *after* the recession had eliminated a sizable proportion of their holdings; Roman Abramovich still owned £7,000 million; the Duke of Westminster, £6,500 million; Simon Keswick and Family, £570 million) (*Sunday Times* 2009).

From 1991 to 2003 the proportion of personal marketable wealth of the top 1 per cent grew from 17 per cent to 21 per cent; the top 10 per cent's share grew from 47 per cent to 53 per cent (see Table 23.1). Although income distribution was somewhat more even in the early period, it was again more unequal during the second term, with incomes skewed even further towards the top 1 per cent (Hills *et al*. 2009: Figure 1, p. 358). Removal of inequalities in terms of outcomes was paramount for neither Conservative nor Labour regimes through the 1990s to the end of the 2000s. On the contrary, the permanent deregulation of financial corporate dealing bolstered New Labour's trade and business policy.

Yet two major empirical studies by Richard Wilkinson have scrupulously documented how societies with high levels of equality produce healthier populations and fewer social problems. Wilkinson's *Unhealthy Societies: The afflictions of inequality* (1996) investigated the impact of inequal-ity upon the levels of health and sickness within a society. The second study, *The Spirit Level* (2009, with Kate Pickett), augmented the analysis to encompass a range of social ills. The degree of affluence or wealth in a society, they found, was *not* the prime determinant of physical or social health problems. Instead, levels of inequality obtaining within a society were much more significant, exerting such dire social and psychological con-sequences that: '. . . modern societies are, despite their affluence, social failures' (Wilkinson and Pickett 2009: 18). And the negative repercussions pervade a whole society:

(The) pressures of inequality and of waiting to keep up are not confined to a small minority who are poor. Instead the effects are widespread in the population.
Wilkinson and Pickett (2009: 25–6)

This occurs through the rise in anxiety, decline in self-esteem, the adversities of social status and their associated shame, with calculable results:

- The fragmentation of community life, decline in trust, and lowering of women's status.
- The rise in incidence of mental illness in the UK.
- Anxiety pertaining to one's position in society produces bodily stress which in turn bears upon life expectancy.
- Performance and behaviour in educational tasks are influenced by how we are perceived. 'When we expect to be viewed as inferior, our abilities seem to be diminished' (Wilkinson and Pickett 2009: 113).
- Violence has become more prominent as competitive behaviour and aggression, con-fronting perceived inequities, has escalated. For example, widening income differentials during the 1980s led to an upsurge in the UK homicide rate.
- Wider inequalities exacerbate social prejudice (downwards), since social status is defended by the deployment of stigma and the demonstra-tion of superiority to those 'beneath' one, flat-tening the possibilities of social mobility. With wider inequalities of outcome, 'equal opportu-nity is a significantly more distant prospect' (Wilkinson and Pickett 2009: 169).

Chapter summary

To summarise, social policy and politics are inextricably connected. Our brief history of social policy demonstrated a growing awareness in the nineteenth century of the utility of government for intervening in citizens' social lives. By the first years of the twentieth century, the British welfare state was in its early stages of gestation. By mid-twentieth century, economic collapse, mass unemployment and war had fuelled acceptance of the cardinal necessity of government intervention and support. Hence, the politics of social policy in the post-Second World War years concentrated on shaping the modern welfare state, which for decades served as a paradigm to Western industrial nations. The radical political reaction to the holistic planning of social welfare occurred in two political phases: the new right conservatism of the 1980s and 1990s; followed by New Labour's managerialism of the late 1990s and the new century, in practice a continuum of applied business methods, performance measurement and privatisation, all inducing a steady erosion of welfare statism. The final section drew attention to key contemporary issues which ostensibly have eluded the grasp of party politics: the catastrophies of inadequate child welfare; renewed breakdown of the modern capitalist engine which has fired social expenditure, and the persistence of a disturbing nexus linking the scale of social problems to economic and social inequalities.

Discussion points

■ To what extent are business management models appropriate for running welfare services?

■ Have the political difference between UK Labour and Conservative strategies in social policy now disappeared?

■ Are UK's social problems invariably rooted in economic and social inequalities?

Further reading

For overviews, Dean (2006) presents a readable, concise and discursive panorama of the subject. Hudson, Kuhner, Lowe (2008) is as it says, a short guide with a distinct comparative focus. Lund (2002) deals with discrete areas of government social policies both empirically and critically. Political and ideological perspectives of social policy are covered by Deacon (2002) a useful, up-to-date analysis of contemporary government welfare approaches; Fyves (2008) connects social policies with their underpinning philosophies; and Ferguson, Lavalette and Mooney (2002) which offers a largely Marxist analysis of contemporary social and welfare policies.

From the historical angle, Thane (1996) delivers a thorough analysis of the period 1870–1945, linking welfare policies to political power structures; Lowe (2005) covers developments in the classic welfare state, and then the subsequent threats to its continued existence; Timmins (2001) is a finely grained account of the postwar welfare state in the UK; Deakin (1994) adopts a historical approach to the politics of welfare; Sullivan (1992) traces the modern politics of welfare, analysing conflict and consensus in UK, USA and Sweden.

Regarding Thatcher and the New Right, Sullivan (1994) coolly charts the swing of social policy to the right in the 1980s and 1990s. Contributors to Powell (ed.) (2002) operate a laser beam scrutiny upon New Labour's social policy performance across the board.

Clarke *et al.* (2002) delivers a sharp set of essays capturing the ideological directions of modern social policies.

Specific areas of social policy

Two clear treatments of modern education policy developments are Chitty (2009) and Tomlinson, (2nd edn 2005). Means *et al.* (2008) is seen as the standard work in the field of Personal Social Services and Community Care. Klein (2006) is still a leading authority on the politics of health; Ham (2004) keeps one up-to-date with UK health policy and institutional structures; Wilkinson (1996) consistently questions common wisdom on health, policy and sickness. Malpass (2005) is a key text covering long-term history of housing and current policy issues. Harrison with Davis (2001) construes discriminatory practice as the prime criterion for evaluating housing policy.

Glennerster (2003) is necessary for grasping the financial aspects of state social policy. George and Wilding (2002) is an extremely accessible volume on globalisation and on social policy perspectives. Deacon (2007) is indispensable for understanding global social policy structures and associated political issues; Alcock and Craig (2009) synthesises an up-to-date set of assessments on welfare in the industrialised world. Hills, Sefton and Stewart (eds) (2009) is crucial evidence in the inequalities and social policy debate, utlising a mass of data to assess New Labour's record on poverty and inequality since 1997; cogently reasoned, and drawing together much empirical research, Wilkinson and Pickett (2009) should stand as the seminal work for a good while into the future.

Useful journals in social policy

British Journal of Social Work
Community Care
Critical Social Policy
European Journal of Housing Policy
Global Social Policy
Health Service Journal
Higher Education Policy
Housing
Housing Studies
Journal of Education Policy
Journal of European Social Policy
Journal of Public Health Policy
Journal of Social Administration
Journal of Social Policy
Professional Social Work
Social Policy Review, Social Policy Association (Annual)

Bibliography

Alcock, C., Daly, G., Griggs, E. (2008) *Introducing Social Policy*, 2nd edn (Pearson Education).

Alcock, P. (2008) *Social Policy in Britain*, 3rd edn (Palgrave).

Alcock, P. and Craig, G. (eds) (2009) *International Social Policy: Welfare Regions in the Developed World*, 2nd edn (Palgrave Macmillan).

Barnes, D. (2009) 'Why Blame Achieves Nothing but Regression', *Professional Social Work*, March.

Beveridge, Sir W. (1942) *Report on Social Insurance and Allied Services*, Cmd.6404 (HMSO).

Bochel, H. (2005) 'Education', in H. Bochel, C. Bochel, R. Page, R. Sykes, *Social Policy: Issues and Development* (Pearson Education).

Bryson, A. (2005) 'Working off Welfare', in H. Bochel, C. Bochel, R. Page, R. Sykes, *Social Policy: Issues and Development* (Pearson Education).

Chitty, C. (1992) *The Education System Transformed* (Baseline Books).

Chitty, C. (2009) *Education Policy in Britain*, 2nd edn (Macmillan).

Clarke, J, S. Gewirtz and E. McLaughlin (eds) (2002) *New Managerialism, New Welfare?* (Sage/Open University Press).

Cole, I. and Furbey R. (1994) *The Eclipse of Council Housing* (Routledge).

Cowen, H. (1999) *Community Care, Ideology and Social Policy* (Pearson Education).

Deacon, A. (2002) *Perspectives on Welfare* (Open University Press).

Deacon, B. (2007) *Global Social Policy and Governance* (Sage).

Deakin, N. (1994) *Politics of Welfare* (Harvester Wheatsheaf).

Dean, H. (2006) *Social Policy* (Polity).

Esping-Andersen, G. (1990) *The Three Worlds of Welfare Capitalism* (Polity).

Esping-Andersen, G. (ed.) (1996) *Welfare States in Transition: National Adaptations in Global Economies* (Sage).

Ferguson, I., Lavalette, M. and Mooney, G. (2002) *Rethinking Welfare: A Critical Perspective* (Sage).

Fergusson, R. (2000) 'Modernising Managerialism in Education', in (eds) J. Clarke, S. Gewirtz and E. McLaughlin, *New Managerialism, New Welfare?* (Sage/Open University Press).

Flynn, N. (2002) 'Managerialism and Public Services: Some International Trends', in (eds) J. Clarke, S. Gewirtz and E. McLaughlin, *New Managerialism, New Welfare?* (Sage/Open University Press).

▶

Forrest, R. and Murie, A. (1991) *Selling The Welfare State: The Privatisation of Public Housing* (Routledge).

Friedman, M. and Friedman, R. (1980) *Free to Choose: A Personal Statement* (Harcourt).

Fyves, A. (2008) *Political and Philosophical Debates in Welfare* (Palgrave Macmillan).

George, V. and Wilding, P. (2002) *Globalization and Human Welfare* (Palgrave).

Giddens, A. (2007) *Europe in the Golden Age* (Polity).

Glennerster, H. (2003) *Understanding the Finance of Welfare: What Welfare Costs and How to Pay for It* (Policy Press).

Glyn, A. and Sutcliffe, B. (1972) *British Capitalism, Workers and the Profits Squeeze* (Penguin).

Guardian (2009) 10 April.

Guardian (2009) 23 April.

Guardian (2009) 24 April.

Ham, C. (2004) *Health Policy in Britain*, 5th edn (Palgrave).

Harrison, M. with Davis, C. (2001) *Housing, Social Policy and Difference: Disabilty, ethnicity, gender and housing* (Policy Press).

Hayek, F. (1944) *Road to Serfdom* (Routledge).

Hewitt, M. (1999) 'New Labour and Social Security', in M. Powell (ed.) *New Labour, New Welfare State? The 'Third Way' in British Social Policy* (Policy Press).

Hills, J., Sefton, T. and Stewart, K. (eds) (2009) *Towards a More Equal Society?: Poverty, Inequality and Policy Since 1997* (Policy Press).

HMRC (2006) *Distribution of Personal Marketable Wealth 1986–2003* (HM Revenue and Customs).

Hudson, J., Kuhner, S. and Lowe, S. (2008) *The Short Guide to Social Policy* (Policy Press).

Johnson, N. (1999) 'The Personal Social Services and Community Care', in M. Powell (ed.) *New Labour, New Welfare State?: The 'Third Way' in British Social Policy* (Policy Press).

Keynes, J.M. (1936) *General Theory of Employment, Interest and Money* (Macmillan).

Klein, R. (2006) *The New Politics of the NHS*, 5th edn (Radcliffe Publishing).

Labour Government (1998) *Modernising Social Services* (The Stationery Office).

Langan, M. (2000) 'Social Services: Managing the Third Way', in (eds) J. Clarke, S. Gewirtz and E. McLaughlin, *New Managerialism, New Welfare?* (Sage/Open University Press).

Lindsay, J. (2009) 'The Refusal to Accept the Limits of What we can do', *Professional Social Work*, March.

Lowe, R. (2005) *The Welfare State in Britain Since 1945*, 3rd edn (Palgrave Macmillan).

Lund, B. (2002) *Understanding State Welfare: Social Justice or Social Exclusion?* (Sage).

Lund, B. (2005) 'Housing Policy', in H. Bochel, C. Bochel, R. Page, R. Sykes, *Social Policy: Issues and Developments* (Pearson Education).

Malpass, P. (2005) *Housing and the Welfare State: The Development of Housing Policy in Britain* (Palgrave Macmillan).

Marshall, T.H. (1963 (1950)) 'Citizenship and Social Class', in *Sociology at the Crossroads and Other Essays* (Heinemann).

McKay, S. (2007) 'Laying New Foundations? Social Security Reform in 2006', *Social Policy Review 19* (Policy Press).

Means, R., Richards, S. and Smith, R. (2008) *Community Care*, 4th edn (Palgrave).

Murie, A. (2007) 'Housing Policy, Housing Tenure and the Housing Market', *Social Policy Review 19* (Policy Press).

Observer (2009) 12 April.

Peckham, S. (2007) 'One, or four? The National Health Service in 2006', *Social Policy Review 19* (Policy Press).

Poole, L. (2000) 'Health Care: New Labour's NHS', in J. Clarke, S. Gewirtz and E. McLaughlin, *New Managerialism, New Welfare?* (Sage/Open University Press).

Powell, M. (2002) (ed.) *Evaluating New Labour's Welfare Reforms* (Policy Press).

PSW (Professional Social Work) (2008) 'What is John Hemming's Problem?', *3 PSW*, November.

Rostow, W.W. (1960) *The Stages of Economic Growth: A Non-Communist Manifesto* (Cambridge University Press).

Sullivan, M. (1992) *The Politics of Social Policy* (Harvester Wheatsheaf).

Sullivan, M. (1994) *Modern Social Policy* (Harvester Wheatsheaf).

Sunday Times (2009) 'The Rich List', 26 April.

Thane, P. (1996) *Foundations of the Welfare State*, 2nd edn (Longmans).

THE (*Times Higher Education*) (2008/2009) weekly.

Timmins, N. (2001) *The Five Giants: A Biography of the Welfare State* (Fontana).

Tomlinson, S. (2005) *Education in a Post-Welfare Society*, 2nd edn (Open University Press).

Toynbee, P. and Walker, D. (2008) *Unjust Rewards* (Granta).

Wilkinson, R. (1996) *Unhealthy Societies: The Afflictions of Inequality* (Routledge).

Wilkinson, R. and Pickett, K. (2009) *The Spirit Level: Why More Equal Societies Almost Always Do Better* (Allen Lane).

Useful websites

Department of Works and Pensions: www.dwp.gov.uk

National Statistics: www.statistics.gov.uk

New Labour: Social Exclusion Unit:
   www.socialexclusionunit.cabinet-office.gov.uk/seu

Eurostat: www.europa. Eu.int/comm./eurostat

CHAPTER 24
Economic policy

Wyn Grant

Learning objectives

- To identify the nature of economic policy.
- To explain the economic policy-making process.
- To explain shifts over time in the conduct of economic policy.

Introduction

Economic policy has a far broader significance than the technicalities of macroeconomic management suggest. It is at the heart of the central question of politics: who gets what, when, how. Decisions on taxation and the budget make citizens poorer and richer. If the market fails, as happened in the global financial crisis, the consequences can be far reaching for everyone.

■ The nature of economic policy

Economic policy seeks to achieve objectives such as a high rate of growth, a low and stable rate of inflation and high levels of employment. These objectives are important to governments both for their own sake and because they influence their chances of re-election. Some critics would question the desirability of a high rate of economic growth as a primary objective because of its effects on the environment, particularly tackling climate change. They would argue that, in any case, conventional measures of national income such as Gross Domestic Product (GDP) per capita are not a good measure of happiness or well-being.

Governments seek to manage the economy through using a number of tools or *policy instruments*. The mix of policy instruments used varies over time both in response to changes in economic thinking and current economic circumstances. For example, in the 1960s and 1970s prices and incomes policies were a favoured policy instrument because these policies were seen as the best available method of reducing the rate of inflation. In the 1990s and the first decade of the twenty-first century, manipulation of the interest rate became the favoured policy instrument. However, with the onset of the global financial crisis (GFC) from 2007 this policy instrument no longer had the desired effect in terms of stimulating the economy and avoiding deflation. Hence, there was a resort to a new policy instrument, quantitative easing, which involved pumping money into the economy.

Over time it has become more difficult for governments to control what happens in their domestic economies because of a process that is often referred to as globalisation. What happens under globalisation is that economies become integrated with each other. This is particularly relevant in the case of Britain which has always been highly integrated in the global economy. Under globalisation trade tends to grow faster than national input, so that a higher proportion of national production is exported and a higher proportion of consumption is imported.

Foreign investment also grows, leading to a growing presence in the economy of multinational companies which often integrate their production across several countries so that, for example, different parts of a car may be made in different locations before being assembled in one country. Multinational companies need new kinds of internationalised financial services to meet their needs. These in turn may acquire a momentum of their own, creating new and often not well understood forms of finance, for example those based on debt which played an important role in the GFC. These developments would not have been possible to the extent that they have occurred without the development of new instantaneous forms of communication of information based on electronic technology.

As economies become more integrated, shocks transmit more rapidly between them so that a crisis in one country can rapidly spread to others. The Asian financial crisis of 1997 started in Thailand, but rapidly spread to other Asian countries. The GFC started with a crisis in the 'sub-prime' housing market in the United States, i.e., mortgages granted to individuals with poor credit histories whose ability to repay was in question. The grant of mortgages to these individuals had wider repercussions because the loans were re-packaged and sold as debt-based financial instruments. Because of the central position of the US in the world economy, and the fact that other economies had also over-borrowed, the crisis rapidly became a global one.

One response to such a crisis is to try and create new mechanisms to coordinate international economic management such as the G-20 summit held in Britain in the spring of 2009. Countries may also come together to coordinate their economic policies on a regional basis, exemplified by the eurozone within the European Union (EU) which seeks to create a zone of regional economic stability organised around the single currency, the euro. Britain has, however, chosen not to become a member of the eurozone, although it does coordinate some aspects of economic policy with other member states in the EU.

However, the development of these forms of global and regional coordination does not mean that economic policy is no longer made at a national level. In particular, national governments make important decisions about taxation and the budget. These affect the distribution of wealth and income in society and the availability of public services such as health and education. Because Britain still controls its own currency, it can also manipulate the exchange rate as a policy instrument. If the pound falls against other currencies, imports become more expensive, but British exports become cheaper and hence more competitive. In the wake of the GFC, Britain was accused by other EU member states of engaging in a competitive devaluation against the euro, an option not available to member states within the eurozone such as Ireland.

The boundaries of economic policy are not entirely clear or fixed. At the heart of economic policy is the management of what are known as the 'macroeconomic aggregates' such as inflation, employment and growth. However, the success of an economy depends on many other factors than how these macroeconomic aggregates are managed. For example, workers in the economy have to have

the right mix of skills and the capacity to develop new ones. There has to be sufficient investment in new plant and machinery and research and development to discover and develop new products, materials and technologies. In the GFC, the Labour government effectively became involved once more in forms of industrial policy that provided funds for particular firms as it sought to secure the future of the motor industry.

Any policy can potentially affect the economy, e.g., environmental policy, but Box 24.1 identifies the policies that are particularly relevant to the management of the economy. There may be tensions between some of these policies and their objectives. For example, industrial or research and development policy may seek to promote European or national 'champion' firms, while competition policy would seek to restrain them. Regional policy generally favours taking work to the workers, while an active labour market policy would prefer taking steps to ensure that workers can move to where there is work.

All forms of economic policy are invariably influenced by the fact that their success or otherwise may have an influence on a government's political fate. Indeed, this is why there has been a trend to take some economic policy decisions away from politicians, often referred to as *depoliticisation*. As a generalisation, it can be said that electorates

---

BOX 24.1 Areas of policy that are related to economic policy

Competition policy – preventing the emergence of monopolies and cartels and removing barriers to the operation of a competitive free market. It also encompasses the regulation of 'natural monopolies' or public utilities.

Industrial policy – providing assistance to firms or sectors in difficulty.

Research and development policy – ensuring that sufficient research and development is undertaken to sustain a competitive economy and that research results are transmitted into commercial innovations.

Regional policy – promoting and developing the economies of less favoured regions which may, for example, be geographically remote, have poor communications links or outdated industrial structures.

Education policy – ensuring that the economy has available to it a workforce with the right mix of

skills and the capability to enhance them in response to changing needs.

Labour market policy – encompasses what was known as training policy (the transmission of vocational skills), but also seeks to ensure that the workforce is flexible and available for work.

Trade policy – negotiating international trade agreements to open up new markets for domestic production and services, but also to secure greater social justice for the Global South.

Transport policy – ensuring that national transport infrastructure is modern and efficient and does not impose costs on the economy through delays or other problems. Its economic significance has grown with the development of 'just in time' manufacturing and new logistical systems for retailers.

punish governments for poor economic performance, but are less inclined to reward them for good economic performance as, after a while, they tend to take good economic times for granted and focus on other issues.

Decisions on economic policy may be distorted by political considerations. Consider, for example, interventions by governments to support firms or sectors in difficulty which were popular with both Conservative and Labour governments in the 1960s and 1970s and have enjoyed something of a revival in the GFC. This type of policy carries with it a number of risks:

1   It enables multinational companies to play one country off against another to extract funds.

2   It is very difficult to demonstrate 'additionality', i.e. that the additional funds made available lead to investment that would not otherwise occur.

3   It is very difficult for politicians and bureaucrats to pick winners (or 'losers').

4   Often decisions are made on electoral grounds, e.g., the sensitivity of a particular constituency or region.

5   Often investments were replicated in different parts of the country for political reasons when there was no good economic case: steel and aluminium provide good examples in the case of Britain.

6   Large companies were generally favoured over smaller companies.

7   Outdated industrial structures were preserved, hindering modernisation.

Economic policy is highly contested because it is at the heart of the central political question of 'who gets what, when, how'. The machinery of economic policy making is not simply a neutral set of procedures for making decisions. It changes in a way that reflects changing perspectives on policy and fluctuations in the distribution of power within government.

■ The machinery of economic policy

The making of economic policy lies at the very heart of the government machine, what is sometimes referred to as the core executive. It involves some of the most powerful figures in politics, in particular the Prime Minister and **Chancellor of the Exchequer**, and much depends on the relationship between them. It also involves powerful individuals outside the machinery of government, most importantly the Governor of the **Bank of England**.

The Prime Minister

Not all Prime Ministers take an active part in the management of economic policy, despite its electoral importance. They may choose to be less involved in economic policy because they have other priorities, doubt their competence to deal with economic matters or because of the nature of their relationship with the Chancellor. When Tony Blair was Prime Minister, he and Gordon Brown operated what was sometimes referred to as a 'dual monarchy' in which Brown was given considerable authority over wide areas of domestic policy and in particular the management of the economy. It has even been suggested that Brown kept the contents of the budget to himself until the very last minute.

Even so, Blair set the general strategy of economic policy which involved the creation of a social market economy in which economic competition was encouraged and the acquisition of wealth was seen as desirable, but where government would intervene to help the less well off in society, e.g., through tax credits and a minimum wage. Blair also sought to pursue his ambition to make Labour 'the natural party of business', meeting frequently with business leaders.

The Prime Minister–Chancellor relationship

This relationship is at the heart of the economic policy making process. If it starts to break down, as it did between Margaret Thatcher and Nigel Lawson, then the whole stability of the government and certainly its capacity to make economic policy is threatened. The average time in office of Chancellors is tending to lengthen. In part this is because it is recognised that it is politically damaging for a Prime Minister to remove or lose a Chancellor. It also reflects the increased emphasis on stability in the conduct of economic policy. There is unlikely to be a repetition of the Macmillan premiership when there were three Chancellors. John Major was damaged by the necessity to remove Norman Lamont as Chancellor after the exchange rate mechanism crisis. Lamont became a thorn in his side, while

The Bank of England, central to the UK's finance governance, was given independence in 1997 to fix interest rates
Source: Copyright © Angelo Hornak/Corbis

BOX 24.2	Involvement of postwar Prime Ministers in the economy

Prime Minister	Level of involvement
Attlee	Moderate
Churchill	Low
Eden	Low
Macmillan	High
Douglas-Home	Low
Wilson (1)	High
Heath	High
Wilson (2)	Moderate
Callaghan	High
Thatcher	High
Major	Moderate
Blair	Moderate
Brown	High

Source: Copyright © Steve Bell cartoon. From the *Guardian*, 23 September 2008. Reproduced with permission

BOX 24.3	Prime Minister–Chancellor relationships	
	Chancellor as political figure in own right	*Chancellor lacks independent political base*
Harmonious relationship	Chancellor enjoys autonomy and support from PM	Chancellor faithfully executes PM's policies
Difficult relationship	Clashes over policy affect work of government	Leads to resignation or dismissal

Major had to be circumspect in his dealings with Lamont's successor, Ken Clarke.

Leaving aside the special case of Iain Macleod, who died after a few weeks in office, there have now been five postwar administrations who have had the same Chancellor for the whole of their period in office (Churchill/Butler; Home/Maudling; Heath/Barber; Wilson and then Callaghan/Healey; Blair/Brown) and there may well be a sixth (Brown/Darling). It is therefore important to consider how this important and often durable relationship works. It should be noted that a harmonious relationship does not mean that a Prime Minister and Chancellor never disagree, or that they are personal friends, but that they can work effectively together and resolve their differences amicably.

In many ways the ideal relationship is where the Chancellor is a political figure in his own right, can challenge the Prime Minister if necessary, but where the relationship is characterised by mutual respect and trust. In general, the relationship between James Callaghan and Denis Healey in the 1970s fits this pattern.

In contrast, over time, the relationship between Tony Blair and Gordon Brown moved from the top left-hand to the bottom right-hand corner of Box 24.3 as it became more strained. This was not because there were significant ideological differences. Both of them were fully signed up members of the New Labour project But Brown's ambition to become Prime Minister, and Blair's reluctance to leave, placed increasing strains on the relationship which affected the whole conduct of government policy. Brown had a significant base of support in the Parliamentary party and although the idea of moving him to Foreign Secretary was mooted, Blair lacked the political confidence to do it.

The relationship in which the Chancellor acts as a loyal servant and helpmate of the Prime Minister does occur from time to time. Derek Heathcoat-Amory was appointed as Chancellor following the resignation of Peter Thorneycroft over policy. He was entirely without ambition and happy to acquiesce in the policies of the Prime Minister. Margaret Thatcher's first Chancellor, Sir Geoffrey Howe, was also fully signed up to her policies, although ultimately he became alienated from her and was instrumental in her downfall.

Nigel Lawson's relationship with Margaret Thatcher deteriorated over time. He had no ambitions to move beyond the post of Chancellor and had not developed his own support base in Parliament. He came to feel that he was being undermined by Mrs Thatcher and her economic adviser, Sir Alan Walters, and resigned.

The Treasury

One of the reasons why the Chancellor is such an important figure is because of the special position of the Treasury in the British policy making process. **The Treasury** wants a strong Chancellor because it is always concerned that the Prime Minister may give way to the pleas of spending departments, placing the public finances under strain.

The role that the Treasury plays in the policy-making process is rather different from that of equivalent departments in other advanced industrial countries. In many such countries, for example Germany and the United States, the roles of raising revenues, overseeing the financial system and economic stability, and making budgetary decisions are split between two different departments. In Britain these functions are all concentrated in one powerful department. This has led to criticisms that the Treasury is too powerful in economic policy making, that it has been insufficiently concerned with economic performance (particularly of manufacturing industry) and that it has contributed significantly to poor economic performance.

Three decision rules in government underpin the ability of the Treasury to exercise control over the conduct of economic policy. A standing order of the House of Commons which dates back to 1713 prevents an MP proposing a measure which would cost the Treasury money without government consent. A second rule, formalised in 1924, requires that no proposal for additional expenditure can be circulated to the Cabinet before it has been discussed in draft with the Treasury. A third rule, dating from 1884, is that any proposal involving an increase in expenditure or any new service requires Treasury sanction. Harold Wilson, in his second term as Prime Minister, promulgated a new ruling to the effect that Treasury ministers could not be over-ruled on financial matters in Cabinet committees which Wilson described as giving the Treasury 51 per cent of the votes. Appeals could only be made to the full Cabinet if the chair of the Cabinet commit-tee agreed. This arrangement was written into the rules for ministers by Margaret Thatcher when she was Prime Minister.

The prestige of the Treasury and its influence on economic policy has fluctuated considerably over time. Before the Second World War, the Treasury was principally concerned with the 'candle ends' task of balancing the budget and exercising restraint in public expenditure. It was heavily wedded to financial orthodoxy and had no solutions to offer to the depression of the 1930s. Indeed, it was the Bank of England which took a more proactive role in seeking to reorganise and stimulate manufacturing industry.

The position of the Treasury was changed by the publication of Keynes' *General Theory of Interest, Employment and Money* in 1936 and the outbreak of the Second World War which required extensive government intervention in the economy. Keynes served as an adviser to the Treasury and his ideas on how a new recession could be avoided gradually won acceptance, although the Treasury never was (or is) monolithic in its views and some officials clung to the view that the restraint of public expend-iture should be paramount.

The economists in the Economic Section of the Treasury played an important role in disseminating and establishing Keynes' ideas (or rather his ideas as interpreted by his disciples after his untimely

death in 1946). The general view in the civil service was that experts should be on tap rather than on top and there was certainly some scepticism about the input of economists among generalist civil servants who at that time were often recruited from a humanities background. Nevertheless, with the establishment of the Government Economic Service economists became more influential both in the Treasury and other departments. By 2009 there were over one thousand of them employed in various branches of government.

The postwar economy in the 1950s and most of the 1960s was characterised by relatively high rates of growth compared with Britain's historical experience, low unemployment and acceptable rates of inflation. Against the background of a fixed exchange rate regime, there were periodic balance of payment crises. Nevertheless, the Treasury was credited with contributing to an economy that was performing better than in the interwar period. Its reputation within the civil service was reinforced by the fact that it was able to recruit the brightest and best among incoming civil servants.

However, the Treasury faced increasing difficulty in keeping inflation under control. Its preferred least bad policy option of prices and incomes policy was insufficient in the face of the rapid rise in commodity prices, especially oil, in the early 1970s. One consequence of rapid inflation was that it lost its ability to keep public expenditure under control and the so-called 'missing billions' of the mid-1970s did considerable damage to the Treasury's reputation. It had to introduce new methods of controlling public expenditure known as cash limits. Although interpretations of these events vary, it is generally accepted that the Treasury used the International Monetary Fund (IMF) intervention in the British economy in 1976 to restore its authority and impose cuts in public expenditure which went beyond what the IMF actually required.

Despite the revival of its authority, suspicions of the Treasury remained. Reformist critics from the left argued that it was short-termist, arrogant, cut off and incapable of seeing the bigger economic picture. However, the Thatcher government which came into office in 1979 was also suspicious of the Treasury mandarins whom (with some justification) it saw as being too wedded to interventionist Keynesian approaches to economic policy. It was only during the Chancellorship of Nigel Lawson that the authority and prestige of the Treasury within the government was restored. The Treasury then

suffered another blow with the exchange rate mechanism (ERM) crisis of 1992 when Britain had to leave the ERM in circumstances not of its own choosing known as 'Black Wednesday'. In fact the subsequent devaluation of the pound provided a stimulus to the economy so an alternative interpretation of the events was that they were 'Golden Wednesday'. After Norman Lamont resigned as Chancellor, Ken Clarke helped to build a new approach to economic policy that saw performance improve and consequently rebuilt the Treasury's reputation.

However, the golden age of the Treasury in modern times was under the Chancellorship of Gordon Brown from 1997 to 2007. Because of the 'dual monarchy' character of the government, the Treasury enjoyed considerable authority over other departments concerned with domestic policy through the use of mechanisms such as public service agreements. Substantial additional funding was made available to public services, but this was made conditional on achieving performance targets with the Treasury, although these targets subsequently became the subject of criticism because of what was argued to be their distorting effect on the way in which services were delivered.

The reputation of the Treasury was also enhanced by a period of good economic performance, made possible in large part by a boom in the world economy that ultimately turned out to be unsustainable. Unemployment declined and, more significantly, employment levels (the proportion of the eligible population in work) increased. Inflation was low and growth rates were good. The one black spot was that Britain's productivity performance continued to be relatively poor, not just in manufacturing but also in services. The Treasury paid considerable attention to this problem and suggested a number of reforms that were controversial because they impinged on the turf of other departments, for example reforms in the planning system. However, productivity performance failed to respond sufficiently, suggesting that the economy displayed structural weaknesses that were to some extent being concealed by a consumer boom fuelled by high levels of personal debt and government spending.

The outbreak of the GFC saw renewed criticism of the role and performance of the Treasury, and in particular the tripartite division of economic management after 1997 between the Treasury, the Bank of England and the Financial Services Authority (FSA) (discussed further below). It was argued that the

Treasury had paid insufficient attention to the stability of the financial system. As part of the continuous search for efficiency savings in the civil service, the size of the Treasury staff had been reduced, making it more difficult for it to conduct detailed surveillance of some areas of policy. Controversy over the place of the Treasury in economic policy making will no doubt continue. Its defenders will portray it as a Rolls-Royce machine which permits an integrated approach to the conduct of economic policy which is paralleled in only one other major advanced industrial country (France). Its critics will argue that it has excessive influence which is informed by a narrow view of economic policy which leads to serious errors.

The Bank of England

An old Treasury joke refers to the Bank of England as the 'Treasury's East End branch', but the Bank of England has always been a power centre in its own right, a role that was enhanced after 1997. The Bank's nationalisation in 1947 made relatively little difference to the way in which it operated: it continued to regard itself as the guardian of the City of London and its representative to government. However, as the City changed and the financial services sector became more differentiated and lost its 'club' atmosphere, the representative role of the Bank came to be shared with professional trade organisations such as the British Bankers' Association. Nevertheless, when the Governor of the Bank speaks, people listen, as they did in spring 2009 when Mervyn King made it known that he did not think that it would be possible to afford another fiscal stimulus to the economy in that year's budget.

Like the Treasury, the Bank's reputation has fluctuated over time. The Bank's reputation was considerably damaged by the way it had handled the deregulation introduced by the 1970–74 Conservative government's White Paper on Competition and Credit Control, and by the secondary banking crisis which followed. This was the most serious crisis in the financial system before the collapse of Northern Rock in 2007 ushered in the financial crisis.

Relations between the Bank and Treasury reached perhaps their lowest ebb in 1976 when the Bank was accused of having mismanaged the foreign exchange markets. A no doubt apocryphal story which has nevertheless entered the folklore is that, having been instructed to bring about a devaluation of sterling, senior Bank officials set sales of the currency in

motion and went out to lunch leaving a junior official in charge. He continued to sell on a falling market which initiated a collapse of the pound. However, the general stance of the Bank in terms of the need to cut public spending and to negotiate an IMF loan to end speculation against sterling was vindicated by events.

Relations between Margaret Thatcher as Prime Minister and the Bank were initially strained. She took the view that her door plate said that she was First Lord of the Treasury and the Governor of the Bank must do as she said, which was not how he understood the relationship to work. Margaret Thatcher could not understand why the monetary indicators were not working as monetarist theory predicted and came to the view that the Bank was either technically incompetent or subversive.

Nevertheless, the emphasis of the Thatcher government on monetary indicators gave the Bank a more central role in the government's economic strategy. Nigel Lawson as Chancellor came round to the view that the Bank's performance would be improved if it had more independence. He made it a feature of his resignation speech and the case for greater central bank independence began to win wider support.

It was argued that politicians were susceptible to a 'political budget cycle', although the empirical evidence for this effect was ambiguous at least. Politicians could not be trusted to run the economy because they would give undue weight to short-term electoral considerations. Central bankers were independent of such considerations, sympathetic to the market mechanism, either possessed or had ready access to relevant expertise and could be trusted to make prudent judgements. Credibility with the markets would thus be established and the chances of success in the fight against inflation increased. An independent central bank could take speedier action to anticipate and choke off the threat of higher inflation.

Politicians and Treasury officials were understandably reluctant to surrender a key policy instrument, the setting of interest rates, to the Bank. John Major's view as Prime Minister was that these decisions should be taken by someone answerable to Parliament. A broader argument was that the Bank would be more cautious (even alarmist) about the prospect of inflation than a politician would be. As a consequence, interest rates would go up relatively quickly and fall slowly.

Nevertheless, Major allowed Ken Clarke as Chancellor to take two small steps towards greater Bank independence which paved the way for the more radical step taken in 1997 by the New Labour government. The minutes of the Chancellor's monthly meeting with the Governor of the Bank, one of the most crucial economic policy-making events, were to be published six weeks in arrears, so that the arguments made by both sides could become public knowledge. It was agreed that the Bank could publish its regular inflation report without prior approval by the Treasury. This was a symbolic recognition of greater Bank autonomy. Clarke, however, continued to set the interest rates, generally a little below the level that the then Governor, 'Steady' Eddie George, thought prudent.

Within a few days of coming into office, the Blair government took one of the most significant economic policy decisions of the postwar period by transferring responsibility for interest rate policy to the Bank. The letter from Gordon Brown announcing the decision is displayed in a glass case in the Bank's museum. It should be emphasised that this policy change gave the Bank operational rather than goal independence. It is government that sets the inflation policy target and it retains emergency powers to intervene and set the interest rate itself, although those have never been used. In practice, the dense network of relationships between the Treasury and the bank allows the Treasury to give some signals about its views on monetary policy. In particular a non-voting representative if the Treasury sits on the Bank committee that sets interest rates, the Monetary Policy Committee (MPC). The Treasury is still responsible for fiscal policy (taxation and spending) and this aspect of policy needs to be coordinated with monetary policy (conventionally pursued through setting the interest rate).

The government influences the appointment of the nine members of the MPC. Candidates for the governorship and deputy governorships of the Bank are recommended by the Prime Minister. These all sit on the committee, along with the Bank's Chief Economist and the Executive Director for Markets. The Chancellor selects the four members appointed from outside the Bank who are generally economists with relevant expertise. The bank has a voting majority, but does not vote as a bloc and financial journalists spend a lot of effort analysing the minutes of the MPC's meetings to determine who can be classified as 'hard' or 'soft' on interest rates.

These arrangements worked well up until the GFC. Inflation was lower and generally more stable, but this was assisted by the benign economic environment. The Bank encountered criticism for failing to anticipate the extent of the GFC, particularly directed at the Governor, Mervyn King. The interest rate policy instrument quickly failed to work as an instrument to regulate the economy with the MPC rate falling to historically unprecedented levels with little immediate effect.

The Bank had to resort from March 2008 to a novel policy of 'quantitative easing' which in effect means printing electronic money and using it to buy up assets such as gilt edged stock (government bonds that pay an interest rate) and corporate bonds. In the first month of this policy the Bank spent £21bn on purchasing securities, principally gilt edged stock. This increases the quantity of money in the economy and should give it a stimulus, although monetarist theory emphasises the velocity at which money is exchanged as well as its quantity. A downside risk of this exceptional policy was that inflation could accelerate as the economy emerged from recession.

These unprecedented events raised questions about the role of both the Bank and the MPC given that the interest rate, for the time being at any rate, no longer had much policy relevance. The MPC was left to discuss the operation of the quantitative easing programme, a much more limited and less high profile role than it had enjoyed. However, this did not mean the importance of the Bank in economic policy making had declined, rather the contrary. The boundary between fiscal and monetary policy has been blurred and it was the Bank that took a major responsibility for reviving the economy. Cooperation between the Treasury and the Bank became more vital than ever and the Governor's role, once he had recovered from some early criticism of his performance, became pivotal.

The Financial Services Authority

The so-called 'Big Bang' of 1986 represented a major step in the liberalisation of financial services in Britain. It ended the traditional demarcation lines in the financial sector. However, it was recognised that there was inadequate protection for investors, something that has been borne out by a number of subsequent scandals in which investors have lost money and found it difficult to obtain compensation. The Conservative government, however, did not want to impose so strict a regulatory regime that it drove business away from London and the tension between investor protection and securing highly mobile business has proved to be a recurrent one. Critics have argued that the interests of domestic investors have been sacrificed to the needs of international financial markets. After the GFC the reputation of the financial services sector was in tatters, it being argued that retail investors paid high fees and were given poor value in return.

Under the 1986 Financial Services Act the Conservatives set up a series of self-regulatory bodies with the Securities and Investment Board (SIB) at its core. This body was accountable to government, but was funded by a series of self-regulatory organisations (SROs) which placed a levy on the firms for which they were responsible. This system was beset by a series of tensions and criticisms and there were many criticisms of its performance. When Labour came into office in 1997 the name of the SIB was changed to the Financial Services Authority (FSA).

The FSA was given statutory powers by the Financial Services and Markets Act 2000. Its principal statutory responsibilities are maintaining market confidence (probably the most important); public awareness; consumer protection; and reduction of financial crime. In legal terms it is a company limited by guarantee and is still financed by levies on the financial services industry. The Treasury appoints the FSA board, which consists of a Chairman, a Chief Executive Officer, three Managing Directors, and nine non-executive directors (including a lead non-executive member, the Deputy Chairman). This board sets our overall policy, but day-to-day decisions and management of the staff are the responsibility of the executive.

With the outbreak of the GFC there was considerable criticism of the FSA's performance, but in particular of the tripartite structure that had been created by the Labour government in terms of the distribution of responsibility for supervision of the financial services sector between the Treasury, the Bank and the FSA. The first stage of the reform of financial services regulation was completed in June 1998, when responsibility for banking supervision was transferred to the FSA from the Bank of England. In May 2000 the FSA took over the role of UK Listing Authority from the London Stock Exchange. The 2000 legislation transferred to the FSA the responsibilities of several other organisations such as the Building Societies Commission. In October 2004 the FSA was given responsibility for mortgage regulation and in 2005 it became responsible for the regulation of general insurance business.

The FSA thus acquired a wide range of additional functions, but concern was expressed about whether it was equipped to deal with them. It was difficult for the FSA to compete with the salaries offered in the financial services sector before the GFC, leading to questions about whether its staff matched the calibre of those employed in City firms. It also lacked the traditional authority and network of contacts of the Bank.

These concerns were reinforced by the collapse of the Dunfermline Building Society, Scotland's largest mutual lender, in the spring of 2009. Mutuals had been seen as a safer part of the financial services sector because they did not pay dividends to shareholders. However, it became apparent that Dunfermline had engaged in highly risky commercial lending and it had to be the subject of a convoluted and expensive rescue operation in which Nationwide took on its savings accounts and the state acquired its more toxic commercial loans. This raised concerns about an apparent failure by the FSA to prevent building societies venturing into more exotic fields during the boom years, driven by a reluctance to regulate business models, even though the FSA argued in its defence that it had performed 'stress tests' on building societies and Dunfermline had been the only one that had failed.

Lord Turner was appointed chairman of the FSA in September 2008 and he admitted that the City watchdog's 'light touch' approach to regulation had been mistaken. In March 2008 a FSA report into its handling of Northern Rock admitted serious errors in the way that it had regulated the lender, although it claimed that this was not reflective of general practice at the FSA. Lord Turner published proposals laying out plans to curb banks' ability to take excessive risks by forcing them to hold more capital and increase their holdings of liquid assets and cash. He pledged to scrutinise any institution that threatened the stability of the financial system. He also gave his support to the creation of a pan-European regulatory body, a move previously opposed by the FSA.

It could be argued that while these steps are laudable and necessary, there is an element of shutting the door after the horse has bolted. The FSA's credibility was tarnished by the collapse in the financial services sector, which seemed to take it by surprise. The underlying problem, which had been present in the regulation of the financial services sector since it was liberalised, was prioritising the international competitiveness of the financial services sector over the protection of consumer investors.

Competition agencies

The competition agencies constitute another set of bodies that have a considerable impact on economic policy. Competition policy has been given a greater emphasis in British economic policy since the 1980s. This is partly a consequence of the need to regulate utilities which have been privatised but enjoy 'natural' monopolies, i.e., a situation where having just one firm is the most efficient solution as in the provision of transmission networks for electricity and gas. However, it also reflects the market-driven emphasis of the Blair government's policies which saw an effective competition policy as an important factor in improved economic performance. Two key pieces of legislation, the 1998 Competition Act and the 2002 Enterprise Act greatly extended the powers of the competition authorities and in particular the range and size of penalties available to them. Some forms of anti-competitive behaviour can now be subject to criminal prosecution leading to prison sentences.

The key body is the Competition Commission (CC) which has around 150 staff, although it works in tandem with the Office of Fair Trading (OFT). The CC has three main functions:

1 To regulate mergers when large companies will gain more than 25 per cent market share and where a merger looks likely to undermine competition.

2 To tackle the prevention, distortion or restriction of competition in particular markets.

3 To oversee the operation of the regulatory system in regulated sectors.

The CC carries out its work in cooperation with the EU competition authorities who have a particular role in dealing with mergers that affect more than one member state, EU-wide cartels and breaches of the EU's state aid rules. The OFT sees its central task as making markets work well for consumers. The CC only initiates inquiries if an issue is referred to it by the OFT or occasionally by the sector regulators or the responsible minister, the Secretary of State for Business, Enterprise and Regulatory Reform.

The GFC has somewhat undermined the effectiveness and credibility of UK competition policy.

The Enterprise Act 2002 was meant to ensure that ministers were largely removed from the merger control process. Ahead of the Act, the government had maintained that decision making would become more predictable if mergers were no longer influenced by political considerations. The old test of whether a merger was in the public interest would be replaced with an independent decision on whether there would be a substantial lessening of competition because rivals had joined forces. Even so, ministers may still intervene in mergers that raise public-interest considerations. Moerover, the minister can redefine the public interest with parliamentary approval. The then Business Secretary John Hutton announced in September 2008 that he would specify the stability of the UK financial system as a public-interest consideration.

The merger between Lloyds Bank and HBOS would not have normally been permitted under competition policy legislation. Moreover, the Banking (Special Provisions) Act of 2008 gave additional powers to government. It means that the Treasury can make an order transferring one bank to another and setting aside UK merger control legislation. This is exactly what happened with the transfer of the assets of Bradford and Bingley to the Spanish bank, Santander. Exceptional circumstances may be said to justify exceptional measures, but the advances made in competition policy were one of the unsung achievements of the Blair government which have now been undermined by the consequences of the GFC.

Sector regulators exist for communications, gas and electricity (previously separate), water, rail, airports and postal services. These 'quangos' have attracted some criticism from the Conservatives because of their cost and the high salaries paid to some of their heads, well above the salary of the Prime Minister. However, some mechanism has to be in place for maintaining competition when public utilities have been privatised. A more telling criticism is that these bodies have been relatively ineffective in promoting market competition and protecting the interests of consumers.

Admittedly, this was partly the consequence of the ways in which the industries were privatised. An emphasis on maximising revenues from privatisation and not offending the existing managements led to the creation of de facto monopolies. A classic example was BAA, the former British Airports Authority, which was given control of the three major airports in the London area. It was not until 2008 that the CC told BA, by then owned by a Spanish company, to sell Gatwick, Stansted and Edinburgh airports to improve competition. In the electricity industry, production is effectively in the hands of a small group of companies again following mergers and acquisitions. In both electricity and gas, it has been argued that companies have made excessive profits, putting prices to consumers up quickly when wholesale prices rise but being slow to adjust them downwards when wholesale prices fall.

■ The changing conduct of economic policy

Four principal phases can be distinguished in postwar British economic policy:

1 A neo-Keynesian phase from 1945 to 1979.

2 The Conservative governments from 1979 to 1997.

3 New Labour from 1997 to 2007.

4 The financial crisis from 2007.

The neo-Keynesian phase from 1945 to 1979

The wartime coalition government accepted a commitment to maintain full employment. Exactly what 'full employment' meant was never defined, but the postwar boom kept unemployment at relatively low levels until the late 1960s. Most unemployment during this period was 'frictional', i.e., it was made up of people changing jobs, although there were some pools of structural, long-term employment in particular localities. Maintaining full employment was essential to the success of the new welfare state as it prevented the cost of unemployment benefit causing too great a burden on the public finances. This is why the term 'Keynesian welfare state' is sometimes used, even though it is somewhat misleading as Keynes, the architect of the full employment economy, and Beveridge, who devised the plan for the welfare state, largely worked separately of each other.

Keynes considered that by a judicious use of government spending it would be possible to run the economy at a higher level of employment than had been possible in the recession of the 1930s. As interpreted by his disciples after his death, this meant 'fine tuning' the economy largely through the fiscal policy instruments of public expenditure and taxa-

tion. (It should be noted, however, that Conservative governments in the 1950s tried to make more use of the monetary policy instrument of the interest rate to regulate the economy.) One of the problems caused by this fine tuning of the economy, which in any case was based on an inadequate set of statistics to measure its performance or the means to analyse such data as was available, was that it tended to produce 'stop go' cycles in the economy. This created uncertainty which made it more difficult for businesses to engage in investment planning.

Another problem with running the economy at near the full employment ceiling was that it tended to create wage push inflation as labour was generally in relatively short supply (one solution was to encourage immigration from the British Commonwealth to fill vacant jobs). Keynes himself admitted that he had no answer to this problem. The solution that was favoured by the Treasury, and employed by both Conservative and Labour governments at various times between 1945 and 1979 was wage restraint in the form of incomes policies. These policies really only had an impact as short-term emergency measures. In the longer run, they increased industrial unrest, particularly by eroding differentials between skilled and unskilled workers. They also tended to be more strictly enforced in the public sector whereas ways were found of them evading them in the private sector. They increased the influence of the trade unions in the running of the economy as their consent was needed to make the policies effective.

By the end of the 1950s it was becoming apparent that the British economy was lagging behind the performance of its major competitors. This led to the 'Brighton Revolution' of 1960 which has been described as an economic *coup d'état*. A conference of the country's economic establishment in Brighton decided that the country needed to move towards a more interventionist economic policy model based on that of France, although it is clear with the benefit of hindsight that the French model was misunderstood at the time. This led to a great reliance on indicative planning in which government set economic targets and the creation of new institutional devices such as the National Economic Development Council (NEDC) which brought together government, the unions and the employer to discuss the management of the economy. There was also a resort to more interventionist forms of industrial policy, particularly under the Labour government from 1964 to 1970.

The high (or low) point of this tripartite (government/unions/employers) model of running the economy was reached under the Conservative government of 1970–74, particularly after its policy 'U-turn' of 1972 which ushered in much more interventionist policies. In effect the trade unions were offered a partnership to run the economy with government. They were tempted, but relations between them and the Government had been soured by controversial industrial relations legislation. The Government lost the 'Who governs?' election which it called in February 1974 amid a miners' strike which had reduced the economy to a three-day week.

The Labour government of 1974–79 continued with interventionist policies, although not as interventionist as some of the left-wing members of the Cabinet such as Tony Benn would have liked. However, it was clear that the neo-Keynesian model was no longer delivering against a background of 'stagflation': high unemployment, historically high rates of inflation and low growth. Alternative monetarist recipes began to be advocated in the financial press. In 1976 the Prime Minister, James Callaghan, made a speech which questioned Keynesian demand management by stating that it was no longer possible for the country to spend its way out of a recession. The government subsequently started to monitor the monetary aggregates, although this was as much to reassure the markets as to guide its economic policy. It persisted with the neo-Keynesian device of prices and incomes policy and opposition to this policy led to widespread industrial unrest in the so-called 'winter of discontent' of 1978–79 and the defeat of the Labour government in the 1979 general election.

The Conservative government, 1979–1997

It is very easy in retrospect to portray Margaret Thatcher, who became Prime Minister in 1979, as someone driven by ideological considerations. In fact, until her final years in office, she was a very shrewd politician who made tactical retreats when she had to. Nevertheless, she did have a clear vision of where she wanted to take the country. In particular, she subscribed to the view held by Sir Keith Joseph that successive Conservative governments had moved away from fundamental Conservative principles and had subscribed to a 'corporatist' version of economic management which had contributed to the country's decline. One of her fundamental principles was that she was not prepared to accept the country's economic decline as an irreversible condition which had to be managed as best as could be achieved. She was determined to reverse that decline by putting new policies in place. She also saw economic management as a means of achieving broader objectives such as a freer society. As she said, 'Economics are the method, the objective is the soul.'

One of the most fundamental changes brought about by the government was the effective replacement of the full employment objective which had prevailed since 1945. The control of inflation was seen as the principal goal and this was to be achieved by control of the money supply and restraint in public expenditure. A rapid appreciation of sterling, which the government did not seek to control, after it came into office made it more difficult for British industry to export its goods and contributed to a rise in unemployment. Unemployment continued to rise for much of the 1980s and reached unprecedented levels for the postwar period. The government's view, however, was that interventions to raise unemployment above its 'natural' level would only further undermine economic performance. Inflation fell, but then rose again, so that by the time Mrs Thatcher left office the 'misery index' that added together inflation and unemployment was higher than when she had become Prime Minister.

A key aspect of the Thatcher government's approach was the emphasis on the supply side of the economy, rather than the manipulation of the demand side as emphasised in the neo-Keynesian model. Contrary to the conventional postwar wisdom, the creation of conditions conducive to growth and employment should be the objective of microeconomic rather than macroeconomic policy. In particular efforts were made to create a more flexible labour market by reducing the power of the trade unions which were seen as having the ability to force up the cost of labour. The influence of the unions was reduced by facing down major strikes, passing new legislation to control them and privatising the nationalised industries which were one of the main bases of union power. The government also sought to encourage entrepreneurship, particularly through smaller firms, by reducing punitive levels of taxation on income and placing greater emphasis on indirect, e.g., Value Added Tax, rather than direct taxation.

The consequences of these policies remain a matter of partisan controversy, but what cannot be disputed is that Margaret Thatcher made a difference to the conduct of British economic policy, in particular emphasising the centrality of sound money. Productivity performance did improve relative to Britain's competitors, although some of this was due to a 'batting average' effect which saw the least efficient firms and plants closed. A more efficient economy was produced, but at some social cost, in particular the creation of an 'under class' of long-term unemployed.

John Major, Mrs Thatcher's successor, consolidated her policies by undertaking further privatisations. He got rid of the last vestige of tripartism by abolishing the NEDC. After Britain was forced out of the ERM, he used an inflation target as the main driver of economic policy. He also placed more emphasis on what are known as active labour market policies designed to cajole those dependent on long-term benefits to enter the labour force, a policy that was developed further by New Labour.

New Labour from 1997 to 2007

New Labour's economic policies built on Thatcherite foundations, but took them in a new direction. They emphasised the value of a competitive market economy, sound money, low and stable inflation and a flexible labour market in which the unions had limited influence on wage bargaining and policy. With the approval of business, the government sought derogations from EU legislation designed to enhance employment rights. The government inherited and put into practice the Private Finance Initiative (PFI), developed by the Major government, which funded major construction projects for hospitals and schools and their subsequent maintenance and operation through agreements with the private sector which critics argued were good deals for firms and poor ones for the taxpayer.

Conservative spending plans were accepted for the government's first two years in office, although the Conservatives would have almost certainly have revised them upwards. In the 2000 Comprehensive Spending Review, however, the government announced substantial increases in public expenditure and the tax take as a share of GDP started to increase. In part this was achieved by maintaining and increasing various indirect 'stealth' taxes introduced by the Conservatives, although the Blair government had to abandon the fuel duty tax escalator after direct action protests. Part of the increase in taxes was brought about by 'fiscal drag', i.e., tax allowances do not increase as fast as wage increases. As wages

and salaries increased, more people found themselves in the higher rate 40 per cent tax band.

The most radical step taken by the government was giving control of the interest rate to the Bank of England. The government generally favoured the 'depoliticisation' of difficult issues, but this was inherently more difficult in the case of fiscal policy. The government did devise a Code of Fiscal Stability. At the centre of the Code were two rules governing fiscal management. The so-called 'golden rule' required that government will borrow only to invest and not to fund current spending. The second rule was a debt rule that required the ratio of GDP to public-sector debt to be held at a prudent and stable level, interpreted somewhat arbitrarily as below 40 per cent.

One consequence of the Thatcher government's policies had been that the Gini coefficient for the UK had risen, i.e., society had become more unequal in terms of the distribution of income. Indeed, Britain was the most unequal advanced industrial country alongside the United States. Labour sought to reverse this trend by introducing a minimum wage and instituting a generous policy of tax credits for working families with particular help for parents with young children. Eliminating child poverty was a long-term New Labour goal. This was often referred to as 'redistribution by stealth', but the Gini coefficient remained stubbornly unresponsive. In large part this was because of the effects of globalisation with international competition and possibly migration adversely affecting the wages of the lower paid. In the absence of New Labour's policies, inequality may have grown even more.

One of the most difficult economic policy decisions Britain faced was membership of the euro. Tony Blair was disposed in favour of membership as he wanted Britain to be at the heart of Europe. However, he had agreed to a referendum on the subject to appease media critics. If this referendum had been held immediately after Labour had won the 1997 election, it is possible that it could have been won. However, Gordon Brown was not in favour of membership and set up the five tests which had to be met before Britain applied for membership. These were essentially a political device to block membership. The only test that mattered was related to convergence between the British and continental European economies, not just in terms of the economic cycle but also structural convergence.

This raised one of the problems about British membership. Britain has much higher levels of home ownership than most other European countries. Consumer activity in the economy more generally is strongly influenced by the housing market. Hence, variations in a 'one size fits all' European interest rate might have broader consequences in Britain than elsewhere. Supporters of British membership of the euro pointed to the boost that the removal of the uncertainty caused by fluctuations of the pound against the euro would give to trade and investment. Transaction costs would be reduced and price comparisons across the internal market would be made easier, delivering benefits to consumers.

Many of the arguments for and against the euro are political rather than economic. Its supporters are concerned that Britain will be excluded from the economic policy-making process at European level that involves the eurozone countries, although Britain had to be brought into decisions about the GFC in the autumn of 2008. Opponents are concerned about what they see as the further loss of British sovereignty. In more practical terms, the UK government would lose a policy instrument, the ability to influence the exchange rate. There were also concerns about the decision-making mechanisms, priorities and accountability of the European Central Bank. There was a revived flurry of interest in British membership of the euro in the most severe phase of the GFC in the autumn of 2008, but the majority of voters remained opposed to membership.

New Labour had promised an end to 'boom and bust' economics. For a time, it seemed as if this might have been achieved. The Government interpreted a rise in tax revenues after 2000 as a permanent one and started to ratchet up public expenditure, failing to put away a sufficient reserve for harder times. The onset of the GFC demanded a range of emergency measures which had to be developed over a short period of time. Many of Labour's economic policy innovations had to be jettisoned, including the fiscal rules.

The financial crisis from 2007

The financial crisis can be dated from the collapse of Northern Rock in September 2007 which saw a run on a bank in Britain for the first time since the nineteenth century. However, the full force of the GFC did not develop until 2008. All the long-run consequences are far from clear, but by 2009 it was evident that the bank bailout would cost the government and the taxpayer at least £50 bn and possibly more. Whatever government comes to power in 2010, it will have to increase taxes and cut public expend-

BIOGRAPHY

George Osborne (1971–)

George Osborne was only elected as an MP in 2001, but was associated with the 'Notting Hill Set' of Conservatives and became Shadow Chancellor in 2005 at the young age of 33. Osborne was the son of a baronet of Anglo-Irish stock and was educated at St Paul's School in London and Magdalen College at Oxford where he took a degree in modern history. While at Oxford he was a member of the Bullingdon Club which had an elitist membership and a reputation for drinking and rowdy behaviour of various kinds. From 1994 he held various posts as a political researcher and adviser, becoming secretary to the Shadow Cabinet and political secretary to the Leader of the Opposition from 1997 to 2001. He was the subject of some controversy in 2008 because of hospitality he had received in Corfu from Nat Rothschild who subsequently criticised him and alleged that he sought a political donation from a wealthy Russian, an allegation that was never substantiated. Throughout this period he received the continuing support of David Cameron as Conservative leader and there is no doubt that Osborne was an effective critic of Labour policies, aided by the events of the GFC. He made it clear that if he became Chancellor he would seek to restore the public finances, exerting stringent control of public expenditure, while protecting the National Health Service.

iture to reduce the massive public debt accumulated in the crisis. Public borrowing was expected to peak at £170–£190 bn. If the Conservatives win the election, they will probably cut public expenditure more and increase taxes less than Labour.

Long time cycles can be discerned in economic policy. For example, between 1945 and 1979 the state's involvement in economic policy tended to increase, more or less regardless of which party was in office. Planning and regulation of the economy was seen as an inevitable feature of modern European societies, although Britain retained aspects of a more liberal outlook that it shared with the United

Source: Copyright © Steve Bell. From the *Guardian*, 27 February 2009. Reproduced with permission

States. After 1979, the state began a long-term retreat from involvement in the economy under the Conservatives and this trend was continued rather than reversed by New Labour.

Following the GFC, there were demands for a renewal of state involvement in the economy. There was a broad consensus that there needed to be tighter regulation of the financial system, at a national, European and global level. There was also much discussion of 're-balancing' the UK economy in favour of manufacturing. Both Labour and the Conservatives signed up to this rather vague notion without offering very much idea of how it was going to be achieved.

Beyond that it was evident that the Labour government wanted to retain a largely hands-off relationship with the economy. It saw its interventions as temporary measures to dealing with an emergency. Even where the state had majority shares in a bank, the government did not want to get dragged into decisions about whether a particular company or individual should receive a loan, although it did involve itself in the storm of complaint about banker's salaries, bonuses and pensions.

The government's 'hands-off' approach to bank ownership is exemplified by the new arm's-length company it set up in November 2008 to manage its shareholdings in banks subscribing to its recapitalisation fund, UK Financial Investments Ltd. The company is required to act on a commercial basis and to ensure management incentives for banks. The board is made up of a private sector chair, three non-executive private sector members with relevant commercial skill and experience and two senior Government officials.

An influential minority within the Labour Party argued for much more extensive intervention in the economy, including the permanent nationalisation of the banks and housebuilders. This body of thinking could become more influential if Labour loses the next general election, but Britain is unlikely to return to extensive and permanent state ownership. Further reliance on regulation of the private sector is more likely, but there is lack of an agreement on an underlying philosophy to determine how much regulation is necessary to protect the market economy without undermining its key competitive features.

Chapter summary

Economic policy went through a period when it was 'depoliticised', particularly after the transfer of the setting of interest rates to the Bank of England. This reflected the influence of the 'rules v discretion' debate in economics which argued that the more policy decisions that were rules-based the better as politicians were liable to be influenced by short-term electoral considerations. The global financial crisis (GFC) has seen a reintroduction of politics into economic policy which has become more central to the political process once again. Depoliticisation analysts would argue that in the long run politicians will want to transfer the responsibility elsewhere for unpopular decisions. There may also be more debate about whether growth should be a central objective of policy, given the importance of mitigating climate change and the questionable relationship between higher income and happiness beyond a level which meets basic human needs.

Discussion points

- What do we mean by 'economic policy'?
- What has been the impact of globalisation on the conduct of domestic economic policy?
- Why is the relationship between the Prime Minister and the Chancellor so important in economic policy making?
- Evaluate the role of the Treasury in economic policy making.
- What has been the effect of the global financial crisis on economic policy making?

Further reading

Although now somewhat dated, Grant (2002) provides an overview of British economic policy within the context of the global economy. Gamble (2009) provides a thorough and authoritative overview of the GFC. Gamble's (1994) book on Thatcherism remains one of the best treatments. Coates (2005) provides an excellent treatment of New Labour policies. Davies (ed.) (2006) allows successive Chancellors to tell their own stories about how they tried to manage the British economy.

Bibliography

Coates, D. (2005) *Prolonged Labour: the Slow Birth of New Labour in Britain* (Palgrave Macmillan).

Davies, H. (ed.) (2006) *The Chancellors' Tales* (Polity Press).

Gamble, A. (1994) *The Free Economy and the State*, 2nd edn (Macmillan).

Gamble, A. (2009) *The Spectre at the Feast* (Palgrave-Macmillan).

Grant, W. (2002) *Economic Policy in Britain* (Palgrave-Macmillan).

Useful websites

The website of HM Treasury is an essential reference point for current developments in economic policy (www.hm-treasury.gov.uk) as is that of the Bank of England (www.bankofengland.co.uk). The Institute of Fiscal Studies provides high-quality independent assessment of the economy and economic policy (www.ifs.org.uk), as does the National Institute of Economic and Social Research (www.niesr.ac.uk), many of whose warnings have been vindicated by events.

CHAPTER 25

British foreign and defence policy

Bill Jones (with some material by Peter Byrd)

Learning objectives

■ To explain the nature of foreign policy and, particularly, the 'idealist' and 'realist' approaches to it.

■ To discuss the idea of an 'ethical foreign policy' and its viability since 1997.

■ To assess defence policy in the post-Cold War world.

■ To analyse relations with the USA and UK's foreign policy options.

We are the ally of the US not because they are powerful, but because we share their values . . . There is no greater error in international politics than to believe that strong in Europe means weaker with the US. The roles reinforce one another . . . There can be no international consensus unless Europe and the US act together . . . We can help to be the bridge between the US and Europe . . . Europe should partner the US and not be its rival.

Tony Blair, quoted in Gamble (2003)

Introduction

I n this chapter, we study British foreign policy (mostly excluding the European issue) since the election of the Labour government in May 1997 under three headings. The first is the government's 'ethical' foreign policy, introduced as part of the FCO mission statement as early as 12 May 1997, days after the election; an extension of this was Blair's policy of 'liberal interventionism'. The second is the Strategic Defence Review, also announced within days of coming into office, conducted by Secretary of State for Defence George Robertson and completed in July 1998. The third heading is the government's relationship with the United States. This is the most familiar theme in foreign policy since the Second World War, although Blair was re-cementing a close relationship that had to some extent atrophied under the Major government.

■ Background

The study of British foreign policy has become increasingly problematical because of the difficulty of defining an arena or 'sphere' of foreign policy that is distinct from domestic policy. The international-isation of government activity means that there are no longer, if indeed there ever were, clearly defined areas of domestic policy and of foreign policy. In the 1960s, this internationalisation was often character-ised by the perceived growth and alleged political influence of the multinational corporation in impact-ing on national political and economic life. In the 1970s and 1980s, the development of the European Community and of the single market blurred enor-mously the boundaries between the British polity and a wider European sphere of policy making. Since the 1990s, the favoured term for this process has been 'globalisation', emphasising the consequences of the revolution in information and communica-tions technology on the behaviour of the money and financial markets. The 'global village' predicted in the 1960s appears to have arrived, although some caution is required in interpreting these develop-ments. For instance, the wars fought in former Yugoslavia throughout most of the 1980s were widely reported on our television screens, and commenta-tors have often referred to these horrors taking place only two hours' flying time from Britain and in areas familiar to British holidaymakers. Nevertheless, at crucial times information about developments on the ground was lacking, air strikes were based on poor information, and the difficulties confronting the Western powers in influencing events were not dissimilar to those confronting the Western allies in 1945.

Practically all departments of government are involved in making European Union policy; the Foreign and Commonwealth Office is not the most important. See Figure 25.1 for a clear diagrammatic chart of the elements involved in making foreign policy.

For instance, policy on British membership of the euro, perhaps the single most important strategic issue facing the government since its election in 1997, has been tightly controlled by the Prime Minister and the Chancellor of the Exchequer. The Chancellor laid down five key criteria to determine the merits of British membership in October 1997, and Foreign Secretary Robin Cook was for long careful not to transgress any of the boundaries established by his colleague, the Chancellor.

'Idealist' versus 'realist' approaches

These two broad categories represent points on a continuum whereby such policies can be analysed. 'Idealist' approaches emerged following the disas-trous Great War. It was felt that the traditional assumptions of foreign policy and practice of diplo-macy which had helped cause such tragic loss of life and that a new approach was required. This would seek to establish international management of dis-putes between nations, to gradually reduce the extent of armaments and conduct relations between states on the basis of moral principles and international law.

The 'Realist' approach represents the inherited wisdom of foreign policy practice over the last several centuries. It is based on the assumption that the key element in foreign relations is security of the state against attack followed by defence of its essential national interests. As inter-state relations

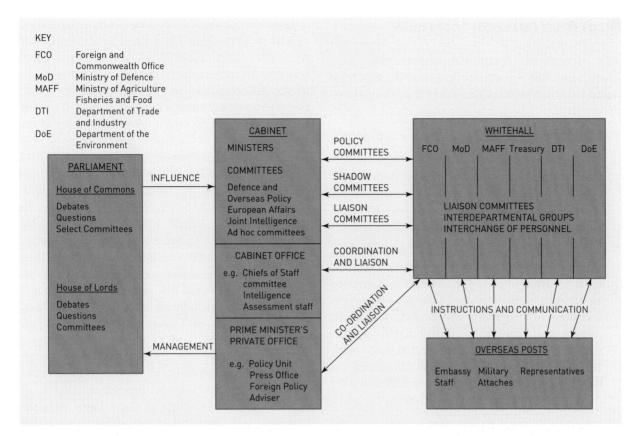

KEY

FCO   Foreign and
       Commonwealth Office
MoD   Ministry of Defence
MAFF   Ministry of Agriculture
       Fisheries and Food
DTI   Department of Trade
       and Industry
DoE   Department of the
       Environment

PARLIAMENT

House of Commons

Debates
Questions
Select Committees

House of Lords

Debates
Questions
Committees

INFLUENCE

MANAGEMENT

CABINET

MINISTERS

COMMITTEES

Defence and
Overseas Policy
European Affairs
Joint Intelligence
Ad hoc committees

CABINET OFFICE

e.g. Chiefs of Staff
     committee
     Intelligence
     Assessment staff

PRIME MINISTER'S
PRIVATE OFFICE

e.g. Policy Unit
     Press Office
     Foreign Policy
     Adviser

POLICY
COMMITTEES

SHADOW
COMMITTEES

LIAISON
COMMITTEES

COORDINATION
AND LIAISON

CO-ORDINATION
AND LIAISON

WHITEHALL

FCO   MoD   MAFF Treasury DTI   DoE

LIAISON COMMITTEES
INTERDEPARTMENTAL GROUPS
INTERCHANGE OF PERSONNEL

INSTRUCTIONS AND COMMUNICATION

OVERSEAS POSTS

Embassy Military   Representatives
Staff   Attaches

Figure 25.1 Schematic representation of the contemporary British foreign policy making process
Source: Michael Clarke, 'The Policy-Making Process' in Michael Smith, Steve Smith and Brian White (eds) *British Foreign Policy: Tradition, Change and Transformation* (London: Unwin Hyman, 1988) p. 86 (Figure 4.1), reproduced by kind permission of Unwin Hyman Ltd; © M. Smith, S. Smith and B. White 1988.

do not operate within a framework which allows rules to be reliably enforced, as in the case of domestic law, every state has to appreciate that they are basically on their own in an anarchic world. States will therefore seek alliances with others to guard against possible threats and to rectify any dangerous balances of power which are perceived. The bottom line of national defence is thus seen to be reliance on good military resources – men in uniform, aircraft, naval forces.

Realists believe they see the world as it is rather than it ought to be and argue that idealism helped allow Hitler to emerge during the interwar years and by exploiting the myths of idealism – including the toothless League of Nations and wishful thinking about Nazi objectives – to establish a momentum of conquest which led to the outbreak of war in 1939. They argue the business of diplomacy is to protect and advance the interests of the state and that if everyone acts in this fashion a kind of stability – albeit fragile at times – is achieved. A basic tenet

of this approach is non-intervention; if everyone cultivates and defends their own gardens there will be peace but intervention might open the door to wider conflicts.

During the Great War the Union for Democratic Control, a body of liberal intellectuals, urged the idealist solution to world conflict. After the Second World War, a similar effusion of idealism occurred resulting in the United Nations, but this improved version of its pre-war League has not been notably successful either. Ernest Bevin, Labour's Foreign Secretary after 1945, had little truck with the Soviet Union, despite earlier claiming that 'left can speak unto left' and substantial support for Russia within his own party. Instead he pursued a fundamentally 'realist' path, allying with the USA to form NATO in defensive alliance against the USSR. The only real legacy of the idealist phase was to clothe foreign policy statements in lip service statements of support for collective security, the need for disarmament and the like.

◼ British national interests

'Our interests are eternal and perpetual' said Lord Plamerston, but was less specific about what they might be. When he was in his pomp they would have included:

1 Security against attack and integrity of frontiers.

2 The primacy of trade. Britain was the world's foremost trading nation in the nineteenth century. It followed that naval supremacy was a prerequisite at that time to protect shipping lanes, especially the English Channel.

3 A favourable balance of power in Europe. Britain feared a dominant power which might encroach upon her trade interests or, at worst contemplate an invasion as Spain under Phillip II or Napoleon had done. The strategy had been to align with powers also opposed to the dominant power, whoever they might be. Palmerston also maintained that, 'We have no eternal allies, and we have no perpetual enemies'; we would side with those who best protected our interests.

4 Peace: a trading nation thrives on peaceful conditions; Britain always regarded war as a last resort.

5 Empire: Britain had created an extraordinary empire comprising one quarter of both the world's landmass and population. Trade within the empire provided an integral part of the home country's prosperity and so defence of the empire was seen as synonymous with the shores of Britain itself.

Modern conditions have caused British interests to change. Peace and security remain clearly as bedrock interests but trade is now a much reduced in extent and its defence is closely related to the worldwide role of the USA. The UK is less concerned about a European balance of power but shifting alliances in the EU continue and British diplomats might find themselves wooing France one year, Germany the next, depending on the evolving politics of the organisation.

The Empire, of course, faded away after 1945 when it became clear an impoverished Britain could no longer defend its far-flung territories. India, the jewel in the imperial crown, was granted its independence in August 1947 and after the 1956 disastrous attempt to seize back the Suez Canal in alliance with France and Israel, the retreat from empire took on the appearance of a rout. By the end of the 1960s all but a few elements of the empire had been granted independence, with Hong Kong transfering back to China in 1997. Accordingly Britain sharply reduced its defence commitments East of Suez in the late 1960s though the percentage of annual expenditure allocated to defence remained higher than most European countries.

In 1962 US Secretary of State Dean Acheson famously said, 'Britain has lost an empire and not yet found a role.' Adjusting to a more modest role proved difficult for British governments. In 1965 Prime Minister Harold Wilson declared, 'We are a world power and a world influence or we are nothing.' However, the only way British leaders were able to maintain the pretence of being a 'world power' was by sticking really close to their American allies. This was the case when Margaret Thatcher had to rely on them for support during the Falklands war and when Tony Blair sought to win Bill Clinton's support for his actions in Kosovo.

| **BOX 25.1** | **A short history of British foreign policy in quotations** |

We have no eternal allies, and we have no perpetual enemies. Our interests are eternal and perpetual, and those interests it is our duty to follow.

Lord Palmerston

The Foreign Office and the Colonial Office are chiefly engaged in finding new markets and in defending old ones.

Joseph Chamberlain (1896)

The general character of England's foreign policy is determined by the immutable conditions of her geographical situation on the ocean flank of Europe as an island state with vast overseas colonies and dependencies whose existence and survival as an independent community are inseparably bound up with the possession of preponderant sea power.

Sir Eyre Crowe (1907)

The policy of England takes no account of which nation it is that seeks the overlordship of Europe. It is concerned solely with whoever is the strongest or the potentially dominating tyrant. It is a law of public policy which we are following, and not a mere expedient dictated by accidental circumstances or likes or dislikes.

Sir Winston Churchill (twentieth century)

Foreign policy isn't something that is great and big, it's common sense and humanity as it applies to my affairs and yours.

Ernest Bevin (1950)

You will realize that I am speaking of the frequent suggestions that the United Kingdom should join a federation on the continent of Europe. This is something which we know, in our bones, we cannot do. We know that if we were to attempt it, we should relax the springs of our action in the Western democratic cause and in the Atlantic association which is the expression of that cause. For Britain's story and her interests lie far beyond the continent of Europe. Our thoughts move across the seas to the many communities in which our people play their part, in every corner of the world. These are our family ties. That is our life: without it we should be no more than some millions of people living on an island off the coast of Europe, in which nobody wants to take any particular interest.

Anthony Eden (1952)

Great Britain has lost an Empire and not yet found a role.

Dean Acheson (1962)

We are a world power, and a world influence, or we are nothing.

Harold Wilson (1965)

British foreign policy is defined as 'first, the commitment to an increasingly integrated Western Europe on as wide a basis as possible, with the European Common Market as its core, and secondly a commitment to a North Atlantic Alliance under US leadership as the main instrument for the conduct of East–West relations . . . Other broad aims on which there is general agreement are the reduction of East–West tension, whenever circumstances in the Soviet bloc permit this without weakening the Atlantic Alliance; the sustaining of Commonwealth links in a form appropriate to contemporary requirements, including our relations with a number of small dependent terri-

tories for which the British Government will continue to be responsible; the improvement of economic conditions in the less developed countries; and the strengthening of international organisations in which an effective dialogue can take place on issues which cause conflicts between nations.'

Duncan Report (1969)

Our destiny is in Europe, as part of the Community. That is not to say that our future lies only in Europe.

Margaret Thatcher (Bruges, 1988)

Foreign and defence policy essentially has to be about the obtaining and management of influence.

Lord Carrington, *Reflect on Things Past* (1988)

My aims for Britain in the community can be simply stated. I want us to be where we belong. At the very heart of Europe. Working with our partners in building the future. That is a challenge we take up with enthusiasm.

John Major (1991)

British foreign policy exists to protect and promote British interests. Despite all the changes in the world that underlying truth has not changed.

Douglas Hurd (1993)

We live in a modern world in which nation states are interdependent. In that modern world foreign policy is not divorced from domestic policy but a central part of any political programme.

Robin Cook (1997)

Robin Cook
Source: Alamy Images / Tim Gander

Our foreign policy must have an ethical dimension and must support the demands of other peoples for the democratic rights on which we insist for ourselves.

Foreign and Commonwealth Office

■ An ethical dimension to foreign policy

A foreign policy based on general principles was not something new as the more idealistic interwar years had shown. Indeed, in 1945 there was some talk that 'Left can talk unto left', in terms of Labour's supposed ability to do business with Stalin but as the latter's designs became clearer, Foreign Secretary Ernest Bevin found himself moving closer to the US in the hope of receiving support against a potentially dangerous enemy. This provoked a discordant protest on Labour's crowded left-wing benches but Bevin steadfastly ignored them and pursued a virtually traditional rather than a 'socialist' foreign policy. Similar eruptions occurred during the 1960s when Wilson supported US actions in Vietnam, though he was careful to stop short of sending any troops.

Nevertheless the belief that Labour could and should offer a different and morally superior direction in foreign policy persisted. Robin Cook, when made Foreign Secretary 12 May 1997, embodied such a concept in his 'mission statement' as a commitment to 'promote the national interests of the United Kingdom and contribute to a world community'. This would include to 'spread the values of human rights, civil liberties and democracy which we demand ourselves'. Senior mandarins in the Foreign office were known to be sceptical of such an approach and others claimed it was in any case an irrelevant sophistry, of no consequence. Certainly the case of arms sales by the UK did not advance the cause.

Sierra Leone

This action was important to Tony Blair as it preceded his Chicago Speech later that year which elaborated the idea of 'liberal intervention'. Sierra Leone had been wracked by a brutal civil war in which Foday Sankoh's Revolutionary United Front (RUF), was raping, mutilating and killing thousands of innocent and helpless people. When they captured 500 members of a UN force in May 1999, Blair ordered a small British force to intervene which they did with clinical efficiency, defeating the RUF, freeing the hostages and preventing the advance on Freetown.

Chicago Speech, 1999

Around the time of the successful military actions in Kosovo and West Africa, Blair was emboldened to elaborate a framework for his ideas on 'International Community' at a speech in Chicago. It is worth quoting from the speech itself:

At the end of this century the US has emerged as by far the strongest state. It has no dreams of world conquest and is not seeking colonies. If anything Americans are

---

BIOGRAPHY

Robin Cook (1946–2005)

Labour Foreign Secretary. Educated at Edinburgh University, MP in 1974, where he made his name as a clever left-winger. Shadowed Treasury, Health and Social Security in opposition but made Foreign Secretary in 1997. Recognised as the best parliamentarian of his party, but chances of leadership said to be impeded, perhaps unfairly, by his unprepossessing appearance. It is hard to say whether his widely publicised affair with his secretary and subsequent divorce damaged him politically, but Blair replaced him after 2001 with Jack Straw, moving Cook to the less prestigious role of Leader of the House, where he proved to be a force for reform of the Commons before resigning over the war against Iraq in March 2003. He died tragically of a heart attack while walking in the Scottish mountains in 2005. Some believed his red hair, spiky Scottishness and less than classical good looks precluded him from ever reaching the premier rank of politics in this image-dominated age and there is probably some truth in this. However, the presentational gifts which made him Parliamentarian of the Year twice over, not to mention his determined insistence on a clear left-of-centre direction to New Labour's administration, mean that his absence will be sorely felt for years to come.

too ready to see no need to get involved in affairs of the rest of the world. America's allies are always both relieved and gratified by its continuing readiness to shoulder burdens and responsibilities that come with its sole superpower status. We understand that this is something that we have no right to take for granted, and must match with our own efforts.

We may be tempted to think back to the clarity and simplicity of the Cold War, but now we have to establish a new framework. No longer is our existence as states under threat. Now our actions are guided by a more subtle blend of mutual self-interest and moral purpose in defending the values we cherish.

The most pressing foreign policy problem we face is to identify the circumstances in which we should get actively involved in other people's conflicts. Non-interference has long been considered an important principle of international order. And it is not one we would want to jettison too readily. But the principle of non-interference must be qualified in important respects. Acts of genocide can never be a purely internal matter. When oppression produces massive flows of refugees which unsettle neighbouring countries then they can properly be described as 'threats to international peace and security'.

Looking around the world there are many regimes that are undemocratic and engaged in barbarous acts. If we wanted to right every wrong that we see in the modern world then we would do little else than intervene in the affairs of other countries. We would not be able to cope.

So how do we decide when and whether to intervene. I think we need to bear in mind five major considerations:

First, are we sure of our case? War is an imperfect instrument for righting humanitarian distress; but armed force is sometimes the only means of dealing with dictators.

Second, have we exhausted all diplomatic options? We should always give peace every chance, as we have in the case of Kosovo.

Third, on the basis of a practical assessment of the situation, are there military operations we can sensibly and prudently undertake?

Fourth, are we prepared for the long term? In the past we talked too much of exit strategies. But having made

a commitment we cannot simply walk away once the fight is over; better to stay with moderate numbers of troops than return for repeat performances with large numbers.

Finally, do we have **national interests** involved? The mass expulsion of ethnic Albanians from Kosovo demanded the notice of the rest of the world. But it does make a difference that this is taking place in such a combustible part of Europe.

Arms sales

Despite UK government condemnation of the Indonesian government's support of the militias terrorising the autonomy-seeking East Timorese, the order for Hawk military aircraft was not cancelled. On 21 July 2002, the *Independent on Sunday* published an investigation that showed Britain selling arms to nearly 50 countries where conflict was endemic. These included Israel, Pakistan, Turkey, China, India, Angola and Colombia. The paper commented: 'Under its "ethical" foreign policy the Government bans arms sales to countries already at war, but instead arms manufacturers actively target countries where ethnic conflict is likely to explode.' For example, sales to Turkey in 2000 approached £200 million: 'Amnesty International has accused Turkey of suppressing its Kurdish minority population and of sustained persecution of orthodox Muslim groups, left-wing opponents and human rights activists.' Even more reprehensible was the suspension of a legal inquiry into allegations that BAE had paid bribes to senior members of the Saudi establishment in order to secure the huge Al Yamamah arms deals stretching from 1985–2006. The official explanation that the decision was in the interests of 'national security' sounded suspiciously like a covering up of very murky dealings.

Kosovo

Kosovo is the most dramatic example of a major foreign policy issue in which there is a strong ethical dimension arising from the prominence given to human rights. The British intervention in Kosovo has been the most important, and arguably most successful, foreign policy initiative of the Labour government. Throughout the Kosovo crisis in 1999, Britain adopted a clear leadership role within the European Union and the Atlantic Alliance, dragging behind it reluctant alliance partners. In Kosovo,

Britain 'punched above its weight' and exercised power within a complex alliance setting.

Throughout 1998, the situation in Kosovo worsened as the Serbian military and political machine exercised increasingly tight control over the province, in which over 90 per cent of the population was Albanian. NATO repeatedly pushed President Milosevic of Yugoslavia towards an agreement with the Kosovar nationalist opposition. Air strikes were threatened, much as they had been earlier in coercing Milosevic into agreement in Bosnia. Eventually, at Rambouillet in January 1999, an agreement was brokered by NATO between Milosevic and his Kosovar opponents to provide for a degree of self-rule within a larger Serbia. The agreement was short-lived. The Kosovar opposition was tentative in its support for the terms, and Milosevic denounced the terms that his negotiators had secured. On 24 March, without seeking UN support, NATO launched a strategic bombing campaign to force Milosevic back to the table.

The bombing, code-named *Operation Allied Force*, lasted until 10 June when, after 34,000 sorties had been flown, President Milosevic signalled that he would accept an allied army in Kosovo and withdraw his own forces. During the air campaign, the war aims of the alliance expanded beyond the Rambouillet settlement to include an international force to be deployed on the ground to guarantee security for the Kosovars. As the scale of the expulsions from Kosovo grew, the British government stated that the removal from power of Milosevic, indicted as a war criminal, had become a necessary guarantee of future stability. Nevertheless, full independence for Kosovo was not a war aim for NATO.

Why did Milosevic agree to NATO's demands and pull out of Kosovo? The continued resolve of the alliance may have persuaded him that eventually he would be forced to give way and that he could not rule out completely the possibility of a land war. However, the British argument that such a war should be planned and threatened was consistently met by American refusal to contemplate such an outcome. Internal opposition to Milosevic may also have played a part. The best explanation is probably that Milosevic was urged to back down by the Russians. His Russian allies could not afford to lose cooperation with the West, despite their opposition to the bombing campaign, and needed an end to the war. In an immediate sense, therefore, it was thus the persuasion of an ally rather than the coercion of an enemy that determined the outcome of the war.

The British government, and its allies, resisted the demands of the Kosovo Liberation Army for an independent Kosovo, preferring weak multinational states in the Balkans to a multiplicity of nation states. Homogeneous nation states would, in any case, require further population movements, probably taking the form of 'ethnic cleansing' in a never-ending cycle of misery.

As in the case of President Carter's human rights policy of 1977, it is possible to argue that the war's consequences, as opposed to motives, for human rights were mixed or even counterproductive. The launch of the bombing campaign precipitated the forcible expulsion of the Kosovars from Kosovo. The expulsion campaign was a macabre, larger-scale version of the ethnic cleansing earlier practised by Milosevic. As the bombing continued, the expulsions escalated. After the successful liberation of Kosovo, the refugees were able to return, in many cases only to find burnt out homes. They paid a very high price for their right to remain. Unfortunately, but perhaps inevitably, the returning Kosovars began to practise similar tactics against their erstwhile Serb neighbours, about 180,000, precipitating a second exodus of refugees from Kosovo.

Nevertheless, it can be argued that, on balance, the consequences of the war are justified in terms of ethical foreign policy. The war improved the human rights situation for the majority of the population of Kosovo by eventually ending the Serb oppression. If the consequences of the war can be justified in ethical foreign policy, can the conduct of the war? There is a complex debate within the tradition of the 'just war' about strategic bombing and, in particular, the requirements under just war to avoid or at the very least to minimise the risk of unintended (collateral) damage to the innocent. Aerial bombardment tends to be indiscriminate unless the attacker accepts very high risks to himself to aim his bombs with precise accuracy. At the start of the air war, NATO attacked the Serb air-defence systems but thereafter continued to minimise the risk of damage to its own forces by confining itself to high-level bombing from about 14,000 feet. The effect of high-level bombing, together with inadequate ground-level information about Serb deployments, certainly minimised NATO's losses (zero in the case of Britain) but on the other hand increased collateral damage from inaccurate bombing or misinterpreted targets. Kosovar refugees were themselves bombed and many killed.

■ The attacks on the World Trade Center, New York, 11 September 2001

When the devastating Osama bin Laden-inspired attacks on the twin towers of the World Trade Center occurred, Tony Blair was quick to stand 'shoulder-to-shoulder' with our American ally. At the Labour Party conference in October 2001, Blair excelled himself with an idealistic speech in which he envisaged a kind of ethical Anglo-US led campaign to make the world better: 'more aid untied to trade'; 'write off debt'; 'encouraging the free trade we are so fond of preaching'. If the world as a community focused on it, 'we could defeat climate change . . . find the technologies that create energy without destroying the planet'. He described Africa as a 'scar on the conscience of the world' that the world could, if it so chose, 'heal'. 'Palestinians', he declared, 'must have justice, the chance to prosper in their own land.' He finished by claiming 'The world community must show as much capacity for compassion as for force.' However, his hopes that the USA would rally to his clarion call were rapidly disappointed: US national interests were paramount for George W. Bush. He had already refused to ratify the hard-won international agreements on climate change signed at Kyoto in 1997. Moreover, he refused to send any representative to the world environment conference in Johannesburg. Tariffs were slapped on European steel products to protect US steel producers, many in regions electorally desirable to the Republicans. And the USA proved unmoved by the continuing refusal of Israel's right-wing government to adopt a conciliatory attitude towards the Palestinians. Progress in resolving this conflict has always been high on the European list of priorities, particularly Britain's.

In the wake of '9/11', Blair made a number of visits to see the President and was, to be fair, received with a warmth denied any other country. But did Blair receive any payoff for his loyalty? Apart from the warmth of his receptions, this was not easy to argue.

Afghanistan

British troops joined in the attack on Afghanistan in October 2001 and shared the deceptive initial sense of victory, despite Bin Laden's escape from pursuing Western forces. However, the country has a long history of resisting conquest, including the Mongols, British and Russians, and suppressing the fundamentalist Taliban, who had supported Al-Qaeda's activities, was always going to be difficult. The Taliban soon recovered their ability to fight, fostered by support of sympathisers over the Pakistan border and began to inflict casualties on NATO (mostly US and British forces) which had come to provide the aegis under which the Western effort was made. The main policy dilemmas related, perhaps, to the objectives of the conflict: was it to support the resistance of the corrupt Karzai government, perceived by some as a Western puppet, or destroy the Taliban as a military force? The latter objective is proving virtually impossible (at the time of writing) while the former is undermined by the fact that Western troops are dying in the cause of an undemocratic and unworthy government. Doubts also exist at all levels as to whether the battle can be won and whether it is worth fighting in the first place. For the UK, this policy area is plagued by: accusations that the Labour government is not providing adequate equipment, especially helicopters and vehicles able to withstand the deadly roadside bombs; open conflict between government ministers and the army top brass; the need to rein back military spending to reduce debt levels; a tragically rising death toll; and demands from President Obama that European forces increase their commitment to win the war.

Gordon Brown would find it hard to withdraw from the fight when so much has already been committed and so many brave young lives have been lost and if Cameron wins in 2010, he is firmly committed to continuing the fight with even more vigour.

Iraq

After Afghanistan, the next on the agenda was the proposed war on Iraq. This created a series of dilemmas: Blair was intent on obtaining UN legitimacy for any invasion but, despite desperate flights to lobby members of the Security Council, he failed, with France playing a distinctly unhelpful role. Everyone agreed Saddam Hussein was a monstrous ruler who should be deposed but to do so would violate international law. The *casus belli* was eventually narrowed down to the fact that Saddam had 'weapons of mass destruction' (WMD) but, despite their best efforts, UN inspectors failed to find any. On 15 February 2003 there were demonstrations all over the world against the war with close on a million people marching in London. Yet this did not

BOX 25.2   Time to withdraw from Afghanistan?

Former Foreign Office minister Kim Howells wrote in *The Guardian*, 4 November 2009, a significant recantation for a senior Labour figure:

It would be better to bring home the great majority of our fighting men and women and concentrate, instead, on using the money saved to secure our own borders, gather intelligence on terrorist activities inside Britain.

This makes some sense in the present situation. The invasion of the country, in the wake of 9/11, was designed to flush out Osama bin Laden: that failed. It was also designed to defeat Al-Qaeda's protectors, the Taliban, but Mullah Omar and his senior colleagues escaped into the Pakistan border areas. The main rationale for the war now remains that if they win, the Taliban might bring back Al-Qaeda and therefore risk death on the streets in the west once again. But, as the *Economist* pointed out 22 August 2009, 'American troops are not really fighting al-Qaeda in Afghanistan because they are not there any more.'

Maybe they would come back if the Taliban won, but al-Qaeda could just as easily re-establish itself in a number of places – Yemen, Somalia, Eritrea, Sudan, Uzbekistan. Stephen Biddle of the American Council on Foreign Relations, comments:

We clearly cannot afford to wage protracted warfare with multiple brigades of American ground forces simply to deny Al-Qaeda access to every possible safe haven. We would run out of brigades long before Osama bin Laden ran out of prospective sanctuaries.

Howells argues that a 'Fortress Britain' strategy, even though it would involve more intrusive surveillance of indigenous Muslims, would be more cost-effective than pouring more treasure and young manhood into an unwinnable war. His argument below is hard to refute:

Sooner rather than later a properly planned phased withdrawal of our forces from Helmand province has to be announced. If it is an answer that serves, also, to focus the minds of those in the Kabul government who have shown such a poverty of leadership over the past seven years, then so much the better.

Seven years of military involvement and civilian aid in Afghanistan has succeeded in subduing al-Qaida's activities in that country but it hasn't destroyed the organisation or its leader, Osama bin Laden. Nor has it succeeded in eliminating al-Qaida's protectors, the Taliban.

There can be no guarantee that the next seven years will bring significantly greater success and, even if they do, it is salutary to remember that Afghanistan has never been the sole location of terrorist training camps.

---

stay the invader's hand: on 20 March 2003 the troops moved in. After a few days fighting Saddam was toppled and Bush indulged in some premature triumphalism when he claimed 'Mission Accomplished' on 1 May 2003.

In fact, his troubles were only just beginning. By disbanding the army and police the invaders were allowing chaos to reign from the start as looters ran wild throughout Iraq. Next came the guerilla attacks on US forces and the murderous feuds between Shia and Sunni Muslims. Moreover, by economising on the initial number of troops, Rumsfeld, the Defence Secretary, had hugely underestimated the numbers required to complete the job. British forces were relatively free of the worst trouble having been given the southern city of Basra to look after. Everyday television brought horrific images into US and UK homes of suicide bombers killing scores of people in Baghdad and elsewhere; reports persisted of night-time murders by one sect against another until the alleged death toll was in the hundreds of thousands.

A democratic framework was introduced by the occupiers and a government elected, but its legitimacy was fragile and its future uncertain. A senior advisory group led by James Baker urged a new multilateral approach but Bush refused and initiated a 'surge' of new troops who actually managed to reduce the killings and begin a process leading to something akin to normalisation.

Jack Straw (1946–)

Foreign Secretary 2001–5. Educated at Leeds University, where he became President of the National Union of Students. Called to the Bar in 1972. Served as councillor for Islington, 1971–8; became MP for Blackburn in 1979. Served in a number of senior Shadow roles before becoming Home Secretary in 1997, where his reputation was as a tough though not illiberal minister. In 2001 he was surprised to be appointed Foreign Secretary, usually regarded as the third most important role in government. Straw has proved an effective supporter of Blair's foreign policy, especially over Iraq, but inevitably was overshadowed by his boss over the big issues and on the big occasions. Former ambassador to Washington, Sir Christopher Meyer, in his memoir *DC Confidential*, damned Straw with faint praise in describing him as 'more to be liked than admired'. He was sacked in May 2005.

It is too early to judge how Iraq will be perceived by history but from the present perspective it still looks like an ill-thought-through policy which was appallingly executed by the US at least and not significantly better by the UK. It was conceived by Blair as a justifiable intervention but its failure has probably scotched any further 'humanitarian interventions' being considered for many a year. Looking back at the Chicago speech of 1999 (see p. 566) can it be argued Iraq met Blair's five criteria?

1 *'Are we sure of our case?'* This has to be a 'no'. The invasion was never endorsed by the United Nations Security Council and the ostensible *casus belli*, the 'weapons of mass destruction', proved to be non-existent.

2 *'Have we exhausted all diplomatic options?'* It seemed clear that many wished the search for a diplomatic solution to continue; it was Bush and his advisers who were keen to get on with a unilateral action; strategic and military factors had made a US invasion inevitable by then anyway.

3 *'Are there military operations we can sensibly and prudently undertake?'* In terms of defeating Saddam 'yes', but it became clear that little thought had been directed towards winning the peace.

4 *'Are we prepared for the long term?'* As events proved, it became crystal clear that neither of the two principal allies had looked into the future and solved problems which in retrospect seem blindingly obvious.

5 *'Do we have national interests involved?'* Britain had scarcely any *direct* economic or military national interests involved yet for Blair there were, on the grounds that Saddam was a leader of a 'rogue state', likely to host terrorists and support their efforts to create mayhem in the world. He and Bush argued that a democratic Iraq would provide a beacon to authoritarian Middle Eastern states and therefore encourage democratic developments in that area, plus a related softening of attitudes to the west.

On 9 October 2009 a service was held in London to commemorate the well-over three figure death toll in Iraq. The Archbishop of Canterbury made some scathing criticisms of Tony Blair's leadership now that UK involvement was at an end; Blair was also snubbed by a father of a soldier killed in the struggle when he refused to shake the hand of someone he accused of being a 'war criminal'.

Defence policy: the Strategic Review

Much is made of 'soft' power in the modern world. The American Joseph Nye invented the term and his book, *Soft Power, the Means to Success in World Politics*, elaborated its scope. The essence of this idea is that states do not necessarily need to achieve their objectives through the threat of military action. Similar results can often be won though the attractions of one's culture, persuasive power, national values and the power of example. Obama right now, for example, exercises considerable soft power through his inspirational life story (of overcoming the disadvantage of racism and winning the presidency); his oratorical abilities which draw upon black religious preaching; and his promise to change things for the better. All this is in addition to America's existing advantages as the perceived land of opportunity, economic freedom and prosperity, not to mention Hollywood, jazz and popular music which have a worldwide reach. Britain is less well equipped

BOX 25.3 The changing pattern of world power

Barack Obama has to decide what to do in a world made unstable by terrorism, economic meltdown and shifts in the balance of power. A report appeared shortly after his election which explained how difficult his foreign policy role would be.

National Intelligence Council (NIC)
A Transformed World: In November 2008 this report revealed just how far-reaching the changes to American status in the world will be: in effect the end of American supremacy.

No longer unipolar
'By 2025 the international system will be a global multipolar one with gaps in national power continuing to narrow between developed and developing countries.' The 'unipolar' world, argues the report, which followed the end of the Cold War and the collapse of the USSR has now passed – arguably an opportunity bungled by George Bush – leaving the USA moving into a relative long-term decline. It is still by far the biggest military power, but as the NIC observes: 'advances by others in science and technology, expanded adoption of irregular warfare tactics by both state and non-state actors, proliferation of long-range precision weapons, and growing use of cyber warfare attacks increasingly will constrict US freedom of action'.

China
China, says the report, is 'poised to have more impact on the world over the next 20 years than any other country'. It is already a major economic power – due to become the world's second-largest economy by 2025 as well as a growing military one. By 2025 it will have replaced Europe as the second most powerful economic region.

Shift of wealth West to East
High oil prices and the growth of manufacturing in the East is causing economic power to shift eastwards. At the same time prosperity has ceased to be associated so much with democracies and more with state-run enterprises: 'state capitalism'. It by no means follows that democracy is bound to extend and take over such countries.

Failed states and failure of international organisations
The NIC predicts more anarchic states like Somalia with a growth of non-state actors like corporations, terrorists and religious groups. Some countries might be taken over by criminal gangs and some states might well wither away, unable to provide for their citizens. Attempts to reform the UN have been tried but it exhibits considerable 'institutional inertia'.

Climate change and scarcity
Finite resources might become a *casus belli* between states, India and China, for example, as their economies continue to grow rapidly. Water and arable land might also become bones of contention – especially in Africa – as states adjust to a less abundant world. James Lovelock recently predicted that once global warming advances, thousands of refugees from Europe will wish to emigrate to our less over-heated climes. This, if it happens, will certainly cause conflict.

but her status as the home of the English language as well as a literary tradition and a leading role in world cinema bestows considerable advantages.

However, the options available to a Foreign Secretary are to some extent defined by what military hardware is available and how many potential troops are on the ground. In his day Palmerston could send a gunboat to achieve his objective but in the present day such a gesture is no longer suggestive of the world's biggest navy, nor are there thousands of troops ready to respond to orders. The 1990 *Options for Change* document foresaw an overall reduction of the military so that by 1998 it had reduced by over 20 per cent as measured by GDP.

By 1997, defence policy had entered a period of relative stability within ever-declining budgets. Three main defence roles had been identified. The first is the defence of the UK and its territories, even when there is no overt external threat. This core defence capability included the retention of the nuclear deterrent, untargeted in the absence of a nuclear enemy. This 'existential deterrent' (deterrence from mere possession) is similar to the traditional French policy of nuclear dissuasion, in contrast to Britain's previous strategy of deterrence through an overt threat of retaliation. The second defence role is insurance against a major attack on the UK or its allies and encompasses the NATO commitment and NATO force structures. The third defence role is the contribution to wider security interests through the maintenance of peace and stability. This is the extended concept of security including peace-keeping and peace enforcement through the UN and NATO, involving British forces even where no national security interests are immediately at stake.

The new Defence Secretary, George Robertson, set in train a Strategic Review in an effort to sculpt a coherent policy to meet Britain's defence needs within a reasonable budget.

Robertson largely confirmed Conservative procurement plans and added one major new project. The order for 386 Challenger 2 tanks would be completed and two armoured divisions established. The major new weapon for the army would be a battlefield helicopter to deploy against armoured forces in the form of the American Apache, to be built under licence in Britain. The Gulf War in 1991 had demonstrated the value of such a capability, at least against a weak opponent and in open desert country, although the American Apache force deployed during the Kosovo war made no impact at all and proved difficult to deploy against the Serbian forces. Robertson committed the government to completion of the full contract for 232 new Euro-fighters. This was the weapon that the RAF had set its heart on. Since the early 1980s it had lacked a specialist air defence fighter aircraft, relying on the ineffective Tornado F3, which had singularly failed to distinguish itself in the Gulf War. The Eurofighter contract had been subject to constant threats since being developed in the early 1980s with Germany, Italy and Spain, with the German government in particular perennially hovering on the point of cancellation.

The Royal Navy would reduce its declining submarine capability still further to a force of only ten nuclear-powered submarines, plus the four Trident ships. Robertson's major new procurement project, and in one sense the main outcome of the whole review, was the proposal to build two new large aircraft carriers, capable of carrying 50 aircraft, to replace the ageing fleet of three small warfare

carriers built in the 1970s. These ships had evolved since the 1970s towards a general air attack role but were too small to carry adequate numbers of aircraft. The two new carriers, together with two new assault ships already on order and the recently completed helicopter carrier *HMS Hero*, would enable rapid deployment of a range of forces by sea. The navy would regain some of its traditional 'blue waters' capability of projecting power globally and flexibly. New naval capabilities complement the army's new emphasis on airmobile forces, in turn supported by heavier forces deployed by sea or by new heavy airlift capabilities.

The rationale for these new capabilities rests on a broad conception of Britain's security interests. What was the case for this? First, there is no immediate direct military threat to British security other than from the IRA, currently signed up to a ceasefire, however, conflicts in one area may spill over into other areas closer to home. Second, the emphasis on an ethical foreign policy and defence of humanitarian interests requires flexible capabilities. Third, it can be argued that Britain benefits by accepting responsibilities and duties that contribute to a stable world, which is itself a British interest. In the short run, Britain could act, like Japan, as a free rider and obtain the benefits of stability without making a military contribution towards ensuring it, but, the government thinks, influence and prestige would decline if such an attitude were adopted. In short, there is an unquestioned assumption within government that, through punching above its weight, prestige and influence are maximised and hence that responsible behaviour brings its own reward. An activist policy increases influence with the United States and Germany and within NATO. NATO remains, on this analysis, the key to security policy, and Britain plans to remain at the centre of NATO.

British forces are highly professional and effective but, given high levels of specialisation, also small and expensive, operating without any economies of scale. Under Robertson's plans, they must also be prepared to take on a variety of roles. Given their small size, one particularly awkward question is raised. Can British military power aspire to be a premier-division force capable of fighting a high-intensity war, or are they now a second-division force whose effectiveness is confined to such lower-intensity wars as Bosnia or Kosovo? Forces capable of high-intensity warfare can be deployed on lower-intensity operations, even if their training and equipment are not exactly suited. On the other hand, forces only capable of lower-intensity warfare cannot be used in a high-intensity battle. British forces have clung persistently to the notion that they are small but capable of high-intensity warfare – in the premier division – and unique among other high-intensity forces in also being trained for low-intensity warfare as a result of the Northern Ireland situation and post-colonial wars. Kosovo does not answer the question. The air force participated on a very small scale, and apparently ineffectively, in an American-led high-intensity bombing campaign. On the ground below, the army prepared for a lower-intensity campaign, though one that was overtly coercive and, potentially, of higher intensity. After two years in office, the government made no radical changes to defence policy. The downward pressure on expenditure remains, but there had been progress in establishing more flexible forces, able to operate within tri-service commands both in Europe and outside. Overstretch remains and has increased with the despatch of a Gurkha battalion to East Timor. Uncertainty remains over whether, in the medium term, it is possible to sustain such a varied defence effort with such small forces.

The Defence White Paper in July 2002 reflected the new realities following the 9/11 attacks on the World Trade Center. New weapons were envisaged for the armed forces that would enable them to identify and strike at terrorist enemies within minutes. Geoff Hoon, the Defence Secretary, explained a scenario where very mobile, lightly armed forces would be able to identify the enemy, acquire authority to act and strike in 'near real time'. Apache helicopters armed with Hellfire missiles would be instrumental in this new capacity. Plans to develop a new pilotless reconnaissance aircraft, the Watch-keeper, would be speeded up. Hoon told the Commons:

Terrorism thrives on surprise and one of the key ways to defeat it is to take the fight to the terrorist. We must be able to deal with threats at a distance: hit the enemy hard in his own backyard – not in ours – and at a time of our choosing – not his – acting always in accordance with international law.

■ Defence overstretch

The Select Committee on Defence, reporting in March 2005, warned that overstretch of resources had reached dangerous levels:

Many frontline units in the army have been experiencing an operational and training cycle whose intensity is unsustainable in the longer term.

MPs also warned that the government may have underestimated the role armed forces may have to play in defending the 'homeland' against international terrorism. Because defence spending had been kept steady at about 2.5 per cent of GDP, a number of measures had been found necessary:

1 Delaying of two new aircraft carriers until the end of the decade or later.

2 Delaying of the Eurofighter (or Typhoon as it is now called) and the Joint Strike Fighter Programme, meaning existing carriers will be at sea without them for a period.

3 Delaying of new helicopters, badly needed by the army and air force.

However, the committee endorsed the decision to merge certain regiments, with some famous single-battalion regiments, like the Black Watch, being merged into bigger regiments.

Cuts continued to achieve economy targets. One journalist, James Meek, reflected in *The Guardian* on 21 January 2004 that the Royal Navy had 900 ships in 1945. In 2010 the number of frigates, destroyers and carriers stands at 36. He went on to question whether even these were needed. Wars fought in recent years had been located in land-locked regions – Afghanistan, Iraq – and even sophisticated high-tech ships like the US Navy's *Cole* had been nearly sunk in 2000 by a few terrorists on a small launch stacked with explosives.

Trident

The one aspect of naval renewal which is guaranteed to cause more controversy is the replacement of the Trident submarine-borne nuclear deterrent. In November 2005 Defence Secretary John Reid was forced to give a pledge that MPs be allowed to vote on the possible purchase of a replacement from the US with a new weapons system estimated to cost £20–25 bn. Reid agreed to hold the debate in a transparent fashion but insisted: 'I defy anyone here to say we will not need a nuclear weapon in 20–50 years' time.' He added that the UK was not planning to place its deterrent into multilateral disarmament negotiations until the US and Russians did likewise.

An opinion poll in November 2005 showed that when told of the cost of replacement, only 33 per cent declared support and 54 per cent opposed. As long as nuclear weapons continue to proliferate – with Iran being perceived as a dangerous impending candidate – retention of the deterrent is likely to be supported by a majority of MPs. However, Labour MPs, with their history of supporting the Campaign for Nuclear Disarmament, will find replacement difficult to accept given the imperative to reduce public spending in the light of the 2008–9 economic crisis which caused government debt levels to multiply. Conservatives too, while officially supporting Trident renewal, contain some dissenting voices on the issue at the time of writing.

Conclusion on Labour's foreign policy

On 10 September 2009 *The Economist* considered how well Labour's declared 'ethical dimension' in foreign policy had been pursued. It argued that 'the assumption that Labour promised much on ethics abroad but delivered little seems overdone'. It went on to point out that: arms sales to Indonesia had terminated in 1999; arms sales were made more transparent; the Kyoto Protocol had been warmly supported; and the International Criminal Court supported together with the Hague trials of war crimes in Yugoslavia.

Mr Blair's 'Chicago Doctrine' was an attempt to insert a norm of ethical intervention into a world long dominated by the principle of state sovereignty. The 'responsibility to protect', an evolving humanitarian concept embraced by the UN, owes something to his words and deeds around the turn of the millennium.

This direction in foreign policy definitely went off track once the Iraq decisions were taken. As David Clark, Cook's adviser noted, it 'shattered the post-Kosovo consensus for ethical intervention'. It seems likely, at the time of writing, that any residual faith in such an ethical dimension, will be obliterated by the painful experience of Afghanistan.

BOX 25.4   BRITAIN IN CONTEXT

Foreign policy in a changing world

Foreign policy is usually founded on defence policy: the ability of a country both to defend itself from harm and to inflict harm in its own right. As defence policy reflects how much a country feels it can afford to pay on military hardware, foreign policy is also based, at root, on economic power. The USA is the world's only superpower and no country can currently match its expenditure on armaments. It spends over $400 bn a year on defence, a sum which has ratcheted up dramatically since the 9/11 attacks. The US spends as much on defence as the rest of the world combined and twice as much as the EU. In addition to this, US arms technology is years ahead of the rest of the world.

But being a superpower militarily is only one facet of US power. America is aided by the huge advantage of a massive economy which stretches out to every corner of the world and a media industry which mass-markets American values and culture to the same places. And yet the superpower is not and does not feel safe. For years it did, and a strong strand of opinion – isolationism – wished to keep it even safer by avoiding major foreign commitments. Indeed George W. Bush himself, when running for President in 2000, expressed mildly isolationist views. But its huge economic strength and international interests made such objectives unachievable for the USA, especially as some elements in the world, especially fundamentalist Muslims, saw the US as the source of great evil and corruption worldwide.

The attacks by al-Qaeda upon the World Trade Center in 2001 signified the opening of a new war which the US could not avoid as this time the fight, traumatic for Americans, had been taken onto their own soil. The 'War on Terror' became the main driver of US foreign policy and, via close association, of UK policy as well. However, the inability of the US to impose its will by brute force and the revulsion of the world at its treatment of prisoners discredited the idea of such a war and the term ceased to be used once Barack Obama was elected president in 2008. Experience in Vietnam in the 1960s and in Iraq since 2003 reveals that mastery of the air and huge military superiority on the ground are no guarantors of successful containment of a determined, irregular enemy armed merely with small arms and suicide bombs.

US foreign policy strategists are highly aware of the changing geopolitical nature of world power. Defending Europe against a predatory USSR used to be its main priority but now the EU is regarded as of waning importance. The new suitors wooed by the USA are all found in Asia. The fastest-rising economic power is China, a country of well over a billion people which has been expanding economically at some 10 per cent a year for the past two decades. It has now left the dark ages of Maoist communism way behind and is beginning to flex its own muscles. It is seen as the major long-term military and economic threat to the USA, already winning manufacturing business from the higher-waged superpower and holding vast sums of US currency which potentially gives it a lever over US economic policy. Bush's visit to India in March 2006 revealed how the US sees the world's biggest democracy – also emerging as an economic superpower in its own right – as a possible counter to China.

In February 2006 Condoleeza Rice announced a major redeployment of diplomatic personnel: 61 posts in the 'old' world of the EU were to be dropped while 74 new posts were to be established in Asia. The UK also has done something similar: Sir Michael Jay, head of the Diplomatic Service, said on 3 March 2006: 'We are making sure our resources are deployed so the right people are in the right places to promote Britain's interests around the world. Among other things, this means shifting resources from our European to our Asian network.' China too has been readjusting to her nascent superpower status, sending scores of diplomats, inevitably, to the USA but also substantial delegations to other countries where she seeks to increase influence: Pakistan, Japan (despite the appalling historical record) and selected African countries like Angola.

■ Relations with the developing world

Since the world banking crisis and subsequent economic recession of 2007–9, the increased importance of the developing world has been recognised by the replacement of the G8 as the world's primary managing group by the G20. It is inevitable that Britain will now seek to establish improved relations with these emergent powers as economic and political power moves from west to east (see Box 25.4).

China

As the most important of the emergent powers and the one destined, perhaps to replace the USA as the world's premier economy, it follows that the UK should have worked very hard to woo for its favours. The Foreign Office has made clear its aim to 'step up our engagement with China across the board. This reflects China's increasing economic weight and political influence and our desire to work with China to tackle the many and complex challenges the international community face today.' Britain has become Europe's largest investor in China and there are more Chinese students in the UK than any other overseas group. In 2004 Tony Blair and premier Wen Jaibao, agreed annual summit meetings between the two Prime Ministers. In addition the *China Task Force*, chaired by the Chancellor and comprising leading business and other public figures provides high-level advice to government. A similar body advises Chinese leaders on the UK. The UK–China Economic and Financial Dialogue is also chaired by the Chancellor and provides a high-level strategic forum; the Sector-specific Ministerial Discussions provide contacts on education and sustainable development; and the UK–China Human Rights Dialogue provides a forum for, given China's repressive record, this more controversial topic. All these efforts help to bring the countries closer but, as its own reserves dry up, Chinese reliance on Iranian oil led to a recent new alliance and explains why China, to the discomfort of the UK and USA, supports Iran's nuclear programme.

India

In September 2005 the UK government spelled out a new strategic partnership with India on Foreign and Defence policy; immigration, counter terrorism, economic and trade issues, sustainable development and educational links. The 2006 White Paper on British Diplomacy stated that 'As the world's largest democracy, India will have a growing influence in international affairs and on the global economy.' This last point is reinforced by the fact that India's economic growth was 9.1 per cent in 2007–8, second only to China's rate of growth. The UK supports India's permanent seat on the UN Security Council and invited her to attend the G8 meeting in Gleneagles in 2005. India is also a significant recipient of overseas aid from the British government and a close collaborator in the fields of education, health, the fight against HIV and Aids and climate change.

Brazil

As the major economic power in Latin America, Britain has been assiduous in establishing educational, sporting and ministerial contacts, as it has with a raft of other emerging nations in Asia, Latin America and Africa.

USA or EU?

Having said all this about the developing nations however, British foreign policy at the end of the first decade of the twenty-first century still grapples with the dilemma which has dominated its concerns since the end of the Second World War: whether to continue seeking to exercise a world role via the proxy of US power, or investing more commitment in a unified EU foreign policy position. Links with the USA since the Second World War have been fondly regarded by Britain's political class as constituting a 'special relationship' but American insistence on debt repayment, the Suez debacle and the 1983 invasion of Grenada without consultation should put this into a wider and less special perspective. Tony Blair seemed almost manic in his desire to please George Bush by joining him in his ill-fated Iraq adventure but received nothing tangible in return. Gordon Brown was keen to draw back somewhat from Blair's position after he became Prime Minister in 2007 but joined in the general lionising of Obama with everyone else after his election in November 2008.

Barack Obama meeting with Brown and Sarkozy
Source: Getty Images/Jim Watson/AFP

Downsizing Britain's role from a world to a medium power has not been easy for Britain. Holding on to her Security Council seat and nuclear weapons have provided two almost credible routes but, for the most part she has sought to manage the transition by adhering, wherever possible, to US policy. Some critics argue that a more fruitful direction for foreign policy would be a serious attempt to engineer a more coherent common EU position. With a population of 500 million and the biggest unified market in the world, the EU is often said to be an 'economic giant but a political pygmy' with no common defence or foreign policy. During the crises caused by the break-up of Yugoslavia, this lack proved embarrassing and harmful as Milosevic's forces operated without scruple. But the UK is hopelessly divided over the EU with a large swath of voters suspicious or hostile of possible federal EU intentions to the extent that support for a unified foreign policy is not even on the distant horizon. Interestingly David Miliband, Foreign Secretary since June 2007, has moved to abandon Blair's idea of the UK being a 'bridge' between the two con-

tinents; it was 'never quite right' he commented dismissively. Contrasting with Blair, again, who took his country to war five times, Miliband stressed soft power and multilateralism in his speech on 12 February 2008 as well as the new primacy of 'citizen issues like climate change global poverty and human rights'. Meanwhile, Iraq is no longer such a divisive issue now that British troops have virtually withdrawn and US troops will do so by August 2010. Significantly Miliband has disavowed the term 'war on terror', as 'misleading and mistaken' (Harvey 2009).

■ Conservative directions in foreign policy

At the time of writing, opinion polls suggest the Conservatives may win the 2010 election. Assuming William Hague is confirmed in his shadow role and becomes Foreign Secretary, what is likely to be their view on the dilemma posed above?

David Milliband
Source: Getty Images/Indigo

William Hague
Source: Getty Images/Wireimage

Firstly, both Hague and Cameron are both Atlanticists and would direct a fair amount of energy to becoming closer to the USA, even with a Democrat in the White House. They would also be likely to reinforce the UK's commitment to the Afghanistan conflict, thus raising questions at home about defence spending. A new defence review would be inevitable.

Secondly, they would likely be far less accommodating to the EU. This question is an exceedingly vexed one for the Conservatives as it caused civil war in their party during the 1990s and was a subject certain to rouse the party's grassroots who tend to view the EU as a conspiracy, possibly inspired by timeless German ambitions, but at any rate antithetical to any British sense of identity and likely to lead to an unelected, supranational, potentially dictatorial super-state. David Cameron is too much of a pragmatist to take a consistently hostile line on the EU – his hands will be more than full with the economy if he becomes Prime Minister – but he took a Eurosceptic line in 2005 to outflank his opponent David Davis in the leadership contest of that year by withdrawing the party from the mainstream EPP grouping containing most centre-right parties. His formation of another anti-federalist grouping with some dubious Polish and Latvian parties was causing him much embarrassment by the summer of 2009, reminding him surely of how toxic this topic was for his wider electoral appeal. Moreover, in September 2007 he pledged *The Sun* a 'cast iron guarantee' he would hold 'a referendum on any treaty that emerges from these (on Lisbon Treaty) negotiations' (Oborne 2009). This proved highly embarrassing for Cameron and Hague but they had to bite the bullet and back down, as Hague explained:

Now that the treaty is going to become European law and is going to enter into force, that means a referendum can no longer prevent the creation of the president of the European council, the loss of British national vetoes . . . . These things will already have happened and a referendum cannot unwind them or prevent them.

The Guardian, 3 November 2009

There can be no doubt Conservatives were hurt by this climb-down and it provides yet another example of how poisonous an issue the EU remains within the party. Furthermore, embarrassment may continue if party zealots insist he dish the EU from early on in his premiership. The problem is that the genuinely Eurosceptic Hague, as Oborne points out, rather like Prescott to Blair, is a senior figure who can deliver party support; but unlike Prescott, Hague is a genuinely formidable politician who could easily be a challenger for the leadership if things go wrong for Cameron. Foreign policy is likely to levitate rapidly up the issue agenda as the election approaches but should Cameron win, it could provide a major hazard in waiting for Cameron's new administration.

Chapter summary

British foreign policy is based upon what it can afford economically and the Strategic Defence Review in the late 1990s did much to adapt defence policy to what could be afforded and what was needed to maintain national security in a rapidly changing world. Labour's attempt to introduce an 'ethical foreign policy' was controversial but was probably justified and successful in terms of the Kosovo crisis. Britain's traditional closeness to US foreign policy was reinforced by Blair when Clinton was president and he was quick to establish close relations with George Bush in 2000. However, the difficulties encountered following the joint invasion of Iraq caused Blair considerable political problems at home.

Discussion points

■ Criticise the 'realist' approach to foreign policy.

■ Should Britain have avoided involvement in Kosovo?

■ Does the world need a new form of international government?

■ Is Britain too keen to support the USA in all situations?

■ Was the Iraq war justified?

Further reading

To be honest there are not many good up to date analyses of this aspect of British policy. Byrd, though dated (1988) is useful for a broad coverage; Little and Whickham-Smith's *New Labour's Foreign Policy: a New Moral Crusade?* is more recent and very useful, especially Chapter 1 by Whickham-Smith, but Chapters 2–6 are all acutely analysed and worth reading. See also the also dated Sanders (1990) and the more recent book by Paul Williams, Britain's Foreign Policy under New Labour. See also Lord Butler's report from 2004 and Sir Christopher Meyer's enjoyably indiscreet memoirs (Meyer 2005).

Bibliography

Butler, Lord (2004) *Review of Intelligence on Weapons of Mass Destruction,* HC 898.

Byrd, P. (1988) *British Foreign Policy Under Thatcher* (Philip Allan).

Carrington, Lord (1988) *Reflect on Things Past* (Collins).

Cook, R. (1997) 'British foreign policy' statement, 12 May.

Economist (2006) 'Fighter Jets: Keeping Secrets', 28 January.

Freedman, C. and Clark, M. (1991) *Britain in the World* (Cambridge University Press).

Gamble, A. (2003) *Between Europe and America: The Future of British Politics* (Palgrave).

Hartley, K. (2002a) 'UK Defence Policy: An Economist's Perspective', www.york.ac.uk/depts/econ/research/documents/defence.pdf

Hartley, K. (2002b) 'UK Defence Policy: A Triumph of Hope over Experience?', www.york.ac.uk/depts/econ/research/documents/ipr.pdf

Harvey, M. (2009) Notes on a Post-Blair Foreign Policy, *New Statesman,* 15 February.

Kampfner, J. (1998) *Robin Cook* (Gollancz).

Labour Party (1997) *New Labour Because Britain Deserves Better* (Labour Party).

Little, R. and Whickham-Smith, M. (2000) *New Labour's Foreign Policy: a New Moral Crusade?* (Manchester University Press).

Martin, L. and Garnett, J. (1997) *British Foreign Policy: Challenges for the Twenty First Century* (Royal Institute of International Affairs).

Meyer, C. (2005) *DC Confidential* (Weidenfeld & Nicolson).

Oborne, Peter (2009) 'Cameron has only Himself to Blame for this Mess on Europe' (*Observer,* 1 November).

Owen, D. (1978) *Human Rights* (Jonathan Cape).

Sanders, D. (1990) *Losing an Empire, Finding a Role* (Macmillan).

Wheeler, N.J. and Dunne, T. (1998) 'Good International Citizenship: A Third Way for British Foreign Policy', *International Affairs,* Vol. 74, No. 4, pp. 847–70.

Williams, P. (2006) *Britain's Foreign Policy under New Labour* (Palgrave).

Useful websites

Amnesty International: www.amnesty.org

Domestic sources of foreign policy: www.apsanet.org/-state

Foreign and Commonwealth Office: www.fco.gov.uk

Ministry of Defence: www.mod.uk

EU common security policy: www.europa.eu.int/pol/cfsp/index-en.htm

NATO: www.nato.int

Organisation for Security and Cooperation in Europe: www.osce.or.at/

CHAPTER 26

Environmental policy

Andrew Flynn

Learning objectives

- To explain the provenance and functions of the Environment Agency; local planning and conservation agencies.

- To elucidate the positions of the main political parties on key features of environmental policy.

- To analyse the role of pressure groups focusing on the environment.

Introduction

Although environmentalism in Britain can be traced back to the nineteenth century with an elite reaction to contemporary urbanism and industrialism, it is only since the late 1960s that the environment as a political issue has engaged the wider public and increasingly become a mainstream public policy concern. Moreover, over the past 40 years the pace of change has quickened in the development of environmental policy ideas and the way in which they are to be administered. Looking back to the late 1960s it is possible to discern a number of key features that have helped to transform the way in which we think about the environment and the content of environmental policy. These include:

- The environment has moved from the political margins to the mainstream. Today all political parties have an environment policy and leading figures in the parties are expected to make references to the environment in set-piece speeches.
- A number of new institutions have been created or reformed to better manage the demands that are made upon the physical environment. These new bodies range from central government departments such as the Department for Environment, Food and Rural Affairs (DEFRA) and the Department of Energy and Climate Change (DECC), to regulatory and advisory bodies such as the Environment Agency and Natural England.
- Policy has metamorphosed over time. As we shall see below, policy has moved from a concern with the physical environment to the more comprehensive and challenging concept of sustainable development in which the goal is the simultaneous realisation of economic, social and environmental goals, and more recently to a preoccupation with climate change.
- The result of such changes is twofold. First, new policies and institutions are layered one upon another. Old ideas, beliefs and ways of working are not simply wiped away but help to inform new thinking and practices. So, despite changes in rhetoric there remain important elements of policy continuity. Second, policy has been stretched. The environment (or climate change) has a legitimacy that allows it to seep into new policy domains. This brings environmental actors (such as pressure groups) into policy domains that would previously have been closed (e.g. business strategy) and brings new actors and perspectives into commenting on the content of environmental policy (e.g. the business community led by the Confederation of British Industry). This in turn reinforces the dynamic nature of environmental policy.

For students of politics the challenge raised by environmental issues to existing administrative structures is of enormous interest. So too is the way in which external pressures on bureaucracies, such as those from the European Union (EU), shape the context of environmental policy making and its implementation. But the nature of the challenge posed by environmentalism goes beyond simply studying bureaucratic structures. It involves questions of how governments respond to environmental issues, how societies articulate their environmental concerns and how political parties and pressure groups seek to represent the environment. These questions will be answered during the course of the chapter, but first we address the impact of Europe on British environmental policy, and then consider what environmental policy might be and how it has become part of the broader debate on sustainable development. (The most recent phase in environmental policy – that of climate change – is analysed towards the end of the chapter.) The third section analyses the impact of devolution on the making and delivery of policy. The fourth section explores the role of key organisations and institutions operating in Britain since it is they who are responsible for much of the delivery of policy, and the fifth examines the part that political parties and pressure groups play when viewed through the lens of transport and energy policy. These are two policy areas where the environmental dimension of policy development cannot be ignored and where climate change implications loom increasingly large.

The impact of Europe on British environmental policy

Membership of the EU has had a profound influence on the content of British environmental policy and also the way that it is made (Lowe and Ward 1998a; Jordan 2005). These two points are addressed in turn.

Policy content

The European Community first began to take a serious interest in environmental issues in the early 1970s (Lowe and Ward 1998a: 11–13, Jordan 2005). Its first Action Programme on the Environment was published in 1973 and aimed to improve people's quality of life, living conditions and their surroundings. At this stage the emphasis was very much on trying to ensure that the people within the Community enjoyed similar standards and that environmental regulations were not used by member states as a means of distorting trade. With regard to the latter there was much work on trying to harmonise product standards, a similar burst of activity being associated with the completion of the Single European Market. Throughout the 1970s the environment continued to rise up the European political agenda and was marked by a growing institutionalisation. An Environment Directorate-General (DGXI) of the Commission was established in 1981, and in 1987 under the Single European Act there was explicitly established a basis for Community action in the environmental field. Until this time environmental legislation had to be justified on the grounds that it was helping to avoid distortions of the market in line with the Community's economic rationale. The EU's responsibilities for environmental protection have been broadened and deepened under the 1993 Treaty on European Union (that amended the Treaty of Rome) and 1997 Treaty of Amsterdam. The former provided a still firmer legal base for EU environmental activities, while the latter has committed the EU as one of its main tasks to promoting sustainable development and a higher quality environment. This involves the EU not only thinking about specific environmental policies but also making sure that environmental concerns are integrated into other policy areas. As we shall see below, Britain has traditionally been regarded as a middle-ranking state with regard to environmental policy. However, in what was clearly designed to give out a quite different message, the Labour government, in hosting its first European Council meeting in Cardiff in June 1998, ensured that there was a reaffirmation of the importance of integrating the environment across the EU's activities.

Articles 174–6 of the Amsterdam Treaty (the latest ratified revision of the founding Treaty of Rome) identified a number of key principles that EU policy should now be based on including the following:

- Precautionary principle – whereas in the past many decisions have been taken only when there is sufficient supporting evidence to justify a course of action this principle justifies action to prevent harm to the environment before such evidence is available.

- Preventative action – recognises that it is better to try to stop environmental problems arising at source rather than to deal with them once they have arisen.

- Polluter pays – those who cause **pollution** should pay for its clean up rather than those who may be most affected by it.

- Policy integration – the environment must play a part in decision making in all policy areas.

The EU's Environmental Action Programmes provide it and the member states with a guide to action, an agenda for change. The Fifth Environmental Action Programme (5th EAP) running for the period 1992–2000 is entitled *Towards Sustainability* (Commission of the European Communities 1992). According to one former senior civil servant it marked the first occasion on which the British government could begin to identify with a European environmental agenda (Sharp 1998: 49). This was both a reflection of the content of the programme and of the way in which ideas in Britain had been developing. The 5th EAP shared the policy principles that were to be found in the Treaty of European Union and suggested that there should be a wider use of policy instruments (e.g. eco-taxes, voluntary agreements with industry) since established command and control measures were no longer sufficient to deal with environmental problems. The document promoted the idea of shared responsibility, that is the solution to environmental problems was not solely the responsibility of government or the private sector but also needed to include the public, voluntary organisations and the public sector. The 5th EAP also identified five key sectors – agriculture, energy, industry, transport and tourism – where there was a particular need to try and make progress to improve their environmental and economic performance. The linking together of the economy and the environment is an important feature of the way in which the environmental debate has broadened into one on sustainable development as we shall see below.

The EU's 6th EAP was published in January 2001 and will run until 2012. Its main goal is to decouple economic growth from environmental damage, once again a theme that the UK government has considerable sympathy with as we shall see below. However, in contrast to the 5th EAP, the 6th is very short on specific commitments or targets. It does reaffirm the 5th EAPs determination to promote shared responsibility for solving environmental problems and of a wish to promote a wider range of policy instruments to achieve goals. There is also less interest than there has been in the past about how goals should be achieved and more attention to the outcomes of policy. A key vehicle for delivery is the identification of thematic strategies, such as air pollution, waste prevention and recycling, the marine environment, the urban environment and soil protection. These themes are in turn underpinned by coordination measures, like implementation (ensuring that member states deliver on policy); integration (promoting sectoral policy complementarity rather than competition); and harnessing the market to achieve environmental goals.

The more modest policy ambitions of the latest EU Environmental Action Plan are a reflection of two key challenges that the EU faces. The first is that earlier Action Plans were able to tackle easier environmental problems. Environmental challenges that have emerged (e.g. climate change) or are still proving difficult to resolve (e.g. the volume and nature of waste production by business and households) do not have straightforward legislative solutions. Tackling waste requires attacking the problem from multiple sources and changing the behaviour of the public – something which is politically sensitive and cannot be secured by traditional forms of regulation alone. Second, the EU is increasingly embracing an economic growth agenda in which environmental issues are clearly less important than they have been in the recent past. Eastward expansion of the EU has further accentuated the growth, rather than the environmental priorities of the EU. In some areas there is a synergy between economic and environmental measures, for example, encouraging more efficient resource use, and where policy progress can be made, but other issues may demand curbs on economic activities, such as tackling climate change.

Policy making

EU law takes precedence over national law and since in the making of environmental policy there has been a shift away from voting by unanimity to majority voting, Britain, like other countries, cannot exercise control over what decisions are made. The environmental field was the fastest-growing EU policy area in the 1980s and by the mid-1990s John Gummer (1994), a former British Secretary of State for the Environment, had estimated that about 80 per cent of British environmental legislation had its origins in Europe. Not surprisingly, therefore, there have been considerable impacts on the British environmental policy process.

Lowe and Ward (1998b: 26–8) identify three dimensions along which it is possible to assess change in the policy process. The first of these is a challenge to Britain's traditional policy style, that is the management and administration of issues. As an important political issue the environment commands the attention of wide swathes of government in a way in which it did not in the past. In tackling problems such as pollution Britain's pragmatic approach in which pollution problems could be dealt with on a case by case basis has been undermined by the elucidation of wide-ranging principles, such as the polluter pays, to govern action. Similarly regulators had liked to be flexible when dealing with polluters to take account of their circumstances, but that is less possible as European legislation is much more target led, meaning that firms and government must meet preset criteria, and so limiting their room for manoeuvre.

Second, there have been changes in the relationships amongst organisations involved in the policy process. As the focus for policy making has moved from London to Brussels it has opened up the process to environmental groups who have found a more receptive audience for their views. Local government meanwhile may have lost some of its authority since it is national governments that engage in negotiations and are held responsible by Brussels for the implementation of policy.

Third, and most difficult of all to assess, what has been the impact of Europe on the substance of policy? Although the evidence is somewhat mixed there is a belief that the EU has meant that Britain has adopted higher standards of environmental protection than it would otherwise have done. What the EU has most certainly done is to help change the terms of the environmental debate in Britain.

While in many cases Britain is an adapter rather than an initiator of environmental policy, government thinking is at least now attuned to that of leading nations such as the Netherlands. This is a point that is explored in greater detail below.

■ From environmental policy to sustainable development

It is easy to suggest that environmental policy was 'discovered' in the 1980s and 1990s. Yet many of the most prominent environmental groups were formed well before then, while Britain has long-standing policies to regulate air quality and land use, two components of any environmental policy. So a first question must be whether the environment is really a new policy area or simply older issues recast in a more fashionable light. In part the answer is determined by the way the environment transcends traditional administrative and policy boundaries leading to, for example, the greening of policies in transport and the environment, agriculture and the environment, etc. rather than existing as a separate policy sector. Rather like the environment itself which is no respecter of borders environmental policy seemingly knows no policy boundaries. In part also perceptions of what counts as the environment are culturally and historically constructed. For example, asked 'When people talk about the "environment", which of the following do you think of first', UK citizens reported pollution in towns and cities (31 per cent) and German citizens protecting nature (27 per cent). Defining the content of environmental policy is, therefore, not easy.

Not surprisingly, therefore, many commentators duck the question of what they regard as environmental policy. It is assumed implicitly that everyone knows what it is and is not. Nevertheless, it is possible to distinguish two popular approaches to defining environmental policy. The first is broad in scope and seeks links to the physical environment: thus environmental policy is 'public policy concerned with governing the relationship between people and their natural environment' (McCormick 1991: 7). Unfortunately this definition is both too narrow, in the sense that it seems to exclude urban areas (as these are difficult to classify as a natural environment), and too general, as it would seem difficult in practice to distinguish it from other policy areas such as rural social policy.

The other approach is much narrower in scope and focusses on 'the use of land and the *regulation* of human activities which have an impact on our physical surroundings' (Blowers 1987: 278–9, our emphasis). This implies a prescriptive element to policy, as politicians should seek a balance in the use of land between its development, **conservation** and ecological functions. In practice this involves working through two regulatory systems, that of the land use planning system (responsible for development and conservation) and pollution control (the ecological function). While providing a framework against which to assess changes in environmental policy, the regulatory definition ignores the wider political and social backcloth, including the activities of political parties and new social groups, against which environmental decisions are made.

Neither was it possible to specify that government action on the environment amounted to an environmental policy. Writing at the end of the 1980s Lowe and Flynn claimed that:

government structures and law relating to environmental protection have been (and largely remain) an accretion of common law, statutes, agencies, procedures and policies. *There is no environmental policy other than the sum of these individual elements, most of which have been pragmatic and incremental responses to specific problems and the evolution of relevant scientific knowledge.*

Lowe and Flynn 1989: 256, emphasis added

However, in 1990 the White Paper This Common Inheritance (Cm 1200) was published, the first ever comprehensive statement in Britain of a government's environmental policy. Criticised at the time for its modest proposals, the document nevertheless marks something of a watershed: the environment was a legitimate and high-profile public policy issue. By the end of the decade the terms of the debate had once again shifted. Increasingly to simply think of the environment as a single policy area is to marginalise it. Successive governments have produced detailed statements of their environmental policy but now they have also sought to integrate the environment with economic and social issues to develop a strategy for sustainable development. So how has such a dramatic shift come about in such a short space of time? Any answer must include at least the following issues: the British government's response to developing agendas in the EU and at the United Nations, the success of pressure groups in the promotion of the environmental agenda, and a growing realisation of the challenges of implementing environmental policy and of the need to ensure that it took account of business and social interests.

■ The sustainable development agenda

One of the classic confrontations of the late twentieth century was that between the environment and the economy. The two were regarded as incompatible: one either had ecological protection and no growth or economic development and environmental degradation. The notion of sustainable development, and the belief of some that we are moving towards a greener society, integrates the economy and the environment and at one stroke sidesteps much of the traditional debate.

Much of the controversy now is over what is meant by sustainable development, for it has become something of a totem, a concept so powerful that no one should question it. But different interests seek to interpret it in various ways. As such sustainable development has become an object of contestation within the environmental debate. Originally developed within the ecological sciences, sustainable development was popularised in *Our Common Future* (more commonly known as the Brundtland Report) (World Commission on Environment and Development 1987) as that which 'meets the needs of the present without compromising the ability of future generations to meet their own needs'. At its minimum this would seem to involve little more than business as usual with a few added-on commitments to environmental protection.

In order to show their commitment to environmental protection and exploit market opportunities businesses have engaged in such measures as environmental management systems and environmental auditing. Purchasing policies, production processes and waste disposal are all now much more carefully monitored. Eco-labelling schemes now exist in many European countries to show that products are produced to a certain standard and an EU-wide labelling scheme – the Flower – first appeared in 1992.

Governments have shown a willingness to co-ordinate and act to address the issue of sustainable development. The Brundtland Report was endorsed by political leaders at the United Nations Conference on Environment and Development (the Earth Summit) in Rio de Janeiro in 1992. The summit produced the following:

1 the Rio declaration, which established a set of principles for action;

2 a programme of action for the next century, Agenda 21;

3 a Climate Change Convention to try to reduce the risks of global warming;

4 a Biodiversity Convention to protect species and habitats; and

5 a statement of principles for the conservation of the world's forests.

Each country was charged with taking forward these points. A follow-up, Earth Summit II, was held in New York in June 1997 and began to expose to a wide audience the difficulties that a number of the developed countries were experiencing in putting into practice the ideas they had endorsed some five years earlier in Rio.

More recently the World Summit on Sustainable Development (WSSD), also known as Rio+10, was held from 26 August to 4 September 2002 in Johannesburg. The sense that Rio had led to tangible achievements heightened the expectations around the Johannesburg summit but the discussions and outcomes showed clearly the tensions that can emerge between governments and between government and NGOs when they seek to bring together trade, economics, social development and environmental protection. While many activists and governments were dissatisfied at the outcomes, and there were few tangible achievements, business for the first time on the world stage did seek to play the role of full partner with governments and NGOs in delivering on sustainability. What was achieved in the great debates conducted by over one hundred heads of government and tens of thousands of citizens? Energy proved to the most contentious issue and little was achieved. More positive were the efforts to promote corporate accountability and sustainable production and consumption and commitments to improve water quality and sanitation for the world's poor. On globalisation, trade and the environment the primacy of the World Trade Organisation was noted. Perhaps not surprisingly the value of such set piece events has been questioned, and Johannesburg may prove to be the last of the great world sustainability summits. Attention is now shifting towards the implementation and monitoring of commitments.

What difference, if any have these major international conferences had in shaping UK policy development? Following the Rio Conference the former Conservative government put some efforts into delivering its promises on implementing its action programme. After a year-long consultation period it published *Sustainable Development: the UK Strategy* (Cm 2426) in January 1994. The document was largely a restatement of existing policies and ideas but did contain some initiatives to promote new ideas. These included a Panel on Sustainable Development comprising five eminent experts who report directly to the Prime Minister on major strategic issues; a Round Table on Sustainable Development made up of thirty representatives drawn from business, local government, environmental groups and other organisations that seek to build consensus about the ways of achieving sustainable development; and a Going for Green programme to carry the sustainable development message to local communities and individuals. From 2000 the Panel and Round Table was subsumed within a new Sustainable Development Commission chaired by a leading environmentalist, Jonathan Porritt.

The government also published proposals on *Biodiversity: the UK Action Plan* (Cm 2428). Again, the policies were modest and often simply consolidated in one document existing actions but did at least represent a positive step forward. In contrast parts of local government have been much more innovative in developing sustainability indicators and action programmes, though they remain hamstrung by lack of resources and powers.

When she returned to Britain from the Johannesburg Summit Environment Secretary Margaret Beckett announced that she had asked Jonathon Porritt, chair of the Sustainable Development Commission, to convene a group of twelve leading figures from business and local and regional government to discuss how to tackle sustainable consumption and production; the role of business in delivering sustainable development; and renewable energy. The direct influence of summits on the development of government policy has, therefore, been rather modest. More important in policy development has been the need to respond to European and domestic agendas.

Many environmentalists argue that a stronger version of sustainable development needs to be put into practice, one in which the state plays a much more positive role in ensuring the equitable distribution of resources through space and time. Attention is switched away from total production to the methods of production of particular goods. A weak version of sustainable development therefore fails to confront the major cause of the ecological crisis, the sheer amount of production and consumption. On this view, sustainable development does not mean no development but much more selective development.

For governments the idea that there should be more selective development is a challenging one as it may alienate voters and their families caught up in those sectors or firms that are seen to be too unsustainable. They have therefore sought to construct defensible policy positions at a point between the weak and strong versions of sustainable development. Shortly after its election to power in 1997 the Labour government announced that it would update the sustainable development strategy of its predecessor. In February 1998 a consultation paper, *Opportunities for Change*, was issued and it was followed by a small number of additional consultation papers on particular aspects of sustainable development, such as business and tourism. A revised sustainable development strategy, *A Better Quality of Life: a Strategy for Sustainable Development for the United Kingdom* (Cm 4345) was published by the government in May 1999.

Interestingly, the government's approach to sustainable development has become ever more interwoven with that of devolution. *A Better Quality of Life* was developed as devolution was coming into force and so would have a limited shelf life. This is because sustainable development has proved to be a key feature of the responsibilities of the Devolved Administrations. So, in the early 2000s it was increasingly recognised within government that a new UK-level strategy would need to be developed that could take account of the impact of devolution on both the formulation and implementation of policy and of the emergence of new issues on the sustainability agenda.

From the outset in developing the new strategy it was recognised that devolution had reshaped the policy context and that it would not be possible to produce a single UK document, like *A Better Quality of Life*, that could embrace both UK policy and that of the Devolved Administrations. Instead, there would be a UK strategy and a UK-wide strategic framework that would cover:

■ 'a shared understanding of sustainable development, a vision of what we are trying to achieve and the guiding principles that we all need to follow to get there;

■ our sustainable development priorities for UK action;

■ our work internationally to help achieve sustainable development; and

■ indicators to monitor and measure performance' (DEFRA 2004: 11).

While the Devolved Administrations and UK government can recognise the need to work cooperatively to pursue sustainability, there is likely to be an underlying tension as the Administrations will develop their own sustainability strategies 'based on their different responsibilities, needs and views' (DEFRA 2004: 11) and these may not always coincide with one another or with UK government. At a political level there is a key challenge for government to develop structures or processes that can operate at multiple levels to deliver common goals.

In the spring of 2005 two high-level policy documents on sustainable development were published simultaneously. One is *Securing the Future* (DEFRA 2005a) which sets out the UK government sustainability strategy but much of whose content does not apply to Scotland or Wales since they have their own authority in this area. From the perspective of the Devolved Administrations the more important document is *One Future – Different Paths* (DEFRA 2005b) as this established a strategic framework for their responsibilities and a common agenda with UK government. One official has explained that it is 'the first properly federal document' in the UK since it says that 'UK policy consists of *One Future – Different Paths* and the documents of the other Devolved Administrations' (which we turn to in the section below). The relationship between the different governments and their key documents is illustrated in Figure 26.1. It is important to note that

the publication of *Securing the Future* may in time come to be regarded as the high point of policy debate on sustainable development. This is because subsequently environmental policy has increasingly been dominated by climate change issues.

Securing the Future recognises that the government's previous sustainable development strategy had largely failed to deliver on its promises. So, the latest document concentrates on delivery rather than aspirational commitments. Among the most important areas for delivery are measures to support businesses to be more sustainable through initiatives on sustainable consumption and production and for consumers to adopt more sustainable lifestyles. A core part of the strategy is also devoted to energy and climate change. Also in *Securing the Future* and repeated in *One Future – Different Paths* are a set of principles and priorities that have been agreed by, and apply to, all governments within the UK (Figure 26.2).

These principles are important since they recognise that living within environmental limits and a strong, healthy and just society are underpinned by a vibrant economy, good governance and basing decisions on scientific evidence. If policy is to be sustainable it must respect and progress all five principles and so moves beyond trade-offs between principles (such as the environment and economy) that have often characterised policy in the past.

Along with the principles the governments have also agreed to four priority policy areas (DEFRA 2005a):

■ *Sustainable consumption and production*: Sustainable consumption and production is about achieving more with less. This means not only looking at how goods and services are produced, but also the impacts of products and materials across their whole life cycle and building on people's awareness of social and environmental concerns. This includes reducing the inefficient use of resources which are a drag on the economy, so helping boost business competitiveness and to break the link between economic growth and environmental degradation.

■ *Climate change and energy*: The effects of a changing climate can already be seen. Temperatures and sea levels are rising, ice and snow cover are declining, and the consequences could be catastrophic for the natural world and society. Scientific evidence points to the release of greenhouse gases, such as carbon dioxide and

* Covers England and all non-devolved issues, including international relations

Figure 26.1 The relationship between different governments and their key documents
Source: DEFRA (2005a)

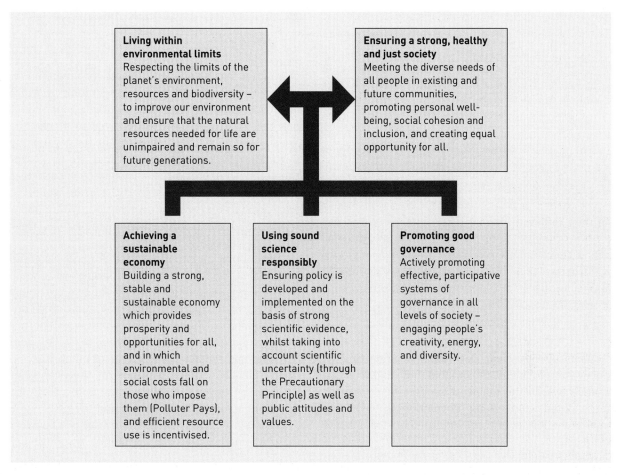

Living within environmental limits
Respecting the limits of the planet's environment, resources and biodiversity – to improve our environment and ensure that the natural resources needed for life are unimpaired and remain so for future generations.

Ensuring a strong, healthy and just society
Meeting the diverse needs of all people in existing and future communities, promoting personal well-being, social cohesion and inclusion, and creating equal opportunity for all.

Achieving a sustainable economy
Building a strong, stable and sustainable economy which provides prosperity and opportunities for all, and in which environmental and social costs fall on those who impose them (Polluter Pays), and efficient resource use is incentivised.

Using sound science responsibly
Ensuring policy is developed and implemented on the basis of strong scientific evidence, whilst taking into account scientific uncertainty (through the Precautionary Principle) as well as public attitudes and values.

Promoting good governance
Actively promoting effective, participative systems of governance in all levels of society – engaging people's creativity, energy, and diversity.

Figure 26.2 UK sustainable development principles
Source: DEFRA (2005a)

methane, into the atmosphere by human activity as the primary cause of climatic change. We will seek to secure a profound change in the way we generate and use energy, and in other activities that release these gases. At the same time we must prepare for the climate change that cannot now be avoided. We must set a good example and will encourage others to follow it.

■ *Natural resource protection and environmental enhancement*: Natural resources are vital to our existence and that of communities throughout the world. We need a better understanding of environmental limits, environmental enhancement and recovery where the environment is most degraded to ensure a decent environment for everyone, and a more integrated policy framework.

■ *Sustainable communities*: Our aim is to create sustainable communities that embody the prin-

ciples of sustainable development at the local level. This will involve working to give communities more power and say in the decisions that affect them; and working in partnership at the right level to get things done. The UK uses the same principles of engagement, partnership, and programmes of aid in order to tackle poverty and environmental degradation and to ensure good governance in overseas communities.

Although the principles and priorities establish a common policy agenda between the different tiers of government, they are pitched at such a general level that the Devolved Administrations retain considerable freedom of manoeuvre. Again, from the perspective of the Devolved Administrations, there is a common perception that having been granted policy responsibility, they would resist policy dictates from Whitehall. So, the agreed principles and priorities had to be broad to secure agreement on them.

The government's sustainable development goal

The goal of sustainable development is to enable all people throughout the world to satisfy their basic needs and enjoy a better quality of life, without compromising the quality of life of future generations.

For the UK Government and the Devolved Administrations, that goal will be pursued in an integrated way through a sustainable, innovative and productive economy that delivers high levels of employment; and a just society that promotes social inclusion, sustainable communities and personal wellbeing. This will be done in ways that protect and enhance the physical and natural environment, and use resources and energy as efficiently as possible.

Source: DEFRA (2005a)

As is already clear devolution is impacting on policy development in variable but highly significant ways. In the following section we explore in more detail what effects devolution is having on environmental policy, including that for climate change.

■ Devolution and environmental policy

Devolution has significant impacts for environmental policy making and its implementation in Wales and especially Scotland. The Scottish government has had far greater powers devolved to it than the Welsh Assembly government: for the former it is the devolution of legislative power and for the latter the ability to exercise responsibility over particular policy areas. Thus, as Table 26.1 shows, while the two legislatures will be concerned with similar topics within the field of environmental policy their authorities are quite different.

Agriculture, an important topic for both Scotland and Wales, has long been an issue with some devolved responsibilities. Energy, though, is a policy area with significant environmental implications but this remains a UK government function. Whether the devolution of responsibilities to Wales and Scotland can remain stable is a moot point. Interestingly, climate change was not on the agenda at the time of devolution but is now a key issue for governments in Wales, Scotland and the UK.

Although Wales has more limited devolved powers than Scotland it does have a unique responsibility

Table 26.1 Key environmental responsibilities and powers of the National Assembly for Wales and the Scottish Parliament

	Welsh Assembly government has responsibility for	The Scottish government has legislative powers over
Transport	Control of the construction of trunk roads in Wales, and the maintenance of existing ones	Passenger and road transport covering the Scottish road network, the promotion of road safety, bus policy, concessionary fares, cycling, taxis and minicabs, some rail grant powers, the Strathclyde Passenger Transport Executive and consultative arrangements in respect of public transport
Planning	Determine policies on town and country planning and issue guidance to local authorities	Land-use planning and building control
Heritage	Determine and implement policy on ancient monuments and listed buildings; allow and encourage visits to ancient monuments and public buildings owned by Cadw	The natural heritage including countryside issues and the functions of Scottish Natural Heritage; the built heritage including the functions of Historic Scotland
The environment	Fund, direct and make appointments to the Countryside Council Wales; fund, direct and make appointments to the Environment Agency (alongside DEFRA); control water quality and river pollution in Wales	The environment including environmental protection, matters relating to air, land and water pollution and the functions of the Scottish Environment Protection Agency; water supplies and sewerage; and policies designed to promote sustainable development within the international commitments agreed by the UK

among all levels of UK government to progress sustainable development. Under the Government of Wales Acts 1998 and 2006 the Assembly government is legally required to make a scheme setting out how it proposes, in carrying out its work, to promote sustainable development. For any legislature such a responsibility if taken seriously is formidable and for a Welsh bureaucracy that has limited experience of policy making (as opposed to policy delivery) and limited resources the challenge is all the greater. What is already clear is that the Assembly is taking its duty seriously. In its internal operations it is addressing machinery of government and policy appraisal issues to ensure that sustainability is considered across all its work, and also rethinking its external relationships so that it can promote a partnership approach to the delivery of sustainable development.

The greater political commitment to devolution in Scotland than in Wales meant that the Scots had done more preparatory work on how they would progress sustainable development within their parliament. So while no duty for sustainable development was imposed upon the parliament in the devolution legislation Lord Sewell, a former Scottish Office minister, argued:

In Scotland, we have moved forward rapidly to make sustainable development a mainstream issue for Government, for local authorities, for business and for the people of Scotland. The cross-linking of issues comes naturally to Scotland; there is a genuine interest in Scotland in delivering on the three arms which make up sustainable development: a sound economy, strong social development, built on a real concern for the environment.

In practice, though, early Scottish efforts to mainstream sustainable development were limited and more linked to political rhetoric than changes of substance. As *Down to Earth*, the first Scottish strategy for sustainable development, put it: 'The Scottish Parliament will choose for itself the form [of sustainable development] which best suits the circumstances of Scotland' (Scottish Office 1999: 5). While the priorities in Edinburgh and Cardiff have not markedly diverged from those in London, and neither should we expect them to given that Wales and Scotland have signed up to common sustainable development principles and priorities (see above), different emphases are apparent. In its second sustainable development strategy, *Choosing our Future*, the then Scottish Executive (2005) (now

the Scottish government) makes it clear that its priority is a more environmentally friendly form of economic growth. The theme of greener growth has been continued in the Scottish government's most recent political strategy, *Greener Scotland* (www.scotland.gov.uk/About/Directorates/Greener), one of five strategic objectives for the government.

Meanwhile in Wales debate moved on to how the Assembly government might enable people to start *Living Differently* (the title of the second sustainable development scheme) by changing structural factors (such as the organisation of communities) and the leadership provided by the Assembly. In its 2009 scheme for sustainable development, *One Wales: One Planet*, the Welsh Assembly Government (2009) adopted a more explicit attempt to identify the environmental impacts of resource use in Wales and to propose ways in which they might be reduced. There are strong parallels here to one of the objectives in *Greener Scotland* to reduce the impacts upon the environment of consumption and production. The focus on one planet living owes much to the influence of proponents of the 'Ecological Footprint' who have pointed out that citizens in the UK are living far beyond the earth's resources, and have received a more sympathetic reception in Wales and Scotland than they have in England.

However, in terms of making a difference to the lives of Welsh citizens the Welsh Assembly government has to work with fewer levers than the Scottish government. In seeking to redirect economic or social forces the Assembly government has the potential to be caught between its own ambitions, the expectations it raises and its ability to shape more sustainable outcomes. One example of the differences in practice between the Scottish and Welsh governments relates to climate change (More on climate change policy at the UK level can be found below, see pp. 606–10). Scotland passed its own Climate Change Act in June 2009 – by far its most ambitious piece of environmental legislation and which illustrates well the emerging nature of competitive politics on the topic. Initially the Bill had proposed that emissions reductions to 2020 would be 34 per cent from a 1990 baseline – the same as that for the UK – but as the Bill went through the Scottish Parliament this figure was raised to 40 per cent and then 42 per cent but with the caveat that the Scottish government can reduce the figure if experience shows it to be too high. In Wales, where there is no provision for primary legislation, a cross-party and multi-sectoral Climate Change Commission for

Wales has been formed to develop a consensus on climate change action.

For the future the ways in which the devolved legislatures meet their own policy agendas and contributions to UK negotiated international environmental agreements, especially in relation to climate change will be an important indicator of the ways in which patterns of devolved governance are operating in the UK. For example, Scottish and UK ministers attend major international climate change conferences, such as that in Copenhagen at the end of 2009. Although meeting GHG reduction targets will be reported at the UK level, there are opportunities for Scotland and Wales to seek to adopt more ambitious targets or to seek to meet targets in distinctive ways. For example, ministers in the Welsh Assembly have not shared the enthusiasm of UK government ministers for a new nuclear power programme but have been more sympathetic to ideas of 'clean' coal.

Europe and policy change

There are two interrelated features that emerge so far from the analysis of policy development in the late 1990s and into the 2000s. The first is that thinking on the environment and sustainability becomes an ever more central concern for government. So, for example, the former Conservative Secretary of State for the Environment, John Gummer, had shown himself to be a keen advocate of policy reform but his ministerial colleagues did not share his enthusiasm. The Labour government has a much greater commitment to environmental issues across government, for example, reflected in administrative improvements to the machinery of government and the content of policy. It is important, though, to remember that politicians will have highly variable interests in the environment. For instance, the Liberal Democrats have consistently advocated high environmental standards. Meanwhile, the former Conservative Party leader, Michael Howard, only made one speech on the environment and concluded 'there is almost no meaningful debate on the environment. It means that politicians like me can trot up to the odd conference, and make a fine and concerned speech, and go away again perhaps coming back in 12 months time to chuck around a few statistics.' Howard's successor, David Cameron, has made more effort to reposition the Conservatives on the environment and move it towards the centre of the Party's concerns by making it a quality of life issue.

The second feature is the changing base of policy. Partly as the result of the process of devolution and the European agenda outlined above, British sustainable development policy has become more attuned to that of its neighbours.

A clear sense of the pace and direction of change can be gained from comparing the development of sustainable development policy in Britain and the Netherlands. The Dutch have dealt seriously with the challenge of the environmental implications of development for a number of years and at the end of the 1980s there was a wide gulf in the thinking of the two nations. Both governments produced documents on their sustainable development strategy in 1994, Britain's as we saw was largely a restatement of existing thinking, while the Dutch engaged in a more fundamental review about the long-term direction of policy. Towards the end of the decade both countries (the Netherlands in February 1998 and Britain in May 1999) once again produced major policy statements. The Dutch remain clear European policy leaders, while Britain remains in the formative stages of its sustainable development thinking (see Table 26.2).

At that time there remained a number of differences of emphasis and some of substance between the two documents that in large part reflect the different social, political and economic circumstances of the two countries. In Britain there is a strong wish to accelerate the rate of economic growth and promote societal renewal, while in the Netherlands there is a more explicit recognition of the need to manage the impacts of industry and consumers on the environment. Within the Netherlands there is also much greater social and political consensus on the principles and content of sustainable development policy. This helps to promote policy continuity and longer term thinking that are so essential in the promotion of sustainable development. In Britain, meanwhile, while there is much agreement on policy aims between the political parties (partly because they are so broad) there tends to be less agreement on means. Since the major opposition party invariably regards it as a duty to oppose government measures, policy can quickly become politicised as the case of road transport explored below shows.

A key aspect of the sustainability strategy of both countries, and one that is now a central theme of the EU's 6th EAP, is that over time the economy should have less impact on the environment. As the British government put it: 'We have to find a new way forward. We need greater prosperity with less

Table 26.2 Britain and the Netherlands sustainable development policies compared in the late 1990s

Feature	Britain	Netherlands
Continuity with previous sustainable development document	Medium – greater emphasis on social issues and that high standards of environmental protection are a prerequisite for future economic growth	High
Overall policy goals	(a) Social progress; (b) effective protection of the environment; (c) prudent use of natural resources; and (d) maintenance of high and stable levels of economic growth and employment	(a) Solve large number of existing environmental problems within one generation (before 2010); (b) to prevent continuing economic growth causing new environmental problems
Programme of action	Emphasis on developing indicators to measure progress towards sustainability in the future and of actions that need to be undertaken	Identification of areas where progress is being made towards sustainability and where activity has been inadequate
Responsibility for action	Key actors to progress sustainable development are noted and their role within the overall framework made clear – a scene-setting exercise rather than the allocation of tasks	Target groups (e.g. industry, agriculture, consumers, government) are identified and they are made responsible for progressing the strategy

environmental damage. We need to improve the efficiency with which we use resources' (Cm 4345: para 1.8). While this is a laudable sentiment that is shared by the Dutch, they term it 'decoupling' (i.e. improving economic growth and at the same time reducing pressures on the environment), they would wish to distinguish between:

■ relative decoupling (when pressure on the environment increases at a slower rate than the economy grows), the position favoured by the British government; and

■ absolute decoupling (when environmental degradation reduces or at least remains constant while the economy grows) (*NEPP3*: 16), which is the perspective that the Dutch government advocates.

The approach of the Dutch government is more ambitious than that of the British government but its emphasis on absolute decoupling has come from its positive experience of breaking the connection between resource use and economic growth. In particular, the Dutch have found that new markets have developed for their industries in, for example, the field of environmental technology and that promoting the highest possible environmental standards within the EU helps create further markets for their companies in other parts of Europe. While the British government may be sympathetic to the approach pursued by the Dutch it will obviously impose additional costs on firms who are currently wasteful of resources. Although there is now some data

(DEFRA 2001) to support claims that the British economy is decoupling, sceptics believe the change largely reflects a switch from coal to gas for electricity generation rather than a shift in resource efficiency. This has also meant that Britain has been able to reduce its GHGs more easily than the Dutch (see below). It will be difficult for British environmental technology firms to quickly catch up with their Dutch counterparts and so issues of competitiveness will play a part in the nuancing of British sustainable development policy.

However, the Dutch have found it less straightforward to apply their modernisation approach so that it becomes an effective climate change strategy. The Dutch policy competence and leadership has been challenged as their emission levels have grown rather than declined as had been expected (Pettinger 2007). The contrasting experiences of emissions levels and political leadership between Britain and the Netherlands is explored further below.

Within both Dutch and UK governments thinking on the environment has now moved forward a further stage, but once again the Dutch remain a step ahead. Debates in the Netherlands have now begun on how governments should manage the transition towards more sustainable societies. The starting point is the recognition that current fossil-fuel-based energy production, intensive farming and transport are unsustainable. Alternative systems must be devised that are environmentally more benign and also beneficial from an economic point of view. The role of government is to help set long-term goals and create a framework in which society can experiment with different means to achieve those goals. In the UK, there is considerable interest in the Dutch approach to innovation and transition and although progress on the long-term reforms to institutional structures and processes has for the most part been sporadic it has undoubtedly influenced the UK's approach to climate change policy (see below, pp. 606–10). There has also been considerable institutional restructuring taking place and it is to this that we now turn. Overall, though, environmental policy goals and mechanisms tend to be rather more cautious than those found in the Netherlands.

■ Central government and its agencies

Department of the Environment, Food and Rural Affairs (DEFRA)

Recurrent themes in the analysis of British institutions for environmental protection are those of integration and fragmentation. As political priorities have changed over time and new problems arisen governments have attempted to solve them through a series of organisational fixes. These fixes, though, become ever more contested as the environment becomes a more important political issue and commentators increasingly turn their attention to the principles and processes for organising to protect the environment. The creation of DEFRA, its predecessor the Department of the Environment Transport and the Regions (DETR) and the original Department of the Environment (DoE) illustrate well the pressures on government and the way in which the pendulum of integration and fragmentation can swing back and forth. The challenge to integrate central government functions to adequately cope with the broad nature of environmental decisions does not change but the political response does.

In an argument that resonates as clearly today as it did when written in 1970 a White Paper on 'The Reorganisation of Central Government' (Cmnd 4506) pointed out that:

It is increasingly accepted that maintaining a decent environment, improving people's living conditions and providing for adequate transport facilities, all come together in the planning of development . . . Because these functions interact, and because they give rise to acute and conflicting requirements, a new form of organisation is needed at the centre of the administrative system.

This new organisation was the Department of the Environment. Headed by a Secretary of State in the Cabinet, it was an amalgamation of the Ministries of Housing and Local Government, Public Building and Works, and Transport. With the benefit of hindsight, however, it is easy to see that while the government may have believed that organisational reform was sufficient to deal with environmental problems, the Department of the Environment was more a rearrangement of the machinery of government than the creation of a department with new powers. It was never going to work as a department of the environment let alone one for the environment because the politics of Whitehall had left key environmental issues with other departments. Thus, responsibility for agriculture and the countryside remained with the Ministry of Agriculture, and energy with the then Department of Energy. In 1976, as political priorities shifted under a Labour government, transport was separated from the department.

Ironically the Labour government elected in 1997 thought it politically important to once again bring transport into the DoE and emphasise the role of regional development (moved from the DTI) and create the DETR. Environmentalists such as Friends of the Earth welcomed the merger of the Departments of the Environment and Transport as it was thought a unified department would be able to think in a more integrated manner. Early on though there were doubts about whether the new department would be more effective than its predecessors. It did not gain significant new powers, some environment responsibilities still lay with other Whitehall departments, and with devolution Edinburgh and Cardiff now also have a more important part to play than in the past. Nevertheless, there was surprise in some quarters that the department should once again be reorganised following Labour's 2001 election victory. There had been disquiet within government at the performance of the Ministry of Agriculture, Fisheries and Food (MAFF) and its demise was expected. The organisation that emerged, DEFRA, was less well anticipated. Alongside the responsibilities of MAFF, DEFRA has also inherited responsibility for sustainable development, environmental protection and water, rural development, countryside, and energy

Energy efficient homes: Beddington Zero Energy Development
Source: Alamy Images/Johnny Greig

efficiency. What had been DETR now became the Department of Transport, Local Government and the Regions, though the following year, in 2002, Transport was separated out to reflect its political prominence. DEFRA will clearly be well placed to attempt the 'greening' of agricultural policy, but in many ways the reforms may not be positive for environmental policy. Planning, a key tool for delivering sustainable development, was initially transferred to the Office of the Deputy Prime Minister and then with its demise to the Department for Communities and Local Government (for England). In Wales and Scotland, planning responsibilities are dealt with by their governments.

The continual repackaging of environment-related responsibilities must raise doubts as to whether bringing together functions does aid integrated policy making. The fundamental tensions between different sectors does not disappear and so what would have been interdepartmental disputes now take place behind the closed doors of one department. In an effort to make sure that the environmental impacts of different policies are incorporated into decision making the Labour government has

built upon the efforts of its Conservative predecessor which had taken two forms. One was to amend the machinery of government and the other was to engage in the environmental appraisal of new policies.

The lead role in formulating the Conservative government's 1990 White Paper This Common Inheritance (Cm 1200) had been taken by the then Department of the Environment but its content had been debated and a number of compromises made in a Cabinet committee set up to oversee its production. Ministers and senior civil servants involved in the process recognised the value of being able to discuss the environment as a policy issue both within and across departments. The White Paper therefore made two commitments to improving the machinery of government: to retain the cabinet committee and the nomination of a green minister in each department who would be responsible for considering the environmental implications of department's policies and programmes. At the time the Conservative Secretary of State for the Environment, Michael Heseltine (1991) proclaimed: 'We now have some of the most sophisticated machinery to be found anywhere in the world integrating environment and other policies.' Commentators have subsequently pointed out that the Cabinet committee was downgraded to a ministerial committee and that the committee 'was an ineffective institutional device, mainly due to the continued territorial preoccupation of departments and hostility within the central government machinery towards the . . . DoE, particularly from the "economic" departments' (Voisey and O'Riordan 1998: 159). The Labour government has upgraded the committee to its original cabinet status, where it is known as the Cabinet Ministerial Committee on the Environment (ENV) but tangible achievements are difficult to detect. Labour has also sought to re-invigorate the green ministers and they now have to report to the ENV Committee and prepare an annual report on their activities. Government has made commitments to put its own house in order. Departments now have to think seriously about introducing environmental management systems and to having their performance appraised against eight criteria, including their business travel and water use. As its own contribution to improving the machinery of government Labour created in 1997 a House of Commons Select Committee on Environmental Audit. The Committee's terms of reference are to evaluate the extent to which the policies and programmes of departments and non-departmental public bodies contribute to environmental protection and sustainable development. However, in a review of the government's progress on mainstreaming sustainable development across Whitehall the Environmental Audit Committee (2004) pointed out that few have met the government's ambitions: few departmental sustainability strategies have been prepared and these have been treated as one-off exercises with little wider relevance.

Government officials routinely engage in policy appraisal. Since 1991 they have been encouraged to broaden their analysis to take into account environmental issues. However, much of the guidance for officials on how to undertake environmental policy appraisals has been skewed towards economic techniques and may not have received a sympathetic response. The Labour government appears to be making renewed efforts to instil environmental appraisal into the routines of decision making (Environmental Audit Committee 1998: paras 89–91). Nevertheless, practice within departments appears to be variable, and while they may be becoming more frequent there is little evidence to suggest that environmental appraisals have made much impact on significant policy issues (Environmental Audit Committee 2004).

Department of Energy and Climate Change (DECC)

As political priorities have changed, so too has the organisation of government. DECC was formed in October 2008 to bring together energy policy (that was formerly the responsibility of the Department for Business, Innovation and Skills) and climate change mitigation policy (previously with DEFRA). DEFRA retains responsibility for promoting a sustainable, low carbon and resource efficient economy and more specifically for reducing emissions for the sectors for which it has responsibility, namely farming and forestry. Much of the responsibility for the delivery of the Climate Change Act 2008 with its commitment to cut carbon emissions will move to DECC. This is because the energy industry is such a key player in emissions reductions. Clearly, though, there were considerable pressures to ensure that DEFRA was not overly weakened with the creation of DECC but it is likely that its influence in Whitehall has been weakened.

The rationale behind DECC is that two-thirds of emissions come from energy use and that since emissions and climate change are inextricably linked the relationship between the two must be thought about in a more integrated manner. While the basis of the new department has a logic, its creation was a surprise and arose out of a wider Prime Ministerial autumn Cabinet reshuffle. Not surprisingly, the new department was welcomed by environment groups who saw it as a mark of the Government's commitment to play a lead role in the international climate treaty negotiations in Copenhagen at the end of 2009 and to deliver on its Climate Change Act targets. Business groups, led by the Confederation of British Industry (CBI) were also supportive of the new department. For the CBI, the department's responsibilities for energy prices and efficiency, particularly with growing concerns about future energy security, were a welcome recognition of the seriousness with which the government is taking these issues and of their implications for the business community.

The organisational and administrative changes noted above certainly indicate some of the ways in which the environment, or particular features of it, has been accorded a higher political priority. While the search for policy integration is certainly a desirable objective and may help to achieve higher levels of environmental protection it should not obscure our gaze from the content of policy. And yet, at times, this seems to have been the consequence of a series of organisational reforms that have affected bodies that administer environmental protection, as we shall see below.

The Environment Agency

The substance of environmental policy presents enormous challenges to decision makers because it defies their conventional timescales and functional divisions. Thus, where politicians' horizons may normally be bounded by that of elections, the environment forces them to think on a quite different scale, of generations for which they cannot possibly receive any political payback. Meanwhile, organisations like to do things in their own way with the minimum of external interference. But environmental policy cross-cuts traditional divisions of government and raises, for those concerned, the unwelcome possibility of turf disputes about who gets to do what. Faced with these dilemmas, decision makers have shown a greater interest in the organisation of environmental protection as a substitute, or at least an alternative focus, for the more challenging issues surrounding the content of policy. Thus recent years have witnessed a flurry of, perhaps, unprecedented organisational reforms. The result has been some grander thinking on structures than is normal and the creation in 1996 of a large, centralised Environment Agency that may fit less easily into Britain's traditional administrative culture. In the past, small, specialised bodies, with for the most part low public profiles, have tended to be favoured.

Demands for the creation of a unified environment body have been long-standing. Since the mid-1970s the standing Royal Commission on Environmental Pollution had argued for a greater integration of the functions of what were at the time a set of disparate organisations. By the 1980s, increasing support from environmental groups, such as Friends of the Earth, and latterly the Labour and Liberal Democrat parties, helped make questions of integration a topic of policy debate. The late 1980s and early 1990s saw the creation of important new bodies, Her Majesty's Inspectorate of Pollution (HMIP), the National Rivers Authority (NRA) and the Waste Regulatory Authorities (WRAs), but still this did not quell the clamour for further reform.

Within a month of the publication in 1990 of the government's White Paper (Cm 1200) on the environment, This Common Inheritance, the opposition parties had issued their own policy documents (*An Earthly Chance* and *What Price Our Planet?* by Labour and the Liberal Democrats respectively), which, in contrast to the Conservatives, committed themselves to major institutional reforms.

Within a year the Conservative government had fallen into line, and in July 1991 John Major, in his first speech on the environment as Prime Minister, argued that 'it is right that the integrity and indivisibility of the environment should now be reflected in a unified agency' and announced the government's intention 'to create a new agency for environment protection and enhancement'.

HMIP, the NRA and the WRAs together form the core of the Environment Agency in England and Wales. The Scottish Environment Protection Agency (the difference in name may be of some significance) has in addition to the three core groups the local authority environmental health officers who deal with air pollution. In terms of the logic creating a unified and all-embracing pollution regulation body, the inclusion of such staff makes sense. That it did not happen in England and Wales indicates the way in which organisational design in the public sector is invariably intertwined with political factors. The then Conservative government had a much greater representation in local government in England than it did in Scotland and knew that it would arouse opposition within its own ranks should it take away responsibility for air pollution from English local authorities.

What does the Environment Agency mean for the work of its core groups and what effects might it have on those they regulate? The functions set out in Box 26.1 are derived from its constituent elements. Of these, HMIP was formed in 1987 as the result of interdepartmental disputes, embarrassment at pollution discharges at Sellafield nuclear power station and pressures from the European Commission. It combined what had been distinct inspectorates in industrial air pollution. It was responsible for regulating discharges to air, land or water for some 2,000 industrial processes with the greatest polluting potential.

The NRA was a much larger and higher profile organisation than HMIP. It has gone on to form the largest part of the new agency and its former staff secured a number of key positions within it. The NRA was created at the same time as the water

BOX 26.1 FACT

Key responsibilities of the Environment Agency and the Scottish Environment Protection Agency

Functions

- Water resource management – conserve and secure the proper use of water
- Water quality – prevent and control pollution and monitor the quality of rivers, estuaries, coastal waters and groundwater
- Integrated pollution control – control discharges to land, air and water for larger and more complex industrial processes
- Air – SEPA alone – control processes which have a medium pollution risk (in England and Wales this task is undertaken by local authority Environmental Health Officers)
- Waste regulation – (a) register and monitor those who carry waste for a business; (b) approve management of waste disposal sites

Achieved by

- Issuing of abstraction licences
- Granting of consent to discharge
- Integrated pollution control authorisation by
  - Regulation of the firm
  - Licence site operators

Dounreay nuclear power station, Caithness, Highlands, Scotland
Source: Alamy Images / archstock

authorities were privatised, under the Water Act 1989, and it took on the pollution control functions and some of the activities of these authorities. The latter were both guardians of the water environment and also major polluters as dischargers of sewage, that is, acting as both poacher and gamekeeper.

Waste collection and disposal has been a traditional local government activity but one where it has lost out to the twin pressures of integration in environmental protection and for contracting out of services. The 1990 Environmental Protection Act created three types of waste authority. Waste Collection Authorities (a local authority or a contractor working for the authority) arrange for the collection of household and commercial waste. Its disposal is the responsibility of Waste Disposal Authority (either a part of local government or a Local Authority Waste Disposal Company). Waste Regulation Authorities, whose staff have been moved from local government to the Environment Agency, are responsible for the safe treatment and disposal of wastes produced by households, mines, quarries and agriculture (so-called controlled waste).

By bringing together in one organisation the control of water pollution, air pollution and commercial waste there is an effort to provide a more integrated approach to environmental management. While structures are important in trying to achieve policy goals, both the English and Welsh and Scottish agencies have had to surmount a number of hurdles. It has taken longer than expected to forge into a cohesive grouping, and the professionals who staff it came with different professional priorities, tactics, and approaches to regulation and (not to be ignored) different career structures. To be seen to be more than the sum of its organisational parts it has been essential for the agencies to prove their independence from government and of those they regulate. The agencies have not been helped in this regard as they have received few additional powers from those that their constituent bodies held. It is unlikely that most businesses will have noticed any practical difference in the way in which they are regulated.

Nevertheless, both agencies have tried to promote a different style and this may lead to a change in substance. For example, the Environment Agency has been actively involved in initiatives to promote waste minimisation in business. Waste minimisation offers a double dividend: a firm reduces its impact on the environment because less material is used in the production process and there is less waste to

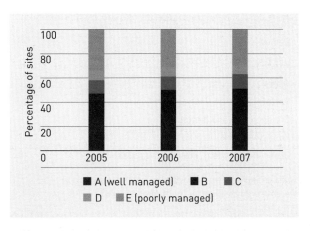

Figure 26.3 Operator performance in all industry sectors
Source: Spotlight on Business: Ten years of improving the environment (Environment Agency, 2008), p. 18

be disposed of, and at the same time becomes more efficient because it is using its materials more efficiently. Here the Agency is able to act as an educator of business encouraging it along a more sustainable route. Where business has proved more recalcitrant the Agency has changed tack and adopted a high profile name and shame campaign of major polluters, for instance, producing an annual *Spotlight on Business* (Environment Agency 2008) that highlights environmental performance (see Figure 26.3). Here the Agency has a role as the citizen's friend through its actions to protect the environment.

Throughout its three terms of office Labour has been sensitive to the potential burden that environmental regulation may place on business. It remains an ongoing challenge for the Labour government to follow through the logic of its sustainable development policy with its implication of rigorous and stringent environmental regulation by the Environment Agency. The Agency has recognised that enforcement action is perceived to be weak and has put in place special enforcement teams to target serious pollution offenders. Table 26.3 provides information on the number of Agency-recorded incidents and shows that waste is the most important area where offenders can make a living from operating illegally.

Over time the Environment Agency data shows that businesses are becoming better managed as their environmental performance is improving. However, where serious pollution incidents do occur the damage to the environment does not appear to be fully reflected by the courts. As the data below shows the fines remain at a low level.

Table 26.3 Pollution incidents caused by businesses

Sector	%
Waste	34
Water	20
Farming	16
Construction and demolition	7
Food and drink	6
Other industry (e.g. industrial estates)	8

Source: *Spotlight on Business: Ten years of improving the environment* (Environment Agency, 2008), p. 18

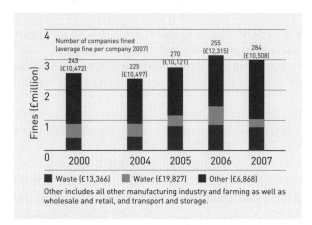

Figure 26.4 Total annual fines by sector
Source: *Spotlight on Business: Ten years of improving the environment* (Environment Agency, 2008), p. 21

An additional challenge for both SEPA and the Environment Agency will arise from the way in which they respond to their responsibilities under devolution. Obviously SEPA will continue to look to Edinburgh for guidance and funding and over time it is possible that its strategy and responsibilities will become still more distinct from those of the Environment Agency. Even in Wales with its more limited devolved responsibilities the relevant part of

the Agency is playing a more active role in trying to formulate a sustainable development strategy for the National Assembly. It is not inconceivable that within a relatively short space of time issues of funding and accountability help to force a separation of the English and Welsh parts of the Agency. These points are considered further above in the section on the implications of devolution for environmental policy.

■ The rural conservation agencies

It is the rural conservation agencies that have the greatest experience of country-specific operations and the fragmentation that it entails. The reforms to the Countryside Agency, English Nature (merged into Natural England), the Countryside Council for Wales and Scottish Natural Heritage are illustrative of the way in which administrative structures influence environmental policy making and government thinking on the environment. The broad remits and size of the different agencies are illustrated in Table 26.4.

All the conservation bodies can trace their origins back to the 1949 National Parks and Access to the Countryside Act. Under the Act two sets of responsibilities were established. The first was for nature conservation, is based on scientific and technical expertise and draws upon an elite tradition of interest in natural history and the preservation of flora and fauna. The other responsibility was for landscape protection. Thus was born a, perhaps, unique organisational division among public sector bodies in Europe of separating landscape and nature protection that has only been fully overcome with the creation of Natural England in 2006. The divide

Table 26.4 Responsibilities and sizes of the rural conservation agencies for 2008–09

Name	Key responsibilities	Number of employees*	Budget £m
Natural England	Landscape protection, nature conservation, economic and social development	2309	273,451,000
Scottish Natural Heritage	Landscape protection and nature conservation	728	70,657,000
Countryside Council for Wales	Landscape protection and nature conservation	482	44,896,000

* Whole time equivalent (including temporary and contract staff where stated)
Sources of information:
Natural England, Annual Report and Accounts 1 April 2008 to 31 March 2009
Scottish Natural Heritage Annual Report and Accounts, 2008–09
Audit Scotland, Scottish Natural Heritage, Report on the 2008–09 Audit, October 2009
CCW Audited Financial Accounts for the year ended 31 March 2009

reflects some of the characteristics of British environmentalism: a strong scientific base to conservation, and a concern for access and notions of beauty in relation to landscape.

The reorganisation of the conservation agencies has taken a different path from that of the pollution control bodies. On the one side, predating devolution, there has been a geographical fragmentation. On the other side there are signs of integration or unification of responsibilities among the bodies, although it has taken different forms and been played out over different time frames. For the conservation agencies the functional integration in 1989 in Wales and Scotland (in which landscape and nature were combined in the Countryside Council for Wales and Scottish Natural Heritage), was not followed in England until 2006. The landscape and recreation functions of the Countryside Agency were joined with English Nature (and DEFRA's Rural Delivery Service) to create Natural England. The Countryside Agency's socio-economic responsibilities have been passed on to the Regional Development Agencies and DEFRA. The remaining functions of the Countryside Agency have been reconstituted as the Commission for Rural Communities, a body that is to act as a rural advocate and expert advisor to government. It is not a situation dictated by organisational logic or adherence to explicit environmental principles. What it represents is the current state of play in an organisational and policy framework that has developed in a largely ad hoc and pragmatic manner, and is a vivid testimony to the weakness of the statutory environmental bodies. Judgements on the conservation bodies tend to be harsh but it is difficult to differ from that of Lowe and Goyder (1983: 67) in writing of the predecessors to the current organisations that they 'have small budgets, little power and limited policy-making initiative, and they are politically marginal'.

Devolution seems to have had a positive impact on the funding of the conservation agencies. The devolved administrations may be more sympathetic to the resource claims of CCW and SNH; they are after all their own organisations, and in the case of Scotland there is now the power to reshape SNH if thought necessary. In terms of policy development the situation is less clear cut. Both organisations may also find that they have better links to policy makers and the policy community more generally, enjoy higher status and are more able to shape strategy, and there are examples of innovative policy development, such as Tir Gofal an all Wales agri-environment

scheme launched in 1989. On the other hand, the bodies for England, Wales and Scotland may become more inward looking and less able to share good practice. There may be much duplication of effort and an inability to develop the high-level scientific expertise that a unified body with all of its resources would be able to bring to bear. Another difficulty that may loom, especially in Wales, is that the conservation bodies will find themselves competing more directly for resources and influence with well-established and highly thought of economic development agencies. Unless The Scottish Government and Welsh Assembly Government are able to formulate sustainable development strategies that do genuinely bring together economic and environmental interests there is a danger that the latter could find themselves marginalised over time.

■ Local government and environmental policy

Another area of interest will be the way in which the devolved governments deal with their local authorities and whether they can share a common environmental agenda. Traditionally, local councils have played a key and wide-ranging role in the UK's system of environmental regulation. They have had statutory responsibilities for waste, air pollution and planning. To this they have added a non-statutory initiative Local Agenda 21 (LA21) that stems from the Rio Earth Summit in 1992. The fortunes of local government in each of these areas have been inextricably tied up with the thinking and actions of central government.

Pollution regulation by local authorities

While the Environment Agency is responsible for emissions from industrial processes scheduled under legislation, district and unitary councils in England and Wales are responsible for those from non-scheduled processes. Scottish councils had held similar powers but these were transferred to SEPA. These responsibilities stem principally from the Public Health Act 1936, the Clean Air Acts of 1956 and 1968 and the Environmental Protection Act 1990. Under the legislation, local authorities control emissions of smoke, dust, grit and odour, and, under the Control of Pollution Act 1974, noise.

As we have seen, however, local authorities play a more important role in waste regulation. Until quite recently local authorities collected, disposed of and were responsible for regulation of the waste that was created in their areas. Under the Environmental Protection Act 1990, responsibility for the collection of household and some commercial and industrial waste is split between the different tiers of government, but the authorities, in this case largely county councils, are required to subject these services to private company bids in a process known as compulsory competitive tendering. The counties, however, remain responsible for waste regulation (Waste Regulation Authorities). (There is a more confused situation in some metropolitan areas where there can be joint responsibility for disposal and regulation.)

Local planning

The planning system is one of the most sophisticated mechanisms for environmental regulation, more specifically for controlling and promoting land use development, in Britain. Although planning decisions are made under the broad supervision of the Department for Communities and Local Government (for England and to a lesser extent Wales), the Scottish Government and Welsh Assembly Government, councils are responsible for both drawing up plans and making decisions on proposed developments. Planning law grants wide discretion to councils to control and promote land-use planning, including the content of plans, the granting of planning permission, the enforcement of breaches of control and the pursuit of positive planning. This discretion and decentralisation makes for both variability and vitality in local planning.

The planning system has been subject to considerable pressure over the past two decades and more. For much of this time planning has been bedevilled by two competing imperatives. On the one side, planning is regarded as a bureaucratic impediment to the operation of the market. Government reforms were therefore designed to reduce the scope of local authority involvement in the planning process and to remove some of the constraints faced by developers in securing planning approval. On the other side, as governments began to embrace the environmental agenda from the 1990s onwards, so any deregulatory instincts had to be tempered. Planning increasingly became heralded as a key means of promoting more sustainable development

because of its ability to engage with economic issues (i.e. the development of land), social needs (what is appropriate development for particular communities) and the protection of valued environments. The ongoing challenge faced by government is, to what extent should the planning system constrain the market? Traditionally the most contentious debates take place in the south-east of England. Here there are major pressures for development, an articulate opposition well able to make their views known through the planning system and a group of councils who are arguing that if the pressures they face for development are not more actively managed then they will become less sustainable. The touchstone around which these debates are taking place is new housing.

In an effort to resolve the perceived tension in the planning system between promoting sustainable development and encouraging development the Labour government introduced two major planning reforms. The Planning and Compulsory Purchase Act 2004 was designed to make planning decisions speedier and more certain in England by amending the public inquiry system for major projects, replacing the structure plans produced by county councils with Regional Spatial Strategies produced by the eight English regions. District councils will produce Local Development Documents rather than the local plans they currently prepare. Both regional and local documents will be subject to sustainability appraisals and the planning system will also have to contribute to sustainable development. The Planning Act 2008 created a new system of development for what were termed 'nationally significant infrastructure projects'. Such projects were those that tended to get close scrutiny within the planning system and might include new airport runways, waste facilities and nuclear power stations. The latter were clearly linked to the government's efforts to promote a low carbon energy system (see below). To ensure that these large and often very controversial projects would not get bogged down in the local planning process a new independent Infrastructure Planning Commission would make the decision. Environmental groups are concerned that both Acts will make the planning system less accountable to local people and too sympathetic to economic interests.

Local authority initiatives

Finally, despite, or perhaps more accurately because of, the criticism and restrictions to which local government has been subject, it has become increasingly involved in a series of measures by which it can promote the environment and at the same time promote itself not only as 'green' but as an active organ of government. The UNCED Conference at Rio, where much of Agenda 21 (the global environmental agenda for the next century) was predicated upon local action, provided a convenient means by which local government could repackage much of what it was already doing and have a justification for extending its work still further. There is no clear agreement on what the content of an LA21 should be since it should be tailored to local circumstances. However, the internal issues that a local authority should expect to cover include: managing and improving its own environmental performance, integrating sustainable development across its activities and awareness raising and education. In its dealings with the wider community the authority should consult the public on LA21, engage in partnerships with the business and voluntary sectors, and measure and report on local progress towards sustainable development. According to O'Riordan and Voisey (1998a: 154) the UK is probably the most advanced nation in taking forward LA21. The Labour government recognised the considerable potential for local government in the delivery of sustainable development and encouraged the production of LA21 strategies. Under the Local Government Act 2000 LA21 Strategies were modified to become Community Strategies, documents that were designed to promote community well being and sustainable development.

Despite their positive comments O'Riordan and Voisey nevertheless made a damning assessment of LA21 and it is one that could also apply to Community Strategies. O'Riordan and Voisey are not convinced that much beyond rhetoric and the production of documentation is taking place. There are a number of difficulties, including the task of taking the sustainable message to those groups such as business who may not be sympathetic to it; overcoming public indifference or even antagonism to local government; broadening the agenda from the environment to include social and development issues; and having to work with limited resources.

■ Pressure groups and government: the case of road transport

Road transport debates and protests illustrate well the changing nature of the environmental movement in Britain, how it can help to change the terms of debate and the challenges that government faces in trying to move policy on to a more sustainable footing (Box 26.2).

Environmental groups

According to McCormick (1991: 34), 'Britain has the oldest, strongest, best-organised and most widely supported environmental lobby in the world.' The foundations of the lobby were laid in the late nineteenth century with subsequent bursts of growth in environmental groups in the late 1920s, the late 1950s, the early 1970s, as well as the late 1980s. The 1970s were distinguished from earlier periods both by the rapid growth of existing groups and the formation of new ones such as Friends of the Earth (formed in the United States in 1969), Greenpeace (formed in Canada in 1972) and Transport 2000. The new groups made a significant impact upon the lobby by highlighting the international nature of many environmental problems, and providing radical analyses of environmental issues which linked them to contemporary social and economic

---

BOX 26.2 IDEAS AND PERSPECTIVES

Transport Act 2000 includes possibility of road charges

The Act introduced the politically controversial idea of charging for road use. Local authorities will be given the power to charge motorists for driving into cities, the idea being that such charging will help reduce congestion and provide funds for the improvement of public transport. The legislation is only permissive, entitling local authorities to introduce such schemes if they so choose, subject to government approval. London's scheme – the largest in Europe – started in early 2003. Motoring organisations are sceptical of the idea and believe that motorists already pay enough tax to use their cars.

Climate change protestors start their march towards Kingsnorth power station, August 2009
Source: Getty Images / David Berehulak

conditions. New tactics also emerged with Friends of the Earth and Greenpeace adopting vigorous, high-profile campaigns to draw attention to a broad range of threats to the environment.

The success of the environmental lobby in increasing its membership, along with a range of other fundraising activities, has had a positive effect on its finances. With greater income, groups have been able to employ more staff to monitor more accurately government activities, engage in more lobbying and prepare better critiques of official policy. Campaigns are much more sophisticated than they used to be, making still greater use of the media and, for the more radical groups, there has been a greater reliance on science and legal evidence to support their positions. The emphasis, therefore, has been, for the most part, on strengthening traditional styles of lobbying.

Greenpeace has confronted a more difficult situation. In some countries the nature of the political system is such that Greenpeace can keep its distance from government and still seek to influence debate. In Britain that is more difficult, and now that many of its concerns have become matters of public policy deliberation, partly as a result of its direct

action tactics, it has to decide whether the same tactics are required for the formulation and implementation of policy.

Road building protests

One of the most bitterly contested areas of government policy has been that relating to road transport. The controversy it has excited has led to set-piece confrontations around proposed new developments, spawned a new wave of environmental activism and challenged successive governments' commitment to sustainable development.

Many local road improvement schemes will arouse little if any controversy. The road-building schemes that have aroused national attention, notably those at Twyford Down, Newbury and Honiton, are significant because of their scale and their impact on nationally important environments. They have thus become a focus, sometimes at a symbolic level, for the arguments for and against the road-building programme. The M3 protest at Twyford Down began in the mid-1980s and initially involved a classic local protest: concerned residents engaged in conventional campaigning tactics, such as lobbying and high-profile events (e.g. protest walks) in which they worked closely with national groups, notably Friends of the Earth.

As all legal avenues of protest disappeared a new form of protester appeared who was committed to non-violent direct action. The latter drew much of their inspiration from the American group Earth First! and disdained conventional politics as failing to protect the environment. The initially small group occupied part of the road-building site known as the Dongas, an area of deep hollows, and became known as the Dongas Tribe. Faced with overwhelming odds the Dongas Tribe could not hope to stop the building of the road. Nevertheless, their courage and commitment provoked enormous interest and inspired other protests such as that at Newbury. The Twyford Down campaign was also significant in another respect. As Barbara Bryant, a leading activist, has written:

almost for the first time . . . [the media] had witnessed middle-class Conservative voters, retired military men, elected politicians and a younger, less conventional group, coming together in an alliance against the Government's road building campaign.

Bryant (1996: 192)

While it is important not to over-emphasise the extent to which a coalition did exist (there were undoubted tensions between the different groups), it does mark a point at which diverse interests could come together to oppose a common policy.

There are many similarities between the Twyford Down protest and that at Newbury. Once again legal avenues of campaigning had been exhausted, leaving the protesters to try to disrupt and delay the building programme sufficiently so that there might be a rethink of policy by a new government. The protests against the Newbury bypass began in earnest in late 1995 with the establishment of six protest camps. At the height of the campaign in the spring of 1996 this had mushroomed to 29. Some of the camps were based in trees, others in tunnels, and led to dramatic media coverage of the evictions of protesters as bailiffs brought in cranes and cherry-picking equipment to dislodge them. Once a site has been cleared for a new road it would be a dramatic event for a government to then halt operations.

Transport protests are now commonplace. Reclaim the Streets, an anti-car pressure group, has organised a number of events in London which have brought traffic to a standstill and in 1996 a street party was held on a stretch of the M41 attended by some 7,000 people, at which parts of the road were dug up and trees planted (see Jordan 1998). A central element to the protest movement now is the extent to which the organisers of different groups seek to link their activities and exchange ideas: a move from competing and exclusive organisations to supportive and overlapping disorganisations.

Government policy and road transport

By helping to raise the profile of transport issues protesters have played a part in creating a climate in which a new agenda can develop. Faced with a massive forecast for increases in traffic, the Conservative government of the 1980s committed itself to a large road-building programme in the suitably titled 1989 White Paper Roads for Prosperity (Cm 693). Within a few years, though, a number of schemes had been dropped or shelved. The reasons for the change in heart are many but, perhaps, three were key. Firstly, the Treasury, desperate to retain a hold on the public finances, had been alarmed at the burgeoning expenditure on roads. Secondly, early in 1994 the government published its strategy on Sustainable Development (Cm 2426) in which, in the cautious language of civil servants, it acknowledged that unlimited traffic growth was incompatible with its environmental commitments. In other words demand would have to be managed, a key argument of the environmental lobby. Thirdly, later in 1994 saw the publication of two key reports on transport. One was by the influential Royal Commission on Environmental Pollution on Transport and the Environment in which it expressed its concern at the implication of current policy on health and the environment. It argued for a halving of the road-building programme and a doubling of the real price of petrol over the decade. The other was by the Standing Advisory Committee on Trunk Road Assessment which concluded that new roads can generate or induce new traffic (i.e. that they may not ease congestion).

The Conservatives' cautious embrace of the need to manage road transport was much more fully embraced by the Labour Party. In government Labour promoted through its White Paper, A New Deal for Transport, the idea of an integrated transport policy to fight congestion and pollution. Essentially, integration means bringing together different types of transport, and ensuring that transport links to other policies such as land use planning. Most attention has focused on three areas: bus quality partnerships to improve services; a strategic rail authority to oversee the privatised companies; and local transport plans. These plans, backed up by the Transport Act 2000, enable councils to introduce charges on some trunk roads and on trunk road bridges more than 600 metres long. The Transport Innovation Fund introduced in 2004 also encouraged councils to develop local road pricing schemes. The money raised from such charges would then be invested in public transport improvements. The proposals, though a modest attempt to manage demand, given the scale of the traffic problem, and voluntary have aroused enormous controversy.

Some indication of the pressures on the government came to a head in the second half of 2000. As we have seen up until this time the Government's transport policy had been reasonably ambitious with a cut in the road building programme and more money for public transport. It was encapsulated in the 1998 White Paper on transport that promised 'radical change'. The government, though, was becoming increasingly sensitive to the charge that it was anti-car or anti-driver and an indication of the shift in policy came in July 2000 when the government launched its much heralded ten-year plan for transport. It promised investments of over £180 billion but a third of the money was to go on motorways and trunk roads, so heralding something of a renaissance in road building and a recognition that supply side measures were also needed. However, the ten-year plan fails to address the fundamental transport problems facing the UK – an over-reliance on the car and the growth in road traffic. Shortly after the publication of the ten-year plan, the government was shocked by the widespread protests in the early autumn of 2000 led by lorry drivers and farmers concerned at the increase in costs of vehicle fuel. The support the protests gathered heightened unease within government that it was alienating drivers, a potentially important part of the electorate (McLean 2008). In his November 2000 pre-budget report the Chancellor of the Exchequer announced cuts in fuel and vehicle excise duty.

The Government's sensitivity to the price concerns of road users did not mean that tax solutions to Britain's congestion and pollution problems disappeared. Rather they took a different form with national government keen to promote local congestion charging schemes. The widespread admiration generated by the introduction of the London congestion charge in 2003, along with the promise of substantial government financial support for investment in public transport, appeared to herald the more widespread use of city centre congestion charging. However, city dwellers have been reluctant to embrace such schemes. For example, in late 2008 in Manchester 79 per cent voted to reject a road pricing proposal. With little support for local road pricing initiatives the Department for Transport has not actively sought to promote charges for the use of motorways. Rather, it intends to overcome congestion of motorways by increasing road space through the use of the emergency hard shoulder during periods of heavy use.

The wider ramifications of the pressure that Labour perceives on transport are apparent. It is sensitive to the charge that it is anti-car, perhaps one reason why it is making implementation of car reduction policies the responsibility of local and not central government. It may also help us to understand why the government has become more cautious about promoting green taxes for transport. Government policy is now focused on reducing the impacts of the car rather than reducing the need to drive. While in the past tensions between seeking to manage demand for the car and the supply of sufficient road space could be largely buried in rhetoric they are becoming ever more acute as the government addresses climate change. For instance, road transports CO_2 emissions rose by 11 per cent between 1990 and 2007 and now account for nearly 25 per cent of total CO_2 emissions.

The difficulties that the Labour government has encountered in tackling car use have spilled over into, and coloured, the government's approach to climate change and energy policy. Road transport is raising key political questions that have to be tackled by governments as they seek to address climate change. These include: can road transport be regarded as a special case that is largely immune from the more stringent climate change targets that apply to other sectors? How do politicians (and pressure groups) seek to engage citizens in behaviour change? How might our individual rights and responsibilities (for example, to consume) need to be rethought to cope with a future-oriented and long-term collective public policy problem?

■ Climate change and energy policy

Climate change policy is proving to be a particularly fascinating area in which to observe how governments seek to deal with a public policy problem that goes well beyond their normal time horizons, and where the actions of a country the size of Britain will have only a marginal effect on global greenhouse gas emissions but where the case for action must be made to meet (or even to lead on) international climate change agreements. What makes action still more difficult to justify is that the evidence for climate change, although becoming ever stronger, still has its sceptics and that the nature of the change is couched in terms of probabilities. From a public policy perspective what is equally interesting is that Britain, which entered the 1980s with a poor reputation for its willingness to support domestic and international environmental policy, has in the 2000s developed a legislative base and emissions reduction targets that make it a world leader. The challenge now will be whether or not those commitments can be met.

Climate change moved to the forefront of international environmental politics with the signing of the Kyoto Protocol in 1997. Industrialised nations including the European Union and Japan (but not the USA) approved a plan to cut emissions of gases linked to global warming to 5.2 per cent below 1990 levels by 2012. The UK, however, set itself more stringent targets and committed itself to reducing its 1990 greenhouse gas emissions by 12.5 per cent by 2010 (and is on course to do so). At the 2001 General Election a stronger manifesto commitment was made to cut carbon dioxide emissions by 20 per cent by 2010. This commitment was later reduced to an aspiration and the target then became to achieve a 60 per cent reduction by 2050 (and EU agreed figure but which is also challenging). As we shall see, though, commitments and targets have continued to change rapidly.

Debates on climate change and energy policy send out numerous mixed messages. While the science of climate change has become ever more certain, governments across the globe have found that tackling the causes of climate change have questioned the basis of fundamental policies and the behaviour of consumers, and thus policies may have high political costs. For the then Prime Minister Tony Blair climate change provided the opportunity to lead international opinion, especially in the UK's role as President of the G8 and of the EU in 2005. Unfortunately the Government's efforts at global leadership were undermined by data showing that Britain was finding it increasingly difficult to reduce its carbon emissions. Climate change debate in the UK has also proved a mixed blessing for environment groups as they are now expected to play an increasing part in devising solutions to deep-rooted problems and not simply raising awareness of the problems.

Nevertheless, there is considerable common ground between groups and government. The government initially had a target of a 20 per cent reduction in CO_2 emissions by 2010 and commitment to an EU-wide greenhouse gas reduction target of 30 per cent by 2020. The Labour government in its presidencies of the EU and G8 sought to promote climate change as an international priority. In a speech on 14 September 2004 Tony Blair told his audience of business people that what 'I believe to be the world's

---

Box 26.3   Climate change is not just another policy problem

'Climate change is not just another environmental problem. Its location at the centre of a nexus of key resource issues that underpin the robustness of the global economy puts into play the current and future prosperity and security of the whole global community. Furthermore, there are two characteristics of climate change that set it apart from other problems facing governments.

First, policy failure is not an option . . . The long lifetime of carbon dioxide in the atmosphere – centuries – means we are committed, irrevocably and indefinitely, to whatever climate is generated by the carbon burden in the atmosphere at the moment of stabilisation. If we fail to stabilise greenhouse gases at a level compatible with staying below a 2 °C average rise we cannot try again to achieve this goal.

Second, action must be taken within a limited timeframe. The build-up of atmospheric carbon is cumulative and in effect irreversible. Climate scientists are confident that for there to be a reasonable chance of keeping the rise in global average temperatures below 2 °C, greenhouse gases should not rise above 450 parts per million of CO_2 equivalent. To remain within this boundary, global carbon emissions must peak during 2015–2020 and then decline.'

Tom Burke, ENDS Report, 415, August 2009: 48

greatest environmental challenge [is] climate change.' All of these commitments are endorsed by environmental groups.

The difficulty is in believing that the policies and government commitment are delivering change sufficiently rapidly. The environmental lobby remains ever watchful of government backsliding. For the Labour government the delivery problem is compounded because key institutions, such as the Intergovernmental Panel on Climate Change (IPCC) have been issuing starker warnings about climate change and domestically the political debate has been heating up. Meanwhile, under the leadership of David Cameron, the Conservative Party have been far more assertive in staking out an environmental agenda (Carter 2008). As Carter (2008) has argued, the more that climate change became part of conventional party politics, the more questions were being asked about how policies were to be implemented.

In moving from contributing to raising awareness of a policy problem to seeking its solution, the Labour government embarked on a small number of key initiatives, some of which it could lead (e.g. the creation of DECC – see above – the Stern Report and energy policy), and some of which was in response to the proposals of others (e.g. the Climate Change Act which was initiated by Friends of the Earth). Government also sought to share responsibility for climate change activities (or the lack of them). These points are explored below.

Sharing responsibility

In an interesting switch in policy responsibility, government is pointing out to environmental groups that policy failures cannot simply be blamed on government and that groups must accept their share of responsibility. One key failing that government is laying at the doors of environment groups is a failure to sufficiently communicate to the public the dangers of climate change. The environmental movement has in part accepted the veracity of the argument and responded in 2005 by forming a new body, Stop Climate Chaos. Stop Climate Chaos draws together influential environmental groups such as Friends of the Earth, Greenpeace and WWF and development organisations like Oxfam. In explaining the reasoning behind the formation of Stop Climate Chaos, its Director Asok Sinha pointed out that 'Individual organisations have done their best, running very good climate or energy campaigns. But the pressure applied didn't bring about the desired changes in policy. Business as usual, in terms of campaigning, was just not working.' Stop Climate Chaos is modelled on Make Poverty History and Jubilee 2000 and aims to turn climate change from an environmental issue into a moral one (in the way in which poverty and international debt relief have been) so that government can feel that the public wants it to take difficult decisions.

However, Stop Climate Chaos has had only limited impact. In a further attempt to mobilise public support in September 2009 the 10:10 campaign was launched. The campaign aims to achieve a 10 per cent cut in the UK's carbon emissions in 2010 and rather than lobbying government seeks to mobilise the public. In a sign of how climate politics had moved up the political agenda within 48 hours of the launch of the campaign the leaders of the three main political parties had signed up, and so too had a host of celebrities, businesses, councils and schools. The campaign is deliberately setting itself apart from the big international climate change conferences, such as Copenhagen, which will be the focus of many of the major environmental groups like WWF and Friends of the Earth, because 10:10 believes that they cannot deliver change sufficiently quickly.

The Stern Report

While the scientific evidence on climate change was mounting governments across the world found it difficult to commit themselves to challenging individual or collective actions. For example, the Kyoto Protocol targets on emission reductions placed only limited burdens upon developed countries. Part of the problem for governments was justifying why they should take action to mitigate climate change when the economic costs would be borne by the current generation (i.e. voters) and the benefits enjoyed by future generations. In an attempt to break the policy impasse, the Labour government commissioned the head of the Government's Economic Service to undertake an analysis of the economic costs of climate change. The report by Sir Nicholas Stern gained worldwide coverage. The review argued that to continue with business-as-usual did not make economic sense since climate change would reduce by at least 5 per cent and up to 20 per cent annual global GDP. Alternatively action to mitigate climate change would cost about 1 per cent of world GDP. Despite some misgivings about the assumptions used by Stern the report was positively received by politicians, environmental groups and economists and helped significantly to shift the terms of debate. Now the question was, what actions should governments take? Here Stern also had an answer: he argued that as the developed world is responsible for about 70 per cent of GHGs in the atmosphere it should bear the brunt of cuts. He thought that the richest countries, including the UK, should commit themselves to reducing their emissions by 60 to 80 per cent by 2050 (the lower figure was one the government was already working towards, the higher one would subsequently inform debate on the Climate Change Bill, see below).

Energy policy

Whether groups and government agree over the outcome of difficult decisions in the area of environmental policy is likely to become an increasingly moot point. In a high-profile energy White Paper published in 2003 (DTI 2003), the government managed to secure a wide-ranging consensus embracing environmental groups, the business community and the renewables industry because it promoted a low-carbon energy economy. For the very first time environmental issues, and specifically climate change, were at the core of energy policy, along with maintaining reliable supplies, promoting competition and ensuring affordable domestic energy. An indication of how climate change had moved to the fore of policy making was the Government's commitment at the time to a 60 per cent reduction in CO_2 (from 1990) by 2050 and the goal was to be achieved by greater energy efficiency, combined heat and power (CHP) projects and renewable energy. To environmental groups such as Greenpeace and Friends of the Earth the White Paper also appeared to signal the demise of the nuclear industry since it noted that the 'economics of nuclear power makes it an unattractive option for new generating capacity'.

By the autumn of 2005 it was becoming clear that the government was concerned that its energy policy was being undermined by internal and external factors. Within government there was increasing concern about the growing reliance on sourcing energy from potentially unstable regions of the world, recognition that energy consumption was continuing to grow, that energy efficiency measures were not delivering, and that renewable energy was not making the contribution that had been hoped for to energy supply. In essence, the argument emerging from government was that by 2020 the UK will

have decommissioned coal and nuclear plants that together generate over 30 per cent of today's electricity supply. Renewable energy, it was claimed, was incapable of meeting the energy shortfall.

Confirmation that the energy debate had shifted from one that was sympathetic to environmental groups to one that they would oppose came in the 2007 energy White Paper and its follow-up, the 2008 nuclear White Paper. In these two White Papers there was a clear turn to the nuclear option. New nuclear power stations had moved to the heart of the government's approach to a lower carbon, more diverse and more secure energy supply. While environment groups could agree with the goals of energy policy the means by which it was to be achieved – the key role for nuclear power – was unpalatable. Nuclear power, though, was now regarded as an important energy source for the government to meet its binding emission reduction commitments (see below).

The Climate Change Act 2008 and carbon reduction

A Climate Change Bill was introduced to Parliament in 2007. The Bill was promoted by a variety of environmental groups, especially Friends of the Earth, and enjoyed cross-party support. Initially, it was proposed that the Bill would make mandatory existing commitments to cut CO_2 emissions by 60 per cent by 2050 on 1990 levels (see above). However, on the Bill's journey through Parliament MPs pushed through an amendment to raise the carbon reduction commitment from 60 per cent to 80 per cent by 2050. This figure was in line with the upper limits of the Stern Report and the recommendations of the recently formed Committee on Climate Change. MPs also agreed that there should be interim, legally binding five-year targets. There was a massive majority for the Bill in the House of Commons.

In order to deliver on the binding targets in the Act in the summer of 2009 the government produced a Low Carbon Transition Plan and set of accompanying documents for a renewable energy strategy, a low carbon industrial strategy and a low carbon transport strategy. The overall Plan and supporting documents are potentially very significant for the government as a whole and for individual ministers and senior civil servants. This is because government departments are now to be responsible for emissions from their own policy area. In a similar way to the financial settlements that are agreed between departments and the Treasury, key departments now have a carbon budget which they must stay within. DECC with its responsibility for the energy has by far the biggest budget (57 per cent of the overall total), followed by Transport (17 per cent), DEFRA (11 per cent) and BIS (7 per cent). To meet its carbon reduction targets DECC will be promoting renewable energy, nuclear energy and clean fossil fuels. Meanwhile, as we have already seen above, the Department for Transport is more sympathetic to technological change than behaviour change and wants to meet its share of the reduction targets through making new cars and vans more efficient and encouraging biofuels. It is likely that the Department for Transport strategy will come under increasingly critical scrutiny from inside and outside of government.

Assessing climate change policy

In order to assess the significance of the changes in British government policy on climate change it is worthwhile once again comparing the British experience with that of the Netherlands, the latter once more having shown itself to be an early international leader. In Table 26.5 key features of climate change

policy are identified and the table clearly shows that Britain has, in a relatively short space of time, moved from being a follower on climate change to a leader and been able to produce innovative legislation, ambitious emissions reductions targets, and that those targets are mandatory. Table 26.5 also shows that in terms of emissions reduction performance Britain is outperforming the Netherlands. However, it would be too simplistic to suggest that Britain's emissions reductions were due to policy success and the Dutch increase to policy failure. In many ways Britain and the Netherlands face similar situations when tackling emissions reductions: both are prosperous, high consumption, energy-intensive societies and changes to consumer behaviour are difficult to achieve. The 'success' for Britain in reducing its emissions, therefore, rests not on consumption but largely on changes in production that had nothing to do with climate change policy. First, the 1980s witnessed a major structural upheaval in the British economy with the demise of much heavy manufacturing industry and the rise of a service sector economy. The latter uses much less energy. Second, there was a significant shift in energy production with the rise of gas-fired power stations that produce far fewer GHGs than coal-fired power stations.

Table 26.5 Britain and the Netherlands compared on climate change, 1980s to 2000s

Feature	Britain	Netherlands
Vulnerability to climate change	Low-lying areas of East Anglia and southern England particularly prone to flood risk	Low-lying and highly vulnerable to sea-level rise
Initial engagement with issue	Initially conceptualised as part of SD agenda; becomes a distinctive policy issue in the lead up to and especially following Kyoto Protocol	Late 1980s (National Environmental Policy Plan (NEPP 1, 1989) identifies climate change as an important issue
Political leadership	Former Prime Minister identifies with and promotes issue	Former Prime Minister identifies with and promotes issue
Policy innovation	Development of national emissions trading scheme for greenhouse gases in 2002; legislation passed to bind future governments to meet GHG reduction targets	Development of national emissions trading scheme for NOx and CO_2 in 2005
Key GHG reduction targets	34% reduction by 2020, 80% by 2050 compared to 1990 (Climate Change Act commitment)	30% reduction by 2020 compared to 1990 (EU commitment)
Meeting targets, 1990–2000	Reduction from 742.5 mte to 649.1 mte	Increase from 210.3 mte to 216.9 mte

Note: mte = million tonne equivalent of CO_2.

Chapter summary

This chapter began by pointing out the forces that make environmental policy a dynamic and changing area. The impact of Europe on the content of British environmental policy and on the policy making process were then described. It was noted that there has been a considerable shift in thinking on the environment so that it now encompasses a very broad area under the term sustainable development. The role of key organisations in central government was set out and the implications of devolution of responsibilities to Cardiff and Edinburgh explored. The part that local government plays in environmental protection and more generally sustainable development was discussed. The role of pressure groups was outlined, how they have contributed to the road transport debate and how in turn government policy has changed. Finally how government addresses climate change was discussed. The chapter shows that issues related to sustainable development and now climate change are amongst the most challenging that any government can face. Not only do they involve all sections of society, different levels of government but also future generations and distant peoples. Moreover, a more sustainable society is a long-term goal but policies to achieve that goal often seem to involve short-term political costs. Little wonder then that at present there often seems to be a mismatch between policies and practice.

Discussion points

■ What is the appropriate contribution of Europe, national government and the devolved administrations to environmental policy?

■ Is sustainable development a meaningful term?

■ Should we try to integrate environmental policy making and its implementation or fragment it among geographically and functionally specialised organisations?

■ Who is best able to promote more environmentally friendly behaviour change, government through regulation or groups through seeking to change the actions of individuals?

Further reading

The best general purpose book on environmental policy and politics is that by Carter (2007). Two other texts are those by Gray (1995) and Connelly and Smith (1999). The former is an edited book with a wide-ranging collection of papers, while the latter is an informative and lively account of contemporary environmental politics. For those interested in studying further how British environmental policy has been shaped by decisions in Europe the book by Lowe and Ward (1998a) is a very good place to start. One of the better books by an environmental activist with insights into the policy process is that by Bryant (1996). There are now a number of good environmental websites. Aside from the media these prove a good means of keeping up to date with what is a fast changing policy area.

Bibliography

Blowers, A. (1987) 'Transition or Transformation? Environmental Policy under Thatcher', *Public Administration*, Vol. 65, No. 3, pp. 277–94.

Bryant, B. (1996) *Twyford Down: Roads, Campaigning and Environmental Law* (E. and F.N. Spon).

Carter, N. (2007) *The Politics of the Environment. Ideas Activism, Policy* (Cambridge University Press).

Carter, N. (2008) 'Combating Climate Change in the UK: Challenges and Obstacles', *The Political Quarterly*, Vol. 79, No. 2, April–June, 194–205.

Cm 693 (1989) *Roads for Prosperity* (HMSO).

Cm 1200 (1990) This Common Inheritance (HMSO).

Cm 2426 (1994) *Sustainable Development: The UK Strategy* (HMSO).

Cm 2428 (1994) *Biodiversity: The UK Action Plan* (HMSO).

▶

Cm 4345 (1999) *A Better Quality of Life: A Strategy for Sustainable Development for the United Kingdom* (The Stationery Office).

Cmnd 4506 (1970) The Reorganisation of Central Government (HMSO).

Commission of the European Communities (1992) *Towards Sustainability: The Fifth Environmental Action Programme* (CEC).

Connelly, J. and Smith, G. (1999) *Politics and the Environment* (Routledge).

DEFRA (2001) *Resource Use and Efficiency of the UK Economy*, available on www.defra.gov.uk/environment/statistics/des/waste/research/index.htm

DEFRA (Department for Environment, Food and Rural Affairs) (2004) *Taking it on. Developing UK Sustainable Development Strategy Together*, a Consultation Paper (DEFRA).

DEFRA (Department for Environment, Food and Rural Affairs) (2005a) *Securing the Future. The UK Government Sustainable Development Strategy*, Cm 6467 (HMSO).

DEFRA (Department for Environment, Food and Rural Affairs) (2005b) *One Future – Different Paths. The UK's Shared Framework for Sustainable Development* (HMSO).

(DTI) Department of Trade and Industry (2003) Energy White Paper: Our Energy Future – Creating a Low Carbon Economy (HMSO).

Environment Agency (2005) *Doing the Right Thing: Spotlight on Business Environmental Performance 2004*, www.publications.environment-agency.gov.uk/pdf/GEHO0706BLBM-e-e.pdf (HMSO).

Environment Agency (2008) *Spotlight on Business: 10 Years of Improving the Environment*, http://publications.environment-agency.gov.uk/pdf/GEHO0708BOFX-E-E.pdf?lang=_e

Environmental Audit Committee (1998) *Second Report, The Greening Government Initiative, Vol. 1* Report, HC 517-1, 2 July 1998.

Environmental Audit Committee (2004) *Eighth Report, Greening Government 2004*, HC 881, 17 July 2004.

Gray, T. (ed.) (1995) *UK Environmental Policy in the 1990s* (Macmillan).

Gummer, J. (1994) 'Europe, what next? Environment, policy and the Community', speech to the ERM Environment Forum organised by the Green Alliance.

House of Commons Environmental Audit Committee (1998) *The Greening Government Initiative*, Vol. 1 (The Stationery Office).

House of Commons Environmental Audit Committee (2004) *The Sustainable Development Strategy: Illusion or Reality?* Vol. 1 (The Stationery Office).

Jordan, A. (2005) *The Europeanisation of British Environmental Policy* (2nd edn) (Earthscan).

Jordan, J. (1998) 'The Art of Necessity: The Subversive Imagination of Anti-road Protest and Reclaim the Streets' in G. McKay (ed.) *DiY Culture: Party and Protest in Nineties Britain* (Verso).

Lowe, P. and Flynn, A. (1989) 'Environmental Politics and Policy in the 1980s', in J. Mohan (ed.) *The Political Geography of Contemporary Britain* (Macmillan).

Lowe, P. and Goyder, J. (1983) *Environmental Groups in Politics* (Allen & Unwin).

Lowe, P. and Ward, S. (eds) (1998a) *British Environmental Policy and Europe* (Routledge).

Lowe, P. and Ward, S. (1998b) 'Britain in Europe: Themes and Issues in National Environmental Policy', in P. Lowe and S. Ward (eds) *British Environmental Policy and Europe* (Routledge).

McCormick, J. (1991) *British Politics and the Environment* (Earthscan).

McLean, I. (2008) 'Climate Change and UK Politics, from Brynle Williams to Sir Nicholas Stern', *The Political Quarterly*, Vol. 79, No. 2, April–June, 184–193.

Ministerie van Volkshuisvesting Ruimtelkjike Ordening en Milieubeheer (VROM) (Ministry of Housing, Physical Planning and the Environment) (1998) *National Environmental Policy Plan 3* (VROM).

O'Riordan, T. and Voisey, H. (eds) (1998a) *The Transition to Sustainability: the Politics of Agenda 21 in Europe* (Earthscan).

O'Riordan, T. and Voisey, H. (1998b) 'Editorial Introduction', in O'Riordan, T. and Voisey, H. (eds) *The Transition to Sustainability: the Politics of Agenda 21 in Europe* (Earthscan).

Pettinger, Mary E. (2007) 'The Netherlands Climate Change Policy: Constructing Themselves/Constructing Climate Change' in H.E. Pettinger (ed.) *The Social Construction of Climate Change* (Ashgate).

Scottish Office (1999) *Down to Earth – a Scottish Perspective on Sustainable Development*, February 1999 (The Scottish Office Sustainable Development Team).

Scottish Executive (2005) *Choosing Our Future: Scotland's Sustainable Development Strategy* (Scottish Executive Publications).

Sharp, R. (1998) 'Responding to Europeanisation: A Governmental Perspective', in P. Lowe and S. Ward (eds) *British Environmental Policy and Europe* (Routledge).

Voisey, H. and O'Riordan, T. (1998) 'Sustainable Development the UK National Approach', in O'Riordan, T. and Voisey, H. (eds) *The Transition to Sustainability: the Politics of Agenda 21 in Europe* (Earthscan).

Welsh Assembly Government (2009) *One Wales: One Planet. The Sustainable Development Scheme of the Welsh Assembly Government.*

World Commission on Environment and Development (1987) *Our Common Future* (Oxford University Press).

Useful websites

Countryside Agency:
http://www.countryside.gov.uk/index.htm

Countryside Council for Wales:
http://www.countryside.gov.uk/index.htm

Department of the Environment, Food and Rural Affairs: http://www.defra.gov.uk/

English Nature: http://www.english-nature.org.uk/

Environment Agency:
http://www.environment-agency.gov.uk/

Friends of the Earth: http://www.foe.co.uk/

Greenpeace: http://www.greenpeace.org.uk/

Scottish Environmental Protection Agency:
http://www.sepa.org.uk/

Scottish Executive:
http://www.scotland.gov.uk/topics/?pageid=1

Scottish Natural Heritage: http://213.121.208.4/

Welsh Assembly Government:
http://www.wales.gov.uk/themessustainabledev/index.htm

CHAPTER 27

Britain, European integration and the European Union

Nicholas Rees

Learning objectives

- To look at Britain's historical relationship with Europe.

- To examine the institutions and policy processes of the European Union.

- To explain the impact of the European Union on Britain.

- To understand Britain's contemporary role in the European Union.

- To examine the challenges facing Britain inside the European Union.

Introduction

The UK's relationship with the European Union (EU) has been marked by a mixture of antipathy and disinterest. This chapter examines how Britain's relationship has evolved and developed over the last 60 years, highlighting key points at which the relationship changed. It suggests that British attitudes to Europe reflect a deep-rooted distrust of all things European, which have not been challenged by British political leaders regardless of party affiliation. The chapter considers the key EU institutions, policies and policy making before moving on to consider the impact of Europe on UK politics, institutions and policy making. The concluding section considers some of the challenges facing Britain, including the implementation of the Lisbon Treaty and other issues of importance to the UK.

■ Britain's historical relationship with Europe

As a 'world' power with a huge empire, a place on the UN's Security Council and nuclear weapons in 1945, Britain saw itself as the equal of the USA and the USSR. The Americans were keen that their Marshall (aid) Plan should be managed directly by cooperation among the European states. There was also considerable discussion in countries such as France, Italy, Belgium and even Britain about what political form Europe should take. As Richard Mayne (1983), reminds us in his seminal work, *Postwar: The Dawn of Today's Europe*, the reconstruction of Europe took many forms with new ideas about Europe taking hold in the different European states. In the context of the atrocities of the war, a number of European politicians and statesmen were concerned with creating political and economic structures that would lessen the likelihood of future wars. From this fermentation of ideas, the vision of a united Europe was born, based upon economic integration.

■ European integration: intergovernmentalism versus supranationalism

In the 1950s Britain maintained its distance from the political developments that had led to the formation of a number of European-level organisations. It was not that Britain was opposed to international cooperation, which it did engage in with other European states, but rather the state's political leaders were not committed Europeanists and were principally concerned with pursuing Britain's economic and political interests on a global stage, building on links with former colonies such as Australia and New Zealand which now formed part of the Commonwealth. Britain's view of Europe was based on support for intergovernmental arrangements that ensured that the government had the final say in any decisions – not European-level institutions.

In contrast, many key European political leaders believed that federal-style arrangements might offer a means of ensuring a lasting peace, while bringing economic and political benefits. Among many committed federalists, there was already a view that Europe had long had a 'unique and identifiable entity', based on its Christian heritage dating back to Charlemagne. At a more pragmatic level, there was a desire to avoid the repetition of a Franco-German conflict, and rampant nationalism, which were seen as the root causes of war, while containing the revived threat of a possibly united Germany.

The creation of such organisations as the Council of Europe, the European Coal and Steel Community and even the move to form a European Defence Community (EDC) illustrated the attempts to create a European political community as the underpinning of West European security and prosperity. The formation of the European Coal and Steel Community provided the first example of a European organisation where political authority was vested by the six founding member states in a supranational institution (the High Authority). In essence, the states agreed to cede decision-making authority to an executive European-level institution (above the nation state) committed to representing a community interest.

BOX 27.1	Key events in European integration, 1945–1958

Winston Churchill's United States of Europe address	September 1946
Marshall Plan for European Recovery	June 1947
Benelux Customs Union established	October 1948
Creation of the Council of Europe	May 1949
French foreign minister Robert Schuman proposes pooling of coal and steel resources	May 1950
Formation of the European Coal and Steel Community	April 1951
French Assembly rejection of the European Defence Community	May 1954
Western European Union	October 1954
Signing of the Treaties of Rome: EEC and Euratom	March 1957
EEC and Euratom come into being	January 1958

After 1949 it became clear that Britain under the Labour leadership of Prime Minister Clement Attlee (1945–51) and Foreign Secretary Ernest Bevin would go no further than participating in the Council of Europe model, which largely consisted of a Consultative Assembly of nominated non-communist parliamentarians, without any executive power. The Labour government declined to join the ECSC negotiations on the grounds that it would be required to accept an element of supranationalism and that it needed to maintain control over key sectors of the economy (leading to nationalisation). Prime Minister Clement Attlee in the House of Commons stated:

We on this side are not prepared to accept the principle that the most vital economic forces of this country should be handed over to an authority that is utterly undemocratic and is responsible to no one.

Palmer and Lambert 1968: 258

The Conservative opposition led by Winston Churchill and Anthony Eden argued that Britain should have participated in the discussions leading up to the formation of the European Coal and Steel Community (ECSC) suggesting it was better to be in the negotiating room than outside it. On his return to power in 1951, however, Churchill refused to contemplate participating in any further attempts at European integration, suggesting that Britain would never have considered joining the ECSC on the same terms as other European states (Denman 1997: 189).

The success of the ECSC surprised the British government and those in it who were sceptical about the possibility of further integration. In December 1955 Britain signed an Association Agreement with the ECSC, providing for further intergovernmental cooperation with the fledgling community. Already by 1955 the European economies had recovered much of their considerable economic strength. Moreover, the ECSC seemed to be an economic success story with the production of iron, crude steel, and sheet metal increased by 20 to 25 per cent and trade within the ECSC registered an increase of 170 per cent between 1952 and 1955. At a political level Jean Monnet and other European political leaders saw this as the first step on the road to European federation. A further sign of Europe's recovery was the doubling of steel importation between 1952 and 1955, while exports increased by 20 per cent. By 1955 to 1957 there seemed to be a favourable political environment with the economies of Europe experiencing a boom.

■ Europe at sixes and sevens

In Britain Anthony Eden, the former Foreign Secretary, succeeded Winston Churchill as Prime Minister in April 1955. Eden was reluctant to commit to Europe, as was his new Foreign Secretary, Harold Macmillan. The British government was not formally invited to participate in the discussions that took place among the foreign ministers of ECSC states in Messina in June 1955. It was, however, consulted by its French counterparts as to the possibility of British attendance but declined to do so. The discussions in Messina (Sicily, Italy) focused on proposals to form a common market and the outcome did not draw much attention. In the aftermath of the discussions a formal committee was convened under the chairmanship of Paul Henri Spaak (Belgian foreign minister) to develop a more comprehensive set of proposals. The British government received an invitation from the ECSC member states to send a delegate to the meetings. In its reply the British government agreed to send a 'representative' (a civil servant), although it noted that Britain could not participate in any such proposals to create a common market given its commitments to its Commonwealth partners, which meant it could not impose tariffs on goods coming from these states to Britain. Later the British government withdrew its representative on the grounds that it would not join a common market.

During the spring and early summer of 1956 the British government slowly began to comprehend the consequences of the successful conclusion of the Spaak committee and the proposals to create a European Economic Community and a European Atomic Energy Community (Euratom). At this point Britain and the other OEEC states began to consider proposals for the establishment of a European Free Trade area linking those European countries outside the EEC to the Common Market. The underlying concern among the other OEEC countries was that the creation of a customs union would discriminate against their products in the marketplace. Yet, at the same time, the EEC was considered by them as an unacceptable alternative. In July 1956 the OEEC Council of Ministers decided to establish a special working party to study possible forms and methods of association between the proposed customs union of the six and the other OEEC countries. A special committee was set up under the then British Paymaster General, Reginald Maudling, and a discussion ensued over the many possible variants of association and details concerning the reduction of tariffs. In January 1960, Britain, Austria, Denmark, Portugal, Sweden, Switzerland and Norway signed the Stockholm Convention leading to the creation of the European Free Trade Association (EFTA). Europe was literally at sixes and sevens between the EEC and EFTA respectively.

■ EEC membership

By the early 1960s there was growing recognition in Britain that EEC membership might provide the best way forward for Britain. There was also growing acknowledgement, following the Suez crisis in 1956, that the world was changing and that Britain was no longer at the centre of an empire and could not always rely on American support. Britain lay between Europe and America with its future depending on its ability to carve out a future role for itself in the Atlantic area. In 1961 the new conservative government of Harold Macmillan, who was himself more pro-European than Eden, announced that Britain intended to apply to join the European Community. However, Britain's bid was opposed by the French President, Charles de Gaulle, who feared that Britain was too closely allied with the United States. This seemed especially to be the case after Britain was offered Polaris missiles by the United States. Thus, de Gaulle exercised the French right of veto in the Council of Ministers thereby terminating the entry negotiations. At a press conference in Paris in August 1963 de Gaulle declared:

England is, in effect, insular, maritime, linked through its trade, markets and food supply to very diverse and often very distant countries . . . [if Britain entered the Community] in the end there would appear a colossal Atlantic Community under American dependence and leadership.

From de Gaulle's perspective while the supranational nature of the European Community was highly undesirable, he was prepared to use the Community to win political advantages for France.

The British application was ostensibly based on the desire to share in the economic advantages that the Community appeared to be bringing to other European countries. For example, the Community's economic growth rate was two-and-a-half times that of Britain. Underlying this was an equally important consideration, namely that Britain should support a cohesive Europe. Britain's decision to seek EEC membership was also backed by the newly elected US President John F. Kennedy, who may have considered Britain as an important counterweight to French influence in the EEC. In any event, Macmillan's decision was a considerable achievement given widespread Conservative opposition to such a move and his decision represented a significant reversal of past policies (or at least tactics). Soon after Britain's application for membership in August 1961, Ireland and Denmark applied for membership, followed by Norway in 1962.

In 1964, a newly elected Labour government came into power under Prime Minister Harold Wilson. It did not initially seek to renew Britain's membership application and espoused no strong European views. In 1966, the Labour government was re-elected to office with an increased majority and in May 1967 decided to renew Britain's application for EEC membership. The Labour government, like its Conservative predecessor, had been forced to recognise that EEC membership was necessary to sustain British trade, the economy and to ensure its political influence. In effect, EEC membership seemed to offer Britain the best chance of ensuring its long-term political influence and economic power. The experiment of EFTA had done little for Britain and there were concerns about Britain's relationship with the USA. However, as on the previous occasion, President de Gaulle once again exercised his state's veto, even before membership negotiations had begun in November 1967. This was in the face of a favourable recommendation by the European Commission in September 1967 and support from the other five member states. Ostensibly the French objection was based on the same reasons as in the past – Britain was too closely linked with the United States – and its membership would have considerably altered the nature of the European Community. There were also broader issues at stake in the European Community, including the reform of the common agricultural policy and the future direction of the European Community (George 1991: 48).

It was not until de Gaulle resigned from office in May 1969 that the political stalemate in the European Community was broken and Britain was able to renew its application, although French policy had begun to change even prior to his departure. The political deadlock over further integration including enlargement was broken at the Hague Conference of European Community Heads of State and Government in December 1969. At this key conference European Community leaders agreed, among other things, to reopen negotiations with European countries interested in European Community membership. In June 1970 negotiations were opened with the four applicant countries (Britain, Ireland, Denmark and Norway) in Luxembourg.

In Britain the June election of a new Conservative government under Prime Minister Edward Heath brought into office a political leader committed to achieving EEC membership. Heath's chief objective was to get Britain inside the European Community and then sort out any British problems that might arise as a result of membership. There was, however, a clear awareness that in so doing the issue of Britain's contributions to the European Community budget were likely to be high, relative to the direct transfers that Britain might expect to receive. This issue was never fully resolved leaving a festering sore that was to haunt the European Community up until the present day. In effect Britain faced a high budget contribution of over £300 million pounds after a transitional period. It had to dismantle its internal customs duties over a number of stages by July 1977 and move towards the application of the Common external tariff beginning in January 1974. It also reluctantly accepted the common agricultural policy (CAP), which was to begin in 1977 and which excluded Commonwealth products. The government secured parliamentary approval for membership in the House of Commons on 28 October 1971, by a vote of 356 to 244 in favour of accession, including that of 69 Labour MPs who defied a three-line whip to support accession. It also passed by 451 votes to 58 in the House of Lords. The treaties of accession were signed in Brussels on 22 March 1972 and came into effect on 1 January 1973 when Britain became a member of the European Community. Britain was the only country of the four applicants not to hold a referendum over membership.

The Heath government was pro-European, but perhaps largely because of the times in which it held power, which suggested its best position was to be in Europe. The changing nature of the international political and economic system in the 1970s, with the US pursuing a distinctly unilateral economic policy and the emerging energy crisis, may have suggested that Europe offered the best option for Britain. In contrast, the Labour party engaged in an anti-market campaign claiming that British terms of entry were unfavourable. It was particularly critical of the cost of the CAP which it considered unacceptable, raised concerns about the impact membership would have on the Common-wealth, and what impact economic integration would have on the regions.

The downfall of the Heath government and the election of Harold Wilson to a second term as Prime Minister brought into power a party in which there were many members who were critical of European Community membership. There were distinct factions in the Labour party, with those on the 'Bennite' left opposed to European Community membership, whereas the social democratic element who were identified with Roy Jenkins (Deputy Leader) and Shirley Williams were supportive of the European Community. The party had, however, pledged at its party conference (1972) and in its election manifesto (1974) that it would renegotiate the terms of European Community membership and hold a referendum on the matter. As a result the new administration called a referendum over European Community membership on 5 June 1975 – the first and only UK referendum over European Community membership. Ahead of the referendum the Labour government had already won concessions from its European counterparts at summits in December 1974 (Paris) and in Spring 1975 (Dublin). These included budgetary concessions via a budgetary correction mechanism, agreement on the setting up of a new regional fund that would benefit British regions and market access for New Zealand's dairy products. It was therefore able to claim to the British public that it had won major benefits for Britain, making it easier for the party leadership to advocate a 'yes' vote in the referendum.

As a result the campaign was not fought along traditional party lines, rather opponents and supporters associated themselves with two umbrella organisations: the Anti-Market National Referendum Campaign and the Britain in Europe Campaign. The opponents included left-wing Labour politicians, Eurosceptic Conservatives and other nationalist parties. The supporters of European Community membership included Labour and Conservative members, as well as the business community, the European Movement, the Anglican Church and elements of the Press. The supporters raised some $1.5 million in comparison to the opponents who only managed to raise $125,000. In the referendum the electorate were asked the following question:

The Government has announced the results of the renegotiation of the United Kingdom's terms of membership of the European Community. Do you think that the United Kingdom should stay in the European Community (Common Market)?

The result was a victory for the Labour party leadership, with 67.2 per cent of the voters endorsing European Community membership with a turnout of 64.5 per cent. The victory, however, was won at some expense to Britain's relationship with Europe. The decision to hold a referendum and the renegotiation of Britain's terms of membership left a lasting impression of Britain in Europe – leading some to brand the country an awkward partner. It also aptly demonstrated how European Community membership had been used as political football in domestic British politics. Europe proved a useful distraction for the new Labour government in light of the prolonged period of social unrest and political turmoil in British politics that had characterised the end days of the Heath administration.

The European Community that Britain joined in 1973 was very different from that of the European Union today. In 1973 the European Community was still relatively underdeveloped with weak institutions and an overwhelming focus on the common market and associated common agricultural policy. The original six members, Germany, France, Italy and the Benelux countries, had prospered inside the EEC, with economic growth rates exceeding those of Britain. However, there remained significant challenges in the European Community, especially over the future direction of European integration. There were also differences of opinion even among the founding states. The French government had already demonstrated in 1965–66 in an incident known as the 'empty chair' crisis that it was willing to veto European plans that were not considered to be in the French national interest. In essence, the experiment of economic integration was based on a number of bargains and compromises made among the member states at the founding of the EEC in 1957. These reflected the differing national economic, political and security interests of those original member states.

■ EU institutions and policy processes

The European Union today is largely still based on much of the key institutional architecture that was provided for in the original EEC and Euratom Treaties of Rome, although the shape of the institutions, their powers and the policies of the European Union are very different some 50 years after the founding of the EEC. Nevertheless, many of the issues that have been discussed in contemporary treaty reforms, such as in the recent debates over the Lisbon Treaty (also known as the Reform Treaty) and its ratification, are not new and reflect the core concerns of the member states. In particular, Britain has been one of the more Eurosceptic states, along with Denmark, the Czech Republic and Poland, cautious about the deepening of European integration and committed to supporting a strongly intergovernmental approach to cooperation with its European

BOX 27.2	EU institutional actors

Institutions	*Other Institutions and Actors*
The European Commission	The Economic and Social Committee
The Council of Ministers	The Committee of the Regions
The European Council	The European Investment Bank
The European Parliament	The European Central Bank
The European Court of Justice	The Court of Auditors
The Court of First Instance	

counterparts. It has, however, as we shall see, been supportive of further enlargement of the European Union. In order to understand Britain's role in Europe we need to first consider the EU's institutional structure and its core policies, and we shall then return to looking at Britain's approach to Europe.

The European Union comprises five key institutional actors which need to be examined: the European Commission, the Council of Ministers, the European Council, the European Parliament and the Court of Justice.

European Commission

The Commission has been variously characterised by scholars as the 'motor of European integration', the civil service, and/or part of a dual executive. The founders of the original European Coal and Steel Community (ECSC) and later the European Economic Community attached considerable importance to this institution having a high degree of autonomy from the state. The Commission was to be independent of the member states and charged with acting in the broader interest of the EC (now EU). The European Commission (or at least the College of Commissioners) comprises 27 commissioners, with one nominated by each member state and each commissioner being responsible for a specific policy area. While a member may often be referred to as the 'British Commissioner' or the 'Irish Commissioner' they are not national representatives and are meant to act in the interests of the EU. In practice, member states clearly see these individuals as key sources of intelligence and influence in Brussels. Moreover, in most cases those appointed as Commissioners have been high-profile national politicians, usually from the ruling party. The Commission is headed up by a President, currently José Manuel Barroso, who was reappointed to a five-year term of office in September 2009. Barroso was a former

prime minister of Portugal, who was chosen in 2004 by the political leaders at a summit and endorsed by the European Parliament following a political deadlock over two other candidates: Chris Patten (Britain) and Guy Verhofstadt (Belgium).

Aside from the individual commissioners, the Commission has a permanent staff in excess of 38,000 officials (2009) based predominantly in Brussels (71.6 per cent), as well as in Luxembourg (12.6 per cent), other member states (10.6 per cent) and outside the EU (5.2 per cent). These officials are selected on the basis of merit and are recruited through annual competitions, although about 3 per cent are seconded national officials. They are drawn from all countries through the EU with the largest number coming from Belgium, France and Italy and the smallest number recruited from the newer member states. The Commission has traditionally been organised around Directorates General (DGs) and Services. These equate with the national ministries in the EU's member states and usually represent functional policy areas, such as regional policy, agriculture and rural development, research and external relations. Each Commissioner is responsible for a specific DG and is supported through a small private office or cabinet of key officials. For example, in the case of Britain the current Commissioner is Catherine Ashton, a former Labour government minister and leader of the House of Lord, who was appointed to replace Peter Mandelson in October 2008. Ashton has responsibility as EU Trade Commissioner for all trade matters, including negotiations at the world trade talks. Her cabinet is typical of many other Commissioners, including about nine senior officials, as well as a smaller number of assistants. In addition to the specific DGs there are a number of other Commission services and bodies. The principal ones include, among others, the Secretariat General, Inspectorate General, the Legal Service, the Spokesman's Service, the Translation

Press conference with Barrosso and Reinfeldt

The Commission

Service, the Statistical Office and Joint Interpretation and Conference Service.

The Commission's formal functions include the initiation and formulation of policy, the supervision of the treaty, and the implementation of EU policy; whereas its informal powers include its standing prestige and legitimacy as an institution and its technical information and expertise. First, the Commission is charged with the responsibility for drawing-up and initiating proposals in consultation

European Commission 2008–09

José Manuel Barroso
Portuguese
President

Margot Wallström
Swedish
Vice-President
Institutional relations and communication strategy

Günter Verheugen
German
Vice-President
Enterprise and industry

Jacques Barrot
French
Vice-President
Justice, freedom and security

Siim Kallas
Estonian
Vice-President
Administrative affairs, audit and anti-fraud

Antonio Tajani
Italian
Vice-President
Transport

Viviane Reding
Luxembourgish
Information society and media

Stavros Dimas
Greek
Environment

Joaquín Almunia
Spanish
Economic and monetary affairs

Danuta Hübner
Polish
Regional policy

Joe Borg
Maltese
Fisheries and maritime affairs

Dalia Grybauskaitė
Lithuanian
Financial programming and budget

Janez Potočnik
Slovenian
Science and research

Ján Figel'
Slovakian
Education, training, culture and youth

Olli Rehn
Finnish
Enlargement

Louis Michel
Belgian
Development and humanitarian aid

László Kovács
Hungarian
Taxation and customs union

Neelie Kroes
Dutch
Competition

Mariann Fischer Boel
Danish
Agriculture and rural development

Benita Ferrero-Waldner
Austrian
External relations and European neighbourhood policy

Charlie McCreevy
Irish
Internal market and services

Vladimír Špidla
Czech
Employment, social affairs and equal opportunities

Andris Piebalgs
Latvian
Energy

Meglena Kuneva
Bulgarian
Consumer protection

Leonard Orban
Romanian
Multilingualism

Androulla Vassiliou
Cypriot
Health

Catherine Ashton
British
Trade

Situation as of November 2008

DG COMM Printed by

NA-30-08-808-EN-P

The Portfolios

with the European Parliament and other groups. It has the right to initiate Community legislation without waiting for instruction from other bodies, such as the Council of Ministers. The Commission has developed an extensive array of advisory committees which precede and accompany Commission policy development (Nugent 1999: 121). Second, the Commission is also the executive organ of the Community, and powers are vested in it to carry through the decisions taken by the Council of Ministers. It is charged with the management of the Community's policies, including financial management and the EU's budget. Third, the Commission is sometimes described as the watchdog of the treaty. In this capacity it watches over the treaty and all subsequent Community legislation making sure it is correctly observed: that individuals, companies and member states do not act in ways which run counter to the treaty or specific policies laid down by the Council. Fourthly, the Commission represents the Union in a variety of international forums ranging from the World Trade Organisation (trade talks) to the Council of Europe and Organisation for Economic Cooperation and Development. It also has an increasing network of diplomatic representations across the globe with other states and international organisations, as well as in international forums. It also examines applications for EU membership, including looking at the implications for the EU and publishes an opinion for consideration by the Council. Finally, the Commission acts as a political broker by mediating between the member states and trying to find solutions acceptable to all parties.

The Council of Ministers

The EC's founding fathers conceived of the Council of Ministers as the body in which decisions would be formally taken and legitimated. The member states would be both negotiators and legislators. At the outset the Council and its president's functions were not clearly defined, although it was conceived that it would be the brake on integration. The founding fathers had hoped that national sovereignty would come to mean less over time with Community considerations becoming more important. This has in fact not been the case and the Council's importance has tended to grow rather than decline relative to that of other EU institutions.

The structure of the Council of Ministers is more complex than the title suggests as there are not one but many forms in which the Council sits. It is the place that brings together the representatives of the various national governments. Under the Treaty, the Council consists of one minister from each member country, although in practice many senior ministers attend the Council sessions. The most important council formation is the so-called General Affairs and External Relations Council made up of the foreign ministers from the member states. The other key formations include the Council of Economic and Financial Affairs (Ecofin) and the Council of Agricultural and Fisheries. This General Affairs Council is concerned with general issues and usually the more politically sensitive ones. In total there are 20 or more sectoral or technical councils in which more specialised matters are considered, such as transportation, agriculture, and industry. The General Affairs Council usually meets one–two days once a month with other Councils meeting less frequently. This system of councils is, however, less than clear-cut in practice where boundaries fade into grey areas and ministers are of varying status.

The Council's role and significance in terms of the European Union varies according to the policy area under discussion. It has also gained influence over the years, as the range of areas in which it is involved has grown, thereby placing it in an increasingly strong position to set the agenda. Its machinery has also grown and its bureaucracy is now in a stronger position *vis-à-vis* the Commission when it comes to looking for assistance and making decisions as it is far more autonomous as a political bureaucracy. In terms of the day-to-day administration of Council business the Council President has become increasingly important over time as the balance of power has shifted from the Commission to the Council of Ministers. The Presidency rotates between the states on a six monthly basis (Jan–June, July–December) and is staffed by a secretariat of desk officers in charge of watching over policy developments. It is supported by a Council General Secretariat with a staff of about 2500 officials of whom 250 are A-grade officials. It is charged with servicing the Council machinery by producing draft agendas, keeping records, legal advice, processing and circulating decisions.

The Council is the main decision taker in the EU and represents the interests of the 27 member states whose representatives sit in its various council formations. As the principal decision-making body it has to decide on the EU's budget, legislation, international agreements and enlargement. In practice it shares its executive role with the European

Commission which is principally responsible for generating the proposals discussed by the Council and the member states. In so doing much of the work of Council meetings takes place through the meeting of the Permanent Representatives of the national governments and their delegations acting for the national governments based in Brussels. Such delegations include a Permanent Representative, a deputy and a staff of some 30 to 40 diplomats plus support staff. They meet in a forum referred to as COREPER (The Committee of Permanent Representatives), which is responsible for preparing the work of the Council and for carrying out the tasks assigned to it by the Council. In fact, there there are two such committees: COREPER II and COREPER I. The former is staffed by the Permanent Representatives and is predominantly concerned with the business of the General Council and EcoFin, while the latter is staffed by their deputies and is less politically important. Often Commission proposals go to COREPER and its subcommittees before they are passed on to the Council. This allows for negotiation and reconciliation before approaching the Council for a final decision. On receipt of a Commission proposal the procedure is to refer it to a committee or working group made up of civil servants. Thus, even the work of the Council, COREPER and SCA is prepared through a system of committees and working parties.

Decisions in the Council are taken on the basis of three voting procedures depending on the issue under discussion. First, under unanimity critical matters concerning the common foreign and security policy, police and judicial cooperation, constitutional and financial issues have been subject to the requirement of obtaining unanimity among the member states in the Council. Second, under a procedure known as simple majority voting all states have one vote. Finally, an increasing number of issues are the subject of qualified majority voting, wherein each state is assigned a weighted vote. The latter procedure means that individual states can be outvoted by a majority of other states, although it is also possible for a group of states to form a blocking minority. As a result of treaty reform dating from the mid-1990s majority voting has been extended to an increasing number of policy areas in an attempt to make decision-making easier and to avoid log jams where individual states had been blocking proposals. By implication, there is a risk that proposals may be adopted with which states have to comply or risk censure including referral to the Court of Justice.

European Council

The European Council, which was established in 1974, was created in response to a perceived need to overcome institutional inertia and that the EC needed a new impetus to drive integration forward and address the problems confronting it. Even prior to this time there had been an increasing number of meetings of the heads of government in response to increasing problems in the Community and outside it in the international environment. (There had been ad hoc summits in 1961, 1967, 1969, 1972, 1973 and 1974.) Today, the European Council comprises the 27 heads of government and state, as well as the foreign ministers and two commissioners (including the President of the Commission), and is usually attended by the President of the European Parliament. It meets at least twice in June and December, as well as usually in March and October for up to two days at a time.

In advance of the meetings much of the preparatory work is undertaken by the General Affairs and External Relations Council, as well as in the Commission and member state delegations (COREPER). Senior officials from the country holding the presidency work in conjunction with the Council of Ministers Secretariat and in liaison with the Commission to identify topics for the agenda. These are then discussed either in COREPER or in the Political and Security Committee. Then, prior to the European Council meeting, the foreign ministers meet to finalise the agenda. This standard working procedure may, of course, be affected by emergencies, previous summit decisions, or a need to take a particular decision. At the European Council meeting participants usually gather over lunch, hold a full plenary in the afternoon, and then two dinners are held: one for heads of government and one for foreign ministers. In the background, and often through the night, conclusions are drawn up by officials on the first day of business. If the meeting extends to the next day, it will include plenary sessions followed by a concluding statement and delegations each hold press conferences usually aimed at their own national audiences.

The introduction of the European Council has had a major impact on the Community decision-making process since it has increased the power of the member states and especially the role of the head of government. It has also, to some extent, undermined the power of the Commission, as well as that of the Council of Ministers as key decision makers.

In the early period it provided a means of getting agreement on key policy measures, such as the European Monetary System, the Single European Act, the Maastricht Treaty, the single currency and further enlargement. It also provided an important forum in which EU heads of government have to coordinate their actions ahead of major international summits, such as in G20 meetings, the UN and with major bilateral partners. It has also proven to be an interesting beauty parade with prime ministers and presidents vying for media attention. More recently, the French EU Presidency in the latter half of 2008 was remarkable for the energy with which French President Nicholas Sarkozy pursued an ambitious agenda during a time of economic and financial turmoil.

European Parliament

The European Parliament's (EP) roots go back before the EEC Treaty of Rome Treaty to its predecessor, the European Coal and Steel Community's Common Assembly, set up in 1952. It was not until 1962 that the name 'European Parliament' was formally adopted by the institution. Today the Parliament comprises 736 directly elected MEPs from the 27 EU member states, of which 72 are from the UK and are elected from 12 multi-member constituencies through a system of proportional representation (see Table 27.1). In 1999 the UK moved from its original first-past-the-post and single member constituencies system to using PR based on a regional basis. These MEPs are elected for a five-year term of office with the most recent election having taken place in June 2009.

As a result of a long-standing agreement among the EU member states, the Parliament holds its plenary meetings in Strasbourg and its mini-plenary meetings in Brussels. In addition, the Parliament's secretariat is divided between Brussels and Luxembourg. Most of the committee work is carried out in Brussels. Under these conditions, it is evident that the EP's work is highly fragmented impacting on its effectiveness as an institution.

Traditionally the European Parliament was the weakest of the EU's institutions whose powers were negligible in comparison to the Council of Ministers and the European Commission. Dating from direct elections in 1979, the EP has increasingly gained powers and influence relative to the other EU institutions. It has also gained considerable influence in the EU institutional system and in formal decision

Table 27.1 UK MEPs by Political Group, 2009–14

Party	EP political group	No.
Conservatives (24) Ulster Unionist Party (1)	European Conservatives and Reformists	25
Labour	Progressive Alliance of Socialists and Democrats	13
Liberal Democrats	Alliance of Liberals and Democrats	11
UK Independence Party	Europe of Freedom and Democracy	13
Green Party (2) Scottish National Party (2) Plaid Cymru (1)	Group of Greens/ European Free Alliance	5
Sinn Féin	European United Left – Nordic Green Left	1
Democratic Unionist Party (1) British National Party (2) Conservative (1)	Non-attached	4

making through treaty change. This dates predominantly from the Single European Act (1986) up until the present Lisbon Treaty (2009). Parliamentarians have constantly sought an enlargement of their role in the EU policy process, as well as greater legitimacy highlighting their democratic mandate relative to the other institutions. Nevertheless, the institution's standing and its image remain problematic with limited public understanding of its role in the policy process. This is also reflected in the low turnout in elections to the European Parliament which have declined since 1979, when it was 62 per cent to 45.5 per cent in 2004, although there is considerable variation across the member states. It has been especially low in the new EU accession states with 26.9 per cent compared to 49.1 per cent in EU 15 in 2004. The low turnout reflects a mix of factors, including the fact that elections do not lead to a change of government or policy at EU level, are largely national events and often reflect how the government in office in the member states is doing relative to the opposition.

In relation to the other institutions the European Parliament has considerably increased its legislative role since the 1980s playing a significant part in the development of EU policy. This is reflected in its early stage discussions with the European Commission prior to the development of legislative proposals. It also has the power to initiate its own work on legislation, can request the European Commission to develop policy and may even seek to influence the Commission's agenda. In the formation of policy, the EP's views must be sought on all important legislation. Until 1987 this was subject to a process known as the consultation procedure, where by the Commission had to seek the EP's opinion on any proposal before it can be passed by the Council of Ministers. There are now four separate procedures that apply to different parts of the treaty articles, including consultation, cooperation, co-decision and assent. The overall effect has been to increase the EP's influence in the legislative process with an increasing range of legislation subject to the co-decision process.

The EP also has an array of other powers including significant influence over the annual EU budget, which it has used on a number of occasions to move its own policy agenda forward. In the past this has included either rejecting the budget or seeking to amend it in those parts which it has the right to do so (i.e. non-obligatory expenditures). It has noticeably increased its influence over the European Commission through its right to approve the nominee for Commission President, its confirmation vote over the appointment of Commissioners, and its formal power to dismiss the College of Commissioners. It also has the ability to exercise some limited power over the Council of Ministers through the President's reports to the Parliament and the EP's questioning of ministers in committee discussions. The EP also has a right to take other Community Institutions to Court. Thus, if the Commission fails to implement a Council regulation then the EP can take it before the European Court of Justice. The EP does also exercise some scrutiny over the work of foreign ministers, such as in relation to external agreements, although it has little say over EU common foreign and security policy.

The European Court of Justice

Above all else the European Union is a legal order based on EU law which is derived from the EU treaties, EU legislation (including regulations, directives, decisions, recommendations and opinions), judicial interpretation, and international law. The most immediate impact of this is felt on the member states, where EU law is said to have 'direct effect' or direct applicability. This means that EU law may confer rights or impose obligations on individuals that national courts are required to recognise and

enforce (Nugent 2006: 292). Furthermore, EU law also has primacy over national law, although this is not explicitly stated in the treaties, and required the European Court of Justice to establish the principle.

In practice, it is the European Court of Justice (ECJ) which has to interpret the treaties and EU legislation as and when called on to do so. The Court, which is based in Luxembourg, comprises 27 judges, one from each member state, with each judge appointed to a six-year term of office. They are assisted by eight advocates general who act in court to make reasoned submissions on the cases brought before the court. They are charged with examining the issue and making a submission to the Court for its consideration. In addition, since the Single European Act, a Court of First Instance was established to reduce the workload of the European Court of Justice. It operates along similar lines to the ECJ, with judges appointed from each state, although there are no advocates general. Between the two courts they have played a key role in developing the EU's legal order, including expanding the policy competence of the European Union, especially in areas such as the single European market, as well as strengthening the role of the EU's institutions (Nugent 2006: 308).

EU policy making

The European Union today has a considerable impact on most aspects the public policy process in the EU's 27 member states. This reflects the manner in which the EU has developed as a policy actor, with its involvement having grown phenomenally since its early days as a fledgling economic actor. In the 1960s the then European Community was predominantly focused on putting in place measures to ensure the free movement of goods, services, capital and peoples between the six founding member states. The objective was to create a common market among the six states by removing barriers to trade, such as tariffs and quotas, while agreeing a common external tariff with respect to all goods imported from outside the European Community. The other main focus of EC policy was on the establishment of the Common Agricultural Policy (CAP), which was designed to ensure both the adequate productions of food stuffs at reasonable prices, while affording a fair living to workers in the agricultural sector. This was especially important in France, where there remained a strong agricultural sector made up of smaller farmers, as well as in (West) Germany where the beef industry was concerned to ensure its future.

Member states of the European Union (2008)

Candidate countries

Map of the EU

BOX 27.3	Enlargements of the European Union	
Britain, Ireland and Denmark	1973
Greece	1981
Spain and Portugal	1986
Austria, Finland, Sweden	1995
Cyprus, the Czech Republic, Estonia, Hungary, Latvia, Lithuania, Malta, Poland, Slovakia and Slovenia	2004
Romania and Bulgaria	2007

The further enlargement of the European Community in the 1970s led to renewed interest in developing new areas of policy, both in response to the new member states, as well as in attempt to deepen the integration process. In the 1970s this included developing new initiatives around European Political Cooperation (foreign policy coordination), regional and social policies, competition policy, and the establishment of a European Monetary System (1979). There was also growing interest in forming association agreements with third countries and regional groupings, including the African, Caribbean and Pacific states, EFTA and other such groups. This reflected the EC's growing role in world trade and particularly the Commission's role in development a Common Commercial Policy; an area in which the treaty empowered it to act on behalf of the member states.

Arising out of subsequent enlargements and treaty reform the EC (now EU's) policy competences were considerably increased during the 1980s and 1990s, including through the development of policy around the Single European Market (Internal Market), Economic and Monetary Union (EMU), the creation of a Single Currency, the Common Foreign and Security Policy (including defence), Environmental Policy and Development Cooperation Policy. In many of these areas the EU shares policy competence with the member states. The member states have also retained exclusive competence in areas such as taxation matters, health and education, which have been areas of great sensitivity. Indeed, even in areas where the EU has developed a shared policy competence, such as common foreign and security policy, the member states remain firmly in control of most of the policy instruments and other resources. Nevertheless, Britain is part of multi-level EU decision making system in which it must work collaboratively with its fellow member states in some areas of policy. The following section explores what this means for Britain and how Britain seeks to shape events in Europe.

■ The EU's impact on Britain

British attitudes to Europe

In Britain, for many among the general public, the EU remains an unwelcome fact of life, reflecting a long standing antipathy to 'things European'. This is reflected in popular sentiment about the EU, which is largely negative, and often stoked by the more popular media, with sensationalist accounts by journalists from the *Sun* and *Daily Mail* (all part of the News International Group) of the European gravy train, concerns over Britain's budgetary contribution to Europe, and scare stories about EU directives challenging core elements of British life (aka the Euro-sausage). On the other hand, papers such as the *Daily Telegraph*, a staunch supporter of the Conservative Party have also pursued a predominantly Eurosceptic line, also reporting negative stories about the EU. There is little doubt that many among the public in Britain have a deep rooted opposition to the EU and harbour concerns that Europe is diminishing British sovereignty. It is noteworthy the European Commission Representation in London has on its website a section on Euromyths, reflecting its awareness of this antipathy.

At a practical level, however, Britain is clearly a part of the European Union and seeks to play a significant role in shaping the direction of EU policy. The dilemma for UK politicians is that there is little public support for Europe and, if anything, being too pro-European can be considered to be an electoral disadvantage. In many respects the substance of British policy towards Europe has been fairly consistent since membership in 1973 (Allen 2005: 120). Successive governments when faced with participating in EU treaty negotiations have continued to argue in favour of a more intergovernmental approach to cooperation, favouring the continuing role of the state, over a more federal-style European entity. Regardless of the party in government in the UK, no political leader has been willing to commit Britain to support the deepening of European integration. In practice, this has meant that Britain has continued to be seen by its European counterparts, especially France and Germany, as an awkward partner in Europe (George 1998). However, UK governments have favoured and supported further enlargement of the EU, reflecting a commitment to support other states engaged in consolidating democracy and economic development, as well as reflecting British interests in developing a more intergovernmental Europe.

Impact on British politics

The lack of a strong permissive consensus in favour of Europe places major constraints on what political leaders can say and do about Europe in Britain. In general, the major political parties have tended to be in favour of Europe, although even here there have been clear divisions within the parties between supporters and opponents of Europe. In the Conservative Party there have been deep divisions over Europe, with a significant minority of MPs opposed to Europe and deeply Eurosceptic. In the past, Margaret Thatcher's staunch defence of Britain's right to reclaim a portion of its budget contribution highlights the strength of this opposition. The most recent examples have included leading members of

the party such as William Hague, a former leader of the party, who has been doggedly anti-Europe. The Labour Party has also been divided on Europe, both in the past with party leaders such as Michael Foot, and the departure of key members to form the Social Democratic Party (SDP), and, more recently, under Tony Blair. In the latter case, his initial enthusiasm for Europe seemed to wane in the face of continuing public unease about all things European. It was noticeable that the commitment both in 1997 and 2001 in the party's manifesto to holding a

BOX 27.4   British Attitudes to Europe

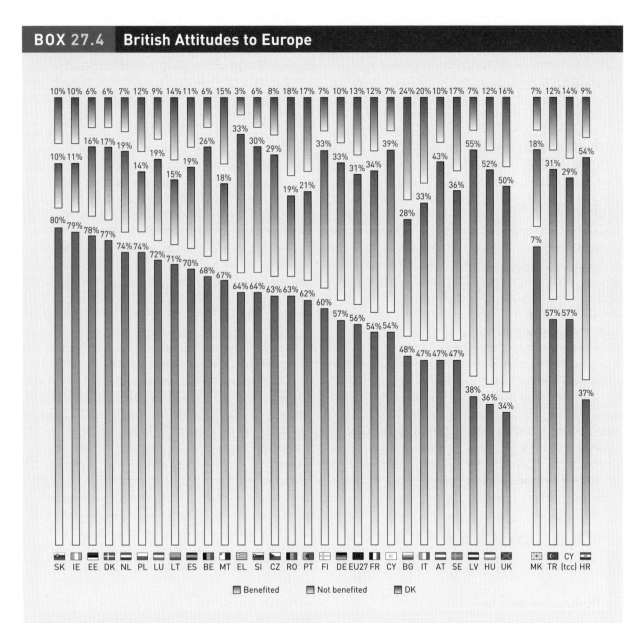

Figure 27.1 British attitudes toward the European Union
Source: Eurobarometer 71, Spring 2009: National Report UK

Key indicators and five-year trends in UK and EU sentiment (in %)

	EB61 Spring 2004	EB62 Autumn 2004	EB63 Spring 2005	EB64 Autumn 2005	EB65 Spring 2006	EB66 Autumn 2006	EB67 Spring 2007	EB68 Autumn 2007	EB69 Spring 2008	EB70 Autumn 2008	EB71 Summer 2009
Trust in the EU											
UK	19	35	27	25	31	26	36	25	29	25	22
EU	41	50	44	45	48	45	57	48	50	47	47
Trust in the European Commission											
UK	26	39	31	26	28	25	29	22	24	27	22
EU	47	52	46	46	47	48	52	50	47	47	44
Trust in the European Parliament											
UK	30	39	35	27	31	25	33	25	27	27	22
EU	54	57	52	51	52	52	56	55	52	51	48
Trust in national government											
UK	19	32	31	33	30	24	34	30	24	29	21
EU	30	34	34	31	35	30	41	34	32	34	32
Trust in national parliament											
UK	25	35	36	37	36	29	41	34	27	30	17
EU	35	38	35	35	38	33	43	35	34	34	32
Support for the euro											
UK	36	31	28	28	28	29	29	24	26	28	27
EU	60	63	59	60	59	60	63	61	60	61	61
Support for enlargement											
UK	31	50	48	43	44	36	41	36	36	40	32
EU	42	53	50	49	45	46	49	46	47	44	43
Number 1 concern of UK											
UK	41 IMM	29 IMM	31 IMM	41 CRIM	41 CRIM	40 IMM	41 CRIM	44 CRIM	38 CRIM	34 EC SIT	41 EMP
EU	16	13	14	24	24	21	24	24	20	37	49
Number 2 concern of the UK											
UK	37 CRIM	28 TERR	31 CRIM	34 TERR	32 IMM	35 TERR	32 IMM	39 IMM	35 IMM	34 CRIM	31 EC SIT
EU	26	16	23	14	14	15	15	15	11	17	42
Membership a good thing											
UK	29	38	36	34	42	34	39	34	30	32	28
EU	48	56	54	50	55	53	57	58	52	53	53
Membership has brought benefits											
UK	30	39	40	37	42	39	43	37	36	39	34
EU	47	53	55	52	54	54	59	58	54	56	56
Number of Member States											
	15	25	25	25	25	25	25	25	27	27	27

Key: IMM = immigration; TERR = terrorism; CRIM = crime; EC SIT= economic situation; EMP = unemployment.

referendum on the single currency did not materialise. In light of public attitudes to Europe, it is hardly surprising that Tony Blair and his government's early enthusiasm for Europe subsided.

In Britain EU issues have never dominated an election, which have usually been fought on national economic considerations and other policy considerations. Indeed, the issue of Europe has tended to be more divisive within the parties than between them reflecting the points discussed above. The only time that the electorate have been asked to vote on Europe has been in relation to EP elections, and these events have tended to arouse limited public interest and have been marked by low turnout. In most past cases these elections have tended to be fought on national issues reflecting either public support for or against the government of the day. In 2009, the rise of the UK Independence Party, which won 13 seats, as well as the British National Party, which won 2 seats, both of which are strongly nationalist parties opposed to Europe, highlights the continuing public disenchantment with Europe. The long-term future of these parties is less than certain, but their members have found bedfellows among the radical right and Eurosceptic parties who are part of the EP party group, Europe of Freedom and Democracy.

Impact on institutions

EU membership has impacted on UK institutions in a variety of ways, reflecting the need to coordinate and manage EU business on a daily basis in Whitehall, Westminster and Brussels. In particular, EU business places considerable burdens on the Prime Minister, Foreign Secretary and Chancellor of the Exchequer and their respective departments. The PM and Cabinet Office are at the heart of EU coordination, with the European Secretariat in the Cabinet Office responsible for policy coordination. In recent years EU business has come to occupy an increasing amount of the PM's time reflecting the growth in the number of formal and informal European Council meetings, as well as the need to attend an array of other high powered summits of European and global leaders. In practice, the Cabinet has tended not to discuss EU matters, leaving these in the hands of a sub-committee chaired by the Foreign Secretary. In practice, it is the Foreign and Commonwealth Office (FCO) that is responsible for coordinating EU policy and maintaining contact with the UK's partners in Europe. Aside from the FCO, the Treasury has maintained control over economic and financial matters, ensuring that it has the final say over matters such as UK membership of the single currency. Other departments, such as the Department of Trade and Industry and the Department of the Environment, Food and Rural Affairs, retain their own independence in respect to their policy areas, and are able define British interests in Europe and negotiate on behalf of the state.

The key actor that links the British government with Brussels is the UK Permanent Representation in Brussels. This is effectively a permanent team of UK civil servants based in Brussels who are charged with representing British interests, negotiating on behalf of the country, and ensuring that the government is kept informed of developments in Europe. The UK Permanent Representative (the equivalent of an Ambassador) plays a key role in this process, including attending on a weekly basis an interdepartmental committee on Europe in the Cabinet Office. In Brussels, the UK Permanent Representative and the Deputy Permanent Representative work closely with their equivalents from the other EU member states in the Committee of Permanent Representatives (COREPER I and II). In essence, this mechanism provides the main means for engaging with the EU Presidency, Council Secretariat and Commission, usually through working groups.

Outside of the executive branch of government, the Parliament is charged with scrutinising EU legislation. In theory, this aims to ensure that nothing detrimental to Britain's interest is passed without the Parliament commenting on it. In order to fulfil this role all EU legislation (including explanatory memorandums) is sent to the House of Commons European Scrutiny Committee for consideration. The Scrutiny Committee has the power to decide which proposals should be debated in the House, as well as being kept informed of ministerial activities. However, in practice, the committee has to deal with a considerable workload and there is limited interest in some of its activities, which do not attract significant attention. In the House of Lords the EU Select Committee has also been very active in undertaking inquiries, receives regular briefings on the outcomes of EU Council Meetings and each EU Presidency. It is regarded by many as a highly authoritative source of high-quality information on European affairs, although it is a specialised arena which receives limited public attention (Allen 2005: 134).

Impact on policy

Today the EU impacts on almost all aspects of policy in its member states. In some areas the EU enjoys the lead role in developing policy, such as in agriculture, whereas in other areas policy competence is shared between the EU and member states, such as in regional and social policy. In other areas, such as education, health and fiscal policy the member states remain the predominant policy actors. As a consequence the EU has a differentiated impact on the policy process in states such as Britain. It is, then, possible to argue that Britain has become increasingly **Europeanised**, with many areas of policy subject to EU-level policy developments. This has raised significant public concerns in Britain where popular sentiment is sceptical of European intentions. There have also been underlying concerns from the early days of membership that Britain did not benefit from policies such as the CAP, given that in the UK farmers already received direct payments which lowered food prices.

The dilemma for the UK is that late EU membership proved to be a costly affair for Britain, with the state having to make large financial contributions to the EU budget of between £2 billion and £4 billion (Allen 2005: 136). This made Britain the second-largest financial contributor after Germany and has proved to be a source of continuing political controversy in the EU. In 2006, the UK paid over £3.9 billion into the EU budget. As a result the UK very early on sought a budgetary rebate from the EU, which was first agreed prior to the 1975 referendum, and then renegotiated by Margaret Thatcher in 1984 at the Fontainebleau Summit. The budgetary issue, however, is as much a political as financial issue, given that the total EU budget is approximately 1 per cent of EU GDP – a relatively small amount.

In many other ways the UK has benefitted from EU membership. Successive British governments have been strong supporters of the common market and then the single European market (or internal market), which has been seen as providing opportunities for exports and investments. The UK exported 62 per cent of its goods in 2006 to other EU states and enjoys significant benefits from being a member of this enlarged market. The Foreign and Commonwealth Office website claim that over 3.5 million jobs in the UK are directly or indirectly linked to the export of goods and services. Furthermore, the abolition of customs duties saves the UK about £135 million a year, with further benefits to

consumers and businesses likely to accrue as a result of the Payments Service Directive. The UK has also directly benefitted from direct EU financial transfers such as through regional, social and cohesion policy instruments (structural funds). In particular, at the time of membership the UK lobbied for the establishment of a European Regional Development Fund, anticipating that regional payments would be beneficial to Britain.

Aside from direct financial benefits EU policy developments have shaped the development of policy in areas as diverse as the environment, consumer affairs, and women's rights and equality. At the same time, UK authorities have taken the lead in some policy areas, such as environmental policy, where they have clearly influenced developments at European level. In contrast, successive UK governments have been reluctant to support Economic and Monetary Union, and have been especially unwilling to commit to joining the single European currency until the time is considered right for the UK economy. Similarly, the UK was initially reluctant to support EU initiatives around the area of justice and home affairs. In recent years, especially since 9/11, there has been an increasing acknowledgement in Britain that intergovernmental cooperation can provide an effective means of addressing transnational security threats posed by terrorism, organised crime and human trafficking.

The UK has also been supportive of attempts by the EU to develop new policy initiatives around the common foreign and security policy and development cooperation with developing states. In the first instance, the UK has been supportive of intergovernmental cooperation in the foreign policy arena, although it continues to exercise considerable independence of action through its own foreign policy initiatives and diplomatic network. It also remains committed to supporting NATO and continues to enjoy strong ties with the United States. At times this leads it to break with other EU member states, as most recently exhibited in Iraq, where it supported the US-led military coalition. It has, however, also been willing to lead and support EU initiatives, including the development of EU Battlegroups and the European Defence Agency, who's first chief executive was Nick Witney (2004–07). The UK government has also supported the Commission's role in development cooperation, coordinating the work of its own Department for International Development with the EU. In 2005 the UK also used its chairing of the EU Presidency to place Africa centrally on the EU agenda, highlighting how the UK has been able to use its position in Europe to achieve its policy objectives.

■ Future issues for Britain in the EU

In looking to the future, the UK faces a number of challenges on the European front which it will have to address if it wishes to play a more prominent role in Europe. On the home front, all governments regardless of their political make-up face the challenge of communicating Europe to the British public. There remains considerable public opposition and/or disinterest to many EU-level developments and this limits what any government can do at a European level. The rise of the UK Independence Party and its success at the last EP elections in 2009 highlights these concerns. This has to be a matter of serious concern for any Prime Minister and the government of the day, as it places limits on what they are

---

BOX 27.5 EU Treaty of Lisbon (2007)

On 13 December 2007, EU leaders signed the Treaty of Lisbon, thus bringing to an end several years of negotiation about institutional issues.

The Treaty of Lisbon amends the current EU and EC treaties, without replacing them. It will provide the Union with the legal framework and tools necessary to meet future challenges and to respond to citizens' demands.

1 **A more democratic and transparent Europe**, with a strengthened role for the European Parliament and national parliaments, more opportunities for citizens to have their voices heard and a clearer sense of who does what at European and national level.

 ■ A strengthened role for the European Parliament: the European Parliament, directly elected by EU citizens, will see important new powers emerge over EU legislation, the EU budget and international agreements. In particular, the increase of co-decision procedure in policy making will ensure the European Parliament is placed on an equal footing with the Council, representing member states, for the vast bulk of EU legislation.

 ■ A greater involvement of national parliaments: national parliaments will have greater opportunities to be involved in the work of the EU, in particular thanks to a new mechanism to monitor that the Union only acts where results can be better attained at EU level (subsidiarity). Together with the strengthened role for the European Parliament, it will enhance democracy and

increase legitimacy in the functioning of the Union.

 ■ A stronger voice for citizens: thanks to the Citizens' Initiative, one million citizens from a number of member states will have the possibility to call on the Commission to bring forward new policy proposals.

 ■ Who does what: the relationship between the member states and the European Union will become clearer with the categorisation of competences.

 ■ Withdrawal from the Union: the Treaty of Lisbon explicitly recognises for the first time the possibility for a member state to withdraw from the Union.

2 **A more efficient Europe**, with simplified working methods and voting rules, streamlined and modern institutions for an EU of 27 members and an improved ability to act in areas of major priority for today's Union.

 ■ Effective and efficient decision making: qualified majority voting in the Council will be extended to new policy areas to make decision making faster and more efficient. From 2014 on, the calculation of qualified majority will be based on the double majority of member states and people, thus representing the dual legitimacy of the Union. A double majority will be achieved when a decision is taken by 55 per cent of the member states representing at least 65 per cent of the Union's population.

 ■ A more stable and streamlined institutional framework: the Treaty of Lisbon creates the function of President of the European Council elected for two-and-a-half years, introduces a direct link between the election of the Commission President and the results of the European elections, provides for new arrangements for the future composition of the European Parliament and for a smaller Commission, and includes clearer rules on enhanced cooperation and financial provisions.

■ Improving the life of Europeans: the Treaty of Lisbon improves the EU's ability to act in several policy areas of major priority for today's Union and its citizens. This is the case in particular for the policy areas of freedom, security and justice, such as combating terrorism or tackling crime. It also concerns to some extent other areas including energy policy, public health, civil protection, climate change, services of general interest, research, space, territorial cohesion, commercial policy, humanitarian aid, sport, tourism and administrative cooperation.

3 **A Europe of rights and values, freedom, solidarity and security**, promoting the Union's values, introducing the Charter of Fundamental Rights into European primary law, providing for new solidarity mechanisms and ensuring better protection of European citizens.

■ Democratic values: the Treaty of Lisbon details and reinforces the values and objectives on which the Union is built. These values aim to serve as a reference point for European citizens and to demonstrate what Europe has to offer its partners worldwide.

■ Citizens' rights and Charter of Fundamental Rights: the Treaty of Lisbon preserves existing rights while introducing new ones. In particular, it guarantees the freedoms and principles set out in the Charter of Fundamental Rights and gives its provisions a binding legal force. It concerns civil, political, economic and social rights.

■ Freedom of European citizens: the Treaty of Lisbon preserves and reinforces the 'four freedoms' and the political, economic and social freedom of European citizens.

■ Solidarity between member states: the Treaty of Lisbon provides that the Union and its member states act jointly in a spirit of solidarity if a member state is the subject of a terrorist attack or the victim of a natural or man-made disaster. Solidarity in the area of energy is also emphasised.

■ Increased security for all: the Union will get an extended capacity to act on freedom, security and justice, which will bring direct benefits in terms of the Union's ability to fight crime and terrorism. New provisions on civil protection, humanitarian aid and public health also aim at boosting the Union's ability to respond to threats to the security of European citizens.

4 **Europe as an actor on the global stage** will be achieved by bringing together Europe's external policy tools, both when developing and deciding new policies. The Treaty of Lisbon will give Europe a clear voice in relations with its partners worldwide. It will harness Europe's economic, humanitarian, political and diplomatic strengths to promote European interests and values worldwide, while respecting the particular interests of the member states in foreign affairs.

■ A new High Representative for the Union in Foreign Affairs and Security Policy, also Vice-President of the Commission, will increase the impact, the coherence and the visibility of the EU's external action.

■ A new European External Action Service will provide back-up and support to the High Representative.

■ A single legal personality for the Union will strengthen the Union's negotiating power, making it more effective on the world stage and a more visible partner for third countries and international organisations.

■ Progress in European Security and Defence Policy will preserve special decision making arrangements but also pave the way towards reinforced cooperation among a smaller group of member states.

Source: http://europa.eu/lisbon_treaty/glance/index_en.htm

willing to do and say in public about the European Union. There is also a risk that Britain's policy in Europe will be used as a domestic soccer ball, kicked around by the political parties to satisfy domestic constituencies while frustrating other European leaders and publics.

In Europe, the UK government is likely to face a number of challenges, including the overall shape of the European Union in the future. The UK remains committed to supporting the EU, although it prefers to see cooperation developing along intergovernmental rather than supranational lines. This is reflected in the UK's support for the open method of coordination in regard to economic matters, whereby there is no one size fits all approach to policy making. The UK will also face the challenge of implementing the new Lisbon Treaty (or Reform Treaty), which as of late 2009 had been ratified by all of the EU member states except for the Czech Republic. This may prove particularly challenging in the UK, where there has been much scepticism about the need for a further treaty, with the Conservative Party even having threatened that they would hold a referendum on the treaty if an opportunity arose. A further challenge lies in managing Britain's financial contribution to the EU, which, while changed as a result of recent enlargements, remains an issue of concern to the public and political leaders.

Conservatives and the Lisbon Treaty

The Conservative Party swung in a radical Eurosceptic direction during the 1980s and 1990s, for a while making it virtually ungovernable and blighting the administration led by John Major. At the leadership contest in 2005 David Cameron wooed this wing of the party by promising to withdraw the party from the mainstream federalist centre-right grouping the European Peoples' Party (EPP). As Cameron's victory in the leadership contest over David Davis owed something to this promise he was obliged to follow it through, via his Eurosceptic foreign affairs spokesman, William Hague. He also promised, via an article in the *Sun* in 2007, a 'cast iron guarantee' he would hold a referendum on the Lisbon Treaty when he came into power. But the treaty was ratified in early November 2009 and Cameron was forced to break his promise; it followed that once the treaty was ratified, it would not make political sense to hold any referendum. Instead he blamed Labour for reneging on its 2005 manifesto promise to hold a referendum and specified the aspects he would wish to renegotiate should he become Prime Minister in 2010. For his pains he faced cries of betrayal from his Eurosceptic wing and his stance was condemned as 'pathetic' 'autistic' and marginalising by the French Foreign Minister, Pierre Lellouche.

The 2008–09 financial and economic crisis also left its mark on British politics with, at the time of writing, the current Labour government under Gordon Brown committed to supporting EU and international efforts to address the underlying causes of the crisis. In effect, Britain enjoyed economic benefits from being a part of the EU during a time of considerable economic uncertainty. Prime Minster Brown was also able to exert pressure on other European leaders and provide considerable leadership at an international level. All of this served to bolster flagging support at home thereby allowing him to address his critics and survive in government. In the future, the UK will almost certainly be willing to agree with its European counterparts new regulations and practices with regard to the banking sector. The challenge will be to ensure that these are effectively implemented in the member states and that there are similar arrangements in place at an international level in other non-EU states. There also remains the unresolved issue of the UK's membership of the euro, which while off the immediate agenda, has to be a long-term consideration. Any future UK government must surely want to be at the heart of EU financial decision making and being excluded from the euro club has to be highly problematic for any such government.

On a pragmatic level the EU27 of today is far closer to what the UK has always wanted Europe to look like than the federal or constitutional arrangements that early European political leaders contemplated in the 1950s. The EU's 'eastern enlargement' has also brought into the EU a number of states that are both more inclined to Britain's view of Europe, as well as being more focused on transatlantic ties. This places Britain in a stronger position to demonstrate European leadership and to play a role in shaping European developments in line with its own interests. In order to accomplish this there will need to be a much stronger emphasis placed on explaining Britain's role in Europe to the public.

Chapter summary

This chapter highlights the ambiguity of Britain's relationship with Europe demonstrating public anti-pathy to the EU while reflecting on Britain's role in Europe. It highlights how Britain chose during the 1950s not to participate in European-level supranational arrangements, and how this policy was reversed during the 1960s, leading after many delays to British EEC membership in 1973. The chapter then examines the key institutions and policies of the European Union, including EU policy making. It considered the impact of Europe on UK politics, highlighting key elements of institutional and policy adaption in the UK system of government and administration. It concludes with a discussion of the key challenges facing Britain in the EU today, focusing especially on the dilemma of public antipathy to Europe in the face of the UK's growing involvement in all things European. This poses a particular problem for UK politicians, who must satisfy a domestic audience while participating at a European level in discussions about the future direction of the EU.

Discussion points

- Why has the UK been so reluctant to participate in European integration?

- Why has the UK been such a reluctant European?

- How and in what ways are UK politicians able to influence EU policy making?

- What type of impact has EU membership had on UK politics?

- What future challenges does the UK face in EU politics?

Further reading

There are a number of key textbooks on the European Union that provide good overviews of the origins and development of the EU, its institutions and policies. Among the many textbooks on this subject the most often consulted are Warleigh (2004), Dinan (2004), Nugent (2006), McCormick (2008) and Cini (2007). For a more detailed discussion of EU policy making consult Wallace and Wallace (2005) and on the EU and the member states see Bulmer and Lequesne (2005). On the origins and development of the European Union Dedman (2009) provides comprehensive coverage and, specifically on history of Britain and Europe, see Foster and Blair

(2002) and Gowland, Turner and Wright (2009). George (1998) and Young (2000) also provide useful accounts of Britain's policy on Europe, while Young (1998) considers the role of key political leaders from Churchill to Blair. In addition to secondary sources, the EU institutions themselves have highly comprehensive entries on the EU website: www.europa.eu. The European Navigator also has much useful historical material on Britain and Europe, including primary source materials: http://www.ena.lu/. Other useful sources on Britain include the UK Office of the European Parliament in London and the European Commission's Representation in the UK. Also, most of the UK institutions, such as the Cabinet Office and the Houses of Parliament, have much information on Britain and the EU.

Bibliography

Allen, D. (2005) 'The United Kingdom: a Europeanised government in a non-Europeanised polity', in *The Member States of the European Union*, pp. 119–41 (Oxford University Press).

Bache, I. and A. Jordan (eds) (2008) *The Europeanisation of British Politics* (Palgrave).

Baker, D. and D. Seawright (eds) (1998) *Britain For and Against Europe: British Politics and the Question of European Integration* (Clarendon Press).

Bulmer, S. and M. Burch (1998) 'Organising for Europe: The British State and the European Union' *Public Administration* 76 (4).

Bulmer, S. and C. Lequesne (2005) *The Member States of the European Union* (Oxford University Press).

Bulmer, S. and M. Burch (2005) 'The Europeanisation of UK Government: From Quiet Revolution to Step-change' *Public Administration* 83 (4).

Cini, M. (ed.) (2007) *European Union Politics* (Oxford University Press).

Dedman, M. (2009) *The Origins and Development of the European Union, 1945–2008*, 2nd edn (Routledge).

Denman, R. (1997) *Missed Chances: Britain and Europe in the Twentieth Century* (Indigo).

Dinan, D. (2004) *An Ever Closer Union*, 3rd edn (Palgrave).

Foster, A. and A. Blair (2002) *The Making of Britain's European Policy* (Longman).

Fletcher, I. (1980) 'The Council of Europe and Human Rights' in K.T. Twitchett (ed.) *European Cooperation Today* (Europa Publications).

Geddes, A. (2004) *The European Union and British Politics* (Palgrave Macmillan).

George, S. (1991) *Britain and European Integration since 1945* (Blackwell).

George, S. (1992) *Britain and the European Community* (Clarendon Press).

George, S. (1998) *An Awkward Partner: Britain and the European Community*, 3rd edn (Oxford University Press).

Gowland, D., A. Turner and A. Wright (2009) *Britain and European Integration since 1945* (Routledge).

Mayne, R. (1983) *Postwar: The Dawn of Today's Europe* (Thames and Hutton).

McCormick, J. (2008) *Understanding the European Union* (Palgrave).

Nugent, N. (1999) *The Government and Politics of the European Union*, 4th edn (Palgrave).

Nugent, N. (2006) *The Government and Politics of the European Union*, 6th edn (Palgrave).

Palmer, M. and J. Lambert (1968) *European Unity: A survey of European Organisations* (Allen and Unwin).

Pinder, J. (2001) *The European Union: A Very Short Introduction* (Oxford University Press).

Pine, M. (2008) *Harold Wilson and Europe: Pursuing Britain's Membership of the European Community* (Palgrave).

Wallace, H. and W. Wallace (2005) *Policy-making in the European Union* (Oxford University Press).

Warleigh, A. (2004) *European Union: The Basics* (Routledge).

Young, H. (1998) *This Blessed Plot, Britain and Europe from Churchill to Blair* (Papermac).

Young, J. (2000) *Britain and European Unity, 1945–1999* (Macmillan).

Useful websites

The EU website: http://www.europa.eu
European Commission Representation in the UK: http://ec.europa.eu/unitedkingdom/index_en.htm
Europe in the UK: http://www.europe.org.uk/info/
UK Office of the European Parliament (London): http://www.europarl.org.uk
Cabinet Office: http://www.cabinet-office.gov.uk/
Prime Ministerial Speeches on Europe: http://www.number10.gov.uk/
The Foreign and Commonwealth Office: http://www.fco.gov.uk
The UK Federal Trust: http://fedtrust.co.uk
Guardian Newspaper: http://politics.guardian.co.uk
Financial Times: http://www.ft.com
University Association for Contemporary European Studies: http://uaces.org
The Archive of European Integration: http://aei.pitt.edu
European Navigator: http://www.ena.lu/
EU Observer daily press service: http://www.EUobserver.com

And another thing . . .

Britain and the World

Jonathan Freedland

Godwin's Law states that the longer an online discussion goes on, the likelier a comparison to Hitler or the Nazis becomes. We could devise a similar, if less eye-catching rule for debates on Britain's place in the world: sooner or later someone will quote either Dean Acheson or Douglas Hurd.

It was the epigrammatic wisdom offered by those two men – one US Secretary of State under Harry Truman, the other British Foreign Secretary under John Major – that has come to represent the two contrasting views of the UK's standing in international affairs (though they are not, in fact, mutually exclusive).

In one corner stands Acheson's 1962 declaration that 'Great Britain has lost an empire and has not yet found a role.' Those terse few words contain the enduring view of Britain as a nation in decline, once proud and muscled, now faded, stumbling and confused: an international has-been.

In the other looms Hurd's 1990s insistence that Britain 'punches above its weight' in world affairs. This conception accepts Acheson's assessment that Britain is not the imperial power it once was, but argues that we matter all the same – indeed that we matter more than other comparable countries (with a tacit nod in the direction of continental Europe).

Which of these is right? The case for Hurd is strong. Britain may no longer be a superpower but, in recent years, it has certainly been a player. For one thing, it still carries serious military heft – spending an annual £35 bn on defence, far more than its European counterparts – and, no less important, it's prepared to use it. In Iraq and Afghanistan, it was Britain that sent the greatest number of troops after the United States. In the first Gulf War in 1991, no fewer than 45,000 British personnel joined the US-led effort. Following the Kosovo war of 1999, the largest national element in the UN peacekeeping force came from Britain.

That conventional muscle is reinforced, if only symbolically, by a nuclear capability that ensured Britain's place at the top table – reserved for atomic powers – in the immediate aftermath of the Second World War. It also helps that Britain has maintained, again at considerable expense, a substantial intelligence apparatus, one that works intimately with its American counterpart.

Which brings us to a crucial element in Hurd's thesis. If Britain punches above its weight, that's in no small part because it's chums with the biggest bruiser in the ring. For Hurd, and most of his predecessors and successors at the Foreign and Commonwealth Office since 1945, it has been the 'special relationship' with the US that has given the British fist more force. In this view, we are heard in the councils of Europe and around the world with extra respect because it is assumed we have the ear of the planet's sole hyperpower. This was the premise on which Tony Blair's entire foreign policy was built: that even to be seen as a glorified ambassador for the US administration – and let's not forget the then Prime Minister's tireless globetrotting in the lead-up to the invasion of Iraq, acting as salesman for George W. Bush's war – is more influential and prestigious than being the mere leader of just another middling European power.

Add to that familiar mix the less obvious sources of influence – a City of London that, until the crash of 2008 at least, seemed to be overtaking Wall Street as the centre of the financial world and a range of cultural exports, ranging from the BBC to British popular music, and a picture emerges of a nation that may no longer rule the waves but which is not reduced to paddling in a backwater either. When a strong individual is at the helm, Britain can still make a serious splash in the world: note the many millions of post-Soviet Eastern Europeans who still revere Margaret Thatcher as a Cold War liberator, regarding her alongside, if not even ahead of, Ronald Reagan.

And yet Acheson's words still sting, nearly 50 years after he uttered them. British politicians know, even if they will seldom say so, that their own decisions rarely matter internationally. Talk even to those at the top of British foreign policy and they concede that their power exists only inasmuch as it is accompanied by an ability to persuade – either their fellow Europeans or, more directly, the Americans. A British decision taken on its own might barely make a ripple.

To take one example, British politicians grumbled throughout the Bush era about the state of the Israeli–Palestinian peace process. They had multiple criticisms of how things were being done and even more numerous suggestions for how things should change. Yet they believed they could do nothing. Only the Americans had the power. The FCO behaved as if its only option was to wait for Bush to be gone and to cross its fingers that something, and someone, better would come along.

If that is true now, the balance seems likely to shift even further in Acheson's direction – and away from Hurd – in the coming years. Pressure to reform the United Nations to reflect the world as it is, rather than as it was in 1945, will surely force the surrender of Britain's permanent place on the security council – the clearest trophy of its above-its-weight influence. No one can justify a Permanent Five that excludes India, Brazil and all of Africa, yet still includes Britain and France.

No less troubling for London, the special relationship which has underpinned Britain's international standing seems less than a fixed point for the ages. Surely Washington will soon regard Delhi and Beijing as more important partners for the twenty-first century than the old pal across the pond. Witness the G20 meeting in April 2009. Yes, it was in London with Gordon Brown in the chair. But, by common consent, the real action was between Barack Obama of the US and Hu Jintao of China, to the point where observers suggested future gatherings should consist solely of the 'G2'. No wonder, then, that British diplomats were so rattled in early 2009 when Obama's press secretary spoke of Britain and the US sharing a 'special partnership', rather than a 'special relationship'. The White House insisted it meant nothing by it. But London heard in

that new formulation a downgrading, which it fears above all else.

Some believe this change in the dynamic between Britain and the US may not be a solely one-way business. They suspect a Conservative administration under David Cameron could do what Labour did not, and strike a new posture, more independent of the United States. As evidence, they cite the speech Cameron gave in his first year as Tory leader, when he marked the fifth anniversary of 9/11 by calling for Britain to be a 'solid but not slavish' ally of the US. They also note the Nixon-to-China possibilities open to a leader of Thatcher's party to make a break from the US, possibilities less available to a Labour party that a generation ago flirted with anti-Americanism and once voted to withdraw from Nato.

One should not hold one's breath. It made sense for Cameron, as part of his rebranding effort, to distance himself from the widely-reviled Bush in 2006. As Prime Minister, he will face plenty of pressures in the opposite direction. First, if Obama remains popular, crude PR dictates that Cameron would want to be at his side. Second, for a British government the only viable alternative to proximity to the US is closer cooperation with the European Union: that is surely the only other foreign policy pole of attraction. But Cameron keeps the right of his party on side by being sceptical, not cosy, towards Europe. And, third, even if he were keen to shift away from Washington, he will be confronted by a noisy right-wing press (especially the Telegraph and Murdoch groups) that believes Britain's place is in lockstep with the US.

That points to a continuation of the status quo and that is probably what Cameron would prefer anyway. But that will be hard to maintain. Punching above its weight has cost Britain money: defence budgets and power projection does not come cheap. Yet Britain is moving into a period of relative austerity, with debts rising and national income falling. If Cameron does not want to raise taxes, and he does not, he will have to cut back in every possible area. He won't want to do that if it means penny-pinching on soldiers and their equipment or medical care, but he may look for big, structural savings that will have a serious effect on Britain's global reach. It is notable that, partly for reasons of fiscal prudence, senior figures on both the Labour and Tory benches are discussing non-renewal of Trident.

In this changed landscape, perhaps Britain could forge a modified role for itself. Still an ally of the US, but one whose help sometimes takes less tangible form than boots on the ground. What if Britain were to exploit the fact that it is not just another arm of the US administration and do what Washington itself might like to do but, thanks to political reality, cannot?

Take the Middle East again. Most involved believe that, eventually, Hamas will have to be brought into the political process but that it is premature for the US to start talks with that group while it has not renounced violence. But Britain – safely at arm's length – could. The same is true when it comes to reaching out to those elements within the Taliban deemed 'reconciliables'. Obama can't be seen speaking to such people, but the same constraints do not apply to a British government.

In other words, Britain could make a virtue of the fact that it wields the second fiddle to the emperor: its own actions simply do not matter as much and, with that, comes a kind of freedom. So let Britain be not just the loyal lieutenant, trudging to war when America calls, but the diplomatic outrider, using what remains of its worldwide reach to avoid conflict. It may not be an empire – but it would certainly be a role.

Glossary

Active minority: that minority of the population which participates to a high degree in political life.

Adversarial politics: a theory popularised by (among others) Professor S.E. Finer in the 1970s which portrayed politics at Westminster as a gladiatorial combat between Labour and the Conservatives with disastrous consequences for the national interest.

Affiliated: the way in which an organisation associates itself with a political party by paying a fee and gaining influence in the party's affairs. In Britain, a number of trade unions are affiliated to the Labour party; members pay the 'political levy' which makes them affiliated members of the party.

Alignment: a situation when the electorate is divided into reliable and stable support for the various parties. The British electorate was said to be aligned in both class and partisan terms from 1945 to 1970.

Anglo-Saxon model: a form of economic organisation dominant especially in the United States and the United Kingdom which stresses the importance of free markets over state controls.

Authority: the acceptance of someone's right to be obeyed.

Backbencher: the name given to all MPs who are not members of the government or the Opposition Front Bench.

Bank of England: the institution concerned with the government's management of all financial markets, and after the Treasury the most important institution in economic policy.

Better Quality Services: the Blair government's rebranding of market testing. Designed to identify the 'best supplier' of a service, BQS obliges departments and agencies to review their systems and consider the possibility of competitive tendering. However, provided real quality improvements can be achieved through internal reviews, there is no compulsion to put services out to tender.

Bicameral legislature: a legislature that consists of two houses. Most Western industrialised countries have a bicameral legislature, with the second or Upper House having a more limited role than the Lower, perhaps being composed of appointed rather than elected members, although in a few countries, most notably the United States, both are of more or less equal significance.

Bipolarity: often used to describe the division of the world between the communist east and the capitalist west after the Second World War, but applicable to any international system in which there are two dominant centres of power.

Block vote: the system under which affiliated trade unions cast votes at Labour Party conferences and in party elections. Unions cast votes on the basis of the numbers of members paying the political levy. These votes may or may not reflect the views of union members.

Bottom-up: the idea that power in the Labour party is dispersed throughout the party, with the final say in the choices of policy and party organisation being vested in the annual conference.

Broadsheets: large-format newspapers, which aim at the better-educated and more affluent readers, with a particular interest in influencing the opinion-formers.

Budgetary instruments of control: those measures that can have an impact on the way in which the economy works, like increasing tax or benefits.

Butskellism: a 'consensus' Keynesian approach to economic policy adopted by postwar Labour and Conservative governments, including full employment, the welfare state and the mixed economy. The term was coined by *The Economist* from the names of R.A. Butler, Conservative Chancellor 1951–5, and Hugh Gaitskell, his Labour predecessor.

Cabinet: the Cabinet consists of the leading members of the government, chosen by the Prime Minister. It is the place where major decisions are taken or ratified and where disagreements within government are resolved.

Cabinet committees: Cabinet committees are appointed by the Prime Minister and are composed of cabinet ministers (sometimes with junior ministers) to consider items of government business. Some are standing committees, some are ad hoc, to deal with specific problems or issues.

Cabinet government: the view that collective government survives and that the Prime Minister is not the dominant force within government. Decisions are taken by a group of colleagues after discussions in Cabinet according to this view.

Capital expenditure: expenditure on long-term projects such as buildings, large items of equipment, etc.

Capitalism: an economic and political system in which property and the means of production and distribution are in private ownership (rather than in the hands of the state) and goods are produced for private profit.

Cause or promotion groups: these groups promote some particular cause or objective, perhaps the protection of some vulnerable section of society, or seek to express the attitudes and beliefs of members. They tend to concentrate on a single issue.

Chancellor of the Exchequer: the political head of the Treasury, and with the Prime Minister the most important elected politician concerned with economic policy.

Charisma: a natural attraction as a quality of leadership.

Charterism: rebranded *Service First* by the Blair government, the Citizen's Charter and its offshoots have the objective of enhancing the quality of public service delivery while emphasising the rights of service users, as 'clients', 'customers' and 'consumers'.

Civil law: the law governing the rights of individuals and their relationships with each other rather than the state.

Civil servants: servants of the Crown, other than holders of political or judicial offices, who are employed in a civil capacity and whose remuneration is paid wholly and directly out of moneys voted by Parliament.

Civility: respect for authority and tolerance of opposing/different points of view.

Class: distinctions made between people on the basis of their social origins, education and occupation.

Cold War: the state of hostility between nations or alliances without actual fighting. Usually applied to USA–USSR relationships after 1945.

Collective responsibility: all members of the government are collectively responsible for its decisions. Members, whatever their private reservations, must be prepared to defend government policy. If unable to do so, they must resign or be dismissed.

Colonialism: the extension or retention of power by one nation over another.

Committee of the Whole House: a sitting of the House of Commons presided over by the Chairman of Ways and Means (Deputy Speaker) which hears the Budget speech and debates the committee stage of important bills, especially those affecting the constitution. It deals with matters where, in principle, any member should be allowed to participate.

Common law: the body of law, distinct from statute law, based on custom, usage and the decisions of the law courts in specific cases brought over time.

Communism: an economic and political system which aimed at the abolition of capitalism, the establishment of the dictatorship of the proletariat and the eventual 'withering away' of the state.

Community charge (poll tax): a flat-rate local tax introduced to replace the rates by the Thatcher government. It was intensely unpopular because of its perceived unfairness, in that the amount paid was not related to income. It was a factor in Mrs Thatcher's downfall.

Competition state: refers to a state intervening to open up society and economy to international market norms.

Compulsory Competitive Tendering (CCT): an aspect of market testing applied to services such as hospital catering and refuse collection. The aims were to improve efficiency and customer responsiveness and to break the power of public sector unions.

Confederation: a loose binding of states.

Consensus: an agreement. In British politics it describes the general continuity and overlap between economic, social, defence and foreign policies of postwar Labour and Conservative governments.

Conservation: care and protection of natural resources.

Consociationalism: power-sharing among political élites, designed to stabilise society.

Constitution: the system of laws, customs and conventions which defines the composition and powers of organs of the state, and regulates their relations with each other and with the citizens. Constitutions may be written or unwritten, codified or uncodified.

Constitutional: doing things according to agreed written or legal authority within the state.

Constitutional monarchy: while the monarch is the titular head of state invested with considerable legal powers, these powers are exercised almost without exception on 'advice' (i.e. by ministers); and the monarch has a largely symbolic role.

Contract state: the system where the state, instead of delivering services by its own institutions, contracts with private institutions for their delivery.

Conventions: unwritten rules of constitutional behaviour; generally agreed practices relating to the working of the political system, which have evolved over time.

Core executive: the group of people and institutions in Whitehall around the Cabinet and Prime Minister who decide most key policies. They include No. 10 staff, the Cabinet Office and senior civil servants, particularly those in the Treasury.

Corporatism: the tendency of the state to work closely with relevant groups in the making of policy. It developed as the state became increasingly interventionist in economic and social affairs.

Cosmopolitan: here meaning a world free from national interests and prejudices.

Council tax: the local tax introduced by the Major government in 1993 to replace the poll tax. It is a property-based tax with reductions and exemptions for a number of categories of residents.

Criminal law: law determining the acts and circumstances amounting to a crime or wrong against society as defined by the terms of law.

Criminalisation: an attempt (in Northern Ireland) to portray and treat convicted members of paramilitary organisations as common criminals.

Cross-borderism: links, in the Irish context, between Northern Ireland and the Irish Republic, mainly in the economic sphere.

Dealignment: a situation when there is a weaker relationship between occupational class and party support and when a declining percentage of the electorate identify with a party.

Decommissioning: removal from use of paramilitary arms in Northern Ireland.

Deference: a propensity to believe that people who have good education or connections with well-established families have more right to be in positions of authority than those who lack these characteristics.

Deindustrialisation: the process by which manufacturing industries decline and close.

Democracy: a political system in which a government is removable by the people, and in which they should be the ultimate decider of who should govern, thus enabling all adults to play a decisive part in political life.

Democratic: a form of decision making in which the wishes of the adult population are claimed to be of decisive importance.

Democratic deficit: the argument that reforms to the management of public services have reduced the accountability of government and diminished the democratic rights available to the citizen.

Department (also known as ministry): the principal organisation of central government, responsible for providing a service or function, such as social security or defence, and headed (usually) by a secretary of state or minister.

Dependency culture: the growth in the sense of dependence by users on the welfare services.

Deviant voting: voting for a party other than the party normally supported by the class to which one belongs.

Devolution: creating government institutions that exercise power locally rather than centrally.

Direct rule: ruling an area directly from the capital of a country rather than through a local or regional government.

Disclaim: under the 1963 Peerage Act, a hereditary peer can give up his or her title (and thus, until 1999, the right to sit in the Lords) without affecting the claim of the next heir.

Divine right: the belief that monarchs derive their power and position from God and that Parliament is dependent on the will of the monarch.

Dominant values: those ideas about the way in which life should be led held by the group in society traditionally exercising most power.

Ecological modernisation: Maarten Hajer (a leading ecological theorist) sees ecological modernisation as pulling together several 'credible and attractive story-lines': a sustainable development in place of 'defining growth'; a preference for anticipation rather than cure; equating pollution with inefficiency; and treating environmental regulation and economic growth as mutually beneficial.

Ecology: an approach to politics centred around the importance of the environment.

Election pacts: an arrangement made at either national or local level between two parties for a mutual withdrawal of candidates in the hope of maximising their strength vis-à-vis a third party.

Electoral college: the body that, in the USA, is legally responsible for the election of the President. In Britain it is best known as the process by which the Labour party elects its leader, with the unions, the constituency parties and the parliamentary Labour Party having one-third of the vote each.

Electoral quota: the average number of electors per constituency. There are separate electoral quotas for England, Wales, Scotland and Northern Ireland. Parliament decides the number of constituencies in each part of the United Kingdom and the *Boundary Commission* is then responsible for drawing constituency boundaries as near the electoral quota as possible.

Electoral register: the list of those entitled to vote. It is compiled on a constituency basis by the Registrar of Electors, an official of the local authority, through forms distributed to homes and by door-to-door canvassing. Although it is supposed to be 100 per cent accurate, there are doubts about its comprehensiveness, an issue highlighted by the poll tax.

Electoral system: a set of rules enabling voters to determine the selection of the legislature and/or the executive. Electoral systems have several often incompatible aims: to produce a legislature that is proportional to the distribution of votes; to produce a government that represents the majority of voters; and to produce strong, stable and effective government.

Emerge: the process by which leaders of the Conservative Party were chosen prior to the adoption of a system of elections in 1965. The new leader would 'emerge' following secret discussions between leading members of the party, with the monarch's private secretary acting as a go-between.

Enabling authorities: the idea that local councils should cease to be solely concerned with the provision of services but should enable those services to be provided by a mixture of in-house and external organisations.

Entitlements: legal rights to welfare services and benefits.

Entrenchment: the idea that the constitution is protected in some way against amendment by a temporary majority in the legislature. There may be provision for judicial review, i.e. that courts can review the constitutionality of statutes.

Environmentalism: the belief that protection of the environment is a political issue of central importance.

Equality: the belief that people should all be treated in the same way and have the same rights.

Equality of opportunity: the idea that there should be no legal or formal barriers to advancement in the world between citizens.

Euro: the short name for the single European currency which since 2002 has been the only currency used in most member states of the European Union. Whether Britain abolishes sterling and joins the eurozone will be the most important issue in British politics in the near future.

European Council: the European Council is made up of all the heads of government of the member states of the European Union.

Europeanisation: a term with a number of meanings, including the impact of membership of the European Union on British society and politics; the European Union expanding its boundaries through enlargement; the development of institutions of governance at the European level; adapting national and subnational systems of governance to Europe-wide institutions and Europe-wide norms; a political project aiming at a unified and politically stronger Europe; and the development of a sense of identity with Europe, the EU, etc.

Eurosceptic: a person with the view that the process of European integration has been moving too fast.

Euroscepticism: a shorthand expression for a set of complex feelings that sees closer economic and political integration in Europe as damaging to national independence. Commonly associated with, but by no means confined to, sections of the Conservative party in the UK.

Executive: the body in a political system responsible for the day-to-day running of the state.

Executive agencies: an office performing a function of government, subordinate to but not wholly controlled by the parent department. They perform the *executive* as opposed to the *policy making* functions of government.

Fascism: the right-wing nationalist ideas espoused by Mussolini and adapted by Hitler as the basis of his own Nazi ideology.

Feminism: the advocacy of women's rights on the grounds of equality of the sexes.

Financial institutions: institutions such as pension funds and insurance companies, identified as the largest holders of shares in British companies.

Financial Management Initiative: a general initiative to enable managers in the Civil Service to identify their objectives and the resources available, to provide methods of measuring performance while clearly identifying responsibilities for performance.

First-past-the-post: the name given to the electoral system used in Britain and a few other Commonwealth countries such as Canada, in which the country is divided into single-member parliamentary constituencies and the winner is the candidate with the largest number of votes, irrespective of whether he or she gains an absolute majority. This can often produce highly disproportionate election results.

Fiscal: relating to public revenue, e.g., taxes.

Flexible constitution: a constitution with no formal method of amendment. The British constitution is amended either by an ordinary Act of Parliament or by a change in convention.

Free market: a doctrine that believes that the economy operates best when it is subject to the 'laws' of supply and demand and when government interferes and regulates as little as possible. The capitalist market system is the best supplier of goods and services and allocator of rewards; the role of government is minimal and is restricted to those things that only it can do, such as national defence and internal law and order.

Front bench: the leaders of the main parties in Parliament, derived from the fact that the leadership groups sit on the front benches of Parliamentary seats in the Chamber.

Frontbencher: the name given collectively to members of the government, who sit on the front bench on their side of the House, and to members of the Shadow Cabinet, who sit opposite.

Full employment: a political and economic doctrine which advocates that everyone seeking work should be able to find a job within their capacities at a wage that would enable them to live an adequate life.

Functional chamber: a legislative body composed of representatives of various interests in society, such as business, trade unions, the churches and so on.

G8: The seven major world economies – G7 (The United States, Japan, Germany, UK, France, Italy and Canada) plus Russia.

Gerrymandering: the practice of rigging electoral boundaries or affecting the social composition of electoral districts to ensure the success of the governing party, whatever level of support it receives. The term derives from Elbridge Gerry, Governor of Massachusetts, who in 1812 drew a congressional district shaped like a salamander so as to maximise the advantage for his party.

Glasnost: the Russian word for freedom of expression, popularised by Mikhail Gorbachev.

Globalisation: the process by which the world is made more interconnected and interdependent, through interregional, transnational and global networks and flows. Especially relevant to the production and marketing of goods which is increasingly organised on a worldwide scale.

Golden Age: the period from 1832 to 1867 when, some commentators claim, there was a balance between the executive and the legislature and when Parliament was a significant influence on government policy and actions.

Governance: the act or manner of governing within or across territorial jurisdictions.

Hegemony: the dominant military and economic state that uses its power to force a world order conducive to its own interests.

Hereditary peers: a member of the aristocracy whose title has been inherited from the nearest relative. Very few peerages are inheritable through the female line.

Home rule: the transfer of independence by a sovereign parliament to former territories.

Hung council: a council in which no party has an overall majority of seats and where business may be conducted by a minority administration or as a result of an agreement between two or more parties.

Identifiers: voters who have a continuing relationship with a party and consider themselves partisans who identify with its beliefs and policies.

Ideology: a system of beliefs embodying political, social and economic ideas and values.

Imperialism: the policy of acquiring power over other countries, usually neighbouring ones, by political and economic exploitation.

Industrial Revolution: the period in the late eighteenth and early nineteenth centuries when mass production techniques were invented and introduced into what became known as factories.

Industrialism: Jonathan Porritt's term for the present attitude of political parties to unlimited production and consumption.

Inequality: differences in wealth and opportunity between different groups in society.

Inflation: the increase in the amount of money in circulation producing rising prices and falls in value.

Influence: the ability to have some bearing on the outcome of a decision.

Inner city: the areas that surround the centres of cities, usually comprising older housing in poor condition and acting as 'reception' areas for immigrant groups.

Integration: full unity of one territory with another. The cooperative process whereby countries move closer together on economic and other areas of policy.

Interest: a stake, or a reason for caring about the outcome of a particular decision.

Interest groups: *see* Sectional or interest groups.

Intergovernmentalism: primacy of national governments in decision making.

Internal market: when an artificial separation between users and providers is invented to try to introduce some of the discipline of the free market into a public service.

International regimes: sets of rules, norms and decision-making procedures that coordinate state activity in particular policy areas.

Internationalism: the view that foreign policy should be based on the idea of cooperation between countries all over the world.

Issue voting: voting on the basis of issues presented at an election rather than on the basis of class or party preference.

Joint authority: the sharing of rule among governments.

Joint sovereignty: ruling an area jointly between two countries, both recognising equal rights to and responsibilities for it.

Judicial review: the ability of the courts to declare illegal any government action that they deem to be unauthorised by the terms of law.

Judiciary: the body in a political system responsible for interpreting and enforcing laws.

Keynesian/Keynesianism: named after the economic theories and prescriptions for government action of John Maynard Keynes (1883–1946). These advocated a role for vigorous government action to stimulate economic growth through high levels of spending and the control of aggregate demand in order to avoid slumps and booms.

Law lords: lords of appeal in ordinary are senior judges who have been given a life peerage so that they can carry out the judicial work of the Lords. There are currently 12 law lords.

Legislature: the body in a democracy responsible for discussing and creating laws.

Legitimacy: the right to govern.

Liberalisation: literally to make freer or less restrictive, as in 'liberalisation of trade'.

Liberty: freedom from slavery, captivity or any other form of arbitrary control.

Life peers: since the 1958 Life Peerages Act, most peers have been created for their lifetime only. Until 1999, life peers constituted around one-third of the nominal membership of the Lords.

Lobby: the general term used to describe the activities of pressure groups, so called because lobbyists seek to waylay MPs as they pass through the lobby of the Commons. It also refers to the off-the-record briefings given by government spokespeople to journalists.

Lords spiritual: the Archbishops of Canterbury and York and the 24 most senior diocesan bishops of the Church of England who sit in the Lords until they cease to hold their post.

Lords temporal: all those peers who are not lords spiritual.

Majoritarian: electoral systems such as the alternative vote which require that the winning candidate receives an absolute majority (over 50 per cent) of the total vote. Although each winning candidate can claim a *mandate*

from his or her electors, it does not prevent disproportionality and other problems.

Mandate: the idea that winning the general election gives the government the authority to put its policies, either as stated in the campaign or as required by circumstances, into effect. It can also mean that the government is expected to put its manifesto into action, that it has made a binding contract with the electors.

Mandatory reselection: the process by which sitting Labour MPs have to face a reselection meeting of the constituency Labour Party to determine whether they will be reselected as candidates for the next election. It was one of the reforms achieved by the Bennite left in the 1980s and is gradually being abandoned.

Manifesto: a document issued by a political party containing a list of policy pledges which will be implemented if the party wins the election.

Manipulation: the ability to influence someone else involved in a decision.

Market failure: instances where the workings of supply and demand in markets fail to provide goods or services that the community desires or needs.

Market testing: the idea that activities provided by government organisations should be tested for cost and effectiveness by subjecting in-house provision to competitive bids from outside bodies.

Means of delivery: the method whereby a particular service is provided.

Media: the collective name for the press, radio and television. Sometimes called the Fourth Estate, to represent its powerful position in the political system.

Mercantilism: the doctrine that state power and security were enhanced by a favourable balance of trade. Popular in Britain between the mid-sixteenth and the mid-eighteenth centuries, when policy was directed to reducing imports and increasing national self-sufficiency at the expense of free trade.

Ministerial responsibility: ministers are responsible to Parliament for their ministerial conduct, the general work of their departments and the actions or omissions of their officials.

Ministry: *see* Department.

Mixed economy: the existence of a substantial public sector in the economy alongside a substantial private one. An economic system combining public ownership (most commonly of certain infrastructure industries and services) with the private ownership of the rest of the economy.

Modernising Government: White Paper published in March 1999, which encapsulates a range of managerial and service delivery themes with a focus on updating and modernising the basic functioning of the government machine. The White Paper and the subsequent implementation programme contained many modish concepts including 'government direct', 'joined-up government' and 'information-age government'.

Monetarism: an economic doctrine adopted by the Thatcherite wing of the Conservative Party which emphasises the control of the money supply as the way to defeat inflation – seen as the main job of the government – rather than ensuring full employment.

Motion of no confidence: a motion tabled (usually by the Leader of the Opposition) stating that 'This House has no confidence in Her Majesty's Ministers'. If passed, the government must, by convention, resign or request a dissolution of Parliament.

Multilateral: agreements between two or more states.

Multilateralism: attempting to solve international problems through collective approaches.

Multinational companies/firms: organisations that operate in a wide range of companies/firms across several national boundaries, shifting economic activity around them in order to exploit the best conditions for producing profit.

Multi-polar: an international system where there are more than two dominant powers, or no dominant powers at all.

National identity: a shared sense by a group of people – usually citizens of a state – as to their own history and character.

National interest: the calculation by its government of what constitutes the best course of action for a nation in international affairs.

Nationalisation: the act of transferring a part of the economy to state ownership, usually by establishing a nationalised corporation. Usually associated with the postwar 'socialist' political device of placing sections of the economy under the control of the government, so that privately owned assets such as buildings, equipment etc., or shares in a company are transferred by law from private into public ownership.

Nationalised corporations: the legal form taken by most publicly owned industries, and until recently the most important form of quasi-government (see below) concerned with economic policy.

Nationalism: the belief that one's country is worth supporting strongly in most situations.

Natural rights: the belief that everyone is born with certain basic rights regarding freedom, citizenship and law.

Negative constitutionalism: a belief in a constitution serving as a constraining mechanism, giving precedence to enduring principles over the transient will of the majority.

Neo-liberalism: in this usage refers to the doctrine which advocates individual autonomy and market principles over state control.

New Labour: the summary label to describe the economic policies devised by the Labour Party in the 1990s to ensure a departure from traditional ('old') Labour economic policies.

'New magistracy': the tendency of governments since 1979 to put functions into the hands of non-elected bodies such as quangos, including health service trusts, responsible for spending large amounts of money with little public accountability.

Next Steps: stemming from the Ibbs, or Next Steps, Report in 1988, a programme of managerial and structural reform which transformed the Civil Service through the creation of new executive agencies to carry out central government services and functions.

Notifiable offences: those offences that are sufficiently serious to be tried by a judge.

Occupational class: the method of assigning individuals to class groups on the basis of their occupational classification – manual working class, and so on.

Oligarchy: a political system in which power is exercised by a group or committee of people.

One member, one vote (OMOV): the process of reform in the Labour Party by which party members vote as individuals instead of having their views represented by unions, constituency parties, etc.

Order: the degree of calm and law-abidingness present in society.

Pacifism: opposition to the conduct of war.

Paramilitaries: groups of supporters for a cause who accept violence as a method, accept military discipline and often wear neo-military dress.

Paramilitary groups: armed organisations not recognised by the state.

Parliamentary lobby: a small group of political journalists from the main media outlets who are given privileged access to ministers and other government spokespeople. They receive highly confidential briefings and in return do not reveal their sources of information.

Parliamentary sovereignty: the doctrine that Parliament is the supreme law-making body in the United Kingdom, with absolute *legal* right to make any law it chooses, subject only to those restrictions imposed by the membership of the EU, itself an expression of parliamentary sovereignty. The sovereignty of Parliament is subject to a host of practical and political limitations.

Participatory democracy: a political system in which everyone is allowed and encouraged to take part in making decisions.

Partisan dealignment: the declining number of voters over the past three decades who are identifying with political parties.

Perestroika: the Russian word for reconstruction, popularised by Mikhail Gorbachev.

Permissive: the alleged characteristic of Labour social policy in the 1960s when it was first believed that anything goes and that 'doing your own thing' was good.

Photo opportunity: a media event where politicians pose for photographs but refuse to answer questions from journalists and where the public is excluded, a technique perfected by Mrs Thatcher.

Pluralism: a political system in which power is diffused into several different centres within society and thus there are competing centres of power and authority rather than one in which the state is dominant. Pluralists argue that power is and should be dispersed in society, thus ensuring that freedom is maintained.

Pluralist: a form of political decision making in which a variety (a plurality) of interests are held to contest outcomes.

Plurality: electoral systems (especially 'first-past-the-post') that require only that the winning candidate has more votes that his or her nearest rival rather than an absolute majority. Such systems tend to produce disproportionate results.

Policy cycle: the process of policy initiation, formulation and implementation.

Political demands: the requirements made upon political systems by the societies they regulate.

Policy directorate: in 2001 Blair combined the No. 10 Policy Unit and some members of the private office into a directorate and it advises him on policy. Since June 2005 the two groups have been reconstituted.

Political entrepreneurship: the activity of promoting political causes, interests or groups in the political marketplace.

Political participation: the act of taking part in politics.

Political party: an organised group of people sharing common policy preferences and a general ideological position. It seeks to possess or share political power, usually by nominating candidates for election and thus seeking a place in the legislature.

Political recruitment: the process by which citizens are recruited into high participation in political life.

Polluted: made unclean, corrupt or defiled.

Positive constitutionalism: a belief in a constitution serving as a mechanism through which the will of the people is paramount.

Power: the ability to make someone do as one wishes.

'Power corrupts': the notion that the ability to get people to behave in a certain way will eventually be abused for selfish ends by the holders of power.

Pragmatism: the belief that problems should be solved on their unique merits rather than according to some pre-ordained ideological pathway.

Prerogative: prior or exclusive privilege often associated with rank or position.

Press barons: newspaper proprietors who have been raised to the peerage either out of gratitude for services rendered to the governing party or because of the hope that they will omit to bite the hand that feeds them.

Pressure group: a body possessing both formal structure and common interests which seeks to influence government at the national, local and international level without normally seeking election to representative bodies.

Primary, secondary and tertiary sectors: the three levels of the economy corresponding to the activities of producing raw materials, producing manufactured goods and delivering services.

Prime ministerial government: the view most associated with Richard Crossman and John Mackintosh that the Prime Minister has become dominant, almost a President, and that the Cabinet has become part of the 'dignified' aspects of the system.

Private bill: a bill brought forward by an individual, company or public body outside Parliament to effect a change in the law of particular interest or benefit to the person or persons promoting it.

Private member's bill: a public bill promoted by a member of the Commons who is not a minister. They have a variety of purposes; several pass into law each year, though most fail. The opposition of the government is usually fatal.

Private sector: the part of the economy that is the product of market forces alone.

Privatisation: the process of transferring state-owned enterprises to the private sector, mainly by the sale of shares. The term also refers to other aspects of the reduction of the economic role of the state, such as liberalisation policies to encourage greater reliance on the market including deregulation of business, contracting out of services and the opening of the public sector generally to market forces.

Professional politicians: the small minority of citizens who devote their whole life to politics, and who make a livelihood from it.

Promotion groups: *see* Cause or promotion groups.

Proportional representation (PR): a system of election that attempts to relate votes cast for the various parties to the number of seats won in the legislature. There are various forms of PR, with widely differing consequences.

Psephology: the study of voting behaviour as shown in elections and opinion polls. The word derives from the Greek word *psephos*, a pebble. Classical Athenians voted by putting a pebble into one of two jars, one for the 'yes' votes, the other for the 'no' votes. It was a form of direct democracy.

Public bills: bills that must relate to a matter of public (general) interest and be introduced by an MP or a peer. Any bill proposed by the government, regardless of its content or intent, is a public bill.

Public corporations: organisations set up to run enterprises and provide services within the public sector or state sector. They include nationalised industries such as coal, gas and electricity and bodies such as the BBC.

Public sector: that part of the economy which is in state ownership and is funded substantially by money originating from taxation of some kind.

Public–Private Partnerships: a range of initiatives designed to bring about greater collaboration between the public and private sectors in the provision of services. The Private Finance Initiative, introduced to facilitate the funding of major public sector capital projects using private funds, is a prime example of public–private partnership.

Quango: a quasi-autonomous non-governmental organisation, independent (at least in theory) from the department that created it, nominally under the control of the minister who appoints its members, sets its budget and establishes its aims, and with little responsibility to Parliament. Quangos are public bodies which advise on or administer activities and which carry out their work at arm's length from government.

Quasi-government: those public institutions that are not formally part of the government but carry out a function central to it.

Rates: a form of local taxation based upon the notional value of a property which was used until replaced by the community charge or poll tax.

Rationality: a belief that the exercise of reason is superior to other ways of finding the truth.

Reactionary: right-wing policies held to be harsh and unfeeling. Strictly speaking support for the status quo ante (that which previously existed).

Realignment: a fundamental change in party structure and voting support for the various parties. An example is the wholesale desertion of the American Republican Party by black voters to the Democratic Party in the 1920s.

Referendum: a ballot in which the people at large decide an issue by voting 'yes' or 'no', although multi-outcome referenda are possible. The matter may be referred to the people by the government, perhaps because it is unable to make a decision, the law or the constitution may require such a reference, or there may be a mechanism by which the people can demand a referendum. Britain's only national referendum, that of 1975 over continued membership of the EC, was *advisory* only.

Regionalisation: the process of interconnection and interaction between groupings of states and societies. The basis for regionalisation may be common history, geographical proximity or common interests.

Regulatory agency: an institution that specialises in a given regulatory task, such as the regulation of competition generally, or of competitive conditions in a single industry or sector, such as the railway industry.

Representation: the notion that those who are governed should be involved in the process of government.

Representative government: government whereby decisions are taken by representatives who are (normally) elected by popular vote. The people do not take decisions directly.

Responsibility: the accountability of government to the people.

Responsible government: the view that government should be held accountable for its actions, initially to the people's representatives and ultimately to the people themselves.

Restructuring the welfare state: changing the balance in spending between different services.

Revenue expenditure: day-to-day expenditure by local authorities on items such as salaries, office supplies and heating.

Rigid constitution: a constitution that contains a provision that it can only be changed by a process different from and more complex than that required for the passage of ordinary legislation. The best-known example is that of the United States.

Royal prerogative: powers that legally are in the hands of the Crown, having been accepted by the courts over time as rightfully belonging to the monarch in his or her capacity as ruler. Most prerogative powers are now exercised by ministers (particularly the Prime Minister) who 'advise' the monarch as to their use.

Rule of law: the idea that human activity should be controlled within a framework of agreed rules.

Secondary sector: *see* Primary, secondary and tertiary sectors.

Sectional or interest groups: these groups represent the interests (particularly economic) of their members. They include business, labour and professional organisations and often have close links with political parties.

Select committee: a committee chosen by the House to work according to specific terms of reference. It may be given special powers to investigate, examine and report its findings to Parliament. Some are concerned with the working of Parliament itself; others scrutinise the activities of the executive.

Selective targeting: the rejection of universalism (see below) in favour of restricting availability of benefits and services to those deemed to be in need by some standard test.

Service sector: *see* Tertiary sector.

Shared responsibility: the solution to environmental problems is the responsibility of government, business, citizens, voluntary organisations and the public sector.

Social capital: The networks and norms of reciprocal trust built up through interpersonal connections. When people associate with one another through voluntary associations they develop better skills of social interaction, treat cooperation as normal and come to rely upon and trust each other.

Social imperialism: an idea involving abandoning the principles of free trade in order to protect British industries and building closer ties with the white dominions of New Zealand, South Africa and Australia, in order to create a closed imperial market. The Tariff Reform Movement under Joseph Chamberlain advocated an elaborate system of imperial preferences, that is, a system of bilateral tariff concessions granted to each other by Britain and the white dominions. The Imperial Conference in 1917 formally approved such a system, but it was not until the 1930s that imperial preference developed to any great extent.

Socialism: an economic system in which everyone benefits from the labour of others.

Soundbite: a brief quote that is intended to make the maximum possible political impact. Research indicates that most listeners and viewers can absorb information for some thirty seconds, a theory that has influenced politicians on both sides of the Atlantic.

Sovereignty: autonomy over national decision making. The ultimate legal authority in a state.

Special relationship: the close feeling between US and British governments based on common culture and alliance in warfare.

Spin doctor: a party official or public relations consultant whose job is to influence the media and put the best possible construction on events, by getting the party or candidate's message over by any possible means.

Standing committee: usually a small group of MPs reflecting party strength in the Commons which takes the committee stage of bills that have received their second reading. They scrutinise the bills and can propose amendments to the House.

State: A commonly governed group of people all living within a defined territory.

Statist-corporatism: is often used to descibe practices in authoritarian and some democratic states and refers to a process by which the state uses officially recognised organisations as a tool for policy making and restricting public participation in the political process, thus limiting the power of civil society.

Statute law: those laws deriving their authority from Acts of Parliament and subordinate (delegated) legislation made under authority of the parent Act. Statute law overrides common law.

Steering the economy: the dominant image used to describe the business of economic management as conducted by government.

Subsidiarity: the general aim of the principle of subsidiarity is to guarantee a degree of independence for a lower authority in relation to a higher body or for a local authority in respect of a central authority. It therefore involves the sharing of powers between several levels of authority, a principle which forms the institutional basis for federal states. When applied in an EU context, the principle means that the member states remain responsible for areas which they are capable of managing more effectively themselves, while the Community is given those powers which the member states cannot discharge satisfactorily.

Subvention: government subsidy.

Suffrage: the right to vote. The extension of the suffrage was a gradual process, culminating in 1969 when 18-year-olds were enfranchised. The suffrage is unusually wide in this country, including British subjects, resident Commonwealth citizens and citizens of the Irish Republic who have been resident for three months.

Supply-side economics: provided the political and theoretical foundation for a remarkable number of tax cuts in the United States and other countries during the 1980s. Supply-side economics stresses the impact of tax rates on the incentives for people to produce and to use resources efficiently.

Supranationalism: the character of authority exercised by European Union bodies that takes precedence over the autonomy of the member states.

Sustainable development: the capability of the current generation to ensure it meets the need of the present without compromising the ability of future generations to meet their own needs.

Sustainable economy or sustainable growth: one in which resources are used more efficiently so that pressures on the environment do not increase as the economy grows.

Swing: the way in which the switch of voters from one party to another on a national or constituency basis can be calculated. It is worked out by adding the rise in one party's vote to the fall in the other party's and then dividing by two.

Tabloids: small format newspapers, usually aimed at the bottom end of the market with an informal style, use of large and often sensational headlines and many photographs.

Tertiary (or service) sector: *see* Primary, secondary and tertiary sectors.

Thatcherism: the economic, social and political ideas and particular style of leadership associated with Margaret Thatcher, Prime Minister from 1979 to 1990. It was a mixture of neo-liberal beliefs in the free market and neo-conservative social attitudes and beliefs about the limited role of government.

The Treasury: the most important department of government concerned with economic policy.

Theological: based upon the science of religion.

Think tanks: the name give to specialist organisations that frequently research and publish on policy and ideological matters.

Toleration: accepting the legitimacy of views with which one does not necessarily agree.

Top-down: the term used to denote power residing in the leading figures of an organisation, control over organisation being exercised by those figures over the ordinary members.

Transfer payments: a method of transferring money from one group of citizens to another: for instance, taxing those in work and transferring the money raised to the unemployed in the form of unemployment benefits.

Transnationalisation: the process whereby politics and other social relations are conducted across and perhaps regardless of national boundaries. There are transnational corporations, such as Wal-Mart, transnational communities, such as religious communities, transnational structures, for example, of finance, and transnational problems like drug trafficking.

Tripartism: a variant of *corporatism* in which economic policy is made in conjunction with business and labour groups to the exclusion of Parliament and other interests.

Turnout: the measure, usually expressed as a percentage, of registered voters who actually vote. The average turnout in postwar elections has been around 75 per cent, generally lower than in most other EU countries.

Tyranny: a political system in which power is exercised harshly without any consideration for the citizenry.

Ulsterisation: the return to front line policing by the Royal Ulster Constabulary, replacing the British Army, undertaken in the mid-1970s, to maintain the image of normality.

Unicameral legislature: legislatures made up of one chamber are to be found mainly in smaller countries such as Israel and New Zealand or in smaller states in federal systems, such as Nebraska in the United States.

Unitary authorities: a local government structure in which all services are provided by a single-tier authority as opposed to a structure in which powers and functions are divided between two tiers.

Universalism: the principle that welfare services should be freely available to all citizens.

U-turn: a fundamental change of policies or philosophy by a political party or leader. The term is used to describe Heath's abandonment in 1971/2 of the free-market policies on which he was elected in 1970.

Washington Consensus: formerly a list of policy prescriptions that were influential in US policy making circles in the late 1980s and early 1990s. The three big ideas at the heart of the concept were macro-economic discipline, a market economy, and openness to the world (at least in respect of trade and FDI).

Welfare mix: phrase invented by Michael Rose to explain his analysis of how welfare services are provided through a wide variety of sources.

Welfare state: the system of comprehensive social security and health services which was based on the Beveridge Report of 1942 and implemented by the postwar Labour government. Often referred to as 'cradle to grave' security.

Welfarism: the idea that the government should take some responsibility for the health and well-being of its citizens.

Whip: this term has several meanings: (a) parliamentary business managers found in all parties, responsible for maintaining party discipline and ensuring a maximum turnout in the division lobbies; (b) the summons to vote for an MP's party, with the importance of the issue indicated by a one-, two- or three-line whip, sent out weekly to members of the parliamentary party; (c) membership of an MP's party – withdrawal of the whip means that the MP concerned is no longer recognised as a member in good standing.

Working peers: peers that are created on the nomination of the political parties to strengthen their representation in the Upper House. This is particularly important to the Labour party, which traditionally was supported by few hereditary peers.

Index

Note: Terms where the page references are in **bold** may be found in the Glossary

The 2010 Election: The End of New Labour

'The country has spoken but we don't know what they've said.'

Paddy Ashdown, BBC interview, 7 May 2010

'Something did go wrong with the Conservative campaign.'

Michael Portillo, *Daily Telegraph*, 8 May 2010

'Cameron has made the most plausible offer. When he and Clegg meet I would predict a brief but torrid affair.'

Simon Jenkins, *Guardian*, 8 May 2010

'Shimmering on the horizon was the chance of a progressive alliance, a rocket about to take off. Then it crashed to earth.'

Polly Toynbee, *Guardian*, 12 May 2010

Introduction

The election of 2010 was one of the most remarkable in most voters' memories. It produced a 'hung parliament', the first since February 1974, and threw the political parties into an orgy of negotiation, secret meetings and a rather public game of political poker. This chapter aims to cover the prelude to the election and the campaign as well as provide some analysis of the results and their unprecedented consequences.

■ The New Labour Years

In May 1997 Tony Blair ushered out the era of 18 years of Conservative rule and ushered in 'New' Labour. The 'newness' related in part to Labour's embrace of market capitalism and the key role played by the City in Britain's economy. Blair's majority was a staggering 179. His first term was characterised by a buoyant economy but spending restraint, courtesy of Chancellor Gordon Brown, who brashly began to claim he had ended the Tory years of 'boom and bust'. In 2001 Labour won another landslide of 178 but on a much reduced turnout of only 59.2 per cent. After the attack on the Twin Powers in New York on 9/11 (11 September 2001), Blair ranged himself alongside US President George Bush in his 'War on Terror' and in 2003 was a partner in the fateful invasion of Iraq. This war soon proved unpopular as it became a military and political disaster and Labour began to decline in the polls with Blair being accused of mendacity via 'spin' or news management.

His attempts to reform the public services to embrace more private sector elements were not assisted by a Chancellor who believed he should really have been prime minister. According to insider accounts, Brown sincerely believed he had been promised by Blair that he would soon resign to allow him a chance to fulfil his ambition of occupying Number 10. However, this second term saw vast amounts of funding poured into health and education; some argued such spending was unfocused and profligate. In 2005 Blair sought to exclude Brown from his election campaign but was forced to include him to ensure a third victory, this time by a majority of 66, though on only 35 per cent of the vote. Throughout this period the Conservatives had 'flat-lined' in the polls at around 30 per cent and were perceived as a divided party, out of touch with the realities of modern society in all its diversity. In

December 2005, old Etonian David Cameron was elected leader and immediately set about rebranding his party and purging it of its extremist 'nasty party' image.

In June 2007, after ten years in power, Tony Blair was finally forced to stand aside for Brown to take over (though without the contest which he once declared he would welcome). Initially Brown enjoyed a 'honeymoon bounce' in the polls as he appeared to handle some minor crises with aplomb. But he fatally allowed speculation about a snap election to extend to the point when it seemed inevitable and then abandoned plans when Tory polls spiked after a conference speech by George Osborne proposing an end to inheritance tax. He denied adverse polls had influenced his decision.

After this turn for the worse – Tories accused him of 'bottling it' – his fortunes never really revived and a succession of disasters attended his government: lost Inland Revenue CDs containing the bank details of millions of people; the failure to deport hundreds of serious overseas offenders who had finished their terms of imprisonment; and his abolition of the 10p tax band in his 2007 budget which, it was revealed, would disadvantage 5.3m of the poorest people in the country. Massive losses in local government elections in 2008 were compounded by by-election defeats and Brown's poll ratings indicated his total failure to win the hearts of voters as his predecessor had once managed.

However, from the autumn of 2008 onwards the banking crisis sparked by the sale of US 'subprime' mortgages began to become desperately serious and Brown was quick to devise a policy of recapitalising British banks; influencing other nations and winning the praise of Nobel prize-winning economist, Paul Krugman. He also tackled the resultant economic recession by the Keynesian solution of injecting substantial amounts of money into the economy. He was also forced to borrow vast sums to maintain his high levels of planned public expenditure: it was calculated that government debt would be in the region of £160–80 billion for a number of years to come. The Conservatives chose to attack Brown's Keynesian approach and argue that expenditure needed to be cut to reduce the deficit and related interest payments. In the spring and summer of 2009 a damaging scandal exploded concerning the way in which MPs exploited their generous expenses. Many MPs were exposed by articles in the *Daily Telegraph* as relying on taxpayers' money to pay for food, regular household upkeep costs, gardening and house repairs. Some had deliberately changed the identification of their 'main residence' to improve flats and houses they subsequently sold on at a profit. Some were even claiming for mortgages which had already been paid off – leading to criminal proceedings. All this induced a powerful 'anti-politics' atmosphere as the election approached.

In the autumn of 2009, despite his spirited attempts to combat the economic crisis, Brown was some 20 points behind Cameron in the polls and the forthcoming election, slated for May 2010, was assumed to be a formality for Cameron by most political commentators. He and George Osborne sought to reinforce their stern message by emphasising how deep cuts needed to be and there was even talk of an 'Age of Austerity' with more specific cuts suggested by Osborne at the 2009 Tory conference. Maybe such talk alarmed voters as the Conservative lead began to narrow and by January 2010 was down to single figures. Labour announced a new 50p in the £ tax on those earning £150,000 and an increase in National Insurance contributions. This set the initial battleground for the election campaign when Brown announced a May election on 6 April. At this point the polls suggested neither Labour nor the Tories would gain an overall majority, with the Liberal Democrats running at 22 or 23 per cent in most polls.

■ The Issues

Economy

Overwhelmingly the issue in this election was the state of the economy. Since 1997 Brown had taunted Tories that he had engineered the end of 'boom and bust' and established a solid economic foundation, exploiting British financial expertise by encouraging the City and super rich individuals to settle in the UK. The banking crisis and the recession in 2008 which saw GDP contract by over 6 per cent, proved Brown had benefitted from a 'boom' and that 'bust', as always, was waiting just around the corner. Brown did his best to argue that these economic travails were the result of events in the USA, and not his responsibility. The Conservatives, however, eager to get their own back, insisted the huge debt mountain was the result of Brown's epic mismanagement of the economy. Given that Conservatives had supported Brown's economic approach and competed to be close friends of the City, this was disingenuous to a degree, but incumbent governments almost always have blame pinned on them for what happens on their watch.

Broken Society

The Conservatives had tried hard to argue that social dysfunction like crime, examples of appalling parenting, and anti-social behaviour were symptoms of a 'broken society' which they alone could fix. To effect this they suggested decentralisation of government, with more local and community control, would improve things immeasurably. In their manifestos Labour suggested a more focussed and benign state, but in theirs the Conservatives essayed the (perhaps) brave idea of the 'Big Society', inviting everyone to join in the running of essential services and take back power from the state. Liberal Democrats argued the 'political' crisis could only be cured by far-reaching reforms to the system and the introduction of a 'new politics'.

Education

It followed, for the Tories, that schools had to be improved, with a proposed adoption of the Swedish practice of allowing parents to form schools and run them on the basis of funding from the state. They supported the expansion of Labour's new 'Academy' schools, a programme they had always thought sensible. Lib Dems also urged decentralisation of power and the encouragement of voluntary energies.

'Playing Field' Changes

The number of seats in the Commons to be contested had been increased by 4 to 650 and a series of Boundary Commission changes had been made creating 13 new seats while 9 disappeared. Rallings and Thrasher of Plymouth University calculated that on the basis of the new boundaries, Labour's majority in 2005 would have been 36 and not 67. This meant that while the Tories would have needed a swing of 2.2 per cent to remove Labour's overall majority, it now became 1.5 per cent. To become the largest single party Cameron needed a swing of 4.6 per cent and to get an overall majority, one of 7.1 per cent; all this assuming a uniform swing across the country. As a result of the expenses scandal a record number of MPs (146) stood down at this election meaning that replacements made the new House, much 'newer' than is usually the case.

■ The Campaign

At the end of March a tanned Tony Blair made a speech in Sedgefield in support of his former friend and bitter rival but it made no special impact. More influential was a televised debate on Channel 4, *Ask the Chancellors*. As the incumbent, Alistair Darling,

addressed what had become the NI debate – Labour wanted to generate £6 billion though raising it, Osborne wanted to abandon such plans – he attacked George Osborne for seeking to have it both ways. By criticising both of them, and raising a couple of laughs, Lib Dem Shadow Chancellor Vince Cable was reckoned to have come off best. Following the official opening of the campaign on 6 April, the wrangle over the NI issue continued. Labour stressed the illogicality of being apparently concerned, initially, about reducing the deficit and then switching to an effective tax cut. Cameron argued NI increases, to be paid by employers too, would be a tax on jobs which would harm the fragile recovery. Brown argued a cut in planned spending would, on the contrary, cause job losses and also threaten the recovery.

These accusations ping-ponged around for some days but Cameron's hand was strengthened by a raft of senior businessmen who publicly came out in support of his line on not imposing the NI increase. Effectively this 'won' the first week for the Conservatives; Labour could not find any point of purchase to attack what was perceived by many as

(Left–right) Chancellor Alistair Darling with Vince Cable and George Osborne in the South Bank Studios in central London for a live televised debate, before the forthcoming 2010 general election
Source: PA Photos.

a postponement of a tax increase: a much more welcome message than the 'austerity' one of the previous autumn.

TV Debates

The second week was transformed by the first televised leaders' debate on 15 April. Ever since the US presidential debates helped John Kennedy win in 1960, there had been pressure for something similar in British elections. To be acceptable there had to be agreement and usually the party expecting to win – e.g. Labour under Blair in 1997 – vetoed the idea to avoid giving a platform to rivals. Perhaps because he had been hounding Gordon Brown so effectively in PMQs, Cameron, despite being the front-runner, agreed to a series of three debates on successive Thursdays during the campaign. Inevitably the Liberal Democrats were excited by the prospect as, for the first time, it gave them exposure equal to the two big parties. Commentators discussed the huge pressure on the youthful Nick Clegg to perform and, in the event, he did, above all expectations, finally stepping out from the shadow of his popular deputy, Cable. Cameron found the sombre format, with no audience reactions allowed, much less congenial than the noisy hub-bub of PMQs. Brown's mastery of policy detail enabled this indifferent television performer to exceed expectations, but the revelation was Clegg.

At PMQs, Nick Clegg, tended to suffer the usual fate of Lib Dem leaders in that he was allowed only small interventions; was patronised by both big party leaders; and shouted down by their respective backbench followers. In the calmer atmosphere of the debate Clegg was able to elaborate an approach which sounded fresher and more hopeful than the two big parties. His youthful good looks and television savvy helped to make him the easy 'winner' according to most polls; Cameron came a distant second and Brown third. Over ten million viewers tuned in – a remarkable figure for 90 minutes of dense political debate. On the strength of Clegg's debating skills the poll position of the Liberal Democrats surged to 30 points and over. The debates had created a three-party contest with all three parties gaining poll ratings of about one third of the electorate. Whilst the Conservatives, polling in the mid-thirties, promised to be the biggest party, any hopes of an overall majority seemed to have faded away. Andrew Rawnsley commented (*Observer*, 9 May 2010):

More fluent and comfortable in the format than an unusually constipated Cameron and a stolid Gordon Brown, Clegg grabbed 'change' from the Tory and 'fairness' from Labour.

The result was 'Cleggmania', a theme which the press took up with gusto. Meanwhile the Conservatives rued the day they had thought Cameron's superiority at PMQs would translate to a format restricted by over 70 rules which punished the kind of aggression on which the Commons thrives. However, one consequence of Clegg's success was smear campaigns delivered by the right-wing press and much closer scrutiny of Liberal Democrat policies which many voters found uncongenial (defence and immigration, in particular). Clegg found himself under attack from both sides in the final two debates and, though defending his corner well, saw Cameron – who had quickly adapted to master the new medium – eventually emerge as the overall victor in terms of public perceptions. Interestingly, Cameron did not find much opportunity in the debates to expand on his 'Big Society' approach.

As polling day on 6 May approached, the polls had settled down to the high-twenties for Labour and Liberal Democrats and the low- to mid-thirties for Conservatives. This focused unflattering attention on the first-past-the-post (FPTP)voting system as it appeared possible that a Labour Party which came third in terms of votes cast might still emerge as the winner in terms of seats won. Needless to say, the Conservatives were mortified that what had appeared a 'shoo-in' during the winter of 2008–9, now seemed to be heading for a hung parliament. Whilst the Lib Dems did not balk too much at such a prospect, the Conservatives bent their efforts to suggest such an outcome would provide only weak and indecisive government when strong leadership was required to reassure the international bond markets which controlled the future of UK lending. All three parties were well aware that the crisis in the EU's euro currency, caused by government spending and huge debt in Greece, might spread to other seriously indebted countries like Spain, Portugal and the UK. The shadow of this threat darkened the whole of the campaign and its volatile aftermath.

The rest of the campaign seemed tame by comparison with the innovation of the debates. It comprised the usual hackneyed staged events for all parties, visits to receptive locations plus the predictable photo-ops. All three party leaders took their wives on the campaign trail – something which now may become a regular feature of such events along with the television debates which have increased the US-style 'presidential' focus on the leading personalities. Labour's campaign was especially lacklustre and one event in particular revealed the shortcomings of Gordon Brown as a campaigner.

'Bigotgate'

On 28 April Brown was served up in Rochdale with a widow, grandmother and life-long Labour voter, Mrs Gillian Duffy, for a chat, live for the television agencies. The chat went along predictably with Brown seeking to exercise the charm at his disposal. However, Mrs Duffy asked a question about immigration which Brown found difficult and when he entered his car he declared to aides the meeting had been a 'disaster' referring to that 'bigoted woman'. Unknown to him, his microphone was still live and his private words were recorded. Aghast, he apologised to the lady, later returning to her house to spend 40 minutes doing so again at length. Mrs Duffy refused to accept his apology in public and when later appearing on Jeremy Vine's BBC radio show, Brown placed his hands over his face in despair – unaware he was being filmed – as the recording of the encounter was played back. It was a PR disaster and cited as further evidence of Brown's poor performance as a candidate for the top job.

However, the damage proved limited as the polls seemed unaffected; maybe voters had already factored in Brown's grumpiness. But the two-faced nature of Brown's treatment of the typical core Labour voter seemed to reinforce a stereotype of politicians who will lie about their feelings to win votes. Brown, however, showed remarkable resilience – a standard feature of his character whatever his misjudgements – in campaigning heroically up to the last minutes of the campaign. Clegg and Cameron also showed great last-minute vigour, with the latter managing a final sustained 36-hour stint. After a campaign transformed by the televised debates, the nation awaited the results on the evening of Thursday 6 May. Interestingly, the poll positions of the three major parties had hardly shifted since

Prime Minister Gordon Brown talks with resident Gillian Duffy on 28 April 2010 in Rochdale
Source: Jeff J. Mitchell/Getty Images

the start of the campaign four weeks earlier. Indeed, the results proved to be quite close to polling six months before the election in November 2009 (see Paul Whiteley, 2010, p7).

■ The Results

The first event in the sequence of results as they fed through into the television companies' elaborate graphic-laden studio sets, was the exit poll, produced jointly by the BBC, ITV and Sky News. It predicted a hung parliament: more particularly 307 seats for the Conservatives, 255 for Labour and only 59 for the Lib Dems. When early returns from Labour seats in the north-west showed swings of 9 and 11 per cent – well above that needed to produce an overall Tory majority – many assumed the exit poll had been wrong (as it was, embarrassingly, in 1992). Tory blogger Iain Dale declared that if it was proved right he would 'run naked down Whitehall' (he later refused to be held to his pledge). Some early swings against Labour, in the north-east exceeded the 7 per cent needed for an overall majority; Cannock Chase even registered 14.2 per cent from Labour to Conservative but other contests showed smaller swings and Scotland even registered a small swing to Labour.

Nevertheless, some Conservatives were confident from their own private polling in the marginals that a pattern would unfold of more and more Tory seats. Yet this did not happen. As the night wore on into the small hours the accuracy of the exit poll became apparent. The final tally of seats is given in Table A1.1.

Table A1.1 The Results

Party	Seats	Poll (%)
Conservative	307	37
Labour	258	29
Liberal Democrats	57	23
Others	28	11

Age

Table A1.2 below shows how age groups broke down for both men and women. It is clear that young men swung heavily to the Conservatives, slightly to the Lib Dems and away from Labour. Women aged 25–54 deserted Labour in some numbers, and young women seemed to take a shine to Nick Clegg.

Table A1.2 Results by age and gender (2005 figures in brackets)

	Conservatives	Labour	Liberal Democrats	Others
Men 18–24	35 (33)	26 (24)	23 (25)	7
Men 25–34	40 (29)	23 (33)	32 (27)	5
Men 35–54	34 (27)	28 (36)	25 (22)	12
Men 55+	39 (40)	27 (33)	18 (20)	15
Women 18–24	25 (22)	33 (43)	36 (26)	6
Women 25–34	27 (21)	37 (43)	25 (28)	10
Women 35–54	35 (27)	32 (40)	26 (27)	7
Women 55+	44 (41)	30 (34)	19 (20)	8

Source: IPSOS MORI, quoted in the *Observer*, 9 May 2010.

Housing

Table A1.3 below shows how occupiers of different types of housing voted. Owner-occupiers and mortgage-holders backed off substantially, but not dramatically, from Labour; the same could be said about social renters, traditionally a Labour constituency.

Table A1.3 Results by Type of Housing

	Conservatives	Labour	Liberal Democrats	Others
Owner	46 (44)	25 (29)	19 (20)	10
Mortgage-holder	37 (31)	28 (36)	27 (25)	9
Social renter	20 (19)	49 (55)	20 (19)	7
Private renter	35 (27)	25 (36)	27 (28)	12

Source: IPSOS MORI, quoted in the *Observer*, 9 May 2010.

Social Class

Traditionally it is the big social groups of C1 and C2 – together comprising more than half the population – whose movements tend to turn elections; this one was no exception. C1, and especially C2, voters swung markedly from Labour to Conservatives as the figures show in Table A1.4.

The biggest desertion of support can be seen to be in C2 voters – often the group which decides UK elections – where a figure of 40 per cent Labour support in 2005 changed to 22 per cent in 2010.

Table A1.4 Results by Social Class

	Conservatives	Labour	Liberal Democrats	Other
AB (upper middle and middle)	36 (37)	29 (28)	28 (29)	7
C1 (lower middle)	42 (37)	26 (32)	26 (33)	6
C2 (skilled working)	39 (33)	22 (40)	24 (19)	15
DE (working, unemployed, benefits)	28 (25)	44 (48)	15 (18)	13

Source: IPSOS MORI, quoted in the *Observer*, 9 May 2010.

Paul Richards, a former special adviser to Labour, posted this assessment on his blog of why Labour lost:

Populus found that it was C2 (the 'skilled manual workers') voters who agreed most strongly with the proposition that 'people who play by the rules always get a raw deal'. It was this section of society who deserted Labour on May 6th. It seems like our version of 'fairness' (more women in top jobs) and C2 voters' version of fairness (my daughter being able to afford a house near me) were not the same thing.

Press

Table A1.5 below shows how the right-wing *Mail* and *Telegraph*, already safe Conservative organs of opinion, had edged further to the right since 2005. *The Sun*, meanwhile, which supported Labour in 2005, swung heavily in the direction media moghul owner Rupert Murdoch pointed the newspaper in the autumn 2009 when he threw his weight behind Cameron.

For a full explanation of how the vote was distributed see Table A1.6.

Table A1.5 Newspaper Readership

	Conservatives	Labour	Liberal Democrats	Others	Swing to Conservatives (%)
Daily Mail	61	14	13	12	6
Telegraph	73	10	10	12	5
Guardian	39	45	39	3	2
The Sun	48	25	19	8	17.5

Source: IPSOS MORI, quoted in the *Observer*, 9 May 2010.

Table A1.6 Distribution of vote

Party	Seats	Gain	Loss	Net	Votes	%	+/–%
Conservative	306	100	3	+97	10,706,647	36.1	+3.8
Labour	258	3	94	–91	8,604,358	29.0	–6.2
Liberal Democrat	57	8	13	–5	6,827,938	23.0	+1.0
Democratic Unionist party	8	0	1	–1	168,216	0.6	–0.3
Scottish National party	6	0	0	0	491,386	1.7	+0.1
Sinn Fein	5	0	0	0	171,942	0.6	–0.1
Plaid Cymru	3	1	0	+1	165,394	0.6	–0.1
Social Democratic and Labour party	3	0	0	0	110,970	0.4	–0.1
Green	1	1	0	+1	285,616	1.0	–0.1
Alliance party	1	1	0	+1	42,762	0.1	+0.0
UK Independence party	0	0	0	0	917,832	3.1	+0.9
British National party	0	0	0	0	563,743	1.9	+1.2
Ulster Conservatives and Unionists – New Force	0	0	1	–1	102,361	0.3	–0.1
English Democrats	0	0	0	0	64,826	0.2	+0.2
Respect-Unity Coalition	0	0	1	–1	33,251	0.1	–0.1
Traditional Unionist Voice	0	0	0	0	26,300	0.1	
Christian party	0	0	0	0	18,623	0.1	
Independent Community and Health Concern	0	0	1	–1	16,150	0.1	+0.0
Trade Unionist and Socialist Coalition	0	0	0	0	12,275	0.0	
Scottish Socialist party	0	0	0	0	3,157	0.0	–0.1
Others	1	1	1	0	319,891	1.1	0.0
After 649 of 650 seats declare				Turnout	29,653,638	65.1	4.0

Source: *Sunday Times*, 9 May 2010.

■ Regions of the UK

Northern Ireland

The biggest shock here – almost a 'Portillo Moment' in the view of some – was the defeat of the DUP leader, Peter Robinson. He had suffered a major scandal involving his wife having an affair with a teenage lover whom she had also used her influence to help financially. The family's collective tax-funded earnings had also received much unflattering attention and Robinson's loss of Belfast East to the non-sectarian Alliance party caused a sensation. Cameron's hope of a new alliance in the province collapsed as his putative allies, the Ulster Unionists, including their leader Sir Reg Empey, failed to win a single seat. The DUP had to be satisfied with eight seats in the end; Sinn Fein, which does not take up its seats, won five; while the SDLP won three. Sylvia Hermon, who rejected the Tory–UUP alliance, was safely returned to the Commons.

Scotland

This country, as it has tended to over the last few decades, voted to reject Conservatism. Compared to its 28 per cent share of the vote in England, Labour won 42 per cent of the Scottish vote, regaining two seats and registering a small swing to them from the Tories. Labour scooped 42 of the 59 contested seats, Liberal Democrats 11, the SNP 6 and the Tories, a forlorn single seat. Scottish voters also voted tactically to keep out Conservatives, as in Perth and North Perthshire where Labour voters backed the SNP's Peter Wishart. SNP leader Alex Salmond's claim that the nationalists in Scotland and Wales had been dealt a 'mighty hand' proved very wide of the mark once the chance of a 'rainbow coalition' bit the dust.

Wales

The sensation of the night in Wales was the loss by a distraught Lib Dem MP, Lembit Opik, of his Montgomeryshire seat, by a huge swing to the Tories. Labour was pleased to win 16 of the 40 seats in Wales; Conservatives increased from three to eight, and Plaid Cymru had to be satisfied with three.

London

Over 70 seats are determined within London and the Conservatives were probably disappointed not to do better than their tally of 28. Labour did well to defend marginals, for example Sadiq Khan in Tooting and Karen Buck in Westminster North. While the Tories did well in the outer suburban 'ring' they had to concede the south-western reaches to the Liberal Democrats, apart from Richmond, which fell to Cameron's fellow old Etonian, Zac Goldsmith.

England

While Scotland showed Labour garnering 42 per cent of the vote and Wales 36.2 per cent, England managed only 28.1 per cent, with 39.6 per cent to the Conservatives and 24.2 per cent to the Lib Dems. Clearly the results reflected a UK where political allegiances have fractured.

■ Expenses Scandal Impact

Prime 'expenses offenders' for the Conservatives – Sir Peter Viggers, Anthony Steen and Julie Kirkbride – all stood down but, surprisingly perhaps, their successors did not suffer any party political guilt by association as they delivered increased majorities in their respective constituencies. However, those tainted in the Labour Party did less well; for example, Geoff Hoon's successor saw a majority of 10,000 cut to a mere 162, and Kitty Usher's seat was lost as was Sylvia Heal's and Barbara Follett's. The infamous Margaret Moran's replacement managed to win Luton, crushing the 'celebrity' candidate Esther Rantzen in the process. Hazel Blears, a highly publicised 'offender' however, was returned by her Salford constituents though Jaquii Smith, former Home Secretary, was not.

■ Fringe Parties

Much was made of the possible success of fringe parties in the election but generally they did not manage to impress.

BNP

Buoyed up by local government success in Barking, party leader Nick Griffin hoped to do well as a parliamentary candidate. However, he trailed in third in the poll, 18,000 votes behind the winning Margaret Hodge. In another key target seat, Stoke Central, the BNP candidate came in fourth with a desultory 2500 votes. Together with a wholesale loss of local government seats, these results put pressure on party leader Nick Griffin and placed a question mark over the future of the party as a whole.

UKIP

The party urging UK's withdrawal from the EU, had aimed to poll 5 per cent of the vote but managed only a disappointing 3 per cent, and no seats. Its former leader, the acid-tongued Nigel Farage, had stood down as leader to fight Speaker John Bercow in his true-blue Buckingham seat. The tradition is for the Speaker's seat not to be contested but Bercow is unpopular with his colleagues for having reneged on his Thatcherite views and moved close to Labour. With an endorsement from Lord Tebbitt, Farage carried many of his party's hopes for a breakthrough. Shortly before the poll he was aloft in a light plane, trailing a UKIP banner when it became entangled in a propeller and caused a plane crash from which he was extremely lucky to walk away relatively unharmed. From his hospital bed, he must have hoped he had won some sympathy votes; he did not, and came a limp third to a Bercow who coasted home with a 12,000 majority.

Greens

A small party with fervent, but thin, national support fares worse than any from first-past-the-post. Green enthusiasts were delighted in 1989 when they polled 15 per cent of the euro elections vote, but have been frustrated that they could not find support sufficiently concentrated to elect a member of parliament. So the victory of the able Caroline Lucas, the party's leader in Brighton Pavilion, has been met with delight by Greens and their wide spectrum of support on the left.

The End of Big Majorities?

Writing in the *Sunday Times* on 9 May 2010, polling expert Peter Kellner argued the 2010 result suggested the age of 'clear-cut victory may be gone for ever'. The key reason was the inexorable rise of the smaller parties:

Labour and Conservative no longer dominate politics as they once did. In 1951 only nine MPs did not take the Labour or Tory whip; in 1979 the number had climbed to 27, but the 70-seat Conservative lead over Labour delivered Margaret Thatcher a 43-seat overall majority. This time even a 70-seat lead would have been insufficient. As well as the 57 contingent of Liberal Democrats, 28 represented eight smaller parties. To secure an overall majority of just two, the Tories would have needed 86 more MPs than Labour.

Cameron's 'A List'

This 'favoured' list of candidates was invented by Cameron to help change the image of his party as too male, too white and too stuffy. A shining list of hopefuls were assembled – not without criticism from those who were excluded from it – and eased into constituencies where they were thought to have a good chance. In the event voters tended not to take to them: Joanne Cash, Annunziata Rees-Mogg, Shaun Bailey, Helen Whateley, Mal Clarke and the like were all rejected with only Zack Goldsmith and author Louise Bagshawe successfully breasting the electoral tape.

Polling Stations Fiasco

During polling night disturbing tales emerged of scores of voters in some constituencies being denied the right to vote because, despite queuing for some time, their votes could not be allowed after the 10 pm deadline had passed. A total of 1200 voters at 27 polling stations were prevented from casting their votes, according to the Electoral Commission's scathing report on 21 May. Other polling stations found they could not take any more voters as they had run out of ballot papers. Manchester Withington suffered this experience as well as polling stations in Leeds, Liverpool, Milton Keynes, Newcastle and other parts of the UK. It seems that the reason, in most cases, was the sudden surge in turnout after two elections when turnout had been low. At a polling station in Birmingham Ladywood, turnout went up from 18 per cent in previous years to 40 per cent. Critics point out that while turnout was indeed up – to 65 per cent on average – it was still way below levels common in the 1980s and 1990s. It seems exceedingly remiss of returning officers that so many people were denied their basic democratic right to vote. Geoffrey Robertson QC echoed this criticism and predicted those who sue are likely to receive £750 or more in compensation. The Electoral Commission recommended that in future electoral law be adjusted so that people queuing at 10 pm be allowed to vote.

Ethnic Minority MPs

The election saw minority ethnic MPs nearly doubling from 14 to 27. These included: Shabana Mahmood, for Birmingham Ladywood, Labour's first Muslim woman; Helen Grant, for Ann Widdecombe's old seat of Maidstone and the Weald, the Conservatives first black woman; Chi Onwurah, the first African woman to win a seat in Newcastle Central for Labour; and Priti Patel, the first Tory Asian female MP, elected in Witham, Essex.

Women MPs

The UK ranks 73rd in the world for female representation and this election's results did not cause much of an upwards climb. In 2005 women represented 19 per cent of the total number of MPs. On 6 May the percentage increased to 21.5; the result of only another dozen new women being sent to the Commons. Amongst them, however, are some notable additions. Bridget Phillipson for Sunderland South is a council estate girl who made it to Oxford; Luciana Berger, criticised in Wavertree for not being local, managed to increase the Labour majority by 2000; and Ashfield, Geoff Hoon's old seat, narrowly elected GMTV's political correspondent, Gloria del Piero for Labour. However, a slew of well-known women lost their seats: former Labour Home Secretary, Jacqui Smith, prominent Lib Dem Susan Kramer and the former Labour Solicitor General, Vera Baird.

Conservatives' New Intake

With so many MPs retiring before the 2010 election the new intake will do much to provide its character, especially in the case of the winning Conservative MPs. The first thing to note is that the number of female Tory MPs has risen from 17 to 49, with 99 male MPs. Four per cent of all Tory MPs are Asian and 2 per cent Black. Educationally, 5 per cent went to Eton, 35 per cent to private schools (up from 32 per cent in 2005), 36 per cent to state schools and 24 per cent to grammar schools. Almost one third are from Oxbridge universities. Sir Peter Lampl of the Sutton Trust commented: 'These results show clearly that the educational profile of our representatives in the 2010 Parliament does not reflect society at large' (*Daily Telegraph*, 10 May 2010).

Over 40 per cent of MPs have worked in finance, business or management; 13 per cent in law; 13 per cent in the public sector; and 8 per cent in the media or public relations. Overall, over a third of MPs have never served in the Commons before (compared with 18 per cent in 2005).

■ Turnout

On 28 April veteran election analyst Professor David Denver (*Guardian*, 27 April 2010), commenting on the hugely disappointing 59 per cent turnout in 2001, quoted a colleague Professor Anthony King's view: 'Just provide the voters with a closely fought election at which a great deal is at stake and, make no mistake, they will again turn out in their droves.' Denver added: 'If we substitute "respectable numbers" for "droves", I suspect he is about to be proved right.'

The 2005 election had not really provided King's conditions – the turnout had been 61 per cent – but 2010 was shaping up to do so. On average the turnout was 65.1 per cent, a reassuring increase on 2005. However, turnout in rural areas was quite frequently as high as 75 per cent, especially in the southern and south-western parts of England. Urban areas, as usual, reflected much lower turnout figures. Renfrewshire East topped the turnout numbers with 77.3 per cent while at the lower end of the scale, only six seats had less than 50 per cent with Hull and Hessle polling the lowest, a desultory 45.7 per cent. However, over 2 million more voters turned out than in 2005.

Do such figures prove Tony King's prediction? To a degree, yes, but until 1997 turnout of 70 per cent and over was commonplace, so in 2010 even a tight race and key economic bones of contention were insufficient to attract voters out in numbers equal to the later decades of the last century. Denver's expectation of 'respectable numbers' sounds about right, especially when the anti-politics mood caused by the expenses scandal is factored in.

The Aftermath: The Road to Coalition

If Gordon Brown's fate has been to resemble not just one but several Shakespearean tragic heroes – cursed in his relationship with Tony Blair by a jealousy worthy of Othello, racked in the first months of his premiership by the indecision of Hamlet – then today he was Macbeth, seemingly playing out his final act. Like the embattled Scottish king holed up in his castle, watching Birnam Wood march on Dunsinane, Brown sat in No 10 knowing that, a few yards away, enemy forces were gathered, preparing to combine and seize his crown.

Jonathan Freedland, *Observer*, 9 May 2010

Party Outcomes

During Friday 7 May, the exhausted principal players in the election drama must have surveyed their respective positions with a mixture of feelings. All must have been disappointed, though Labour must have felt a combination of emotions. Since mid-2009 most Labour people, apart from the congenitally naive or optimistic, had expected the coming election to end in defeat. Pessimistic supporters feared a wipe-out, Labour perhaps destroyed for a generation. To return 260 seats, therefore, gave substantial reassurance that the party was still in business.

The Conservatives, conversely, had long expected to cruise grandly into office, with a tidy majority. To end up in a hung parliament therefore appeared a disaster to some, a condemnation of Cameron and Osborne's campaign strategy to others. The decision to allow televised debates when well ahead in the polls was especially the object of derision by some disaffected Conservatives. Most of them tended to be of the more traditional variety who thought Cameron's 'Big Society' theme had sounded impractical and was impossible to sell on the doorstep.

But maybe it was the Liberal Democrats who were most keenly disappointed. After steady but unspectacular progress after 1992, the party had played very much a peripheral role in British politics, seeking hard to make an impact and leaning mostly towards support for Labour. Their expectations however had been electrified by the televised debates. From being a 20 per cent polling element in a 'two-and-a-half party system', they suddenly were an equal part of a three-way contest. Of course, the voting system would not deliver them power unless they won over 40 per cent of the vote – almost unthinkable – but a 30-plus share would have given them a slew of more seats and a more powerful moral case to demand voting reform.

The end result however revealed that 'Cleggmania' had delivered virtually nothing: only 1 per cent more of the vote than in 2005 and several seats lost besides. It was 'so unfair and undemocratic' many party members must have raged. But the arithmetic of the election had created a number of intriguing possibilities.

Constitutional rules

In the event of a 'hung parliament', where no party has an overall majority, the rules drawn up, based to some extent on the last time this occurred back in February 1974, lay down that the prime minister *remains* in office while he seeks to form a government which can command the House of Commons.

In practice this means the PM tries to do a deal with another party which will facilitate a majority in the House. In 1974, Tory prime minister Edward Heath – having polled the most votes but still four seats short of Labour's total – tried to persuade Jeremy Thorpe's Liberals to add their weight to the Tories.

Thorpe was interested but when his party insisted on voting reform as a condition, Heath backed off and Labour's Wilson took over at the head of a minority administration. Gordon Brown, therefore – accused of 'squatting' in Number 10 by *The Sun* – was in fact performing his proper role to the letter. But, as he pondered his quandary, the numbers did not look promising for Mr Brown.

Box A1 How Much Difference Would Voting Reform Make?

Much sound and fury after the election focused on reforming the voting system. Alan Travis in the *Guardian*, 11 May 2010, examined the difference various types of voting reform might make.

The Alternative Vote

Would make it possible for voters to rank their preferences among the candidates, ensuring that the winner needs to command the support of over half of all voters. Lib Dems criticise AV as insufficiently proportional and inadequate for fair votes in a proper democracy. Had it been applied in 2010 the results would has been estimated as: Conservatives 281 instead of 307; Labour 262 instead of 258, Liberal Democrats 79 instead of 57 and Others, 28 as under FPTP. Scarcely 'fair voting' from the Lib Dem perspective.

Alternative Vote Plus

This is the system, based on the German model, called the Additional Member System (AMS), and recommended by the 1998 Jenkins Report, which gives voters two votes, one for a constituency MP and another for parties in a 'top-up pool' used to improve proportionality between them. This would have produced results of: Conservatives 275. Labour 234, Liberal Democrat 110 and Others 31.

Single Transferable Vote

This is the system used in Ireland with large multi-member constituencies where candidates are ranked according to preferences and elected when a quota of preferences is achieved. Candidates do not need a majority to be elcted, just the known share of the vote. This is the system favoured by the Lib Dems and would have produced: Conservatives 246, Labour, 207, Liberal Democrats, 162 and Others, 35. It is easy to see why the Liberal Democrats believe this is the system which should be introduced to the UK.

The Post-Election Arithmetic

The figures ended up as: Conservatives, 307; Labour, 258; Lib Dems 57; and Others, 28. This meant that, with no overall majority available to any party, two main options offered themselves: an agreement, ranging from a pact not to vote down major bills to full coalition; or a minority administration in which the Conservatives, as the largest party, sought to pass their major measures, while daring the other parties to precipitate a second election in which they might be punished by the voters for bringing down the government. This feat had been achieved by Wilson in 1974 when his minority government had held on until the autumn when a second election delivered him a small majority of six.

Coalition Options

Conservative–Liberal Democrat

This was easily envisaged as both sets of MPs added up to a comfortable 364, easily able to survive all but the most massive backbench revolts. On the plus side: Clegg and Cameron, both public school and Oxbridge, seemed to get on well personally; both believed in robust approaches to dealing with the deficit; and both shared an antipathy to Labour's record on human rights. Against it however was a formidable list of disadvantages: Lib Dem and Conservative activists, whilst they co-operated on some councils, were frequently at daggers drawn over bitterly disputed local issues; most of the former were naturally closer ideologically to Labour; and many Lib Dem MPs had only been elected through persuading Labour voters to vote for them in order to keep Conservatives *out*, not put them *in*.

Moreover, Lib Dems feared a coalition might absorb their smaller party via a new realignment of centre-left and centre-right – as had happened to the 'National Liberals' in 1931. In addition, the Conservatives were mostly opposed to the EU while the Lib Dems were essentially committed to it. But the most crucial bone of party contention was reform of the voting system. Once again the 'third party' had done badly, garnering nearly a quarter of the popular vote yet winning less than 10 per cent of the seats. Lib Dems were desperate to achieve a more proportional system of voting while the Conservatives, aware that some 60 per cent of voters were left-of-centre, feared such a system would lock them out of power, possibly indefinitely.

Labour–Liberal Democrat

The possibility of a Conservative–Liberal Democrat alignment was too dangerous for Labour to just sit back and watch happen, especially as there was the chance it might become permanent.

Tony Blair and Paddy Ashdown had both wanted such a 'progressive alliance' in 1997 but it had been vetoed by senior figures in Labour's Cabinet. At the end of election night, thirteen years on, a number of Labour Cabinet ministers – such as Business Secretary Lord Mandelson, Welsh Secretary Peter Hain and Home Secretary Alan Johnson – were openly suggesting a deal could be done on voting reform. The Lib Dems knew Labour was more sympathetic than the Tories but were wary of a number of factors: Clegg had declared he did not think he could work with Labour as long as Brown was their leader; a number of Labour's influential figures, like Ed Balls, were not happy about voting reform (Brown, in addition, was believed to have been the main opponent back in 1997); and both parties disagreed on things like ID cards. But the biggest disadvantage lay in the arithmetic.

To assemble a majority, Labour would need to construct a 'rainbow' coalition comprising themselves, the Lib Dems, plus the nationalists and the single Green to achieve a very slim and probably unworkable majority. The DUP might have been persuaded but their natural allies lay in the blue not red corner. Hard-headed realists on both sides doubted if such a coalition could be sustained for long. The SNP would be likely to demand a high price and any major reform of the voting system might have led to revolts in the Labour ranks. Finally, a referendum cobbled together by such an assorted collection of forces might have been perceived as opportunistic and voted down.

Box A2 The Rival Offers

Tory offer to Lib Dems

- Referendum on Alternative Vote for elections to Commons.
- Cabinet seats and other ministerial jobs for Lib Dems.
- Agreement on schools, environment and, possibly, taxation.

Labour offer to Lib Dems

- Guaranteed Alternative Vote for elections to Commons.
- Possible future referendum on 'full PR' of single transferable vote.
- Full coalition with Cabinet seats.
- Broad agreement on deficit reduction.
- New leadership for Labour once binding deal with Lib Dems agreed.

Based on Patrick Wintour, *Guardian*, 11 May 2010

The End Game

The day after a desperately close-fought election campaign must have left Nick Clegg exhausted. And he must have been hugely disappointed when viewing the wreckage of his hopes for a massive increase in seats turned into a net loss of five. But, so baffling and confusing had the whole process been, he suddenly found himself the much courted object of a bidding war. Gordon Brown, still prime minister in Downing St remember, announced he would offer a referendum on the Alternative Vote (AV) system and Cabinet seats to Clegg's party. He said he was prepared to talk to the leaders of 'all parties' and provide civil servant support for any negotiations other parties might pursue.

Cameron countered by announcing a 'big, open, comprehensive offer' to the Liberal Democrats, recognising the differences but emphasising the common ground, plus an 'all-party inquiry into electoral reform'. Clegg had said before the election that if he held the balance of power after it, he would talk to the party with the biggest mandate. Clearly the Conservatives were this party and negotiations ensued with William Hague spokesman on the Conservatives' side. The media interest was intense with 24-hour news channels providing continuous broadcasts. Rumours abounded that the EU and voting reform were proving to be sticking points but Hague and other Tory voices spoke of great good will and a substantial meeting of minds.

The next day the right-wing press were aghast to hear that Clegg had been talking secretly to Labour on Sunday. This was followed by Brown's final attempt to keep Cameron out of what had been his home for the past three years; however, once he realised that a deal with the Lib Dems was not going to happen he announced his resignation as Labour leader, offering to step down after a period of five months once a new Labour leader had been elected by the party. It was rumoured senior figures had urged Brown to stand down with dignity having effectively lost the election. Clegg thereupon announced he would enter into negotiations with Labour, while the country waited on tenterhooks. The day before the *Observer* had followed the likes of Polly Toynbee in Saturday's *Guardian* in urging the negotiation of a 'rainbow coalition'. 'To Seize this Historic Moment, the Lib Dems Must Turn to Labour', cried the Sunday's editorial, backed up by columnists Will Hutton and Nick Cohen.

Leader of the Labour Party, Gordon Brown, with his wife Sarah and children John and James, walk to his car, after he announced his resignation as Prime Minister; Downing Street, on 11 May 2010.
Source: Ben Stansall / AFP / Getty Images.

Clegg carried the hopes of the left-of-centre with him, his ears ringing with cries of betrayal from the Conservatives; though Hague, for one, was careful to withhold criticism of someone he knew might still be his coalition colleague. Hague's caution proved prescient as the talks with Labour soon broke down with both sides blaming the other of not really wanting to come together – both sides were sceptical – and an extraordinary series of attacks on the proposed deal by a number of senior Labour figures, including former Home Secretary John Reid, Lord Falconer, Andy Burnham Diane Abbott, and several others. Their objections ranged from an opposition to changing the voting system to a strong sense that a 'coalition of the losers' would be unstable, undemocratic, short-lived and against the party's long-term interests. Clegg and his colleagues fled to the open arms of his first suitor and a coalition agreement was soon announced.

Perhaps stung by the thought Labour might still capture the prize, Cameron upped his offer on voting reform to a promise of a referendum on the AV system. Shortly afterwards a new coalition Conservative–Liberal Democrat government was announced. Gordon Brown came out of 10 Downing Street to resign with dignity and walked off with his wife and family to return to Scotland before beginning a new life, presumably not so focused on politics.

David Cameron followed Brown to the palace to 'kiss hands' and become Britain's 52nd prime minister. On Wednesday 12 May Cameron and Clegg appeared at a joint press conference in the garden of Number 10 Downing Street, displaying an almost indecent degree of enthusiasm for each other and the new coalition (the *Economist* on 15 May called them a 'startlingly lovely couple').

Prime Minister David Cameron (left) welcomes Deputy Prime Minister Nick Clegg (right) to Downing Street for their first day of coalition government on 12 May 2010.
Source: Matt Cardy / Getty Images.

What did the Liberal Democrats get out of the deal?

Clegg became Deputy Prime Minister with responsibility for political reform – a key part of the deal which is likely to be contentious as the referendum approaches. Four Cabinet posts were given to the smaller party: Chris Huhne became Energy secretary, Vince Cable Business Secretary, Danny Alexander Scottish Secretary and David Laws Chief Secretary to the Treasury.

Coalition Government's Programme

The programme of the new government emerged as including:
1. A five-year fixed parliament which can only be dissolved through a 55 per cent vote in parliament.
2. A mutual agreement to drop increase of inheritance tax threshold to £1 million by Tories and 'mansion tax' by Lib Dems.
3. Abandonment of Labour's planned rise in National Insurance rates but some relaxation of income tax thresholds for the lower paid.
4. Referendum if any further pledging of powers to EU is proposed and no entry to euro during the life of the current parliament.

5. The Tory proposal of £150 marriage tax allowance will go ahead as planned with Lib Dems abstaining.
6. Lib Dems will drop their opposition to the replacement of Trident nuclear missiles.
7. The government deficit to be reduced by £6 billion in 2010.
8. Referendum on AV to be held and a three-line whip applied to coalition MPs.
9. A move to an elected House of Lords.
10. A commission to review party funding.
11. A new 'pupil premium' for children from poor homes to help close gap in school results.

The 55 per cent requirement for the dissolution of parliament caused immediate controversy but at the time of writing, in May 2010, this will surely be only a curtain raiser to the conflicts likely to be caused by cuts in public spending required to solve the problem of the government's massive debt obligations. All political parties will take their time to digest the election results. On the fringe, the BNP has to consider if it even has a future after a disastrous wipe-out of its hopes. Labour has been plunged into a leadership contest with the two Miliband brothers competing against each other and several other candidates. The party will also seek to renew itself and conduct itself as a competent opposition. The Conservative party, in May 2010, was still smarting at being denied its expected easy majority and there were pockets of strong disaffection at the coalition with Nick Clegg. The same could also be said for the Liberal Democrats with some activists claiming the coalition would destroy the party's radical appeal for the foreseeable future. Clegg himself, on 15 May, offered this defence:

There are those on both the left and right who are united in thinking this should not have happened. But the truth is this: there was no other responsible way to play the hand dealt to the political parties by the British people at the election. The parliamentary arithmetic made a Lib–Lab coalition unworkable, and it would have been regarded as illegitimate by the British people. Equally, a minority administration would have been too fragile to tackle the political and economic challenges ahead. (Guardian)

55 Per Cent Rule

Voters and MPs learnt soon after Nick and Dave's 'civil ceremony' that their marriage had a built in anti-divorce device proposed: to dissolve the five-year fixed term a majority of 55 per cent would be required. On the face of it Cameron has relinquished one of the PM's major powers: that of choosing the election date, often criticised as allowing a time to be chosen when the economy is good or can be made to seem so. But the new rule suggests Cameron could be defeated on a vote of no confidence by 51 per cent yet still continue in power to try and form a new coalition. The rationale here is that neither party in the coalition would be able to withdraw, as the Conservatives have 47 per cent and the Opposition plus the Lib Dems 53 per cent. So neither side can pull the rug out within the next 5 years just because, say, they are ahead in the opinion polls and think an election would do them a power of good. 'Sounds good' some thought, but others had their doubts.

Critics argue that whereas previously the PM would have been bound to face the voters if he lost a no-confidence motion, he can now carry on and if MPs want to bring about a vote of no confidence, they have to muster more supporters than the Opposition currently numbers. So, in theory, this 'locks in' the coalition and makes it invulnerable to adverse votes. Many – like David Blunkett, Andrew Adonis and Jack Straw – feel that this is merely a cynical 'fix' to keep Nick and Dave cosy and safe in power. The US government has fixed terms, they say, but if the executive party loses its majority in the legislature, it just has to struggle on as best it can. However, there is a precedent within the UK: the Scottish Parliament has a threshold of 66 per cent, set by the Labour–Lib Dem coalition, and if a new first minister cannot be found within 28 days then an election must be held. Wales has a similar system.

Britain's new coalition Cabinet. Front row (left–right): Work and Pensions Secretary, Iain Duncan Smith; Defence Secretary, Dr Liam Fox; Chancellor of the Exchequer, George Osborne; Foreign Secretary, William Hague; Prime Minister, David Cameron; Deputy Prime Minister, Nick Clegg; Conservative Party Chairman, Baroness Sayeeda Warsi; Welsh Secretary, Cheryl Gillian; Environmental Secretary, Caroline Spelman; Justice Secretary and Lord Chancellor, Ken Clarke; Treasury Secretary, David Laws. Back row (left–right): Chief Whip, Patrick McLoughlin; Home Secretary, Theresa May; Minister for Universities and Science, David Willetts; Minister of State and Policy, Oliver Letwin; Business Secretary, Vince Cable; Minister for the Cabinet Office, Francis Maude; Communities Secretary, Eric Pickles; Leader of the Lords, Lord Strathclyde; Health Secretary, Andrew Lansley; Leader of the Commons, George Young; Education Secretary, Michael Gove; International Development Secretary, Andrew Mitchell; Transport Secretary, Philip Hammond; Energy and Climate Secretary, Chris Huhne; Culture Secretary, Jeremy Hunt; Northern Ireland Secretary, Owen Paterson; Scottish Secretary, Danny Alexander; Attorney General, Dominic Grieve; Cabinet Secretary, Gus O'Donnell. Taken in the garden of Number 10 Downing Street, 13 May 2010.
Source: Andrew Winning – WPA Pool / Getty Images.

Reaction to Coalition from Former Lib Dem Leaders

Former Lib Dem leader Charles Kennedy, could not bring himself to support the deal and so abstained in the vote by fellow Lib Dem MPs on whether to accept the coalition. He regretted the loss of the 'progressive alliance' of Labour and his party which had so attracted Liberal leaders from Jo Grimond onwards. Other former leaders, David Steel and Paddy Ashdown, also expressed severe doubts for similar reasons plus the fear that their smaller group would be 'rolled up' eventually into the bigger right-wing party. However, both the latter finally came down on the side of support on the basis this was the best deal *available*.

Mori Poll Supports Coalition

According to the Mori poll in the *News of the World*, 16 May 2010, the ordinary public had fewer doubts. According to the poll: 59 per cent thought it 'good for the UK'; 72 per cent thought Cameron 'right to form the coalition'; and 66 per cent thought Cameron 'fit to be prime minister'. Moreover, 89 per cent of Tory voters were happy Cameron had formed the coalition, according to the poll.

Whether this coalition of Conservatives with Lib Dems, can survive the challenges of major underlying policy differences, the backlash against inevitably unpopular cuts and the unforeseen crises which affect all governments, remains, tantalisingly, to be seen. The Tantalising prospect for the Conservatives is that, if seen to be successful, the coalition might become permanent and a realignment of British politics occur between the centre right and a major element of the centre left, instead of the re-alignment within the centre-left of which Blair, Ashdown and Kennedy had dreamed. The nightmare downside of such a development for the Lib Dems would be the absorption of their party into the bigger grouping and maybe, in any case, the desertion of their voters to Labour and other parties.

The coalition received its first big hit, 2 June 2010, when David Laws, the brilliant Liberal Democratic Chief Secretary to the Treasury, was forced to resign following revelations he had used £40,000 of public money 2004–10 to pay rent to his male partner. Fellow Liberal Democrat Danny Alexander took over his role but few thought that Laws could be effectively replaced.

Further reading

This chapter has been informed by a wide range of contemporary press articles plus television and radio broadcasts. The following books were also useful:

Callus, G. and Dale, I. (2009) *Total Politics Guide to the 2010 General Election* (Total Politics).

Lee, S. and Beech, M. (eds) (2009) *The Conservatives under David Cameron* (Macmillan).

Maitland, J. (2010) *Jonathan Maitland: The Complete and Utter Guide to the 2010 Election* (Metro).

Paul Whiteley, 'Can Labour Win?, Poliutical Insight, April 2010 pages 5–8.

Rallings, C. and Thrasher, M. (2006) *British Electoral Facts* (Total Politics).

Source: The Sunday Times, © Gerald Scarfe.